10/95

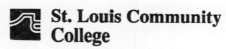

The United States in the First World War

MILITARY HISTORY OF THE UNITED STATES (VOL. 3)

GARLAND REFERENCE LIBRARY OF THE HUMANITIES (VOL. 1205)

The United States in the First World War
An Encyclopedia

Editor
Anne Cipriano Venzon

Consulting Editor
Paul L. Miles

GARLAND PUBLISHING, INC.
New York & London
1995

Library of Congress Cataloging-in-Publication Data

The United States in the First World War : an encyclopedia / editor, Anne
    Cipriano Venzon, consulting editor, Paul L. Miles.
                p.   cm. — (Garland reference library of the humanities ;
    vol. 1205. Military history of the United States ; v. 3)
        Includes bibliographical references and index.
        ISBN 0-8240-7055-0
        1. World War, 1914–1918—Encyclopedias.   I. Venzon, Anne Cipriano,
    1951–   . II. Series: Garland reference library of the humanities ; vol. 1205.
    III. Series: Garland reference library of the humanities. Military history of the
    United States ; v. 3.
        D510.U65   1995
        940.3'03—dc20   95-1782
                                                                          CIP

Cover illustration courtesy The Bettmann Archive
Cover design by Lawrence Wolfson Design, New York.

Printed on acid-free, 250-year-life paper
Manufactured in the United States of America

Contents

Introduction

The First World War was the first total war in modern times, and virtually every aspect of American society felt its impact to some extent. Industry shifted—in some cases lurched—to a war footing. Women entered the work force in unprecedented numbers and redoubled their call for equal rights. Revenues had to be collected to finance the struggle. Food and fuel conservation measures were instituted. A chaotic railroad system was nationalized. Civil liberties were threatened. There was strident opposition to United States participation in the conflict. Relations with other nations underwent profound changes. War, that most unpredictable of solvents, was at work in every corner of society, not just the battlefield. Therefore, the editors of this encyclopedia concluded that domestic issues such as preparedness, foreign relations, industrial mobilization, tax policy, regulatory agencies, civil rights, the woman's movement and the peace movement, as well as military topics, should be covered to provide a realistic overview of the United States at war in 1917. Given space and time constraints, not every pertinent topic could be included. Likewise, the purely practical consideration of length led us to focus, quite literally, on the *United States* in the First World War. Only those foreign issues and personalities which had substantial bearing on the conduct of the U.S. war effort have been included. However, we have tried to provide a reasonably comprehensive survey of the important issues, individuals, and technologies which directly affected the United States during the Great War.

Of great assistance in the selection process were our contributors. Our first and preeminent note of thanks must go to this group of experts who gave their time and talent so generously. The Office of Research of the History Department at the United States Air Force Academy was instrumental in recruiting contributors to our ranks. In addition to writing a number of essays, George B. Clark made rare and invaluable source materials available and introduced us to other scholars who were interested in the project. Professor Paul Braim was of tremendous assistance in securing maps for the volume and sharing his great expertise on the war. Michael J. Knapp guided us through the labyrinthine collections at the National Archives and prepared several major articles. Shirley Cobert, our copy editor and Helga McCue, managing editor of Garland Publishing, made significant suggestions which improved both the content and style of the book. Finally, we recognize the late Professor Richard Blanco, general editor of this series. His vision and wisdom will be sorely missed.

Abbreviations

AEF	American Expeditionary Forces
Adm.	admiral
BGen.	brigadier general
Capt.	captain
Cmdr.	commander
Col.	colonel
Commo.	commodore
Cpl.	corporal
Ens.	ensign
Gen.	general
Lt.	lieutenant
LtCmdr.	lieutenant commander
LtCol.	lieutenant colonel
LtGen.	lieutentant general
Maj.	major
Pvt.	private
Q.M.	quartermaster
R.N.	Royal Navy
S.O.S.	Service of Supply
USA	United States Army
USCG	United States Coast Guard
USMC	United States Marine Corps
USN	United States Navy
VAdm.	vice admiral

Contributors

Addington, Larry
The Citadel (emeritus)
Charleston, SC

Alford, Dora
Abilene Christian University
Abilene, TX

Ambrosius, Lloyd E.
University of Nebraska
Lincoln, NB

Annunziata, Frank
Rochester Institute of Technology
Rochester, NY

Aronsen, Lawrence
University of Alberta
Canada

Arnold, Allan A.
U.S. Merchant Marine Academy
Kings Point, NY

Ashkenas, Bruce
National Archives & Records Administration
Washington, DC

Bacevich, Andrew J.
The Paul Nitze School of Advanced
   International Studies
The Johns Hopkins University
Washington, DC

Bailey, Fred Arthur
Abilene Christian University
Abilene, TX

Barbeau, Arthur
West Liberty State College
West Liberty, WV

Barrett, Michael B.
The Citadel
Charleston, SC

Beaver, Daniel R.
University of Cincinnati
Cincinnati, Ohio

Biskupski, M. B.
St. John Fisher College
Rochester, NY

Bittner, Donald
Command & Staff College
United States Marine Corps
Quantico, VA

Blackburn, Charles
Appalachian State University
Boone, NC

Blewett, Daniel K.
Loyola University of Chicago
Chicago, IL

Boemke, Manfred F.
German Historical Institute
Washington, DC

Bogacz, Theodore †
United States Naval Academy
Annapolis, MD

Boxerman, Burton A.
Independent scholar
St. Louis, MO

Boyer, Harold N.
Independent scholar
Aston, PA

Braim, Paul F.
Embry-Riddle Aeronautical University
Daytona Beach, FL

Broadwater, Jeffrey
Barton College
Wilson, NC

Brodhead, Michael J.
University of Nevada-Reno (emeritus)
Reno, NV

Brown, Jerold
Hartwick College
Oneonta, NY

Byrne, Kevin B.
Gustavus Adolphus College
St. Peter, MN

Campbell, D'Ann
Austin Peay University
Clarksville, TN

Carpenter, Robert A.
Independent scholar
New Orleans, LA

Carr, Michael
Independent scholar
Mukwonaga, WI

Challener, Richard D.
Princeton University (emeritus)
Princeton, NJ

Chambers, John Whiteclay II
Rutgers University
New Brunswick, NJ

Chapman, Richard N.
Francis Marion College
Florence, SC

Christian, Garna L.
Houston Community College
Houston, TX

Christiensen, Lawrence O.
University of Missouri
Rolla, MO

Clark, George B.
Independent scholar
Pike, NH

Clements, Kendrick A.
University of South Carolina
Columbia, SC

Clifford, J. Garry
University of Connecticut
Storrs, CT

Coker, Katherine R.
U.S. Army Signal Corps
Fort Gordon, GA

Coletta, Paolo E.
United States Naval Academy (emeritus)
Annapolis, MD

Collins, James L., Jr.
Independent scholar
Middleburg, VA

Conner, Valerie Jean
Florida State University
Tallahassee, FL

Controvich, James
Independent scholar
Springfield, MA

Cook, Bernard A.
Loyola University
New Orleans, LA

Cooper, Jerry
University of Missouri
St. Louis, MO

Cordier, Sherwood S.
Western Michigan University (emeritus)
Kalamazoo, MI

Cornebise, Alfred E.
University of Northern Colorado (emeritus)
Greeley, CO

Cox, Gary P.
Gordon College
Barnesville, GA

Curtis, Susan
Purdue University
West Lafayette, IN

Danielson, Elena
The Hoover Institution on War, Revolution,
   and Peace
Stanford, CA

Davis, Colin
University of Alabama
Birmingham, AL

Davison, Joan
Rollins College
Winter Park, FL

Debauche, Leslie Midkiff
University of Wisconsin
Stevens Point, WI

DeGraff, Leonard
Edison National Historic Site
National Park Service
West Orange, NJ

Dorley, Albert
Villanova University
Villanova, PA

Dowless, Donald
Independent scholar
Louisburg, NC

Drake, Frederick C.
Brock University
Canada

Dubofsky, Melvyn
State University of New York
Binghamton, NY

Dubovoj, Sina
Independent scholar
Washington, DC

Durham, Weldon B.
University of Missouri
Columbia, MO

Edwards, John C.
University of Georgia
Athens, GA

Eltscher, Louis
Rochester Institute of Technology
Rochester, NY

Endress, Charles A.
Angelo State University
San Angelo, TX

English, Thomas R.
The George School
Newtown, PA

Esposito, David
Shippensburg University
Shippensburg, PA

Faber, Peter R.
United States Air Force Academy
Colorado Springs, CO

Ferrell, Robert H.
Indiana University (emeritus)
Bloomington, IN

Fisher, William E., Jr.
United States Air Force U.S.—R.O.K.
   Combined Forces Command
Seoul, Korea

Garry, Patrick
Saint John's University
Collegeville, MN

Gelfand, Lawrence E.
University of Iowa (emeritus)
Iowa City, IA

Gillett, Mary
U.S. Army Center of Military History
Washington, DC

Ginther, James
Texas Tech University
Lubbock, TX

Gough, Terrence J.
U. S. Army Center of Military History
Washington, DC

Graham, Sally Hunter
Louisiana State University
Baton Rouge, LA

Grandstaff, Mark R.
Brigham Young University
Provo, UT

Greene, John R.
Cazenovia College
Cazenovia, NY

Gregory, Ross
Western Michigan University
Kalamazoo, MI

Grimes, Vincent P.
National Defense Magazine
Arlington, VA

Grubbs, Frank L.
Meredith College
Raleigh, NC

Grumelli, Michael
United States Air Force Academy
Colorado Springs, CO

Hallas, James
Independent scholar
Portland, CT

Hanigan, William
University of Illinois College of Medicine
Peoria, IL

Harris, Ruth
Independent scholar
Washington, DC

Harrison, Richard A.
Lawrence University
Appleton, WI

Heath, James
Portland State University (emeritus)
Portland, OR

Heidenreich, Donald E., Jr.
Kemper College
Boonville, MO

Heiser, Matthew
University of Wisconsin
Milwaukee, WI

Helmreich, Jonathan E.
Alleghany College
Meadville, PA

Hendricks, Charles
U.S. Army Corps of Engineers
Fort Belvoir, VA

Hillman, Rolfe
Independent scholar
Arlington, VA

Hirst, David W.
Princeton University (emeritus)
Princeton, NJ

Hogue, James
Princeton University
Princeton, NJ

Holley, I.B. Jr.
Duke University (emeritus)
Durham, NC

Holmes, William F.
University of Georgia
Athens, GA

Houchin, Roy
Auburn University
Auburn, AL

Hourihan, William J.
U.S. Army Chaplain School & Center
Fort Monmouth, NJ

Imber, Michael
University of Kansas
Lawrence, KA

Imholte, John
University of Minnesota
Morris, MN

Irwin, Manley R.
University of New Hampshire (emeritus)
Durham, NH

Irwin, Patricia
Independent scholar
Durham, NH

Jackson, Michelle
U. S. Navy Mobile Mine Assembly Group
Charleston, SC

Jenson, Carol E.
Independent scholar
Minneapolis, MN

Johnson, Charles
Independent scholar
Del Ray Beach, FL

Johnson, Douglas V.
U.S. Army War College, Carlisle Barracks
Carlisle, PA

Johnson, Judith
Wichita State University
Wichita, KA

Johnson, Robert E.
University of Alabama (emeritus)
Birmingham, AL

Kauffman, Christopher J.
Catholic University of America
Washington, DC

Keene, Jennifer
Independent scholar
Washington, DC

Kehrberg, Richard
University of Wisconsin-Madison
Madison, WI

Kells, Laura
Independent scholar
Washington, DC

Keylor, William
Boston University
Boston, MA

Kist, Glenn J.
Rochester Institute of Technology
Rochester, NY

Klunder, Willard C.
Wichita State University
Wichita, KA

Knapp, Eric W.
United States Air Force Academy
Colorado Springs, CO

Knapp, Michael J.
Independent scholar
Middlebury, VT

Knock, Thomas J.
Southern Methodist University
Dallas, TX

Kostic, Jeffry
Independent scholar
Wayne, NJ

Kraft, Barbara S.
Independent scholar
Washington, DC

La Forte, Robert S.
University of North Texas
Denton, TX

Lauderbaugh, George M.
U.S. Air Force Air University
Maxwell Air Force Base, AL

Laurie, Clayton D.
U.S. Army Center of Military History
Washington, DC

Lee, David D.
Western Kentucky University
Bolling Green, KY

Levering, Ralph B.
Davidson College
Davidson, NC

Lindley, John M.
West Publishing Co.
St. Paul, MN

Little, John E.
Independent scholar
Princeton, NJ

Long, John W.
Rider University
Lawrenceville, NJ

Lowry, Bullitt
University of North Texas
Denton, TX

McBride, William M.
James Madison University
Harrisonburg, VA

McCaffrey, James
University of Houston-Downtown Campus
Houston, TX

McCallum, Jack
Independent scholar
Fort Worth, TX

McCarthy, Joseph M.
Suffolk University
Boston, MA

McCarthy, Michael J.
Marshall University
Huntington, WV

McCartin, Joseph
State University of New York
Geneseo, NY

McDevitt, Theresa
Indiana University of Pennsylvania
Indiana, PA

McEwen, John M.
Brock University
Canada

MacGregor, David
Rochester Institute of Technology
Rochester, NY

McKinley, Edward H.
Asbury College
Wilmore, KY

Maddox, Robert J.
Pennsylvania State University
University Park, PA

Mangusso, Mary Childers
University of Alaska
Fairbanks, AK

Marshall, R. J.
North Carolina Museum of History
Raleigh, NC

Mathes, William L.
Seton Hall University
South Orange, NJ

Mayrhause, Richard T. von
Slippery Rock University
Slippery Rock, PA

Melton, Buckner F. Jr.
Independent scholar
Burlington, NC

Melton, Carol Kingsland Willcox
Elon College
Elon College, NC

Messimer, Dwight R.
Independent scholar
Mountain View, CA

Miller, J. Michael
Senior Archivist
Marine Corps University Archives
Quantico, VA

Miller, Jennifer
State University of New York
Binghamton, NY

Mjagkij, Nina
Ball State University
Muncie, IN

Molloy, Scott
University of Rhode Island
Kingston, RI

Moore, David W.
Loyola University of New Orleans
New Orleans, LA

Morse, Walter T.
Independent scholar
Sarasota, FL

Murphy, Justin D.
Howard Payne University
Brownwood, TX

Murrell, Robert T.
80th Division Veterans Association
Pittsburgh, PA

Nash, Betsy
Stennis Oral History Project
Mississippi State University
Mississippi State, MS

Nash, Gerald D.
University of New Mexico
Albuquerque, NM

Nash, Lee
Independent scholar
Banbury, England

Nazzaro, Pellegrino
Rochester Institute of Technology
Rochester, NY

Nelson, John T.
U.S. Army War College
Carlisle Barracks
Carlisle, PA

Neu, Charles E.
Brown University
Providence, RI

Nichols, Gary
The Citadel
Charleston, SC

Nielson, Jonathan M.
El Camino Community College District
Torrance, CA

Nolt, James H.
Center for International Affairs
Harvard University
Cambridge, MA

Norris, Vincent
Pennsylvania State University (emeritus)
University Park, PA

Ohl, John K.
Mesa Community College
Mesa, AZ

Olitzky, Kerry M.
Hebrew Union College
Jewish Institute of Religion
New York, NY

Peterson, Barbara Bennett
University of Hawaii
Honolulu, HI

Pierard, Cynthia K.
University of Kansas, Library
Lawrence, KA

Pierard, Richard V.
Indiana State University
Terre Haute, IN

Pisano, Dominick A.
National Air & Space Museum
Smithsonian Institution
Washington, DC

Pohl, James W.
Southwest Texas State University
San Marcos, TX

Ramsey, Robert D. III
Independent scholar
Leavenworth, KS

Recken, Stephen L.
University of Arksansas
Little Rock, AR

Resh, Richard W.
University of Missouri
St. Louis, MO

Richards, Miles S.
University of South Carolina
Columbia, SC

Robrock, David
James R. Dickinson Library
University of Nevada
Las Vegas, NV

Rohfeld, Rae Wahl
Florida International University
Miami, FL

Roshwald, Aviel
Georgetown University
Washington, DC

Roth, Brenda
U.S. Air Force Institute of Technology
Patterson Air Force Base
Wright, OH

Roth, Irvin M.
Foothill-DeAnza Community College (emeritus)
Los Altos Hills, CA

Saltmarsh, John
Northeastern University
Boston, MA

Samerdyke, Michael
Clinch Valley College of the University
of Virginia
Wise, VA

Schnakenberg, Jeffrey D.
Independent scholar
Richmond, VA

Scheller, Robert J.
Naval Historical Center
Washington, DC

Sharp, Sarah
Rosemont College
Rosemont, PA

Sheehy, Edward J.
LaSalle University
Philadelphia, PA

Shilcutt, Tracy
Museums of Abilene at the Grace Cultural
    Center
Abilene, TX

Shirley, Noel
Independent scholar
San Jose, CA

Shorrock, William
Cleveland State University
Cleveland, OH

Shrader, Charles R.
Independent scholar
Carlisle, PA

Sondhaus, Lawrence
University of Indianapolis
Indianapolis, IN

Speed, Richard B.
California State University at Hayward
Hayward, CA

Steele, Elizabeth
Clinch Valley College of the University of
    Virginia
Wise, VA

Steinson, Barbara J.
DePauw University
Greencastle, IN

Stokes, Carol E.
U.S. Army Signal Corps
Fort Gordon, GA

Streckfuss, James
Independent scholar
Cincinnati, OH

Tepe, Dawn A.
Abilene Christian University
Abilene, TX

Theoharis, Athan
Marquette University
Milwaukee, WI

Thomas, Donna Gates
Cazenovia College
Cazenovia, NY

Thompson, Gregory L.
Florida State University
Tallahassee, FL

Tischler, Barbara L.
Columbia University
New York, NY

Toerpe, Kathleen
Loyola University of Chicago
Chicago, IL

Toguchi, Michael
United States Military Academy
West Point, NY

Towne, Ruth M.
Northeast Missouri State University (emeritus)
Kirksville, MO

Trask, David F.
Independent scholar
Washington, DC

Travers, T.H.E.
University of Calgary
Calgary, Canada

Tull, Charles
Indiana University
South Bend, IN

Vander Meulen, Jacob
Dalhausie University
Nova Scotia, Canada

Vandiver, Frank E.
Mosher Institute for Defense Studies
Texas A & M University
College Station, TX

Venzon, A.C.
Independent scholar
Darnestown, MD

Victory, James
Illinois Mathematics & Science Academy
Aurora, IL

Votaw, John F.
Cantigny First Division Foundation
Wheaton, IL

Wadleigh, John R.
Independent scholar
Newport, RI

Walz, Ralph C.
Seton Hall University
South Orange, NJ

Weizhong Lee
Brigham Young University
Provo, UT

Westheider, James E.
Northern Kentucky University
Highland Heights, KY

Weyant, Jane
Georgia Institute of Technology
Atlanta, GA

White, Lonnie
University of Memphis (emeritus)
Memphis, TN

Williams, Jeffrey
Northern Kentucky University
Highland Heights, KY

Williams, Vernon
Abilene Christian University
Abilene, TX

Williams, William
U.S. Air Force Academy
Colorado Springs, CO

Wilson, Dale E.
Valley Forge Military Academy
Valley Forge, PA

Witcover, Jules
Baltimore *Sun*
Baltimore, MD

Wood, Laura Matysek
Tarrant County Junior College
Northwest campus
Fort Worth, TX

Woodman, Harry
Independent scholar
London, England

Worthington, Daniel E.
University of Illinois
Urbana, IL

Wright, Steven
Independent scholar
Cincinnati, OH

Yang, Jennifer
Independent scholar
Pasadena, CA

Yerxa, Donald A.
Eastern Nazarene College
Quincy, MA

Young, Arthur P.
Northern Illinois University Library
Chicago, IL

Zehnder, R.D.
Augsburg College
Minneapolis, MN

Zeiger, Susan
Regis College
Weston, MA

Zimmerman, Phyllis
Ball State University
Muncie, IN

Abbeville Conference

The first move toward a unified Allied command in the First World War came on March 26, 1918, in Doullens, France, when the British and French governments charged Gen. Ferdinand Foch with the coordination of the two armies on the Western Front. A week later, at Beauvais, Foch was entrusted with the strategic direction of military operations, and on April 14, he was appointed commander-in-chief of the Allied armies in France.

At Abbeville, on May 1 and 2, the Supreme War Council met to review the decisions of Doullens and Beauvais in light of new developments. Italy's premier, Vittorio Orlando, had raised the question of Foch's position with regard to the Italian Army, while the arrival of units of the American Army demanded agreement on their deployment and their place in the Allied chain of command.

Present at the conference were the prime minister of Great Britain, David Lloyd George, the premier of France, Georges Clemenceau, and the premier of Italy, Vittorio Orlando. Representing the United States was Arthur H. Frazier, first secretary of the American embassy in Paris, and also representing Great Britain were Lord Milner, the British war minister, and Sir Maurice Hankey, the secretary of the British War Cabinet. In addition, some twenty-four naval and military officers attended, including General Foch and the commanders-in-chief of the British, French, and American armies.

The council was mainly occupied with discussions about the incorporation of the American troops who were arriving in France in increasing numbers. On May 1, there were seven American divisions and parts of two others, in all about 430,000 men on French soil. Because of the terrible losses of March and April, both the French and British wanted the Americans to be brigaded by battalions or smaller units into existing Allied formations, thus filling the ranks of their armies, which had been decimated by the German spring offensive.

A heated debate followed because of the demands made by the American commander-in-chief, Maj. Gen. John J. Pershing. Pershing insisted on an independent U.S. army under its own commander and its own flag. The Europeans worried that the Americans would not be ready in time and that the war would be lost before they were an effective fighting force. But Pershing had great faith in his soldiers and the courage of his convictions. He was willing to allow his allies to fall back, believing he could recover any lost territory and defeat the Germans unaided if necessary. Described by both Hankey and Haig in their works as persistent in his demands for American forces in Europe, Pershing to make his points pounded the table and would not settle for anything less than an American army fighting under the American flag with American commanders.

Finally, it was agreed that the program of transporting infantry and engineer troops, without their heavy equipment, should be continued through June. The British government would furnish the transportation necessary with the understanding that the first contingent would go to the British for training and service and that troops arriving in June would be allocated as Pershing might determine.

The Supreme War Council also formally resolved that in order to carry the war to a successful conclusion, an American army be formed as early as possible under its own commander and under its own flag. General Pershing had won his first battle.

The council passed several additional resolutions. In view of the powers conferred on Foch, it dissolved the Executive War Board. It arranged for the immediate withdrawal of some British troops from Salonika, agreed to urge the Italian government to accept arrangements for an increase of naval forces in the Aegean, approved the plans for the transport of Czech troops from Russia, and, finally, extended Foch's power of coordination to the Italian front.

Irvin M. Roth

See also BEAUVAIS AGREEMENT; CZECH LEGION; FOCH, FERDINAND; PERSHING, JOHN JOSEPH; SUPREME WAR COUNCIL

Bibliography

Edmonds, BGen. Sir James. *History of the Great War, Military Operations France and Belgium 1918*. Vol. 3. London: Macmillan, 1939.

Haig, F.M. *The Private Papers of Douglas Haig 1914–1919*, ed. by Robert Blake. London: Eyre and Spottiswoode, 1952.

Hankey, Sir Maurice. *The Supreme Command 1914–1918*. 2 vols. London: Allen and Unwin, 1961.

Lloyd George, David. *War Memoirs*. 2 vols. London: Odhams Press, 1942.

Addams, Jane (1860–1935)

The noted social worker and pacifist Jane Addams was born on Sept. 6, 1860, in the small town of Cedarville, Illinois. Growing up, she was profoundly influenced by her idealistic yet practical father. One of the first generation of American women to attend college, Addams graduated in 1881, the valedictorian of her class at Rockland Seminary (now Rockford College). In the 1880s, she traveled to Europe. In London, she was greatly impressed by the work at Toynbee Hall, the pioneering settlement house founded in 1884, and on her return to Chicago established in 1889 Hull House, which was to become America's best-known settlement house.

Influenced by her experiences in the immigrant and working-class neighborhood in Chicago where she worked and lived and by her reading of Tolstoy, Addams became a pacifist. After the Spanish-American War she joined the Anti-Imperialist League in Chicago and began to seek what she called "a moral substitute for war." Addams believed that in the new industrial age, with the growth of democracy and woman suffrage, war would be impossible.

The outbreak of war in 1914 was a severe blow to her theories of peace and progress. Undaunted, in January 1915, she called a conference of women's organizations, which adopted a Peace Platform and from which was formed the Woman's Peace Party. Addams, one of the most famous and respected women in the United States due to her work at Hull House, chaired the conference and was made chairman of the new party. She called for "continuous mediation," for a convention of neutral nations to establish peace, and for President Woodrow Wilson to initiate a mediation conference. A few months later she chaired an International Congress of Women. The congress called for liberal peace terms, the establishment of a permanent international court, no transfer of territory without the consent of the people, and the representation of women in both national and international political life. Addams was chosen as a delegate to present these resolutions both to belligerent and neutral nations and to the President of the United States, which she did. Her efforts brought mixed reviews. Some congratulated her, others criticized her participation in the "peace at any price" group; most seemed to think she was well meaning but foolish. This general tolerance of Addams's naivete turned to denunciation following a remark she made before a Church Peace Union about soldiers being given drink or stimulants to steel them to the horrible task of the bayonet charge.

Disturbed by the vilification and frustrated by her critics, Addams became more militant in her pacifism. Henry Ford had purchased a "peace ship" to carry delegates of neutral nations to a conference in Stockholm to promote mediation. Though it was ridiculed in the press, Jane Addams, who had been asked to participate, was reluctant to pass up even the slimmest opportunity to promote peace. She consented to go but was too ill to make the December 1915 voyage. The adventure was a debacle, and Addams's name was associated with it. That, added to the "drugged soldiers" comment, and her testimony before Congress in January 1916 against preparedness, provoked further criticism of Addams for wrongheadedness and operating out of her depth.

She supported Wilson for reelection in 1916 as the peace candidate and took heart in his January 1917 "Peace Without Victory" speech. However, she despaired over the break in diplomatic relations with Germany in February and the declaration of war in April 1917. Despite the fact that many in the peace movement now supported the President, Addams remained a pacifist, convinced that fighting and bloodshed solved nothing. The attacks on her grew more heated and personal; her patriotism was questioned, she was called "unAmerican," a "traitor." Her solution was to work for Herbert Hoover's Food Administration. In this way she could be "patriotic," help the starving, and return to her earlier ideas of women as providers and protectors. She recorded her wartime experiences and her philosophy of pacifism in her book, *Peace and Bread in Time of War* (1922).

Promoting food rather than peace helped rehabilitate her reputation, but not everyone forgave or forgot. War's end brought not only peace but also the Red Scare, and pacifists, Jane Addams among them, were seen as Bolsheviks and dangerous radicals. Meanwhile Addams worked to rebuild the women's peace movement. The result, in 1919, was the Women's International League for Peace and Freedom, which elected her president, a post she filled until ill health forced her to resign in 1929.

Even winning the Nobel Peace Prize in 1931, which she shared with the pro-war Nicholas Murray Butler, did not eliminate the attacks by the self-anointed keepers of the patriotic flame. And Jane Addams would never again, in her lifetime, regain the public stature and respect she had enjoyed before World War I. Jane Addams died in Chicago on May 21, 1935.

David W. Moore

See also FORD PEACE EXPEDITION; WOMAN'S PEACE PARTY

Bibliography
Davis, Allen F. *American Heroine: The Life and Legend of Jane Addams*. New York: Oxford University Press, 1973.
Farrell, John C. *Beloved Lady: A History of Jane Addams' Ideas on Reform and Peace*. Baltimore: Johns Hopkins University Press, 1967.
Linn, James W. *Jane Addams, A Biography*. New York: Appleton-Century, 1935.

A

Aerial Warfare

When President Woodrow Wilson led the United States into war on April 6, 1917, what passed for the nation's air arm consisted of an uneven assortment of some 200 obsolete aircraft and approximately 1,200 officers and enlisted men. The actual number of rated pilots, observers, and aerial gunners within this organization was less than 60. More importantly, the American military establishment possessed no significant operational experience in aerial warfare, while the nascent domestic aviation industry was still far too small, inexperienced, and factious to match the production capacity of its European counterparts. Despite all of these handicaps, by studying the performance of their principal allies, coupled with a Herculean organizational effort, America's airmen were able to produce a timely and significant air effort.

In the spring of 1917, the United States embraced the idea of a great struggle in the air over Europe with enthusiasm and expectations for success that far outdistanced current military capabilities. To a large extent, this response represented some deeply rooted aspects of the nation's popular culture. In particular, a long fascination with the history, myths, and traditions of the American West found another outlet in the marvelous exploits of a new "cavalry of the clouds" or breed of "top guns."

More importantly, the European ground war had proven to be primarily a contest of mass—armies, artillery bombardments, and casualties. Even though the conduct of this conflict contained some striking similarities to the American Civil War, the indistinguishable massive struggle in the trenches that marked the "Great War" in Europe ran counter to the public's romantic attachment to the notion that rugged individualism was the only appropriate response to adversity. Since the ground war was seemingly bereft of individual heroes, it held little appeal for America in 1917. Air fighting, however, had just the opposite effect on the nation. The skies over Europe had already produced a host of rugged air fighters the public could easily identify with and admire. Among their ranks was the dashing American adventurer Raoul Lufberry, an ace in the famous Lafayette Escadrille.

Large manufacturing enterprises had also been a continuing source of national pride. With encouragement from its new European allies, the American public quickly came to believe that one of its most important contributions to the overall war effort would be the construction of a vast aerial force. The country that had given the world powered heavier-than-air flight was now prepared to demonstrate the strength of its industry.

Given the romantic appeal of air fighting and the need to create a gigantic new machine industry, it was not difficult for the daily press and a host of overzealous aeronautical supporters to drive the public's air war frenzy to new heights. Starting in April 1917 and continuing on into the summer of that year, the nation's daily newspapers and popular periodicals carried one sensational story after another about how the United States was going, in short order, to gain aerial dominance and darken the skies over Germany with thousands upon thousands of airplanes. Popular expectations for a devastating aerial campaign became increasingly unrealistic.

Journalists were not the only culpable actors in this national vanity pageant. Numerous military experts, civic leaders, and politicians made similar claims. Critical to the process of convincing the public that America was capable of producing 25,000 planes a year, sending 1,000 aviators across the Atlantic every month, or operating at least 10,000 airplanes in France before the end of the year were such notables as Secretary of War Newton D. Baker; Howard Coffin, chairman of the Aviation Commission of the Council of National Defense; RAdm. Robert Peary, executive director of the Aerial League of America; and Allen Hawley, president of the Aero Club of America. In addition, there was BGen. George O. Squier, commanding officer of the U.S. Army Signal Corps and a military expert of considerable standing on aviation matters, who predicted American airmen would sweep the German aviators from the sky—this before the first dollar had been spent to train, equip, or deploy an air force.

The upshot of all this uniformed air war hyperbole was disappointment and great outrage when, a year after war had been declared, the first few American air units entered combat in French airplanes. This led to widely publicized allegations of rampant corruption among the ranks of the Aircraft Production Board, the organization charged with overseeing the dis-

bursement of an unprecedented $640 million congressional appropriation for aviation equipment and supplies. The investigations that naturally followed, one of which was conducted by renowned sculptor Gutzon Borglum, produced much talk but little understanding of the problem inherent in creating a viable aviation industry capable of supporting a massive war effort from scratch.

American aircraft companies produced some 7,000 planes during the First World War, more than half of which were intended for frontline service. Less than 1,200 of these machines, however, actually made their way to training and combat units in Europe before the Armistice was signed on Nov. 11, 1918. In retrospect, it can be argued that this was a remarkable achievement for such an embryonic industry. Nevertheless, with actual production figures so far below public expectations the resulting shock to American pride cast a deep pall over the entire U.S. air war effort, especially the Liberty engine and the DH-4 "Liberty plane."

As the nation's industrial resources began to mobilize for war in 1917, the youth of America also responded enthusiastically to President Wilson's call "to make the world safe for democracy." Some of those rushing off to enlist in the Great War chose to take their chances in the air instead of the trenches. One of these young men was Henry W. Dwight, the eldest son of an upper-middle-class Brookline, Massachusetts, family. He interrupted his undergraduate studies at Williams College to join some classmates serving in the United States Naval Reserve. Bored by the prospect of spending the entire war guarding Boston harbor, Dwight managed to transfer to the United States Army Air Service on Aug. 23, 1917, in hope of seeing action in France. A year later he was serving as a pilot with the 12th Aero Squadron, one of the finest U.S. observation units operating over the American section of the Western Front.

Another young man, with an entirely different social background who flew for the United States in France was Walter S. Williams. A machinist with the Midvale Steel Company of Philadelphia, Williams enlisted in the United States Army Signal Corps on April 23, 1917. Much to his surprise, he was transferred six days later to its aviation section because of his noted mechanical aptitude for repairing automobile engines. After pilot training, Williams was assigned to the 27th Aero Squadron on

June 27, 1918. His unit would prove to be one of the best fighter outfits in the American Air Service. It was also home to Frank Luke, Jr., the famous "Arizona Balloon Buster."

Whether an urban industrial worker, Ivy League college student, or midwestern farmer, the air war usually began with an extensive course in flight fundamentals and theory at one of the eight United States Schools of Aeronautics. The next step for those successful aviation cadets was assignment to a primary flying field for actual flight training. Advanced training was most often taken overseas either at an American aviation instruction center, such as the large complex at Issoudon, France, or at one of the special aviation schools operated by British, French, and Italian airmen.

While America quickly moved to equip, arm, staff, and train an aviation force to darken the skies over Germany, the long awaited air war began when the U.S. 103d Aero Squadron commenced combat operations on Feb. 18, 1918. The squadron was primarily made up of American aviators who had served in either the Lafayette Escadrille or British Flying Corps. The 103d Squadron provided the expanding United States Air Service with an important source of experienced combat aviators and leaders. Many of the airmen initially assigned to this organization were later selected for command positions in other American squadrons. Moreover, the nation's first aerial victory of the Great War was gained by a pilot in the 103d. On March 11, 1918, 1st Lt. Paul F. Baer brought down a German single-seat aircraft near La Noblette, France. Baer survived the war with eight confirmed air victories.

The first air unit to reach Europe from the United States was the 1st Aero Squadron, which had seen some active service in the summer of 1916 with Gen. John J. Pershing's command in Mexico. Although the squadron had arrived in France by the first week of September 1917, it was not fit to fly over the lines until the middle of April 1918. Nevertheless, it represented the start of an American air buildup that continued to gain momentum right up to the last day of the war.

The spring and summer of 1918 was the key period of organizational growth for the United States Air Service as a combat force. It was then that the foundations for the 1st Pursuit Group, the 1st Day Bombardment Group, and the 1st Corps Observation Group were firmly established and tested. In the region around Toul, one of the few "quiet" areas on the Western Front, American airmen gained the initial experience and confidence which proved invaluable in subsequent air operations over Château-Thierry, St. Mihiel, and the Meuse-Argonne region.

The months spent in the countryside near the ancient fortress town was also a time of firsts for America's new air arm. The 94th Aero Squadron, the "Hat-in-the-Ring" Squadron, became the first of the newly arrived outfits to see combat and achieve an aerial victory. On April 14, Lts. Alan Winslow and Douglas Campbell, flying French Nieuport 28s, shot down two German airplanes in the vicinity of their airfields. On June 12, the 96th Aero Squadron completed its first bombing mission of the war in French Breguet 14–B1s with a successful raid on the railroad yard at Dommary-Baroncourt, an important transportation hub northwest of the city of Metz. Perhaps the most significant "first" achieved by the young Air Service occurred on August 7 when the 135th Aero Squadron made its initial operational sortie in American-built De Haviland-4 Liberty (DH-4) airplanes. A tangible expression of the nation's industrial commitment to air power, the flight provided the hard-pressed Wilson administration with a greatly needed success in military aviation. Before the Armistice brought an end to operations on the Western Front, a total of seven DH-4 squadrons served over the lines with the U.S. Air Service.

The relatively quiet period of adjustment enjoyed in the Toul sector came to an abrupt close at the end of June. America's airmen were hurriedly committed to severe air fighting in the Marne region when the German Army attempted to breach the Allied line at Château-Thierry. These first elements of the U.S. Air Service encountered a formidable concentration of enemy aircraft in the offensive phase of the battle and during the Allied counterattack in the second half of July. German fighter units were particularly effective. Battle-tested, well-trained, and flying the new Fokker D VII fast scout plane, they posed a deadly menace to the less-experienced Americans with their inferior equipment. However, with the employment of new tactics, such as tiered flights and mass employment of combat aircraft, coupled with an emerging core of skillful air warriors, such as Frank Luke, Jr., and Eddie Rickenbacker, the U.S. Air Service was able to hold its own by the end of July 1918.

A

Château-Thierry was an important turning point for America's airmen. Previously, the U.S. Air Service existed as an unstructured aggregation of small units, whose operational existence was marked by numerous exciting but unfocused individual exploits. Over the Marne, the nation's nascent air arm received a true baptism of fire and matured as a combat capable force. The organizational nucleus for American air power in the First World War was also firmly established during this battle with the creation of the 1st Air Brigade.

Most importantly, the need for inspirational and energetic leadership was met in the person of Col. William ("Billy") Lendrum Mitchell. Mitchell had obvious talent for directing air operations, and despite a volatile personality he rose out of the shifting milieu of senior American aviation officers in France to become the principal air leader at the front. He ultimately provided the air organization with managerial expertise, a sound grasp of aerial warfare, decisive leadership, and panache.

The Air Service entered a period of dramatic expansion in the month preceding the great offensive drives that the Allied high command planned to open before the summer of 1918 was over. Initially, Pershing's First Army would be committed to eliminating German positions in the St. Mihiel salient as a prelude to an important attack in the region extending between the Meuse River and Argonne Forest.

At St. Mihiel, Billy Mitchell lead a coalition force of more than 1,400 American, British, French, and Italian aircraft in a concerted campaign to dominate the skies over the battlefield and beyond. It was the largest single concentration of air power in the First World War; as a result, Mitchell emerged as one of the premier air commanders of the entire conflict. During the campaign, American pursuit pilots fought to gain air superiority and in the course of events established for themselves a formidable reputation as aggressive combatants. Meanwhile, the observation units adjusted artillery fire on enemy forward positions, provided timely intelligence, and maintained a vital command link with the advancing ground forces. American bomber squadrons were given the job of striking at the important lines of communications supporting German forces in the salient.

The ground campaign was successfully concluded in four days. For America's airmen, however, the start of the St. Mihiel offensive on Sept. 12, 1918, heralded an intense period of bitter aerial warfare. The pace of air operations continued to increase until the end of the war, interrupted by only a few weather-induced periods of inactivity.

During the remaining six weeks of the war, as the fighter units continued to gain air victories, the observation and bomber aircrews flew a never ending series of less-glamorous but critical photographic reconnaissance, artillery regulation, infantry contact, harassment, and interdiction missions. The four observation squadrons equipped with Liberty planes—the 8th, 50th, 135th, and 168th Aero squadrons—flew more than 3,000 sorties alone in support of the great offensives in the fall of 1918. The 11th, 20th, and 166th Aero squadrons engaged in bombardment work with American-built de Havilland-4s, completed sixty-two raids and dropped over seventy tons of high explosives on rear area targets in the same period. Unfortunately, the greatest misery encountered in this first American air war fell on the bomber crews. The two Liberty bombardment units had suffered a total of thirteen aircraft destroyed and twenty-six aircrew casualties in the two weeks that separated the openings of the St. Mihiel and Meuse-Argonne campaigns. The worst blows fell on September 18 when five out of seven planes from the 11th Squadron failed to return from a run on the Conflans railroad yard, and on September 26 when the 20th Aero Squadron suffered a similar fate over Dun-sur-Meuse.

In fact, the entire U.S. 1st Day Bombardment Group had been decimated by the end of September. The 96th Bombardment Squadron, now flying French-built Breguet 14–B2s, had sustained equally severe losses in personnel and equipment—fourteen planes and sixteen aviators. Given the grueling pace of operations and the maelstrom of steel encountered in the air over their targets, it was no surprise that morale within the group plummeted and a growing sense of fatalism set in. The fact that missions continued to be flown under such adverse conditions can only be credited to the courage of the surviving aircrews.

By the end of the war, Gen. Billy Mitchell had become chief of the Air Service Army Group, directing the operations of forty-five frontline squadrons in the zone of the advance. More than 1,300 American aviators had been committed to the air battle before hostilities came to an end on Nov. 11, 1918. Their proven combat record indicates a timely and significant contribution to the Allied war effort.

America's first air war has been parenthetically subordinated in military history to the massive aerial effort mounted by the United States in World War II, Korea, Vietnam, and, more recently, the Persian Gulf. If the statistics seem insignificant in comparison to these later air campaigns, it should be remembered that the effort generated in the First World War started from a state of abject unpreparedness when the United States entered the war in 1917. The building of an air arm capable of engaging in a protracted campaign in less than sixteen months was in itself a miracle. Indeed, this first experience in aerial warfare would provide the nation with a cadre of air leaders, men like Henry ("Hap") Arnold, Carl Spaatz, and Clayton Bissel, and valuable lessons in industrial mobilization for the next great air war.

Unquestionably, the First World War provided aviation with an inescapable allure. The pursuit pilot, in particular, captured the public's imagination with his dogfights above the dismal slaughter in the trenches, while the "ace" was seen as the embodiment of the medieval knight-errant. In the heady weeks that followed the Armistice, many foreign journalists, such as Elizabeth Frazier in the *Saturday Evening Post,* captivated their readers with the glamour of aerial combat. Killing the "Hun" in the air was romantically portrayed as a contest of acrobatic skill and daring. More importantly, America's troubled wartime aviation program at home had been redeemed by the valor and achievements of its aviators at the front. The popular magazines were filled with feature stories exploiting the public's intense interest in the war's aerial exploits.

Hollywood was quick to cash in on the public's postwar interest in aeronautics. Aviation war movies were among the most popular films in the 1920s, and motion picture companies were quick to use war heroes in their flying extravaganzas.

Publishing houses and popular magazines turned out an incredible mass of aviation works. Much of what was offered tended to be repetitive or vapid, but the reading public did not seem to tire of stories about aeronautics or winged warriors. Initially, the mainstay of the aeronautical genre was the war reminiscence. It was not long before there were literally hundreds of such personal narratives of the air war in print. Even the prestigious university presses churned out a spate of airmen's memoirs. Publishers were also quick to target young readers or "young moderns" who were perceived as being even more aeronautically attuned than their parents.

The subject of aeronautics was examined more seriously in numerous modern aviation primers and treatises on the importance of air power to national defense. These works found their greatest outlet in popular periodicals, although publishing houses were not shy about producing a book with a catchy title and a message, especially if the author was the outspoken and controversial BGen. William L. Mitchell. Indeed, in this realm of aeronautical writing few surpassed the prolific assistant chief of the Army Air Service and former leader of America's air combat effort in the First World War.

Michael Grumelli

See also AIRCRAFT; BORGLUM, GUTZON; LAFAYETTE ESCADRILLE; LIBERTY ENGINE; MITCHELL, WILLIAM LENDRUM; RICKENBACKER, EDWARD V.; UNITED STATES AIR SERVICE

Aircraft

Trenches, mud, massive artillery barrages, and no-man's-land are the common impressions conjured up when discussing the First World War. But as in most conflicts, the war produced great strides in military technology. Only eleven years before the cataclysmic events of August 1914, the Wright brothers made the first powered flight at Kitty Hawk, North Carolina. The advances in aeronautics since that time had not been substantial, but in the opening days of the First World War, the plane was still viewed as a novelty—little better than a captive balloon and an innovation that would scare the horses. That perception soon changed. In the course of the war, over 400 planes were developed by the Allies and Central Powers, always improving speed, maneuverability, and armament. Ironically, the United States, birthplace of manned flight, lagged behind the European powers in aircraft development and production. Although the Curtiss Aeroplane Company did develop its Model R series for war use, for much of the war the U.S. Air Service was forced to rely on French- or British-designed and built planes.

Bristol F2A and
F2B Fighter-Reconnaissance Biplane

Following the heavy losses of Royal Flying Corps (RFC) crews during the early part of the war, the British government changed its policy of relying exclusively on Royal Aircraft Factory machines and began to invite designs from private companies. As a result, Capt. Frank Barnwell (RFC) was given unpaid leave to rejoin the Bristol Company as chief designer. He set about designing a two-seat reconnaissance and artillery spotter to replace earlier aircraft.

Barnwell's first design, the Bristol R2A, was an equal-span biplane powered by a 120-hp Beardmore engine. Various features were incorporated to provide the crew with the best all-around view and defensive capability. The pilot was placed in front with the observer behind. When attacked, they would be back to back, close enough to communicate by hand signals, and each armed with a machine gun. The unusual location of the fuselage midway between the wings brought the upper wing near to the pilot's eye level, ensuring a good view forward and upward. This low position of the top wing also gave the observer a wide field of fire forward, and the top of the fin was designed to be low to ensure a clear field of fire to the rear. During the early months of 1916, the design was modified as more powerful engines became available, culminating in the first flight of the prototype F2A in September. Barnwell had changed the label R to F to indicate his revised concept of the aircraft as a fighter. Deliveries of the F2A began in late 1916.

In February 1917, No. 48 Squadron began replacing its BE12 aircraft with the F2A, and after training with the new type, the squadron went to France in March 1917 to take part in the forthcoming Battle of Arras. On the morning of April 5, six F2As led by Capt. W.L. Robinson, left Bellevue Airfield, France, on their first operational patrol. Only two returned. The patrol was attacked by five Albatross D IIIs led by the legendary Baron Manfred von Richthofen, and four Bristols were shot down. Much has been written since World War I concerning this disastrous debut of the new fighter, condemning the tactics and the fighting spirit of the crews. However, other patrols that day with the same plane encountered enemy aircraft and returned to base without loss. Also during the weeks that followed, the old two-seat defensive tactics were changed, and the Bristol was flown more like a single-seat fighter with the front gun in use as the main weapon of attack. The aircraft became so successful that in July 1917 the British War Office ordered 800 more aircraft to reequip all fighter-reconnaissance squadrons. These aircraft were the F2B, with more improvements, including the more powerful 275-hp Rolls-Royce Falcon III. By the spring of 1918, it was said that German fighters would not take on more than two Bristols at a time.

Compared to single-seat fighters of its day, the Bristol was huge. Although some pilots described it as being heavy on the controls, it was very maneuverable and could be looped, spun, and even flick-rolled. It could also dive faster than any other fighter on the Western Front. Capt. J.H. Hedley, flying as an observer with No. 20 Squadron, would certainly have testified to the aircraft's maneuverability. During an attack by enemy fighters his pilot threw the aircraft into a steep dive. So violent was this evasive action that Hedley was thrown out of the cockpit. As the pilot recovered the aircraft to level flight, he felt a thump on the rear fuselage. Captain Hedley had had the amazing luck to land back on the aircraft, and there he stayed, clinging on, until the plane was landed.

The F2B equipped six Western Front squadrons. Two aircraft were allocated to transport Lawrence of Arabia between General Allenby's headquarters and the Arab force. Four Home Defense squadrons were also equipped with Bristols. In all, just over 3,000 aircraft were delivered to the British forces. Plans were made for large-scale production in the United States. Toward the end of 1917, the task was undertaken of redesigning the F2B to accept the Liberty-12 engine, against advice that it was unsuitable and too heavy. Final results were disastrous. A contract with Curtiss was canceled following a series of crashes caused by structural failure. Of the 2,000 aircraft ordered from the American company, only 27 were built. By contrast, such was the success of the Rolls-Royce-powered F2B that it became one of the most famous fighters of its day, remaining in RAF service long after the war, finally retiring in 1932.

Lee Nash

Bibliography

Barnes, C.H. *Bristol Aircraft Since 1910.* London: Putnam, 1964.

Robertson, Bruce. *British Military Aircraft Serials 1912–1963*. London: Ian Allan, 1964.

Curtiss Floatplanes—Model R

Early in 1915 the Curtiss Aeroplane Company developed a larger, more advanced aircraft than its earlier J and N models that was to become the Model R used by American and British services during World War I. After the war it would be further developed through the R-9 model.

The original Model R was an observation aircraft with a pilot and an observer. Designed with a speed of 86 mph and a six- to seven-hour endurance, it was essentially an enlarged version of the Curtiss Model N. Tested as both a landplane and single-float seaplane, it had equal span, staggered wings, no dihedral, and a single, long cockpit with the pilot in the rear seat.

The Model R was sold to both the United States Army and Navy from 1915 to the end of the war and was also flown by Britain's Royal Flying Corps. By the end of 1915, Curtiss had refined the plane extensively, producing the Model R-2. The modified version included two separate cockpits, redesigned landing gear, unequal wing spans, ailerons in the upper wing and a dihedral, and a nose radiator in the production models. In August, 1915, Curtiss pilot Raymond V. Morris, along with three passengers, set an American altitude record of 8,105 feet in an R-2A aircraft. Twelve planes were sold to the United States Army and 100 to the Royal Flying Corps equipped with 200-hp Sunbeam Arab II engines.

When the United States Navy expressed an interest in the model, Curtiss designed a seaplane version—the R-3. It had twin floats and longer wings to carry the weight of these floats. Two R-3s were delivered to the navy in 1916. Since the navy was not entirely satisfied with it, Curtiss designed the R-6 in 1917. This differed from the R-3 in having a more powerful 200-hp V-2-3 engine and three degrees of dihedral on the outer wing panels. It cost $15,200 per plane.

Forty R-6s were converted to R-6L configuration in 1918 to serve as the U.S. Navy's first torpedo bombers. These had 360-hp low-compression Liberty engines, a maximum speed of 100 mph, 565-mile range with pilot and observer, and carried one 1,026-pound torpedo. R-6Ls served the United States Navy until 1926.

Operationally, the R-6 was the first American-built aircraft to serve United States forces overseas in World War I. On Jan. 9, 1918, the U.S. Marine Corps First Aeronautic Company embarked from Philadelphia for the Azores Islands equipped with ten R-6s and two N-9s. Later it received six HS-2L flying boats. The company's mission was patrolling the waters surrounding the Azores and antisubmarine warfare.

The Curtiss Model R with its serial modifications provided a number of aviation milestones, including the R-2A's altitude record in 1915 and being the first American-built aircraft to see service overseas in World War I for both the United States Army and Navy and the Allies.

Model N-9

The Curtiss N-9 (Model N, production model #9) provided realistic training to the hundreds of U.S. Navy and Marine Corps student pilots and became the primary seaplane trainer of World War I and the early 1920s.

Curtiss provided a JN-4B "Jenny" model to the navy, which after modifications became the N-9. Equipped with a 100-hp Curtiss OX-6 150-hp Hispano-Suiza (N-9H) engine, the N-9 had a single centerline float and smaller wingtip floats, five-foot wing extensions on each side of the fuselage, a lengthened center fuselage section, and an enlarged vertical fin. These modifications changed its original JN-4B appearance considerably. With two pilots aboard, the N-9C had a maximum speed of 70 mph and a range of 200 miles. A total of 560 N-9s were built, and many remained in U.S. Army and Navy service until 1927.

On May 23, 1917, the United States Joint Technical Board on Aircraft recommended the N-9 and R-6 aircraft as the most satisfactory aircraft for training and squadron use. With this official approval, N-9s went into service in 1917 as primary trainers for U.S. Navy and Marine Corps units.

N-9 aircraft played a prominent role in two aviation developments that had significance for the future. The first was as a remote-controlled "flying bomb." On May 17, 1917, Elmer and Lawrence Sperry met with Secretary of the Navy Josephus Daniels to discuss the possibility of converting an N-9 into what is called today a remote-piloted vehicle (RPV). It was decided to proceed with this project using five N-9 aircraft and six sets of Sperry automatic gear. In mid-November thirty–mile test flights were made with an error in range of about two miles. It was planned to have the N-9 carry 1,000 pounds of explosive to a range of fifty miles at 90 mph. However, the complex engineering problems encountered were not resolved, and the project never reached the production stage.

The second role for the N-9 lay in aviation safety and occurred fortuitously on Feb. 13, 1917. Maj. Francis T. Evans claimed that he could "loop" a tractor-type seaplane such as the N-9. This had never been accomplished before. At Pensacola, Florida, he attempted this maneuver while flying an N-9 at 3,500 feet. The maneuver failed, the aircraft stalled, and went into a spin. Previous to this no American aviator had worked out a procedure for recovering from a spin, although several had died in the attempt to do so. Evans instinctively pushed his control column forward to gain speed while controlling the spinning motion with the rudder. This procedure recovered the N-9 from the spin, and Evans went on to loop the aircraft that day. He thus solved a major aviation safety problem and was sent on a tour of military air bases to teach his method to fellow aviators. On June 10, 1936, Evans received the Distinguished Flying Cross for his solution.

The N-9 also saw limited combat service with the 1st Marine Aeronautic Company when on Jan. 9, 1918, ten Curtiss R-6s and two N-9s left Philadelphia for deployment in the Azores. The two aircraft were N-9Hs with a rear-cockpit machine gun added for antisubmarine warfare missions.

The major significance of the N-9 lies in its service as a primary trainer for U.S. Navy and Marine Corps pilots. It also played a key role in the early development of remote-piloted vehicles, a development that is usually attributed to World War II research and development. Lastly, the N-9 was the aircraft inadvertently used to solve the problem of spin recovery, which has saved the lives of countless aviators ever since. These three developments alone are sufficient to ensure this aircraft a place in aviation history.

Harold N. Boyer

See also LIBERTY ENGINE

Bibliography

Bowers, Peter M. *Curtiss Aircraft, 1907–1947.* London: Putnam, 1979.

Johnson, Edward C. *Marine Corps Aviation: The Early Years, 1912–1940.* Washington, DC: Government Printing Office, 1977.

Van Wyen, Adrian O. *Naval Aviation in World War One.* Washington, DC: Government Printing Office, 1969.

de Havilland 4

The de Havilland 4—better known in Britain as the D.H. 4—was designed in 1916 by Geoffrey de Havilland in direct response to a request by the British government for an airplane with reconnaissance and day bombing capabilities. It became one of the most successful planes of World War I and is claimed by some to have been without peer among all the aircraft of its type flown in the Great War. Large-scale production took place in both Great Britain and the United States. It was the only airplane produced in the United States to be manufactured in quantity and to see combat in the war. The D.H. 4 was also used extensively in postwar aviation on both sides of the Atlantic.

The Aircraft Manufacturing Company (Airco), where de Havilland was employed, initiated design work immediately upon receipt of the government request, and completed the prototype D.H. 4 by the summer of 1916. Its maiden flight took place at Hendon in August, with official trials conducted at the Central Flying School from September 21 to October 12. From the beginning, the D.H. 4 could be flown with ease by a novice pilot. It had excellent stability in all axes, was light on the controls, comfortable to fly, and easy to land. Moreover, when first introduced into combat, the D.H. 4 surpassed all aircraft in its class with a superior rate of climb and top speed, even outperforming many scout planes, though this advantage declined as other, more advanced aircraft entered service.

The first D.H. 4s reached France with the No. 55 Squadron, Royal Flying Corps (RFC) on March 6, 1917, and they went into combat for the first time in a bombing attack at Valenciennes on April 6. Ultimately, thirty-one squadrons of the RFC, Royal Air Force (RAF), and the Royal Naval Air Service (RNAS) flew the plane in various missions, which included day bombing, photographic reconnaissance, gunnery spotting, plus antizeppelin and antisubmarine warfare. It performed well in each of these missions. Used in great numbers on the Western Front, the D.H. 4 also saw service in

Italy, Russia, Macedonia, the Aegean Sea region, Palestine, and Mesopotamia. A total of 1,449 British-built D.H. 4s were produced in 1917 and 1918 by several manufacturers.

With America's entry into the war, the Bolling Mission, sent to Europe to select appropriate aircraft designs for manufacture in the United States, chose the D.H. 4 among others. The U.S. government ordered the D.H. 4—known in America as the DH-4, or Liberty plane—into production on Oct. 18, 1917. Three firms, the Dayton-Wright Company of Dayton, Ohio, the Fisher Body Division of General Motors at Cleveland, Ohio, and the Standard Aircraft Corporation of Elizabeth, New Jersey, manufactured the Liberty plane in America.

The first of the American-produced aircraft reached France in May 1918. By July, American DH-4s began arriving in quantity, and a month later the 135th Aero Squadron flew them over the front for the first time. They remained in continual service as day bombers and, more successfully, as observation aircraft until the Armistice.

Figures for the total number of American Liberty planes produced from February to November 1918 vary, with the most authoritative source listing 4,151 units. Close to 1,000 ultimately entered frontline service. Between July 1918 and May 1919, the 11th, 20th, 96th, 100th, 155th (night), 163d, and 166th Bombardment squadrons, and the 8th, 50th, 85th, 135th, 168th, 278th and 354th Observation squadrons of the U.S. Army Air Service were equipped at one time or another with Liberty planes. They were also flown in Belgium by four squadrons of a combined U.S. Navy-Marine Corps Northern Bombing Group.

Regretfully, the Liberty plane was obsolete by 1918 standards. One design weakness, initially disregarded, had become a lethal problem and required a significant modification. It was the unprotected gasoline tank, located between the two cockpits. Not only did it place the pilot and observer too far apart for adequate communication, but it also became a target for every attacking enemy aircraft. The problem was exacerbated by a pressure feed system that caused the tank to explode when hit by a bullet. Moreover, the tank tended to break loose in a crash landing, crushing the pilot against the engine. Critics in the United States vilified the DH-4 as a "flaming coffin" and ultimately embroiled the airplane in a postwar controversy that resulted in an investigation of the entire American aviation industry. Much of the controversy was caused by unrealistic production estimates combined with unavoidable delays in the manufacturing process.

In the summer of 1918, a modified Liberty plane, the DH-4A, appeared. Outwardly, it was indistinguishable from the original model but incorporated a number of internal changes, including a revised fuel system. A second revised model, the DH-4B, was introduced in October 1918 and featured several major improvements in the original design. Most significantly, the front cockpit and fuel tank exchanged places, improving not only communications between pilot and observer, but also pilot safety and visibility. Additionally, the landing gear was moved slightly forward, thus reducing the tendency of the aircraft to nose over on landings. The signing of the Armistice on November 11 prevented the DH-4B from entering combat, but its career as a civil aircraft was about to begin. Many original Liberty planes were subsequently revised to the DH-4B configuration and were used in a variety of civil and military roles. It is perhaps best known as a mail plane for the U.S. Post Office. Later revisions allowed the DH-4 to continue in civil and military service long after it had become almost hopelessly obsolete, surviving in the U.S. Army Air Corps until 1932.

Louis Eltscher

See also BOLLING MISSION

Bibliography
Boyne, Walter J. *De Havilland DH4: From Flying Coffin to Living Legend.* Washington, DC: Smithsonian Institution Press, 1984.

Hudson, James T. *Hostile Skies: A Combat History of American Air Service in World War I.* Syracuse, NY: Syracuse University Press, 1968.

HS-2-L Flying Boat

With their unique ability to operate from the surface of the ocean, the Curtiss HS-2-L flying boats were among the first American aircraft to undertake missions both overseas and along the East Coast of the United States during the First World War. This ability led to a multimission capability consisting of patrol, search, and rescue (SARR) and antisubmarine (ASW)warfare.

Originally a Curtiss-designed, twin-engined flying boat designated H-14, the HS-2-L (hydroplane, single-power plant, Liberty engine) resulted from the decision to redesign the H-14 as a single-engined, pushed-type flying boat known as the HS-1. With the United States entry into the war, the U.S. Navy placed orders for a modified version of the HS-1, which was designated HS-2-L. Modifications included increased wing span, enlarged vertical tail, and enlarged rudder. By the standards of the day, performance of the HS-2-L was respectable. With a three-man crew, maximum speed was 82.5 mph, patrol endurance was four and a half hours, and armament consisted of one .303-caliber Lewis gun and two 230-pound bombs or depth charges to being carried on missions.

With an average unit cost of $30,000, a total of 1,092 HS flying boats were produced by Curtiss and other licensed subcontractors, with the majority of models being the HS-2-L. They served throughout United States involvement in the First World War and continued in naval service until 1928. Civilian use in both the United States and Canada continued well past 1928.

The first HS flying boat assigned to naval service was delivered on March 16, 1918, to the Miami, Florida, Naval Air Station for coastal patrol missions. The HS-2-L was the first American-built aircraft sent overseas during the war. On May 25, 1918, the first six of 182 HS-type flying boats were placed aboard the USS *Houston* for shipment to American naval aviation units in France. They arrived at Naval Air Station Pauillac, and the first flight took place on June 13. Eventually replacing French flying boats then in service with American units, the HS-2-L was operated out of naval air stations in Ireland, Italy, and France and by the Marine Corps units based at Ponta Delgada, the Azores. By Nov. 11, 1918, there were twenty-seven aviation bases overseas and twelve bases in the United States supporting HS-2-L flying-boat operations.

Flying boats were an integral part of the prosecution of the war at sea. Their primary mission was antisubmarine warfare, which at this time was in its infancy both in terms of aviation and surface warships. HS-2-L flying boats possessed sufficient speed and endurance to patrol large expanses of ocean, but 180-pound depth charges originally carried for destruction of surfaced or partially submerged submarines were inadequate, so a 230-pound

depth charge was developed. One of the reasons for the modification of the HS-1 to the HS-2-L was its inability to carry the heavier charges.

Failure to detonate was a common ordnance problem as evidenced by an attack on the German *U-156* on July 21, 1918, off Cape Cod. The submarine was surfaced when the HS-2-L attacked it from an altitude of 400 feet. It was struck by a bomb that failed to detonate. The HS-2-L was joined by an R-9 aircraft, which bombed the submarine from 500 feet. This bomb too failed to detonate. *U-156* returned fire at the aircraft and submerged unscathed.

No enemy submarines are known to have been sunk as a result of attacks by HS-2-L flying boats. The United States Naval Air Service recorded thirty attacks on submarines during the war with ten considered to have been partially successful. Cooperation between aircraft and ships was essential to the successful prosecution of the campaign against submarines. HS-2-L flying boats laid the groundwork for this type of cooperation in spite of primitive radio communication equipment and the widespread use of messenger pigeons for aircraft-to-shore communication.

The significance of the HS-2-L lies in its effect on submarines and in aircraft-warship cooperation in the prosecution of attacks. While the plane was not responsible for destruction of U-boats, its deterrent role should not be underestimated. More significantly, this flying boat presaged the highly successful flying-boat operations conducted in World War II by American Catalina, Mariner, and British Sunderland flying boats.

Harold N. Boyer

Bibliography

Bowers, Peter M. *Curtiss Aircraft, 1907–1947*. London: Putnam, 1979.

Johnson, Edward C. *Marine Corps Aviation: The Early Years, 1912–1940*. Washington, DC: Government Printing Office, 1977.

Knott, Richard C. *The American Flying Boat: An Illustrated History*. Annapolis, MD: Naval Institute Press, 1979.

Roseberry, C.R. *Glenn Curtiss: Pioneer of Flight*. Syracuse, NY: Syracuse University Press, 1991.

Van Wyen, Adrien O. *Naval Aviation in World War One*. Washington, DC: Government Printing Office, 1969.

Nieuport 28

The French Nieuport 28 series followed the same basic design as its predecessors—a wire-braced wood fuselage with fabric covering, wood frame wings and tail, and aluminum tube undercarriage. Yet this new Nieuport radically differed from the familiar line of sesquiplane V-strutters comprising its ancestry.

A prototype underwent trials in June 1917. After some modification, there were further tests of additional prototypes during the second week of November. At least two of these had full dihedrals. They were compared to a prototype having the upper wing raised with no dihedral and to a prototype having a small dihedral. The latter prototype was accepted and went into production as the Nieuport 28.3. The tail surfaces were identical to those of the Nieuport 23/24/27, but the fuselage was almost four feet longer than that of the V-strutters, and the longitudinal stringers carried the rounded cross section under the fuselage instead of leaving a flat section. However, the major design change was in the wings. Both were two-spar with the chord of the lower nearly matching the upper, and both were fitted with elliptical wingtip bows in contrast to the angular raked tips of the V-strutters. The power plant was the nine-cylinder Gnome 9-N rotary engine of 150–170 "questionable horsepower," the first Gnome used on a production Nieuport since 1914. In its original form, the new model carried only a single Vickers .303 machine gun outboard of the center-section struts. This was soon considered inadequate. On the production models, the upper wing was raised and a second Vickers was placed on top of the fuselage and a bit left of the centerline.

Although ordered into production by the French, the Nieuport 28 did not prove to be a desirable combat plane, in spite of its improved performance over its predecessors. Other designs, notably the SPAD XIII, proved more suitable, and had it not been for the American Expeditionary Force (AEF), Nieuport would have found itself out of the fighter plane business. Some 297 Nieuport 28s were delivered to the AEF. The U.S. Air Service found it serviceable as a chase plane, and given the dearth of aircraft available to American forces early in the war, Nieuports were a welcome addition to the service's arsenal.

The shortcomings of the Nieuport 28 were myriad, including problems with the engine, airframe, and armament. In certain high-speed maneuvers the fabric frequently separated from the wing; motor-induced vibrations often caused cracks in the fuel line, which could lead to in-flight fires. Problems with the Vickers guns centered around American ammunition, which was three millimeters wider than either French or British rounds, requiring modification of the Nieuport's ammunition boxes and breeches of the machine guns to reduce the incidence of jamming. Eventually, improvements and refits solved those problems, but the modifications were not complete before the Armistice.

American pilots utilized the strengths and weaknesses of their French-built Nieuports to their best advantage against an equally equipped enemy, but the plane's useful life was short and the nimble Nieuport was soon outclassed by newer, more advanced aircraft, particularly by the SPAD XIII. Confidently, the men of the 94th Aero Squadron—the first to fly the Nieuport 28 in combat—weathered the storms of nature and combat.

Roy Houchin

Bibliography

Bowers, Peter M. "The Nieuport N.28c-1." In *Profile Publication*. London: Hills and Lacy, 1966.

Bruce, Jack M. *Nieuport Aircraft of World War One*. New York: Arms and Armour Press, 1988.

Cavanagh, Robert L. "The 94th and Its Nieuports: 15 April–11 June, 1918." *Cross and Cockade* (Autumn 1980).

Lamberton, W.M., and E.F. Chessman. *Fighter Aircraft of the 1914–1918 War*. Fallbrook, CA: Aero Publishers, 1964.

S.E. 5 and S.E. 5a

Early in 1917, the Imperial German Air Force, flying Albatross fighters and led by the redoubtable Manfred von Richthofen (popularly known as the Red Baron), reigned supreme in the skies over the Western Front. To recapture air superiority, the Allies brought into action in the spring and summer of 1917 the S.E. 5, Sopwith Camel, and French SPAD XIII warplanes. Flying these new machines, British and French airmen wrested mastery of the air from their German opponents.

Designed and developed by the Royal Aircraft Factory in Farnborough, England, during 1916 and early 1917, the single-seat biplane S.E. 5 suffered a series of vexing problems, ranging from a clumsily designed windscreen to

A

struts that pulled out of the wings. Powered by a Hispano-Suiza water-cooled power plant, the S.E. 5 and subsequent S.E. 5a were beset by engine difficulties. But the eight-cylinder 200-hp Hispano-Suiza possessed one of the best power-to-weight ratios of its time, and units from the French manufacturer Emile Mayen proved reliable.

The angular S.E. 5 did not possess the superlative maneuverability so characteristic of the Sopwith Camel and SPAD XIII. A Vickers .303 machine gun was fixed on the port side of the fuselage. A Lewis .303 machine gun on a sliding mount was set above the center section of the upper wing. But it was quite difficult while in flight to change the ammunition drums of the Lewis gun and shove the weapon back into firing position.

Nonetheless, the S.E. 5 and 5a proved to be formidable warplanes. They were fast, capable of 138 mph, possessed a good rate of climb, reaching 10,000 feet in ten minutes and twenty seconds, and featured an exceptional endurance of three hours. The S.E. 5 was outstanding in the dive and zoom climb, and its ruggedness became legendary. The machine absorbed substantial damage and brought its pilots back alive. Exceptionally stable and steady, it proved an ideal gun platform. The S.E. 5 was light on the controls, easy to fly, and had no vices, welcome features indeed to fledgling pilots flying into combat after short and rudimentary training. Visibility, a key element in aerial combat, was superb.

In March 1917, the Royal Flying Corps formed a new squadron, No. 56, of elite pilots who took the new S.E. 5 fighter to France and successfully challenged Richthofen and his "Flying Circus" for supremacy in the skies. Included in the unit were such notable English fliers as Albert Ball, James McCudden, Cecil Lewis, and A.P.F. Rhys-Davids. Accustomed as they were to light, rotary-engined, and nimble machines, the English pilots had to adopt new tactics to obtain full advantage from the capabilities of the new S.E. 5. Even so, the S.E. 5 was a favorite of such aces as Edward "Mick" Mannock, Canadian William Bishop, and the second-ranking American ace, William Lambert. In the number of enemy aircraft shot down, the S.E. 5 was second only to the Sopwith Camel.

At the end of the First World War, some 2,700 S.E. 5a's were in service with twenty British, one Australian, and two American squadrons. Some 5,138 were built in the course of the

conflict. The S.E. 5 and S.E. 5a will always be remembered as key fighters that enabled Great Britain to secure and hold air superiority over the Western Front.

Sherwood S. Cordier

Bibliography
Bruce, J.M. *The S.E. 5a*. London: Profile Publications, n.d.
Clark, Alan. *Aces High*. New York: Ballantine, 1973.
Connors, John F. *S.E. 5a in Action*. Carrollton, TX: Squadron Signal Publications, 1985.
Lewis, Cecil. *Farewell to Wings*. London: Temple Press Books, 1964.
Taylor, John W.R., ed. *Combat Aircraft of the World from 1909 to the Present*. New York: Putnam, 1969.

SPAD Aircraft

SPAD (sometimes S.P.A.D. or Spad) was originally an acronym for Société pour les Appareils Deperdussin, a pioneering French aircraft manufacturing firm founded by Armand Deperdussin in 1910. Deperdussin's chief designer, Louis Bechereau, quickly learned how to design excellent airplanes. They won numerous races and awards, and the company received contracts from the French, British, and Russian governments. In 1913, the firm went into receivership, but at the outbreak of World War I, a corporation headed by Bechereau bought the company. The name was changed to Société pour l'Aviation et ses Dérives, still preserving the acronym SPAD. Louis Blériot became chairman of the board, while Bechereau busied himself designing war planes.

Military authorities on both sides viewed an airplane as a device for observing behind enemy lines. Consequently, when pilots attempted to prevent the observation of their own armies by enemy airmen, their first battles were fought by firing revolvers or rifles at each other. There are even reports of rocks being thrown, and an imaginative Russian pilot trailed an anchor at the end of a cable to snag and dismember enemy aircraft. Despite a few astonishing successes of such practices, it soon became clear that fighting airplanes must carry machine guns. Soon guns were mounted in a fixed position, safely firing off to the side, but aiming them by maneuvering the airplane was not easy. The huge advantage of being able to shoot straight ahead, greatly simplifying the aiming of the gun, was clear, but until the development of an apparatus to prevent severing one's own propeller, this challenge was met by designing "pusher" aircraft on which the engine and propeller were mounted behind the pilot or by mounting a Lewis machine gun atop the center section of the upper wing and firing straight ahead above the propeller arc. The gun also could be tilted to fire upward, but it was virtually impossible to replace empty ammunition drums in the heat of battle.

Bechereau's attempt to provide a better solution was imaginative but not successful. Designated the A.2, the aircraft was a tractor biplane similar in most respects to later SPADs and other fighters, with the pilot seated in the fuselage behind the propeller, engine, and wings. However, a second crewman, armed with a machine gun, was perched in a "pulpit" in front of the propeller, supported by struts connected to the wings and landing gear. Thus the zone of fire of the observer in the pulpit was virtually the entire hemisphere ahead of the airplane. However, the mounting of the machine gun significantly limited its movement and the pulpit itself hampered movement of the propeller. Only 100 of the airplanes were built, and their service life was brief.

The "improved" A.3 and A.4 models were even less airworthy. A much more successful design, the SPAD VII, was first flown in April 1916. Designed around a Hispano-Suiza V-8 liquid-cooled engine capable of producing 140 hp, it was highly dependable and remarkably light, weighing only two-thirds as much as the German Mercedes of comparable horsepower. A single-seater with one synchronized forward-firing Vickers .303-inch machine gun, it was strong as well as fast, although not as maneuverable as the lighter but more fragile Nieuport fighters.

The Allies immediately ordered 268 of them; soon eight French factories and two in Britain were manufacturing SPAD VIIs. Completed aircraft were delivered to French squadrons by Sept. 12, 1916. No. 60 Squadron of the British Royal Flying Corps (RFC) evaluated the SPAD in October and early in 1917 the machine was ordered for both the RFC and the Royal Naval Air Service (RNAS), but as it turned out, all the SPADs went to the RFC, the RNAS getting Sopwith Triplanes instead. The SPADS replaced the RFC's B.E. 12s, which were not very maneuverable and hence were being badly mauled by superior German fighters.

Eventually, about 6,000 SPAD VIIs were built by a number of manufacturers to equip British, Italian, Belgian, Russian, and American squadrons. The U.S. Air Service purchased 189 SPAD VIIs, outfitting seven squadrons and shipping the remainder to the United States for training. Some Italian pilots flew SPAD VIIs until the Armistice, as did one RFC unit stationed in Mesopotamia. At the U.S. Army's Kelly Field, SPAD VIIs flew training missions until 1926.

The SPAD XI, which first flew in September 1916 and entered service in 1917, was a two-seat observation and light bombing aircraft. It looked much like the SPAD VIII, from which it was developed, but weighed about 800 pounds more and had ten-foot longer wings, swept slightly back to balance the weight of the observer in the rear seat. It could carry 154 pounds of bombs. It was not very successful, being considered difficult to land and tending to spin out of tight turns.

The SPAD XVI was an improved SPAD XI with a 236- and then a 250-hp Lorraine-Dietrich engine and with two forward-firing synchronized guns and two free-swinging Lewis guns for the observer in the rear cockpit. Although it was a dozen miles per hour faster than the SPAD XI, it was scarcely an improvement.

The U.S. Air Service received thirty-five SPAD XIVs and sixteen SPAD XVIs. One of the latter was flown by the chief of the United States Air Service (USAS) in Europe, Col. William "Billy" Mitchell, during the battles of Château-Thierry, St. Mihiel, and the Argonne.

One year after the appearance of the SPAD VII, the slightly larger but similar appearing single-seat SPAD XIII was introduced. The resemblance was only superficial. With two Vickers guns instead of one and a 220-hp Hispano-Suiza engine, it was twenty miles per hour faster than the SPAD VII and had a service ceiling 4,000 feet higher. The SPAD XIII first flew in April 1917; in May, it began replacing the SPAD VII. More than 8,000 of the planes were built; eventually, the SPAD XIII became virtually the only machine flown by *escadrilles de chasse*. It was the best of the French fighters and is considered by some the best Allied fighter of the war.

The United States purchased 893 SPAD XIIIs from the French to equip sixteen squadrons. Some of them, such as those flown by the Second Pursuit Group, based at Souilly, were rigged to carry two twenty-pound bombs.

A

SPADs could also be armed with Le Prieur rockets mounted on the interplane struts. Although not very accurate, these rockets were useful primarily for attacking large targets, such as observation balloons. After the war a number of SPAD XIIIs were shipped to the United States, where they were reengined with Wright-built Hispano-Suizas of 180 hp and given the designation SPAD XIIIE. A further 2,000 had been ordered during the war by the Bolling Mission, to be built by Curtiss, but at the Armistice the order was canceled.

The SPAD XIV made its debut in November 1917, equipped with twin Tellier floats for the French Forces Aeriennes de la Mer and the British Royal Naval Air Service. It was eventually followed by the SPAD XXIV, with wheels, designed for aircraft carrier service. Tested only six days before the Armistice, it was too late to see war service.

In June 1918, the SPAD XVII, an improved SPAD XIII, was tested with a 300-hp Hispano-Suiza engine. Only twenty were built. They were sent to Escadrille Spa.3, one of the squadrons of the famous French fighter group known as Les Cigognes.

Vincent Norris

Bibliography

Angelucci, Enzo. *The Rand McNally Encyclopedia of Military Aircraft, 1914–1980.* New York: Military Press, 1983.

Chadeau, Emmanuel. *De Bleriot á Cassault: Histoire de l'Industrie Aeronautique en France, 1900–1950.* Paris: Fayard, 1987.

Christienne, Charles, and Pierre Lissarague. *A History of French Military Aviation.* Washington, DC: Smithsonian Institution Press, 1986.

Laux, James M. "The Rise and Fall of Armand Deperdussin." *French Historical Studies* (1973).

Taylor, John W.R. *Jane's Fighting Aircraft of World War I.* New York: Military Press, 1990.

Sopwith Aircraft

Sir Thomas Octave Murdoch Sopwith founded the firm that designed and built several of the most successful Allied aircraft of World War I—and eventually of World War II. On Sept. 18, 1910, returning to England from a Channel cruise aboard his yacht, Sopwith heard that a Bleriot airplane had landed nearby after a Channel crossing from Paris. Going to see it, he was immediately fascinated by flying. He soon bought a Howard Wright monoplane, taught himself to fly, and began entering races on both sides of the Atlantic.

On Feb. 1, 1912, Sopwith advertised the formation of the Sopwith School of Flying, located at Brooklands, a racetrack at Weybridge, Surrey, popular with early fliers. With his flying school staff, he soon built a biplane, adapted from a Wright design, capable of carrying a pilot and two passengers, thus entering the aircraft business. Leaving the flight-training business to others at Brooklands, Sopwith phased out his flying school to concentrate on aircraft design and construction, setting up shop in a former skating rink at Kensington-on-Thames. Sopwith soon sold an early Bat Boat and three floatplane versions of his biplane to the Royal Navy, and the Royal Flying Corps (RFC) ordered four land plane versions.

Sopwith was shortly building the Tabloid, the progenitor of a line of successful World War I fighters. When the British Expeditionary Forces sailed for France, four Tabloids went along—unarmed and in packing crates, though two were assembled in time to enter, still unarmed, the Battle of Le Cateau. More planes soon arrived and began to raid enemy installations.

The firm was also building aircraft, including Tabloids and "Folder" seaplanes (equipped with folding wings to save space) to serve on the HMS *Ark Royal*. When the *Ark Royal* departed England on Feb. 1, 1915, to participate in the Dardanelles campaign, these planes were to serve as gunfire spotters and for antisubmarine patrol. Plagued by engine trouble and other problems, they performed in mediocre fashion.

Design work had already begun on the Sopwith two-seat biplane, also designated the Sopwith military tractor and identified in the Royal Naval Air Service (RNAS) as Type 9700. It was test flown in February 1916. The upper wing was attached to the lower wing by interplane struts and to the fuselage by two sets of cabane struts resembling a widespread letter W as seen from the front or rear. This feature led to the craft's being known as the "1 1/2 Strutter." Before production of this craft ceased, over 5,000 more would be built by Sopwith and nine other firms in order to meet the urgent demand of both the Royal Navy and the RFC.

Because of its excellent performance, it was the first RFC machine chosen to be equipped with a forward-firing synchronized Vickers machine gun operated by the pilot; a free-swinging Lewis gun was used by the observer in the rear seat to fend off attacks from behind. Innovative in other ways, the plane was equipped with landing flaps and a variable incidence stabilizer so that the pilot could "trim" for hands-off level flight.

Type 9700 reached France on April 24, 1916, and proved to be an effective weapon for two years. Some single-seat models were built as bombers; with the weight of the observer eliminated, they were capable of carrying four sixty-five-pound bombs within the fuselage. On Sept. 24, 1916, two French pilots flying Strutters bombed Essen, and on Nov. 16, 1916, one of them took a Strutter from Luxeuil, flew to Munich where he bombed the railroad station, and then flew on to land in Italy after eights hours in the air.

Like all military hardware, the Strutter eventually was rendered obsolete and its loss rate began to climb as improved German fighters appeared. The Strutter was phased out, its place taken by the R.E. 8, the D.H. 4, and the Bristol F2A and F2B, the latter so excellent in design that it would continue to serve for more than a decade.

Soon after the appearance of the Strutter, the Sopwith company developed the Scout Tractor (designated Sopwith Type 9901 in the RNAS). A single-seat fighter, it looked very much like a small Strutter. When Col. Sefton Brancker of the War Office went to Brooklands to see the first one being tested, he exclaimed, "Good God, your 1 1/2–Strutter has had a pup!" Despite the disapproval of officialdom, the name "Pup" stuck.

First used by the RNAS at Dunkirk in May 1916, the Pup is widely regarded as one of the most delightful airplanes ever to fly. With only 80 hp it was not fast; top speed was 106.5 mph at sea level and only 94 mph at 15,000 feet. But it could climb to 10,000 feet in fourteen minutes; its ceiling was 17,500 feet. It was light and light on the controls. RFC Pups carried one Vickers gun with a Sopwith-Kauper synchronizer. Navy Pups carried, in addition, one Lewis gun mounted to fire upward at an angle. Highly maneuverable, the Pup could turn inside a formation of German fighters and was superior to the Albatross D III, which had twice the horsepower. Eventually, 1,806 Pups were built. By the end of the war, 877 were still on the RAF rolls.

Recognizing the inherent shortcomings of seaplanes, their performance lessened by the weight and drag of the large floats, the Royal Navy was interested in the possibilities of launching and retrieving landplanes aboard ship. In the spring of 1917 the light cruiser HMS *Yarmouth* was fitted with a twenty-foot-long deck specifically for a Pup to take off from, which it did successfully. By July of that year, the HMS *Furious* was fitted with a deck at the bow for launching aircraft and one at the stern for recovering them. The ship's superstructure, however, caused so much air turbulence that landings were rendered almost impossible. Further redesigns of the *Furious* and the *Argus* led eventually to the development of the flush-deck carrier of the sort that played a major role in World War II.

Quickly following the Pup into production was the single-seat Triplane fighter, often called the "Tripehound," which began its service in April 1917. It looked very much like a Pup but with an extra wing. Early models had a 110 hp engine; later models with a 130-hp Clerget rotary engine were capable of 116 mph. The Triplane could climb to 10,000 feet in thirteen minutes and had a ceiling of 22,000 feet. It was issued to several RNAS fighter squadrons, in which it performed superbly.

Despite its successes, the Triplane was phased out after only 144 were built so that production could be concentrated on an even more successful aircraft—in fact, the most successful fighter of the war, the Camel, which first flew in December 1916, and entered service on the Western Front in June 1917. The Camel destroyed more enemy aircraft—1,294—than any other warplane until the Battle of Britain in World War II. By November 1918, half of all RAF aircraft in service were Camels.

The original Camel, the F.1, was armed with two Vickers synchronized guns forward of the pilot in a slight "hump" that gave the machine its name. The Camel was extremely maneuverable. This was due in part to the gyroscopic forces generated by its rotary engine and in part to its being short-coupled—only eighteen feet eight inches long, with the pilot sitting immediately aft of the engine and guns so that turning moments were minimized. But a number of fledgling pilots were killed before they learned how to handle those gyroscopic forces. Many others cringed at the prospect of trying. Eventually, Sopwith produced a two-seat trainer version of the Camel to introduce novice pilots to the airplane. The first F.1 Camels reached the front in July 1917, assigned to No. 70 Squadron. As soon as more could be built, Camels began to replace Pups, Triplanes, and other single-seat scouts in RFC squadrons.

Meanwhile, Sopwith Aviation concentrated on design work while other firms built the aircraft. Of 5,497 Camels built, Sopwith produced only 503. A number of Camel variations emerged, including a naval Camel, which had slightly shorter wings and an upward-firing Lewis gun in addition to the two Vickers. Rather than folding wings to save storage space aboard ship, the rear fuselage—which carried four air bags as flotation devices—could be detached. More than two dozen ships of the Royal Navy were equipped with Camels. Six Camels from the HMS *Furious* raided Tondern in July 1918, destroying two airships.

The T.F. 1 (Trench Fighter 1) was a Camel carrying 700 pounds of steel armor plate; in addition to the two Vickers guns mounted in the usual fashion, there were two other guns mounted to fire downward at a 45-degree angle for the purpose of strafing enemy trenches. This plane would evolve into the T.F. 2 Salamander. It was decided, however, that forward-firing guns, because of their more nearly horizontal trajectory, were more effective against enemy infantry, and only three Salamanders reached the front.

The 5F.1 Sopwith Dolphin fighter, which entered service in February 1918, was a significant departure from the line of successful fighters descended from the Tabloid. It was powered by a 200-hp Hispano-Suiza liquid-cooled engine, not the rotary engine Sopwith usually chose. Its wings displayed "negative stagger"— that is, the upper wing was placed slightly behind the lower. The pilot sat with his head projecting through a gap between the right and left upper wing panels, just behind the engine and in front of the fuel tank. The machine was disliked at first for that reason, and there were, in fact, a number of fatalities when Dolphins flipped onto their backs during landings. Incorporation of a crash pylon to protect the pilot's head and an escape hatch in the side of the fuselage reduced pilots' objections; eventually, those who flew the Dolphin developed a high regard for it.

The Dolphin had extraordinary visibility and more firepower than found on any other single-seat scout. In addition to two fixed Vickers machine guns firing through the propel-ler arc, there were two free Lewis guns. Pilots found, however, that the twin Lewis guns were more than they could manage in the heat of combat; often one or both were removed, in some cases to be mounted on the lower wings outside the propeller arc. Despite its heavy armament, the Dolphin displayed outstanding high-altitude performance, often flying top cover for other Allied types.

The final wartime development of the Sopwith line of single-seat scouts was the 7F.1 Snipe. It reached the front only in September 1918, equipping three RAF squadrons. It performed magnificently.

Although those aircraft described above achieved a degree of fame, a number of other lesser designs emanated from the Sopwith shops during the war, such as the T.1 Cuckoo, the L.R.T., the Tr. Scooter, the Swallow, and the Bee.

With the end of the war, orders for aircraft were canceled. Worse, the British government adopted a tax policy that virtually guaranteed that aircraft manufacturing firms would not survive. Thomas Sopwith liquidated his company while he was still able to pay his creditors, and in 1920, he created the H.G. Hawker Engineering Company. It would produce, barely in time, the Hurricane, the first "modern" cantilevered low-wing monoplane fighter with retractable landing gear and multiple guns. Although assisted magnificently by the Supermarine Spitfire, it was this aircraft in World War II that won the Battle of Britain, destroying even more German planes than had its distant ancestor, the Camel.

Vincent Norris

Bibliography

King, Peter. *Knights of the Air: The Life and Times of the Extraordinary Pioneers Who First Built British Aeroplanes*. Iowa City: University of Iowa Press, 1989.

Lewis, Peter T. *The British Fighter since 1912: Fifty Years of Design and Development*. London: Putnam, 1965.

Penrose, Harald. *British Aviation: The Great War and Armistice*. New York: Funk and Wagnalls, 1969.

Robertson, Bruce. *Sopwith—The Man and His Aircraft*. Letchworth, UK: Air Review, 1970.

Raleigh, Walter, and H.A. Jones. *The War in the Air: Being the Story of the Part Played in the Great War by the Royal*

Air Force. 6 vols. London: Oxford University Press, 1922–1937.

Air Service, United States

See UNITED STATES AIR SERVICE

Aisne-Marne Offensive

See MARNE, SECOND BATTLE OF THE

Albert I, King of the Belgians (1875–1934)

Albert I reigned as King of the Belgians from Dec. 23, 1909, until his death in a climbing accident on Feb. 17, 1934. Nephew of King Leopold II, Albert became crown prince through the deaths of Leopold's son and of Albert's older brother. Tall and quiet, Albert studied at the École Militaire and took interest in engineering and Alpinism. From 1893 to 1898, he served in the Belgian Senate and traveled widely. Marriage in 1900 to Elisabeth, Duchess of Bavaria, brought three children: Leopold (the future Leopold III), Charles, and Marie Jose.

The Belgian constitution of 1831 required that a minister countersign the sovereign's decrees. But it also declared the king to be commander-in-chief with supreme command in time of war. Early in his reign Albert reorganized the General Staff and in 1913 supported a military bill intended to strengthen the Belgian Army. Throughout World War I, despite those in government who believed the king should seek the advice and approval of his ministers regarding his actions as commander, the king clung to his prerogative. He also cited his duties under the constitution when resisting French and British pressure for a unified command of all forces opposing Germany.

As war rumors mounted in 1914, Albert ordered full mobilization of the still weak army. Though the General Staff favored withdrawal of the field army to the central redoubt at Antwerp, Albert preferred defensive operations farther forward: his decision that the 3d Division remain at Liége later slowed the German advance. On August 1, Albert wrote to William II of Germany requesting assurance of German respect for Belgium's neutrality. Albert presided over the Crown Council held on August 2 that rejected Germany's ultimatum requesting free passage of troops.

Upon the outbreak of hostilities in August 1914 and the German invasion of Belgium, Albert took formal command of the Belgian Army, as it fell back from Liege to Louvain and then Antwerp. He directed a brief counterattack toward Louvain intended to relieve French and British troops fighting on the Marne. He chose not to remain in Antwerp as the Germans breached its defenses; the king and his soldiers retreated south and fought well at the Yser, gaining eventual support from the French. The Germans were blocked from the channel ports, but only a strip of Belgium remained independent. The ministers fled to Le Havre, France while Albert stayed with his troops in the Belgian village of La Panne.

The separation of king and ministers, Albert's observation of the sufferings of his army and people, and his belief that Allied victory over the well-drilled Germans was improbable led to some differences of opinion between king and cabinet. Albert resisted any premature abandonment of neutrality, and he softened replies to German notes lest the enemy be provoked into occupying the remainder of Belgium. He did not let the remnants of his army be absorbed by the French or British and jealously protected his troops from being squandered in pointless offensives that would devastate his homeland. The king saw compromise as the likely course to end the war and thought the war aims and attitudes of the French and British prolonged the devastation. Though on Aug. 9, 1914, Albert had rejected German peace feelers, in November 1915 and early in 1916, he secretly responded to a German approach. He apparently feared infeudation to the French and British, saw Germany as the strongest military power, and was willing to abandon neutrality for a defensive agreement that assured Belgium's territory and political and economic independence. But German demands were extensive, and rumors of the talks brought British and French pressure on Belgium; the negotiations withered.

When in late 1916 a German peace overture was floated, Albert wished Belgium's negative reply to be separate from that of Britain and France. He failed in this but did gain a special paragraph; and he won a separate response to a note from President Woodrow Wilson. When approached by the new Emperor Charles of Austria in 1917 regarding a peace settlement, Albert declined any initiative and referred the Austrians to Paris and London. Only in 1918, as the balance of forces appeared to shift, did Albert alter his position regarding joint command. He accepted leadership of the Allied offensive in South Flanders, aided by a French chief of staff, and achieved success. He returned to Brussels on Nov. 22, 1918.

Albert's decision to remain with his troops earned him heroic status not only within his country, but also in the Western world where he was hailed as a leader of a noble nation. His inspirational role during the war carried over to the chores of domestic reconstruction and the bridging of differences between Walloons and Flemings. But an appearance at the Paris Peace Conference in April 1919 had little success in persuading the Great Powers to give more consideration to Belgian aspirations. In Belgium, the king's prestige knew no bounds; his unexpected death in 1934 was a deep shock at a time when his nation faced challenges both at home and abroad.

Jonathan E. Helmreich

See also PARIS PEACE CONFERENCE

Bibliography

Cammaerts, E. *Albert of Belgium, Defender of Right.* New York: Macmillan, 1935.

Galet, E. *Albert, King of the Belgians, in the Great War.* Boston: Houghton Mifflin, 1931.

Van Overstraeten, R., ed. *The War Diaries of Albert I, King of the Belgians.* London: Kimber, 1954.

Willequet, J. *Albert Ier, roi des Belges.* Paris: Delarge, 1979.

Alexander, Robert (1863–1941)

Although a lawyer by profession, Robert Alexander enlisted as a private in the 4th Infantry on April 7, 1886, and was commissioned a second lieutenant in 1889. Alexander participated in the expedition against the Sioux in 1890–1891, helped maintain order during the railroad strikes in 1894, and fought the Spanish in Puerto Rico, insurgents in the Philippines, and Villistas in Mexico. He also attended the Army School of the Line and the Army Staff College and served as inspector-instructor of the Maryland National Guard.

Following the declaration of war against Germany by the United States, LtCol. Alexander helped organize National Guard units and the 17th Infantry for overseas duty.

He went to France in November 1917 and became inspector of the line of communications for the American Expeditionary Force (AEF). Shortly afterward, Alexander was promoted to the rank of brigadier general in the National Army, commanding the 41st Division. In early 1918 he became commander of the 63d Infantry Brigade, and in late August, with the rank of major general in the National Army, he was given command of the 77th Division, which was originally made up of draftees from the New York City area.

Morale in the unit was low as a result of major command changes and losses suffered in fighting along the Vesle River. Alexander immediately set out to turn the division into a first-class unit. A "fierce mustang" noted for his gruffness, he transferred a regimental commander who had a defeatist attitude, made frequent visits to the front, and carried out several minor operations to build confidence. Alexander's measures soon proved their worth, for in the Allied advance from the Vesle to the Aisne River in early September 1918, the 77th Division outran its flanking divisions and displayed a fighting spirit that many of its critics thought impossible.

During the Meuse-Argonne campaign, Alexander was charged with clearing the Argonne Forest, from whose bluffs the Germans commanded much of the defile through which the Americans had to advance in their push to the vital Sedan-Mézières railroad. Despite formidable terrain and fierce resistance, Alexander expelled the Germans from the Argonne in bitter fighting that lasted from Sept. 26 to Oct. 10, 1918. Driving his men hard, he forbade the yielding of any ground and took stern measures to minimize straggling. Casualties were heavy. But the 77th Division, reflecting Alexander's pride and aggressive spirit, fought with great determination. During the last days of the war, the division helped spearhead the Allied advance on Sedan.

After the 77th returned home in the spring of 1919, Alexander reverted to his rank of colonel in the Regular Army. In 1921, he was promoted to the rank of brigadier general and named commander of the 3d Field Artillery Brigade. He remained in this post until retiring in October 1927 with the rank of major general.

John K. Ohl

See also MEUSE-ARGONNE CAMPAIGN; UNITED STATES ARMY: 77TH DIVISION

Bibliography
Alexander, Robert. *Memories of the World War, 1917–1918*. New York: Macmillan, 1931.
History of the Seventy-seventh Division, August 25th, 1917–November 11th, 1918. New York: Winthrop, Hollenbeck & Crawford, 1919.
Stallings, Laurence. *The Doughboys: The Story of the AEF, 1917–1918*. New York: Harper & Row, 1963.

Alien Property Custodian

The inviolability of private property during war, a principal of international law dating from the Magna Carta in the thirteenth century, ended during the twentieth century because of the large amounts of private investment crossing international borders. In the United States, violation of private property rights took the form of the Trading with the Enemy Act of Oct. 6, 1917, which called for the sequestration of enemy property during hostilities.

The Alien Property Custodian (APC) was directed to take possession of property of enemy citizens. The first custodian, A. Mitchell Palmer, established offices in Washington, D.C., New York City, and the Philippines and after a short witch-hunt—during which no person of German extraction could feel secure—organized his work to aid the war effort. Confiscated German property was sold to Americans, and the proceeds went to financing the war.

The history of the APC was replete with scandal. Its most notorious case was that of the Chemical Foundation, a quasi-public institution owned by drug and chemical companies. The second custodian, Francis P. Garvan, sold 5,000 seized German chemical patents to the foundation while serving as the group's president. In a statement to the Senate Finance Committee on Dec. 13, 1919, Garvan maintained that he did not benefit personally from the sale.

A limited return of seized property, begun after the war, was stopped in 1921 when the Knox-Porter Joint Peace Resolution was passed by Congress and incorporated in the Treaty of Berlin. The resolution maintained that the United States should retain seized property until the German, Austrian, and Hungarian governments satisfied American claims for losses during the war. The Mixed Claims Commission was established in 1922 to adjudicate these losses.

The magnitude of the seizure of enemy property during World War I can be realized in a statement from the annual report of the custodian of Jan. 4, 1922: "Some 33,000 active trusts are held representing property scattered from the Philippine Islands and Hawaii to the coast of New England and consisting of industrial plants, such as chemical and woolen mills, steamship lines, banks, land and cattle companies, salmon factories, gold, silver, and other precious mines of metal, and other miscellaneous industrial plants, to say nothing of thousands of parcels of real estate.

Bruce Ashkenas

See also PALMER, ALEXANDER MITCHELL; TRADING WITH THE ENEMY ACT

Bibliography
Gathings, James A. *International Law and American Treatment of Alien Enemy Property*. Washington, DC: American Council of Public Affairs, 1940.
Miller, Thomas W. *Alien Property and its Relation to Trade, Commerce, and American Claims*. Washington, DC: Government Printing Office, 1922.

Allen, Henry Tureman (1850–1930)

Henry Tureman Allen graduated from the United States Military Academy in 1882 and accepted a commission in the cavalry. In the mid–1880s, he led an exploring party into the Alaskan interior, and during the 1890s, he served as the military attaché to Russia and Germany. Following the Spanish-American War, he organized and led the Philippine Constabulary, a paramilitary police force responsible to the new civil government.

When war erupted between the United States and Germany in 1917, the War Department quickly promoted Allen to major general and gave him command of the 90th Division at Camp Travis, Texas, which primarily was composed of draftees from Texas and Oklahoma and had to be turned into a trained, efficient military outfit. Allen faced shortages of everything from housing and uniforms to rifles and artillery, even men. By the spring of 1918, the 90th Division was short over 10,000 men. Nevertheless, Allen maintained a training program that stressed basic infantry skills and physical fitness. In May he received word that the division would join the American Expeditionary Force (AEF) within a month. Almost immediately, troops began pouring in, and Allen expanded the training schedule to run fifteen hours a day, seven days a week. Despite the resulting confusion at the base, the division sailed for France during the third week of June.

After further training in the countryside northeast of Dijon, the 90th Division entered a quiet sector of the front on the eastern end of the St. Mihiel salient on August 24. However, General Pershing was preparing his first major offensive—pinching off the salient—and Allen's division was to form the right pivot. The offensive began in the early hours of September 12. Preceded by a rolling barrage, the 90th pushed ahead and within nine hours captured its objectives. Over the next three days Allen continued to press his two brigades forward. By September 16, the Americans had reduced the salient.

With the St. Mihiel salient eliminated, Pershing began shifting American troops west for an attack in the Meuse-Argonne. At first, Allen and his men remained near St. Mihiel, consolidating their positions and covering sectors vacated by units that had already moved west. As the fighting in the Meuse-Argonne stiffened, Allen's troops entered the lines near Bantheville. Allen pushed his men hard and ruthlessly relieved officers who he thought were weak or incompetent. Fighting was intense, and the division advanced slowly. Nevertheless, the division managed to cross the Meuse River near Stenay just a few days before the Armistice.

In July 1919, Pershing appointed Allen commander of the American Forces in Germany (AFG) after the first two commanders, Joseph T. Dickman and Hunter Liggett, ran afoul of the Allies. For the next four years, Allen acted as military governor of the American occupation zone around Coblenz and served as a member of the Inter-Allied Rhineland High Commission. Allen tried to represent the interests of the United States, although both the War and State departments habitually failed to provide him specific instructions or guidance. Increasingly, he found himself acting to restrain French ambitions in the region.

With the withdrawal of the AFG in 1923, Allen retired from the military. For the next seven years he spoke and wrote on international politics and his own experiences in the Rhineland, and dabbled in Democratic Party politics. He died on Aug. 29, 1930.

Richard Kehrberg

See also UNITED STATES ARMY: 90TH DIVISION

Bibliography

Allen, Henry T. *My Rhineland Journal.* Boston: Houghton Mifflin, 1923.
———. *The Rhineland Occupation.* Indianapolis: Bobbs-Merrill, 1927.
Bullard, Robert L. *Fighting Generals.* Ann Arbor, MI: Edwards, 1944.
Twichell, Heath, Jr. *Allen: The Biography of an Army Officer, 1859–1930.* New Brunswick, NJ: Rutgers University Press, 1974.

Allied Maritime Transport Council

The Allied Maritime Transport Council (AMTC) was established in order to make the most effective use of Allied merchant shipping tonnage. The AMTC was a product of an important Allied conference held at Paris from Nov. 29 to Dec. 3, 1917. The Special Committee for Maritime Transport and General Imports agreed that it was vital that Allied merchant shipping be brought under a new organization that could maximize use of all available merchant tonnage.

On Feb. 15, 1918, representatives of the United States, Britain, France, and Italy met at the British Foreign office to plan the organization. The first meeting of the AMTC took place on March 11 and continued through March 14.

Each of the four nations involved eventually appointed two representatives to the AMTC—Raymond Stevens, the vice-chairman of the Shipping Board, and George Rublee, a public-spirited lawyer who had served on the Federal Trade Commission, for the United States; Lord Robert Cecil and Sir John Maclay, the minister of shipping, for Great Britain; Etienne Clémentel and Louis Loucheur for France; and Silvio Crespi and Giovanni Villa for Italy. Each country retained control of its own shipping. The AMTC was purely advisory, but its decisions were generally followed.

The AMTC officially convened just four times during the course of the war; consequently, it was inevitable that most of its work was performed by committees. Twenty committees were functioning by the time of the Nov.

11, 1918, armistice. The bulk of the work, however, was performed by the Main Committee, which consisted of George Rublee, Sir J. Arthur Salter of Great Britain, Bernardo Attolico of Italy, and Jean Monnet of France.

At the start, President Woodrow Wilson was opposed to the United States having representatives on any Allied war councils, fearing that any American representative would initially find himself so carried away by the wartime atmosphere that he would become pro-European, or more specifically, pro-British. United States Shipping Board Chairman Edward N. Hurely takes credit in his memoirs for changing the President's mind. At first Wilson would only permit one American member, but he later permitted Hurley to name Rublee as the second American member in addition to Stevens.

Unfortunately, but not surprisingly, the goal of full Allied cooperation in shipping matters was never reached. The United States and Great Britain never totally trusted one another. Each thought the other was sacrificing the common war effort to commercial advantage. The American delegation was embarrassed to discover that the United States had several ships engaged in non-essential commercial trade at the very time when there was an urgent need to supply additional tonnage for the rapidly expanding AEF.

A study made at the end of the war indicates that the British were actually more forthcoming than their American counterparts. The study revealed that, at the insistence of P.A.S. Franklin, chairman of the Shipping Control Committee of the U.S. Shipping Board, the United States had used many valuable ships in a profitable, but unnecessary trade with the West Indies and Central America.

Edwin Gay, director of the Division of Planning and Statistics of the Shipping Board openly confronted Franklin at a meeting of the Tonnage Committee on Oct. 4, 1918, and Franklin belatedly ordered all suitable vessels removed from these trade routes and placed in the Army's service.

The AMTC ended on March 24, 1919, when the Supreme Economic Council formed a separate shipping committee to deal with tonnage problems.

Charles Tull

Bibliography
Hurley, Edward N. *The Bridge to France.* Philadelphia: Lippincott, 1927.
Salter, Arthur. *Allied Shipping Control: An Experiment in International Administration.* Oxford, UK: Clarendon Press, 1921.

Allied Naval Council

It was the problem of overcoming submarine warfare in the Mediterranean Sea that prompted British Prime Minister David Lloyd George to call an Interallied Naval Conference at London in January 1917. The conference, at Italy's behest, established a commission to study the advisability of replacing antisubmarine patrols with the convoy system. Compared with the Atlantic and the Mediterranean, the Adriatic Sea appeared to the British and French to be a backwater area that could be entrusted to Italy. The Italians disagreed, and on the ground that Britain and France had not delivered naval forces promised in the Treaty of London of 1915, Italy refused to undertake offensive action in that sea. The best thing that came out of the conference was the statement by Lloyd George that "unless we show a disposition to pool our resources as common, we shall not achieve victory." RAdm. William S. Sims, commanding the American naval forces in Europe, seconded Lloyd George in seeking "maximum cooperation with the Allies in defeating a common enemy." The same objective was sought by RAdm. Henry T. Mayo, commander-in-chief, U.S. Atlantic Fleet, during a visit to Europe in August 1917. However, Mayo reported that the Allies continued to stress matters that concerned their countries alone and lacked the will to cooperate fully on common objectives. Finally, agreement was reached on the grand naval strategy that the Allies would pursue to the end of the conflict. The United States would provide new and more powerful mines for the North Sea Mine Barrage, more ships for antisubmarine warfare, cruisers for convoy duty in the Atlantic, and a battleship squadron to operate with the British Grand Fleet. Italy was appeased by the adoption of the convoy system in the Mediterranean, increased coal and merchant ship tonnage, plans to establish a ship and mine barrier at the Otranto Straits, and increased supplies from the United States. However, the formation of an Allied Naval Council (ANC) was postponed for a month following the creation of the Supreme War Council in November 1917.

Establishment of the Supreme War Council that would coordinate Allied political-military operations set a precedent for Allied cooperation. Why not create a similar organization for naval affairs? When the General Board of the United States Navy endorsed the creation of an interallied naval agency, the way was cleared for the establishment of the Allied Naval Council. Comprised of the naval department heads and chiefs of staff of Britain, France, Italy, and Japan, with Sims representing the United States, the ANC watched over the general conduct of the naval war, offered recommendations to the member governments, oversaw the execution of plans agreed upon, and reported as necessary to the home governments. The council would not write war plans or interfere in tactical matters. However, since Allied naval forces were not placed in a common pool and Italy would not let foreigners command its naval force, it proved impossible to appoint a supreme naval commander as the Supreme War Council had done in tapping Ferdinand Foch as the Allied commander.

On November 29 and 30, the ANC drafted its constitution. In January 1918, in its first meeting, members considered such topics as what could be done to crush the U-boat, improve mine barrages, and energize the Italian Navy. Sims later said that his work on the council was the most important he performed during 1918.

At the second meeting of the ANC, in London, on March 12–13, antisubmarine warfare still rated first priority, but the Adriatic question was a close second and consumed more time than any other matter. To Sims, the British, and the French, it seemed that Italy preferred defensive to offensive action and harbored imperial rivalries with Britain and France that were as threatening to the success of the war as the Austro-Hungarian Navy. When Adm. Sir Rosslyn Wester Wemyss recommended the pooling of resources in the Mediterranean, the Italian fleet commander, Adm. Paolo Thaon di Revel, countered with a demand for more destroyers. Sir Eric Geddes, the British first lord of the Admiralty, supported by Sims, replied that the Mediterranean should be considered as a whole, that no nation should look upon any part of it as its particular domain. Di Revel agreed that a naval mission be formed to investigate conditions in that sea. The commission met in Rome on February 8 and 9 and recommended helping Italy build a mine barrage at Otranto Strait. Finally, the Allies decided to grant Italy additional naval support and urged di Revel to assume a more offensive attitude toward the Austrians. As a first step, Sims offered a plan to cut rail communications between Pola and Cattaro and destroy the latter, used as a U-boat base. The United States would provide the ships, equipment, and an admiral to command the operation. As expected, di Revel opposed the plan, in part because an Italian must be in command. Sims launched into di Revel, saying that he did not care who commanded the operation as long as he was a fighter. Although a committee appointed by the ANC unanimously favored the operation, Sims gave up in disgust when faced with di Revel's stubborn opposition.

Italy's refusal to cooperate with its allies was referred to the Supreme War Council. Although eager to please his fellow premiers, the most Vittorio Orlando would agree to was a supreme Allied naval commander for the Mediterranean—but not for the Adriatic—and to send some Italian ships to strengthen the French at Corfu—but not to place them under French command. The heated debate ended only when the British gave up on a supreme commander and said they would make their arrangements with the French. Sims reported home that "the Italian representatives take the position that the Adriatic is Italy's particular field."

The third meeting of the ANC, held in Paris April 25–27, 1918, dealt mainly with the building of the Otranto barrage, a subject also discussed at the fourth meeting, also held at Paris, on September 13–14. With the end of the war in sight, a fifth meeting produced little of importance beyond promising Italy additional antisubmarine craft. At its sixth and final meeting, held in Paris and Versailles between October 28 and November 4, the ANC provided the Supreme War Council with its input into the naval peace terms to offer Austria and Germany. Austria accepted di Revel's terms, but Italy itself later violated them by seizing all Dalmatian territory that it could. Further meetings of the ANC were postponed because, as Sims put it, "There is no urgent matter to be discussed . . . which cannot be settled by correspondence."

In the operation of the ANC, the British and French cooperated with the Americans, but the Italians let their statecraft impede their naval cooperation. No better example can be found of how the personal jealousies, political susceptibilities, and national prejudices and interests of the Allied civil and military leaders made naval cooperation impossible.

Paolo Coletta

See also NORTH SEA MINE BARRAGE; OTRANTO BARRAGE; SIMS, WILLIAM SOWDEN

Bibliography
Coletta, Paolo E. *Sea Power in the Atlantic and Mediterranean in World War I.* Lanham, MD: University Publications of America, 1989.
———. "The United States Navy in the Adriatic in World War I." In *Ships, Seafaring, and Society: Essays in Maritime History*, ed. by Timothy J. Runyan. Detroit: Wayne State University Press, 1987.
Lloyd George, David. *War Memoirs of David Lloyd George.* 6 vols. London: Nicholson & Watson, 1933–1936.
Po, Guido. *Il Grande Ammiraglio Paolo Thaon di Revel.* Turin: n.p., 1936.
Trask, David F. *Captain and Cabinets: Anglo-American Naval Relations, 1917–1918.* Columbia: University of Missouri Press, 1972.

American Alliance for Labor and Democracy

The American Alliance for Labor and Democracy (AALD) was the prowar propaganda organization of the American Federation of Labor (AF of L). It was created by AF of L President Samuel Gompers and the prowar federation's affiliates in New York City and Chicago after antiwar labor agitation in those cities during the summer of 1917.

On Sept. 4, 1917, the AALD held its first convention in Minneapolis. Gompers assumed the presidency, and Robert Maisel, a prowar socialist and director of the National Labor Publicity Organization, became director. When the Wilson administration agreed to finance the AALD through George Creel's Committee on Public Information, the labor organization in effect became an arm of the administration's prowar propaganda machinery.

The AALD held prowar rallies, published propaganda, and attracted a few prowar socialists, such as J.G. Phelps Stokes and John Spargo.

But during the summer of 1918, the administration cut back drastically on AALD funding, and the war's end, on Nov. 11, 1918, removed the AALD's objectives. Attempts to keep it active as a labor watchdog agency failed during the postwar period.

While the AALD may have influenced many antiwar workers to support the war effort, its greatest achievement was as a symbol of labor loyalty.

Frank Grubbs

See also AMERICAN FEDERATION OF LABOR; GOMPERS, SAMUEL

Bibliography
Grubbs, Frank L., Jr. *Samuel Gompers and the Great War: Protecting Labor's Standards.* Wake Forest, NC: Meridional Publications, 1982.

American Civil Liberties Union

See CIVIL LIBERTIES BUREAU

American Expeditionary Force

See UNITED STATES ARMY: AMERICAN EXPEDITIONARY FORCE

American Expeditionary Force University

The American Expeditionary Force University (AEFU) was the apex of a broad educational system for soldiers in World War I. The University was organized in Beaune, France between January and March 15, 1919 and operated from March 15 to June 7. Classes began with 309 instructors and about 5,000 students studying in twelve colleges. At the height of its operation, it enrolled 9,571 participants. Upon conclusion, every participant received a certificate indicating the courses taken, the length of time, the grades, and the instructors.

The army's non-military educational programs in World War I were under that auspices of the Y.M.C.A. (Young Men's Christian Association). As the Armistice approached, "Y.M.C.A." and army officials began planning activities for the American soldiers who would serve in Europe during the post-war period. No one knew exactly how long American troops would have to remain abroad, but planners worked under the assumption of a long occupation. The Y.M.C.A. asked Anson Phelps

Stokes of Yale University, who was working in Europe, to help design an educational plan for the troops after the war. Stokes recommended a wide range of courses from literacy programs through university-level courses. He also realized such an enterprise would require increased staff and support. To help achieve this, he recommended the creation of an Army Educational Commission of three educators who could organize instruction.

The Y.M.C.A. adopted Stokes' recommendations and appointed the Army Educational Commission with John Erskine, a professor of English from Columbia University, as chair. The other members were Frank E. Spaulding, superintendent of the Cleveland Public Schools, and Kenyon L. Butterfield, president of Massachusetts Agricultural College. Each member assumed responsibility for a particular area of education. For university and professional education, John Erskine was the leader.

The American Expeditionary Forces Headquarters had designated the A-5 section of the General Staff to be the Army's liaison with the "Y.M.C.A." Army Educational Commission. Officers were to assign students and generally provide support to Y.M.C.A. programs. In April, 1919 the Army officially took over responsibility for the Army Educational Commission and its programs and organization. By then, however, the Commission and Army personnel involved had long been working as though the transfer had taken place.

General Robert I. Rees had military authority for the educational programs. As he and Erskine observed the heavy response from American soldiers to invitations from British and French universities to study in their facilities, they decided the army had to establish its own university. The other commissioners objected that such an undertaking would diminish the Commission's role in the total educational system of the army. Eventually, however, the full Commission agreed to create the American Expeditionary Forces University.

In January, 1919 the Commission began to implement the plan. Gen. Rees assigned Col. Ira Reeves to inspect the hospitals at Allery and Beaune as possible locations. In early February, Reeves recommended Beaune as the site for the American Expeditionary Forces University and Allery as the site for the agricultural school. Rees appointed Reeves, who had once been President of Norwich University in Vermont, as the military commander—later changed to superintendent— of A.E.F.U. John Erskine became the Educational Director. They quickly moved to requisition materials, remodel facilities, gather books, and assign instructors.

On February 26 AEF Headquarters sent a telegram to commanding officers announcing that the University at Beaune would begin to receive students on March 6 for the classes beginning on March 15. All officers and soldiers who were high school graduates were eligible. The Army continued to provide full pay and allowances to the soldiers who became students. Participants also received tuition, texts, and supplies without charge. Students did not have to stay until the end of the term if their units were ordered home unless they chose to remain.

Erskine and Reeves described the institution as one devoted to adult education. By necessity and belief, they chose a self-selection process for admission. Any high school graduate who wanted to attend could do so; the test of ability would come in the course work, not beforehand. Erskine observed that many of the soldiers had discovered their need for education in the course of their war experiences and hoped the AEFU experience would encourage a habit of life-long study. Secretary of War Newton D. Baker, a post-war leader in the adult education movement, believed that the AEFU experiment demonstrated the hunger of adults for education throughout life and presaged the rapid expansion of evening colleges that occurred in the 1920s.

Rae Wahl Rohfeld

Bibliography

Erskine, John. *The Memory of Certain Persons*. Philadelphia: J.B. Lippincott, 1947.

Erskine, John. *My Life as a Teacher*. Philadelphia: J.B. Lippincott, 1948.

Rohfeld, Rae W. "Preparing World War I Soldier for Peacetime: The Army's University in France." *Adult Education Quarterly*, 39 (4), Summer 1989, 187–198.

American Federation of Labor

The American Federation of Labor (AF of L) was organized in 1886 from the Federation of Organized Trades and Labor Unions of the United States and Canada. The man most responsible for its founding was English-born Samuel Gompers of the International Cigarmakers Union. The AF of L grouped together a wide range of independent unions, mostly craft unions, both local and international, ranging from conservative to socialist in tone.

By 1914, the federation was the largest trades organization in the United States. Even so, it had developed slowly since its founding. With fewer than 1 million members it had to oppose antagonistic state and federal courts, unsympathetic presidents, and a laissez-faire business community.

The outbreak of the First World War severely disoriented the federation. Most of its unions opposed the war, for they feared that it would destroy any labor gains made up to 1914. The federation's concern became how to protect its prewar gains from the inevitable wartime federal regulations and to obtain for its unions fair wage and hour contracts. As the American war effort developed, the liberal unions in the AF of L became militant in demanding concessions from the Wilson administration. However, the majority conservative-moderate unions followed the leadership of President Samuel Gompers, who, in 1916, laid down a nationalistic, moderate course for the federation. During the war years Gompers became convinced that the AF of L could trade off its wartime support for future labor gains, chief among which would be obtaining the good will of both the government and the public so that after the war labor would have equal status with management in the nation's economy. Because of its nonpartisan and nationalistic position, the federation had succeeded in gaining, by 1915, President Woodrow Wilson's tentative endorsement of its program and the choice of William B. Wilson, a United Mine Worker official, as the first secretary of labor. Nevertheless, when President Wilson proposed a preparedness program in 1916, AF of L unions were divided over the proposition due to their large membership of Irish- and German-American workers, who tended to be anti-British and pro-neutrality. But Gompers's support of the war, his appointment to the Labor Committee of the Council of National Defense (CND), and Wilson's assurances that labor's gains would be protected for the duration allowed the federation's conservative-moderate unions to carry the day for the preparedness effort.

When the United States entered the war, the AF of L generally supported the declaration. The federation's wartime loyalty was based on the government's willingness to protect its prewar gains and to meet its wartime contract de-mands. However, the Selective Service Act caused great consternation among the unions, who saw the draft as weakening their membership. The AF of L lobbied intensely to gain exemption for its skilled workers but with little success. The Espionage Act further alienated the federation's liberal unions. Yet, the administration gave organized labor enough to keep the AF of L behind the war effort. Wilson's dedication of the new federation headquarters in Washington, D.C., the Keating-Owen Child Labor Act, the Adamson Act, and other legislation gave labor a portion of what it wanted. In addition, President Gompers's presence on the CND's Labor Committee was an ever present comfort to the majority of the AF of L membership. But the Wilson administration's "carrot and stick" labor policies kept the AF of L in a state of constant uncertainty during the war. For example, the War Industries Board and the War Labor Board were generally welcomed by labor, but the Lever Food and Fuel Control Act was not, because of the fear that rationing would cause unemployment. Wilson's nationalization of the rails greatly pleased most of the federation, but his failure to name AF of L members to policy-making positions on the Coal Production Board and the U.S. Shipping Board, among others, angered much of the federation. Likewise, the government's freeze on all existing labor standards alarmed the federation. The Federal Mediation Commission pleased the AF of L, but the American Alliance for Labor and Democracy, although headed by Gompers, displeased the liberal unions, whose membership rolls were filled with antiwar workers. Basically, Wilson's labor policies and Gompers, with the support of his loyal executive committee, kept the federation behind the war effort.

In the area of foreign affairs, the AF of L enjoyed its greatest wartime prestige. From 1914 on, Gompers and several executive council members were in constant contact with Allied labor leaders. As the war developed, President Wilson allowed Gompers to play an increasingly important role in gaining Allied labor's support for his Fourteen Points announced on Jan. 8, 1918. Lobbying by Gompers for Wilson's foreign policy made him Wilson's foremost labor diplomat. But Wilson never took seriously the Federation's Resolution 104, demanding a say in the peace negotiations, even though Gompers was allowed to attend the International Labor Legislative Commission in Paris. Still, no American labor organization had been allowed previously to dabble in foreign policy with the government's blessing.

When the war ended, Gompers and the executive council believed the AF of L's wartime loyalty would pay off handsomely in new peacetime gains. The federation now had almost 3 million members. This vision of a new day for labor seems to have been prevalent among most of the Federation except the most liberal segments, such as the United Mine Workers, the Teamsters, and the Carpenters unions. The dream came to a quick end. The rapid removal of federal wartime regulations left labor unprotected once again vis-à-vis capital. The Red Scare turned the nation against the most harmless unions, and the return to normalcy incorporated a return to laissez-faire capitalism. As the federation's unions saw their wartime relationship with the government dissolve, leaders of the liberal unions began to challenge Gompers's leadership. John L. Lewis, Daniel Tobin, and William L. Hutcheson were foremost in charging federation leaders with selling out to the government during the war. Despite its loss of influence after the war, the AF of L remained a moderate federation that refused to accept socialism or communism or to advocate violence against the government.

Frank Grubbs

See also AMERICAN ALLIANCE FOR LABOR AND DEMOCRACY; COUNCIL OF NATIONAL DEFENSE; ESPIONAGE ACT; FOURTEEN POINTS; GOMPERS, SAMUEL; LEVER FOOD AND FUEL ACT; NATIONAL WAR LABOR BOARD; SELECTIVE SERVICE; WAR INDUSTRIES BOARD

Bibliography

Gompers, Samuel. *Seventy Years of Life and Labor.* New York: Dutton, 1925.

Grubbs, Frank L., Jr. *Samuel Gompers and the Great War: Protecting Labors' Standards.* Wake Forest, NC: Meridional Publications, 1982.

Lorwin, Lewis L. *The American Federation of Labor: History, Politics, and Prospects.* Washington, DC: Brookings Institution, 1933.

Taft, Philip. *The A.F. of L. in the Time of Gompers.* New York: Harper, 1957.

Watkins, Gordon S. *Labor Problems and Labor Administration in the United States During the World War.* Urbana: University of Illinois, 1920.

American Legion

Initially, the American Legion was an organization of persons who served in the United States military from April 5, 1917, until Nov. 11, 1918, the period of American participation in the Great War. At its zenith during the interwar period, over 1 million men and women belonged to the association. After the nation entered World War II, veterans of the armed forces from other eras were included.

The legion's design, purpose, and nomenclature reflected a variety of forces in American history. Veterans' organizations date back in the national past, starting with the Society of the Cincinnati, a fraternal group for officers of the Continental Army. More immediate influences on the legion were the Veterans of Foreign Wars, the United Spanish-American War Veterans, and the Civil War's Grand Army of the Republic (GAR).

Composed of ex-Union Army soldiers, the GAR served as something of a model for the legion; although the legion eschewed involvement in party politics, early leaders were impressed by the political power that the Grand Army exercised within the Republican Party and by the lavish benefits gained by Civil War veterans from a grateful government. To win and keep southerners who fought in World War I, members of the United Confederate Veterans were invited to all American Legion national conventions and despite some criticism were accorded a status equal to GAR veterans.

Other influences on the American Legion included a group formed in 1915 by Arthur Sullivant Hoffman, editor of *Adventure* magazine. Called the American Legion, the organization was open to all former soldiers, sailors, and marines interested in preparing for the war that many anticipated the United States would enter. Endorsed by former President William Howard Taft and various secretaries of war, this group provided the government's Council of National Defense with a list of approximately 50,000 members, and their military and technical abilities, in 1916.

Hoffman's American Legion likewise endorsed the Training Camps Movement, or Plattsburg Movement, when that program began in May 1915 following the sinking of the *Lusitania*. The Plattsburgers were interested in preparing the country for war and included among its membership were men who would spearhead the founding of the American Legion of 1919: Theodore Roosevelt, Jr., Eric Risher Wood, George A. White, and William J. ("Wild Bill") Donovan.

The 97th Overseas Battalion of the Canadian Expeditionary Force, composed of volunteers from the United States, also called itself the American Legion. It had this name on badges it wore, and in bivouac the Yanks raised the Stars and Stripes and sang the "Star Spangled Banner," activities British officers disliked. In 1920, this unit and the American Legion of 1915 waived all rights they may have had to the name.

The Boy Scouts of America, along with other patriotic organizations, also influenced the formation of the American Legion. The legion motto "For God and Country" echoes the Boy Scout's oath, which begins, "On my honor I will do my best to do my duty to God and my country." The Salvation Army and Young Men's Christian Association, which were present in U.S. military camps and overseas, also had an impact on legionnaires and their early program.

The American Legion itself was created in 1919 in two caucuses of veterans. The Paris meeting, which was held first, set the tone for the new organization. The occasion for calling a caucus was the concern by Gen. John J. Pershing and others for the morale of the American Expeditionary Force, which, according to the historian Marquis James, had deteriorated considerably since the Armistice, causing a fear at General Headquarters in Chaumont that the soldiers might be "going bolshevist."

Obviously, concern over radicalism making inroads into the American forces played a role, but so did the ambitions of Theodore Roosevelt, Jr., Wood, White, and Donovan. An organization for veterans of the Great War had been Roosevelt's objective prior to Pershing's approval of a "morale conference." Roosevelt had convinced the general that this was the way to combat growing dissatisfaction in the ranks. The February morale meeting of twenty officers, eight of whom came from New York, resulted in a call for a Paris meeting to be held from March 15 to 17, 1919. Roosevelt's organizational efforts were given effective support by the American forces' newspaper in Europe, *Stars and Stripes*.

Pershing did not favor the Roosevelt-inspired group, but he felt he could not oppose the March meeting. Both the general and President Woodrow Wilson had endorsed another veterans' fellowship, Comrades in Service, founded by Ora D. Foster of Iowa and the Very Reverend Charles H. Brent, a bishop of the Episcopal Church and senior chaplain of the American Expeditionary Force. Its religious affiliations may have doomed Comrades as the main veterans' organization of the war. In an action he later rued, Brent agreed to merge the Comrades with the American Legion.

The Paris Caucus, as the meeting was called, opened at the American Club, an old French residence. Because this accommodation was too small, on the second day the meeting was held at the Cirque de Paris, a large amusement hall, which was arranged much like an American political convention with bunting and banners.

The meeting worked through four committees that were concerned, respectively, with a permanent organization, constitution, name, and site for an American caucus. After allaying fears that the legion would be used as a vehicle for aspiring politicians, and after somewhat satisfying the forty-seven enlisted men who were delegates and were concerned that the officer corps would dominate the new organization, committee reports were heard, and the delegates adopted the name American Legion and provided for a stateside caucus. (Roosevelt had already sailed for the United States to prepare for that gathering.) A brief constitution, which allowed for a national body and subsidiary branches for each state, territory, and foreign possession of the United States, was accepted, and an executive committee was named to guide the organization until its American meeting could be held.

Among the approximately 450 delegates in Paris from AEF units were men who, in the coming years, would attain fame for a variety of reasons. Journalists present were Harold D. Ross, who founded *The New Yorker*, and John T. Winterich, who edited *Saturday Review of Literature*. Also in attendance were Ogden Mills, who would later be a secretary of the treasury, and A. Piatt Andrew and Ralph D. Cole, both of whom served in Congress. Alvin M. Owsley, future minister to Rumania, Ireland, and Denmark, and Frank D'Olier, later president of the Prudential Insurance Company, were there, as were John G. Winant, who would be governor of New Hampshire, ambassador to England and first head of the Social Security Board, Dwight F. Davis, future secretary of war and tennis great for whom the Davis Cup is named, and "Wild Bill" Donovan, who organized the Office of Strategic Services in World War II, were positive forces in the meeting.

Even before the Paris Caucus adjourned, Roosevelt was busy in New York City planning for the American caucus. Largely through his effort, over 1,000 delegates from across the nation met in the Shubert-Jefferson Theater in St. Louis on May 8 and elected Henry D. Lindsley of Texas as convention chairman. Roosevelt had vigorously and successfully resisted the effort to have him chair the meeting.

Because of difficulty in devising a workable method of choosing delegates from the several states, the legion was generous in extending participation to almost all who came. The only delegates not allowed votes were members of a radical group called Private Soldiers and Sailors Legion of the United States of America or The Soldiers' and Sailors' Council, or, simply, World War Veterans. They were associated with the Industrial Workers of the World (IWW, "Wobblies"). This organization and its members were disliked by many soldiers. Although one of their number was allowed to address the caucus, he was roundly booed by the attendees.

In fact, considerable time was spent listening to speeches denouncing radicals, Bolsheviks, and "slackers," men who had evaded the draft. Although its middle-class origins explain in part the antiradical attitude of the American Legion, the major reason for this hostility stemmed from the belief that while legionnaires were overseas successfully defending the nation and its form of government, at home they were being betrayed by antidemocratic, anti-American Wobblies and other radicals.

The first two days of the St. Louis Caucus were spent listening to speeches. On the third day, committee reports were delivered and voted upon. Legion leaders succeeded in avoiding disruptive issues such as prohibition or ratification of the League of Nations, which might have compromised the young organization's growth. In addition to asking that IWW members and Bolshevik aliens be deported, the assembly called upon the government to help veterans get jobs and receive medical care and to provide pensions for widows and orphans of their dead comrades. Its objectives, as stated in the preamble of its constitution, included the maintenance of law and order, preservation of the memories of the Great War, combating autocracy and safeguarding the principles of justice, freedom, and democracy, and promoting peace and good will throughout the world.

That initial convention chose Franklin D'Olier as the first national commander. By then a paid membership of approximately 648,000 existed. Before the next meeting in Minneapolis on Nov. 11, 1919, George White had begun publishing the *American Legion Weekly* from temporary national headquarters in New York. Congress granted the legion a national charter on Sept. 16, 1919.

Legion posts in some instances had become active in combating radicalism, contributing to what had become the "Red Scare." It has been suggested that there were several hundred incidents where legionnaires broke up radical or socialist gatherings, interfered in labor-management disputes, stopped German music concerts, etc. The most serious clash occurred between legionnaires and the IWW in Centralia, Washington, in 1919. During an Armistice Day parade shots fired from a building occupied by the Wobblies killed several marchers. In the ensuing trial several IWW members were acquitted and several imprisoned for second-degree murder.

While eschewing party politics, American Legion groups did oppose some third-party organizations, including the Non-Partisan League, Farmer-Labor Party, and La Follette's 1924 Progressive Party. For the most part, the legion concentrated on veteran benefits and involved itself in matters of national defense. It could claim responsibility for creation of the Veterans Administration in the 1930s, the GI Bill of Rights (Servicemen's Readjustment Act) in 1944, the Korean GI Bill in 1952, and its later extension. The legion, likewise, was concerned with child welfare programs and promoted a full-range of Americanism activities that included a national legion baseball tournament, Boys' State and Nation, and sponsorship of Boy Scout groups, as well as other such programs.

Indianapolis became the site of the national headquarters in 1919, when the adjutant, Lemuel Bolles, assumed quarters provided by the chamber of commerce in the Meridan Life Building. Subsequently, the offices moved to a $3 million memorial building constructed for them. A branch of the national headquarters is also located in Washington, D.C.

The organization's membership peaked at nearly 3 million members in the post-World War II era. It continues today as an advocate for what members see as "Americanism" and has remained an organization for veterans to use for mutual association.

Bullitt Lowry

Bibliography

Gray, Justin, and Victor H. Bernstein. *The Inside Story of the Legion.* New York: Boni and Gaer, 1948.

James, Marquis. *A History of the American Legion.* New York: William Green, 1923.

Jones, Richard Seelye. *A History of the American Legion.* Indianapolis: Bobbs-Merrill, 1946.

Pencak, William. *For God and Country: The American Legion, 1919–1941.* Boston: Northeastern University Press, 1989.

Wheat, George Seay. *The Story of the American Legion.* New York: Putnam, 1919.

American Library Association

Several weeks after the United States entered World War I, the American Library Association (ALA) began preparations for the worldwide distribution of library materials to American soldiers. Its Executive Board, following an invitation from the War Department's Commission on Training Camp Activities, appointed a permanent War Service Committee in June 1917 to oversee what became known as the Library War Service. Herbert Putnam, twice president of the ALA and Librarian of Congress, became general director of the Library War Service. He defined jobs, recruited personnel, set wages, and negotiated contracts. A formidable administrator and an excellent judge of character, Putnam moved rapidly to centralize functions and to employ such first-rate assistants as Carl H. Milam, Malcolm G. Wyer, and Joseph L. Wheeler.

Fund raising, book drives, and personnel recruitment proceeded with deliberate speed. The first finance campaign was conducted by the ALA alone and netted $1.7 million by late 1917. A year later the ALA participated in a massive United War Work Campaign, which brought in a total of $205 million, with the ALA receiving $3.8 million. Despite the substantial sums generated, there was never enough to purchase an adequate supply of books and magazines. To supplement book purchases, the ALA conducted three book drives. Approximately 1,200 library workers served in ALA-sponsored libraries by war's end. Competition from the draft and the rapid turnover of camp library staff were persistent problems. Blacks, German Americans, and women encountered varying degrees of discrimination in their attempt to join the Library War Service.

The association constructed forty camp library buildings with seating for 150 people. The typical library was staffed by three full-time employees and contained 25,000 volumes. Barriers between books and soldiers were minimal. The ALA adhered to an honor system without fines. Attendance and circulation figures confirm the heavy use of camp libraries, and they provide a barometer of soldiers' reading interests. Many libraries experienced attendance rates of 1,000 or more soldiers per day and a daily average of 500 loan transactions. Nonfiction was more popular than fiction by a ratio of two to one. Some books, however, never reached the camp libraries, and if they did, were promptly removed by the librarian. The War Department issued several lists of banned titles, concentrating on pacifist and pro-German items. These lists, together with considerable self-censorship on the homefront, found complacent assent within the library community.

Extension of the ALA's war work to Europe and other foreign locations in the spring of 1918 introduced new problems and created new opportunities. The transportation of library materials to England and France became a logistical nightmare due to the poor control of books on the ships and the mobile character of the troops in Europe. Relations between the ALA and its partner, the Young Men's Christian Association, were sometimes fractious. Yet by the summer of 1918, the ALA overseas library program was fully operational. Six overseas dispatch offices distributed more than 2 million books and magazines between January 1918 and January 1920 to 1,500 European locations. Headquarters for the European library service was the Paris American Library directed by Burton C. Stevenson. One of its most popular services was an innovative books-by-mail program to remote locations, sometimes operating at the rate of 2,000 deliveries per day.

The Library War Service had immediate and long-term consequences. Librarians were proud of their contribution to the war effort, soldiers appreciated library facilities away from home, and military departments assimilated the ALA programs following the Armistice. Similarly, the hospital library service continued, first under the U.S. Public Health Service and then under the sponsorship of the Veterans Bureau. Creation of the American Merchant Marine Library Association and the American Library in Paris were permanent legacies. The European phase of the war work and the destruction of great libraries highlighted the interdependence of the world's libraries. The library destruction in particular aroused great sympathy from American librarians, and financial aid and other forms of assistance were offered to many libraries.

The American Library Association and many of the nation's librarians embraced the singular opportunity to serve military personnel during the Great War. Librarians, together with their emerging professional association, joined with the federal government to do what they had always done best: select, organize, and disseminate the printed word for education and entertainment.

Arthur P. Young

Bibliography

Koch, Theodore W. *Books in the War: The Romance of Library War Service.* Boston: Houghton Mifflin, 1919.

Thomison, Dennis. *A History of the American Library Association, 1876–1972.* Chicago: American Library Association, 1978.

Young, Arthur P. *Books for Sammies: The American Library Association and World War I.* Pittsburgh: Beta Phi Mu, 1981.

American National Red Cross

At the outbreak of war in 1914, American National Red Cross (ANRC) President Mabel Boardman hurriedly cabled the 267 chapters of the ANRC requesting supplies for war-torn Europe. Wires were also sent to the warring European states, including Germany, with an offer of ANRC aid. The departure of the mercy ship *The Red Cross* from New York in September 1914 was accompanied by much fanfare. On it, and on several others vessels, were 170 doctors and nurses, divided into teams, who were headed for England, France, Germany, Austria-Hungary, Serbia, and Russia. Except for the team that arrived in Serbia in time to

combat a devastating typhus epidemic, most of the doctors and nurses exacerbated rather than eased tensions. Hence, for the first three years of World War I, the ANRC's direct involvement was limited to sending supplies to its sister societies in Europe.

During this period the feeling grew that the United States might become involved in the European conflict. Preparations had to be made. By 1917, the ANRC had on its rolls 8,000 nurses and had established twenty-six base hospitals. Its operating budget stood at $200,000, and its paid staff totaled 167. The entry of the United States into the war in April 1917 dramatically transformed the American National Red Cross. President Woodrow Wilson, who hitherto had concerned himself little with the Red Cross, now called a meeting of top businessmen and bankers to discuss a major expansion of the ANRC. The outcome of this meeting was the appointment of a new directing body of the ANRC, the War Council, which in effect ended the organization's neutrality. Henceforth, the ANRC would be an arm of the government and as such would adhere to American policy abroad.

Henry P. Davison, a Wall Street banker and a Republican, directed the War Council and exercised total control over the ANRC. He was an affable man, with a keen sense of humor, who listened to people's advice. His friends scoffed when he pledged to raise $100 million for the ANRC's coffers. Disbelief turned to amazement when, by the end of 1917, this goal had been exceeded. The American National Red Cross became not only the largest relief society in the world, but also the best endowed.

How to assist the 3-million-man American Expeditionary Force (AEF) and their dependents, as well as civilian war victims in Europe, and provide supplementary medical services to the armed forces, became the question of the hour for Davison and his War Council. None of these problems could even begin to be resolved without the devotion of American women. They flooded to join local Red Cross chapters. From 267 chapters in February 1917 their number exploded to 2,279 by August. Largely fundraising organizations before the war, chapters now were transformed into efficient units of mass production with 8 million female volunteers. During the eighteen-month-long war, they tirelessly churned out vast quantities of surgical dressings (300 million), supplies for soldiers and sailors such as sweaters, socks, and mittens

(23 million), and refugee garments (6 million). This civilian army became an indispensable source of supplies for the armed forces. Approximately 12,000 women also were the drivers for the Motor Service, established in February 1918, which chauffeured sick and wounded soldiers from trains to hospitals, hauled Red Cross supplies, and drove nurses to and from work.

Besides chapter work and Motor Service, the ANRC developed three new branches: Canteen Service, Home Service, and the Junior Red Cross. Canteen, or food service, emerged swiftly when it was realized that soldiers often were forced to wait for hours for troop trains. A doughnut and a cup of coffee helped morale, and canteens, at first simple affairs on wheels, expanded in some cases to full-menu restaurants, with reading rooms and showers. Again, the typical canteen worker, in a crisp Red Cross uniform, was female. Home Service arose out of the need for counseling the raw recruits at base camps, young men who were away from home possibly for the first time or who had marital and other family problems. Its work was not limited to base camps, however, but included the family members of the soldier, or it could be simply an information booth at a railway junction, where a soldier could gather information about his family, his pay, or his leave, or send long-distance messages.

Even children were recruited and drilled to do their part. In 1918, the Junior Red Cross enrolled more than 8 million children in 60,000 schools nationwide and in American communities abroad. World War I was the heyday of recycling, and children collected used paper, toothpaste tubes, even apricot pits. An elementary school in Los Angeles earned as much as $1,000 a month from recycling. Fund raising and the making of millions of simple refugee children's garments were not the least of the achievements of the Junior Red Cross. By the end of the war, membership in the ANRC totaled 33,000,000.

Gen. John J. Pershing, commander of the AEF, was anxious to get the American National Red Cross to Europe as quickly as possible, since U.S. forces would not be fully trained and ready for action until well into 1918. French morale in 1917, the year the United States entered the war, was at its lowest point and a strong showing of American National Red Cross personnel and supplies would be a morale booster. ANRC canteens went into action.

Financially hard-hit families of French soldiers received assistance, huge amounts of supplies began to arrive, and the ANRC immediately donated $1.5 million to the French Red Cross. Paris was the headquarters of the ANRC overseas, and the Commission to France was the first of many ANRC commissions to arrive in Europe. Red Cross neutrality was already a thing of the past (to be reinstated at the end of the war), and American National Red Cross officials bore military titles and donned army uniforms.

The biggest problem during and after the war was the masses of refugees. The ANRC was put in sole charge of the refugees in Paris, and provided them with shelter, food, and medical care free of charge. Most miserable of all were the thousands of refugees whom the German government allowed back into unoccupied territory in 1917 and 1918. Most of the children had been orphaned and were suffering from tuberculosis. The ANRC hospitalized many of them, established orphanages, and helped the elderly locate relatives while providing them with food, clothing, and shelter. Elsewhere in France the ANRC cooperated with other agencies in establishing numerous hospitals, convalescent homes, and dispensaries. In the tiny corner that was left of unoccupied Belgium the ANRC developed an extensive child welfare program, and helped to relocate 10,000 Belgian children in Holland.

Unlike the aid in France, ANRC assistance to the Italian military was limited to an ambulance corps of 135 men and 104 ambulances. In the face of the massive Austro-Hungarian offensive in Italy in the spring of 1918, this ambulance corps removed 60,000 sick and wounded soldiers to base hospitals. In the end, the Italian government decorated all of the drivers, one of whom was Ernest Hemingway, for heroism.

The main priority of the ANRC's Commission to Italy when it arrived in January 1918 was civilian relief. In cooperation with the Italian government and the few local relief organizations still functioning, the ANRC assisted 300,000 Italian families with food and other supplies. It also donated medications and equipment to approximately 1,800 Italian hospitals and sent nurses to stricken villages at the height of the worldwide influenza epidemic. In the fall of 1918, the ANRC entered each village immediately after it was liberated and began food distribution. So deep was Italian gratitude to the ANRC that at the end of the war an impressive ceremony was staged in the Coliseum in Rome to honor the American National Red Cross.

The ANRC did not end its overseas assistance programs in 1918. From 1917 to 1922, the American National Red Cross expended $90 million in civilian relief overseas. It also spearheaded the founding, in April 1919, of the International League of Red Cross Societies.

In Russia

During the first three years of the war, because of its remoteness and the fact that the autocratic tsarist government was in disfavor in Washington, Russia received virtually no outside humanitarian assistance. After the February 1917 revolution, when a Provisional Government replaced the tsar, Congress and President Wilson were anxious to render the new democratic regime all possible aid. Henry P. Davison, former Wall Street banker and head of the War Council of the American National Red Cross, approved the first ANRC mission to Russia, sending with it $200,000 worth of supplies. Its principal goals were to strengthen the Provisional Government's ties with the United States and to encourage the faltering Russians to stay in the war. Medical assistance earmarked for Russia was designated for the Russian Army.

William B. Thompson, a multimillionaire friend of Davison's, headed the first ANRC Commission to Russia; indeed, he paid for the entire twenty-nine-man staff. Upon arrival in Petrograd in July 1917, Thompson ensconced himself in a luxurious hotel suite and distanced himself from Red Cross work. The actual head of the commission, Dr. Frank G. Billings, left Russia in disgust one month later, but not before he obtained from Red Cross headquarters in Washington an additional $238,000 worth of medical supplies as well as 125 badly needed ambulances for the Russian Army.

When, in November 1917, the Bolshevik Party overthrew the Provisional Government, the cigar-chomping Thompson left Russia in dismay. Though reduced to a skeletal staff, the ANRC commission remained in Petrograd under Raymond Robins. After the Bolsheviks concluded peace with the Germans in March 1918 and moved the capital to Moscow, the ANRC commission followed suit.

Robins's aims were political as well as humanitarian. A charismatic, self-made man, he was popular with the Bolsheviks and used this as leverage to persuade them to continue the war. Davison realized that Robins had over-stepped the bounds of his mission and in May 1918 recalled him.

The three-man ANRC mission that remained in Moscow was virtually the sole relief agency in Russia, but it accomplished a staggering amount of work. Allen Wardwell, who succeeded Robins, was a veteran Red Crosser and deliberately nonpolitical. Huge problems loomed in the summer of 1918. The infant mortality rate was 50 percent due to poor nutrition and the dearth of milk. That sparked an ANRC plan to ship 450,000 cans of condensed milk from America to Russia, doubtless saving many lives before the project was abandoned in May 1918. In addition to food, clothing, and medical shortages, the Russians were faced with the return of Russian prisoners of war from Germany, most of them ill and undernourished. The ANRC joined with the YMCA in Moscow to help the overcrowded hospitals with food and medicine. These had to be shipped overland in unreliable, decrepit trains from northern Russian ports to Moscow. The ANRC also distributed large amounts of clothing and cloth to orphanages. Sanitation was so bad in the cities that cholera epidemics broke out in Moscow and Petrograd. Quantities of disinfectants were rushed to Petrograd from ANRC storehouses in Moscow. By June 30, total ANRC expenditures for food, medicine, and other supplies amounted to $666,003.85.

On Aug. 30, 1918, an assassination attempt against Lenin led to an orgy of Communist terror against unarmed civilians that lasted for weeks. Despite the daily arrests and prevailing atmosphere of fear, Wardwell and his aides stayed on until, in October, the entire staff of the YMCA was arrested and imprisoned. This signaled the end of Red Cross work in Communist Russia. From then on, the ANRC concentrated its efforts in areas of northern Russia and Siberia dominated by anti-Communists and occupied by U.S. and Allied troops.

As soon as the ANRC's North Russian Commission arrived in Archangel in July 1918, it began widespread civilian relief. For the next twelve months, expeditions constantly traveled from Archangel throughout the area with supplies of food, clothing, and medicine. Accompanied by a few assistants, Major Kirkpatrick, a physician attached to the North Russian Commission, traveled across Allied-occupied northern Russia, attending the sick and leaving medicine behind. All destitute Russian families in Archangel received food and clothing from the ANRC. One million rubles worth of medicine was donated by the ANRC to the localities. The Red Cross also devoted considerable resources to caring for school children and orphans, distributing hot lunches to school children and equipping every orphanage in the district as well as providing them with regular issues of food. With the Kola Peninsula and Archangel finally in Allied hands, at least until the following summer, the ANRC resumed food shipments to Petrograd even though it was under Communist control.

In its twenty-month stay, the Siberian Commission of the ANRC, with a staff of 2,667, operated eighteen hospitals and ministered to 13,300 U.S. officers and men. The ANRC dispatched hospital trains at once to care for the 50,000 Czech troops still en route along the Trans-Siberian Railroad (TSRR) to Vladivostok. However, the ANRC's greatest challenge in Siberia, as in northern Russia, was the immediate relief of a desperate civilian population. Refugees fleeing Soviet-controlled Russia clogged the streets of Vladivostok. The ANRC built refugee barracks for 2,000 people, with medical help and food provided free of charge. The condition of these unfortunates could not compare to the gruesome misery of refugees encountered along the 4,000 miles from the Ural Mountains to Vladivostok. To reach them, the ANRC sent trains along the Trans-Siberian Railroad with over 8,000 tons of desperately needed supplies and medicines.

The journeys westward from its warehouses in Vladivostok were perilous and slow, averaging twenty-five days. The ANRC's "typhus train" was a typical example of medical relief via the Trans-Siberian Railroad. Shuttling between Vladivostok and Perm, the train bathed 105,000 people, disinfected 1 million items of clothing, issued 500,000 articles of new clothes and operated a free clinic and drug dispensary. There was also an ANRC dental clinic and a "hospital on wheels," which covered a distance of 18,000 miles.

No doubt one of the most extraordinary adventures of the ANRC in Russia was the rescue of some 1,200 Russian children stranded in the Urals. Relief workers gathered the children, conveyed them via the TSRR to Vladivostok, where the ANRC fed, sheltered, and educated them for many months. The children left with the ANRC volunteers on a Japanese ship bound for America and from there, returned to Petrograd (a far longer but safer route than the dangerous trip overland through Siberia), where their parents were sought and found.

The Red Army's defeat of White Adm. Aleksandr Vadil'evich Kolchak's forces in the fall of 1919 signaled a gradual withdrawal of the U.S. Army and the American National Red Cross from Siberia. Until the last possible moment, the ANRC assisted the continuous flood of refugees. But by the spring of 1920, the Red Army controlled the Trans-Siberian Railroad and most of Siberia, and Washington headquarters ordered the remaining ANRC staff to return home. The entire Siberian operation had cost the American National Red Cross $23 million, most of the funds going to combat typhus and to provide refugees with food, clothing, and medical care.

Sina Dubovoj

Bibliography

Bicknell, Ernest P. *With the Red Cross in Europe, 1917–1922.* Washington, DC: American National Red Cross, 1938.

Davison, Henry P. *The American Red Cross in the Great War.* New York: Macmillan, 1919.

Dulles, Foster R. *The American Red Cross, a History.* Westport, CT: Greenwood Press, 1971.

Lamont, Thomas W. *Henry P. Davison, the Record of a Useful Life.* New York: Harper, 1933.

Miller, Floyd. *The Wild Children of the Urals.* New York: Dutton, 1965.

American Social Hygiene Association

Efforts to combat venereal disease through sex education led, in 1913, to the formation of the American Social Hygiene Association (ASHA), the first major organization to favor sex education for youth outside the home. However, despite the support of John D. Rockefeller, Jr., and an influential membership led by Charles Eliot, president emeritus of Harvard, ASHA's pre-war efforts produced much negative reaction and were largely ineffective. The public's attitude toward venereal disease was generally apathetic and the government took little notice of ASHA's work.

However, the coming of war brought widespread fear that venereal disease posed a serious threat to military efficiency. Cursory examinations at mobilization camps found more than 5 percent of all inductees infected, with seven states reporting rates above 10 percent. During 1917, more than 15 percent of American soldiers were treated for syphilis or gonorrhea. Although these percentages were not really much higher than those compiled earlier in the century, they received a good deal more publicity as the health of the nation's young men was now a national priority. The American government plunged headlong into an extensive anti-venereal disease campaign. In May 1917, the General Medical Board of the Council of National Defense provided a scientific foundation for prostitution laws by declaring that "continence is not incompatible with health and is the best preventive of venereal disease."

Two weeks later, Congress passed the Selective Service Act, which included a provision forbidding prostitution within five miles of a military post. Inspired by this law and desiring to cooperate in the war effort, all state legislatures passed related ordinances during the next two years. The Public Health Service claimed that by the war's end, vigorous enforcement of these new laws had succeeded in closing more than 90 percent of the red-light districts around the country, though many reopened soon after hostilities ceased.

Although they applauded these ordinances, no one in ASHA expected to control venereal disease purely by legal means. However, ASHA viewed the government's new interest in fighting venereal disease as an opportunity for large-scale implementation of sex education and other programs. At the suggestion of William F. Snow, a highly respected public health physician and ASHA's general director, the entire male staff of the association volunteered for active military duty in order to participate in the battle against the venereal enemy.

With the association in uniform, Secretary of War Newton D. Baker named a Commission on Training Camp Activities to coordinate military anti-venereal disease and anti-vice work and designated ASHA's lawyer, Raymond Fosdick, as chairman. Under Fosdick's leadership, the commission developed a program of prompt medical treatment for soldiers infected with venereal disease, legal suppression of prostitution, provision of wholesome recreational opportunities, and sex education stressing the dangers of venereal disease for all recruits. This program was designated the "American Plan" to distinguish it from those in effect in Europe, where the emphasis was on control of venereal

disease through medical supervision of prostitution.

On July 9, 1918, Congress passed the Chamberlain-Kahn Act as part of the Army Appropriation Act for the fiscal year 1919. Among other provisions, the act established the Venereal Disease Division of the United States Public Health Service and an Interdepartmental Social Hygiene Board to implement the American Plan.

Whether this war within a war was won or lost is not clear. According to the Surgeon General's report for 1919, venereal disease was the second greatest cause of absence from duty during the war, far ahead of battle wounds and injuries. Only the worldwide epidemic of Spanish Influenza in 1918 nudged venereal disease from its customary position as the leading cause of military disability. On the other hand, this same report claims that the venereal disease rates within the army during the war were actually lower than those for civilian communities surrounding military bases. However, neither government reports nor ASHA records contain reliable statistics to support these claims.

Michael Imber

See also COMMISSION ON TRAINING CAMP ACTIVITIES; FOSDICK, RAYMOND BLAINE

Bibliography

Imber, Michael. "The First World War, Sex Education, and the American Social Hygiene Association's Campaign Against Venereal Disease." *Journal of Educational Administration and History* (January 1984).

———. "Toward a Theory of Curriculum Reform: An Analysis of the First Campaign for Sex Education." *Curriculum Inquiry* (Winter 1982).

———. "Toward a Theory of Educational Origins: The Genesis of Sex Education." *Educational Theory* (Summer 1984).

American Union Against Militarism

The American Union Against Militarism's (AUAM) roots go back to autumn 1914 when members of the Henry Street Group, composed of social workers, journalists, ministers, and professors, met informally to discuss means to prevent the United States from becoming involved in the recently declared European war. By November 1915, Lillian D. Wald, Crystal

Eastman, Jane Addams, Paul Kellogg, Oswald Garrison Villard, Emily Balch, and others had formed the Anti-Preparedness Committee, which became the AUAM in April 1916. From the outset, its members opposed military preparedness because it would stifle progress toward domestic reform and the realization of social justice.

The AUAM had 1,000 to 1,500 dues-paying members. There were probably another 60,000 volunteers and friends who could be called upon to help or support the organization. The AUAM was a radical but, nonetheless, mainstream group. Known as the "brains" of the peace movement because of the number of intellectuals who were members, the AUAM opposed conscription, supported conscientious objectors, and advocated the nationalization of the armaments industry to remove the profit motive from the manufacture of munitions.

The AUAM's effectiveness was hampered by its ambivalent attitude toward President Woodrow Wilson. Many of its leaders were strong supporters of Wilson's Progressive reform agenda and therefore were unwilling to oppose him or the politics he advocated for expediting the war effort. Others believed that stronger, more radical positions had to be taken in opposition to many of the government's war measures. A turn to the left occurred shortly after Roger Baldwin joined the AUAM and after the entry of the United States into the war in April 1917. Baldwin set up the Civil Liberties Bureau, first called the Bureau for Conscientious Objectors and later the American Civil Liberties Union, within the AUAM to provide support for conscientious objectors and for others opposing the government's infringement of their civil liberties. AUAM President Lillian Wald and Paul Kellogg opposed Baldwin and the bureau. The actual break between moderate and radical board members occurred when a majority decided to participate in a conference sponsored by the People's Council, an antiwar Socialist group. Although the decision was reversed later, it was too late to heal the rift. The AUAM disintegrated soon after. Members drifted off to other organizations more compatible with their beliefs or simply withdrew from active opposition to the war. The organization was officially dissolved on Feb. 1, 1922.

John Imholte

See also ADDAMS, JANE; CIVIL LIBERTIES BUREAU; EASTMAN, CRYSTAL; WALD, LILLIAN D.

Bibliography
Balch, Emily G., ed. *Approaches in the Great Settlement.* New York: Hubesch, 1918.
Chatfield, Charles. *The American Peace Movement.* New York: Twayne, 1992.
Cook, Blanche W. "Democracy in Wartime: Antimilitarism in England and the United States, 1914–1918." In *Peace Movements in America,* ed. by Charles Chatfield. New York: Schocken Books, 1973.
Johnson, Donald. *The Challenge to American Freedoms.* Lexington: University of Kentucky Press, 1963.
Link, Arthur S. *Wilson: Campaigns for Progressivism and Peace, 1916–1917.* Princeton, NJ: Princeton University Press, 1981.

American Volunteer Squadron, French Air Service

See LAFAYETTE ESCADRILLE

Andrews, Avery Delano (1864–1959)

Avery Delano Andrews graduated from the United States Military Academy at West Point in 1886 and was commissioned as a second lieutenant in the 5th Artillery. Following duty at Fort Columbus, Governors Island, New York, and at headquarters, Division of the Atlantic, Andrews served as aide-de-camp to LtGen. John M. Schofield, commanding general of the U.S. Army from 1889 to 1892. While stationed in Washington, D.C., Andrews earned a law degree from Columbia University. A year later he received a law degree from New York University Law School.

In 1893, Andrews resigned his commission and began practicing law in New York City. He was also a member of the Board of Police Commissioners of New York City. During the Spanish-American War he served as a lieutenant colonel of volunteers on the staff of MajGen. James H. Wilson at Camp Thomas, Chattanooga, Tennessee. After working for a year as chief of staff for Governor Theodore Roosevelt of New York and as adjutant general of the state of New York, Andrews concentrated on a business career.

Shortly after the United States entered World War I, Andrews became director of military service for the Committee of Public Safety of Pennsylvania. In October 1917, he was commissioned as a colonel of engineers in the National Army and sent to France, where he served as deputy director of transportation, deputy chief of utilities, and deputy assistant chief of staff of the Service of Supply of the American Expeditionary Force. During his tenure with the Service of Supply, Andrews was a member of a five-man board chaired by Col. Johnson Hagood that, in February 1918, laid out the organization of the headquarters, general staff, and supply services of the AEF that would be in effect, with slight changes, until the war's end.

In August 1918, Gen. John J. Pershing, a close friend since their days at West Point, appointed Andrews assistant chief of staff of the AEF General Staff. In this position he supervised a wide variety of administrative functions including the organization and equipment of troops, the establishment of priority for troop shipments, and the replacement of men and animals. By the end of the war Andrews, now a brigadier general, had requisitioned more than 500,000 men from the United States for the AEF to replace losses and meet emergency requirements.

Following the war, Andrews resumed his business career. He retired in 1930, and nine years later published a laudatory biography of Pershing entitled *My Friend and Classmate, John J. Pershing.* Andrews died on April 19, 1959.

John K. Ohl

Bibliography

Hagood, Johnson. *The Services of Supply.* Boston: Houghton Mifflin, 1927.

Harbord, James G. *The American Army in France, 1917–1918.* Boston: Little, Brown, 1936.

Anglo-American Relations

Before and after the United States entered the First World War, the Wilson administration's determination to keep militarism and selfish nationalism from dominating the world, and thus from threatening American interests and American ambitions, was the major influence upon a foreign policy that ultimately required cooperation with the Allies and especially with the United Kingdom.

It was Wilson who defined that policy. His adamant assertion of traditional neutral rights between 1914 and 1917 arose from his conviction that exigencies of war must not be allowed to nullify precepts of international law. Wilson understood that many of those precepts, and particularly the rules governing the conduct of war, were obsolete. His purpose was to insure that their revision would be accomplished in an orderly way as part of the establishment of a new approach to international relations rather than in haphazard changes dictated by the success of arms. As a scholar of government, he understood the utility and importance of registering protests in preventing the unilateral revision of customary rules. By objecting to British war measures, Washington reserved its right to refuse to accept them as precedents. So long as the grievances identified in those protests remained amenable to subsequent rectification through negotiations, and so long as there was in the objectionable conduct no implicit rejection of the eventual redefinition of the international order along the lines Wilson sought, none of the problems dividing the United States and Great Britain during the period of neutrality was irreconcilable. Thus the President's differentiation between German conduct that imperiled human life and British conduct that complicated American commerce was neither disingenuousness nor sophistry. Only when British behavior seemed to reflect a determination never to subscribe to the new standards Wilson sought did the strain on Anglo-American relations become dangerous.

London's conduct of the war at sea and its responses to Wilson's efforts to end the fighting short of absolute victory always bore the potential for serious division. From the outset, Britain's reliance on its naval power led to confrontations with American claims of neutral rights, for London refused to abide by the unratified Declaration of London of 1909, leaving the nineteenth-century rules of maritime warfare as the only standards against which to measure the conduct of navies. These the British immediately transgressed by expanding the list of absolute and conditional contraband beyond traditional limits and then by applying the doctrine of continuous voyage more ambitiously than ever before. The result was a challenge to virtually all neutral commerce with the Central Powers and to commerce between neutrals as well.

Foreign Secretary Sir Edward Grey, while a fervent exponent of the naval stranglehold on Germany, ultimately sympathized with Wilson's aspirations for change. For that reason, and because he appreciated Britain's increasing dependence upon American financial and material resources, he did his best to maintain American goodwill. He championed compensating American exporters for seized cargoes, and his influence was paramount in London's decision to buy an adequate supply of American cotton to maintain a price high enough to quiet complaints about the stifling of cotton exports to European neutrals. Ambassador Sir Cecil Arthur Spring-Rice was not, however, the best advocate the British might have had in Washington, for his close friendship with American industrial and financial magnates and leaders of the Republican Party had long antagonized the administration.

Likewise, the American case was jeopardized by the clearly unneutral attitude of Ambassador Walter Hines Page in London, who diluted even the initial protests that did little more than warn of the danger to the American public's attitude toward the Allies should the draconian restrictions on trade remain in effect. Page's reluctance to appear less than friendly to Whitehall constantly frustrated Wilson. Unable to find a suitable replacement for the ambassador, Wilson held the reins of Anglo-American relations tightly in his own hands, and communication between the two governments on the most important matters was thus often left to the President's personal envoys, notably Col. Edward M. House, on whom the President particularly relied to explore any chance for American mediation to end the war.

Unlike Wilson, Secretary of State William Jennings Bryan did not question the possibility of complete neutrality under antiquated rules. It was he who urged Wilson to ban all loans by Americans to belligerent governments when the war began, seeking to avoid any commitments that might deflect the United States from its course of absolute uninvolvement. As they considered American protests against their maritime restrictions and certain legislative proposals designed to increase American merchant tonnage, the British regarded the ban on loans as pro-German. London interpreted all such measures as attempts to negate Britain's most important advantages as a belligerent. The ban on loans, however, lasted only two months. Its reversal, thinly disguised as permission for private citizens and firms to extend credit, was an early indication of the decline of Bryan's influence as well as of the growing importance of

Britain's wartime market to a depressed American economy.

The administration continued to protest the inclusion of foodstuffs and other raw materials on the contraband lists, such onerous restrictions as the designation of the entire North Sea as a war zone, and the requirement that all ships wishing to traverse those waters put in at British ports (where they could most easily be searched) for charts or pilots. Technically, there was no blockade, for Britain chose not to test the aged legal definition against the requirements of modern war. But Grey referred to the restrictions as a blockade, and since they remained in effect, almost all American seaborne trade was diverted to Britain and its allies. The result was a commercial relationship of vital importance to both countries.

That trade was not, however, the most important factor in Wilson's decision not to press his protests to the point of rupturing Anglo-American relations. German countermeasures, which included the indiscriminate use of contact mines and then the recourse to submarine warfare, regularly deflected American rage from London to Berlin. These actions gave credibility to British propaganda accounts of German barbarism generally and encouraged the turn of American opinion in the Allies' favor. In marked contrast to his stern-but-patient reaction to Britain's "blockade," Wilson immediately declared that Germany would be held to "strict accountability" for its actions against American citizens. German policy narrowed the gap between London and Washington by underscoring what they had in common.

When Anglo-American relations were at a low point after Britain's suppression of the Easter Rebellion in Ireland, including the execution of its leader, Sir Roger Casement, which profoundly offended American public opinion— the torpedoing of the unarmed *Sussex* passenger ship in the English Channel in March 1916 turned the spotlight on Germany. Comparing his situation to that of James Madison in 1812, Wilson also likened the kaiser to Napoleon. In both cases, Britain opposed the most dangerous threat to peace and freedom. Too rigorous American insistence upon neutral rights had effectively put the country on the wrong side a century before, and the President did not mean to repeat the mistake.

London overestimated the license the *Sussex* affair provided to tighten its noose around Germany, for Berlin's prompt pledge to abandon unrestricted submarine warfare once again raised the visibility of British offenses in American eyes. Thus the British proclamation of a blacklist of American firms to be boycotted for trading with the Central Powers, the refusal to provide bunker coal to merchantmen that did not abide by British maritime regulations, and especially the interference with trans-Atlantic mail, produced the moment of greatest tension between the United States and Britain during the autumn of 1916. Wilson was already impatient with London's failure to implement the House-Grey Memorandum of the previous February, which promised that the Allies would attend a conference to negotiate a settlement, for British inaction denied the President an opportunity to intercede to bring peace. And the rhetoric of the presidential election campaign, in which the Democratic Party's boast that "He Kept Us Out of War" accentuated strict neutrality, both limited the President's flexibility and antagonized Britons, who resented the implication that their cause was no better than Germany's.

Such stands by the two sides in moral terms also help explain Britain's unhelpful replies whenever Wilson offered to mediate the conflict between 1914 and 1917. Indeed, the President's call for war aims in December 1916, which followed quickly upon a heavily conditional German proposal for a peace conference, looked far too much like support for Berlin to suit Whitehall. Neither belligerent was prepared in those first years of war to consider a peace that did not include victory, which was the essence of Wilson's appeals even before he coined the phrase "Peace Without Victory" in January 1917. Yet it was a major strength of British diplomacy that London's responses, even when negative, seemed to come closer to the President's desires than did the declarations from Berlin.

While Germany's resumption of unrestricted submarine warfare ended American neutrality, it did not guarantee harmony between the United States and its new partners at war. Determined to avoid even the appearance of being the tail of the British dog, Wilson resented London's habit of taking initiatives on its own and expecting American cooperation. In military and naval affairs, there was little the President could do to change that pattern, and in most cases the United States accepted British leadership on questions of grand strategy throughout the war. Relatively minor differ-ences over naval building programs and the American role in antisubmarine warfare were uniformly resolved according to British desires. Even on the controversial question of whether American troops were to be "brigaded" with Allied armies or given an independent mission with an independent command, Wilson ultimately compromised General Pershing's insistence upon autonomy.

There were two strategic issues on which the President and the British government differed irreconcilably. One was the purpose and extent of Allied intervention in Russia. Refusing to countenance participation in the Russian Civil War, Wilson delayed the intervention and limited it, although he failed to prevent the futile attempt to unseat the Bolshevik government. Americans may have been the first international troops to leave Russia, but they had been engaged in that attempt. The other, less consequential difference involved Prime Minister David Lloyd George's effort to engage the United States in persuading his own military commanders to shift the main military effort from the Western Front to an attack on the Austrian Empire and through southeastern Europe. Since American generals, like their British counterparts, opposed the idea, it came to nought.

The entry of the United States in the war meant salvation for Britain, whose treasury, stocks of munitions and materiel, and pools of troops had reached their last reserves by April 1917. American financial aid to London was substantial and timely, although there were several threats to limit it and although it was bound up with conditions and strings that would come back to haunt Anglo-American relations after the war. Nor did it come cheaply at the time: the British government had to reduce its gold reserves to critical levels and mortgage most of the securities it held in the United States.

Wilson, and most Americans, assumed at first that the American contribution to the war effort would be limited to money and supplies. In April 1917, Foreign Secretary Arthur J. Balfour disabused the President of that assumption when he arrived (uninvited) in Washington on a special mission. Balfour explained the Allies' urgent need for all manner of aid and support, including troops.

Ambassador Spring-Rice's ineffectiveness led to the dispatch of the mercurial newspaper magnate Lord Northcliffe as head of a British purchasing and financial mission in New York, but this division of Britain's official voice only complicated matters. A young intelligence officer, Capt. Sir William Wiseman, managed to ingratiate himself sufficiently with House and then Wilson to become a crucial conduit of information and ideas. He helped bring about the consolidation of the British voice in Washington even before Lord Reading replaced Spring-Rice in early 1918, and then provided an efficient diplomatic backdoor for Anglo-American consultation that influenced important decisions throughout the war.

Though Wilson named House as his representative to the Allied Supreme War Council in response to Lloyd George's pleas, House in fact attended only two council meetings, one of them at the end of the war. The President had no objection to General Tasker Howard Bliss participating in the council's military deliberations, but his determination to keep the United States an "Associated Power" meant that he would not be tied to Allied plans for the political structure of the peace. Thus, not participating in the political deliberations of the Supreme War Council preserved American independence, but it may also have put the United States at a disadvantage when the peace conference began.

On his mission to Washington, Balfour adopted a posture of candor with the administration and, as evidence of British openness, offered to show Wilson the treaties, including the Treaty of London of 1915, in which the Allies had exchanged promises about the postwar settlement. Though the President was cordial and appreciative, he declined to examine the treaties then, a decision perfectly consistent with his refusal to sign a formal alliance with Britain. For while Britain had clear advantages in determining military strategy, American entry into the war gave Washington immense leverage in dictating the terms of the peace which would increase with the American contribution to the war.

Postwar planning was the major source of friction between the United States and Britain during the war, for Wilson suspected British motives and distrusted Britain's commitments to old-fashioned international arrangements, including its traditional interpretation of the freedom of the seas. He opposed London's obvious intention to punish Germany after the war, and he refused even to discuss British proposals for a league of nations, first, because he

understood that the nature of the league would depend on whether Germany was truly defeated and, second, that the league would be a version of the Holy Alliance against the former enemy powers. The President had important supporters in the Liberal and Labour camps in Britain, in response to whom Lloyd George finally pledged his support for a new world system in his Trades Union Congress speech of January 1918. Wilson's Fourteen Points address, delivered less than a week later, galvanized reformers in Britain and on the Continent behind the President's approach.

Wilson's unilateral handling of the German appeal for an armistice in the fall of 1918, during which he succeeded in making the Fourteen Points and a league integral parts of the peace settlement, infuriated British leaders. But the threat of a separate peace compelled Lloyd George to accept Wilson's achievement, with the sole reservation that the definition of freedom of the seas had yet to be decided. The President was surprisingly flexible on that issue and on the question of the fate of German colonies when he arrived in Europe for the peace conference.

Ultimately, it was the prospect of Anglo-American entente that dictated British openness to Wilson's postwar plans, but even that was not universally celebrated in London. Avid Atlanticists among commonwealth leaders had significant territorial ambitions in direct conflict with the President's intentions. Foreign Office professionals were strongly averse to abandoning Britain's historic partnership with France. Conservatives, increasingly resentful of Wilson's constant recourse to principle, were outraged by American insistence upon dictating the conditions of relief and recovery programs in Europe. After the American election of 1918, encouraged by the vigorous lobbying of Senator Henry Cabot Lodge, Wilson's opponents in Britain dismissed the President as a lame duck who did not speak for his own government. There was, therefore, no certainty to Anglo-American unity in the peace conference.

Like all the issues that had separated the two nations since 1914, however, the difficult question of how to structure the postwar world was ultimately less significant than their mutual commitment to the general principle that the world required a new structure. The Anglo-American diplomatic tradition insured their common interest in limiting the influence of militarism and in guaranteeing the dominance of a rule of law in international affairs. These left ample room for bitter differences, which were exacerbated by the decline of British power and the ascendancy of the United States. But they would be differences between governments working together for the same ultimate purpose.

Richard A. Harrison

See also HOUSE, EDWARD MANDELL; HOUSE-GREY MEMORANDUM; SUPREME WAR COUNCIL

Bibliography

Coogan, John W. *The End of Neutrality: The United States, Britain, and Maritime Rights, 1899–1915*. Ithaca, NY: Cornell University Press, 1981.

Egerton, George W. *Great Britain and the Creation of the League of Nations: Strategy, Politics, and International Organization, 1914–1919*. Chapel Hill: University of North Carolina Press, 1979.

Fowler, Wilton B. *British-American Relations, 1917–1918: The Role of Sir William Wiseman*. Princeton, NJ: Princeton University Press, 1969.

Link, Arthur S. *Wilson: Confusions and Crises, 1915–1916*. Princeton, NJ: Princeton University Press, 1964.

Trask, David F. *Captains and Cabinets: Anglo-American Naval Relations, 1917–1918*. Columbia: University of Missouri Press, 1972.

Woodward, Sir Llewellyn. *Great Britain and the War of 1914–1918*. London: Methuen, 1967.

Ansell, Samuel Tilden (1875–1954)

Educated at the United States Military Academy, Samuel Tilden Ansell began his commissioned service with the infantry in 1899. He also earned an LL.B. from the University of North Carolina in 1904.

Ansell served in the Philippine Insurrection, as an instructor in law at West Point, and as an attorney before the federal courts of the United States for Puerto Rico and the Philippines. After the United States entered World War I, he was promoted to lieutenant colonel and then to the temporary rank of brigadier general in October 1917. He served as the acting judge advocate general of the army during Gen. Enoch H. Crowder's absence while serving as provost marshal general to administer the draft.

For two years Ansell dealt with the shortcomings and problems of the Articles of War as applied to an army of about 4 million civilian draftees serving at home and overseas. Confronted by court-martial cases that involved excessive sentences and other injustices, Ansell established a system of review in the Office of the Judge Advocate General and sought other changes in court-martial procedures that would bring military practices into closer conformity to civilian criminal procedures.

Ansell presented his ideas to the Senate Military Affairs Committee in 1919. This public criticism of the court-martial system precipitated a controversy over the Articles of War and hostile rebuttals from Crowder, Secretary of War Newton D. Baker, and other senior army leaders.

Ansell received support for reform of the military justice system from Senator George E. Chamberlain and Representative Royal C. Johnson, but the opposition of his army superiors and reversion to his permanent rank of lieutenant colonel following demobilization forced Ansell to resign from the service in July 1919 to enter private law practice. With the help of Senator Chamberlain, Ansell continued to press for reform in late 1919 and 1920. Congress subsequently included some of Ansell's reforms relating to review of serious court-martial sentences in the National Defense Act of 1920.

John M. Lindley

See also NATIONAL DEFENSE ACT OF 1920

Bibliography

Lindley, John M. *A Soldier Is Also a Citizen: The Controversy Over Military Justice in the U.S. Army, 1917–1920*. New York: Garland, 1990.

Antisubmarine Warfare

Antisubmarine warfare was the decisive naval contest of World War I. As an island nation, Great Britain was extremely vulnerable to economic destruction and even starvation should an adversary gain control of the sea. Stalemated on land and unable to defeat the British in a fleet action, Germany gambled on an all-out campaign to blockade the British Isles with submarines. Had it been successful, Britain could not have continued the war, and the United States would not have been able to deliver and supply the American Expeditionary Force (AEF) across the Atlantic.

In 1914, the submarine was a new and largely untested naval weapon that both sides employed primarily against enemy warships. In September, a single German submarine sank three British cruisers in one hour, dramatically demonstrating the striking power of the new weapon. After that the submarine menace loomed large in the minds of British admirals and imposed severe restrictions on fleet movements in submarine-infested areas. However, warships were not actually easy targets for submarines due to their generally high speed and heavy destroyer escorts after 1914. German submarines increasingly concentrated on merchant shipping, which offered much easier targets and struck directly at Britain's most vulnerable point—its overseas supply lines. After the Battle of Jutland in 1916 convinced the Germans to abandon hope of a victorious fleet action, their submarines focused entirely on the destruction of shipping. British losses increased sharply, from less than 37,000 tons in June 1916 to over 180,000 tons in December. Once Germany declared unrestricted submarine warfare in February 1917, attacking all targets without warning, British losses jumped again to over 300,000 tons in February and over 500,000 tons in April.

In the nick of time, the entry of American escorts and aircraft into the war and the adoption of the convoy system turned the tide. The American Expeditionary Force arrived safely in France, with the loss of only one troopship and less than a hundred men. Monthly shipping losses remained above 100,000 tons until October 1918, but they were within the Allied capacity to replace them, while submarine losses rose quickly to levels that the German Navy could not endure.

The desperate struggle between submarines and antisubmarine escorts for the Allies' vital sea lanes of communication involved a continuous tactical as well as technical contest. Each side attempted to gain an advantage through improved methods, improved weapons, or a combination of both, and the tide turned many times before the Allied effort eventually was successful. Antisubmarine tactics were essentially of three types: barriers, hunting patrols, and convoys. One of the earliest techniques employed by the Royal Navy against the U-boats was a mine barrage intended to close "choke points" and prevent the enemy

from reaching its patrol areas. The Dover Straits, leading from the North Sea to the Atlantic, were relatively simple to guard with mines and destroyer patrols once sufficient resources were devoted to that purpose, and by the summer of 1918, this route was essentially closed. However, the other North Sea exit, between Norway and Scotland, was too vast, and the Royal Navy was never able to close it successfully, even after the United States Navy joined the effort in 1917. Mines laid in the Dover Straits, North Sea, and off the German coast sank fifty-two submarines, more than any other single weapon, but were unable to prevent the U-boats from continuing their devastating campaign.

If U-boats could not be penned into their home waters, they would have to be hunted down, the Royal Navy concluded early in the war. To this end, the British dedicated hundreds of antisubmarine craft, large and small, ranging from major warships to frail civilian trawlers conscripted and armed for the duration, that patrolled choke points and known submarine operating areas. Unfortunately, these hunting patrols found the oceans vast and the submarines all but invisible, and once again huge resources proved unequal to the task.

An interesting variant of the hunting method was the Q-ship. This was a decoy vessel with a naval crew and concealed guns made to look like an unarmed civilian ship in order to lure a submarine into approaching on the surface. When the submarine was at point-blank range, the Q-ship would raise its naval colors, uncover its guns, and sink the helpless submarine before it could escape. Q-ships had some success early in the war before Germany adopted unrestricted submarine warfare and sank targets on sight without approaching on the surface. Beyond some deterrent effect on submarine attacks upon apparent stragglers, the Q-ships sank few submarines and suffered heavy losses. The British had abandoned the tactic by the time the United States entered the war, but the U.S. Navy still employed a Q-ship of its own, with similarly meager results.

The tactical answer to the U-boat problem came from another direction entirely. If confining or hunting the submarines was hopeless, all that was left was to guard their targets so closely that attack would be suicidal. This escort policy had been applied to main fleet units all along, but merchantmen had been allowed to sail independently because the Royal

Navy lacked the resources to escort them all individually and wide dispersal seemed the next best alternative. Not until 1917 did the Admiralty admit that concentrating merchant shipping in convoys was a viable alternative.

Opposition to convoy, a tactic against commerce raiders for centuries, had several sources. The highly organized British Admiralty doubted the ability of merchant captains to navigate in a crowded convoy without massive collisions. Cautious admirals also worried that there were too few escorts to defend a convoy effectively, and a poorly defended convoy was just a rich U-boat feast concentrated in one place. Finally, naval officers disliked in principle supposedly "defensive" techniques such as convoys, much preferring an active chase method such as the hunting patrols.

The adoption of convoy in 1917, which spelled the end of effective submarine warfare, resulted from a combination of circumstances. First, the situation in early 1917 was so desperate that the Admiralty was ready to try any method, no matter how distasteful, and the British civilian government was pressing it to do so. Second, the entry of the U.S. Navy into the war in April 1917 added the escorts and escort construction capacity of the world's second largest naval power to Britain's, largely eliminating the resource constraint. And finally, an experimental convoy to Gibraltar and others to Scandinavia demonstrated that merchant captains could indeed sail in convoy and that such formations did not offer happy hunting to submarines—but rather left them impotent.

Convoys proved to be not only an effective defense, but also the most effective offensive tactic against the submarine. No matter how effective they were at hiding from hunting patrols, U-boats had to come out of hiding to attack their targets. Convoy escorts did not have to face long, fruitless searches for their quarry; the enemy came to them. With convoys as bait, British and American antisubmarine craft began sinking U-boats wholesale and by late 1918 had driven them from the seas.

The actual technology used against submarines had a similarly prolonged course of development during four years of war. When the war began, a fully submerged submarine was quite undetectable. The only means of spotting a submarine was to catch it on the surface or sight its periscope while it was submerged. Since submarines needed periscope observations to attack and could not remain submerged for very long,

this was not a hopeless proposition. However, submarines not actually engaged in an attack could always elude their pursuer by diving below periscope depth and moving off fully submerged.

Antisubmarine escorts needed a more reliable means of detection, and they found one in 1916 in the hydrophone, a listening device that allowed escort vessels to locate submarines by listening for their engine and propeller noise. This, too, was an imperfect solution, since the oceans were full of extraneous noises, not the least from the escorts' own engines and propellers, which helped to mask the sound of any submarines. The best apparatus for detecting submarines arrived just as the war ended, with the development of sonar (sound navigation and ranging), or asdic in British parlance from the initials of the Allied Submarine Detection Investigation Committee, the team of scientists that developed the technology. This device produced an underwater sound wave that echoed off any solid object it met. By timing the travel of the sound and echo, the transmitting ship could calculate the position, range, and movements of an underwater object invisible from the surface. Unfortunately, it entered service too late to make a difference in World War I but proved vital in the next antisubmarine war twenty years later.

The most effective means of locating submarines during World War I, however, was the airplane. Airplanes and seaplanes flying from shore bases could scan much larger areas of ocean from the air than were visible from the surface, making sightings of surfaced U-boats more likely. Moreover, they actually could see a submerged submarine underneath them if it was close to the surface, rendering their quarry even more vulnerable. Aircraft escorted convoys and patrolled known submarine operating areas, with devastating effect. Aircraft bombs sank only one submarine directly, but aircraft helped surface escorts to sink numerous others and, most important, ensured that submarines could not escape detection. As a result, U-boats avoided air patrols like the plague, and in the entire war only five ships were lost from air-escorted convoys.

At the beginning of the war, there was no way to kill a submerged submarine. If one was caught on the surface or at periscope depth, a surface vessel could ram it or sink it with gunfire. The fragility of a submarine made it unnecessary to inflict heavy damage, but its small size and ability to submerge before an attacker came within range made ramming or surface fire inadequate weapons. The Royal Navy needed a weapon capable of hurting a submerged submarine; in 1916, it developed the depth charge to accomplish this. The depth charge was a contained charge about the size of an ash can (hence the nickname), filled with a few hundred pounds of explosive and triggered by a hydrostatic detonator which set off the explosives when the charge reached a preset depth. The "ash cans" were rolled off the stern of an escort or fired several dozen yards from launchers, singly or in patterns. It was necessary to know the target location and depth with some precision in order to employ the depth charge effectively, but even a near miss was often sufficient to rupture a thin submarine hull and force it to surface or sink. Depth charges killed twenty-nine submarines by the end of the war, more than any other weapon except mines, and brought many more to the surface, where they could be sunk with gunfire.

Signals intelligence also contributed to the success of the antisubmarine campaign. Royal Navy codebreakers in Room 40 of the Admiralty learned to decipher the radio communications that directed German submarines to their patrol areas and reported their target sightings. Using this information, Room 40 could reroute convoys away from danger areas and direct escorts to where German submarines could be found. Although coordination between the codebreaking and operations sections was not as smooth in World War I as it was in World War II, antisubmarine forces received vital information, which simplified their task substantially.

By November 1918, the Allies were confident that the submarine menace had been blunted for good by convoy tactics, aircraft, depth charges, and sonar. However, German submarine captains developed several countermeasures that might have renewed their success had the war continued. In the Mediterranean, German submarines began to operate in groups, or "wolfpacks" which allowed them to outnumber and overwhelm a small convoy escort. They also learned to attack at night on the surface, where the darkness concealed them from aircraft and their surface position concealed them from sonar. Both these tactics produced dramatic results for their World War II successors.

David MacGregor

See also MINES; NORTH SEA MINE BARRAGE; OTRANTO BARRAGE; Q-SHIPS; SIMS, WILLIAM SOWDEN

Bibliography

Beesly, Patrick. *Room 40: British Naval Intelligence, 1914–1918*. London: Hamish Hamilton, 1982.
Hackman, Willem. *Seek and Strike: Sonar, Anti-Submarine Warfare and the Royal Navy*. London: Her Majesty's Stationery Office, 1984.
Marder, Arthur J. *From the Dreadnought to Scapa Flow*. London: Oxford University Press, 1978.

Arabic and *Sussex* Pledges

The episodes of the *Arabic* and *Sussex* were a part of the long struggle between the United States and Germany over the use of submarine warfare from 1914 to 1917, the period before the United States entered the First World War. The incidents tested the ability of President Woodrow Wilson to protect the rights and interests of the United States while keeping the country out of the conflict. They tested the strength of German Chancellor Theobald von Bethmann Hollweg in fighting factional battles within the German government and ultimately whether or not Germany would go to war with the United States. Both episodes represented an extension of the controversy over the sinking of the British liner *Lusitania* on May 7, 1915. When the American government sent three notes of protest and demands, the German government proceeded to haggle, and as the summer of 1915 wore on, it was not clear where matters stood on the sinking of the great British liner or on submarine warfare in general.

Into this unsettled state of affairs came the sinking of the *Arabic*, a British passenger ship of 15,000 tons. It was torpedoed by a German submarine on Aug. 15, 1915. The fact that the vessel was bound westward from England made the issue of contraband superfluous. Two Americans were killed in the incident. The sinking seemingly clarified the issue of submarine warfare in all too dramatic a fashion and presented President Wilson with a terrible dilemma. If it went unprotested, it meant that Germany could pursue its own course on the Atlantic Ocean, regardless of the consequences for the United States. On the other hand, to force acceptance of American demands—essen-

A

tially that Germany must stop all submarine activity that threatened American lives and property—probably would entail a threat to break relations and possibly more. It could lead to war. The case of the *Lusitania* had narrowed the President's options, and he knew he had to act. Rather than issue a public threat, however, he had Secretary of State Robert Lansing use quieter diplomatic channels to convey his message that Germany must yield or face a break in relations.

Bethmann Hollweg took the threat seriously. He believed that American intervention on the enemy's side would mean defeat for Germany, and he was determined to prevent it. But concessions on submarine warfare meant a showdown with naval officials who were anxious to use U-boats without restriction. Bethmann Hollweg thereupon formed an alliance with German Army chief of staff, Erich von Falkenhayn, in a quest for approval from the final voice on policy: Kaiser Wilhelm II. The tactic succeeded. Defeat for the navy led to the firing of Gustav Bachmann, head of the German Admiralty, and almost to resignation of Grand Admiral Alfred von Tirpitz, the navy's leader within the government. On Sept. 1, 1915, the German ambassador to the United States, Johann von Bernstorff, submitted to Lansing a promise that submarines thereafter would not sink passenger ships without warning. Germany later repudiated the sinking and offered an indemnity. These concessions, especially the promise to spare passenger liners, became known as the *Arabic* Pledge. It represented a first victory on submarine warfare for President Wilson.

The torpedoing of the *Sussex* some seven months later, on March 24, 1916, again highlighted the submarine controversy and political struggles within the German government. An unarmed English Channel steamer that carried passengers, the *Sussex* did not sink, but some eighty persons lost their lives in the incident. While several Americans were aboard, none were killed. The commander of the German U-boat probably made a mistake of identification, although the navy generally was looking for an opportunity for a more liberal use of submarine activity. The incident, in any case, appeared to be a violation of the recent *Arabic* promise; it perhaps indicated a new round of submarine activity and certainly presented a new challenge to Wilson. The disheartened president saw but two options at his disposal: he must break re-

lations with Germany at once or he must openly threaten a break pending a virtual German surrender to all American demands. Choosing the second approach, he dispatched, on April 18, a message that demanded an end to submarine warfare against all "passenger and freight-carrying vessels." Wilson made the note and the threat public, fully understanding that he might be setting in motion events that could lead the United States to war.

Bethmann Hollweg's response to the crisis over the *Sussex* was identical to his attitude toward the case of the *Arabic*. He was determined to prevent submarine warfare from bringing Germany into war against a new enemy. The chancellor fortunately was equipped to meet the challenge. In the weeks before the attack on the *Sussex,* he had fought off a new naval effort to promote expanded submarine activity against enemy and neutral shipping. By challenging the navy's claims about the effectiveness of submarines and by emphasizing the potential American contribution to the Allied war effort, he not only had acquired support from a whimsical monarch, but also had maneuvered the resignation of his chief rival in the government, Grand Admiral Tirpitz. Concession in the incident of the *Sussex* logically followed. It came on May 4, 1916. The settlement of the case of the *Sussex* differed from that of the *Arabic* in that the German renunciation of sudden submarine attacks in the second case was extended to merchantmen, enemy or neutral, as well as passenger ships. There was to be no genuine submarine warfare, as least not for the immediate future. Submarines could continue to operate as cruisers, stopping ships at sea and searching them. Germany did leave itself liberty of action, pending similar concessions from the Allies to the United States.

Taken together, the pledges in the cases of the *Arabic* and *Sussex* represented a remarkable victory for President Wilson in the spring of 1916. He received virtually everything he asked for and for the time being did manage to keep the country out of war. The pledges also represented a victory for Chancellor Bethmann Hollweg over adversaries in the German government. Because the victory was never complete, however, Bethmann Hollweg would be subject to new pressures and challenges as the war continued. The promises represented only a temporary answer to the vexing submarine question. Failure to find a permanent solution to the problem would hold fateful consequences for Germany, for the United States, and for both nations' leaders.

Ross Gregory

Bibliography

Gregory, Ross. *The Origins of American Intervention in the First World War.* New York: Norton, 1971.

Link, Arthur S. *Wilson: The Struggle for Neutrality 1914–1915.* Princeton, NJ: Princeton University Press, 1960.

———. *Wilson: Confusions and Crises 1915–1916.* Princeton, NJ: Princeton University Press, 1964.

———, ed. *The Papers of Woodrow Wilson.* 69 vols. Princeton, NJ: Princeton University Press, 1993.

May, Ernest R. *The World War and American Isolation, 1914–1917.* Cambridge: Harvard University Press, 1959.

Armed Neutrality

Persuaded by the arguments of his military and naval advisers, Kaiser Wilhelm II decided on Jan. 9, 1917, to break the *Sussex* Pledge by engaging in unrestricted submarine warfare, effective Feb. 1, 1917. German leaders knew that the decision would probably bring the United States into the war on the Allied side, but they concluded that their U-boats could destroy sufficient British tonnage over the following five or six months to force her out of the war. With Britain removed, the war would end. The U.S. contribution would be too little and too late. Some Germans even hoped that the United States would remain neutral. After all, Woodrow Wilson had only recently won reelection as President by wooing voters with the slogan, "He kept us out of war."

The German note announcing unrestricted submarine warfare stated that all navigation, including neutrals, was forbidden in a zone around Great Britain, France, and Italy and in the eastern Mediterranean. Any Allied or neutral vessel, merchant or naval, would be sunk on sight by the German Navy. It did stipulate one exception—a single American merchant ship without contraband aboard could sail to and from Falmouth, England, each week, provided that three one-meter vertical stripes of alternating red and white were painted on the hull. The ship must fly red and white checkered flags from its stern and masthead, be lighted at night, and follow a course determined by German authorities.

These terms were totally unacceptable to the American government. When published by Germany in American newspapers, the American public interpreted them as a blatant effort to humiliate the United States.

Two American merchant ships were sunk by U-boats in February, but in each instance a warning was given and no lives were lost. Nonetheless, American shippers were concerned. They demanded that naval guns and gun crews be placed on their ships for protection. At first, Wilson was opposed to armed merchantmen because he felt it could ultimately lead to direct American participation in the war. But, on February 25, he learned of a telegram that the British had intercepted from Alfred Zimmermann, the German foreign minister, to the Mexican government. It proposed an alliance between Germany and Mexico in return for the restoration of territory that the United States had obtained as a result of the Mexican War (1846–1848).

The following day, Wilson requested approval from Congress to arm American merchant ships. The House of Representatives approved his appeal by a 403–14 vote, but Robert La Follette and George Norris led a group of senators in a filibuster that prevented the bill from being considered prior to the required adjournment of the 64th Congress on March 4. After consulting with Secretary of State Robert Lansing, Attorney General Thomas W. Gregory, and others, Wilson indicated on March 9 that in spite of congressional inaction, he would authorize the placement of guns and gun crews on merchant ships. He based his decision on a 1797 statute that had been used to arm American ships in the undeclared war with France in 1798. On March 18, three American merchant ships—the *City of Memphis*, *Illinois*, and *Vigilancia*—were sunk, and American lives were lost. Although Wilson realized that his armed neutrality policy would probably lead to war, he had hoped that Germany would refrain from committing an overt action. The March 18 sinkings made American participation in the war inevitable. Armed neutrality ended on April 6 when the United States joined the Allied powers as a belligerent.

John Imholte

See also ARABIC AND *SUSSEX* PLEDGES; LANSING, ROBERT

Bibliography

Link, Arthur S. *Wilson the Diplomat: A Look at His Major Foreign Policies*. Baltimore: Johns Hopkins Press, 1957.

Lowitt, Richard. "The Armed-Ship Bill Controversy: A Legislative View." *Mid-American* (January 1964).

May, Ernest R. *The World War and American Isolation, 1914–1917*. Cambridge: Harvard University Press, 1959.

Smith, Daniel M. *Robert Lansing and American Neutrality, 1914–1917*. Berkeley: University of California Press, 1958.

Armistices of 1918

Between Sept. 29 and Nov. 13, 1918, all the Central Powers signed armistices with the Allies and the United States. Before World War I, an armistice may have meant a temporary cease-fire for some particular purpose, such as rescuing the wounded from a battlefield. In contrast, the armistices at the end of World War I were surrenders in which the Allies and the United States achieved the greater number of their war aims, at least temporarily.

The collapse of the Central Powers began when the Germans were unable to make their March 1918 Offensive a decisive military action. After it ground to a halt in mid-summer, the Allies and the United States steadily drove the Germans backwards. Equally worrisome to German's allies—Bulgaria, the Ottoman Empire, and Austria-Hungary—was that German military assistance all but stopped.

The Allied Army of the East, facing Bulgaria in the Balkans, launched a new attack on Sept. 15, 1918. On Sept. 25, with their front lines crumbling, the Bulgarian leaders decided to seek an armistice. The French commander of the Army of the East sketched out the terms of the armistice and had them approved in Paris and London (the United States was not at war with Bulgaria). Bulgarian delegates signed the Salonika Armistice on Sept. 29, 1918.

The Salonika Armistice required Bulgarians to evacuate Greek and Serbian territory. More important, this armistice gave Allied forces the right of transit through Bulgaria. The Bulgarians had to demobilize all but three divisions and surrender military equipment to the Allies. Finally, German and Austro-Hungarian troops were given four weeks to withdraw from Bulgaria. The Bulgarian surrender isolated the Ottoman Empire. It gave the Allies access to Rumania, and the Allied right of transit through Bulgaria made possible an eventual attack on Hungary or southern Austria.

Bulgaria's collapse also seems to have precipitated a crisis of nerves in Erich von Ludendorff, who shared command of the German army with Paul von Hindenburg. By Sept. 28, Ludendorff was demanding that the Germans seek an armistice. The German government was reorganized with Prince Max of Baden as chancellor, and on Oct. 3, 1918 the Germans sent the First German Note to President Woodrow Wilson, asking him to arrange an armistice for the purpose of making peace on the basis of Wilson's Fourteen Points.

The Allied prime ministers were meeting in Paris to discuss the Bulgarian situation when they learned of this German overture. The Central Powers had made peace overtures in the past, and the Allied leaders had no confidence that this German proposal would lead to an end of the war. Nevertheless, the Allied leaders thought it was necessary to deal with the matter in case anything came of it. They eventually drafted several sets of terms, the most important being one prepared by Marshal Ferdinand Foch, the Commander-in-Chief of the Allied Armies on the Western Front.

President Wilson, meanwhile, in the First Wilson Note of Oct. 8, avoided specific commitments, by asking whether the Germans accepted his Fourteen Points without reservations and whether the German government truly spoke for the German people. The Second German Note of Oct. 12 stated that the Germans accepted the Fourteen Points and asked for assurances that the Allies accepted Wilson's peace program as well. The Second Wilson Note of Oct. 14 said that military terms of armistice must be left to the Allied and American military advisers, but that any arrangement reached must maintain Allied military supremacy. At this time, too, Wilson sent his friend and adviser, Col. E.M. House, to Europe to represent the United States in discussions over armistice terms. The Third German Note of Oct. 20 accepted all of Wilson's conditions, and Wilson thereupon formally asked the Allies to draw up armistice terms for Germany.

On Oct. 29 the Allied prime ministers and Col. House began meetings which continued through Nov. 4. Four elements shaped their talks. First, the Allied leaders wanted to include many of their war aims directly in the armistice terms. Second, the Allied nations were jockeying for position in a postwar world and did not want to let any opportunities escape. Third, the Allies wanted to render Germany militarily helpless, and they wanted to be certain that the terms of the armistice met that requirement.

The fourth and last element was the most complicated. President Wilson had charged House with gaining full Allied acceptance of his Fourteen Points. The Allies had no great objection to most of the Wilsonian program, but they did not want their hands tied in the peace settlement. In general terms, Allied objections had less to do with what the Fourteen Points included than with what they omitted. They were particularly concerned with the lack of reparations. The British rejected the idea of freedom of the seas, and the Italians feared that Wilson's program might block them from territorial gains they hoped to make in the Balkans and southern Austria.

Marshal Foch's draft of military terms, prepared early in October and slightly revised later, became essentially the military terms of the armistice with Germany. His terms required that the Germans evacuate Belgium, France, and Luxembourg quickly, which would force the Germans to abandon military equipment. In addition, the Germans had to surrender about one-third of their artillery and one-half of their machine guns.

The Germans were required to withdraw their military forces from German territory as well. This included the evacuation of Alsace and Lorraine, the French "Lost Provinces" of 1871. Foch's draft required the Germans to evacuate the left bank of the Rhine, which the Allies would occupy, along with bridgeheads across the Rhine at Mainz, Coblenz, and Cologne. The Germans also had to withdraw from a neutralized strip on the right bank of the Rhine. Furthermore, Foch's draft required the Germans to surrender most of their railroad engines and cars, as well as a large number of motor trucks. Finally, it called for the blockade of Germany to continue.

While the Allied leaders and House were meeting in Paris to discuss terms for Germany and Wilson's Fourteen Points, German's remaining wartime partners accepted separate armistice terms with the Allies. The Turks signed an armistice that was essentially a British document. Indeed, the British excluded French officers from participation in direct negotiations with Ottoman representatives.

The Mudros Armistice with Turkey was signed on Oct. 30. Through the Mudros Armistice, the Straits were opened, and the Allies got the use of Turkey's ports and waterways, thus allowing Allied forces to move through the Black Sea to the Danube. The Mudros Armistice also required the Turks to demobilize their army, surrender their warships, and allow occupation of any strategic point named by the Allies. It was a crushing defeat, and with it the second of Germany's allies had fallen.

The third was Austria-Hungary. The Dual Monarchy was disintegrating. On Oct. 15 the Poles announced their independence. On Oct. 20 the Hungarians demanded control over Hungarian units in the army, and the following day the Czechs announced their independence. This accelerating internal chaos drove Emperor Charles to seek terms. The trouble lay with the Allies. The Italians expected to make great gains from the war, gains granted them in part in the Treaty of London (1915), but Italian ambitions had grown beyond even the promises made in that treaty. Unfortunately for Allied unity, Serbia, or Yugoslavia, expected much of the territory that Italy had wanted. The Allied leaders and House had to decide between the irreconcilable claims of two Allied nations. On balance, the Italians won this first round, partly because the various factions of Slavs did not present a united front.

On Nov. 3, Austrian representatives signed the Villa Giusta Armistice. The military terms for Austria-Hungary required the Austro-Hungarian army to demobilize the greater part of its men and surrender arms and equipment. The Allies, which for all practical purposes meant the Italian army, would occupy Austro-Hungarian territory that paralleled the gains promised in the Treaty of London. The blockade would remain in force. The Allies would have the right of transit across Austria-Hungary, which would let them develop an attack against Germany's vulnerable southeast frontier. Finally, the Allies and the United States would seize the greater part of the Austro-Hungarian fleet.

The Allied leaders wasted no time in planning an attack through Austria against Bavaria. The plan called for several armies to converge on Munich. Although the Allied military leaders were optimistic about the eventual decisive nature of that attack, it would have taken some time to develop—given the lateness of the year, it would be well into 1919 before such an offensive could take place.

The Villa Giusta Armistice left many problems unsettled. Not only were there sharp divisions between the Italians, Serbs, and Yugoslavs, but it was not clear whether the Austro-Hungarian central government spoke for very much of the army.

As is turned out the Hungarians required a separate protocol. Hungarian leaders hoped to get separate armistice terms, thus possibly receiving treatment similar to that accorded the Poles and Czechs. On Nov. 1, the Hungarians declared peace unilaterally, but the Allies refused to accept it. The Allied commander of the Army of the East met in Belgrade with the new Hungarian leaders on November 7. The Hungarians were promised that their territory would not be subject to immediate Rumanian or Czechoslovakia annexation. The Military Convention of Belgrade, signed on Nov. 13, applied the relevant clauses of the Villa Giusta Armistice to Hungary.

Meanwhile, in Paris, House was pushing the Allied leaders to accept Wilson's Fourteen Points. Despite cabled orders from President Wilson that he refuse any amendments to the Fourteen Points, House eventually agreed to reservations on the freedom of the seas and reparations, which he advised Wilson to accept. Grudgingly, the President accepted a compromise that left freedom of the seas undefined and allowed the Allies claim reparations for war damages.

Balancing the terms caused problems. The Allies thought the Germans would refuse the terms at first. Indeed, during talks between Oct. 29 and Nov. 4, most of the Allied leaders believed the war was likely to continue into 1919. There was, however, a possibility that Germany might accept the terms immediately, and each of the European Allies wanted to lure Germany by softening terms that some other nation found indispensable. For example, the French wanted to have little or nothing in the way of naval terms, and the British wanted to ease some of the military exactions upon which the French depended.

The British admirals drove the demand for harsh naval terms. They wanted the surrender of all submarines and most of the German surface fleet. The British politicians were less stubborn than their admirals and supported less brutal naval terms than those demanded by their admirals. The British politicians wanted the surrender of all German submarines, but they saw no need to do more than intern the German battle fleet in a neutral port. The French wanted naval terms that were even less rigorous.

The final draft of the naval terms reflected the middle position also supported by British politicians: the surrender of all German submarines, the internment of the battle fleet, and the continuance of the naval blockade. At the last moment, however, the Allied leaders worried that neutrals might refuse the responsibility of overseeing the internment of the German battle fleet, so they added a provision that German warships might be interned in an Allied port. After the Germans signed the armistice, the Allied leaders made no effort to get a neutral to accept the ships, and instead interned them in the great British naval base at Scapa Flow.

The Allied leaders and House accepted Foch's military terms. They worried about what would happen on the Eastern Front, where the Russian Empire was deep in revolution and civil war, but they still required the Germans to withdraw from Russian, Rumania, and Turkey.

With agreement on these matters reached on Nov. 4, the Allied leaders adjourned, telling Wilson to advise the Germans to send delegates to meet with Allied military representatives, which he did on Nov. 5. He also forwarded to the Germans the Allied note accepting the Fourteen Points with reservations on freedom of the seas and reparations.

The Allies still were not certain the Germans would accept the terms, but internal events in Germany were leaving the Germans with few options. Revolution, which had broken out at the end of October, was spreading rapidly through the German army and navy as well as from one German city to another. On Nov. 9, Emperor William II abdicated, and the Germans in Berlin proclaimed a republic.

In the meantime, the Germans had sent four delegates to meet with Marshal Foch, who represented the Allied and American armies, and Admiral Sir Rosslyn Wemyss, who represented the Allied and American navies. Matthias Erzberger, Center Party leader and principal architect of the Reichstag Peace Resolution, lead the German delegation. His friend Captain Ernst Vanselow, represented the navy. Minister to Bulgaria Count Alfred von Oberndorff represented the Foreign Office. The German army had no direct representation; the only ranking army member of the German delegation was Maj.-Gen. Detlev von Winterfeld, the liaison officer between the Supreme Command and the Emperor.

Negotiations over the Compiègne Armistice began on the morning of Nov. 8 in railroad cars between Compiègne and Rethondes. The Germans sought easings of the terms, but got little. They wanted the Allies to relax the blockade when hostilities ended; they got a statement that the Allies might furnish foodstuffs to German's hungry population at some later date. The Germans wanted to keep more arms and railroad equipment than allowed by the draft terms. Foch did let the Germans surrender only 25,000 machine guns, not the 30,000 demanded by the original draft terms. He rejected any lessening of the requirement to surrender railroad material.

Foch reduced the speed with which the Germans were required to evacuate Allied territory and withdraw behind the Rhine. He gave the Germans a total of thirty-six days, six more than specified in the original terms, to withdraw across the Rhine to a designated positions.

He also made an important change in the clauses dealing with the Eastern Front. The Germans argued that immediate withdrawal from Russia would expose the inhabitants there to Bolshevism. Foch rewrote that clause to have the Germans remain in Russia until some later date when the Allies would order them to withdraw.

Finally, Foch lengthened the duration of the armistice from thirty to thirty-six days, at which time it would either be denounced or renewed.

At 5:10 A.M. on Nov. 11, Foch, Wemyss, and the Germans signed the Compiègne armistice. It went into effect that same day at 11 A.M.

The German withdrawal took place. By Dec. 12, Allied and American forces reached the Rhine. By Dec. 17, they completed the occupation of the three specified bridgeheads. The British escorted the ships of the German battle fleet to their internment on Nov. 21.

The armistice was renewed three times, each time with slight modifications. The last renewal was at Trèves (Trier) on Feb. 14, 1919, and that version of the armistice stayed in force until the signing of the Versailles Treaty, June 28, 1919.

People have argued that the Compiègne Armistice was signed either too soon or too late; too late assumes that presenting the document earlier would have saved lives. It is hard to see how the process of preparing the armistice might have been appreciably shortened, and it is unlikely that the German government would have accepted the terms before the outbreak of revolution within their nation.

The argument that the armistice was signed too soon stems from the 1920s and 1930s, when right-wing propagandists, like Adolf Hitler, claimed that the German army had been stabbed in the back with the signing of the armistice. The Allies might have blunted that claim by waiting to grant an armistice until their armies were deep inside Germany or by requiring von Hindenburg to sign the articles.

At the time, no German army leader truly believed there was any wisdom in, or possibility of, continuing the war. The German army was a beaten army, and it was difficult to see what symbol or ritual might have confirmed that defeat more effectively in the public eye than the actual armistice terms could do. The Germans had to give up their navy, surrender a large proportion of their army's equipment, and allow the occupation of the vital western strip of their nation. From the Allied point of view there was no reason to fight on, or to ask for terms any more degrading than those that were already contained in the Compiègne Armistice.

The Compiègne Armistice already assured the greater portion of Allied war aims. The British had wanted the destruction of the German battle fleet, the end of the submarine threat, and the economic crippling of Germany. They won all that in the Compiègne Armistice. The French had wanted an end to the German menace, the return of Alsace and Lorraine, and the establishment of the Rhine as a strategic frontier. For the moment, they had all that. Those were not only military items; they were war aims, and insofar as those matters were dealt with in the Compiègne Armistice, the document established a preliminary peace treaty with Germany.

Bullitt Lowry

Bibliography

Maurice, General Sir Frederick Barton. *The Armistices of 1918.* New York and London: Oxford University Press, 1943.

Rudin, Harry R. *Armistice, 1918.* New Haven: Yale University Press, 1944.

Renouvin, Pierre. *L'Armistice de Rethondes, 11 Novembre 1918.* Trente Journeés qui ont fait la France. Paris: Gallimard, 1968.

Weintraub, Stanley. *A Stillness Heard Round the World. The End of the Great War: November, 1918.* New York: Truman Talley Books/E.P. Dutton, 1985.

Armor

See BODY ARMOR

Army, United States

See entries under UNITED STATES ARMY

Atterbury, William Wallace (1866–1935)

William Wallace Atterbury studied mechanical engineering at Yale University, graduating in 1886. He then joined the Pennsylvania Railroad, advancing rapidly through the railroad's management ranks. In 1912, he was named vice president in charge of the Pennsylvania's operations. He was elected president of the American Railway Association in 1916, and in that post he assisted the War Department in moving troops and supplies to the Mexican border in support of the Punitive Expedition into Mexico. He also helped place the nation's railroads on a war footing following the American entry into World War I in April 1917.

Atterbury's work with the American Railway Association soon led to his service overseas with the American Expeditionary Force (AEF) in France. As the American buildup in France began in the summer of 1917, Gen. John J. Pershing, commander of the AEF, quickly discerned that the railroads the French had designated for transporting American men and supplies desperately required drastic improvement if they were to meet the immense demands of the AEF. Many roadbeds had to be relaid and new yards and facilities constructed to accommodate the additional traffic. Moreover, the railroads lacked sufficient operating personnel, locomotives, and rolling stock, and the French did not appear up to the task of running the lines effectively. Therefore, Pershing persuaded the French to place these railroads under American control, and in July 1917, he asked the War Department to send him the "ablest man in the country" with "large experience in managing commercial railroads" to direct the AEF's rail operations. The department selected Atterbury, and at its request the Pennsylvania Railroad released Atterbury to become director general of transportation for the AEF on the understanding that he should have a free hand and deal directly with Pershing.

Upon his arrival in France in late August 1917, Atterbury quickly impressed Pershing with his businesslike approach, and in September Pershing created a separate Transportation Department under Atterbury, charging him with operating and maintaining the railroads and canals in France that had been turned over to the AEF. Pershing also commissioned Atterbury a brigadier general.

Atterbury faced a plethora of obstacles in fashioning an efficient rail system, including shortages of men and equipment and organizational difficulties. He and the railroad executives he had sent over from the United States to man the key slots in his department preferred to operate according to their own methods rather than those of the army, even though they were now in uniform. This created many snags in the Transportation Department's relations with other AEF departments and prompted complaints from Regular Army officers. As a result, in the summer of 1918, Atterbury agreed to the militarization of his department through the detailing of a Regular Army officer as deputy director general of transportation and the issuance of orders clearly placing it on the same footing as the other AEF departments.

Despite the obstacles, Atterbury steadily improved the efficiency of the AEF's rail system so that it was able to move an ever increasing flow of men and supplies eastward from the French ports to the combat zone. By the war's end his empire included four railroads—the Paris-Orleans, the Paris-Lyon-Mediterranean, the État, and the Est—and 1,500 miles of railroads around docks, terminals, and depots. To operate this system, he had 1,906 locomotives, 22,385 cars, and more than 60,000 men. While still short of personnel and equipment, the Transportation Department was delivering 300,000 men a month and 30,000 tons of supplies a day to their destinations. For this achievement, Atterbury won the high praise of Pershing and was awarded the Distinguished Service Medal.

Atterbury returned to the Pennsylvania Railroad in 1920 in his former capacity, and in 1925, he was promoted to the railroad's presidency. One of the outstanding railroad men of his generation, Atterbury retired in April 1935 and died on September 30 of that year.

John K. Ohl

Bibliography

Burgess, George H., and Miles C. Kennedy. *Centennial History of the Pennsylvania*

Railroad Company, 1846–1946. Philadelphia: Pennsylvania Railroad Company, 1949.

Forbes, B.C. "Give a Good Man Authority." *American Magazine* (March 1920).

Hagood, Johnson. *The Services of Supply: A Memoir of the Great War*. Boston: Houghton Mifflin, 1927.

Pershing, John J. *My Experiences in the World War*. 2 vols. New York: Stokes, 1931.

Wilgus, W.J. *Transporting the A.E.F. in Western Europe, 1917–1919*. New York: Columbia University Press, 1931.

Auchincloss, Gordon (1886–1943)

Gordon Auchincloss achieved prominence through his friendship with Col. Edward Mandell House, President Woodrow Wilson's close friend and trusted adviser. A graduate of Yale University and Harvard Law School, he married House's daughter Janet in September 1912. Auchincloss practiced law in New York City, but he shared many political and social interests with his famous father-in-law, and their lives soon became intertwined. House relied on Auchincloss to handle many of his business affairs and to serve as an intermediary to Democratic Party leaders in New York. He also introduced his son-in-law to the President and to other leaders of the Wilson administration.

Auchincloss admired House and envied the life that he led. After the outbreak of World War I, House became deeply involved in the diplomacy of the Wilson administration toward the European belligerents. Auchincloss followed House's diplomatic activities with growing fascination, reading his correspondence and diary entries and concluding that his father-in-law was destined to be a major actor on the world stage. In May 1917, he moved to Washington, D.C., to become an assistant to Frank L. Polk, counselor of the Department of State. There Auchincloss conducted a wide variety of diplomatic business and served as a channel of communication between House, the diplomatic corps, and high-level officials in the Wilson administration.

In late October 1917, he accompanied House to London and Paris as secretary of the American War Mission (House Mission) to Great Britain and France. He served as House's secretary once again during the Armistice negotiations in October and November 1918 and during the Paris Peace Conference. Auchincloss functioned as much more than a secretary, for House built up his own personal organization at the Versailles conference and used Auchincloss as the prime mover within it. Auchincloss consulted with the President, mingled with Allied leaders, and sought to advance his father-in-law's position on the peace settlement. He became convinced that House was a great diplomat, far superior to the President in his judgment of men and issues. Auchincloss promoted House assiduously, but he lacked his mentor's subtlety and tact. His brash and officious conduct offended the President, his wife, and his personal staff, which no doubt contributed in a small way to Wilson's loss of confidence in his long-time adviser.

In August 1919, Auchincloss returned to New York, where he resumed the practice of law. He remained close to House, interested in Democratic Party politics, and prominent in New York legal and social circles, but never again would he be near the center of power in Washington.

Charles E. Neu

See also House, Edward Mandell

Bibliography

Floto, Inga. *Colonel House in Paris: A Study of American Policy at the Paris Peace Conference of 1919*. Princeton, NJ: Princeton University Press, 1980.

Walworth, Arthur. *America's Moment: American Diplomacy at the End of World War I*. New York: Norton, 1977.

———. *Wilson and His Peacemakers: American Diplomacy at the Paris Peace Conference, 1919*. New York: Norton, 1986.

Austro-Hungarian-American Relations

In the decades before World War I the United States and Austria-Hungary (commonly called the Dual Monarchy) enjoyed relatively good relations, thanks to the absence of common economic or strategic interests that could have caused conflicts. This mutual indifference continued after the start of the war in 1914, as pro-Entente sentiment in the United States naturally focused on Germany, not Austria-Hungary, as the greatest danger to American principles and interests.

This situation changed in the summer of 1915, when Woodrow Wilson's reaction to the German torpedoing of the *Lusitania* strained the President's relationship with his secretary of state, the staunch neutralist William Jennings Bryan. After Bryan disclosed to Constantin von Dumba, the Austro-Hungarian ambassador in Washington, that he did not share Wilson's views of the sinking, Dumba tactlessly betrayed his confidence and helped make the serious differences between the secretary and the President a matter of public record. Bryan's pro-Entente replacement, Robert Lansing, distrusted Dumba from the start. It did not help matters that the ambassador subsequently became involved in clumsy German plots to impede the flow of American armaments to the Entente countries. In November 1915, Dumba returned home in disgrace, recalled at the request of the United States government. Austria-Hungary never appointed a new ambassador, leaving the Washington embassy in the hands of a chargé d'affaires until the final breach of relations between them two years later.

By the time Dumba departed, the relationship between the two powers had deteriorated markedly, thanks to the Habsburg Navy's participation in the Central Powers' campaign of submarine warfare. While the Austro-Hungarian Navy had an undersea fleet only a fraction the size of the German (there were never more than nineteen Habsburg submarines in service at any given time, and only twenty-seven saw action in the war), its active support of the German submarine campaign ultimately dragged the Dual Monarchy into the broader dispute over the practice of attacking passenger liners on the high seas.

Austria-Hungary's more intimate involvement in the German campaign began on May 23, 1915, just two weeks after the sinking of the *Lusitania*, when Italy declared war on the Dual Monarchy but not on Germany. The Italians would not declare war on the Germans until fifteen months later; in the meantime, German submarines active in the Adriatic and Mediterranean seas resorted to the expedient of attacking Italian shipping under the Habsburg flag. Ultimately, the two navies formulated a policy under which many German submarines in the theater were double-numbered, becoming "Austrian" as of the dates that they had first passed through the Straits of Gibraltar. Between June 1915 and October 1918, fifty-one double-numbered German submarines saw action in

the Mediterranean; only two were ever actually turned over to the Austrians. Other German submarines never received Austrian numbers but still flew the Habsburg flag while surfaced, either to attack Italian vessels or simply to keep the enemy fleets confused about the actual number of German U-boats deployed in the Mediterranean. The growing German presence in the theater during 1915 warranted the formal creation of special German submarine commands in Pola (Pula) and Cattaro (Kotor), the two principal bases of the Austro-Hungarian Navy.

The double-numbering and flagging practices caused no great diplomatic complications until November 1915, when the German *U–38* (aka Austro-Hungarian *U38*) torpedoed the 8,210-ton Italian passenger liner *Ancona* while hunting off the Tunisian coast. The ship, en route from Messina to New York, was fully booked and over 200 lives were lost; the dead included nine Americans. Coming six months after the torpedoing of the *Lusitania* off the Irish coast, the *Ancona* sinking only added to the growing outrage in the United States over unrestricted submarine warfare. With Wilson's approval, Lansing sent a sharply worded protest to Vienna.

After receiving little satisfaction from the Austro-Hungarian foreign minister, Count István Burián, the United States in December 1915 demanded that the Habsburg government denounce the sinking and punish the captain of the submarine responsible for it. The Germans, at that stage eager to keep the United States neutral, advised Burian to give in to the American demands. Ultimately, Vienna agreed to pay an indemnity and also assured Washington that the captain would be punished, although because the captain was, in fact, a German officer, this promise was meaningless. Once the affair was settled, Austria-Hungary formally requested that German submarines refrain from torpedoing passenger vessels when flying the Austrian flag.

Burian's diplomatic retreat angered Grand Admiral Anton Haus, commander of the Habsburg Navy, who had advocated a harder line after the *Ancona* sinking. Haus justified the targeting of the passenger liner on the grounds that on its return voyage from the United States, the ship could have been used to transport arms or Italian emigrants returning home for military service. Germany's decision, in April 1916, to cancel its unrestricted submarine warfare temporarily suspended the debate within the

Habsburg leadership over Austria-Hungary's role in the undersea campaign.

In January 1917, after the Germans resolved to resume unrestricted submarine warfare, Foreign Secretary Arthur Zimmermann led a delegation from Berlin to Vienna to secure Austro-Hungarian collaboration. Grand Admiral Haus wholeheartedly supported the German proposal, but Count Ottokar Czernin, Burian's successor as foreign minister, had grave misgivings, as did the new emperor, Charles I. Haus and the Germans finally swayed them, in part by citing several examples of Entente submarines sinking unarmed Austro-Hungarian vessels in the Adriatic. The ensuing German-Austrian negotiations over the terms of the campaign in the Mediterranean were greatly simplified by the fact that Italy finally had declared war on Germany on Aug. 28, 1916, making it unnecessary for German submarines to pretend to be Austrian when attacking Italian targets. To supplement the German effort, the Austro-Hungarian Navy promised to deploy some of its own submarines in the central Mediterranean.

The resumption of unrestricted submarine warfare provided the pretext for the American declaration of war against Germany on April 6, 1917, but in the renewed campaign Habsburg submarines had caused no losses in American lives or property and at least initially there was little sentiment in Washington for war with Austria-Hungary. Six weeks before the onset of hostilities with Germany, Wilson and Lansing made a secret overture to Vienna for a separate peace that would have detached the Dual Monarchy from its German alliance. Delivered through formal diplomatic channels, the scheme did not make it past Czernin, the staunchest defender of the German alliance within the circle of Austro-Hungarian leaders. Ironically, at the same time Charles I was pursuing a peace overture to the Entente through a private envoy in Paris, an initiative unknown to Czernin or the Americans.

The American attitude changed in the autumn of 1917 after the Habsburg Army, with German support, handed the Italians a serious defeat at Caporetto. British and French leaders, fearful that Italy would leave the war, persuaded Wilson that the sagging Italian effort against the Dual Monarchy required the material and moral support of the United States. Czernin, buoyed by the success at Caporetto, conveniently provided belligerent statements of his country's fidelity to the German alliance and determination to pursue a victorious peace. On Dec. 7, 1917, Congress declared war on Austria-Hungary.

A month later Wilson issued his Fourteen Points, four of which directly concerned the future of Austria-Hungary. Point ten called for "the freest opportunity of autonomous development" for the nationalities of the Dual Monarchy; point nine, an adjustment of the Italian border "along clearly recognizable lines of nationality"; point eleven, a Serbian outlet to the sea; and point thirteen, the establishment of an independent Poland. The governments of the Central Powers did little to respond to Wilson's unilateral declaration of American peace principles, but the Fourteen Points were quickly embraced by proponents of peace in both Germany and Austria-Hungary. When the Habsburg fleet at Cattaro mutinied on Feb. 1, 1918, the political points of the rebels' manifesto embraced the concepts of democratization and national self-determination, and called upon the government of Vienna to open negotiations with the United States based on Wilson's points.

The Cattaro mutiny shared similar roots with the concurrent unrest in the German Navy at Wilhelmshaven and Kiel. The Habsburg fleet had been bottled up in the Adriatic for the entire war; other than the submarines and smaller surface vessels, its warships rarely ventured out of port. But fear of submarine attack alone had prompted the British, French, and Italians virtually to concede the Adriatic to the vastly inferior Austro-Hungarian fleet, while they used their overwhelming numbers to blockade the mouth of the sea. After the United States declared war on the Dual Monarchy, American officials were harsh in their criticism of their allies' Adriatic policy. The American commander in the Mediterranean, VAdm. William S. Sims, proposed an offensive in the Adriatic to shut down the submarine bases of the Central Powers. He offered five American battleships and 20,000 marines for an assault on Cattaro, but his scheme also required troops from the Allied armies and unfortunately there were none to spare, especially after March 1918, when the German Army launched its final offensive on the western front. With the bulk of American resources also earmarked for the campaign in France, Sims abandoned his plans.

During the summer of 1918 the United States Navy reinforced the blockade of the mouth of the Adriatic with three dozen "submarine chasers," seventy-five-ton boats equipped with primitive underwater listening devices and depth charges. American commanders were very enthusiastic about their effectiveness, but a postwar investigation revealed that the boats in fact had little impact on the flow of German and Austrian submarine traffic in and out of the Adriatic. On Oct. 2, 1918, eleven submarine chasers supplemented an attack by British, French, and Italian warships on Austro-Hungarian vessels in the harbor of Durazzo (Durres), Albania. It was the last engagement ever fought by the Habsburg Navy, and the only occasion in which American forces were so actively involved against the Austro-Hungarians. Two days after the battle, Germany and Austria-Hungary formally requested an armistice based on the terms of Wilson's Fourteen Points.

The last plan to preserve the unity of Austria-Hungary, Emperor Charles's "People's Manifesto" of Oct. 16, 1918, attempted to satisfy the "autonomous development" requirement of Wilson's tenth point by promising to convert the Austrian half of the Dual Monarchy into a federal state with German, Czech, South Slav, and Ukrainian components. In response to points nine and thirteen, the predominantly Italian seaport of Trieste would be granted some sort of special status and the Poles of Galicia would be freed to join a united Poland. None of the nationalities involved accepted the offer, and it also had no impact in the United States or elsewhere in the international arena, even though it was followed, on October 17, by another good-will gesture, the end of Habsburg participation in the unrestricted submarine warfare campaign. On October 20, Wilson confirmed the degree to which he now supported the dismemberment of the Dual Monarchy, informing Austria-Hungary that the United States had made irrevocable commitments to the South Slavs and to the Czechoslovak national committee, even recognizing the latter as a belligerent government. In the last days of October, the various national committees started to issue their declarations of independence and the Habsburg armed forces finally collapsed. On November 3, the Dual Monarchy signed an armistice with Italy, and eight days later Charles renounced his voice in the political affairs of Austria.

The anti-Versailles revisionists of the postwar years accused Wilson of complicity in the destruction of Austria-Hungary and the "balkanization" of Eastern Europe. After World War II the onset of the Cold War and the extension of Communist rule into most of the former Habsburg lands prompted further questioning of the wisdom of American policy toward Austria-Hungary during World War I. Such broader criticisms aside, even his staunchest defenders would be hard pressed to demonstrate that Wilson followed a consistent policy toward the Dual Monarchy. As late as December 1917, as the United States issued its declaration of war, Wilson vowed not to pursue the breakup of Austria-Hungary, but as early as January 1917—a full year before the Fourteen Points—his open support of Polish independence had implied at least a partial dismemberment.

In the interwar years, as Wilson's own countrymen repudiated his policies and embraced isolationism with a new fervor, the peoples freed from Austro-Hungarian rule continued to revere Wilson as a great hero. One may question the degree to which he deserved to be honored as a gravedigger of the Dual Monarchy. Nevertheless, it cannot be denied that the hopes of the various breakaway national groups, dealt a serious blow by the demise of their initial mentor, Imperial Russia, were revived, encouraged, and strengthened by the public pronouncements of Wilson and by the subsequent American intervention in the war.

Lawrence Sondhaus

See also CZERNIN, OTTOKAR; FOURTEEN POINTS

Bibliography

Czernin, Ottokar. *In the World War*. London: Cassell, 1919.
Halpern, Paul. *The Naval War in the Mediterranean, 1914–1918*. Annapolis, MD: Naval Institute Press, 1987.
Mamatey, Victor S. *The United States and East Central Europe, 1914–1918: A Study in Wilsonian Diplomacy and Propaganda*. Princeton, NJ: Princeton University Press, 1957.

Ayres, Leonard Porter (1879–1946)
Leonard P. Ayres studied at Boston University, where he received an A.B. M.A., and Ph.D. He directed the departments of education and sta-

tistics at the Russell Sage Foundation during the period 1908–1920. At the outbreak of the First World War, Ayres became director of the Division of Statistics of the Council of National Defense, but the division exercised no control over the statistical offices of the supply bureaus and had no authority to establish a record-keeping system. As the work expanded, Ayres organized and became director of the Division of Statistics of the War Industries Board, the Priorities Committee, and the Allied Purchasing Commission.

Eventually, Ayres became a lieutenant colonel in charge of the statistical section of the purchasing service in the Office of the Chief of Staff. The most important work of the branch was preparation of a weekly fifty-page report of diagrams and tables covering more than 1,000 elements of supply and purchasing. Another, and still more confidential report, went to the President.

News of Ayres's work reached General Pershing, who requested that statistical personnel familiar with supply bureau operations supervise an exchange of information between the War Department and the AEF. Chief of Staff Peyton C. March sent Ayres with seven officers and nine field clerks to France, where the unit collected and collated data on procurement, transportation, and distribution of supplies both for Pershing's headquarters at Chaumont and for the Service of Supply at Tours.

In the summer of 1918, Ayres represented the United States Army in joint conferences held by the Supreme War Council to determine the nature of information to be exchanged among Allied governments. Ayres accompanied President Woodrow Wilson to Paris as chief statistical officer of the American Commission to Negotiate the Peace. At the direction of Secretary of War Newton D. Baker, Ayres prepared in 1919 a compilation of facts and figures recording United States participation in World War I entitled *The War With Germany—A Statistical Summary*.

Ayres served as vice president for economics and statistics at the Cleveland Trust Company from 1920 until his death. In 1924, he was an economic adviser to the United States delegation to the Dawes Commission, established to examine problems of postwar reparations and German finance.

Ayres returned to active duty in October 1940 as Coordinator of Statistics in the Office of the Undersecretary of War. He was promoted to brigadier general in July 1941. From March until his retirement from military service in June 1942, Ayres was assigned to the Service of Supply in Washington, D.C. He served as a consultant to the War Manpower Commission from 1943 until 1945 and died in 1946.

Phyllis Zimmerman

Bibliography

Ayres, Leonard P. "The War with Germany, a Statistical Summary." In *Source Records of the Great War,* ed. by Charles F. Home. 7 vols. Indianapolis: American Legion, 1931.

B

Baker, Newton Diehl (1871–1937)

Newton Diehl Baker became secretary of war in March 1916 at a critical moment when traditional American military policies were being questioned seriously for the first time in almost a century. Before he left office in March 1921, he helped shape legislation to reform the armed forces to meet new realities. He was caught up in the First World War and faced issues of War Department command and control, civil rights and liberties and civil-military relations not confronted since the Civil War. To many observers his career was a paradox. A man of peace and a confirmed antimilitarist, he became a celebrated war leader. A constructive conservative and middle-class professional, he had a reputation, made when he was city solicitor and later mayor of Cleveland, Ohio, as something of a radical reformer as well as one of the significant architects of the Progressive movement. He died a successful corporate lawyer.

Baker entered the Wilson administration as part of an effort to cool a political situation that had become so heated during the preparedness debates of 1915 that it threatened the unity of the Democratic Party and jeopardized the President's reelection. In February 1916, Secretary of War Lindley M. Garrison resigned to protest Wilson's failure to support a new military manpower scheme, which its supporters labeled "The Continental Army." The plan called for a federally controlled reserve of 400,000 volunteers. This reserve threatened the role of the state-controlled National Guard as the organized reserve of the country. Baker had given little thought to such matters and found it easy to accept the compromises worked out in the National Defense Act of 1916. The "Dual Oath" imposed on the

National Guard retained the soldiers of the states as the primary reserve force of the nation, while it made them immediately available for federal service in an emergency. The voluntary Reserve Officer's Training Corps (ROTC) reorganized the old military instruction program embodied in the Morrill Land-Grant Act to give systematic training and commissions to college men who completed the course of study successfully. For the first time the importance of the civilian economy in wartime was recognized through a rider attached to the 1916 military appropriations act, which created a Council of National Defense in the executive branch.

Baker would have been content to retire once the preparedness crisis was over, but the declaration of war against Germany on April 6, 1917, made such an option politically impossible. Immediate issues of war direction and management of unprecedented scope replaced those of long-range national military policy. Secretary of War Baker was a cautious administrator. He chose to maintain traditional relationships between the General Staff and the bureau chiefs in the War Department rather than risk controversy. He opposed every effort made during the war to lodge independent authority in civilian superagencies such as Bernard Baruch's War Industries Board. But he could move very effectively when he had to. Forced during the winter of 1917–1918 to act in haste, he strengthened the War Department's control over industrial mobilization and consolidated the management of military supply and procurement in the General Staff Division of Purchase, Storage and Traffic under canal builder Gen. George W. Goethals. At the end of the war the civilian agencies had eroded the War Department position, but it still controlled the mobilization process in most important areas.

Baker was less successful in resolving purely military command questions. From the time Gen. John J. Pershing arrived in France in June 1917, there were two American armies: one abroad and one in the United States. And it was never clear who commanded what. There was little difficulty until early 1918, when the reorganized General Staff under the relentless leadership of Chief of Staff Gen. Peyton Conway March began to insist that full policy control must be lodged in Washington. Pershing declared that the commander in the field should not be constrained in any way. Baker avoided a decision on the matter and attempted to act as a facilitator between the general in France and the chief of staff at home. The war was almost over when a controversy over the ultimate size of the American Expeditionary Force (AEF) brought Baker to the support of March. The issue was not settled at the time, and it remained for Henry L. Stimson and Gen. George C. Marshall to resolve it twenty years later.

The greatest innovation of the war was systematic conscription. The Wilson administration had opposed even the mention of such a notion before the war. In April 1917, however, for reasons both practical and political, it executed a complete about face. Baker pivoted with the President. Indeed, his conversion was particularly important because it persuaded many of his antimilitarist associates (traditional opponents of the power of government over the individual), who feared "Selective Service" would become permanent policy, that such a temporary expedient might be risked in a war for democracy. Other issues, the most important of which were army racial policy and the civil rights and liberties of drafted citizens, were involved in the conscription decision. Little of the racism and anti-civil libertarianism that rose during the conflict can be traced directly to the secretary of war's office, but Baker did little to control the zeal of soldiers in the training camps, in conscientious-objector centers or in the field. He chose to deflect and, if possible, dilute the impact of bigots and witch-hunters rather than confront them forthrightly. Accordingly, he was condemned by African Americans and civil libertarians for the acts of subordinates and got little credit for avoiding the cruder excesses that undoubtedly would have occurred if he had done nothing at all.

The secretary was always the President's man, and Wilson's confidence in him grew during the war. Baker already had astutely handled his part of the Mexican crisis of 1916–1917 in such a way as to reduce public hysteria and help keep control of events in administration hands. After the war began, he revealed exceptional diplomatic skills. In conferences with the French and British, he effectively protected the independence of the American forces and prevented it from being absorbed piecemeal into the deteriorating Allied fighting forces. During two critical wartime trips to Europe, Baker negotiated agreements that determined American troop strength and assured the shipping necessary to move the AEF to France. When he disagreed with the President, as he did in the debates over intervention in Russia during the summer of 1918, he loyally carried out administration policy once it had been established. Near the end of the war, he was prepared, if necessary, to relieve General Pershing from command of the AEF if Pershing continued, as he had been doing, to interfere with efforts to secure an armistice with the Germans.

Experience at war modified Baker's views substantially. He supported Chief of Staff March's postwar efforts to give the Regular Army its own reserves through a program of universal military service. He tried to make the consolidation of bureau management in the General Staff, so painfully achieved during the war, permanent. However, the National Defense Act of 1920 rejected all such organizational innovations and settled for incremental rather than revolutionary change. In 1930, Baker assessed his war record in a letter to his biographer Frederick Palmer: "My own responsibilities and performances in the War Department were such that it would be impossible for me to have any illusion about them. Each day of twenty-four hours had a week's work packed into it, and that there were errors and shortcomings is not only not surprising, but also inevitable. I was conscious of them at the time, as I am now, but I have been comforted by the feeling that we all did and gave it our best."

Baker retired in 1921 and never held public office again. After a generation of public service he owed his family, he wrote, at least, "a roof to keep out the rain, a few more windows to lock at night, and an additional dozen frail porcelain gods and goddesses which my romping babies may break." He did far better than that. His law practice flourished. Professional success during the twenties allowed him time to render outstanding philanthropic and educational service to the community. Still active in national politics, his plea for the League of Nations at the Democratic convention of 1924 was remembered forty years later by Ambassador to the United Nations Adlai Stevenson as the greatest speech he had ever heard. Baker was nominated among others, by anti-Roosevelt Democrats for the presidency in 1932. During the thirties he served the U.S. Army on various boards, including the "Baker Board" on the reorganization of the Army Air Corps. During his career he had been honored many times in both the public and private arenas. He died at his home in Shaker Heights, Ohio, on Christmas Day, 1937.

Assessments of Baker's life and work written at the time and later reflect the deep national political and moral divisions over the nature of progressivism and the impact of the First World War. Critics have made clear his inadequacies as an organizer and administrator. All too often he let the soldiers have their way. He neither resolved the command conflicts between March and Pershing nor brought the bureau chiefs under permanent central control. Former friends and associates charged correctly that he did not support civil rights and liberties in the military as effectively as he should have. But Baker was an ameliorator, not a crusader. He could influence strong-minded and contentious people to subordinate, at least temporarily, their personal ambitions to higher goals. In those subtler areas of leadership Baker was gifted; he allowed greatness to emerge in others. Finally, as secretary of war, he interpreted the military to the country in such a way that the army retained, at least for the duration of the war, the support of certain segments of the Progressive movement who had grave doubts about the conflict. As long as Baker was at the War Department, they supported the Wilson administration, admittedly half-heartedly at times, in a cause to which their commitment could easily have been lost entirely. Baker was never one to shake society from the top to the bottom. To ask that from him was to ask in vain. He was simply a competent, humane, and compassionate man who—like his contemporaries Henry L. Stimson, Charles Evans Hughes, Elihu Root, and Woodrow Wilson—abhorred extremes and entwined commitment to social and economic amelioration with profound concern for decency and order.

Daniel R. Beaver

See also MARCH, PEYTON CONWAY; PERSHING, JOHN JOSEPH

Bibliography

Beaver, Daniel R. *Newton D. Baker and the American War Effort 1917–1919.* Lincoln: University of Nebraska Press, 1966.

Chambers, John W., II. *To Raise an Army: The Draft Comes to Modern America.* New York: Free Press, 1987.

Coffman, Edward M. *The Hilt of the Sword: The Career of Peyton C. March.* Madison: University of Wisconsin Press, 1966.

Hewes, James E. *From Root to McNamara: Army Organization and Administration 1900–1963.* Washington, DC: U.S. Army Center of Military History, 1975.

Schaffer, Ronald. *America in the Great War: The Rise of the War Welfare State.* New York: Oxford University Press, 1991.

Balfour, Arthur James (1848–1930)

As a member of one of Britain's greatest political families and the nephew of late-nineteenth-century Conservative Prime Minister Salisbury, Balfour enjoyed a swift ascent in politics. Educated at Cambridge, he entered Parliament in 1874 at the age of twenty-six. Balfour held minor offices and was dismissed by some as a lightweight politician with only his uncle's favor protecting him from a mediocre career as a backbencher. But he defied that easy characterization by the combination of courage and imagination he brought to his tenure as chief secretary for Ireland (1887–1891). He steadfastly opposed home rule for Ireland and moved resolutely against militant Irish resistance, but his sensitivity to the roots of Irish resentment against English control led him to modify his normal conservatism to the point of advocating progressive measures of agrarian reform. The Conservative Party recognized Balfour as the legitimate political heir to Lord Salisbury, and he served as leader of the party in the House of Commons from 1891 until 1902, at which time he assumed the premiership on the retirement of his uncle.

Balfour's only stint as prime minster (1902–1905) included some noteworthy achievements, such as extension of the national educational system, further modest reforms of the Irish land tenure law, and correction of some of the deficiencies in British military policy and

B

structure revealed during the Boer War. Balfour also presided over the initiation of the Anglo-French Entente of 1904. But his party split bitterly over the issue of free trade. Balfour's government resigned in 1905 and suffered a devastating defeat in the election of 1906. Until 1911, Balfour led the Conservative Party's resistance to the great reform measures of the Liberal government of Herbert H. Asquith. Always a pessimistic opponent of social and economic reforms that might undermine the established class system, which he felt obliged to defend, Balfour used his party's huge majority in the House of Lords to block reform measures from the House of Commons until the former's veto power was stripped from it during the constitutional crisis of 1909–1911. Balfour's interest in the leadership declined as the intensity of political battles increased, and his natural predilection for a philosophical viewpoint ill-equipped him for party leadership in an age of ruthless partisanship. His patrician concept of gentlemen politicians combining public service with other pursuits had little place in the increasingly professional world of twentieth-century politics, and he resigned as party leader in 1911 at the age of sixty-three. Relieved from the rancor of politics, he pursued his serious interest in philosophy.

Soon after the Great War began, Prime Minister Asquith appointed Balfour to an advisory role as the only Conservative member of the War Council. Then, in 1915, when Asquith's Liberal government lost the confidence of wartime Britain, a coalition government was formed, and Balfour was persuaded to return to office, initially as first lord of the Admiralty and subsequently as foreign secretary (1916–1919). Balfour's willingness to collaborate with Liberal politicians for whom he had earlier expressed much contempt led Winston Churchill to compare him to a "powerful graceful cat walking delicately and unsoiled across a rather muddy street." His reputation for fair-mindedness, steadiness of spirit, and logical thinking made him the most attractive senior Conservative to represent that party in any coalition.

In his Admiralty post, Balfour presided over the humiliation of British withdrawal from the abortive Gallipoli expedition. Moreover, in the opinion of many naval historians, Balfour failed to move decisively enough to correct deficiencies in naval leadership and preparation that led to the eventual failure to achieve complete victory at the Battle of Jutland in May 1916. Balfour also argued, unsuccessfully, against national conscription. His contention that conscription would weaken Britain's economic productivity and hence its ability to prosecute a modern industrial war was rejected by its advocates, who argued that only massive offensives on the Western Front would win the war, a strategic policy for which Balfour had much skepticism. It was with some relief, therefore, that Balfour shifted from a primarily military responsibility to the foreign secretaryship when Lloyd George replaced Asquith. Though often overshadowed by his prime minister in the realm of foreign policy, Balfour worked with unobtrusive patience to gain such personal goals as Anglo-American cooperation in 1917. That year he journeyed to Washington in April where his success in arranging for the rapid deployment of American destroyers as merchant convoy escorts significantly helped to end the U-boat threat to Britain's food supply.

Balfour's most famous action as foreign secretary was undoubtedly the issuance in November 1917 of the declaration bearing his name that expressed the British government's support of "the establishment in Palestine of a national home for the Jewish people." Balfour's sympathy for Zionism stemmed from his philosophical and religious interest in Hebrew civilization and made him the logical articulator for the collective belief of Lloyd George's government that Jewish self-determination was justified. It was hoped that the declaration would rally Jews worldwide to the Allied cause, win favor with Jewish leaders in the Russian Bolshevik government as it considered withdrawal from the war, and preempt French claims in Palestine, which threatened British control of Egypt. That Arab nationalists would so sorely resent this imposition and that implementation of the declaration would prove so complex seem not to have troubled the normally cautious Balfour.

At war's end Balfour played a secondary role at the Paris Peace Conference, accepting with characteristic self-effacement the domination of Lloyd George in negotiating the terms of the Treaty of Versailles with other Allied leaders. But after its completion in June 1919, when Lloyd George returned to Britain, Balfour became deeply involved in the drafting of the Treaty of St. Germain determining the Allied settlement with the defunct Austro-Hungarian Empire. Already past seventy years of age,

Balfour announced his retirement upon his return to Britain in October 1919.

Nonetheless, throughout the first postwar decade, the British government continued to call upon him to serve as elder statesman. In this capacity, Balfour represented Britain from 1920 until 1923 in the Council of the League of Nations, and he was Britain's chief delegate to the 1921 Washington Conference on naval disarmament. In both venues, his apparently effortless grasp of detail, unfailing courtesy, and elderly dignity gave him a prestige and power that he expertly used to resolve disputes through artful compromise.

Ennobled in 1922 as the first earl of Balfour, he was in a Conservative cabinet again by 1925, serving as lord president of the council under Prime Minister Stanley Baldwin until 1929. Balfour took a leading role in the Imperial Conference of 1926, throwing his prestige and support behind the redefinition of the British Empire, and he remained remarkably active in public affairs until the illness that ended his life in 1930.

Jeffrey Williams

See also BALFOUR MISSION

Bibliography

Dugdale, Blanche E.C. *Arthur James Balfour*. New York: Putnam, 1937.

Egremont, Max. *Balfour*. London: Collins, 1980.

MacKay, Ruddock F. *Balfour*. New York: Oxford University Press, 1985.

Zebel, Sydney H. *Balfour*. Cambridge, UK: Cambridge University Press, 1973.

Balfour Mission

In late March 1917, the British War Cabinet, recognizing that war between the United States and Germany was imminent, determined to send a commission to the United States after America declared war. Prime Minister David Lloyd George was assured by American Ambassador Walter Hines Page that such a mission would be welcomed. Page was wrong. President Woodrow Wilson feared that the public might think Foreign Secretary Arthur J. Balfour would make the United States a junior partner in the coalition. He was finally persuaded by Col. Edward M. House, his friend and confidante, that there was no way to refuse politely.

Balfour's party included Gen. G.T.M. Bridges, RAdm. Sir Dudley de Chair, Lord Cunliffe of Headley (governor of the Bank of England), plus numerous lesser diplomats and military experts. The mission arrived in Washington on April 22 to a warm popular reception. The British foreign secretary then engaged in a month-long propaganda tour, laying a wreath on George Washington's tomb; visiting Richmond and Chicago; paying his respects to Theodore Roosevelt; and making a number of speeches, including addresses to the House of Representatives on May 4 and the Senate on May 8. Balfour also met privately with Wilson, who explained the United States government's refusal to sign a treaty of alliance or to discuss possible peace terms. The President was already aware, in a general way, of the secret treaties binding the Allies together, and while disapproving of them, wished to see exactly what the Allies promised each other. Balfour supplied Wilson with copies, which he later denied seeing when asked by the Senate Foreign Relations Committee. The foreign secretary also agreed to steer secret intergovernmental communications away from British Ambassador Spring-Rice, who had lost the confidence of House and Wilson, and through William Wiseman whom the Americans trusted.

In discussions with American officials, Balfour and General Bridges asked for ships, food, and financial aid and received assurances from their hosts that all would be forthcoming. However, neither Briton initially asked for American troops. It was only when the Viviani mission arrived from France, and Marshal Joffre, its military representative, made an overt appeal for an American expeditionary force, that Bridges conceded that some few thousand American soldiers might be allowed to enroll in English units. Since Joffre was quite willing to let American troops carry American-made arms and fight under their own flag, the British proposal was rejected. Having already secured their primary objectives—material and financial commitments—and having laid the groundwork for future cooperation, the Balfour mission departed without ceremony at the end of May.

Although members of the Balfour and Viviani missions were critical of America's war preparations, Secretary of War Newton D. Baker thought the two Allied missions demonstrated a considerable lack of coordination in the war effort. He observed later that they entered the United States at different points on different days, came asking for different things, and left separately.

David Esposito

Bibliography
Bridges, Sir Tom. *Alarms and Excursions: Reminiscences of a Soldier.* London: Longmans, Green, 1938.
Dugdale, Blanche E.C. *Arthur James Balfour,* New York: Putnam, 1937.
Halsey, Francis W., ed. *Balfour, Viviani and Joffre: Their Speeches and Other Public Utterances in America.* New York: Funk and Wagnalls, 1917.
Long, Kenneth. *Arthur James Balfour: The Happy Life of the Politician, Prime Minister, Statesman, and Philosopher, 1848–1930.* London: Bell, 1930.

Balloons

Although the tethered balloon was used for organized military observation before and during the American Civil War, it was in World War I that the concept matured. The balloon was well suited to the stagnant nature of combat on the Western Front from 1914 through the Armistice in 1918. Big and unmoving like the lines themselves, the balloons offered a perfect stationary platform from which an observer could spy on the enemy on behalf of his brothers in the infantry and artillery.

Basic equipment of the Allied balloon services during the war was the Caquot balloon, an egg-shaped craft filled with hydrogen, which sported three stabilizing fins on the narrow end that hung limp on the ground and acted like windsocks, pointing the main body of the airship into the wind when the balloon was aloft. Designed by the French engineer Albert Caquot, it represented a vast improvement over the conventional spherical balloon, which swayed unmercifully in the wind, often making its observer too airsick to report anything of military value. Germany eventually copied the Caquot for its own use. From its basket, one or two observers telephoned their reports to the ground or dropped them in weighted envelopes, during a duty shift that sometimes lasted all day. Dangling from the side of the cramped crew quarters, in megaphone-shaped containers, parachutes waited to be used, for despite antiaircraft guns, light machine guns, and nearby friendly fighters, attacks occasionally came. When they did, the balloon

observer had a privilege not shared with other World War I aircrews until the conflict's final months when parachutes were issued to German airmen—he could bail out.

Fighter pilots who specialized in "balloon busting" were regarded as foolhardy or suicidal by their comrades due to the necessity of running the gauntlet of heavy defensive fire protecting the "flying sausages." However, some—including the Belgian ace of aces, Willi Coppens; the first American airman to win the Medal of Honor, Frank Luke; Germany's Fritz Ritter von Roth; and the war's most successful "buster," France's Michel Coiffiard—made a career of it.

Balloons were as cumbersome on the ground as they were in the air. Necessary equipment in a balloon company included gas wagons and cylinders to transport the hydrogen, several thousand feet of steel cable, a motorized winch, radio and telephone equipment, living accommodations for the personnel and horses (sometimes nearly as many as humans) to pull it all from base to base. All this paraphernalia contributed to a serious lack of mobility.

Being tied to one spot had its advantages however. Balloon observers became extremely familiar with their part of the front. On a clear day the trained observer could view and report on an area spanning fifteen miles or more. While aloft, the observer would report enemy troop movements, trains leaving and entering stations, new trench construction, approaching aircraft, and, perhaps most importantly, the position of the enemy's artillery. On the artillery-happy Western Front, the balloon observer's chief value lay in his ability to tell the gun commander whether his shells were landing long or short, or to the right or left, of their intended targets.

For this purpose a clock code was devised and used both by balloon and airplane observers. The code enabled each small section of the front to be assigned an identity by means of a grid marked on the official map in the form of an imaginary clock. When the observer wanted to change the direction of fire, he would simply report by means of the code where his battery's shells were landing, and the commander would know what sort of correction to make to the position of his gun before launching the next round.

During the war, the United States formed thirty-six balloon companies. The first contingent to leave the United States (the 1st, 2d, 3d, and 4th companies) departed on Dec. 8, 1917.

The 14th Company was the last to return from overseas duty, and it arrived in the United States on Aug. 4, 1919.

By the opening salvo of World War II, the balloon was no longer technologically efficient as a military observer, and it was relegated to barrage duty in that conflict. One Caquot used in this way has been preserved with its World War I markings at the United States Air Force Museum—a humble yet honorable end for a brief but distinguished career.

Robert A. Carpenter

Bibliography

Kennett, Lee. *The First Airwar 1914–1918.* New York: Free Press, 1991.

Morris, Alan. *The Balloonatics.* London: Jarrolds, 1970.

Ovitt, S.W., ed. *The Balloon Section of the American Expeditionary Forces.* New Haven: n.p., 1919.

Vittali, Paul. "Balloon Commander." *Over the Front,* trans. by Peter Kilduff. Vol. 6, No. 3 (Fall 1991).

Ballou, Charles Clarendon (1862–1928)

Charles Clarendon Ballou was born in Troy, New York. In 1882, he entered the United States Military Academy and graduated with the class of 1886. Lieutenant Ballou was assigned to an infantry regiment that was involved periodically in armed skirmishes with the various Great Plains Indians, most notably the Sioux. He remained in the Far West until 1891 when he temporarily resigned his commission. For the next three years, Ballou was professor of military science and tactics at Florida State Agricultural College in Tallahassee. He returned to active duty with the rank of captain in 1895. From 1899 until 1905, Ballou served with the American occupation forces in the Philippines. In 1901 during the bloody Philippine Insurrection, he was awarded the Silver Star; subsequently, he received a field promotion to lieutenant colonel.

On May 29, 1917, Lt. Col. Ballou assumed command of the Colored Officers Training Camp at Camp Des Moines, Iowa. Beginning on June 18, the course lasted three months. During this period Ballou was promoted to the rank of brigadier general. In October 1917, brevet Major General Ballou was appointed to command the all-black 92d Infantry Division of VI Corps, which was stationed at Camp Upton

on Long Island, New York, despite the fact that Ballou did not approve of the proposed use of African-American soldiers in combat. He was very committed to maintaining the Jim Crowism that was so rampant in American society during that era. Most certainly, the general was greatly influenced by several white staff officers who came from the Deep South.

Quite early in his command of the 92d, Ballou issued Command Bulletin 35, which stated that in cases of conflict between black and white soldiers the burden of proof always lay with the former to prove their innocence. Various black troopers later recalled that Ballou repeatedly condoned acts of racism made against his command by soldiers from nearby white outfits. It was common knowledge that Ballou and his cronies referred to the 92d as the "Rapist Division." He consistently refused to allow photographers to record the activities of the 92d Division in France. On Nov. 11, 1918, Ballou forbade the official army photographers from covering the bestowing of Distinguished Service Crosses on several members of the division at Villers-en-Haye. Instead, he dispatched them to nearby Belleville, where a black soldier was to be executed for rape.

Despite the efforts of Col. James A. Moss and other critics, the Allied high command was loathe to move against Ballou. During the last weeks of the fighting, reports circulated that the regiments of the 92d were about to mutiny and that the enlisted men had placed a bounty on Charles Ballou. Accordingly, he was removed from his post—but only when his very physical safety appeared to be threatened.

It seems that the War Department remembered Ballou's questionable record in France. During the demobilization following World War I, Ballou reverted to his prewar rank of colonel. Whether he ever reconsidered his basic attitude toward African-American soldiers is not known. He retired from active duty in August 1926, and died on July 23, 1928, in Spokane, Washington.

Miles S. Richards

Bibliography

Du Bois, W.E.B. "The Black Man in the Revolution of 1914–1918." *Crisis* (March 1919).

———. "The History of the Black Man in the Great War." *Crisis* (June 1919).

MacGregor, Morris J., and Bernard C. Nalty, eds. *Blacks in the United States Armed*

Forces: Basic Documents. Wilmington, DE: Scholarly Resources, 1977.

Bandholtz, Harry Hill (1864–1925)

Harry Hill Bandholtz fought in the Spanish-American War of 1898 and served in the Philippines from 1900 to 1913. He was chief of staff of the New York National Guard division sent to the Mexican border in 1916 and remained with it in New York through 1917. He then became commander of the 58th Infantry Brigade of the 29th Division. The brigade went to France in June 1918 and served on the Meuse-Argonne front through September. Gen. John J. Pershing appointed Bandholtz provost marshal general of the American Expeditionary Force on Sept. 27, 1918, a position he held until August 1919, at which time he was appointed as the American representative on the Inter-Allied Military Mission to Hungary.

The Supreme Council of the Paris Peace Conference instructed Bandholtz and his British, French, and Italian counterparts to supervise the disarmament of Hungarian military forces and the withdrawal of Rumanian and Serbian armies of occupation from Hungary. In practice, the four generals dealt with a much wider range of military, political, and economic questions, and the energetic and forceful Bandholtz tended to dominate the mission and its activities. Bandholtz and his colleagues were repeatedly angered and frustrated by the refusal of the Rumanians to evacuate Hungary and by their looting of Hungarian economic resources. Ultimately, they did withdraw, and Bandholtz resigned from the mission in mid-December. He left Budapest on Feb. 9, 1920, for his return to the United States.

John E. Little

Bibliography

Bandholtz, Harry Hill. *An Undiplomatic Diary by the American Member of the Inter-Allied Military Mission to Hungary, 1919–1920*, ed. by Fritz-Konrad Kruger. New York: Columbia University Press, 1933.

Barnett, George (1859–1930)

Born in Lancaster, Wisconsin, George Barnett entered the United States Naval Academy in 1877. In an era when most of the academy's graduates would not receive commissions, Barnett opted for a commission in the Marine Corps, exercising a provision in the Naval Personnel Act of 1882 that enabled academy graduates to join the corps. He was commissioned a second lieutenant in 1883.

Barnett's early career was one of slow promotion and traditional postings with marine detachments afloat and service at marine barracks ashore. He commanded the marine detachment aboard USS *New Orleans* during the Spanish-American War. After the war he commanded three expeditionary battalions: in Panama (1902), the Philippines (1903–1905, while also serving as fleet marine officer with the Asiatic Squadron), and Cuba (1906). Between 1908 and 1910, he commanded the marine legation in Peking, China. From 1911 until 1914, Barnett was based in Philadelphia as commanding officer of the marine barracks. He also commanded the 1st Marine Regiment, and took this ad hoc force to Cuba in 1911, 1912, and 1913 in support of American policy on that island. During this period, the Marine Corps was pioneering amphibious warfare, and Barnett participated in the earliest development of this type of expeditionary duty. In 1914, he commanded the 1st Advanced Base Force Brigade, whose mission was to secure temporary forward bases necessary for the replenishment of the fleet, and his unit participated in the Culebra maneuvers, where aspects of amphibious warfare were tested.

In 1914, Barnett, a colonel with less than four years seniority, was selected as the major general commandant of the Marine Corps. He was the first commandant appointed under the provisions of a 1913 law that limited the term of office to four years, with a possibility of reappointment. In 1916, he was promoted to permanent brigadier general.

As commandant, Barnett coped with three major issues: (1) the continued refinement of amphibious warfare, (2) the deployment of marine units in Mexico, Haiti, the Dominican Republic, the Philippines, and China, and (3) the possibility of U.S. involvement in the war in Europe. Barnett chaired a board devoted to increasing the efficiency of the Marine Corps and helped draft pertinent legislation to achieve this goal. He also served on the secretary of the navy's Advisory Council and was the first commandant to serve as an ex-officio member on the General Board of the Navy.

Between 1914 and 1917, Barnett's task increasingly became to prepare the Marine

Corps for its role in Europe in the First World War. His greatest accomplishment was to raise, equip, train, and dispatch two brigades of marines to France to serve in that war, while continuing to meet the corps' other commitments. In the process, Barnett's Marine Corps grew from just over 10,000 men in 1914 to 17,000 in 1917 and over 75,000 in 1918. To implement his goals, Barnett expanded the headquarters staff, ensured talented officers held the proper assignments, established a major base at Quantico, Virginia, and further developed the bases at Parris Island, South Carolina, and San Diego, California.

With a war in Europe, Barnett realized that the Marine Corps would have to be involved in that conflict. His hope to create a Marine Corps division in Europe was dashed by General Pershing's opposition, rooted in a concern about the Navy Department's influence in the affairs of the American Expeditionary Force (AEF). The AEF commander allowed marines in France and let them fight. He permitted marine officers to command both marine and army troops, but there would be no marine division. Barnett accomplished what he could under these orders. The 4th Marine Brigade was sent to France, where it became part of the U.S. Army's 2d Infantry Division. The 5th Brigade followed but saw no combat as an organized entity. One unforeseen side effect of Barnett's success with the 4th Brigade was its continued identification as a marine unit. While Pershing's censors would not permit the specific identification of units in news releases, the 4th Brigade continued to be identified as "marine." The resulting publicity created a discordant note in army-marine relations that lasted into World War II.

Because of the war, President Wilson reappointed Barnett as commandant in 1918. However, Secretary of the Navy Josephus Daniels demanded that Barnett sign an undated letter of resignation. He refused, stating that he served at the pleasure of the President and if the chief executive requested him to leave, he would do so. This response possibly alienated Daniels. Furthermore, in 1918, the commandant backed legislation, against the secretary's wishes, to raise the rank of commandant to lieutenant general. This became a politically divisive issue, debated on the floor of the House of Representatives with Barnett and his wife in the gallery.

The net result was the controversial removal of Barnett as commandant on June 30, 1920, and his replacement by MajGen. John A. Lejeune, who had actually been Daniels's first choice for commandant in 1913 but who was too junior at that point. Barnett was given half a day's notice to decide whether to retire at the grade of major general or to continue to serve on active duty, revert to his permanent grade of brigadier general, and request his preferred next assignment. Barnett's request for the command at Quantico could not be honored, since that post had been promised to someone else. So the new commandant created the Department of the Pacific, based in San Francisco, for his predecessor. Lejeune also supported Barnett's promotion to major general, which occurred in March 1921. Barnett thus remained on active duty until 1923, when he attained the mandatory retirement age of sixty-four. He died on April 27, 1930.

In addition to various campaign medals, Barnett was awarded the Legion of Honor by the French government and the Distinguished Service Medal by the United States.

Donald Bittner

Bibliography

Bartlett, Merrill L. *John A. Lejeune: A Marine's Life.* Columbia: University of South Carolina Press, 1991.

Frank, Benis M. "The Relief of General Barnett." *Records of the Columbia Historical Society.* Washington, DC: The Society, 1973.

McClellan, Edwin N. *The United States Marines in the World War.* Washington, DC: Historical Division, U.S. Marine Corps, 1968.

Schmidt, Hans. *Maverick Marine: General Smedley D. Butler and the Contradictions of American Military History.* Lexington: University of Kentucky Press, 1987.

Shulimson, Jack. "First to Fight: Marine Corps Expansion, 1914–1918." *Prologue* (Spring 1976).

Baruch, Bernard Mannes (1870–1965)

One of the most colorful characters in the world of finance and politics at the turn of the century, Bernard Mannes Baruch was born on Aug. 19, 1870, in Camden, South Carolina. The family moved to New York City in 1880, where his father was a successful physician who became influential in public health issues. Upon graduation from the City College of New York, Baruch joined the Wall Street firm of A.A. Houseman and Co. as a clerk. With an extraordinary grasp of facts and market data, he quickly became a successful investor for his clients and himself. By 1903, he had purchased a seat on the New York Stock Exchange and opened his own brokerage house. During this period, Baruch belonged to the "Waldorf crowd," a group of shrewd financiers and investors who gathered at the bar of the old Waldorf Astoria Hotel.

He was rapidly amassing a substantial fortune with relative ease and began to look for other stimulating projects. Baruch was strongly attracted to politics. His warm, outgoing personality and abundance of self-confidence were attributes that fitted him well for politics. He had become an admirer of Woodrow Wilson, who, as president of Princeton University, had opposed the chartering of fraternity chapters at the university. In 1912, Baruch met Wilson, who was then the Democratic candidate for president, and he became an enthusiastic backer of the professorial candidate, investing both his talent and treasure in Wilson's campaign.

In the early years of the Wilson administration, Baruch was happy to strengthen his ties to the seat of power by doing minor political errands. Then in 1915, as the war in Europe settled into a bloody stalemate, Baruch became increasingly involved in the preparedness movement. He joined the National Security League, which promoted preparedness, patriotic education, and universal military training and contributed to the Navy League, actions that were useful counters to the early Republican claim of Democratic inaction and pacifism. He also met privately with Wilson to discuss the formation of a "Businessmen's Commission" to study industrial preparedness in light of the continuing conflict in Europe.

Wilson responded to the mounting threats from a warring Europe with a preparedness campaign of his own, which included formation of a Council of National Defense (CND) and an Advisory Commission reminiscent of Baruch's Businessmen's Commission, in August 1916. Baruch, along with a distinguished group of industrialists and academics, was appointed to the Advisory Commission. With no designated responsibility, the commission floundered about trying to define its duties and responsibilities. In February 1917, the commission formed seven divisions, with Baruch heading the raw materi-

als section. Although lacking in the organizational skills of a bureaucrat, he excelled in interpersonal relationships, so he drew on his vast pool of talented friends and acquaintances to provide the technical expertise required by the division.

Two months later the United States was at war with the Central Powers, and tentative issues of preparedness changed to immediate demands for mobilization. At the behest of businessmen who looked for some coherence in the areas of supply, price, and procurement, Wilson created the War Industries Board (WIB) in May 1917 and named Baruch, then a member of the Allied Purchasing Commission and the General Munitions Board, to the new WIB. Like the CND, the WIB initially had little authority and vainly worked to centralize control of production in the hands of the producers rather than the War Department. After nearly a year of ineffectual efforts, Wilson appointed Baruch chairman of the WIB in March 1918. Along with the new title came the authority to do whatever was necessary to achieve production goals without permanently disrupting the economy. The Wall Street gambler had become one of Wilson's closest advisers and confidants. Under Baruch's direction the energized agency fixed prices, quotas, wages, hours, and allocation of raw materials. Again, his success at the WIB lay in his ability to find " a few good men" and then give them the freedom to do their jobs.

At the same time as Baruch's appointment as chairman of the WIB, Wilson created an unofficial "War Cabinet" of those most responsible for the prosecution of the war. Baruch, Secretary of the Treasury and Railroad Administration Director William G. McAdoo, Secretary of the Navy Josephus Daniels, Secretary of War Newton D. Baker, Fuel Administrator Harry A. Garfield, Food Administrator Herbert C. Hoover, Shipping Board and Emergency Fleet Corporation Chairman Edward N. Hurley, and War Trade Board Chairman Vance C. McCormick met with Wilson every Wednesday to resolve questions affecting the war effort. Though Baruch was not a professional politician, his instinctive political acumen, congenial attitude, and his total devotion to Wilson won for him the President's absolute trust.

While actively overseeing massive shifts in industrial production for the war effort, Baruch and his fellow agency heads, particularly Herbert Hoover, were already developing a philosophy, if not actual policies, for demobilization. Baruch and others looked toward a Europe in the throes of reconstruction as a vast potential market. Their goal, therefore, became rapid demobilization and a return to peacetime production in order to take advantage of post-war trading opportunities. As a first step, the WIB was disbanded almost immediately after the Armistice.

Baruch was well aware of the impact of any peace settlement on the American economy and was anxious to participate in the negotiations in Paris. Besides, he had become accustomed to being among Wilson's inner circle and was loathe to lose his place to another. Wilson, in turn, was happy to have this trusted member of the War Cabinet with him in Paris.

As a member of the peace delegation, Baruch was once again faced with the task of defining his role, now in the peace delegation. His plate seemed full. He was a member of the Supreme Economic Council, chairman of its Raw Materials Division, member of the drafting committee of the Economic Council, a representative on the Economics and Reparations Commission, and an economic adviser to the American Peace Commission. Even so, he seemed to be something of a supernumerary. In truth, he was at the conference because Woodrow Wilson wanted him there, and he gave Wilson his complete support even when other advisers and confidants were second guessing the President and falling from his favor.

Upon the delegations' return to Washington, the major issue of the day, and one upon which hinged the success or failure of American efforts at the peace conference, was passage of the treaty by the Senate. It was of particular importance to Baruch, for he felt that passage of the treaty and full participation in the League of Nations would put American commercial interests in a strong position for decades. However, the debate on the treaty quickly became polarized between the Wilsonians and the so-called Reservationists led by Senator Henry Cabot Lodge of Massachusetts. Committed to the passage of the treaty, Baruch assumed the role of honest broker between the two groups. Despite the urgings of Baruch and others, Wilson refused to compromise, and the treaty went down to defeat in March 1920. Even though the financier had disappointed Wilson by urging compromise, he remained one of the frail President's closest associates for the rest of his life.

Baruch's association with presidents did not end with the election of Warren G. Harding. President Calvin Coolidge was anxious to have his assistance in securing bipartisan support for various legislative proposals, and Baruch shared an easy rapport with Herbert Hoover. While personally friendly with Franklin Roosevelt, theirs was not a close relationship, for FDR's administration tended to place the onus for the Great Crash on Wall Street and investors like Baruch. During World War II, many of Baruch's days were spent on a bench in Lafayette Park opposite the White House, a genial elder statesman frequently assisting the administration. His last official service for the government was in 1946 when President Truman appointed him as the United States representative to the United States Atomic Energy Commission. Baruch also maintained a lifelong friendship with Winston Churchill, whom he had first met during the Great War and again at the Paris Peace Conference.

A well-known philanthropist, Baruch contributed generously to the Red Cross, several universities and medical schools, and endowed the Baruch School of Business and Public Administration at his alma mater. Baruch died on June 20, 1965.

A.C. Venzon

See also COUNCIL OF NATIONAL DEFENSE; WAR INDUSTRIES BOARD

Bibliography
Schwarz, Jordan A. *The Speculator, Bernard M. Baruch in Washington, 1917–1965.* Chapel Hill: University of North Carolina Press, 1981.

B

Beauvais Agreement
After almost four years of war, the British and French armies in 1918 were still operating independently with all cooperation on a purely voluntary basis subject to the judgment and prejudices of the respective commanders-in-chief. The great spring 1918 offensive of the German Army, which broke through the lines of the British Fifth Army and endangered the very existence of the Allied forces, revealed the weakness of the arrangement and motivated the two governments to meet at Doullens on March 26, where French General Ferdinand Foch was

tapped to coordinate the action of the Allied armies on the Western Front.

A week later, when it was apparent that the German attack was faltering, General Foch wanted a more precise definition of his powers. He had concluded that the situation had changed and that the question of future strategy and coordination for anticipated actions demanded a commander with authority to command and not merely coordinate or advise.

It was to resolve this question that a conference was held in Beauvais on April 3, 1918. It was attended by British Prime Minister David Lloyd George, French Premier Georges Clemenceau, as well as a number of military leaders including General Sir Douglas Haig, General Foch, and General John J. Pershing, the American commander.

At Beauvais, Foch explained that the military situation was far different than it had been on March 26. At that time it was a question of coordinating action during a battle imposed on the Allies by the Germans, but now Foch was thinking of initiating action and wanted to be certain that future strategy was in his hands. He wanted the power of a commander-in-chief with authority over all Allied armies and commanders.

Haig agreed that there should be only one head in France and that he, Haig, would accept Foch as that commander. Since the American Expeditionary Force (AEF) was about to take its place alongside those of Britain and France, General Pershing was asked by Lloyd George to give his opinion.

The American commander said that the war had reached a point where the entire cooperation of the Allied armies should be assured and that the only way to ensure that cooperation would be to have a single command. He believed that success from then on depended upon the Allies having a single leader.

Since there was general agreement for an Allied commander-in-chief, and since all agreed that General Foch should be that officer, the conferees drew up a formula for its implementation. The British, French, and American governments charged General Foch with the coordination of the action of the Allied armies on the Western Front. All powers necessary for effective realization of this cooperation were conferred on him. The three governments entrusted Foch with the strategic direction of all military operations. The formula did give to each of the other army commanders the right of

appeal to his government if, in his opinion, the safety of his army was compromised by any of Foch's orders.

The Beauvais Agreement gave great power to General Foch, but his authority did not extend beyond the Western Front. Later augmented by the Abbeville Conference, it did give to the Allied armies a unified command, which was instrumental in the final Allied military victory.

Irvin M. Roth

See also ABBEVILLE CONFERENCE

Bibliography

Foch, Ferdinand. *The Memoirs of Marshal Foch*, trans. by Col. T. Bentley Mott. Garden City, NY: Doubleday, Doran, 1931.

Hankey, Maurice. *The Supreme Command, 1914–1918*. 2 vols. London: George Allen and Unwin, 1961.

Lloyd George, David. *War Memoirs*. 2 vols. London: Odhams Press, 1942.

Belfort Ruse

In mid-August 1918, the newly formed First American Army was preparing to launch its first independent operation of World War I, a pincer movement on the St. Mihiel salient southeast of Verdun. In an effort to preserve secrecy, conceal U.S. intentions from German intelligence, and divert the enemy's attention to other sectors, American intelligence launched a major *ruse de guerre* in the Belfort sector 125 miles south of the actual target.

As one of the traditional invasion routes into France, the Belfort Gap, as it was known, was a logical place to feign an offensive. With the French-held seventeenth-century city of Belfort on one side of the gap and the German-held Mulhouse on the other, the area was the nearest Allied point threatening the Rhine and the only point from the east of Metz to Switzerland where an Allied army could advance over level ground.

On August 10, U.S. intelligence (G-2) had purposely leaked false information that the First Army would operate in the Marne area. A week later, when the U.S. 5th Division pinched out a minor German bulge in the Vosges sector, G-2 tried again. The official communiqué made much of the action, and news correspondents were asked to do likewise in hopes that the German High Command would shift troops away from St. Mihiel to cover an apparent threat in the Belfort area.

A French liaison officer at American press headquarters coyly suggested that an offensive at Belfort might be in the works. Some reporters proceeded to write stories on that possibility. Pershing drove down to the sector ostensibly to inspect the 29th Division, then holding a section of the line there. His visit was followed by a similar tour by Gen. Henri Pétain. The 29th Division doughboys were ordered to increase the number and intensity of their raids in this otherwise quiet sector.

On August 28, Gen. Omar Bundy, commanding a primarily paper VI Corps at the Bourbonne-les-Baines Training Area about seventy-five miles northeast of the gap, was ordered to take key members of his staff to Belfort and make detailed plans for an attack. Bundy was told that the St. Mihiel buildup was a feint and the real attack would take place through the Belfort Gap to Mulhouse. He would not learn the embarrassing truth—that he was the diversion—until after the St. Mihiel operation commenced.

Col. Arthur L. Conger, assistant to AEF Chief of Staff James McAndrew, was assigned as a field operative, spurring Bundy on. Bundy needed little spurring. By September 1, his inspections and reconnaissances had whipped the whole region into a frenzy. The city of Belfort, with its numerous blond, German-speaking Alsatians, was a hot bed of spies and agents. The Grand Hotel et du Tonneau d'Or, where Bundy and his staff took up quarters, quickly filled with painfully nonchalant tourists, Swiss businessmen, and other shadowy characters who bribed waiters for gossip and purchased the contents of wastebaskets from chambermaids.

Only two days after Bundy's arrival, U.S. intelligence began to receive reports that a German hospital and large numbers of civilians were being moved to the other side of the Rhine. Conger acquired a couple of old tanks that he sent rattling around the countryside for the benefit of German reconnaissance planes. German intelligence was also alarmed by the sudden appearance of a new corps-sized radio net in the sector. The net, another of Conger's schemes, was made up of borrowed French wireless sets that sent out thousands of fake coded messages for the benefit of German monitoring stations.

The ingenious Conger also managed to "lose" a carbon of a message to General Pershing. The message informed Pershing that everything was ready for the big attack through the Belfort Gap. All Pershing had to do was set the date. The carbon went into the wastebasket at Conger's quarters at Hotel Tonneau, and the colonel went out for a quick stroll. When he returned, the wastebasket was empty.

German intelligence monitored these goings on carefully. The ranking German intelligence officer in the region informed his superiors that the activity might well be a *ruse de guerre* "intended to mislead us to the real point of attack." However, he felt extra divisions should be sent just in case. Ludendorff's headquarters acceded and sent three more divisions into the area. A French agent in Geneva reported that the Germans were also evacuating villages in the gap area, filling munitions dumps and bringing in more artillery.

Conger himself doubted the Germans were completely fooled; there were not enough real battle preparations to be convincing. In addition, the troop movements around St. Mihiel, the real point of attack, were simply too big to hide.

In the end, the Belfort Ruse may have been more valuable as a training exercise for American intelligence operatives than as an actual diversion. The St. Mihiel attack on September 12 was an enormous success. At its conclusion a highly successful charade was conducted to conceal surprise attacks on the Meuse-Argonne, and this success drew heavily on the lessons learned at Belfort. Indeed, Belfort, with its fictitious "wireless army corps" could be said to have been the seed of the whole fictitious army created twenty-six years later before the Normandy invasion of World War II.

James Hallas

See also BUNDY, OMAR

Bibliography

Johnson, Thomas M. *Without Censor.* Indianapolis: Bobbs-Merrill, 1928.
U.S. Army. *United States Army in the World War.* Vol. 8., St. Mihiel. Washington, DC: U.S. Army Historical Division, 1948.

Belknap, Reginald Rowan (1871–1959)
Reginald Rowan Belknap was born in Malden, Massachusetts. He was graduated from the United States Naval Academy in 1891. In July

1893 he was commissioned an ensign after two years at sea as a naval cadet aboard the USS *Chicago.* He was promoted through the ranks to captain, and by special act of Congress on May 3, 1927, he was promoted to rear admiral for his war service.

Belknap served in the Spanish-American War, the Boxer Rebellion, and the Philippine Insurrection and was detailed to the Bureau of Navigation from 1902 to 1904. He held the post of naval attaché in Berlin in 1907 and 1910 and in Rome and Vienna from 1908 to 1909. While in Rome he directed the American relief operations following the devastating Messina earthquake, which included the construction of housing for 16,000 homeless people. In 1919, he served as naval aide to former president Theodore Roosevelt and acted as special ambassador at the funeral of King Edward VII of England. Belknap was assistant chief of the Bureau of Navigation from 1912 to 1913 and from August to October 1914 served as an observer in Germany.

Belknap's service during the First World War included a stint in the Office of Naval Operations in 1917 and as senior officer at Santiago de Cuba. His most significant contributions came in 1918, when he invented and patented a collapsible antisubmarine net. Belknap also organized, trained, and commanded the United States Mining Squadron, which operated in the North Sea from June to October 1918. The squadron laid a 230-mile net of mines, some 70,000 in all, which accounted for the destruction of seven German submarines and the damaging of nine others.

He was awarded the U.S. Navy Distinguished Service Medal in 1919, as well as the Belgian Order of Leopold and the French Legion of Honor. In 1920, he published *The Yankee Mining Squadron,* which described his operations during the war. Belknap was director of the strategy department of the Naval War College from 1921 to 1923. He retired from the navy in 1926. Belknap died on March 30, 1959.

Michael J. Knapp

See also NORTH SEA MINE BARRAGE

Bibliography

Belknap, Reginald R. *The Yankee Mining Squadron: or, Laying the North Sea Mine Barrage.* Annapolis, MD: Naval Institute Press, 1920.

Bell, George, Jr. (1859–1926)

George Bell, Jr., was born at Fort McHenry, the son of brevet BGen. George Bell. Appointed by President Grant to the United States Military Academy with the class of 1880, Bell, Jr., was commissioned a second lieutenant upon graduation and assigned frontier duty in the Montana Territory for the following eight years. After an assignment at Fort Snelling, Bell served as professor of military science and tactics at Cornell University, where he earned an LL.B. degree in 1894. During the Spanish-American War, Bell saw combat in Cuba at the Battle of El Caney and near Santiago. He then served in a variety of capacities over the next fifteen years, including quartermaster, infantry company and battalion commander, and inspector general at posts in the United States and overseas. During this period, Bell earned distinction by participating in the capture of the Philippine Insurrection leader Vincente Lukban. In 1913, Bell took command of the 16th Infantry at the Presidio at San Francisco. He remained there until promoted to brigadier general and transferred to head the El Paso District along the Texas border. Although arriving at his new duty station the day the American Punitive Expedition advanced into Mexico in search of Pancho Villa, Bell did not actively participate in that campaign. In August 1917 Bell became commanding general of the 33d Division, an Illinois contingent, later known as the "Prairie Division," at Camp Logan, Texas.

The division arrived in France in May 1918 and entered the trenches near Albert the following month, fighting alongside the British. Bell's skillful leadership as commander of the only American division to fight in three sectors (under British, French, and American corps), and the division's success during the Meuse-Argonne offensive, earned the rotund, goateed general the nickname "Do-It-Now" Bell. Returning with his division to the United States in 1919, Bell assumed command of Camp Grant, near Rockford, Illinois, and later in the year took charge of the VI Corps Area, headquartered in Chicago. He remained associated with the Prairie State for the rest of his life. Retiring from active duty in 1922, Bell became president of a local bank, holding that post until his death in October 1926.

William E. Fisher, Jr.

Bibliography
Coffman, Edward M. *The War to End All Wars: The American Military Experience in World War I*. New York: Oxford University Press, 1968.
Illinois in the World War: An Illustrated History of the Thirty-third Division. 2 vols. Chicago: States Publications Society, 1921.

Bell, James Franklin (1856–1919)

James Franklin Bell was born near Shelbyville, Kentucky. After attending the Shelbyville school, he was appointed to the United States Military Academy with the class of 1878. Reporting for duty on Sept. 1, 1874, he struggled for four years with the academic and disciplinary programs. His affable and cheerful disposition made him very popular with his classmates. On graduation he was commissioned a second lieutenant and assigned to the 9th Cavalry, but before joining it, he was reassigned to the 7th Cavalry at Fort Lincoln, Dakota Territory.

On the frontier he trained troops, escorted wagon trains, and later guarded the construction of the Northern Pacific Railroad west of the Missouri River. In 1886, he became professor of military science at Southern Illinois Normal University at Carbondale. In addition to his regular duties, he studied law and was admitted to the bar. Bell rejoined the 7th Cavalry, now at Fort Riley, Kansas, in August 1889.

In 1890, after twelve years as a second lieutenant, Bell began to be discouraged about ever receiving a promotion. When an opportunity arose to visit Mexico to look into the possibility of a business connection, he took a leave of absence from the army and missed the battle at Wounded Knee, which his regiment fought against the Sioux. He returned shortly after the fight and became secretary of the School of Cavalry and Light Artillery at Fort Riley until 1894, when he served successively in California and at Fort Apache, Arizona. In April 1898, he was detailed as acting judge advocate of the Department of Columbia. However, as soon as war was declared with Spain, he sought relief from this detail and was ordered to the Philippines with Gen. Wesley Merritt's expedition. This began five years in which he covered himself with glory, winning the Medal of Honor, being promoted to brigadier general, and gaining a reputation as a fearless combat leader and a gifted civil administrator. Returning to Fort Leavenworth in 1903, Bell became commandant of the General Service Schools, where he served with distinction until named chief of staff of the U.S. Army in April 1906.

As chief of staff, he made a great record as the father of the Army School System and in effecting a general reorganization of the U.S. Army. In 1911, Bell returned to the Philippines as commander-in-chief. He took command of the 2d Division in Texas in 1914, became commander of the Western Department in 1915, and took command of the Eastern Department at Governor's Island, New York, in May 1917. He relinquished this post in August 1917 to lead the 77th Division of the National Army in the hope that he would be able to take it to France. In December 1917, he went to Europe to observe Allied actions and returned in March 1918. Much as he wanted a combat command, his friend Gen. John J. Pershing recommended that due to his precarious health he remain in the United States. Greatly disappointed, Bell relinquished command of the 77th Division and reverted to command of the Eastern Department, where he remained until his death of a heart attack on Jan. 8, 1919.

James L. Collins

Bibliography
Dawes, Charles G. *A Journal of the Great War*. Boston and New York: Houghton Mifflin, 1921.
Marshall, George C. *Memoirs of My Service in the World War 1917–1918*. Boston: Houghton Mifflin, 1976.
Pershing, John J. *My Experiences in the World War*. New York: Stokes, 1931.
Smythe, Donald. *Pershing*. Bloomington: Indiana University Press, 1986.

Belleau Wood, Battle of

Belleau Wood was the general name given to an area in which the U.S. 2d Division fought in the Château-Thierry sector from June 1 to June 26, 1918. Actually, the wood was just a relatively small section of the entire territory occupied by the division. It was roughly one mile in length and one-half mile at its widest point. The entire engagement received the rather vague identification of the Aisne-Marne defensive. It was considered a rather inconsequential affair that had little effect upon the participation and eventual success of the American Expeditionary Force (AEF) and the Allies in France.

The 2d Division was composed of two infantry brigades: the 3d, which included two Regular Army regiments, the 9th and 23d Infantry plus the 5th Machine Gun Battalion, and the 4th Marine Brigade, which included the 5th and 6th Marine regiments plus the 6th Machine Gun Battalion. The other division troops, artillery, engineers, and train were composed of Regular Army (USA) units. MajGen. Omar Bundy (USA), commanded the division, and in May 1918, BGen. James G. Harbord (USA) relieved ailing Marine BGen. Charles A. Doyen as commander of the 4th Brigade.

In late May 1918, the German armies launched a very successful attack upon the French Army in the area known as the Chemin des Dames, moving rapidly toward the Marne River line. It was the third German assault since the beginning of the year and was the most serious for the Allies. French troops scattered before the onslaught of as many as fifty German divisions. On May 31, 1918, the 2d Division, having been assigned by Pershing to French command, received orders to board camions and head eastward in the general direction of Meaux and the farming country between Château-Thierry and Soissons. The division was to supplement the French forces still engaged in that section. Their general orders were to form a "brick wall" for advancing German armies and at all cost to keep them as far away as possible from Paris, the hub of France.

The division traveled most of May 31, and many units had still not arrived at their specific location before the afternoon of June 1. Almost immediately the division's infantry, both the 3d Infantry Brigade and the 4th Marine Brigade, were engaged in defending the general position that the division had been assigned by their Sixth French Army commander, Gen. Denis Duchêne. By a quirk of fate, and contrary to the original division orders, the 4th Marine Brigade occupied the left flank of the division's flank and the 3d Brigade the right. The marines faced troops of five German divisions on an arc running northward from Triangle Farm, where the 3d Brigade's left flank terminated, to the right flank of the French 167th Division at a point just north of Marigny and perhaps a mile southwest of Torcy. During the period between June 1 and June 5, the division's various infantry units met the oncoming Germans and handily defeated them, using mainly aimed rifle fire.

The Germans finally had enough when their attempts to take Les Mares Farm were defeated by Capt. John Blanchfield's 55th Company of the 2d Battalion, 5th Marine Regiment, which battalion was led by a marine officer of the old school, LtCol. Frederick M. (Fritz) Wise. The farm was at the extreme left of the division's sector and just thirty or so miles from Paris, the closest the Germans were able to get to that target since 1914. Never again during the war would the German Army be as near victory as they were at this point in time. All roads led to Paris, and if the capital had fallen, the French would have been unable to continue the war, leaving the British no alternative but to retire to the home island. The AEF would have been in a very tenuous position if that had happened. It would have been impossible to continue the war and a complete surrender was the probable outcome.

The few French troops still in front of the 2d Division's line continued to fall back through those lines until nothing stood between the Americans and the advancing German Army. Finally, the German probes of the American lines ceased except for normal patrol activity. The French commander, Gen. Joseph Degoutte, who had been at the receiving end of the German onslaught, decided that he now had two relatively unscathed divisions, the 167th and the 2d; therefore it was time to turn on the Germans. Very late on June 5, he ordered the U.S. 4th Marine Brigade to launch an attack on the morning of June 6. Maj. Julius S. Turrill's 1st Battalion, 5th Marine Regiment was to lead off in an attack northward upon a promontory known as Hill 142, which poked its nose nearly between the towns of Torcy and Bussiares, both occupied by the enemy. Maj. Benjamin Berry's 3d Battalion, 5th Marine Regiment was to support Turrill's right flank in the early morning advance. During the late afternoon Berry's men would have their "show." The hunting preserve known as Belleau Wood was its main target. Maj. Berton Sibley's 3d Battalion, 6th Marine Regiment, the battalion that flanked Berry to the southeast, would join in the assault upon the south end of the woods. While this was in progress, LtCol. Thomas Holcomb's 2d Battalion, 6th Marines would cover Sibley's right flank and advance toward and take the town of Bouresches, which lay at the southeastern edge of the woods, and effectively outflank the occupants of the woods. Actually, the local French intelligence services had proclaimed the woods "Boche free." Unfortunately, the in-experienced Americans were not able to verify that for them-

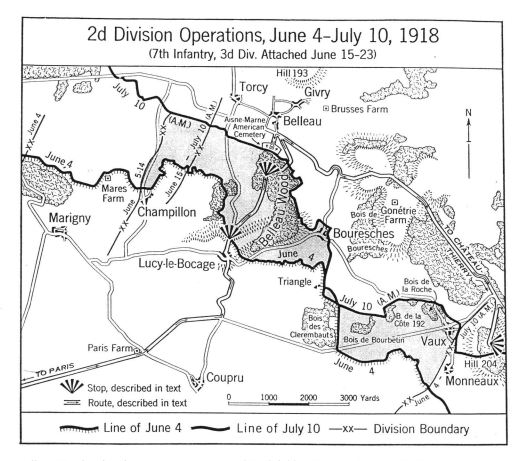

2d Division Operations, June 4–July 10, 1918
(7th Infantry, 3d Div. Attached June 15–23)

Belleau Wood. *Taken from* American Armies and Battlefields in Europe, *American Battle Monuments Commission, Government Printing Office, 1938.*

selves, a major error that they would rue for many a day afterward. The absence of artillery preparation, a severe shortage of maps available to the field commanders, and the fact that the orders did not come down from brigade headquarters until very late on the morning of June 6 compounded the Americans' difficulties. Another, and not inconsequential matter, was the fact that Turrill's battalion was missing two of its four companies, which were on loan to Wise's battalion at or near Les Mares Farm. So was most of the regiment's own 8th Machine Gun Company, and it was not until very late after the assault began that a few guns and crews from the 6th Machine Gun Battalion would be in position to provide barrage support for the assault. All in all, the division's first attack began under rather inauspicious conditions.

Turrill's two companies—the 49th led by Capt. George W. Hamilton and the 67th led on this occasion by 1st Lt. Orlando Crowther—started their offensive at 3:45 A.M. They immediately received a heavy concentration of machine gun and artillery fire, forcing the marines to take what little cover was available. Captain Hamilton immediately moved along his front line and talked his men into leaving their cover and to continue the advance against the German lines. A battery of at least thirty-six German Maxim's poured fire into their ranks. But soon the marines had penetrated the German line, and the few remaining Americans utilized their bayonets with murderous precision to silence most of the guns. Hamilton and elements of his 49th Company went far beyond the elongated sector of the woods assigned to them, plunging downward toward Torcy, which lay not far ahead. However, they retired back up the hill, not knowing that three enlisted marines had actually made their way into the town. (These three brave men were to meet their death at Torcy within hours of their entering the town.) Meanwhile the 67th Company, which was on the left flank, headed down into Belleau's deep ravine and lower slopes, meeting exceptionally heavy fire in so doing. By 7 A.M. the remnant of the two companies, with added support from platoons of the 17th and 66th companies, which were just arriving from duty with the 2d Battalion, managed to create a defensive line on the hill and cover the slopes on each side. Casualties were very severe, especially in the 67th Company: Crowther was dead, and only one officer remained on his feet. Hamilton temporarily assumed responsibility for both companies, and Turrill did yeoman's duty providing direction and stability to the badly used marines still alive on the hill.

Meanwhile, the 3d Battalion, 5th Marines provided some support on the right flank during the advance and had suffered a few casualties doing so. But their opportunity for glory came soon enough. Col. Albertus Catlin, commander of the 6th Regiment, was placed in overall command of the afternoon's attack. LtCol. Logan Feland, assistant to Col. Wendell Neville, was to command the left of the line, where the 3d Battalion, 5th Marines would be. The 96th Company, with support from the 79th Company, both from the 2d Battalion, 6th Marines, would attack and take Bouresches, which they did. Bouresches was one of the few early successes of the campaign, albeit with great losses, including that of Capt. Donald Duncan, the skipper of the 96th.

Belleau Wood was a most difficult position for attacking infantry. It has been described by one U.S. Army historian, Maj. R.M. Johnston, as "a mass of underbrush covering the roughest sort of a rock formation. It is as wild and difficult as any tract in the White or Appalachian Mountains. Broken by one very deep ravine, it afforded endless positions for small groups of riflemen and machine gunners." Trees lined the edges, but enormous boulders within the woods provided protection to occupants from almost everything the marines could throw at them.

The attack was launched. The Germans were waiting in the woods. Their machine guns and artillery zeroed in on both battalions. The 3d Battalion, 5th Marines had a wheat field to cross, and that caused them the most immediate damage. Some of the marines managed to enter the woods but were so badly shot up, losing many of their officers and noncoms, that

they became disoriented, and it was some time before they could be effectively withdrawn. Berry himself was soon incapacitated, losing his hand a short time after entering the woods.

While the 5th Marine Brigade was so occupied, the 3d Battalion, 6th Marines, found the southern edge of the woods permeated with German machine gun nests. Despite heavy casualties, the battalion managed to enter the fringes of the woods, though with little overall success. While the two battalions were assaulting the woods, elements of the 2d Battalion, 6th Marines were advancing across open ground toward Bouresches and taking heavy casualties in the process. The commander of the 96th, Duncan, was severely wounded almost at the beginning; shortly thereafter he and several other officers and men fell mortally wounded when a shell landed in their midst. Then 1st Lt. James Robertson assumed command and continued the advance toward the town. Eventually, twenty men led by 2d Lt. Clifton B. Cates entered Bouresches and fought off the Germans there, holding on until reinforcements arrived to support their very weak position. More men had been killed by the end of that most bloody day for the U.S. Marine Corps than had fallen, collectively, in combat in the entire 143-year history of the corps.

The situation at the end of the day was that the 1st Battalion, 5th Marines still tenuously controlled Hill 142, one of the three main objectives; an ever growing number of marines weakly held Bouresches, but the main goal, Belleau Wood, was still held almost completely by the well-entrenched Germans.

The 4th Marine Brigade had paid a very heavy price for the objective on June 6, and it would continue to do so during the next twenty days, when launching another five attacks. During the next few days, the marines made several attempts against the woods but with little success. At 4:30 A.M. on June 10, Maj. Johnny "the Hard" Hughes was leading the 1st Battalion, 6th Marines when the next major effort was launched against Belleau. A few local and minor successes were all that came from this effort, but there were more casualties. The 6th Marines retained Bouresches and a very sketchy foothold on the southern edge of the woods, nothing more.

On June 11, another major, and almost successful, assault was led by LtCol. Wise in the same spot in which Berry's men had been slaughtered, and they too paid a heavy price for their courage and tenacity. The battalion did manage to enter the woods, but because of considerable confusion and disorientation they lost much of what had been gained that day. Still they retained a foothold within the woods, which would be expanded slowly as the days went by.

The following evening at 6 P.M. Wise and his battalion made another assault, gaining a few more yards of woods before grinding to a halt. The 4th Marine Brigade had been on the move and engaged in unsuccessful attacks upon a well-defended objective since May 31, nearly two weeks of contentious activity. They were exhausted; for the most part they had received not more than one hot meal in that time and very little rest. The veterans had welcomed many replacements, most of whom were barely out of boot camp but who, if they survived would uphold the honor of their corps in the days to follow. At this point even the high command of the brigade and division acknowledged that the marines were unable to take any more punishment, without at least a brief rest. And they got it with the arrival of the 7th Infantry of the 3d U.S. Division, who relieved elements of the various marine battalions. During the following few days, the marine brigade tried to collect itself in a modest reserve position. The Germans also had been taking a lot of punishment themselves and were not too anxious to start any trouble during those few days of respite.

Rejuvenated, the 4th Marine Brigade launched another attack upon the woods at 7 P.M. on June 23. Maj. Maurice Shearer, now in command of the 3d Battalion, 5th Marines, made some valuable gains, and at 5 P.M. on June 25, the same battalion again advanced into the northern tip of Belleau Wood, which resulted in the final clearing of all Germans from the wood. Shearer, in a message to headquarters, was finally able to state jubilantly "Woods now U.S. Marine Corps entirely."

Nearly 4,600 officers and men were casualties, at least 50 percent of the entire marine force, but still Belleau Wood was not considered more than a "local engagement" by the AEF command. The French were ecstatic and renamed the wood Bois de la Brigade de Marine. Plaudits from every political and military organization in the Allied world flooded the headquarters of the Marine Corps as well as that of Pershing's. The French populace was convinced that the marines had saved not only Paris but France as well. But not only the French believed so. Gen. Robert L. Bullard wrote in his book *American Soldiers Also Fought*, "The marines didn't 'win the war' here. But they saved the Allies from defeat. Had they arrived a few hours later I think that would have been the beginning of the end: France could not have stood the loss of Paris. So today at Belleau Wood stands perhaps America's finest battle monument." But the 2d Marine Battalion commander Fritz Wise succinctly described the price the marines paid when, in response to his wife's query "How are the Marines?" he responded "There aren't any more Marines."

The 4th Brigade went on to other, equally bloody combats but none have the lasting reputation of Belleau Wood. The determination of the marines, combined with their unbelievable courage and the need for an American victory against an unyielding German defense with an obstinacy designed to crush the Americans early in the game, forced the situation into the path it took. It was the beginning of the end for the Germans.

George B. Clark

Bibliography

Asprey, Robert B. *At Belleau Wood*. New York: Putnam, 1965.

Catlin, Albertus W., and Walter A Dyer. *With the Help of God and a Few Marines*. Garden City, NY: Doubleday, 1919.

McClellan, Edwin. *The United States Marine Corps in the World War*. Washington, DC: Historical Branch, U.S. Marine Corps, 1968.

Stallings, Laurence. *The Doughboys: The Story of the AEF, 1917–1918*. New York: Harper & Row, 1963.

Benedict XV (1854–1922)

Benedict XV, or Giacomo Della Chiesa, was pope from Sept. 3, 1914, until his death on Jan. 22, 1922. He succeeded Pope Pius X, who supposedly died of a broken heart with the outbreak of the Great War. Benedict was an experienced diplomat, having served as the personal secretary to Rampolla del Tindaro, the secretary of state under Pope Leo XIII. Not only was Benedict faced with the challenge of bringing peace to a world gone insane, but he was also working toward the advancement of traditional papal interests: asserting papal independence from the Italian state and regaining the extensive confiscated church holdings in Italy.

Upon the outbreak of hostilities, Benedict immediately declared neutrality for the papacy, but this was somewhat tainted by the composition of the two alliances. The Vatican did not see the victory of an alliance composed of Protestant England, a France under an extremely anticlerical Third Republic, and an Orthodox Russia as furthering its interests.

On the other hand, the Vatican, like the rest of the Continent, simply could not imagine a Europe without the ancient Habsburg Empire and its deep Catholic roots. The papacy harbored little love for the German Empire after the *Kulturkampf,* the struggle between Bismarck and the Catholic Church, but the German state was still home to millions of Catholics. Despite this bias, Benedict maintained such an honest stance of neutrality that he drew criticism from both sides. The English called him the "Boche" (swine) Pope, the Germans called him the "Franzozenpapst" (French pope), and the Italians called him "Maledetto" (ill-spoken) rather than "Benedetto" (well-spoken).

Benedict made continual though unsuccessful efforts to inspire peace. The most notable attempt was the famous letter to "the leaders of belligerent peoples," also known as the 1917 Peace Note, issued on Aug. 1, 1917, to an extremely war-weary Europe. It called for a peace without victory that preserved Austria-Hungary, reestablished an independent Poland, and returned occupied territories to their rightful states.

Benedict's impartiality allowed him to participate in numerous charities for both sides. The Vatican became a second Red Cross as it tracked prisoners and contacted families. Twice during the war Benedict secured an exchange of prisoners. The papacy spent an estimated 82 million gold lire, including the majority of Benedict's personal wealth, for the relief of refugees. This continued after the war as Benedict sought to relieve famine in Europe and Spanish Influenza victims.

After the war Benedict petitioned the Big Four for a role in the peace treaties but only obtained one place as an observer at Versailles. He disagreed with the harsh terms against Germany, fearing that they would lead to another war. However, Benedict's humanitarian efforts and accomplishments were recognized by the Great Powers as evidenced by the increase in the number of diplomatic representatives accredited to the Papal Court. Benedict's neutral diplomacy was greatly misunderstood during the war and would not be appreciated until compared with the papal cooperation with fascism after his death.

Mathew Heiser

Bibliography
Falconi, Carlo. *The Popes in the Twentieth Century.* Boston: Little, Brown, 1967.
Holmes, J. Derek. *The Papacy in the Modern World.* New York: Crossroad Publishing, 1981.
Peters, Walter H. *The Life of Benedict XV.* Milwaukee: Bruce, 1959.

Beneš, Edvard (1884–1948)

Edvard Beneš was the principal lieutenant of Thomas G. Masaryk from the First World War until the latter's retirement as president of Czechoslovakia in 1935, a post Beneš then assumed. Trained as a sociologist, Beneš began his political career during World War I when he attached himself to the far older Masaryk, then in exile in Switzerland, becoming his most devoted and trusted aide. His first role was to act as liaison between Masaryk and his Czech political allies in Prague, the so-called Mafie. Beneš joined Masaryk in France in late 1915 and worked tirelessly to advance the Czech cause. To Beneš belongs much of the credit for the gradual and hard-won diplomatic success of the Czecho-Slovak National Council on which he served as secretary general under Masaryk's presidency. With the Armistice, Beneš returned to Prague to be the first foreign minister of newly created Czechoslovakia, serving as his nation's spokesman at the Paris Peace Conference.

The architect of Czechoslovakia's interwar foreign policy, Beneš replaced Masaryk as president in 1935. He resigned after the dismemberment of his country by the Munich Pact in 1938 and went into exile in England. During World War II Beneš created a government in exile under his presidency. He was allowed to return to Czechoslovakia as president by the Russians but resigned following the Communist coup of 1948.

A controversial figure, Beneš had remarkable diplomatic skills and rare energy and industry. However, his vaunted political "realism" is often condemned as a euphemism for a lack of both vision and courage.

M.B. Biskupski

See also MASARYK, TOMÁŠ GARRIGUE

Bibliography

Beneš, Edvard. *My War Memoirs,* trans. by Paul Selver. Boston: Houghton Mifflin, 1928.

Taborsky, Edward. *President Edvard Beneš between East and West, 1938–1948.* Stanford, CA: Hoover Institution Press, 1981.

Wallace, William V. "An Appraisal of Edvard Beneš as a Statesman." *Historical Studies* (Dublin) (1971).

Wandycz, Piotr S. "The Foreign Policy of Edvard Beneš, 1918–1938." In *A History of the Czechoslovak Republic, 1918–1948,* ed. by Victor S. Mamatey and Radomir Luza. Princeton, NJ: Princeton University Press, 1973.

Benson, William Shepherd (1855–1932)

William Shepherd Benson was one of the first Southerners to enter the Naval Academy after the Civil War, graduating with the class of 1877. His early naval career was marked by nondescript ship and shore assignments and slow, steady advancement through the officer ranks. His first command came in 1908 with the protected cruiser *Albany,* then engaged in gunboat diplomacy duty off the Pacific coast of Central America. In 1909, he was promoted to the rank of captain and became the chief of staff to the commander-in-chief of the Pacific Fleet. Captain Benson held the coveted command of a new battleship, the *Utah,* from 1910 through 1913. From 1913 until 1915, he served as commandant of the Philadelphia Navy Yard and supervisor of the Third, Fourth, and Fifth Naval districts.

In May 1915, Benson became the first chief of naval operations (CNO) with the rank of rear admiral. While some colleagues complained that he was not the most qualified officer for this important new post, Benson was certainly not unqualified, and he was removed from the political maneuverings of some of the naval reformers who objected to his appointment. Admiral Benson, however, quietly gained the confidence of most of his fellow officers within the Navy Department as well as his civilian boss, Secretary of the Navy Josephus Daniels. To his credit, Benson used the new office to centralize the navy's administration, no easy task given the secretary's suspicions of an overly centralized naval high command. Benson got all bureau chiefs to submit their reports to the Navy Department through the CNO's office, and after 1916, the CNO issued orders to the fleet in the name of the secretary of the navy.

Admiral Benson's primary concern while CNO was preparing the fleet for war. This involved him in war planning and strategic matters as well as in efforts to expand the size of the navy. He labored hard to secure passage of the important Naval Appropriations Act of 1916, which authorized the building of an American navy second to none.

Benson, who was promoted to the rank of full admiral in 1916, was the navy's administrative manager during World War I. In the first months of American participation, he clashed with Admiral William S. Sims, who believed that the navy should suspend capital-ship construction in favor of antisubmarine vessels and strip the American battle fleet of most of its destroyers for service as convoy escorts. Without them, he argued, Britain would fall. Benson's reluctance to accept this assessment prompted opponents and historians to charge him unjustly with Anglophobia. The CNO's thinking was shaped by the teachings of Alfred Thayer Mahan, which emphasized the deployment only of a balanced fleet in wartime. Benson also was concerned with the postwar strategic implications of suspending capital-ship building, especially in the light of the long-term American goal of constructing a navy second to none. He later concluded that the German submarine menace was indeed the navy's top priority, but he also pushed for the Allies to adopt more active measures to prosecute the naval war: the North Sea mine barrage and the attack of U-boat bases.

During the war Admiral Benson forged the Office of Naval Operations into an effective administrative organization, efficiently handling the details of a modern wartime navy. To assist in war planning, his office included a Plans Division and an Intelligence Division. To guide fleet operations, there was a Division of Operating Forces.

After the war Benson was the principal American naval adviser at the Paris Peace Conference. There he did his best to prevent the defeat of Germany from unduly benefitting the British Royal Navy. He argued against any measures that would lead to American naval inferiority. Admiral Benson retired in 1919 but continued to serve on the U.S. Shipping Board until 1928.

Donald A. Yerxa

See also NORTH SEA MINE BARRAGE; SIMS, WILLIAM SOWDEN

Bibliography

Klatchko, Mary. *Admiral William Shepherd Benson: First Chief of Naval Operations.* Annapolis, MD: Naval Institute Press, 1987.

———. "William Shepherd Benson: Naval General Staff American Style." In *Admirals of the Steel Navy: Makers of the American Naval Tradition*, ed. by James C. Bradford. Annapolis, MD: Naval Institute Press, 1990.

Reynolds, Clark G. *Famous American Admirals.* New York: Van Nostrand Reinhold, 1978.

Trask, David F. "William Shepherd Benson." In *The Chiefs of Naval Operations,* ed. by Robert W. Love, Jr. Annapolis, MD: Naval Institute Press, 1980.

Berchtold, Leopold (1863–1942)

Count Leopold Berchtold's career in the Austro-Hungarian Foreign Service reflected his background as a member of the extremely wealthy landed Habsburg magnate-class aristocracy. Unlike many of the great families that retreated from state service with the rise of democratic politics in the nineteenth century, the Berchtolds remained active and set an example of duty and Habsburg loyalty for Leopold. His father Sigmund was an active member of both the Moravian legislature and the central Austrian parliament in Vienna. His maternal grandfather, Count Trauttmansdorff, had been ambassador to Prussia; an uncle was president of the House of Lords. Leopold, born in Vienna, was tutored at home and proved an able student. After a year as a reserve lieutenant in the army, he passed the state civil service exam with distinction in 1883 and began a career in the Moravian civil service.

In 1892, he married Countess Karoli, daughter of the late ambassador to Great Britain and a member of the Hungarian aristocracy. This expanded his connections with the great families of Hungary. He now transferred to the Habsburg Foreign Service with an unpaid position as attaché in Paris. Refusing a promotion to St. Petersburg at the behest of his wife, Berchtold was assigned to London as first secretary. Finally, in 1903, he accepted a posting to Russia at the express request of Ambassador Count Alois Aehrenthal. A man of tact and routine, Berchtold was an ideal diplomat for this embassy at a time when foreign policy was still made by the great families at rounds of parties.

Berchtold had no particular interest in politics. In May 1905, he retired briefly, but in December 1906, Aehrenthal became foreign minister and wanted Berchtold as his replacement as ambassador at the crucial Russian post. Berchtold stayed on until 1911 at the cost of the death of his frail second son.

In retirement again in 1911, Berchtold returned to his farms and horses and followed a new interest in auto and air racing. Qualified by wealth and title to sit in either the Hungarian or the Austrian House of Lords, he opted for the Hungarian body, reflecting an apolitical desire for aristocratic company. Again it was not to be.

In January 1912, Emperor Franz Joseph asked Berchtold to become foreign minister. Berchtold refused, saying he had no aptitude for the post. In this he was correct. The qualities that had made him a good ambassador—affability, charm, and tact—were not sufficient for the death struggle about to begin. However, because of Berchtold's good Hungarian and Austrian connections, Franz Joseph preferred him to several others who were perhaps more skillful, energetic, and ambitious politicians, and the emperor prevailed on Berchtold to accept. Berchtold's goals were peace and the status quo—and a retreat from the policies of Aehrenthal.

It was too late for Berchtold. Italy had attacked Turkey in Libya in 1911 in reaction to French moves in Morocco. In October 1912, a Balkan alliance crafted by Russia attacked the weakened Turks. Their unexpected early collapse completely changed Austria-Hungary's Balkan position and required extensive, and it must be said successful, damage control by Berchtold. He resisted the Habsburg war party led by General Conrad, chief of the General Staff. The dangerous Balkan League was broken up although an alliance with disaffected Bulgaria was not achieved by July 1914. Dynamic Serbia, now doubled in size and seen as Austria-Hungary's greatest enemy in the Balkans, was denied access to the Adriatic Sea by the creation of a large Albanian state out of the ruins of Turkey in Europe. This limited success orchestrated by Berchtold required all of Austria-Hungary's energies, including mobilization of a large part of the army and the threat of war with Russia, patron of recalcitrant Serbia and Montenegro.

Equally disquieting, Austria-Hungary's long-time German ally often did not support the Habsburg Balkan position. In November 1913, Berchtold again had to threaten force to make Serbia evacuate Albania. At this point, he was convinced that his peace policy was perceived as weakness by Austria-Hungary's foes and only encouraged their predations. He now thought war with Serbia was inevitable, and numerous minor successful diplomatic inroads in the Balkans brought no improvement.

From the Habsburg perspective, the June 28, 1914, assassination of Franz Ferdinand, heir to the throne, was just one more Serbian provocation. Berchtold was not bullied into war against his better judgment. Rather he and the emperor had long since joined the consensus of the Crown Council that only war would solve the Serbian problem. Peace was a sign of weakness.

Despite the German lack of support for the Habsburg Balkan policies, the interlocking treaty system buttressing a fragile balance of power in Europe, coupled with Kaiser Wilhelm's bellicose ambitions, led Germany to join the conflict. The treaty system gave way to elaborate, minutely detailed mobilization and war plans. Failure of the German Schlieffen Plan to knock out France and the Habsburg defeats by both Serbia and Russia in 1914 led to a dangerous stalemate, which tempted the neutrals to enter the fray. Most serious for Berchtold was the position of the Habsburg's old ally, Italy, which was being wooed by France and Great Britain. In January 1915, Berchtold tried to buy Italy's continued neutrality by offering it the Italian-speaking South Tyrol. Although encouraged by Germany in this move, both the Austrian and Hungarian governments and Franz Joseph were opposed. Without support for his policy, which might have won the war if Italy had agreed, Berchtold resigned.

In the summer of 1915, he joined a cavalry regiment as a reserve officer. Later he became court steward and chamberlain for Charles I, who became emperor in 1916. These were largely ceremonial posts. After the war he lived on his estates, then reduced by land reform and managed by his sons. He worked on his memoirs in a desultory manner. At his death in 1942 they remained unfinished.

R.D. Zehnder

See also CONRAD VON HOTZENDORFF, FRANZ

Bibliography
Hantsch, Hugo. *Leopold Graf Berchtold.* Graz, Austria: Verlag Styria, 1963.

Berger, Victor Louis (1860–1929)

Victor Louis Berger was born in Austria. He moved to the United States in 1878, eventually settling in Milwaukee, Wisconsin, where he taught German in the public schools. He participated in Socialist politics and in 1892 was made editor of the *Wisconsin Vorwarts,* the Milwaukee German daily of the Socialist Labor Party. He later became the editor of the (Milwaukee) *Warheit,* the *Social Democratic Leader,* and the *Milwaukee Leader,* a Socialist daily, which he directed until his death in 1929.

Berger began his political career as a delegate to the People's Party Convention held in St. Louis in 1896. The following year, along with Eugene V. Debs, he helped found the Social Democrats, and in 1898, he was one of the organizers of the Social Democratic Party, later known as the Socialist Party.

In 1904, Berger unsuccessfully sought a seat in the U.S. House of Representatives on the Socialist ticket. He was elected a member of Milwaukee's charter commission and alderman-at-large. In 1910, with the backing of Socialists, German Americans, and organized labor, Berger was elected to the U.S. House of Representatives—the first Socialist to be elected to Congress. In Congress, he supported such reform measures as the eight-hour day, child labor laws, federal farm relief, and old-age pensions. He served from 1911 to 1913; he was defeated for reelection in 1912 and again in 1914 and 1916.

Berger vehemently opposed American entry into World War I and published numerous antiwar articles, cartoons, and editorials in the *Milwaukee Leader* expressing his concerns. Although he was elected to Congress again in 1918, the House refused to seat him because of his opposition to the war and the virulent nature of his writings. In 1919, he was indicted under the Espionage Act of 1917 for giving aid and comfort to the enemy and was sentenced to twenty years in prison. While awaiting appeal of his sentence, Berger was reelected to the congressional seat he had been denied a year earlier. Once again Congress refused to seat him. His constituents nominated him a third time, but the governor refused to call a special election.

In 1921, the United States Supreme Court reversed Berger's conviction, and in 1923 he was once more elected to the House of Representatives. This time he took his seat without opposition. He was reelected for two additional terms but was defeated for a third term in 1928 when he supported Alfred E. Smith for president.

On July 16, 1929, Berger was struck by a streetcar in Milwaukee and died on August 7.

Burton A. Boxerman

Bibliography
Miller, Sally M. *Victor Berger and the Promise of Constructive Socialism, 1910–1920*. Westport, CT: Greenwood Press, 1973.

Berkman, Alexander (1870–1936)

Alexander Berkman was born in Vilna, Russia, of middle-class Jewish parents but was influenced by Russian populist thought at an early age. He immigrated to the United States in 1888 and was soon active in Jewish anarchist organizations in New York City. He met Emma Goldman in 1889 and formed a political and personal relationship with her that was to last until his death. Berkman attained great notoriety following an abortive attempt to assassinate Henry Clay Frick on July 23, 1892, during the Homestead steel strike. Berkman served fourteen years of a twenty-two-year prison sentence for this deed. Following his release in 1906, he returned to anarchist activities and wrote his *Prison Memoirs of an Anarchist.*

From 1914 to 1917, Berkman strongly opposed the entrance of the United States into World War I and tirelessly promoted the pacifist cause both in his journalist and in public-speaking tours. Following American involvement, he and Emma Goldman actively opposed the draft. On June 15, 1917, both were arrested on the charge of conspiring to obstruct the operation of the Selective Service Act. Though they insisted at the trial that they had not actually incited men to evade the draft, they were convicted on July 9, 1917. Following the rejection of an appeal by the Supreme Court, Berkman was sent to the federal prison in Atlanta in February 1918. Immediately following his release on Oct. 1, 1919, he and Goldman were subjected to deportation proceedings as undesirable aliens, Berkman having never become a citizen and Goldman's citizenship being found defective. On December 21, they and 247 other persons were deported to Russia on an old military transport derisively dubbed the "Red Ark." Berkman never returned to the United States.

John E. Little

Bibliography
Berkman, Alexander. *The Bolshevik Myth.* London: Pluto, 1989.
———. *Life of an Anarchist: The Alexander Berkman Reader,* ed. by Rene Fellner. New York: Four Walls Eight Windows, 1992.

Bernstorff, Johann Heinrich von (1862–1939)

Count Johann Heinrich von Bernstorff spent his first ten years in London, where his father represented Prussia (from 1871 Germany) at the Court of St. James. After the elder Bernstorff's death in 1873, the family returned home, and the son received the customary academic high school education. Bernstorff initially pursued an officer's career in the 1st Guard Field Artillery, but military life did not appeal to him and his eight-year military career in Berlin was uneventful. It did provide him with numerous social contacts, however, and resulted in his marriage to the American-born descendant of a prominent merchant family, Jeanne Luckmeyer, in 1887. Soon after this, Bernstorff was posted as a military attaché to the embassy in Constantinople, and this opened the way to a diplomatic career. He rapidly advanced through the ranks with various positions in Europe, eventually becoming counselor of the embassy in London and counsel general in Cairo.

The diplomatic capabilities that he demonstrated during the Moroccan crisis of 1905, and the personal support of Chancellor von Bülow, resulted in Bernstorff's appointment as ambassador to the United States in the fall of 1908. He was well received in his new post, and through a combination of personal charm, intelligence, and savoir faire gained many friends over the course of his nine-year stay.

Bernstorff was convinced that a Western-oriented foreign policy combined with liberal politics at home would be the best path for Germany. He was particularly strong in his view that England, not Russia, would be the best ally of Germany, but this amity would only result if Germany did not attempt to compete with England as a sea power. That, of course, is precisely what Germany under Wilhelm II attempted to do.

When Bernstorff learned of the disaster at the Battle of the Marne in September 1914, he abandoned hope of a German victory and agreed that a compromise peace must be sought. These views brought him closer to the neutrality policies of President Woodrow Wilson, Col. Edward M. House, and Secretary of State William Jennings Bryan. After the sinking of the *Lusitania* in May 1915, Bernstorff played the difficult role of mediator. He advised Berlin to accept responsibility for the attack, while simultaneously justifying the torpedo attack to the Wilson administration as retribution against the British blockade. His efforts, however, were only temporarily successful because in August 1915, the *Arabic*, a British mail and passenger ship was also sunk. While Bernstorff was permitted to tell Wilson that there would be no further attacks on passenger liners, he recognized that this would never satisfy an outraged American public and so allowed the new secretary of state, Robert Lansing, to make his statement public.

Bernstorff's quick thinking may have diffused the immediate crisis; unfortunately, his recognition of the volatility of the situation was not shared by Berlin. Neither were his solitary and largely symbolic gestures persuasive to an increasingly hostile American public. In particular, Bernstorff did not share the German Navy's optimism about unrestricted submarine warfare. In fact, in 1916 and early 1917, he warned the Foreign Office that this would bring the United States into the war and would result in an Entente victory. Unlike the leadership in Berlin, Bernstorff firmly believed that Wilson's commitment to neutrality and peace was serious. So firm were his convictions that on several occasions he personally reinterpreted orders from Berlin to make them more acceptable to the United States.

Eventually, Bernstorff's hopes for peace vanished in the face of the combination of military enthusiasm in Germany and increasing U.S. hostility. In retrospect, it is somewhat surprising that relations between the United States and Germany lasted as long as they did. The subma-rine attacks of 1915 were closely followed by the Dumba affair, which diverted attention from Bernstorff's mediation attempts to German intelligence operations in the United States, and embittered public opinion all the more. The situation became even more grave with the expulsion of the military and naval attachés Franz von Papen and Karl Boy-Ed in December 1915 on allegation of munitions trade conspiracies. Finally, the sinking of the unarmed *Sussex* in March 1916 left both parties unsatisfied. The Americans perceived the episodes as a cold-blooded German policy and the Germans, as evidence of Wilson's Allied sympathies. Once again, the immediate crisis was alleviated because of Bernstorff's maneuverings and Berlin's inaction, but the broader issues involving submarine warfare were never resolved. When Germany resumed submarine attacks in January 1917, following a ten-month pause, Wilson broke relations and Bernstorff's diplomatic career in the United States ended.

The ambassador's return to Germany in March proved as uncomfortable as the situation he had left behind in America. No one would give him credit for his efforts to maintain peace with the United States. General Ludendorff denounced him before the parliament, popular sentiment labeled him as a weak "democrat," and even Wilhelm II refused to receive his ambassador. Bernstorff agreed to accept the ambassadorship to Constantinople in September, with the understanding that newly appointed Chancellor Michaelis and Secretary of State Kuhlmann were intent on reaching peace. He remained there for the rest of the war.

The November revolution of 1918 in Germany found Bernstorff supportive of the efforts of the Social Democrats, but he was reluctant to assume a greater role in diplomatic affairs. In 1919, he declined Friedrich Ebert's offer to serve as foreign minister, insisting that his former role as ambassador had tainted him in the eyes of the German public and that his presence would complicate the efforts to secure peace at Versailles.

Bernstorff then turned to domestic politics, but he never swayed from his internationalist convictions. He joined the left-liberal Democratic Party and was elected to the Reichstag in 1921. There, he continued to influence foreign affairs and argued for the acceptance of the unpopular London reparations ultimatum and for Germany's admission to the League of Nations.

Bernstorff called the League of Nations a "battlefield of two epochs, on which the historic action will be fought out between the new and the old conceptions of politics." For Bernstorff, the "new" and favorable course was undoubtedly that of anti-imperialism, disarmament, and international rapprochement, but these hopes were far from achievement. When the National Socialists assumed control of the government in January 1933, Bernstorff realized there was no future for him in Germany and fled to Switzerland, where he died six years later, ignored and forgotten.

Cynthia K. Pierard

See also ARABIC AND SUSSEX PLEDGES

Bibliography

Bernstorff, Johann Heinrich von. *The Memoirs of Count Bernstorff*. New York: Random House, 1936.

———. *My Three Years in America*. New York: Scribner, 1920.

Dorries, Reinhard R. *Imperial Challenge: Ambassador Count Bernstorff and German and American Relations, 1908–1917*. Chapel Hill: University of North Carolina Press, 1989.

Bethmann Hollweg, Theobald von (1856–1921)

The grandson of a distinguished liberal jurist and opponent of Bismarck, Theobald von Bethmann Hollweg was born in 1856 on the estate of Hohenfinow northeast of Berlin, which his businessman father had recently purchased. Thus, though he was from a well-to-do family, he was not really of the Junker aristocracy. He had a good education, including university training in law at Strasbourg, Leipzig, and Berlin, and after completing his doctorate in 1884, Bethmann entered the Prussian civil service. He advanced rapidly, becoming governor of the Mark Brandenburg in 1899 and secretary of the interior in 1905. Two years later he was appointed vice-chancellor and secretary of the interior in the Imperial German government, and on July 14, 1909, he became the chancellor, replacing Prince von Bülow, who had fallen from favor with Kaiser Wilhelm II.

Bethmann was an enigmatic figure. Although he lacked charisma and was unskilled in public relations, he was a hard-working administrator and effective political infighter. He was a sincere German patriot but did not share the expansionistic vision of the Pan-Germans and other extreme nationalists. In both the 1911 Moroccan crisis and naval arms negotiations, he hoped for rapprochement with Great Britain. He also pursued the Bismarkian policy of friendly relations with Russia as a counterweight to French hostility and in the Balkan Wars of 1912–1913 adopted an even-handed approach to the problems there.

In the crisis following the assassination of the Austrian archduke at Sarajevo on June 28, 1914, Kaiser Wilhelm sided with the military leaders who regarded this as a golden opportunity for a preventive war, and he pledged full support to Austria in a showdown with Serbia. Bethmann saw a chance for breaking the grip of encirclement by realigning the powers in southeastern Europe, and he too endorsed action by Austria, fully realizing that his "leap into the dark" could lead to war with Britain. He feared that inaction would have even worse consequences, and thus he took the diplomatic gamble of backing Austria. With war becoming more likely by the hour, he made a bid for British neutrality by promising no annexation of French and Belgian territory, but Foreign Secretary Sir Edward Grey rejected the overture. At last realizing the seriousness of the situation, Bethmann tried to persuade Austria to back down in Serbia and also courted public support for a policy of peace by informing the Social Democratic parliamentary leaders of the threat posed by a Russian mobilization in support of their Balkan ally. By delaying the German mobilization until after Russia had acted on July 31, he achieved the appearance of a defensive war.

Actually, Bethmann opposed a declaration of war against France, but the kaiser's will prevailed, and the chancellor yielded, even though the German war plan required the violation of Belgian neutrality. Vainly Bethmann hoped that Britain would not enter the conflict, and in his Reichstag speech on August 4, Bethmann defended the "wrong" that Germany had committed as a military necessity and promised no annexations or attacks on commercial shipping. Speaking to the British ambassador, Sir Edward Goshen, the chancellor lamented that just for a word "neutrality, just for a scrap of paper," the island kingdom "was going to make war on a nation who desired nothing better than to be friends with her." This off-the-cuff remark would later become a keystone in British propaganda.

Bethmann often said that Germany did not want war, but clearly he was only one voice around the kaiser, and the military leaders and public opinion prevailed in the decision for war. Once that had been made, being a traditional nationalist he wholeheartedly supported it.

As the war chancellor, he pursued the illusory goal of permanent security. He helped articulate a set of war aims that included German domination of central Europe, territorial annexations to keep France and Russia weak, the creation of a vast colonial empire in Africa, and achieving equality with Britain in the realm of economic power. However, unlike many in the military and right-wing pressure groups, Bethmann was not an exponent of boundless expansionism. Also, he engaged in attempts to split the Entente Powers and secure peace through the negotiations promoted by the United States and other neutrals, especially in late 1916. From 1915, he struggled with military and naval chiefs over unrestricted submarine warfare, a policy that he viewed as extremely unwise. In 1916, he urged the emperor to replace the ineffective Falkenhayn as chief of the army command with the popular team of Hindenburg and Ludendorff, but this only made things worse for him, as they too became champions of U-boat warfare. Finally, in January 1917, he yielded to the demands of the military, even though he knew full well this would bring America into the war, and civilian government for all practical purposes came to an end.

Caught between the pressures of the left for a compromise peace and democratic reforms and of the right for annexation, submarine warfare, and no reforms, Bethmann's position deteriorated. The moderates in the parliament realized that the increasing domestic unrest, stalemate on the Western Front, continuation of the war in the east in spite of the February Revolution in Russia, and failure of the all-out submarine offensive provided the opportunity to take action to secure peace and political reform. When in early July they pushed through the nonbinding peace resolution and Bethmann persuaded the kaiser to allow suffrage reform in Prussia and true parliamentary government in the empire, conservatives in the Reichstag declared their lack of confidence in the chancellor, and Hindenburg and Ludendorff threatened to resign if he remained in office. Desiring to avoid the humiliation of being fired, on July 13, Bethmann submitted his resignation and retired to private life to watch the disasters of defeat and then revolution that he had long feared would take place.

After the war, Bethmann encouraged his former conservative supporters to participate in the new Weimar Republic in order to stabilize it and keep it from falling under the control of the left. In various writings he defended his and the empire's policies and accepted responsibility for his own failures, but he categorically rejected any idea of German war guilt. However, it must be conceded that his halting implementation of a progressive conservative program had proven to be inadequate in solving the problems of Imperial Germany.

Richard V. Pierard

Bibliography

Bethmann Hollweg, Theobald von. *Reflections on the World War*. London: Butterworth, 1920.

Fischer, Fritz. *Germany's Aims in the First World War*. New York: Norton, 1967.

———. *War of Illusions: German Policies from 1911 to 1914*. New York: Norton, 1975.

Jarausch, Konrad H. *The Enigmatic Chancellor: A Political Biography of Theobald von Bethmann Hollweg, 1856–1921*. New Haven: Yale University Press, 1973.

Stern, Fritz. "Bethmann Hollweg and the War: The Limits of Responsibility." In *The Responsibility of Power*, ed. by Leonard Krieger and Fritz Stern. New York: Doubleday, 1967.

Biddle, John (1859–1936)

Appointed to West Point at the age of eighteen, John Biddle graduated second in the class of 1881 and received his commission as a second lieutenant of engineers.

Between 1891 and 1911, he served in various engineering posts around the nation and as chief engineer of U.S. Volunteers during the Spanish-American War. From 1911 until the outbreak of war in Europe, Biddle was a member of the War Department General Staff in Washington. In 1914–1915, Biddle was an observer with the Austro-Hungarian Army in Austria and Poland. Soon after his return to the United States, Biddle, by then a colonel, was appointed superintendent of the United States Military Academy.

When the United States entered the war in April 1917, Biddle took command of a brigade of American engineers stationed with the British in northern France. Between Oct. 30 and Dec. 17, 1917, and again between Jan. 10 and Mar. 4, 1918, he was acting chief of staff in Washington. He served in that position well and in the tradition of his two predecessors, Hugh L. Scott and Tasker H. Bliss.

After leaving his post in Washington in 1918, Biddle returned to Europe and oversaw the deployment of troops in Great Britain and Ireland. After the Armistice, he returned to the United States and commanded Camp Travis, Texas, and later Camp Custer, Michigan. After serving in the American military for forty-three years, Brigadier General Biddle retired on Dec. 1, 1920.

Biddle received a Silver Star for gallantry against Spanish forces in Puerto Rico in 1898; the Distinguished Service Medal in 1919 for his efficiency in handling troops in Great Britain; and the Knight Commander of the Bath (military) and the Commander of the Victorian Order, of Great Britain. Biddle died at Fort Sam Houston on Jan. 18, 1936.

Michael J. McCarthy

Bibliography

"John Biddle." In *Annual Report of the Association of Graduates of the United States Military Academy at West Point, New York*, n.p., 1936.

Bisbee Deportations

The deportation of strikers from Bisbee, Arizona, was one of the most blatant cases of industrial violence and denial of civil liberties to occur during the First World War. It resulted from the unpopularity of labor, especially the Industrial Workers of the World (IWW), the xenophobia and jingoism of local citizens, and the desires of industrialists to maximize profits and break unions.

On June 27, 1917, a copper strike was called by the International Union of Mine, Mill and Smelter Workers and the Metal Mine Worker's Industrial Union No. 800. Its aims were improved working and living conditions, wage increases, and an end to antiunion practices. The nonviolent strike closed pits in the Clifton-Morenci, Globe-Miami, Bisbee-Warren, and Jerome districts of southwest Arizona.

Bisbee, population 8,000, contained five mining firms dominated by the Phelps-Dodge Company. Its manager, Walter Douglas, vowed not to negotiate. He believed, as did most town residents, that German agents caused the strike and that the offenders had to be expelled. Following the example set in nearby Jerome, town businessmen decided to arrest and deport all strikers and aliens.

On July 12, 1917, a posse of 2,000 members of Bisbee's Workman's Loyalty League and Citizen's Protective League, led by Cochise County Sheriff Harry Wheeler and directed by Phelps-Dodge, Calumet, and Arizona Mining Company executives, made mass arrests. Over 1,000 residents suspected of being union men, strike supporters, or aliens were herded at gun point to waiting boxcars of the El Paso and Southwestern Railroad, a Phelps-Dodge subsidiary, for deportation.

The train went to Columbus, New Mexico, but angry residents refused to allow the prisoners to disembark, forcing them to move on to Hermanas, New Mexico, where they were dumped without food, water, or shelter. Two days later the group was taken into custody by federal troops and escorted back to Columbus, where they remained until October. Most never returned to Bisbee.

A United States Army survey showed that 20 nationalities were represented in the group, including 199 Americans, 141 Britons, 82 Serbians, 179 other Slavs, 268 Mexicans, and 200 "enemy aliens." Of the prisoners, 468 were American citizens, 520 were property owners, 472 had registered for the draft, 433 were married with families, 351 were AF of L members, 426 were members of the IWW, 205 had purchased liberty bonds, 520 had subscribed to the Red Cross, and 62 were veterans.

The deportation caused an outcry from the AF of L, IWW, civil liberties groups, and Mexico's ambassador. President Wilson appointed a commission to investigate the incident. It reported that the deportations were unprovoked, unjustified, and illegal. Civil rights suits were filed in state courts against the railroad, copper companies, and several individuals, but none were tried. The federal government's indictment of Wheeler and twenty-four others for violating the civil rights of deportees was struck down by the U.S. Supreme Court. When tried on state charges, the defendants were acquitted.

Clayton D. Laurie

Bibliography

Byrkit, James W. *Forging the Copper Collar: Arizona's Labor-Management War of 1901–21.* Tucson: University of Arizona Press, 1982.

Taft, Philip. "The Bisbee Deportation." *Labor History* 13 (Winter 1972).

Black Americans

Black America faced greater challenges during the tenure of Woodrow Wilson than it had since the first years of Reconstruction. Five members of the ten-man cabinet were from the South, as was Wilson himself. His administration, strongly supported by southern racists such as Senators James K. Vardaman and John Sharpe Williams of Mississippi, Colman Blease of South Carolina, and Hoke Smith of Georgia nearly eliminated black-American carry-forward federal jobholders. The administration permitted the introduction of racist bills in Congress and took no active federal stand against lynching. Whenever the administration was approached with demands that the government suppress such blatant abuses, the responses were always the same—states rights prevailed to the exclusion of federal laws in every state. Given the negative attitudes of the administration, it is a wonder that any support for U.S. participation in the European war was forthcoming from the black community.

Surprisingly, black leaders such as W.E.B. Du Bois, always an outspoken opponent of war, especially for black Americans, supported the entry of the United States into the conflict and urged black Americans to become involved with their dollars and with their lives. He was not alone. Many blacks came forward to join, or urge others to join the army in the hope that doing so would secure for them the equal rights denied them since their arrival in Virginia in 1619. Some black intellectuals, like some white intellectuals, were all for getting into the war, even before Wilson asked for a declaration from Congress in April 1917. On a few occasions, blacks were even permitted to attend mixed-race liberty bond rallies. At other bond rallies, they were excluded, such as the rally in Jacksonville, Florida, where a black British composer's music was to be played. Nonetheless, black Americans were as patriotic as their white contemporaries and bought bonds to the limit of their means.

During the initial decade of the twentieth century, blacks from various parts of the South began a massive migration northward, in the search for jobs, schools, and other public facilities that they might use and enjoy. The migration increased enormously after the war began in Europe in 1914. In all northern industry during the decade of 1910–1920, there was an increase from 550,000 black workers in 1910 to nearly 1 million by 1920. They were engaged in all aspects of American industry, from meatpacking houses in Chicago to shipbuilding on the East Coast and, particularly after 1917, in all forms of war work. Employers found the traditionally unskilled black workers to be as easy to train and as productive as any European immigrants. They worked at war jobs, bought war bonds, sent their sons and husbands to fight, and did whatever was expected of any other Americans at the time.

As in all things, the white majority was divided upon the matter of black participation in the military. There was, for some length of time, a very vocal white southern group, especially in Congress, which wanted all African Americans proscribed from any military service whatsoever. Their major fear was that black Americans would gain self-respect that would make them less docile and more assertive in their dealings with whites in the South. However, it certainly was not unusual for black Americans to serve as soldiers in the U.S. Army. They had fought, mostly as volunteers, in every war this nation had been engaged in since the Revolution. They had provided two fine Regular Army infantry regiments, the 24th and 25th, in addition to two well-known cavalry regiments, the 9th and 10th. The three black officers graduated from West Point prior to World War I were guaranteed posts in one of those regiments.

There were three major groups from which black soldiers for the expeditionary forces could come. One was the four Regular black regiments. Professionals all, they were the most obvious candidates for an army desperately in need of trained soldiers. However, these regiments were not allowed to see combat in Europe because army commanders did not consider them to be up to the standards set by the army and feared they might reflect badly on the United States. Nor did the national consciousness envision the possibility of a black American showing his ability as a soldier, especially as a trained leader, commissioned or noncommissioned. Those regiments were destined to remain stateside throughout the war.

The second group from which combat personnel could be drawn was the various black National Guard units. They were from Illinois, New York, Ohio, and other northern states with large black populations. These organizations were reasonably well led and had long, often illustrious, histories of serving their country. Their great enthusiasm made up for a lack of training. They needed reequipping and modern training. Eventually, they comprised two full infantry brigades ready for action in France.

Black Americans who could be drafted were the last possible source for the armed forces. The draft presented greater problems for blacks than for whites. The southern black was generally from a rural environment and often the chief source of labor for the white southern farmers. These farmers strongly opposed drafting this relatively cheap available labor force. Naturally, most draft boards in the South were made up of white men, and most of those boards showed little or no sensitivity to the black inductee. Due to southern economic realities and the persuasions of the boards, blacks owning their own farms were much more apt to be drafted than the laborers who were so much a part of southern agriculture.

African Americans living in the North were usually employed in heavy industry. They were generally better educated and in better physical condition than southern blacks and more likely to take umbrage at ill treatment. But whether he hailed from the North or South, the average drafted black man was going to spend his days as a laborer. Although blacks made up less than 10 percent of the general population, they comprised over one-third of the laborers in the army. The army decision makers were convinced that blacks would never make soldiers, and assigning them to labor units was one way to secure desperately needed support troops while freeing more "acceptable" troops for combat.

Black draftees initially were not properly clothed, fed, or housed. Many were left to fend for themselves under trees when there was no shelter. If tents were available, they usually lacked flooring of any kind. During the winter months, these same soldiers were often without stoves. Since mess halls for black soldiers were scarce, they usually had to bring their food back to their quarters. Water for sanitation was severely restricted. Black professionals, whether doctors or dentists, were refused commissions in their callings, often being drafted and used as laborers, despite the critical need for medical professionals.

Military training was not considered necessary for black soldiers because the army had decided they were to be what most were in civil life: laborers. A very serious problem was the inability of many black Americans to read or write properly, and they were therefore unable to complete the necessary paperwork in company or regimental offices. That predicament was evident in all black regiments and the two black (92d and 93d) divisions.

Joel Spingarn, a white leader of the National Association for the Advancement of Colored People (NAACP), was the first person to make a major effort to create a black officer corps. Speaking at Howard University, he made it clear that he was not making this a mission of the NAACP but rather one of his own. Although most black college men vehemently opposed segregation, they developed a plan for a segregated training camp for black officers in the spring of 1917. The idea had its supporters, but Spingarn and W.E.B. Du Bois, a founder of the NAACP and a leading black educator and editor, initially opposed it. Both eventually came around; in fact, in his publication, *Crisis*, Du Bois actually lent considerable support to the project. He went so far as to write an editorial entitled "Close Ranks," in which he suggested that black Americans should forgo, for the duration of the war, any further attempts to push forward their "equal treatment" agenda. Since it was well known that he was being considered for a commission in the army, he received harsh criticism from antisegregationists.

Finally, the army established a camp to train black officers at Fort Des Moines, Iowa, in May 1917. African Americans involved in the camp's development pressed for the appointment of Col. Charles Young, the third black graduate of West Point, as its commander. Unfortunately, the army did not want any black Americans to be so highly placed. In the ensuing controversy, Young was found to have high blood pressure and therefore was retired. Another officer, LtCol. Charles C. Ballou, was named to head the training camp since he had led the famed all-black 25th Infantry. However, while slightly more positive toward black Americans than most army officers, he by his attitude conveyed the opinion that no one should expect too much from the camp's graduates. Their training was inadequate, almost farcical. Since the young black men were expected to fail, they were trained with that in mind and many did just that.

In the first month that the camp was open, 1,250 men arrived at Fort Des Moines for training. About 40 percent were college graduates; some were members of the faculty at Howard University; 50 percent had professional or business training. In addition, 250 were noncommissioned officers from the Regular Army, selected especially to add experience to the group, but experience alone was not enough.

When their training was over, the new officers were presumed to be ready for battle. The majority of early graduates were assigned to a newly formed division, the 92d, which was to be the second all-black division (except for white officers in the highest ranks). An early unit made up of black National Guard troops had already been formed as the 93d Division; after being shipped to France, it was assigned to the French Army, which was very happy to receive it. The 93d's regiments were scattered throughout French formations and ultimately made a fine reputation for themselves, earning many French citations.

The 92d Division did not do as well in combat. The division, as already noted, was badly trained as well as poorly led. Its white officers were just as inefficient as the black officers, many having been assigned to what professional soldiers considered an onerous task. At any rate, the division spent far too little time in the front lines to establish itself after a few failed exercises in the Meuse-Argonne campaign. A number of its junior officers were accused of cowardice. It eventually was decided that a few of them should be charged and tried, then placed in confinement.

But what of the majority of black soldiers? They, in fact, became the laborers on the docks and rail lines, unloading ships, loading trains and trucks, and doing sanitary duty. The interaction of black-American soldiers with the French populace was, overall, positive. Unfortunately, many white officers created difficulties that caused the black soldiers much distress. The efforts of some whites to change French attitudes toward black Americans made life unbearable for them.

After the Armistice, the largely untested 92d Division was one of the first units returned to the United States because General Pershing wanted the division out of the AEF as soon as possible. Members of the 93d Division were reassigned into the AEF, and they too were sent home, but with a better overall battle reputation and, consequently, higher morale. Unfortunately, when the returning black soldier arrived home, he found a nation that, if possible, was more racist than when he left.

George B. Clark

See also BALLOU, CHARLES CLARENDON; BALLARD, EUGENE JACQUES; CAMP MCARTHUR RIOT; HOUSTON RIOT; UNITED STATES ARMY: 92D DIVISION; UNITED STATES ARMY: 93D DIVISION

Bibliography

Barbeau, Arthur E., and Florette Henri. *The Unknown Soldiers. Black American Troops in World War I*. Philadelphia: Temple University Press, 1974.

Ellis, Mark. "'Closing Ranks' and 'Seeking Honor': W.E.B. Du Bois in World War I." *Journal of American History* (June 1992).

Patton, Gerald W. *War and Race. The Black Officer in the American Military, 1915–1941*. Westport, CT: Greenwood Press, 1981.

Black Tom Explosion

In the early morning hours of Sunday, July 30, 1916, while the East Coast of the United States slept secure in the knowledge that a vast ocean separated it from the Great War then raging in Europe, huge explosions took place on Black Tom, a promontory that juts into New York harbor from the New Jersey waterfront. It was the site of the principal depot for the shipment of munitions to the Allied Powers. The blasts rocked the harbor, illuminating the dark Manhattan skyline in the eerie light of exploding armaments. The blast pierced the postmidnight quiet with screeching shells, while shrapnel tore holes in the Statue of Liberty and Ellis Island. The Brooklyn Bridge swayed perilously from the blast's shock waves; plate-glass windows by the thousands in Lower Manhattan's financial district gave way and crashed to the streets below.

As far south as Philadelphia and into Maryland, local police fielded calls from petrified citizens who heard the explosions, felt tremors, and feared an earthquake or worse. The immediate assumption, held for years thereafter, was that a tragic accident had occurred at the munitions depot, probably caused by careless security guards who might have lit fires to drive away New Jersey's notorious mosquitoes. The *New York Times,* indeed, reported an accidental cause but editorialized that the destruction of massive amounts of war materiel must have delighted the Central Powers.

In fact, the devastation of Black Tom, resulting in the loss of many millions of dollars in munitions, was the work of saboteurs in the employ of Imperial Germany. Although under the neutrality laws all combatant countries were eligible to buy armaments from the United States, as a practical matter the British and their allies controlled the Atlantic seaways and thus shipments to Germany. So Germany felt obliged to inhibit the munitions flow from America by whatever means possible.

Unable to smuggle more than a handful of professional saboteurs into the country, Germany used interned German sailors and recruited sympathetic German Americans and Irish English-haters to carry out its mission. The sabotage ring conducted its forays under the direct authority of the German ambassador, Count Johann Heinrich von Bernstorff. His prime diplomatic assignment was to keep the United States neutral, but at the same time his principal embassy associates were overseeing, bankrolling, and directing the sabotage effort, of which the Black Tom explosions were only the most spectacular.

Several years after the Armistice, the United States and the new German government agreed to negotiate legitimate war claims, including those damages sustained at Black Tom. But only after World War II, when confronted with irrefutable evidence of German responsibility, did the new Federal Republic of Germany agree to pay the American interests in the Black Tom case. The whole affair underscored the vulnerability of the United States to foreign mischief, and in part as a result of the Black Tom episode, the United States began to construct an intelligence apparatus against foreign escapades in this country.

Jules Witcover

Bibliography

Witcover, Jules. *Sabotage at Black Tom: Imperial Germany's Secret War in America, 1914–1917.* Chapel Hill, NC: Algonquin Books, 1989.

Blanc Mont Ridge

In early October 1918, the American 2d Division, experienced in hard and costly combat in the Belleau Wood area, at Soissons, and at St. Mihiel, and the newly arrived 36th Division, formed from the Texas and Oklahoma National Guards, were loaned from Gen. John J. Pershing's American First Army to Gen. Henri Gourard's French Fourth Army to attack the key terrain of the German stronghold at Blanc Mont Ridge, located in the Champagne area between Reims and the western edge of the Argonne Forest. The battle took place within the context of the general Allied offensive, begun on September 26, that extended from the Swiss border to the English Channel, a huge converging attack with, north to south, the British moving toward Cambrai, the French moving east and west of Reims toward the Aisne River, and the Americans advancing toward Sedan and Mézières.

At this time, the Americans had fielded twenty-nine combat divisions. Two were with the British, three being brought to readiness in quiet sectors, seven left in the St. Mihiel area, and fifteen planned for the initial phase of the Meuse-Argonne campaign. The two other divisions, the 2d and the 36th, had been reluctantly set aside by Pershing to serve as a special reserve in anticipation of the French difficulty in keeping abreast of an American advance. Although the Blanc Mont Ridge itself, elaborately fortified over a four-year span, did not actually overlook the American First Army zone, continued control by the Germans gave them observation and artillery control over the French zone. The terrain also represented the Germans' last natural defensive line south of the Aisne River, sixteen miles to the north.

For the Meuse-Argonne attack, the Americans moved north in their zone that extended from the Meuse River in the east through and beyond the massive tangle of the Argonne Forest in the west. The French in the zone adjacent to the left (west) made initial gains but stalled south of Somme. It was, as anticipated, time to commit the Americans.

The 2d Division on loan to the French was unique in the American Expeditionary Force, having a brigade of two marine regiments—the

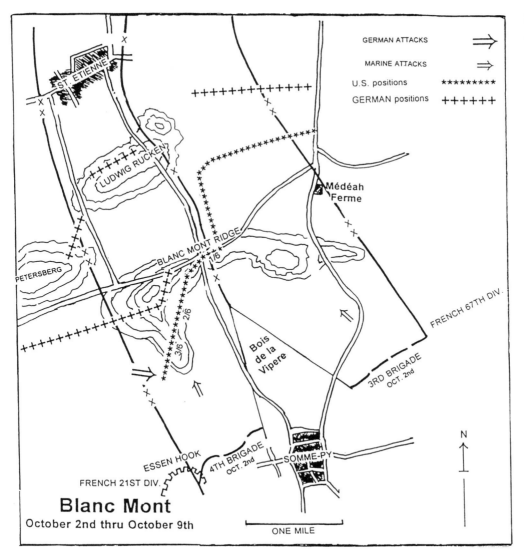

GERMAN ATTACKS ⟹
MARINE ATTACKS ⟹
U.S. positions ✴✴✴✴✴✴✴✴✴
GERMAN positions ++++++

ST. ETIENNE

LUDWIG RUCKEN

Médéah Ferme

PETERSBERG

BLANC MONT RIDGE

1/6

2/6

3/6

Bois de la Vipere

FRENCH 67TH DIV.

3RD BRIGADE OCT. 2nd

N

ESSEN HOOK

4TH BRIGADE OCT. 2nd

SOMME-PY

FRENCH 21ST DIV.

Blanc Mont
October 2nd thru October 9th

ONE MILE

Blanc Mont. Taken from The Marine Brigade at Blanc Mont Ridge *by George B. Clark.*

5th and 6th—combined with its brigade of two army regiments—the 9th and 23d. Its command evolution was likewise unusual. On May 5, Pershing had given command of the 4th Marine Brigade to his trusted chief of staff, Gen. James G. Harbord, who, in June, commanded that brigade through the historic early display of American determination and fighting ability at Belleau Wood (often inaccurately referred to as Château-Thierry). On July 15, Harbord, promoted to major general, was named to command the division, just days before the short, searing, successful but calamitous experience of Soissons on July 18 and 19, during which the division sustained a total of 3,700 total casual-

ties. Pershing then called upon Harbord to unsnarl the logistical turmoil in the Service of Supply, and the command of the 2d Division was given, on July 28, to Marine Corps MajGen. John A. Lejeune. Lejeune showed his merit in leading the division's spearhead attack at St. Mihiel on September 12.

In conference with Gourard and the French XXI Corps commander, LtGen. Andre Naulin, Lejeune learned that the French planned to separate his two brigades and place them under French command. To this he responded with a bold and confident counterproposal: if left intact and given a narrow zone, his division would deliver Blanc Mont

Ridge. Afterward, Lejeune would write to his men, "To be able to say, when the war is over, 'I belonged to the Second Division, I fought at Blanc Mont Ridge' will be the highest honor that can come to any man." But the honors were to come at a high cost for, in just four days of combat, 4,075 men killed, wounded, or missing, almost equally spread among the four combat regiments.

Lejeune proposed an unusual converging attack that would move the marine brigade, commanded by Marine BGen. Wendell C. Neville, directly north toward the objective of the Medeah Farm–Blanc Mont road. The infantry brigade, commanded by BGen. Hanson E. Ely, situated to the east about a mile beyond, would converge and connect on the objective, which included 660-foot Blanc Mont Ridge, 200 feet above the valley. The troops would advance over a devastated terrain of chalky limestone with scrub pine and rolling ground with some steep slopes.

Jump-off was designated for 5:50 A.M. on October 3. Each brigade was assigned a battalion of French tanks. There would be generous artillery support, with a rolling barrage moving 109 yards in four minutes. Both brigades would attack in columns of regiments, and within regiments would be the usual column of battalions—assault, support, and reserve at 500-yard intervals. In accord with the tactics of the time, in effect two battalions, each with four companies abreast, would attack on a total front of two miles.

On the left flank of the marine brigade, connecting with the French XI Corps, a particular trouble spot was a curved line of German trench, called the Essen Hook, that if controlled by the Germans, would give flanking fire at the time of departure and beyond. It had not been cleared by French troops in preliminary operations. In this left flank area, the 6th Marines had achieved their assigned objective by 8:30 A.M. However, the French 21st Division had not advanced on the left and the entire flank was exposed, now subjected to murderous fire from Essen Hook and from strong German positions on the western slopes of Blanc Mont Ridge. Elements of the 5th Marines were moved forward and faced west, while Essen Hook remained in contention. A further advance on this first morning of battle was by no means possible, but the 5th Marine Brigade did move up units to make connection, in the evening, with the 23d Infantry Brigade to the east.

On the right, to reach their line of departure the infantry brigade of the 9th and 23d regiments had made a night march for five miles, initially under German observation and without the expected French guides. In the confusion, the 9th Infantry had two battalions in the assault position, but the regiment took Medeah Farm and its entire objective by 8:40 A.M. without serious loss except for heavy indirect barrages of machine gun fire. Late in the afternoon, the 23d Infantry passed through the 9th and gained another mile, but it then had both flanks exposed to particularly powerful artillery fire, from the front. Two battalions of the 9th were brought up on the right to bend back and connect with the French at Medeah Farm.

The situation for the 2d Division on the night of October 3 was dangerous. The front line formed a thrusting northward salient a mile and a half deep, a mile wide at the base, but only 500 yards wide for the last half mile. The higher levels of command, however, viewed the situation as a huge success to be exploited immediately; accordingly, orders and exhortations were passed down the line. Thus, on the morning of October 4, the 5th Marine Brigade moved toward St. Étienne, making contact with the 23d Infantry in their isolated penetration. Further progress was halted by the heavy fire from the Germans' virtual fortress in the village and cemetery of St. Étienne. The Allied advance was saved from disaster when a reserve battalion of the 5th Marines, taking heavy losses, thwarted a strong counterattack on the west flank. During the morning of October 4, the two regiments of the infantry brigade were fully occupied by heavy German counterattacks on their right and on their rear.

In the late morning or early afternoon, General Naulin was in Lejeune's command post at the time when Col. Logan Feland, commanding the 5th Marines, called to say that his regiment was almost surrounded by a ring of machine guns, especially vicious on his left rear, and at the same time was being subjected to intense artillery fire from the front. Lejeune repeated the conversation to Naulin, pointing out emphatically the fact that his troops were being shot up by machine guns located some distance to the rear of locations that Naulin had just stated as being held by the French. General Gourard happened by at this sensitive time and revoked Naulin's order for further advance.

At 3 P.M. the chief of staff of the 2d Division informed the operations officer of the XXI Corps that further advance could not be made because the divisions on its flanks had failed to stay abreast and the French 22d Division on the left had advanced west instead of north. He stated the division could not hold positions north of Blanc Mont and Medeah Farm unless its flanks were covered. Nevertheless, in midafternoon one battalion from the 23d Infantry and one from the 9th attacked. The troops came under fire from the Orfeuil-St. Étienne road and retired to their attack line with severe losses. Late in the day, another try was made on the right of the 23d Infantry, but at 8 P.M. the battalion was ordered back to Medeah Farm.

By any standard, the fighting on October 4 between determined Americans and desperate Germans had been of exceptional severity. On the morning of October 5, the third day of combat, the 3d Battalion, 6th Marine Brigade moved out at 6 A.M. following intense artillery support against the hornet's nest of German machine guns on the west of Blanc Mont. At no cost in casualties, the battalion brought back from their foray 65 machine guns and 205 prisoners, the remnants of a German regiment that had occupied that sector. Contact was then made with the French 22d Division, which was of considerable additional importance.

In the afternoon, the 6th Marines again passed through elements of the 5th to attack the ridge southeast of St. Étienne, but they were held up before Hill 160. This contingent of the 6th also made contact with the French 22d Division. During this day, no orders were given for the 3d Brigade, its flanks still exposed, to attempt further advance.

On October 6, fighting was limited to local actions that advanced the line slightly to the Orfeuil-St. Étienne road. The major actions of the 2d Division had been completed, although contributions by individual battalions of infantry and engineers were yet to come. Lejeune wrote in his memoirs, "On that day, the situation of the Division had greatly improved, as only one flank—the right—was then exposed. The men, however, were physically exhausted. Constant fighting, almost no sleep, and the difficulties of supplying food because of the salient position, combined with heavy casualties, caused me to recommend that the Division be relieved." He was soon informed that the 71st Brigade of the 36th Division would join the division temporarily.

The 36th Division, with its shoulder patch of a black "T" on an Indian arrowhead, known as the Lone Star or Panther Division (informally as the "cowboys and Indians" from its ethnic mixture), was formed in the summer of 1917 and had trained extensively at Camp Bowie, Texas, until deployment to Europe in the summer of 1918. At the time of its commitment as a reserve for the French Fourth Army, the division had no field artillery. On October 5, the division's 71st Brigade, consisting of the 141st Infantry and the 142d Infantry and the 111th Field Signal Battalion, were assigned to the French XXI Corps "for the purpose of reinforcing the 2d and of relieving part of that division should the occasion arise." On October 6, these units were placed at the disposal of the 2d Division, and the two infantry regiments were moved into the line during the night of October 6–7, with the provision that the 2d Division leave one battalion and fire support unit in each of its brigade areas. Guides from the 2d Division were not in prescribed locations, maps were scarce, and the movement was poorly handled; nevertheless, on the morning of October 7, the units of these two divisions on the front lines were, from left to right, the 3d Battalion, 6th Marines and, rearward, the 1st Battalion, 6th Marines in the woods south of St. Étienne; the 142d Infantry with its battalions in depth; the 141st Infantry; and, on its right, the 2d Battalion, 9th Infantry and 4th MG Battalion. A gap, inherited from the 2d Division, existed between the 141st and 142d infantries.

French Corps Commander Naulin informed Lejeune on the morning of October 7 that a general attack would be renewed on the morning of the eighth, saying that he anticipated the fresh brigade would achieve a success equal to that gained by the 2d Division on October 3. Of this Lejeune later wrote, "I explained to him that he was expecting the impossible of untried troops, and urged that the 71st Brigade not be required to engage in an attack until it had a few days' training under fire. He was insistent, however, and on leaving said, 'Tomorrow will be another great day for the 21st Corps.'" The attack at 5:15 A.M., October 8, supported by 2d Division artillery and two battalions of French light tanks, made initial progress on the strength of the fresh determination of new troops, but, with misplaced friendly artillery and fierce German resistance, the columns of attacking battalions telescoped into the vulnerable forward areas and became mixed beyond the margins of tactical control. By 8:45 A.M., based on hasty and exaggerated reports indicating 50 percent casualties, General Whitworth of the 71st Brigade requested reinforcement by his sister brigade, the 72d, and Lejeune ordered all 3d and 4th Brigade battalions back into line. As the situation clarified, these reinforcements were not considered necessary. Composite units were formed as the situation permitted, and, on the morning of the ninth, the attacks continued with, from unit to unit, ground gained then lost to counterattack. The 71st Brigade lost 1,300 casualties on October 8 and another 300 on October 9.

The 2d Division was officially relieved in this sector on the morning of October 10, leaving its artillery brigade, the engineer regiment, and some supply and sanitary units and material with the 36th. The front lines then ran from, on the left, a point just north of St. Étienne then west parallel to and north of the Orfeuil-St. Étienne road. Hill 210 on Blanc Mont Ridge lay about two hard-earned miles to the south. This can be considered the end of the engagement known as Blanc Mont.

The 36th Division, now employing both brigades, remained in line to move north against lessening resistance to a respite on reaching the Aisne River; then, in a well-planned and executed action on October 27, it took Forest Farm, a German pocket of resistance just south of the Aisne.

Rolfe Hillman

See also ELY, HANSON EDWARD; HARBORD, JAMES GUTHRIE; LEJEUNE, JOHN ARCHER; NEVILLE, WENDELL CUSHING; UNITED STATES ARMY: 2D DIVISION; UNITED STATES ARMY: 36TH DIVISION

Bibliography

American Battle Monuments Commission. *2d Division Summary of Operations in the World War*. Washington, DC: Government Printing Office, 1944.
———. *36th Division Summary of Operations in the World War*. Washington, DC: Government Printing Office, 1944.
Lejeune, John A. *The Reminiscences of a Marine*. New York: Dorrance, 1930.
Spaulding, Oliver L., and John H. Wright. *The Second Division American Expeditionary Force in France 1917–1919*. New York: Hillman Press, 1937.
U.S. War Department, War Plans Division, Historical Branch. *Blanc Mont Monograph No. 9*. Washington, DC: Government Printing Office, 1921.

Bliss, Tasker Howard (1853–1930)

General Tasker Howard Bliss, U.S. Army chief of staff in 1917, the U.S. military representative to the Supreme War Council, 1917–1919, and an American commissioner plenipotentiary to the Paris Peace Conference in 1919, was born on Dec. 31, 1853, in Lewisburg, Pennsylvania. His father was a Greek professor at Bucknell University, and Bliss, a bright and well-read youth, graduated eighth of forty-three in the class of 1875 at West Point.

Although commissioned into the artillery, Bliss spent most of his military career in staff positions, not line commands. From 1876 to 1880, he taught at West Point.

In 1888, Bliss, still a lieutenant, became the aide-de-camp to the army's commanding general, John M. Schofield. Four years later, still serving in that post, he was promoted to the rank of captain, but in the Commissary Department, where there was a vacancy. When Schofield retired in 1895, the secretary of war kept Bliss on at the War Department, and in 1897, he went to Spain as military attaché. Bliss did well in his quasi-diplomatic duties in the difficult environment that preceded the Spanish-American War. He left Madrid when the war broke out and saw active service in Puerto Rico.

Following the Spanish-American War, Bliss became the collector of customs for Cuba, in which post he distinguished himself for hard work and impeccable honesty. In 1901, he was appointed a brigadier general of volunteers, and the next year, he was made a regular brigadier general. He served on the newly created General Staff, and in 1903, he became the founding president of the Army War College.

Many of Bliss's appointments involved instruction of some kind. All his life, too, he kept up his classical languages, reading regularly from the great writers of antiquity, a pastime he tried unsuccessfully to hide from his peers.

In 1905–1906, Bliss commanded the Department of Luzon in the Philippines, and from 1906–1909, the Moro Province (Mindanao). Leaving the Philippines, he became president of the Army War College again, and from 1910 to 1911, he commanded the army's Department of

California. He briefly commanded a brigade on the Mexican frontier during a period of unrest in Mexico. From 1911 to 1913, Bliss commanded the Department of the East and then a brigade on the Texas border, once more in response to unrest in Mexico.

In February 1915, Bliss became assistant chief of staff under Hugh L. Scott. Dealing successfully with preparedness issues, Bliss, now a major general, became acting chief of staff in May 1917 and chief of staff from September to December 1917, when he reached mandatory retirement age, sixty-four. In October 1917, Bliss received two more stars.

At the end of October 1917, just before his retirement, Bliss was named the senior military member of Col. Edward M. House's mission to Europe. Thus, he was on the spot when the Supreme War Council, after the Rapallo Conference of Nov. 7, 1917, created the committee it named the Military Representatives to the Supreme War Council, and Bliss became the United States representative. At the beginning of 1918, that committee was the most important of all the inter-Allied military bodies. It provided the coordination that before had come only from liaison officers and direct contact between the chiefs of the various armies. Because President Wilson chose not to have regular United States participation on the Supreme War Council, Bliss, the military representative, had greater responsibilities than his Allied military colleagues. He dealt with, and earned the respect of every Allied leader.

During the early months of 1918, Bliss opposed the amalgamation of United States forces into the Allied armies, but he was a strong supporter of other efforts to promote military unity among the Allied and Associated Powers. During the crisis of the German March, or Ludendorff offensive, he was prepared to support limited amalgamation, or at least more prepared to do so than General Pershing. Except on that point, his relations with General Pershing were efficient and proper, but not cordial, and the two generals kept to their respective spheres. Bliss generally deferred to the wishes of the commander of the American Expeditionary Forces when there were differences between them.

After the Allied leaders created a single overall command to meet the German March offensive, naming Ferdinand Foch as commander-in-chief of the Allied armies on the Western Front, the military representatives declined in importance. However, thereafter, they continued to do valuable work in preparing technical studies and in providing inter-Allied cooperation.

Bliss was essentially a "Westerner," opposing diversion of strength to secondary theaters of war. Early in 1918, he did support Allied intervention in revolutionary Russia, but he turned ever more strongly against it as the year wore on.

By the fall of 1918, Bliss was the senior general among the military representatives. On Nov. 30, 1918, he learned that he would be one of the five American commissioners plenipotentiary to the upcoming Paris Peace Conference. One of his biographers claims that Bliss received the appointment because of the support of Secretary of War Newton D. Baker, but Bliss was a logical choice. By November 1918, he had more experience working with the Allied leaders than any other American.

During the Paris Peace Conference, Bliss campaigned fruitlessly for disarmament. "Has this war not made us ready for general Disarmament?" he wrote to a newspaper editor. "If not, God help us." Bliss also consistently opposed intervention in Russia. On other issues as well, he showed himself to be an idealist, believing in the necessity of establishing justice and liberty in the world if the terrible slaughter of the war was to have any meaning.

His influence at the beginning of the peace conference was not great, but as time went on, particularly after President Wilson broke with Colonel House in March 1919, Wilson began to pay very close attention to the tightly reasoned memoranda General Bliss circulated. Bliss particularly advised Wilson of the dangers inherent in proposals for perpetual Allied control over Germany.

Even more important to Bliss in the short run was the need to bring about an early peace, so that Germany could become a stable bulwark against unrest in Europe. What the world needed, he believed, was a quick peace and the reestablishment of trade, and the story of Bliss at the peace conference is one of progressive disillusionment.

In the winter of 1919, Bliss came home from Europe and then served two terms as governor of the Soldiers' Home. His interest in disarmament involved him in the Kellogg-Briand Pact of 1928, but he played no major role. He died on Nov. 9, 1930.

Bullitt Lowry

B

See also SUPREME WAR COUNCIL

Bibliography

Palmer, Frederick. *Bliss, Peacemaker: The Life and Letters of General Tasker Howard Bliss*. New York: Dodd, Mead, 1934.

Trask, David F. *General Tasker Howard Bliss and the "Sessions of the World," 1919*. Transactions of the American Philosophical Society, N.S., No. 56. Philadelphia: American Philosophical Society, 1866.

———. *The United States in the Supreme War Council: American War Aims and Inter-Allied Strategy, 1917–1918*. Middletown, CT: Wesleyan University Press, 1961.

Body Armor

Since men have fought each other, they have sought ways to protect themselves from their enemies' weapons. This led to the creation of armor. During World War I, the most common piece of protective equipment was the steel helmet. However, as the war progressed, body armor was also introduced to protect the soldiers in the trenches from shell fragments, shrapnel, and expended bullets.

With the introduction of trench warfare, there was a general increase in the number of head wounds. The French Army was the first to introduce the steel helmet. The first model, developed by Sous-Intendant-General August-Louis Adrian, was a steel cap liner that fit inside Adrian's képi (peaked military cap). Eventually, the French army ordered 700,000 of these protective devices. The design of a real protective helmet proceeded rapidly, and Adrian's helmet was replaced by one modeled on that worn by French fire-fighters.

In November 1915, the British began the manufacture of the Mark 1 steel helmet. Originally to be made of light steel, it was changed to steel containing 12 percent manganese. The helmet's wide brim provided protection from shell fragments and shrapnel that came raining down during enemy bombardments. Over 7 million of the helmets were produced, of which 1.5 million were used by American forces.

The Germans introduced their first helmet at the beginning of 1915, but it was not widely distributed until they issued the M16 Stahlhelm in November of that year. Made of a very hard silicon-nickel steel alloy, it was very expensive and difficult to produce. It was deeper than the British and French models, therefore giving greater protection to the head, ears and neck. This extra protection increased the weight of the Stahlhelm to 2 pounds, $10^{1}/_{2}$ ounces, as opposed to 1 pound, 11 ounces and 2 pounds, $2^{1}/_{2}$ ounces for the French and British models respectively. Over 8.5 million Stahlhelm's were produced by the end of the war.

Besides protection for the head, the armies developed armor to protect other parts of the body. The armorer, however, ran into the classic problem of trading weight and protection for lightness and comfort. Men did not wish to wear the more protective models because of their weight, yet were reluctant to wear the lighter models, which were not as effective. Nonetheless, the French and German armies did produce some types of body armor that were often heavy and cumbersome. Only limited quantities were produced, and these were issued to men whose responsibilities required them to be continually exposed to enemy fire—particularly snipers and sentries.

The British conducted the most extensive research on body armor. Researchers experimented with three different types, which might be referred to as hard, intermediate, and soft. Hard armor generally weighed from 5 to 10 pounds and offered the same type of protection as the Mark 1 helmet. The British Munitions Inventions Board issued a standardized model in 1917. Weighing $9^{1}/_{2}$ pounds, this model consisted of a breast plate, back plate, and groin protector. It provided protection against fragments and could resist a .45 round at 800 feet per second or a rifle round at 1,000 feet per second.

The intermediate type was formed from small square plates of metal, which were then attached to a canvas foundation. The garment that was created could be worn under a soldier's uniform. This type of armor was very close fitting and regarded as comfortable by those who wore it. Unfortunately, this lower grade of body armor could only stop low-velocity projectiles; as such, it was not very effective.

The so-called soft armor was formed from fibrous materials of all types. Instead of stopping a round, soft armor works by slowing down and dissipating the force of the projectile, trapping it in the garment. This type of armor did not afford the same protection against bullets and bayonet thrusts as the hard variety, but neither did it deform the bullet when penetrated. An undeformed bullet enters a body more cleanly than a deformed one, thus lessening the severity of the wound. The soft body armor was effective against low-velocity objects such as shrapnel, grenade fragments, and shell splinters. An original issue of soft armor made from silk proved to be subject to rapid deterioration in the field and was soon replaced with the 6-pound Chemico Body Shield. Using a technology known to the Assyrians over 3,000 years ago, it was formed from multiple layers of tissue, linen scraps, cotton, and silk which were bonded together with a resinous material.

Research continued throughout the war and, while far from perfect, the armor and helmets devised made significant contributions to the survival of those in the trenches.

Albert Dorley

Bibliography

Dean, Bashford. *Helmets and Body Armor in Modern Warfare*, n.p., n.d.

Dunstan, Simon. *Flak Jackets: 20th Century Military Body Armour*. London: Osprey, 1984.

Shepard, R.G. *Helmets and Body Armour Development in the 20th Century*, n.p., n.d.

Bolling, Raynal Cawthorne (1877–1918)

Raynal Cawthorne Bolling was born in Hot Springs, Arkansas, and educated at Harvard University. In 1903, he began a law career with United States Steel, becoming general solicitor in 1913. Bolling took up flying in 1915, advocated American military preparedness, and was commissioned a major in the United States Army in 1917. He headed the 1917 Aeronautical Mission (Bolling Mission) to Europe to determine those aircraft to be produced in the United States and to seek joint production efforts with the Allies. Bolling was appointed to the mission because, in addition to his aviation experience, he had the business and legal skills needed to negotiate prices and royalties with European suppliers.

The Bolling Mission departed on June 17, 1917. Bolling's report, dated August 15, argued for America's role as a supplier of materials, engines, parts and trainers to the Allies rather than combat aircraft. He stressed the need to retain final authority over the aircraft program among officers in France. General Pershing promoted Bolling to the rank of colonel and made him head of air power supply for the American Expeditionary Force. In December, Bolling was relieved of his supply position and appointed to represent the United States on air matters at the Supreme War Council. Bolling became discouraged as his work and proposals were undone by competing officers and administrative delays. On March 26, 1918, while touring the front near Estrées, his car was stopped by the enemy. Rather than surrender, he drew his pistol and was killed by a German officer. In Bolling's memory, an army airfield in the District of Columbia was named after him in July 1918.

Jacob Vander Meulen

See also BOLLING MISSION

Bibliography

Pearson, H.G. *A Business Man in Uniform*. New York: Duffield, 1923.

Bolling Mission

When the United States entered the First World War in 1917, its aviation capability consisted of little more than a handful of obsolete, or at best obsolescent, aircraft assembled to reconnoiter the Mexican border. None of these aircraft was capable of military service in Europe. To its credit, the American government was quick to realize its predicament and to take steps to rectify it. The first reaction to the problem was a record-setting congressional appropriation. A more reasoned course was the formation of the Aeronautical Mission of the Aircraft Production Board under the command of then Maj. Raynal C. Bolling.

The mission was charged with the responsibility of going to Europe to study aircraft then in use by the Allied powers, to recommend those types that should be put into production in the United States for its infant air service, and to determine what types should be purchased in Europe. Bolling was as qualified to head the group as anyone in the United States could have been fourteen years after the first successful heavier-than-air flight. He had commanded the First Aero Squadron of the New York National Guard and was a senior attorney at United States Steel. Consequently, he possessed the aviation expertise as well as the international business acumen to conduct the sensitive negotiations in which the mission would be involved.

Talks with the Allied representatives in June–August 1917 were later recalled more for their emphasis on financial matters than for their spirit of cooperation, more for the interest of the Europeans in royalty payments than for any genuine enthusiasm for winning the war. In Great Britain, the American team found discussions stalled over availability of the Rolls-Royce engine. Though the matter was appealed all the way to the prime minister, Rolls-Royce would not budge on its insistence that a royalty be paid. In France, the situation was little different. French manufacturers managed to postpone delivery of promised sample aircraft until the United States government promised, and paid, $100,000 to each of them. Only in Italy did the mission's staff find a genuinely cooperative attitude. The Italians requested only a good supply of American raw materials for their aircraft industry.

At the end of its tour, the mission recommended that several Allied aircraft types be put into production in the United States. As it developed, however, the rapid technological advances in aviation equipment, which had characterized the entire war, outpaced the ability of American industry to deliver most of the aircraft recommended, and the majority of aircraft used by the American Air Service were purchased abroad. By the end of the conflict only the famous Liberty-engined de Havilland-4, a fast two-seat day bomber, had emerged from American factories and made it all the way to the Western Front.

James Streckfuss

See also AIRCRAFT; BOLLING, RAYNAL CAWTHORNE

Bibliography

Gorrell, Edgar S. "What—No Airplanes?" *Journal of Air Law and Commerce* 12 (January 1941).

Mauer, Mauer. *U.S. Air Service in World War I. The Final Report and A Tactical History.* Washington, DC: Office of Air Force History, 1978.

Rawlinson, A. Douglas. "Failure of the U.S. Aircraft Industry." *Cross and Cockade Journal* 9 (Winter 1968).

Bolsheviks and Bolshevism

The Bolsheviks were the forerunners of the contemporary Communist Party of the former Soviet Union. In the October Revolution of 1917, under the leadership of Vladimir Ilyich Lenin, they overthrew the Provisional Government of Russia. They hoped to take advantage of the disruption caused by the World War and begin a wave of revolutions across Europe that would overthrow the capitalist system and create a socialist order. They considered themselves the heirs of Karl Marx.

The word "Bolshevik" means "men of the majority" and was applied to Lenin's followers at the Second Congress of the Russian Social Democratic Workers' Party (RSDWP), held in London in 1903. Differences of opinion between Lenin and his fellow Russian Marxists led to a split in the party. Lenin claimed the title Bolshevik because his faction had won a vote on control of the party's newspaper. His opponents accepted the title Mensheviks ("men of the minority") despite the fact that most members of the RSDWP did not share Lenin's views at the time. In 1918, the Bolsheviks changed their name to the Russian Communist Party.

Under Lenin's guidance, the Bolsheviks distinguished themselves from the rest of Europe's Socialists by the uncompromisingly harsh positions they held. Since the 1890s, many Socialists had largely abandoned the idea of revolution and hoped to change society through gradual reform. Lenin scorned such ideas as weakness, if not heresy. His opponents, the Mensheviks, believed that Russia's Marxists should form a mass party and cooperate with the liberals against the tsar. The Bolsheviks, however, adhered to the plan set forth by Lenin in *What Is To Be Done?* which called for a tightly controlled elite party of professional revolutionaries. Only such a party, Lenin believed, could guide the working class to a socialist revolution. Left to its own devices, the working class, in Lenin's view, would become distracted by economic concerns, such as higher pay and shorter hours, and fail to seize power. Lenin's position came under bitter attack by Leon Trotsky, a Russian Marxist who stood aloof from both Bolsheviks and Mensheviks. Trotsky predicted that the only result of Lenin's centralized party organization would be a dictatorship.

Lenin also differed from the Mensheviks in believing that the peasants of Russia could be co-opted into a socialist revolution. Instead of seeing the peasantry as a conservative class, Lenin hoped to turn them against the government by promising to nationalize the land. Lenin also sought to mobilize the resentment of the non-Russian nationalities of the empire by promising them self-determination.

The years between 1903 and 1917 proved trying ones for Lenin and his followers. The exiled Bolshevik failed to play a major role in Russia's 1905 Revolution. Appeals for unity from persecuted Marxists in Russia led to a half-hearted reconciliation with the Mensheviks, which finally collapsed in 1907, largely because of Lenin's intransigence, and in 1912 the Bolsheviks became a separate party. Besides fighting the Mensheviks, Lenin found himself assailed by dissenters from within his own party, despite the value the Bolsheviks placed on discipline and obedience. Finally, irregularities in Bolshevik fund raising, particularly the use of armed robbery and extortion, had turned most European Socialists against Lenin by the eve of the World War.

Despite all these challenges and setbacks, Lenin maintained his position at the head of the party and developed a corps of skilled and devoted followers. These included Grigory Zinoviev and Nikolai Bukharin, who lived, like Lenin, in exile, and Lev Kamenev and Josef Stalin, who remained in Russia. All four would play important roles in the first decade of post-Tsarist Russia.

The outbreak of the World War created another difference between Lenin and Europe's Socialists. Most of the latter patriotically supported their countries in the summer of 1914, but Lenin called for the defeat of Russia and wanted the war between nations turned into a war between classes. In his view, Socialists who supported the war betrayed the working class, and Lenin poured scorn on them from his exile in Switzerland. At the antiwar Socialist conferences of Zimmerwald and Kienthal, Lenin won European supporters to his position, thus laying the foundation for what would become the Communist Internationale.

The overthrow of the tsar in the February 1917 Revolution caught the Bolsheviks by surprise. Under Kamenev and Stalin, the Bolsheviks in Russia urged support for the Provisional Government's efforts to continue the war. This outraged Lenin, who realized that a revolutionary moment had come not only for Russia but also for war-weary Europe. A socialist revolution in Russia, Lenin reasoned, would begin a wave of revolutions across the continent, as workers rebelled against being cannon fodder in an imperialist war. Unfortunately for himself, Lenin was trapped in Switzerland, far from any revolution.

Unconcerned with the long-term implications of Lenin's ideas, the German government transported Lenin to Russia, hoping that he would destabilize the war effort and knock the country out of the conflict, so Germany could concentrate its forces in the West. Upon arriving in Petrograd, Lenin issued his "April Theses," which attacked the Provisional Government and called for the transformation of the World War into an international class war. Pleased that Lenin had seen the link between revolution in Russia and in Europe, Leon Trotsky joined the Bolsheviks when he returned to Russia in May. Trotsky's oratory and organizational skills proved vital to the Bolsheviks in the coming years of conflict.

Growing disillusionment with the war and the reluctance of the Provisional Government to address the land question, while Lenin and Trotsky promised "Peace, Bread, and Land" led to a continual growth of support for the Bolsheviks in the summer of 1917, particularly among workers and soldiers. By autumn, Lenin was urging his party to seize power before the moment slipped away. On Nov. 6, 1917, the Bolsheviks took control of Petrograd and toppled the ineffective Provisional Government. In March, the Bolsheviks would take the country out of the World War, only to plunge it into civil war.

Michael Samerdyke

Bibliography

Haimosn, Leopold H. *The Russian Marxists and the Origins of Bolshevism.* Cambridge: Harvard University Press, 1955.

Keep, J.L.H. *The Rise of Social Democracy in Russia.* Oxford, UK: Oxford University Press, 1963.

Schapiro, Leonard. *The Communist Party of the Soviet Union.* New York: Vintage Books, 1971.

Ulam, Adam. *The Bolsheviks.* New York: Macmillan, 1965.

Wolfe, Bertram D. *Three Who Made a Revolution.* New York: Dial, 1948.

Borah, William Edgar (1865–1940)

William Edgar Borah was born and raised on an Illinois farm. At twenty he moved to Kansas to live with an older sister whose husband was an attorney. Borah read law and passed the bar examination in 1887. After practicing with his brother-in-law for three years, Borah headed west to Boise, Idaho. There he quickly attained a reputation as an excellent trial lawyer and became involved in politics. Although Borah was something of a maverick, his shrewdness and superb oratorical talents eventually won him election on the Republican ticket to the United States Senate in 1907.

As a senator, Borah was a Progressive, although an erratic one. He wanted to curb corporate interests but was reluctant to enlarge governmental powers in order to do so. This often left him in the position of having nothing to offer except verbal condemnation. In foreign relations, he generally opposed American interference in the affairs of other nations, particularly in Latin America, but became a militant nationalist whenever "honor" was concerned.

When war broke out in Europe in 1914, Borah applauded President Woodrow Wilson's appeal to Americans to remain neutral in thought and deed. Borah regarded the struggle as a clash of imperial blocs from which the United States should remain aloof. At the same time, Borah urged a stronger response to German submarine depredations. He voted in favor of war against Germany in April 1917 but stated that he did so solely in defense of national interests and not in behalf of some idealistic crusade. He supported most wartime legislation, though he repeatedly denounced profiteering by big business. He stoutly upheld civil liberties in an atmosphere of wartime hysteria, in which dissent was often equated with disloyalty.

When the first Russian revolution occurred in March 1917, Borah echoed Wilson's approval of the tsar's downfall. He parted company with the administration after the Bolshevik revolution when Wilson refused to recognize the new government. Through the years Borah campaigned for its recognition until it was finally extended during the early months of Franklin D. Roosevelt's administration.

Borah's most extended argument with the Wilson administration came over the latter's endorsement of the League of Nations. Well before World War I ended, the senator had made it clear that he opposed American entry into an international organization, no matter what its form. He believed that the United States should retain complete independence in foreign affairs and predicted that League of Nations membership would enmesh the United States in endless struggles around the world. Borah's popularity, his speaking skills, and his impregnable political position in Idaho, made him one of the leading figures in the struggle that climaxed in 1919–1920 with the Senate rejection of the treaty and the League of Nations.

Borah exercised strong influence on American foreign policy during the 1920s, particularly after he became chairman of the Senate Foreign Relations Committee in 1924. His influence waned during the Great Depression, but in the late 1930s he became one of the most outspoken critics of Roosevelt's foreign policies, which, Borah believed, would drag the nation into another conflict. On Jan. 16, 1940, he suffered a massive stroke and died three days later.

Robert J. Maddox

Bibliography

Johnson, Claudius O. *Borah of Idaho.* New York: Longmans, Green, 1936.

Maddox, Robert J. *William E. Borah and American Foreign Policy.* Baton Rouge: Louisiana State University Press, 1969.

Borglum, (John) Gutzon (1867–1941)

Gutzon Borglum was born in the Idaho Territory. He moved to New York in 1890, then on to Paris, where he studied under the sculptor Auguste Rodin at the Academie Julian. As a sculptor, Borglum was widely acclaimed in Paris salons and in London. He traveled extensively, living in Spain, London, and San Francisco, before settling in New York in 1901. There he completed commissions for the Cathedral of St. John the Divine and other public buildings. Later he turned to creating large-scale public monuments, such as the bust of Lincoln which is now in the rotunda of the Capitol in Washington, D.C.

In 1912, Borglum became involved in national politics, stumping Connecticut in support of Theodore Roosevelt, Bull Moose (Progressive) candidate for president. When the United States entered World War I in 1917, Borglum, a long-time member of the Aeronautical Club of America, began to probe the aircraft industry, looking for waste, mismanagement, and inefficiency. His investigation convinced him that the aircraft industry was in a shambles. He set about transmitting his findings to President Woodrow Wilson, who remembered Borglum as an outspoken critic during both the 1912 and 1916 elections. Wilson did not see Borglum but directed him to present his findings to the National Aeronautical Board. Borglum wrote a note to the President that this board was a large part of the problem and reflected badly upon his presidency.

The sculptor/investigator later recommended a presidential investigation as to why no planes had yet been produced by the American aircraft industry. Borglum volunteered to be on a panel appointed by the President to lead the investigation. Although Wilson did not appoint the panel, Borglum worked, at his own expense, to probe America's aircraft industry.

Borglum alienated many of those who were sympathetic to him when he presented his well-documented report as an exposé and by asking for unlimited power to subpoena witnesses and aircraft personnel to appear before the Senate Military Affairs Committee. The administration frowned on such tactics. Borglum refused to step down from his post at the President's request, and Wilson dismissed him publicly.

Irate over Borglum's public challenges, Wilson called upon Charles Evans Hughes to head a committee to investigate the aircraft industry along the lines encouraged by Borglum. Hughes's reports vindicated Borglum and his findings.

During and after World War I, the sculptor pursued a number of projects, including an impressive sculpture of Gen. Robert E. Lee at Stone Mountain, Georgia. The United States government commissioned him to carve the heads of Washington, Jefferson, Lincoln, and Theodore Roosevelt in Mt. Rushmore National Memorial in South Dakota. The work began in 1927. Borglum died in 1941, the year the monument was completed.

Barbara Bennett Peterson

Bibliography

Dean, Robert J. *Living Granite: The Story of Borglum and the Mount Rushmore Memorial.* New York: Viking Press, 1949.
Taft, Lorado. *The History of American Sculpture.* New York: Macmillan, 1924.

Bourne, Randolph Silliman (1886–1918)

B

Undaunted by severe birth defects, Randolph Silliman Bourne entered Columbia University in 1909. Bourne came of age intellectually just as Europe was plunged into war. Everything he believed caused him to reject war and see the United Sates as able to present an alternative to the failed European nation-state. He wrote in 1916 of a "trans-national America" as an alternative to European nationalism—and war. He worked for peace, editing a symposium of peace proposals and programs, *Towards an Enduring Peace*, for the American Association of International Conciliation; led the committee for Democratic Control, which supported the need for a popular referendum to declare war; and joined forces with the new Woman's Peace Party.

The United States entry into the war came as a terrible blow to Bourne. Dissenting from the claim that this war would "make the world safe for democracy," he believed that the war was its own master, that it would lead to its own ends. He scoffed at John Dewey's perception of "the social possibilities of war." Bourne proclaimed that if intellectuals were unable to prevent the war, they would be unable to influence the peace. He believed that someone, necessarily outside the mainstream, had to insist that "the real enemy is war rather than Imperial Germany," that this was not a holy crusade. Writing for the new literary monthly, the *Seven Arts*, Bourne put these and other ideas together in a series of bitter articles. The benefactress of the *Seven Arts*, a Mrs. Rankine, grew more troubled with each article that Bourne published. Accused by her friends of bankrolling spies and traitors, then snubbed by them, she withdrew her subsidy to the journal and committed suicide a few weeks later.

The Great War both broke and made Randolph Bourne's reputation, but he would not live long enough to see that many of his predictions about the postwar world would come true. He died in New York on Dec. 22, 1918, of bronchial pneumonia, a complication of the deadly influenza epidemic of that winter.

David W. Moore

See also WOMAN'S PEACE PARTY

Bibliography

Bourne, Randolph S. *The Letters of Randolph Bourne.* Troy, NY: Whitston, 1981.

————. *War and the Intellectuals, 1915–1919,* ed. by Carl Resek. New York: Harper, 1964.

Bowman, Isaiah (1878–1950)

A Canadian by birth, Isaiah Bowman achieved renown as one of America's pioneer geographers, as a foremost academic administrator, and as a distinguished internationalist who served the United States government during both World Wars. Born near Waterloo, Ontario, in 1878, his family soon thereafter moved to Michigan. After graduating from Harvard University in 1905, Bowman accepted an instructorship in geology at Yale University, while also matriculating in Yale's doctoral program in geology, specializing in the geography of South America. Bowman joined the "Yale South American Expedition of 1907," where he conducted research for his dissertation. He soon won recognition in his growing profession of geography and participated in numerous expeditions to the Andes. On one of those treks, Bowman came to realize the special value of large-scale base maps. Out of this concern emerged Bowman's passionate commitment to construct the "Millionth Map for Hispanic America," a project he would lead in the United States for the next three decades.

In 1915, Bowman was appointed director of the American Geographical Society in New York. After American entry in the World War, he was invited to serve as an officer of The Inquiry, an independent, classified commission, established by President Wilson in September 1917, for the purpose of laying the groundwork for American participation in the eventual peace settlement. Bowman not only served as executive director under the titular leadership of Col. Edward M. House and Dr. Sidney Mezes, but also had The Inquiry housed on the third floor of the Geographical Society's building in New York.

By the summer of 1918, Bowman's influence in The Inquiry had risen to the extent that he was, practically speaking, making decisions on priorities and allocation of funds. Although conclusive evidence is lacking, it seems likely that Bowman authorized expending funds for numerous reports concerning Latin America that had little or no relationship to The Inquiry's official mission. Apparently, these allocations, which are revealed in the organization's financial records, were never questioned at the time.

Bowman accompanied President Wilson and his entourage to the Paris Peace Conference in December 1918. As chief territorial specialist, Bowman served on the American Commission to Negotiate Peace. In this capacity, he sat on several commissions and subcommissions concerned with Poland and Rumania. In May 1919, Bowman returned to the United States, but in September of that year, President Wilson requested him to return to Paris and assist with problems affecting treaties with Austria, Hungary, and Bulgaria. When the American commission finally withdrew from the peace conference in December 1919, Bowman returned to the United States.

He then turned his attention to writing *The New World: Problems in Political Geography,* which quickly became a classic treatise on how the war and the peace conference had transformed the political globe. His career proceeded in several directions simultaneously. From 1935 to 1949, he served as president of the Johns Hopkins University. He continued a long involvement with the work of the Council on Foreign Relations. Two years before his death in 1950, Bowman was awarded the Gold Medal of the Royal Geographical Society in London.

Lawrence E. Gelfand

See also INQUIRY, THE

Bibliography

Bowman, Isaiah. "The American Geographical Society's Contribution to the Peace Conference." *Geographical Review* 7 (1919).

————. *The New World: Problems in Political Geography.* New York: World Book, 1921.

Gelfand, Lawrence E. *The Inquiry: American Preparations for Peace 1917–1919.* New Haven: Yale University Press, 1963.

Martin, Geoffrey J. *The Life and Thought of Isaiah Bowman.* Hamden, CT: Archon Books, 1980.

Brandeis, Louis Dembitz (1856–1941)

Louis Dembitz Brandeis, whom Woodrow Wilson nominated to the Supreme Court in 1916, was born in Louisville, Kentucky, and graduated from Harvard Law School in 1877. He rose to prominence as a New England political activist with an extraordinary reputation for judicial progressivism based on his ground-breaking sociological brief in 1908, *Muller v. Oregon*. His relationship with Wilson began during the 1912 campaign when he helped Wilson formulate a trust strategy and the animating principles of the New Freedom.

Brandeis assisted many government officials to staff the expanding bureaucracy caused by America's participation in the war. Most notable, however, among all the activities he engaged in while commencing his first year's service on the Supreme Court was the guidance he gave Wilson on the formulation of Britain's Balfour Declaration. Brandeis and his close friend Professor Felix Frankfurter of the Harvard Law School were crucial liaisons for Wilson to British Foreign Secretary Arthur Balfour in 1917. Brandeis was the energizing center of the Wilson administration's deliberations over the establishment of a viable Jewish state in Palestine.

Frank Annunziata

See also BALFOUR DECLARATION

Bibliography

Lash, Joseph P. *From the Diaries of Felix Frankfurter.* New York: Norton, 1975.

Mason, Alpheus Thomas. *Brandeis: A Free Man's Life.* New York: Viking Press, 1961.

Paper, Louis J. *Brandeis.* Englewood Cliffs, NJ: Prentice-Hall, 1983.

Strum, Philippa. *Louis D. Brandeis: Justice for the People.* New York: Schocken Books, 1984.

Urofsky, Melvin I., and David W. Levy, eds. *Letters of Louis D. Brandeis.* Albany: State University of New York Press, 1971–1978.

Brent, Charles H. (1862–1929)

Charles H. Brent, the Episcopal bishop of the Philippines, was the most influential chaplain in World War I. It was Bishop Brent who was asked by General John J. Pershing in January 1918 to take charge of all chaplain activities in the American Expeditionary Force (AEF). Commissioned as a major, he was appointed as senior general headquarters chaplain. He would be known as chief of chaplains, and, indeed, that title is engraved over his tomb in Lausanne, Switzerland.

Bishop Brent's connection with Pershing was a close one and of long duration. They first knew each other in the Philippines in 1901, and it was Brent who baptized Pershing and his family, confirmed the general and his wife into the Episcopal Church, and then consoled him when Frances Pershing and three of their children died in a fire at the San Francisco Presidio. Brent's relationship with Pershing was that of both friend and pastor, and it was to Brent that Pershing turned for help in organizing the chaplains into an effective component of the AEF.

Brent, like the more famous chaplain, Francis Duffy of the Rainbow Division, was originally Canadian. Born in Newcastle, Ontario, he graduated from Trinity College, Toronto, in 1884. Ordained in 1887, he came to the United States and became a citizen in 1891. After ministering for a decade in Boston, Brent was elected as the first Episcopal missionary bishop of the Philippines in 1901, a position that he would hold until 1918.

Pershing invited Bishop Brent, who was in France as a special agent for the Young Men's Christian Association, to work out a plan of organization for the chaplains under his command. Bishop Gwynne, deputy chaplain general of the British forces, visited headquarters and explained the British Army system. Several of its features were adopted in the American plan.

General Pershing favored the formation of a chaplain "corps" with Brent as its head. Brent convinced him that a better plan was the appointment of a permanent executive committee of chaplains, with Brent serving as chairman, to study conditions and make direct recommendations to the general. This committee included a Catholic chaplain, a clergyman of a Protestant church with the Episcopal plan of organization, and one of a body that followed the Congregational system. Their duties included assignment of chaplains to units and installations in the European theater, visits to chaplains in the field, investigation of situations affecting the moral welfare of troops, and supervision of the chaplain's school in France.

Following the war this system of administration was modified and continued among occupation forces by the senior chaplain of American forces, Edmund Easterbrook. After the Armistice, Brent stayed on in France for some time to help make plans for the welfare of the troops during the irritating delays before they could be brought back home. He left the army and returned to the United States in the spring of 1919. Brent was appointed bishop of Western New York and served in that position until his death on March 27, 1929.

William J. Hourihan

See also CHAPLAINS

Bibliography

Stover, Earl F. *Up From Handyman: The United States Army Chaplaincy, 1865–1920.* Washington, DC: Office of the Chief of Chaplains, 1977.

Brest Litovsk, Treaty of

The Treaty of Brest Litovsk was the first treaty of peace between former antagonists in World War I. It illustrated the complete victory of German forces on the Eastern front and humiliated Russia militarily and diplomatically. In March 1917, the forces of Imperial Russia had crumbled and Tsar Nicholas II had been forced to abdicate the throne. A new Provisional Government led by Alexander Kerensky tried to continue the war, a miscalculation which eventually allowed Lenin and the Bolsheviks, with their promises of "Peace, Land and Bread," to gain power and popularity with the masses of Russian peasants. In his first address to the All Russian Congress of Soviets after the successful coup, Lenin delivered the October Peace Decree, holding out an offer of peace based on no annexations, no indemnities, the right of self-determination for all peoples, and a promise to publish and repudiate all secret treaties.

Negotiations between Russia and the Central Powers began on Dec. 22, 1917, at Brest Litovsk. The German delegation included MajGen. Max Hoffman, chief of staff to the commander-in-chief in the East; Foreign Secretary Richard von Kühlmann, and Baron Frederic von Rosenberg, of the German Foreign Office. The Austro-Hungarian Empire was represented by Colonel Pokorny, Turkey by General Zekki Pasha, and Bulgaria by General Gantcheff. The Soviet delegation was initially led by Adolf Joffe, who was accompanied by Leo Kamenev, Leo Karakhan, secretary general of the Soviet mission, and Anastasia Bitsenko. Additional representatives were chosen to reflect all the revolutionary classes—soldiers, sailors, workers and peasants—although these delegates had limited powers. The Soviets intentionally attempted to slow down the deliberations, hoping to wear down the Germans and buy time for a general proletarian revolution to sweep through Europe.

By Jan. 18, 1918, after little progress in the deliberations, the German delegation sought to divide the Soviet delegation by granting independence to the former Russian Baltic states, to Russian Poland, and to the Ukraine. Upon the urgings of Leon Trotsky, who now headed the Soviet delegation, Lenin's government partially capitulated. Trotsky's scheme was to agree to end the state of war but reach no final terms of peace, a situation that he termed "neither peace nor war." Upon returning to the negotiating table after meeting with Lenin in Petrograd, Trotsky again attempted to stall any final peace agreement. The Ukrainian delegation now bolted and signed a separate peace with the Germans on Feb. 9, 1918. To force the Soviets to conclude a treaty, the Germans resumed fighting in February. On March 3, 1918, Lenin's government concluded the peace.

The 1918 treaties signed at Brest Litovsk allowed the Germans to annex large portions of former Russian territory, and represented the apex of German expansion in Europe during World War I. It signified Lenin's desire to buy time to reorganize Russia and his realization that the new Soviet state was too weak to continue military involvement in the war.

Under the terms of the treaty, Russia was to end all anti-German propaganda. The Germans were allowed to occupy the Ukraine as far as Baku, and Russia surrendered all claims to the territories west of a line running from Riga to the northwest corner of the Ukraine, an area that included Poland, Courland, and Lithuania. The fate of these detached areas was to be determined by Germany and Austria-Hungary in agreement with their populations. In reality, the Central Powers intended to dominate these areas completely. Russia acknowledged the independence of the Ukraine and its right to make a separate treaty. Russian forces were to evacuate the Ukraine, Estonia, Livonia, Finland, and the Aaland Islands.

Russia's army was to be demobilized immediately; its navy was to remain in Russian ports and completely disarm. German forces would leave those areas of Russia not previously mentioned after Russian disarmament was complete. Ardahan, Kars, Batum, and eastern Anatolia were returned to Turkey, and Russia was forbidden to concentrate any armed forces in the region of the Caucasus that might threaten Turkey. The return to Turkey of Batum, which controlled the oil fields of Baku and Azerbaijan, allowed the Central Powers to exploit these resources.

Technically, the treaty contained no provisions for reparations, but each country was to reimburse the other for the costs of incarcerating their prisoners. Since the number of Russians captured was much larger than the number of German POWs, Russian payments would likewise be substantial. The treaty provided for favorable commercial arrangements between Russia and the Central Powers and stipulated that no export tax would be levied by Russia on lumber or ores. Through this treaty, Germany extended its control of Eastern Europe to the Arctic Ocean and the Black Sea and opened resources, especially Ukrainian wheat and oil, to the German war machine.

Despite the fact that the treaty was very unpopular in Russia and was criticized by friends and enemies alike, Lenin accepted it, knowing that the alternative was continued war, which he could ill afford if he were to mold Russia into a worker's paradise.

The greediness of the Central Powers in forcing upon the Russians the devastating provisions of Brest Litovsk hardened the Allies' resolve to push for the ultimate defeat of Germany, for they viewed the treaty as evidence of the impossibility of achieving a negotiated peace with the Germans. However, the treaty served Lenin's purposes, allowing him to work his will on the masses of Russian people.

Barbara Bennett Peterson

Bibliography

Lloyd George, David. *The Truth About the Peace Treaties.* 2 vols. London: Gollancz, 1938.

Mayer, Arno J. *The Political Origins of the New Diplomacy, 1917–1918.* New Haven: Yale University Press, 1959.

———. *The Politics and Diplomacy of Peacemaking.* London: Weidenfeld & Nicolson, 1968.

Wheeler-Bennet, John W. *Brest-Litovsk, the Forgotten Peace, March, 1918.* London: Macmillan, 1956.

Brett, Sereno (1891–1952)

An aggressive and courageous leader, Sereno Brett, probably more than any other officer besides George Patton, was a driving force be-

hind the AEF Tank Corps' light tank brigade's battlefield success.

Captain Brett, an infantry officer who was expert with the 37-mm cannon, applied for assignment to the Tank Corps in early 1918. Patton, impressed by Brett's desire to get out of the AEF schools at Langres and into a combat command, encouraged Col. Samuel Rockenbach to pull the necessary strings to obtain Brett's release. After much bureaucratic maneuvering, the request was approved, and Brett reported for duty at the Light Tank School on March 28, 1918. He initially served as Patton's senior instructor, but a month later, when the 1st Light Tank Battalion was formed, he became commander of Company B and later succeeded Patton as battalion commander, a post Brett retained through two numerical redesignations of the unit and for the remainder of the war.

As the senior of the two battalion commanders, Brett became Patton's "right-hand man." His aggressive leadership earned him a Distinguished Service Cross during the St. Mihiel offensive. Less than two weeks later, on the first day of the Meuse-Argonne campaign, Major Brett assumed field command of the 1st Tank Brigade when Colonel Patton was seriously wounded while supporting 35th Division troops near Cheppy. Patton's wounds kept him out of action for the remainder of the brigade's field service, and Brett earned plaudits from senior commanders for his battlefield leadership.

After the war, Brett returned to Camp Meade, Maryland, with the remnants of the AEF Tank Corps. There he joined LtCol. Dwight D. Eisenhower, who had commanded the Tank Corps' largest stateside training center, Camp Colt, Pennsylvania, and the two served as Tank Corps representatives on the Army's First Transcontinental Motor Convoy in 1919.

Brett became the World War I Tank Corps' only major figure to maintain his allegiance to tanks during the troubled 1920s and 1930s. He commanded the Expeditionary Tank Force in Panama in 1923–1924, was executive officer of the Experimental Mechanized Force in 1930–1931, and was a member of the Infantry Board for the balance of the 1930s. Brett joined the newly created Armored Force at Fort Knox as chief of staff in 1940 and commanded the 31st Armored Regiment in 1941. He joined the staff of the 5th Armored Division in 1942–1943 but was forced to retire as a colonel because of physical disability before that unit deployed overseas. He died on Sept. 9, 1952, at the age of 61.

Dale E. Wilson

See also PATTON, GEORGE SMITH, JR.; TANKS

Bibliography

Blumenson, Martin, ed. *The Patton Papers, 1885–1940.* Boston: Houghton Mifflin, 1972.

Wilson, Dale E. *Treat' Em Rough! The Birth of American Armor, 1917–1920.* Novato, CA: Presidio Press, 1989.

Bristol, Mark Lambert (1868–1939)

One of the twentieth century's foremost naval diplomats, Mark Lambert Bristol's early career in the navy was marked by typical assignments to modest vessels on station in foreign and domestic waters. In 1896, however, he was transferred to the battleship *Texas* as a member of the gunnery crew, and he saw action during the Spanish-American War at Guantanamo Bay and Santiago. Following the war, he emerged as one of the navy's top ordnance specialists, working on mines and torpedoes in the Bureau of Ordnance, designing gun sights while serving in the North Atlantic Fleet, and commanding the naval torpedo facility at Newport, Rhode Island.

After two years of commanding vessels assigned to the Asiatic Fleet (1911–1913), Bristol was promoted to the rank of captain and given command of the navy's fledgling air service. With little funds and lukewarm support, he attempted to expand naval aviation and hoped to integrate it into the battleship fleet. While his ambitious plans did not materialize, he laid the essential administrative and political groundwork for advancing naval aviation. In 1916, he took command of the cruiser *North Carolina,* which was outfitted as an experimental aviation station ship, and continued his efforts to make naval aviation at sea a reality. His direct association with naval air ended in 1917 when he began a course of study at the Naval War College.

World War I cut short Captain Bristol's War College assignment, and once again he found himself in command of the *North Carolina,* which was involved in the convoy of troop ships to Europe. In March 1918, he assumed command of the Ireland-based battleship *Okla-homa.* Four months later he was promoted to the rank of rear admiral. Just days prior to the Armistice of November 1918, Bristol was given command of the U.S. naval base at Plymouth, England, a billet he would hold for only a few weeks.

In January 1919, the Navy Department assigned Admiral Bristol to command a small naval detachment charged with protecting American interests in the eastern Mediterranean, particularly in Turkish waters. Because of his diplomatic acumen and humanitarianism, Bristol soon became the principal American diplomatic voice in the region. He was appointed U.S. high commissioner to Turkey in August 1919, a post he held until 1927. He won the friendship of the Turks by adhering to a unilateral open-door type of policy, in stark contrast to the bankrupt imperial policies of the victorious European powers, who were intent on carving up the old Ottoman Empire among themselves.

In mid-1927, the navy promoted Bristol to the rank of full admiral and appointed him commander-in-chief of the Asiatic Fleet, an assignment that also required considerable diplomatic skill. Most of his attention was focused on protecting American interests during the Chinese civil war and on altering the Asiatic Fleet's mission from gunboat diplomacy to fostering good will and, in extreme instances of physical threat, protecting American nationals.

Admiral Bristol ended his distinguished naval career with assignment to the General Board (1929–1932), a body he chaired from March 1930 to May 1932. He died on May 13, 1939.

Donald A. Yerxa

Bibliography

Braisten, William R. "Mark Lambert Bristol: Naval Diplomat Extraordinary of the Battleship Age." In *Admirals of the Steel Navy: Makers of the American Naval Tradition,* ed. by James C. Bradford. Annapolis, MD: Naval Institute Press, 1990.

Reynolds, Clark G. *Famous American Admirals.* New York: Van Nostrand Reinhold, 1978.

Brittany Patrol

See SUICIDE FLEET

Brown, Preston (1872–1948)

Preston Brown was born in Lexington, Kentucky. He was graduated from Yale University in 1892. In 1894, he enlisted in the Regular Army and rose to the rank of corporal before being commissioned a second lieutenant of infantry, just prior to the Spanish-American War. A veteran of the 1897 campaign against the Cheyenne Indians as well as of the Battle of Santiago, he served in the Philippine Insurrection campaigns of 1900 and 1901.

When the United States entered World War I, Major Brown was an observer with the Austrian Army. He returned immediately to the United States. He helped form the 2d Infantry Division and in April 1918 became its chief of staff. He participated with the division in engagements near Verdun in March and April 1918 and northeast of Château-Thierry from May to July. He then played a primary role in preparing his division for the attack on Vaux on July 1, 1918. This action was characterized by senior French officers as one of the few "perfect attacks" of the war. Brown was promoted to brigadier general on Aug. 25, 1918.

In September, he left the 2d Division to become the chief of staff of the IV Army Corps located in the quiet sector near the old St. Mihiel battlefield. There, he was instrumental in preparing the corps for the feint on September 26 designed to mask the main American attack between the Argonne Forest and the Meuse River. This offensive rapidly bogged down. The Americans failed to take the commanding heights of Montfaucon on the first day as planned, and German reinforcements streamed into the area. Impatient with the slow progress, General John J. Pershing relieved three of the division commanders, including the commander of the 3d Division, replacing him on Oct. 18 with BGen. Preston Brown.

The 3d Division fought on through October. On October 20, it captured the Bois Claire Chenes, but lost it to a fierce German counterattack and then regained it in very heavy fighting. On October 22, the division cleared the Bois de Fôret and essentially reached its objective for this phase of the battle. This in effect ended the 3d Division's fighting, for it was placed in the V Corps reserve and the Armistice soon followed.

After the end of hostilities BGen. Brown was made assistant chief of staff of the American Expeditionary Force and was stationed in Germany until his return to the United States to attend the Army War College, class of 1920, in Washington, D.C. He later commanded the 2d Division in Texas and was promoted to major general. He then commanded the 1st Division, the I Corps Area, headquartered in Boston, the Panama Canal Department, and the VI Corps Area at Chicago, from whence he retired after forty years of service on Nov. 30, 1934. He died in 1948.

James L. Collins

Bibliography

Marshall, George C. *Memoirs of My Services in the World War 1917–1918*. Boston: Houghton Mifflin, 1976.

Pershing, John J. *My Experiences in the World War*. New York: Stokes, 1931.

Smythe, Donald. *Pershing*. Bloomington: Indiana University Press, 1986.

Bryan, William Jennings (1860–1925)

William Jennings Bryan, three times the unsuccessful presidential nominee of the Democratic Party, served Woodrow Wilson as secretary of state from 1913 to the summer of 1915. He resigned, as a matter of principle, over Wilson's second *Lusitania* note, convinced that Wilson's demands on Germany would lead to unnecessary war. Thereafter he took his case for peace to the country, leading an unsuccessful campaign not only against the preparedness movement but also against any presidential action that appeared to threaten absolute neutrality. But his resignation was widely misinterpreted; some, indeed, charged him with betraying Woodrow Wilson. While Bryan was, to be sure, partially responsible for the near success of the Gore-McLemore resolutions, which would deny passports to American citizens wishing to sail on ships of belligerent nations, he was soon outflanked by Wilson's "He kept us out of war" campaign in 1916 and had become, by 1917, an irrelevant voice preaching in the wilderness.

A pacifist and anti-imperialist who had unsuccessfully tried to turn the 1900 campaign against William McKinley into a referendum on imperialism, Bryan, the Great Commoner, came to office in 1913 committed to the idea of negotiating a series of "cooling-off" treaties. Nations would agree to submit all disputes, including those involving "national honor," to impartial investigation and pledge not to go to war for at least twelve months while the issues were being resolved. He was convinced—and remained convinced even after the guns of August 1914 had begun their murderous thunder—that his treaties would end the scourge of international war forever. He promised, when he took office as secretary of state, that there would be no war during his watch, and when war broke out in Europe, he was even more committed to American neutrality than the President. But for Bryan neutrality meant not insistence upon neutral rights but, rather, absolute and unwavering impartiality. At the heart of his disagreement with Wilson was his conviction that the President should treat Germany no differently than England—indeed, should protest British violations of American neutrality at the same time that he was protesting German submarine policy.

Yet in Latin America Bryan sanctioned, even furthered, the many direct interventions that Wilson initiated in the Caribbean. He approved the ill-fated operations at Tampico and Veracruz in Mexico, raised few if any objections to Wilson's Mexican policy, and assiduously pursued the navy's search for bases in Haiti and Santo Domingo. An unabashed supporter of the spoils system, Bryan soon became notorious for staffing American embassies and consulates with "deserving Democrats" whose only qualifications for appointment were their political loyalties and whose achievements, by even the most charitable standards, were minimal.

Bryan's record was an inconsistent one. His greatest virtue—love of peace—was also his greatest liability. A Christian pacifist, Bryan simply believed that peace was always preferable to war. He was a reductionist who dealt in blacks and whites, and he had no appreciation for the complexities of international relations or the tensions that led to conflict. In a very real sense, he represented the Populist agrarian past of the Democratic Party and not its Progressive urbanized future. Moreover, convinced that America was truly "the city set upon the hill" and that American democracy represented mankind's greatest political achievement, he easily concluded that the United States had a moral mission to spread its ideals into the Caribbean and a Christian duty to mediate the European conflict. On the other hand, his lack of detailed knowledge meant that he could be influenced by semipermanent officials in the Department of State who were wedded to the preservation of American hegemony in the Caribbean.

Yet there is abundant evidence that Woodrow Wilson did value Bryan's advice, realizing that he was a vital link between the wings of the party. And, in such matters as getting the Federal Reserve Act through Congress, Bryan did play such a role. But Wilson was ever his own secretary of state, and he himself always handled the big issues—Mexico and American neutrality. Bryan, to be sure, was not intellectually equipped to influence a president with Wilson's convictions and determination. But Robert Lansing, his successor and a man of far greater ability and experience, encountered the same difficulties and resistance in his dealings with the President. Besides, Bryan, for all his limitations, did offer some common-sense solutions—ideas that would resonate again in the 1930s—to the problem of preserving American neutrality. Believing that money was the greatest of all contrabands, he opposed any loans to the belligerents, and he argued, without success, that Americans who knowingly booked passage on a belligerent passenger ship in the face of the submarine danger had been guilty of contributory negligence. Moreover, his resignation demonstrated that Bryan had the courage of his convictions; few American public officials, before or since, have been willing to give up high office as a matter of conscience.

Despite his resignation from the cabinet, Bryan supported Wilson for reelection in 1916, and a year later he did not oppose the American war effort. After the war, he maintained an active speaking career on the Chautauqua circuit. As a proponent of fundamentalist Christian ideals, he opposed the theory of evolution. He was one of the prosecuting attorneys during the famous trial of John Scopes for teaching the theory of evolution. Opposing counsel was Clarence Darrow. The prosecution prevailed, but the trial took its toll on Bryan, who died suddenly on July 26, 1925, just days after the conclusion of the trial.

Richard D. Challener

Bibliography

Bryan, William J., and Mary B. Bryan. *The Memoirs of William Jennings Bryan.* Philadelphia: Winston, 1925.

Challener, Richard D. "William Jennings Bryan (1913–1915)." In *An Uncertain Tradition,* ed. by Norman A. Graebner. New York: McGraw-Hill, 1961.

Coletta, Paolo E. *William Jennings Bryan.* 2 vols. Lincoln: University of Nebraska Press, 1969.

Levine, Lawrence W. *Defender of the Faith. William Jennings Bryan: The Last Decade, 1915–1925.* New York: Oxford University Press, 1965.

Buck, Beaumont Bonaparte (1860–1950)

Beaumont Bonaparte Buck was graduated from the United States Military Academy at West Point in 1885. Buck's prewar military career included service with several Volunteer and Regular Army units and was marked by a rapid rise through the ranks of the Volunteer and Regular Army officer corps. His first duty assignment was with the 16th Infantry Regiment as a newly graduated second lieutenant. In 1889, Buck began a four-year stint as the commandant of cadets at the University of Missouri. On May 4, 1892, he was promoted to the rank of first lieutenant and posted to the 19th Infantry Regiment, where he remained four months before transferring back to the 16th. In 1893, he became commandant of cadets at Baylor University in Waco, Texas. He was promoted to the rank of major in May 1898 and joined the 2d Texas Infantry, serving with this regiment until he was honorably discharged from the army on Nov. 9, 1898.

Buck returned to the army in March 1899, receiving a commission as a captain in the Regular Army. He was assigned to duty in the Philippines, where he served until 1902. Between 1902 and 1914, Buck climbed with remarkable speed to the rank of brigadier general, serving with various infantry units in the Philippines, Mexico, and Massachusetts.

Buck's experience in World War I began with his assignment as commander of the 28th Infantry Regiment, 1st Division, American Expeditionary Force (AEF) on June 12, 1917. On Aug. 5, 1917, Buck assumed command of the 2d Infantry Brigade, 1st Division. The brigade fought near Château-Thierry on May 19 during the opening days of the German's third spring offensive. At one point Buck, after the loss of all his field officers, rallied his troops by making sweeps along the front lines, waving his helmet and rallying the brigade like a platoon leader. In four days of fighting, his men, and those of the 1st Division, captured 3,500 prisoners and 68 guns, suffered 7,200 casualties, and earned the praise of the French Army officers serving with them.

Later, Buck's brigade bore the brunt of the fighting in the first all-American infantry offensive of the war, leading the attack on Cantigny, May 28–29, 1918. Buck's old regiment, the 28th Infantry, captured 250 German prisoners in the attack. Buck also commanded troops in the St. Mihiel and Meuse-Argonne offensives.

On Aug. 5, 1918, he was promoted to the rank of major general and three days later took command of the 3d Infantry Division, AEF. On Oct. 17, 1918, Buck moved to the 34th Division, a reserve and replacement unit, serving there until his return to the United States on Nov. 15, 1918.

During the war, in addition to two promotions, Buck received the Distinguished Service Cross, the French Chevalier and Commander Legion of Honor, and the Croix de Guerre with two palms as well as the Italian War Cross.

After the war, Buck commanded Camp MacArthur, Camp Meade, and the Laredo district along the Mexican border. His final assignment was as acting chief of staff of the 90th Division Organized Reserves at San Antonio, Texas.

Buck retired to San Antonio in 1921 and died there on Feb. 10, 1950.

James Ginther

See also CANTIGNY; CHÂTEAU-THIERRY SECTOR; MEUSE-ARGONNE CAMPAIGN

Bibliography

Stallings, Laurence. *The Story of the Doughboys: The AEF in World War I.* New York: Harper & Row, 1966.

Bullard, Eugene Jacques (1894–1961)

Eugene Jacques Bullard, America's first black aviator, who served with the French not the Americans in World War I, was born on Oct. 9, 1894, in the Rose Hill district of Columbus, Georgia. His father, a former slave, frequently told him stories of his French ancestors from the island of Martinique and France, which had abolished slavery before America. The boy encountered racial injustice in its most virulent form when his father was hunted by a white mob for defending himself against an abusive white employer. His brother, Hector, died at the hands of a Georgia lynch mob for attempting to retain title to rich farmland.

It was after these events that Bullard decided to go to France, which he believed was the land of freedom. He sold his pet goat for $150 and began his odyssey. The adolescent's wanderings throughout the South on his way to the Continent were full of adventure. He traveled with a gypsy caravan and learned how to care for horses and steal food from neighboring farms. He also worked as a jockey and stable manager.

Bullard finally arrived in Great Britain in 1904. Years later, he crossed the English Channel to France, proclaiming that America was his mother but France was his mistress. On Oct. 19, 1914, he enlisted in the French Foreign Legion. Bullard participated in four major campaigns and was severely wounded. Following a subsequent tour of duty with the 170th Franco-American Infantry Regiment, he earned his pilot's license in the spring of 1917.

The twenty-three-year-old aviator underwent preliminary flight training in the Bleriot and Caudron G–3 at the French flying school Tours, and received his brevets on May 5 and May 17, 1917. Bullard participated in advanced combat flight training in the Caudron G–4 at Avord and Châteauroux, and in the Nieuport series at the Plessis Belleville, from June through August 1917. He flew the SPAD VII in combat with Spa. 93, Group Brocard from Aug. 27 to Sept. 13, 1917, and Spa. 85, Group c–15 from Sept. 13 to Nov. 17, 1917. He claimed two victories in November 1917, destroying a Pfalz and a Fokker DR-1 in the vicinity of Verdun. In the air Bullard was always recognized by the wounded heart painted on his SPAD VII's fuselage.

Bullard was discharged from the French Army on Oct. 24, 1919. His World War I decorations included the Legion of Honor, Chevalier, Medal Militaire, Croix de Guerre, Croix de Combattant 1914–1918, Medaille Commemoration Francaise 1914–1918, and Medaille Verdun. Gene Bullard died on Oct. 12, 1961, and was interred in the Federation of French War Veterans Cemetery, Flushing, New York.

John C. Edwards

Bibliography
Carisella, P.J., and J.W. Ryan. *The Black Swallow of Death; the Incredible Story of Eugene Jacques Bullard, the World's First Black Combat Aviator.* Boston: Marlborough House, 1972.

Bullard, Robert Lee (1861–1947)

Born William Robert Bullard in Yonges-borough, Alabama, Bullard at age six prevailed upon his parents to change his name to Robert Lee Bullard. In 1885, he graduated from the United States Military Academy at West Point. His first post as a second lieutenant was at Fort Union, New Mexico. He remained on frontier service with the 10th Infantry until 1898, when, using political influence, he requested a transfer to the Quartermaster Corps, which transfer would automatically bring him his captain's bars. Like most officers of the time, he had languished in his lieutenancy for many years, and he did whatever he could to promote himself. His attempt at self-promotion was more blatant than usually occurred in the officer corps of the day and was one of the most controversial episodes of his military career.

Before the transfer could be approved, the Spanish-American War broke out, and First Lieutenant Bullard, still on duty with the 10th Infantry, was on his way to war. The fastest way into action was to become an officer of a volunteer unit, and the governor of Alabama appointed him a major of Alabama (black) volunteers. Though the unit did not get to Cuba, Bullard built a reputation for successful troop handling, which was useful in his future career. After the war, he was appointed colonel of the 39th U.S. Volunteer Infantry, a unit raised to fight the insurgents in the newly acquired Philippine Islands. He commanded his troops successfully through 1901, when, after again using political influence, he arranged to transfer to the Regular Infantry at his current rank of major. Although he was a brilliant officer, his use of influence created a particularly bad impression among his colleagues.

Bullard subsequently served as an official in the provisional government in Cuba, as a spy in Mexico, a National Guard instructor in California and Hawaii, a student at the Army War College in 1912, and commander of the 26th Infantry. He and his regiment became part of the 2d Division based in Texas during a period of great tension along the border with Mexico.

During his many years of service he and General John J. Pershing had developed a cordial relationship. When the United States entered the World War in April 1917, Bullard was slated to command an officers' training camp, but in June 1917, he received new orders to command the 2d Brigade of the newly formed 1st Division, which sailed for France that same month. His first assignment in France was as officer in charge of the AEF's officer and specialist school, where he served until December 1917. He then returned to the 1st Division to replace Gen. William L. Sibert. By this time Bullard had been promoted to major general. For the next five months, he and his staff created a first-class division, and in late April 1918, they undertook the first major attack of the AEF at Cantigny. It was a great success and showed the British and French, as well as the Germans, that American troops were capable of performing well as an offensive as well as a defensive force.

One of Bullard's strong points was his ability to get along with the French military. He was fluent in their language, and he used good sense in dealing with what often was an exhausted ally, with frayed tempers. In mid-July 1918, after the Château-Thierry campaign, he assumed command of the III Corps, part of the French Tenth Army. His two divisions were included in a French corps with a Moroccan division between them. The Americans had arrived well after Gen. Charles Mangin, the commander of the Tenth Army, and his staff had made their plans for the Soissons attack, of which Bullard was neither aware nor prepared. Nonetheless, with a staff that was "the newest thing I ever saw—except what the stork brings," Bullard directed Gen. Charles P. Summerall and the 1st Division and Gen. James G. Harbord, leading the 2d Division, in a successful but bloody operation. After Soissons, Bullard resumed command of the III Corps, now composed of the 3d, 28th, and 32d divisions, all of which had been in combat with the French Sixth Army.

During August 1918, the III Corps continued its attack on the Velse during the Aisne-Marne counteroffensive and advanced after the Germans retreated to the Aisne. The III Corps then moved into the Meuse-Argonne offensive, doing well enough to earn Bullard promotion to the command of the newly formed Second Army, AEF. His new army, composed of about 180,000 men, saw combat for just two days before the Armistice.

Bullard never became as well known as Pershing, Liggett, and others of his peers, but, with few exceptions, he maintained his professionalism throughout his service. He made the transition from serving in a frontier cavalry army to a modern field army, and he was one of the major players in that progression. Though he seemed to be resistant to academic military training schools, he consistently supported continuing military education. His stron-gest suit was always to be his troop training and handling.

Following the war, Bullard wrote several books. These created quite a stir, particularly *Personalities and Reminiscences of the War.* Although his appraisal of the entire AEF led to much censure, the various African-American organizations were extremely distressed by his description of the difficulties that black officers in particular and the entire 92d Division as a whole endured in training and at the front. Bullard died on Sept. 11, 1947.

George B. Clark

See also HARBORD, JAMES GUTHRIE; SOISSONS; SUMMERALL, CHARLES PELOT

Bibliography

Bullard, Robert Lee. *American Soldiers Also Fought.* New York: Longman, Green, 1936.

———. *Personalities and Reminiscences of the War.* Garden City, NY: Doubleday, Page, 1925.

Millett, Allan. *The General: Robert L. Bullard and Officership in the United States Army, 1881–1925.* Westport, CT: Greenwood Press, 1975.

Bullitt, William Christian (1891–1967)

William Christian Bullitt was born in Philadelphia on Jan. 25, 1891, to a wealthy, prestigious family. Nurtured in the progressive ideas of the period, Bullitt acquired a deep feeling for the rights of man and a professed dislike for the rigidity of the ruling classes. His family traveled extensively, and he became familiar with Russia and the western European countries at an early age. When war broke out in 1914, Bullitt became a special correspondent for the Philadelphia *Public Ledger* reporting on events in Germany and Austria. His experience in Europe and his knowledgeable reporting led to a position in 1917 with the State Department's Western European Division. A friendship with Col. Edward M. House prompted an invitation in 1918 to join the American Commission to Negotiate Peace, where he was to give political and military updates to the American commissioners. In light of the Bolshevik Revolution in Russia, Secretary of State Robert Lansing ordered Bullitt to go to Russia to study conditions there and to determine what terms the Soviet government was ready to accept to become a part of the peace process.

An enthusiastic Bullitt, accompanied by his friend Lincoln Steffens, made his way to Russia, where the two soon obtained an audience with Lenin. Bullitt laid out to Lenin the conditions set forth by the peacemakers in Paris, which included the proposition that representatives of the Soviet government should be brought to Paris along with representatives of the other Russian governments, an immediate armistice among the Russian factions, the reestablishment of economic relations between the Allies and Russia, and a withdrawal of all Allied troops from Russia. Lenin's counterproposals were similar to the proposals Bullitt had offered—all Allied armies as well as support for the White Army would be withdrawn, and the blockade of all Russian ports would stop. In return, White Army members would be granted a general amnesty and at least a portion of the debts owed to foreigners would be repaid. The offer had to be accepted by April 10, 1919.

From his previous conversations with Secretary Lansing and communications with Philip Kerr, British Prime Minister Lloyd George's confidential secretary, Bullitt was convinced that the Allied chiefs in Paris would certainly accept the terms offered by Lenin. Bullitt was shocked and disillusioned when Woodrow Wilson decided not to make Bullitt's report public. Lloyd George, likewise, completely refuted any knowledge of Bullitt's mission to Russia.

Deeply hurt by this apparent betrayal of his efforts, Bullitt resigned from the State Department on May 17, 1919. He would later testify before the Senate Foreign Relations Committee to denounce the treaty the Allied leaders had made in Paris and to rebuke bitterly the leadership of President Wilson.

Bullitt remained out of the public eye until President Franklin D. Roosevelt called upon him to represent the United States in Moscow while the United States was negotiating the recognition of the Soviet Union. As the first ambassador to the Soviet Union (1933–1936) Bullitt looked forward enthusiastically to his work with his Russian friends. Within a few months, however, Bullitt again was terribly disillusioned by the intransigence he found among the Soviet diplomats and with Joseph Stalin. He rapidly became a hard-line anti-Communist, and, in 1936, he gladly accepted his appointment as ambassador to France. He then served as ambassador at large (1941–1942) and as special assistant to the secretary of the navy in 1942. He retired from public service and died on Feb. 15, 1967.

Charles Blackburn

See also PARIS PEACE CONFERENCE

Bibliography

Brownell, Will, and Richard Billings. *So Close to Greatness: A Biography of William C. Bullitt*. New York: Macmillan, 1987.

Bullitt, Orville H., ed. *For the President. Personal and Secret Correspondence between Franklin D. Roosevelt and William C. Bullitt*. Boston: Houghton Mifflin, 1972.

Bullitt, William C. *The Bullitt Mission to Russia*. Westport, CT: Hyperion Press, 1977.

Bundy, Omar (1862–1940)

Omar Bundy attended Asbury College, now DePauw University, for a year before entering West Point. He graduated in 1883 with a commission in the infantry and went to serve on the frontier, first against the Crows in Montana and then the Sioux in South Dakota. During the Spanish-American War, Bundy was brevetted major at the siege of Santiago. He then served in the Philippines and at Fort Leavenworth. In 1905, Bundy returned to the Philippines where he distinguished himself leading a column against the Moros on Jolo Island. Returning to the United States, he was promoted to lieutenant colonel in March 1911 and then entered the Army War College. In 1914, he was promoted to the rank of colonel and assigned to command the 16th Infantry in El Paso, Texas. Bundy was promoted to brigadier general in 1917 and ordered to France to command the 1st Infantry Brigade, 1st Division.

In November 1917, he assumed command of the newly formed 2d Division, having already been promoted to the rank of major general. It was to be his good fortune to command the division that helped stem the tide of the third German offensive of 1918 at an area just north and west of Château-Thierry. His men performed remarkably at Belleau Wood but sustained enormous losses in the process, particularly the 4th (Marine) Brigade. Bundy and Gen. James Harbord, the army officer who commanded the 4th Brigade, gained reputations that would stand both well in the days ahead. When Bundy protested the promotion of Robert L. Bullard as III Corps commander over him in the summer of 1918, Pershing placed Bundy in command of the VI Corps. In September 1918, he moved to the VIII Corps and in November Bundy returned to the United States to command Camp Lee in Virginia.

In September 1920, Bundy took command of the VII Corps Area at Fort Crooks, Nebraska. In 1922, he reassumed the rank of major general in command of the Philippine Division. Two years later he was transferred to the V Corps Area at Columbus, Ohio, which he commanded until his retirement in 1925.

George Clark

Bibliography

"Omar Bundy." In *Annual Report of the Association of Graduates of the United States Military Academy of West Point, New York.*

Bureau of Investigation

On July 26, 1908, Attorney General Charles Bonaparte drew upon his department's "miscellaneous expense" fund to create an investigative division within the Department of Justice, the Bureau of Investigation. Staffed by twenty-four agents, the newly created bureau was assured neither continued existence nor future growth, for, in the preceding year, Congress had adopted riders to appropriations bills for the Treasury and Justice departments prohibiting the attorney general from contracting, as had been done heretofore, for the temporary investigative assistance of Secret Service agents. Congressional proponents defended their action by commenting darkly on the inherent threat to constitutional government posed by a national police force, citing the case of the secret police of tsarist Russia.

Inevitably, Bonaparte's decision invited congressional opposition. He was invited to testify before a House Appropriations Committee in January 1909, at which time he assured committee members that the bureau would not monitor political activities but would only investigate violations of interstate commerce and antitrust laws. The attorney general stressed the need for administrative flexibility and assumed personal responsibility to ensure that bureau activities were properly conducted. Committee members accepted these assurances and accordingly recommended full funding for the bureau.

The bureau profited from the new consensus that had evolved during the Progressive era that supported an increased federal regulatory role over business and personal misconduct. Having increased to 100 agents by 1914 following passage of the Mann Act of 1910, the number of bureau agents rose to 300 by 1917 because, after the outbreak of war in Europe, the bureau began to investigate suspected violations of the neutrality laws of the 1790s. Legislation in 1916 authorized the bureau to investigate suspected foreign agents if directly requested by the secretary of state. This concern about foreign agents intensified after the United States entered World War I in April 1917, with the result that bureau investigations focused on radical and antiwar dissent. Pacifist, socialist, anarchist, and communist groups were suspected of aiding the nation's adversaries. Alien radicals in particular became the target of a specially created alien enemy registration section within the Department of Justice, headed by a recent George Washington University Law School graduate, J. Edgar Hoover.

Bureau investigations no longer focused exclusively on economic crimes. They also scrutinized suspect associations and activities—whether seeking to identify so-called "slackers," monitoring the speeches and publications of antiwar liberals and radicals or planning and conducting the highly publicized raids during which thousands of alien radicals were arrested in 1919 and 1920. Nor were investigations confined to law enforcement. Agents were also motivated by a desire to contain the influence of dissident organizations and their leaders. In this effort bureau officials established questionable relations with politically conservative activists.

In March 1917, when faced with budgetary limitations and a shortage of agents, Attorney General Thomas W. Gregory approved a plan proposed by a Chicago-based business group, the American Protective League (APL). Under this arrangement, APL members were to provide transportation to bureau agents and to forward to their bureau contacts any information they secured about suspected pro-German activities. Given the conservative orientation of this group, APL reports invariably focused on the political and labor union activities of the nation's sizable immigrant community. Bureau officials welcomed these reports, and, in concert

B

with APL members, they planned and executed a series of mass draft raids in major cities, notably Minneapolis, Chicago, and New York, ostensibly to identify draft violators, during the summer of 1918.

The resulting adverse publicity raised questions about the bureau's adherence to the law and respect for due process. This furor did not result in any restrictions on the bureau's authority, however, owing to the prevailing conviction that the nation confronted a serious internal security threat. The Wilson administration's sole response was to prohibit APL members from representing themselves as Secret Service agents, implying that the abuse stemmed from overzealousness by these patriotic volunteers.

These publicized abuses, moreover, were not aberrations. Indeed, bureau investigations targeted radical activists, not necessarily because their actions suggested a willingness to act as German agents, but because of their political dissent, whether during the prewar period opposing United States involvement in the war or after April 1917 opposing the administration's mobilization and conscription policies. In September 1917, for example, bureau agents simultaneously raided and arrested the local and national leadership of the Industrial Workers of the World (IWW), ostensibly for participating in a conspiracy to violate the Selective Service and Espionage acts.

Despite postwar retrenchment, bureau officials did not abandon their antiradical mission. During the 1920s, bureau agents continued, if more cautiously and circumspectly, to monitor radical activities, as the duties and responsibilities of the agency expanded to meet new challenges, and grew into today's Federal Bureau of Investigation.

Athan Theoharis

See also INDUSTRIAL WORKERS OF THE WORLD

Bibliography

Jensen, Joan. *The Price of Vigilance.* Chicago: Rand McNally, 1968.
Murray, Robert. *Red Scare: A Study of National Hysteria, 1919–1920.* New York: McGraw-Hill, 1964.
Powers, Richard Gid. *Secrecy and Power: The Life of J. Edgar Hoover.* New York: Free Press, 1987.
Theoharis, Athan, and John S. Cox. *The Boss: J. Edgar Hoover and the Great American Inquisition.* Philadelphia: Temple University Press, 1988.
Williams, David. "The Bureau of Investigation and Its Critics, 1919–1921: The Origins of Federal Political Surveillance." *Journal of American History* 68 (December 1981).

Burleson, Albert Sidney (1863–1937)

When Woodrow Wilson became the twenty-eighth President of the United States in 1913, he chose Albert Sidney Burleson to be his postmaster general. Burleson was perhaps the most controversial member of the President's cabinet, primarily because of his strict enforcement of the Espionage Act of 1917.

Burleson, a Democrat, was first elected to Congress in 1898. He effectively represented the interests of his constituents from Texas—farmers and small businessmen. On Capitol Hill, Burleson tended to vote along party lines and gained influence with Democratic leaders. At the 1912 Democratic Presidential Convention in Baltimore, he played an important role in helping Wilson secure the nomination. He owed his appointment as postmaster general to this and to the support of his longtime friend Col. Edward M. House, Wilson's confidant.

As Wilson's postmaster general, Burleson served as an intermediary between the President and Congress. A superb professional politician, he effectively used patronage to help win support for the administration's legislative proposals. His power was expanded on June 5, 1917, when Congress passed the Espionage Act in response to America's entry into World War I. Under this act, the postmaster general was given virtual dictatorial powers to prohibit from the mails publications that he deemed to be "advocating or urging treason, insurrection, or forcible resistance to any law of the United States." Burleson interpreted this legislation liberally and used the act to retract the mailing privileges of certain ethnic groups, such as German Americans, radical labor organizations, and left-wing political parties. The American Socialist Party became his first, and primary, target. A large organization, with over 600,000 members, the party was vehemently antiwar. Its members promised to resist conscription, censorship, and the curtailment of labor's right to strike.

Burleson acted quickly to stop Socialist mailings, denying postal access to several Socialist newspapers even before Wilson signed the Espionage Act into law. The first publication he removed from the mails was the Socialist paper the Halletsville, Texas, *Rebel*, which, interestingly, had exposed the eviction of tenant farmers and their replacement by unpaid prison labor on land Burleson owned. During the summer of 1917, Burleson withdrew mailing privileges from more than a dozen other Socialist publications. He said that he would not ban Socialist material unless it contained treasonable or seditious matter, but he believed that most Socialist papers were seditious.

Burleson's tactics did not stop with Socialist newspapers and periodicals. For example, he banned a single issue of the *Masses*, a left-wing radical publication, because he felt it contained "offensive" matter; he then refused to restore the magazine's second-class mailing permit on the ground that the magazine had skipped an issue—the issue he had banned—and was therefore ineligible for a second-class mailing permit. Burleson suppressed another journal because it published a suggestion that the President should finance the war through higher taxes and less borrowing, yet another because it reprinted Thomas Jefferson's opinion that Ireland should be a republic, and still another for expressing doubt that Britain would keep its promise to make Palestine an independent Jewish state. He even banned from the mails Thorstein Veblen's *Imperial Germany and the Industrial Revolution*, a publication George Creel's Committee for Public Information wanted to use to show the inferiority of German society. These methods of enforcing the Espionage Act soon came to be characterized as "Burlesonism" and led Colonel House to remark that Burleson was the most belligerent member of the cabinet.

President Wilson did little to curb Burleson's actions, but he did show concern over the zeal displayed by his postmaster general. Late in 1917, the President suggested to Burleson that he act with caution in censorship activities. But Burleson did not alter his tactics. When Wilson later confronted Burleson with complaints about censorship, the stubborn postmaster general threatened to resign and the President relented. Moreover, Burleson apparently had support in Congress, which extended his powers by passing the Trading with the Enemy Act later in 1917. This act required all foreign-language newspapers and publica-

tions to submit English translations to the Post Office of all news and editorial articles concerning the United States government. Although it stipulated that the President could waive this requirement for publications with proven loyalty, Wilson delegated this function to Burleson.

Throughout the period of American participation in World War I—and for a time after the Armistice—Burleson had broad powers to censor and suppress publications using the United States mails. Congress and the U.S. courts, for the most part, supported his activities. Newspapers and magazines determined by Burleson to be in violation of the Espionage or the Trading with the Enemy acts, were cut off from their subscribers and frequently went out of business. This process continued as late as 1921, when the Supreme Court upheld the postmaster general's decision to deny second-class postal privileges to the *Milwaukee Leader*. Although Burleson's influence lessened somewhat after the war, he remained at the head of the Post Office until Wilson left office in 1921. However, his wartime activities helped fuel the "Red Scare" that spread throughout America after World War I.

However harsh and rigid Burleson appeared to his critics, he did make many positive changes in postal service, such as expanding rural mail service and the parcel post system, centralizing many department functions, and initiating air-mail service. While Burleson's censorship tactics did not bring him fame or make him a national hero, Wilson relied on his leadership to help encourage national unity during the uncertain and often confusing times of World War I.

Brenda Roth

See also CENSORSHIP; ESPIONAGE ACT; TRADING WITH THE ENEMY ACT

Bibliography

Kennedy, David M. *Over Here: The First World War and American Society*. New York: Oxford University Press, 1980.

Link, Arthur S. *Woodrow Wilson and the Progressive Era: 1910–1917*. New York: Harper, 1954.

Peterson, H.C., and Gilbert C. Fite. *Opponents of War*. Madison: University of Wisconsin Press, 1957.

B

Scheiber, Harry N. *The Wilson Administration and Civil Liberties, 1917–1921.* Ithaca, NY: Cornell University Press, 1960.

Walworth, Arthur. *Woodrow Wilson.* New York: Norton, 1978.

Butler, Smedley Darlington (1881–1940)

Smedley Darlington Butler was born in West Chester, Pennsylvania. He left high school at the onset of the Spanish-American War and was commissioned a marine second lieutenant at age sixteen. After three weeks training at basic school in Washington, D.C., he was posted to Guantanamo Bay. He later served aboard the USS *Newark* and participated in the Philippine Insurrection and the Boxer Rebellion, as well as marine landings in Honduras, Panama, Nicaragua, Veracruz, and Haiti.

After besieging headquarters with requests for duty abroad, Butler finally obtained command of the 13th Regiment. He sailed for Brest, France, in September 1918. There the regiment was ordered to guard various posts and depots nowhere near the front, and Butler became the commander of Camp Pontanezen, the embarkation camp at Brest.

The camp was in a disastrous state when he assumed command, but within hours he began a massive effort to reorganize and revitalize every aspect of life at Pontanezen. His nickname "Old Gimlet Eye," was changed to "General Duckboard" after his request for surplus duckboards stored at Brest was denied. Butler mustered the inmates of the camp and proceeded to "liberate" the duckboards and other supplies that were needed to rebuild Pontanezen. His efforts, and those of his permanent staff, to turn the camp around made Butler a hero to both its occupants and headquarters and saved the lives of many doughboys who passed through the camp during the raging Spanish influenza epidemic. His drive and organizational ability earned him both the Army and Navy Distinguished Service Medals and the French Order of the Black Star.

Butler returned to the United States in August 1919. He assumed command of Quantico in 1920 and held a variety of posts both stateside and in China until his retirement in 1931. Butler carried on a second career as a writer and lecturer until his death in Philadelphia in 1940.

George B. Clark

Bibliography

McClellan, Edwin N. *The United States Marine Corps in the World War.* Washington, DC: Government Printing Office, 1920.

Schmidt, Hans. *Maverick Marine, General Smedley Butler and the Contradictions of American Military History.* Lexington: University of Kentucky Press, 1987.

C

Cadorna, Luigi (1850–1928)

Luigi Giovanni Antonio Carlo Giuseppe Cadorna was born in Pallanza, Italy, son of General Raffaele Cadorna. He entered the Military Academy of Turin in 1865 and in 1870, under his father's command, took part in the occupation of Rome. From 1880 to 1890, Cadorna was promoted from captain of the Bersaglieri to major and division commander of the army. His was one of the most admired careers in the history of the Italian military.

On July 11, 1914, King Victor Emmanuel III appointed Cadorna chief of the General Staff and commander of the Italian Army. He took command of a poorly trained force and reorganized it. When Italy entered the war on May 24, 1915, there were 400,000 Italian soldiers on the front. Cadorna detailed his strategy in a manual entitled Attacco Frontale in which he called for siegelike attacks against the enemy's positions.

Cadorna applied his strategy against the Austro-Hungarians in four offensives along the Isonzo River (June–December 1915). The results were extremely costly to the Italian Army: 280,000 men dead, wounded, or missing. The fifth offensive on the Tolmino produced no success. Then, in May 1916, the Austro-Hungarians and Germans launched a joint offensive which decimated some 140,000 Italian troops. Cadorna's strategy again proved ineffective and costly. Nonetheless, he launched the seventh offensive on the Isonzo, and Italian troops occupied the city of Gorizia. Even this partially successful offensive cost the Italian Army 20,000 additional casualties. From October 1916 to August 1917, Cadorna launched the eighth, ninth, tenth, and eleventh offensives against the enemy. The results were insignificant, and the cost in human lives and military equipment was extraordinarily high.

In September 1917, the German General Staff laid out the plan for operation Waffetrennen, which ultimately led to the defeat of the Italian Army at Caporetto that October. From October 24 to November 4, the Italians retreated to the line of the Piave River. The defeat, the worst of the war, and the rout of the army, a national catastrophe, ended Cadorna's military career. On Nov. 9, 1917, Gen. Armando Diaz replaced him.

General Cadorna then served as the Italian representative to the Inter-Allied Council in Paris. However, in January 1918, he was summoned to Rome to appear before a special commission of inquiry. The commission's final report found Cadorna and other military commanders "responsible" for the disaster at Caporetto. With the advent of fascism, Luigi Cadorna was "rehabilitated" as a national leader, and on Nov. 3, 1924, King Victor Emmanuel III named him Marshal of Italy. Cadorna died on Dec. 21, 1928.

Pellegrino Nazzaro

See also CAPORETTO, BATTLE OF

Bibliography

Cadorna, Luigi. *Altre pagine sulla Grande Guerra*. Milan: Treves, 1925.
———. *La guerra all fronte italiana fino alla linea d'arresto del Piave e del Grappa, 24 maggio 1915–9 novembre 1917*. Milan: Treves, 1923.
———. *Pagine polemiche*. Milan: Garzanti, 1950.
Camera die Deputati. *Comitati Segreti sulla Condotta della Guerra, giugno–dicembre*

1917. Rome: Archivio Storico, Camera dei Deputati, Segretariato Generale, 1967.

Capello, Luigi. *Caporetto, perché.* Turin: Einaudi, 1967.

Cameron, George Hamilton (1861–1944)

George Hamilton Cameron was born in Illinois. He graduated from the United States Military Academy in 1883 and accepted a commission in the cavalry. After serving on the Great Plains, he fought in the Philippine Insurrection and then commanded the Big Bend District on the Texas-Mexican border. In addition, he taught at West Point, the Mounted Service School, and the War College and served on the General Staff.

With the entry of the United States into the First World War, Cameron became a temporary brigadier general, commanding the 40th Division's 80th Infantry Brigade made up of California National Guardsmen at Camp Kearney, California, throughout the fall of 1917. In December, the War Department ordered him east to take command of the newly activated 4th Division at Camp Greene, North Carolina, and promoted him to major general. In March 1918, over 10,000 men joined the division and the following month the 4th sailed for France.

From May until July, the division trained with the British and French armies. In mid-July, Cameron's men moved into the frontlines with the French. At first the division was in reserve or held only small sections of the front. As the Allied Aisne-Marne offensive developed, however, the 4th relieved the U.S. 42d Division near the town of Mareuil-en-Dole in early August and entered into its first division-sized attack. Inexperience, especially among the junior officers, hampered operations at first, but Cameron kept the division moving forward. After two days of fighting, his men reached the Vesle River near the village of St. Thibault.

The commander of the American Expeditionary Force (AEF), John J. Pershing, was very pleased with Cameron's performance and promoted him to command the V Corps. With this command came enormous new responsibilities. Pershing planned to use the corps in his drive to pinch off the St. Mihiel salient. Cameron had to complete the organization of his staff and make his headquarters ready for battle in less than a month. The V Corps' objective was the town of Vigneulles to the southeast, where it was to link up with the U.S. IV Corps advancing from the opposite direction. The attack began in the early hours of September 12 and moved quickly against sporadic German resistance. By 2:15 A.M. the following morning, Cameron's 26th Division was in the outskirts of Vigneulles and by 6:00 A.M. had linked up with the leading elements of the IV Corps.

Within just a few days of the seizure of Vigneulles, Cameron shifted his corps headquarters to the Meuse-Argonne sector to take part in the offensive about to be unleashed there. Cameron's Corps held the center position in the U.S. First Army's line with orders to penetrate three German defensive lines and seize the town of Romagne. To accomplish this mission, the First Army gave him four American divisions, none of which had ever been under his command. Worse still, two of the four had never been in combat before and a third had only seen service in quiet sectors.

The infantry began its attack on September 26. Fighting all along the First Army front was severe, and Cameron's corps inched forward but failed to take its objectives on schedule. Stiff fighting continued into October and only after bringing two veteran divisions into the line did Cameron begin to make satisfactory progress. Pershing, however, had expected much more from Cameron and removed him from command of the V Corps on October 11. Cameron never fully understood the reasons for his relief and blamed his fall on the ill will of First Army Chief of Staff Hugh Drum.

Cameron briefly led the 4th Division once more, but late in October he returned to the United States to command Camp Gordon, Georgia. Following the war, he reverted to his prewar rank of colonel and assumed command of the Cavalry School. From 1921 until his retirement in 1924, he served as the chief of staff of the 76th Division, Organized Reserve. George Cameron died in 1944.

Richard Kehrberg

Bibliography

Pershing, John J. *My Experiences in the World War.* 2 vols. New York: Stokes, 1931.

Smythe, Donald. *Pershing: General of the Armies.* Bloomington: Indiana University Press, 1986.

Camouflage

Deception has always been a military tool, but most forms of what we call camouflage today had their roots in the First World War. As early as November 1914, the French began working on camouflage in an effort to employ the country's artists for military services other than combat. In England, the British camouflage service was formed in January 1916 under the camouflaged title, "Special Works Park, R.E." By the end of the war, camouflage had proliferated into a multitude of forms used by both the Allies and Central Powers in almost every military endeavor.

The French claim the development of painted camouflage. To conceal soldiers and equipment from rapidly improving air reconnaissance, the French painter and military telephonist Victor Lucian Guirand de Scevola suggested concealing artillery with new "painted-in-earth" colors. Soon after the First Battle of the Marne, Marshal Joffre and President Poincaré approved Scevola's idea and, in February 1915, created the first official *service de camouflage*.

The British are credited with the invention of naval "dazzle paint," a style of painted camouflage unique to World War I. Before the war zoologist Sir John Graham Kerr had recognized that all-gray ships are easily seen. In 1914 he suggested to the British admiralty that they paint ships with multicolored patterns instead of one uniform color. Although the Admiralty rejected the idea at first, it was accepted in 1917 and carried out by LtCmdr. Norman Wilkinson. The goal of dazzle paint was not to render a ship invisible but rather to confuse the image seen through a submarine's periscope. The striking and bizarre patterns of dazzle paint worked with the reflections of sun and sky on water to break up the vertical and horizontal contours that identify a ship. Dazzle paint foiled enemy attempts to determine an individual ship's location and direction, but it was especially effective for whole convoys of ships. Because of dazzle paint, destroyers were sometimes mistaken for merchant or fishing boats—with unfortunate consequences for the observers.

By 1916, the Germans were discovering as many ingenious forms of camouflage as their opponents. One German camouflage painter was the expressionist Franz Marc, who served almost continuously in the war and died in the Battle of Verdun in 1916.

Camouflage projects brought a great variety of people into the war effort. American women, for instance, worked on camouflage in New York and formed the Women's Reserve Camouflage Corps, part of the National League for Women's Service. But most "camoufleurs" as they were called, were male artists. By 1918, France had over 3,000 artists working on camouflage, and not all of them were painters. Listed in the French camouflage corps in February 1917, for example, were 190 painters, 74 carpenters, 6 sculptors, 5 moldmakers, 5 cartoonists, and 5 architects.

In the United States, a research center for naval camouflage was established at the Eastman Kodak Company Laboratory in Rochester, New York. George de Forest Brush, Sherry Fry, Wilford Conrow, and Homer Saint-Gaudens were among the American artists enlisted for camouflage work.

By the end of the war, camoufleurs from all sides had created an abundant array of concealments. Besides the painting of materiel and vehicles, airstrips and the roofs of buildings were often painted to look like fields. Hangars and other buildings were painted so that the shadows they threw would not make them stand out. Earlier in the war, painted linen was thrown over trenches that were under construction, though later the threat of fire led troops to use garnished wires instead of canvas, linen, or netting.

Decoys and dummies were also important parts of camouflage. False observation posts and trenches were constructed to convince the enemy that they were being watched. False batteries, dummy tanks, and dummy infantrymen deceived the enemy as to troop strengths or locations; the fakes could also lead the enemy to reveal their defensive organization. When a lookout post was needed, camoufleurs would choose a dead tree that stood near the trenches and construct a replica of it. They would then wait until night and remove the real tree, replacing it with the iron-plated duplicate. An imitation branch could contain a periscope, and the tree might even be equipped with a telephone. The same trick was used with papier-mâché imitations of dead horses. A whole village could be concealed at night by extinguishing its lights and constructing lights and landmarks nearby as decoys for night raids. Both the Allies and the Central Powers built raised construction that looked like roads from the air but allowed the troops beneath to move undetected.

Both sides also used forms of what might be called "auditory camouflage." Troops wrapped cloth around wagon wheels or horses hooves to dampen the sounds of their movements. The Canadians used dummy radio signals to confuse their opponents at the Battle of Amiens. At Cambrai, the first mass tank attack of the war, the British masked the sound of the gathering tanks with the sound of low-flying airplanes over their enemy's lines for two days before the attack.

One of the war's most popular means of camouflage was the smoke bomb. Smoke screens were used on both land and sea. Troops or ships would emerge from a smoke screen to make a surprise attack; but if the wind shifted and blew away their cover, the attack would no longer be a surprise. At Cambrai, the British feigned attacks on the Germans by placing dummy infantrymen in smoke clouds. Smoke screens also played a part in the Somme and Loos battles and—unsuccessfully for the Allies—at Zeebrugge harbor.

Patricia Irwin

Bibliography

Behrens, Roy R. *Art and Camouflage: Concealment and Deception in Nature, Art and War.* Cedar Falls, IA: North American Review, 1981.

Crutwell, C.R.M.F. *A History of the Great War.* Oxford, UK: Clarendon Press, 1934.

Edmonds, James E. *History of the Great War: France and Belgium, 1914.* London: Macmillan, 1932.

Kern, Stephen. *The Culture of Time and Space, 1880–1918.* Cambridge: Harvard University Press, 1983.

Shapiro, Theda. *Painters and Politics: The European Avant-Garde and Society, 1900–1925.* New York: Elsevier, 1976.

Campbell, Douglas (1896–1990)

Douglas Campbell was born in San Francisco in 1896. He entered Harvard University in 1913 and with the outbreak of war in 1917 enlisted in the U.S. Army Air Service. Following flight training in the fall of 1917 at the American flying school at Issoudon, France, he joined Eddie Rickenbacker's outfit, the 94th Squadron, 1st Pursuit Group in March 1918. On April 14, 1918, during his first day of combat operations, Campbell, flying a French Nieuport 28, entered into the first dogfight between German and American AEF pilots. Within minutes of takeoff, Campbell shot down his first plane, an Albatross. While his friend Lt. Alan Winslow actually shot down a German flier a few seconds before Campbell, Winslow had been trained by the French. Hence, Campbell became the first American-trained pilot to score a kill.

Campbell did not think of himself as a good shot and thus had to maneuver his plane as close as twenty-five to fifty feet to the enemy before he fired. In World War I, pilots were fighting other men, not distant weapon systems and targets. Campbell's rise to air ace went rapidly. On May 18, a little over a month after his first kill, he shot down a second plane. The next day, while engaging another German biplane, his guns jammed. Campbell had to avoid the German and repair his machine guns. He did both, and after a short, violent action, the enemy plane caught fire and plunged to the earth. Two weeks later, on May 27, Campbell found three German monoplanes flying in a loose formation over Montsec, France. He attacked all three, scoring one kill and forcing the other two back across German lines. The following day, he engaged another formation, shooting down one (unconfirmed) and causing the other five planes to retreat. On May 31, the twenty-two-year-old shot down his fifth confirmed plane and earned the title of "ace." His last major action came on June 5, when he attacked two planes. Although he was shot in the back, he managed to drive one aircraft to the ground and send the other fleeing for its lines. He was hospitalized, and the war ended before he was released from the hospital.

After the war, Campbell went to work for W.R. Grace and Co. In 1935, he joined the South-American-owned Pan American Grace Airways (PANAGRA), and in 1948, he became its general manager. Campbell died on Oct. 18, 1990. Among his treasured possessions was the Croix de Guerre awarded to him by the French for his heroism, skill, and dedication to duty over their skies in the spring of 1918.

Mark R. Grandstaff

Bibliography

Adjutant General of the Army. *American Decorations.* Washington, DC: Government Printing Office, 1927.

Rickenbacker, Eddie. *Fighting the Flying Circus.* New York: Stokes, 1919.

Thayer, Lucien. *America's First Eagles*. Mesa, AZ: Champlin Fighter Museum Press, 1983.

Camp MacArthur Riot

The so-called Camp MacArthur Riot occurred on the night of July 29, 1917, when members of the 1st Battalion, 24th Infantry, fired shots in downtown Waco, Texas, after protesting racial segregation and alleged police brutality. Although without casualties, the incident resembles in motivation and execution the notorious Camp Logan riot in Houston one month later and intensified prejudice against black soldiers in World War I.

The soldiers had arrived that morning at the central Texas city of approximately 33,000 to guard the construction site of Camp MacArthur, one of sixteen National Guard training sites selected by the War Department. Although the regiment had performed with distinction in the American West, Cuba, the Philippines, and Mexico, the stationing of black troops in a southern community with recent experiences of racial violence presented inherent difficulties.

Military and community leaders sought to contain the potentially explosive situation. The chamber of commerce, press, and city administration muted criticism of the black garrison, emphasizing its expected brief stay. The army command repeatedly reminded the troops en route from Columbus, New Mexico, to obey all ordinances and laws. Upon arrival at the Waco depot, Capt. C.F. Andrews, battalion commander, conferred with local civic and peace officers. Police Chief Guy McNamara consented to the provost guard patroling the town nightly and delivering to Andrews any soldier arrested for disturbing the peace. That evening Andrews dispatched six provost guards to the police station, limited passes to 50 percent of the 600 infantrymen, and imposed an 11:00 P.M. curfew.

The precautions proved insufficient. Soldiers complained of racial insults from civilians and harassment by police, who overshadowed the compliant provost guards. Merchants, in turn, charged servicemen with flaunting segregation ordinances and adopting a defiant attitude. Tensions escalated when Private Willie Jones was struck in the head while police cleared a sidewalk in front of a black establishment. As an angry white crowd gathered, some of Jones's comrades whisked him to safety and plotted an armed return.

Perhaps a dozen soldiers gathered weapons from the camp, with about half that number continuing into town. Alerted by a corporal, Andrews sealed off the camp, conducted roll call, and ordered an arms inspection. Capt. James Higgins, Company C commander, led a security force after the missing men. When a policeman sighted the soldiers in an alley, Higgins received permission to move his detail alone to the opening. This drew a volley of erratic fire from the alleyway, the renegades escaping into the night. Meanwhile, police apprehended Jones, who revealed to Higgins the identity of the culprits.

A loud public outcry, an army investigation, and a series of court-martials followed. Col. G.O. Cress, inspector general of the Southern Department, filed a report on August 1 blaming young inexperienced enlistees. Discrediting allegations of police brutality or conspiracy as motivations for the shooting, he judged the incident spontaneous and noted that neither police nor provost guards had considered prior activities worthy of report. Cress acknowledged the existence in Waco of some disreputable whites who could inspire future problems.

The military trials, concluded on August 21, convicted six defendants. James Johnson, Howard Hood, Walter Lusk, Willie Lewis, and James Mitchell received dishonorable discharges and five years at hard labor. Luther Briggs, cited by some participants as the organizer, drew a dishonorable discharge and ten years at hard labor, later reduced to five years. The First Battalion departed Waco on August 25.

Though frightening in its potential and destructive to race relations, civil-military cooperation, the decision by Higgins to approach the alley with only military personnel, and the errancy of the firing precluded a more serious confrontation between Camp MacArthur and Waco.

Garna L. Christian

Bibliography

Christian, Garna L. "The Ordeal and the Prize: The 24th Infantry and Camp MacArthur." *Military Affairs* (April 1986).

Canadian-American Relations

The unforeseen effects of war on the course of United States foreign policy are of particular relevance to an understanding of twentieth-century relations with Canada. At the beginning of the First World War, officials in the Wilson administration did not realize in what ways the war would mark a departure from the past and set a precedent for future relations with Canada. With the decline of Britain as the world's leading commercial and financial center, new trade and investment opportunities opened up in Canada for the United States. The war also highlighted Canada's contribution to Allied industrial defense production and its importance to American defense policy in the North Atlantic. During the course of the war the United States began to view Canada as an autonomous dominion rather than as a semiautonomous colony and this posed new challenges and opportunities for American postwar foreign policy.

Prior to the First World War, Canada frequently had been subjected to coercive diplomacy, the threat of annexation, and the possible use of military force to settle boundary disputes. Until the negotiation of the 1871 Treaty of Washington, Canada was perceived as the last bastion of British military power in North America and was therefore thought to pose a potential threat to the existing territorial integrity of the United States and to future westward expansion. In the period from 1871 to 1914, War and State Department officials no longer perceived Canada as a threat to the United States. Before 1917, U.S. national security planners assumed that Britain and Canada would look after the defense of the northern frontier and the North Atlantic sea lanes. The border with Canada, so often referred to at the time as the "longest undefended frontier" in the world, required only routine patrols. Relations between the two countries were amicable though not intimate.

Between 1914 and 1917, the course of United States relations with Canada was defined by President Wilson's larger objectives with regard to the war in Europe and his concerns about how to deal with an empire that imposed a colonial status on its overseas subjects. As to Canada, Wilson quickly realized that he was dealing with a special case insofar as Canada was a semiautonomous dominion within the British Empire. At first he believed that relations with his northern neighbor should

be in keeping with his neutrality guidelines outlined in August 1914. It should be emphasized, however, that Wilson in his first term of office was not as well informed about Canada as were his predecessors, Presidents Roosevelt and Taft. Wilson's benign neglect was of some advantage to Canada because the President did not attempt to continue the policy of previous administrations, which aimed at either weakening Canada's ties to the British Empire or developing an interlocking economic system in North America that could lead to political annexation.

During the early stages of the First World War, Canada became a notable example of how the policy of neutrality would be put into practice. Two weeks after Woodrow Wilson issued his proclamation of neutrality, the President asked American citizens to be impartial in thought as well as in deed. Over the next three years however, that policy was interpreted in such a way that it had little impact on loans, raw material exports, and arms sales to Canada. On the eve of the British declaration of war, a Seattle shipbuilder made arrangements for the sale of two submarines to the province of British Columbia, which in turn immediately sent them to the federal Canadian government. In 1915, a deal was worked out between Bethlehem Steel and Canadian Vickers Shipbuilding whereby submarine components manufactured in New Jersey would be sent to the Vickers yard in Montreal for final assembly. Certain compromises with regard to American neutrality were also made regarding the export of Canadian goods to the United States. For example, in an effort to prevent the Germans from acquiring Canadian nickel purchased south of the border, the Wilson administration allowed French and British consulate officials to name which companies would be permitted to buy nickel refined by companies in the United States.

It was during the First World War that the American government adopted specific financial measures to improve trade relations with Canada. In so doing, the Wilson administration not only provided new opportunities for American businessmen, but also made it clear that it saw the expansion of Canadian defense industries as important to the security of the United States. In contrast to its former indifference to the state of its northern neighbor's economy, the American government in 1915 approved a private loan designed to facilitate Canada's defense production; additional assistance followed in 1916 and 1917. When the War Industries Board imposed controls on steel and coal exports, which had the unintentional effect of disrupting Canadian defense production, satisfactory adjustments were made. According to Secretary of the Treasury William G. McAdoo, Canada was singled out for "distinctive assistance" with regard to the regulation of fuel controls, wheat marketing, and steel and coal exports in accordance with the dominion's requirements. The secretary recommended a continentalist approach to American defense production that involved "pooling our resources and our endeavors." These measures marked the beginning of the policy of "exemptionalism" that was to be the hallmark of continental relations during and after the Second World War.

The policy of exemptionalism was reflected in the efforts made to improve the trade balance within the North Atlantic trading triangle—Canada, Great Britain, and the United States. By 1915, the British Treasury Board had reached the point where it was unable to maintain the convertibility of the pound sterling into dollars, and this had repercussions on the Canadian balance of payments with the United States. Historically, Canada had exported more to Britain than it imported and in turn converted the pounds sterling into dollars to offset its trade deficit with the United States. The problems posed by scrapping convertibility were compounded by the growing demands of the Canadian war economy for American imports.

Canada's increasingly unfavorable trade balance with the United States coincided with a decline in British war contracts as the war continued. A crisis developed in September 1917 when some Canadian war industries began to close their production lines. Robert L. Borden's Conservative government in Ottawa concluded that new arms markets abroad were desperately needed. In response to an appeal by Joseph Flavelle, director of the Imperial Munitions Board, the United States Ordnance Department offered to sidestep existing tariff regulations and increase munitions imports from Canada. As a result, by November 1918, Canada's shipments to its southern ally included not only shells and light ammunition but limited quantities of JN4 fighter aircraft, the F5 flying boat, and a number of civilian vessels. The United States placed orders for $178.4 million in military equipment overall, and the figure was expected to rise over $200 million if the war continued into 1919.

Apart from the War Department's approval of the transfer of classified arms production technology in 1917, the Wilson administration did not play a direct role in the expansion of branch plants and subsidiaries north of the border. The northward flow of investment capital was of some importance to American war production, and hence to national security, but there were no specific policies adopted by the United States to encourage capital flows northward. American corporate expansion into Canada during the war was determined by other considerations, such as the absence of investment opportunities in war-torn Europe and the favorable conditions offered in Canada owing to that government's mobilization program. Aetna Explosives and the Nichols Chemical Company, for example, moved into Canada in 1915, while Canadian Explosives Ltd., a Du Pont subsidiary, expanded its operations for making gun cotton, cordite, and TNT. Two new additions to the Canadian automobile industry in 1916 were Chalmers Motors, a predecessor of Chrysler, and the Willys-Overland Company. At this time their main competitor, Ford of Canada, increased its vehicle production threefold by filling government contracts. In 1916, Willys-Overland formed a joint venture with the Canadian Russell Motor Car Company to produce engines for the JN4 fighter.

The First World War also altered the course of military relations between the United States and the northern dominion. Shortly after Wilson's declaration of war, a continental division of labor was established to coordinate air and sea patrols off the Atlantic coast. With the assistance of the United States, antisubmarine aircraft stations were set up in Halifax and Sydney, Nova Scotia. At the same time, Canada's armed forces moved through the United States en route to Europe, as did Americans through Canada. American aviators were trained in Canada, and the two countries shared their intelligence data. Termination of the war in 1918 brought to an end these efforts at forging a continental defense system. Some historians have also suggested that Canada's status as a partially autonomous British dominion prevented the negotiation of further bilateral agreements. An anomaly in this climate of improving relations was the contingency planning of the Canadian and American armies for war against each other. These plans, however, were never more than academic exercises for younger officers, and it was unlikely that American or

Canadian political leaders were even aware of their existence.

The First World War marked a turning point in American diplomatic relations with Canada—a transitional period from an era of indifference to one of formal alliance beginning with the signing of the Ogdensburg Agreement of 1940. The Wilson administration recognized Canadian aspirations for greater autonomy in relation to Britain and where possible accommodated its northern neighbor. For example, although Canada did not have official diplomatic status in Washington, a Canadian War Mission was officially received in February 1918. At times, however, Canadian interests were not well received, such as when Wilson initially rejected a Canadian proposal for separate and independent representation at the Versailles peace negotiations. Nevertheless, Canada proved to be diplomatically useful to the United States on the whole. On several occasions the Canadian government during and shortly after the Versailles peace negotiations acted as a mediator between the United States and Britain. More importantly, Canadian officials, seeking greater autonomy from Britain, became enthusiastic supporters of the Wilsonian vision based on collective security and the economic open door. Postwar economic statistics provide further evidence of Canada's receptiveness to Wilsonian open-door policies.

In conclusion, then, it was during the First World War that American economic and military power superseded that of Great Britain. This shift was reflected primarily in America's new economic relationship with Canada and to a lesser extent in military relations. Twenty years later Canada's cooperation during the First World War was seen by American national security planners as a precedent to the highly successful 1941 Hyde Park defense production agreement. On the Canadian side, these First World War developments in military and economic relations reversed the long-standing anti-American sentiment in Canada arising from the Alaska boundary dispute and the rejection of reciprocity in 1911. Canadian cooperation stemmed largely from a calculation of its own national interest, which converged with U.S. economic and national security interests. This pattern would become the defining characteristic of the Canadian-American relationship later in the twentieth century.

Lawrence Aronsen

Bibliography

Cuff, Robert D., and J.L. Granatstein. *Canadian-American Relations in Wartime: From the Great War to the Cold War.* Toronto: Hakkert, 1975.

Keenleyside, Hugh L. *Canada and the United States.* New York: Knopf, 1952.

Mahant, Edelgard E., and Graeme S. Mount. *An Introduction to Canadian-American Relations.* Toronto: Nelson Canada, 1984.

Preston, Richard A. *The Defence of the Undefended Border: Planning for War in North America, 1867–1939.* Montreal: McGill-Queens University Press, 1977.

Stacey, C.P. *Canada and the Age of Conflict: A History of Canadian External Policies, 1867–1921.* Vol. 1. Toronto: University of Toronto Press, 1977.

Cantigny

When the United States entered World War I in April 1917, its miniscule army was unready to deal with a competent Eurasian force. Therefore, some assumed that the nation would limit its war effort to naval and economic measures, but President Woodrow Wilson soon decided to mobilize a huge army that would fight under its own flag with its own commanders and staffs, develop its own logistical system, conduct operations according to its own doctrine, and fight in its own sector of the Western Front.

Wilson took considerable risk; the Central Powers might win before the United States could join the battle. An independent U.S. army could not enter the battle in full panoply until 1919 or perhaps even 1920 because of the extended period needed to mobilize an independent army. The alternative to an independent army was to insert small American units in the French and British armies as replacements, an expedient, known as "amalgamation," that would be feasible within a few months. The President and his military advisers never seriously considered amalgamation except as a temporary measure during a desperate crisis. Perhaps they hoped that victory would come before it became necessary to commit American troops in large numbers, but other compelling motives led in the same direction. Public opinion would instantly oppose amalgamation, and so would the army. Of equal importance was President Wilson's desire to dominate the peace settlement. He could anticipate a powerful post-

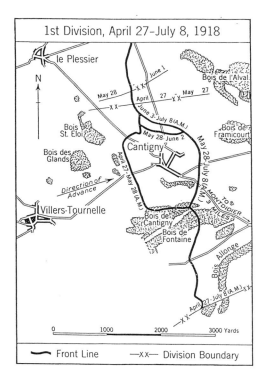

Cantigny. Taken from The American Armies and Battlefields in Europe, *American Battle Monuments Commission, Government Printing Office, 1938.*

war position provided that the U.S. Army, operating independently in strength, had made a vital contribution to the defeat of the Central Powers.

The ambitious American mobilization plan meant that the War Department could transport only four divisions to Europe by January 1918, when it was recognized that Germany, using divisions withdrawn from the Eastern Front after the defeat of Russia, planned a great offensive to force a decision in France before the American Expeditionary Force (AEF) under the command of Gen. John J. Pershing could arrive in sufficient numbers to influence the outcome.

The impending crisis of 1918 led to a considerable inter-Allied controversy over amalgamation. French and British leaders urged Pershing to consider temporary amalgamation for training and even for operations during the emergency. Pershing proved intransigent, assuming that any such measures would cause serious delays in creating an independent army. The German offensives started on March 21 with a powerful attack toward Amiens that drove a deep salient into the British lines. A second thrust against the British began on April

9 in Belgium and created another deep salient. These events led to the appointment of Gen. Ferdinand Foch as overall commader in chief, finally establishing inter-Allied unity of command in France.

The desperate situation on the Western Front forced Pershing to permit the temporary attachment of a few American divisions to the British and French armies. One of these units was the 1st Infantry Division, "The Big Red One," commanded by MajGen. Robert L. Bullard. Its first contingent accompanied General Pershing to France in June 1917. After parading in Paris on July 4, it began training, a necessarily extended experience because most of the officers and men were recruits. The division included two infantry brigades of two regiments each and an artillery brigade, constituting a "square division" that with its support troops numbered about 28,000 men. The organization went into the line near the small town of Cantigny in the French zone of operations on the night of April 24–25, 1918. To the north was the French 45th Division and to the south was the French 162d Division, both from the French X Corps, MajGen. Charles A. Vandenberg commanding, a component of the French First Army under Gen. Marie Eugene Debeney. The American movement into the line led to the first battle of the AEF in France.

Cantigny was located about three miles west of Montdidier in a German salient about 3,300 feet deep and 4,950 feet wide. A major German attack had ended just west of the town, giving the enemy control of the road junction at Cantigny. The German Eighteenth Army commanded by Gen. Oskar von Hutier held the salient. One of the divisions, the 86th Reserve Division, part of the 26th Reserve Corps, occupied the line at Cantigny. The 272d Reserve Infantry Regiment held the middle; the 270th Reserve Infantry Regiment was on its right and the 271st Reserve Infantry Regiment on the left. The latter force held Cantigny and also an area just to the south that included a significant terrain feature, Hill 104. The 86th Division, which had served earlier on the Eastern Front, had not seen action for two years and was not highly regarded.

Debeney contemplated a major attack in the area, but threatening German movements to the north led to a much more modest plan. Bullard prepared a regimental-size attack to achieve a limited goal—the reduction of the Cantigny salient. General Pershing hoped that this attack would demonstrate the competence of the AEF and justify his stubborn commitment to an independent army. In tactical terms, the attack would improve the defensive dispositions of the X Corps and also prepare for future offensive operations.

Bullard designated the 28th Infantry Regiment commanded by Col. Hanson E. Ely, part of the 2d Brigade commanded by BGen. Beaumont B. Buck, to conduct the assault on Cantigny. Bullard issued Field Order No. 18 on April 20, prepared by LtCol. George C. Marshall, the division's G–3, and by the artillery commander, BGen. Charles Summerall. The tactical emphasis was on surprise. Three infantry battalions abreast, less one infantry company, would advance to defensible positions east of Cantigny. Two companies of the 18th Infantry Regiment became the reserve for the 2d Battalion, which, accompanied by twelve French tanks and a flame-thrower section, would seize Cantigny. Elsewhere the 3d Battalion would move forward on the left to cover the main assault, and a company of the 1st Battalion supported by a battalion of the 26th Infantry Regiment would occupy positions south of the salient, commanding a road between Cantigny and Fontaine-sous-Montdidier. This measure would prevent the enemy from reinforcing the Cantigny area. One company of the 1st Battalion served as the regimental reserve. Each of the three attacking battalions would receive a machine gun company to help maintain control of the objective. A company of combat engineers was assigned to support the assault. A formidable artillery force of 173 guns, including 50 heavy pieces, was assembled to support the attack. The 18th Artillery Regiment contributed about a third of the guns, and the French provided the rest. The artillery would fire a brief preparation followed by a rolling barrage ahead of the infantry advance and then bombard the town and associated positions, conducting counterbattery fire and interdicting counterattack routes.

The 28th Infantry rehearsed the attack twice before H-hour, which was finally scheduled for May 28. On May 27, however, another major German offensive began to the south—an attack toward the Marne River, which had a significant consequence. It meant that the supporting French artillery would depart after the first day of the Cantigny operation. Nevertheless, Bullard decided to persevere, and Pershing supported him. The infantry assault

began at 6:40 A.M. after preparatory artillery fire at 4:45 A.M. and heavy artillery fire at 5:45 A.M. It was immediately successful, the advance companies having little difficulty overwhelming the few German troops in the town who survived the intense artillery bombardment. American casualties were less than 100; about 200 Germans were made prisoners of war. The five assault companies quickly established defensive positions east of the town.

Unfortunately, the supporting movements on the right and the left were not nearly as effective. The German command decided that the operation was aimed at Hill 104 and Fontaine-sous-Montdidier, the gateway to the important town of Montdidier. To frustrate this presumed operation, counterattacks and artillery fire were ordered against the American positions, which were easily observed. German howitzer and machine gun fire exacted many casualties, about a third of the troops in the front line, but the 28th Infantry repulsed German counterattacks on the evening of the first day. Colonel Ely requested either relief or permission to withdraw, citing heavy losses, but Bullard decided to keep the 28th Infantry in place.

The easy early victory turned into an extended bloody defense. The withdrawal of the French artillery and the deficiencies of the supporting American attacks north and south of Cantigny brought on two difficult days for the 28th Infantry. Ely was forced to deal with further German counterattacks and to engage the enemy's artillery. He and Lieutenant Colonel Marshall attributed the unexpected resistance to the enemy's desire to repulse the first American attack of the war, but postwar investigation revealed that von Hutier reacted strongly because he feared that the American attack was the beginning of an attempt to recapture Montdidier, a far more important location than Cantigny.

German efforts to recapture Cantigny ended on May 30, when von Hutier decided that Montdidier was not in danger. Units of the 16th Infantry and the 18th Infantry relieved the shattered 28th Infantry on the nights of May 30–31 and May 31–June 1. Ely had lost 38 officers and 903 men, about a third of his complement. The defenders suffered more severely, losing over 1,750 officers and men.

General Pershing interpreted the outcome at Cantigny as a brilliant success that vindicated his optimistic evaluation of American troops and American tactical doctrine. This verdict ignored the fact that the assault did not test the central American doctrinal principle, open warfare, and that the enemy had fought well after recovering from the surprise attack. The leading authority on Cantigny, Allan Millett, concluded that this minor battle illustrated the normal course of such struggles on the Western Front. Attacking troops were able to advance while receiving effective artillery support, but they had difficulty dealing with retaliatory enemy artillery fire, especially when they moved beyond supporting guns.

David F. Trask

See also BULLARD, ROBERT LEE; ELY, HANSON

Bibliography

Millett, Allan R. "Cantigny, 28–31 May 1918." In *America's First Battles: 1776–1965*, ed. by Charles E. Heller and William A. Stofft. Lawrence: University Press of Kansas, 1986.

Cantonments

As soon as the United States decided to commit troops to France, the War Department set the wheels in motion to raise, train, and deploy a large army. Initial planning was for a force of 500,000 men. The first decisions had to be made quickly and without firm information or guidance. Troop housing available on April 6, 1917, totaled 124,000 units; by the end of 1917, there would be shelter for 1.5 million soldiers. The best estimates of the moment led to the decision to build sixteen cantonments each for the National Guard and the National Army. On May 4, 1917, the War College Division of the General Staff recommended that department commanders be authorized to select camp sites within their departments. There was fierce competition from surrounding communities for location of the camps, and the last one was finally approved on July 6. The secretary of war directed that all National Army camps be completed by September 1—in essence, a ninety-day building program!

As construction got underway following standardized plans, a major problem arose. At issue was the size of the organizations to be housed and trained in these facilities. The authority to determine the final structure of the American Expeditionary Force (AEF) had been delegated to its commanding general, John J.

Pershing. Yet the War Department, which was responsible for initiating construction of the cantonments, found that it had to begin construction before the AEF had settled upon the exact size and composition of the divisional structure. Therefore, the department based construction upon the prewar structure in which the company, the basic unit, contained 150 men. There was an accompanying assumption that these cantonments would train only divisions, which, as BGen. Fox Connor observed after the war, were only a small part of the entire force.

Camp construction began quickly in order to be ready to house the first inductees. As a consequence, the camps were built to hold approximately 40,000 soldiers. This was large enough to accommodate an entire division plus a replacement training organization and provided for divisional schools and various other activities. As luck would have it, as soon as the standardized plans were sent to the 200,000-man construction force, Pershing announced his decision to raise the strength of the infantry company from 150 to 250 men. There were other changes that modified the internal division structure and eventually raised the final divisional strength to 28,059 from a prewar anticipated minimum of 20,002. This caused building to be continued beyond the scheduled deadline, and further changes kept many men employed well into the new year.

Under the organization of the War Department on April 6, 1917, the quartermaster general was in charge of the Cantonment Division. This division was activated on May 19, 1917, with a core of personnel from the Construction and Repair Division, which remained responsible for the work on permanent installations. Construction of National Army camps began in June; work on National Guard camps started in July. It was remarkable that construction was largely completed by October 5. Since the first draft call did not go out until July, the installations were basically ready to receive the recruits before their arrival. All originally planned construction, as well as additional structures for morale and welfare activities, was completed by Nov. 30, 1917.

Secretary of War Newton Baker had made an early decision that the National Guard cantonments would be tent cities and those of the newly forming National Army would be of wooden construction. Each camp was to be self-contained. Since metal was in short supply, some camps were equipped with wooden water pipes. During that hectic summer, the construction army consumed an estimated 30,000 tons of construction materials every day.

Camp Devens, Massachusetts, is a good example of one of these cantonments. The facility, planned to house 37,416 men, was electrified by August 5 and handed over to the government, essentially complete, on August 28. It had taken 9,000 men nine weeks to finish the 600 buildings, 25 miles of underground sewers and waterpipes, 400 miles of electric wiring, and 20 miles of paved roads. Devens had an 18,000-foot-long railroad spur to handle the arrival and distribution of the hundreds of train loads of materials arriving each week. Wells with a 3 million gallon capacity had been dug to service the camp's needs. Those 600 buildings included 199 company barracks of two sizes, reflecting the change in company strength, 74 officers barracks, 300 lavatories, including 2,200 showers, 10 regimental headquarters buildings, 1 division headquarters, 10 quartermaster warehouses, 15 medical buildings, 4 artillery buildings, 41 company storehouses, 1 refrigerating plant capable of producing twenty tons of ice per day, 1 bakery, 3 fire stations, chapels, and post offices and all the other facilities necessary to operate a self-contained city. Infantry barracks were somewhat self-contained with billets on the top floor and mess and instructional facilities on the first. Adjacent to each barracks was a cement-floored lavatory building containing its own boiler for hot water showers.

As the construction army grew and the payroll increased to approximately $400,000 per week, the 3d Battalion, 15th York Colored Infantry arrived at Camp Devens to provide a police detail. The first draftees arrived on Sept. 5, 1917.

As ambitious and successful as the cantonment construction program in the United States was, there was a belated recognition that a similar program would be required in France. During the time between the arrival of the first troops and the construction of cantonments in France, American soldiers slept in barns, pig styes, hay lofts, equipment sheds, and any other place they could be under cover. Units arriving later spent a portion of their precious training time in construction of their own billets.

The decision to allow the National Guard troops to move into tent camps was based partly on their southern location. As it turned out, the winter of 1917–1918 in the South was terrible, causing considerable hardship in those camps and contributing to the outbreaks of several epidemics of measles, mumps, tuberculosis, smallpox, meningitis, and other diseases. As for the National Army, the insufficient canvas available to meet that army's needs and the generally more northern locations of the army's camps settled the issue of tents or permanent construction. National Guard tent camps cost an average of $4.5 million each, while the wooden construction of the National Army camps ran $12.5 million.

The cantonment construction program was a masterpiece of organization, planning, and dedication. No soldier's training was inhibited for lack of living space or training facilities in the United States.

Douglas V. Johnson

Bibliography

Batchelder, Roger. *Camp Devens*. Boston: Small, Maynard, 1918.

Center for Military History. *Order of Battle of the United States Land Forces in the World War*. Washington, DC: Government Printing Office, 1988.

Kreidberg, Marvin A., and Merton G. Henry. *History of Military Mobilization in the United States Army 1775–1945*. Washington, DC: Government Printing Office, 1955.

Caporetto, Battle of

The Battle of Caporetto (October-November 1917) marked the disastrous culmination of Italy's efforts to drive the Austro-Hungarian Army from its positions along the Isonzo River on Italy's northeastern border. Instead, a combined Austrian-German force routed the Italians and almost forced that nation out of the war.

Although a member of the Triple Alliance, Italy remained neutral until May 23, 1915, when she joined the Allies and declared war on Austria-Hungary. At that time the Italian Army totaled approximately 900,000 men organized into thirty-six infantry and four cavalry divisions. Italy had few options for military actions as northern Italy is bordered on all sides by the Alps. Army Chief of Staff Gen. Luigi Cadorna decided that Italy's best strategy was to advance across the Isonzo River, on the northeast border with Austria, and seize the port of Trieste.

The valley of the Isonzo, which runs north-to-south, is marked by broken ground and towering mountains that form ideal defensive terrain. The weak Austrian Fifth Army under General Svetozar Boroevic defended the valley. Boroevic had about 100,000 troops initially, though he was quickly reinforced following Austro-German successes on the Eastern Front in the summer of 1915. Cadorna concentrated his forces for the Isonzo attack under two army headquarters, the Second and Third. He launched four offensives against the Isonzo on a fifty-five-mile front in 1915, gaining little territory and suffering 280,000 casualties. In these battles the Italians outnumbered the defending Austrians as much as two to one, though they were deficient in artillery, having only 212 guns to support their first offensive.

In eleven offensives, or "battles," along the Isonzo front from 1915 to 1917, the Italian Army suffered over 725,000 casualties and advanced less than ten miles. In spite of these massive losses the army expanded from forty-eight divisions in 1916 to sixty-five in 1917. Cadorna massed the bulk of the army on the Isonzo front.

The eleventh battle of the Isonzo (August–September 1917), set thirty-eight Italian divisions and 2,600 guns against eighteen Austrian divisions backed by 1,400 guns. Surprisingly, the Italian Second Army, under Gen. Luigi Capello, almost pushed the Austrians out of their last defenses along the Bainsizza plateau at the northern end of the Isonzo Valley. Austria, fearing the loss of its positions on the Isonzo and being too weak to undertake an offensive alone, requested German assistance. Though hard pressed on other fronts, the Germans dispatched seven divisions under Gen. Otto von Below to aid their ally.

Italian intelligence detected the arrival of German forces, and, recognizing the growing demoralization of his forces, Cadorna went over to the defensive. On paper, his forty-one divisions outnumbered the combined Austro-German force of thirty-five divisions, but his troops were greatly demoralized after two years of bloody and seemingly pointless offensives. Cadorna believed that the upper Isonzo region, covered by the Second Army and including the town of Caporetto, was too rugged for an Austro-German offensive and so concentrated his reserves behind the Third Army along the lower Isonzo.

The Austro-German offensive began on the morning of October 24 in the Caporetto sector. The German Eleventh Army employed what were then the novel tactics of short, massive artillery barrages followed by rapid infantry advances; points of resistance were bypassed to be mopped up later by reserve units. The fact that General Capello, not expecting an attack, failed to establish defenses in depth further aided the offensive. The storm of artillery and attacking infantry soon overwhelmed the Italian Second Army, and the entire Italian line was in retreat by October 27.

Cadorna ordered his forces to fall back to the Tagliamento River, thirty miles west of the Isonzo. Von Below had planned to halt his advance along that river, but on the night of November 2, two divisions of his army gained a bridgehead and outflanked the defending Italians. On November 4, Cadorna ordered a retreat to the Piave River.

Von Below pursued, but resupply problems slowed his advance. The Italian forces were behind the Piave River by November 10, seventy miles from the Isonzo. The Italian Second Army had suffered heavy losses and was taken out of the line. The Third Army fell back in good order and joined with the First and Fourth armies to defend the river. Increasing Italian resistance was bolstered by the arrival of six French and five British divisions, and the Austro-German force was fought to a standstill along the Piave River.

The Battle of Caporetto was a military disaster that almost led to the collapse of the Italian Army. Although the Italians suffered 340,000 casualties, including over 275,000 prisoners, they eventually held the Austro-German advance. The near disaster led to the replacement of Cadorna by General Armando Diaz, a man more amiable to the politicians and who recognized the importance of improving the morale of his men. Perhaps the most important, though unintended result of the battle was that it brought the Austrian forces out from easily defended terrain along the Isonzo River to the open country of the Piave, where they were routed the following year in the Battle of Vittorio-Veneto.

David Robrock

See also CADORNA, LUIGI; VITTORIO-VENETO, BATTLE OF

Bibliography

Capello, Luigi. *Caporetto, perché*. Turin: Einaudi, 1967.

Gathorne-Hardy, J.F. "A Summary of the Campaign in Italy and an Account of the Battle of Vittorio Veneto." *Army Quarterly* (October 1921).

Carnegie Endowment for International Peace

The Carnegie Endowment for International Peace was established in 1910 by Andrew Carnegie, former head of the United States Steel Corporation. He subsidized the endowment with $10 million of U.S. Steel bonds. Its purpose was to promote international peace and good will through education and research. A conservative, some might even say an elitist organization run by prominent, successful, and wealthy businessmen, the endowment provided financial support for research on internationalism to academics and other intellectuals whose views were at least generally compatible with those of the endowment. The endowment was also generous in providing subsidies and assistance to active peace organizations, such as the American Peace Society.

An example of the organization's conservative nature was its adoption in January 1917 of the "Recommendations of Havana." They called for a third Hague peace conference, for holding periodic meetings thereafter, and for the appointment of a committee to obtain and register all declarations and conventions dealing with internationalism in order to bring them to the world's attention. The endowment also favored an international court of justice and the use of mediation, arbitration, or conciliation in settling international disputes. However, it opposed stringent enforcement procedures.

The endowment backed American participation in World War I. Indeed, it adopted the slogan "Peace through Victory" to make its support unequivocally clear. It also turned over its Washington, D.C., offices to the Creel Committee on Public Information, the official propaganda arm of the government.

The endowment never pretended to be an advocate for pacifism. It wanted to raise mankind up to the point where it would support internationalism, and it wanted to enhance the efforts of scholars to better understand and promote internationalism. Although the Carnegie Endowment did not support the League of Nations at the end of the war, it continues to this day to work for international peace.

John Imholte

Bibliography

Butler, Nicholas M. *Across the Busy Years: Recollections and Reflections*. New York: Scribner, 1939.

Chatfield, Charles. *For Peace and Justice*. Knoxville: University of Tennessee Press, 1971.

DeBenedetti, Charles. *The Peace Reform in American History*. Bloomington: Indiana University Press, 1980.

Kuehl, Warren F. *Seeking World Order*. Nashville: Vanderbilt University Press, 1969.

Patterson, David S. *Toward a Warless World*. Bloomington: Indiana University Press, 1976.

Catlin, Albertus Wright (1863–1933)

Albertus Wright Catlin was born in New York City. Graduating from the Naval Academy in 1890, he was commissioned a second lieutenant in the Marine Corps in 1892. In 1898 he was commanding officer of the marine detachment aboard the battleship USS *Maine* when that vessel exploded and sank in Havana harbor. He later served in the Philippines, China, Hawaii, Cuba, and Mexico, commanded the Naval prison at Portsmouth, and served in Buffalo, New York, on recruiting duty. His most notable achievement before 1918 was as commanding officer of the 3d Marine Regiment at Veracruz, Mexico, in 1914, for which he was awarded the Medal of Honor. Between 1915 and 1917, Catlin attended the Army Service Schools, Fort Leavenworth, and the Army War College, after which he was promoted to colonel.

Shortly after the United States entered the First World War, Catlin assumed command of the new marine barracks at Quantico, Virginia, and the newly raised 6th Marine Regiment. In October 1917, he led his regiment to France. Early in June 1918, he took his men into the front lines on the Paris-Metz road through Lucy-le-Bocage to Hill 142. There the marines helped repulse German attacks. On June 6, 1918, Catlin led two battalions, one each from the 5th and 6th Marines, in the initial attack on Bois de Belleau (Belleau Wood). In this attack, a German sniper shot him through the chest. He was evacuated, moved to a hospital in Paris, and subsequently returned to the United States.

Upon his return home, he was promoted to brigadier general, served at the headquarters of the Marine Corps, and then again commanded Quantico. Between 1918 and 1919, he commanded the 1st Provisional Marine Brigade in Haiti. Due to the effects of his war wound, Catlin retired on Dec. 10, 1919. He died on May 31, 1933.

For his services in the First World War, the French government awarded him two Croix de Guerre (one with gilt star and the other with palm) and made him an officer in the Legion of Honor for his performance at Belleau Wood.

Donald Bittner

Bibliography

Catlin, Albertus W. *With the Help of God and a Few Marines*. New York: Doubleday, Page, 1919.

McClellan, Edwin N. *The United States Marines in the World War*. Washington, DC: Government Printing Office, 1920.

Millett, Allan R. *Semper Fidelis: A History of the United States Marine Corps*. New York: Macmillan, 1980.

Catt, Carrie Clinton Lane Chapman (1859–1947)

Obtaining woman suffrage was always Carrie Clinton Lane Chapman Catt's first priority and although vehemently opposed to wars as "man-made" atrocities, she was extremely cautious about mixing woman suffrage with the peace cause. Rather than taking the lead herself, Catt urged Jane Addams to convene a national meeting of women in January 1915 to launch a woman's peace movement. Catt attended the meeting, made the motion to form the Woman's Peace Party, and helped organize a New York branch, but that was the extent of her peace activism until after the Armistice. She concentrated on the New York suffrage campaign and, after resuming the presidency in 1915, on revitalizing the National American Woman Suffrage Association (NAWSA) and developing a nationwide strategy for obtaining a federal woman suffrage amendment. Adopted by NAWSA in 1916, Catt's "Winning Plan" called for combining support for a federal amendment with continuing efforts to expand the number of states in which women could vote.

Three weeks after the Feb. 3, 1917, break in diplomatic relations with Germany, Catt led NAWSA's Executive Council in pledging the service of its 2 million members to the government in the event of war. Catt announced that suffragists would support their country and continue their suffrage work. She hoped women's war service might be used to further the goal of woman suffrage, and thus she was untroubled by criticism from the National Woman's Party and by her ouster from the New York City branch of the Woman's Peace Party.

When the United States declared war on Germany on April 6, 1917, Catt urged that suffrage organizations register women for war service. Appointed to the Woman's Committee of the Council of National Defense, Catt viewed this as another opportunity to advance the suffrage cause, especially because suffragist Anna Howard Shaw had been appointed its head. Unlike Shaw, however, Catt continued to devote her attention almost exclusively to suffrage. She presented suffrage as a war measure by arguing that women would have more time to devote to the war effort if they were not forced to continue campaigning for suffrage. Although a harsh critic of the Woman's Party White House pickets, she supported their argument that it was impossible to claim the United States was itself a democracy when women were denied the right to vote. Although the House passed the federal amendment giving women the vote for the first time in January 1918 and President Wilson personally urged its passage before the Senate the next fall, it was not until June 1919 that the Senate passed the Nineteenth Amendment. Catt was in the forefront of the ratification drive and spent several weeks in Tennessee, the last state to ratify the amendment in 1920.

After the Armistice, Catt became concerned about the role of women in obtaining world peace. She lobbied Wilson to appoint women to the treaty delegation, she resumed her work in the International Woman Suffrage Alliance, and, in 1925, she convened a conference on the Cause and Cure of War. Catt chaired the group until 1932. She died in 1947.

Barbara Steinson

See also WOMAN'S PEACE PARTY

Bibliography

Flexner, Eleanor. *Century of Struggle, The Woman's Rights Movement in the*

United States. New York: Atheneum, 1973.

Fowler, Robert B. *Carrie Catt: Feminist Politician*. Boston: Northeastern University Press, 1986.

Peck, Mary Gray. *Carrie Chapman Catt: A Biography*. Westport, CT: Hyperion Press, 1976, reprint of 1944 edition.

Steinson, Barbara J. *American Women's Activism in World War I*. New York: Garland, 1982.

Van Voris, Jacqueline. *Carrie Chapman Catt: A Public Life*. New York: Feminist Press, 1987.

Censorship

The wartime cohesion needed for a nation to defeat an enemy invariably collides with the constitutional exercise of individual liberties. Soon after America's entry into World War I, the Wilson administration supported measures that restricted civil liberties on an unprecedented scale. Four legislative acts authorized the federal government to monitor and control domestic opinion, speech, and publications: the Espionage Act (May 1917), the Trading with the Enemy Act (October 1917), the Alien Act (October 1918), and the Sedition Act (May 1918). Collectively, these statutes and various executive orders prohibited spying, sabotage, and commerce with the enemy; empowered the postmaster to suspend the mailing privileges of publications deemed objectionable; conferred broad powers of deportation; and specified penalties for disloyal or profane speech or publication. Accompanying the suppression was a sweeping program of propaganda to inculcate patriotic values.

Coordination of the administration's censorship activities was achieved by creation of the Censorship Board in late 1917, a body composed of the Post Office Department and representatives from the War and Navy departments, the War Trade Board, and the Committee on Public Information. Although advisory in nature and without separate funding, this forum provided an opportunity for sharing information throughout the war. Postmaster General Albert S. Burleson used his powers with special vigor, invoking the standard that any publication which impugned the government's motives could be withheld from distribution through the mail. Publications that questioned American intervention or the President were subject to a mail embargo. Two such cases involved Charles A. Lindbergh, Sr.'s *Why is Your Country at War?* and Tom Watson's magazine the *Jeffersonian*. Other prominent examples of banned newspapers and magazines were the *American Socialist,* the *Masses,* the *Milwaukee Leader,* and the *New York Call.* More than 400 periodical issues fell victim to the censor's hand.

Surveillance of American reading habits was exercised by government agencies, state organizations, and patriotic societies. George Creel's Committee on Public Information contacted authors and referred suspect materials to other federal departments. Various state agencies affiliated with the Council of National Defense called for libraries and the public to be alert to pro-German and pacifist titles. Public librarians readily embraced the war effort and the opportunity to demonstrate their professionalism. Materials considered seditious or propagandistic were removed from libraries or not purchased at all. In several extreme instances, librarians burned offending books and pamphlets. The public library committee believed that they were protecting patrons from disloyal literature and did not resist censorship or question underlying assumptions. Censorship in the civilian sector mirrored the firm control exercised by military officials.

The military acted early to control the reading matter available to the soldiers and sailors. Initially, a secret list of nearly 100 titles prepared by the War Department's Military Intelligence Branch and Morale Division, the "Army Index," was released in late September 1918. The American Library Association, responsible for library service within the camps and cantonments, readily supported this program to remove objectionable books from the training environment. The *New York Tribune* reported that the books had been carefully read by military censors, who pronounced some titles as "vicious German propaganda" and others as either "salacious" or "morbid." Among the banned books were *Understanding Germany* by Max Eastman; *War and Waste* by David Starr Jordan; *The Neel of War* by George B. McClellan; *England or Germany?* by Frank Harris; and *Why War?* by Frederic C. Howe. Apart from the alleged pro-German or pacifist bias of the books, no pattern is discernible. Neither the authors' backgrounds nor the publishers themselves fully explain why certain titles appear and others do not. Hundreds of pro-German titles published since 1914 were not cited, and even similar books by listed authors did not appear in the index.

The influence of motion pictures on public opinion was considerable, and they became a special target of the censors. Film producers were cautioned to observe four elements that could trigger censorship: false representation of U.S. life or ideals; derogatory remarks about the United States or its allies; mob scenes that could be distorted; and failure to convey a favorable impression of America and its people. These criteria were generally assimilated by the filmmakers, and few films were actually withdrawn or seized. The most celebrated case involved the Los Angeles seizure of Robert Goldstein's *The Spirit of '76*, a revisionist production about the American Revolution. The United States Circuit Court of Appeals affirmed the decision of the lower court and Goldstein received a ten-year jail sentence. U.S. films exported to Europe and foreign films entering the United States were subject to the full measure of censorship. Unlike the library community, the motion picture producers took a firm stand against the censorship of movies on the editorial pages of the *Exhibitor's Trade Review*.

Censorship was but one manifestation of a government policy to regulate the freedom of expression. Banned books, dissident professors, pacifists, and suspect movies all qualified for state surveillance and punishment. The Wilson administration's ambivalence on the issue of social control reflects the competing demands of wartime solidarity and a democratic form of government. President Wilson occasionally intervened to curb his zealous postmaster general, as in the resumption of mail delivery for the *Nation*, but Wilson otherwise accepted the restrictions as necessary for the exceptional situation of war. And there were others who periodically recommended more draconian measures, such as the application of courts-martial to civilians, an idea firmly opposed by the President. Finding the balance between the competing rights of the state and the individual eluded national leaders during World War I, and the resulting struggle was probably inevitable.

Arthur P. Young

See also COMMITTEE ON PUBLIC INFORMATION; COUNCIL OF NATIONAL DEFENSE

Bibliography

Martin, James J. *An American Adventure in Bookburning: In the Style of 1918.*
Colorado Springs, CO: Ralph Myles, 1988.
Mock, James R. *Censorship 1917*. Princeton, NJ: Princeton University Press, 1941.
Schaeffer, Ronald. *America in the Great War: The Rise of the War Welfare State.* New York: Oxford University Press, 1991.
Wiegand, Wayne A. *"An Active Instrument of Propaganda": The American Public Library During World War I.* Westport, CT: Greenwood Press, 1989.
Young, Arthur P. *Books for Sammies: The American Library Association and World War I.* Pittsburgh: Beta Phi Mu, 1981.

Chafee, Zechariah, Jr. (1885–1957)

Civil liberties, particularly free speech, became one of the first domestic victims of America's entry into the First World War. The national paranoia and insecurity generated by the war and the Bolshevik Revolution, in turn, fostered a repressive campaign against political dissidents. In addition to public pressure, laws such as the Espionage and Sedition acts were used to silence critics of the government's war policies. Consequently, the war period marked the beginning of an extensive use of federal power in controlling speech and in harassing critics and suspected radicals. Such a national campaign against civil liberties had not occurred since the Alien and Sedition Act of 1798; and few defenders of free speech came forward.

Zechariah Chafee, Jr., was an exception. He criticized the social intolerance reflected by the wartime excesses of the Wilson administration in the civil liberties area. Chafee particularly tried to steer the courts on a more pro-civil libertarian approach when ruling upon convictions brought under the Espionage and Sedition acts. In so doing, Chafee became the first major American scholar of the First Amendment.

Chafee had begun to explore the law of civil liberties as a Harvard Law School professor in the immediate prewar period and had found it almost nonexistent. At the time of America's entry into the war and its subsequent campaign against political dissent, the Supreme Court had never applied nor interpreted the First Amendment; nor had it ever considered the constitutionality of federal legislation in relation to the right of free speech. Indeed, since the ratification of the Constitution, the nation

C

had had little experience with applying and defining free speech.

This void of First Amendment precedent left free speech with undeveloped defenses in the face of strong wartime public demands for restrictions. Consequently, free speech was sacrificed for the sake of a vague and undefined sense of national security.

Chafee criticized the judicial disregard of the First Amendment and advocated a more sensitive law of civil liberties. He strongly opposed the Supreme Court's wartime decisions in which it upheld convictions of political dissenters under the Espionage and Sedition acts and failed to recognize any First-Amendment rights of those dissenters. Chafee argued that speech should be free in wartime unless it clearly threatened to cause direct and dangerous interference with the conduct of the war.

Believing that free speech was vital for the survival of democratic society, Chafee argued that the social interest in the attainment of truth required a system of free expression. Thus, he warned that the restrictive government behavior was corrupting a primary value underlying democratic processes—freedom of speech.

Chafee was widely criticized for his views, and he was unable to convince the Court, during the war and immediate postwar period, to adopt his views. Yet, Justice Holmes, in the first defense of the First Amendment by a Supreme Court justice, did incorporate Chafee's free-speech theory into his eloquent dissent in *Abrams v. U.S.* articulating the need for free speech. By the early 1930s, however, Chafee's views regarding free speech came to be embraced by the Supreme Court in several of its First-Amendment decisions.

Patrick Garry

Bibliography

Chafee, Zechariah, Jr. *Free Speech in the United States*. New York: Harcourt, Brace & Howe, 1920.
Smith, Donald L. *Zechariah Chafee, Jr., Defender of Liberty and Law*. Cambridge: Harvard University Press, 1986.

Chamberlain, George Earle (1854–1928)

George Earle Chamberlain attended Washington and Lee University, graduating in 1876. He headed west to Oregon, first teaching school there, then serving as a county clerk, and eventually being elected to the Oregon House of Representatives and then winning election as district attorney for the Third Judicial District (1884–1886). Chamberlain subsequently served as Oregon attorney general (1891–1895) and twice was elected governor. In 1909, the strongly Republican legislature elected Chamberlain, a Democrat, as United States senator, largely on the strength of his popularity in the state and the public support he received from President Theodore Roosevelt.

Reelected in 1915 by popular vote under the newly ratified Seventeenth Amendment, Chamberlain quickly became a national leader and prominent supporter of exempting United States ships from the payment of tolls for use of the Panama Canal. By the time war broke out in Europe in 1914, Chamberlain had become chairman of the Senate Military Affairs Committee and an outspoken advocate of military preparedness in the United States. When President Woodrow Wilson called for American entry into the war in 1917, Chamberlain led in the formulation and passage of legislation establishing selective military service, food control, and financing of the war.

But Senator Chamberlain was independent enough of the Wilson administration to criticize publicly the War Department in early 1918 for its initial handling of mobilization, training of draftees and its failure to furnish troops with adequate guns, uniforms, and other equipment. President Wilson sharply denied Chamberlain's charges in a public statement and subsequently excluded Chamberlain from his circle of confidential advisers on the war.

In 1919, a Senate subcommittee chaired by Chamberlain held hearings on the army's court-martial system and investigated charges by soldiers that the Articles of War were ill suited for an army of draftees called to service against Imperial Germany. With the help of the army's former acting judge advocate general, Samuel T. Ansell, Chamberlain advocated reform of the existing military code to provide more safeguards for the accused and judicial review of serious sentences. This proposed legislation failed to gain congressional support, but the National Defense Act (1920) that did pass included some reforms to the Articles of War that provided for review of serious court-martial sentences.

Chamberlain initially supported Wilson's Treaty of Versailles, but he later switched his position and backed Senator Henry Cabot Lodge's reservations to the League of Nations.

Wilson, in turn, singled out Chamberlain for public criticism in 1920 when he urged Oregon's voters to defeat the senator for reelection. Chamberlain lost in the Harding landslide.

After a brief period of service on the United States Shipping Board, Chamberlain left politics for the practice of law. He subsequently was counsel for former Attorney General Harry M. Daugherty during the Senate investigation of mismanagement of the Department of Justice during Daugherty's tenure. Chamberlain died in 1928.

John M. Lindley

Bibliography
Lindley, John M. *"A Soldier Is Also a Citizen": The Controversy Over Military Justice in the U.S. Army, 1917–1920.* New York: Garland, 1990.

Chaplains

"Chaplain" is the name given to a member of the clergy assigned to meet the spiritual needs of armed services personnel. The United States Army, including air units, and Navy had chaplains corps.

When America entered the First World War, there were seventy-four Regular Army and seventy-two National Guard chaplains. A congressional act of May 1917 increased the number to 194 for the Regular Army, but subsequently this number was found to be insufficient. In September 1917, the General Committee on Army and Navy Chaplains, a board of the Federal Council of Churches, requested that the army, which heretofore had assigned one chaplain for every 3,600 soldiers, or one per regiment, establish a new ratio of one chaplain for every 1,200 soldiers. Based on the Canadian model of one chaplain for every 1,000 soldiers and backed by Gen. John J. Pershing, this proposal was passed by Congress and went into effect in May 1918. By war's end, this ideal ratio had not been met; instead, there was one chaplain for every 1,690 soldiers.

Army chaplain appointments were overseen by the adjutant general's department, which selected chaplains on a proportionally based scale. Army totals for the war were as follows: 2,363 served; 23 died in service; 27 were wounded; 28 received American decorations, including five Distinguished Service Medals; and 57 were awarded foreign decorations. A granite monument was placed in Arlington National Cemetery in Washington, D.C., to commemorate the sacrifice of those chaplains who died in the war theater.

In the navy, the ratio had been one chaplain for every 1,250 service personnel, and in early 1917, there were forty navy chaplains. Navy recruitment came under the aegis of Chaplain John Frazier, a Southern Methodist and chief of the Navy Chaplain Corps. As a preliminary trial, Frazier required all Protestant candidates to preach a twelve-minute sermon. Between 1917 and 1918, 162 more chaplains joined the Navy Chaplain Corps.

The army did not appoint a chief of chaplains until 1920. During the First World War, Charles H. Brent, a former missionary to the Philippines, served as senior chaplain.

Prior to the war, requirements for appointment as a military chaplain were simple. Candidates had to appear before an examining board, which had the power to approve appointments. The lone requirement for approval was "good standing in a denomination," substantiated by five letters of recommendation from other ministers. With the organization and development of ecclesiastical endorsing agencies, the recruitment and appointment of potential military chaplains became more efficient. Educational institutions also attempted to find qualified young men for military service. Three days after America's entrance into the war, Harvard University began registering male students for military service. One of the areas for which they could apply was the chaplaincy. Prospective chaplains to army air units were supposed to have air training, but due to a large number of aviation volunteers and a severe shortage of chaplains, the mandate was not enforced.

Chaplains were not addressed by their military rank—that of first lieutenant—but were referred to simply as "chaplains" in an attempt to emphasize office rather than rank and because many chaplains felt that enlisted soldiers might respond to them more favorably if rank were not used in address. In regard to insignia, chaplains wore both their rank and chaplain's insignia (a Latin cross) on their shoulder loops at the outset of the war. To aid in the deemphasis of rank and promotion of ecclesiastical office, Congress approved a bill directing chaplains to wear the cross alone on their shoulder loops, a situation that sometimes caused confusion in that chaplains were sometimes mistaken for brigadier generals, who

C

wore a lone star on their shoulder loops. Rank insignias were restored in 1926. Jewish chaplains, the first of whom was Rabbi David Goldberg, resisted wearing the Latin cross, to them a symbol of a different faith. They were allowed to wear their own distinctive badge—a shepherd's crook—that had been used in the nineteenth century by the army chaplaincy instead of the cross. After much deliberation, Jewish chaplains were allowed in late 1918 to wear a symbol of the tablets of the Ten Commandments surmounted by the Star of David.

In order to train would-be chaplains, the army in March 1918 established a chaplaincy school at Fort Monroe, Virginia. It was later moved to Camp Zachary Taylor in Kentucky. The five-week course included instruction in military and international law, army regulations, first aid, drill, rules of warfare, and the art of horsemanship, or equitation. Chaplains were not commissioned as first lieutenants until successful completion of the regimen. Until that time, they received the pay and allowances of a private, first class. Those deemed unfit for service could be dropped from the school at any point in the course of study and training. Drill sergeants could not use profanity when instructing candidates, even in drill and calisthenics. The school held seven sessions throughout the war; more than 1,300 men attended and 915 graduated. Some failed to complete the training because they were judged unfit by the faculty, while others did not finish because of illness or academic failure. The school was deactivated in January 1919. Notable graduates included John W. Bricker, a United States senator, and John M. Thomas, former president of Middlebury College.

By order of General Pershing, a second chaplain's school was opened in France in July 1918 southeast of Paris near Chaumont. Later the school with a faculty of seven was relocated to Le Mans. This school was established in order to train chaplains already serving in the war zone who had not been able to benefit from stateside training. The course of instruction lasted two weeks and was similar to the stateside school—notable exceptions were courses in French language and history. There were also classes in gas defense drill, map reading, the chaplain at the front, and censorship. Because of a wide diversity of beliefs among the chaplains and because time was limited, there was no instruction in theology. It was assumed that the chaplains had obtained adequate profes-

sional education. The military schools were geared to prepare them for the rigors of military duty. Before closing in June 1919, the Le Mans faculty had trained more than 600 chaplains.

Manuals and instructional materials were also important for the military chaplain, especially for organizational purposes. Some of the more popular manuals used were Alva J. Brasted's *Suggestions for Newly Appointed Chaplains* (1918), Orville J. Nave's *Handbook on the Army Chaplaincy* (1917), and George J. Waring's *Chaplain's Duties and How Best to Accomplish His Work* (1912).

The duties and responsibilities of the chaplains were many and were not always associated with the traditional ecclesiastical service. Generally, duties included military responsibilities in addition to the ministry. Chaplains held religious services wherever they could, including huts, tents, ships, libraries, dugouts, under trees, and in the open air. Most of the time, there was a "general" or nonsectarian service for soldiers of all denominations and religious persuasions. Thus chaplains had to be flexible and willing to lead services for faiths other than their own. Attendance was generally voluntary, although compulsion was sometimes used. Favorite sermon topics covered such themes as Loyalty, Honesty, and Fear, among others. Popular hymns included "Onward, Christian Soldiers," "Trust and Obey," "Nearer, My God, To Thee," and "What a Friend We Have in Jesus." At times, services were also held for enemy prisoners of war. Chaplains occasionally preached in local churches when requested by local clergy.

Some of the chaplain's nonministry-related duties included serving as officer of the post exchange and mess, heading special funds, participating as athletic leaders, being mail censors, as well as acting as defense counsel in courts-martial. The latter responsibility was especially dreaded by many chaplains, who had very little legal training.

Other duties of the chaplain consisted of performing marriages; visiting barracks, hospitals, and guardhouses; providing counseling; conducting Bible classes; writing letters for servicemen; and providing general moral and morale support. Serving as burial officers was also part of the chaplain's obligation. This task involved organization and supervision of burial of soldiers, insuring they received military honors as well as rites of their faith. In order to attend services at both front-line and rear positions, chaplains used various methods of travel. When a car was not available or proved impractical, chaplains rode horses or walked to their service sites.

Chaplains were often assisted in their work by nonmilitary service organizations, for example, the American Red Cross, Salvation Army, YMCA, the Knights of Columbus, and stateside churches. These organizations provided books, Mass materials, communion sets, typewriters, hymnals, and various religious literature for distribution.

Donald Dowless

Bibliography
Cox, Harvey, ed. *Military Chaplains*. Nashville, TN: Abingdon Press, 1969.
Honeywell, Roy J. *Chaplains of the United States Army*. Washington, DC: Department of the Army, 1958.
Jorgensen, Daniel B. *The Service of Chaplains to Army Air Units, 1917–1946*. Vol. 1. Washington, DC: Office, Chief of Air Force Chaplains, 1961.

Charles I (1887–1922)

Charles I, the last emperor-king of the Dual Monarchy of Austria-Hungary, was born at Schloss Persenberg, the first child of Archduke Otto of Habsburg-Lorraine and Princess Maria Josepha of Saxony. Known as Archduke Charles Francis Joseph until his accession to the throne, he spent his childhood far removed from the limelight of the court and imperial politics. As a great-nephew of Emperor Francis Joseph, he became heir to the throne only through a remarkable chain of events. He was two years old when his cousin, Crown Prince Rudolf, committed suicide at Mayerling. In 1896, the death of his grandfather, Charles Ludwig, next in the line of succession, made his uncle Francis Ferdinand the heir, but Francis Ferdinand's marriage to Countess Sophie Chotek was a morganatic union, placing Charles's father next in line after Francis Ferdinand. Otto died in 1906 at the age of forty-one. Thereafter, as second in line to the throne, the young archduke remained in his uncle's shadow until the assassination at Sarajevo on June 28, 1914, elevated him to the position of Francis Joseph's heir.

The young Charles received a strong Catholic upbringing and studied at the prestigious Schottengymnasium in Vienna. He entered military service in 1905 as a cavalry of-

ficer and remained on active duty until 1912, retiring one year after his marriage to Princess Zita of Bourbon-Parma. Charles returned to the army at the start of World War I and served in the central headquarters at Teschen. In March 1916, he received his only major field command, as head of the XX Army Corps on the Italian front. He remained there until the summer of 1916, when he was reassigned to the Eastern Front in a reshuffling of commanders following heavy Austro-Hungarian losses caused by Russia's Brusilov offensive. The eastern army, plagued by sinking morale and a shortage of reserves, made a strong impression on Charles. As early as August 1916, in discussions within the inner circle of the Habsburg leadership, he raised the possibility of a compromise peace.

Because Francis Joseph entrusted his young heir with no responsibilities other than his army duties, Charles inherited the throne on Nov. 21, 1916, as a political novice. During his two-year reign his strongest influences were the former political associates of the late Francis Ferdinand and his own assertive wife. The empress allegedly was responsible for a series of "humanitarian" orders issued by Charles shortly after his accession, including a requirement of specific imperial authority for the use of poison gas on the battlefield and an end to all aerial bombardment that might endanger civilians. Habsburg military leaders opposed these unrealistic measures from the start, and in the spring of 1917 persuaded the emperor to rescind them.

After ascending the throne Charles assumed personal command of the armed forces, moving the headquarters from Teschen to the town of Baden, just south of Vienna, where he could remain directly involved in military decision-making without leaving the capital. In May 1917, he reconvened the Austrian parliament, inactive since 1914, and attempted to spur long overdue political reforms in the kingdom of Hungary by firing the powerful Hungarian minister-president, István Tisza. Two months later Charles proclaimed an amnesty for political prisoners and relaxed wartime censorship, measures that quickly backfired in a wave of antigovernment agitation by various nationalist groups. But by far his most significant departure from the policies of Francis Joseph came in the so-called "Sixtus Affair," his secret peace initiative to the French government.

In the spring of 1917, Charles initiated contact with the French through his brother-in-law, Prince Sixtus of Bourbon-Parma, an officer in the Belgian Army. Sixtus visited Raymond Poincaré and continued to serve as an agent between the emperor and the French president for two months before talks collapsed, mostly because Charles was prepared to offer little that would satisfy Italy's war aims. In Austria the small circle of people aware of the initiative excluded even Count Ottokar Czernin, the Habsburg foreign minister. The contact remained secret until April 1918, when French Premier Georges Clemenceau made the startling revelation. Charles denied the reports from Paris and reassured William II of his fidelity to the German alliance, but their personal relationship and the overall alliance of the Central Powers remained strained for the duration of the war. Public opinion in both Germany and Austria-Hungary doubted the veracity of the emperor's denials, and he never recovered from the loss of credibility. Czernin resigned shortly after the scandal broke.

Charles's last attempt to preserve his empire took the form of the "People's Manifesto" of Oct. 16, 1918, which promised to convert the Austrian half of the Dual Monarchy into a federation of autonomous nation-states. By then, however, national committees had been formed to represent most of the nationalities in question, and some had secured the formal recognition of the Entente Powers. On October 21, even the German Austrians formed their own provisional national assembly, laying the foundation for the future Austrian republic. Ten days later Charles made the first official acknowledgment of the breakup of Austria-Hungary, turning over the Habsburg Navy to the Yugoslav National Committee. Ironically, his throne survived longer than that of William II. On November 11, two days after the abdication of the German emperor and four hours after the final armistice went into effect on the Western Front, Charles renounced his voice in the political affairs of Austria without formally abdicating or forswearing the rights of his heirs.

Charles spent the winter of 1918–1919 at Schloss Eckartsau, east of Vienna on the Hungarian border, before retiring to Switzerland in March 1919. Having never issued a statement regarding his Hungarian rights, he welcomed the rise to power in Budapest of his old friend Miklós Horthy, a former Habsburg admiral, who became regent of Hungary in March 1920. Nevertheless, the two attempts by Charles to claim the Hungarian throne, in March and October of 1921, both failed because of the resistance of Horthy, who opposed Charles on the grounds that Hungary's neighbors would never accept a Habsburg restoration. After the second attempt Charles was turned over to the commander of the British Danube flotilla; the British Navy then transported the former emperor and his family to exile on the Portuguese island of Madeira. At the Paris Peace Conference, the victors had reserved the right to treat William II as a war criminal but made no such claims against Charles. His deportation and captivity rested on shaky international legal ground and must be viewed as a pragmatic move by the Great Powers to preserve the postwar peace of Central Europe.

Charles died on April 1, 1922, succumbing to pneumonia after only five months on Madeira.

Lawrence Sondhaus

Bibliography

Brook-Shepherd, Gordon. *The Last Habsburg*. London: Weidenfeld & Nicolson, 1968.

Feigl, Erich, ed. *Kaiser Karl: Personliche Aufzeichnungen, Zeugnisse und Dokumente*. Vienna: Amalthea, 1984.

Hoyer, Helmut. *Kaiser Karl I und Feldmarschall Conrad von Hötzendorff*. Vienna: Verlag Notring, 1972.

Rieder, Heinz. *Kaiser Karl, 1887–1922*. Munich: Callwey, 1981.

Château-Thierry Sector

From March 21, 1918, to July 15, 1918, Germany mounted five offensive operations on the Western Front as the General Staff tried to end the war before the American Expeditionary Force could effectively reinforce the beleaguered Allies. The Treaty of Brest-Litovsk with Russia allowed the German Army to transfer enormous numbers of troops to the Western Front facing the British and French armies. Recognizing that American forces would soon create insurmountable odds for Germany, Field Marshal Erich Ludendorff rushed to engage the Allies before Pershing's forces were strong enough to resist the German assault.

The first two attacks at the Somme and the Lys river were not decisive. On May 27, 1918, Ludendorff launched the third—the most damaging and the most successful—offensive across the Chemin des Dames where the French were spread quite thinly, the weakest link in the Allied line. The Germans opened up with a major artillery barrage all along the line, shattering the French defenses, particularly at the juncture of the British and French armies, crushing whatever opposition might have delayed their forward movement. Upwards of fifty relatively fresh German divisions were massed for this offensive. Many were soon across the Aisne and then the Vesle rivers, using bridges left intact by the retreating French. The Germans held nine miles of line at the end of the first day of the offensive.

The following day the Germans advanced beyond the town of Soissons, and by June 1 they had exceeded their objectives, reaching the banks of the Marne River. They were now in a position to envelop the town of Château-Thierry and advance along the south and north banks of the river toward Paris, a mere forty miles to the west. Along the way, German units had captured 60,000 prisoners, 650 guns, 2,000 machine guns, and enormous quantities of materiel.

When it became obvious to General Pershing that the Germans were launching an offensive that the French could not hope to contain, the American commander of the American Expeditionary Force offered his modest resources to Field Marshal Ferdinand Foch. The 1st Division (Regular) was already committed at Cantigny, where they had just performed successfully. The 26th "YD" New England National Guard Division and the 42d "Rainbow" National Guard Division, composed of troops from all over the United States, were also assigned to other areas. Pershing had but two other divisions with which he could help stem the German tide. They were the 2d and 3d Divisions.

Lt. John T. Bissell and a small advance unit from the 7th Machine Gun Battalion (Motorized), 3d Division, left for the front to establish defensive positions at the wagon bridge at Château-Thierry and in the town proper, arriving on May 31. On the morning of June 1, Bissell's unit, which was posted at the first crossroad just north of the main bridge in order to protect the north and east approaches to Château-Thierry, covered the retreat across that bridge of what was left of a French Senegalese division. At approximately 10:00 P.M., French pioneers prematurely demolished the bridge, killing both the oncoming German soldiers and the Senegalese rear guard as they reached the

middle of the span. Lieutenant Bissell and his platoon, who had been cut off by the explosion, managed to make their way to the railroad bridge—and in the dark that was a notable feat. Through the bravery of a Lieutenant Cobby, who heard their distress call, the platoon managed to make their way across to safety. During the night of June 3–4, that railway bridge was also blown, cutting off all ties to the northern bank. For the French it was a fitting end to what had been a catastrophic rout of the past four days.

The German forces, which were still advancing north of the Marne, ran into the U.S. 2d Division, composed of infantry (Regular Army), marines, and supporting troops, along a line running north and eastward from Château-Thierry. The Germans, having already occupied the town of Belleau, noted for its magnificent spring and its small hunting preserve (the Bois de Belleau), were now catching their collective breath and reorganizing for the final push to Paris. The 2d Division would stop them permanently, effectively saving Paris, and quite likely the Allied cause.

By June 2, 17,000 infantrymen of the 3d Division arrived and established positions along the south bank of the Marne across from the occupied town. The main parts of the division were the 5th Brigade, composed of the 4th and 7th Infantry units plus the 8th Machine Gun Battalion. The 6th Brigade was composed of the 30th and 38th Infantry and the 9th Machine Gun Battalion. The 7th Machine Gun Battalion was the division's own battalion. The 3d Division would remain essentially in the same positions for nearly two months, being credited with four separate engagements, and they helped to stem two German offensives during that period.

During the next few weeks, troops from the 3d Division controlled the bridges at Château-Thierry, successfully repelled German attacks on the town, and counterattacked. This was the defensive period of the Château-Thierry action, and for the 2d Division it ended on June 5. For the 3d Division it dragged on for some weeks and did not end until after the Germans tried to cross the Marne on June 15. In the meantime, one regiment of the 5th Brigade was assigned a different role during the month of June. The 7th Regiment joined the marines in and around Belleau Wood itself during the middle of June so that elements of the 5th Marine Brigade could get a respite from their con-

C

stant engagement during the previous fifteen days. During their period at Belleau Wood, the 1st Battalion, 7th Infantry participated in an attack, which was ordered by Col. Wendell C. Neville, USMC, commanding the 5th Marines, on June 19, and again on June 20. Both attacks were unsuccessful, with about 25 percent of the unit killed or wounded. Back at the Château-Thierry river line, the 4th Infantry was having some difficulty, "shifting about a good deal," as the division commander later said, but by June 19, it was occupying a portion of the line just east of Château-Thierry in good order.

The 6th Brigade was stretched out to cover much of the seven-mile front from Château-Thierry to Varennes, with its two infantry regiments and machine gun battalion. Later, when both the 4th and 7th Infantry regiments returned to their parent division, they would take the western portion of the river while the 6th Brigade moved toward the right flank. The 30th Infantry returned from its supporting role at Vaux and was next in line after the 7th Infantry; the 38th Infantry was on the far right of the line. In mid-July, the 28th National Guard Division from Pennsylvania would come up on the 38th's right.

The month of July moved along quietly until the 15th when a well-planned German alternate offensive, designed to widen the Château-Thierry front, was launched across the Marne directly at the 6th Brigade. All of the German endeavors in the west against the 2d Division had been successfully resisted, forcing the Germans to take what appeared to be an easier course toward Paris. They were wrong.

The German forces included both their 10th Division on the west and the 36th Division on the east flank. The attack began with an artillery preparation at 12:10 A.M., followed by infantry units crossing the Marne in pontoon boats. At 3:50 A.M. a rolling barrage was followed by the main infantry attack. The U.S. 5th Brigade was saturated with gas and high-explosive shells but faced no infantry crossings of consequence. However, the 30th, 38th, and 28th divisions faced determined assaults by experienced German units.

Between Mezy and Sauvigny there is a huge northward bend in the river. It was there that the 38th Infantry earned the sobriquet "Rock of the Marne," which endures today. A French division, the 125th, which was east of the 38th Infantry, folded up almost as soon as the Germans arrived and only managed to re-

form, somewhat, about five miles south of its starting point. Its retirement completely exposed the right flank of the 38th. Company F, 38th Infantry, which was situated just opposite the town of Varennes, was subjected to the German assault on both flanks and to its front, making a very unpleasant few hours for that small unit and its mother battalion. The balance of the 38th was similarly engaged and, though outflanked on three sides for several miles, repulsed the enemy, making the other German successes impossible. When General Pershing wrote his final report of World War I, he commented, "A single regiment of the 3d Division wrote one of the most brilliant pages in the annals of military history in preventing the crossing at certain points on its front, while on either side the Germans, who had gained a footing, pressed forward." The 30th held fast, as did the 4th and 7th; therefore the outcome of the German attack was decided almost before it had begun.

In early June, the 2d Division was already in place to the northeast, but some of its units were still somewhat disorganized with many still on the road. The 4th Brigade, composed of the 5th and 6th Marines and their 6th Machine Gun Battalion were on the north end of the line, whereas the 3d Brigade, which was composed of the 9th and 23d U.S. Infantry and their 5th Machine Gun Battalion, held the south end, based with their right flank opposite Hill 204, a major observation point for the occupying German Army. The marines would have the impenetrable forest, Belleau Wood, at the center of their portion of the line, whereas the 3d Brigade, Infantry, would have the town of Vaux to their center.

The major activity for the 4th Marine Brigade was the continued assault, which began on June 6, of the hunting preserve of Bois de Belleau, an assault that fell more than half the marine brigade and did not end until June 25. The 3d Brigade was busy, as was the 3d Division with the 23d Infantry during the month of June, taking up part of the 4th Brigade's front as their numbers decreased, with modest readjustments to the 9th Infantry's line as well. The American 2d Division's offensive in that part of the sector during the three weeks of the engagement was at great cost to both sides. The German losses exceeded 9,500 men; the 2d Division losses were nearly 9,800.

Meanwhile, the 3d Brigade of the 2d Division, although relatively inactive compared to its sister brigade, the 4th, was busy throughout the month of June. The division suffered casualties of nearly 1,800 officers and men, mostly from gas attacks. The official division history states that "the 2d Division had consistently maintained that it should conduct only one operation at a time, and therefore nothing should be undertaken here until the Bois de Belleau was clear." The wood was finally cleared on June 25 when the Bois de Belleau was declared "U.S. Marine Corps entirely." Finally, the infantry was given its chance to prove to everyone, especially the marines, that the army too could launch and sustain a successful attack on an important position, the town of Vaux. Orders were issued on June 30, and the assault began on July 1 at 6:00 P.M., preceded by a twelve-hour bombardment. By daybreak of July 2, the infantry was in complete control, and the 23d Infantry was able, the following night, to withdraw from the front line. The 26th Division relieved the 2d Division on July 5–6, giving that overworked division a short rest until the next action.

The 26th Division became part of the Allied defensive of the region and, with the 3d and other U.S. divisions, would participate in the offensive, which began on July 18, as far north as Soissons and south to Courthiezy, approximately nine miles in a direct line east of Château-Thierry, where the 28th "Keystone" Division would also be fully committed.

Germany's third offensive had failed because of the High Command's failure to recognize the consequences underlying the initial dramatic German success. The drive deep into France and the prospect of taking Paris mesmerized Ludendorff, who committed the grievous error of overextending his supply lines; at the same time, he failed to grasp the significance of fresh American forces along the front. As the 2d Division successfully began offensive operations against the Germans in the Belleau Wood region, the American 3d Division held the German advance in June and later blocked new German offensives to the east of Château-Thierry, preventing any breech of the Marne River line. By September, American forces in France had reached a total of eight divisions, organized primarily in American corps, as the Germans were driven back all along the front. The American success at Château-Thierry had shifted the war's momentum permanently.

Vernon Williams

See also BELLEAU WOOD, BATTLE OF

Bibliography
Liddell Hart, B.H. *The Real War, 1914–1918.* Boston: Little, Brown, 1930.

Matloff, Maurice, ed. *American Military History.* New York: McKay, 1988.

McClellan, Edwin N. *The United States Marine Corps in the World War.* Washington, DC: Headquarters, U.S. Marine Corps, 1920.

Millett, Allan R. *Semper Fidelis: The History of the United States Marine Corps.* New York: Macmillan, 1980.

Stallings, Laurence. *The Doughboys.* New York: Harper & Row, 1963.

Chemical Warfare

See UNITED STATES ARMY CHEMICAL WARFARE SERVICE

Children's Bureau

President William Howard Taft established the Children's Bureau on April 9, 1912, as a division of the Department of Commerce and Labor. The purpose of the bureau was to investigate and report upon all matters—education, social development, labor, family life, and nutrition—that affected children's lives. Taft chose former Hull House worker Julia Lathrop as its first director. During the pre-World War I years, Lathrop and her fifteen-person research staff concentrated on compiling statistics on maternal/infant mortality and conducted the first nationwide census of babies.

Director Lathrop, concerned that the war would divert attention away from the growing needs of America's children, pushed the Children's Bureau into the forefront of the war effort. She explicitly linked the democratic war aims of the Allies with the right of children to live in a stable, nurturing home and school environment. To this end, the bureau created programs to benefit both the temporarily fatherless and the permanently orphaned dependents of American soldiers.

At Lathrop's urging, Congress passed the Military and Naval Insurance Act in October 1917. Similar to a plan enacted by Canada, the act provided for supplemental pay for soldiers with families, direct salary deductions paid to the soldier's families, and the availability of war-risk insurance. Among other things, the insurance provided that upon the death or disability of a soldier monthly benefits would be paid to the family until his children reached eighteen years of age.

The wartime bureau provided the basic research underlying the first federal child labor law, which went into effect in September 1917. The employment of children had actually decreased throughout the early 1900s, but as the United States embarked on its military-preparedness campaign, the number of children employed in heavy-manufacturing industries rose. The flood of enlistees and conscripts into the armed forces created a labor shortage and encouraged the return of children to the workforce. While the Child Labor Law was later declared an unconstitutional infringement on interstate commerce and personal liberty, the bureau continued to insist on the abolition of child labor contributed to the passage of the first constitutionally viable child labor law, the Fair Labor Standards Act, in 1938.

In May 1917, the Children's Bureau established National Baby Week to increase public awareness of the needs of the children. The recent declaration of war overshadowed the message of Baby Week, and on April 6, 1918—the one-year anniversary of American participation in the war—Director Lathrop announced Children's Year specifically intended to establish national child welfare as an American war aim. The impetus for the creation of a Children's Year came from the war itself as the physical examinations of thousands of young American draftees revealed the poor state of child medical care in the United States. Easily correctable maladies or the side effects of untreated childhood diseases left thousands scarred and sickly each year and contributed to high numbers of medically unfit draftees. Lathrop, in cooperation with the Women's Committee of the Council of National Defense and independent physicians' groups, organized a campaign to weigh, measure, and physically examine American preschoolers throughout the country, both to gauge the overall health of American children and to offer early preventive care for childhood diseases.

Throughout the war, the Children's Bureau believed that the needs of children were being overshadowed by the exigencies of war. To counteract that perceived imbalance in national priorities, the bureau pushed to have the field of civilian public nursing officially recognized as a legitimate form of wartime service. This discouraged public health nurses from being co-opted by the Red Cross and sent overseas. The bureau also repeatedly emphasized the need to train high-school-age youth in athletics, both to improve the health of future soldiers and to serve as an outlet for restless youths bereft of a male role model at home. The bureau's earlier commitment to maternal and infant health care was also maintained during the war years. Lathrop deserves credit for the eventual passage of the 1920 Sheppard-Towner Act, which established the first federal grant-in-aid program to subsidize state efforts at decreasing maternal and infant mortality.

The final achievement of the Children's Bureau during World War I was the push for a 1919 White House conference devoted to establishing enforceable standards of national child care in the United States. The gathering addressed all the major children's issues of wartime America—health and physical fitness, juvenile delinquency, and child labor legislation—and sought to create national standards to end the disarray and confusion of child-related legislation at the state and local levels.

Kathleen Toerpe

Bibliography

Lathrop, Julia. "The Children's Bureau in War Time." *North American Review* (November 1917).
Four Decades of Action for Children: A Short History of the Children's Bureau. Washington, DC: Department of Health, Education, and Welfare, 1956.

Chinese-American Relations

On the eve of World War I, even as President Woodrow Wilson steered a course of non-involvement in European affairs, he recognized the need to intervene in China (as well as Mexico and the Caribbean). Wilson's interventionist policies seemed well intended but at times were controversial, full of self-righteousness, often contradictory, and smacked of self-interest. His policy toward China included maintaining open trade, inhibiting Japanese expansionism, and helping China become a democracy. Despite good intentions, by the end of the Paris Peace Conference in 1919 Wilson found his China policies teetering on disaster. Many Chinese began to view Wilson's policies toward their nation as a betrayal of trust. Renouncing its ties with the United States, China, rather than embrace democracy, eventually looked toward the doctrine of Karl Marx for direction. Furthermore, Japanese expansionism continued during the 1920s and 1930s jeopardizing U.S. security and world peace.

Much of American policy toward China prior to the First World War was predicated upon desires for unrestrained commercial and hopes that China would become a Christian democracy. Even as early as 1783, American diplomats and businessmen sought to exploit the China market. When Britain forced China to relax trade barriers in the early 1840s, Americans, motivated by their own belief in Manifest Destiny and desires for East Asian trade, sought similar entitlements. In 1844, a special trade treaty, the Treaty of Wanghai, granted the United States both commercial and extraterritorial rights. Between 1840 and 1890, businessmen and Christian missionaries worked to spread American influence throughout China, proclaiming the gospel of democracy, capitalism, and Christian beneficence.

As American industrial productivity increased in the 1890s, businessmen actively sought expanded foreign markets in the Far East. Significantly aiding their quest was President William McKinley's interventionist policies. For instance, military interventions in Cuba as part of the larger Spanish-American War led to the United States emerging with a protectorate over Cuba and an island empire consisting of the Philippines, Puerto Rico, and Guam. The United States also annexed the Hawaiian Islands in 1898, thus completing the connections to the Far Eastern markets.

By the late 1890s, with European powers seeking to bring East Asia within their spheres of influence, America's need to be included in the China market took on a new urgency. Many, like McKinley's secretary of state, John Hay, believed that those who understood China "had the key to world politics for the next five centuries." During his tenure alone American exports to China nearly quadrupled. Cries from American businessmen demanded an open door to China—"and a big one at that." The problem was that European powers and Japan were attempting to partition China into separate and exclusive spheres of influence. Fearing that the United States was increasingly being cut off from trade with China, Hay set out the "Open Door" policy in two notes of 1899 and 1900. The notes pledged America's support for Chinese independence as well as equal access for all nations to China's markets.

Presidents Theodore Roosevelt and William Howard Taft showed great interest in maintaining the Open Door. Nevertheless, Roosevelt, who mediated the Portsmouth Treaty, which ended the Russo-Japanese War, recognized that Japan would never be satisfied with an open trade agreement. Based on Japan's earlier successful war (1894–1895) with China in which China recognized Korean independence and ceded Taiwan, the Pescadores, and the Liautiang Peninsula of Manchuria to Japan, combined with Japan's recent military defeat of Russia, Roosevelt believed that Japan eventually would dominate China. In 1908, hoping to forestall the inevitable, Roosevelt secured the Root-Takahira Agreement with Japan, which pledged Tokyo to respect the Open Door in China in return for America's recognition of Japan's preeminence in southern Manchuria. Symptomatic of much of U.S. policy toward China was Roosevelt's failure to consult the Chinese before entering agreements involving China's rights and sovereignty with third-party nations, especially Japan. Taft, on the other hand, hoped that American money would keep China's trade routes open and good will flowing, while at the same time hold off Japan's acquisitiveness. Both presidents would agree, however, that only the unified efforts of the United States and the European powers could keep Japan's aggressive expansionism in check.

With the coming of the World War in 1914, however, the United States found itself as the only major power capable of constraining the often violent relationship between Japan and China. Both Asian countries were undergoing agonizing changes that would have profound effects on their relationships with each other. In Japan, the Meiji emperor, who had successfully guided colonial acquisitions and strengthened the military, died in 1912. The beginnings of the Taisho era witnessed rigorous opposition to colonization and a large military. Yet with the war in Europe, Japan—believing that China was of vital economic value and strategic concern—took advantage of the vacuum created by the exodus of European powers and began to threaten China's territorial integrity.

As it was also undergoing a revolutionary transformation, China was susceptible to Japan's threats and pressure tactics. A 1911 revolt, largely spurred by nationalist and anti-imperialistic factions, brought 268 years of

Ch'ing dynastic rule to an end. In 1912, Yuan Shih-K'ai, a faction leader, arranged the peaceful abdication of the Ch'ing emperor and created the Republic of China, appointing himself as provisional president.

For the next four years, Yuan attempted to unify the nation by establishing central control over the rebellious provinces and winning foreign recognition. Even before his death in 1916, various provisional leaders who had opposed the Yuan administration had already developed their own military bases, became warlords, and divided the new republic into competing subunits. Wedded to political instability was the emergence of a new politico-intelligentsia who were embarrassed by China's ineffectiveness in international affairs and determined to end the country's record of weak foreign policy. Japanese demands often demonstrated China's ineffectiveness against aggression and produced a nationalistic response, which made it almost impossible for the government to submit to Japan's threats.

It was in such a volatile environment that the Wilson administration found itself becoming more involved in Asian affairs than it had anticipated. Although United States economic ties with Japan were much stronger than with China, Americans had a greater affinity for the Chinese people. Wilson's perception of the Chinese was shaped by his beliefs about God, ethics, the nature and purposes of government, human rights, and the role of the United States in advancing democracy throughout the world, as well as by his own Presbyterian background.

The former Princeton professor detested the imperialistic system that allowed government-backed financiers to exploit underdeveloped nations. Thus, he firmly believed in the Open Door policy that provided the "slow and steady improvement of mankind through the spread of a reformed and socially responsible democratic capitalism." In Wilson's opinion, China should have been left alone to establish its own government, which he assumed would have eventually become democratic. Obvious in his approach toward the Mexican revolution, Wilson saw wisdom in letting a nation's people settle their own internal affairs, for it did not "lie with the American people to dictate to another people what their government should be." Wilson justified his later intervention into Mexico on the basis that all peoples could self-govern "when properly directed." He firmly believed that America could provide that "direction."

Moreover, Wilson's secular thinking on political and economic affairs in China was circumscribed by his belief that China was on the verge of becoming a Christian country. In fact, those who advised him in Chinese relations were often former Christian missionaries who had served in China and believed, as did Wilson, that the "most amazing and inspiring vision" was the "vision of that great sleeping nation suddenly awakened by the voice of Christ." Central to Wilson and his advisers' motivations were the desire to do justice, to advance world peace, and to offer humanity the blessings of democracy and Christianity.

The secular and religious roots of Wilson's thinking formed an important paradigm from which he made decisions about his policy toward China. Even before taking office, Wilson had strong sympathies toward the developing "sister republic" and wanted to promote American influence there. Two weeks after his inauguration, and in line with his thinking about imperialism, Wilson announced the cancellation of a proposed American bankers' loan, denouncing the international banking consortium as potentially compromising of Chinese independence.

Another important decision was his selection of a minister to China. Wilson wanted a person of "pronounced Christian character" who could guide "the men now most active in establishing a new government and a new regime for China in the Christian, democratic tradition." Wilson's first choices included Charles W. Eliot, a former president of Harvard University, and John R. Mott, a leader of the YMCA and chairman of the Student Volunteer Movement for Foreign Missions. Wilson's final choice was perhaps the best person for the job—Paul S. Reinsch, a professor of political science at the University of Wisconsin and one of the few Far Eastern experts in the United States. Wilson also sent Frank Goodnow of Johns Hopkins as a special adviser to Yuan Shih-K'ai.

Perhaps Wilson's most important decision in his early presidency was granting recognition to China's new republic. Although Yuan had formed the republic in 1912, no Western nation had formally recognized it. Wilson was concerned that Russia and Japan were withholding recognition in order to gain commercial and territorial concessions from China. Furthermore, he believed that for the vision of a Christian democracy to flourish, China needed a strong stable government—something that some great powers would try to prevent. On May 2, 1913, Wilson was the first world leader to grant unilateral recognition to the new government. Such action not only shocked some in his own administration, but also suggested to Europe and Japan that the U.S. concern for China was, in reality, a ploy to exact economic and political influence. Because the Japanese hoped to dominate China themselves, Wilson's action only served to heighten Japanese fears and suspicions about American intentions.

The Chinese government, on the other hand, was elated to know that it had an American friend to which it could turn in perilous times. With the outbreak of World War I, that friendship was soon put to the test. Because the Western powers were preoccupied with the war, Japan declared war on Germany. By so doing, Japan could enter the German leaseholds in China and later claim them as spoils of war. Japan easily secured the German leasehold of Shantung Province. And on Jan. 18, 1915, Japan presented China with its "Twenty-One Demands," which, according to some, would have made much of China a Japanese protectorate. The list required China to renew the lease of the southern Manchurian bases, the transfer of the German rights in Shantung to Japan, and Japanese supervision of the Chinese constabulary. Four days later, a tearful Chinese minister visited Paul Reinsch in Peking and informed him that "Japan had made categorical demands which, if conceded, would destroy the independence of his country and reduce her to a servile state."

Despite the apparent seriousness of the situation, the Wilson administration was slow to respond to China's plea for help. Even as early as November 1914, the administration had begun backing away from entangling itself in East Asian affairs, for "it would be quixotic in the extreme to allow the question of China's territorial integrity to entangle the United States in international difficulties." For all its rhetoric about Christian democracy and self-government, there were practical limits on what the administration was willing to do. After reports of the Twenty-One Demands reached Washington, Secretary of State William Jennings Bryan waited several months before objecting mildly to some of the more outrageous aspects of the dictum. Still, as an ardent believer in the Monroe Doctrine, Bryan acknowledged to Japan that its "territorial contiguity create[d] special relations between Japan and these districts."

By May 1915, even though the Japanese significantly toned down their "requests," Woodrow Wilson became convinced that yielding anything to the Japanese was a mistake. On May 5, Wilson sent a note to the Japanese objecting to almost every concession still requested, even some to which Bryan had previously consented in March. In the face of British warnings, and internal power struggles, Japan significantly altered its demands, which were accepted by the Chinese on May 9. Many Chinese were angered and outraged by their government's acceptance of the revised demands. Chinese students and merchants warned their government that surrender to Japan would make China a second Korea. Wilson in effect ignored China's capitulation to the Japanese and responded with a note on May 11. The note argued that the United States could not recognize any agreement between Japan and China that violated American treaties or rights of American citizens, China's political and territorial integrity, or the Open Door policy.

With the disrupted Great Power balance in China due to the war, Wilson's toughened approach in diplomacy spoke to his own decreasing confidence in competition and the belief that America could economically compete with Japan and China. By 1916, Wilson reversed his policy toward financial consortiums and began to explore the possibility of having American bankers rejoin the international loan consortium they had left in 1913. He believed that the conditions of the new consortium would protect China from imperialistic designs of the other major powers, for, as the United States became more involved in the war in Europe, the administration found that it could not contain Japanese expansionism alone.

On April 6, 1917, the United States entered the war in Europe. In August 1917, China declared war on Germany largely at the encouragement of President Wilson. By declaring war, China could confiscate enemy properties, cancel old treaties, and consider members of the Central Powers as enemy aliens. Entry into the war also gave China a needed place at the postwar peace conference in order to reclaim the former German leasehold at Shantung. Though initially opposed by Japan, Tokyo eventually saw the wisdom of allowing China to declare war on Germany. Since Peking was under the control of warlords (some of whom were pro-Japanese), Tokyo reasoned that China's entry

C

into the war would only smooth a path for better relations between the two nations.

With America's entry into the war, Japan also sought to consolidate its position in China. Guaranteed through secret treaties with the Allies, Japan claimed postwar title to the German islands in the North Pacific and to German concessions in Shantung Province. Japan hoped that the United States, which was not a party to those treaties, would also recognize its interest. In June 1917, Tokyo proposed a general affirmation of its rights in China, which had already been accepted by the United States in March 1915 but had since come under renewed scrutiny. Secretary of State Robert Lansing, Bryan's successor, wrote to Japanese officials explaining that the United States recognized "special relations between Japan and the districts of Shantung, Southern Manchuria and East Mongolia," but it might not in the future. In September 1917, a Japanese delegation, led by the former foreign minister Viscount Kikujiro Ishii, met with Lansing to settle the two nations' differences.

After much heated debate, both men sought a resolution that would project an impression of harmony. The result was a memorandum of agreement that recognized Japan's special interests in China in return for a reiteration of both governments' adherence to the tenets of the Open Door. The agreement was so loosely constructed that it did little except allow each country to justify its interests. Many saw it as a reversal of the American Open Door policy in China. Wilson, however, argued that there was no change in policy but rather "a distinct gain for China" because Japan agreed not "to take advantage, commercially or industrially, of the special relations to China created by geographical position." Few Chinese saw it as a panacea for Japanese acquisitiveness, and many protested the Lansing-Ishii Agreement vehemently. Especially annoying to the Chinese was the fact that they were excluded from the negotiation process. They disliked the notion that the Chinese government and people were passive victims of international realities.

As a war measure, the agreement may have harmonized relations between America and Japan for the moment, but ultimately it failed to restrain Japanese expansionism in China. Late in 1917, Japan began to tighten its rein on Shantung; in 1918, it offered loans for additional concessions. Japan cited the Lansing-Ishii Agreement as justification for its actions.

Shortly after the Bolshevik Revolution of November 1917 forced Russia out of the war, Japan also sought to establish influence in Siberia. Wilson saw it essential to maintain harmony with Tokyo, even while taking measures to curtail Japanese expansion.

When Russia began separate peace negotiations with the Germans in the spring of 1918, the Allies wanted Japan to intervene in Siberia, a move which they believed would bring the Russians back into the war. Despite Wilson's misgivings, it became apparent that the Japanese would send troops to Siberia regardless of what the other powers wanted or did. Japan was intent upon strengthening its position in the region adjacent to Manchuria (something Japan had hoped to do with the Twenty-One Demands). Wilson reacted to the determined Japanese by demanding that an international coalition join Japan in an expedition to Siberia. According to the Allies' agreement, Japan was to send only 8,000 soldiers; by November 1918, Japan had over 72,000 troops in Siberia. Although the Europeans left in 1919, over 6,000 American troops remained in Siberia until 1920, keeping a watchful eye on the Japanese. Japan withdrew its troops from Russia in 1922, having failed in obtaining either Russian or Chinese territories.

When the Allies met at the Paris Peace Conference from January through June 1919, the Japanese were determined to keep the German islands in the Pacific and to obtain Germany's rights and concessions in Shantung. Of course, China opposed such measures, and for its participation in the war desired to reassume the former German and Austrian rights in its country. Wilson had agreed with Peking, although tense negotiations made it clear that the Japanese would rather pull out of the peace talks and spoil Wilson's desire for a League of Nations than recant their position on China. Wilson eventually capitulated to Japanese demands, but not until he exacted assurances from Tokyo that Japan's rights would not exceed those of the Germans. Moreover, Wilson received assurance that Shantung would be given back to China in "full sovereignty" and that the Japanese would evacuate the area in a reasonable time.

By the end of the conference, Wilson had lost not only his dream of a unified league, but negotiations on the question of concessions had also caused a tremendous rupture between the United States and China. In fact, on May 4,

1919, thousands of politically active students held large demonstrations in Peking to protest the Japanese-American deal and the groveling of the warlords. Many Chinese felt shocked and betrayed by America and the West. Despite its good intentions, American foreign policy seemed fraught with self-interest and indecision. Notwithstanding Wilson's recognition of China, his breaking up of the six-power banking consortium in 1913, his turning back of Japan's aggression toward China in 1915, and his exhausting work at Versailles on behalf of China's needs, much of his East Asian policy ultimately failed. Japanese expansion continued, China became neither Christian nor democratic, and East Asian relations with the United States became only more strained.

Espousing antiforeign sentiments, along with internal cultural and political reform, the Chinese began to look beyond the United States for help in establishing governmental stability. Despite the Washington conferences of 1921 and 1922 as well as the Five-Power and Nine-Power treaties that addressed China's political and territorial integrity, China's new nationalistic ideologues found little room for Western assurances. In 1928, the Communist Party came under the leadership of Mao Tse-tung, who offered the Chinese people hope for a brighter future devoid of Western interference and empty promises. Furthermore, in 1931, the Japanese began a series of incursions into Manchuria that resulted in the Sino-Japanese War beginning in July 1937. Indeed, China's own internal instability combined with the American and European failure to stop Japan's expansion and growing militarism during World War I and after eventually led to the Sino-Japanese War and later to the events at Pearl Harbor on December 7, 1941.

Mark R. Grandstaff and *Weizhong Lee*

See also JAPANESE-AMERICAN RELATIONS; LANSING-ISHII AGREEMENT; TWENTY-ONE DEMANDS

Bibliography

Jiang, Arnold X. *The United States and China*. Chicago: University of Chicago Press, 1988.

La Fargue, Thomas E. *China and the World War*. New York: Fertig, 1973.

Link, Arthur S. *Woodrow Wilson: Revolution, War, and Peace*. Arlington Heights, IL: Harlan Davidson, 1979.

Reed, James. *The Missionary Mind and American East Asian Policy, 1911–1915*. Cambridge: Harvard University Press, 1985.

Schaller, Michael. *The United States and China in the Twentieth Century*. New York: Columbia University Press, 1990.

C

Christy, Howard Chandler (1872–1952)

Howard Chandler Christy was an illustrator, portraitist, and mural painter. He is best known for his paintings, the most famous of which, "The Signing of the Constitution," now hangs in the United States Capitol. From 1910 to 1920, Christy gained fame for his magazine illustrations and especially his World War I public service posters.

Christy, born in Morgan County, Ohio, moved to New York as a young man to study art. In 1895, he abandoned fine art for a lucrative career in magazine illustration. During the Spanish-American War, he also served as a war correspondent, accompanying Teddy Roosevelt's "Rough Riders" to Cuba. He returned from the war with a reputation as a military artist, but he soon grew tired of drawing soldiers. He then developed the "Christy Girl," which became a popular fixture of his magazine illustrations and World War I posters.

A fervent patriot, during World War I Christy donated his talents to the war effort. Receiving assignments from the Division of Pictorial Publicity, Christy created posters for war bond drives, recruiting campaigns, and the Red Cross. His best-known poster, titled "Gee I Wish I Were a Man," struck a chord with the male population, and the winsome "Christy Girl" lured thousands of young men into naval recruiting centers.

In 1921, the United States Naval Academy graduating class elected Christy an honorary class member in recognition of his public service. The only civilian ever to receive this distinction, he proudly wore his class ring for the remainder of his life. Christy retired from illustration in the same year and devoted himself to portraiture, but his patriotism led him to continue creating public service posters. Christy died in New York City on March 4, 1952.

Dawn A. Tepe

Churchill, Marlborough (1878–1947)

An American soldier with two classic names from modern military history was destined to succeed. Marlborough Churchill made his mark in the field of military intelligence. Born in Andover, Massachusetts, young Churchill was the son of a professor of sacred rhetoric at Andover Theological Seminary. He studied at Phillips Academy and graduated from Harvard University in 1900. He received a commission as a second lieutenant in the coast artillery in 1901 and served at Fort McHenry and Fort Howard for four years, then spent two years in the field artillery at Fort Riley, Kansas, Fort Sam Houston, Texas, Fort McKinley, Philippine Islands, and Fort Sill, Oklahoma. From 1907 to 1910, 1st Lt. Marlborough Churchill served as aide-de-camp to BGen. Albert L. Myer. Captain Churchill was an instructor at the field artillery school at Fort Sill from 1912 to 1914 and edited the *Field Artillery Journal* from 1914 to 1916.

Major Churchill served as an observer with the French Army from January 1916 to June 1917, when he was detailed to General Pershing's staff. After promotion to the rank of colonel, Churchill served as acting chief of staff of the U.S. First Army's artillery from February to May 1918, then returned to the United States, where he assumed duties as assistant chief of staff for military intelligence at the War Department, succeeding Col. Ralph Van Deman, who had been ordered to France. This exchange of duties improved the strained relations between the War Department intelligence arm and the G–2, American Expeditionary Force (AEF).

Churchill was promoted to the grade of brigadier general in August 1918 and served as the director of army intelligence until June 1920. From December 1918 until March 1919, Churchill served as general military liaison coordinating officer for the Peace Commission. General Churchill had presided over a military intelligence establishment that was shrinking quickly during postwar demobilization, and his successor, BGen. Denis E. Nolan, continued the essential reorganization of the agency.

General Churchill died on July 9, 1947, in New York City.

John F. Votaw

Bibliography

Bidwell, Bruce W. *History of the Military Intelligence Division, Department of the Army General Staff: 1775–1941.* Frederick, MD: University Publications of America, 1986.

Van Deman, Ralph H. *The Final Memoranda,* ed. by Ralph E. Weber. Wilmington, DE: Scholarly Resources Books, 1988.

Civil Liberties Bureau

The Civil Liberties Bureau (CLB) was formed by Roger N. Baldwin and Crystal Eastman on July 1, 1917, as a subsection of the American Union Against Militarism (AUAM) to provide legal counsel for conscientious objectors and to pose a legal challenge to conscription laws. Many CLB members were noted progressives, social reformers, conservative lawyers, and clergymen. The bureau's methods consisted of lobbying congressmen and making personal appeals to government leaders for changes or clarifications in federal laws and wartime policies.

Within months of the CLB's formation Baldwin began to support unpopular radical groups and their causes, alienating many of the bureau's more moderate members. The CLB/AUAM partnership disintegrated, and Baldwin formed the National Civil Liberties Bureau (NCLB) on Oct. 1, 1917.

Although the NCLB remained involved with conscription cases, it expanded its role to include defending conscientious objectors in court, challenging prosecutions under the Espionage and Sedition acts, publicly speaking out against vigilante and mob violence directed toward dissenters and aliens, and seeking due process and fair trials for those people Baldwin and his staff deemed were victims of government oppression.

Along with its new emphasis the NCLB changed its tactics. Members openly distributed literature reaffirming the right of free speech for all and decrying government repression and vigilante actions by liberty leagues and ultrapatriotic groups. They publicly spoke out against censorship and held mass meetings to show their opposition to conscription.

When the NCLB began aggressively to defend the rights of members of the Industrial Workers of the World (IWW), the government's cooperative attitude toward the bureau changed dramatically. Because the government viewed the IWW as a revolutionary organization composed of radicals, German agents, and saboteurs, the NCLB was similarly categorized as a left-wing organization that championed pacifist, antiwar, and obstructionist causes. In late 1917, the U.S. Army Military Intelligence Division and the Bureau of Investigation began to compile dossiers on bureau members, tap their phones, raid NCLB headquarters, and step up seizures of bureau publications. The movement to support radical rights and subsequent censure by the federal government cost the NCLB much of its remaining moderate and liberal support, especially in the media. It also caused internal controversy as prominent NCLB members abandoned the organization. The government campaign against the activities of the NCLB climaxed in November 1918, when Roger Baldwin was sentenced to eleven months in prison for refusing military induction.

The war ended by the time Baldwin was released from jail in late 1919, but the federal government's assault on the civil liberties of radicals, aliens, and dissenters continued and actually intensified. Baldwin decided to carry on his wartime work. On Jan. 19, 1920, the NCLB was reorganized and became the American Civil Liberties Union (ACLU). Instead of focusing on pardons for conscientious objectors, the ACLU now began pushing for a general amnesty for all political prisoners. The ACLU was an early and outspoken critic of the tactics and deportations carried out by the Justice Department and Bureau of Investigation during the Palmer Raids and Red Scare of 1919–1920. The group raised funds and publicly supported those arrested during the raids and offered many defendants legal representation at their deportation trials. This continued support of unpopular groups and causes further cemented the ACLU's reputation as a radical organization that supported revolutionaries and those deemed "un-American." In fact, however, the ACLU was a unique private organization that did not represent any particular special interest; rather, it impartially defended the civil liberties of all groups, especially the right of free speech.

Clayton D. Laurie

See also AMERICAN UNION AGAINST MILITARISM

Bibliography

Johnson, Donald. *The Challenge to American Freedoms: World War I and the Rise of the American Civil Liberties Union.* Lexington: University of Kentucky Press, 1963.

Murphy, Paul L. *World War I and the Origins of Civil Liberties in the United States.* New York: Norton, 1979.

National Civil Liberties Bureau. *War-Time Prosecutions and Mob Violence.* New York: National Civil Liberties Bureau, 1919.

Walker, Samuel. *In Defense of American Liberties: A History of the ACLU.* New York: Oxford University Press, 1990.

C

Clark, James Beauchamp (Champ) (1850–1921)

Prior to entering Congress as a Democrat, James Beauchamp Clark was president of Marshall College, edited two newspapers, and practiced law. He was elected from Missouri's 9th District to the United States House of Representatives in 1893 and, except for one term (1895–1897) remained there until his death on March 2, 1921, although he was not reelected in 1920.

Clark was chosen minority leader by the Sixtieth Congress (1907), rose to the speakership in the Sixty-second Congress (1911), and returned to head the minority again when his party lost control of the House in 1919. He was the Democratic front-runner for president in 1912 but eventually lost the nomination to Woodrow Wilson.

As Speaker of the House when the United States entered World War I, Clark neither took part in the short debate nor voted on the declaration of war on April 5, 1917. Thus, one can only surmise his position. Reportedly, he reflected his constituency's views by opposing the declaration. His silence was the result of his position within the Democratic Party and the government.

In May 1917, however, when President Wilson requested imposition of the military draft, Clark took the floor to oppose it, arguing that the nation had fought foreign wars earlier with volunteers and should do so again. He added that young men deserved the right to serve their country of their own free will and that "in the estimation of Missourians there [was] . . . precious little difference between a conscript and a convict." A noted orator, he closed his speech by saying that he had given his son, Bennet Champ Clark, permission to join the military and that, while he prayed for his safe return, should the younger Clark fall in battle, his father wished to have "the privilege of carving on his tombstone these words: 'This man, a Missouri volunteer, died fighting for his country.'"

Despite Republican suggestions later that Clark was less than patriotic because of his earlier attitudes, during the war he worked for almost all measures the administration thought necessary to prosecute it. He did, however, assail the censorship provision and other aspects of the Espionage (1917) and Sedition (1918) acts. He favored Wilson's war aims as stated in the Fourteen Points message but was not a warm supporter of the Treaty of Versailles in 1919.

Clark was considered by his contemporaries as a simple, strong, impulsive, yet scholarly man without pretensions or affectations.

Robert S. La Forte

Bibliography

Clark, Champ. *My Quarter Century of American Politics.* New York and London: Harper, 1920.
Morrison, Geofrey F. "A Political Biography of Champ Clark." Ph.D. dissertation, St. Louis University, 1972.

Clemenceau, Georges (1841–1929)

After a life that encompassed medicine, journalism, and politics, Georges Clemenceau rose to supreme power in the darkest hours of France's ordeal. His indomitable spirit and determination to mobilize and employ his country's last resources to gain victory earned him the sobriquet *Père-la-Victoire* from his countrymen in their hour of victory. Like Winston Churchill a generation later, Clemenceau came to symbolize France's heroic contribution to the Allied victory.

"The Tiger," as he came to be known for his ferocity in the internecine fighting that characterized the politics of the Third Republic, was naturally drawn to politics by his family and its origins. The Clemenceau family came from the Vendee, the region perhaps most divided by the Revolution of 1789. Vendeean royalists had waged a bitter civil war against the revolutionaries, and republican armies had devastated the region to bring it under the central government's control. In the mid-nineteenth century, the province was still divided between royalists and republicans. Clemenceau's family was staunchly republican. His father, Benjamin, whose ardor for republicanism was as fierce as his hatred for organized religion, was the major influence on Clemenceau in his formative years.

Not surprisingly, these beliefs played a crucial role in Clemenceau's development. Like his father, he studied medicine but quickly gravitated to journalism and politics. He enjoyed the heady days of the "liberal empire" period of Napoleon III's reign. Clemenceau spent one month in jail because of his political activities, but it was a broken friendship with radical Auguste Blanqui, and a failed romance, not governmental oppression, that sparked his decision to go to the United States.

He spent four years in America, earning his livelihood as a journalist and chronicling the triumphs and problems of Reconstruction. The young journalist met many of the republic's most important figures; perhaps not surprisingly, he developed a lively admiration for Thaddeus Stevens, the champion of "radical" Reconstruction. While earning money as a French instructor, he met and married, after an involved courtship, an American woman, Mary Plummer. The marriage produced three children, but it was not a happy one and ended in divorce.

Clemenceau returned with his new wife to France in 1870, where he was almost immediately swept up in the tumultuous events of *L'Année Terrible.* At age twenty-nine he was appointed provisional mayor of the XVIII Arrondissement of Paris and was elected to the post during the siege of Paris in November 1870. Although he was elected to France's National Assembly, Clemenceau's most crucial role during the "Terrible Year" came in Paris in the famous uprising, the Commune, which began in his district when the army attempted to seize artillery that the national guard had parked in Montmartre. Though attacked by both sides, Clemenceau seems to have done his best to defuse the confrontation between the army and the people. But his intervention came too late, and when two generals commanding the troops attempting to spirit away the guns were arrested and shot by *communards,* Clemenceau found himself in personal danger. He succeeded in leaving his district, then resigned from the National Assembly when the radicals won a majority and officially proclaimed the Commune. He left Paris and thus missed the Commune's bloody denouement.

Clemenceau returned to local Paris politics following the Commune. Indeed, politics and journalism now became his life. He won a seat in the new Chamber of Deputies in 1876 and quickly earned a reputation as a duelist, a fearless and implacable journalist, and a wrecker of governments. Although he never outgrew this reputation, Clemenceau's political program was ambitious and reflected the goals and beliefs of his generation of republicans. Clemenceau and his supporters were most interested in solidifying the separation of church and state, including the suppression of the monastic orders, instituting civil divorce, and guaranteeing free, obligatory, and secular primary schools. "The Tiger" also strongly advocated improved civil liberties in France and the abolition of the death penalty. His was a republicanism firmly rooted in the traditions of the Great Revolution of 1789.

Clemenceau found himself at the center of all the important controversies that enlivened the first three decades of the Third Republic. He helped sponsor General Boulanger's appointment to the ministry of war, then helped bring down this "man on horseback" when the danger of a coup d'état became apparent. Clemenceau's prominence in the gaudy lifestyle of *Tout Paris* gave credence to charges that he had profited from the Panama scandal and ultimately cost him his seat in parliament. At age 52, his political career seemed over.

Like most Frenchmen, Clemenceau had little interest in the beginning of the Dreyfus Affair in 1894. But as more information emerged suggesting that Jewish army captain Alfred Dreyfus had been falsely charged and convicted of espionage and that the army was attempting to cover up its complicity in a grossly improper investigation and trial, Clemenceau swung his considerable journalistic talents to examining "the Affair." Indeed, for more than two years he scarcely wrote about anything else, turning out over 600 articles that would comprise seven volumes. From his post on the newspaper *L'Aurore* he composed the headline "*J'accuse . . .*" to introduce Emile Zola's sensational open letter to the president of the republic charging the army with systematic obstruction of justice. When Dreyfus was retried, again convicted, and then offered a pardon, Clemenceau urged him to spurn this offer and continue his fight for complete vindication, although privately he understood the Dreyfus family decision to accept the pardon.

The Dreyfus Affair intruded into almost every aspect of French political, intellectual, and cultural life, and it placed great strains on the fragile links that kept the Third Republic from collapsing into its rival constituencies. For Clemenceau, however, "the Affair" marked his return to politics; he would go on to win a Senate seat in 1902. He also became editor-in-chief of *L'Aurore* in 1903. He seemed set to pursue his domestic political program, first by finally accepting a cabinet post, the interior ministry, early in 1906, then by becoming premier in October. For thirty-three months, the Clemenceau ministry, which included five future premiers, ruled France. In an increasingly tumultuous period marked by social unrest and labor activism, Clemenceau was censured by all sides for his tough but even-handed dealing with these problems. Increasingly, however, Clemenceau, his government, and France found themselves drawn into the vortex of international politics that led to the outbreak of the Great War.

Clemenceau understood France's weakness in comparison to Germany; nevertheless, he wrote defiantly of his country's determination to resist German pressures. This tough-minded stance toward Germany won respect and support from conservatives who found his domestic politics an anathema. As a nobleman told Maurice Paléologue, "That Jacobin all of a sudden appeals to me. Danton must have talked like that!" His realism compelled him to help obtain loan guarantees for the tsar—the price of Russian support at Algeciras—money that allowed Russia's autocrat to prorogue the Duma. As premier, he worked hard to strengthen the new Entente Cordiale with Britain and won high marks for his handling of the Bosnian crisis of 1908–1909. It was also during his premiership that France finally established a Conseil Superieur de Guerre. Surprisingly, he also appointed Ferdinand Foch, a deeply religious man with a Jesuit brother, as director of the war college.

Clemenceau's government fell in the summer of 1909. For the five years preceding the "cataclysm," he resumed his familiar role as "the Tiger," the breaker of governments. Joseph Caillaux's ministry collapsed when Clemenceau demonstrated that Caillaux had lied about informal contacts he had initiated to improve relations with Germany in 1912.

The coming of war in 1914 brought a *union sacrée* to French politics, a coalition that

Clemenceau pointedly refused four times to join. His critics asserted that it was unbridled ambition that kept him from serving France in her hour of greatest need. While ambition doubtlessly played a role, it ought to be added that Clemenceau had spent much of his career opposing this kind of compromise—a wishy-washy suppression of essential differences he felt all too characteristic of French politics—and he felt that the "sacred union" of all political parties could not successfully prosecute the war.

Outside the cabinet, Clemenceau served on the Senate's Army Commission, which was charged with providing direct government oversight of the battlefield, and the Foreign Affairs Commission. These posts gave him information and a rostrum, and he spent the war's first three years criticizing what he viewed as the government's ineffective prosecution of the war and army commander Joffre's bloody, ineffectual offensives on the Western Front. It is not at all certain that Clemenceau ever said that "war is too important to be left to the generals"; it is clear, however, that he believed this strongly. From the beginning of the war, he wanted it prosecuted to the bitter end. He was also a confirmed "westerner," opposing what he viewed as the dissipation of France's fragile strength by opening fronts in Greece or the Dardanelles.

Clemenceau also continued his journalistic career during the war. His newspaper, *L'Homme libre*, proved so bitterly critical of the government and its policies that the authorities invoked the provisions of military censorship to suppress it. Quickly Clemenceau founded a new paper, *L'Homme enchaîné*, which became a publishing success and immediately earned the censor's wrath. The paper's ever present bold-faced concluding line, "The Boches are at Noyon," reminded all France just how close the German lines were to Paris.

The great French crises of 1916–1917 thus found Clemenceau ideally placed to make his views known forcefully. In 1916, the year of Verdun, he criticized Joffre's failure to prepare the garrison adequately for its ordeal. He then turned his attention to the government, which earned his censure for its failure to clamp down on rising antiwar and antigovernment propaganda spread by defeatist groups. In 1917, against the background of the Russian Revolution, the disastrous Nivelle offensive, and rising domestic unrest in France, Clemenceau focused on the government's failure to rally the country, and he called for a supreme effort by France to win the war. He specifically wanted the country's leadership to show its soldiers that their sacrifices were not in vain and that the country's leaders meant business.

The deadly series of crises in 1917 brought about an end to the *union sacrée* and ultimately swept Clemenceau into power. On Nov. 20, 1917, French President Raymond Poincaré, putting the country's efforts above his own preferences—like most politicians he had often crossed swords with Clemenceau—called the old man to supreme power.

Clemenceau's government carried France to victory. While national morale inched up only slowly, there is little doubt that the sight of the country's premier, at seventy-six, visiting the front, meeting the embattled poilus, being under fire, and at least once risking capture stirred Frenchmen during their great ordeal. At the same time, "the Tiger's" claws remained sharp. The career journalist maintained a tight military censorship and initiated prosecution of one of his former cabinet members, Joseph Caillaux, for treason. Still Clemenceau's "reign of terror," as it was sometimes called, encompassed only three executions and 1,700 arrests.

In 1918, Clemenceau played a truly pivotal role as France staggered to victory. He galvanized a wavering government, shivering in dread of a massive German offensive, with his most famous philippic—that whatever the situation, "I wage War!" His presence and pressure helped achieve a unified military command structure among the Allies on the Western Front. His realism helped bridge the differences between the eternal optimism of the new Allied commander, Ferdinand Foch, and the deep pessimism of the army's commander, Henri Pétain. He defended both men before the French parliament; at the same time he made it clear that the army High Command was no longer a law unto itself, but would follow the government's direction. In the closing months of the war, Clemenceau "bagged" one more Ottonian ministerial scalp: Austrian Foreign Minister Count Ottokar Czernin resigned when the French premier publicized the secret negotiations Emperor Charles I had initiated to extract the battered Austro-Hungarian Empire from the war.

France lay prostrate and exhausted in her hour of victory, and Clemenceau's understanding of his country's plight shaped his goals for the peace negotiations of 1918–1919. Although seriously wounded in an assassination attempt on Feb. 19, 1919, "the Tiger" had recovered enough to pursue French goals at the Versailles conference. France needed protection from German aggression. Never again could she hope to face Germany alone. This meant, in turn, that whatever her other demands, France required allies. Clemenceau failed in this at Versailles. Neither Britain nor the United States wanted a long-term alliance with France, nor would either country agree to the kind of absolute security arrangements—a Rhine frontier, permanent occupation of the Rhine bridgeheads, or the establishment of separate states along that river—that France believed were required by the collapse of the wartime coalition. Although the differences between the "realist" Clemenceau and the "idealist" Wilson over the peace treaties have often been emphasized, it seems clear, as Clemenceau noted, that the two men agreed on goals, but they were very far apart on the ways and means to achieve them.

Clemenceau's failure at the peace conference completed the circle of his enemies. The Left, which still condemned his treatment of socialists and pacifists during the war, was now joined by the Right, which pounded on his failure at Versailles. After failing to win the presidency, Clemenceau retired from public life early in 1921. He died in Paris on Nov. 24, 1929.

In many ways Clemenceau's volcanic career prefigured that of his younger contemporary, Winston Churchill. Clemenceau held power during the supreme crisis of the Great War; had France faltered in 1918, it is difficult to see how the Allies could have won the war. Like Churchill, it was Clemenceau's task to rally his country to face this crucial year. His long career prepared him for this task—his implacable stare and ferocity in debate caused his contemporaries to fear him, and doubtlessly aided him in his lonely leadership post.

Gary P. Cox

Bibliography

Bruun, Geoffrey. *Clemenceau.* Cambridge: Harvard University Press, 1944.

Duroselle, J.-P. *Clemenceau.* Paris: Fayard, 1988.

Newhall, Davis S. *Clemenceau: A Life at War.* Lewiston, NY: Edwin Mellen Press, 1991.

Watson, David R. *Georges Clemenceau: A Political Biography.* London: Fyre Methuen, 1974.

Coffin, Howard Earle (1873–1937)

Howard Earle Coffin was born on Sept. 6, 1873, near Milton, Ohio. He studied engineering at the University of Michigan but never completed his course work. Still, his experiments with automobiles led to his appointment as head of development at the Olds Motor Works in 1902. In 1922, he and Roy D. Chapin established the successful Hudson Motor Car Company.

Coffin wrote extensively on design and production techniques and became identified with a movement among trade associations, engineers, and scientists that hoped to rationalize production systems through standardization of specifications and materials, uniformity of procedure, and the dissemination of data.

Coffin's vision and connections made him well suited to survey the capacity of the nation's industry for war production, which he did for the Naval Consulting Board in 1916. In the same year, he was appointed to the Council of National Defense, and in 1917, he became chairman of the Aircraft Production Board. Coffin's efforts were critical in building national commitment to a large-scale air power program.

Suspicions by Congress and the military of Coffin's auto interests, as well as chronic delays in aircraft production, left him with a minimal role in production management once the program was funded in July 1917. In March 1918, he resigned from the board, defending himself against unsubstantiated charges of corruption.

In 1919, Coffin became president of the Society of Automotive Engineers and of the National Aeronautical Association in 1923. He was a founder, president, and chairman of the board of the National Air Transport Company, which later evolved into United Airlines. He died on Nov. 21, 1937.

Jacob Vander Meulen

See also COUNCIL OF NATIONAL DEFENSE; NAVAL CONSULTING BOARD

Collins, James Lawton (1882–1963)

James Lawton Collins was born in Algiers, Louisiana. Upon graduation from the United States Military Academy at West Point in June 1907, he was commissioned a second lieutenant of cavalry. His initial assignment was at Fort Robinson, Nebraska, with the 8th Cavalry, where he distinguished himself by organizing and commanding one of the first machine gun platoons in the cavalry.

In 1910, his regiment went to the Philippines, and he served with it at Batangas, Luzon, and Jolo. He was detailed as aide-de-camp to Gen. John J. Pershing, the commander of the Department of Mindanao in early 1911. While at Jolo, Collins led the first detachment sent out by the 8th Cavalry against hostile Moros and personally commanded the American forces at the Bagsak operation for the last two days of the battle.

Returning to Pershing's headquarters as the general's aide in January 1914, Collins briefly commanded a troop of the 11th Cavalry in December 1915. However, in March 1916, he was recalled by General Pershing to serve as his aide during the Punitive Expedition into Mexico.

When Pershing sailed for Europe as commander of the American Expeditionary Force (AEF) on May 28, 1917, Collins accompanied him as his aide. In June 1917, he was detailed as an observer with the First French Army at Verdun to report back to Pershing on trench warfare and the French organization for combat. In September 1917, having transferred from the cavalry to the field artillery, Collins attended the Field Artillery School at Saumur; on completion of the course, he rejoined General Pershing as aide with the rank of colonel. On May 1, 1918, he was appointed secretary of the General Staff, headquarters of the AEF, where he remained until assuming command of the 1st Battalion, 7th Field Artillery of the 1st Division on October 8. Colonel Collins led his battalion in the Meuse-Argonne campaign where he earned a Silver Star for gallantry.

After the Armistice, Collins was recalled for duty as secretary of the General Staff of the AEF. He was a member of the General Staff board to study and report on the General Staff organization best suited to the United States Army. Its findings and recommendations had considerable influence on the later reorganization of the War Department General Staff.

Collins returned to Washington, D.C., on Aug. 1, 1919, and attended the Army War College there. He later served on the War Department General Staff and was military attaché in Rome, 1928–1932. In 1937, he attended the coronation of King George VI, again as aide to General Pershing. He held various commands until his retirement as a major general on Aug. 31, 1946. Collins died on June 30, 1963.

James L. Collins, Jr.

Bibliography
Marshall, George C. *Memoirs of My Services in the World War 1917–1918*. Boston: Houghton Mifflin, 1976.
Pershing, John J. *My Experiences in the World War*. New York: Stokes, 1931.
Smythe, Donald. *Pershing*. Bloomington: Indiana University Press, 1986.

Commission for Relief in Belgium

Herbert Hoover founded the Commission for Relief in Belgium (CRB) in London in October 1914 as a private organization to provide food for German-occupied Belgium. Belgium's attempts at resistance to German military demands at the outbreak of the Great War had aroused much popular sympathy in England and the United States. A densely populated, industrialized country, Belgium depended on imports for three-quarters of its normal food supply. When the German Army began to requisition local foodstuffs and the British blockade cut off imported sources, 7 million Belgians faced severe hunger as the winter of 1914–1915 approached. When the American ambassador in London, Walter Hines Page, met with Belgian representatives, they concluded that Herbert Hoover was the best choice to administer some emergency relief action. The comprehensiveness of the program, however, was the result of Hoover's personal determination to feed the entire nation.

The CRB conducted its humanitarian work on an unprecedented scale and with a unique administrative organization. The official CRB documentary history cites a British characterization of the commission as a "piratical state organized for benevolence." Like a pirate state, the CRB flew its own flag, negotiated its own treaties, secured special passports, fixed prices, issued currency, and exercised a great deal of fiscal independence. Its bold acts of benevolence were accomplished with an efficiency and integrity that later became a model for modern foreign aid.

The basic facts hint at the scope and complexity of the undertaking. Between 1914 and 1919, the CRB dispensed nearly $1 billion in order to feed 9 million Belgian and French citizens behind German lines. Strictly maintained accounting records, provided pro bono by a prestigious accounting firm, present a clear picture of the CRB's finances. Funding was secured through a complex combination of guaranteed loans and subsidies from the Belgian, British, French, and United States governments combined with an outpouring of charitable contributions, as well as considerable donated transportation and services. About 78 percent of the money came from direct governmental subsidiaries. Initially, most funds came from the Allied governments, and then after 1917 primarily from United States congressional appropriations. In the final accounting report, administrative overhead came to less than 1 percent.

About sixty full-time American administrators, most unpaid, supervised over 130,000 Belgian, French, and American volunteers. The CRB purchased about 5 million tons of food in the United States, Canada, and Argentina and then shipped it through the war zone to Belgium and northern France. The Americans, who as neutrals were allowed to travel freely in Belgium, coordinated distribution with thousands of local Belgian volunteers and members of the Comité National de Secours d'Alimentation (known as the CN).

Political obstacles were far more daunting than the logistical problems. CRB ships loaded with grain were repeatedly threatened by both German submarines and hostile British admirals. Hoover tirelessly negotiated with such wartime leaders as British Prime Minister Herbert Asquith, David Lloyd George, Winston Churchill, German Chancellor Theobald Bethmann Hollweg, President Wilson, Col. Edward House, and Senator Henry Cabot Lodge to keep the CRB operating.

Hoover's motivation for initiating the CRB was very complex and grew out of his experiences as a successful international mining engineer based in London. In 1914, at the age of forty, Hoover was at the peak of his business career. He served as a director of eighteen financial and mining companies with total capital in the range of $55 million. He controlled investments in major Australian, Burmese, South African, and Russian mines. In terms of sheer size, his Russian mining and forestry holdings had a combined area larger than Belgium. He had amassed a substantial fortune, although much of it was not in liquid assets. More importantly, he had acquired formidable experience in the use of money and power, deploying men and equipment, and in negotiating with foreign governments. He was anxious to put his restless energy and managerial skills to use for the public good. Already he was exploring possibilities such as the purchase of a newspaper or perhaps

even serving as the president of his alma mater, Stanford University.

While the outbreak of war threatened to throw his far-flung mining operations into disarray, he used the crisis as an opportunity for service. Hoover appointed several close business associates, including his trusted brother Theodore, to oversee his business ventures and then devoted himself with intense and almost ruthless concentration to the emergencies created by the international crisis. Transportation was disrupted, banks closed, normal financial transactions across borders were abruptly halted. As a result, tens of thousands of American travelers and tourists were stranded at the outbreak of the war. Just as fourteen years earlier as a young mining engineer in China, he and his wife, Lou Henry Hoover, had set up a field hospital for victims of the Boxer Rebellion, now in wartime London he and Lou used their private means and considerable initiative to create a self-help organization, the Committee of American Residents in London for Assistance of American Travellers. The committee, already in full operation by Aug. 6, 1914, coordinated scores of volunteers to assist thousands of American tourists and travelers fleeing the Continent, many of whom were cut off from their normal source of funds. During the first two months of the war, Hoover, with the support of the American ambassador, distributed $400,000 in loans and gifts, including some $150,000 in U.S. government funds. This experience shaped Hoover's views about the best means of organizing an effective humanitarian response to a political crisis. He was highly critical of bureaucratic waste, especially the teams of governmental officials traveling in luxury at public expense to inspect a situation that Hoover had already reported on in depth.

The characteristics of the committee were shaped by Hoover's improvisation during the chaos of impending war. He was forced to pull together funding from all available sources, including private and public sectors, loans, and charitable donations. He established the authority of his committee by working with high-level government officials but preserved the charitable nature of the work by keeping it officially private. Working without compensation, Hoover made the disinterested humanitarian nature of the work clear. He built a team of pragmatic volunteer administrators, many engineers. The charity was based on hard-headed logic rather than traditional appeals to sentiment. Above all, he insisted on personal administrative control. Two months later these same traits were codified on a larger scale for the working arrangements of the CRB.

The plight of the hungry Belgian children in particular took his attention. Hoover felt the need for quick action since he was very aware that malnutrition in growing children can cause lasting physical and mental damage. He founded the CRB in October 1914 with a group of trusted friends from his circle of mining engineers and businessmen. Like the London-based committee, it was an essentially private enterprise. A private volunteer organization was free of the corruption of expense accounts, maintained low administrative overhead, and enjoyed the prestige of a charitable institution. Also like the London American committee, the CRB secured high-level governmental support. Both Walter Hines Page and Brand Whitlock, American minister in Brussels, supported the CRB and gave it the legitimacy to negotiate with German authorities. Technically, President Wilson considered the ambassadors to be acting as private citizens in this matter. This ambiguous mix of private prestige and governmental legitimacy came to be the hallmark of a long series of organizations established by Hoover. The pattern was set by the circumstances of the American Committee, expanded to serve the CRB, and later replicated many times in the U.S. Food Administration, American Relief Administration, and presidential conferences.

A third feature of the CRB, which also set the tone for later Hoover organizations, was its monopoly on relief. This can be traced to the hectic days of the London American committee when Hoover competed with other committees for control over travelers' aid. Hoover used a number of mechanisms from well-timed newspaper articles to connections with high-level diplomats to assert his control over relief in Belgium. He insisted that all donations from whatever sources be administered through his organization in order to eliminate waste, competition, and redundancy. Competitors would be rapidly dispatched, including the independent and well-funded Belgian Relief Committee which had been established in New York some weeks prior to the founding of the CRB. Hoover was also able to persuade the prestigious Rockefeller Foundation that his organization should take precedence in receiving fund allocations. His organizational genius was acknowledged by the Allied authorities and the still neutral United States.

Hoover played the role of the pivot in an intricate diplomatic balancing act that required constant adjustments. For each of the countries involved, the CRB posed serious problems while it provided handsome benefits. Hoover fought for the preservation of the CRB on many fronts simultaneously. In each country he had to keep his opponents in check in order to insure a continuous flow of food supplies to the German-occupied territory, whose welfare he essentially adopted as his own.

The CRB posed difficult public relations problems for Britain. Clearly, Britain had a vested interest in the continued strength and resolve of its occupied ally. The British population, like the American public, was very sympathetic to the plight of the Belgians and contributed large sums for their relief. The government certainly wanted to prevent the Belgian workforce from serving the German military in exchange for daily rations. As citizens of a neutral country, American administrators, given Hoover's ability to secure guarantees from the Germans, were able to distribute British funds in Belgium. Despite these natural sympathies for the Belgians, Hoover never received unqualified support from the British. Sharp divisions in the cabinet over the utility of the CRB resulted in rapidly shifting policies toward what Hoover viewed as a human response to an emergency.

When the CRB was founded in October 1914, Prime Minister Herbert Asquith and Foreign Secretary Sir Edward Grey initially approved the concept of food shipments from neutral ports on neutral ships to land in Rotterdam for overland transport to Belgium, provided the Germans did not seize the food. Asquith immediately faced a rebellion from his cabinet, including Lord Kitchener, Lloyd George, Churchill, and Reginald McKenna, all of whom objected to humanitarian aid. Their reasoning followed traditional military thinking, which was totally alien to Hoover. In this view, as the invading force, the German army had the complete responsibility for provisioning the population in occupied territory. This situation would force Germany either to divert funds to feed the country or face food riots and world condemnation. Food relief would only be diverted to feed German troops. By maintaining a tight blockade of the Continent, Britain could use the hunger in Belgium to undermine the German military machine. In an effort to sound less cynical, the British cabinet maintained that relief in Belgium would prolong the war and lead to more suffering in the long run.

Hoover was well aware that public opinion did not accept this cold logic and that the British cabinet, unlike the German High Command, was very sensitive to public pressure. While he succeeded in securing official British approval of the CRB, he never overcame the resistance of the British military, which presented a continuing series of obstacles from bureaucratic inertia to a formal investigation of Hoover on trumped-up charges of espionage, at Churchill's instigation. Each time the Germans evaded their agreements and profited from Hoover's shipments, the British responded with new demands and conditions for permitting food through the blockade. Hoover, caught in the middle, played each side against the other. Over the long run, British support for the CRB strengthened as the moral idealism of the CRB proved to have unexpected advantages in modern warfare. Hoover won over a major ally in the Foreign Office, Lord Eustace Percy, who facilitated the interests of the CRB with increasing finesse throughout the war.

The most problematical country in Hoover's geopolitical balancing act was Germany. For the Germans, outside food subsidies presented the strong advantage of relieving the occupation authorities of any financial responsibilities toward feeding the population of 7 million Belgians and later 2 million Frenchmen. Without that subsidy the German occupation army faced food riots and civil disturbance, perhaps outright rebellion, that would divert energy from the front lines. In addition, the Germans exploited any loopholes in their agreements and weaknesses in security to divert Belgian-produced food to the German Army. The scale of thefts was kept very small by Hoover's consistent efforts to plug any holes in security as they appeared. Despite assurances to the British to the contrary, Hoover was well aware of the benefits of his program to the German occupation forces under the command of Governor-General von Bissing, and he freely used this card in negotiations with him.

Von Bissing for his part played a very cautious game. For the strong strategic advantage of incoming food relief, he was keenly aware of the dangers involved in the programs. Not least of these was the effect of fifty energetic American administrators freely touring the Belgian countryside, in new imported cars—greeted with cheers and applause. Several were accused of subverting their neutral role and spying for the British, a charge later revealed to be fictitious. Nonetheless, from the German military's point of view the potential was alarming. There were other disadvantages for the Germans. By feeding unemployed Belgians, the CRB indirectly cut off a source of cheap labor for the German Army as well as supporting the passive resistance of the population. As the war dragged on, a domestic liability became apparent when the German population began to complain that the Belgians were better fed than the citizens of Imperial Germany.

In a steady succession of crises in negotiations with von Bissing and his deputy, Oscar von der Lancken, Hoover fought to maintain hard-won agreements for the safe passage of CRB ships, passports for his administrators, security from requisition for his food supplies. Several well-marked CRB ships were torpedoed with the loss of crew members. Some American administrators were expelled. Food shipments were occasionally diverted for German use. Hoover met each threat to his program with aggressive threats and deals of his own.

At one point in 1915 he stabilized the CRB's guarantees by negotiating directly with Chancellor Theobald von Bethmann Hollweg in Berlin. Later Hoover rescued the CRB from an apparent attempt to cancel its guarantees by negotiating with General von Sauberzweig, the officer responsible for the execution of British nurse Edith Cavell. With a certain audacity, Hoover initially attempted to secure partial funding for the relief from the German government itself, a bold initiative that eventually failed but one that served Hoover well as a lever to secure funding from the Allies. Hoover did succeed in maintaining German tolerance for the American supervised relief, from October 1914 to 1919. At several points the Germans made it clear that relief efforts would only be permitted if supervised by neutral Americans under Hoover. Even Hoover's adversaries conceded that only his bold tactics could accomplish such a feat.

For the Belgian people caught between the German occupation and the British blockade, Hoover's personal determination to provide for them in the time of need came as a totally unexpected boon. Thousands of spontaneous letters of thanks poured in to the Brussels office of the CRB each week. Expressions of gratitude were often creative, taking the form of children's artwork. Hundreds of emptied flour sacks from American mills were covered with Belgian embroidery and fine lace and given to relief workers or sold to raise funds.

Even while the benefits to Belgium were self-evident, relief politics inside Belgium were far from straightforward. The logical person to coordinate distribution of food inside Belgium was Emile Francqui, a director of the main bank, one of the wealthiest men in the country, a veteran of establishing the Belgian Congo, and a participant in other international ventures. Hoover and Francqui had met thirteen years before in China, where they clashed over conflicting business interests. In fact, Hoover had once testified against Francqui in court. When they met again on Oct. 19, 1914, they had to overcome deep personal animosity in order to found their historic joint enterprise of the CRB and the Comité National, which oversaw the Belgian side of the operation. Francqui returned to Belgium and spoke to Brand Whitlock, the American minister in Brussels, of Hoover's managerial genius.

The old animosity between the two resurfaced later in the course of the relief work as Hoover pressured Francqui's organization to keep better records, provide better security, and enforce sanctions against cooperation with the Germans. Hoover held the Comité National responsible for the illegal diversion of food to the German Army and for the difficulties those leaks caused with the British cabinet. Francqui, for his part, countered in kind. In fact, at one point in February 1916, Francqui went to London with letters of assurances from the Germans in an attempt to eliminate the role of the Americans altogether and place the Comité National in complete control. The British rejected this proposal given the CN's vulnerability to pressure from the occupation army. Both Francqui and Hoover became concerned that their disputes threatened to overshadow the historic significance of their joint undertaking. Eventually, a more cordial relationship evolved.

Compared with Britain, Germany, and Belgium, the French government posed relatively few problems for Hoover and the CRB. Once the German Army secured northern France, appeals came to Hoover for aid. He considered the expansion of the CRB into northern France to be inevitable, the only obstacle was funding. Obtaining German cooperation for supplying northern France was one of

the main purposes of his trip to Berlin in January 1915. The French government was at first reluctant to finance the relief directly, thinking the work of the CRB might lend legitimacy to the German occupation. Hoover engaged the assistance of a French mining engineer, an old acquaintance, Louis Chevrillon, to expedite negotiations. To save face, the French subsidies were initially funneled through the Belgian government in exile in Le Havre. This arrangement maintained the flow of food into occupied France until funding ran short in 1917, and the American government took over the primary financial responsibility.

There was both a positive and a negative side to the American response to the CRB. Hoover's friends in the press, such as Ben S. Allen of the Associated Press office in London, interpreted the mission of the CRB to the American public and served as a conduit for Hoover's carefully timed press releases. The spontaneous response in the United States was enthusiastic. At the outset of the war, Mrs. Hoover returned to California with instructions from her husband to send a shipload of supplies to Belgium. With a capacity for organization very similar to her husband's, she easily succeeded in raising funds in California and organized a boatload of food, one of the first to reach Rotterdam, en route to Brussels. A letter to the governor of Kansas was all it took to secure another shipload. Charity for Belgium was a very prestigious activity for American society women and occupied the time of Edith Wharton as well as Alma Spreckels. It soon became apparent, however, that charity would not be sufficient.

Engaging American administrative talent proved to be one of the easiest aspects of the effort. Hoover drew on former classmates, old business associates like Edgar Rickard, and American diplomats such as Hugh Gibson. This core of devoted supporters helped the Chief, as he was known, develop a series of charitable international institutions. Hoover's popularity in the United States seemed assured.

It was an unexpected blow to the organization when a former mining associate and once loyal friend of Hoover's named Lindon Bates, the man in charge of the New York CRB office, accused Hoover of violating the Logan Act of 1793. The Logan Act prohibits private citizens from negotiating treaties with foreign governments in controversial matters. Senator Henry Cabot Lodge was prepared to investigate the allegations. In October 1915, Hoover traveled to New York to deal with this challenge. Both Woodrow Wilson and Theodore Roosevelt assisted Hoover in reestablishing the solid reputation of the CRB. Hoover personally met with Senator Lodge to calm his fears, and the investigation was dropped. Bates had lost his son when the Germans sank the *Lusitania,* and Hoover attributed the trouble Bates caused the CRB to the emotional turmoil resulting from this family tragedy.

The need for a larger financial base became obvious by the end of 1916. In January 1917, Hoover, with Wilson's support, began to lobby for U.S. congressional appropriations. The entry of the United States into the war altered the fundamental nature of the organization. No longer neutral, the United States substituted massive financial support for its former administrative assistance. As the Americans were forced to withdraw from Belgium, they arranged for neutral Dutch and Spanish administrators to assume the direct supervision of relief.

Until the spring of 1917, Hoover had been directly involved in the European arena. He had observed the front lines, sailed through mine-infested waters on some forty voyages, was subjected to body searches by hostile military officers, witnessed zeppelin raids and aerial bombardment. He had fought political battles at the highest levels on all fronts. With the U.S. entry into the war, Hoover was under consideration for several possible roles. Ultimately, he was tapped by Wilson for the position of U.S. food administrator. In that capacity he was able to continue oversight of the relief in Belgium from his Washington office. The Food Administration permitted him to expand on his recent experiences in creative ways within the United States. Then at the end of the war he used this base to build the American Relief Administration, eventually providing for Soviet relief in 1921.

From all accounts, Hoover thrived on the challenges posed to the CRB and welcomed the openings they provided into postwar politics. The moral justification of the relief work coincided completely with his drive for public influence. His contentious personality was an asset in overcoming opposition in England, Germany, Belgium, and the United States. His basic objectives were clear to himself and the American public. From the outset, the CRB was an "absolutely new thing in History," accord-

ing to Professor E.D. Adams. The ultimate dimensions became clear only with the conclusion of the war as events played themselves out. In a very real sense the CRB fundamentally changed American assumptions about its role in the world and its obligations to Europe.

Elena Danielson

See also FOOD ADMINISTRATION; HOOVER, HERBERT CLARK; PAGE, WALTER HINES; WHITLOCK, BRAND

Bibliography
Burner, David. *Herbert Hoover: A Public Life.* New York: Atheneum, 1984.
Gay, George I., and H.H. Fisher. *The Public Relations of the Commission for Relief in Belgium: Documents.* Palo Alto, CA: Stanford University Press, 1929.
Hoover, Herbert Clark. *Memoirs of Herbert Hoover: Years of Adventure, 1874–1920.* New York: Macmillan, 1961.
Nash, George. *The Life of Herbert Hoover: The Humanitarian, 1914–1917.* New York: Norton, 1988.
Whitlock, Brand. *Belgium under the German Occupation: A Personal Narrative.* London: Heinemann, 1919.

Commission on Training Camp Activities

On the eve of America's entry into the European war, Secretary of War Newton D. Baker recalled Raymond B. Fosdick's report on the army's morale problems on the Mexican border in 1916. Baker now proposed to address the homesickness, liquor, prostitution, and motion pictures, all of which seemed to be the major causes of discipline and morale problems. Although the General Staff wanted to close training camps to civilian social workers, Baker, at Fosdick's behest, asked welfare organizations to enrich camp life with their ideas, money, and manpower. Fosdick, an investigator for the Rockefeller-supported Bureau of Social Hygiene (BSH), became chairman of the War Department's newly created Commission on Training Camp Activities (CTCA), serving as a volunteer while the BSH paid his salary. Fosdick also chaired a similar commission, created in July 1917 by Secretary of the Navy Josephus Daniels.

Camp reforms were born of idealistic as well as practical concerns. While President Wilson and Secretaries Baker and Daniels believed military training could promote progressive social ideas and sustain middle class virtues, they also realized that soldiers and sailors debilitated by drunkenness, disease, and boredom made poor crusaders. They saw camps and naval stations as potential models of the planned use of leisure time as well as proving grounds for prohibition, sex education, and vice control, reforms only tentatively adopted in some of the nation's cities. The CTCA was a means whereby a progressive social reform agenda and its embracing cultural paradigm could be more deeply inserted into American life.

Seven volunteer organizations—the YMCA, YWCA, Knights of Columbus, Jewish Welfare Board, Salvation Army, War Camp Community Service, and the American Library Association—vigorously assayed the task of supplying educational and recreational services. CTCA's specially created agencies focused on restricting the trainees' access to liquor and prostitutes, though they provided some educational, recreational, and environmental services. Five of the "Seven Sisters," as they were dubbed, represented religious sects.

The YMCA assured Fosdick that its social halls would serve all regardless of faith; however, the "Y" allowed no Catholic representation on its National War Work Council. Catholics contended that the YMCA intended to proselytize, so the War Department sanctioned the Knights of Columbus and the Jewish Welfare Board (JWB) to provide programs paralleling those of the YMCA. YMCA social centers supplied, free of charge, nearly a quarter million motion picture programs and other entertainments and published *Trench and Camp*, a weekly herald of association and camp events in thirty-five editions. The YWCA operated about 100 "Hostess Houses," whose sitting rooms, cafeterias, verandas, and nurseries teemed with men and women on visiting days. Long popular with the British and American Expeditionary Forces in France, the Salvation Army was allowed in 1918 to dispense in American camps their hallmark coffee and doughnuts.

Services provided by two nonsectarian groups touched many lives. The War Camp Community Service (WCCS) promoted hospitality and friendliness in the 600 communities adjacent to the camps and naval stations. The American Library Association circulated almost 3 million books and maintained 24,500 periodi-cal subscriptions in library buildings erected by the CTCA in thirty-six camps and naval stations as well as in branch libraries located in other service buildings.

The Military Draft Act prohibited liquor sales to soldiers and outlawed prostitution in a zone around each military installation. CTCA coordinated enforcement, monitored conditions in communities near the camps and naval stations, and informed civic officials of their findings. Local police could enforce federal law or see their cities inundated by military police and Justice Department agents. The War Department also closed uncooperative communities to soldiers and sailors on leave and publicized violations. Women arrested for prostitution in camp zones were confined in CTCA detention houses before trial (their right of habeus corpus thereby suspended) and given medical treatment for venereal disease. Sanitary Corps personnel educated soldiers, sailors, and marines about the danger of venereal disease and urged those infected to seek immediate treatment. At the war's end, Fosdick claimed that CTCA police work had closed the red-light districts in American cities near the camps and naval stations and that selective prohibition had dried up the zones around them.

CTCA promoted the wholesome use of leisure time. Athletic directors trained soldiers to play football, baseball, and soccer, while boxing, wrestling, swimming, and sailing coaches physically conditioned soldiers and sailors and helped them develop skills and an aggressive nature. Song leaders organized competitive music festivals and encouraged recreational singing. Soldiers and sailors saw motion pictures and plays performed by professional touring companies in "Liberty Theaters" at most camps and naval stations. The War Department's CTCA sent dramatic directors to the camps to train the men to organize their own entertainments. CTCA offered millions of lower-class Americans unprecedented access to middle-class culture, but programs designed to replicate aspects of the social life of urban America were simply not congruent with the experience of conscripted soldiers or sailors. CTCA recognized and accepted engrained patterns of racism in the military and in communities adjacent to the camps and stations, providing, for instance, segregated seating in camp theaters and auditoriums.

Funding disparity suggests the degree to which the volunteer programs overshadowed the commission's own efforts. The YMCA alone solicited $162 million for its war work; the Knights of Columbus about $31 million. Gifts, fees, and federal appropriations totaling about $6.6 million supported CTCA, a pittance in comparison to the resources available to the Seven Sisters. The volunteers provided comfort, education, and recreation, but with these consolations came aggressive efforts to attract soldiers. Power, prestige, and privilege accrued to conspicuously successful programs, but the spectacle of sectarian competition, with its attendant jealousy and discord, demoralized rather than uplifted. The commission's own ventures into athletics, music, and theater suggested that the army of the future should and could manage its own recreation and entertainment programs. Indeed, the Morale Division of the General Staff absorbed the functions of the CTCA in September 1919.

Weldon B. Durham

See also AMERICAN LIBRARY ASSOCIATION; FOSDICK, RAYMOND BLAINE; JEWISH WELFARE BOARD; KNIGHTS OF COLUMBUS; SALVATION ARMY; WAR CAMP COMMUNITY SERVICE; YM/YMCA

Bibliography

Beaver, Daniel R. *Newton D. Baker and the American War Effort, 1917–1919.* Lincoln: University of Nebraska Press, 1966.

Davis, Allen F. "Welfare, Reform, and World War I." *American Quarterly* (Fall 1967).

Durham, Weldon B. "'Big Brother' and the 'Seven Sisters': Camp Life Reforms in World War I." *Military Affairs* (April 1978).

Fosdick, Raymond B. *Chronicle of a Generation: An Autobiography.* New York: Harper, 1958.

U.S. War and Navy Departments. *Commissions on Training Camp Activities.* Washington, DC: Government Printing Office, 1918.

Committee on Patriotism Through Education

The declaration of war on April 2, 1917, inspired the National Security League (NSL), the country's foremost civilian patriotic society, to seek to reeducate the American people on the meaning of patriotism. In existence since the winter of 1914, the NSL's character and focus changed overnight. Blaming Congress and the American people for the passage of the anemic National Defense Act of 1916—legislation that compromised the concepts of a large standing Regular Army, a two-ocean navy, and universal military training and service—the NSL leadership founded the Committee on Patriotism Through Education to arouse an apathetic populace.

With Harvard Professor Alfred B. Hart as his new educational director, NSL President S. Stanwood Menken obtained pledges from over a score of colleges and universities to donate faculty temporarily for the league's propaganda work. On Aug. 29, 1917, forty-two-year-old Princeton historian Robert M. McElroy succeeded Hart as educational director. McElroy's early enlistments included A.O. Lovejoy of Johns Hopkins, Franklin H. Giddings of Columbia, William Bennett Munro of Harvard, William H. Schofield of Harvard, Claude H. Van Tyne of Michigan, Walter P. Hall of Princeton, Melancthon F. Libby of Colorado, and Ephraim D. Adams of Stanford. These eight scholars were charged with policing primary, secondary, and higher education in their respective districts of the United States. E.D. Thompson of Princeton's mathematics department agreed to serve as McElroy's educational secretary and Etta V. Leighton, a member of the Passaic, New Jersey, Board of Education, assumed the title of civics secretary. To her fell the responsibility of all matters pertaining to the instruction of foreigners.

McElroy's first major propaganda program was a statewide speaking campaign in New York under the supervision of Vassar's President Henry S. MacCracken. The committee slated thirty-six speakers who during a six-day tour covered every county, drawing crowds as large as 10,000 people. In New York City McElroy conducted a "Speakers' Plattsburg" to refine forensic techniques and to recruit new participants. Outside New York McElroy sent his academicians to more than 250 summer schools in forty-three states, conducting sessions that lasted from a few days to several weeks. Emphasizing patriotism and an end to alien influence, these scholars assisted teachers in applying league Americanization programs to local classrooms and community conditions. This ambitious project reached over 300,000 teachers with an incredible twenty-eight tons of printed matter. A striking feature of the NSL

C

summer sessions was the appeal to black colleges. McElroy established league workshops in African-American colleges in Virginia, North Carolina, Alabama, and Texas, while Dr. Lewis B. Moore, dean of Howard University, organized special adult education classes in Louisiana and Mississippi under the league's aegis. The New York Board of Education yielded to NSL pressure and banned the instruction of all foreign languages in elementary schools after Feb. 1, 1918. McElroy's committee also clamored for an end to all newspapers circulated in the languages of the Central Powers. On June 3, 1918, the NSL petitioned its 281 branches and 100,000 members to push the Wilson administration for a five-year grace period legislated for these alien subscribers wherein they might learn English and become naturalized citizens or else be deported. Menken's successor-elect, Charles E. Lydecker, coordinated these efforts with McElroy through the newly created Committee on Foreign Language and Foreign Press. Lydecker's policies resulted in the systematic probes into the loyalty of all college teachers even suspected of sympathizing with the enemy and summary dismissals of those thought to be disloyal.

In the summer of 1918, the committee sponsored the Bartlett and Lawrence programs in Massachusetts in order to "Americanize" the primary school children of Lowell and Lawrence. In this instructional setting immigrant children were urged to convince their parents to become naturalized citizens while steering clear of labor unrest and Bolshevik agitators. Despite the energetic leadership of Ephrian D. Adams of Stanford University, the New England experiment failed due to growing factionalism within the league and the dark prospect of an impending 1918 congressional investigation.

During the winter of 1918–1919, organizational relations between McElroy's committee members and Menken's old guard regulars deteriorated to the point where day-to-day business seemed impossible. Overworked, understaffed, and frightfully short of funds, McElroy decided to quit his post in mid-summer. He and his captains carried the summer school lectures to completion, and on Sept. 27, 1919, the Committee on Patriotism Through Education ceased to exist.

John C. Edwards

See also NATIONAL SECURITY LEAGUE

Bibliography
Edwards, John C. *Patriots in Pin-Stripe: Men of the National Security League.* Washington, DC: University Press of America, 1982.

Committee on Public Information

As the United States entered the First World War in April 1917, the administration of President Woodrow Wilson faced the challenge of mobilizing public opinion in support of U.S. involvement. Although Congress had passed its declaration of war by a large majority, the legislative debate had been protracted, lasting thirteen hours in the Senate and even longer in the House of Representatives, and support had not been unanimous. Some questioned the dedication of German and Irish Americans, who might still hold reservations about fighting against the kaiser or allying with Great Britain. Although many Progressives had thrown their support behind American involvement, some vocal intellectuals and labor organizers still expressed misgivings. Above all, if the American public were to endure the coming months of sacrifice, Wilson would have to elevate a distant war to primacy in the American mind. On April 14, a little more than a week after the declaration of war, Wilson signed the executive order creating the government agency that would address these pockets of ambivalence and spearhead the American propaganda effort: the Committee on Public Information (CPI).

Journalist George Creel was named to head the CPI, but no specific guidelines were given for the structure of the agency. Under the executive order the CPI was charged with the task of directing the release—and suppression—of government news to promote the "absolute justice of America's cause, the absolute selflessness of America's aims." With only this overriding purpose, and with no preestablished program, Creel and the CPI set to work.

The Executive Division of the CPI coordinated and guided the committee's efforts. In October 1917, the Business Management Division was added to administer the wartime budget totaling $9,675,670.23. The remainder of the CPI fell into two sections, Domestic and Foreign. The larger of the two, the Domestic Section, included several divisions. The Division of News, created immediately with the formation of the CPI, was responsible for disbursing a total of 6,000 news releases. The Official

Bulletin Division published the official daily newspaper of the United States government between May 10, 1917, and March 31, 1919, reaching a peak circulation of 118,008. The Civic and Educational Cooperation Division enlisted the help of nationally known scholars to produce 105 publications with a total circulation of 75 million. The Film Division, which incorporated the Picture Division, the Bureau of War Expositions, and the Bureau of State Fair Exhibits as well, worked to bring home visual images of the war by producing and distributing slides and moving pictures and by staging public exhibits of captured war machinery. More than 2 million people in twenty cities witnessed the displays of the Bureau of War Expositions, and an estimated 7 million Americans visited the booths of the Bureau of State Fair Exhibits promoting wartime conservation.

Among the other divisions of the Domestic Section was the Labor Publications Division, which distributed literature appealing to working-class Americans but which later was transferred to the Department of Labor. The Services Bureau acted as the information arm of the CPI, and from its booths in Union Station in Washington, D.C., and elsewhere answered more than 86,000 queries about various government agencies. The Advertising Division and the Pictorial Publicity Division managed the posters and promotions for the Liberty Loans and other campaigns throughout the war and succeeded in securing for the government a reported $1,594,814.71 worth of free advertising space. The Speaking Division, which merged with the Four-Minute Men in September 1917, directed the efforts of all government lecturers and the more than 75,000 volunteer speakers, who delivered a total of 755,190 fervent, four-minute talks to an estimated 314,454,514 listeners at movie theaters, schools, civic groups, and other public gatherings across the country. The periodicals of the Syndicate Features Division—which recruited the help of the nation's leading novel, essay, and short-story writers—reached an estimated 12 million readers every month. Until congressional budget cutting eliminated the Women's War Work Division on June 30, 1918, such well-known women activists as Carrie Chapman Catt, Ida Tarbell, and Anna Howard Shaw, helped to inform and motivate the nation's women by preparing 2,305 news stories and 292 pictures concerning women's work during wartime and by writing 50,000

letters to assuage concerns about conscription and conservation. The Division of Work with the Foreign Born, which subsumed the responsibility of the Foreign Language Newspaper Division in March 1918 but which was not formally created until May, sought to ensure the loyalty of "hyphenated" Americans. In so doing, this division worked closely with the divisions of the Foreign Section of the CPI.

Three separate groups comprised the CPI's Foreign Section, which was in part responsible for assisting American diplomatic representatives abroad. With the help of the Domestic Section's News Division, the Wireless and Cable Service prepared and disseminated daily reports across the globe, with some even appearing in German newspapers. The Foreign Press Bureau sent photographs and articles from the Domestic Section's Division of Syndicate Features and Film to U.S. agents overseas. Finally, the Foreign Film Division administered the export of movies made by the Domestic Section.

Much controversy surrounds the nature of the CPI's activities. Creel himself maintained that the CPI always "dealt in the positive," emphasizing "expression, not suppression" and seeking "the verdict of mankind by truth telling." Conscious of the connotations of the word "propaganda" and hence avoiding that label, Creel claimed that the work of his committee "was educational and informative only, for we had such confidence in our case as to feel that only fair presentation of its facts was needed."

The credibility of Creel's claims is open to debate. The CPI avoided the strict censorship proposals of the War Department, the State Department, and other official agencies, promoting instead a system of voluntary censorship and self-restraint by the nation's media. But behind this elective system lay the threat of government enforcement to ensure compliance. The CPI's "Preliminary Statement to the Press of the United States," issued on May 28, 1917, warned that "the printed word has immeasurable power, and the term traitor is not too harsh an application to the publisher, editor, or writer who wields this power without full and even solemn recognition of responsibilities." Although having no specific powers of enforcement, the CPI's agents were authorized to report to other government agencies those individuals or publications who flouted the proscriptions of the Espionage, Sabotage, and Sedition acts.

The CPI's work was tainted as well by Creel's position as an official member of the Censorship Board. All magazines in the United States were required to submit articles for board approval weeks prior to publication. Creel also sought to limit the import and export of those publications that might portray the United States in a bad light or contain ideas too dangerous for the American public. Similarly, he praised the board's decision to disallow books favorable toward Germany. Creel's involvement with the Censorship Board and the CPI's frequent publication of arguments by Clarence Darrow, William Jennings Bryan and others in favor of the restriction of free speech and press suggest that those Americans tasked with the dissemination of news did not view free expression as absolute, particularly during the crisis of wartime.

Although behind Creel's claims of "expression, not suppression" lay a rather ominous power to control information, and while the CPI was used to promote Wilson's ideas, there is no evidence that it served as a partisan vehicle. Republicans filled some of the highest positions in the CPI. Nor was it a springboard to advance Creel's own career. Perhaps, as historians James R. Mock and Cedric Larson suggest, Creel's reluctance to expand his powers even further is a strong testament to the CPI's sincerity.

Despite numerous hurdles, the CPI was phenomenally successful in its mission. Hindered by poor relations with Congress, and hence a paltry appropriation of only $1,250,000, Creel garnered the remainder of his budget from $2,800,000 in sales of CPI literature and $5,600,000 in presidential discretionary funding. In an era before radio or television, delivering a message throughout America proved challenging, but through an innovative and concerted use of pictures, printed words, and speeches, Creel managed to broadcast the Wilsonian ideal around the world.

Michael McCarthy

See also CREEL, GEORGE; FOUR-MINUTE MEN

Bibliography

Blakey, George T. *Historians on the Homefront: American Propagandists for the Great War.* Lexington: University of Kentucky Press, 1970.
Cornebise, Alfred. *War As Advertised.* Philadelphia: American Philosophical Society, 1984.
Mock, James R., and Cedric Larson. *Words that Won the War: The Story of the Committee on Public Information, 1917–1919.* Princeton, NJ: Princeton University Press, 1939.
U.S. Committee on Public Information. *Complete Report of the Chairman of the Committee on Public Information, 1917; 1918; 1919.* Washington, DC: Government Printing Office, 1920.
Vaughn, Stephen L. *Holding Fast the Inner Line: Democracy, Nationalism and the Committee on Public Information.* Chapel Hill: University of North Carolina Press, 1980.

Conger, Arthur Latham, Jr. (1872–1951)

Arthur Latham Conger, Jr., was born at Akron, Ohio, on Jan. 30, 1872. The son of a prominent Ohio industrialist and politician, he graduated in 1894 from Harvard University, where he developed a lifelong interest in music, religion, and philosophy. Conger began his military career in May 1898 by enlisting in Company M, 12th New York Volunteers. He quickly rose to the rank of sergeant, and on Sept. 9, 1899, he was commissioned as a second lieutenant in the 18th Infantry, Regular Infantry. He saw active service with his regiment in the Philippine Insurrection and won a Silver Star for his role in the Battle of Dunanjao. From May 1901 to April 1903, Conger served as aide-de-camp to MajGen. R.P. Hughes in the Philippines and California. He returned for another tour of duty in the Philippines in 1903–1905.

In 1905–1907, Conger was a student at the Infantry and Cavalry School and the Staff College at Fort Leavenworth, Kansas. In July 1907, he began his first tour on the faculty of the Leavenworth schools as an instructor in the Department of Military Art. Between August 1910 and February 1911, Conger was a student at the University of Heidelberg and at the University of Berlin, where his mentor was the famed German military historian Hans Delbrück. Following a short tour of regimental service, Conger was assigned for a second time to the Leavenworth faculty, serving from August 1912 to May 1916. This tour at Fort Leavenworth was a period of great productivity for him as a military historian. He introduced the so-called "scientific historical method" learned from his German mentors, conducted a seminar in military history at

Harvard Summer School in 1915, and became actively involved with the American Historical Association. He also produced several historical monographs, and in August 1915, he joined with Robert M. Johnston and Mark H. Wentworth to establish a new scholarly journal, the *Military Historian and Economist*, which had significant impact before its premature demise in 1918.

After Mexican border service with the 26th Infantry in 1916–1917, Conger sailed for France on the SS *Baltic* with General Pershing and the staff of the American Expeditionary Force (AEF). He was chief of the Information Division under AEF G-2 BGen. Denis Nolan and subsequently served as G-2 of the 2d Division in June–July 1918. Promoted to colonel in July 1918, Conger played a key role in the "Belfort Ruse," a complex deception operation which successfully masked preparations for the American offensive at St. Mihiel in September 1918. Conger's wife, Margaret Loring Guild Conger, who took up residence in Paris during the war, was apparently also involved in American intelligence work as a private agent for General Pershing.

In September–October 1918, Conger commanded the 56th Infantry Brigade, 28th Division, in the Meuse-Argonne offensive before being reassigned to confidential duties with GHQ AEF. The first American officer to enter Germany in the closing days of the war, Conger coordinated the repatriation of Allied prisoners of war, assisted German authorities in suppressing incipient revolution, and arranged transit of the Polish Army under Gen. Józef Haller through Danzig. He worked diligently to avoid a resumption of the war and is said to have nearly persuaded the German cabinet to adopt the U.S. Constitution. Conger returned to the United States in August 1919. After a number of routine assignments in Washington, D.C., Texas, Oklahoma, and Ohio, he returned to Germany in December 1924 as military attaché in Berlin. He remained in Berlin until June 1928 and was instrumental in advising German officers struggling to reform the armed forces of Weimar Germany.

Following his retirement from active military service on Oct. 31, 1928, Conger became more deeply involved in the activities of the Theosophical Society, which he had joined at Harvard in 1892. In January 1932, he was elected president of the American section of the society but was forced to resign for reasons of ill health in December of that year. In 1945, he became the international leader of the theosophical movement and continued in that position until his death on Feb. 22, 1951.

Charles R. Shrader

See also BELFORT RUSE

Bibliography

Conger, Arthur L. *Historical Research*. Fort Leavenworth, KS: Army Service Schools, 1916.

Nenninger, Timothy K. *The Leavenworth Schools and the Old Army: Education, Professionalism and the Officer Corps of the United States Army, 1881–1918*. Westport, CT: Greenwood Press, 1978.

Paschall, Rod. "Deception for St. Mihiel, 1918." *Intelligence and National Security* 5 (July 1990).

Reardon, Carol. *Soldiers and Scholars: The U.S. Army and the Uses of Military History, 1865–1920*. Lawrence: University Press of Kansas, 1990.

Shurlock, Aileen B. *Biographical Sketch of Colonel Arthur Latham Conger, Fifth Leader of the Theosophical Society, Point Loma-Covina, California, [and] Diplomat, Statesman, Philosopher, Scholar, Soldier, Author, Musician, Composer, Humanitarian*. Oakland, CA: n.p., 1955.

Conner, Fox (1874–1951)

A native of Slate Sprints, Mississippi, Fox Conner was the son of a Confederate Army veteran. He graduated from the United States Military Academy in 1898 and was commissioned a second lieutenant of artillery. In his first tour of duty he was involved in the occupation of Cuba and then was assigned to routine garrison duty in the United States. In 1901, Captain Conner received command of a company of the newly organized Coast Artillery Corps.

Conner was a close student of his profession, reading widely in military history and doctrine. He graduated from the Staff College at Fort Leavenworth, Kansas, in 1906. While serving on the General Staff in Washington, 1907–1911, he also taught at the Army War College. In 1911, he was assigned to a French artillery regiment. This experience improved his fluency in French and gave him a thorough acquaintance with the French Army; both were soon to prove useful.

In 1916, Conner was again sent to France, this time as an observer on the Western Front. After American entry into World War I, he served as coordinator of the visit of Joffre's French commission to the United States. He accompanied General Pershing to France, having been personally selected by the commander of the American Expeditionary Force (AEF) to be a member of the advance staff. For most of America's involvement in the war, Colonel Conner performed brilliantly as Pershing's chief of operations (G–3). In this capacity he played a major role in the planning of successful American actions, notably the St. Mihiel offensive. His performance attracted the attention of his superiors and that of younger officers, such as George C. Marshall. In recognition of Conner's wartime achievements, he was promoted to brigadier general and awarded the Distinguished Service Medal; he also received the Purple Heart for wounds received at Seicheprey during an inspection of the 1st Division.

The American experience in the war did much to shape his later thinking on military matters, and his thoughts were to have an impact on army policy and doctrine in the years between the two world wars. Conner was selected to write the AEF's after-action report, and many of his views on army reorganization expressed therein were embraced by Pershing, particularly those calling for reducing the size of divisions and integrating heavy weapons within infantry units at all levels of a division. Years later, the army adopted his suggestion for lighter, more mobile "triangular" divisions.

Convinced that the Versailles settlement made a second world war inevitable, he urged the army to prepare for it. He was equally convinced of the need to develop leaders who could learn from the mistakes and weaknesses of the World War's coalition leadership. Seeing in Dwight D. Eisenhower, a junior officer in the brigade Conner commanded in Panama, the potential for a successful commander of coalition warfare, he groomed Eisenhower with a rigorous program of reading and discussion. He influenced many other officers through publications in professional journals. Some of his thinking reached civilians by means of an article, "The National Defense," published in the *North American Review* in 1928.

In 1925, Conner became a major general and deputy chief of staff. He ably commanded the Hawaiian Department from 1928 to 1930,

then the I Corps Area from 1930 until his retirement in 1938. Conner was disappointed in not being appointed chief of staff, a position for which many others felt he was admirably qualified.

Michael J. Brodhead

See also EISENHOWER, DWIGHT DAVID; ST. MIHIEL

Bibliography

Brown, Charles H. "Fox Conner: A General's General." In *Journal of Mississippi History*, ed. by J.R. Skates. Jackson: Department of Mississippi Archives and History, 1987.

Conner, Virginia. *What Father Forbad*. Philadelphia: Dorrance, 1951.

Eisenhower, Dwight D. *At Ease: Stories I Tell to Friends*. Garden City, NY: Doubleday, 1967.

Kingseed, Cole C. "Mentoring General Ike." *Military Review* (October 1990).

Vandiver, Frank E. *Black Jack: The Life and Times of John J. Pershing*. College Station: Texas A&M University Press, 1977.

Connor, William Durward (1874–1960)

William Durward Connor was born in Rock County, Wisconsin. He graduated from the United States Military Academy at the head of the class of 1897 and was commissioned a second lieutenant of the Corps of Engineers. After brief service in the United States, he went to the Philippines during the Spanish-American War. Initially stationed at Cavite Arsenal and Camp Dewey, in August 1898 Connor was assigned as the Manila city engineer. Despite the apparently sedentary nature of this position, he participated in various engagements during the Philippine Insurrection and earned a Silver Star for heroism in combat.

On his return to the United States in August 1900, Connor attended the Engineer School and after graduation served at various posts as an engineer officer. In 1908, he attended the Army War College and in the years that followed assumed positions of increasing responsibility.

In November 1916, he returned to Manila as chief engineer of the Philippine Department, but was recalled to Washington in March 1917 for duty with the office of the chief of engineers.

With the entry of the United States in the First World War, he was sent to Europe in July 1917. There he joined the Operations Section of the American Expeditionary Force (AEF) General Staff. In August, he became assistant chief of staff, Supply Division, AEF, where he faced the myriad logistical problems of an army training and fighting an ocean away from its supply bases and dependent upon inadequate shipping and port capacity. As General Pershing stated in the citation awarding Connor the Distinguished Service Medal, "As Assistant Chief of Staff and head of the Coordination Section of the General Staff, AEF, he showed unusual ability and tireless energy."

Like most of the officers of the AEF staff, he longed for a field command, and in April 1918, his wish was granted. Connor was posted to the 32d Division as chief of staff. In July, he was promoted to brigadier general and given command of the 63d Brigade of the 32d Division. While General Connor commanded the 63d Brigade, it was involved in heavy fighting around Château-Thierry and in the reduction of the Marne salient. He earned another Silver Star for gallantry in action. Since his supply experience was badly needed, on August 7, he took command of the Bordeaux District, Base Section No. 2 of the Service of Supply. In November 1918, he became chief of staff, Service of Supply and its commander in May 1919. On July 28, 1919, Connor was appointed commanding general, Headquarters, France, until January 1920. On his return to the United States, he became the commander of the Engineer School at Camp Humphries, Virginia, for eight months until his assignment in the office of the quartermaster general, followed by duty as the assistant chief of supply, War Department General Staff until November 1922.

Assignments in Hawaii and China followed, and in 1926 and 1927, he commanded the 2d Division and the post of Fort Sam Houston, Texas. He was commandant of the Army War College from December 1927 to April 1932, when he was appointed superintendent of the United States Military Academy. He retired from there in February 1938 but was recalled to active duty in the Pentagon from 1941 to 1942. He died in Washington, D.C., on June 16, 1960.

James L. Collins, Jr.

See also UNITED STATES ARMY SERVICE OF SUPPLY

Bibliography
Pershing, John J. *My Experiences in the World War.* New York: Stokes, 1931.
Dawes, Charles G. *A Journal of the Great War.* Boston: Houghton Mifflin, 1921.
Smythe, Donald. *Pershing.* Bloomington: Indiana University Press, 1986.

Conrad von Hötzendorf, Franz (1852–1925)

Franz Conrad von Hötzendorf was born in Pensing, a suburb of Vienna. Without preferments or connections, Conrad fortuitously pursued a military career during a period of military reform when advancement was based on merit. After graduation from the Wiener Neustadt Military Academy as a second lieutenant, he joined the prestigious 11th Feldjager Light Infantry. The light infantry flare and mentality imprinted all his later ideas on tactics, operations, and strategy. By his own admission very ambitious, Conrad, in 1874, entered the Kriegsschule General Staff College in Vienna. He excelled, finishing first in his class. He then joined the staff corps, which had a separate, faster career track than a line post. He participated in the Balkan campaigns of 1878 and 1882, the only combat he ever saw. His tactical ideas were based on this experience against a foe with low cohesion and fire capability. Conrad developed and published his theories when he returned to the staff college to teach from 1888 to 1892. At this point he abandoned a promising General Staff career to return to troop duty.

He became colonel of the important Silesian 1st Regiment, whose honorary colonel was Emperor Franz Josef. It was here that Conrad met Archduke Franz Ferdinand. After brigade command in Trieste, Conrad commanded the crack Tyrolean 8th Division (1903–1906), developing an interest in Alpine warfare. In 1906, now a protégé of Franz Ferdinand, Conrad became chief of the General Staff. Although he had a reputation in Central Europe based on his several books on infantry battle training, he had been away from the General Staff for eighteen years. Conrad saw Austria-Hungary ringed with foes and hampered by internal enemies. The Habsburg Army, which had been one of the largest and finest in Europe, had been unable to participate in the arms race (a demographic impossibility against Russia) and had fallen behind the other great powers.

Conrad's solution was to train vigorously for the war he knew was inevitable. As he had done in the past with students and troops, he now energized and raised the morale of the General Staff and High Command with his deep sense of urgency. Motivating the entire army, let alone the moribund state, was more difficult. He expanded the heavy artillery and technical troops and founded the best Alpine units in the world. Once he had begun to reestablish Habsburg military credibility through rigorous training, Conrad reactivated the alliance with Germany, which had decayed under his aged predecessor. Conrad sought out and befriended the German General Staff chief Gen. Helmuth von Moltke, nephew of the famous field marshal. A tightly developed joint war plan in the event of the dreaded Russian war could compensate for Habsburg inferiority.

Conrad wished to keep the initiative in a war rather than wait for the enemy to attack. During the Bosnia annexation crisis of 1908 and the Balkan Wars of 1912 and 1913, Conrad advocated preventive war. However, while Franz Joseph and Franz Ferdinand had encouraged Conrad to energize the army as a symbol of "great power status," they had no intention of actually using it. Conrad never understood this and was dismissed in November 1911.

After a tour as an army field commander, Conrad returned as chief of the General Staff in December 1912 during the Balkan Wars. He felt prospects for victory were not as good as the earlier lost opportunities, and now that the legislatures, reacting to the crisis, had finally supported the long requested military expansion, he was content to wait for the army to be reequipped and supported by the new reserve formations that would not be ready until the 1920s. During this period Conrad fell out with his old sponsor, Franz Ferdinand, who began to assume more powers from the eighty-three-year-old emperor. In the autumn of 1913, Conrad attempted to resign, but his reputation was such that Franz Ferdinand felt obliged to keep him on. Conrad agreed to stay only out of loyalty to Franz Joseph.

This was Conrad's position when the June 28, 1914, assassination of Franz Ferdinand created the war crisis and simultaneously removed one of the key opponents of war. By this time everyone in the Crown Council had come around to Conrad's earlier stand, while Conrad felt the chance for victory against a ring of foes was now slight. The mobilization, concentra-

tion, and deployment of July–August 1914, was the test of the years of peacetime preparation for the general staffs of the European powers. It established Conrad's postwar reputation as a brilliant strategist. His complex multifront war plans were the only ones of the belligerents to compare with the Schlieffen Plan for daring.

The key had been Conrad's plan for a cooperative battle with German assistance against the Russian "steamroller" in the Polish salient. This bold offensive, based in large part on Conrad's personal relationship with von Moltke, was obviated by Moltke's nervous breakdown at the beginning of combat. Always suspicious of the German ally, Conrad was unable to develop a good rapport with Gen. Erich von Falkenhayn, Moltke's successor as chief of the German General Staff. The failure of the Central Powers to cooperate more closely, at least part of which must be attributed to Conrad, was a major cause of their final defeat.

As with all the other countries, Austria-Hungary started the war in a tactical offensive posture. Based on prewar thinking that only the offensive could bring victory, this position ignored the tremendous defensive power of the new weapons. By October 1914, the original cadre armies of all the belligerents were destroyed. Two of Conrad's four sons were casualties in the early fighting.

After a very expensive winter attrition campaign against the Russians in the Carpathian gateways to the interior of the empire, Conrad showed his skill as a strategist in the breakthrough at Gorlice in May 1915. With crucial German help, by the end of the summer the Russian army was completely driven out of Poland. This brilliant success did not come in time to prevent Italy from entering the war on the other side. Although the Italians were halted during the summer in the Alpine frontier, Austria-Hungary avoided a three-front war only by destroying Serbia in the fall of 1915 with German and Bulgarian help.

These victories gave the Central Powers some prospect of victory in 1916. After extensive and acrimonious debate with Falkenhayn over a joint plan for 1916, Conrad decided on his own to knock out Italy and independently pulled troops from the Russian front. Conrad stopped the June 1916 attack in the Tyrol short of its objectives when Russia launched the Brusilov offensive. Conrad was mortified by underestimating the Russians who were driven back at the end of the summer only with substantial German assistance. By the time Russia collapsed in the late winter of 1916–1917, Conrad had been demoted to a field command in the Tyrol by the young Emperor Charles, who wished to pursue a separate peace.

In the fall of 1917, again with German assistance, Conrad's planned Isonzo offensive won a stunning victory at Caporetto. Italy was almost knocked out of the war. One last offensive was attempted against Italy in June 1918 by greatly weakened Habsburg forces. After its defeat, Conrad was retired.

After the war, his empire gone, stripped of his titles by the new Austrian republic, which he loathed, Conrad retired to Innsbruck. He supported himself by writing what many consider the best, most candid of the war memoirs, *Aus Meiner Dienstzeit*. They were unfinished when he died in 1925.

R.D. Zehnder

See also Caporetto, Battle of

Bibliography

Fiala, Peter. *Il Feldmaresciallo Franz Conrad von Hötzendorf*. Vecenzia, Italy: Edizioni Gino Rossato, 1990.
Peball, Kurt. *Conrad von Hötzendorf*. Vienna: Amalthea, 1977.

Conscientious Objectors

Conscientious objectors (COs) are people who oppose war and whose beliefs prohibit them from bearing arms in their nation's military services. While these beliefs are often rooted in a religious faith, some COs base their objections on philosophical, humanitarian, or political grounds. If called upon to serve when their country goes to war, the range of views among conscientious objectors of what is permissible is quite broad. One might agree to serve in the military, though as a noncombatant, while another might regard any association with the military, including registering for the draft, as a violation of conscience.

War and conscientious objection to participation in it have presented a challenge to governments and individuals in North America from the time of English settlement to the present. Religious pacifists such as the Quakers were granted exemptions from the colonial militia. The Revolutionary and Civil wars presented more serious governmental claims on citizen participation, but in both situations the conscientious objector was able to find some legal refuge. It was in the context of universal military conscription and the total war of 1917, when the United States entered World War I, that the U.S. government and the conscientious objector found their conflicting claims most difficult to resolve. In a struggle characterized as being for civilization itself, *all* were expected to participate. To this end, Congress enacted the Selective Service Act, signed into law by President Wilson on May 18, 1917. It called for the registration of all able-bodied adult males and, for the first time on the national level, exempted conscientious objectors from combat duty. This act, however, too narrowly defined the conscientious objector, giving CO status only to members of "some well-organized religious sect or organization whose existing creed or principles forbid" participation in war "in any form." And those who were granted CO status would still be required to do noncombat duty in the military. By the end of 1917, Secretary of War Newton D. Baker had expanded the definition of conscientious objector to include all men who had "personal scruples against war," giving official recognition to nonreligious objectors. There was a considerable gap, however, between recognition of the legitimacy of a conscientious objection to service in the military (and ordering, as Baker did, that the COs should be treated with tact and consideration) and the actual experiences of the COs and the treatment they received.

The first group of conscientious objectors to be officially recognized, the religious objectors, included denominations or sects such as the Quakers, Mennonites, Molokans, Dukhobors, Dunkards, Seventh-Day Adventists, Jehovah's Witnesses, Russellites and Christadelphians, and the Hutterian, Plymouth, and River Brethren. Nonreligious objectors, which included humanitarians, socialists, and syndicalists, were slower to be recognized and faced greater difficulties in gaining recognition, a situation expressed by CO Louis Fraina who wondered why a person had to belong to a church in order to have a conscience.

Of the millions of men who registered between May 1917 and November 1918, only 64,693 claimed conscientious objector status. Of these, just over 20,000 of those judged to be "sincere" by the local board were found eligible, passed the physical, and were inducted. This was when the real problem began, for all

C

COs—religious, nonreligious, absolutist, and nonabsolutist—were put under the jurisdiction of the military. Even those who refused to register were arrested, turned over to the military, drafted, and tried in a military court, often receiving sentences of twenty years or more. Indeed, the military seemed to take the position that the CO, like any other inductee, was to be prepared for combat duty—the only difference being that the conscientious objector had to be converted to this view first. Shaming, taunting, physical abuse, threatening court-martial, and a variety of other tactics were used to convince the objector of his "patriotic duty." Roughly 16,000 succumbed to the pressure and abuse and agreed to accept combat roles. Some 1,300 others bowed to the pressure enough to accept noncombatant status from the army, although even this was not defined for them until March 1918 when President Wilson, in an executive order, designated certain noncombatant activities.

However, nearly 4,000 COs remained adamant in their refusal, and to them the worst abuses occurred. Many of these COs were subjected to tactics by camp commanders and their officers that included being taunted, beaten, dunked, bayoneted, handcuffed in a standing position for nine hours a day in solitary confinement, and put on a bread and water diet. While treatment varied from camp to camp, it was generally bad, with the most notorious cases occurring at Camp Funston and Camp Riley, camps under the command of Gen. Leonard Wood, who established an atmosphere in which abuse and mistreatment aimed at "breaking" the CO appeared to be permissible. For 540 "absolutist" COs who refused to cooperate in any way with the military, court-martials were held, and they were found guilty. These trials, sometimes stemming from incidents provoked by the military and often held to serve the purposes of a camp commander, seemed to emphasize speed—one CO was tried and sentenced in eighteen minutes. For obeying the dictates of their consciences rather than the orders of military officers, 17 COs were given death sentences, 142 were sentenced to life imprisonment, and 345 were given sentences with an average term of sixteen and one-half years. None of the death penalties was carried out and 185 of the sentences were eventually reduced, but it was not until 1933, with a pardon by President Franklin D. Roosevelt, that the last CO of World War I was released. At least 17

conscientious objectors died in prison as a direct consequence of physical abuse or prison conditions. Psychological abuse took its toll as well; the constant ridicule to which COs were subjected caused at least one to commit suicide. He had hoped his death would call attention to the plight of the conscientious objector; instead it was ignored by the press and by officialdom.

Conscientious objectors, especially the nonreligious, were generally seen by the military—and public—as slackers and cowards; unpatriotic at best, traitors at worst. For the most part, the family and friends of the men engaged in combat did not sympathize with the CO; nor, in general, did religious denominations other than those historically associated with opposition to war. Many prominent Americans, including Theodore Roosevelt, criticized conscientious objectors, denouncing them as mostly cowards and pro-German traitors. In general, military officers did not accept any CO as sincere. And War Secretary Baker seemed to sanction that attitude when, in April 1918, he ordered the army to court-martial any CO whose sincerity was questionable, who was "sullen and defiant," or who engaged in propaganda. In this atmosphere even the religious objector met with intolerance and misunderstanding. The Mennonites and the Molokans, who came to the United States from Russia for the single purpose of avoiding participation in war, found themselves in quite a dilemma with the passage of the Selective Service Act. One group of Molokans in Phoenix turned themselves in to authorities rather than submit to the draft. They were turned over to the military, court-martialed, and sent off to prison. Twelve Mennonites who had obeyed the civil law and registered as conscientious objectors were sent to Camp Riley where they got in trouble for refusing to obey a military order, in this case to cut down a sunflower ten feet from their camp. They were court-martialed and sentenced to twenty-five years in prison. Refusal to wear the army uniform cost forty-five COs, mostly Mennonites, twenty-five years each in prison, and in a separate incident another man lost his life. Jane Addams provided a moving description of this young man, a Dukhobor, who contracted pneumonia and died from the prolonged dunking and then exposure in freezing temperatures he had suffered at the hands of military authorities who were determined to force him, against his religious beliefs, to wear the military uniform. His widow, when she went to claim his remains, found, to her horror, that the body had been dressed in a soldier's uniform.

Conscientious objectors during World War I found themselves in a very difficult situation, and being found "sincere" and being granted CO status did not resolve their difficulties. Their problems arose because they were placed under the authority of the military. The military did not know what to do with them except try to turn them into soldiers. The COs, forced to register and be drafted, were put in the position of having to establish to the military their ethical objections to everything the military stood for and, what was worse, do it from within the service. They did not, in general, get a sympathetic hearing. However, though they were few in number, and their views were hardly mainstream, they did have their defenders. Many pacifists spoke out on their behalf, and a number of groups were formed to defend the right of conscientious objectors to live by their principles. One such group was the National Civil Liberties Bureau (CLB), at one time a part of the American Union Against Militarism (AUAM). Roger N. Baldwin, its director, was also its most active and prominent member. Having served ten months in jail himself for refusing to register for the draft, Baldwin, a man of tremendous integrity, won the respect of people on both sides of the issue. The most important work he and the CLB did was to document and publicize the mistreatment of objectors and protest these abuses to the government. His, and others' advocacy did have a positive impact, and to the extent possible within a faulty structure, some government officials indeed tried to find ways to provide civilian jobs for conscientious objectors. In addition, Quaker historian Rufus Jones sparked the formation of the American Friends Service Committee (AFSC) in April 1917. Ultimately supported by the Wilson administration, the AFSC was organized to provide Quaker noncombatants with work in war relief and reconstruction. Its efforts continued in war-torn Europe long after the fighting had ended. And finally, in response to the protests of the COs and their defenders, on June 1, 1918, Secretary Baker established a Board of Inquiry and gave its three appointees the near impossible task of traveling to all the camps, interviewing the COs, judging their sincerity, and making recommendations regarding their service. Fortunately for everyone, the war would soon be over.

David W. Moore

See also CIVIL LIBERTIES BUREAU; SELECTIVE SERVICE ACT

Bibliography

Chatfield, Charles. *For Peace and Justice: Pacifism in America 1914–1918*. Boston: Beacon Press, 1971.

Peterson, H.C., and Gilbert C. Fite. *Opponents of War, 1917–1919*. Seattle: University of Washington Press, 1957.

Schlissel, Lillian, ed. *Conscience in America*. New York: Dutton, 1968.

Thomas, Norman. *The Conscientious Objector in America*. New York: Huebsch, 1923.

Conscription

See SELECTIVE SERVICE

Continental Army Reserve Plan

Rudely awakened to America's lack of preparedness by the sinking of the *Lusitania* in May 1915 and hoping to preempt a Republican attack on the country's weak military posture, President Woodrow Wilson asked his secretaries of war and the navy, on July 21, 1915, to draft defense programs that he could submit to Congress in his next annual message. The War Department already had the skeleton of such a policy because earlier in the year Secretary of War Lindley M. Garrison had requested that the General Staff revise its 1912 report, "The Organization of the Land Forces of the United States." Garrison modified this report slightly and submitted it to the President.

Garrison believed that a minimum force of 500,000 soldiers, available for immediate call, was necessary to meet the defense needs of the United States. However, neither Wilson nor the American public was willing to accept a standing army of that size, and the army itself had no means of feeding, clothing, and housing such a force. The resources then available to the Regular Army permitted an increase to a force of no more than 140,000. War Department planners viewed the National Guard as inadequate to provide the remaining soldiers; its employment was restricted by the Constitution, and military leaders doubted its capabilities. As a solution, Garrison suggested the creation of the Continental Army, a federal reserve force available in times of crisis.

The proposed Continental Army was to be raised in annual increments of 133,000 men until a force of 400,000 was established. Those who volunteered under this plan would commit to periodic training over three years without obligation except that they return to the army in the event of war or a serious threat to national security. The training was spread out to avoid disrupting the schedule of the Regular Army. Although the exact amount of training was never explicitly determined, a period of two months per year was used to figure the costs of the proposal.

The Continental Army Plan had several weaknesses. First, the War Department had no existing program to recruit the necessary number of soldiers. In the previous fiscal year, the army had recruited only 35,941 men—a figure far short of the annual goal of 133,000. It was unlikely that large numbers of able-bodied recruits would sacrifice their full-time jobs for two months out of the year to receive the Regular Army pay of fifty cents a day. Conscription was the only feasible means of enlisting the required number of troops, but finding supporters of the draft outside of the War Department—especially within the President's own party—was difficult. House Speaker Champ Clark of Missouri claimed that there was little difference between a conscript and a convict. Southern James Hay, chairman of the House Military Affairs Committee, warned Wilson that many representatives from his region would resist conscription because they feared it would arm large numbers of African Americans. With a peacetime draft in America hardly likely, the Continental Army did not appear to be a reasonable means of raising the fighting force that Garrison desired.

More importantly, the Continental Army Plan stepped on the toes of the existing National Guard. The War Department had little faith in the poorly trained and fragmented state militias and desired a cohesive force solely under federal control. Attempting to undermine the power of the National Guard did not sit well with its powerful supporters in Congress, especially southern states' rights advocates such as Hay. In a confrontation between legislators who favored the existing structure of the militia and the military professionals whose plan smelled strongly of conscription, Garrison's Continental Army would likely lose.

On Feb. 5, 1916, Hay informed Wilson that his committee would reject the Continental Army. Hay instead suggested federalizing the militia, a plan that could provide the numbers of men the War Department sought, but one that was unacceptable to Garrison because it still failed to yield a force under a single command. On Feb. 9, 1916, Garrison told Wilson that if they were not in agreement on the fundamental principles of army expansion, he could not remain in his post. In attempting to force Wilson to confront Congress, Garrison sealed his own fate. While committed to preparedness as a concept, Wilson himself had few preconceived ideas of how to achieve it, and he would not risk his relationship with his own party to secure a plan to which he was not dedicated. Wilson responded to his secretary of war the next day, warning Garrison not to try to impose his personal views on the administration. Upon receipt of Wilson's letter, Garrison submitted his resignation and, together with Assistant Secretary of War Henry Breckinridge, walked down the halls of the War Department and out of the building.

Following Garrison's departure, Wilson endorsed Hay's plan of a federalized militia. But while dead in name, the idea of a national volunteer reserve force remained alive in concept. At the suggestion of Judge Advocate General Enoch Crowder, Senator George Chamberlain of Oregon, chairman of the Senate Military Affairs Committee, included in his Army Reorganization Bill of March 1916, a proposal for a volunteer reserve plan more flexible than the Continental Army. This attempt at compromise met with the same objections as had its predecessor, and although it managed to survive five weeks of committee hearings, it died on the floor of the House in May 1916. The influence of the National Guard, combined with America's reluctance to accept anything that hinted at peacetime conscription, again killed any thoughts of a national reserve force.

Michael J. McCarthy

See also GARRISON, LINDLEY MILLER

Bibliography

Chambers, John W. *To Raise an Army: The Draft Comes to Modern America.* New York: Free Press, 1987.

Derthick, Martha. *The National Guard in Politics.* Cambridge: Harvard University Press, 1963.

Finnegan, John P. *Against the Specter of a Dragon: The Campaign for American*

Military Preparedness, 1914–1917.
Westport, CT: Greenwood Press, 1974.
Link, Arthur S. *Woodrow Wilson and the
Progressive Era, 1910–1917*. New York:
Harper, 1954.

Council of National Defense

Part of the response to World War I in the United States was the preparedness movement of the years 1914 to 1917. While much of the preparedness agenda was vague, the movement did result in some specific institutional developments in the U.S. government. In 1916, Congress passed what Russell F. Weigley calls "the most comprehensive military legislation" the country had yet seen—the National Defense Act of 1916 and the army appropriations act of the same year. A rider attached to the appropriations act (which passed on Aug. 29, 1916) created the Council of National Defense (CND) and an advisory commission; together these agencies were to focus on the problems of economic mobilization. The European war had made clear that these problems were of an unprecedented scale and complexity, so the possibility of U.S. involvement in the war certainly justified this effort to coordinate policy. The council consisted of the secretaries of war, navy, agriculture, commerce, interior, and labor, with the secretary of war as chairman. An Advisory Commission consisted of seven private citizens to be named by the President.

From the beginning these efforts to coordinate policy struggled against political resistance. The Council of National Defense lacked specific authority beyond investigating and making recommendations. Who, if anyone, would have any stronger authority was not clear. The National Defense Act had limited the size of the Army General Staff to three general officers and fifty-two junior officers, no more than half of whom could be on duty in or near Washington, D.C., at the same time. Furthermore, the General Staff's duties were specifically limited to nonadministrative functions. Thus the secretary of war would undertake his duties as chairman of the Council of National Defense without any significant number of military professionals to help him.

Much of the assistance that the Wilson administration eventually found in its efforts to coordinate industrial mobilization came from private individuals and especially businessmen. The members of the Advisory Commission, as President Wilson announced them in October, were Howard Coffin, president of the Society of Automotive Engineers and vice president of the Hudson Motor Car Company; Holliss Godfrey, president of the Drexel Institute (now University) of Philadelphia; Samuel Gompers, president of the American Federation of Labor; Franklin H. Martin, director general of the American College of Surgeons; Julius Rosenwald, president of Sears, Roebuck and Company; Daniel Willard, president of the Baltimore and Ohio Railroad; and Bernard Baruch, a Wall Street speculator. Of this group, Baruch, Coffin, Godfrey, and Martin were outspoken campaigners for preparedness. Their efforts in that campaign indicate the ideas that would motivate the Advisory Commission and the CND in their first efforts.

In the summer of 1914, Martin attended a professional meeting in London. When war broke out, he traveled to the Continent to rescue a friend's daughter stranded in Munich. He returned to the United States deeply convinced that doctors had to prepare for what would soon be an American war. As a highly respected gynecologist, Martin sought to include physicians of all specialties in his efforts. In April 1916, a Committee of American Physicians for Medical Preparedness formed and undertook a survey of the medical resources of the country. An advisory committee consisted of representatives from the medical societies in each state.

Coffin had been more directly involved with the armed forces, but otherwise his work was similar to Martin's. As president, he had made the Society of Automotive Engineers a well-organized and active body, and he had promoted the idea of standardizing automobile parts among all of the small manufacturers of the industry. In 1915, Secretary of the Navy Josephus Daniels, responding to comments by Thomas Edison, set up the Naval Consulting Board (NCB), composed of two representatives from each of the eleven largest engineering societies. The NCB would be an advisory group of scientific experts working on a variety of naval mobilization problems. At Coffin's suggestion, the board formed several subcommittees, giving each one the authority to set its own goals. Both Coffin and Martin reflected the turn-of-the-century efforts of newly organized professionals to win public recognition. Both men saw increased status for their own profession and patriotic service to the country as a natural combination.

At the NCB, Coffin directed Walter S. Gifford, a young statistician from the American Telephone and Telegraph Company, to direct a survey of industrial resources, undertaken through the state committees of engineers. In an effort that foreshadowed some of the work of the Council of National Defense, this information gathering met with some support from industry, some opposition from peace-minded engineers, and much indifference from the public. While CND members amassed a great body of data, information alone did nothing for preparedness because the nature of the future problems was unknown. This statistical survey was eventually handed over to a section of the Council of National Defense, which never made much use of it.

Nevertheless, Gifford moved with Coffin to the Advisory Commission of the Council of National Defense, so it is not surprising that the council's approach to its work began with efforts to gather information. The council met for the first time in the office of Secretary of War Baker on Sept. 18, 1916, while the Advisory Commission held its first meeting in a Washington hotel room on Dec. 6, 1916. According to David M. Kennedy, a leading historian of the homefront, Hollis Godfrey submitted a proposal for mobilization that would have taken five years to implement fully, and the Advisory Commission as a group felt only a little more need for haste. It planned a three-year effort, spending the first year on a comprehensive study of existing industries, the second examining the particulars of specific industries in military planning and procurement, and the third attempting to implement its program. This emphasis on the importance of complete and accurate information as the basis for addressing problems was completely consistent with the methods of the Progressive Era reformers.

The Council of National Defense organized itself geographically. It encouraged the creation of defense councils in every state; these in turn were to encourage county and community councils of defense. The goal was to have an organization of volunteers that could connect the national government with all its citizens through personal contact. This structure, reminiscent of the geographic departments of the nineteenth-century army, proved in David Kennedy's words, "spectacularly irrelevant to the economic character of an industrial nation" such as the United States. Once the war was

underway, economic mobilization quickly passed into the hands of a series of functionally organized agencies responsible for specific economic sectors. These agencies generally ignored the state councils, leading Secretary Baker to complain about the practice to President Wilson. The Chief Executive suggested to the agencies that they try to work through the state councils, but in practice nothing changed. The state councils became primarily propaganda agencies to generate public support for the war effort, including occasional attempts to stifle dissent.

As Robert D. Cuff comments in his study of economic mobilization in World War I, the CND and its Advisory Commission meant different things to different people, even the people who were members. The political process that created these institutions had been very contentious, and both Daniels and Baker had favored calling the CND the Council of Executive Information, thinking that such a title was more appropriate for the work they had in mind. On the other hand, with no clear mission or authority, the work of the council could be expanded in almost any direction. As the council and commission members began to meet and decide what to do, they quickly ran into conflict over these very problems.

During the winter of 1916–1917, the members began to structure their tasks. Godfrey presented his plan for a slow survey of resources. Most of the other members of the Advisory Commission, as might be expected of men at the heads of their various professions, grew impatient. What they were able to agree on was to define several subject areas for further research: creating an industrial reserve, establishing methods of determining costs and profits on war contracts, collecting information on mineral resources, and deciding upon the proper responses to the growing number of suggestions from private citizens. As the different members of the Advisory Commission pursued their particular interests through this structure, some of them sought to involve a broad sector of the public, while others, Baruch in particular, favored an approach that dealt only with the leading men in each industry.

Baruch's energy came to dominate both the Council of National Defense and the Advisory Commission. Secretary Baker tried to use the two institutions to support the work of the War Department, but the department was working through the conservative men and traditional methods of the supply bureaus, and the scale of the mobilization effort, once war was declared, dwarfed any experience the bureaus could call on. Committees multiplied to try to keep up with the needs of mobilization. By July 1917, according to Baker's biographer Daniel Beaver, "over 150 separate committees, attached in various ways to the Army and the Council of National Defense, were engaged in military purchasing and requisitioning." By law, contracts could only be placed by officers from the bureaus of the War Department, a situation that led to some awkward arrangements. For example, the Committee on Supply under the general direction of Julius Rosenwald or his vice chairman, Charles Eisenman, virtually controlled the purchase of military clothing, but the contracting office of the Quartermaster Corps actually signed the contracts, essentially doing what it was told by Rosenwald. Another area where the Wilson administration walked into a political crossfire was coal, where the largest producers dominated the Coal Committee of the Advisory Commission, a situation that quickly led to charges of price gouging and conflict of interest. In both the coal and clothing industries, organized labor greeted the role of industry leaders in mobilization with great suspicion.

Along with the political tangle at home, the vast mobilization effort had to be superimposed upon an industrial base that was already committed to producing supplies for the Allies. By the summer of 1917, it was becoming clear to many members of the administration that mobilization would not succeed unless the federal government undertook a much stronger effort to organize the entire economy. In mid-May, Frank A. Scott, chairman of the Munitions Board (which was subordinate to the Advisory Commission), called upon the Council of National Defense to grant him direct executive power over production. Scott's request prompted discussions about a possible reorganization of the Advisory Commission, but Secretary Baker firmly opposed any such changes. As Daniel Beaver puts it, if Baker had to choose between delays in the initial mobilization program or regimentation, he would choose delay. He especially opposed creating a single, unifying director of purchases. At the same time, congressional criticism of economic mobilization was growing, even among Democrats. To try to improve the supervision and control of the mobilization effort, the Council of National Defense in July 1917 created the War Industries Board with Scott as chairman.

The War Industries Board at this time was still subordinate to the Council of National Defense, and it still had only advisory powers, a situation that Secretary Baker was determined to maintain. Frank Scott soon collapsed physically under the strain of the work, and after a prominent shipbuilder declined the appointment, Daniel Willard tried to direct the board's activities but resigned after two months. By this time it was mid-January of 1918, and even Senator George E. Chamberlain of Oregon, the Democratic chairman of the Senate Military Affairs Committee, was outspoken in his criticism of the conduct of mobilization. President Wilson had little choice but to overrule Secretary Baker and grant Bernard Baruch the power to control the mobilization effort. Eventually, Baruch would be given the legal powers to be the controlling figure of economic mobilization. As Army Chief of Staff Peyton C. March put it, "He could do things, instead of recommending them."

Though the Council of National Defense remained in existence throughout the war, its functions became less and less important as it yielded power to what had originally been its creation, the War Industries Board. The history of the CND and its Advisory Committee serves as a reminder of the reluctance with which many Americans, even many leaders in big business and the professions, accepted the demands of total war. The culture of American individualism was yielding to the demands of organization and mobilization for war.

Thomas R. English

See also BARUCH, BERNARD; COFFIN, HOWARD; EDISON, THOMAS; NAVAL CONSULTING BOARD; ROSENWALD, JULIUS; WAR INDUSTRIES BOARD

Bibliography
Beaver, Daniel R. *Newton D. Baker and the American War Effort, 1917–1919.* Lincoln: University of Nebraska Press, 1966.
Cuff, Robert D. *The War Industries Board: Business-Government Relations during World War I.* Baltimore: Johns Hopkins University Press, 1973.
Kennedy, David M. *Over Here: The First World War and American Society.* New York: Oxford University Press, 1980.

C

Council of National Defense: Woman's Committee

The Woman's Committee of the Council of National Defense (WCCND) was appointed by the Council of National Defense (CND) in April 1917 in response to pressure created by the eagerness of women's organizations to assist the government in a time of emergency. Anna Howard Shaw, former National American Woman Suffrage Association president, headed the eleven-member committee. Lacking clear directions from the Wilson administration, the Executive Committee decided it should serve as a clearing house for women's organizations involved in war service activities, develop an educational propaganda department to be concerned with Americanization and patriotism, cooperate in organizing food conservation efforts, consider the need for a registration of women, study problems of camp life and moral standards in wartime, and suggest legislative measures to the CND. The women projected an organization that was not simply advisory but would direct and coordinate women's activities in every state, and serve as the only channel between the government and women. The government, after the women had already launched their organizing efforts, indicated that it envisioned a much more circumscribed role. Secretary of War Newton D. Baker told Shaw that the main purpose of the WCCND was to bring the CND into closer contact with women's efforts in order to avoid duplication. He viewed it as an advisory body to the CND, not a clearing house and not the only group for directing women's war work. These fundamentally different perceptions of the role of the WCCND led to considerable frustration and conflict.

There was serious friction between the WCCND state divisions and the state councils of the CND. Since the state legislatures funded the state councils, but not the WCCND, the WCCND state organizations had to request financial support from their male counterparts. The men, in state after state, refused to support the WCCND because the women were not directly under their control, but received instructions from the executive committee of the WCCND in Washington. Thus, women in the state divisions had to raise money for their activities.

The first tasks of the WCCND were the food conservation pledge campaign and the registration of women for voluntary service. Herbert Hoover, the national food administra-

tor, presented plans for a food drive at a mid-June 1917 conference of representatives of national women's organizations called by the WCCND. The scheme, devised without consulting the WCCND, called for women to sign pledge cards between July 1 and July 15 in which they promised to carry out the instructions of the government on food conservation. The WCCND was in charge in thirty-one states, and despite inadequate preparation time, only ten states did not complete the campaign. The hastily launched registration drive, on the other hand, was successful in only sixteen states. The state divisions received some guidelines and could decide when the registration would occur. The WCCND came into conflict with the National League for Women's Service (NLWS) in the registration drive. In some states the WCCND absorbed the NLWS, but in most states the two organizations competed with one another and both carried out registrations.

The WCCND made important contributions to the Liberty Loan campaigns, but there was dissension over lines of authority between the WCCND Liberty Loan Department and the Woman's Liberty Loan Committee (WLLC). Confusion resulted because state WCCND leaders thought they should be responsible for directing all government-related women's activities in their states, while state WLLC leaders thought that the WCCND should have no authority over state Liberty Loan committees. Despite the fact that the WCCND had provided valuable support for the Liberty Loan campaigns on state and national levels, the WLLC was ultimately given authority to operate independently of the WCCND.

The WCCND sought out some of its own projects and was most successful in promoting general social reform in cooperation with the Children's Bureau of the Department of Labor. The bureau designated 1918 as Children's Year and through the WCCND launched a massive campaign to weigh and measure all children under school age. With about half the preschool children tested, the campaign led to increased awareness of children's health issues and in several states to the development of new agencies concerned with children's health. The WCCND state divisions also cooperated with the bureau in drives to increase recreational facilities for children and in a back-to-school drive.

Anna Howard Shaw was probably as effective as any leader could be given the nature of the WCCND. She persisted in her criticisms of the shoddy treatment of the WCCND by the government. She also kept the committee from becoming yet another vehicle of wartime hysteria and intolerance. She opposed universal military training and lowering the draft age, and she refused to attack others like Jane Addams who were being condemned as unpatriotic. Frustrated by the inefficient use of women in the war effort, she suggested the conscription of women for war service once they had received the vote.

A major conference was held in May 1918 to discuss the role of the WCCND and the state divisions. The conference approved resolutions calling for improved cooperation between state councils and the WCCND state divisions and requesting that the CND and other government agencies work through the WCCND. Shortly after the conference, the Executive Committee resigned in order to give the CND complete freedom in restructuring the men's and women's CND work in the states. Refusing to accept their resignations, the CND finally recognized that the WCCND needed more authority in the states. The result was a merger of the WCCND and the CND on state matters with a joint organization of men and women to direct state councils and state divisions. Since this plan came late in the war, however, it had little practical effect in most states, and the Wilson administration provided little direction to those men and women attempting to work together through the newly created Field Divisions.

The WCCND did not see its task ending with the Armistice, but the only important task given to the states by the Field Division was to help find jobs for returning servicemen. Shaw requested that the state divisions be continued under the direction of a federal board to aid women workers in the conversion to a peace-time economy, but there was no reply. Women hoped for some further responsibilities for reconstruction, but the state councils decided there was no reason to continue with so little work left for them after the war. In some states far more women had participated in the WCCND work than in any other woman's organization, and the WCCND leaders in these states did not want to see this activism cease. Although some women active in WCCND state divisions were able to continue their activities by cooperating with other agencies or by turning their divisions into private organizations, the WCCND Executive Committee in February 1919 offered its resignation to the government because they did not believe the committee could function without official authorization.

Barbara J. Steinson

See also COUNCIL OF NATIONAL DEFENSE

Bibliography

Blair, Emily N. *The Woman's Committee, United States Council of National Defense, An Interpretive Report.* Washington, DC: n.p., 1920.

Breen, William J. *Uncle Sam at Home: Civilian Mobilization, Wartime Federalism, and the Council of National Defense, 1917–1919.* New York: Greenwood Press, 1984.

National American Woman Suffrage Association. *Woman Citizen.* n.p., 1917–1918.

O'Neill, William L. *Everyone was Brave, the Rise and Fall of Feminism in America.* Chicago: Quadrangle Books, 1969.

Steinson, Barbara J. *American Women's Activism in World War I.* New York: Garland, 1982.

Craig, Malin (1875–1945)

Born in Missouri, Malin Craig grew up on military posts as the son of an army officer. He graduated from the United States Military Academy in 1898. Commissioned in the infantry, he immediately transferred to the cavalry, his father's branch, and participated in the invasion of Cuba. He subsequently served in the Philippines and the China Relief Expedition. Upon returning to the United States, Craig attended the army's service and staff schools and displayed a genuine talent for staff work. In fact, his fine record at the Army War College led to his appointment as an instructor there upon his graduation in 1911.

When the United States declared war on Germany in the spring of 1917, Craig was working in the office of the chief of staff. He applied for duty in the field, and in September the War Department detailed him to be the 41st Division's chief of staff and promoted him to lieutenant colonel. Initially, Craig's principal task was to establish and train his own division staff. Soon, however, he had to turn to reorganizing the division's various National Guard units and to instituting a uniform program of instruction. Throughout this period, Craig worked closely with MajGen. Hunter Liggett, the division commander, and soon earned his confidence and respect. After only a few weeks of training, the division sailed for Europe in November 1917.

Upon arriving in France, the American Expeditionary Force (AEF) headquarters designated the 41st a replacement division and began transferring its men to other units. In January 1918, Liggett took command of I Corps and had Craig accompany him to be his chief of staff. During the spring, the corps was largely involved in training and administrative matters. In July, Craig became a temporary brigadier general, and the corps moved into combat for the first time. Initially in a defensive sector west of Château-Thierry, I Corps went on the offensive on July 15. It performed well in the Champagne-Marne and Aisne-Marne offensives, and Liggett was quick to give part of the credit to Craig's efficient handling of the corps' staff.

In September, the corps participated in the St. Mihiel offensive. The attack began on September 12, and I Corps quickly moved forward. Craig's job, like all chiefs of staff, was to oversee the day-to-day operations of the corps in order to allow Liggett to concentrate on fighting the Germans. In this regard, Craig coordinated the activities of the supply and operations staffs, made sure the subordinate divisions received and understood their orders, and supervised the corps' correspondence. Furthermore, he acted as an adviser to Liggett and helped formulate operations.

As soon as fighting subsided on I Corps' front, Liggett and Craig moved their headquarters west to join the American offensive in the Meuse-Argonne. The corps occupied the American left wing in the Argonne Forest, and fighting proved much tougher than St. Mihiel. When the attack bogged down in mid-October, AEF commander John J. Pershing promoted Liggett to command the First Army. MajGen. Joseph T. Dickman then assumed command of I Corps. Craig and Dickman, another cavalryman, worked well together, and got the corps moving forward again after Liggett had straightened out the First Army. Despite the difficulties of the campaign, bad roads, poor communications, ill-trained troops, and stiff German resistance, both Liggett and Dickman lauded Craig's performance.

Following the Armistice, Dickman left I Corps to command the Third Army, and he took Craig along as his chief of staff. After participating in the occupation of Germany, Craig returned to the United States in the fall of 1919

and reverted to his prewar rank of major. He held a number of school and troop commands before becoming a major general and chief of cavalry in 1924. In 1926, he served as the army's assistant chief of staff for operations and training. After a series of top field commands, Craig became army chief of staff in the fall of 1935. As chief of staff, he worked to modernize the army's equipment and training and to add realism to its planning. He retired from the Army in 1939 but served briefly again during World War II. Malin Craig died on July 25, 1945.

Richard Kehrberg

Bibliography

Pershing, John J. *My Experiences in the World War.* 2 vols. New York: Stokes, 1931.

Smythe, Donald. *Pershing: General of the Armies.* Bloomington: Indiana University Press, 1986.

Crane, Charles Richard (1858–1939)

Charles Richard Crane was a plumbing supply manufacturer and philanthropist. After selling his interest in the Crane Company in 1912, he devoted himself primarily to world travel, philanthropy, and sporadic public service. He was active in the Progressive Movement and became the largest single contributor to the presidential election campaign of Woodrow Wilson in 1912. Wilson and Col. Edward M. House seriously considered Crane for various positions in the cabinet and as ambassador to Russia, but he was not appointed to the former and declined the latter.

Through his extensive travels, Crane had become something of an expert on Eastern Europe, the Russian Empire, and the Middle East in an era when few Americans knew much about those areas. It was probably this expertise that led President Wilson to appoint him to the Root Mission to Russia in April 1917. Unfortunately, there is little evidence to indicate what role Crane played within the mission. He certainly knew many of the leaders of the Russian Provisional Government of 1917, and he was unquestionably sympathetic to that regime. There is nothing to indicate that he was aware of the possibility of the Bolsheviks seizing power, as they did in November 1917, three months after the Root Mission had returned to the United States.

In March 1919, Wilson chose Crane and Henry Churchill King, the president of Oberlin College, both of whom were then in Europe, as the American members of an international commission to visit the Near East in an effort to determine the attitudes of the various ethnic groups toward possible mandates in the region. After two months of delay, during which the British, French, and Italian governments decided not to participate in the commission, the two Americans with a small support staff left Paris on their own fact-finding mission on May 29.

The King-Crane Commission spent six weeks from June 10 to July 21 traveling in Palestine and Syria and conducting extensive interviews with residents of the area. They spent nearly another month in Constantinople holding additional interviews and working on their final report. They arrived back in Paris on August 27. Crane cabled a summary of the commission's report to Wilson on August 31. They recommended that the unity of Syria, including Palestine and Lebanon, be preserved and that a mandate over that area should be offered to the United States. They also recommended Great Britain as an alternative mandatory power, should the United States not accept that responsibility. Finally, they suggested that the United States accept mandates over a separate Armenian state, the new Turkish state, and an internationalized city of Constantinople.

A copy of the complete report of the King-Crane Commission was delivered to the White House in late September 1919. However, President Wilson, because of his critical illness, in all probability never read it. The United States did not accept any of the suggested mandates.

John E. Little

See also ROOT MISSION

Bibliography
Howard, Harry N. *The King-Crane Commission: An American Inquiry in the Middle East*. Beirut: Khayat, 1963.

Cravath, Paul Drennan (1861–1940)
Paul Drennan Cravath was born in Berlin Heights, Ohio. He earned his B.A. from Oberlin College in 1882 and received his LL.B. from Columbia Law School in 1886. In 1891, he became senior partner in the firm of Cravath and Houston in New York City.

When war broke out in 1914, Cravath, like most Americans in the Northeast, sided with the Entente. In fact, his law firm represented several banks and industries that financed and supplied the Entente war effort. In the summer of 1916, Cravath traveled to Britain where he inspected a variety of military facilities. He also conferred with General Sir Douglas Haig and visited the British Expeditionary Force in northern France. Cravath returned from the front convinced that an Allied victory was vital to the security of the United States.

When America entered the war, President Woodrow Wilson named Cravath as a member of the American mission to the Inter-Allied War Conference, a meeting called to coordinate the war efforts of the United States and its allies. The conference, attended by representatives of the United States, Great Britain, France, Italy, Belgium, Japan, and other allied nations, sat both in London and Paris in November and December 1917. The conference established both the Supreme War Council and the Inter-Allied Council on War Purchases and Finances. Cravath served as legal counsel to Oscar T. Crosby, the American delegate to the Council on War Purchases and Finances.

Continuing his interest in world affairs after the conclusion of the war, Cravath was among those Republicans who were initially sympathetic to the League of Nations. However, conflict broke out in October 1920 between the leading Republican supporter of the League of Nations, Senator Selden P. Spencer of Missouri, and President Wilson. The dispute centered around Article X of the Covenant. When Wilson refused to withdraw his pledge to send troops to Rumania and Serbia in case of invasion, Cravath and the internationalist faction of the Republican Party joined with the isolationists to resist joining the league and endorsed the presidential bid of Warren G. Harding.

For his activities during the war, Cravath received the United States Distinguished Service Medal in 1919. He died in New York on July 1, 1940.

Jennifer Yang

Creel, George (1876–1953)
George Creel was an outstanding exemplar of a Wilsonian progressive. Reared in midwestern progressivism, he was an early Wilson enthusiast. Wilson's own respect and affection for Creel

were based on the rhetorical skills he displayed during Wilson's two presidential campaigns.

In both 1912 and 1916, Creel worked as a writer for the Democratic National Committee. His spirited defense of Wilson's policies, *Wilson and the Issues* (1916), reflected his flair for advocacy. Suffusing the book was Creel's enthusiasm for Wilson's "passionate idealism." Americans had a choice, in his estimate, "between a proved democrat and the captains who served under Hanna; between equal justice and special privilege." He equated democracy with spiritual progress and denounced "property rights" as a perversion of "human rights" and a denial of the "Brotherhood of Man." Wilson embodied the authentic reform spirit in the national character for he knew it inherited in the "idealism of the Declaration of Independence, not in the cautious phrases of the Constitution."

It was during the 1916 election campaign that Creel had gained what Kenneth Davis has properly described as Woodrow Wilson's "rarely-bestowed personal affection." When Wilson selected Creel, on April 14, 1917, as chairman of the Committee on Public Information (CPI), he had already become, in Arthur Link's estimation, a leading figure "of the advanced wing of the Progressive Movement in the United States."

While the *New York Times* protested Wilson's appointment because of Creel's "radicalism," there was, in fact, an extraordinary complementarity between the position and the personality, for Creel possessed a passionate, partisan spirit and an unswerving devotion to Wilson—a temperament so oriented to offering justifications for Wilson's leadership that a year after his appointment, Creel provided this apologia for the President's prewar leadership: "I would rather be an American filled in the unpreparedness that proved devotion is to declared principles than a German living as the result of years of lying, sneaking, treacherous preparation, for a wolf's spring at the throat of an unsuspecting world."

From April 1917 through March 1919, Creel directed the federal government's policies, programs, and personnel to enhance the image of the United States abroad and to oversee the dissemination of news and information. Books and pamphlets, posters, and press releases were distributed worldwide.

Creel's frenetic pace and the imperatives of mobilization led to severe and substantial criticisms of what H.L. Mencken called the "star-spangled men." Despite these critiques of Creel's style and tactics, he retained Wilson's esteem and approval. "I want to say how much it has gratified me," wrote Wilson to Creel in January 1918, "and how entirely the work being done by the Committee meets with my approval."

Creel's leadership of the CPI led to significant sales of war bonds, subscriptions to Liberty Loans, and other manifestations of intensified nationalism. He remained an intimate, devoted friend and adviser to Wilson in the President's retirement years on S Street and a fierce guardian of the Wilsonian legacy.

Creel's later career involved service in FDR's New Deal, a failed bid for the 1934 Democratic gubernatorial nomination in California, and a repudiation, in the last decade of his life, of New Deal fair liberalism, which he came to see as a violation of Wilsonian progressivism. As a strident Cold-War opponent of "international communism," his last years were dedicated to supporting right-wing Republican efforts to combat what he regarded as the malign departure Democrats had taken in the 1940s from authentic World War I progressivism. Creel died in San Francisco in 1953.

Frank Annunziata

See also COMMITTEE ON PUBLIC INFORMATION

Bibliography

Creel, George. *Rebel at Large: Recollections of Fifty Crowded Years*. New York: Putnam, 1947.
———. *Wilson and the Issues*. New York: 1916.
Davis, Kenneth. *FDR: The Beckoning of Destiny, 1882–1928*. New York: Putnam, 1972.
Link, Arthur S. *Woodrow Wilson and the Progressive Era, 1910–1917*. New York: Harper & Row, 1963.
Mock, James R., and C. Larson. *Words that Won the War: The Story of the Committee on Public Information, 1917–1919*. Princeton, NJ: Princeton University Press, 1939.

Croly, Herbert (1869–1930)

From 1914 to 1917 progressive essayist and journalist Herbert Croly expressed foreign policy views that paralleled or reinforced the publicly stated policies of Woodrow Wilson. Croly was, however, profoundly disillusioned with the results of the Great War. He denounced the Treaty of Versailles because, to his mind, it legitimized a vindictive peace settlement and insured further destruction.

From 1900–1906, he was editor of the *Architectural Record*. In 1909, Croly published *The Promise of American Life,* which established its author as one of the country's leading progressive intellectuals. In it, Croly argued for strong nationalist policies. Individualism was irrelevant and perhaps impossible in an industrial age. His views on foreign policy were a logical extension of his domestic politics. Theodore Roosevelt and Woodrow Wilson both read the book, which seemed to influence both the New Nationalism and the New Freedom.

Croly also promoted his ideas when, in 1914, he founded the progressive journal the *New Republic*. Croly invited like-minded intellectuals to join the staff, including journalist Walter Lippmann and economist Walter Weyl. The journal was established through the sponsorship of a wealthy New York couple, Willard and Dorothy Straight, who were greatly attracted to Croly's message of a robust national government.

The outbreak of World War I provided an opportunity for Croly to apply his progressive philosophy to foreign policy. In an editorial in the first issue of the *New Republic,* Croly asserted that traditional American isolation must end. He further argued that if the United States hoped to take a leading role in peacemaking, it should remain neutral. Like most Americans, however, Croly privately sympathized with the Entente. During the first months of the conflict, he and his colleagues avoided blaming Germany for the war. They questioned the rumors of German atrocities and criticized the British blockade. Initially, Croly envisioned a limited role for the United States, perhaps eventually establishing a "league of neutrals."

As the war continued, Croly and his colleagues gradually moved away from moderation. After the United States entered the war, Croly met informally on a weekly basis with Wilson's adviser, Col. Edward M. House. These exchanges gave Croly the mistaken impression that his ideas were influencing Wilson's policies and created the public impression that the *New Republic* was an unofficial voice of the Wilson administration. This connection seemed to be confirmed, however, in Wilson's Jan. 22, 1917, speech when he used the phrase "Peace without Victory"—a phrase that had first appeared in the journal a month before.

When the terms of the peace treaty were announced in May 1919, Croly was shattered. In his May editorial, Croly expressed a feeling of personal betrayal. He attacked the treaty because it served only to guarantee the Allies the spoils of victory and represented a repudiation of the internationalist position. Croly's editorial rejection of the treaty cost the *New Republic* half of its subscribers. The experience of World War I irrevocably split the voices of a "new liberalism" and the potential for a national reform movement that Croly had envisioned before the war began.

Stephen L. Recken

Bibliography

Forcey, Charles. *The Crossroads of Liberalism: Croly, Weyl, Lippmann, and the Progressive Era, 1900–1925.* New York: Oxford University Press, 1961.

Levy, David W. *Herbert Croly of the New Republic: The Life and Thought of an American Progressive.* Princeton, NJ: Princeton University Press, 1985.

Crowder, Enoch Herbert (1859–1932)

Enoch Herbert Crowder was born in Edinburg, Missouri. A member of the class of 1881 at the United States Military Academy, he was commissioned a second lieutenant in the cavalry. Crowder served on the frontier in the Indian campaigns, although he did not see combat. When not occupied with military duties, he studied law, and in 1886, he earned a law degree from the University of Missouri, where he was professor of military science and tactics. In 1895, Crowder transferred from the cavalry to the judge advocate general's department, which brought him promotion to major.

Crowder served as a staff officer in the Philippines during the Spanish-American War and the Philippine Insurrection and was a member of the War Department General Staff after its creation in 1903. He was an observer in the Russo-Japanese War and a member of the executive staff of Provisional Governor Charles E. Magoon during the Cuban intervention of 1906–1909. While in Cuba, Crowder supervised the elections of 1908 and headed the advisory commission that drafted many of the

C

organic laws of the Cuban republic. In all of his assignments, Crowder displayed an outstanding legal mind, administrative ability, and the capacity for completing a prodigious amount of work. As a result, in 1911, he was appointed judge advocate general of the army with the rank of brigadier general, a post he held for the next twelve years.

As judge advocate general, Crowder reformed and modernized the military judicial and penal systems. Combining an understanding of law and politics with a thorough knowledge of the military, he gained great power in the War Department. In the eyes of many progressive military officers, however, Crowder did not always use his power constructively, for he strongly advocated the traditional practice of the military bureaus controlling the War Department at a time when the General Staff was attempting to expand its authority over those bureaus. In interpreting the National Defense Act of 1916, he suggested that the supervisory and coordinating role of the General Staff had been curtailed by the legislation and that the General Staff should be restricted to planning functions and advising the secretary of war. Chief of Staff Gen. Hugh L. Scott staunchly opposed that opinion. After carefully studying the question, Secretary of War Newton D. Baker decided that Crowder was wrong and approved the supervisory role of the General Staff.

In the period preceding American entry into World War I, Crowder was a major participant in the War Department's deliberations concerning compulsory military training and service. Because of the strong antimilitary bias in Congress and the nation's historical commitment to volunteerism in raising armies, he was unwilling to recommend any form of conscription before the nation entered the war. However, once President Woodrow Wilson decided in February 1917 to utilize conscription to raise a national army if the United States entered the war, Baker called upon Crowder to play a key role in preparing the proposed legislation for selective service. After the declaration of war in April 1917, Baker directed Crowder to develop the mechanism for implementing the draft.

Crowder was guided by the experience of the Union Army's draft during the Civil War. An army-run draft, it had directly produced only 6 percent of Union troops. Besides being inefficient, its inequitable system of exemptions and often arbitrary and high-handed enforcement by provost marshals had provoked wide resent-

ment and reinforced the sentiment for volunteerism. Determined to avoid these mistakes, Crowder provided for a small federal agency headquartered in Washington that would be responsible for policy making and supervision and placed day-to-day administration of the draft, particularly the distasteful task of actually selecting men for military service, in the hands of local civilian authorities. The government thus avoided the stigma of military control of the draft and made it more palatable to Congress and harmonious with the nation's long-standing penchant for localism. At the same time, Crowder's assistants worked out the details for the first draft, so that by the time Congress passed the Selective Service Act in May 1917, the machinery for selecting hundreds of thousands of men for the army was ready to function.

On May 22, 1917, Baker named Crowder provost marshal general and charged him with administering the Selective Service Act. Under his direction, over 9 million men were registered for the draft in June with only minor problems. In July, the first great lottery for determining the order in which men were to be selected was conducted, and by September, the initial "driblet" of the 687,000 men selected in the first draft began reporting to training camps. Meanwhile, Crowder concluded that a new selection process would speed up the induction of men and insure a rational allocation of manpower between the military and the industrial sector as the nation geared up for total war. Working closely with local officials, Crowder's office in the fall of 1917 devised new procedures that went into effect in December 1917. This was supplemented in the spring of 1918 by a "work or fight" order in which Crowder informed deferred men who were idle or engaged in nonessential work that they risked reclassification and induction if they did not find work in essential industries. New legislation proposed by Crowder in the summer of 1918 extended the age limits for the draft from eighteen to forty-five and ended voluntary enlistments for all services. With these steps he made the draft the basis of military recruitment as well as a vehicle for allocating labor to war industries.

Once the draft was firmly established, Crowder, now a major general, sought an overseas command. His frail physical condition ruled out this prospect, and he had to content himself with fighting the war from Washington. As it was, during the winter of 1917–1918, Crowder's public stature grew steadily, and he emerged as the symbol of the draft. More importantly, he became the dominant figure in the War Department as Baker, confronted with a weak chief of staff, increasingly turned to Crowder for advice and support. This situation changed after MajGen. Peyton C. March was appointed chief of staff in March 1918 and given a virtual free hand to bring order to the floundering War Department. A long-time foe of Crowder, the relentless March determined to assert the authority of the General Staff over the bureaus, and in a showdown in the summer of 1918, he significantly curbed Crowder's power and influence both as judge advocate general and provost marshal by limiting his access to the secretary of war and reaffirming the supremacy of the General Staff in military matters.

Following the war, Crowder served as special representative, minister, and, after his retirement from the army in 1923, ambassador to Cuba. After resigning his ambassadorship in 1927, Crowder opened a law office in Chicago, representing several sugar and public utility corporations. Remembered as the father of the modern Selective Service system, he died in Washington, D.C., on May 7, 1932.

John K. Ohl

See also NATIONAL DEFENSE ACT OF 1916; SELECTIVE SERVICE

Bibliography

Chambers, John W., II. *To Raise an Army: The Draft Comes to Modern America.* New York: Free Press, 1987.

Coffman, Edward M. *The Hilt of the Sword: The Career of Peyton C. March.* Madison: University of Wisconsin Press, 1966.

Crowder, Enoch H. *The Spirit of Selective Service.* New York: Columbia University Press, 1920.

Dickinson, John. *The Building of an Army: A Detailed Account of Regulation, Administration and Opinion.* New York: Century, 1922.

Lockmiller, David A. *Enoch H. Crowder: Soldier, Lawyer and Statesman.* Columbia: University of Missouri Studies, 1955.

Crowell, Benedict (1869–1952)

Benedict Crowell was born in Cleveland, Ohio, on Oct. 21, 1869, the son of William and Mary Benedict Crowell. He graduated from Yale University in 1891 and in 1918 received his M.A. from Yale. After graduation in 1891, Crowell became a prosperous builder and contractor in Cleveland. In 1917, he became affiliated with the General Munitions Board in Washington, working to accelerate steel production and shipment abroad. At that time he was commissioned a major in the Ordnance Department and also in the Corps of Engineers. In November 1917, he was named assistant secretary of war with responsibility for the engineering and munitions phase of the country's war preparations, including providing weapons and munitions for all armed forces. In 1918, he was named director of munitions.

After the war, Secretary of War Newton D. Baker sent Crowell, who had been an early proponent of aviation and former president of the Aero Club of America, to Europe on a fact-finding trip to assess the organization, development, and production of aircraft in those countries and recommend a course of action for the United States. Called the American Aviation Mission, or the Crowell Commission, the group recommended strongly that air activities in the United States, civil and military, be placed under a "single Government agency created for the purpose, co-equal in importance with the Departments of War, Navy, and Commerce. . . ." Although Secretary Baker rejected the commission's findings, Crowell's summary *Report of American Aviation Mission* resulted in a flurry of legislative proposals for an independent government office to regulate aviation in the United States.

Crowell was a prolific writer concerning America's role in mobilizing for World War I. With Robert Forrest Wilson, he authored six books on mobilization and an important volume on munitions production during the war. In 1922, Crowell's life took an unfortunate turn when he and six assistants, all members of the Emergency Construction Committee of the Council of National Defense, were indicted by a special grand jury on charges of price fixing. In 1925, these charges were dismissed by Attorney General Harlan F. Stone because he claimed there was no evidence to support them.

During the 1930s, Crowell held several positions in Franklin D. Roosevelt's administration, was state director for the National Emergency Council in Ohio, and president of the National Central Bank in Cleveland. In 1931, he was made a brigadier general in the U.S.

Army. He was appointed as a special consultant on defense by Secretary of War Henry L. Stimson and asked to make a preliminary survey of the nation's defense program. Crowell died on Sept. 8, 1952.

Dominick A. Pisano

Bibliography

Komons, Nick A. *Bonfires to Beacons: Federal Civil Aviation Policy under the Air Commerce Act, 1926–1938*. Washington, DC: Smithsonian Institution Press, 1989.

Crozier, William (1855–1942)

William Crozier was born in Carrollton, Ohio, to Judge Robert and Margaret Atkinson Crozier. He graduated from the United States Military Academy in 1876. Lieutenant Crozier was assigned to the 4th U.S. Regiment of Artillery. After service against the Sioux and Bannock tribes, he was commissioned in the Ordnance Corps. In 1899, he was appointed as the military delegate to the International Peace Conference at the Hague. Crozier served in the Philippines during the insurrection that followed U.S. occupation of those islands. He was later assigned as the chief of ordnance of the 1900 China Relief Expedition.

In late 1901, at the recommendation of the Secretary of War Elihu Root, President Theodore Roosevelt selected Crozier to be chief of ordnance. He was to serve in that post for almost seventeen years, longer than any one officer in the U.S. military. In 1912, although a permanent staff officer, he was appointed head of the Army War College. In that post he took a prominent part in the discussions resulting in the "Report on the Organization of the Land Forces of the United States," a historic study out of which came the first tactical organization of an American army in time of peace.

Early in his career, General Crozier recognized the complete interdependence of ordnance and civilian science, engineering, and industry. He became an advocate for industrial preparedness. With limited resources, he organized the Ordnance Department for emergency service in the field long before the United States entered World War I.

When the United States did enter the Great War, Crozier was one of those primarily responsible for turning civilian factories into ordnance-producing operations. President Woodrow Wilson named him to the U.S. War Council. In January 1918, Crozier visited British, French, and Belgian units along the Western Front to study the performance of modern ordnance in actual combat operations. When the Supreme War Council was organized at Versailles, General Crozier and the minister of munitions of Great Britain, Winston Churchill, developed the basis for the complete and effective pooling of ordnance equipment for the Allied armies.

General Crozier was one of the first American officers to visit the Italian front during the war. At the request of King Victor Emmanuel III, Crozier toured practically the entire Italian front in a demonstration of United States support. This effort at improving troop morale took place just after the Italian defeat at Caporetto. Upon his return from Europe in July 1918, he was appointed major general and relieved of his position as chief of ordnance. From that day until his retirement on Jan. 1, 1919, Crozier served as commander of the Northeastern Department.

In 1919, General Crozier was a founder of the Army Ordnance Association (AOA), the predecessor of the American Defense Preparedness Association. He continued to be a strong supporter of the AOA during the remainder of his life. In 1941, the AOA established the Crozier Gold Medal Award for outstanding service in the field of American ordnance. Crozier died on Nov. 10, 1942.

Vincent P. Grimes

Bibliography

Sterling, Keir B. *Serving the Line with Excellence*. Washington, DC: U.S. Army Ordnance Center and School, 1987.

Curtiss, Glenn Hammond (1878–1930)

Glenn Hammond Curtiss was born in Hammondsport, New York. When Curtis was twelve, the family moved to Rochester, where Curtiss worked as a messenger for Western Union and assembled cameras in the Eastman Kodak plant. The "Great Bicycle Craze" began sweeping the nation just as Curtiss was entering his teens, and Curtiss began racing. He soon became bicycle champion of western New York. Returning to Hammondsport, he eventually owned and operated three bicycle shops.

Before long, Curtiss attached to a bicycle a small engine that he had assembled from parts purchased through an advertisement in *Scien-*

tific American, with a carburetor he made from a coffee can. He began to manufacture motorcycles, continuing to win races and set speed records to stimulate the demand for his machines. Curtiss sold one of his engines to "Captain" Thomas R. Baldwin for his airship, the *California Arrow*, which, in November 1904, won the grand prize at the Louisiana Purchase Exposition in St. Louis. Baldwin and Curtiss went on to collaborate on the U.S. Army's first airship.

In 1907, Curtiss visited Alexander Graham Bell to demonstrate an engine Bell had purchased. While there, the two formed the Aerial Experiment Association (AEA), along with J.A.D. McCurdy, F.W. Baldwin, and Lt. Thomas E. Selfridge, U.S. Army, who was assigned to observe advances in aeronautics. The group agreed that each member should design a flying machine that the group would build and test. Between 1907 and 1908, the AEA developed and built seven planes of varying designs and success. Bell applied for several patents for the innovations resulting from the AEA's experiments, but the Wright brothers challenged one of those applications. This dispute dragged on for years, while Curtiss continued to design and build airplanes.

The AEA came to an end on March 31, 1909, and Curtiss joined with Augustus M. Herring to form the Herring-Curtiss Company. However, in 1910, Curtiss was able to reorganize his business as the Curtiss Motor Company. Its subsidiaries were the Curtiss Aeroplane Company, which manufactured aircraft and engines, and the Curtiss Exhibition Company.

Curtiss has been called the "Father of Naval Aviation." He recognized the suitability of bodies of water for launching and recovering aircraft, and a number of his early aircraft were designed to operate from water. He also conceived of the possibility of using ships as "flying fields." The U.S. Navy offered him the use of the cruiser USS *Birmingham* to test his ideas. A platform was built on the ship, and on Nov. 14, 1910, Eugene Ely flew a plane from the ship, anchored at Hampton Roads, Virginia, to shore.

On Nov. 19, 1910, Curtiss sent offers to the secretary of war and the secretary of the navy: he would provide flight training, free and without conditions of any kind, to officers of the army and navy. While he was in California making arrangements for that training, a plat-

form 120 feet long and 30 feet wide was built on the quarterdeck of the USS *Pennsylvania*, sloping downward toward the stern. Ropes tied to sandbags at each end were placed at intervals across the deck. On Jan. 18, 1911, Ely took off from the parade ground at the Presidio, flew out to the *Pennsylvania* anchored in San Francisco Bay, and landed successfully. The machine was turned around and Ely took off from the platform and returned to land at the camp of the 30th Infantry Division. The aircraft carrier was born. The navy bought fourteen Curtiss aircraft by 1914. By 1917, Curtiss Aeroplane Company had become the leading American aircraft manufacturer; in fact, it was the only firm producing significant numbers of aircraft when the United States entered the war, and it held its lead throughout the conflict. At the same time, Curtiss began work on a successful "flying boat," which landed *in* rather than on the water.

At the outbreak of World War I, Cmdr. J.C. Porte, R.N., who had worked extensively with Curtiss, became commanding officer of the Naval Air Station at Felixstone, England. At his urging, the Admiralty bought two Curtiss flying boats in August 1914. Fifty more were ordered in March 1915. Later another fifty larger boats were ordered. Despite some problems with their engines, the Curtiss boats performed valuable services. Guided by radio direction-finding stations in England, a Curtiss flying boat tracked down and destroyed zeppelin *L 22* with a single burst of fire. A few weeks later another flying boat destroyed the *L 43*. Those attacks taught the Germans that they must conduct their zeppelin patrols at altitudes above the ceilings of the flying boats—about 11,000 feet—thus minimizing the German ability to detect British submarines and mines.

In a cooperative effort, the U.S. Navy and Curtiss began design work on flying boats that could reach Europe by flying the Atlantic instead of crossing aboard ship, thus avoiding losses to U-boats. In December 1917, construction began on a series of the NC (for Navy Curtiss boats. Only the NC-1 was completed by the Armistice, but construction went forward with the NC-2, NC-3, and NC-4. The NC-4 safely reached Plymouth, England, on May 31, 1919.

Curtiss went to England and Europe in 1913 to observe developments there. Visiting the Sopwith Aviation Company, he met B. Douglas Thomas, whom he persuaded to resign from Sopwith and design an airplane for the Curtiss firm to build. It was called the Model J.

During the winter, Thomas, working in England, sent Curtiss design materials, and construction began. By the time Thomas himself arrived in Hammondsport in April 1914, the plane was almost ready. After tests were conducted, work was begun on a Model N, in hope that the new machine would meet army specifications. It was an unstable plane that barely met army requirements. Further refinement led to a hybrid of the J and N, designated the JN series—the Jennies—which first saw duty with General Pershing and the Punitive Expedition into Mexico. Virtually all Jennies produced after that served as trainers. Curtiss already had established a flying school at Long Branch, Ontario, just west of Toronto, and more than 95 percent of Canadian as well as American World War I pilots learned at least some of their flying skills in Jennies. The British ordered large numbers as well.

When the United States entered World War I, the great demand for planes led to the construction of a second Curtiss plant, at Buffalo, New York. It became the largest airplane factory in the world. New management was brought in from the automobile industry to apply "mass production" know-how to the building of airplanes. Under wartime contracts, Curtiss delivered twenty H-12 and 125 H-16 flying boats, 4,895 Jennies, and 5,000 aircraft engines. After the end of the war, Curtiss repurchased from the government $20 million worth of aircraft for 13 percent of the price the government had paid for them. This was considered scandalous by critics of the war effort, who also charged aircraft firms with incompetence and wartime profiteering. Subsequent investigations, however, produced evidence that the firms had been closely supervised by government agencies and had merely followed orders.

In the years following the war, surplus Curtiss Jennies and Curtiss OX-5 engines dominated domestic aviation. Used Jennies could be purchased for as little as $50 and were widely used by "barnstormers" until eventually they just wore out. The army flew its Jennies until 1927. Glenn Curtiss died on July 23, 1930.

Vincent Norris

See also AIRCRAFT

Bibliography
Bowers, Peter M. *Curtiss Aircraft, 1907–1947*. Annapolis, MD: Naval Institute Press, 1979.
Casey, Louis S. *Curtiss: The Hammondsport Era, 1907–1915*. New York: Crown, 1981.
Curtiss, Glenn H., and Augustus Post. *The Curtiss Aviation Book*. New York: Stokes, 1912.
Hatch, Alden. *Glenn Curtiss, Pioneer of Naval Aviation*. New York: Messner, 1942.
Lincke, Jack R. *Jenny Was No Lady: The Story of the JN-4D*. New York: Norton, 1976.

Czech Legion

The odyssey of the Czech Legion is one of the remarkable operations in military history. For two years, 45,000 Czechs and Slovaks comprised the only effective military force in Russia, controlled that country's only artery between the Urals and the Pacific, and stayed in the forefront of wartime diplomacy.

In 1914, there were approximately 100,000 Czech citizens in tsarist Russia. One thousand of these joined the Russian Army as the Druzina or Czech regiment. Pan-Slavist sentiments contributed to the surrender of tens of thousands more Czechs early in the war and two months after Tsar Nicholas abdicated in March 1917, the Russian government, with the encouragement of the French, allowed those prisoners to form two Czech divisions based at Kiev.

The Czech division fought in the July 1917 offensive. They were especially effective in the Battle of Zborov. However, when the offensive failed, and the Russian government seemed ready to collapse, Tomáš Masaryk arranged to have the Czech Legion, as it had become known, join France on the Western Front. He received encouragement in December 1917 when France recognized the legitimacy of a Czech state and the legion as its army. Further support came in January 1918 when Woodrow Wilson made formation of a Czech state one of his Fourteen Points.

Meanwhile, the Czech Legion's situation had become desperate. In January 1918, the Ukraine declared its independence and the German Army was approaching Kiev from three directions. Masaryk's Czech government in Paris declared war on the Central Powers and the Czech Legion moved from Kiev north to Bakhmach, where, in March, they defeated the Germans who were trying to deny them access to the railway. The legion then moved east from Bakhmach toward Moscow, tearing up the rails behind them.

Moscow was the hub of the Russian rail system; lines ran north to Petrograd and east in two branches—a northern line through Perm and Ekaterinburg and a southern route through Samara and Chelyabinsk. The lines joined at Omsk and continued as a single track to China and far eastern Siberia. At China, the line again divided into a southern route through northern China and Harbin and a northern road through Kharbarovsk before coming together outside Vladivostok.

As the Czechs moved toward Moscow, the conflicting interests of the warring powers came into play. The French wanted the Czechs in Europe to fight Germany. The British wanted to move them north to guard the port and supplies at Murmansk and Archangel. The new Bolshevik government, besides having a treaty obligation with Germany not to allow foreign troops on Russian soil, looked with trepidation on the Czechs, who were the only functioning military organization in Russia. Leon Trotsky was torn between wanting the Czechs out of his country and wanting to co-opt them into the Red Army.

The Czechs gave up most of their arms in return for access to the Trans-Siberian Railway and were nearly defenseless, besides being scattered from Penza to Chelyabinsk. Then on May 14, 1918, an Austrian prisoner of war killed a Czech legionnaire, an incident that led to open conflict between the Bolsheviks and the Czechs. The Czechs took Chelyabinsk, organized themselves into an independent, self-governing force and attacked the Bolsheviks. In less than six weeks, the legion controlled the entire Trans-Siberian Railway from the Volga to Vladivostok.

On July 6, 1918, Wilson decided to join the French, British, and Japanese intervention in Russia. Although he claimed that the intervention was to save the enormously popular Czech soldiers, the President was actually alarmed at the possibility of Germany and Japan coming from opposite directions to divide the immense Russian land mass. Wilson also worried about the return to the European theater of hundreds of thousands of German and Austrian prisoners held in Siberia.

On July 23, an independent Siberian republic was declared, buttressed by the presence of a strong Czech Army. By August 3, a combined Czech, Cossack, White Russian, British, Japanese, and American force occupied Vladivostok. The Czech Legion was ordered to move west, to occupy the banks of the Volga, and to establish a link with Allied forces in Archangel and Murmansk.

Trotsky then took personal command of four Russian armies and defeated the Czechs at Kazan on Sept. 5, 1918. The legion, wanting to be home in Europe, was badly demoralized. When Czechoslovakia declared its independence and elected Masaryk president, he ordered the Czechs to stay in Siberia, hoping that their efforts would provide a bargaining chip for the new government in postwar peace negotiations.

The Armistice of Nov. 11, 1918, applied only to the Western Front and left the Czechs stranded and still fighting the Bolsheviks. The legion struggled on through the Siberian winter, but, by August 1919, the Red Army had pushed them back to Omsk. The White Russian government in Siberia collapsed in December, and the Americans withdrew the following month. January 1920 saw the majority of Czechs west of Lake Baikal.

Now the Czech Legion had to fight its way east, past the remains of the Russian counter-revolutionaries who wanted to keep them in the west to delay the advancing Red Army. Over the next six months, the Czech Legion defeated Ataman Semyenor's Cossacks and gathered in Vladivostok, where ships chartered by the Red Cross and American Czechs took them to San Francisco. From there, they returned to Europe and eventually formed the nucleus of the new Czechoslovak Army.

Jack McCallum

See also FOURTEEN POINTS; MASARYK, TOMÁŠ GARRIGUE

Bibliography

Unterberger, Betty Miller. *America's Siberian Expedition, 1918–1920.* New York: Greenwood Press, 1968.
———. *The United States, Revolutionary Russia, and the Rise of Czechoslovakia.* Chapel Hill: University of North Carolina Press, 1989.

Czernin, Ottokar (1872–1932)

Count Ottokar Czernin of Chudenitz was born at Dimokur, in Bohemia, of a wealthy family of the Czech aristocracy. After initial service in a cavalry regiment, he decided upon a career in diplomacy. He earned a law degree at the University of Prague and then served in the Austro-Hungarian diplomatic corps in various capitals, including Paris, from 1895.

In 1903, Czernin entered politics and was elected to the Bohemian provincial assembly. Between 1908 and 1913, he was a close adviser to Archduke Franz Ferdinand, who found the count's political philosophy particularly congenial. It was at the request of the archduke that Czernin was appointed to the Austrian upper house in 1912. In October of that year, he was appointed Austro-Hungarian minister to Bucharest. During the early months of World War I, he strove successfully to keep Rumania neutral, a policy in which he was supported by the aged King Carol, a Hohenzollern by birth. Czernin understood that Carol's strong pro-German sentiments were not shared by most Rumanians, and he urged the Austro-Hungarian government to promise territorial concessions to keep Rumania neutral. In that he was opposed by the Hungarian prime minister, István Tisza. Czernin remained in Bucharest until Rumania declared war on Austria in August 1916.

After the death of Emperor Franz Joseph, the new Austrian emperor, Charles I, on Dec. 23, 1916, appointed Czernin as his minister of foreign affairs. Charles had been deeply influenced in political matters by his uncle, Franz Ferdinand. The fact that Czernin had belonged to the inner circles of the slain heir presumptive undoubtedly contributed to his selection as foreign minister.

In his memoirs, Czernin stated that even before 1914 he had come to believe that time had run out for the empire. That did not stop him from accepting the post of foreign minister in 1916. He quickly discovered that Austria's increasing wartime dependence on Germany rendered a truly independent foreign policy impossible. He tried unsuccessfully to oppose Germany's decision to wage unrestricted submarine warfare on the ground that it would bring the United States into the conflict. Czernin's efforts in 1917 to persuade the German government of the need for a peace by compromise also proved unsuccessful. Moreover, those efforts were partially undermined by the erratic ambiguity of his own policies. At a

meeting with the German chancellor in Vienna in March 1917, Czernin asked Bethmann Hollweg to yield to France on the matter of Alsace-Lorraine in exchange for territorial concessions in the East. Simultaneously, Czernin sought Germany's agreement to the extension of Austria's sphere of influence in the Balkans and territorial gains at Rumania's expense. Though these negotiations led ultimately to the Kresznach Accord (May 17, 1917), Bethmann Hollweg did not know about Austria-Hungary's secret negotiations with France. The ambiguity of Czernin's policies was further reflected in his public opposition in the summer of 1917 to the cession of Galicia to Germany, a scheme that he had privately initiated.

Early in 1918, Czernin represented Austria at the peace negotiations at Brest Litovsk and Bucharest. Largely in response to dangerous food shortages, Czernin reluctantly agreed to cede to the newly created Ukraine republic the province of Chelm. The settlement with Ukraine, the "bread peace," of Feb. 9, 1918, did not solve the food supply problem, but, as Czernin feared, it did earn him the undying hatred of the Austrian Poles, who laid claim to the ceded province. Similarly, the Brest Litovsk settlement with Russia of March 3, 1918, brought Austria no lasting benefit.

It was the famous Sixtus Affair that led to Czernin's fall from office. Czernin had agreed to Emperor Charles's suggestion to use Prince Sixtus of Bourbon-Parma as an intermediary in secret negotiations with France. What Czernin did not know was that the emperor had given the prince a confidential letter on March 24, 1917, in which Charles assured President Poincaré that he would support France's "just claims in Alsace-Lorraine." A year later, in a public speech on April 2, 1918, Czernin cited French intransigence on the question of Alsace-Lorraine as the reason for the failure of peace negotiations with Austria. Clemenceau was quick to retaliate by publishing the emperor's secret letter. Czernin, feeling betrayed by Charles, resigned on April 15, 1918.

After the war, Czernin broke with what he had previously stood for and sponsored the democratic movement in the Austrian republic. Subsequently, at the beginning of the 1930s, he made one final political switch, repudiated parliamentary democracy, and joined the fascist Heimwehr movement. He died in Vienna on April 4, 1932.

William L. Mathes

See also BETHMANN HOLLWEG, THEOBALD VON; BREST LITOVSK, TREATY OF

Bibliography
Czernin, Ottokar. *In the World War*. New York: Harper, 1920.

Kann, Robert A. "Count Ottokar Czernin and Archduke Francis Ferdinand." *Journal of Central European Affairs* (July 1956).

C

D

Daly, Daniel (1873–1937)

Perhaps the most famous marine in the history of the Marine Corps, Dan Daly personified its ideals of courage, professionalism, leadership, and modesty. Born in Glen Cove, New York, Daly enlisted in the Marine Corps on Jan. 10, 1899, and his career exemplified the colonial infantry tasks of the marines in the early twentieth century. Between 1900 and 1915, he served in China, the Philippines, Mexico, and Haiti and had won two Medals of Honor: the first in Peking during the Boxer Rebellion in 1900 and the second in Haiti in 1915.

By June 1918, Daly was in France as first sergeant of the 73d Company, 6th Marines, 4th Marine Brigade. Custom has it that during the attack at Belleau Wood he came across a platoon pinned down by German machine gun fire and allegedly exhorted his marines to advance, yelling "Come on, you sons of bitches! Do you want to live forever?" Daly denied ever using such language. He actually participated in three actions for which he received the Distinguished Service Cross and later the Navy Cross and the French Medaille Militaire and the Croix de Guerre with Palm. On June 5, 1918, he extinguished a fire, caused by German bombardment, in an ammunition dump at Lucy-le-Bocage; on June 7, while enemy artillery bombarded his company, he visited all of the gun crews, which were dispersed over a wide area; then, on June 10, he alone attacked a German machine gun position and, armed only with hand grenades and his pitol, captured it. Later that day, he was wounded during the German attack on Bourseches and medically evacuated under protest. Returning to duty, he was twice wounded during the 4th Marine Brigade's attack on Blanc Mont ridge near Somme-Py in Champagne.

In 1920, at his request, the Marine Corps placed Daly on the inactive list, and he retired in 1929. After his service, he worked for a banking firm on Wall Street. Daly died on April 27, 1937.

Donald Bittner

Bibliography

Hough, Frank O. "Dan Daly." *Marine Corps Gazette* (November 1954).
Millett, Allan R. *Semper Fidelis: A History of the United States Marine Corps*. New York: Macmillan, 1980.
Skelly, Anne. "Dan Daly, Legendary Marine 'Devil Dog'." *Leatherneck* (November 1985).

Daniels, Josephus (1862–1948)

A Democratic national committeeman from North Carolina in 1912 and publisher of the *Democratic News and Observer,* Josephus Daniels supported Woodrow Wilson for president in 1912 and was rewarded for his assistance by being named Wilson's secretary of the navy.

Daniels was determined to keep the power to direct naval policy at his own desk. However, his administration of the U.S. Navy and his unwillingness to improve its preparedness after the Great War began in August 1914 led to difficulties, especially with his primary military adviser, the aide for operations, RAdm. Bradley A. Fiske.

Seeing naval officers as aristocrats and enlisted men as an extension of his own brood of "boys," Daniels improved the lot of the enlisted man while restricting the prerogatives of officers. Disliking the navy's aide system, he let it die as the aides completed their tours. To many officers, especially Fiske, Daniels used military discipline as a cloak for sumptuary despotism.

As Daniels saw it, preparing for war violated U.S. neutrality; consequently, he halved the shipbuilding programs recommended by the Navy General Board, thus making it impossible for it to fulfill its goal of forty-eight battleships by 1920. Nevertheless, some improvements came in the Naval Act of 1915. Among these were authorization for the creation of the Office of Chief of Naval Operations (CNO)—which Daniels did not want—the establishment of a naval reserve, and the granting of additional funds for naval aviation. Meanwhile, by obtaining authority to build the navy's own armor plate plant, Daniels forced down prices charged by civilian manufacturers. Changes he made in navy-yard management reduced overhead costs for new construction by 30 percent, and he blocked legislation permitting private producers to obtain oil from the navy's petroleum reserves. He also approved the creation of a National Advisory Committee for Aeronautics, the establishment of an Office of Aeronautics in the Office of the Aide for Operations and a flight school at Pensacola, Florida, and augmented funding for naval air operations.

When Congress passed the law that created the Office of CNO, Admiral Fiske wanted its chief to control the navy. However, Daniels was able to amend the law so that the secretary retained management control and the bureaus remained uncoordinated. To Fiske's repeated suggestions that a naval general staff would be even better, Daniels replied that such a staff was not consonant with the principles of a democracy. Daniels also disapproved Fiske's suggestion that an administrative plan be adopted by which the bureaus could report their progress in preparing for war and that a council of national defense be created. Having run up against a stone wall, in December 1914, Fiske decided to go over the secretary's head and appeal to Congress and the public. Daniels ignored him thereafter, and in April 1915, he accepted Fiske's resignation. Because no rear admiral would serve as CNO, Daniels chose Capt. William S. Benson, who was no strategist and dabbled with details rather than delegate authority. However, he was "obedient."

With Europe at war, Daniels proposed converting cruisers to carry passengers, mail, and freight to South America and Europe, acquiring ships of German and Austrian registry interned in American ports, and enlarging the merchant marine. Congress disapproved the first, the Allies objected to the second, and Congress waited until September 1916 to approve the third.

To keep his pledge of neutrality, President Wilson kept defense spending for 1915 close to that of 1914, whereupon Daniels cut to twenty the forty-eight new ships recommended by the General Board. However, a preparedness step came with the establishment of the Naval Consulting Board, which particularly sought ways to fight U-boats. Daniels also had the board make an inventory of the nation's industrial capacity. Moreover, although he had opposed Fiske's call for a council of national defense, such a council was created on Aug. 29, 1916. As one of the six cabinet members Wilson appointed to it, Daniels tried to "coordinate industry and resources for the national security and welfare."

To put force behind his attempt to mediate the European conflict, on July 21, 1915, Wilson directed his service secretaries to draft an "adequate defense program." Accordingly, the General Board on July 30 recommended spending $6 billion for a six-year program including ten battleships and six battle cruisers that would give the U.S. Navy parity with the Royal Navy by 1921. In addition, it recommended $6 million for naval aviation. Daniels cut the timetable to five years.

On May 18, 1916, the House Committee on Naval Affairs rejected the five-year program in favor of the normal one-year plan. However, Republicans preferred speedier progress. In the end, agreement was reached upon a three-year program that would produce 153 ships, of which 148 would be combatants, with work on 3 battleships, 4 battle cruisers, and 47 other ships to begin immediately. The bill Wilson signed on Aug. 29, 1916, in addition, granted the CNO fifteen assistants to draft war plans and increased the number of both regular and reserve personnel. On that same day, Daniels advertised bids for those ships to be built immediately.

Because of a reconstitution of the Democratic National Committee and his objection to promoting Cary Travers Grayson, Wilson's personal physician, to the rank of admiral, a serious attempt was made in 1916 to remove

Daniels from office. Wilson would not hear of it, for Daniels had supported both his neutrality policy and the strengthening of the navy.

Then Germany announced that neutral as well as belligerent ships found within an extensive zone would be sunk without warning beginning Feb. 1, 1917. On February 3, Wilson broke diplomatic relations with Germany and began to prepare for a war he still hoped to avoid. On the fourth, Daniels set his department to work on plans for full mobilization. That was followed on the nineteenth with a directive from Wilson that the navy's bureau chiefs report to him on the status of their preparedness and his service secretaries "get and keep" the ablest men they could for their departments. The Naval Appropriation Bill for fiscal year 1918, though again loaded with capital ships, also called for fifty-two destroyers and a fleet of submarine chasers and other small craft.

Spurred in part by the Zimmermann Telegram and the overthrow of tsarism in Russia, Wilson, on February 26, asked Congress not for war but for an armed neutrality that allowed the arming of merchantmen. However, upon learning on March 18 that three American ships had been torpedoed by German U-boats, he decided upon war, which was declared on April 2.

On May 24, Wilson asked Daniels to establish confidential liaison with the British. The nod went to RAdm. William S. Sims, president of the Naval War College. Sims cooperated cordially with the British and demanded from Washington support for decisions he made as "the man on the spot" in command of American naval forces in Europe. After learning in London on April 10, 1917, that no Allied methods currently used were effective against U-boats, he prompted the British to implement the convoy system. Meanwhile, at Wilson's urging, Daniels sent across the Atlantic all the destroyers that could be spared from defending home waters. By November 1917, convoys had proved the answer to the submarine threat. Wilson and Daniels also approved the laying of the North Sea mine barrage and the naming of Sims as the American member of the Allied Naval Council created in December 1917.

Due in part to stupendous efforts by Daniels, the 113 American naval vessels in European waters on Jan. 1, 1918, grew to 338 by October of that year. However, most of the ships authorized in 1917 and 1918 were not completed until after the war, and poor administration of the aviation effort resulted in having American pilots use French and occasionally British planes.

Although the war was winding down by October 1918, Daniels and Congress agreed that during the postwar years a powerful navy would be needed to support America's interests. Building programs, however, would be cut if Britain agreed to grant the navy parity and cooperated with the United States in policing the world in the name of a "League of Nations." Then Congress, determined upon retrenchment, set limits on what Daniels could do by restricting naval personnel to 120,000 men effective Jan. 4, 1921.

During hearings held by a Senate subcommittee on whether Daniels had correctly handled the awarding of wartime decorations, Sims revealed that on Jan. 7, 1920, he had written a letter to Daniels on "Certain Naval Lessons of the Great War." In new hearings beginning March 9, Sims charged that the navy "failed for at least six months to throw [its] full weight against the enemy." During the critical months of the German submarine campaign, from April to October 1917, he said, the department had violated the strategic principle of concentration of maximum force in the critical area of the conflict—the western approaches to the British Isles. The result was that for the first six months of the war the Navy Department had "cost the Allied cause 2.5 million tons of shipping, 500,000 lives, and $15 billion." Daniels retorted that what counted was "results" and charged that the admiral's objective was to advocate military rather than civilian control of the navy. In 1921, with Daniels out of office, a majority report signed by three Republicans of the Senate committee confirmed most of Sims's contentions, while two minority reports written by Democrats rejected them. If Sims established that there was room for improvement in the department, he failed to prove that its shortcomings stemmed from its administration by Daniels. To his supporters, Daniels had for eight years performed a "great job greatly done."

His former civilian assistant—now President of the United States—Franklin D. Roosevelt called him back to government service as ambassador to Mexico (1933–1941). He died in 1948.

Paolo Coletta

D

See also BENSON, WILLIAM SHEPHERD; FISKE, BRADLEY ALLEN; NATIONAL ADVISORY COMMITTEE FOR AERONAUTICS; NAVAL CONSULTING BOARD; ZIMMERMANN TELEGRAM

Bibliography
Coletta, Paolo. *Admiral Bradley A. Fiske and the American Navy.* Lawrence: University of Kansas Press, 1979.
Cronon, E. David, ed. *The Cabinet Diaries of Josephus Daniels, 1913–1921.* Lincoln: University of Nebraska Press, 1963.
Daniels, Josephus. *The Wilson Era.* 2 vols. Chapel Hill: University of North Carolina Press, 1946.
Morison, Elting E. *Admiral Sims and the Modern American Navy.* Boston: Houghton Mifflin, 1942.
U.S. Senate. Naval Affairs Committee. *Naval Investigation.* 2 vols. Washington, DC: Government Printing Office, 1921.

Daylight Saving Time

The concept of daylight saving time was popularized during the early twentieth century by an Englishman, William Willett. After the commencement of the First World War, belligerents on both sides adopted what the English referred to as "fast time" to conserve fuel. In the United States, the National Daylight Saving Association, with the support of Samuel Gompers of the American Federation of Labor, successfully lobbied Congress to move the clocks forward one hour on March 31, 1918. The daylight saving law also gave statute authority to the five time zones established by the railroads in 1883. Opposition to daylight saving time from rural communities and rank-and-file industrial workers led to its repeal over President Woodrow Wilson's veto in August 1919. It was reinstituted as "war time" in 1942 and is currently used by all states except Arizona and Indiana.

Willard C. Klunder

Bibliography
O'Malley, Michael. *Keeping Watch: A History of American Time.* New York: Viking Penguin, 1990.

Debs, Eugene Victor (1855–1926)

Eugene Victor Debs, a product of the social ferment of the Gilded Age and Progressive Era, underwent an apostolic transformation to socialism after a long conservative career in the Brotherhood of Locomotive Engineers. Titular head of the Socialist Party and its perennial presidential candidate, he had also attended the founding of the Industrial Workers of the World in 1905. At a time when the government, with unlimited resources, orchestrated a comprehensive propaganda campaign to energize the American people for war, the only major political force to resist that indoctrination was Debs's domestic Socialists. (Their leftist counterparts in Europe succumbed to nationalistic appeals and enlisted to fight neighboring working-class soldiers.)

The Socialist Party, although internally fractured and externally hounded, held firm. Debs and surrogate speakers fanned out across the nation to oppose American intervention in the already raging European conflagration. Debs scathingly attacked the conflict in various speeches; after U.S. intervention, he accelerated the vitriol. He arrived for a fateful speaking engagement in Canton, Ohio, on June 15, 1918. Before a large outdoor audience he pounded at the hypocrisy of a war to buttress democracy abroad while government agents were imprisoning protestors at home.

Federal authorities in Ohio decided to charge Debs under the Espionage Act. Ironically, officials at the Justice Department were reluctant to prosecute, fearing that they would make a martyr out of Debs. A physically and emotionally exhausted Debs, now in his sixties, seemingly welcomed the charge and perhaps a chance at a prison respite after a stressful career.

Debs was indicted and tried in September 1918. He refused to contest the charges but gave two impassioned speeches to the jury, not unlike his original talk in Canton but laced with the symbolism of the American Revolution and Bill of Rights. Nonetheless, Debs was found guilty and sentenced to ten years in prison. The war would be over in two months.

Arriving at the federal Atlanta penitentiary in April 1919, he organized his last campaign for the presidency from his cell. Campaign buttons pictured the candidate in jail garb and admonished supporters to vote "FOR PRISONER 9653." He received 1 million antiwar protest votes. During his incarceration, the government intensified its hunt for domestic radicals, ushering in a decade of labor repression and a continuation of First Amendment restraints that had originated during the war.

In an unusual gesture, President Warren G. Harding pardoned the aging but unrepentant leftist on Christmas Day 1921. Debs died in 1926.

Scott Molloy

See also ESPIONAGE ACT

Bibliography
Ginger, Ray. *The Bending Cross: A Biography of Eugene Victor Debs*. New Brunswick, NJ: Rutgers University Press, 1949.
Salvatore, Nick. *Eugene V. Debs: Citizen and Socialist*. Urbana: University of Illinois Press, 1982.

Decorations

When the United States declared war on the Central Powers in April 1917, the only medals authorized by the American government to reward valor were the Medal of Honor, the Certificate of Merit, and the Distinguished Service Medal (navy). The Medal of Honor was instituted by Congress in December 1861 for award to the navy, and in July 1862 it was extended to include the army as well. The medal was awarded by the President, in the name of Congress, to enlisted men for bravery in action involving actual conflict with the enemy, and then only to those who distinguished themselves conspicuously above and beyond the call of duty. The award of the Medal of Honor was only made after a full inquiry with supporting recommendations from several sources was completed. In 1863, the army broadened the scope of the award to include officers. The navy did not make the award available to officers until 1915.

The design of the medal varied for the two services. The army award was a five-pointed bronze star set upon a green enameled laurel wreath. The center of the star has the head of the Roman goddess Minerva in a circle bearing the words "United States of America." It hangs from a bar bearing the word "Valor," which is surmounted by an eagle with spread wings clutching arrows and oak leaves in its talons. It is suspended on a light blue ribbon with thirteen white stars. It was worn pinned to the breast with other awards but later changed to hang around the neck. The navy award, redesigned in 1919, was a gold cross superimposed on a laurel wreath. An anchor was on each arm of the cross and in the center the Great Seal of the United States was placed in an octagon surrounded by the words "United States Navy, 1917–1918." The cross hung from the ribbon by a ring, and at the top of the ribbon was a brooch bar with the word "Valor" on it.

The Certificate of Merit was created in 1847 by Congress for award to private soldiers who distinguished themselves. It was subsequently extended to noncommissioned officers, and in 1905, a medal was created to accompany the award of the certificate. It was not limited in its scope to acts of valor in the face of an enemy. It was a bronze medal with a Roman war eagle surrounded by the words "*Virtutis et Audaciae Monumentum et Praemium*" (Virtue and Courage [are their own] Monument and Reward). Its reverse had the words "For Merit" within an oak wreath inside of a larger circle with the words "United States Army" on the upper half and thirteen stars on the lower half. The ribbon had blue edges with white stripes inside the blue and in the center two broad stripes of red divided by a narrow stripe of white. In 1918 the award of this medal was discontinued, and the Distinguished Service Medal was issued in its place.

As the role of the American Expeditionary Force (AEF) expanded from training behind the lines to actual combat, the instances of gallant action on the part of its soldiers increased. Commanders began to forward names of men who distinguished themselves so that these men might receive some form of recognition. The very high standards which had come into use governing the award of the Medal of Honor would not allow each man whose name was sent forward to be awarded the medal. This paucity of suitable awards for acts of valor less than that required for the nation's highest award led to the creation of the Distinguished Service Cross and of the Distinguished Service Medal. Both medals were instituted in January 1918, and AEF General Order 26, dated Feb. 11, 1918, published the requirements of the two new awards. The Distinguished Service Cross was to be awarded to any person who, while serving in any capacity with the army, distinguished himself by extraordinary heroism in operations against the enemy that did not justify the award of the Medal of Honor. The requirements for the Distinguished Service Medal were similar. However, one need only have distinguished oneself by exceptionally meritorious service and not necessarily in actual combat.

The Distinguished Service Cross consisted of an American spread eagle superimposed on a cross. Beneath the eagle was a scroll with the words "For Valor" all done in bronze. The ribbon was blue with narrow red and white stripes at either side. The Distinguished Service Medal was a bronze coat of arms of the United States surrounded by a circle of blue enamel with the words "For Distinguished Service" and the date "MCMXVIII." The ribbon was white with a wide red stripe and a narrow blue stripe on either side.

The Navy Distinguished Service Medal was created to award those members of the naval service who had distinguished themselves by exceptionally meritorious service to the government in a position of great responsibility. Initially proposed in August 1913 to be an equivalent of the Certificate of Merit, it was an award for those who did not meet the criteria for the award of the Medal of Honor. The medal was of gilded bronze bearing an American eagle surrounded by a blue enameled circle bearing the words "United States of America" and at the bottom "Navy," all within a gold border. The reverse had a trident with a blue circle with the words "For Distinguished Service." It was suspended by a white enamelled star with a gold anchor superimposed. The ribbon was blue with a central gold stripe.

Established in 1919, the Navy Cross was awarded to any member of the naval service who, since April 6, 1917, had distinguished himself by heroism or distinguished service not of a degree to justify the award of the Medal of Honor or the Distinguished Service Medal (navy). It was a dark bronze cross with laurel leaves between the arms of the cross. In the center was a figure of a navy ship. The reverse showed crossed anchors with the letters "U.S.N." The ribbon was dark blue with a central white stripe.

Soldiers and marines serving with the AEF who performed gallantly but did not meet the criteria for any of the established awards were cited for gallantry in action in the orders from headquarters of any force commanded by a general officer. This could be the division, corps, army, or AEF headquarters. This Citation for Gallantry in Action was a paper certificate listing the names of the soldier, the date and location of the action, and sometimes a brief description of the act. Award of this citation entitled the individual to wear a silver star three-sixteenths of an inch in diameter on the ribbon

of a campaign medal, in this case the World War I Victory Medal. When the Silver Star Medal was created in 1932, those holders of Citations for Gallantry in Action were eligible for the new award.

For those members of the AEF who were wounded, the army created a wound chevron to be worn on the lower half of the right sleeve of the uniform coat. AEF General Order 110, dated July 7, 1918, specified a v-shaped bar of gold lace, with arms two inches long and one-fourth inch wide. Subsequent wounds each entitled the soldier to additional chevrons. Being gassed would count as a wound if it required treatment by a medical officer. The award of the Purple Heart was not made to wounded soldiers until 1932, when Douglas MacArthur reinstituted the award, which had fallen into disuse following the Revolutionary War. Those men who had received wound chevrons in the First World War were then eligible to receive the award.

Following the cessation of hostilities, the Allied countries decided upon the creation of a Victory Medal to be awarded to all their troops. The basic design consisted of a figure of Victory, and the American version depicts a winged Victory holding a shield and sword. The reverse has the shield of the United States with the letters "U.S." and is surrounded by the names of all the Allied countries. The ribbon is rainbow colored. There were fourteen separate battle clasps for combat operations, and five clasps for service in foreign countries that were not awarded to those men who had earned battle clasps. These clasps were worn on the ribbon of the full-sized medal. When the ribbon was worn alone, small bronze stars were worn to signify an award of the battle clasps. No stars were worn for the country clasps. The navy had an additional nineteen clasps that denoted types of service in addition to the battle clasps and country clasps. The navy had the further distinctions that any man who had received a letter of commendation signed by the secretary of the navy was entitled to wear a small silver star on the ribbon, and those men who had served with the AEF but were not entitled to a battle clasp were authorized to wear a small Maltese cross on the ribbon. This medal was awarded to all members of the armed forces whether or not they served overseas.

Many states and cities created victory medals and commemorative medals to award their citizens following the war. These medals, however, were never recognized as United States decorations. The average serviceman, after enduring the hardships of the war, was most often rewarded with the World War I Victory Medal. Those who had been cited for valor might have received another medal, but for the vast majority the experience of the Great War was embodied by the rainbow colored ribbon and winged victory. In November 1941, Congress authorized a medal for the Army of Occupation (Germany) for those men who had served in Germany or Austria-Hungary following the war. During and after the war, a few American soldiers were awarded decorations by Allied countries.

Michael J. Knapp

Bibliography

Above and Beyond: A History of the Medal of Honor from the Civil War to Vietnam. Boston: Boston Publishing Company, 1985.

Kerrigan, Evans E. *American Medals and Decorations.* Noroton Heights, CT: Medallic Publishers, 1990.

Purves, Alec A. *The Medals, Decorations and Orders of the Great War 1914–1918.* London: Seaby, 1981.

Demobilization

The Armistice on Nov. 11, 1918, came much more quickly than any U.S. Army official had predicted just a few months earlier. As recently as July, Gen. John J. Pershing, commander of the American Expeditionary Force (AEF), advised the General Staff that he expected the war to last at least another year, during which time he would require approximately 100 divisions to defeat the Germans. Therefore, the German capitulation in the fall of 1918 took most army officials by surprise. The sudden Armistice obviously benefitted the nation by reducing potential loss of life among servicemen and by limiting the financial drain on the country. Instantaneously, however, numerous unexpected problems arose for those army and government officials responsible for developing manpower policies in the wartime army.

With their attention focused on creating an army large enough to endure another year of bloody stalemate along the Western Front, these policymakers had given little thought to disassembling their vast wartime organization. The army's success in mobilizing close to 4 million men into sixty-four divisions and transporting over 2 million of them to France within a span of eighteen months underscored how well the officials had fulfilled their primary task. Yet their failure to plan for the eventual demobilization would prove costly for both the army and the nation.

Policymakers realized immediately that a bungled demobilization could create havoc for the economy, society, and the government. The administration responded to the news that hostilities had ceased by immediately canceling numerous munitions and ship contracts, eliminating the jobs of tens of thousands of workers. The postwar employment scenario only worsened when one realized that 4 million unemployed soldiers were also about to return home. Fears that this unsettled economic environment would become a breeding ground for political radicalism preoccupied officials. These were the opening months of the nation's first Red Scare, a time when practically every dissenting voice was linked to an anarchist plot to overthrow the American government. Officials feared that exposure to the political upheaval then sweeping through Germany, France, and England might make unemployed Americans receptive to radical programs for redistributing wealth and power in American society. Finally, officials' greatest fear originated from the precedent that Civil War veterans had set with their incessant pension demands from the federal government throughout the late nineteenth century. The government wanted to sever its relations with World War I soldiers immediately and dissuade them from believing that any further monetary or medical benefits were due them.

Besides these broad societal considerations, army and government officials were concerned about the purely logistical problem of mustering men out of the service in the most orderly and fair way possible. Logistics required that the 1.5 million men in domestic training camps be released before officials could even begin to tackle the problem of how to commandeer enough Allied shipping to bring the other 2 million men home from France in a timely fashion. As training camps were transformed into demobilization centers, commanders needed time to train a staff to handle the cumbersome paperwork associated with releasing men from the service. Finally, the army had to decide the order of demobilization. Yet before going any further in designing a demobilization program, the army had to decide which logistical, eco-

D

nomic, political or societal factor would become its basic governing principle.

It was questionable how appropriate it was for the army to formulate this national policy because it had such far-reaching economic, political, and social significance. But at this time, President Woodrow Wilson was obsessed with the campaign to incorporate his Fourteen Points into the Versailles Peace Treaty. Due to this preoccupation, Wilson essentially abdicated any responsibility for devising a coherent demobilization program. Two governmental agencies that supervised the wartime workforce, the Council of National Defense (CND) and the Department of Labor, were similarly ineffective in offering solutions to the complicated questions facing the army. When civilian volunteers in the CND resigned from their wartime posts within weeks of the cease-fire and the Labor Department lost the federal funding that supported its initial soldier reemployment bureaus, these agencies were rendered mute. It fell to the War Department, therefore, not only to create a viable demobilization policy for the nation, but also to do its best to find jobs for returning soldiers.

The army considered four basic demobilization programs. One was to release soldiers who had served the longest first, but officials knew that processing this kind of detailed information on every soldier was beyond their organization's capacities. The next was to release soldiers according to their occupation as jobs opened up for them at home. Though this plan was as bureaucratically cumbersome as the first, the proposal was appealing because it took into account the economic ramifications of demobilization. Yet though the British organized their initial demobilization process around this principle, the Americans rejected it as too unwieldy; in fact, the British government abandoned this plan a few months later. The War Department also rejected a third recommendation to let local draft boards call their men home when the community was ready to receive them because it ignored the fact that only the army could determine when a soldier's services were no longer needed. Officials finally embraced the plan that met the army's needs the best, which was simply to release units when the military rationale for their existence expired.

This plan called for the immediate release of most stateside troops by February 1919, at which time soldiers would return from overseas in the following order: casuals, surplus and special service troops (including divisions which had been skeletonized to create replacements for front-line combat units), troops in England, U.S. Air Service personnel, troops in Italy, combat divisions, then finally Service of Supply troops. Army officials hoped these few months would give them enough time to build the large debarkation centers needed near French ports to process troops before they returned home. Completing the physical exams, final pay sheets, and personnel files of stateside soldiers went smoothly for the army. The tendency of some released soldiers to head immediately for nearby metropolitan areas with their pockets full of money alerted officials that they needed to take additional steps to insure that masses of veterans did not descend on the nation's cities. In the winter, the army began to encourage soldiers to purchase discounted train tickets before they left the demobilization camp so they would return to their original communities within a few days of being mustered out of service.

This minor snag in the domestic demobilization operation paled in comparison to the vast problems that soon materialized when troops began moving into overseas debarkation camps. The AEF channeled overseas troops through ports in Brest, Saint Nazaire, and Bordeaux. Soldiers waited for their final shipping date in satellite camps that served each port and in the meantime completed the administrative formalities that preceded the trip home. Officials boasted publicly about the efficient debarkation procedure established at the "Bordeaux Mill" where tired, dirty, and louse-infested soldiers were transformed into clean, disinfected, and rested men within twenty-four hours. These personal benefits aside, the Bordeaux system also set an admirable standard by moving the soldier through his physical exam, to a records inspection officer, and to a payroll officer in one day. Acquiring complete final records was of utmost importance to the government because they would become the basis upon which the government defended itself from any future claims by former soldiers. The army tried to publicize the Bordeaux image of productive efficiency as representative of the demobilization experience, but instead the horrendous ordeals that soldiers who debarked through Brest encountered dominated public perceptions of the demobilization process in the winter of 1919.

During the fall and winter, the terrible Spanish Influenza epidemic had swept through the world, exacting a devastating toll both in the United States and in Europe. Oddly, however, the flu virus remained isolated in the rear areas of France, where it ravaged American noncombatant units. The majority of American combatants were spared as long as they remained in the front lines, but when these units began to trek back to the hastily built debarkation camp in Brest, they lost their immunity. Close to 1 million men, over half of the AEF, debarked through Brest during the brutally foul winter weather. Camp administrators were woefully unprepared to handle hoards of impatient men, the pervasive mud and cold, or the flu that resulted from unsanitary and crowded conditions. Americans became furious when soldiers who had survived a year in the front lines died while waiting for a ship home, and these returning troops soon informed the public and Congress of conditions. These reports led to a change in command of the camp, and under BGen. Smedley D. Butler, USMC, conditions were vastly improved in a matter of weeks.

Congress became the forum in which daily public attacks were launched against the army's perceived mismanagement of the demobilization process. Besides the horrible conditions in Brest, soldiers and their families queried their congressmen about the long delays in bringing men home, the supposed favoritism in the process which determined the order of returning units, and the army's failure to pay troops in full until they left the service. As Congress launched one investigation after another into these charges, both the secretary of war and the chief of staff tried to defend the army's actions and to explain the rationale behind the army's program in detailed letters that they sent to every member of Congress. Gen. Peyton C. March, the chief of staff, refused, however, to answer letters from individual congressmen or to brief Congress routinely on the state of the army's demobilization. By failing to enlist Congress as a partner in the demobilization process, March seriously miscalculated. Creating a positive image of the army in the public mind was crucial if the army wanted to parlay its tremendous victory along the Western Front into increased funding for the peacetime military establishment. By ignoring the importance of good public relations, army officials received little public credit for how quickly they did in fact return soldiers to their homes. Instead, Army officials would begin hearings on the federal budget the following year with a tarnished reputation.

The future was equally uncertain for the returning soldier. When civilian governmental agencies abdicated any responsibility for finding returning soldiers jobs, the War Department established the Office of Assistant to the Secretary of War to offer some assistance. Col. Arthur Woods, the agency's director, sent agents from the Agriculture Department to encourage rural soldiers back to their farms and established employment boards for city-bound troops. The agency claimed that out of 1,332,494 soldiers who registered with these employment boards over 70 percent were placed in jobs in over 500 cities. Besides actually finding soldiers employment, the agency organized a vast propaganda campaign which encouraged servicemen to return to their homes immediately and to take the first job which became available. The agency used the slogan "Local Jobs for Local Men" to encourage employers to rehire men who had left their jobs to serve and to urge communities to hire veterans for public works projects. "No service man will be considered completely demobilized until a job has been found for him," Woods claimed, but then the government considered its responsibility to the returning soldier fulfilled.

When conscripting the wartime army, the government feared that draft riots might break out as they had during the Civil War. During World War I, however, the public overwhelmingly supported the government's decision to conscript a national army, and the mobilization of this army proceeded smoothly. Conversely, while regional units had drifted back quietly to their communities after the Civil War, demobilization was a much more cumbersome and contentious process once hostilities ceased along the Western Front. In the end, the army's failure to justify its response to the various economic, political, and logistical problems of demobilization damaged its postwar public image. This was a lesson army policymakers would remember well during the Second World War.

Jennifer Keene

Bibliography

Crowell, Benedict, and Robert F. Wilson. *Demobilization: An Industrial and Military Demobilization after the Armistice, 1918–1920.* New Haven: Yale University Press, 1921.

Kennedy, David M. *Over Here: The First World War and American Society.* New York: Oxford University Press, 1980.

Sherry, Michael. *Preparing for the Next War: American Plans for Postwar Defense, 1941–45*. New Haven: Yale University Press, 1977.

Sparrow, John C. *History of Personnel Demobilization in the United States Army*. Washington, DC: Department of the Army, 1952.

Wecter, Dixon. *When Johnny Comes Marching Home*. New York: Greenwood Press, 1970.

Dernburg, Bernhard (1865–1937)

Bernhard Dernburg had a successful career in banking and became a director of the Darmstadter Bank in 1901. From 1906 to 1910, he managed Germany's colonial administration. Because Dernburg had studied in the United States and traveled there frequently, he was known and respected, especially in the business community. After the outbreak of the war, he went to the United States ostensibly to seek donations for the German Red Cross. However, his real mission was to secure a loan to cover the costs of goods being obtained in the United States by Heinrich Albert, the agent of the German Central Purchasing Agency. Arriving in New York on Aug. 23, 1914, Dernburg soon found that the general anti-German mood and the close economic ties between Britain and the United States was frustrating the quest for credits.

In October, Dernburg opened the German Information Service in New York. The office was adjacent to that of the leading German-American propagandist, George Sylvester Viereck. Working with Dernburg were a dozen consular officials, attachés, and businessmen who were inexperienced both with public relations and the United States. Dernburg, surprised by the degree of anti-German feeling in the United States, did his best to defend his country's position. In dozens of speeches, articles, and pamphlets prepared during his nine months in America, he refuted charges of German militarism, by pointing to British naval chauvinism, insisted symbols of bellicosity such as Bernhardi and Treitschke actually had little influence, and suggested the song "Deutschland über Alles" was no more menacing to peace than "Rule Britannia." His country had to maintain a large military establishment because it lay exposed in the center of Europe and for centuries had been a battleground for foreign armies. Peace-loving Germany had spent more money on manufacturing, commerce, and social security measures for its people than it did on its military.

At first Dernburg was quite well received in the United States, and the *New York Times* in September 1914 labeled him, next to Ambassador Johann von Bernstorff, as the most important German in America. His attempts to counter Allied arguments and to justify German behavior only seemed to confirm the anti-German prejudices held by most of the population, while tensions developed between him and Bernstorff, who feared he was being upstaged by the banker/propagandist. Dernburg's fixation on economic questions and his inability to comprehend the nature and depth of the American ties with Britain seriously limited his impact. Then the wave of public indignation following the *Lusitania* sinking sealed the fate of his mission, and on June 12, 1915, he returned home. From this point on, the effectiveness of German propaganda steadily declined.

Richard V. Pierard

See also PROPAGANDA

Bibliography

Alphaud, Gabriel. *L'Action allemande aux Etats-Unis de la mission Dernburg á l'incident Dumba (2 aout 1914–25 septembre 1915)*. Paris: Payot, 1915.

Dernburg, Bernhard. *Search-lights on the War*. New York: Fatherland Corp., 1915.

Deutschland, The

The German merchant U-boat program was an attempt by the German government to break the British blockade. Disguising the project as a private capital venture, the German Navy set up a complex organization of dummy firms and interlocking corporate directorships to operate the program. The principal front company was the newly created German Ocean Navigation Company, but the parent firm was the old North German Lloyd Shipping Line.

Despite the civilian appearance, the entire venture was a naval operation. The crews were selected from experienced U-boat crews and given phony discharges, then redesignated merchant seamen. The officers were all naval reservists on active duty with the fleet. In every case, the officers were former merchant officers who had served with North German

Lloyd before the war. The *Deutschland*, built at the Krupp Works in Kiel, was commissioned in April 1916 and underwent sea trials that month. It departed Kiel on its maiden voyage on June 14, 1916, sailing "north about" around Scotland and into the North Atlantic. After a frightening start that included near sinking and a crash dive to avoid a British destroyer, the *Deutschland* settled down to a dull routine trip.

The *Deutschland* arrived in Baltimore, Maryland, on July 9, 1916, to a tumultuous welcome. But its presence in a United States port quickly caused an international controversy. Under international law, a merchant vessel could remain in a neutral port to discharge and take on cargo. But a warship could only remain twenty-four hours or be interned for the war's duration. The question was—was the *Deutschland* a real merchant ship or a disguised U-boat?

The British and French argued that a U-boat by any other name was still a U-boat and subject to internment. Submerged it was immune from the international rules of stop and search, and it could be quickly converted to a warship. The United States Navy sent several inspectors aboard the *Deutschland* to determine if it was, in fact, armed or would it be possible to convert the ship to a war boat quickly. Their conclusion was an unqualified "no" on both points.

But the British suggested that the *Deutschland*, with its huge cargo and fuel capacity, could easily become a seagoing gas station and supply vessel for U-boats in the Atlantic. The American government adopted the view that this was possible, but it would not act on the mere possibility. The official United States opinion was that the *Deutschland* was a cargo vessel.

On Aug. 2, 1916, loaded with 800 tons of cargo, which included nickel, rubber, and 550 gallons of fuel oil, the ship started its homeward voyage. There is evidence to support the rumor that it also carried $4 million in gold smuggled aboard from the interned steamer *Kronprinzessin Cecilie*. From the German viewpoint, the *Deutschland*'s first visit to the United States was an unqualified success. The accomplishment had polished Germany's badly tarnished image, the United States government had recognized the boat as a merchant vessel, and American businessmen were anxious to trade with Germany.

The *Deutschland*'s second, and last, trip to the United States was marred by racial strife, violence, and a tragic sinking. The *Deutschland* arrived in New London, Connecticut, on Nov. 1, 1916. The Germans' heavy-handed insistence on using only black stevedores to handle the cargo sparked an angry response from the white community. Amidst the uproar, a German crewman got into a bar fight and stabbed the American bartender.

After a series of bureaucratic delays, the ship left its dock for home on Nov. 17, 1916. But near Fisher's Island in Long Island Sound, it rammed and sunk the tug *T.A. Scott, Jr.*, killing the five-man American crew. The public was outraged.

The *Deutschland* returned to dock and remained there for several days while the legal questions were resolved. Finally, it was exonerated by the Bureau of Navigation and allowed to return to Germany.

By the time it reached Bremen on December 10, the merchant U-boat program was effectively finished. Following a six-year period of indecision, the ship went into drydock for conversion. It emerged from the yard as *U–155*, armed with two huge deck guns and six torpedo tubes. As a war boat, it was a great disappointment. *U–155* was too slow on the surface to overtake most Atlantic freighters and was so lightly built that the recoil from the guns tore up the decks. Its externally mounted torpedo tubes wobbled, and its torpedoes were faulty. It suffered repeated engine breakdowns, steering failures, and equipment malfunctions.

The *U–155* made undistinguished war patrols to the Azores and along the U.S. Atlantic coast. At the end of the war, it was turned over to the British, who quickly sold it to a showman as a maritime novelty. However, its showboat career was short and unprofitable. In 1920, it was sold for scrap.

Dwight R. Messimer

Bibliography

Messimer, Dwight R. *The Merchant U-Boat: The Adventures of the Deutschland, 1916–1918*. Annapolis, MD: Naval Institute Press, 1988.

Diaz, Armando (1861–1928)

Armando Diaz was born in Naples to Ludovico Diaz and Baroness Irene Cecconi. At the age of seventeen, Diaz was admitted to the Military

Academy of Artillery and Engineering in Turin. In 1883, he was promoted to the rank of lieutenant of artillery and served in a number of posts. As colonel of the 93d Infantry Regiment, Diaz, in May 1912, devised the plan for the campaign that resulted in the Battle of Zanzur in the Italo-Turkish War. Severely wounded, he returned to Rome. In 1914, Diaz was promoted to major general and collaborated with Gen. Luigi Cadorna in reorganizing the Italian Army. At the outbreak of World War I, Diaz was appointed director of operations at staff headquarters in Rome. In June 1916, he was made a lieutenant general and placed in charge of the 49th Division operating in the area of Carso, where he distinguished himself in a number of actions. In the eleventh battle of the Isonzo, Diaz led the offensive that made the deepest penetration of the war by Italian troops into enemy territory. However, the advance was not exploited, and on Nov. 8, 1917, following the Italian defeat at Caporetto, King Victor Emanuel appointed Diaz commander-in-chief of the army, replacing Cadorna.

Diaz took over an army that had lost more than 700,000 men and a staggering quantity of materiel. The Italian Army appeared powerless and on the verge of total collapse. But Diaz planned to resist the enemy at any cost. The first German-Austrian offensive against Diaz was launched on Nov. 10, 1917, and stretched from the Asiago Altipiano to the Grappa. The Italians prevented the enemy from crossing the Piave River, and the offensive ended on November 27. A second enemy offensive was launched on Dec. 6, 1917. Again, the Italians were able to hold their own, and the offensive halted at the end of December. Diaz calculated that the enemy would launch another offensive in the spring of 1918 concentrated on the Piave front. Indeed, on June 15, 1918, the enemy's massive assault, known as the Battle of the Piave, began. By June 23 it was evident that the valiant Italian defense had broken the back of the offensive.

On Sept. 18, 1918, Diaz met with the commander of the American Expeditionary Force, John J. Pershing. The two agreed that from a military and strategic point of view, a counteroffensive on the Italian front would be very important, and on Oct. 21, 1918, the Italians launched the Battle of Vittorio Veneto, which raged for four days (October 26–30). Diaz engaged fifty-seven divisions: fifty-one Italian, three British, two French, one Czechoslovak, plus the 332d American Infantry Regiment.

Diaz combined Napoleonic crushing maneuvers and a maximum thrust in one direction. The ultimate objective of the strategy was to split the enemy's army and outflank it. The strategy worked, and the Austro-Hungarian army crumbled. Hostilities ended with the signing of the Armistice of Villa Guisti on Nov. 3, 1918.

Armando Diaz died in Rome on Feb. 29, 1928, and was buried in the Basilica of Santa Maria Degli Angeli.

Pellegrino Nazzaro

See also CADORNA, LUIGI; CAPORETTO, BATTLE OF; VITTORIO VENETO, BATTLE OF

Bibliography

Albertini, Luigi. *The Origins of the War of 1914,* trans. and ed. by Isabelle M. Massey. London: Oxford University Press, 1952–1957.

Baldini, Alberto. *Diaz,* trans. by W.F.M. Humphrey Toulmin. London, n.p., 1935.

Mangone, Angelo. *Diaz. Da Caporetto al Piave a Vittorio Veneto.* Milan: n.p., 1987.

Dickman, Joseph Theodore (1857–1927)

Joseph Theodore Dickman was appointed to the United States Military Academy in 1876, but because of disciplinary demerits, he was suspended for a year, returning to graduate with the class of 1881. He was commissioned in the cavalry and served in the West, fighting Indians, outlaws, and Mexican revolutionaries. Dickman attended the Infantry and Cavalry School at Fort Leavenworth, Kansas, graduating with honors in 1883. After more service in the West, he returned to the Leavenworth school as an instructor, serving there from 1895 to 1898.

During the Spanish-American War, he was on the staff of Gen. Joseph Wheeler in the Santiago Campaign in Cuba. Dickman was sent to the Philippines in 1899, where he commanded an infantry regiment in the Panay campaign. He also participated in the International Relief Expedition to China during the Boxer Rebellion. In the early years of the twentieth century, Dickman again served on the faculty of the Infantry and Cavalry School and spent much of his off-duty time studying military affairs and foreign languages. His peers recognized him as an intelligent and diligent military scholar. He also served as a member of the first

War Department General Staff, as a member of various military boards, and as an inspector general in several commands. In 1904, Dickman attended the Army War College, graduating in 1905. After that he was promoted rapidly and by 1917 held the rank of brigadier general.

In April 1917, Dickman was given command of the 3d Division at Camp Greene, North Carolina. Despite his portly figure, he actively and vigorously guided the training of his division. He and his troops went overseas in May 1918. Shortly after arriving in France, the division was sent into action against the German spring offensive of 1918. Dickman's training paid off, for the green troops withstood the offensive, with their backs to the Marne River. In July, the 3d Division again stopped the German offensive (the second major German effort) with a flexible defense designed by Dickman in violation of instructions from his Allied commanders. The stalwart defense of the Marne by the soldiers of the 3d, after French units on their flanks were driven back, earned the division the sobriquet "The Rock of the Marne." Gen. John J. Pershing, commander-in-chief of the American Expeditionary Force (AEF), impressed with Dickman's drive and spirit, selected him to command IV Corps, which was formed in July 1918, to participate in the St. Mihiel offensive. The corps, consisting of the experienced 1st and 42d divisions and the newly arrived 3d and 89th divisions, jumped off on September 12, attacking the east face of the defenses of the St. Mihiel salient. The advance was rapid against dwindling German resistance. IV Corps linked up with elements of V Corps on the second day of the operation, closing the gap on the retreating enemy forces. The number of enemy prisoners was large, but Dickman was disappointed, as the bulk of the German forces had escaped.

When the U.S. First Army's offensive in the Meuse-Argonne sector was stalled in mid-October 1918, Dickman was called from St. Mihiel to command I Corps, replacing Gen. Hunter Liggett, who took command of the First Army. Dickman's corps was on the left of the army and had been most seriously engaged in the heavily defended Argonne Forest. Dickman himself directed local attacks during the first two weeks of command in order better to dispose the corps for resuming the offensive. When the First Army again attacked on Nov. 1, 1918, Dickman's corps advanced rapidly and oper-

ated more professionally than in previous campaigns. Dickman was dynamic and exultant in command as his forces drove the retreating Germans from the Bois de Bourgogne and surrounding areas. As the corps advanced to the heights south of Sedan, Pershing sent a message that was interpreted as authorizing the disregard of corps boundaries in order to seize Sedan. This resulted in a race for Sedan, in which the 1st Division of V Corps advanced into I Corps' zone without specific approval. Dickman became furious over this violation of authority; his choler concerning this incident provoked the animosity of his peers and may have cooled Pershing's support for Dickman following the Armistice.

Dickman took command of the newly formed Third Army in November 1918. Its primary responsibility was participation in the Allied occupation of the Rhineland. The army took up duties in a bridgehead over the Rhine at Coblenz. Promoted to major general in the Regular Army in January 1919, Dickman remained at odds with Pershing, who disliked Dickman's "pompous manner." Pershing replaced Dickman with Hunter Liggett at the end of April 1919. Dickman returned to the United States to command the Southern Department until his retirement on Oct. 6, 1921. For his outstanding service in World War I, Dickman was awarded the Distinguished Service Cross and a number of foreign awards. After his retirement, he wrote *The Great Crusade* on his experiences in the war. He died in Washington, D.C., on Oct. 23, 1927.

Paul F. Braim

See also SEDAN INCIDENT

Bibliography

Braim, Paul F. *The Test of Battle: The AEF in the Meuse-Argonne Campaign.* Newark: University of Delaware Press, 1987.

Dickman, Joseph T. *The Great Crusade: A Narrative of the World War.* Boston: Appleton, 1927.

Smythe, Donald. *Pershing.* Bloomington: University of Indiana Press, 1986.

Dollar-a-Year-Men

"Dollar-a-year-men," mainly from business, served federal mobilization agencies during World Wars I and II and the Korean War. They held their positions under an expedient designed to secure quickly for the government the nation's best organizational and industrial expertise while maintaining individuals at salary levels well beyond government pay scales. Continuing in their private-sector affiliations and salaries, they received one dollar for full-time federal employment. Thus, a legal employee/employer relationship was established. The expedient was also designed to circumvent a statute prohibiting volunteer work for the government and to reassure newcomers that their private positions and seniority would not be threatened.

During World War I, dollar-a-year-men—such as Bernard Baruch, Robert S. Brookings, Herbert B. Swope, and many others—staffed the Advisory Commission to the Council of National Defense (CND) and comprised the majority of personnel at the War Industries Board. In these positions they helped set policy on how the armed services dealt with suppliers, many of which were represented by the dollar-a-year-men. Members of the Committee on Automotive Transport of the CND, for example, advised on prices and contract distribution while retaining the highest positions in the auto industry. Advocates of the dollar-a-year men stressed the efficient use of private talent for the war emergency in their support of the system. But critics in Congress, the press, and the military limited the power of the dollar-a-year-men, citing conflicts of interest not only in particular dealings, but also on social and political values that would prevail in a war-mobilization system overseen by representatives of large corporate enterprises. Despite these concerns, most dollar-a-year-men focused on the tasks at hand and made valuable contributions to the war effort.

Jacob Vander Meulen

Bibliography

Reagan, Michael D. "Serving Two Masters: Problems in the Employment of Dollar-a-Year and Without Compensation Personnel." Ph.D. dissertation, Princeton University, 1959.

Donovan, William Joseph (1883–1959)

William Joseph ("Wild Bill") Donovan was born in Buffalo, New York, and received a B.A. and LL.B. from Columbia University. After establishing a promising law practice in Buffalo, Donovan helped organize Troop One of the First Cavalry, New York National Guard in 1912, and he served as a captain with the unit during the 1916 Punitive Expedition in Mexico. Donovan was sent to Europe in 1916 by the Rockefeller Foundation to assist in relief work in Poland.

When the United States entered World War I, Donovan quickly joined up. He first served with the 27th Division of the American Expeditionary Force (AEF). He also was part of the 51st Brigade and later commanded the 165th Infantry Division (formerly the 69th New York Infantry Regiment). In his first engagement with the enemy in March 1918, Donovan received the Croix de Guerre for bravery under heavy enemy bombardment. He had been promoted to colonel by the time of the Meuse-Argonne operations, and in early September, he led the division in heavy fighting at Ourcq, for which he was awarded the Distinguished Service Cross. Donovan's action on Oct. 14 and 15, 1918, earned him the Medal of Honor. During fighting at Landres and St. George's, while badly wounded in the leg, Donovan remained in command and in the front ranks, exposing himself as a target to the enemy while encouraging his men. The unselfish Donovan later donated his medal to his unit, which he felt really deserved it. For the same two-day action Donovan was also awarded two wound chevrons, a bronze oak leaf cluster to his Distinguished Service Cross, and more than twelve foreign decorations. In all, Donovan received more combat awards than any other American soldier in World War I.

After the war, Donovan served as an unofficial observer in the anti-Bolshevik force of Admiral Kolchak in Russia. He performed the same duties in 1935 in Ethiopia and in Spain in 1936. During the 1920s and 1930s, he worked in a variety of posts in the Justice Department. With the outbreak of World War II in 1939, Donovan went to Britain to observe military preparations. His knowledge of European military capabilities brought him to the attention of President Roosevelt, who appointed him coordinator of information, and when the Office of Strategic Services (the forerunner of the Central Intelligence Agency) was created in June 1942, Donovan was made the director and headed it until 1945. In 1953–1954, he again served his country as ambassador to Thailand. He died on Feb. 8, 1959.

Laura M. Wood

Bibliography

Dunlop, Richard. *Donovan: America's Master Spy.* New York: Rand-McNally, 1982.

Ford, Corey. *Donovan of OSS.* Boston: Little, Brown, 1970.

Troy, Thomas F. *Donovan and the CIA.* Washington, DC: CIA Center for the Study of Intelligence, 1981.

Doyen, Charles Augustus (1859–1918)

Charles Augustus Doyen was born in New Hampshire and was graduated from the United States Naval Academy in 1881. He was commissioned a second lieutenant of the Marines Corps in 1883. Doyen's early career was typical of his era: tours with marine detachments aboard ship, barracks assignments, and service ashore in foreign lands. In the Philippines, from 1905 to 1906, he commanded a battalion, then the 2d Marine Regiment, and finally the 1st Marine Brigade. He returned to the islands, serving in 1913 and 1914, again as commanding officer of the 1st Marine Brigade. In 1914, he commanded the 5th Marine Regiment in Cuba and the Dominican Republic and later was commanding officer of the marine barracks in Washington, D.C.

After the United States entered World War I, Doyen was selected to command the 5th Marine Regiment, the first marine unit sent to France. The unit arrived there in June 1917, and shortly thereafter, Doyen was promoted to brigadier general. With the arrival of the 6th Marine Regiment and the 6th Machine Gun Battalion in France, the 4th Marine Brigade was formed, and Doyen assumed command of it on Oct. 24, 1917. The 4th Brigade became part of the 2d Division, which assembled in France in the autumn of 1917. A skeleton headquarters was established at Bourmont, France, and as the division's senior officer present, Doyen temporarily assumed command from Oct. 26 to Nov. 8, 1917. Doyen then became the first marine to command a division.

General Doyen had a reputation as a superb instructor and trainer of men. While in France, he worked so hard in preparing the 4th Brigade for the arduous duties he knew would be coming that his health was severely impaired. He remained in command of the brigade until May 7, 1918, when a medical board declared him unfit for further service in Europe. The 4th Brigade's performance in combat in the Château-Thierry sector and at Belleau Wood shortly after his departure was a tribute to Doyen's efforts to prepare it for action. He returned to the United States where, upon his arrival, he assumed command of the new Marine Corps Training Camp and the Marine Barracks at Quantico, Virginia. His experience in France was invaluable in training officers and men for service overseas. He was struck, like so many others, by the Spanish Influenza epidemic and died of bronchial pneumonia on Oct. 6, 1918.

Shortly after his death, Doyen's wife was presented with the first Distinguished Service Medal awarded by the Navy Department. The citation specifically noted his efforts at training the 4th Brigade, the effect his tour of command had on his health, and the brigade's subsequent performance in battle.

Donald Bittner

Bibliography

Heinl, Robert D. *Soldiers of the Sea: The United States Marine Corps, 1775–1962.* Annapolis, MD: U.S. Naval Institute, 1962.

McClellan, Edwin N. *The United States Marine Corps in the World War.* Washington, DC: Historical Branch, U.S. Marine Corps Headquarters, 1920.

Metcalf, Clyde H. *A History of the United States Marine Corps.* New York: Putnam, 1939.

Millett, Allan R. *Semper Fidelis: A History of the United States Marine Corps.* New York: Macmillan, 1980.

Drum, Hugh Aloysius (1879–1951)

Hugh Aloysius Drum was born at Fort Brady, Michigan, the son of Capt. John Drum, who had received a Regular Army commission after the Civil War. Drum attended post schools, but most of his education was gained informally from association with army personnel and observing military life. He did not attend college.

Captain Drum was killed at the Battle of San Juan Hill in Cuba in 1898. President William McKinley, on September 9, offered his son, the eighteen-year-old Hugh, a commission as a second lieutenant in the Regular Army. On September 21, just after his nineteenth birthday, Hugh accepted and was sworn in, at the time one of the youngest Regular officers in the army.

After only five months service with the 12th Infantry, Drum sailed with that regiment for combat duty in the Philippine Insurrection, where he participated in numerous engagements. In 1899, he joined the 25th Infantry and commanded an expedition that captured a notorious guerilla leader. Subsequently, he saw action against the Moros, warlike Islamic inhabitants of the southern Philippine Islands. During this period he won a brevet captaincy and a Silver Star citation for bravery. The Moro expedition was commanded by Col. Frank D. Baldwin and Captain Drum so impressed him that when Baldwin was promoted to brigadier general, he appointed Drum as his aide-de-camp.

After further service in the United States and the Philippines, completion of the Army School of the Line as an honor graduate, and graduation from the General Service and Staff School at Fort Leavenworth, Kansas, Drum became assistant commandant at Fort Leavenworth and director of both schools. There he wrote many articles on tactical subjects. One particular essay on the attack of cities brought him to the attention of MajGen. Frederick Funston, who commanded the U.S. Expeditionary Forces in the Mexican port city of Veracruz. Funston appointed Drum assistant chief of staff of the expedition in early 1914. After the return of the forces in September of that year, Drum again served at Fort Leavenworth and at El Paso, Texas. Drum had also come to the attention of Gen. John J. Pershing, and when Pershing was named to command the American Expeditionary Force (AEF), he chose Drum as one of the six General Staff officers to accompany him to France.

In August 1917, Drum was promoted to lieutenant colonel and was named to a group studying the needs of the AEF for training areas, rail communications, and ports. Drum was also a member of the Operations Section of General Headquarters of the AEF, which was studying the future organization of American forces. It was the consensus of observers, both American and European, that the organization of the existing infantry division was not suited to the war being fought in Western Europe. Drum's contribution to this study was substantial, and General Pershing accepted the majority of its conclusions and recommendations. These increased the division to roughly twice the strength of the British or French division and gave it great staying power. This so-called "square division" remained the basic structure of the American infantry until the Second World War.

On July 30, 1918, Drum was promoted to colonel and detailed as chief of staff of the newly activated First Army. In that position, he was responsible for organizing the staff of the headquarters and overseeing the development and execution of the plans for the St. Mihiel and Meuse-Argonne offensives. On October 1, 1918, he was promoted to brigadier general and as such supervised the First Army's participation in the final offensive of the war.

Following the Armistice, General Pershing directed General Drum, among others, to make lecture tours of divisional camps to brief the troops on the accomplishments of the American forces. Then in April 1919, Drum was named assistant to the chief of staff of the Service of Supply of the AEF. In that capacity, he oversaw the redeployment of the American forces to the United States.

Upon returning to the United States, Drum reverted to his permanent rank of major but was soon promoted again to brigadier general in 1920, to major general in 1930, and lieutenant general in 1939. He held many important assignments during the interwar period and in 1939 was the principal rival to Gen. George C. Marshall for assignment as chief of staff of the U.S. Army.

General Drum retired in 1943 and died on Oct. 3, 1951.

James L. Collins, Jr.

Bibliography

Dawes, Charles G. *A Journal of the Great War*. New York: Houghton Mifflin, 1921.

Fredericks, Pierce G. *The Great Adventure*. New York: Dutton, 1960.

Marshall, George C. *Memoirs of My Service in the World War 1917–1918*. Boston: Houghton Mifflin, 1976.

Pershing, John J. *My Experiences in the World War*. New York: Stokes, 1931.

Smythe, Donald. *Pershing*. Bloomington: Indiana University Press, 1986.

Duffy, Francis Patrick (1871–1932)

The most celebrated U.S. Army chaplain of World War I, Father Francis Patrick Duffy, a Roman Catholic priest, was born in Cobourg, Canada, and was ordained in 1896. He then attended Catholic University of America in Washington, D.C., and was appointed professor of psychology and ethics at St. Joseph's

Seminary in New York. Father Duffy's career as an army chaplain began with a brief tour of duty during the Spanish-American War when he was stationed at Montauk Point, Long Island. In 1912, he became pastor of Our Savior parish in the Bronx, New York City. It was not until 1914 that he was appointed chaplain of the 69th Infantry Regiment of the New York National Guard.

The "Fighting Sixty-Ninth," a basically Irish regiment, had served with distinction during the Civil War. It was called up briefly during the Spanish-American War and also in 1916 when it served on the Mexican border during General Pershing's Punitive Expedition. When the United States entered the Great War, the regiment was renumbered the 165th Infantry and assembled at Camp Mills, New York. Assigned to be part of the new Rainbow (42d) Division, its members continued to refer to it by its traditional sobriquet.

Chaplain Duffy, now a major and the senior chaplain of the 42d Division, became an inspirational focus for the division and later the AEF. The poet Joyce Kilmer writing of the voyage across the Atlantic observed that every day there could be seen a line of soldiers, "as long as the mess-line," waiting their turn to have Duffy hear their confessions. Every morning, Kilmer noted, a large crowd would gather amidship on the transport where Chaplain Duffy said Mass at an altar made from a long board resting on two nail kegs. Arriving in France in November 1917, the division spent the winter in training and in late February 1918 took over frontline trenches from French Chasseurs at Luneville in the Lorraine sector. At dawn on March 20, Duffy and the men of the 42d received their baptism of fire when mustard gas shells burst among them. The bombardment lasted two days and over 400 men were injured, the majority of them blinded.

For Chaplain Duffy, the next few months were to be filled with such scenes. He was most often found along the front lines hearing confessions and saying Mass, as well as visiting and counseling the soldiers. It was by this "ministry of presence" that he had his greatest influence. Once the fighting began, he often traveled with a unit first-aid station, providing physical and spiritual care of the wounded and dying. His presence on the battlefield was inspirational. Duffy was always near the heaviest fighting, exposing himself as he moved from unit to unit. He was awarded the Distinguished Service Cross and the Distinguished Service Medal. Duffy ended the war as a lieutenant colonel.

After the war, Father Duffy returned to a new parish in New York City. As pastor of Holy Cross Church on 42d Street, just off Broadway, the "actor's church," Duffy added to his already great popularity. In 1919, he published a best-selling book, *Father Duffy's Story,* detailing his experiences in the war. He died on June 26, 1932.

William J. Hourihan

Bibliography
Duffy, Francis P. *Father Duffy's Story.* New York: Doran, 1919.

Dulles, John Foster (1888–1959)

John Foster Dulles, who was to become Dwight D. Eisenhower's secretary of state, first emerged as a minor actor on the American diplomatic stage in World War I. A young Wall Street lawyer just beginning his long, successful career with the prestigious firm of Sullivan and Cromwell, Dulles came to Washington in 1917 under the sponsorship of his uncle, Robert Lansing, by this time Woodrow Wilson's second secretary of state. Dulles performed several minor diplomatic missions in Panama, Costa Rica, and Nicaragua, all related to thwarting presumed German machinations in Central America. He then moved, as a major in the U.S. Army, into the War Trade Board, where his work impressed Vance McCormick and Bernard Baruch, the influential head of the War Industries Board. As a result, Dulles went to Paris as a junior member of the American delegation to the Paris Peace Conference of 1919, where he served as legal adviser to Baruch on the troubling issue of German reparations.

At Paris, Dulles vigorously defended the American position, laid out in the pre-Armistice agreement, that German reparations should be strictly limited to actual war costs—even, on one occasion, disagreeing with Wilson on its interpretation. Indeed, had the Senate ratified the Versailles Treaty, Dulles, most likely, would have been asked to serve as the American representative on the Reparations Commission. Ironically, he was one of the authors of the notorious, ill-starred Article 231—the "war-guilt" clause—which assigned responsibility for the outbreak of war in 1914 to the German Empire. He would, to be sure, always insist that

D

the intent had been solely to fix the legal basis for reparation and not to assign moral guilt.

His experiences at Paris influenced his later thinking about international affairs. In the twenties, he became a recognized authority on and critic of the economic settlement at Paris, above all of the way in which Allied war debts and German reparations had been handled. By the thirties, with the rise of Hitler and a new war on the horizon, he would insist that the United States should steer clear of future involvements with the French and British, the victors of 1918, because they had become "status quo" nations committed only to preserving the advantages they had won at Versailles. They ignored Wilson's commitment to a peaceful change and rejected Article XIX of the treaty, which called for the peaceful revision of treaties when they no longer corresponded to international realities. Wilson's principles, he argued in a major speech in 1936, had not failed; they had never been tried.

Richard D. Challener

Bibliography
Beal, John R. *John Foster Dulles, a Biography*. New York: Harper, 1957.

Guhin, Michael A. *John Foster Dulles, a Statesman and His Times*. New York: Columbia University Press, 1972.

Pruesson, Ronald. *John Foster Dulles*. New York: Free Press, 1982.

E

Eagle Boats

Drawing their name from a December 1917 *Washington Post* editorial that wished for an eagle to pounce upon German submarines, the U.S. Navy's Eagle Boats were 500-ton steel escort vessels designed to fill the gap between the 75-ton, wooden subchaser built for coastal patrol and larger, more expensive fleet destroyers. The Eagle Boat design was strongly influenced by automotive industrialist Henry Ford, who had offered the manufacturing resources of the Ford Motor Company to the U.S. Navy in February 1917. By the time Ford accepted membership in the U.S. Shipping Board in November 1917, he had become convinced that warships could be mass-produced. Ford claimed he could build submarine-detecting ships at a savings of 80 percent compared to the cost of traditional ship construction.

In January 1918, the navy's Bureau of Construction and Repair finalized the preliminary design for the Eagle Boat, which was to be 204 feet in length with a 25-foot beam. It was designated "PE" for patrol escort, and Ford submitted a bid incorporating the navy specifications at a cost of $265,000 per ship. The first vessel was to be delivered in July 1918, ten in August, twenty more by mid-September, and then twenty-five per month thereafter. On January 17, 1918, Secretary of the Navy Josephus Daniels authorized Ford to construct 100 Eagle Boats. In concert with Ford engineers, the navy refined the Eagle design to enhance its mass production at Ford's new River Rouge facility. Easily fabricated straight components replaced rolled structural members and curved hull plating wherever possible. Although a full-sized model was constructed to provide manufacturing jigs, the rate of construction never approached assembly-line speed. The main problems were the shortage of skilled riveters in Ford's employ and the lack of appreciation by Ford engineers and production managers for the time-consuming installation of integrated piping and electrical systems in a modern warship.

The first Eagle Boat was finally launched on July 11, 1918, two months after its keel was laid, but it took almost four more months to install machinery and equipment to place the ship in commission. Despite Ford's promise to deliver twenty-five ships per month by September 1918, only seven were in commission by the end of 1918. Due to the poor quality of riveting at Ford, the first ships had leaky hulls and contaminated fuel tanks; some had machinery defects. The navy reduced the total order from 100 to 60 ships with all to be delivered by November 1919. Ford met the deadline, but he discovered that complex technological systems, such as ships, were exceedingly more difficult to produce than automobiles. Three Eagle Boats sank at sea, and the ships were considered unseaworthy within some naval circles. As a result, the navy readily sacrificed the Eagle Boats to the federal economy drive of the New Era. By 1924, thirty were decommissioned, five were transferred to the U.S. Coast Guard, and the remaining twenty-two trained naval reservists.

William M. McBride

See also Shipping Board

Bibliography

Cianflone, Frank A. "The Eagle Boats of World War I." U.S. Naval Institute *Proceedings* 99 (June 1973).

Furer, J.A. "The 110-Foot Submarine Chasers and Eagle Boats." U.S. Naval Institute *Proceedings* 45 (1919).

Hounshell, David A. "Ford Eagle Boats and Mass Production during World War I." In *Military Enterprise and Technological Change: Perspectives on the American Experience*, ed. by Merritt Roe Smith. Cambridge, MA: MIT Press, 1988.

Eastman, Crystal (1881–1928)

Crystal Eastman, a Socialist and feminist, sister of activist Max Eastman, was one of the most influential activists in the American antiwar movement that developed during World War I. After the outbreak of war, Eastman, who held a masters degree in sociology and a law degree, began organizing opposition to militarism and to American involvement in the hostilities. She believed that war jeopardized social justice and democratic rights. This led her to work with some of the nation's leading social reformers, such as Lillian D. Wald, Paul U. Kellogg, and Jane Addams. The group, subsequently known as the American Union Against Militarism (AUAM), became an antipreparedness organization late in 1915, largely due to Eastman's influence as its executive secretary. Her "Platform of Real Preparedness" called on peace forces to develop a definite antipreparedness program to push when Congress convened in December 1915.

In addition to shaping the AUAM, Eastman was influential in the Woman's Peace Party (WPP). After considerable debate, the national WPP adopted an aggressive antipreparedness program, which drew heavily from Eastman's platform. During 1916, members of the WPP and AUAM testified before Congress in opposition to preparedness and in support of international peace.

Following Wilson's preparedness tour in late January and early February 1916, Eastman organized an AUAM "Truth about Preparedness" tour that began on April 6, 1916. An AUAM delegation that met with President Wilson after the tour concluded that he failed to grasp the dangers perceived by the preparedness movement.

Eastman believed that the AUAM should wage an anticonscription campaign and defend the rights of conscientious objectors. Together with Norman Thomas and Roger Baldwin, she organized a new committee in the AUAM, the Civil Liberties Bureau, which later became the American Civil Liberties Union. Despite her efforts to hold the AUAM together, many did not share her views that protection of civil liberties in wartime was the logical culmination of AUAM efforts and the membership split over this issue. Passage of the Espionage (1917) and Sedition (1918) acts made it illegal for Eastman and other activists to continue most of their antiwar efforts.

With Eastman as its president, however, the New York City branch of the WPP continued some work during the war. Eastman made it clear that the WPP had never urged resistance to the Selective Service Act and that it had not called for immediate peace, only that the government respond in some way to the peace proposals put forward by revolutionary Russia. Such disavowals did little to assuage concerns of more conservative WPP members, who feared Eastman's radicalism and tried unsuccessfully to prevent her from attending the Second International Congress of Women in Zurich after the war. Her final WPP activity was to organize the First Feminist Congress in the United States in March 1919. Eastman's postwar efforts focused on promotion of feminism and socialism.

Barbara J. Steinson

See also AMERICAN UNION AGAINST MILITARISM; CIVIL LIBERTIES BUREAU; WOMAN'S PEACE PARTY

Bibliography

Cook, Blanche W. *Crystal Eastman on War and Revolution*. New York: Oxford University Press, 1978.

Marchand, C. Roland. *The American Peace Movement and Social Reform, 1898–1918*. Princeton, NJ: Princeton University Press, 1972.

Steinson, Barbara J. *American Women's Activism in World War I*. New York: Garland, 1982.

Eastman, Max (1883–1969)

Max Eastman, brother of feminist Crystal Eastman, graduated from Williams College in 1905 and entered Columbia University, where he completed the work for the Ph.D. but chose not to receive the degree. Living in Greenwich Village in New York City, Eastman met many radical young artists and writers who were consumed with creating a new cultural framework for America. Eastman mixed easily with these bohemians, virtually all of whom were Socialists. In August 1912, he received a letter from John Sloan, Art Young, Louis Untermeyer, and five other artists and writers. "You are elected editor of *The Masses*. No pay." Less a magazine than a movement, *The Masses* promoted both art and revolution.

Eastman was surprised and dismayed by the outbreak of war in Europe in 1914. With the hope of a unified international proletariat now dashed, he still felt that some good could come from the war: the advancement of democracy in Germany and the freeing of the proletariat to rebel. He traveled to Europe for two months in 1915 to see the war firsthand, but he was unable to get to the front. Eastman published a book, *Understanding Germany,* in 1916. In it he found fault on both sides and saw patriotism, or nationalism, as the source of war. Not a strict pacifist—he supported the Russian Revolution, for example—he opposed militarism, and nationalism. Eastman spoke with President Woodrow Wilson in the summer of 1916 as one of several representatives of the American Union Against Militarism, which had been organized by Eastman's sister Crystal. He supported Wilson as the peace candidate in the 1916 election and testified against intervention before a congressional committee in January 1917. He continued to call for mediation and "peace without victory" in March and April, after Wilson had abandoned these positions, for Eastman saw no assurance that democratic war aims would be realized just because the United States entered the war. After the United States declared war on Germany, Eastman was among the critics of intervention who believed that progressive gains would not follow the prosecution of the war. American entry made a negotiated peace less likely and, following Germany's defeat, would leave that country embittered and the seeds sown for a future war.

The government, however, was in no mood to tolerate dissent. After passage of the Sedition and Espionage acts, Washington prosecuted, and vigilante groups persecuted those viewed as obstructing the war effort. But Eastman refused to be intimidated. Speaking at a huge rally at Madison Square Garden in New York City on Aug. 1, 1917, he called for support of the peace proposals being made by the new Kerenskii government in Russia and attacked civil rights violations at home.

The Masses became the major vehicle of protest against U.S. intervention. Through poetry, art, essay, and journalism *The Masses* kept up a steady attack on the government at war, quickly attracting official attention. The Justice Department secured a court order delaying the August 1917 issue. This permitted the Post Office to charge that *The Masses*, because it had not appeared on schedule, was not a periodical as defined by law and therefore it should lose its second-class mailing privileges. This doomed *The Masses*, but not before, ironically, Eastman endorsed a Wilson position paper in which the President outlined what would become his Fourteen Points. Throughout this period of war hysteria, and despite the personal attacks on him, Eastman continued to speak out against militarism and for mediation and a "hands-off" policy toward Russia. Eastman did take a conciliatory approach toward Socialists and intellectuals who supported U.S. intervention in the war. This attitude was clearly expressed in the new magazine Eastman founded, the *Liberator*. Eastman wanted to find areas where he could support the government so that his views, especially those regarding Russia, might have some impact. This is well illustrated by his support for the Fourteen Points in the first issue of the *Liberator* in March 1918. But when Wilson failed to recognize the Soviet government and sent American troops to join Allied forces in Archangel, Eastman concluded that he was little more than another tool of the capitalists.

Prior to this, and despite his efforts at conciliation, Eastman and six others from *The Masses* were indicted for conspiracy to promote mutiny and obstruct the draft. Max Eastman was treated as the central figure of the trial. He avoided attempts to force disloyal admissions in his testimony and managed to make his points, including his belief that there should be a free press and free speech even in time of war. The trial ended with a hung jury. A second trial in October also turned on Eastman's articulate defense of his right to express dissenting views, and his masterful summation to the jury produced the same result as the first trial. With the war over the government dropped the charges. Now Eastman had the unwelcome satisfaction of seeing many of his predictions for the postwar world come true.

David W. Moore

See also AMERICAN UNION AGAINST MILITARISM; FOURTEEN POINTS; MASSES, THE; RUS-

Bibliography
Eastman, Max. *Enjoyment of Living.* New York: Harper, 1948.
———. *Love and Revolution: My Journey through an Epoch.* New York: Random House, 1964.
O'Neill, William. *The Last Romantic: A Life of Max Eastman.* New York: Oxford University Press, 1978.
———, ed. *Echoes of Revolt: The Masses, 1911–1917.* Chicago: Quadrangle Books, 1966.

East St. Louis Race Riot, 1917

The East St. Louis riot of July 1917 was the most serious of eighteen outbreaks of racial violence occurring in the United States between 1915 and 1919. This riot, like most others of the period, was caused by tensions associated with the wartime movement of large numbers of poor southern blacks into previously white-dominated northern industrial cities which lacked adequate housing, transportation, employment, and recreational facilities. The migration itself was the result of recruitment campaigns conducted by northern employers seeking to meet expanded wartime production, pay lower wages, and to stymie labor organization efforts and strikes.

Troubles began in East St. Louis, Illinois, in April 1917 when unionized white workers at an aluminum-processing plant were fired and replaced by strikebreakers. The strike, which company officials blamed on the Industrial Workers of the World (IWW) and German sympathizers, was crushed by state militia units supported by court injunctions. The union blamed black strikebreakers for the defeat, even though most strikebreakers were white. Bitter about their loss of jobs and alarmed by the increasing numbers of black migrants to the city, union leaders met with municipal officials in late May and demanded that East St. Louis be kept a "white town." A riot immediately followed in which blacks were assaulted and several buildings were demolished. Random violence continued through June 1917.

Tensions were still high on the night of July 1 when a group of whites drove through the black district of town randomly firing into residences. When the police came to investigate in a car similar to the first vehicle, a crowd of several hundred armed blacks fired on the car, killing two white officers. As word of the shooting spread, white mobs began pulling blacks off trolleys, beating, stoning, lynching, and shooting them. Other mobs numbering in the thousands roamed the city beating and shooting blacks while chanting racist slogans and burning houses. Most blacks did not resist, but one group of 100 armed men did barricade themselves in a building until a National Guard unit succeeded in negotiating a cease fire and escorted the group from the city. Upward of 6,000 blacks fled East St. Louis, the majority never to return. While the most intense rioting occurred on July 2, sporadic looting, beatings, and shootings continued for several days.

Official casualty figures showed that 9 whites and 39 blacks were killed, although unofficial police estimates claimed that over 100 people died. Hundreds were wounded and injured. At least 300 buildings were burned, mainly in black residential areas, and property losses totaled more than $350,000. Approximately 100 people were arrested, but only 4 whites and 11 blacks were convicted of homicide, and 41 others, mainly whites, paid small fines or served short jail terms.

The riot stunned the nation, prompting a month-long congressional inquiry into its causes and a state investigation into the biased role of the Illinois National Guard. The subsequent congressional report strongly condemned the East St. Louis white community and blamed the actions of city politicians, employers, and labor leaders for creating a situation that made racial violence between the 10,000 black and 60,000 white residents of the city inevitable.

Clayton D. Laurie

Bibliography
Du Bois, W.E.B., and Martha Gruening. "Massacre at East St. Louis." *Crisis* 14 (1917).
"Report of the Special Committee authorized by Congress to Investigate the East St. Louis Riots," House of Reps. Doc. No. 1231, 65th Congress, 2d Session, July 15, 1918.
Rudwick, Elliot M. *Race Riot at East St. Louis, 2 July 1917.* New York: Atheneum, 1972.

Edison, Thomas Alva (1847–1931)

Thomas Alva Edison played several important roles during World War I. Recognizing that science and technology, particularly the submarine and airplane, were rapidly changing the nature of warfare, he became an ardent proponent of military and industrial preparedness. In a *New York Times* interview published on May 30, 1915, Edison outlined a preparedness plan based on the belief that the training of military personnel and the procurement of war materiel should be organized along industrial lines. He wanted large stockpiles of airplanes, battleships, and munitions to be kept in storage until needed and a large army of reservists trained by industry. He also called for the creation of military research laboratories to develop new inventions quickly.

In July 1915, Secretary of the Navy Josephus Daniels asked Edison to head an advisory board to evaluate technical ideas submitted by the public. Edison agreed to serve as president of the Naval Consulting Board, provided that he did not have to handle administrative matters and that he would be free to pursue his own research on military technology.

At the request of Secretary Daniels, Edison laid aside his own business and laboratory affairs in January 1917 to work on a number of war-related technical problems. At this time, Germany was preparing to resume unrestricted submarine warfare, and the prospects for United States entry into the war were high. Edison devoted much of his attention in 1917 to the problem of protecting Allied ships from submarine attack.

The inventor outfitted a vacant building near his West Orange, New Jersey, laboratory with equipment to conduct tests for locating gun positions by sound. In the spring and summer of 1917, Edison chartered an eighty-foot yacht, equipped with a variety of electrical devices, to conduct experiments on detecting submarines by sight, sound, and magnetic field. He also studied ship camouflage problems and recommended that steamships burn anthracite coal to lessen smoke emissions.

In the fall of 1917, Edison spent several weeks in Washington collecting data on Allied shipping losses. Edison discovered that the Allies were using old routes and that many ships passed through danger zones during daylight. He recommended that the Allies change their shipping schedules and routes to avoid German submarines.

The war also presented challenges and opportunities for Edison's business interests. As a manufacturer, Edison was heavily dependent on German chemicals, particularly phenol, which was used in the production of phonograph records and explosives. Cut off from his German suppliers, he developed a process to make synthetic phenol at a plant near Johnstown, Pennsylvania. At its peak, the plant produced six tons of phenol a day, allowing Edison to sell the surplus to other customers.

Edison developed a phonograph for troops in the field, while the Edison Phonograph Works manufactured bombsights and gas masks. He was less successful in marketing his alkaline storage battery, which Edison hoped to sell to the navy's submarine fleet. These hopes were dashed on Jan. 15, 1916, when the E–2 submarine exploded at the Brooklyn Navy Yard, killing four men. The explosion was attributed to the release of hydrogen gas from Edison's batteries, which had been placed aboard the vessel for a series of tests.

Leonard DeGraff

See also NAVAL CONSULTING BOARD

Bibliography

DeGraff, Leonard, and Edward Wirth. "Thomas A. Edison and the Exploding Submarine." *Seaport Magazine* (Winter/ Spring 1991).

"Edison's Plan for Preparedness." *New York Times Magazine*, May 30, 1915.

Millard, Andre. *Edison and the Business of Innovation.* Baltimore: Johns Hopkins University Press, 1990.

Scott, Lloyd N. *Naval Consulting Board of the United States.* Washington, DC: Government Printing Office, 1920.

Edwards, Clarence Ranson (1860–1931)

Clarence Ranson Edwards was graduated from West Point in 1883. He then held a number of posts on the frontier, taught military science at Fordham University, commanded the guard at President Garfield's grave in Cleveland, and served with the adjutant general's office. With the outbreak of the Spanish-American War, Edwards accompanied the 23d Infantry to New Orleans, later serving as adjutant general of the army's VI Corps. Earlier, Edwards had come to the attention of MajGen. Henry W. Lawton, and in early 1899 Lawton selected him to act as the general's chief of staff in the Philippines. He served in that capacity until Lawton was killed on Dec. 19, 1899. On four occasions, Lawton mentioned Edwards in his reports for conspicuous gallantry and administrative ability and recommended him for four brevets.

In 1902, Edwards was promoted to colonel and chief of the Bureau of Insular Affairs, which dealt with policy and administration in America's colonial possessions. Edwards was promoted to brigadier general in 1906. He was transferred to the line at his own request in 1912 and did a tour of duty at Fort D.A. Russell in Wyoming before assuming command of a brigade in Texas. He was later stationed in Hawaii and in 1915 became commander of U.S. troops in the Panama Canal Zone. He remained there until 1917 when he was appointed commandant of the newly created Department of the Northeast.

General Edwards organized the 26th "Yankee" Division from New England National Guard units and sailed for France in command of the division in September 1917. His division was the first fully complete National Guard Division to arrive in France. He commanded it through virtually all of its major campaigns, including early defensive sectors, the Champagne-Marne defensive, Second Battle of the Marne, St. Mihiel, and a good part of the Meuse-Argonne campaign.

His tenure did not go completely uncriticized. In early 1918 he had a spat with the officers of the 1st Division when the 26th relieved the "Big Red One" in the Toul sector and complained that the 1st had left the defenses in poor condition. During the Second Battle of the Marne, it was charged that the 26th Division's leaders lost track of units, failed to launch attacks on time, and suffered breakdowns in liaison.

On a personal level, General Pershing considered Edwards "contentious," and Regular Army officers claimed he was too emotionally involved with the New England guardsmen. In fact, he was generally adored by the guardsmen of the Yankee Division, who referred to him as "Daddy Edwards," and, by extension, by New England as a whole. As a result, his relief on Oct. 22, 1918, in the midst of the Meuse-Argonne campaign was widely resented, both by his division and by the New England media. Aside from the fact that corps commander Hunter Liggett, as well as Pershing himself, did not like Edwards, there was no obvious reason

for his being relieved of command. It has been speculated that it may have been sparked by an incident of fraternization between men of his division and some enemy soldiers.

Upon returning from France, Edwards was again placed in command of the Department of the Northeast until 1920; he was later promoted to major general and made commander of I Corps area headquarters army base at Boston. He held that post until his retirement in 1922. For his services, France awarded him the Croix de Guerre with palm and made him a commander of the Legion of Honor. He also received the Grand Cross of the Order of Leopold from Belgium.

Edwards and his wife stayed in their adopted New England, settling on a farm he named "Doneroving" outside Boston. His death in 1931 brought a tremendous outpouring of grief and eulogies throughout New England. After lying in state in the Hall of Flags of the Massachusetts State House—the first man to be accorded such an honor in almost twenty years—he was buried in Arlington National Cemetery.

James Hallas

See also MARNE, SECOND BATTLE OF THE; MEUSE-ARGONNE CAMPAIGN; ST. MIHIEL; UNITED STATES ARMY: 26TH DIVISION

Bibliography
Sibley, Frank P. *With the Yankee Division in France*. Boston: Little, Brown, 1919.
Taylor, Emerson G. *New England in France*. Boston: Houghton Mifflin, 1920.
"Yankee Doings." Boston: Yankee Division Veterans Association, March 1931.

Eisenhower, Dwight David (1890–1969)

An infantry officer and 1915 West Point graduate, Dwight David Eisenhower volunteered for service in the newly formed U.S. Tank Corps in early March 1918. He was assigned to the 1st Separate Tank Battalion at Camp Meade, Maryland. Captain Eisenhower so impressed Col. Ira C. Welborn, Tank Corps director in the United States, with his organizational abilities while coordinating the battalion's overseas movement at the port of embarkation in New York that Welborn ordered him to remain stateside and establish the first Tank Corps Training Center at Camp Colt in Gettysburg, Pennsylvania.

Camp Colt became the largest Tank Corps training post in the United States, reaching a peak strength of 10,600 officers and men in September 1918. Some twenty light and heavy tank battalions were activated and underwent initial entry training under Eisenhower's command before the war ended.

Training at Camp Colt was limited to little more than basic soldiering skills as there were no tanks with which to operate. Eisenhower showed a great deal of ingenuity in developing a training program, however, begging and borrowing machine guns from various units and mounting them on trucks to simulate firing on the move from tanks. He also acquired a swivel-type navy three-pounder while on a trip to Washington. Although unable to get ammunition for it, having the gun allowed crewmen to at least familiarize themselves with the characteristics of light cannon by conducting dry-firing drills.

Eisenhower advanced to lieutenant colonel by mid-October 1918 and was ordered to France in early November, but the war ended before he could get overseas. Shortly after the Armistice, Eisenhower began demobilizing the units he had so hastily organized. He participated in the army's 1919 Transcontinental Motor Convoy as a Tank Corps observer with Maj. Sereno E. Brett before returning to Meade to take command of a heavy tank brigade and later the 301st Tank Battalion. During this period Eisenhower cultivated a close relationship with Col. George S. Patton, Jr., commander of the 304th Tank Brigade at Meade. The pair worked closely developing new tactical concepts for the employment of tanks and wrote articles published in the *Infantry Journal* in 1920, which earned the censorship from their respective branch chiefs.

Eisenhower reverted to his permanent rank of captain in June 1920. Although he tried to get out of service with tanks in the summer of 1920, Col. Samuel D. Rockenbach refused to release him to the infantry branch. Finally, BGen. Fox Conner was able to obtain Eisenhower's transfer to his infantry brigade in Panama in January 1922. The relationship Eisenhower forged with Conner in Panama helped propel him on his path to Allied Commander in World War II. In June 1942, he took command of the American forces in Europe and later that year directed the Allied invasion of North Africa. A year later, Eisenhower planned and directed the invasion of Sicily and the Ital-ian peninsula. Then, in 1944, he directed the momentous Allied invasion of Normandy, which began the long-awaited defeat of Germany in Europe.

Eisenhower replaced Gen. George C. Marshall as the U.S. Army chief of staff in 1945. Upon his retirement in 1948, he became president of Columbia University. But his retirement was short-lived, and he returned to uniform in 1950 when President Truman requested that he become supreme commander of NATO forces. He resigned from that post in July 1952 and in November 1952 was elected the thirty-fourth President of the United States and won reelection in 1956. Eisenhower died on March 28, 1969.

Dale E. Wilson

See also ROCKENBACH, SAMUEL; TANKS

Bibliography

Ambrose, Stephen E. *Eisenhower: Soldier, General of the Army, President Elect, 1890–1952.* Vol. 1. New York: Simon & Schuster, 1983.

Blumenson, Martin, ed. *The Patton Papers, 1885–1940.* Boston: Houghton Mifflin, 1972.

Eisenhower, Dwight D. *At Ease: Stories I Tell to Friends.* Garden City, NY: Doubleday, 1967.

Wilson, Dale E. *Treat 'Em Rough! The Birth of American Armor, 1917–20.* Novato, CA: Presidio Press, 1989.

Eltinge, Leroy (1872–1931)

Leroy Eltinge entered the cavalry after graduating from the United States Military Academy in 1896. He fought in the Philippines and saw considerable service as a line officer but was best known in the army as an instructor at the staff school at Fort Leavenworth, Kansas. Soon after the United States entered the First World War, he left Leavenworth and joined the American Expeditionary Force (AEF) General Staff in July 1917.

As part of the Operations Section, Eltinge helped draft plans for the training and disposition of American troops arriving in France. Additionally, he worked on several projects aimed at increasing the efficiency of the AEF's General Staff, especially in regard to liaison activities. Another important part of his job was preparing assessments of the military situation in Europe and making recommendations about where American operations should be focused. It was one of these studies that suggested the St. Mihiel salient as an area for large-scale American operations.

After briefly serving with the headquarters of the U.S. Army's I Corps in May 1918, Eltinge became a temporary brigadier general and the AEF's deputy chief of staff. In his new position, he worked closely with both the AEF's chief of staff, James W. McAndrews, and its commander, John J. Pershing. As deputy chief of staff, Eltinge often accompanied Pershing to inter-Allied conferences as a representative of the AEF General Staff, ran the headquarters whenever McAndrew's was away, and kept Pershing informed of the situation at headquarters at that time. Furthermore, he oversaw a number of special projects, most notably the reorganization of the Service of Supply in the summer of 1918.

Following the Armistice, Eltinge remained as deputy chief of staff until July 1919. Upon returning to the United States, he reverted to his prewar rank of major and began the cycle of school, staff, and troop assignments over again. In 1924, he regained his wartime rank of brigadier general and became head of the U.S. Army War Plans Division. After this tour in Washington, LeRoy Eltinge commanded a succession of brigades until his death at Fort Omaha in 1931.

Richard Kehrberg

Ely, Hanson Edward (1867–1958)

Hanson Edward Ely graduated from the United States Military Academy in 1891. He then served with infantry units at various posts in the United States. In February 1899, he was sent with the 22d Infantry to the Philippines. There he participated in numerous engagements during the Philippine Insurrection and was awarded a Silver Star citation for gallantry in action. In 1901, Ely was assigned as regimental recruiting officer at Des Moines, Iowa, and later served at Fort Sam Houston, Texas. He was an excellent rifle marksman and captained the Southwestern Division Rifle Team in 1904.

In 1906, after graduating with distinction from the Infantry and Cavalry School and the Army Staff College at Fort Leavenworth, Kansas, Ely was granted a leave of absence for three months to attend, as an observer, German maneuvers and to study various European armies. After this assignment, he joined the 26th Infantry and returned with it to the Philippines for

another five years. He went with Gen. Frederick Funston on the Veracruz Expedition in 1914 and on his return to the United States, Ely attended the Army War College.

Ely sailed for Europe on June 1, 1917. There he was a member of a mission to study the organization and equipment of the British and French armies. This group, at General Pershing's request, worked closely with the Operations Division of the General Headquarters, American Expeditionary Force (AEF). Promoted to colonel, Ely was selected to organize the Military Police Corps and laid the foundation for this branch. However, at his own request, he was soon relieved of this duty and joined the 1st Infantry Division.

Initially, he was detailed as the division's chief of staff, but in December he was given command of the division's 28th Infantry. This regiment captured Cantigny on May 28, 1918. This was the first major attack of the 1st Division—indeed, of the AEF. Colonel Ely's careful preparation for the attack paid off in quick victory with few American casualties and relatively heavy enemy losses, including about 100 prisoners. During the ensuing heavy German counterattacks, the regiment, reinforced by a battalion each from the 18th and 26th infantries, repulsed the attackers, although at great cost. While it had taken only fifty casualties to capture Cantigny, the division lost almost a thousand men in defending it. For this action, Colonel Ely received another Silver Star Citation.

In July 1918, Ely was promoted to brigadier general and took command of the 3d Infantry Brigade of the 2d Division. Soon his brigade was on the move from the Château-Thierry sector to the line of departure for the Soissons attack. After a grueling night march, the brigade barely made it in time for the jump off at dawn on July 18. The fighting was hard, and General Ely distinguished himself during the battle, for which he was awarded the Distinguished Service Cross.

On October 15, Ely was promoted to major general and became commander of the 5th Division in the middle of the Meuse-Argonne offensive. In the first week of November, the 5th Division, in a maneuver that General Pershing characterized as "brilliant," forced a crossing of the Meuse.

After the Armistice, Ely remained in the Army of Occupation with his division until his return to attend the General Staff College in Washington, D.C. Subsequently, he served at

Fort Leavenworth, commanded the 2d Division, was commandant of the General Service School and the Army War College. From December 1927 until his retirement in November 1931, he commanded the Second Corps Area at Governor's Island, New York. He died in 1958.

James L. Collins

See also CANTIGNY; MEUSE-ARGONNE CAMPAIGN; SOISSONS

Bibliography
Harbord, James G. *The American Army in France.* Boston: Little, Brown, 1936.
Marshall, George C. *Memoirs of My Service in the World War 1917–1918.* Boston: Houghton Mifflin, 1976.
Pershing, John J. *My Experiences in the World War.* New York: Stokes, 1931.
Smythe, Donald. *Pershing.* Bloomington: Indiana University Press, 1986.
Weigley, Russell F. *History of the United States Army.* Bloomington: Indiana University Press, 1984.

Emergency Fleet Corporation

The United States Shipping Board, in accordance with the provisions of the Shipping Act of 1916, formed the Emergency Fleet Corporation on April 16, 1917. This government-owned corporation, with an original capital stock of $50 million, was established for the "purchase, construction, equipment, lease, charter, maintenance, and operation" of American merchant vessels during the Great War. As the conflict progressed, additional legislation and executive orders greatly increased the funding and powers of the corporation. Eventually, it was authorized to spend almost $4 billion on wartime ship construction and operation, and it gained far-reaching authority to requisition merchant tonnage, seize control of shipyards, and even build housing and transit systems for shipworkers.

Unfortunately, a bitter controversy arose between the corporation's first general manager, MajGen. George W. Goethals, and William Denman, who held a dual position as chairman of the U.S. Shipping Board and president of the Emergency Fleet Corporation. To deal with the shipping crisis caused by Germany's unrestricted submarine warfare, Denman proposed that the corporation concentrate on turning out large numbers of small wooden steamers.

Goethals saw this scheme as impractical and insisted that steel tonnage be the centerpiece of the shipbuilding program. This dispute severely hampered the functioning of the corporation and eventually led President Wilson, in July 1917, to dismiss both men.

Wilson replaced Denman with Edward Nash Hurley, a Chicago businessman who had previously served in the administration as chairman of the Federal Trade Commission. Replacing Goethals was RAdm. Washington Lee Capps, a renowned naval architect. These two men laid the groundwork for a massive shipbuilding program that emphasized steel construction, but which also continued the wooden ship effort begun by Denman, since both types of tonnage seemed necessary. Their first major act was to commandeer for the government, on Aug. 3, 1917, all merchant tonnage under construction or contract in American shipyards; a total of 431 vessels, aggregating over 3 million tons. Two months later, the corporation took control of all the ships in service in the American merchant marine.

To operate this fleet, Hurley established a Division of Operations, which was efficiently headed by Edward F. Carry, a businessman whom Hurley brought in from Chicago. Hurley, along with Capps, also took steps to enlarge the nation's shipbuilding capacity; the two men encouraged the expansion of existing shipyards, assisted in the building of new ones, and proceeded with a proposal Goethals had made for the establishment of "fabricated shipyards." The latter plan called for the mass production of steel vessels at huge government-owned shipbuilding plants, where workers would rivet together standardized shapes fabricated at mills throughout the country. Three of these fabricated shipyards would eventually be built: two on the Delaware River and one on Newark Bay. The largest of these was Hog Island, near Philadelphia. When it was completed, it was, by far, the world's biggest shipyard, boasting fifty shipways, twenty-eight fitting-out berths, and a workforce of almost 35,000 men. It was designed, when operating at full capacity, to launch a ship every other day. Unfortunately, the contracts for these fabricated yards would not be signed until September 1917, due largely to disputes between Capps and the contractors over price. As a consequence, construction of these innovative shipbuilding plants did not begin until autumn, and by the time these facilities were built and ready to launch vessels, the Armistice was rapidly approaching. The ambitious fabricated ship scheme would thus have no positive results in 1918; although if the war had continued into 1919 or 1920, the output from these yards would have been prodigious.

The slowness with which Capps negotiated the three fabricated shipyard contracts, and the delays in review of other contracts, along with health problems that affected the admiral's performance, convinced Hurley that his general manager could not efficiently run the shipbuilding program. As president of the corporation, Hurley decided to create a new position, that of vice president, and fill it with another of his Chicago acquaintances, Charles Piez, president of the Link-Belt Company. Hurley's plan was to have Piez, an efficient manager, run the corporation in place of Capps; changes to the bylaws now emasculated the power of the general manager. Capps, upset at this challenge to his authority, resigned in November 1917, but he did so without public protest, citing his poor health as the reason. Hurely replaced Capps with another naval officer, RAdm. Frederic R. Harris, who became general manager on November 24.

Confusion developed over who had real authority in the corporation: Piez, the vice president, or Harris, the general manager. Harris, taking the initiative, decided to act on his own and made key decisions without coordinating through Hurley or Piez. Infuriated, Hurley demanded Harris's resignation, which he got on December 17. Piez now became both vice president and general manager. Harris's "resignation," the third by a general manager in less than five months, led to an imbroglio in the press and a Senate Commerce Committee investigation. The congressional hearings, however, did not reveal any serious mismanagement or improprieties at the corporation. In fact, under Piez's efficient direction, the ship construction effort picked up momentum. Results, though, were not readily visible, for it took time to produce ships. In March 1918, the Emergency Fleet Corporation came under stiff political attack for not producing tonnage quickly enough. Hurley replied that the groundwork had been laid for vastly increased production by mid-1918, but the public seemed unimpressed.

This led Hurley and Piez, in an effort to improve the corporation's image, to invite one of America's best-known industrialists, Charles M. Schwab, the head of Bethlehem Steel, to join the Emergency Fleet Corporation. Schwab was not enthusiastic about leaving Bethlehem but patriotically agreed to take the newly created position of "director general," which gave him practically unlimited power over the merchant shipbuilding program. From a public relations standpoint, he proved to be a perfect choice: his appointment was universally acclaimed by the press, and congratulatory telegrams flooded into the corporation's main office. Schwab, moreover, spent his first day on the job, April 18, publicly praising the work that Hurley and Piez had done. His appointment thus gave a much needed boost to the corporation's reputation. Schwab, though, did not take an active role in running the shipbuilding program, a job he left mostly to Piez, whom he recognized to be an exceptionally talented manager. Schwab's only major decision was to move the corporation's headquarters to Philadelphia, which was closer to shipbuilding centers, and less overcrowded, than wartime Washington. A superb speaker, Schwab also spent a good deal of time visiting shipyards to urge management and workers to speed up production.

During the summer and fall of 1918, Hurley, Schwab, and Piez took pride in their accomplishments: in June, American shipyards set a new work record for monthly ship production in one country and then did so again in August, September, and October. The nation, which only had 37 steel shipyards and 24 wooden plants when it entered the war, now possessed 71 steel yards and more than 100 wooden plants. The number of shipways in the country had multiplied during the same period from 235 to 890. By the time of the Armistice, the Emergency Fleet Corporation had accepted delivery of over 380 steel ships aggregating 2,350,000 tons, and over 90 wooden steamers aggregating 350,000 tons. If the war had continued into 1919 or 1920, these numbers would have been far more impressive. As it was, the Armistice forced the corporation to reverse gears suddenly and begin the difficult task of cutting back on the more than 17 million tons of shipping it had under contract in November 1918.

William Williams

See also GOETHALS, GEORGE WASHINGTON; HURLEY, EDWARD NASH; SCHWAB, CHARLES MICHAEL

Bibliography

Ferrell, Robert H. *Woodrow Wilson and World War I, 1917–1921*. New York: Harper & Row, 1985.

Hurley, Edward N. *The Bridge to France*. Philadelphia: Lippincott, 1927.

Mattoc, W.C. *Building the Emergency Fleet*. Cleveland: Penton Publishing, 1920.

Safford, Jeffrey J. *Wilsonian Maritime Diplomacy, 1913–1921*. New Brunswick, NJ: Rutgers University Press, 1978.

Smith, Darrel H., and Paul V. Betters. *The United States Shipping Board: Its History, Activities and Organization*. Washington, DC: Brookings Institution, 1931.

Espionage Act of 1917

With the support of the Wilson administration, Congress passed the Espionage Act (40 *Statutes at Large* 217) on June 15, 1917. The act provided for imprisonment up to twenty years and/or a $10,000 fine for individuals found guilty of aiding the enemy, obstructing recruiting, or causing insubordination, disloyalty, or refusal of duty in the armed forces. The act also gave the postmaster general the power to deny the use of the mails for any materials that in his opinion advocated treason, insurrection, or forcible resistance to the laws of the United States.

Directed at the opponents of American participation in World War I, the Espionage Act led to a ban from the mails of several Socialist publications such as the *American Socialist*, *The Masses*, and Victor Berger's *Milwaukee Leader*, as well as anti-British and pro-Irish publications, and other radical papers. Eugene V. Debs, leader of the Socialist Party, was convicted of violating the Espionage Act when, in 1918, he publicly opposed the United States war effort. Debs was sentenced to ten years in prison.

In 1919, the Supreme Court upheld the constitutionality of the act in the case of *Schenck v. United States* (249 U.S. 47, 39 S.CT. 247, 63 L.Ed. 470). Charles T. Schenck had admittedly prepared and mailed leaflets to men eligible for military service in which he asserted that the draft violated the Thirteenth Amendment's prohibition of slavery.

In his appeal to the Supreme Court, Schenck argued that the Espionage Act violated his right to free speech. Justice Oliver Wendell Holmes, Jr., wrote the unanimous opinion of the Court, rejecting this argument by applying the "clear and present danger" test to Schenck's actions. Congress, Holmes wrote, had the power in wartime to limit speech that, although permissible in peacetime, constitutes a hindrance to the war effort such as resistance to the draft. Subsequently, in a 1944 case (*Hartzel v. United States*), the Supreme Court substantially limited the enforcement of the Espionage Act by requiring the government to prove specific intent to obstruct the war effort in obtaining a conviction.

John M. Lindley

See also BERGER, VICTOR; DEBS, EUGENE VICTOR; *Masses, The*

Bibliography

Chaffee, Zechariah, Jr. *Freedom of Speech in the United States*. Cambridge: Harvard University Press, 1941.

———. *The Guide to American Law*. Vol. 9. St. Paul, MN: West Publishing, 1985.

Link, Arthur S. *American Epoch: A History of the United States Since the 1890's*. New York: Knopf, 1955.

F

Farnsworth, Charles Stewart
(1862–1955)

Charles Stewart Farnsworth was born in Lycoming, Pennsylvania, and graduated from the United States Military Academy in 1887. Commissioned a second lieutenant of infantry, he served with the 25th Infantry Regiment at outposts in the Dakota Territory, Montana, and North Dakota and took part in the last of the Indian Wars. He was an instructor in military science at the University of North Dakota and served with the 7th Infantry Regiment in Colorado. During the Spanish-American War, Farnsworth went to Cuba as acting quartermaster of the 2d Division and participated in the Santiago campaign before becoming an aide on the staff of MajGen. Adna R. Chaffee. The next year he led an infantry company in Alaska, where he assisted in building the Alaskan telegraph system. During the early years of the new century, Farnsworth rose to the rank of colonel and served with the 7th and 16th Infantry regiments or on detached service as a constructing quartermaster and as a post adjutant general throughout the West and in the Philippines. From 1911 to 1913, he was an instructor with the Pennsylvania National Guard. He graduated from the Army School of the Line and Staff College at Fort Leavenworth in 1910 and the Army War College in Washington, D.C., in 1916. Farnsworth was also a battalion commander in the 16th Infantry, which participated in the 1916 Punitive Expedition into Mexico in pursuit of Pancho Villa.

Shortly after the United States entered World War I, Farnsworth was named commandant of the Infantry School of Arms at Fort Sill, Oklahoma. He was promoted to the temporary rank of brigadier general in the National Army in August 1917 and took command of the 159th Infantry Brigade, then training at Camp Lee, Virginia. In May 1918, Farnsworth, now holding the temporary rank of major general, became commander of the 37th Division. During the summer of 1918, he led the division to France, where it completed its training and later took part in the occupation of the quiet sectors at Baccarat and St. Mihiel.

In late September 1918, Farnsworth led the 37th Division in the assault by the American V Corps against the German stronghold at Montfaucon during the first phase of the Meuse-Argonne offensive. Given that this was the first real combat for the division, they performed about as well as could be expected. But after several days of fierce fighting the division, like the others in the initial assault, was so spent that it was pulled out of the line so that losses could be replaced. At the end of October, Farnsworth and his division were attached to a French corps and saw considerable action in Belgium during the Ypres-Lys campaign until the war ended on Nov. 11, 1918.

Following the return of the 37th Division to the United States in the spring of 1919, Farnsworth was made commander of Camp Benning, Georgia, with the responsibility of organizing and constructing the new Infantry School, of which he was the first commandant. In 1920, he was appointed chief of infantry, a post he held until his retirement at the rank of major general in 1925. An officer who was highly regarded for his abilities as an infantry tactician, Farnsworth died on Dec. 19, 1955, at Corona, California.

John K. Ohl

Bibliography

Cole, Ralph D., and W.E. Howells. *The Thirty-Seventh Division in the World War, 1917–1918*. Columbus, OH: N.p., 1926.

Stallings, Laurence. *The Doughboys: The Story of the AEF, 1917–1918*. New York: Harper & Row, 1963.

Van Every, Dale. *The A.E.F. in Battle*. New York: Appleton, 1928.

Federal Trade Commission

The Federal Trade Commission (FTC), an independent administrative agency of the federal government, was established by the Federal Trade Commission Act of 1914 and charged by Congress with regulation of the business practices of firms engaged in interstate commerce.

The concept of a federal agency to supervise business conduct was a result of public concern about the size and power of large corporations and of business concern about the injurious effects of unrestrained competition. At first, President Woodrow Wilson opposed the creation of a powerful interstate trade commission but later changed his mind and in the summer of 1914 threw his support behind a bill to establish such a federal agency. In September 1917, the Federal Trade Commission Act became law. Composed of five presidentially appointed commissioners, the FTC was authorized to conduct investigations, to demand reports from corporations, to publish findings, and to issue cease and desist orders, subject to judicial review by federal courts, to stop unfair methods of competition.

Largely because of Wilson's choice of pro-corporation commissioners, in its early years the FTC proved a disappointment to those who hoped it would control big business. With the entry of the United States into World War I in April 1917, the FTC became involved in war-related activities, chiefly investigating the prices of food and other materials. Several of these investigations found evidence of corporate wrongdoing and profiteering and generated considerable controversy.

Perhaps the most important FTC investigation during World War I involved the meatpacking industry. On Feb. 7, 1917, President Wilson had directed the FTC to study the food industry in the United States. Accordingly, the commission examined the business practices of the major meat-packers: Swift, Armour, Wil-son, Morris, and Cudahy. The FTC report on the meatpacking industry, submitted to Congress on Aug. 24, 1919, revealed that the large meatpacking firms had formed an illegal combination to control prices and sales of meat products.

The meatpacking investigation triggered a backlash against the FTC in Congress, which was now controlled by the Republican Party and much more sympathetic to corporate interests than had earlier been the case. The large meatpacking firms engaged in strenuous lobbying of Congress, and their spokesmen on Capitol Hill, such as Senator James E. Watson, an Indiana Republican, denounced the Federal Trade Commission as hopelessly biased against big business. Watson and others charged that the staff of the FTC included socialists and communists and introduced a Senate resolution to investigate the commission. Although the resolution was defeated, Congress reduced the appropriation of the Federal Trade Commission and compelled the dismissal of FTC personnel who had been involved in the meatpacking investigation. Furthermore, Congress eliminated FTC jurisdiction over the meatpackers by passing the Packers and Stockyards Act of 1921, which transferred oversight to the Department of Agriculture. The outcome of the meatpacking episode forced the Federal Trade Commission to recognize the power of large corporations and their congressional spokesmen. During the 1920s, a much chastened FTC proved exceedingly reluctant to challenge the giant firms of the American economy.

Richard N. Chapman

Bibliography

Blaisdell, Thomas C. *The Federal Trade Commission: An Experiment in the Control of Business*. New York: Columbia University Press, 1932.

Henderson, Gerard C. *The Federal Trade Commission: A Study in Administrative Law and Procedure*. New Haven: Yale University Press, 1924.

Holt, W. Stull. *The Federal Trade Commission: Its History, Activities, and Organization*. New York: Appleton, 1922.

Stone, Alan. *Economic Regulation and the Public Interest: The Federal Trade Commission in Theory and Practice*. Ithaca, NY: Cornell University Press, 1977.

Wagner, Susan. *The Federal Trade Commission*. New York: Praeger, 1971.

Fellowship of Reconciliation

On Nov. 11 and 12, 1915, American Protestant clergymen, Quakers, members of the YMCA, and other individuals met in Garden City, New York, with Henry T. Hodgkin, one of the founders of the British Fellowship of Reconciliation (FOR) movement established one year earlier. The group discussed the war in Europe and possible American antiwar efforts. Out of this meeting grew not only the American FOR, but also much of the leadership of peace activism in the United States for the next several decades. American FOR membership would number over 1,000 by World War I's end. Between 1916 and 1919, FOR members, each of whom pledged Christian pacifism, campaigned against national conscription legislation, attended peace conferences to gain new members, interceded with President Woodrow Wilson and Congress regarding the severe handling of conscientious objectors in American prisons, assisted enemy nationals living in the United States, and published magazine articles, pamphlets, and sermons to keep the Christian pacifist alternative before the American people. Early FOR members included Gilbert A. Beaver, Henry Sloane Coffin, John Nevin Sayre, and Norman M. Thomas. At the war's end, FOR lobbied against President Wilson's signing the Treaty of Versailles because of its harsh treatment of Germany.

Sarah Sharp

Bibliography

Brittain, Vera. *The Rebel Passion: A Short History of Some Pioneer Peace-makers.* London: N.p., 1964.

DeBenedetti, Charles. *The Peace Reform in American History.* Bloomington: Indiana University Press, 1980.

Howlett, Charles F. "John Nevin Sayre and the American Fellowship of Reconciliation." *Pennsylvania Magazine of History and Biography* (July 1990).

Film in the First World War

When the United States entered the First World War in April 1917, Hollywood was already the headquarters of the motion picture industry. Feature-length narrative films were a staple item in the entertainment repertoire of the American middle class. Stars like Mary Pickford and Charlie Chaplin earned more than $1 million a year while they and their celestial colleagues were playing influential roles in shaping the popular culture of the United States. One index to the pervasiveness and persuasiveness of this relatively new popular art form was the amount of legislative interest in censoring its content. Legislators, social workers, reformers, and church folk all expressed concern over the effects of the movies on the manners and morals of the poor, children, and society at large.

The film industry, dominated by such names as Paramount, Fox, and Goldwyn, was quick to enlist in the war on the homefront. Only days after the United States entry, links were forged between the National Association of the Motion Picture Industry and the federal government. War cooperation committees comprised of leaders within the Hollywood film establishment—Adolph Zukor, D.W. Griffith, Lewis Selznick, Mary Pickford, Cecil B. De Mille—were attached to departments including the War Department, Treasury Department, Food Commission, and Committee on Training Camp Activities. The film industry saw an opportunity to help disseminate government propaganda while at the same time improve its image with those who might wish to interfere in its business affairs. Practical patriotism was the order of the day. The government, for its part, recognized the ability of movies and of movie theaters to reach a broad cross section of the American public.

The motion pictures produced by the American film industry during the country's involvement in World War I were a mixed lot. Westerns and romances, comedy and drama, literary adaptation and original scenarios, serials, animated films, and newsreels, some scripts with war-related content and most with no narrative relation to the war—all were offered by the film producer and distributor to the exhibitor and by the film exhibitor to his local clientele. The war as content for the movies, and the movies made utilizing that content, occupied an alternative position within the film industry's regular production schedule during the war. The major producers, such as Paramount, included war-related pictures among their standard releases in increasing numbers over the months of U.S. involvement in World War I but never to the exclusion or even the diminution of nonwar-related entertainment. Likewise, the virulent "Hate the Hun" films—*The Kaiser, The Beast of Berlin*, released in March 1918; *To Hell with the Kaiser*, June 1918; *The Prussian Cur*, September 1918; and *Kulture*, September 1918—were generally cited to characterize "the films of World War I." They were released relatively late in the war. Instead, Mary Pickford's filmography for this period is more typical of film industry production. Pickford starred in seven films between April 1917 and November 1918. Two of these, *The Little American*, a drama that contains all the elements of the Hate-the-Hun genre including a threatened rape of "America's Sweetheart" by a Prussian colonel, released in the summer of 1917, and *Johanna Enlists*, a comedy in which Pickford comes of age when a regiment camps on her family's farm, released in September 1918, were war-related works. Pickford's other work during this period included *Romance of the Redwoods, Rebecca of Sunnybrook Farm, The Little Princess, Stella Maris,* and *How Could You, Jean?*

While war-related narrative films did not dominate the bills of movie theaters during World War I, the most popular and the most prestigious film released in 1917–1918 was D.W. Griffith's *Hearts of the World*. This film opened in New York City on April 4, 1918, and played, at legitimate theater prices, until Oct. 5, 1918. It enjoyed similarly long runs across the country. *Hearts of the World* was made with the cooperation of the French and British governments and was partially shot on the battlefields of France. It received rave reviews. A *Milwaukee Journal* editorial is typical: "Every Milwaukeean should see it, partly because it is great Art, but even more because its plot is such as will uncover a deeper vein of patriotism in every man, woman, and child with eyes to see and a heart to feel." While the use of the war as a subject of the movies may be the most apparent connection between the film industry and World War I, it is not the only way the movies participated in the war on the homefront.

The movie theater itself functioned as a medium for the government's message. Four-Minute Men spoke during the reel changes of films, recruiters set up tables in theater lobbies, "peach-stone matinees," where part of the price of admission was a peach pit to be used in the construction of gas masks, were all common occurrences during this time. Exhibitors also programmed their entertainment to include war-related offerings, even when the film being featured was not a war movie. For instance, in December 1917, the new, elegant Rivoli Theater opened in New York City. The film that was chosen for this occasion was a Douglas Fairbanks feature, *The Modern Musketeer*. This was not a war film; however, the Fairbanks feature was preceded by a pageant entitled "Victory for Democracy." Other examples of such war-related programming included sing-alongs of patriotic songs before the film played, screening of advertising for Liberty Bonds, and linking of film advertising with war-related activities like the Red Cross. The Food Aministration had a set of slides made and distributed to theaters throughout the United States urging movie-going citizens to participate in the Second Food Pledge Card Drive of October 1917. There were also newsreels, chock full of war-related stories, and short war-related documentaries—*How Uncle Sam Prepares, Tanks at the Battle of Ancre,* and *Manning our Navy*—that made up the program at the neighborhood or downtown movie theater. Thus, while most of the feature films of World War I were not war films, the programming introducing those films was frequently war-related.

With the Armistice in November 1918, the popularity of war-related feature films declined. There was a resurgence of interest in the war film in the mid-to-late 1920s when such features as *Four Horsemen of the Apocalypse, What Price Glory? The Big Parade,* and *Wings* opened to critical and popular acclaim.

Leslie Midkiff Debauche

Bibliography

Brownlow, Kevin. *The War, the West and the Wilderness*. New York: Knopf, 1979.

Campbell, Craig. *Reel America and World War I: A Comprehensive Filmography and History of Motion Pictures in the United States, 1914–1920*. Jefferson, NC: McFarland, 1985.

Merritt, Russell. "D. W. Griffith Directs the Great War: The Making of *Hearts of the World*." *Quarterly Review of Film Studies* (Winter 1981).

Mould, David. *American Newsfilm 1914–1919: The Underexposed War*. New York: Garland, 1980.

Ward, Larry W. *The Motion Picture Goes to War; the United States Government Film Effort during World War I*. Ann Arbor, MI: University Microfilms International, 1985.

Fish, Hamilton (1888–1991)

Hamilton Fish attended the Plattsburg, New York, military training camp in 1915 and 1916 and later joined, as a white officer, the 369th Infantry Regiment, an all-black unit that became known as the "Harlem Hellfighters." While training in Spartanburg, South Carolina, a southern regiment threatened to beat up members of the 369th. Fish, who was devoted to his men, informed the adjacent regiment that the 369th would fight "to the death . . ." if attacked. No interregimental brawl ensued.

As a captain in the American Expeditionary Force, Fish and his regiment fought with distinction in the Meuse-Argonne offensive of 1918. His valor in the capture of the French village of Sechault on September 29 earned him the Silver Star and the French Croix de Guerre. He was promoted to major and served with the Army of Occupation in 1919.

Following the Armistice, Hamilton Fish was instrumental in organizing the American Legion and coauthored the Preamble to the legion's constitution. In 1920, Fish was elected to the House of Representatives from New York's 26th Congressional District and served in that capacity until 1944. He sponsored legislation giving benefits to veterans, civil rights for African Americans, establishing the Tomb of the Unknown Soldier, making Armistice Day a legal holiday, and adopting the "Star Spangled Banner" as the country's national anthem. Hamilton Fish died in 1991.

Manley R. Irwin

Bibliography

Fish, Hamilton. *Memoir of an American Patriot*. Washington, DC: Regnery Gateway, 1991.

Fiske, Bradley Allen (1854–1942)

When the Great War began in Europe, Bradley Allen Fiske had served the navy for thirty years. The greatest naval inventor of his generation, he served as second in command of the Atlantic Fleet and also in the war plans section of the General Board. As the aide for operations to Secretary of the Navy Josephus Daniels since February 1913, Admiral Fiske filled the navy's top professional billet. With the other aides—materiel, personnel, and inspections—he advised the secretary and sought to coordinate the work of the naval bureaus. Most important, he was responsible for war plans and efficient fleet operations.

Fiske found Daniels to be unfailingly polite but bereft of technical knowledge or familiarity with naval customs and traditions. While he supported civilian supremacy, Fiske wanted to create a naval general staff that would improve organization and administration. It appeared to Fiske that Daniels failed to see that his primary mission was not to democratize and "dry up" the navy but to maintain the service as a fighting machine. Daniels paid him no heed except to approve the creation of an Office of Aeronautics within Fiske's own office.

When war broke out in Europe, Daniels concluded that augmenting the navy's defensive strength would violate the administration's neutrality policy; therefore, he halved the recommendations of the General Board for fiscal years 1914 and 1915, making it impossible for the board to implement its policy of building forty-eight battleships by 1920. Nor would Daniels approve either realistic fleet war games or Fiske's administrative plan to have the bureaus prepare for war.

Rather than seeking Fiske's advice, moreover, Daniels relied upon his civilian assistant, Franklin D. Roosevelt, and upon some of Fiske's subordinates and failed to inform service personnel of administration policy. Furthermore, because of misunderstandings on the part of Daniels and Adm. Frank F. Fletcher, Fiske was denied the billet of commander-in-chief of the fleet. Fiske therefore felt that his position as aide for operations was becoming "excessively disagreeable."

The "disagreeableness" of Fiske's position increased after Daniels rejected the General Board's building and personnel programs for fiscal year 1916. Following additional attempts to have Daniels realize "[the] gravity of . . . unpreparedness of [the] fleet," Fiske concluded that Daniels wanted him out of the way but was not quite ready to press the point. While President Wilson kept the service estimates for fiscal year 1916 close to those of 1915, Daniels continued to reject Fiske's importunities to improve naval efficiency and particularly to create a naval general staff. As he saw it, no "emergency" existed.

On Dec. 3, 1914, Fiske noted in his diary, "I am liable to be bounced any day." Yet, he continued to push for an increase in personnel and concentration of the fleet. When Daniels, in his annual report, provided what he held was proof of the preparedness of the navy, Fiske decided he must go to Congress and to the American people. After telling Congress how he would operate the navy at war, Fiske shocked it, and the nation, by saying that it would take the United States five years to prepare for war and that a naval general staff would operate better than the aide system. Daniels overlooked him thereafter, his formerly cordial attitude changing to one of cold formality.

On Jan. 3, 1915, Fiske joined with five fellow officers and drafted legislation calling for an Office of Naval Operations whose chief of naval operations (CNO) would be "responsible for the readiness of the Navy for war and be charged with its general direction." Fifteen assistants would draft war plans. Fiske knew that passage of the bill would end his career.

Daniels said that he would "go home" if Fiske's bill passed but then stated he would aid its passage through the House. However, he got the Senate to change Fiske's wording—"A Chief of Naval Operations . . . who shall . . . be responsible for the readiness of the navy for war and be charged with its general direction"—to read instead "A Chief of Naval Operations . . . who shall be charged . . . with the operations of the fleet, and with the preparations and readiness of plans for its use in time of war." Daniels thus retained control in the hands of the secretary of the navy. Further, the bill deleted the fifteen assistants to draft war plans. On March 25, Fiske told Daniels that he wished to be relieved of his duties and, on April 1, submitted his letter of resignation. Daniels made it effective on May 11, after he had chosen Capt. William S. Benson, USN, to serve as the first CNO.

Despite his difficulties with Daniels, Fiske left Washington happy with the thought that he had awakened Congress to naval needs. Moreover, Daniels quickly accepted two of his suggestions: (1) a Navy Department agency for recognizing and developing new inventions and (2) the administrative section of the general war plan.

Ironically, three weeks after Fiske reported as president of the Naval War College at Newport, Rhode Island, President Wilson asked his service secretaries to draft an "adequate national defense" program for him to present to Congress in November. In mid-January 1916, Daniels offered Congress several recommendations that Fiske had made about improving the navy, although the secretary made no mention of the need for a naval general staff or powerful CNO. Fiske remained content with the knowledge that, even if the bureaus remained uncoordinated, the Office of Chief of Naval Operations, created by law, could be changed only by Congress.

On Aug. 29, 1916, Congress adopted the "reasonable" defense program President Wilson had presented the previous November. Included were several items Fiske had long called for: a Council of National Defense, a three-year building program to include 156 ships, a naval experiment laboratory, increased funding for naval aviation, augmented enlisted strength, a naval reserve, and staff aid for the CNO. Fiske thereupon commented that "I feel that I have not lived in vain."

In October 1916, Fiske published *The Navy as a Fighting Machine*, a fine exposition of the place of the navy in the nation's armory and of the missions it could perform. He also spoke of the many missions aircraft could perform at war and to this end worked hard to make a torpedo plane he had patented in 1912 efficient so that it could countermine defensive minefields and destroy enemy ships in their own harbors, which warships could not do.

On March 25, 1917, he obtained Daniels's permission to continue working on the plane, and interest in the plane grew markedly after the declaration of war in April 1917. It was the familiar story of "too little too late." Although tests were slated for Nov. 5, 1918, the Armistice was signed on the eleventh and plans for the plane were scrapped.

Some of Fiske's innovations remain valid today. He devised the strategic war game still employed. In organization and administration, he developed the Office of the Chief of Naval Operations, the Office of Aeronautics, and the administrative plan by which the bureaus report on their preparedness for war, the basis of modern supplementary and operational logistics plans. If Fiske failed, it was in his attempt to have military men rather than civilians responsible for conducting war.

Paolo E. Coletta

See also DANIELS, JOSEPHUS

Bibliography

Coletta, Paolo E. *Admiral Bradley A. Fiske and the American Navy.* Lawrence, KS: Regents Press of Kansas, 1979.

Cronan, W.P. "The Greatest Need of the United States Navy: Proper Organization for the Successful Conduct of War."

United States Naval Institute Proceedings 42 (July–August 1916).

Daniels, Josephus. *The Wilson Era.* 2 vols. Chapel Hill: University of North Carolina Press, 1946.

Morison, Elting E. *Admiral Sims and the Modern American Navy.* Boston: Houghton Mifflin, 1942.

Fiske, Harold Benjamin (1871–1960)

Harold Benjamin Fiske was graduated from the United States Military Academy in 1897. From then until the outbreak of the First World War, he served at a variety of posts in the United States and the Philippine Islands. In August 1909, he attended the Army School of the Line, where he became the honor graduate. He then moved directly to the Army Staff College as an instructor, where he served, with one short interruption, until he sailed for France with the 1st Infantry Division (Provisional) on June 12, 1917. During that "interruption," then Major Fiske served as the chief of staff of the U.S. Army's only provisional division.

During his tenure at the Staff College, Maj. Fiske delivered a lecture to a class of new second lieutenants. This lecture, the only published writing he ever produced, reveals a great deal about him as a professional officer. Despite the fact that the lecture was delivered in January 1917, when the authorized strength of a U.S. Army infantry company was 150 men, Fiske argued that the exigencies of the new war in Europe demanded that the figure be raised to 250. In an army where peacetime strength had been allowed to drift down to 50, this was a radical statement. It demonstrated, however, that at least some officers were paying close attention to events in Europe. The lecture also noted other changes in the armament of European armies, including the extensive use of grenades and a very large increase in the number of machine guns. Fiske recommended that the U.S. Army examine and consider adopting the machine gun ratio used by the Germans on the Eastern Front, where the war was more mobile. It would be mid-July 1917 before General Pershing's General Organizational Project was submitted to the War Department recommending, among other things, that the strength of the infantry company be raised to 250 men. It would be very much later before the impact of that change, and the weapons changes Fiske had noted, would be appreciated in the U.S. Army or its training bases.

On Aug. 7, 1917, Lieutenant Colonel Fiske was assigned to the newly created Training Section, G–5, Headquarters, American Expeditionary Force (AEF). He became chief of G–5 on Feb. 18, 1918, replacing Col. Paul B. Malone.

Fiske struggled against increasing odds to implement the training program demanded by General Pershing. The accelerating arrival of troops, the unplanned requirement for huge labor details, sickness (including the devastating influenza epidemic), and, finally, the quickening pace of combat all conspired to defeat an otherwise sensible training program. Unable to control the flow of troops through the training program, the G–5 section gathered many first-hand observations of troop performance in combat and fed those observations into a system that, had there been more time, would have rapidly improved training. Now Brigadier General Fiske was himself an observer with three different divisions in combat during critical periods. The deficiencies in infantry training noted in Pershing's final report are lifted directly from Fiske's final report.

Fiske's "After Action Report" on the activities of the G–5 section reflect the strongly expressed desires of the commander-in-chief. The report criticizes the War Department and unit commanders for the inability to fulfill the requirements of the AEF training system, but there is no criticism of the disrupting changes directed by the commander-in-chief or the lack of realism of the G–5 section. The most serious criticism of AEF training was Fiske's insistence that all unit officers attend AEF staff and specialist schools upon arrival in France regardless of when the parent unit was scheduled to enter combat. As a consequence, some units on arrival in France, were stripped of their officers and some noncommissioned officers, and, because of the demands of combat, were sent into the line under the command of strangers.

By August 1919, along with hundreds of other career officers, Fiske once again found himself a major. He did eventually recover his wartime rank and, following successful command of the Panama Department, retired a major general.

Douglas V. Johnson

Bibliography

Fiske, Harold B. *Notes on Infantry*. Ft. Leavenworth, KS: Army Schools Press, 1917.

Johnson, Douglas V. "A Few 'Squads Left' and Off to France." Ph.D. dissertation, Temple University, 1992.

Pershing, John J. *My Experiences in the World War*. New York: Stokes, 1931.

U.S. War Department. *Report of the Commander-in-Chief of Services and Staff Sections*. Vol. 14 of *The American Expeditionary Forces in the World War, 1917–1919*. Washington, DC: Government Printing Office, 1948.

Flamethrowers

Modern flame projection weapons were invented in 1906 and introduced in World War I by the German Army in 1914–1915. The first successful use by the Germans was during an attack west of Verdun on Feb. 26, 1915, in the Avocourt forest. Britain and France quickly followed with their own devices, the French using them liberally and the British more selectively. The U.S. Army did not deploy a portable flamethrower until World War II. In World War I the American Expeditionary Force (AEF) relied on the French to provide flamethrower support.

The flamethrower is essentially simple in its design, consisting of a container of flammable mixture of light and heavy oils, a container of propellant gas (usually nitrogen or carbon dioxide under pressure), a discharge tube with a nozzle, and an igniter device in the nozzle. In order to achieve man-portability, it was necessary to limit the weight of the apparatus, the duration of burn of the flammable contents, and the range that the mixture could be thrown, all of which restricted the combat usefulness of the flamethrower. Additionally, the operator could not distance himself from the flammable contents, thereby risking immolation if his tanks were ignited by rifle fire or some other enemy action.

Soldiers had an innate fear of death by fire because it was a weapon against which one could not easily defend. If confined to a hole, cave, or other restrictive space, there was no escape from the searing heat and the sudden consumption of all available oxygen. Flame as a weapon was not new in warfare, but its appearance as a mechanical device in World War I was facilitated by experimentation with volatile fuels that could be projected in a stream of fire.

The Germans used flamethrowers (*flammenwerfer*) in their many assaults on the fortifications of Verdun in 1916. Those weapons were capable of projecting a jet of flame about twenty yards beyond the nozzle with a duration of about two minutes. Each firing required a new ignition device for the nozzle.

Many attacks against British positions in the Somme sector by German flamethrower teams had mixed results. According to a British officer, whose anonymous account was published in 1917 in *The Times History of the War* (Vol. X, p. 425), the effects of the flame weapons "may be very easily exaggerated. When you see it for the first time, it rather gives you the jumps. It looks like a big gas jet coming towards you, and your natural instinct is to jump back and get out of the way. A man who thinks nothing of a shell or a bullet may not like the prospect of being scorched or roasted by fire." He went on to explain that the weapons had very limited range and the operator was exposed to return rifle fire or grenades. The soldiers nicknamed the flamethrower "devil's fire" but quickly got over their first fears. "The actual cases of burning by devil's fire have been very few," according to this eyewitness. Although the burning liquid would saturate and set fire to soldiers' clothing, as well as burn down the wooden revetments of the underground dugouts, the true value was both tactical and psychological.

British author Denis Winter noted in his book *Death's Men* that a burst from a portable flamethrower was accompanied by a "huge noise and vast black clouds [that] hid a jet which swelled to an oily rose six feet in diameter at its burning end." Soldiers lying flat on the ground might escape injury, but they were usually terrified the first time they came under flamethrower attack. Even if the operator of the flamethrower survived his own attack, his fuel was quickly exhausted, leaving himself exposed to the angry return fire of those who had just been the targets of his attack.

After the 28th Infantry Regiment of the U.S. 1st Division seized the village of Cantigny in the Picardy region north of Paris on May 28, 1917, French flamethrower teams were invaluable in driving the enemy out of their positions in basements and dugouts within the ruined village. The 28th Infantry's history noted that the French flamethrowers expedited the mopping up.

During the German attack on British lines at Ypres in August 1917, the British troops "fell back before the flames" but then rallied when "rifle bullets and flashing bayonets proved better than burning flames." The account from *The Times History of the War* continued, noting that as German flame bearers fell, the canisters pierced by British rifle fire, the burning liquid often set fire to German troops "who were seen to burn briskly. . . . It was a terrible sight to see these human torches writhing in the agony they had hoped to inflict on the British."

An American inventor, Joseph Menchen, presented the British War Office with a design for a heavy flamethrower device in March 1915. Initial attempts to mount the device in a caterpillar tractor, thus becoming a mobile flamethrower tank, were met with apathy by both the British commanders in France and the team developing the fighting tank for the Admiralty.

Tactically, all three belligerents using portable flamethrower weapons in World War I—Great Britain, France, and Germany—assigned them to the engineers. Flamethrowers were gluttons for petroleum products; the very high consumption rate of that precious commodity was an important constraint to their use. Trucks, tanks, and airplanes, only slightly more efficient in their consumption, demanded the priority on fuel oils. Despite all the drawbacks, the portable flamethrower survived attempts to outlaw it as an inhumane weapon of war, and it was used extensively by tactical units in World War II.

John F. Votaw

Bibliography

Langer, William L. *Gas and Flame in World War I.* New York: Knopf, 1965.
The Times History of the War. 22 vols. London: The Times, 1914–1921.
Winter, Denis. *Death's Men: Soldiers of the Great War.* London: Penguin Books, 1979.

Foch, Ferdinand (1851–1928)

Ferdinand Foch was the French Army's most important officer and military theorist in the First World War. He served as an army commander at the Battle of the Marne and in March 1918 was appointed supreme commander of the Allies and in August a marshal of France. He was the Allied military representative who dictated the terms of the Armistice to the Germans in November 1918.

Foch was born to a Catholic family in Tarbres in 1851. He was educated in a series of Jesuit schools, where he was an excellent student and a passionate believer, a faith that lasted his entire life and often brought him into conflict with his secular political masters. Despite his convictions, he chose a military career and attended the elite École Polytechnique in Paris, graduating in 1873 and receiving a commission in the field artillery. He saw only brief action in the Franco-Prussian War in 1870, but the sight of French military humiliation and the annexation of Alsace and Lorraine by the Germans affected him deeply. From then on, he was personally and professionally devoted to overturning both the psychological and material wounds that Germany had inflicted on France.

Even before the beginning of the war in 1914, Foch had achieved prominence within the army. His graduation from the École Supérieure de Guerre (the French war college) in 1887 marked him as a candidate for higher command. From 1895 to 1901, he served as an instructor of military theory at the college, a position that served to make him well known and influential to an entire generation of French officers. As a lecturer, Foch was spellbinding, brilliant, and charming. To the future generals of France, he ranged with ease and eloquence over the campaigns of Napoleon, the Prussian victories of 1862–1870, and the prospects for future wars. Foch diagnosed France's military ills as stemming primarily from a loss of will and spirit at all levels. The antidote, he felt, was to reinvigorate the French Army with the doctrine of the offensive. He defended his belief in the power of the attack despite the growing contradictory evidence that modern weaponry had made charges with bayonets and horse cavalry against machine guns and quick-firing artillery obsolete.

In 1908, he was appointed to head the École Supérieure de Guerre, a position of great influence within the army. It also brought Foch into contact for the first time with Prime Minister Georges Clemenceau, the man who approved his assignment. It was the beginning of a long and stormy relationship in which each needed the other but despised the other with equal fervor. Clemenceau, "the eater of clerics," was prominent within France for views opposing the institutional influence of Catholicism. As a journalist, he had defended Alfred Dreyfus in the long affair that divided France. Clemenceau was personally indifferent to religion. Foch, on the other hand, raised in a family of devout Catholics, was himself a believer and had a brother, Germaine, who was a Jesuit priest. Foch probably believed that France had fallen on hard times because its modernism had caused it to fall away from its historic faith. Perhaps the only thing that united Foch and Clemenceau was a love of France and a hatred of what Germany had done to it.

As head of the nation's war college, Foch made an impact on the French preparation for war in the last critical years before 1914. In 1910, he inaugurated a crucial dialogue with the head of the British staff college, General Sir Henry Wilson, over the proposed deployment of a British expeditionary force to France in case of war with Germany. The two became close personal friends, and through Wilson, Foch gained a voice in British military affairs that would be important to his own career in World War I and help cement the entry of Britain into the land war on the Continent. In 1911, Foch also worked behind the scenes to help engineer the promotion of General Joseph Joffre to the position of commander-in-chief of the French Army. Foch and his disciples on the General Staff believed that Joffre would be a pliable candidate in their determination to remold French war plans into a more offensive cast, and they were right. One of Foch's own students at the college, Louis Loyzeau de Grandmaison, became Joffre's chief of operations, rewriting the French Army's field manual and designing the operational scheme that became Plan XVII, France's war plan for 1914. Another, Maurice Gamelin, was appointed as Joffre's principle military aide and years later became commander of the French Army in the disastrous campaign of 1940.

In August 1914, Foch commanded XX Corps, the most elite formation of the army and the designated spearhead of the attack to retake Alsace and Lorraine. When war broke out, Foch immediately assembled his corps and proceeded according to plan. Prewar optimism of victory over the Germans was soon shattered, however. On August 20, just inside the border of Lorraine, XX Corps suffered a devastating defeat at Morhange that threw Foch back onto the defensive. He rallied his divisions around Nancy and defended against further attacks until called by Joffre to head a newly forming Ninth Army east of Paris.

During the critical Battle of the Marne in September, Foch maintained his determination to repulse the Germans, arguing against any further retreat and ordering attack after attack against the German Third Army. When the Germans finally withdrew, he advocated further attacks to outflank them in the so-called "Race to the Sea." From 1914 until the end of the war, Foch tirelessly promoted new attacks to break through the German defenses on the Western Front, believing that final victory could only be achieved by a German defeat in the West. In 1915, he was appointed commander of Army Group North, again building on his good relations with the British to try to achieve breakthroughs in May and again in September. Both failed with heavy losses. In 1916, Foch was designated to command French forces for the "Big Push" on the Somme, which the Allies again hoped would break through when the full weight of the British Army was thrown into the fray. This offensive also ended in failure and at great cost in casualties. For a while at the end of 1916, Foch was in disgrace, relieved of all command. France's political leaders by this time had begun to reassert themselves and now began to demand that generals begin to show real progress for the millions of lives being lost in the endless war of the trenches.

In 1917, Foch was recalled to duty after the failed Nivelle Offensive and the subsequent mutinies within the French Army. He was appointed chief of the general staff, and though still the consummate optimist, he now became more cautious and calculating in his approach to the war. When the commander of the British Expeditionary Forces, Sir Douglas Haig, revealed new plans for another great trench offensive at Ypres in 1917, Foch opposed them, arguing that terrain and the Germans would prevent any significant advance. This time he proved correct, and David Lloyd George, prime minister of Great Britain, noted approvingly his analysis of the military situation.

In November 1917, Foch was appointed chief of the Inter-Allied General Staff, his first step toward eventual appointment as supreme commander. In October, using their newly perfected infiltration tactics, the Germans had broken through the Italian front at Caporetto, menacing Venice and threatening to force Italy out of the war. At an Allied meeting in Rapallo on November 5, Foch argued vigorously for a stiffer defense and the firing of the incompetent Italian commander, Gen. Luigi Cadorna. When the Italians vacillated, Foch insisted on a meeting with King Victor Emmanuel III, where he secured Cadorna's dismissal and promised French troops and heavy artillery to shore up the front.

With the Italian front stabilized by year's end, attention returned to the Western Front. The German High Command of Gens. Paul von Hindenburg and Erich Ludendorff had finally forced Russia out of the war with the Treaty of Brest Litovsk and could now turn the full weight of the Germany Army to the West. Over the course of the winter, they assembled more than 200 divisions in France and Belgium, the first time since 1917 that they could muster such numerical superiority over the Allies. With the American divisions still arriving in France at a trickle, a window of opportunity existed in the spring of 1918 for Germany to win the war.

The success of the German attack against the British Fifth Army on the Somme caught all the Allies off guard and opened the way for Foch's elevation to supreme commander. Within several days the attack threatened to drive a wedge between the French and British armies, with General Haig's British forces falling back on the Channel ports to defend their link to Britain and with General Pétain shifting forces to guard the approaches to the French capital. Neither was willing to give troops to help the other. Finally, a conference was called on March 26, 1918, at the little village of Doullens and Foch was given the cumbersome title of "commander for the coordination of the British and French armies near Amiens" with the full support of Haig and Gen. John J. Pershing, the American Expeditionary Force commander. Pétain was more grudging in ceding authority but finally agreed. Foch immediately ordered French troops to act as reserve for the British seeking to restore the front. The next month the role was reversed as the Germans struck toward Paris and British and American troops were ordered into the line to prevent a German breakthrough. In all, the Germans launched five major offensives in the first half of the year. In each instance, Foch's ability to shift forces from one sector to another was critical in defeating each German advance.

Foch was not content, however, merely to stay on the defensive. By June, he felt that the Germans must be running out of combat strength. With divisions from all three of the major Allies, he assembled a counterattack under French Gen. Charles Mangin to pinch off the bulging German salient between Paris and Reims. The launching of this attack on July 18 threw the Germans onto the defensive and forced Hindenburg and Ludendorff to call off their offensives altogether. In August, Foch, who by now had been named marshal of France as well as commander-in-chief of the Allied armies in France, agreed with Haig that final victory in 1918 was possible. His general plan for the remainder of the war consisted of launching one offensive after another by French, British, and now American troops in such rapid succession that the Germans could no longer cover the front with their dwindling reserves. From August to November, the Germans gave up ground all along the front. Progress was slow but constant, and casualties, although high for the Allies, now seemed to be having a positive result.

With the cracking of the Hindenburg Line in September and the American offensive in the Meuse Argonne, the German government began to look for a way out of the war. Foch was empowered as the Allied military representative to state the military terms for an armistice. After some confusion on both sides over the details of the arrangements, the German delegation signed the Armistice to end the war at 5 A.M. on Nov. 11, 1918. The effective date of the Armistice was 11 A.M., November 11. The war was over, and the difficult problems of peace took the fore.

Foch had gained very favorable terms for France in the Armistice, but it was also the beginning of the unravelling of the war-winning alliance. Foch insisted that the entire left bank of the Rhine be evacuated by the Germans and that bridgeheads be established over the Rhine at key points to prevent a resumption of German hostilities. The British and Americans began to wonder, with some reason, whether the French had designs over traditionally German territory. Foch argued publicly with Clemenceau over the terms of the Treaty of Versailles, arguing prophetically that it was no peace treaty but only an armistice for twenty years. In the end, both men went into rather unhappy retirements, watching events turn against France in the 1920s. In 1928, shortly after attending the funeral of his old friend Douglas Haig in a driving rain, Foch came down with pneumonia and died at the age of seventy-seven. He was buried with full military honors in Les Invalides in a side chapel near the tomb of Napoleon.

Foch's greatest contribution to the war effort was his ability to create the unified command that had eluded the Allies from the beginning of the war. His theories about modern warfare proved to be far off the mark, and his perennial pressing for offensives nearly drove the French to defeat in 1914 and exhaustion later in the war. At the right moment in 1918, though, he was the right man for the job of pulling all the Allies together. He had excellent relations with the British throughout the war, and after it became clear that Pershing was not going to allow any amalgamation of the American soldiers into European armies, he settled into a fairly smooth relationship with the Americans. He clearly possessed the talent for command of an alliance army, understanding that the armies of different and proud nations had to be led by persuasion and inspiration rather than abrupt orders. His bitter disputes with Clemenceau tarnished his reputation within France after the war, but his concerns about France's security, always foremost in his mind, were borne out within the next generation.

James K. Hogue

See also CLEMENCEAU, GEORGES; JOFFRE, JOSEPH

Bibliography

Barnett, Correlli. *The Sword Bearers*. New York: Morrow, 1964.

Foch, Ferdinand. *The Memoirs of Marshal Foch*, trans. by T. Bentley Mott. Garden City, NY: Doubleday, Doran, 1931.

Liddel Hart, Basil. *Foch: Man of Orleans*. Boston: Little, Brown, 1932.

Toland, John. *No Man's Land: 1918—The Last Year of the Great War*. Garden City, NY: Doubleday, 1980.

Food Administration

See UNITED STATES FOOD ADMINISTRATION

Food and Fuel Control Act

See LEVER FOOD AND FUEL ACT

Ford Motor Company

Prior to the entry of the United States into the Great War in April 1917, Henry Ford had been a strident pacifist, adamantly prohibiting the sale of Ford Motor Company products to any of the belligerents and underwriting the ill-conceived Ford Peace Ship. Despite his efforts, Britain obtained Ford cars through unauthorized suppliers. Fords proved to be excellent ambulances and utility vehicles and saw service in France. Upon his country's declaration of war, however, Ford abruptly changed his mind, pledging, "Everything I've got is for the government and not a cent of profit." By war's end, Ford would make significant contributions in the production of tractors, vehicles, aircraft engines, and submarine chasers. His nonprofit pledge would become a matter of controversy.

Ford's first contribution to the Allied war effort came in the form of tractors. The Fordson Tractor was put in production in late 1917, and 7,000 were delivered to Britain the following April. The Fordson boosted Britain's agricultural output and lessened dependence on imported foodstuffs.

It was not difficult for Ford to convert civilian automobile production to military specifications. The famous Model T was a durable machine, easily adapted to the muddy conditions of the Western Front. By war's end, about 39,000 Model T's of various types saw service in France and Belgium.

Henry Ford also turned his attention to aircraft production, vowing to mass-produce 150,000 airplanes for the Allied effort. It was a task he grossly misread, and his company did not produce a single plane during this period. Production of the American-designed Liberty engine proved to be a more realistic challenge for the industrialist. Ford engineers solved a critical problem with Liberty cylinders, cutting both the time and cost of production. Ford Motor manufactured all the cylinders for the Liberty, delivering 415,377 in 1918. The company followed Packard and Lincoln in production of complete engines, delivering 3,940 by the end of the war.

As part of the war effort, Ford also entered the unfamiliar realm of shipbuilding. The task was to build fast submarine chasers called Eagle Boats. With government financing, Ford built a new plant on the Rouge River to produce the craft, which was 204 feet in length with a 25-foot beam. Despite the fact that he did not have an experienced workforce, Ford turned out sixty Eagles. The ships proved seaworthy, but they did not see action in the war.

Another enterprise, more in line with Ford Motor Company's expertise, was the design of a new weapon—the tank. Ford designed and tested several models of tanks and won an army contract for production of a two-man six-ton tank costing $6,000 per unit. The contract was signed in early November 1918, but the signing of the Armistice a week later led to its cancellation.

Like most American industries, Ford Motor Company was unable to convert to war production as easily as anticipated. Unrealistic goals were set, especially in aircraft production. Nevertheless, Ford made significant contributions to the Allied war effort. Not surprisingly, its most important achievement was the production of highly reliable cars, trucks and tractors at low cost. On the other hand, Ford's ventures into shipbuilding, aircraft engine manufacture, and the supply of other war fighting materials that were not related to the automobile industry were astonishingly successful.

George M. Lauderbach

See also EAGLE BOATS; FORD PEACE EXPEDITION

Bibliography

Lacey, Robert. *Ford: The Men and the Machine*. New York: Ballantine, 1986.
Nevins, Allan, and Frank E. Hill. *Ford: Expansion and Challenge, 1915–1933*. New York: Scribner, 1957.

Ford Peace Expedition

The eruption of the European war in August 1914 stunned and shattered the American peace movement. Although most members waited for the war to end before renewing their peace efforts, a small group of pacifists did decide to act. The Ford Peace Expedition sought through personal diplomacy to end the war by peaceful means. Members of the expedition and their European sympathizers, believing that the fighting could be ended through reason rather than by military victory, in 1915 called the Neutral Conference for Continuous Mediation to take place in 1916 in Stockholm, the first unofficial gathering of concerned neutrals that ever tried to mediate an ongoing war.

In the first months of the war, Hungarian-born feminist and journalist Rosika Schwimmer and others held mass peace meetings that sent thousands of petitions to President Wilson asking him to mediate among the warring nations. Julia Grace Wales, a Canadian English instructor at the University of Wisconsin, formulated a detailed plan calling for delegates from neutral countries to meet at a conference for continuous mediation and act as a clearinghouse, receiving and disseminating peace proposals to and from the belligerents. Through this process, the pacifists hoped to create a just and lasting settlement. Miss Wales's plan was passed by the Wisconsin state legislature and by the newly formed Woman's Peace Party and was approved by the International Congress of Women (later known as the Women's International League for Peace and Freedom) in May 1915. When Wilson declined to act, the pacifists planned to establish an unofficial conference, which they hoped would be taken over by the neutral governments.

Learning that Henry Ford had agreed to fund educational peace efforts, the pacifists persuaded him, in late November 1915, to finance their venture in Stockholm. Within ten days, Ford chartered space on the *Oskar II* and sailed for Norway with more than 160 hastily gathered delegates, mainly ministers, teachers, suffragists, and lecturers. Ford, seeking publicity for his educational venture, invited journalists, almost all of whom mocked the endeavor, to attend as well as a group of college students, who came as observers. Most prominent Americans were also asked. All declined. Schwimmer's authoritarian control, marked in part by her unwillingness to discuss her plan of action, caused dissension among the passengers on the *Oskar*. Ford, ill and impatient with the resulting tension, took the next boat home as soon as they landed in Christiania.

The peace pilgrims held mass meetings in Norway, Sweden, Denmark, and Holland and invited peace societies in these countries and Switzerland to send national delegations to the Stockholm conference; then the Ford expedition disbanded. The Neutral Conference, comprised of approximately thirty delegates from six countries, sat from the end of February through May 1916. Few of the delegates were international experts, and though all opposed the war, they seldom agreed on what their role should be in ending it.

Still, the conscientious delegates, mindful of the possible historic importance of their work and of its immediate significance, strove to overcome their differences and, through an elaborate committee system, produced two appeals.

The first, addressed to the neutral nations, urged them to initiate mediation among the belligerents without delay. The second, addressed to the belligerents, suggested a permanent peace based on self-determination of populations, disarmament, freedom of the seas, parliamentary control of foreign policy to prevent secret diplomacy, the establishment of an international organization to mediate disputes between the states, and other principles later included in the Fourteen Points. These appeals were published in the world press and presented to the concerned government officials, who listened but gave no formal approval.

Ford's associates, regarding the entire peace conference as an unprofitable arm of the automotive company, decided too much money had been spent for value received; by the end of August, only six delegates from the Ford group were organizing various educative activities. After Wilson called on the belligerents to seek "Peace Without Victory" in January 1917, Ford abruptly ended his peace work and pledged his fortune to the manufacture of war materiel.

Although it failed in its immediate objective, the peace mission dramatized the hope of peace by daring, in the name of the people, to ask warring nations to settle their disputes, not on the basis of conquest but according to the principles of justice and humanity.

Barbara S. Kraft

Bibliography

Kraft, Barbara S. *The Peace Ship: Henry Ford's Pacifist Adventure in the First World War*. New York: Macmillan, 1978.

Nevins, Allan, and Frank E. Hill. *Ford: Expansion and Challenge, 1915–1933*. New York: Scribner, 1957.

Fosdick, Raymond Blaine (1883–1972)

A student at Princeton University while Woodrow Wilson was its president, Raymond Blaine Fosdick acquired from Wilson a strong commitment to public service and a belief in the perfectibility of a morally ordered society. Fosdick earned a B.A. and an M.A. in history, then studied law in evening classes at the New York School of Law, where he earned an L.L.B. in 1908. For a year the penniless law student taught history classes in exchange for a room at New York's Henry Street Settlement.

Service with New York City's watchdog commission monitoring city government established Fosdick's reputation as a dauntless opponent of corruption and inefficiency. Fosdick's assistance to John D. Rockefeller, Jr., chairman of a grand jury investigating prostitution and police corruption in New York City, began what was to be a lifelong association with the young oil magnate and led, in 1913, to Fosdick's appointment as an investigator for Rockefeller's Bureau of Social Hygiene (BSH). Fosdick and Rockefeller believed that policy efficiency and incorruptibility bore directly on the problem of eradicating prostitution.

In 1916, Fosdick reported to Secretary of War Newton D. Baker on the organizational causes of, and possible remedies for, the plague of alcoholism and venereal disease disabling the troops sent to Mexico in the Punitive Expedition. After studying Canadian army training camps, Fosdick recommended, and Baker established a committee of leaders of social service agencies to oversee welfare and recreation in U.S. Army and National Guard training camps. Fosdick chaired the Commission on Training Camp Activities (CTCA), focusing his energies and expertise on suppressing prostitution and the sale and use of liquor in zones around the army camps and naval and marine stations.

Conditions in France made control of liquor and prostitution much more difficult than in the United States, and so, in 1918, Secretary of War Baker sent Fosdick to tour the front as his special representative to study the situation and make recommendations. Closer cooperation among the civilian agencies operating within the American Expeditionary Force resulted, as did a unified fund-raising campaign for war-work organizations. Fosdick's tour also sharply altered his perceptions of war and prepared him for a deeper commitment to international organization and conflict resolution through diplomacy, sanctions, and collective military action. After the Armistice, he returned to France as a special aide to General Pershing, once again to promote harmony among the social service agencies.

After serving briefly as undersecretary-general of the League of Nations, Fosdick entered private law practice. He was founder, member, and president of the League of Nations Non-Partisan Association from 1923 to 1935, during which time he wrote and spoke in support of United States membership in the League. He was a trustee of the Rockefeller Foundation from 1921 to 1935 and its president from 1936 to 1948. When he retired from public life in 1949, he then devoted himself to the perpetuation of the memory of Woodrow Wilson by supporting the publication of *The Papers of Woodrow Wilson*.

Weldon B. Durham

See also COMMISSION ON TRAINING CAMP ACTIVITIES

Bibliography
Fosdick, Raymond B. *Chronicle of a Generation: An Autobiography*. New York: Harper, 1958.

Foulois, Benjamin Delahauf (1879–1967)

Benjamin Delahauf Foulois enlisted in the United States Army before the Spanish-American War and served in Puerto Rico and the Philippines, where he was commissioned in 1901. He was detailed to aviation duty in 1908. His first assignment was with lighter-than-air craft, but in 1909, he flew as the navigator (and observer) on the final acceptance flight of the army's first airplane. The plane was wrecked, however, before Foulois had any pilot training.

Lieutenant Foulois was ordered to take the repaired plane to Fort Sam Houston, Texas, and thus became the army's first assigned aviator. With written instructions from the Wright brothers and the aid of a small ground crew, he taught himself to fly. He was in his element among fliers and ground crews. It was in this environment that Foulois excelled. Always on the alert to improve plane safety, he replaced the Wright "B" landing skids with wheels and installed both the first safety belt and the first air-to-ground wireless set. In 1915, he took command of the army's first tactical air unit, the 1st Aero Squadron. Its support of the Punitive Expedition to Mexico in 1916, though only marginally effective, was, nevertheless, the first aviation support of ground operations.

With the United States entry into World War I, Major Foulois was promoted to brigadier general and in November went to France as the Chief of the Air Service, American Expeditionary Force (AEF). Foulois and his staff were resented by those already in the theater of operations, particularly by BGen. William "Billy" Mitchell. Unfortunately, Foulois lacked the administrative skill needed to create an efficient operation. As a result, he was reassigned as chief of the Air Service, First Army, and then on Aug. 1, 1918, at his own request, he relinquished this post to Mitchell to become deputy chief of the Air Service under Gen. Mason Patrick.

In the postwar years, Foulois became a leading advocate of an independent air force. He became the assistant chief of the U.S. Air Corps in 1927, having for the second time in his career advanced to the rank of brigadier general without having been a colonel. He directed the air maneuvers of 1931 and in December was promoted to major general and became the chief of the U.S. Air Corps.

His advocacy of a separate air arm, which began in the 1920s, finally resulted in congressional approval for a general headquarters air force, a consolidated headquarters to control air operations. In the process, however, Foulois had made many enemies in Congress, in the Department of the Navy, and on the Army General Staff. In February 1934, President Roosevelt, during a confrontation with the commercial airlines over airmail contracts, directed the U.S. Air Corps to deliver the mail. He took this step on the ill-considered advice of MajGen. Foulois, who had only a week to begin this service. The result was poor mail service, many dead pilots, and an embarrassed president. The outspoken general became embroiled in a congressional investigation with no allies except the general public. Realizing that the Air Corps would be dragged down with him if he continued, he retired on Dec. 31, 1935. He died on April 25, 1967.

Charles A. Endress

Bibliography
Foulois, Benjamin D., with Carroll V. Glines. "Early Flying Experiences." *Air Power Historian* (April, June 1955; April 1956).
———. *From the Wright Brothers to the Astronauts: The Memoirs of Major General Benjamin D. Foulois*. New York: McGraw-Hill, 1968.
Shiner, John F. "Benjamin D. Foulois: In the Beginning." In *Makers of the United States Air Force*, ed. by John L. Frisbee. Washington, DC: Office of Air Force History, 1987.
———. *Foulois and the Army Air Corps*. Washington, DC: Office of Air Force History, 1983.

F

Four-Minute Men

Four-Minute Men were volunteers for the propaganda effort on the home front in World War I who brought the message of patriotism, sacrifice for the war effort, and "100% Americanism" to the diverse populations of the United States. Organized under the auspices of the Committee on Public Information (CPI), 75,000 Four-Minute Men (along with a Women's Division and a group for children) were an integral part of what CPI director George Creel called "a vast enterprise in salesmanship, the world's greatest adventure in advertising."

Throughout the country, at public gatherings and in local movie houses, the Four-Minute Men presented inspirational and instructional speeches composed in Washington in support of the war effort. Their talks were designed to cover briefly (about four minutes being the time it took to change reels of silent films) such topics as food conservation, morale at home, and the various Liberty Loan campaigns.

By September 1918, the Four-Minute Men had discovered the ease with which the patriotic message could be spread through popular song. Armed with slides containing the words to the latest hit songs composed for the war effort along with familiar popular and patriotic tunes, speakers used their four minutes to urge audiences to new heights of patriotic enthusiasm, if not to a high standard of musical performance. These brief interludes encouraged active participation by the audiences, and the most popular songs included "The Star Spangled Banner," "Columbia, Gem of the Ocean," and "Keep the Home Fires Burning." The Four-Minute Men asserted the effectiveness of group singing in their efforts with the declaration that "the Singing Army, whether it be a fighting army or a working army, cannot be beaten." Their enthusiasm and spirit, if not their musical leadership abilities, were appropriate to the crusade for "100% Americanism" during the war years.

Barbara L. Tischler

Bibliography

Creel, George. *How We Advertised America, The First Telling of the Amazing Story of the Committee on Public Information that Carried the Gospel of Americanism to Every Corner of the Globe.* New York: Harper, 1920.

Fourteen Points

Woodrow Wilson's Fourteen Points Address of Jan. 8, 1918, as the *New York Herald Tribune* described it at the time, is "one of the great documents in American history." The most important statement of war aims advanced by any leader during the First World War, the address was a series of proposals for territorial settlements and a timely reiteration of what is often referred to as the New Diplomacy. The President's utterance was in part intended as a response to V.I. Lenin's peace decree of late 1917 and the Bolshevik government's publication of the Allies' secret treaties for parceling out captured territories after the war; however, the Fourteen Points also had roots in Wilson's peace efforts prior to American involvement in the war in April 1917.

In 1914–1915, practically all European political parties, on both the Left and the Right, supported their respective government's war efforts in great displays of national unity. But by 1916, that unity had begun to crack under the weight of unending mass slaughter at the Marne, Tannenburg, the Somme, and Verdun. In all of the Allied countries (and in Germany as well), increasing numbers of liberals, laborites, and socialists wavered in their previous views on the war; they began to hope for a peace based not on outright victory but rather on one grounded in principles that would put an end to territorial conquest, secret diplomacy, militarism, and atavistic nationalism. It was in this context that the so-called New Diplomacy emerged.

During the first two years of the war, the United States struggled to maintain neutrality in the face of the British naval blockade of Europe and German submarine warfare. American neutrality was always a very fragile thing, and President Wilson came to realize that the best way to keep the country out of war was to try to bring about a negotiated settlement. Twice, in 1915 and 1916, he sent his personal emissary, Col. Edward M. House, to Europe for direct parlays with the heads of all the belligerent governments. House was not successful. Then, after his reelection in 1916, Wilson issued a peace note asking the warring nations to state under what terms they might be willing to come to the peace table. This appeal, too, proved unavailing. Thereupon he decided on a bold stroke—to go before the United States Senate on Jan. 22, 1917, and call for a "Peace Without Victory." Wilson derived most of the ideas for this address from several liberal, pacifist, and socialist groups in the United States and their counterparts in Europe. The "Peace Without Victory" address advanced a penetrating critique of European imperialism, militarism, and balance-of-power politics—the leading causes of the war, the President maintained. In their stead, he advocated the creation of a "community of nations," sustained by procedures for the arbitration of future disputes between nations, a dramatic reduction of armaments, adherence to the principles of the equality of nations and self-determination, freedom of the seas, and collective security. The chief instrumentality of the new world order was to be a league of nations. The intellectual precursor of Wilson's more famous pronouncement of a year later, this initial synthesis of the New Diplomacy was, in a very real sense, *the* Wilsonian manifesto of the Great War.

The "Peace Without Victory" formulation met with an unprecedented outpouring of praise from progressive groups at home and abroad. When it was read aloud to the annual conference of the British Labour Party, the delegates stood and cheered Wilson's name for five minutes. One American commentator hailed the President for having rendered "a service to all humanity that it is impossible to exaggerate," while another stated that the address was "destined to an immortality as glorious as that of the Gettysburg Address." Even so, the governments of both opposing coalitions still hoped for a decisive victory and either ignored the speech or greeted it with contempt. Then, a week later, Germany announced the resumption of unrestricted submarine warfare, beginning on Feb. 1, 1917. By the end of March, Wilson had concluded that war had been thrust upon the United States. In his war address, however, he said that his goals were the same as before and implied that Americans would be fighting to establish some measure of "Peace Without Victory," a program attainable now, apparently, only through the crucible of war.

In exchange for American belligerency, Wilson did not impose any conditions on the Allies; in light of their self-aggrandizing territorial ambitions, then, considerable divergence in avowed purposes remained unreconciled as Congress voted on the war resolution. Though a day of reckoning was inevitable in any case, the problem would soon become exceedingly vexatious owing to epochal upheavals in Russia.

In March 1917, the repressive autocracy of Tsar Nicholas II had been overthrown by an ostensibly social democratic coalition led by Aleksandr Kerenskii. The United States was the first major power to recognize Kerenskii's Provisional Government. In the meantime, while the new regime affirmed its commitment to the war, the starving and poorly equipped Russian Army had begun to mutiny. In May, the soldiers' and workers' councils of Petrograd issued proclamations on behalf of peace based on self-determination and prevailed upon the peoples of Europe to demand that their governments repudiate plans for conquest. By autumn, the Provisional Government teetered on the brink of collapse. On November 7, the Petrograd Soviet, led by Lenin and Leon Trotsky, overthrew Kerenskii; the new Bolshevik government issued a peace decree, calling for the "immediate opening of negotiations for a just and democratic peace." Two weeks later, to expose the unholy lie of Allied war aims, the Bolsheviks published the secret treaties to which Nicholas II had been a party. Shortly afterward, Russian representatives engaged the Central Powers in peace negotiations at Brest Litovsk. For all practical purposes, Russia had left the war.

In conjunction with the October defeat of the Italian Army at Caporetto as well as the growing disenchantment among many groups in Great Britain and France, these developments in Russia dealt the Allied position a potentially mortal blow. In view of all the foregoing circumstances—including the Allies' persistent disinclination to embrace ideologically progressive war aims—Wilson decided to respond to the Bolshevik challenge and thereby remove the suspicions hanging over the Allied cause.

In late December 1917, the President instructed Colonel House to put to work the special team of experts known as "The Inquiry." Over the next two weeks, they drew up specific recommendations on a wide variety of economic, political, and territorial matters. On their own, Wilson and House hammered into shape a series of (as it turned out, fourteen) concise, categorical paragraphs on war aims on January 5. Three days later, Wilson delivered his Fourteen Points Address to a joint session of Congress. He began by asserting that the Central Powers were merely exploiting the precepts of the New Diplomacy in order to absorb Russia. Even so, there was no good reason not to respond to the Bolsheviks' earnest invitation to the Western powers to state their terms. The conception of the Russian people "of what is right, of what is humane . . . must challenge the admiration of every friend of mankind," he said. Whether the Bolsheviks believed it or not, it was his "heartfelt desire" that America might "be privileged to assist the people of Russia to attain their utmost hope of liberty and ordered peace." The American people saw clearly that unless justice were done to others, it would not be done to them. "The programme of the world's peace, therefore, is our programme; and that programme, the only possible program, as we see it, is this."

The first five of the Fourteen Points were fairly familiar to most progressive internationalists: covenants openly arrived at and the abolition of secret treaties; absolute freedom of the seas; the removal of all economic trade barriers and the establishment of the equality of trade conditions; the reduction of all national armaments to the lowest point consistent with domestic safety; and the impartial adjustment of all colonial claims in observance, in part, of the principle of self-determination.

The sixth point demanded the evacuation of all Russian territory and the "unembarrassed opportunity for the independent determination of her own political institutions." Points seven through thirteen specified the evacuation of Belgium; the return of Alsace-Lorraine to France; the readjustment of Italian frontiers along clearly recognizable lines of nationality; autonomous development for the peoples of Austria-Hungary, the Balkans, and the Turkish portions of the Ottoman Empire; and the creation of a Polish state assured of free and secure access to the sea. The fourteenth point, for Wilson, was the most important one of all: "A general association of nations must be formed under specific covenants for the purpose of affording mutual guarantees of political independence and territorial integrity to great and small states alike."

It was for these things that the United States and its associates were fighting, he said in conclusion. Before serious discussions could begin, however, the United States must know for whom Germany's representatives spoke—whether for the Reichstag majority or for the military party whose creed was imperial domination. The single thread that ran through the whole program (as Wilson had said many times before) was "the principle of justice to all peoples and nationalities and the right to live on equal terms of liberty and safety with one an-other, whether they be strong or weak." This was the only principle upon which the American people could act. "The moral climax of this the culminating and final war for human liberty has come, and they are ready to put their own strength, their own highest purpose, their own integrity and devotion to the test."

Since the height of the Cold War in the late 1950s and 1960s, the preponderance of historical interpretations—most notably those of Arno J. Mayer, William Appleman Williams, N. Gordon Levin, and Lloyd C. Gardiner—have emphasized the degree to which Wilson's program was formulated in response to, and the degree to which its provisions were influenced by the revolution in Russia. Yet, save the very one on Russia, Wilson did not define a single point that was in any way inspired by the Bolsheviks. The seven proposals for territorial adjustments would have been advised in any circumstances. The remaining six constituted a reprise of Wilson's pronouncements before the United States had entered the war—and long before revolutionary upheaval in Russia appeared imminent. Neither was the address the opening salvo of a counterrevolutionary campaign. Not until the spring of 1918, when a German victory became a distinct possibility, did Wilson's historical appreciation of the Russian upheaval begin to show signs of wear and hostility toward Lenin. Then, too, one of the most striking aspects of the Fourteen Points, in its restatement of the "Peace Without Victory" address, was its uncompromising anti-imperialism. Wilson did not consider liberalism and socialism, practically speaking, as irreconcilable—not in the sort of community of nations he envisioned, in which such contending forces would naturally audit and regulate one another.

In any event, Lenin himself reportedly hailed the address "as a great step toward the peace of the world" and arranged for its publication in *Izvestiya*. American representatives and Bolsheviks worked together to circulate millions of copies in Petrograd and Moscow and among German soldiers inside Russia. The entire French Left, along with most of the French press, greeted the Fourteen Points with unqualified approval—despite the circumspect attitude of Georges Clemenceau's government. In Great Britain, whereas the London *Times* commented that the speech presumed "that the reign of righteousness upon earth is already within our reach," the London *Star* implored British politicians "to emulate . . . the greatest

American president since Abraham Lincoln." Without actually endorsing its contents, Prime Minister David Lloyd George said he was "grateful" that his and Wilson's peace policies were "so entirely in harmony."

In the United States, the approbation heaped upon the address approached phenomenal proportions. Although a few Republicans took sharp exception to the point on free trade, praise from both parties was generous. The headline that the New York Times ran above its main editorial, "The President's Triumph," was indicative of the general reaction across the country. Wilson had articulated "the very conscience of the American people," said Hamilton Holt in the Independent. The social reformer Jane Addams acclaimed the address "the most profound and brilliant formulation as yet put forth by any responsible statesman of the program of international reorganization." Socialist party leader Eugene V. Debs pronounced the Fourteen Points "thoroughly democratic," deserving of "the unqualified approval of everyone believing in the rule of the people, Socialists included."

If Wilson's objective was to rally doubters to see the war through to the bitter end—and if these kinds of responses to the Fourteen Points were any guide—then it seemed that he had succeeded magnificently. His championship of the New Diplomacy, like a miraculous cure, breathed new life into the hope that a better world could come of the violent and complicated spectacle through which humanity was passing. Moreover, some ten months later, Prince Max of Baden, chancellor of Germany, appealed to Wilson to take steps for the restoration of peace based on the Fourteen Points. The Germans thus had decided to put their fate in Wilson's hands; it is probable that the address helped to bring the fighting to an end sooner than might have otherwise been the case.

In the ensuing Armistice negotiations of October 1918, it quickly became apparent that the Allies, nonetheless, held serious reservations about the American program. For example, the British refused to consider "freedom of the seas" until after the peace treaty was signed. The French demanded that their army be permitted at least temporarily to occupy the east bank of the Rhine. Both governments said that Germany must compensate civilians for all damage she had inflicted upon them and their property. At the Paris Peace Conference itself, Wilson confronted additional difficulties. Virtually all the great Allied powers intended to annex one former German or Turkish colony or another, in violation of the fifth of the Fourteen Points. Because his concern about getting the League of Nations established was so great, Wilson felt compelled to compromise on these and other principles embodied in his address.

The results were most unfortunate. Many influential American liberals and supporters on the left now believed that the President had betrayed his own program. When he returned to the United States with the League of Nations as part of the Treaty of Versailles, many of them joined Wilson's die-hard conservative opponents, to prevent ratification of the treaty and American membership in the League.

In fairness to Wilson, it should be emphasized that at Paris, as in the bitter parliamentary struggle with the Senate, he had confronted a uniquely herculean task. His devout hope was that, once the passions of war had dissipated, the League of Nations would be in a position to rectify most of those injustices in the peace settlement for which the progressives reproached him. Although his great dream ended in supreme tragedy, Wilson would in time ascend to a position of central importance in the history of international relations in the twentieth century. And the Fourteen Points would continue to stand, as a disillusioned former Wilsonian once put it, as "a great inspiration to the believers in democracy in all lands."

Thomas J. Knock

See also BREST LITOVSK; INQUIRY, THE; PARIS PEACE CONFERENCE

Bibliography

Gardner, Lloyd C. *Safe For Democracy: The Anglo-American Response to Revolution, 1913–1923.* New York: Oxford University Press, 1984.

Knock, Thomas J. *To End All Wars: Woodrow Wilson and the Quest for a New World Order.* New York: Oxford University Press, 1992.

Levin, N. Gordon. *Woodrow Wilson and World Politics: America's Response to War and Revolution.* New York: Oxford University Press, 1968.

Link, Arthur S., et al. *The Papers of Woodrow Wilson.* 69 vols. Princeton, NJ: Princeton University Press, 1966–1993.

Mayer, Arno J. *The Political Origins of the New Diplomacy, 1917–1918.* New Haven, CT: Yale University Press, 1959.

Francis, David Rowland (1850–1927)

David Rowland Francis was born in Richmond, Kentucky, and earned a B.A. in the classics in 1870 at Washington University in St. Louis. For six years Francis worked at his uncle's St. Louis commission house. Then he and his brother Sidney opened their own firm, D.R. Francis and Brother, Grain Merchants. Francis attended the 1884 Democratic National Convention as one of Missouri's delegates-at-large. From 1885 to 1889, he served as the St. Louis mayor, cutting spending, obtaining reduced interest rates on the city's debt, and collecting $1 million owed to the city by the Missouri Pacific Railroad. He fought special-interest measures and improved municipal services. His reputation as a reform mayor won him the Missouri governorship from 1889–1893. As governor, he cut spending and taxes and shepherded an Australian ballot act through the legislature.

Francis became secretary of the interior during the closing months of Grover Cleveland's second administration. On his recommendation, Cleveland withdrew 21 million acres of public land as forest reserves and vetoed a bill that would have allowed future presidents to modify or reverse such withdrawals. Distaste for William Jennings Bryan's 1896 presidential candidacy caused Francis to withdraw from politics, but he remained active in civic affairs, concentrating upon the Louisiana Purchase Exposition and World's Fair (1903–1904) in St. Louis.

Francis returned to politics in 1908, although he never again held elective office. In 1916, he reluctantly accepted the post of United States ambassador to Russia. State Department officials apparently felt that his business acumen would enable him to negotiate a new commercial treaty to replace the agreement that Russia had terminated in 1912. His failure to obtain the desired treaty was a result of war and revolution, not his inadequacies as a diplomat.

Nevertheless, Missouri politics had not prepared Francis well for diplomacy. His wife remained in the United States, and he took little part in Petrograd's social life, preferring in general to limit his contacts to members of the American community. After the United States entry into World War I, American officials seemed to recognize Francis's limitations and frequently bypassed him, often relying upon American National Red Cross officials for information. President Woodrow Wilson sent Edgar Sisson, a journalist and associate of George Creel, to investigate conditions in Russia and to disseminate anti-Bolshevik propaganda. Sisson and the Red Cross representatives each believed themselves to be independent of and superior to Francis. They undercut each other as well as the ambassador. Sisson even launched an ineffective campaign to remove Francis.

Francis initially welcomed the Russian Revolution and supported Kerenskii's Provisional Government. He distrusted the Bolsheviks; although soon after they seized power, he recommended that they be accorded diplomatic recognition in the hope that the United States could then favorably influence the terms of their proposed peace settlement with Germany. But as their radical policies became clear, Francis came to support the policy of nonrecognition and rejected all Bolshevik requests to move his residence to their new capital, Moscow.

As Russia's political situation deteriorated, the ambassador's Missouri-honed talents proved more appropriate. He once faced down a mob threatening to occupy the American embassy, warning that he would shoot the first man who came through the door. When the Germans approached Petrograd in early 1918, Francis, then the dean of the diplomatic corps, organized the diplomats' evacuation to Vologda and later to Archangel. By that time he welcomed Allied intervention in Russia.

In late 1918, Francis's health broke. A United States warship took him for medical treatment to London, whence he returned to the United States. He never fully recovered, although he lived until Jan. 15, 1927.

Mary Childers Mangusso

Bibliography

Cockfield, Jamie H., ed. *Dollars and Diplomacy: Ambassador David Rowland Francis and the Fall of Tsarism.* Durham, NC: Duke University Press, 1981.

Francis, David R. *Russia from the American Embassy.* New York: Scribner, 1921.

Kennan, George F. *Soviet-American Relations, 1917–1920.* Princeton, NJ: Princeton University Press, 1956–1958.

Stevens, Walter B. *David R. Francis, Ambassador Extraordinary and Plenipotentiary.* St. Louis: N.p., 1919.

U.S. Department of State. *Papers Relating to the Foreign Relations of the United States.* Supplement, *The World War, 1916; 1917, Russia.* Washington, DC: U.S. Government Printing Office, 1918.

Franco-American Relations

"Lafayette, we are here," proclaimed an American officer at the tomb of the Revolutionary War hero as the first units of the American Expeditionary Force (AEF) arrived in France in 1917. Such a bold statement might indicate a long history of mutual friendship between the United States and France, but in actuality, Franco-American relations were seldom as smooth as the Lafayette legend would suggest. The only major instance of cooperation between the two countries between 1792 and 1940 was their joint military effort against Germany in World War I. And even that fell apart shortly after the Armistice, a victim of rival visions of Europe and the world.

Throughout the nineteenth century, tensions between France and the United States were in evidence. Napoleon's Continental System nearly led to war; only Great Britain's more stringent policies diverted the United States from a showdown. Relations again came close to the breaking point in the 1830s during the presidency of Andrew Jackson. Another period of serious tension occurred in the 1860s during Napoleon III's adventure in Mexico. Around the turn of the century, a number of irritants strained relations between the two republics. France, for example, offered diplomatic support to Spain during the Spanish-American War. French colonial adventures in West Africa appeared to threaten the U.S. client nation of Liberia. The French, in turn, became alarmed by the economic expansion of the United States, fearing a loss of markets to this increasingly aggressive competitor.

When World War I began, the United States adopted an official stance of neutrality. Much debate has ensued about whether the United States was truly neutral in that struggle. But whether or not President Woodrow Wilson was emotionally pro-Entente is less important than the actual nature of the war itself. The most important fact was that the Entente Powers controlled the seas and were therefore in a position to maneuver neutrality practices and maritime customs to their own advantage.

Between 1914 and April 1917, the United States loaned more than $2 billion to Britain and France, a financial infusion that rescued the Entente states from a dire economic situation and made possible their prosecution of the war. This economic policy also stimulated American industry, since much of the money loaned to Britain and France was used to purchase American goods and supplies. At this point in time, Germany was also free to contract American loans. But since the Entente Powers controlled the high seas, German leaders saw little point in borrowing money to purchase goods that could not be delivered. It might, therefore, be argued that American economic policy gave the United States an increasingly vested interest in an Entente victory. It is not possible to assert, however, that this situation influenced President Wilson's decision to enter the war in April 1917. The determining factor was Germany's decision to break the Entente blockade and to drive for victory through the use of unrestricted submarine warfare—a tactic that subjected United States ships and sailors to attack.

The period of United States participation in the First World War marked a high point in Franco-American cooperation. Shortly after the United States declared war on Germany, French president Raymond Poincaré appointed André Tardieu as high commissioner for France in the United States. Tardieu envisioned the pooling of all resources among the Entente and the United States. During the next eighteen months in Washington, he worked closely with American officials to organize the purchase and transfer of millions of tons of sugar, grain, steel, artillery shells, and soldiers to France. The American manpower contribution to the war effort was perhaps the most remarkable. In April 1917, the United States Army was composed of only 200,000 officers and men. By the end of the war, the American Army had increased to 4 million soldiers, half of whom had gone to France for combat duty. Some 50,000 U.S. servicemen were killed in the war, and an additional 230,000 were wounded; direct costs to the United States for prosecuting the war came to around $21 million. Although miniscule compared to France's human and economic sacrifice, in the end American manpower and economic resources served to shorten the war and guarantee victory over the Central Powers.

Even before the Armistice of Nov. 11, 1918, the spirit of Franco-American cooperation began to fade as President Wilson's vision of the postwar order in Europe collided with that of French Premier Georges Clemenceau. Wilson advocated a peace without annexations or indemnities, whereas Clemenceau sought a settlement that would guarantee future French security against its materially and demographically stronger German neighbor. Wilson's Fourteen Points, articulated in an address to Congress on Jan. 8, 1918, called for the return to France of the "lost provinces" of Alsace-Lorraine. But his principle of national self-determination clashed at virtually every point with initial French proposals for a settlement with Germany. Clemenceau proposed, in addition to the repatriation of Alsace-Lorraine, a very substantial reparation settlement, restoration to France of Rhenish territory lost in 1815, French ownership of the Saar coal basin, an independent Rhineland state to serve as a buffer between France and Germany, and inter-Allied occupation of the bridges across the Rhine River. In Eastern Europe, Clemenceau's insistence upon containing Germany through the recognition of strong and economically viable frontier nations made it virtually inevitable that the new Poland and Czechoslovakia would contain substantial German minority populations. The two heads of government also differed over the nature of Wilson's proposed League of Nations. Whereas Wilson saw it as an impartial arbiter of international disputes, to which Germany would ultimately belong, Clemenceau viewed it as a continuation of the wartime alliance to preserve the eventual peace settlement.

These opposing viewpoints led to frequently acrimonious exchanges at the Paris Peace Conference. During negotiations over the settlement with Germany, both Wilson and Clemenceau were forced to retreat from their maximum positions. In the end, Germany was punished, but not as severely as she might have been had Wilson remained in Washington. Alsace-Lorraine was returned to France; Germany was limited to a defensive military force of 100,000 men; the Saarland's coal mines were ceded to France for fifteen years; the Rhineland remained German but would be occupied by Allied forces for fifteen years to insure Germany's fulfillment of the terms of the settlement. The Treaty of Versailles also called for creating the League of Nations and diverted the controversial question of the magnitude of German reparations by establishing a special commission for its resolution; the commission deliberated another year and a half before submitting a bill for war damages to Germany.

Questions of imperial rearrangement also agitated Franco-American relations in the immediate aftermath of World War I. The Fourteen Points had called for an "absolutely impartial adjustment of all colonial claims" and for "an absolutely unmolested opportunity for autonomous development" for the nationalities of the Ottoman Empire. France's secret wartime understandings with Britain, Italy, and Russia, however, envisioned a wholesale partition of Asiatic Turkey. Furthermore, Germany's defeat raised the question of the disposition of her colonies in Africa and the Pacific. Differences were resolved with the adoption of the Mandate System, a scheme whereby trusteeship of the Ottoman nationalities and German colonies was vested in the League of Nations; the latter in turn assigned administrative mandatory responsibility to one of the large victorious powers. France thus acquired additional African territory and political control of Syria and Lebanon.

Even though victorious, the French entered the postwar period in a highly insecure frame of mind, painfully aware of Germany's economic potential and of the fact that Germany's population was half again that of France. The Treaty of Versailles, therefore, was presented to the French Parliament for ratification not as a huge success but rather as the best that could be had under the circumstances. In order to win French acceptance of the settlement, Wilson and British Prime Minister David Lloyd George offered France a joint treaty of military guarantee. According to its terms, the United States and Britain were obligated to come to France's aid immediately should the latter be the victim of unprovoked aggression by Germany.

The Anglo-American Treaty of Guarantee has been criticized on a number of grounds. Wilson, for example, was probably unwise to have proposed such an old-style treaty without first consulting the Senate; the French were naive to accept such a promise guaranteed only by the whims of American and British public opinion. It may be concluded, however, that the proposed treaty represented a reasonable method of achieving compromise among the Allied and Associated Powers under the pressures of the peace conference. In any case, evidence indicates that Wilson saw the treaty only as a temporary measure to reassure the French until the League of Nations became fully operational.

In many respects, the most interesting reaction to the Treaty of Versailles occurred in the United States. The fact that the United States emerged from the First World War as the wealthiest and most powerful nation on earth meant little to the American people. To the latter, the end of the struggle did not mean the acceptance of new worldwide responsibilities but rather an opportunity to return to the temporarily interrupted course of domestic concerns. Here is where Wilson's vision conflicted with that of the majority of the American people, for Wilson had insisted that the Covenant of the League of Nations be written into all the treaty settlements. Thus, ratification of the Treaty of Versailles by the Senate implied an American leadership role in the League. In the Senate, debate over the treaty focused squarely on the Covenant. Given the temper of American public opinion, Wilson's uncompromising, all-or-nothing stance virtually guaranteed that the Senate would fail to ratify the treaty.

The Anglo-American Treaty of Guarantee to France was to have been considered at the same time as the Treaty of Versailles. But in the heat of the debate and ultimate rejection of the latter, the former never even reached the floor of the Senate. Although that instrument was quickly forgotten by Americans, from the French perspective an important part of the peacemaking bargain had fallen by the wayside. The failure of the Anglo-American guarantee, coupled with Washington's insistence on the full repayment of France's war debts (which the French believed ought to be written off or reduced as part of the U.S. contribution to victory) created a legitimate sense of grievance among France's postwar leaders. The search for alternative methods to preserve its economic and military security became an important feature of France's postwar diplomacy.

William Shorrock

Bibliography

Blumenthal, Henry. *Illusion and Reality in Franco-American Diplomacy, 1914–1945*. Baton Rouge: Louisiana State University Press, 1986.

Kaspi, André. *Le temps des Americains: le concours Americain á la France, 1917–1918*. Paris: Université de Paris I, 1976.

Nere, Jacques. *The Foreign Policy of France from 1914 to 1945*. London: Routledge & Kegan Paul, 1975.

Zahniser, Marvin R. *Uncertain Friendship: American-French Diplomatic Relations Through the Cold War*. New York: Wiley, 1975.

Franklin, Phillip Albright Small (1871–1939)

Phillip Albright Small Franklin served as the head of the Shipping Control Committee of the United States Shipping Board from February 1918 until December 1918. He was born in Ashland, Maryland, the son of Col. Walter S. and Mary Franklin. At age eighteen, he went to work for the Atlantic Transport Corporation in Baltimore as an office boy. By 1903, he had worked his way up to vice president and director of the International Mercantile Marine (IMM) in New York. In 1916, Franklin became president of the firm. In this position he managed the American Pioneer Line, the Panama Pacific Lines, and the American Merchant Line. At a later period, IMM also controlled the White Star Line, the Red Star Line, and Leyland Lines.

In April 1917, the Council of National Defense appointed Franklin as an adviser to William Denman, chairman of the United States Shipping Board. When Denman's successor as Shipping Board chairman, Edward N. Hurley, needed an experienced shipping man to untangle the congestion at American and French ports in early 1918, it was only natural to turn to Franklin, who was recognized as one of the leading shipping authorities in the United States. At this point, Franklin was already serving as chairman of the advisory committee approving the design of the fabricated ship and as chairman of the committee to advise the United States Shipping Board on the style and type of ship to be built for war purposes.

As a condition for taking the chairmanship of the Shipping Control Committee, Franklin demanded full authority to allocate merchant tonnage as he saw fit. In November 1918, Chairman Hurley decided he had made a mistake in abdicating so much of the Shipping Board's authority. Accordingly, the board passed a resolution calling for Franklin to be subject to the board's guidance. Shortly thereafter the war ended, and Franklin resigned on Dec. 11, 1918.

Edward Hurley, in his memoir, *The Bridge to France*, credits Franklin with making a valuable contribution to the war effort by greatly reducing the turn-around time of cargo ships in service to France. Even President Wilson praised Franklin for serving his country so well. Franklin was honored for his war services by receiving the Distinguished Service Medal from the United States, the Legion of Honor from France, and the Order of Leopold from Belgium. He died on Aug. 14, 1939.

Charles Tull

See also SHIPPING CONTROL COMMITTEE

Bibliography

Hurley, Edward N. *The Bridge to France.* New York: Ozer, 1974.

Heaton, Herbert. *A Scholar in Action: Edwin F. Gay.* Cambridge: Harvard University Press, 1952.

Franz Ferdinand, Archduke (1863–1914)

Franz Ferdinand's birth on Dec. 18, 1863, placed him fourth in line to the throne of the Habsburg Empire. By 1896, however, with the murder-suicide of the Crown Prince Rudolf and his mistress Maria Vetsera, Franz Ferdinand had emerged as the heir apparent to the Habsburg throne. His superficial education, which emphasized Habsburg history intermixed with doctrinaire Catholicism, had prepared him inadequately for succession to the throne. He possessed little power of concentration with subjects that bored him, and he developed a pronounced intolerance for Jews, Protestants, Freemasons, Social Democrats, liberals, and ethnic Magyars. Around people with whom he was not comfortable, Franz Ferdinand seemed aloof. He did maintain Habsburg tradition and served as an officer in the army, a tradition with which he seemed quite comfortable. A major general at age twenty-eight, Franz Ferdinand intended to pursue a strictly military career and diligently avoided matters of state.

In 1900, Franz Ferdinand married a Czechoslovakian commoner, Sophie Chotek. Emperor Franz Joseph, never close to his nephew and disgusted with his choice of a wife, forced a morganatic marriage. Feeling ostracized from power, Franz Ferdinand devoted his time to his wife and children and concentrated on his rose garden, antique collecting, and hunt-

ing, only gradually becoming involved in governmental policies.

Despite his many reactionary attitudes, the heir presumptive grew into something of a reformer, particularly in questions of the internal structure of the empire and army affairs. Franz Ferdinand was terribly concerned with the disruptive influence of the Magyars in Hungary, holding them responsible for the rise of nationalism among the other ethnic minorities within the empire. He worked to curtail Magyar influence in imperial affairs, limiting Magyar importance outside Hungary whenever possible.

In Austria-Hungary's Balkan provinces, nationalism had become a serious issue—generally known as the South Slav question. Franz Ferdinand and others within the government, as well as many Serbs and Croats, favored an arrangement called "trialism," under which a third state would be created within the empire. It would play a role equal to that of Austria and Hungary in governing the empire and would grant similar autonomy on local issues. Had the scheme been proposed twenty or thirty years sooner, it might have delayed or somehow prevented the disintegration of the Habsburg empire, but at that late date nothing short of independence would satisfy the growing number of nationalists in the Balkan provinces.

Franz Ferdinand had always believed that while the South Slav question was in flux, the army would be a useful tool to govern the Balkans, fostering loyalty toward the dynasty and mitigating the disruptive influences coming out of Hungary. However, to accomplish those goals, there had to be substantial changes within the military establishment. The archduke was a strong backer of the reforms pushed by the chief of staff, Conrad von Hötzendorf. Franz Ferdinand even engineered the latter's return to office when he fell into the emperor's disfavor. Finally in 1913, the emperor named Franz Ferdinand General Inspector of all the armed forces. In effect the heir now commanded all Habsburg forces.

As inspector general of the army, Franz Ferdinand accepted an invitation to review the troops engaged in summer maneuvers near Sarajevo in June 1914. Unofficially, he hoped to improve relations between Vienna and the restive provinces. Unfortunately, his arrival coincided with the 525th anniversary of St. Vitus's Day, and to radical Bosnian groups like the Black Hand, Franz Ferdinand was the reincarnation of their former Turkish ruler. Led by Col.

Dragutin Dimitrijevic, chief of intelligence of the Serbian army, a group of young nationalists planned to kill the heir. The plot was an open secret within the Serbian government as early as a month prior to the visit, but officials did little to warn the Austrian government or prevent implementation of the plan. An assassination attempt in the morning of June 28, 1914 failed, but while driving from the Town Hall to a military hospital to visit those wounded in the morning attack, the Archduke and his wife met their assassin, Serbian extremist Gavrilo Princip, eye to eye. Two shots were fired. The Archduke and his wife died within the hour. Ironically, the Serbs had killed the most influential opponent of a preventive war with Serbia in the entire empire and plunged the world into war.

Steven Wright

Bibliography

Cassels, Lavender. *The Archduke and the Assassin*. New York: Stein & Day, 1984.
Dedijer, Vladimir. *The Road to Sarajevo*. New York: Simon & Schuster, 1966.
Kann, Robert A. *Erzherzog Franz Ferdinand Studien*. Vienna: Verlag fur Geschicte und Politik, 1976.
Kiszling, Rudolf. *Erzherzog Franz Ferdinand von Österreich-Este: Leben, Pläne und Wirken am Schickslasweg der Donaumonarchie*. Graz: Hermann Bohlaus Nachfolger, 1953.
Remak, Joachim. *The Story of a Political Murder: Sarajevo*. New York: Criterion Books, 1959.

Franz Joseph, Emperor (1830–1916)

Franz Joseph was born in Schönbrunn Palace near Vienna and became emperor of Austria in 1848, and king of Hungary in 1867, when he divided his empire, creating the Dual Monarchy known as Austria-Hungary. At eighteen, he was proclaimed emperor of Austria during the revolution of 1848, which forced the abdication of Ferdinand I. Franz Joseph was able to hold on to his royal prerogatives and Austrian lands throughout the revolutions which rocked all of western Europe at this time, and in 1851, he witnessed a further centralization of his absolute powers with the promulgation of a new constitution engineered by his interior minister, Albert Bach. In 1854, Franz Joseph married the Duchess Elizabeth of Bavaria, who remained a forceful influence on his policies until she was assassinated in Geneva in September 1898.

Rooted in the thesis of the divine right of kings and Roman Catholicism, Franz Joseph's reign lasted sixty-eight years. Under his leadership, in 1859, Austria slipped into war against the Italian kingdom of Piedmont-Sardinia and France over control of Lombardy in northern Italy and was defeated. In 1866, Austria lost control of Venezia, its final possession in Italy. These losses and growing demands for liberalization within Austria forced Franz Joseph to experiment with new constitutional charters, but he never met the expectations of liberals and various ethnic minorities for greater regional autonomy. Austria's defeat by Prussia in the Seven Weeks' War in 1866 and growing animosity toward Austria in Hungary were the backdrops for the creation of the Dual Monarchy, which gave equal status to both halves of the former empire. The emperor controlled foreign policy for both parts and ruled as emperor of Austria and king of Hungary. Each half of the empire had its own parliament and legislated its own internal affairs, while a higher parliament, composed of sixty representatives from both Austria and Hungary, met to determine policies common to the entire Dual Monarchy.

Austria's military reverses precipitated a significant diminution of Habsburg prestige, particularly in the eyes of Russia. In addition, Franz Joseph had antagonized Russia during the Crimean War. In light of these conditions, his foreign minister, Count Gyula Andrássy, encouraged collaboration with a united Germany, and Franz Joseph formed the Dual Alliance in 1879. Engineered by German "Iron" Chancellor Bismarck, this alliance remained a central pillar in Austrian foreign policy until the death of Franz Joseph. The emperor was more reserved toward Italy, which joined this pact, thus creating the Triple Alliance in 1882.

Essentially a feudalist-centralist and conservative who rejected parliamentary rule, Franz Joseph never resolved the problems or claims of the many minorities within his empire. The Slavs did not share equally in the privileges granted to the German Austrians; the Bohemians (Czechs) and Poles felt underrepresented in the government, while the South Slavs, Croats, Magyars, and Slovaks felt deprived in the Hungarian half of the empire. Pan-Slavism, encouraged by Russia, fanned separatist movements within the empire. Tensions grew to a fevered pitch over the Austrian annexation of Bosnia-

Herzegovina in 1908. Nearby, the small independent state of Serbia felt itself threatened by the policy of trialism advanced by the heir to the throne, the Archduke Franz Ferdinand. Trialism would allow Austria to annex Slavic Serbia and the crown of Serbia would be joined to the Dual Monarchy. Since the advent of Pan-Slavism, Serbia had become increasingly bent on separation from Austria-Hungary and was bitterly opposed to trialism. Then, on June 28, 1914, Franz Ferdinand and his wife, the Archduchess Sophie, were assassinated in Sarajevo by Gavrilo Princip, a Serbian terrorist. Franz Joseph, now eighty-four, received the news in Ischl by telegram, and his aide-de-camp reported that the emperor was deeply shaken. He feared divine retribution for Franz Ferdinand's morganatic marriage had caused the assassination.

After the deaths, Austria responded with an extraordinarily harsh ultimatum to Serbia drafted by Count Leopold Berchtold, the foreign minister, who earlier had proposed a preventive war against both Serbia and Italy. Encouraged by Germany, Austria issued a forty-eight-hour deadline with the ultimatum on July 23, 1914. Although Franz Joseph had formerly cultivated a peace policy, he allowed Berchtold and his cabinet to persuade him to deal harshly with the obstreperous Serbs, and public opinion in Austria supported that stance. The ultimatum began by restating the 1909 agreement by which the Serbs promised not to interfere with the Austro-Hungarian annexation of Bosnia, heretofore opposed by the Greater Serb movement. It went on to demand the supression of all anti-Austro–Hungarian propaganda, the dissolution of all Greater Serbia organizations, and the elimination of the illicit arms traffic along the Serb-Bosnian border. Even more intrusive was the insistence that Austro-Hungarian police and judicial officials deal with the conspirators. After the Serbs refused to satisfy the terms of the ultimatum, which would have seriously impaired their sovereignty, the Austro-Hungarian representative in Belgrade, Baron Vladimir von Giesl, returned to Vienna. But Franz Joseph, moving cautiously, remarked that breaking off diplomatic relations did not necessarily mean war.

Two events then occurred shifting the difficulties between Austria and Serbia from the local to the international level. Russia openly supported Serbia and began to mobilize its armed forces, while Germany sent a "blank

check" to Austria promising military aid in the crisis. Serbia, while conciliatory, would not compromise its sovereignty, and Franz Joseph reluctantly allowed war to be declared on Serbia, with the rest of Europe dividing into two camps like a series of falling dominoes.

The emperor, who had had a heart attack in the spring of 1914, appointed Gen. Conrad von Hotzendorf to command Austria's armies. However, Franz Joseph attempted to maintain control over the war effort by insisting that all decisions of the General Staff have his blessing. Initially, the Austrians suffered very heavy casualties at Lemberg at the hands of the Russians and Serbs. However, the German and Austrian armies enjoyed impressive successes on the Eastern Front and in the western Balkans. Yet Austrian troops did not measure up to German standards, a source of acute embarrassment to Franz Joseph when he was visited by Kaiser Wilhelm II in Vienna in November 1915.

Events began to sour for the emperor with the Austrian failures in Italy and against the Russians in Galicia. Franz Joseph became more of a recluse at Schönbrunn, not taking part in the strategic decisions made at military headquarters at Teschen in eastern Silesia. His old friend, General von Bolfras, kept him apprised of all military decisions. The emperor was becoming increasingly pessimistic about the outcome of the war. However, Franz Joseph continued to collaborate with the German high command, agreeing that Poland should be unified and independent in a union with Austria and Germany. When his advisers pointed out the contradictions in this plan, he would tolerate no criticism, seeking to support fully the German military leaders.

The heir apparent, Archduke Charles, who worked with the High Command at the beginning of the war, was called home to Schönbrunn with his family. The presence of the heir's children playing in the palace lightened Franz Joseph's declining spirits. While the emperor did not bring the heir into decision-making circles, he did instruct his cabinet ministers to instruct Charles about the operations of their various departments to familiarize him with his future duties and responsibilities.

By November 1916, Franz Joseph was in failing health, suffering from respiratory ailments. In his final days, he was encouraged by news from the front that General Falkenhayn's German and Austrian forces had taken Transylvania and were about to capture

Wallachia and Bucharest. He died in the evening of Nov. 21, 1916, and his body lay in state on November 30 at the Cathedral of St. Stephen. Mourning was led by the new Emperor Charles, and his wife, Empress Zita. Franz Joseph had been the last powerful monarch of the Austro-Hungarian Empire, an empire that reached back to Charlemagne's coronation in Rome, and an empire that very shortly would be forever split asunder.

Barbara Bennett Peterson

See also CHARLES I

Bibliography
Crankshaw, Edward. *The Fall of the House of Hapsburg.* New York: Viking Penguin, 1963.
Hantsch, Hugo. *Die Geschichte Österreichs, 1648–1918.* Graz: Verlag Styria, 1953.
———. *Die Nationalitätenfrage im Alten Österreich.* Vienna: Herold, 1953.
Redlich, Joseph. *Emperor Francis Joseph of Austria, A Biography.* New York: Macmillan, 1929.

F

G

Garfield, Harry Augustus (1863–1942)

Harry Augustus Garfield, director of the U.S. Fuel Administration in World War I, was a distinguished political scientist, educator, and college administrator. He was born in Hiram, Ohio, the first son of President James A. Garfield. In 1879, his father sent him to the exclusive St. Paul's School in Concord, New Hampshire, where he remained for two years before entering Williams College. In fact, he was accompanying Garfield to the President's twenty-fifth class reunion at Williams when the assassin Charles J. Guiteau shot his father, who later died.

Upon graduating from Williams in 1885, Garfield returned to St. Paul's School for a year to teach Latin and Roman history. He then studied at Columbia University Law School in New York, All Soul's College at Oxford, and the Inns of Court in London.

Garfield was admitted to the Ohio bar and opened a legal practice in Cleveland with his brother, James R. Garfield. Between 1892 and 1895, Garfield also taught courses on contracts at the law school of Western Reserve University. His practice was eminently successful, as were his business ventures in railroading and coal mining. But Garfield was not content with amassing money or with a hectic law firm. A rather reserved and formal man who cherished books and reading, he personified the patrician gentleman-scholars of the Gilded Age. Like them, he also dabbled in reform politics. In 1896, he organized the Cleveland Municipal Association to fight political corruption.

Despite the success of his reform movement, he jumped at the opportunity to return to education when, in 1903, the new president of Princeton University, Woodrow Wilson, offered him a chair of politics. Wilson was assembling a young and reform-minded faculty. When, in 1908, the presidency of Williams College became available, Wilson had no reservations about recommending his friend Garfield. Garfield modeled his administration at Williams on Wilson's programs at Princeton, inaugurating curriculum reforms designed to raise academic standards.

When Wilson was organizing his war administration, therefore, he readily turned to Garfield. On Aug. 23, 1917, the President appointed Garfield director of the U.S. Fuel Administration, whose responsibility it was to allocate and coordinate coal and oil resources in wartime. Like many of the agency's 18,000 workers, Garfield served without pay. As administrator, he sought to stimulate coal production by offering various incentives, including subsidies. He also undertook stabilization of fuel prices by coordinating government purchases of bituminous coal, and by assuring a balance between civilian and military requirements. At the same time he conducted effective public relations campaigns to reduce coal consumption by various means such as heatless Thursdays. Enjoying a close relationship with Bernard Baruch, chairman of the War Industries Board, Garfield was often able to secure compliance with his policies because Baruch could withhold priorities for scarce materials from business people who were uncooperative. Since petroleum became increasingly important in wartime and was absorbing a considerable share of his attention, Garfield delegated most of his responsibilities concerning oil to a new Oil Division in his agency which President Wilson had established on Jan. 11, 1918. Mark

Requa, a successful mining engineer, was appointed to head the unit.

After the war, Garfield returned to Williams College, where he remained as president until 1934. His wartime experiences convinced him more than ever of the need for government officials who held high ideals of good citizenship and public service. In pursuance of that goal at his own college he persuaded Bernard Baruch to finance the establishment of an Institute of Politics at Williams that would bring public leaders to the campus. Garfield retired in 1934 and moved to Washington, D.C., where he died on Dec. 12, 1942.

Gerald D. Nash

Bibliography

Botsford, Eli Herbert. *Fifty Years at Williams.* Pittsfield, MA: Eagle Printing and Binding, 1940.

Garfield, Harry A. *Lost Visions.* Boston: N.p., 1944.

U.S. Fuel Administration. *Final Report of the U.S. Fuel Administration.* Washington, DC: Government Printing Office, 1921.

Garrison, Lindley Miller (1864–1932)

The son of a physician who had abandoned medicine to become an Episcopal priest and professor of canon law, young Lindley M. Garrison also decided to prepare for the ministry; however, after a year at Harvard and then graduation from the University of Pennsylvania Law School, he turned his attention to jurisprudence. By 1888, the able, young attorney became senior partner in his own firm in Camden, New Jersey, and later senior partner in yet another firm in Jersey City. His natural proclivity for the law, his unquestioned ability, and an astounding capacity for hard work caused his rise and prominence in his profession.

Because of his skill in legal matters as well as his dedicated activity within the Democratic Party, he was selected for the position of secretary of war in President Woodrow Wilson's newly formed cabinet in 1913. An eleventh-hour selection, he nosed out James Luther Slayden, member of the House of Representatives from San Antonio. Garrison was a popular choice with the army in general and the General Staff in particular, and he proved to be an able administrator and organizer. He was an inspiration for many in the military who were stationed in the District of Columbia. Unfortu-

nately, he also proved to be a political lightning rod and an embarrassment to Wilson, who occasionally complained of his secretary's absolute forthrightness. In short order, Garrison found himself on a collision course with the leadership of both the House and Senate Military Affairs committees, James Hay (D., Virginia) and Francis Warren (R., Wyoming), respectively.

The difficulty centered about Garrison's advocacy of the Continental Army Plan whereby the Regular Army, reserve force, volunteers, and militia would be raised to a strength fluctuating between 400,000 and 500,000. There was at once an outcry from those opposed to preparedness, including many in the Democratic Party, such as William Jennings Bryan and Claude Kitchin. Robert LaFollette also opposed the measure although George Chamberlain (D., Oregon), a rising figure in military matters in the Senate, generally supported the proposal. Among the most vocal and effective opponents were the National Guard and its public spokesman, the National Guard Association, an enormously powerful lobby with influence in every state in the Union.

Earlier, Wilson supported the plan, but his enthusiasm waned as the opposition, particularly in the Democratic Party, grew. In the end, the President withdrew his support in favor of Hay's and the National Guard's plan, which was passed as the National Defense Act of 1916. Garrison, whose bad temper and plain-spoken words had caused problems with Congress, abruptly resigned. In a show of solidarity, Assistant Secretary of War Henry Breckinridge also resigned. Courageous, blunt, and determined, Garrison was sorely missed by many on the General Staff, but Wilson was not sorry to see him go. The President replaced him with a former student and Democrat, Newton D. Baker of Cleveland, Ohio. After his resignation, Garrison returned to private practice in New York City. He died in Sea Bright, New Jersey, on Oct. 19, 1932.

James W. Pohl

See also CONTINENTAL ARMY RESERVE PLAN

Bibliography

Houston, David F. *Eight Years with Wilson's Cabinet.* New York: Doubleday, Page, 1926.

Link, Arthur S. *Wilson.* 5 vols. Princeton, NJ: Princeton University Press, 1947–1965.

Pohl, James W. "The Congress and the Secretary of War, 1915." *New Jersey History* (Fall 1971).

———. "Slayden's Defeat." *Military History of Texas and the Southwest* (1972).

———. "Woodrow Wilson Chooses a Secretary of War." *Historical Musings* (Fall 1971).

George V (1865–1936)

As hereditary monarch in a parliamentary democracy, King George V of Great Britain was more a symbol of sovereignty than a wielder of political power. His direct involvement in the conduct of policy was therefore minimal, and he played only a marginal role in the crisis leading up to the outbreak of war in 1914. When Prince Henry of Prussia (the German kaiser's brother) paid him a social call at the end of July, King George expressed dismay over the descent toward armed conflict. The prince misinterpreted these words as a promise of British neutrality in the event of conflict. The incident was substantially used by the Germans as a propaganda point against "perfidious Albion" in the contest to win American support, or neutrality, in the conflict.

George's role in the actual conduct of the war was similarly circumscribed. He did not generally intervene in the policy-making process; instead, his function was to serve as a symbol of national unity transcending party politics and the divisions of class. Much of his time and energy was taken up with visits to naval bases, the armies in France, hospitals, industrial areas, munitions factories, areas in Britain hit by zeppelin attacks, and the like. On Oct. 28, 1915, during one such inspection tour of the troops in France, the horse he was riding reared in fright at the cheering of the men and slipped on the mud. The king suffered two fractures of the pelvis and had to be hospitalized.

To the extent that he did try to play a role in policy making, George focused on upholding ethical standards and common decency in the conduct of warfare. He was concerned that enemy prisoners of war be accorded fair and humane treatment while in British custody and objected to the imposition of unusually harsh conditions on captured members of German submarine crews. He protested the internment of British conscientious objectors in Dartmoor, a particularly grim criminal prison. He was aghast over the slander campaigns launched against prominent public figures who were unjustly accused of harboring pro-German sympathies (such as Lord Battenberg, first lord of the Admiralty, and Lord Haldane, the lord chancellor—both of whom were finally obliged to resign their posts). In general, the king tried to dissociate himself from the atmosphere of unbridled Germanophobia which characterized public rhetoric in Britain during the war. Indeed, he went so far as to resist the suggestion that the German kaiser and his family should have their prewar honorary commands of British regiments revoked. King George's stance on these issues reflected a combination of commitment to moral and legal principle and a somewhat anachronistic sense of chivalry that struck many as out of place in the context of total war. In any case, his interventions in these matters usually proved unsuccessful.

Not all of King George's wartime actions were noble-minded and statesmanlike. In the wake of the March 1917 revolution in Russia, he proved most reluctant to take in the overthrown Russian tsar and his family for fear of damaging the image of the British royal house. This led to the British government's withdrawal of an asylum offer; soon thereafter, the Bolsheviks came to power and had the Russian royal family executed.

George V generally displayed considerable sensitivity to the importance of cultivating good relations with the United States and occasionally appeared to possess more subtle understanding of the American outlook on the war than did some of Britain's professional politicians. This was particularly evident during the months leading up to American entry into the war, when President Wilson was making one last attempt to broker a solution to the conflict. When the American initiative elicited a vaguely worded peace note from the German government on Dec. 12, 1916, the king warned Prime Minister David Lloyd George against phrasing the official British response in overly harsh terms, lest the Americans be alienated. When the United States government responded with a peace note of its own on December 18, George V took deep offense at its apparently even-handed tone; however, he expressed his sentiments to U.S. Ambassador Walter Hines Page by openly weeping and speaking of his disappointment rather than through recriminations. Upon the arrival of American troops on the Western Front in 1918, the king induced Lloyd George to eliminate a line in his welcoming

G

message referring to the unseasoned condition of the American soldiers.

As in many other issues, and despite his understanding of the issues, George V was occasionally prone to fits of almost childish petulance in his relations with the United States. Thus, in the wake of the Armistice, when informed on short notice by Lloyd George that President Wilson would be paying a state visit on the day after Christmas 1918, the king objected that this would interfere with his own holiday plans. To this, his prime minister responded bluntly to the effect that the Imperial War Cabinet had overruled the king. Wilson and his wife duly arrived on Boxing Day and were honored by a state banquet in Buckingham Palace. Here it was Wilson who made a *faux pas* by failing to make any reference in his toast to Britain's wartime sacrifices. The king later confided to a friend that he found Wilson to be an unbearably cold, odiously academic man.

If his encounter with the President was a chilly one, George's warm relationship with Ambassador Page and his cultivation of friendship with a number of prominent Americans over the years served to sensitize him to the idiosyncrasies of American public opinion. Within the narrow limits of his authority, George V contributed actively to the cultivation of Great Britain's crucial wartime relationship with the United States.

Aviel Roshwald

Bibliography
Gore, John. *King George V. A Personal Memoir*. London: Murray, 1941.
Nicolson, Harold. *King George the Fifth. His Life and Reign*. London: Constable, 1952.
Rose, Kenneth. *King George V*. New York: Knopf, 1984.

Gerard, James Watson (1867–1951)

James Watson Gerard was born in Geneseo, New York. As a child, he went to school in England and traveled with his family throughout Europe. He studied at Columbia University and Columbia University Law School. Following admission to the New York bar in 1892, he entered his grandfather Gerard's New York City law firm and eventually became a partner.

At his father's suggestion, Gerard joined the Tammany Society and became active in Democratic Party politics. Elected to the New York Supreme Court in 1907, he served from 1908 until 1913, when he resigned to accept appointment as United States ambassador to Germany.

Gerard embarked upon his new career energetically, renting a building in downtown Berlin to house the American embassy at his own expense (customary practice at the time) and setting out to learn the German language and as much as possible about German politics and culture. His initial diplomatic task was to obtain Germany's approval of Secretary of State William Jennings Bryan's "cooling-off" treaty. He failed. However, he successfully represented American interests in other routine matters.

The outbreak of war took Gerard by surprise, as it did dozens of other Americans in Germany, many of whom were without their passports. Gerard issued passports and arranged transportation for those who wished to return to the United States. His efforts to expedite the departure of persons who lacked adequate proof of American citizenship provoked occasional reprimands from the State Department, although these did not noticeably dampen his enthusiasm for quick and effective action. Gerard also acted as diplomatic liaison for some of the nations at war with Germany, including Great Britain, Japan, Serbia, and Rumania. In this capacity he supervised repatriation of those countries' civilian nationals interned by the Germans at the start of the war. He also inspected prisoner-of-war camps and worked aggressively and effectively to improve prisoners' living conditions and medical care.

The issue of neutral rights proved particularly troublesome for Gerard. He fielded a stream of complaints from German officials about American arms sales to Britain and France while at the same time negotiating exchanges of German dyestuffs for American cotton. Escalating anti-American sentiment in Germany alarmed him, as did Germany's use of unrestricted submarine warfare. He did not participate directly in most of the negotiations surrounding Germany's use of submarines, although he voiced American protests as instructed and faithfully reported to Washington disagreements within the German government over submarine policy. During the *Sussex* crisis, Gerard met with Kaiser Wilhelm II and forcefully reiterated the United States position. He believed this meeting to have been instrumental in Germany's renunciation of unrestricted submarine warfare soon thereafter.

In September 1916, Gerard journeyed to Washington to confer with President Wilson about the likelihood of German resumption of unrestricted submarine warfare and about a possible new presidential peace initiative. He returned to his post in December. The following month Germany did announce resumption of unrestricted submarine warfare, and the United States consequently broke diplomatic relations. On Feb. 3, 1917, Gerard received instructions to close the embassy.

By the time he returned home, the United States had entered the war. Gerard undertook a nationwide speaking tour to generate support for the war effort. He also wrote two books, *My Four Years in Germany* and the more propagandistic *Face to Face with Kaiserism*.

Following the war, Gerard returned to his law practice. He acted as President Franklin D. Roosevelt's representative at George VI's coronation in 1936, although he turned down Roosevelt's offer of formal ambassadorships to Argentina and Russia. He undertook some additional work for the government, serving on the New York Industrial Survey Commission and on President Harry Truman's Point Four Program advisory board. From 1920 until 1932, he served as treasurer of the Democratic Finance Committee, which he also chaired in 1933–1934, and 1940. He died on Sept. 6, 1951, shortly after his autobiography appeared.

Mary Childers Mangusso

Bibliography

Gerard, James W. *Face to Face with Kaiserism*. New York: Doran, 1918.
———. *My First Eighty-Three Years in America—the Memoirs of James W. Gerard*. Garden City, NY: Doubleday, 1951.
———. *My Four Years in Germany*. New York: Doran, 1917.
U.S. Department of State. *Papers Relating to the Foreign Relations of the United States*. Supplements, *The World War*, 1914, 1915, 1916, 1917. Washington, DC: Government Printing Office, 1915–1918.

German-American Relations

The traditional approach of the American people and their government has been to avoid entanglements in European affairs. The violation of this long-held rule, and the emergence of the United States as a world power, reflects the monumental effect of the Great War.

In particular, the United States enjoyed a cordial relationship with the German principalities until German unification. One of the first major events in Central Europe to capture diplomatic attention in America were the revolutions of 1848. In the German principalities, the failure of the revolutionaries resulted in a wave of immigration to the United States that established a link between the two peoples.

The 1860s were tumultuous for both nations, as Prussia fought the three wars of German unification and the United States became engulfed in its Civil War. When the Civil War ended in 1865, American attention returned to foreign affairs, and Europe became much closer to the New World with the completion of the first trans-Atlantic cable in 1867. America passively supported Prussia in the Franco-Prussian War of 1870 because of recent French anti-Americanism and meddlesome intervention in Mexico by Napoleon III. While the United States criticized Chancellor Otto von Bismarck for taking Alsace-Lorraine after the defeat of France, the government never directly opposed it.

Upon the formation of the German Empire in 1871, the United States and Germany enjoyed good relations for the remainder of the decade. Although he did not view America as a great power because of its relatively small military, Bismarck liked the United States and maintained pleasant contacts with American diplomats. At the end of the decade, though, that relationship began its long downward spiral. The first hint of deterioration began when, during the economic depression of the mid-1880s, Bismarck became interested in building a colonial empire and Germany began seeking territory in Africa and the Pacific. The United States was concerned about German interests in South America and was particularly wary of the possibility of a large German naval base in the Caribbean.

In 1890, another crucial step was taken when Wilhelm II sacked Bismarck and assumed a more authoritative role in German diplomacy. Wilhelm's arrogant, blustering temperament ruined the international image of Germany, and his sabre-rattling politics supported the stereotype of German militarism. Wilhelm's character made it very difficult for anyone to deal with

Germany diplomatically, for the empire challenged the existing international power structure. If his attitude had been in question before 1898, it was clarified when he ordered his chief admiral, Alfred von Tirpitz, to build a world-class navy—an announcement which shocked the United States and clearly threatened traditional British naval supremacy.

Historians characterize the ten-year span from 1895 to 1905 as one of hyperimperialism. This period saw a number of conflicts and confrontations between the imperial powers as Germany's aggressive entry into the competition produced a new fervor on all fronts. For the United States, jostling for territory reached a peak during the Spanish-American War. During that conflict, it appeared that the German Navy was trying to interject itself in the lopsided struggle between Admiral Dewey's fleet and Spanish forces at Manila Bay. Current historiography indicates that was not actually the case, but at the time the actions of Vice Admiral von Diederichs aggravated relations with the United States. The Manila incident was followed by a crisis in the Samoan Islands in 1899. This was only resolved when Great Britain relinquished its right in the archipelago and allowed it to be divided between the two rising imperial powers, Germany and the United States. In addition, German participation in the multinational force sent to quell the Boxer Rebellion of 1900 in China was criticized for being too heavy-handed.

The German effort to improve its relationship with the United States produced a flow of gifts and gratuities to America around the turn of the century. One of the warmest displays was a visit by the kaiser's brother, Prince Henry of Prussia, in February 1902, who was accompanied by Admiral von Tirpitz. The tour was specifically designed to allay misgivings arising from a conflict between the United States and German fleets in Manila in 1898. Unfortunately, Henry's stay occurred just as a crisis over Venezuela began. It was this additional perceived threat in Latin America, not Prince Henry's presence, that captured the attention of the American media, public, and government.

The controversy over Venezuela ensued when the practices of the country's rather sleazy Venezuelan dictator, Cipriano Castro, threatened to ruin European investors, a group dominated by British and German financial interests. In December 1902, the British and Germans, along with the Italians, placed a "pacific"

blockade around Venezuela, during which the British sank a number of gunboats, and German vessels sank two of them. Although the dispute was ultimately settled peacefully, it now appears that Theodore Roosevelt, while not viewing the blockade as a threat to the Monroe Doctrine, did exert pressure on the kaiser behind the scenes to bring the affair to a peaceful conclusion.

German-American relations experienced a slight improvement in 1905 when the German Empire, realizing its encirclement and diplomatic isolation, supported Roosevelt's efforts at mediation in the Russo-Japanese War. Berlin remained cordial even through the Algeciras Conference of 1906 at which Roosevelt had favored the French and British positions toward Morocco. Roosevelt's role in the Algeciras Conference was of particular significance because it set a precedent for American interest and involvement in European affairs.

As the diplomatic climate in Europe darkened during the first thirteen years of the twentieth century, America and Germany were economic competitors and naval rivals, and the United States was still concerned about German interests in South America, especially near the site of the construction of the Panama Canal. On the other hand, Berlin had been wooing the United States in hopes of an alliance that would break Germany's encirclement. The sore spots between Germany and the United States look mild when compared to the crises that were erupting in Europe.

As tensions in the Balkans seemed to forecast a confrontation in Europe, the German government seriously misjudged the strength of its link to the United States The friendship that supposedly existed between the kaiser and Roosevelt was a result of German efforts for a German-American alliance that simply had not penetrated the formidable tradition established by George Washington in the Farewell Address. Berlin's reliance on millions of German Americans to sway American support for German interests was a mistake because the German Americans were divided in their desire to assimilate into American society and, regardless of their loyalty to the old country, as a group they could influence public opinion very little.

When the war began, United States-German diplomacy was shaped by a number of forces. As Wilhelm's personality had played a dominant role after 1890, now Woodrow Wilson's persona set the pace for American neutrality. Wilson himself had to struggle to overcome his own pro-British leanings. Col. Edward M. House, a trusted adviser to Wilson, was anti-German, as was the American ambassador to the German Empire, James W. Gerard. Only Secretary of State William Jennings Bryan was truly open-minded, and he resigned in 1915 during the controversy over the sinking of the *Lusitania*. He was replaced by Robert Lansing, who was also anti-German. Despite this bias, Wilson was determined to maintain a strict neutrality, a policy that drew criticism from both sides. The Germans were angry that Wilson did not oppose the Allied blockade of Germany, while the British considered Wilson diplomatically impotent because he could not thwart the German use of the submarine. By the end of 1915, though, both sides were convinced of Wilson's favoritism toward the Allies.

Several factors influenced Wilson's gradual shift to the Allies. The German Empire proved completely inadequate in the propaganda war; the British quickly captured the American press and with it American public opinion. In addition, the United States was economically tied to the success of the Allies because of its massive support of the Allied war machine. The blundering sabotage campaign carried out by Germany in America did not improve relations. Ultimately, though, the single largest factor that made the situation between the United States and Germany irreconcilable was the German submarine policy.

Both the Allies and the Central Powers pursued a dual goal when dealing with the "Great Neutral." Their first priority was to maintain a healthy relationship to ensure open supply lines across the Atlantic. Second, they wished to deny their enemies access to the cornucopia of American goods and financing. Unfortunately, pursuing the latter meant sacrificing the former.

While the Allied surface blockade of the Central Powers angered the United States because cargos were confiscated, it was viewed only as loss of property. Ships were not sunk. The vulnerability of the U-boat, however, necessitated an underwater attack, and limited space on a submarine prevented the rescue of survivors. Thus, the German blockade cost not only cargos, but also entire vessels and precious human lives.

The German Empire announced a counterblockade to be enforced by U-boats in February 1915. The first American ship sunk without warning was the tanker *Gulflight* on May 1, 1915. Six days later a disaster occurred when the passenger liner *Lusitania* was sunk, killing 1,198 people, including 124 Americans. It is generally believed that only Wilson's calm and rational response avoided war at this point. He sent a note to Berlin on May 13 demanding reparations for lost cargo and assurance that it would never happen again. The Germans waited two weeks to answer, and then they blamed the British for the entire event. Wilson sent a second note in June and a third in July, each one in a progressively harsher tone.

The German ambassador to Washington, Count Johann von Bernstorff, worked hard to convince his superiors that the American government was sincere. On August 19 of that same year, the passenger liner *Arabic* was sunk, drowning forty-four, including two Americans. Again, Washington replied immediately and aggressively, and Bernstorff secured a promise from the German government that German U-boats would no longer attack passenger vessels.

In February 1916, Germany announced that all armed merchantmen would be sunk without warning. On March 25, the *Sussex* was sent to the bottom and some Americans were injured. Washington threatened to sever diplomatic relations unless the submarine threat to neutrals was harnessed. Berlin replied on May 4 with the "Sussex Pledge" in which they promised to warn merchant vessels and provide within their limited ability for the safety of survivors.

During 1916, the German military and government evaluated the nation's rapidly dwindling supplies of raw materials. Gen. Erich Ludendorff estimated that the Allied blockade gave the Allies a ten-to-six material advantage over the Central Powers. The Allied blockade had to be broken.

On Jan. 31, 1917, the German government once again announced unrestricted submarine warfare to begin the next day. As promised, the United States severed diplomatic relations on February 3, but the Wilson administration waited for an event to actually bring America into the war. The Germans provided a ludicrous event around which the Americans could rally.

German Foreign Minister Arthur Zimmermann wired a message to the German ambassador in Mexico. He was to offer the Mexican government territory lost to the United States, and German assistance in fighting, if they would attack the United States. Brit-

G

ish intelligence intercepted the message and released it to Washington on Feb. 26, 1917. On April 6, 1917, the United States declared war on the German Empire.

Peace efforts by Wilson were sporadic and became more rigid as American military participation expanded. Wilson made his famous speech to Congress espousing the Fourteen Points on Jan. 8, 1918, which was a benevolent peace proposal. As more American soldiers died in the war, Wilson's benevolence faded. In September 1918, Wilson made it clear that he wanted changes in the German government before he would make peace. On October 3, Prince Max von Baden, representing a supposedly reformed government, made an initial inquiry into a peace based on the Fourteen Points. Wilson did not believe the claims of the prince, and on October 14 and October 27, he demanded an even greater degree of reform before he would make peace. Wilson's desires were satisfied on November 10 when the Kaiser abdicated. The following day the guns fell silent in Europe.

Mathew Heiser

See also ARABIC AND SUSSEX PLEDGES; FOURTEEN POINTS; ZIMMERMANN TELEGRAM

Bibliography

Gatzke, Hans W. *Germany and the United States. A "Special Relationship?"* Cambridge: Harvard University Press, 1980.
Fischer, Fritz. *Germany's Aims in the First World War.* New York: W. W. Norton, 1967.
Jonas, Manfred. *The United States and Germany.* Ithaca, NY: Cornell University Press, 1984.

Gibbons, Floyd (1887–1939)

Floyd Gibbons seemed to land on his feet right in the middle of all of the turmoil of the early twentieth century with his pencil scratching out the next story. He witnessed nine major conflicts, from chasing Pancho Villa in 1915–1916 through the Spanish Revolution of 1936. Had he not died in 1939, he undoubtedly would have packed his knapsack and found the action on some far-away battlefield in World War II.

Gibbons, who was born in Washington, D.C., attended the preparatory school in Georgetown University but was dismissed prior to graduation for misconduct. He traveled around the country, and it was in Minneapolis in 1907 that he first ventured into reporting on the staff of the *Daily News*, well aware that his father considered all reporters to be drunks and bums. After gaining some experience, he landed a job with the *Chicago Tribune* in 1912.

Ordered to the Mexican border in 1914 by Robert R. McCormick and Joseph M. Patterson, his bosses at the *Tribune*, Gibbons managed to interview Pancho Villa on the battlefield, then accompanied the bandit army on campaign in his own private railway boxcar with "*The Chicago Tribune*—Special Correspondent" painted on the side in Spanish. By June 1915, Gibbons was back in Chicago ready for his next adventure.

After accompanying BGen. John J. Pershing into Mexico in pursuit of Villa in 1916, Gibbons was posted in February 1917 to London as the *Tribune*'s correspondent to cover the events of World War I. He began his assignment with a bang, surviving the sinking of the S.S. *Laconia* off the Irish coast on February 25. His story, filed the next day from Queenstown, burst like a rocket over metropolitan America. When the United States entered the war on April 6, Gibbons again marched toward the sound of the guns. He accompanied Pershing to France and witnessed the arrival of the 1st Division at Saint Nazaire in June. Gibbons and seventeen other accredited reporters were controlled by the American Expeditionary Force (AEF) staff in a "press pool."

Gibbons did not adapt well to censorship, so he "disappeared" and joined a 6th Field Artillery gun crew training at Le Valdahon. He got to the front in October 1917 in time to see the Americans in their first action while his fellow correspondents were detained at a French checkpoint. Later, while accompanying the 5th Marine Brigade at Belleau Wood in June 1918, Gibbons was wounded three times and lost his left eye. He was treated at Military Base Hospital No. 1 near Paris and received his famous white eye patch. Cited by Marshal Ferdinand Foch and General Pershing, Gibbons sailed for home on Aug. 15, 1918. A marine corps honor guard met him at the dock in New York on August 22 with news that he had been awarded the Croix de Guerre with Palm by the French government for valor at Belleau Wood.

Gibbons was something of a celebrity when he set out on the lecture circuit in the fall of 1918, well before the Armistice of November 11. During a respite in the tour schedule that fall—caused by the influenza epidemic—he wrote *And They Thought We Wouldn't Fight* in Atlantic City. His later books, *The Red Knight* and *The Red Napoleon*, the latter a fictional account of future warfare, were serialized in *Liberty Magazine* published by Joseph M. Patterson.

For the rest of his very active life, Floyd Gibbons hobnobbed with adventurers, politicians, and royalty, even flirting with the new science of radio broadcasting as a commentator. He sided with the Bonus Marchers in 1932 and won the enduring friendship of thousands of veterans. Death caught up with the retired gentleman farmer at age fifty-two on his Stroudsburg, Pennsylvania farm.

John F. Votaw

Bibliography

Crozier, Emmet. *American Reporters on the Western Front 1914–1918*. New York: Oxford University Press, 1959.

Gibbons, Edward. *Floyd Gibbons: Your Headline Hunter*. New York: Exposition Press, 1953.

Gibbons, Floyd. *And They Thought We Wouldn't Fight*. New York: Doran, 1918.

Knightly, Phillip. *The First Casualty: From the Crimea to Vietnam: The War Correspondent as Hero, Propagandist, and Myth Maker*. New York: Harcourt Brace Jovanovich, 1975.

Gibbons, James Cardinal (1834–1921)

James Cardinal Gibbons, archbishop of Baltimore, was a leading spokesman for the Roman Catholic Church in the United States in the early twentieth century. In spite of the strong ethnically motivated sympathies of many American Catholics at the outbreak of the war in Europe, Cardinal Gibbons avoided actions that might embarrass the Wilson administration's policy of neutrality. When the *Lusitania* sank in May 1915, Gibbons counseled caution and restraint. A year later, the cardinal supported President Wilson's campaign for preparedness and the movement for universal military service.

With the United States entrance into the war in April 1917, Gibbons called on American Catholics to support their government. The cardinal based his position on patriotism, his conviction that citizens were bound by a moral obligation to support the legitimate authority of a constitutional government, and his desire to give no ground for allegations that Catholics had failed in their duties as American citizens. In November 1917, to coordinate the Catholic war effort, he endorsed the formation by the American bishops of the National Catholic War Council.

During the war, the Holy See called upon Cardinal Gibbons to represent Pope Benedict XV's position to the Wilson administration. In August 1917, the Vatican urged Gibbons to use his influence to secure United States support for the papal peace plan that had been circulated among the belligerents. Gibbons publicly defended the pope against charges of being pro-German and praised the pontiff's motives in seeking an end to the conflict. He did not, however, attempt to discuss the peace plan with the President. Again, in October 1918, when Austria sought an armistice, Benedict XV urged Gibbons to persuade President Wilson to give favorable consideration to the Austrian proposal. The cardinal chose simply to write to Wilson. His response to these two papal initiatives probably reflected a realistic assessment of both the government's position and American public opinion.

In early 1918, Cardinal Gibbons complied with a request of the papal secretary of state and petitioned the British government to reject the exclusion of the Vatican from the peace conference as provided for by the 1915 secret Treaty of London. Again, at the behest of the papal secretary of state, Gibbons called upon participants in the Peace Conference to recognize the independence of the Vatican. He couched his request in the context of the Peace Conference's work to remove areas of conflicts between peoples.

Convinced by the horrors of the war that the best hope for a lasting peace was a league of nations, Cardinal Gibbons readily supported Wilson's efforts in the postwar years to establish the League of Nations and to secure United States acceptance of the league.

Glenn J. Kist

Bibliography

Abrams, Ray H. *Preachers Present Arms: The Role of the American Churches and Clergy in World Wars I and II, With Some Observations on the War in Vietnam*. Scottsdale, PA: Herald Press, 1969.

Dohen, Dorothy. *Nationalism and American Catholicism*. New York: Sheed & Ward, 1967.

Ellis, John T. *The Life of James Cardinal Gibbons: Archbishop of Baltimore, 1834–1921*. Milwaukee: Bruce, 1952.

Hennesy, James. *American Catholics: A History of the Catholic Community in the United States*. New York: Oxford University Press, 1981.

Piper, John F., Jr. *The American Churches in World War I*. Athens: Ohio University Press, 1985.

Gleaves, Albert (1858–1937)

The naval officer largely responsible for developing the antisubmarine measures by which American troops and supplies reached Europe in vast numbers during 1918, Albert Gleaves was an 1877 graduate of the United States Naval Academy. His early career was marked by extensive sea duty on a variety of warships, ranging from the screw sloops *Hartford* and *Plymouth* during the late 1870s to the protected cruiser *Boston* and the new battleship *Texas* in the 1890s. His first command came in 1897 aboard the torpedo boat *Cushing*. During these early years of his career, Gleaves wrote articles for the United States Naval Institute *Proceedings* stressing the need for naval reforms. He also formed a close friendship with Theodore Roosevelt, then serving as assistant secretary of the navy.

Between the Spanish-American War and World War I, Gleaves advanced through the ranks, while serving in a variety of sea and shore billets.

Following American entry into World War I, RAdm. Gleaves assumed command of the Atlantic Fleet's Cruiser and Transport Force. In this capacity, he was charged with the task of devising transportation and convoy techniques to enable the American Expeditionary Force (AEF) to cross the Atlantic safely. According to one estimate, the navy delivered safely ashore in Europe on the average seven soldiers and their equipment per minute in the summer of 1918. Losses to German submarines were kept to a minimum; only 8 of 450 transports that Gleaves used were lost due to enemy action.

After the war, Gleaves was promoted to vice admiral (1918) and admiral (1919) and briefly given command of the Asiatic Fleet, during which service he came to the conclusion that Japan and the United States would likely drift into war. His last command was the Boston Navy Yard (1921–1922). He retired in 1922; though in retirement, he served as governor of the Philadelphia Naval Home. He died on Jan. 6, 1937.

Donald A. Yerxa

Bibliography

Coletta, Paolo E. *Sea Power in the Atlantic and Mediterranean in World War I*. Lanham, MD: University Press of America, 1989.

Reynolds, Clark G. *Famous American Admirals*. New York: Van Nostrand Reinhold, 1978.

Goethals, George Washington (1858–1928)

George Washington Goethals was born in Brooklyn, New York. He spent three years at City College of New York and then transferred to West Point, where he graduated second in the class of 1880. The capstone of his career in the Corps of Engineers was appointment by President Theodore Roosevelt as chief engineer in the construction of the Panama Canal. In addition to the monumental engineering problems of lock construction and mud slide recurrences, Goethals also faced vast administrative challenges: the housing and feeding of 4,500 men of various nationalities and the organization of an efficient, self-sustaining supply system. Vested with nearly dictatorial powers, he managed through diligence and intelligence to complete the canal in 1913, and it was opened the following year—six months ahead of schedule. Goethals became a national hero and was promoted two grades, from colonel to major general.

From April to July 1917, Goethals was general manager and chairman of the Executive Committee of the United States Shipping Board's Emergency Fleet Corporation. Charged with creating enough wooden ships, in the shortest possible time, to carry an American army and its supplies to France, Goethals encountered complex technical and administrative problems. He did not oppose wooden ships but questioned their seaworthiness and postwar commercial value. Goethals preferred a curtailed wooden program and reliance on the larger and commercially feasible steel ships. He lacked, however, the power to translate his program into tonnage. Unlike his canal experience of absolute authority, Goethals now shared decision-making power with Shipping Board President William Denman, who preferred wooden ships. Their repeated clashes over the type of ship and general authority to let contracts made the Denman–Goethals controversy the talk of Washington. Since they could not resolve the dual authority issue and President Woodrow Wilson refused to give Goethals ultimate power, both men resigned in July 1917. Little tonnage came down American ways in 1917 or 1918. Some blamed the paralysis in the shipping program on the lack of centralized authority.

Recalled to active duty as acting quartermaster general on Dec. 18, 1917, Goethals replaced Henry G. Sharpe, who was at the storm center of controversy over supply blunders during the bitter winter of 1917–1918. Within nine days Goethals also became director of the new Storage and Traffic Division of the War Department. Goethals clearly wanted to restructure the Quartermaster Corps so that, in coordination with the other bureaus, it could supply the army through a mobilized economy. He had to solve problems of inadequate personnel, decentralized organization, and diverse functions. Following a personnel shakeup, Goethals organized the corps along civilian lines. He hired military men who could get along with industrialists and capable, energetic, young businessmen. Goethals changed the cumbersome decentralized organization by establishing centralized procurement control. He stripped the corps of extraneous functions. No longer would it be a catchall for duties not assigned other bureaus. Goethals reorganized it along functional lines, fashioning the corps into a purchasing agency. By April, the Quartermaster Corps controlled the purchase of all classes of standard supplies.

As director of the Storage and Traffic Bureau, Goethals supervised storage, inland water transportation, and embarkation. He had to overcome seemingly insurmountable problems: overburdened railroads, eastern seaboard congestion, and uncoordinated shipments of men and supplies. Goethals tackled each in turn. He required shippers of freight to obtain releases from both the Inland Transportation Service and the Embarkation Service for overseas shipments. He coordinated the work of supply bureaus not merely in inland and overseas traffic activities, but also in storage.

Further reorganization of the General Staff in April 1918 led to the creation of the Pur-chase, Storage, and Traffic Division, with Goethals as director. For the first time in the World War, one individual was expected to supervise and coordinate supply bureau policies. Largely independent of each other and government supervision, the uncoordinated supply bureaus had competed for the nation's resources. Competition increased government costs, disorganized industry and labor, congested transportation facilities and inevitably slowed down input of war supplies. Through the Purchase, Storage, and Traffic's four divisions (purchase and supply, storage, inland transportation, and embarkation) Goethals expected to rein in bureau excesses, correct inefficiencies, and create uniformity.

He expected complete control over supply. Instead, he operated uncomfortably in a confused chain of command. When dealing with the business world, he was subordinate to Assistant Secretary of War Benedict Crowell. In military activities, Peyton C. March, army chief of staff, had authority over Goethals. In this awkward, complicated system, Goethals built a new staff composed of bright, aggressive businessmen like Robert Thorne and Gerard Swope as well as BGens. Robert Wood and Hugh Johnson. They succeeded in establishing a system of interbureau procurement and standardization of bureau recordkeeping, priority, and requirement schedules.

Goethals also found bureau financial practices haphazard. He worked toward consolidation payment for purchases, proper accountability, and uniform machinery to prepare congressional appropriation estimates. By the end of summer 1918, his organization could supervise, coordinate, and standardize bureau finances but lacked operational control. The disgruntled bureau chiefs jealously guarded their power to prepare and present estimates to Congress.

Linking the General Staff with the War Industries Board (WIB) became imperative. Goethals knew hard feelings existed between the two. The army tried to do within itself what the WIB undertook as an independent agency. The War Department lacked access to WIB data on tonnage and plant capacities as no agency existed to link the two on a working basis. Goethals built liaisons with the WIB through a parallel committee system. His director of purchases and supply, Brigadier General Johnson, served as the army link with the WIB, and

G

Goethals for a time served on the WIB priorities committee.

As a result of criticism of AEF handling of supply and congestion at French ports, a plan known as the "Goethals Proposal" emanated from the War Department and General Staff to appoint Goethals to command supply in France from a headquarters of equal rank with that of General Pershing, thus restricting Pershing to field command. Claiming the prerogative of the theater commander to control supply, Pershing headed off division of his command by revamping his Service of Supply. For Goethals, therefore, hope of going to France was a closed chapter.

By late summer, however, Goethals had turned his attention to merging his supervisory and coordinating powers into a bold attempt to establish his division as the army's sole purchasing agent. On Aug. 26, 1918, reorganization of the Purchase, Storage, and Traffic Division gave Goethals executive as well as supervisory powers. He worked it out so that the General Staff moved into bureau domain and took over supply functions. He believed that the Purchase, Storage, and Traffic Division should assume responsibility and control of all supply operations. The bureaus fought back. They resisted procurement consolidation inch by inch. They refused to provide the necessary information for a full statistical picture. Control over the bureaus never materialized. With the end of the war in sight, many ambitious projects remained on paper.

In 1918, Goethals was awarded the Distinguished Service Medal for conspicuous service in reorganizing the Quartermaster Corps. On March 4, 1919, he returned to civilian life as head of an engineering firm. He died in 1928 and was buried at West Point.

Phyllis Zimmerman

See also EMERGENCY FLEET CORPORATION; SHIPPING BOARD

Bibliography

Beaver, Daniel R. "George W. Goethals and the Problem of Military Supply." In *Some Pathways in Twentieth Century History*. Detroit: 1969.

Bishop, Joseph B. *Goethals, Genius of the Panama Canal*. New York: Harper, 1930.

Hewes, James E., Jr. *From Root to McNamara: Army Reorganization and Administration 1900–1963*. Washington, DC: Center for Military History, 1975.

Risch, Erna. *Quartermaster Support of the Army: A History of the Corps 1775–1939*. Washington, DC: Office of the Quartermaster General, 1962.

Zimmerman, Phyllis. *The Neck of the Bottle: George W. Goethals and Reorganization of the United States Army Supply System, 1917–1918*. College Station: Texas A&M University Press, 1992.

Goldman, Emma (1869–1940)

Sometimes called "Red Emma," "the mother of anarchy in America," and "the most dangerous woman in the world," Emma Goldman was born in Kovno, Lithuania. In 1885, she immigrated to the United States. She worked briefly in a clothing factory in Rochester, New York, and began to attend socialist meetings. When she moved to New Haven, Connecticut, Goldman met a number of young Russian socialists and anarchists. The celebrated Haymarket trial of Chicago anarchists deeply stirred Goldman. She became an anarchist in 1889 and moved to New York City to participate in radical activities.

In New York, she worked closely with Alexander Berkman, a young Russian anarchist who, in 1892, attempted to assassinate Henry C. Frick, head of United States Steel, during the Homestead Steel Strike. Berkman went to prison, and Goldman, a charismatic speaker, rose to prominence within the anarchist movement. The following year she was sentenced to a year in prison for inciting a riot among unemployed workers at a mass meeting in New York City.

In 1901, a young anarchist, Leon Czolgosz, assassinated President William McKinley. Czolgosz claimed that he was inspired by Emma Goldman's speeches. Although there was no evidence linking her to the crime, she was taken into police custody. The harassment she received for her defense of Czolgosz's act led her to seek temporary seclusion from the public. By 1906, Emma Goldman was back in the public eye when she founded an anarchist monthly journal, *Mother Earth*, which she edited until its suppression in 1917.

With the outbreak of World War I, Emma Goldman attacked Wilson's preparedness program. After America's entry into the war, she and Berkman were convicted of conspiracy to obstruct the operation of the selective service law. Each was sentenced to two years' imprisonment and fined $10,000. After her release in 1919, Emma Goldman was ordered deported to Russia during the "Red Scare."

Although Goldman had originally supported the Bolshevik Revolution, she became disillusioned with the despotism of Lenin and Trotsky. Goldman left the USSR in 1921 for Riga, Latvia, and in 1923 wrote *My Disillusionment in Russia*. Goldman became deeply involved in supporting the anti-Franco revolutionaries in the Spanish Civil War in 1936. In May 1940, she suffered a fatal stroke in Toronto, where she was working for refugees from Fascist Spain and Italy.

Burton A. Boxerman

Bibliography

Drinnon, Richard. *Rebel in Paradise: A Biography of Emma Goldman*. Boston: Beacon Press, 1970.

Goldman, Emma. *Living My Life*. New York: Knopf, 1951.

Wexler, Alice. *Emma Goldman—An Intimate Life*. New York: Pantheon, 1984.

Gompers, Samuel (1850–1924)

In 1914, Samuel Gompers was considered the grand old man of organized labor. Gompers had been a founder and president of the American Federation of Labor (AF of L) since its establishment in 1886. He was born in London and immigrated with his family to the United States in 1863, where he became a member of the International Cigarmakers Union. He largely determined the AF of L's policies of trade unionism, nonpartisan politics, nationalism, and rejection of socialism. A pacifist until 1914, he was a firm believer in American democracy and an absolute nationalist.

With the outbreak of war in August 1914, Gompers became alarmed over the prospects of the AF of L's demands, which he had been pressing on President Woodrow Wilson since the election of 1912. Gompers had swung the majority of the federation's unions behind Wilson in return for the President's tentative support of the AF of L's programs. But Wilson had done little for the federation except to appoint William B. Wilson, a United Mine Workers union official, as the first secretary of labor. Gompers watched Wilson's swing toward war with increasing anxiety in 1915 and in 1916. During these years, his foremost concern became the protection of the AF of L's standards if war

came. Consequently, he led the federation in a vigorous lobbying campaign to realize as many labor demands as possible before the United States entered the war.

In January 1916, Gompers openly declared his support for preparedness and in March joined with the League to Enforce Peace in advocating a world government. His support of Woodrow Wilson's foreign policy and his value to the administration as the single most important American labor leader gained for him an appointment to the Committee of Labor of the Advisory Commission to the Council of National Defense (CND). In this position, Gompers represented the interests of American workers during the war. His closeness to the administration allowed him to lobby labor leaders of the Allied nations for Wilson's Fourteen Points; in 1918, Gompers attended the British Trades Union Congress. In 1917, he demonstrated his intense nationalism by accepting the presidency of the American Alliance for Labor and Democracy, a federation of prowar unions opposing all antiwar sentiment and especially the People's Council of America.

Despite Gompers's support of the war effort, he failed to gain all he wanted from the administration. While protecting most of the AF of L's prewar gains, he never succeeded in placing labor leaders in policy-making positions on the numerous agencies that controlled hours and wages through the War Labor Board. Moreover, liberal unions constantly attacked Gompers for suppressing threatened strikes and not demanding more concessions from the administration. The year 1918 saw Gompers at his peak of influence both at home and abroad. That year brought forth increased administration support for the AF of L's wage and hour demands and increased contacts with Woodrow Wilson.

At the war's end, Gompers supported the Versailles Treaty and represented American labor on the International Labor Legislative Commission in Paris. However, the Senate's failure to ratify the Versailles Treaty, President Wilson's stroke, the resurgence of laissez-faire capitalism and the Red Scare all destroyed Gompers's ability to lead the federation into a new era of equity with capital.

Samuel Gompers spent his remaining years as AF of L president physically ailing and almost blind. He came under increasing attacks from the liberal unions, such as the United Mine

Workers, for selling out to the government during the war years. He held the presidency until his death in 1924 only through the good will and loyalty of the moderate unions.

Frank L. Grubbs

See also AMERICAN ALLIANCE FOR LABOR AND DEMOCRACY; AMERICAN FEDERATION OF LABOR

Bibliography

Gompers, Samuel. *Seventy Years of Life and Labor*. New York: Dutton, 1925.

Grubbs, Frank L. *The Struggle for Labor Loyalty, Gompers, the A.F. of L. and the Pacifists, 1917–1920*. Durham, NC: Duke University Press, 1968.

———. *Samuel Gompers and The Great War: Protecting Labors' Standards*. Wake Forest, NC: Meridional Publications, 1982.

Taft, Philip. *The A.F. of L. in the Time of Gompers*. New York: Harper, 1957.

Grain Corporation

Established by executive order on Aug. 14, 1917, the Grain Corporation began operation on Sept. 14, 1917, under the direction of Julius H. Barnes and Frank G. Crowell. Its primary responsibility was to facilitate the purchase, sale, and storage of grain and cereal commodities. In addition, the Grain Corporation enforced and maintained the price controls for wheat that had been established by the Lever Food Control Act.

Because of record grain harvests in 1914 and 1915, the United States became the largest supplier of wheat and flour to the Allies and the neutral countries. Poor crops in 1916 and 1917, however, forced the government to take action to protect United States food requirements while still supplying the Allies with all the grain they required. An increasing demand for wheat and flour by United States consumers, coupled with a falling supply, sent grain and flour prices upward and led Congress to adopt the Food Control Act on Aug. 10, 1917. The act corrected the large discrepancy between the prices received by farmers and the prices paid by consumers by guaranteeing a minimum price to producers of $2.20 per bushel of wheat for the 1917 wheat crop and $2.26 for the 1918 and 1919 harvests. Upon establishment of a minimum fair price, Food Administrator Herbert

Hoover oversaw the organization of a Grain Corporation that would act as an intermediary between the farmers and the grain exchanges to enforce and maintain the authorized price. It also served as a commercial agency for the buying, selling, and distributing of wheat. The Grain Corporation's responsibilities included licensing grain terminals and flour mills, thus ensuring that federal regulations for storage and handling were followed, and enforcing the Food Control Act's prohibition on trading in wheat futures.

To guarantee cooperation between terminal markets in the United States, the country was divided into fourteen zones, each centered around a large grain terminal. A second vice president for each zone was named to act as the Grain Corporation's buyer of wheat. Allotments to flour mills within each zone were established upon a proportional basis: wheat delivered to each mill was averaged for the three years 1914–1916 to establish a mill's 1917 allocation of wheat. Two-thirds of the country's 21,600 country elevators entered into the Grain Corporation's wheat distribution agreement.

The Grain Corporation, acting also as the middleman for overseas grain sales, dealt directly with the Wheat Export Company, which was responsible for supplying Allied countries with cereal grains during the war. The corporation's total sales of cereal grains to the Wheat Export Company for the years 1917 to 1921 was 9,602,683.7 metric tons, worth $952,091,853.71. Wheat and flour made up the largest percentage of commodities.

With the signing of the Armistice on Nov. 11, 1918, the food situation in the United States changed immediately. Except for the regulations on wheat and sugar, many of the Food Administration rules and regulations were relaxed or repealed. In order to maintain the 1918 guarantee of a minimum price for wheat until March 1919, the Grain Corporation briefly remained in operation. At the same time, millions of people in Europe faced starvation as a result of the war. The responsibility of feeding these peoples rested upon the shoulders of the Allied governments, including the United States. President Wilson authorized the Grain Corporation to act as the fiscal agent of the American Relief Administration in the purchase, transportation, and handling of grain products and in the collection of accounts. On Dec. 23, 1918, the corporation established an office in London under the directorship of Edward M. Flesh. The

London office was responsible for all the shipping and delivery of foodstuffs in European waters, for all necessary accounting, and for the monetary settlements with the Eastern European governments.

The Food Administration officially ceased operations on June 30, 1919. President Wilson issued an executive order on May 14, 1919, creating the position of "wheat director," to which he appointed Grain Corporation Director Julius Barnes, and a new organization, the United States Grain Corporation, was formed. It operated on the same basis as its predecessor and was responsible for carrying out the 1919 wheat price guarantee. On May 31, 1920, the United States Grain Corporation ceased its buying operations. It then disposed of the 7,197,133 bushels of wheat and 3,188,925 barrels of flour it had on hand, settled all outstanding accounts and claims, and officially ceased operations on Jan. 31, 1921.

The Grain Corporation purchased approximately 492 million bushels of wheat and 57.6 million bushels of flour between 1917 and 1920. The total value of all grain products purchased amounted to approximately $3.75 billion. The organization made an important contribution to the Allied victory by channeling American foodstuffs to Allied armies and civilians.

Betsy Nash

Bibliography

Eldred, Wilfred. "The Wheat and Flour Trade Under Food Administration Control: 1917–1918." *Quarterly Journal of Economics* (November 1918).

Morgan, Dan. *Merchants of Grain: The Power and Profits of the Five Giant Companies at the Center of the World's Food Supply.* New York: Viking Press, 1979.

Mullendore, William C. *History of the United States Food Administration, 1917–1919.* Stanford, CA: Stanford University Press, 1941.

Surface, Frank M. *The Grain Trade During the World War.* New York: Macmillan, 1928.

———, and Raymond L. Bland. *American Food in the World War and Reconstruction Period: Operations of the Organizations Under the Direction of Herbert Hoover, 1914 to 1924.* Stanford, CA: Stanford University Press, 1931.

Graves, William Sidney (1865–1940)

William Sidney Graves entered the United States Military Academy at West Point in 1884. Although he missed his plebe year as a result of pneumonia, Graves graduated forty-second in the class of 1889.

Following graduation, he was commissioned in the infantry and served with the 7th Infantry Regiment at Fort Logan, Colorado. In 1899, Captain Graves joined the 20th Infantry for service in the Philippines, where he was cited for bravery in action during the Philippine Insurrection. He remained with his regiment, except for short periods of detached service, until 1914 when he was assigned to the War Department General Staff in Washington, D.C.

In 1917, Lieutenant Colonel Graves served a second tour of duty as secretary of the General Staff and accompanied Secretary of War Newton D. Baker to France as part of a mission to determine the requirements and composition of an American expeditionary force. He was promoted to brigadier general in December 1917 and appointed assistant to Chief of Staff Gen. Tasker H. Bliss. In June 1918, after frequently requesting assignment to France, he was promoted to major general in the National Army and assigned to command the 8th Division at Camp Fremont, California. But General Graves was not destined to command his division in France.

At a confidential meeting at the Kansas City train station in August 1918 with Secretary Baker, Graves learned that he was to command the American Expeditionary Force to be sent to Siberia. The secretary handed him a sealed envelope containing the policy of the United States in Russia and his instructions, then departed saying "Watch your step; you will be walking on eggs loaded with dynamite." Thus began the most unusual assignment of Graves's career.

The War Department designated two regiments of infantry from the Philippines, the 27th and 21st, with 5,000 men from Graves's 8th Division, to fill vacancies in the two regiments, plus support units, to form the force that sailed from San Francisco for Vladivostok on Aug. 14, 1918. For the next twenty-one months, Graves found himself and his command in the middle of a whirlpool of international intrigue. His vague orders were to guard military stores and assist the efforts of the Czech Legion without intervening in the internal affairs of Russia. He quickly discovered that his principal protagonists were the commanders of the other foreign contingents and agents of his own State Department who were in Russia attempting to influence the outcome of the civil war. Clearly, the small American force, devoid of artillery, could not influence much. Perhaps the real reason for the American presence in Siberia was to deter Japanese attempts at aggrandizement.

Following his return to the United States in April 1920, Major General Graves commanded the 1st Division, then the VI Corps Area at Chicago. He later commanded the Panama Canal Department until his retirement from active duty in 1928. General Graves died at his home in Shrewsbury, New Jersey, on Feb. 27, 1940.

John F. Votaw

See also CZECH LEGION; RUSSIA: AMERICAN INTERVENTION IN NORTH RUSSIA

Bibliography

Graves, William S. *America's Siberian Adventure 1918–1920.* New York: Cape and Smith, 1931.

Unterberger, Betty Miller. *America's Siberian Expedition, 1918–1920: A Study of National Policy.* New York: Greenwood Press, 1969.

———. *The United States, Revolutionary Russia, and the Rise of Czechoslovakia.* Chapel Hill: University of North Carolina Press, 1989.

Great Britain

See ANGLO-AMERICAN RELATIONS

Gregory, Thomas Watt (1861–1933)

Thomas Watt Gregory, son of a Confederate soldier killed in the Civil War, was born in Crawfordsville, Mississippi. Following early training in his native state, he graduated from Southwestern Presbyterian University at Clarksville, Tennessee, and attended the University of Virginia as a special student. He received a law degree from the University of Texas and was admitted to the Texas bar in 1885. Gregory practiced law at Austin, Texas, over the next twenty-eight years and served as assistant city attorney. With Robert L. Batts, he founded the legal firm of Gregory and Batts in 1900, which acted as special state counsel to prosecute Waters-Pierce Oil Company and other corporations for violating antitrust laws. The litigation

brought Gregory national attention and earned him an appointment as special assistant attorney general in 1908.

A lifelong Democrat, Gregory served as a delegate to the national conventions of 1904 and 1912. Although never a candidate for elective office, he, with Thomas Love and George Armistead, opposed the Joseph Weldon Bailey machine in Texas and enthusiastically endorsed Woodrow Wilson's prospective candidacy in 1911. Gregory persuaded Edward M. House to support the New Jersey governor, creating a long-lasting tripartite alliance. After Wilson's election, Gregory became special assistant attorney general to U.S. Attorney General James McReynolds. Gregory obtained a dissolution decree that ended the Union Pacific's control over the Southern Pacific Railroad, and he spent the summer and fall of 1913 preparing civil and criminal suits against the New York, New Haven, and Hartford Railroad, for monopolistic practices in New England. With the elevation of McReynolds to the United States Supreme Court the following year, Wilson named the Texan his attorney general.

The outbreak of World War I cast many of Gregory's decisions in terms of national defense. With a half-dozen antitrust suits pending in the Supreme Court, the President and Attorney General Gregory decided to curtail further prosecutions until the end of the war. Gregory and House successfully turned back an attempt by Secretary of the Interior Franklin K. Lane to permit private leasing of government oil lands, thereby reserving their use for the navy. Although criticized by civil libertarians for his influence on the passage and enforcement of the Espionage and Sedition acts, detention of 2,300 enemy aliens, and prosecution of more than 2,000 critics of the war, Gregory often expressed the voice of moderation. He cautioned against hysteria, sought to exempt Austrians from harsh alien regulations, and opposed a declaration of war until Germany's renewal of unrestricted submarine warfare resulted in the loss of American ships. Yet he was unrelenting against "slackers" and vowed to prosecute every rich man's son sent abroad to escape the draft. Gregory refused a Supreme Court appointment on the basis of poor hearing but did accept the role of adviser to the Versailles Peace Conference. In a rare criticism of his leader, Gregory later stated that Wilson had erred in calling for a Democratic Congress on the eve of the conference and in failing to invite Republican Senators to attend.

Gregory returned to private law practice after the war, though he served on the President's Second Industrial Conference, 1919–1920. He strongly backed the nomination of Louis Brandeis to the Supreme Court and opposed the modern Ku Klux Klan. Contrarily, he remained conservative on the racial issue, cautious on woman's suffrage, and ambivalent toward big business. Consistent with his station, Gregory served on numerous educational, civic, and religious boards and received several honorary degrees. Maintaining his interest in Democratic politics, Gregory was visiting New York City to confer with President-elect Franklin D. Roosevelt when he died of pneumonia on Feb. 26, 1933.

Garna L. Christian

Bibliography

Anders, Evan. "Thomas Watt Gregory and the Survival of His Progressive Faith." *Southwestern Historical Quarterly* (July 1989).

Baker, Ray Stannard. *Woodrow Wilson, Life and Letters.* New York: Scribner, 1939.

Webb, Walter Prescott, ed. *The Handbook of Texas.* Austin: Texas State Historical Association, 1952.

Grenades

See HAND GRENADES; SMALL ARMS

Grew, Joseph Clark (1880–1965)

Joseph Clark Grew was a member of a prominent family in Boston. Growing up, he attended Groton and Harvard, from which he graduated with an A.B. in 1902. Following two years of European and Far Eastern travels, he entered the foreign service and diplomatic life, which he and others of his social class regarded as a calling rather than an occupation.

Beginning with his first postings in Cairo, Mexico City, St. Petersburg, Berlin, and Vienna, Grew established his reputation and those connections that constituted, in his words, "a pretty good club." As chargé d'affaires and counselor of the embassy in Vienna, Grew provided valuable analyses of the European situation before returning to the United States after the severing of relations between the United States and the Austro-Hungarian imperial government in 1917. Because of the absence of reliable American intelligence sources in Europe, Col. Edward M. House suggested to President Wilson that Grew be appointed a special representative of the State Department to inform the American government of post-Armistice developments in Europe. In November 1918, he was appointed chief of the Division of Western European Affairs in the State Department and, in December, was appointed secretary-general of the American Commission to Negotiate Peace. Grew proved adept at facilitating the complex proceedings and internal dynamics of the peace negotiations and the American delegation. He also served as United States secretary on the international secretariat of the Peace Conference. For several months following the signing of the Treaty of Versailles, Grew remained in Europe as counselor of the American embassy in Paris.

After the war, he continued a distinguished diplomatic career, serving as U.S. minister to Denmark and Switzerland, undersecretary of state, ambassador to Turkey, and ambassador to Japan at the outbreak of World War II. He died in 1965.

Jonathan Nielson

Bibliography

Gelfand, Lawrence. *The Inquiry: American Preparations for Peace, 1917–1919.* New Haven: Yale University Press, 1963.

Grew, Joseph C. *Turbulent Era: A Diplomatic Record of Forty Years, 1904–1945.* Boston: Houghton Mifflin, 1952.

Heinrichs, Waldo H., Jr. *American Ambassador: Joseph C. Grew and the Development of the United States Diplomatic Tradition.* Boston: Little, Brown, 1966.

H

Haan, William George (1863–1924)

Born in Indiana, William George Haan accepted a commission in the artillery after graduating from the United States Military Academy in 1889. He fought in the Philippines during the Spanish-American War and Philippine Insurrection and served on the staff of the military governor. Upon returning to the United States, he became a part of the original General Staff in 1903. Thereafter, he was heavily involved in coast defense work.

In August 1917, after the United States had entered the First World War, Haan became a temporary brigadier general and took command of the 32d Division's 57th Field Artillery Brigade at Camp McArthur, Texas. He became acting division commander when the 32d's commander, MajGen. James Parker, left for an inspection tour of the Western Front. He was made permanent division commander and a temporary major general in December 1917.

The division was sent overseas in 1918. Upon arrival in France, the 32d was designated a replacement division and began transferring its men to other units. The German spring offensive and Haan's protests saved the division from complete dismemberment, however. The Allied need for new units had become critical by April 1918, so the 32d moved to a quiet sector in Alsace for further training.

In late July, Haan led the 32d into its first major battle in the Aisne-Marne offensive. The division entered the Allied line north of the Ourcq River near the town of Ronchères on the night of July 29. Over the next nine days, Haan's men battered their way through to the Vesle River at Fismes and captured the important German strongpoints at Bellevue Farm and in the Bois de Jomblets along the way. Ameri-

can Expeditionary Force (AEF) commander John J. Pershing praised Haan's aggressive leadership and vigor with which he had pursued the retreating Germans. The French, under whose command the 32d had fought, were also pleased and lauded the division's elan.

In late August, the French Tenth Army was attempting to turn the German line along the Vesle River with an offensive north of Soissons. Haan's mission was to seize the heavily defended town of Juvigny. The attack began on August 28. Haan skillfully encircled the town and captured it after three days of hard fighting. Thereafter, the 32d beat back two strong German counterattacks and continued to advance until relieved on September 2.

After Juvigny, Haan moved his men southwest to Joinville and joined the United States V Corps. Here they went into reserve and enjoyed a few days rest as the Meuse-Argonne offensive began on September 26. German resistance was strong, and the 32d moved to the front on September 30 to relieve another badly battered division. Casualties climbed in stiff fighting, but Haan kept the division inching forward. On October 14, the division captured Côte Dame Marie, the important heights near the town of Romange, and pierced the German's main defensive line. On October 20, after three weeks of continuous combat, the First Army pulled the division out for a rest. In early November, the 32d was back in action east of the Meuse River and fought there until the war's end.

Pershing was delighted with Haan's performance in the Meuse-Argonne, especially the capture of Côte Dame Marie. Following the Armistice, he made Haan the commander of the VII Corps and promoted him to brigadier general in the Regular Army. Within a few days,

Haan led his new unit into Germany as part of the Army of Occupation. After returning to the United States in the spring of 1919, he became head of the War Department's War Plans Division and was promoted to major general in 1920. Ill health forced him to retire two years later. He moved to Milwaukee and started a second career in business and writing. Haan died on Oct. 26, 1924.

Richard Kehrberg

Bibliography
Bullard, Robert L. *Fighting Generals*. Ann Arbor, MI: Edwards, 1944.
Pearson, Le Roy. "Major General William G. Haan." *Michigan History Magazine* (1925).

Haig, Douglas (1861–1928)

Field Marshal Sir Douglas Haig, commander-in-chief of the British Expeditionary Force (BEF) from 1915 until 1919, has remained a highly controversial figure in the literature of the First World War. He has been accused of being callous, bungling, incompetent, incapable of changing, unimaginative, and stupid. Most recently, the list has expanded to include being an intriguer and a falsifier of documents, and having engineered a massive cover-up, with British government assistance, of his worst blunders. On the other hand, Haig's supporters have seen him as the embodiment of the British nation during the war, sternly following an undeviating course to victory on the Western Front. If casualties were high, this school of thought argues that there was not any other way of winning the war: the German Army had to be worn down before it could be defeated.

Born to a wealthy Scottish family, Douglas Haig was the youngest of eleven children. His father was often absent and died in 1878. Haig was therefore largely brought up by his mother, who doted on him and was very ambitious for him. This sense of ambition, which she instilled in her son, became a dominant feature of Haig's personality. Together with the drive for success was a feeling that forces and individuals were opposed to him. This combination of personality traits led Haig to fight hard for promotion and to use whatever channels of influence were open to him. At the same time, when few took the business of soldiering seriously, Haig did and worked hard at his profession. These factors—added to his contacts with the royal family and with important senior officers and politicians, such as Lord Kitchener, Sir John French, Sir Evelyn Wood, and Lord Esher—eventually led to promotion to senior rank for the ambitious Haig. In fact, Haig made good use of the patronage system of the Edwardian British Army, whereby promotion through the influence of powerful patrons was a surer route to the top than seniority or merit.

After leaving Sandhurst, the British military academy, he joined the 7th Hussars as a junior cavalry officer in 1885. He was soon posted to India, then attended the Staff College in 1896–1897, and shortly thereafter served in the Sudan campaign as a staff officer. He also served in the Boer War as a staff officer and as commander of the 17th Lancers. At this point, Haig's career took off, and in fairly rapid succession he became inspector general of cavalry in India (1903), director of military training at the War Office (1906), director of staff duties at the War Office (1907), chief of the General Staff, India (1909), and chief of the Aldershot command in 1912. Thus, when war broke out in 1914, it was reasonable that he be given command of I Corps under Sir John French, commander-in-chief of the BEF.

By 1914, Haig's strong cavalry background, his previous combat experience in the Sudan and South Africa, and the lessons learned at the Staff College had combined to produce a fixed concept of warfare in his mind. This image of war focused on mobility and the need to fight structured battles, which would follow an inevitable threefold classical sequence: preparation and wearing down; a rapid, decisive offensive; and, finally, exploitation. In this scenario, the artillery bombardment need only last for half an hour before the decisive offensive, while the cavalry would undertake the key exploitation phase. Thus, the morale of the army and the determination of the commanding officer were of much greater importance than either technology or innovative ideas in winning battles. Finally, of importance for the planning of the two major BEF offensives of the Somme and Passchendaele, Haig understood that the commander-in-chief could make strategic plans but should then step aside and let the army and corps commanders deal with the tactics of the battle. It is also worth noting that Haig had spent most of his career before 1914 as a staff officer, both junior and senior, and his distant, detached methodical style of command reflected this staff background. All in all, Haig's military experience before 1914 was a distinctly poor preparation for the transitional nature of the First World War.

As I Corps commander, Haig was involved in the retreat from Mons on Aug. 24, 1914, and on August 25, his headquarters at Landrecies was surprised by German advance guards. Haig barely escaped, and he vowed to fight to the end. He was apparently shaken, but he had recovered by the next day when II Corps' stand at Le Cateau did much to save the BEF. The BEF's two corps retreated for the next thirteen days, mostly out of touch with each other, a situation that was not ideal. When the French Army and the BEF turned to launch an offensive in early September, Haig's I Corps was ordered to seize crossing points at the Aisne River, but it proved slow in doing so. Again this was not outstanding leadership; however, it should be noted that Haig's troops were very tired and probably could not have taken their objectives anyway. By mid-September, the front line stabilized, and at the end of October, the first defensive battle of Ypres, on the Belgian-French border, was fought in a salient. It resulted in severe casualties to both the British and French forces.

On Dec. 26, 1914, the BEF was divided into two armies, with Haig appointed to command the First Army. The next year was to be a learning time for Haig. In March 1915, he launched four divisions in a battering-ram style breakthrough offensive at Neuve Chapelle, supported by large amounts of artillery, which fired a thirty-five-minute surprise bombardment. The concept of surprise was good, but the barbed wire of the front line was not cut, reserves were slow to exploit, and 12,000 casualties were incurred in advancing some 1,000 yards. A rather similar assault on Aubers Ridge in May 1915 led to much the same result, another 11,500 casualties for very little ground gained. Indeed, this was part of the problem. Haig was trying to break through ever improving German defenses without considering the tactical nature of the ground involved. Instead, he should have attacked where the ground favored the offensive. The same mistake was made at Loos in September 1915, when Sir John French and Haig, under pressure from the French for an offensive, attempted to attack over unpromising ground. As a surprise, Haig intended to use chlorine gas, but on the day of the offensive the wind was barely favorable and was not sufficient to get the gas through the second line of German defenses. Moreover, the BEF reserve

did not come up soon enough to push through the initial gaps. Afterward, Haig accused his colleague Sir John French of holding back the reserves and thus losing the battle, although, in fact, they had been placed in positions selected by Haig himself. Nevertheless, this accusation by Haig, together with much behind-the-scene maneuvering, was sufficient to unseat French, and Haig was appointed commander-in-chief of the BEF in December 1915.

Haig's thinking in early 1916 was that the earlier battles had failed because while the enemy's first line of defenses had been captured, their reserves had prevented a breakthrough. Hence, it was necessary to wear down the enemy reserves before putting in the decisive offensive. Thus in planning the Somme offensive of summer 1916, Haig wanted a preparatory battle some ten days before launching the decisive offensive. A recent interpretation argues that Haig actually meant the Somme attack itself to be the short preparatory battle before launching the decisive BEF offensive elsewhere in the Flanders area. However, Haig also seemed to view the earlier but ongoing German Verdun offensive as contributing to the wearing down of the German reserves before his own offensive, and on July 1, 1916, fifteen BEF divisions and five French divisions attacked on both sides of the Somme River. The BEF suffered 57,000 casualties on the first day and another half million or more before the campaign ended in November 1916. Haig has been criticized for lack of communication with his army commander, Rawlinson, before the Somme and for forcing more ambitious objectives on Rawlinson than the latter wanted, thus resulting in a mixed plan that was neither a breakthrough nor a limited objective attack. The main reason for the heavy casualties on July 1, however, was not so much Haig's planning but the BEF's artillery, which could not properly cut wire, destroy dugouts, eliminate machine guns and artillery, or take the assaulting troops through the German trenches as they advanced.

Leaving aside smaller operations in 1917, the next major offensive planned by Haig and his staff was the Passchendaele offensive of July 31, 1917. If problems at the Somme could be blamed on inexperience or technical inability, Passchendaele was another matter. Here the poor choice of battlefield, lack of communication with the army commander, Gough, before the offensive, confusion over whether the offensive was to be a breakthrough or a step-by-step

H

advance, and failure to recognize the difficulty of assaulting the right flank of the Passchendaele ridge all contributed to the problems of the initial attack for which Haig and his staff can be held responsible. The continuation of the campaign into November also did not make much sense, and although the Cambrai tank-infantry-artillery attack at the end of 1917 promised much, the German counterattack ten days later should have been anticipated.

By 1918, Haig's conception of wearing down the enemy and then launching the decisive offensive that would lead to mobile warfare and the end of the war had not materialized. Instead, the German Army was able to transfer troops from the Eastern Front and launch a massive attack against the BEF on March 21, 1918, which Haig and his staff generally anticipated as to date and place but not as to style and method. Thus, Haig lost control of the BEF's retreat, so that the BEF was very nearly separated from the French Army, which would have meant defeat and retreat to the Channel ports as in World War II in 1940. As a result, Haig came close to being replaced, and at the end of March, he was subordinated to Marshal Ferdinand Foch as the supreme commander on the Western Front. From this time forward, Foch managed allied strategy, and Haig found that his own army commanders were becoming more independent. Thus the triumphs of the last 100 days on the Western Front until November 11, which have often been seen as offsetting criticisms of the attrition of 1916 and 1917, cannot be particularly ascribed to Haig.

However, sufficient evidence is available to argue that Haig really entered the conflict in 1914 with a fixed idea of what warfare was about and that he did not change his mind throughout four and a half years on the Western Front. He continued to believe in the structured three-phase offensive and in the centrality of infantry on the battlefield. Although Haig was willing enough to use gas, tanks, Lewis guns, aircraft, and other inventions, he did not think through their value and always considered them as auxiliary to the infantry. Haig believed the way to victory was to use his infantry, and cavalry, supported by artillery, to wear down the manpower available to the enemy. This is, in fact, exactly what did occur for the Allied victory in the First World War. In this sense, Haig achieved the victory he sought, although there never was a decisive offensive.

In terms of command, Haig continued to see his role as the rather distant chief strategist who laid plans and left subordinates to carry them out. This concept, combined with his aloof personality and inarticulate manner, made communication difficult with his commanders, and he tended to lose touch with what was actually going on. Indeed, his detachment from the battlefield required reliance on liaison officers for details of the front line—but, unfortunately, these officers in 1916 and 1917 often told him what he wanted to hear. Haig was not an imaginative commander; his key staff were generally not chosen for independence of mind, and the innovations that the BEF produced usually came about through ideas filtering upward from lower levels. Even when one major change in defensive tactics was introduced by Haig and his staff—the defense-in-depth concept before March 1918—this was borrowed from the German Army, and it did not actually work. On the offensive side, Haig preferred the straightforward artillery-infantry offensive, and his staff remained cool to the tank well into 1918. Hence, victory arrived in late 1918 more through weight of manpower and traditional technology, plus German mistakes and previous attrition, than through new ideas or strategy introduced by a relatively less powerful Haig. After the war, Haig served as commander-in-chief of Great Britain's Home Forces. He retired in 1921.

T.H.E. Travers

Bibliography

Bidwell, Shelford, and Dominick Graham. *Fire-Power: British Army Weapons and Theories of War, 1904–1945*. London: Allen & Unwin, 1982.

de Groot, Gerard. *Douglas Haig, 1861–1928*. London: Unwin Hyman, 1988.

Terraine, John. *Douglas Haig: The Educated Soldier*. London: Hutchison, 1963.

Travers, Tim. *The Killing Ground: The British Army, the Western Front, and the Emergence of Modern Warfare, 1900–1918*. London: Allen & Unwin, 1987.

Winter, Denis. *Haig's Command: A Reassessment*. New York: Viking, 1991.

Hand Grenades

The hand grenade had been used in the fifteenth century and perhaps saw its widest use prior to World War I in the seventeenth century when grenadiers were the elite shock troops of most European armies. It fell into disuse, however, in the eighteenth century and by 1914 had all but disappeared from the arsenals of Europe. Although its use in the Russo-Japanese War did show its value, it was not until 1914 that it regained prominence as a weapon. As the stagnation of trench warfare took hold, the grenade—the rifle as well as the hand grenade—again became commonplace. While European armies stumbled through the process of rediscovering and inventing hand grenades, the American Army because of its late entry into the war was able to plan ahead and model its grenades on those that had already proved most successful in trench warfare. It developed several types to meet different needs.

Defensive Hand Grenades

Perhaps the best-known grenade was the defensive hand grenade, Mark II. It was based on the French Le Blanc and British Mills hand grenades, both of which have segmented cast-iron bodies. The Mark II is about the size and shape of a large lemon, although often referred to as a "pineapple grenade." The World War I model weighed about twenty-two ounces. Screwed into the top of the body is the bouchon, or fuse, assembly of die-cast metal. This bouchon assembly consists of a tube containing a fuse projecting into the core of the grenade body. At the bottom of the fuse is a detonator of fulminate of mercury; at the top, a primer and a striker that is held cocked by a sheet-metal lever. This lever covers the top of the bouchon in such a way as to prevent the striker from falling on the primer and igniting the fuse. The lever is held in place by a pin that has a ring attached to allow it to be pulled free.

To use the grenade, one held the lever against the body of the grenade with one hand while pulling the safety pin out by the ring provided. When the grenade was thrown or released, the striker, which was spring-loaded, struck the primer. This caused the lever to fly off, and the primer, when struck, ignited the fuse. It burned for five seconds, at which point it exploded the detonator, which, in turn, ignited the explosive charge inside the body of the grenade. The segmented body broke into fragments with a blast radius of eighty feet. It was a defensive grenade because it had to be thrown from a position where the thrower was protected against the fragments. The Mark II saw service with the U.S. Army well into the 1960s.

Offensive Hand Grenade

The offensive hand grenade consists of a cylindrical body made of laminated cardboard. The base is plugged with cardboard covered with an asphalt layer. It uses the standard bouchon assembly screwed into a conical die-cast cap on top and is filled with four ounces of high explosive. It is operated in the same manner as the defensive grenade. The grenade's total weight is twelve ounces.

Because it has no fragmentation owing to its cardboard body, it can be used by troops in the open who are assaulting a position or counterattacking. Its purpose is to create a violent concussion that will stun any enemy, thus allowing the attacker to close in and overcome the foe.

Phosphorus Hand Grenade, Mark II

The phosphorus hand grenade, which has a total weight of twenty ounces, has a sheet-metal body shaped somewhat like a barrel that is three and a half inches long and two and one-quarter inches in diameter. The body is filled with four ounces of phosphorus. An electrical weld around its circumference creates a raised ridge. A steel tube, or thimble, is screwed into the center of the body. The bouchon is attached to this thimble, and the fuse and detonator are contained inside it, out of contact with the phosphorus.

This grenade works in the same manner as the grenades already described as far as the fuse is concerned. When the detonator explodes, however, there is only a small explosion, which is enough to rupture the steel shell of the body and release the phosphorus. Upon coming into contact with the air, the phosphorus ignites and covers a radius of thirty feet. This grenade is used to create smoke clouds to screen movement of individuals or, when used in quantities, to conceal movements of small units. Since it contains no high explosives, it causes little physical effect to the enemy unless he is within the blast range of the phosphorus.

Gas Grenade, Mark II

The gas hand grenade employs the same sheet-metal body as that of the phosphorus grenade. The only difference is the addition of two annular corrugations on the lower half of the body below the weld ridge. These corrugations serve to distinguish the gas grenade from the phosphorus grenade. The gas grenade body is filled with twelve and one-quarter ounces of stannis tetrachloride. When used, the small explosion of the detonator ruptures the body and allows the gas to escape. This grenade was designed for use in clearing out dugouts, cellars, pillboxes, or any small, enclosed, strong point that would not allow the gas to dissipate. If used in the open, it has a very limited local effect. This grenade weighs twenty-two ounces.

Thermit Hand Grenade, Mark I

A copy of a French design, the Thermit hand grenade consisted of a tin cylinder with tin plates closing the top and bottom. Into the top was screwed a striker bouchon. This was a die-cast plug to which was attached a brass tube with a cap that closed it. Inside was a die-cast holder that suspended a primer above a sheet-steel striker. Beneath the striker was a length of fuse. The fuse led to two lengths of quick match encased in a paper tube of priming powder. The entire assembly was set in the middle of the filling of the grenade's body, which was Thermit, a trade name for thermite, a mixture of aluminum powder and iron oxide. When ignited, this mixture burns at extremely high temperatures. The weight of this grenade is approximately thirty ounces.

To use the grenade, one removes the cap of the bouchon and strikes the primer holder onto the striker, thus igniting the primer and fuse assembly. There is a five-second delay until the priming powder ignites the thermite charge. Once ignited, the charge has to burn itself out. This grenade was used to seal shut the breechblocks of captured or abandoned artillery pieces by igniting and placing it in the breech or down the barrel. It could also be used to burn captured stores.

Incendiary Hand Grenade, Mark I

The rifle grenade used by the American Army in the First World War was intended to fill the gap between the range available to the hand grenade and that of the light trench mortars. It was modeled on a French design by Viven and Bessiéres, and for this reason it was called the VB rifle grenade. The grenade is two and one-quarter inches long and two inches in diameter and weighs seventeen ounces. The body is made of a malleable iron with a rounded top, smooth sides, and a flat base. There are grooves cut on the side of the body to ensure proper fragmentation when exploded. It has a central tube that runs longitudinally through it. When used, a bullet is fired from the rifle and the bullet passes through this tube. At the end of the tube, a striker sits obliquely over the opening. As the bullet exits the tube, it hits the striker, which folds back against the fuse container and fires the primer. This in turn ignites the fuse, which burns for eight seconds until it reaches the detonator. The fuse and detonator are housed in a chamber within the body of the grenade, parallel to the central bullet tube. When the detonator explodes, it causes the filling, one and three quarters ounces of high explosives, to detonate and the body fragments.

The grenade is projected by the VB rifle grenade discharger, Mark IV. This is a steel cylinder, tapering below its middle to less than half its largest diameter. Slots run most of the length of this narrow part allowing it to be slid onto the front of the barrel of the service rifle. There is a steel shim securing it to the barrel. When the rifle is fired, the gases escaping behind the bullet create pressure that forces the grenade out of the discharger. The principle is that of a piston. When the rifle is held at forty-five degrees from the ground, the normal range of the VB rifle grenade is 200 yards.

Michael J. Knapp

Bibliography

U.S. Army. Ordnance Department. *Handbook of Ordnance Data*. Washington, DC: Government Printing Office, 1919.

Harbord, James Guthrie (1866–1947)

James Guthrie Harbord was born on a farm near Bloomington, Illinois. The family moved to Missouri and then, in 1878, to Kansas. Harbord received a B.S. from Kansas State Agricultural College in 1886. Failing to gain an appointment to West Point, he taught in the public schools and at Kansas State University before enlisting as a private in the 4th Infantry in January 1889. Rapid promotion to regimental quartermaster sergeant followed. In March 1891, he placed first among fourteen NCOs selected to compete by examination for commissions. He was commissioned a second lieutenant on July 31, 1891, and assigned to the 5th Cavalry. He graduated from the Infantry and Cavalry School at Fort Leavenworth, Kansas, in 1895, and the same year earned an M.S. from his alma mater.

During the Spanish-American War, Harbord served as a major in the 2d Cavalry (U.S. Volunteers) in Florida and, briefly, in

Cuba. Reverting to Regular Army status, he was promoted to first lieutenant in July 1898. Assigned as quartermaster for the 10th Cavalry at Huntsville, Alabama, he met and for a few weeks in December 1898 shared a tent with 1st Lt. John J. Pershing. During this period, he sorted out Pershing's equipment shortages occasioned by the regiment's hasty deployment to Cuba the preceding year. Harbord was promoted to captain in 1901 and was assigned to the 11th Cavalry.

Harbord served as an assistant chief of the Philippine Constabulary in the rank of colonel from August 1903, to January 1914. The position gave him command responsibility for maintaining law and order over a large district, an invaluable experience for an officer of his rank. Coincidentally, his acquaintance with Pershing grew into friendship when their tours of duty overlapped for seven years. Upon Harbord's return to the United States, he was promoted to major and assigned to the 1st Cavalry.

When the United States declared war on April 6, 1917, Harbord was a student at the Army War College. On May 15, 1917, General Pershing selected him to be his chief of staff. He began working for Pershing the same day and was promoted to lieutenant colonel on the General Staff. Pershing's command group sailed for France at the end of May, and on June 17, 1917, his headquarters opened in Paris. Harbord played a significant role in the formation of the American Expeditionary Force (AEF). Most prominent among the concerns Harbord recorded in his war diary were the creation of an independent role and structure for the American Army alongside its battle-seasoned allies, selecting the best-qualified general officers to direct the rapidly expanding force, and establishing the training and supply base to bring the AEF to combat readiness. As the transition from buildup to combat took place in the spring of 1918, Pershing carried out sweeping replacements in his staff and rewarded his faithful subordinates.

Harbord was given command of the 4th Brigade (5th and 6th Marines) of the 2d Division on May 5, 1918. Though he had been promoted to brigadier general in August, he was apprehensive that as a regular lieutenant colonel he would not be welcomed by his regimental commanders, both of whom were marine colonels and holders of the Medal of Honor. His fears proved groundless. He developed a close professional and personal relationship with the marines of his command as the 2d Division took up positions on the Paris-Metz highway to stop the hemorrhage in the Allied lines. The 4th Brigade took up position south of Belleau Wood at Lucy-le-Bocage. By June 4, retreating French troops had passed through the 2d Division lines, which now constituted the front.

The Marine 4th Brigade launched a counterattack into Belleau Wood on June 6 and after nineteen days of continuous fighting secured the wood. The 2d Division, which had played a major part in stopping the German attack and sustained massive casualties in the process, was withdrawn from the line at the beginning of July. Harbord was promoted to major general on June 26, 1918, but only received official notification on July 11. He assumed command of the 2d Division on a day's notice on July 15 and was immediately called upon to participate in a major offensive operation.

The Aisne-Marne offensive (Second Battle of the Marne), planned for July 18, was designed to drive the Germans out of the newly created Marne salient. The attack of the Allied counteroffensive was to destroy the salient's viability by striking high on its western face, driving east to seize the key rail junction at Soissons and cutting the highway between Soissons and Château-Thierry. Harbord's division was administratively under III (U.S.) Corps, but for the purposes of this attack, it was under the operational control of XX (French) Corps, which placed the 2d Division on the right (south) flank of the corps attack.

The plan, fairly straightforward in its conception, was figuratively and literally breathtaking in its execution. Harbord learned of the general idea of the attack as his first official duty at a commander's conference on the morning of July 15. Before he arrived to take command, his division had already begun to scatter. The previous evening his divisional artillery and trains had been set in motion from south of Château-Thierry; their movement and subsequent location were unknown to Harbord until July 17. With only an hour's notice in the afternoon of July 16, the division's infantry boarded buses and began moving west and north with no knowledge of their destination or mission. Harbord, of course, knew they were moving toward battle, but it was not until he located corps headquarters late in the evening of July 16 that he was given attack orders for the morning of July 18, a scant thirty-five hours later. Although French movement officers were supposed to insure a timely delivery of 2d Division troops to their assembly points, XX Corps headquarters could give Harbord no information concerning their transit, destination, or location. In the early morning hours of July 17, he was able to obtain maps and a written terrain analysis of his zone of operations from III (U.S.) Corps but was unable to reconnoiter before the attack. After dawn on July 17, Harbord and his staff began the search for his scattered division. Secrecy, officious French liaison and transit officers, drenching rain, and a primitive road network through a dense forest conspired against the operation. His infantry units were unloaded an average of twelve to fifteen miles from their lines of departure. Harbord and his staff spent the day and the predawn hours of July 18 attempting to direct and coordinate the units struggling to reach their attack positions. Leading elements of all three attacking regiments ultimately double-timed across the line of departure at 4:25 A.m., July 18.

Despite heavy casualties, the attack went surprisingly well. On a mile and a half front the division advanced five miles against increasingly stiff resistance. An advance of an additional mile and a half on July 19 left division troops just short of the offensive objective. The 2d Division went into the attack 5,000 men under strength and took 5,000 casualties in these two days of heavy fighting.

Out on the line for only six days, Harbord was unexpectedly summoned to general headquarters (GHQ) by Pershing. Within minutes of his arrival at Chaumont on July 26, Pershing requested that Harbord relinquish command of the 2d Division to take command of the Service of Supply (S.O.S.), the AEF's vast support organization. Harbord had only commanded the 2d Division for two weeks and had hopes of higher combat command. Certainly being assigned to a supply organization with a reputation as a dumping ground for failures, misfits, and civilians in uniform was not his idea of a promotion. Nevertheless, he immediately acquiesced to Pershing's request.

This unexpected turn of events hinged on two considerations. The first was the increasing supply problem faced by the rapidly expanding AEF. The second was a threat to Pershing's overall command from Washington. On July 6, Secretary of War Newton D. Baker had requested that Pershing consider accepting MajGen.

George W. Goethals as the commanding general of the S.O.S. responsible directly to the War Department. Pershing saw behind the suggestion a scheme by Army Chief of Staff Peyton C. March to diminish his status and authority. Pershing moved quickly to solve both problems by appointing Harbord. Pershing knew his close friend would bring a competent dynamism to the S.O.S. while simultaneously covering the AEF's Washington flank.

Harbord assumed command of the S.O.S. at his headquarters in Tours on July 29, 1918, and, with Pershing, began a one-week tour of the vast, and widely scattered, command. Harbord ultimately did little to change the structure of the organization. But the tour, followed over the next months by Harbord's driving, hands-on leadership style, raised morale and invigorated the S.O.S. He gained control of the AEF's routine supply operations and received permission to communicate directly with the War Department instead of through GHQ. Typical of his leadership style was the creation of a rolling headquarters. Using a seven-car train, he moved through the S.O.S. with his principal staff officers, adminitrative aides, telegraph equipment, staff cars, and living accommodations. In the first 100 nights of his command, Harbord spent 55 on the train, constantly moving through his vast domain. His efforts in supporting the fighting units in the last three months of the war were a major contribution to victory, and his achievements during this period were unsurpassed by Pershing's other major subordinates.

Harbord remained in command of the S.O.S. until May 1919. Following a brief encore as Pershing's chief of staff, he headed a presidential military mission to Armenia. Promoted to major general in September 1919, he briefly commanded the 2d Division in Texas before returning to Washington for a final tour as deputy chief of staff, U.S. Army from July 1, 1921, to Dec. 29, 1922, when he retired from active duty.

Only fifty-six years old at the time of his retirement, Harbord began a long and distinguished career in private industry. He served as president of the Radio Corporation of America from 1923 until 1930 and chairman of the board from 1930 to 1947. He was also a board member of the Atchison, Topeka, and Santa Fe Railroad, New York Life, and NBC among other large corporations.

He was promoted to lieutenant general on the retired list on July 9, 1942. Harbord died at his home in Rye, New York, on Aug. 20, 1947, and was buried at Arlington National Cemetery.

Charles A. Endress

See also MARNE, SECOND BATTLE OF THE; UNITED STATES ARMY SERVICE OF SUPPLY

Bibliography
Hagood, Johnson. *The Services of Supply; A Memoir of the Great War.* New York: Houghton Mifflin, 1927.

Harbord, James G. *The American Army in France, 1917–1919.* Boston: Little, Brown, 1936.

———. *Leaves From a War Diary.* New York: Dodd, Mead, 1925.

Pershing, John J. *My Experiences in the World War.* New York: Stokes, 1931.

Haskins, Charles Homer (1870–1937)

Charles Homer Haskins was perhaps the foremost American historian of Medieval Europe, specializing in early Norman and Saxon England. He had received his Ph.D. from Johns Hopkins University in 1890 and by 1914 was Gurney Professor of History at Harvard. A conservative "old-school" intellectual, Haskins was a close friend of Woodrow Wilson.

With the coming of the war, Haskins responded enthusiastically to the government's call to historians and other intellectuals and joined the Committee on Public Information (CPI), or "Creel Bureau," in 1917. He was also a key member of the National Board for Historical Service, which was responsible for writing and disseminating government war propaganda, so important in marshaling public opinion in support of intervention in Europe.

In September 1917, Haskins joined a select group of scholars and university academics in what constituted America's first "think tank," The Inquiry. This group, formed at President Wilson's request, was charged with formulating America's war aims as a basis for peace in Europe. Haskins headed the Northwest Europe Research Division of The Inquiry, whose dozens of reports were complied under his direction, many by Haskins himself, and their analyses served as the basis for Wilson's Fourteen Points.

In December 1918, Haskins was asked to accompany several dozen historians and other members of The Inquiry sailing with President Wilson to France as the American Commission to Negotiate Peace (ACNP). For the next seven months, the commissioners were deeply involved in presenting the American position on the territorial, economic, political, and military clauses of the Treaty of Versailles. As America's expert on France and Belgium, Haskins sat on the key commissions considering complex territorial issues. His influence in shaping the final clauses of the treaty regarding Belgian claims, Alsace-Lorraine, the Saar, and the Danzig Corridor was significant. He worked closely with Wilson as an intimate adviser and friend during the Council of Ten and Big Four negotiations, and he more than held his own with his British and French counterparts.

After the war, Haskins continued to support Wilson's achievements at Paris and authored, with colleague Robert H. Lord, a defense of his policies in *Problems of the Paris Peace Conference.*

Jonathan M. Nielson

See also INQUIRY, THE

Bibliography
Gelfand, Lawrence. *The Inquiry: American Preparations for Peace, 1917–1919.* New Haven, CT: Yale University Press, 1963.

"Charles Homer Haskins." *American Historical Review* (July 1937).

Haskins, Charles H., and Robert H. Lord. *Some Problems of the Paris Peace Conference.* Cambridge: Harvard University Press, 1920.

Herron, George Davis (1862–1924)

During World War I, George Davis Herron, a former Christian minister and American expatriot in Italy, became an outspoken advocate of United States entry into the European war. Formerly a member of the Social Gospel movement in American Protestantism, he believed that the United States had a chance to create a "Christly world order" by fighting in the war and negotiating the peace. Like many American ministers, Herron favored the war because he hoped it would help usher in the Kingdom of God on earth.

Born in Montezuma, Indiana, the only son of William and Isabella Davis Herron, he grew up in a deeply religious home. In 1883, while working for a newspaper in Ripon, Wisconsin, he experienced a religious conversion that impelled him into the Congregational ministry. During the 1890s, he became a prominent spokesman for the Social Gospel, asserting the need for social reform and social justice as the basis for salvation. Departing from the individualistic view of most nineteenth-century evangelical Protestants, social gospelers like Herron criticized industrial capitalism in America for its exploitation of workers and its destruction of the Christian spirit. His career was cut short, however, by a scandal and divorce in 1901, and the Congregational Church's decision to defrock him. He then moved to Italy with his second wife.

Herron did not address American audiences again until after 1914, when he published several books intended to inspire Americans to support the war. Volumes such as *The Menace of Peace* and *Germanism and the American Crusade* appropriated the language of the Social Gospel to argue in favor of war. He believed that the war gave Americans a "divine chance to rescue the world from the clutches of "Germanism" and to erect a world order based on democracy and cooperation.

By the end of the war, he had regained some of his credibility. He joined Woodrow Wilson in Paris and worked as a special emissary to the Germans to convince them of Wilson's efforts to negotiate an equitable settlement. When events in Russia threatened to impede the peace process, George Herron was one of two representatives sent by Wilson to the Prinkipo Conference to work out an arrangement with the Bolshevik regime.

Disheartened by the outcome of negotiations and dismayed by angry reactions to his role in the process, Herron once again retreated to Italy, where, in 1921, he published *The Defeat in the Victory*. It recounted Wilson's heroic efforts at the peace conference and explained the ultimate failure of the Versailles Treaty. Herron died in 1924.

Susan Curtis

Bibliography

Briggs, Mitchell P. *George D. Herron and the European Settlement*. Stanford, CA: Stanford University Press, 1932.

Crunden, Robert M. *Ministers of Reform: The Progressives' Achievement in American Civilization, 1889–1920*. New York: Basic Books, 1982.

Curtis, Susan. *A Consuming Faith: The Social Gospel and Modern American Culture*. Baltimore: Johns Hopkins University Press, 1991.

Herron, George D. *Woodrow Wilson and the World's Peace*. New York: Kennerley, 1917.

Hindenburg, Paul von (1847–1934)

Paul von Hindenburg was Germany's most renowned hero of World War I. The name Hindenburg graced battleships and battle lines, buildings and dirigibles. His countenance appeared on millions of postage stamps, and to this day, visitors are still drawn to his final resting place. His fame in war laid the foundation for a controversial political career, and after a second retirement lasting six years, he was elected president of the Weimar Republic in 1925. Seven years later, at eighty-five, he defeated Adolf Hitler for the same post, only to feel compelled to appoint the latter as chancellor in January 1933. For all of his importance, Hindenburg's consequential historical role did not begin until 1914, when he had reached the age of sixty-seven.

Paul von Hindenburg belonged to the fabled caste of Prussian landed aristocrats, which numbered some 26,000 families. He was born in Posen, deep in Prussian Junkerdom. His descent from a long line of nobles made it all but inevitable that he would serve as an officer in the army of his king. His career, until the Great War, was without distinction, although he served in both the Seven Weeks' War against Austria in 1866 and in the Franco-Prussian War in 1870. He was wounded in the former and decorated for valor in the latter. In January 1871, Hindenburg had the honor of representing his regiment at the proclamation of the German Empire in Versailles. From this point until his retirement in 1911, he was a soldier serving in a peacetime army. The old veteran seems to have been looking forward to retirement for he laid aside his epaulettes before reaching the mandatory age. He had stepped down at his own request and disappeared into a leisured life, pursuing the interests suitable to his age and station.

A telegram from Berlin on Aug. 22, 1914, brought Hindenburg's leisure to an abrupt end.

The message informed him that he had been appointed to command the 8th Army in East Prussia and that he would be joined by MajGen. Erich Ludendorff, who was to serve as his chief of staff. Facing the 8th Army was an invading Russian force already standing on German soil. Panic gripped Germany and diverted national attention, as well as troops desperately needed for the drive on Paris, to the east. The two generals set off immediately for the front. A pair of bloody contests, the Battle of Tannenberg and the Battle of Masurian Lakes, ensued almost upon their arrival, and by the end of the first week of September, the invader had been routed. Russia's losses were so staggering and demoralizing that the country never fully recovered, though it gamely stayed in the war as it had promised the Western Allies it would. Credit for the German victory went to Hindenburg, and he became a hero overnight. At the time it was widely believed that his successes had saved Germany from the ordeal of a Russian invasion. More importantly, they also strengthened the unfounded hope that the war would be a short and victorious one for Germany.

The resounding triumphs on the Russian front during the late summer of 1914 launched Hindenburg's lustrous reputation, but they also masked an unpleasant truth. The stark fact of the matter was that the victories had failed to eliminate Germany's greatest disadvantage—the two-front war. Though Russia had been badly hurt, it remained in the war. With two fronts to cover, Germany was still forced to divide its limited resources, no matter how weak the foe on one side had become. And as before, its enemies enjoyed the formidable option of synchronizing and timing their operations.

Not only did Hindenburg's early successes fail to solve Germany's basic strategic dilemma, but they also may have cost Germany whatever chances there had been for victory in the first place. The war plan formulated by the chief of the General Staff, Gen. Alfred von Schlieffen, in 1907, rested on the simple assumption that the German armies were incapable of waging successful offensives on eastern and western fronts simultaneously. Therefore, he called for the concentration of forces in the west in order to bring victory there in the shortest possible time, while maintaining a minimum guard against the Russians. After success in the west, German forces there were to be sent to the east in order to achieve the same result. Von Schlieffen's

strategy, which was called the Schlieffen Plan, was bequeathed to his successor, Helmut von Moltke, who departed from Schlieffen's concept by subtracting a crucial force from the west just when it was most needed in order to provide Hindenburg with troops to win in East Prussia in 1914. For this reason, France was never brought to its knees, the two-front war continued, and Germany drifted into a long, stagnant war, the one kind it could never win. However encouraging they may have been at the time, if Hindenburg's victories were made possible at the expense of delivering the knockout blow to France, they can be regarded as disastrous for Germany.

Hindenburg could not deliver the final blow against the Russians because of the weakness of the Austro-Hungarian forces holding the right flank of the Eastern Front. Further limiting Hindenburg's initiatives were the insatiable demands for manpower on the Western Front to which chief of the General Staff Gen. Erich von Falkenhayn, von Moltke's replacement, attached a higher priority. As if to compensate him for his frustrations, Kaiser Wilhelm II, in November 1914, appointed Hindenburg commander-in-chief of all German forces in the east and accompanied this honor with a promotion to field marshal.

The year 1915 brought very modest victories for the Central Powers on the Eastern Front, among them a slow withdrawal by the Russians and the evacuation of Warsaw. But the destruction of the Russian Army was out of the question as long as Falkenhayn regarded the war in the east as secondary and accordingly deprived Hindenburg of the manpower he needed to launch a final offensive operation.

Matters went from bad to worse for the Central Powers in 1916. It was Falkenhayn's plan to force a decision in the west by launching a great German attack against Verdun. Hindenburg, who disagreed with the logic of Falkenhayn's strategy, was required to relinquish precious manpower from his own forces in order to insure its success. Since he had long lamented that the number of troops in his command was too few to begin with, Hindenburg emerged from the dispute as a critic and a rival of Falkenhayn. Despite the reduction in manpower, Hindenburg was able to block a Russian offensive timed to relieve the German pressure on Verdun. The Austrians on the southern flank were less successful and their lines buckled under the Russian pressure. As a result of this menacing development, Hindenburg was given command of the entire Eastern Front, and in this capacity he distinguished himself again by stabilizing the lines across the entire sector.

The setbacks for the Central Powers in 1916 were many and painful. Even Hindenburg's latest success on the Russian front could not conceal the fact that Germany's situation was grim. The attack at Verdun had failed, the Italians were making headway at the expense of the Austrians at Gorizia, the offensive on the Somme by the Western Allies was producing much consternation in Germany, and Rumania had entered the war as an ally of the Entente. General von Falkenhayn paid the price for these setbacks, and the kaiser turned to Hindenburg, appointing him chief of the General Staff in August 1916. The crisis not only changed military leadership, but amounted to a constitutional turning point in German history as well, for Hindenburg was simultaneously granted the discretionary powers of supreme war lord in the name of the kaiser himself. General Ludendorff remained in Hindenburg's entourage and was invested with the designation "first quartermaster general." In this capacity he was able to exercise the virtually unlimited powers bestowed upon his superior.

The original Hindenburg-Ludendorff partnership worked as smoothly on the new, greatly elevated level of power as it had before. The relationship between the two, however, underwent a change. The senior officer gradually slipped into the role of figurehead, while Ludendorff, his junior, aggressively assumed more power and responsibility. However, Ludendorff never lost the confidence of his nominal superior. Ludendorff's brisk and inspired use of Hindenburg's sweeping powers gave rise to complaints about a "military dictatorship." This charge, however, could not tarnish the revered Hindenburg, who was protected by his legend. His imperturbable calm and his paternal benignity were the perfect complements to the volatile and energetic Ludendorff. The division of labor within the Supreme Command left the older officer with a vague and general overlordship and provided the command with the spell of his magic name and presence. The actual use of power, however, fell to Erich Ludendorff.

The broadening powers of the military triggered a bitter test of strength between civilian institutions and the generals during the last two years of the war. The Foreign Office, the Chancellory, the Reichstag, and even the imperial crown itself, found the military encroaching on their defined spheres of authority. Though it was Ludendorff who usually instigated these encroachments, he invariably enjoyed the unswerving support of his Junker patron. Again and again, Hindenburg used the threat of resignation as his ultimate weapon in order to assure the triumph of his abrasive subordinate. The soldiers forced Chancellor Theobald von Bethmann Hollweg, whom they regarded as irresolute, to step down. His replacement, Georg Michaelis, was their nominee. They fought the moderation of the Foreign Office by demanding annexationist war aims. They insisted on creating a puppet kingdom of Poland, thereby ending all hope for a separate peace with Russia, and they rode roughshod over the Reichstag by sabotaging its irenic peace resolution. War production was increased by imposing a quasi-military regimentation (known as the Hindenburg Program) at the expense of labor unions. The kaiser himself was rendered as harmless as a titular monarch and relegated to the sidelines, where he waited to be summoned for ceremonial duties or to lend the dignity of his office to endorse the moves of his supposed retainers.

It was from this panoramic vista afforded from the citadel of the Supreme Command that Hindenburg came to a full and sobering appreciation of Germany's bleak situation. Also, he could now understand von Falkenhayn's preoccupation with the Western Front and that, if defeat or stalemate were to be avoided, if Germany were to impose its will on the Allies, it would be necessary to concentrate all of Germany's resources in the west. Time clearly was not on Germany's side. Its strength was slowly ebbing as the noose of the blockade and the stagnant fronts tightened around the nation. To deal with this predicament, the Supreme Command proposed a grand plan. It not only involved high risk but also included a critical timing element in order to achieve success. In fact, it would make or break Germany.

The final gamble of the Supreme Command contained several elements. The first called for the resumption of unrestricted submarine warfare. This was aimed at Britain, which depended on a bridge of ships coming mainly from North America to feed its population and to supply its armed forces. With new submarines, the German Admiralty believed it could interdict or discourage enough shipping to force Britain to sue for peace. The objection that the renewed use of submarines would bring the United States into the war was met with the rejoinder that the American colossus was already doing everything that it could to aid the Allies, short of sending ground forces. To build up such forces would require the United States to start almost from scratch and then bring them to France. The estimate was that this would require close to two years, by which time the other elements of the Supreme Command's plan would have decided the issue. Thus, the plan took into account the fact that still another country would likely be added to the already formidable list of Germany's foes.

The second part of the Supreme Command's plan for bringing the war to a victorious conclusion called for the elimination of Russia as a belligerent by fomenting revolution. The Russian Revolution of March 1917 produced the impetus for this far-fetched idea. The March Revolution had brought constitutionalism, but not peace, and there was ample reason to believe that the war-weary nation was ripe for a second revolution. Lenin, the leader of the Bolsheviks, then living in exile in Switzerland, was counted on as the man who could make it happen. That Lenin's call for peace was based on the need to consolidate his power, rather than on any pacific principles, affected this thinking not at all. The hope was that Lenin, once in power, would take Russia out of the war and give Germany relief from the debilitating burden of fighting on two fronts. Although the plan was obviously a risky expedient, especially in view of what was to happen later, it appealed to Ludendorff, and Hindenburg gave it his perfunctory approval. Both men were oblivious to the danger from the Bolshevik extremist, just as they disregarded the fact that Lenin's radical political principles contradicted everything that they stood for. The urgent need of the moment was to end the war with Russia and not to worry about whatever disruptive effects bolshevism might unleash later in Germany, Europe, or the world. The German forces that would no longer be needed to fight in Russia were to be sent to France. Once a numerical improvement had been achieved there, the final component of the Supreme Command's plan called for breaking France's will to fight by launching a last, crushing offensive. Timing was critical to the plan, for it was urgent that the submarine force capitulation on Britain, that Lenin sue for peace, and that the German armies defeat France in the field before the Americans arrived in Europe. It would certainly be close in any event.

The declaration of war by the United States upon Germany and its allies in April 1917 came as no surprise and caused little dismay at Hindenburg's headquarters. More attention that month was focused on Russia. Lenin had just been whisked across Germany and into Petrograd and the General Staff watched anxiously as he began his revolutionary agitation. By November the Bolsheviks were in power. Lenin's Soviet Russia immediately defected from the Entente and asked for an armistice. Peace negotiations were begun at once at Brest Litovsk, and German hopes for victory were suddenly revived. Conversely, those of the Western Allies were greatly weakened. Ostensibly, the Supreme Command's gamble was beginning to pay off. Russia's defeat seemed to nullify the fact that the United States had associated itself with the Entente. As Germany waited for its submarines to produce the intended effects on Britain, preparations were made for the great final offensive in France by capitalizing on the manpower dividend that was expected from victory in Russia. No notice was taken of the irony that a regime which was the very antithesis of what Imperial Germany stood for had just been fastened upon hapless Russia, nor that the Bolsheviks immediately set about to instigate another revolution in Germany itself.

With high hopes and expectations, the great German spring offensive of 1918 began on March 21. Hindenburg and Ludendorff both understood that they were playing Germany's last card. Initially, the attack made dramatic headway and lifted German spirits accordingly. The first wave of attacks, hitting at the point where the British and French sectors of the front joined, tore an opening that was mended with only the greatest effort. The consequence of this near calamity was the creation of a much needed unified command under French General Ferdinand Foch, which henceforth controlled all Entente forces in the west. Meanwhile, the onslaught continued into July, at which time German forces stood once again on the Marne. But even as the Allied armies retreated, there was no panic and their lines never broke. The Allied forces made the enemy pay dearly for every yard of ground gained. Thus, as the Germans were expending their very last strength, the Entente powers never contemplated surrender but rather bided their time, knowing that relief from America was on the way.

Germany's last offensive was brought to a halt on July 18, 1918. A vigorous counterattack by French and American forces then pushed the exhausted Germans back from the Marne. Manpower ratios of the two opposing forces were already unfavorable for the Germans when the "Emperor's Campaign" began in March. Since that time, German losses had been unusually heavy and were in fact unsustainable. Moreover, 1 million Americans were now disembarked in Europe, with more on the way. Not a single troop transport had been lost to submarines on the voyages across the Atlantic. Besides, the manpower dividend expected from the victory over Russia was disappointingly small. Of the 1 million German troops on the Russian front at the time of the Armistice, 500,000 remained there to maintain and exploit the newly won influence in East Central Europe. These same contingents, however, were desperately needed for the great final effort in the west. Whether the manpower shortfall resulting from the Treaty of Brest Litovsk cost Germany its victory in the west in 1918 is one of history's imponderables. What is clear is that the Central Powers continued to suffer the disadvantages of their encirclement even after their victory over Russia and that the Hindenburg command had not found a solution to this persistent problem.

Hindenburg and Ludendorff were slow to see the hopelessness of Germany's situation. It was not until Aug. 8, 1918, when a British tank offensive could not be halted, that Ludendorff came to the conclusion that German forces were no longer able to provide an effective defense. Ludendorff described that day as the "darkest day" of the German armed forces and concluded that Germany now had no choice of imposing its will on its enemies and that therefore the war should be ended. But neither he nor Hindenburg took any immediate action to bring this about. The sudden and almost simultaneous collapse of the other Central Powers— Austria-Hungary, Bulgaria, and Turkey—during September and October, finally forced both Hindenburg and Ludendorff not only to concede that the war was lost, but also to call for an immediate armistice based on Wilson's Fourteen Points.

Wilson's insistence that he would only negotiate an armistice with a government that had democratic and parliamentary forms meant that Germany could not expect an armistice unless it made fundamental constitutional changes. At the urgent behest of the Supreme Command, the long-debated constitutional changes were swiftly made in Prussia and the empire. At the same time, Prince Max of Baden, an advocate of a peace with victory, was named chancellor. He formed a new government that reflected the composition of the majority parties in the Reichstag. Again, citing the imminence of a military collapse, Hindenburg and Ludendorff put extreme pressure on the new government to send a request for an immediate cease-fire to Washington. The generals were accommodated on October 4. Wilson, seeing the daily improvement in the Entente's situation and allowing time for negotiations with his allies, did not respond until October 23. Instead of offering an armistice, he required an unconditional capitulation. The news drove Ludendorff to resign. With great misgivings, a German delegation was sent to Compiègne to receive the terms from General Foch. Hindenburg admonished the delegation to ask the enemy for moderation, but if none was shown, to accept whatever was offered.

The humiliation of defeat was not the only bitter pill that Hindenburg had to swallow in the final days of the Great War. President Wilson's communications with the German government had made it clear that one of the conditions of peace was the abolition of the monarchy in Germany. As difficult as it was for the field marshal, himself a monarchist by conviction and dedicated to a lifetime of service to the Prussian dynasty, to accept this condition, it was immeasurably more painful to carry out the duty of persuading the reluctant Wilhelm that he had no choice but to abdicate. The war-weary population, as well as the armed forces themselves, had come to understand that the monarchy constituted the only remaining obstacle to peace, and it was this which triggered mutiny and revolution throughout Germany. With a heavy heart, Hindenburg personally undertook the responsibility of pointing out to his lord that the army would no longer obey his commands and that the consequence of obstinacy would be civil war and chaos in Germany. He furthermore urged Wilhelm to seek asylum in Holland, a step taken on November 9, the day on which the Weimar Republic was proclaimed.

The end of the war and the abolition of the monarchy placed Hindenburg in an awkward and uncertain situation. It could be argued that the kaiser's abdication had released him from the bonds of his soldierly oath and that he was morally and legally free to wash his hands of all responsibilities and return to private life. The new first quartermaster general, Wilhelm Groener, presented his superior with another alternative, however. Groener was well aware of the troubles facing the provisional *Reichspresident,* Friedrich Ebert. No sooner had Ebert assumed his new office in Berlin than he faced the threat of revolutionary upheaval from the Bolsheviks, whose aim it was to establish a Marxist dictatorship of the type foisted upon Russia a year earlier. At this point, Ebert's sole source of institutional support was the trade unions, strong in numbers but otherwise short of tangible power. Reaching the desperate leader of the new republic by wire from his headquarters, Groener offered a bargain that Ebert accepted immediately. The arrangement was simple enough. In exchange for the army's defense of Ebert's Provisional Government against the Bolsheviks, the republic would adopt the orphaned army. The linchpin in the bargain was Hindenburg, whose name had lost none of its magic and whose acceptance of the plan Groener vouchsafed without even troubling to consult the field marshal. When the septuagenarian warrior was informed, he endorsed the pact without expressing misgivings or reservations. The power of the defeated army with the revered and legendary Hindenburg at its head not only sufficed to face down the immediate threat coming from the Left and thus to save the young democratic republic, but it also made the new government legitimate and acceptable to soldiers, patriots, and conservatives who were otherwise not disposed to endorse the new political order in Germany.

By the summer of 1919, the Weimar Republic had shed its provisional character. Not only had it stabilized itself by fending off the violence coming from the Left, but it had also been legitimized through the process of democratic elections based on the widest franchise known in the world. A constitution that would have satisfied the most fastidious Wilsonian had been adopted, and a peace settlement, however unsatisfactory, had been signed with Germany's former enemies. Hindenburg, then approaching his seventy-second birthday, at last considered his service to his country and to the new republic to be completed and embarked upon his second retirement. If he had failed to bring victory to Germany in war, at least his calming presence had contributed significantly to the arduous transition from war to peace and from monarchy to republic. His place in the hearts of his countrymen was as secure as it had been ever since his victories in the summer of 1914, as the welcome given to him upon his return to his home in Hanover amply demonstrated. No one could have dreamed then that the old man would be called to serve his country as *Reichspresident* in 1925, much less that he would eventually hoist Adolf Hitler into the German chancellery and thus set the stage for an even greater disaster than the one Hindenburg himself had lived through.

Ralph C. Walz

See also LUDENDORFF, ERICH

Bibliography
Asprey, Robert B. *German High Command at War.* New York: Morrow, 1991.
Goldsmith, Margaret L. *Hindenburg: The Man and the Legend.* New York: Morrow, 1930.
Hindenburg, Paul von. *Out of My Life.* New York: Harper, 1921.
Schultze, Pfaelzer. *Hindenburg: Peace, War and Aftermath.* New York: Putnam, 1932.
Wheeler-Bennett, John W. *Wooden Titan; Hindenburg in Twenty Years of German History, 1914–1934.* New York: Morrow, 1936.

Hines, John Leonard (1868–1968)

John Leonard Hines was born in White Sulphur Springs, West Virginia. He won a competitive examination for a congressional appointment to the United States Military Academy at West Point. There he had a hard time maintaining passing grades but persevered and graduated with his class in 1891. While at West Point he took a great interest in athletics and was a member of one of the academy's first football teams.

As a new second lieutenant, his first assignment was with the 2d Infantry at Fort Omaha, Nebraska. This was followed by service at Fort Harrison, Montana, and in 1898, he went to Cuba with the 25th Infantry. There he landed at Siboney and served with distinction throughout the campaign. He was cited in War Department orders for gallantry at the Battle of San Juan Hill. After duty in Cuba, Captain Hines went on the first of several assignments to the Philippines, where he saw more combat in the Insurrection and later in the campaign against the Moros.

In 1916, Hines joined Gen. John J. Pershing as adjutant of the Punitive Expedition against Pancho Villa. This close association led to his inclusion in the first group of officers to go to France with General Pershing to form the nucleus of the general headquarters of the American Expeditionary Force (AEF). In October 1917, he was given command of the 16th Infantry of the 1st Division. During the harsh winter of 1917–1918, Colonel Hines put his green regiment and its inexperienced officers through rigorous training. This paid off as demonstrated by the regiment's stellar performance in the fierce fighting in May 1918 in the Cantigny-Montdidier area, the first offensive by U.S. forces in France. Promoted to brigadier general, Hines led the division's 1st Brigade in the battle at Soissons and the occupation of the Saizerais sector. His division commander, MajGen. Charles Summerall, stated, "The success of the 1st Division in the desperate fighting at Soissons is due in great measure to the qualities General Hines displayed in the operations."

After the Aisne-Marne counteroffensive Hines was promoted to major general and assigned to command the 4th Division. He led it in the reduction of the St. Mihiel salient and in the Meuse-Argonne offensive. His success prompted General Pershing to give him command of III Corps. The successful crossing of the Meuse and, after the Armistice, the occupation of the Rhineland demonstrated the general's tactical and administrative skills. He kept the corps command until late 1919, when he returned to the United States. In 1922, General Pershing called him from the command of VIII Corps Area to be his deputy in Washington and to succeed him as chief of staff of the army in 1924.

After completion of his four years as chief of staff, he served as commander of IX Corps Area headquartered in San Francisco and then as head of the Department of the Philippines. He retired in 1932 as a major general, but Congress in 1940 promoted him again to four-star rank. General Hines died in Washington, D.C., on Oct. 13, 1968 at the age of 100.

James L. Collins

Bibliography

Marshall, George C. *Memoirs of My Services in the World War 1917–1918*. Boston: Houghton Mifflin, 1976.

Pershing, John J. *My Experiences in the World War*. New York: Stokes, 1931.

Smythe, Donald. *Pershing*. Bloomington: Indiana University Press, 1986.

Hines, Walker Downer (1870–1934)

In January 1918, William G. McAdoo, secretary of the Treasury and railroad czar, appointed Walker Downer Hines to serve as his assistant director general of the Railroad Administration (RA). A Kentucky-born lawyer, Hines had risen through management ranks to become chairman of the Santa Fe Railroad in 1916. During 1917, however, he had not been associated with the Railroads' War Board, formed voluntarily by the industry to meet the war emergency.

With McAdoo frequently absent due to travel and ill health, Hines effectively ran the daily operations of the RA. Upon McAdoo's resignation at war's end, Hines became director general of the RA. The appointment of this reserved, spare, hard-working advocate of efficiency pleased neither reformers nor railroad management. The former saw Hines as a pawn of owners, while the latter feared he was a renegade who would support permanent government operations of the lines. In fact, Hines was neither.

Hines held his post until May 18, 1920, guiding the RA through the rocky postwar period. Fearing inflation, he opposed raising either wages or rates. He was influential in framing an antilabor stance within the Wilson administration during a coal miners' strike in 1919, but he also led a bruising battle with steel manufacturers over the cost of their product. Originally supporting McAdoo's call for a five-year continuation of federal control of the railroads, Hines subsequently offered a three-year plan, which unsuccessfully urged government consolidation of the nation's railroads into twenty or fewer major regional systems, replacing the "inefficient" competition of the prewar years.

Following his resignation in 1920, Hines returned to private law practice, and wrote a history of the Railroad Administration for the Carnegie Endowment, entitled *War History of American Railroads*.

Kevin B. Byrnes

See also RAILROAD ADMINISTRATION

Bibliography

Hines, Walker D. *War History of American Railroads*. New Haven, CT: Yale University Press, 1928.

Kerr, K. Austen. *American Railroad Politics, 1914–1920: Rates, Wages and Efficiency*. Pittsburgh: University of Pittsburgh Press, 1968.

McAdoo, William G. *Crowded Years, The Reminiscences of William G. McAdoo*. Boston: Houghton Mifflin, 1931.

Hoover, Herbert Clark (1874–1964)

Herbert Clark Hoover was one of the major American figures to emerge from the home front in World War I. While careful study of an historical figure usually reveals a personality different from the public image, rarely is that discrepancy as great as with Hoover. Since Hoover has been indelibly etched in the public mind as the president during the dreary failures of the Great Depression of the 1930s, few Americans are aware of his larger-than-life reputation during the Great War. Hoover's main contributions to the war effort and later reconstruction were the organization of the Commission for Relief in Belgium (CRB), the U.S. Food Administration (USFA), and the American Relief Administration in Europe and later the Soviet Union (ARA). These three vast organizations, unprecedented in scale and concept, built a humanitarian response to war, without ignoring the realities of the new global politics.

The CRB was begun largely on Hoover's own initiative in the fall of 1914. With the cooperation of American diplomats and Belgian civic leaders, he developed the idea of feeding millions of children and other civilians in German-occupied Belgium and later northern France. Compliance with the Logan Act, cooperation from President Wilson, and allocations from Congress were secured after the organization was already underway. In 1917, Hoover became the immensely popular "Food Administrator." He rejected plans for rationing and instead launched a volunteer conservation program that mobilized American households to create surpluses of food, fuel, and other crucial wartime commodities. The success of the U.S. Food Administration rested on millions of housewives who signed pledges to observe Meatless Mondays and Wheatless Wednesdays in support of Hoover's call for a simpler way of life to assist American allies abroad. The scale of volunteerism in the Food Administration has rarely been duplicated. Hoover then expanded his wartime achievements by implementing a far-flung feeding program throughout devastated Europe—the American Relief Administration. In a final postscript to the Great War, he fed the starving Russians in 1921 after years of war and revolution had completely undermined the economic structure of their country.

Joan Hoff Wilson, in her counterintuitive biography entitled *Herbert Hoover: The Forgotten Progressive* provides examples of Hoover's pragmatic mix of political views that defy easy political categories of right or left wing. As a mining entrepreneur, he represented big business interests coping with strikes and labor disputes, yet in his widely read mining textbook he emphasized the importance of unions for mine workers. From experience he felt that the mines were simply more profitable in the long run when the workers' welfare was protected. As secretary of commerce, he did not believe in heavy government regulation, yet he worked tirelessly through trade conferences to develop voluntary standardization of hundreds of manufacturing parts to facilitate the growth of American industry. A firm believer in free commerce, he, nonetheless, watched emerging technology carefully, such as radio and early television, and provided for control of the common airwaves. In matters of race relations he was more enlightened than most of his contemporaries of either party. His general demeanor was quiet and decidedly uncharismatic, yet his early years brimmed with glamor and adventure. Often depicted by political enemies as a plutocrat, Hoover, even after acquiring a substantial fortune himself, had a lifelong contempt for snobbery.

Biographer David Burner reconciles these apparent contradictions in Hoover's character by examining his early years spent under Quaker influence in *Herbert Hoover: A Public Life*. While Hoover did not actively practice his parents' religion in adult life, many of the themes of Hoover's public career can be found in the mixed idealism and plain pragmatism of the Quaker community of West Branch, Iowa, where Hoover was born the night of August 10, 1874. The Quaker emphasis on building sound schools and active church meetings developed a broader perspective among West Branch's farming community than one would expect in an isolated provincial village of a few hundred people. Burner convincingly links Quaker charity with Hoover's later devotion to humanitarian programs. The doctrine of plain living and hard work made a virtue of simple necessity.

Hoover's father Jesse was a tinkerer and blacksmith who sold farm implements. His shop provided a basic living and for the children an introduction to the world of machinery. Jesse Hoover died in 1880 when his son was six. Hoover seems to have inherited his facility for mathematics and engineering from his father. His mother, Hulda, gained a reputation as a preacher at Friends' meetings. As a young widow responsible for the care of three children, she handled the family finances with great care, once delaying sending a letter until she felt she could afford a stamp. Reflecting on her situation, she came out in support of woman's suffrage, a radical position for her times. Like her husband, she also died young, in 1884, leaving Hoover orphaned before he turned ten. Due to their mother's resourcefulness, the three Hoover children had a surprisingly large inheritance of $2,000, which with careful management served to see them through to adult life. Even before her death, the children had spent months at a time with various relatives. In later life Hoover's memory of his parents was very dim. At the age of eleven he was sent to live with his uncle, Dr. John Minthorn in Newberg, Oregon, another Quaker community. Dr. Minthorn was a physician, one-time Indian agent, founder of the Friends Pacific Academy, and a real estate developer. As a youth, Hoover was expected to work for his uncle in exchange for his room and board, first as a laborer and later as an office assistant. He learned typing, accounting, and other office skills but never completed a formal high school education. It was a well-ordered but overworked and somewhat lonely childhood. Hoover's experience in his uncle's Oregon Land Company was his first taste of capitalism. The company, which undertook large and complex dealings, eventually went bankrupt during the recession of the 1890s.

Despite academic deficiencies, Hoover was able to enroll in the first class of the new university dedicated by Senator Leland Stanford to the children of the West. Stanford, having made his fortune building the first transcontinental railroad, envisioned a university that would educate practical engineers and businessmen. Hoover was in the student audience when Stanford opened the university on Oct. 1, 1891 with the words "You are here to fit yourself for a useful career." Hoover's temperament was well suited to this vision of robust but idealistic pragmatism. The most dynamic teacher on the new faculty was John Casper Branner, a geologist who trained a generation of American mining engineers. The utility of a mining career was clear to Hoover after his work in land development in Oregon.

A shy personality and blunt speech did not hamper Hoover's social life. At Stanford, he made lifelong friends, served as student-body treasurer, and managed the athletic teams. Here he met his future wife, Lou Henry, who had been recruited by Professor Branner to study geology. In addition to studies, a social life, and student politics, Hoover was faced with earning his way through school, which he accomplished through a number of enterprising schemes, such as a student laundry service, and through summer jobs with the U.S. Geological Survey. The incongruous combination of restless activity and a retiring manner that marked his entire career became firmly set at Stanford; more importantly, he acquired his sense of direction in life. Quite simply he believed, "Stanford is the best place in the world."

After Hoover graduated from Stanford in 1895, he spent the summer studying gold deposits in the Sierras. This academic work was followed by a brief stint as a mine laborer, working ten hours a day, seven days a week for about $1.50–2.50 a day. By February 1896, he secured a clerical position with Louis Janin, a mining expert in San Francisco. Within a few months Janin helped Hoover publish his first article and find a more promising position with the British partnership of Bewick, Moering, and Company. For a salary of $450 a month, he was sent to Western Australia to help develop new gold mines. He was twenty-two.

After meeting with Moering in London, Hoover traveled to Coolgardie and Kalgoorlie in Western Australia, an area characterized in Hoover's words by "red dust, black flies, and white heat." Hoover's detailed technical reports led Bewick and Moering to purchase the highly profitable Sons of Gwalia mine, and Hoover's reputation and salary increased accordingly. The rough, unstructured frontier life allowed Hoover to experiment with all aspects of mining, from technical innovations and labor relations to financing and public relations.

By 1898, Moering was investigating opportunities in China and offered Hoover the job of developing them. With a secure income in hand, Hoover traveled to California where he married his former Stanford classmate, Lou Henry, on Feb. 10, 1899. The following day the young couple boarded a ship for China. He examined and invested in a variety of mining interests there. The largest was the Kaiping coal mines, managed by Chang Yen-Mao. Chang needed the help of a well-funded British concern to counteract the Russian commercial interests in northern Chinese coal. Competing British, Russian, German, American, Japanese, and Belgian colonial business interests quickly introduced Hoover to the complexities of turn-of-the-century global politics. When the Boxer Rebellion broke out, Herbert and Lou Hoover responded quickly by building barricades, establishing emergency hospitals for the wounded, and ensuring a supply of food and water. Lou, who was a good shot, carried a pistol and served as watch along with the men. The young couple's quick response to the crisis set a pattern for reacting to the emergencies unleashed in 1914.

Hoover's work in China led to a partnership in Bewick, Moering. While Hoover left China in October 1901, after two years of intense work under difficult circumstances, he retained a financial interest in the Chinese mines until 1912. Of the greatest significance for his role in World War I was the experience Hoover gained in China dealing with an international group of financiers, including Emile Francqui, with whom he would later work on the Commission for Relief in Belgium. Since the Kaiping mines were in the Russian sphere of influence, he became increasingly aware of the strengths and weaknesses of the tsarist empire that would be played out in 1917.

Based in London from 1902 to 1914, Hoover traveled restlessly around the world and reorganized mines in Australia, South Africa, Burma, and tsarist Russia. The Bawdwin silver mine in Burma proved immensely profitable. After leaving the firm of Bewick, Moering, Hoover turned his attention to a variety of investments in Russia that also held great potential, primarily in iron, copper, gold, and oil deposits. Together with his brother, Theodore, also a mining engineer, and often accompanied by Lou, Hoover spent many months traveling throughout Russia. Although his adult life at this point was almost entirely spent abroad, he was developing a philosophy of American individualism and efficiency. He preferred to hire managers trained in the geology departments and mining schools of American universities.

Herbert Hoover's private life in these years was as rich as his business experiences. The Hoovers' first son, Herbert, was born in London in 1903 and their second son, Allan, in 1907. Despite a growing family and months-long trips, the Hoovers found time to pursue an interest in the history of mining that was sparked by their education at Stanford. They drew up a list of early mining books and purchased as many as could be located, including some very fine incunabula.

With the outbreak of war in August 1914, both Herbert and Lou Henry Hoover threw themselves into war relief efforts, first to help stranded American travelers showing up in London, whose normal sources of funds were cut off by the disruption of banking. With the German invasion of Belgium, Hoover responded quickly to the threat of hunger that the populace faced. His career up to this point had accustomed him to operating in an international arena with unclear legal boundaries, where negotiating skills made the difference between success and failure and where speed was of the essence. With the backing of American and other neutral diplomats in Europe, Hoover established the Commission for Relief in Belgium (CRB). He secured promises (sometimes flimsy ones) of funding from the Belgian, French, and British governments to purchase wheat for the Belgian civilians. He brashly negotiated the right to travel in occupied territory and gained official promises of security for the food shipments from the German government, sometimes dealing with the occupation forces and other times dealing directly with the authorities in Berlin, whichever seemed more expedient. He challenged the British cabinet's opposition to the feeding program and dealt with the tightening blockade of the Continent to get his shipments through Rotterdam and then to Brussels. When the legality of the CRB was challenged, he secured the support of President Wilson and even Theodore Roosevelt. In all, the CRB handled about $1 billion, distributing 5 million tons of food and supplies over a period of four years.

Although initially ambivalent to U.S. entry into the brutal hostilities that he knew from firsthand experience, by 1917 Hoover recognized that American involvement was inevitable. In May, he sailed for New York, and within a few days Woodrow Wilson appointed Hoover the head of the U.S. Food Administration (USFA). By devising an extraordinarily

H

successful conservation campaign, he was able to avoid rationing programs common in Europe. With the passage in August of the Lever Food Control Act, the USFA was able to implement a variety of price guarantees, taxes on excess profits, licensing schemes, and volunteer programs to manage the food supply, set prices, and hold speculation to a minimum. The USFA became one of the most efficient of the many wartime agencies.

In November 1918, Wilson and Hoover transformed the USFA into a new agency for the relief and reconstruction of Europe—the American Relief Administration (ARA). Hoover immediately sailed for Europe, where he served as director of the ARA and economic director of the Supreme Economic Council, working closely with the peace delegation. In a now familiar pattern, Hoover insisted on tight personal control of the ARA, free of European boards. By February 1919, Congress appropriated an initial $100 million for the ARA. Providing the food was only the first step. Hoover and his team of aggressive American administrators had to rebuild much of the devastated transportation system of Europe in order to distribute goods.

The ARA operated throughout Europe. The primary beneficiaries of American aid were Great Britain, France, Italy, Belgium, Poland, Germany, Austria, and Czechoslovakia. The organization is generally credited with spending $3.5 billion to distribute 19 million tons of food. Hoover, in Volume II of *An American Epic*, estimates that over the course of nine years of war and reconstruction the United States supplied $6 billion in aid as outright gifts and unreimbursed loans to forty-five nations.

Feeding the European population served both humanitarian and political goals, the latter by fortifying the new geopolitical configuration against both Bolshevik revolutionary influence and extremist right-wing movements. At this point in his career, Hoover believed that a well-fed population was the best defense against political unrest. Communism in this view was not viable in the long run. During the brief Communist regime of Béla Kun in Hungary, Hoover argued against the widespread proposal for military intervention, considering force unnecessary.

Massachusetts Senator Henry Cabot Lodge, who had tried to investigate the Commission for Relief in Belgium as being in violation of the Logan Act and who caused embar-rassment to the USFA, now succeeded in passing a bill to prohibit direct loans to former enemy states. In this he had much popular support. Despite all of the warnings Hoover had issued about the dangers of German nationalism, he, nonetheless, preferred diffusing Austrian and German militarism with economic support rather than with punitive measures, which could, and did, backfire. Hoover ingeniously obviated the bill by channeling funds to Austria through Serbia and Hungary and to Germany through the offices of the American Friends Service Committee and the European Relief Council.

On July 1, 1919, congressional authorization for the ARA expired, and Hoover continued the organization as an essentially private charity, similar to the status of the CRB from 1914–1917, an arrangement with certain advantages because it enabled Hoover to operate with great independence. Hoover hoped that assistance would combat the disturbing extreme left and right radical movements in Germany, but he carefully discouraged publicizing his work in those countries because of the widespread public contempt for the defeated.

Poland, on the other hand, enjoyed great international sympathy, which permitted Hoover to operate more openly. As early as October 1915, a Warsaw charity organization had appealed to Hoover to provision Poland during the German occupation. One of his most trusted associates in the CRB, Vernon Kellogg, investigated the Polish situation in detail. The German General Staff and the British cabinet could not come to terms about appropriate guarantees for the food shipments. Once the United States entered the war, feeding Poland had to be delayed until the Armistice. In December 1918, Hoover secured permission from Secretary of State Robert Lansing for Kellogg to head an American delegation to study conditions in Poland and propose a relief program.

Hoover instructed his staff to concentrate on relief and avoid politics. Hoover himself followed the political situation closely and structured relief to support Wilson's plan for building strong nation-states out of the disintegrating empires of Eastern Europe. Hoover's special relationship with Poland dated back twenty-five years to his student days at Stanford when he audaciously booked the most celebrated concert artist touring America, Ignacy Jan Paderewski, a great Polish patriot. In 1919, the relationship was renewed when Hoover worked behind the scenes to elevate the cultured Paderewski to the position of prime minister of Poland as a balance to the new chief of state, Józef Piłsudski, who had the support of the army. The United States was the first power to recognize the newly independent Poland, and encouraged other countries to follow its example. Both Hoover and Wilson were key factors in the success of reestablishing a Polish state after more than a hundred years of partition.

The European Allies worked to reduce their participation in the Allied Commission for Poland, and as a result most of the relief work was financed by a combination of American and Polish governmental appropriations. The ARA in Poland helped coordinate an impressive amount of private charity from groups such as the Red Cross, Quakers, the YWCA, and the Jewish Joint Distribution Committee. In August 1919, Hoover visited both Austria and Poland, avoiding all publicity in Austria but reveling in the adulation afforded him in Poland. In 1922, a public square in Warsaw was named after him. Although the memory of Hoover Square faded during the German occupation of World War II and the Communist era that followed, the name was restored in 1992.

The ARA in Poland provided food equally to the diverse ethnic groups and religions, including Roman and Orthodox Catholics, Jews, and Muslims. The situation was most serious in the underdeveloped borderlands in eastern Poland. This is precisely the area where Piłsudski fought the Red Army in the Polish-Russian war of 1920. Clearly, the ARA support of Poland was one contributing factor in Piłsudski's military success.

The ARA was only one aspect of Hoover's efforts in the immediate postwar period. His observations from two decades of world travel had crystallized into a vision for building postwar democracy. He privately held a black pessimism about the future of Europe if regional conflicts and chaotic economic conditions were not stabilized, but publicly he championed a positive Wilsonian program for reconstruction. He worked tirelessly to promote American membership in the League of Nations and the World Court. He favored both arms reduction and reparations reductions, in a consistent political view that has been termed "liberal internationalism." By 1920, the deepening isolationist tendencies of the American public and the failure of the Senate to ratify the League of Nations Treaty forced him to retreat from his ideal of international cooperation.

His war work had made Hoover a presidential prospect for a brief period in 1920. In recognition of his proven ability and growing influence, Warren G. Harding appointed Hoover secretary of commerce, a post he held through the Coolidge administration as well. Hoover transformed the once largely ceremonial office into an engine for modernizing American industry.

For some years Hoover had wanted to extend the ARA into Soviet Russia. He hoped that a well-fed population would be better able to cope with the political and social turmoil unleashed by the revolution and civil war. Hoover's faith in American enterprise and his contempt for socialism were so well known that he took both friends and enemies by surprise when, in 1921, he responded to Maxim Gorky's plea to feed the starving masses in Soviet Russia. The Russian famine of 1921 was severe enough to threaten the newly established Bolshevik regime. Though initially reluctant to ask for outside help, Lenin pragmatically shifted his position as conditions worsened. He allowed Gorky to issue an appeal addressed to "all honest people," on July 13, 1921. Secretary of Commerce Hoover responded with an offer by July 22.

Walter Lyman Brown of the ARA met at Riga with Soviet Deputy Foreign Minister Maxim Litvinov, who was known for his skepticism about accepting help from the United States. Despite the lack of diplomatic relations, Brown and Litvinov were able to reach an agreement within a few days. The Americans promised not to interfere in internal Soviet politics, and the Russians agreed to release American political prisoners still held in Soviet jails. The experienced ARA organization quickly established offices and began the process of purchasing, shipping, and distributing vast quantities of food. Hoover used the same type of funding structure that had served his previous relief programs. Under the careful administration of William Haskell, the ARA as a private organization managed about $20 million in United States congressional appropriations, $10 million from Soviet gold reserves, and a diverse combination of private and governmental donations that eventually totaled about $60 million. The original agreement stipulated that the program would feed 1 million Russian children. At the height of the effort, the ARA was feeding 18 million Russians, children and adults, on a daily basis. An attempt was made to provide seed as well as food to foster self-sufficiency, and the program was concluded in 1923 with the new Russian harvest.

Between 1920 and 1928 Hoover devoted most of his energies to developing the Department of Commerce. War relief had started him on what he later termed "the slippery road of public life." The role as secretary of commerce enabled Hoover to apply some of the lessons of wartime economics to the peacetime U.S. economy. The postwar slump, with high unemployment and overproduction, was his first challenge. He sought to combat unemployment by expanding public works during the 1920–1921 recession, then postponing such projects when construction revived.

Hoover saw the role of government as synchronizing business forces so that private companies would cooperate for their mutual benefit. In this spirit, the Commerce Department increased its research arm and began to publish timely industrial statistics to encourage rational planning. Hoover continued to advocate the practical benefits of efficiency, simplicity, and honesty that had worked so well in the war effort. The appeal to enlightened self-interest worked best in the area of standardization. He used the prestige of the cabinet to convene conferences in various sectors of manufacturing to pool ideas about the optimum sizing for key items. Government recommendations were issued for voluntary reduction in the numbers of sizes and types of manufactured goods, from screws to bed springs. Compliance was encouraged by governmental purchasing of these standardized parts. Hoover's program of standardization greatly facilitated domestic trade.

Other areas of note were the promotion of new industries such as radio and aviation. Again Hoover fostered a pattern of free enterprise supervised by governmental standards. One of his most ambitious undertakings in this broad range of activities was taming the Colorado River to prevent floods, provide water for irrigation, and generate electricity. In 1921, simultaneously with the relief program in Soviet Russia, President Harding appointed Hoover to negotiate the Colorado River Commission. It took years of lobbying in seven state legislatures to achieve the agreement that led to the construction of Hoover Dam.

Not all of his projects were unqualified successes. The older industries of steel, coal, and the railways presented thorny labor and production problems. It is notable that Hoover promoted the eight-hour day for steel workers and unions for mine workers. Another intractable area was foreign trade, complicated by the postwar economic disarray. Hoover also made little headway in restraining stock speculation, which he vigorously complained about in 1925.

In 1927, President Coolidge appointed Hoover to oversee the Mississippi Flood Committee that coordinated relief for the 600,000 people dislocated by the disastrous flood. The publicity from this repeat performance of his war relief programs positioned him for his successful bid for the White House. Shortly after the flood program, Coolidge made his famous announcement that he did not choose to run.

Despite its seeming inevitability, Hoover's election to the presidency in 1928 ran counter to standard political patterns. He had operated largely outside the Republican Party machinery; his work with Congress was generally restricted to expert testimony; he had never before run for public office; and the Old Guard viewed him as alarmingly progressive. However, the public respected his war record and knew that both Harding and Coolidge depended on his energetic work in the domestic as well as international spheres. Most historians agree that Hoover was elected because the general public felt American economic interests would be safe with a man of his special abilities.

As president, Hoover's hard-won image as master of emergencies served him poorly. The economic crisis of the Great Depression proved intractable and the American public became deeply embittered. During the Great War the newly coined verb "to Hooverize" had an idealistic ring, conserving food for the benefit of world peace. In the 1930s, it meant the humiliating descent into poverty.

Hoover's efforts to control the stock market before and after his election are well documented. He criticized the lax policies of the Federal Reserve Bank throughout the 1920s. Just two days after assuming the presidency in March 1929, he conferred with Federal Reserve officials about controlling stock speculation. Financial experts such as Andrew Mellon, secretary of the treasury under both Coolidge and Hoover, considered Hoover's worries unwarranted and alarmist. The stock market crash may have surprised the financial community, but it did not surprise Hoover. It was the duration of the depression that he did not foresee.

Anticipating a year-long slump such as occurred in 1920–1921, he prescribed the same cure, congressional appropriations for public works. Past remedies no longer helped. Most disappointing of all, the personal qualities that had served Hoover so well as an international war relief administrator now failed him in the domestic peacetime arena. Neither the engineering approach to problem solving nor the appeals to the idealism of a simpler age affected the economic situation in any meaningful way. Tiresome fights with Congress over tariff legislation, unhappiness with the restrictions of prohibition, and then the tragic events of the World War I Veterans' Bonus March created a downward spiral for his presidency.

From his defeat for reelection in 1932 until his death at age ninety, Hoover devoted himself to the study of twentieth-century politics. He amassed a huge library on the subject at Stanford University, the Hoover Institution on War, Revolution and Peace. He wrote multivolume memoirs of his experiences, analyses of the problems of lasting peace, and hundreds of articles and speeches. History came full circle in 1946–1947 when President Truman asked him to evaluate the food situation around the world, and he was able to help hungry children again. This time it was legal to feed the children of the defeated enemy states such as Germany. He took special pleasure in the tokens of appreciation from German children. His final public service focused on improving governmental efficiency through the Hoover Commission. He died on Oct. 21, 1964, and was buried at his birthplace, West Branch, Iowa, on the grounds of his presidential library.

Elena Danielson

See also COMMISSION FOR RELIEF OF BELGIUM; UNITED STATES FOOD ADMINISTRATION

Bibliography

Burner, David. *Herbert Hoover: A Public Life.* New York: Atheneum, 1984.
Hoover, Herbert. *An American Epic.* 4 vols. Chicago: Regnery, 1959–1964.
———. *Memoirs of Herbert Hoover.* 3 vols. New York: Macmillan, 1951–1952.
Nash, George. *The Life of Herbert Hoover.* 2 vols. New York: Norton, 1983, 1988.
Wilson, Joan H. *Herbert Hoover: The Forgotten Progressive.* Boston: Little, Brown, 1975.

Hoover, J(ohn) Edgar (1895–1972)

J. Edgar Hoover was born in Washington, D.C., the son of Dickerson N. and Annie Sheitlin Hoover. From his father, an engraver for the Commerce Department, Hoover developed a deep appreciation for the federal bureaucracy's polity. He studied law at George Washington University's night campus while working days at the Library of Congress. Receiving his degree in 1917, he joined the Justice Department as a clerk assigned to the Alien Enemies Bureau.

Ambitious and efficient, Hoover was soon promoted to the post of attorney. Given great latitude to determine the fate of resident German citizens during World War I, he learned that an efficient bureaucrat was not strictly limited by concerns for civil liberty. This attitude made him the ideal assistant to Attorney General A. Mitchell Palmer, who determined to use administrative techniques to suppress unpopular political beliefs. Caught up in the xenophobia of the postwar "Red Scare," the two planned for the expulsion of alien communists, socialists, anarchists, and other radicals.

Following a would-be assassin's bombing of Palmer's residence on June 2, 1919, the attorney general elevated Hoover to head the Justice Department's newly created Radical Division (changed to the General Intelligence Division in 1920). He quickly developed a list of 60,000 "radically inclined" aliens who were potentially liable for deportation under the Immigration Act of 1918. Hoover-inspired raids led to hundreds of arrests in the waning months of 1919, culminating in a nationwide roundup of approximately 10,000 radicals on Jan. 2, 1920. Some 6,500 were released without prosecution, but many spent days and even weeks incarcerated without due process of law. Several hundred—most notably the anarchist Emma Goldman—were eventually deported.

His fame assured, Hoover was appointed director of the Federal Bureau of Investigation (FBI) in 1924. He organized the FBI as a body to combat domestic and foreign enemies, and eventually emerged as one of Washington's more powerful figures. While his admirers argue that he created the world's most efficient law enforcement agency, his critics claim he established a fiefdom dedicated to a social order devoid of adequate safeguards for liberty. He headed the bureau until his death in 1972.

Fred A. Bailey

See also BUREAU OF INVESTIGATION

Bibliography

Messick, Hank. *John Edgar Hoover*. New York: McKay, 1972.

Murray, Robert K. *The Red Scare: A Study in National Hysteria, 1919–1920*. New York: McGraw-Hill, 1955.

Powers, Richard G. *Secrecy and Power: The Life of J. Edgar Hoover*. New York: Free Press, 1987.

Theoharis, Athan G., and John S. Cox. *The Boss: J. Edgar Hoover and the Great American Inquisition*. Philadelphia: Temple University Press, 1988.

House, Edward Mandell (1858–1938)

Edward Mandell House was the son of T.W. House, one of the leading citizens of Texas, a wealthy merchant, banker, and landowner. He led a privileged youth, meeting many prominent people who visited the large family homes in Galveston and Houston and enjoying the colorful life of his father's sugar plantation. House attended Houston Academy and later the Hopkins Grammar School in New Haven, Connecticut, where he and his closest friend, Oliver T. Morton, the son of Senator Oliver Perry Morton of Indiana, became absorbed in the crisis following the Hayes-Tilden election of 1876.

In the autumn of 1877, House entered Cornell University, where he remained until his father's death in January 1880. House decided to stay in Texas and help manage his father's estate. On August 4, House married Loulie Hunter of Hunter, Texas. After a year in Europe, they returned to Texas, where he became a prominent member of Austin society and pursued a variety of business activities, including farming and land speculation.

House was drawn into state politics through his friendship with James Stephen Hogg, who in 1892 faced a formidable challenge for renomination and reelection from conservative Democrats and Populists. House directed Hogg's campaign, creating a network of local, influential Democratic leaders, manipulating the electoral machinery, and bargaining for the votes of black and Mexican Americans. Hogg triumphed in a bitter three-way race and rewarded House with the title "Colonel."

Concerned more with the process than with the substance, House proceeded to build his own faction—"our crowd," as he called it—which became a powerful force in Texas politics. He was an ambitious political operator, skilled in organizing and inspiring others. He worked largely behind the scenes, developing ties of loyalty and affection with his close associates and using patronage to rally party workers behind his candidates. From 1894 to 1906, House's protégés served as governors of Texas. He and his associates managed the gubernatorial campaigns of Charles A. Culberson, Joseph D. Sayers, and Samuel W. Lanham. House was especially close to Culberson, directing his elevation to the United States Senate in 1898. He served as the chief political counselor of all three governors, dispensing advice and controlling patronage.

By the turn of the century, House was bored with his role in Texas politics and restlessly searched for broader horizons. He sought further wealth, attempting to profit from the discovery of oil at Spindletop in 1901, and in 1902 with the backing of eastern financiers, forming the Trinity and Brazos Valley Railway Company. He also felt the pull of the East. For years he had summered on Boston's North Shore, and gradually he began to winter in New York, severing most of his ties with Texas and only occasionally visiting the state. After 1904, he was never again involved in a gubernatorial campaign.

As a youth, House dreamed great dreams, yearning for a place on the national political stage. A conservative, sound-money Democrat, he disliked the platform of William Jennings Bryan and in 1904 supported Alton B. Parker for the presidential nomination. Discouraged by the prospects of the Democratic Party after Parker's defeat and Bryan's loss in 1908, House found solace in leisurely tours of Europe and in spiritualism, believing that he would have another chance in life after death. He continued his search for a Democratic presidential candidate amenable to his advice. For a time he cultivated Mayor William J. Gaynor of New York but found him too independent and unreliable. In November 1911, he met Woodrow Wilson, forming a close friendship that would last for years. While House was on the periphery of Wilson's campaign for the Democratic nomination and the presidency, after his election he played a key role in patronage decisions, eventually placing five personal friends in the cabinet.

During the winter of 1912–1913, House joined the circle of intimates around the President who were dedicated to advancing his political career and maintaining his physical health and emotional stability. House was a shrewd political infighter, one who liked people and understood how to move them. He performed all sorts of political tasks the President found distasteful. House also catered to many of Wilson's personal needs, recognizing his yearning for male companionship and his vulnerability to emotional stress. House's gentle, deferential manner, his lack of assertive masculinity, and his frequent assurances of affection and support helped to satisfy some of the President's deepest desires. Soon he was Wilson's most trusted confidant.

House developed a deep and genuine admiration for Wilson, both as a person and as a political leader. He believed that inspired leadership could solve the nation's problems and bring its spiritual regeneration, and in Wilson he found a leader who embodied his moral and political values; one who could move the American people toward these higher goals. The two men's conversations moved far beyond the realm of politics, as the President confided his dreams, nightmares, fears and aspirations, and family problems. The President's first wife, Ellen Axson Wilson, had a keen insight into her husband's emotional makeup and a wise tolerance of his political associates. She had welcomed House into her family, seeking his advice on both personal and political matters. Her death in August 1914 left Wilson in a state of despair and caused him to lean even more heavily on House for companionship and emotional support.

Wilson's second wife, Edith Bolling Galt, whom he met in March 1915 and married in December, was a different sort of person. She was lively and attractive but poorly educated and intolerant of some of the President's closest advisers, including House. Wilson had imprudently drawn her into his work, showing her House's letters and many important state papers, encouraging her to believe that her judgment was as good as that of his experienced advisers. In turn, House resented Wilson's transference of affection to Edith and the extent to which she changed his relationship with the President. After Wilson's remarriage, the remarkable intimacy between the two men lessened. They would remain dependent on one another, but the extraordinary closeness of those early years would gradually fade.

In 1913 and 1914, as Wilson pushed his New Freedom agenda through Congress, House served as a high-level political intermediary, quieting Democratic factional squabbles and helping to fuse the needs of many special-interest groups into a coherent, moderate legislative program. He collaborated with Wilson in moving the Democratic Party away from its traditional advocacy of states rights and limited government toward an extension of federal authority over the nation.

With the outbreak of World War I, House was the first member of the administration to inform himself about the complexities of the struggle and to grapple seriously with the dangers and opportunities the war posed for the United States. As Wilson's mind came to grips with the magnitude of the conflict and the difficulties of America's position, he turned to House for advice and also chose him as his chief emissary to the European capitals. Strongly pro-Ally from the start, House saw no prospect for peace until the belligerents had lost their hope for total victory. Moreover, House wanted American mediation to be based on a previous agreement with the Allies and believed it must be an instrument for achieving moderate Allied success.

Wilson's choice of House gave a strange quality to American attempts to end the war. He was a curious combination of shrewdness and naiveté, driven by the spur of fame to seek a great place in the history of his times. During his wartime missions to Europe, House sent back vivid, detailed letters, full of valuable information on every phase of the war. But he also dramatized these missions, exaggerating their possibilities and his influence on other men. Although his diplomacy had a veneer of realism, he often misjudged British and French leaders and assumed that in the end reason, calmness, and idealism would triumph over the passions generated by the war.

Prior to American entry into the war, House undertook two missions to Europe. During the first, from January to June 1915, he realized that the Allies were not prepared to think seriously about ending the conflict and sought to cultivate their good will. After the sinking of the *Lusitania* on May 7, tension heightened between the United States and Germany, and Wilson and House realized the precariousness of American neutrality. House now viewed the war as a struggle between democracy and autocracy, and he was convinced that American intervention was virtually inevitable. One way or another, House wanted to guaran-

H

tee a limited Allied victory, while Wilson genuinely viewed American mediation as a way in which to end the war. He still believed that the United States might keep out and was not willing to use American military powers to ensure an Allied triumph.

House accepted another mission to Europe, although it is clear that the two men had quite different notions of what was to be achieved. During his second trip, from January to March 1916, House negotiated a memorandum with British Foreign Secretary Sir Edward Grey in which the two statesmen agreed that, on a signal from the Allies, Wilson would propose a peace conference to put an end to the war. If Germany refused to attend the conference, or, once there, insisted on unreasonable terms, the United States would probably enter the war on the side of the Allies. Since the Allies refused to invoke the House-Grey Memorandum, the scheme embodied in it was never put to the test and the differences between House and Wilson never rose to the surface. On Jan. 31, 1917, Germany's announcement that all vessels, enemy and neutral, found near British waters would be attacked ended all hopes for peace and virtually assured America's entry into the war.

After United States intervention in the European conflict on April 6, 1917, House continued as Wilson's closest foreign policy adviser, consulting with the President over his plans for peace and serving as his special emissary. In September 1917, Wilson directed House to assemble a group of experts, eventually known as The Inquiry, to study war aims and to plan for peace negotiations. In late October, House traveled to Europe to participate in inter-Allied military discussions and to seek agreement on war aims. In the summer of 1918, Wilson assigned to House the responsibility for preparing a constitution for a league of nations, which they called a covenant, and he and the President exchanged drafts in ensuing months. In October, when Germany sought peace on the basis of the President's Fourteen Points, Wilson again dispatched House to engage in prearmistice negotiations with the Allies. The apparent success of these efforts led Wilson and House to overestimate American influence and to remain convinced that out of the chaos of war a new community of nations would emerge, based on a league of nations and a sweeping reconstruction of the international order.

As the Paris Peace Conference unfolded, differences between the President and his confidential adviser emerged. House had grown impatient, eager to dominate the discussions and bring about the fulfillment of his dreams. He surrounded himself with sycophants and lost touch with the direction of Wilson's thought. His arrogance and ambition gradually became apparent to Wilson and to other members of the American Commission to Negotiate Peace. At first during the drafting of the Covenant of the League of Nations, House and Wilson worked together, but a gap became apparent when Wilson returned to the United States in mid-February and House took his place on the Council of Ten. House lacked the President's deep convictions, as well as his distrust of the Allies, and he was far more willing to concede to British, French, and Italian demands. Despite the President's clear instructions to the contrary, during Wilson's absence he sought to speed up the negotiations and, in the process, seriously weakened Wilson's position. In mid-March, when Wilson returned and became aware of House's conduct, he lost confidence in his intimate adviser. For the remainder of Wilson's presidency, House found himself on the sidelines.

During the 1920s, House made frequent trips to Europe and energetically supported American membership in the League of Nations and World Court. He also sought to mediate the bitter quarrels within the Democratic Party and to strengthen the party's organization. In 1932, he supported Franklin D. Roosevelt for the nomination and, with Roosevelt's election, sought to reestablish his role as a presidential confidant. While House influenced some diplomatic appointments, he was excluded from the President's inner circle. As for domestic policy, as the years passed he became increasingly unsympathetic with the New Deal. His long, unique career as a confidential adviser ended in frustration. He died in 1938.

Charles E. Neu

See also House-Grey Memorandum; Inquiry, The

Bibliography

Floto, Inga. *Colonel House in Paris: A Study of American Policy at the Paris Peace Conference, 1919.* Princeton, NJ: Princeton University Press, 1980.
George, Alexander L., and Juliette L. George. *Woodrow Wilson and Colonel House: A*

Personality Study. New York: Dover, 1956.

Heckscher, August. *Woodrow Wilson: A Biography.* New York: Macmillan, 1991.

Neu, Charles E. "Woodrow Wilson and Colonel House: The Early Years, 1911–1915." In *The Wilson Era: Essays in Honor of Arthur S. Link,* ed. by John M. Cooper, Jr. and Charles E. Neu. Arlington Heights, IL: Harlan Davidson, 1991.

Seymour, Charles. *The Intimate Papers of Colonel House.* Boston: Houghton Mifflin, 1926.

Weinstein, Edwin A. *Woodrow Wilson: A Medical and Psychological Biography.* Princeton, NJ: Princeton University Press, 1981.

House-Grey Memorandum

The House-Grey Memorandum, initialed in London by Col. Edward M. House and British Foreign Secretary Sir Edward Grey on Feb. 22, 1916, has been variously interpreted as a significant initiative toward American mediation to end the war or as a subterfuge to engage the United States on the Allied side.

In early summer 1915, German-American relations were badly strained by the *Lusitania*'s sinking and Anglo-American relations were sorely tested by the British blockade. Convinced neither side was open to his unprejudiced mediation, Wilson feared that without it the momentum of the war would drag the United States into the hostilities. As the *Arabic* Pledge eased anti-German pressure on the administration, Grey encouraged Washington to consider diplomatic intervention, not only to end the war, but also to lay the basis for a league of nations committing all states to the end of militarism, an objective Grey certainly equated with the curtailment of German power.

Grey was acutely aware of Britain's dependency upon American money and materiel and advocated clearer ties with the United States rather than moderation of British war aims. He played adroitly on House's pro-Allied inclinations and Wilson's determination to make over the international system. On Oct. 8, 1915, House urged Wilson to offer his good offices to both sides, with the understanding that if Germany did not agree, the United States would sever relations with Berlin and might go even further. In a letter House told Grey he would come to Europe to offer Wilson's mediation.

House thought he might persuade the Germans to agree, but if they did not, he wrote, Washington would throw in its lot with the Allies. Wilson amended House's pledge to say that if Germany refused, the United States would "probably" side with Britain.

House warned that his mission was urgent: a military setback to the Allies would make it impossible for Washington to commit itself to their cause. He did not tell Grey he feared a disaster if the ill-prepared United States was actually forced to fight. Nor did he mention the problems Wilson was likely to face in the election of 1916 if the constant tensions with both belligerents were not resolved. For the Germans, House offered assurances of American disinterest in territorial issues. Washington's concern was to end militarism and guarantee freedom of the seas.

British officials doubted that Wilson could deliver on any promise to support the Allies. Grey asked whether the President's goal of eliminating "militarism" and "navalism" meant Wilson was prepared to participate in establishing a league of nations, but even when House answered that it did, the foreign secretary expected little to come of the American initiative. House left for Europe in December with instructions to demand only an end to militarism, freedom of the seas, and creation of a league of nations. If either side accepted those terms, Wilson wrote, the duty of the United States would be to compel the other side to agree.

The principle of freedom of the seas was too much for British statesmen, who still set their hopes on victory without making such a concession. Though he hoped to insure American participation in the peace settlement, Grey did not believe House's plan could win the support of his colleagues or the other Allies. In Berlin, House portrayed Anglo-American relations as so troubled that Germany's renunciation of submarine warfare and acceptance of American mediation would align the United States with the Central Powers. But he found the German government intransigent about submarines and adamant about its territorial demands. House told French officials in Paris that their acceptance of American mediation on Wilson's terms would make it possible for Washington to side with the Allies because Berlin was sure to reject those terms. Still, the French would not consider such mediation until they had the advantage on the battlefield.

On hearing the colonel's account of his talks in Berlin, and fearful that Britain might appear to be the obstacle to peace, Grey initialed the memorandum endorsing a peace conference summoned by Wilson, with the understanding that if Germany refused, the United States would probably enter the war on the Allied side. But House had mistaken Grey's certain interest in Anglo-American cooperation for disinterest in conventional victory, and he ignored the hostility of other members of the British government. He thus gave Wilson the false impression that the foreign secretary agreed with the President's purposes and was able to carry the cabinet and the other Allies with him. With that confidence Wilson adopted a sterner line toward Germany. The *Sussex* crisis of March 1916 very nearly led to the break with Berlin that would have pleased British leaders but destroyed Wilson's hopes to achieve peace through American mediation, and, in addition, might have cost the President reelection.

House had urged Grey to implement the memorandum quickly to prevent just such an eventuality, but the British did not move. Wilson's public commitment in May to a postwar league of nations was part of his strategy to induce Grey to act, but it had no more effect than his several earlier appeals. Whatever Grey's personal attitude toward the memorandum, he was not disposed to champion it in a war cabinet that doubted Wilson could fulfill his promises and wondered whether "probably" meant he never intended to do so. While Allied armies planned the Somme offensive that spring, the British government discussed and dismissed the House-Grey Memorandum. Grey's departure from the Foreign Office soon thereafter insured it would not be reconsidered. Convinced he had been betrayed, Wilson resolved that the American pursuit of a just peace would thereafter be conducted independently.

Richard A. Harrison

Bibliography

Cooper, John M., Jr. "Note: The British Response to the House-Grey Memorandum: New Evidence and New Questions." *Journal of American History* (1973).

Devlin, Patrick. *Too Proud to Fight: Woodrow Wilson's Neutrality.* New York: Oxford University Press, 1975.

Link, Arthur S. *Wilson: Confusions and Crises, 1915–1916.* Princeton, NJ: Princeton University Press, 1964.

Seymour, Charles, ed. *The Intimate Papers of Colonel House.* Boston: Houghton Mifflin, 1926.

Williams, Joyce G. *Colonel House and Sir Edward Grey: A Study in Anglo-American Diplomacy.* Lanham, MD: University Press of America, 1984.

Houston, David Franklin (1866–1940)

Born in Monroe, North Carolina, David Franklin Houston earned a B.A. degree from South Carolina College in 1887. At only twenty-two years of age, he became superintendent of the Spartanburg, North Carolina schools, serving in that post until 1891. He left Spartanburg to earn an M.A. degree from Harvard in 1892.

In 1894, Houston became adjunct professor of political science at the University of Texas. The university promoted him to associate professor in 1897 after he published *A Critical Study of Nullification in South Carolina* as Volume III in the *Harvard Historical Studies*. He stayed in Austin until 1900, when Texas A&M University selected him as its president. After eight years of administering that institution, Washington University in St. Louis appointed him chancellor, a position he held officially until 1917, but in reality only until 1913, when President Woodrow Wilson selected him as secretary of agriculture.

During Houston's years in Texas, he became acquainted with Col. Edward M. House. According to Houston's memoirs, House approached him about a cabinet post not long after Wilson's election to the presidency. Houston expressed interest in the post of secretary of agriculture because of the importance of agriculture to the nation and his admiration for his fellow academic (Wilson) who represented the "principled" men in government.

When the United States entered World War I, the significance of agriculture became clear, and Houston and the nation moved quickly. Congress appropriated more than $11 million for the Department of Agriculture to improve health and to increase the production, conservation, and utilization of livestock and plants. This charge included provisions to supply seeds to farmers and to extend and enlarge the availability of market news to them. Both Congress and Secretary Houston sought to develop further the cooperative agricultural extension service. Houston's department surveyed the country's food supply, gathered and disseminated information about farm products, and conserved food by preventing losses in storage and transit. The department provided farmers with advice about market conditions and the distribution of perishable foods. It sought to maintain the quality of agricultural products by investigating and certifying their condition. It helped farmers to secure an adequate labor supply, and increased its research role. The department also directed the administration of stockyards and supervised producers of ammonia, other fertilizers, and farm-equipment manufacturers.

While Houston's department worked with agricultural production, Herbert Hoover and the Food Administration controlled and regulated the commercial distribution of food and promoted conservation and the elimination of waste. The two agencies worked well together. Finally, Houston and Hoover created a National Advisory Committee, which provided the administration with the perspective and advice of farmers and their organizations. In addition, 5,000 extension workers linked this elaborate federal machinery to individual farmers. Houston wrote that these agents "constituted the . . . intimate touch with the millions of people in the farming districts."

Houston served as secretary of agriculture throughout the war and ended his federal service with his appointment as secretary of the treasury in 1920–1921. He then moved to New York and became chairman of the board of the Mutual Life Insurance Company. Houston died in New York on Sept. 2, 1940.

Lawrence O. Christiansen

See also UNITED STATES FOOD ADMINISTRATION

Bibliography

Houston, David F. *A Critical Study of Nullification in South Carolina.* New York: Longmans, Green, 1896.

———. *Eight Years with Wilson's Cabinet, 1913 to 1920: With a Personal Estimate of the President.* Garden City, NY: Doubleday, Page, 1926.

Selby, P.O. "David F. Houston." In *Missouri College Presidents: Past and Present.* Kirksville, MO: N.p., 1971.

Shoemaker, Floyd C. "Hn. David F. Houston." *Official Manual of the State of Missouri, 1919–1920.* Jefferson City, MO: Secretary of State, 1920.

Houston Riot

Often termed the Camp Logan riot, the mutiny in Houston, Texas, of members of the 3d Battalion, 24th Infantry, on Aug. 23, 1917, caused the deaths of at least twenty people, resulted in the largest court-martial in American military history, and severely damaged deteriorating race relations during World War I.

Black troops representing a distinguished regiment that had served gallantly on the American frontier, in the Spanish-American War, the Philippine Insurrection, and the Punitive Expedition into Mexico were garrisoned about one and a half miles from the National Guard camp in western Houston to guard the construction site at Camp Logan. The battalion, consisting of companies J, K, L, and M, arrived in the city on July 28, anticipating a seven-week tour of duty.

Although Houston actively sought the training center for prestigious, patriotic, and pecuniary reasons and the War Department considered it a choice location, the city and the army shared apprehension about stationing black soldiers in the area. Houston had experienced fewer contacts with black servicemen than San Antonio and Del Rio, which had recently witnessed racial turmoil over segregating soldiers, and Houston continued to enforce racial separation.

There was an uneasiness within the black community, which considered Houston police racist and uncontrollable. The East St. Louis riot, the most violent racial confrontation of the century, was still a topic of conversation, blending with memories of the Brownsville raid of 1906, in which the 25th Infantry reputedly attacked the south Texas town. Ominously, the 1st Battalion of the 24th Infantry, which was, like the 3d Battalion, on guard duty, had rebelled against racial restrictions and indignities on July 29, its first day in camp at Waco.

To limit areas of tension in Houston, Police Chief Clarence Brock and Battalion Commander William Newman conferred. The chief agreed to allow the army to punish its own violators of segregation ordinances and permitted provost guards to assist policy in patrolling sections frequented by off-duty troops. Newman promised to disarm the provost guards and to restrict the number of servicemen gathering off post. The colonel scheduled social events at the camp to attract black citizens and reduce the necessity of soldiers entering the city for recreation.

Despite these efforts, soldiers complained of verbal and physical abuse and occasionally flaunted racial regulations on streetcars. Frustration escalated on the morning of August 23 as police arrested a black woman for gambling and beat and jailed a soldier, Alonzo Edwards, for protesting. Early that afternoon Corporal Charles Baltimore visited the arresting officers, Lee Sparks and Rufus Daniels, on behalf of Edwards. Angered, Sparks struck Baltimore and fired several shots at the fleeing figure before apprehending him. Rumors spread to the camp that a policeman had killed a black soldier. Baltimore's comrades plotted vengeance after the corporal's return.

Shortly after 8:00 P.M. various conspirators created diversions to cover their trail. Sergeant Vida Henry told the new battalion commander, Maj. Kneeland Snow, of reports of trouble in the ranks. Private Frank Johnson shouted falsely that a white mob was approaching the base. Frightened soldiers seized rifles and ammunition and fired indiscriminately. Henry rallied 75 to 100 men to march on the city, though many dropped out at the first violence.

By the next morning the carnage in west Houston resembled a war zone. Five policemen, including Daniels, lay dead or dying, along with eight white civilians, one Hispanic, two National Guardsmen, and four black soldiers, including Henry, an apparent suicide. From Galveston 350 coast guardsmen and from San Antonio 602 infantrymen answered the appeal of Acting Mayor D.M. Moody for protection against a threatened white riot. Order was restored to the city.

Massive courts martial followed. In the first round of trials, thirteen defendants received death sentences by hanging and forty-one drew life imprisonment. The army subsequently sentenced sixteen others to death and twelve to life terms, though appeals from the black community persuaded President Woodrow Wilson to commute ten death sentences to life imprisonment. Presidents Warren Harding and Calvin Coolidge later released most of the surviving prisoners, closing the bloodiest chapter in American military-civilian relations.

Garna L. Christian

Bibliography
Foner, Jack D. *Blacks and the Military in American History*. New York: Praeger, 1974.
Haynes, Robert V. "The Houston Mutiny and Riot of 1917." *Southwestern Historical Quarterly* (April 1973).
———. *A Night of Violence: The Houston Riot of 1917*. Baton Rouge: Louisiana State University Press, 1977.
McComb, David G. *Houston: A History*. Austin: University of Texas Press, 1981.

Howze, Robert Lee (1864–1926)

Born in Texas, Robert Lee Howze joined the cavalry after graduating from the United States Military Academy in 1888. During his first battle, the Pine Ridge campaign against the Sioux Indians in 1890–1891, he earned the Medal of Honor and gained a well-deserved reputation for courage and efficiency. He fought in Cuba and the Philippines, earning more citations for gallantry and another nomination for the Medal of Honor. He graduated from the Army War College, served as tactics instructor at West Point, and later was commandant of cadets.

When the United States entered the First World War, Howze was a colonel and chief of staff of the Northeastern Department based in Boston. In February 1918, he assumed command of the 2d Cavalry Brigade at Fort Bliss, Texas. As brigade commander, Howze had to balance the often contradictory tasks of training his men to fight in Europe and simultaneously patrolling the U.S.-Mexican border. In May, he took charge of the District of El Paso which placed not only his old brigade but also all American troops stationed in the region around the city of El Paso under his control.

Howze now supervised the creation and training of dozens of new units destined for Europe as well as the protection of the volatile border. Nevertheless, he was anxious to get a command in France, and on Aug. 30, 1918, he did receive the command of the 38th Division and a promotion to temporary major general.

The division, originally composed of National Guardsmen from Indiana, Kentucky, and West Virginia, had been training for over a year and was preparing to move overseas when Howze joined it. In mid-October, the division moved into the training area around Nantes, but within just a few days of arriving, the American Expeditionary Force headquarters ordered it broken up and its men shipped out as replacements. Howze was greatly disappointed. Within a few weeks his division shrank from over 27,000 officers and men to only 8 officers and 102 men. Soon after the Armistice, however, Pershing ordered Howze to take charge of the crack 3d Division. He led that division into Germany with the Third Army and remained on occupation duty until August 1919.

Upon returning to the United States, Howze reverted to his prewar rank of colonel and once again headed the District of El Paso. During the summer of 1920, he became the first commander of the new 1st Cavalry Division and received a promotion to brigadier general. In December 1922, he became a major general. In July 1925, after five years on the border, Robert L. Howze assumed command of V Corps Area based at Columbus, Ohio. He died there the following year.

Richard Kehrberg

Huebner, Clarence Ralph (1888–1972)

Clarence Ralph Huebner enlisted as a private in the Regular Army on Jan. 17, 1910. Thirty-eight years and one week later he was promoted to the grade of major general in the Regular Army. "The Coach," as he was known to his World War II soldiers, learned his military skills in an army in transition from a provincial to a modern fighting force.

Born in Bushton, Kansas, Huebner worked as a court reporter for the Chicago Burlington and Quincy Railroad. But an administrative life fit him like a badly tailored suit, and at twenty-two he enlisted in the Regular Army.

Field service at former frontier posts in Colorado and Wyoming was to Huebner's liking, but the routine of army life often called on those same administrative skills he had honed in civilian life. He was smartly dressed and efficient in his many duties, traits that soon brought him to the attention of his officers. Persuaded by them to take the examinations for a commission, Huebner pinned on the gold bars of a second lieutenant in the infantry on Nov. 26, 1916. After completing the course of instruction at the Infantry Service School at Fort Leavenworth, Kansas, in April 1917, Captain Huebner joined the 28th Infantry Regiment and soon was on his way to France with the 1st Division, later known as the "Big Red One" in recognition of its distinctive shoulder insignia.

Clarence Huebner was an extraordinary soldier. He commanded Company G, 2d Battalion, 28th Infantry in the battle to seize Cantigny, a small village fifty miles north of Paris. On May 28, 1918, he led his men against the German soldiers of the 82d Reserve Division who were defending Cantigny. The 2d Battalion, with French Schneider CA.1 heavy tanks and flamethrowers attached, had the mission of taking the village. Performing as they had learned in the earlier rehearsals, Huebner's men jumped off in the attack at 6:45 A.m. behind a thunderous rolling barrage and took the village 2,000 feet away by 7:20 A.M. When his battalion commander was mortally wounded, Huebner led the battalion and was awarded the Distinguished Service Cross (DSC) for heroism under fire.

At Soissons, Huebner, a major since June 21, 1918, and wounded for the second time, was cited for gallantry with his second DSC. After recovering from his wounds, he led his battalion in the attack near Saizerais, then at the St. Mihiel salient. He was promoted to lieutenant colonel on Oct. 25, 1918, and given command of the 28th Infantry Regiment, which he led in the final offensive of the war, the Meuse-Argonne. He received the first of three Distinguished Service Medals that he earned during his forty years of service for exemplary performance of duty in positions of great responsibility during World War I—a remarkable achievement for a young field-grade officer. Again his conduct and efficiency brought him to the attention of his superiors, who rewarded him with choice assignments.

Lieutenant Colonel Huebner commanded the 1st Battalion, 28th Infantry and the 16th Infantry Regiment during the occupation of Germany following the Armistice. In 1919, after returning to the United States, he reverted to his permanent rank of captain. But the army was not through with Huebner. On Feb. 16, 1942, he was promoted to brigadier general. At the end of the battle for Troina, Sicily, in August 1943, Major General Huebner took over his beloved 1st Infantry Division from his old friend MajGen. Terry de la Mesa Allen. Ahead of the new division commander lay Omaha Beach and an honored place in the history of World War II. General Huebner retired from active duty on Nov. 30, 1950, and died on Sept. 23, 1972, in Washington, D.C.

John F. Votaw

Bibliography

Blumenson, Martin, and James L. Stokesbury. "Huebner." In *Masters of the Art of Command.* Boston: Houghton Mifflin, 1975.

Buck, Beaumont B. *Memories of Peace and War.* San Antonio, TX: Naylor, 1935.

Coffman, Edward M. *The War to End All Wars: The American Military Experience in World War I.* Madison: University of Wisconsin Press, 1986.

Patch, Joseph D. *A Soldier's War: The First Infantry Division A.E.F. (1917–1918).* Corpus Christi, TX: Mission Press, 1966.

Society of the First Division. *History of the First Division During the World War 1917–1919.* Philadelphia: Winston, 1922.

Hurley, Edward Nash (1864–1933)

Edward Nash Hurley was born in Galesburg, Illinois. The son of a railroad mechanic, he quit high school to follow his father's trade. He later became active in Chicago's Democratic Party politics, which earned him several patronage positions in Cook County, but he soon left these to become a traveling salesman. He prospered modestly, but his big break came in 1896 when he made the acquaintance of a man whose brother had invented a piston air drill. Seeing the potential for this invention, Hurley mortgaged his home to obtain capital and formed the Standard Pneumatic Tool Company. Sales rapidly grew, the company prospered, and after six years Hurley sold his interest in the business for over $1.25 million. Several years later, he founded the Hurley Machine Company in Chicago, which manufactured household electrical appliances and became one of the most successful firms of its kind in the country.

Still interested in Democratic politics, Hurley played a small role in Woodrow Wilson's successful campaign for governor of New Jersey in 1910, and he supported Wilson in the 1912 presidential election. After Wilson entered the White House, he appointed Hurley to the newly organized Federal Trade Commission, where the Chicago businessman served as vice-chairman and then chairman. During this time, Hurley developed a great admiration for the President, which Wilson reciprocated, leading to a lifelong friendship between the two men. Hurley left the Federal Trade Commission in February 1917 and was working for the Exports Council when a crippling controversy at the Shipping Board led to the resignation of the board's chairman, William Denman. Wilson asked Hurley to take Denman's place, which he reluctantly agreed to do, protesting that he did not know much about shipping or shipbuilding. Hurley, nonetheless, was an effective chairman of the Shipping Board and also served as president of its subsidiary, the Emergency Fleet Corporation. He found a chaotic situation at both agencies and restored order with the help of Edward F. Carry and Charles Piez (two business associates from Chicago) and Charles Schwab (the head of Bethlehem Steel).

Hurley saw the huge merchant fleet the United States was creating as useful not only in wartime, but also after peace was restored, when he felt it would facilitate a dramatic expansion of American trade. During the war, however, his primary concern was to provide the merchant tonnage needed for victory. After the Armistice, Hurley went to Europe to negotiate postwar shipping arrangements. Upon returning to the United States, he suffered a collapse due to exhaustion. He resigned his government positions in August 1919 and returned to Chicago, where he remained until his death in 1933.

William Williams

See also SHIPPING BOARD

Bibliography

Hurley, Edward N. *Awakening of Business.* Garden City, NY: Doubleday, 1916.

———. *The Bridge to France.* Philadelphia: Ozer, 1927.

———. *The New Merchant Marine.* London: Century, 1920.

Safford, Jeffrey J. *Wilsonian Maritime Diplomacy, 1913–1921.* New Brunswick, NJ: Rutgers University Press, 1978.

I

Income Tax

The advent of American involvement in World War I brought with it the problem of financing the first major war fought by Americans on foreign soil. Estimates ranged as high as $10 billion to cover salaries and supplies for the first year of the war alone. Because the length of America's involvement could not be determined at the outset, there was great disagreement regarding the total amount of money needed to be raised and the timetable and methods for raising it.

The debate focused on whether loans or taxes should be the primary source of funds used to finance the war effort. Proponents of loans cited the danger that would result from the removal of tens of millions of dollars from consumers' pockets. These economists feared that removing money from circulation before it could be spent would lead to an overall decline in purchases, both by individual consumers and businesses. This, they feared, would lead to a cessation of growth and maintenance in the industrial sector and to a halt in the development of new technology as the absence of disposable income would make speculation virtually impossible.

Proponents of taxation as the primary source for funding the war cited the willingness of citizens to pay more taxes during wartime, when patriotism would be at an abnormally high level. It was claimed that increased production of war-related materials would lead to an overall rise in wages for American workers. Because most raw materials would be used for the war effort, however, these workers would be left with disposable income. Protaxation economists predicted that patriotic American workers would willingly return this "surplus" to their government.

Many proponents of exclusive taxation favored a "conscription-of-wealth" approach. They attempted to draw a parallel between the lower and middle classes (who comprised the bulk of America's fighting force) with the wealthy, whom they predicted would sacrifice their money during wartime as members of the lower classes sacrificed their lives. This idea was not widely accepted, however; many felt that taxing the wealthy to excess would prove injurious to the businesses they owned, which would ultimately hurt their employees.

Although a portion of war expenses were financed through loans, a taxation scheme that weighed heavily upon Americans, especially wealthy ones, was adopted. The plan became effective on Jan. 1, 1918. It called for an increase of 2 percent in the existing income tax rate for all taxpayers, and for a graduated increase beyond that for those who earned $5,000 or more per year. Those who earned less than that paid between 2 and 4 percent; earners of $5,000 and $7,500 paid 5 percent. Rates increased as high as 65 percent for earners of over $1 million. This scheme resulted in many Americans having to pay an income tax for the first time. It also indicated that proponents of the "conscription-of-wealth" approach had scored at least a partial victory.

Although taxes would be paid quarterly, citizens were encouraged to pay the entire amount by June 15. Interest on advance payments was credited toward tax paid as an incentive to pay in one lump sum.

The new income tax imposed to finance World War I inflated the number of American taxpayers to 7 million in 1918, far above the 500,000 who had paid taxes the previous year. The government tried to make the process as easy as possible by simplifying forms and procedures and by presenting the program to Americans as a "Liberty Tax," similar to the sale of the already popular Liberty Bonds. It was hoped that by taking a positive approach to an unpleasant chore, patriotic Americans would pay taxes willingly as a "sacrifice for victory." The early success of the program, coupled with the relatively short period of American involvement, made it possible for tax revenues adequately to finance much of the American war effort.

Jeffry Kostic

See also LIBERTY LOANS; REVENUE ACT OF 1917; REVENUE ACT OF 1918

Bibliography

Bullock, Charles J. "Conscription of Income." *North American Review* (June 1917).

Seligman, Edwin R. "Borrowing Must Supplement Taxes in War Finance." *New York Times* (April 15, 1917): 5.

Industrial Workers of the World

The Industrial Workers of the World (IWW) was founded in Chicago in 1905 by labor radicals who dedicated themselves to making a revolution in the United States. During its first four years, the IWW suffered a series of internal schisms that left it bereft of members and influence. Between 1909 and 1913, however, the radical organization, whose members had become better known as "Wobblies," enjoyed a resurgence. In 1912 and 1913, such famous Wobblies as William D. "Big Bill" Haywood and Elizabeth Gurley Flynn led tumultuous mass strikes among textile workers in Lawrence, Massachusetts, and Paterson, New Jersey. By then, the IWW had come to exemplify American syndicalism, a radical revolutionary doctrine that disdained political action and craft unionism, preferring direct action at the point of production by industrial unions. The Wobblies argued that only workers themselves taking direct action at the factory, mine, etc., eventually culminating in a national general strike, could make a real revolution. The IWW, however, watched its dream of revolution dissolve as an economic contraction between 1913 and 1915 paralyzed it, caused membership to decline substantially, and left the organization a shambles.

The outbreak of World War I in 1914 created a situation in which the IWW could again grow. Wartime labor scarcity and demand by European belligerents for American products gave workers greater power against their employers. After 1915, under the leadership of Haywood, the IWW discarded much of its revolutionary verbiage, concentrating instead on recruiting new members, winning higher wages, and improving working conditions. It proved especially successful in attracting members among the migratory wheat harvesters of the Plains states, the lumber workers of the Pacific Northwest, and the copper miners of the Rocky Mountain states.

After the United States entered the war in April 1917, the IWW's influence among western workers rose. As industrial conflict spread across western agriculture, copper mining, and the lumber industry, public officials came to believe that the IWW threatened the war production effort. At the same time, business people and conservative politicians sought to identify the Wobblies with the German enemy and treason, one U.S. senator condemning the organization as "Imperial Wilhelm's Warriors."

State officials in the West and their corporate allies persistently pressured the national government to repress the IWW. In the summer of 1917, President Woodrow Wilson appointed a special mediation commission to investigate the causes of labor unrest and conflict in industries vital to the war effort. The commission recommended that the influence of the IWW be reduced by improving working conditions and enabling AF of L unions to represent workers in the conflict-ridden industries. Because employers refused to recognize any unions or to improve wages and conditions significantly, industrial conflicts and the presence of IWW continued to plague agriculture, mining, and the timber industry. As a result, public officials and private business people in western states continued to urge the federal government to suppress the IWW.

In the fall of 1917, Wilson authorized the Justice and War departments to act against the IWW. In September, agents from the Justice Department raided IWW headquarters in Chicago, Wichita, Omaha, Sacramento, and elsewhere. Shortly afterward, the government charged all the leaders of the IWW with violating the Espionage and Sedition acts. At a series of trials in 1918 in Chicago, Sacramento, Wichita, and Omaha, juries found almost all the indicted Wobblies guilty of violating the federal wartime statutes. Sentenced to long terms in the federal penitentiary in Leavenworth, Kansas, more than 100 IWW leaders were incarcerated. As a Justice Department attorney had earlier promised, "Our purpose being, as I understand it, very largely to put the IWW out of business."

As a radical labor organization, the IWW never recovered from the blows it suffered at the hands of national authorities during World War I. After the raids, it operated more as a legal defense organization than as a militant labor organization. Some of its top leaders drifted away toward the new Communist Party; others, like Haywood, jumped bail and fled to the Soviet Union; most served out their terms in Leavenworth.

Melvyn Dubofsky

Bibliography

Dubofsky, Melvyn. *"Big Bill" Haywood.* New York: St. Martin's Press, 1987.
———. *We Shall Be All: A History of the Industrial Workers of the World.* Chicago: Quadrangle Books, 1969.
Foner, Philip S. *History of the Labor Movement in the United States.* Vols. 4 and 7. New York: International Publications, 1965, 1987.
Preston, William, Jr. *Aliens and Dissenters: Federal Suppression of Radicals, 1903–1933.* Cambridge: Harvard University Press, 1963.

Inquiry, The

Six months after America's entry into the European war, President Woodrow Wilson determined the need for a planning commission to study and recommend an American program for eventual peace. By September 1917, the White House and the State Department had already been apprised of the Allied secret treaties whereby Britain, France, Italy, Russia, and Japan had arranged to divide among their countries specified territories belonging to the Central Powers, assuming of course an Allied military victory in the war. Such aggrandizement was clearly contrary to President Wilson's public pronouncements during 1916–1917. Therefore, Wilson sought to focus Col. Edward M. House's attention on how best the United States should respond to the Allied governments' demands. By placing House in charge of this planning commission, Wilson was circumventing

the State Department; by indicating that he could rely on funds already at his disposal, Wilson seemed determined to keep House's new responsibility secret, even from Congress. It was also evident that Wilson was aware that Britain and France were already involved in similar planning pursuits.

If Wilson was aware of the scope of the work to which he was inviting Colonel House, there is no indication. Soon after House took on this new assignment, it became clear that the commission's work would be universal, covering the entire political world. Implicit in Wilson's directive to House was the underlying assumption that there existed in America, presumably in academic institutions for the most part, a corpus of persons competent in the historical, economic, and geographic knowledge of Europe, Africa, the Middle East, South and Eastern Asia, Latin America, and the Pacific Islands areas, which would all plausibly enter the agenda of a future peace conference.

Colonel House proceeded speedily with his new assignment. By the end of October, the organization then known by its code name The Inquiry, had its offices in place and was beginning to function. Starting out in quarters located at the New York Public Library, The Inquiry soon moved to larger offices at the American Geographical Society's building in New York City. As director, House selected his brother-in-law, Sidney Mezes, a philosopher of religion and then president of the City College of New York; as deputy, Isaiah Bowman, the respected director of the American Geographical Society; as secretary, Walter Lippmann, then the youthful editor of the recently founded liberal journal, the *New Republic*; as treasurer, David Hunter Miller, a lawyer associated with the law firm at which House's son-in-law, Gordon Auchincloss, was also a partner; and as director of research, James T. Shotwell, professor of European history at Columbia University. In the formative weeks, it became clear that the rank and file of The Inquiry's personnel would not be specialists or experts on their assigned subjects. Rather, the organization would recruit mainly scholars of repute or great promise who would be given the opportunity to develop the requisite knowledge and competence.

At its height, The Inquiry's personnel numbered about 150 members drawn mainly, but not exclusively, from well-established historical and social science faculties of eastern and midwestern colleges and universities. William Westermann, an ancient historian; Dana G. Munro, a medievalist; Charles H. Haskins, a medievalist; William Lunt, a medievalist; and George Louis Beer, an historian of the seventeenth- and eighteenth-century British Empire were among those recruited. These historians soon realized that their knowledge of earlier centuries was useful but would not suffice; they would require considerable retraining for the twentieth century. For areas such as Eastern Asia, The Inquiry relied on Wolcott H. Pitkin, a lawyer and former political adviser to the government of Siam, a person whose knowledge of China and Japan was admittedly very thin. For Russia and East-Central Europe, The Inquiry fared much better, utilizing the services of Archibald Cary Coolidge, Robert J. Kerner, Charles Seymour, Clive Day, and Robert Lord. Recruitment of able personnel was no simple matter. Academicians were often unable to obtain leaves with salary from teaching duties even when important public service in wartime was the issue. Some members of The Inquiry received no remuneration other than expenses from the government; some received stipulated salaries. Deferments from military service were not automatic for Inquiry staff members, and when the existence of The Inquiry eventually leaked out into the print media, charges of disloyalty led to investigations resulting in certain individuals failing to receive appointments while others, who had earlier won appointments, were summarily dismissed. As the need for specialized personnel mounted toward the war's end, members of other government agencies, including the State Department, the Central Bureau of Statistics, and the Geological Survey, were asked to prepare reports on miscellaneous topics that were anticipated to be of importance at the peace conference.

During its existence, The Inquiry prepared some 3,000 reports, which had varying degrees of influence on the later peace negotiations. In December 1917, Colonel House transmitted two memoranda that served as the bases for several of President Wilson's Fourteen Points in his address of Jan. 8, 1918. The Inquiry produced a surprisingly large number of reports pertaining to Latin America. Most reports focused on national boundaries, the postwar status of colonial dependencies, and economic conditions. Virtually no attention was given to the formation of international organizations, including the League of Nations.

When President Wilson and his official party departed for the peace conference in Europe in December 1918, only a handful of The Inquiry's personnel was included. Once in Paris, members served as advisers to the American plenipotentiaries and as negotiators on the nearly sixty commissions and subcommissions that conducted much of the important work of the peace conference. According to the account books, The Inquiry's life came to an end officially at the end of January 1919, though members informally often referred to themselves as members of The Inquiry while serving with the American Commission to Negotiate Peace. Clearly, The Inquiry's staff, reports, and maps did provide the United States government with important advantages during the difficult peace negotiations at Paris in 1919.

Lawrence E. Gelfand

See also AUCHINCLOSS, GORDON; HASKINS, CHARLES HOMER; HOUSE, EDWARD MANDELL

Bibliography

Gelfand, Lawrence. *The Inquiry: American Preparations for Peace, 1917–1919.* New Haven, CT: Yale University Press, 1963.

Ireland, Merritte Weber (1867–1952)

Merritte Weber Ireland was born at Columbia City, Indiana, the son of Martin and Sara Fellers Ireland. He received an M.D. from the Detroit College of Medicine in 1890, followed by a year of postgraduate training at Jefferson Medical College in Philadelphia.

On May 4, 1891, Ireland joined the United States Army and was appointed a first lieutenant and assistant surgeon. After service at Fort Riley, Kansas, Fort Apache, Arizona Territory, and Fort Staunton, New Mexico, he was promoted to captain in 1896. Taking part in the Santiago campaign during the Spanish-American War, Ireland was recommended for brevet major for gallantry in action. In 1899, he transferred from the 7th Cavalry to the 45th Infantry and sailed with his regiment to the Philippine Islands. The following year he joined Wheaton's Expeditionary Brigade and served in several campaigns throughout the archipelago.

From 1902 to 1912, he served as assistant to Surgeons General Robert M. O'Reilly and

George H. Torney, stationed in Washington, D.C. In June 1915, Ireland was placed in charge of the base hospital at Fort Sam Houston, Texas, and accompanied Gen. John J. Pershing during the Punitive Expedition into Mexico in 1916.

Ireland transferred to Pershing's staff in 1917, was promoted to the rank of colonel, and was named assistant chief surgeon of the American Expeditionary Force (AEF). Soon after arrival in France, he organized the sanitary facilities in French ports for the debarkation of American troops. At Pershing's request, he was appointed executive officer to General Bradley, the chief surgeon of the AEF. As such, Ireland was responsible for the principle organization of the Medical Department's services. On May 1, 1918, he was promoted to brigadier general, Medical Corps, National Army and made chief surgeon, AEF. On August 8 of the same year, he was temporarily appointed surgeon general of the AEF. Ireland became surgeon general, United States Army, with the rank of major general, on October 30. He was reappointed in 1922 and 1926 and retired on May 31, 1931.

General Ireland's lengthy service experience and training established his reputation as one of the army's ablest physicians. His command in France numbered 33,000 commissioned officers and a large number of enlisted personnel. A popular officer, he was acclaimed on both sides of the Atlantic for the efficient care of wounded American soldiers. After the Armistice, he directed the return of the sick and wounded and provided for equipment, facilities, and long-term rehabilitation of the permanently disabled. Ireland died on July 5, 1952.

William Hanigan

Isolationism

Although the term "isolationism" would not come into vogue until the 1920s, the essence of this tradition in U.S. foreign relations shaped the American response to World War I. Prior to 1914, the United States had sought to stay out of the Old World's politics and wars. The purpose of avoiding entanglement in Europe was to preserve the independence that Americans had declared in 1776. The new nation that emerged from the American Revolution had struggled to isolate itself from the Old World in order to preserve its newly acquired independence. Yet Americans had never wanted to cut all ties to Europe. They maintained commercial

and cultural contacts and established diplomatic relations with European countries. They also expanded their nation across North America and extended its influence into the Caribbean and Latin America and across the Pacific to Asia.

Isolationism expressed a fundamental belief in exceptionalism that characterized American political culture. President Woodrow Wilson, like other Americans before and since, thought that the United States was unique. Combining religion and patriotism, Americans viewed the country as God's "chosen nation." Paradoxically, while believing in its uniqueness, Americans also thought that their nation should serve as the model for the world. Isolationism expressed the traditional American desire to withdraw from the corrupt Old World, but its legacy also appeared in Wilson's liberal internationalism during World War I.

When Europe erupted into war in 1914, Wilson proclaimed American neutrality on August 4. He followed the tradition that President George Washington had established in 1793. Seeking to escape the deadly conflict between the Allies and the Central Powers, the United States concentrated on protecting its own maritime and commercial rights. Both sides threatened these rights with their new forms of naval warfare. The British established an off-shore blockade and promulgated a definition of contraband that enabled them to control neutral traffic to Germany and the other Central Powers. The Germans, in turn, began to use the submarine against Allied and neutral shipping. Assisted by the State Department, with William Jennings Bryan and then Robert Lansing as secretary of state, Wilson asserted the neutral rights of American citizens to engage in commerce and travel across the Atlantic Ocean.

The President also offered American mediation between the Allies and the Central Powers in the hope of ending the war. His friend and adviser, Col. Edward M. House, went to Europe in early 1915 and again in early 1916 to find a way to restore peace. Emphasizing that the United States was not interested in the exact terms of the European settlement, but only in restoring peace, House and Wilson revealed their isolationist attitudes toward the Old World. They thought that the United States did not have a vital stake in the European balance of power. A primary motivation for offering mediation was to end the war before German submarines further threatened U.S. neutral rights and forced the United States into the war. Wilson did not request the European belligerents to state their war aims until his December 1916 peace note.

In 1915 and 1916, Wilson promoted Pan-Americanism as a way to unite the Western Hemisphere and protect the Monroe Doctrine. Although unsuccessful because the Latin American nations wanted to avoid U.S. hegemony, his Pan-Americanism exemplified Wilson's commitment to isolationism. The lack of military preparedness during this period also revealed his reluctance to entangle the United States in the Old World. Even the President's emerging idea for a postwar league of nations reflected the same orientation. Prior to 1917, he reconciled his vision for a postwar league with his dedication to U.S. neutrality. Only later did Wilson use the league idea as a rationale for U.S. involvement in the war.

After Germany's unrestricted submarine warfare forced the United States into the European conflict on April 6, 1917, Wilson continued to manifest the attitudes long associated with isolationism. He insisted on distinguishing the United States from all the Allies. The United States became an Associated Power rather than one of the Allied Powers, resulting in the official title of the Allied and Associated Powers for the coalition. He instructed Gen. John J. Pershing to keep the American Expeditionary Force separate from the Allied armies. Even as the United States was breaking its tradition of avoiding entanglement in Europe's wars and politics, the exceptionalism of American political culture continued to shape the relationship between the Old and New Worlds.

In his famous Fourteen Points speech on Jan. 8, 1918, Wilson announced his principles for the future peace settlement. For the first time in U.S. history, he stated an official policy toward the political and territorial questions in Europe. He applied the principle of national self-determination to the Old World, making it the basis for redrawing the map of Europe and the Middle East. Yet he did so only in a tentative way. He was still more concerned with commercial and maritime rights for the United States and with global plans for open diplomacy and a postwar league of nations than with Europe's problems. At the time of the Armistice on Nov. 11, 1918, he distinguished between the points that were essentially American and the remainder that dealt with the settlement in Eu-

rope. This distinction was consistent with the tradition of isolationism.

Wilson's internationalism, which culminated in the drafting of the League of Nations Covenant at the Paris Peace Conference of 1919, expressed the exceptionalism that had characterized American isolationism. The President viewed the new League of Nations as the worldwide expansion of the Monroe Doctrine. Expecting that the United States would exercise global hegemony through the League, he intended to reserve the unilateral right for himself and future presidents to decide when and whether to act for the collective security. The unilateralism that was at the core of isolationism thus manifested itself in Wilson's internationalism.

The fight in 1919–1920 between the President and Republican senators over the Versailles Treaty occurred within the political culture that emphasized American exceptionalism. Wilson and the Republican leader, Henry Cabot Lodge, pursued what each of them regarded as the interests of their nation. While the President and Democratic senators wanted the United States to enter the League of Nations without reservations, Lodge and his fellow Republicans insisted on strong reservations to protect American independence. Otherwise, they intended to defeat the treaty. Wilson thought that the League would never threaten American independence because he expected the United States to control it, but Lodge doubted this control and sought other protections. Both agreed, however, that the United States should preserve its independence, which had been the essence of isolationism since the American Revolution. In that sense, the treaty fight was not over whether to end isolationism, but only over how best to achieve it.

Wilson and his supporters denounced Lodge and his colleagues as isolationists. Because of the President's ability to shape the debate over U.S. foreign policy, the term "isolationism" came into vogue during the 1920s in the aftermath of Wilson's defeat. The rejection of the League of Nations, now identified with internationalism, appeared as the triumph of isolationism. However, this partisan terminology failed to acknowledge that all Americans, whether they favored or opposed the League, wanted to preserve U.S. independence and thus affirmed the essence of isolationism.

Lloyd E. Ambrosius

See also LEAGUE OF NATIONS

Bibliography

Adler, Selig. *The Isolationist Impulse: Its Twentieth-Century Reaction*. New York: Abelard-Schuman, 1957.

Ambrosius, Lloyd E. *Woodrow Wilson and the American Diplomatic Tradition: The Treaty Fight in Perspective*. Cambridge, UK: Cambridge University Press, 1987.

Cooper, John Milton, Jr. *The Vanity of Power: American Isolationism and World War I, 1914–1917*. New York: Greenwood Press, 1969.

May, Ernest R. *The World War and American Isolation, 1914–1917*. Cambridge: Harvard University Press, 1959.

Widenor, William C. *Henry Cabot Lodge and the Search for an American Foreign Policy*. Los Angeles: University of California Press, 1979.

Italian-American Relations

From 1870 to World War I, Italy's foreign policy and diplomacy focused on two main objectives: to make Italy a great power and to liberate the Italian *terre irredente* still under Austro-Hungarian control. Foreign Ministers Marquis Emilio Visconti-Venosta, Marquis Antonino Paterno' Castello-Di San Giuliano, and Baron Sidney Sonnino, among others, demonstrated determination in pursuing Italy's objectives. Italy signed the Treaty of the Triple Alliance with Germany and Austria-Hungary in May 1882 and renewed it four times. The Triple Alliance was meant to be solely defensive, promising reciprocal friendship and peace among the three partners. In case of an unprovoked attack against one of them by a nonsignatory, all would go to war against the aggressor. In addition, Austria-Hungary and Italy agreed that the Balkans and the Adriatic were of mutual interest. Hence, the Second Treaty of the Triple Alliance (1887) stipulated that in case the status quo in the Balkans and Adriatic could not be maintained, and Austria-Hungary and Italy deemed necessary to change it, the modification would be based upon reciprocal compensation. These agreements were reiterated and inserted in a separate treaty between Austria-Hungary and Italy signed in Berlin on Feb. 20, 1887, in the Third Treaty of the Triple Alliance (1891) and again in the Fourth Treaty of the Triple Alliance signed in Vienna on Dec. 5, 1912. However, to allow some flexibility and future independent diplomatic action, Italy in 1896 notified Germany and Austria-Hungary that it would not participate in any armed conflict against France or England.

On July 24, 1914, the day that Austria-Hungary sent its ultimatum to Serbia, Italian Foreign Minister Di San Giuliano spelled out Italy's future course of action. He informed Italian Ambassadors Riccardo Bollati in Berlin, Giuseppe d'Avarna-Gualltieri in Vienna, and Andrea Carlotti-Riparbella in St. Petersburg that, under the terms of the Treaty of the Triple Alliance, Austria-Hungary was obligated to consult with Italy before taking action against Serbia. Having failed *intentionally* to do so, the ultimatum to Serbia did not constitute a legitimate cause for war. Consequently, Italy would not be a cobelligerent. Furthermore, in case Austria-Hungary modified the existing territorial status quo in the Balkans, then, under the terms of the Triple Alliance, it was obligated to compensate Italy. Finally, Italy reserved the right to intervene in the conflict. Di San Giuliano informed King Victor Emmanuel III of his decision toward Austria-Hungary and referred it to Prime Minister Antonio Salandra. Both the king and the prime minister endorsed Di San Giuliano's action. On August 2, 1914, the king authorized the official Declaration of Neutrality.

Italy's neutrality was seen as a potential gain for the Entente. The idea that Italy might join the Entente was set forth by Russia and entertained by England and France. It was also the "trump card" in Di San Giuliano's diplomatic deck. On Aug. 23, 1914, Thomas Nelson Page, American ambassador to Italy, told Secretary of State William Jennings Bryan that Italy was steadily preparing to intervene against Austria-Hungary in the Balkans. In light of the deteriorating relations between Italy and Austria-Hungary, Di San Giuliano, on September 17 and 19, instructed his ambassador in London, Guglielmo Imperiali, that Italy intended to look for an excuse to enter the conflict.

Upon Di San Giuliano's death, Sidney Sonnino became Italy's foreign minister, and between December 1914 and May 1915, he and Count Leopold Berchtold, the Austro-Hungarian foreign minister, exchanged proposals and counterproposals to keep Italy out of the conflict. However, when Rome became convinced that Vienna was not going to comply with Italy's territorial requests, the Italian government announced the cancellation of the Triple

Alliance and turned to secret negotiations with the Entente. The Treaty of London, signed on April 26, 1915, embodied most of Italy's territorial ambitions in the Adriatic, although certain points, such as control of Fiume, were not specifically delineated, a situation that led to great tension and debate at the peace conference.

From 1915 to 1920, diplomatic relations between Italy and the United States deteriorated. Several factors contributed to this situation. The United States suspected that Italy had entered the war solely for self-interest and that the nation had sold itself to the highest bidder. Italy's entrance to the hostilities at that particular juncture made President Wilson's efforts to restore peace in Europe through diplomatic channels all the more difficult. Then too, Italy at war would curtail emigration and revive the old dispute over dual citizenship.

The June 1915 appointment of Robert Lansing as U.S. secretary of state seemed to ease the tension between the two countries. But in August, the American government sent an official protest to Italy, condemning the blockade of the coasts of neutral Albania. Italy's decision was interpreted as an act against neutral rights in the Adriatic. On Nov. 2, 1915, the U.S. Department of State sent another protest to the Italian government warning it against any attempt to blockade the Adriatic. In the meantime, the Italian ambassador in Washington, D.C., Count Vincenzo Macchi di Cellere, expressed to Sonnino his constant concerns about American feelings toward Italy. In particular, Macchi di Cellere was concerned that U.S. entry into the war would give Wilson a voice in the peace settlement.

On Jan. 22, 1917, Wilson's address on the "Bases of a Durable Peace" to the U.S. Senate proclaimed the principle of "Peace Without Victory." Sonnino was visibly agitated and reiterated that the Allies had never encouraged Wilson's "dangerous polemics" or his obvious bid for participation in the peace conference. On July 21, 1917, Wilson confided to Col. Edward M. House that he expected to win over the Entente to his political theories because by the end of the war all of Europe would be in debt to the United States.

When, on Dec. 7, 1917, the U.S. Congress voted to declare war on Austria-Hungary, Italy's hope and confidence soared momentarily. Only two months before, the Italian Army had been routed at Caporetto by the Austro-Hungarians.

The whole nation was overjoyed on America's entry into the war.

On Jan. 8, 1918, Woodrow Wilson announced in Washington his Fourteen Points for European peace. Suddenly, he had become the *deus ex machina* of European diplomacy. Expressing his reaction to the address to Sir James Rennel Rodd, British ambassador to Italy, Sonnino described Wilson as a kind of cleric. Rodd, however, warned that if contradicted, Wilson could become "fanatically malignant, believing himself absolutely right." Arthur S. Link, Wilson's biographer, had observed, "There was much truth in a British contemporary's quip that Wilson sounded more like an arbitrator than a belligerent."

It was Wilson's idealism that troubled Sonnino. His concern was that Wilson concentrated more on European imperialism than on the principle of the balance of power. Ambassador Page explained to Lansing that Sonnino believed that Italy's future as an independent power was irrevocably tied to security from Austrian domination. Italy's hegemony in the Adriatic was necessary for its safety, but other interests claimed by Italy were essential and were guaranteed by the earlier Pact of London.

The developing conflict between Italy's realpolitik and Wilson's idealism can be clearly traced. Sonnino articulated to Macchi di Cellere his views on Wilson's Fourteen Points on Jan. 10, 1918. He stated that President Wilson considered Italian claims limited only to the ethnic component. However, Sonnino held that it was of vital importance to Italy's existence and security, and he, therefore, pursued Italy's quest for the balance of power in the region. Throughout his *Carteggio: 1916–1922* and *Diario: 1916–1922* it is evident that Sonnino rejected the allegations that Italian belligerency was motivated by imperialistic aims. He expressed constant disappointment and outrage over Wilson's intentions to limit Italian territorial claims exclusively to ethnic questions. Sonnino was convinced that there were many concrete geographical, historical, and strategic reasons for Italy's supremacy in the Adriatic as stipulated in the Treaty of London.

On Jan. 21, 1918, Macchi di Cellere told Sonnino that he had met with Wilson and queried him firmly. Wilson had assured him that in the event that the League of Nations did not successfully resolve issues of Italy's strategic and territorial borders, the Great Powers would reconsider them.

On Feb. 11, 1918, Wilson addressed a joint session of Congress. He stated that the United States had "no desire to interfere in European affairs or to act as arbiter in European territorial disputes." However, he underlined that self-determination was "an imperative principle of action" and that the principle of balance of power was "forever discredited." Sonnino feared that Wilson was totally disinclined to accept any plans based on the principle of balance of power. His concerns were reinforced by the many conflicting reports that reached the Italian Foreign Ministry. On March 5, 1918, he informed Macchi di Cellere that U.S. Secretary of State Robert Lansing had declared that the American government was not going to support Italy's territorial claims in Dalmatia. On June 21, Sonnino informed Premier Vittorio Orlando and Macchi di Cellere that, according to the *Daily News* of Chicago, the peace conference was going to deal with complex and difficult problems in the Adriatic and the Balkans. Then, in his July 4 address at Mount Vernon, Wilson again condemned the principle of balance of power.

To make things worse, the United States decided in July to send the bulk of its troops to the French front and only a small contingent, the 332d Infantry Regiment, to Italy. The Italians were deeply disappointed, and Macchi di Cellere complained to Wilson that the American decision had placed Italy in an inferior position to the rest of the Entente. In reality, the contribution of the American regiment was irrelevant. The American presence was limited to boost the morale of Italian troops. At the end of the hostilities, the Americans reported one killed and seven wounded. Even without massive reinforcement, the Italian soldiers continued to demonstrate great patriotism and bravery in the battles of the Piave and Vittorio Veneto.

Then, on September 22, Wilson delivered an address in the Metropolitan Opera House in New York. Speaking about the tasks of the League of Nations, he condemned any arbitrary "compromise or adjustment of interests."

The dispatches that Macchi di Cellere sent to Sonnino and Premier Orlando in November and December 1918 indicated that President Wilson manifested an increasing vacillation over the legitimacy of Italian territorial claims. On the one hand, the President expressed his enthusiasm for the Italian victory and sought Italian support at the peace conference, insinuating that France and England were working to demolish the Treaty of London; on the other hand, the President manifested indecisiveness and inconsistency over the peace program that he intended to propose in Paris. The ambassador attributed Wilson's position to total ignorance of the details of the Adriatic question.

That the Treaty of London was not in consonance with the principle of self-determination was something that Woodrow Wilson had known all along. In a confidential letter to Wilson of Jan. 29, 1918, Ambassador Page reminded the President that his principle of recognized lines of nationality "would eliminate a considerable part of what the Italians have been led to believe they might justly claim on the conclusion of the conference." The ambassador continued: "The extent of those claims is, of course, known to you and the aspirations are set forth in the secret treaty of the 26th of April between Italy and the Allies, which was published in England in the 'New Europe' and had been published in America, I understand in the 'Denver Post.'"

Wilson certainly knew that his Fourteen Points had created dissatisfaction and disappointment in Italy. On Jan. 25, 1918, Lansing reported to Wilson: "I fear that if Italy gains the impression that she is not to strengthen her position in the Adriatic, the Italian people will become discouraged and feel that the war has no actual interest for them. . . . Such an impression would be most unfortunate and might be disastrous."

Italy demanded and expected the full implementation of the Treaty of London, and the reciprocal mistrust growing between Sonnino and Wilson led, eventually, to the major conflict between the two at the Paris Peace Conference. There, Sonnino seemed to detect in Wilson a stern and almost contemptuous indifference for all Italian arguments that tried to prove the inconsistencies between his Fourteen Points and Italy's territorial claims as stipulated in the Treaty of London. During the conference, the conflict between the legality of the Treaty of London and the utopianism of the Fourteen Points ran deep.

Whereas the Italian delegation saw in the Treaty of London the legitimization of Italy's national aspirations and supremacy in the Adriatic, Wilson and his advisers saw peace in Europe as the triumph of self-determination over imperialism, of idealism over realpolitik. Consequently, territorial claims based on balance of power appeared Bismarckian, imperialistic, and antidemocratic. The differences between the Italian and American delegations at the peace conference remained unresolved. Col. Edward M. House miscalculated the true intention of the Italian delegation. He alleged that Italy's refusal to sign the peace treaty, unless Fiume was assigned to Italy, was a bluff. Consequently, Wilson issued a most serious statement on April 23, 1919. According to René Albrecht-Carrié, it eliminated the possibility of a future compromise. The following day Orlando replied. He dismissed the argument that the downfall of the Austro-Hungarian Empire implied a reduction of the Italian aspirations. Above all, Orlando castigated Wilson for his inconsistency. That same day, Orlando and Sonnino abandoned the peace conference and returned to Italy. The turn of events produced widespread protests against Wilson in Italy. Even Gaetano Salvemini and Leonida Bissolati, outspoken critics of the Treaty of London and supporters of Wilsonianism, joined in the protest. Orlando and Sonnino returned to Paris on May 6, 1919, but Wilson remained unyielding.

The Nitti-Tittoni-Scialoja delegation that replaced Orlando and Sonnino in June 1919 found Wilson more uncompromising than ever. The issue of Fiume remained unresolved only to be concluded by the Treaty of Rapallo of Nov. 12, 1920, between Italy and Yugoslavia. It established the Free State of Fiume, an idea that the Italians had advocated but Wilson had rejected.

It was paradoxical that the Italian claims in the Adriatic and the Balkans, as stipulated in the Treaty of London, became the test case of Wilsonian standards. France, on the contrary, imposed its own standards on the territorial settlements with Germany, and Wilson yielded. It was also interesting, as Harold Nicolson points out in *Peacemaking 1919*, that Wilson agreed to place 230,000 Tyrolese under Italian rule in violation of the principle of self-determination, but when the Adriatic question was debated, Wilson became "obstinate and professorial, transforming it from a minor issue into the nervous peaks of a world crisis."

In Paris, the conflict between the legitimacy of the Fourteen Points and the legality of the Treaty of London remained deep and substantive. Woodrow Wilson impugned the legality of the Treaty of London, and the Italians did not feel bound by Wilson's idealism and his Fourteen Points. As far as Italy was concerned, its territorial claims had been legitimized in the Treaty of London, which represented the triumph of fifty years of Italian foreign policy and diplomacy.

Pellegrino Nazzaro

See also ORLANDO, VITTORIO EMANUELE; PARIS PEACE CONFERENCE; SONNINO, SIDNEY

Bibliography

Albrecht-Carrié, René. *Italy at the Peace Conference.* Hamden, CT: Archon Books, 1966.

Link, Arthur S., ed. *The Papers of Woodrow Wilson.* Vols. 43, 45, 46, 47, 49, 51, 53. Princeton, NJ: Princeton University Press, 1983–1986.

Nicolson, Harold. *Peacemaking 1919.* New York: Harcourt, Brace, 1939.

Sonnino, Sidney. *Carteggio, 1916–1922.* Bari: Laterza, 1975.

U.S. Department of State. *Papers Relating to the Foreign Relations of the United States, The Lansing Papers: 1914–1920.* 2 vols. Washington, DC: Government Printing Office, 1939–1940.

J

Japanese-American Relations

As a result of its dramatic and decisive victory in the Russo-Japanese War (February 1904 to April 1905), Japan emerged as a regional power with international aspirations and proceeded to expand its interests in the Far East and the Pacific. Ironically, despite its overwhelming defeat of tsarist Russia, the Japanese government was compelled to accept unpopular peace terms in the 1905 Treaty of Portsmouth mediated by the United States. Under its provisions, Japan received Russia's leasehold on the Liaotung Peninsula, including the railway concession, and the southern half of Sakhalin Island, but it was denied its demand of a large war indemnity from Russia. Thus, Japan ended the war victorious but with a nearly crippled economy and a debt of roughly £83 million owed to British interests. Because of severe economic depression and the accompanying political instability, Japan of necessity adopted a cautious foreign policy in the years immediately preceding the war in Europe. For their part, both the United Kingdom and the United States supported Japanese militarism to the extent it diminished Russian power on the Chinese mainland.

Japan occupied, then annexed its former ally, Korea, in August 1910. At the same time, Japan acquired a concession over the South Manchurian Railway, which bolstered its claim to the region, and accelerated a program of economic development and expansion. Japan also entered into treaties with its former adversary, Russia, with the Entente powers in Europe, and with its main Pacific rival, the United States. On Nov. 30, 1908, Secretary of State Elihu Root and Japanese Ambassador Baron Kotaro Takahira signed an instrument known as the Root-Takahira Agreement. Both parties agreed to maintain the status quo in the Pacific and to respect each other's territorial acquisitions, such as Formosa and Korea for Japan and the Philippines and Hawaii for the United States. They also pledged to maintain the Open Door policy in China and to support Chinese independence. The agreement assuaged U.S. fears of Japanese designs on the Philippines and China and represented tacit U.S. approval of Japan's occupation of Korea and domination of Manchuria.

Of great importance to Japan's relations with the United States and its role in the Great War was the Anglo-Japanese Treaty and Alliance of 1902, renewed in 1905 and 1911. Initially, it obligated each signatory to maintain neutrality in the event the other went to war defending its Far Eastern interests. If the partner were attacked by an outside power, the other would come to its aid. By 1911, all mention of neutrality was dropped, and each promised to join the other in the event of war. These agreements, however, did not extend to Europe and, more importantly, did not bind Britain in the event of a Japanese war with the United States. For Japan, the treaty confirmed its major power status; for Britain, the Japanese alliance was a matter of strategic necessity. Alone, Britain could no longer protect its far-flung interests in Asia, where Germany had dramatically expanded its presence since the 1890s.

In 1898, Germany had acquired a ninety-nine year lease on Kiachow, a 200-square-mile territory on the south coast of China's Shantung Peninsula. The German Far Eastern Naval Squadron was based at its main port, Tsingtao, as was a garrison of 4,000 German marines and some 2,600 Austrian and German militia. Tsingtao was well fortified by heavy naval guns covering the isthmus and by defensive fortifications covering the land approaches to the peninsula. By 1914, Germany had expanded its colonial empire to over 1 million square miles. With holdings in the Bismarck Archipelago, Kaiser-Wilhelmsland (northeast New Guinea), Western Samoa, parts of the Solomon and Mariana Island groups, and the Marshall and Caroline islands, Germany inevitably clashed with Japanese, and potentially with American interests.

When Britain declared war on Germany in Europe on Aug. 4, 1914, the belligerents endeavored to maintain the status quo in the Far East. Three days prior to the declaration of war, British Foreign Secretary Sir Edward Grey informed the Okuma government in Tokyo that Whitehall did not expect to require Japanese military intervention. Likewise, the German ambassador, Count Rex, assured the Japanese that Germany would initiate no hostile action provided Japan remained neutral. Upon these assurances, the Okuma government informed Grey that Japan would observe strict neutrality—unless Britain subsequently asked Japan to intervene.

However, within three days of the declaration of war, Britain reversed its policy. The British Admiralty determined quickly that German naval power in the Far East was sufficient to require limited Japanese intervention in support of the Royal Navy. Grey informed the Japanese on August 6 that Britain wished to invoke the Anglo-Japanese Treaty. Following considerable debate in the cabinet and only after receiving approval from the emperor's personal advisers, the Genro complied with the request. Japan declared war on Germany on Aug. 23, 1914.

The most persuasive voice in the Japanese cabinet was Baron Komei Katō the foreign secretary. He convinced opponents that Japan would benefit from the war regardless of the outcome in Europe, but it would be most advantageous if Germany could be eliminated as a power in the Pacific and China, where it threatened to encircle Japanese interests. Moreover, entering the war would not violate agreements with the United States, or the other powers, regarding China. Indeed, on August 18, Premier Okuma gave formal, albeit vague, assurances that Japan had "no design for territorial aggrandizement" in China.

The British government's initially favorable response to the Japanese cabinet's decision was tempered by Japan's intention not to be limited to a supporting role. The Foreign Office hurriedly attempted to withdraw its request of the sixth. Failing that, it tried to exact a promise from Japan to limit its military actions to the China Sea—but to no avail. Japan issued an ultimatum to Germany for total liquidation of its mainland and insular possessions. Japan then struck quickly at Tsingtao and Germany's island outposts, just missing an opportunity to destroy the German Far Eastern Squadron, which barely escaped to safety.

Japan joined with the Entente Powers in declaring war on the Central Powers in August 1914, exhibiting the same aggressive nationalism and territorial aspirations of its counterparts in Europe. This became eminently clear when, in January 1915, Tokyo presented its Twenty-One Demands to the Peking government. While Japan tried to keep the terms secret, the Chinese promptly turned to the United States, the traditional protector of the Open Door. Secretary of State William Jennings Bryan, a firm supporter of the Monroe Doctrine in the Western Hemisphere, conceded that there was a special relationship between Japan and China, but he would not agree to any change in Chinese territorial integrity or to the Open Door policy, particularly as it affected the United States. It was not the decisive response hoped for by the Chinese. However, in a half-hearted attempt to lessen the impact of Japanese expansion in China, Woodrow Wilson supported plans for a four-power bank consortium to improve the Chinese economy.

Shortly after the United States entered the war, Viscount Kikujiro Ishii opened negotiations with Robert Lansing, the new American secretary of state, and by November they had reached an understanding. According to the Lansing-Ishii Agreement, both parties acknowledged Japan's "special interests" in China, although in a secret protocol attached to the agreement they promised not to take "advantage of the present conditions to such special rights or privileges in China which would abridge the rights of the subjects or citizens of other friendly states."

Japanese ambition surfaced once again when, after the Bolshevik Revolution in Russia, Japan sent 72,000 troops to Siberia, ostensibly to protect Allied military stores in Vladivostok but in reality to seize territory in Siberia and northern Manchuria. Although opposed to the venture, President Wilson found himself forced to send U.S. troops as well. The mission's public goals were the protection of U.S. property in

Siberia, and the assistance of the evacuation of the Czech Legion. In private, though, Wilson hoped the Americans would act as a restraining influence on the Japanese. Interest in the occupation petered out, and the United States withdrew its forces in 1920. The Japanese followed two years later, with nothing to show for their effort and expense. Clearly, Japanese policy prior to and during the First World War confirmed the fears of the British and American governments that Japan was a power in the Far East and Pacific to be reckoned with.

Jonathan Nielson

See also CHINESE-AMERICAN RELATIONS; LANSING-ISHII AGREEMENT; RUSSIA: UNITED STATES INTERVENTION IN SIBERIA; TWENTY-ONE DEMANDS

Bibliography

LaFargue, Thomas E. *China and the World War.* New York: Fertig, 1973.

May, Ernest R. "American Policy and Japan's Entrance into World War I." *Mississippi Valley Historical Review* 40 (1953).

Morley, James W. *The Japanese Thrust into Siberia, 1918.* New York: Columbia University Press, 1957.

Nish, Ian H. *Alliance in Decline: A Study in Anglo-Japanese Relations, 1908–1923.* London: Athlon Press, 1972.

Unterberger, Betty M. *America's Siberian Expedition, 1918–1920.* Durham, NC: Duke University Press, 1956.

Jewish Welfare Board

Three days after America's entry into World War I, a conference was convened to organize a program/body to minister to Jewish men and women being mobilized for active war service. This meeting was held at the initiative of Cyrus Adler, Louis Marshall, and Felix Warburg in reaction to the apparent lack of coordination of services by Jewish agencies when American troops were assembled on the Mexican border in 1916. The major religious groups in the Jewish community sent representatives to the conference—the United Synagogue of America (Conservative), the Union of American Hebrew Congregations (Reform), the Union of Orthodox Jewish Congregations, and the Agudath ha-Rabbonim (Orthodox rabbis), as well as the major Jewish lay organizations such as the Jewish Publication Society and the Council of Young Men's Hebrew and Kindred Association. The delegates originally set up the Jewish Board for Welfare Work in the United States Army and Navy. The name was then officially changed to the Jewish Welfare Board (JWB).

Initially, the JWB was, in effect, an expansion of the Army and Navy Branch of the Young Men's Hebrew Association (YMHA), which had been in existence since 1913 and was already working at army posts and on the Mexican border. Other Jewish social service agencies had been in operation since the middle of the nineteenth century. Unfortunately, these organizations proved ineffective in meeting the needs of Jewish soldiers and sailors in wartime.

It soon became clear that an independent Jewish organization needed to be recognized as the official agency of the Jewish community to work with the War Department through its Commission on Training Camp Activities.

While there was no precedent for such an organization in Jewish life, the Jewish Welfare Board presented itself as such to President Woodrow Wilson and was so recognized by Secretary of War Newton D. Baker. In a short period of time, the JWB built up an organization and trained and placed personnel for field work in the United States and abroad, often financing its work through the American Jewish Relief Committee. Until personnel could be properly recruited, adequately trained, and then placed, the JWB sent congregational rabbis to serve as chaplains for several months at a time. Rabbis had never before served as chaplains in the United States Army, but the Committee on Chaplains rapidly became the primary instrument for service delivery.

Col. Harry Cutler of Providence, Rhode Island, chaired the executive committee from 1917 until his death in 1920, and Chester Teller, formerly of the Bureau of Municipal Research of New York, served as the first executive director. The "Star of David Men," as the early Jewish workers were often called, provided support to the men and women of the armed forces through religious and social services. Since many soldiers had come to the army and navy without an adequate education, general education and Americanization courses were held as well. The JWB also served Jews from other countries who were in the Allied forces, as well as members of other denominations. For instance, the JWB reached out to the non-Jewish Slavic and Russian immigrants in the armed forces through the activities of its Russian Aid Bureau.

Adapting the models of the Young Men's Christian Association (YMCA) and the Knights of Columbus, the JWB eventually built buildings and stocked libraries on army installations and distributed books, articles, Bibles, and prayerbooks supplied through its affiliation with the Jewish Publication Society. In addition, the JWB, through the Bureau of Statistics of the American Jewish Committee, prepared an accounting of the participation of Jews in the American military and naval forces. These services were extended to the Jewish legionnaires enlisting in America for service in Palestine under the British flag.

The JWB established community branches throughout the United States to support activities at local army installations as well as to assist soldiers returned home on leave. In addition, it sought to serve the families of servicemen left behind. Through its work in the "second line of defense," the JWB supported Jewish workers in the shipyards, arsenals, and other military plants and factories, as well as hospitals and universities where the government had taken over under military regulations.

Community branches provided the foundation for the JWB's peacetime efforts following the Armistice in 1918. In 1920, in compliance with Navy Department orders, the JWB transferred its efforts to veterans' hospitals and community service in the form of Jewish centers. Impressed by the cooperative work it had undertaken during the war, the secretaries of war and of the navy supported the efforts of the JWB and requested that it continue its efforts on behalf of servicemen. In the Jewish community, these enlarged centers provided a full opportunity for self-development and social activity. The JWB developed these centers in various areas of the country without advocating a particular religious point of view in order to furnish a common meeting ground for all the Jews of the community. These centers also strove to contribute to the welfare and development of their Jewish consciousness as a constructive force in American life.

The organization has been actively involved in subsequent American war efforts. Now called the Jewish Community Center Association (JCCA), it continues to maintain its commitment to serve the religious and social needs of Jewish men and women in the armed forces, but it has, especially in peacetime,

broadened its emphasis on youth and Jewish center work.

Kerry M. Olitzky

Bibliography

Adler, Cyrus. *Lectures, Selected Papers, Addresses.* Philadelphia: Privately printed, 1933.

Marcus, Jacob. *United States Jewry, 1776–1985.* Detroit: Wayne State University Press, 1989.

Sachar, Howard. *A History of Jews in America.* New York: Knopf, 1992.

Joffre, Joseph Jacques Césaire (1852–1931)

Joseph Jacques Césaire Joffre, marshal of France and chief of the French General Staff from July 1911 until December 1916, was one of the most controversial of all the commanders of 1914. Joffre has emerged in the Anglo-Saxon world as almost a cartoon character; his paunch, legendary appetite, and aloofness from his subordinates have generally been featured in unflattering portraits of his years of command. A more balanced assessment, while not diminishing Joffre's responsibility for the unfolding of the conflict, would stress the problems he inherited in preparing France for war and his undoubted contributions to the crucial French victory at the First Battle of the Marne in September 1914.

The son of a barrel maker, Joffre attended the École Polytechnique, interrupting his schooling to fight in the Franco-Prussian War in 1870. After France's defeat, Joffre returned to the military school to complete his studies, receive his commission, and enter the engineering corps. His early career was almost equally divided between service in metropolitan France and in the colonies. His service overseas gained him a reputation as one of the army's leading engineers.

Joffre returned to France a brigadier general in 1900 and for the next decade progressed steadily up the army hierarchy. In 1906, he commanded an infantry division; by 1910, he was a corps commander. His elevation to chief of the General Staff in 1911, almost as a compromise caretaker commander, was the product of bitter doctrinal divisions inside the army and of Joffre's own noncontroversial nature rather than his brilliance or innate suitability for command. In an army where an officer's political affiliation and religious practices were closely monitored, Joffre had the reputation of a "good republican," supportive of the regime, and thoroughly secular in his outlook. He was thus acceptable to a government deeply suspicious of its own officers' loyalty to the Third Republic.

The doctrinal debates Joffre inherited centered around the best way for France to fight a war against an increasingly powerful German Empire. Since the 1870s, the French General Staff had been responsible for formulating a war plan for such a conflict, and in 1911 Joffre inherited Plan XVI, the sixteenth revision of this campaign plan. Plan XVI was fundamentally defensive with the bulk of the army mobilizing south of the Paris-Metz line in order to launch a counterattack once they had identified the German center. Such a maneuver surrendered large areas of northeast France to German occupation. More importantly in view of the commonly perceived lessons of the wars that preceded 1914, it allowed the Germans to assume offensive operations virtually unhindered by the French armies—seemingly a sure recipe for defeat.

Joffre was alarmed by these aspects of Plan XVI, especially in light of the intelligence reports that suggested a limited German violation of Belgian territory to outflank the French armies and their fixed defenses. He wanted to preempt such a thrust by an offensive of his own into Belgium (precisely the maneuver that the Allies would undertake in 1940), but the government, specifically Premier Raymond Poincaré, was adamantly opposed, fearing complications in the Anglo-French Entente. Joffre's solution to this thorny problem was the controversial Plan XVII. While moving the French armies closer to the threatened frontier, it saddled the country with a war plan that called for a massive offensive conducted by an army that, by its own inspection reports, was poorly trained for such operations, and lacked the weight of artillery that might compensate for its other inadequacies.

In the face of an increasing German threat to move through Belgium, Joffre planned to sever the German right and left wings with a massive assault toward the northeast, in the general direction of Berlin. The French did not underestimate the problems of offensive operations on the modern battlefield; far from it—the latest studies of French tactical doctrine, *offensive à l'outrance*, emphasized that it was the product of the conundrum caused by the realization that offensive operations were crucial to victory, yet among the most difficult tactical problems of modern war. But the French mistakenly believed that the Germans would use few if any reservists in frontline formations. Had this been true, then French confidence that the invasion of Belgium meant that the German line had to be weak elsewhere might have had merit. Instead, the German decision to commit reserve formations to the front lines meant that the French offensive would not be directed at a weakened German center but into the teeth of strong German forces.

In his memoirs, Joffre admitted that the French gravely miscalculated the strength of the German right wing. He did emphasize, however, that the decision to take the offensive was politically popular and was necessary to shore up civilian morale and support for the army. In Joffre's defense, it should also be noted that the German campaign plan, the famous Schlieffen Plan, was scarcely more practical than Plan XVII.

Joffre's chief contribution to the 1914 crisis was his pressure on the government to mobilize its forces and protect the endangered frontiers. By mid-August Joffre launched Plan XVII with assaults into Alsace and Lorraine while simultaneously diverting a reserve army to the north to stop the German thrust emerging through Belgium. French attacks were everywhere repulsed with cruel losses; as many as 300,000 French soldiers were lost in the war's first six weeks. At the same time, the forces deployed against the German thrust through Belgium found themselves outnumbered and pushed back toward Paris.

The collapse of Plan XVII made Joffre and his generalship the focus of the crisis. He coolly used France's lateral railroads to regroup his armies and launch a counterattack against the German armies when they made their famous wheel above Paris. The resulting battle, the First Battle of the Marne, while tactically indecisive, was a strategic success of the highest order, preventing Germany from winning the quick victory that it desperately required, but dooming all the combatants to a war of attrition.

Joffre commanded French forces until December 1916, but the Marne remained his only real success. He launched great offensives in 1915 that produced meager results and horrific casualties. France's losses in 1915 are estimated at 1.5 million; with the exception of the ill-fated Gallipoli campaign, most of these occurred on

Joffre's offensives on the Western Front. His explanation of these operations—jokingly asserting that they were *grignotage* (nibbling away at the enemy)—rightly or wrongly has come to symbolize the attitude of the commanders toward the men they led. In 1916, he was deceived by German operations and thus contributed to the unpreparedness of the Verdun fortress when the great German blow struck. While presiding over the bloodletting at Verdun, Joffre also threw French forces into the great battle of the Somme alongside British forces in July. French losses in 1916 totaled more than 800,000.

The year 1916 proved to be the great watershed year of the war. The general malaise and war weariness that affected all the warring parties helped bring Joffre down. Once the war started, he grew unpopular with the politicians, who disliked his imperious handling of the war and whom he had barred from the war zone. Joffre was "kicked upstairs" and made marshal of France in December. For the remainder of the war he played a largely ceremonial role, visiting the United States in 1917 after it joined the Allies.

Joffre died in Paris on Jan. 3, 1931. His memoirs were published after his death. Generations of students of the Great War have seen in Joffre the epitome of the callous incompetence that doomed a generation in the trenches. Rehabilitating his reputation has proven difficult. Generally these efforts have pursued two lines of argument: that the essence of modern war between great powers is attritional, as ultimately illustrated by World War II, and that given the ill-trained French Army, Joffre did well to save the country in 1914 and was compelled to launch the bloodbaths of 1915 in order to liberate the occupied portions of the country. Joffre had little choice but to attack. These arguments, essentially true, have done little to dispel Joffre's image as an uncaring, out-of-touch commander whose ill-conceived attacks killed a generation of Frenchmen.

Gary P. Cox

See also SCHLIEFFEN PLAN

Bibliography

Joffre, Joseph-Césaire. *The Personal Memoirs of Joffre, Field Marshal of the French Army.* Bently Mott, trans. New York: Harper, 1932.

Liddell Hart, Basil H. *Reputations Ten Years After.* Boston: Little, Brown, 1928.
Porch, Douglas. *The March to the Marne: The French Army 1871–1914.* Cambridge, UK: Cambridge University Press, 1981.
Williamson, Samuel R., Jr. *The Politics of Grand Strategy: Britain and France Prepare for War, 1904–1914.* Cambridge: Harvard University Press, 1969.

Johnson, Hiram Warren (1866–1945)

Hiram Warren Johnson was born in Sacramento, California, to Grover and Annie Johnson. He attended the University of California and became an attorney in 1888, practicing in Sacramento and San Francisco. Two high points marked his early political career. The first was his two successful terms as the Progressive Republican governor of California (1911–1917); the second was his run for vice president with Theodore Roosevelt on the Bull Moose ticket in 1912. In 1916, he won a seat in the United States Senate, where he would assume an important role during World War I and in votes on the Treaty of Versailles and the League of Nations.

Johnson took office on March 16, 1917, immediately prior to the United States entry into World War I. His experiences as governor did not prepare him for his future role as a wartime leader. It was his relationship with Theodore Roosevelt that helped give him direction.

Johnson was a supporter of Roosevelt's efforts to raise and have recognized a volunteer army division for use in Europe. Wilson's refusal to accept Roosevelt's offer helped embitter Johnson toward all Wilson's efforts during his presidency. He became a leading opponent of Wilson during the war and afterward a vocal leader of the "Irreconcilables" in the Senate.

Johnson's concerns about executive policy led him to fear the influence of war profiteers and excessive presidential power. His fear of big business, which he saw as the moving force behind the Wilson policies, led him to propose an excess profits tax of 80 percent on war industries. He also opposed the Espionage Act of 1917 and the Sedition Act of 1918, both of which he believed attacked the traditional liberties of American citizens.

Finally, he was a leading opponent of the Treaty of Versailles. Early in the national debate, Johnson felt that the treaty would be ratified with amendments, but that attitude did not last. In the fall of 1919, he refused to vote for the treaty with or without reservations. By December 1919, he decided that Senator Henry Cabot Lodge's reservations could be used to get Wilson to oppose his own treaty and thus supported their passage. Wilson was unwilling to compromise with Senate Republicans on the treaty, which fell short of ratification on March 19, 1920. Congress finally ended the war on July 2, 1921, by joint resolution.

Johnson continued as an important member of the Untied States Senate until his death on Aug. 8, 1945.

Donald Heidenreich

Bibliography
Howard, DeWitt. "Hiram W. Johnson and Economic Opposition to Wilsonian Diplomacy: A Note." *Pacific Historian* (Spring 1975).
———. "Hiram Johnson and World War I: A Progressive in Transition." *Historical Society of Southern California* (Fall 1975).
Lincoln, A. "My Dear Senator: Letters between Theodore Roosevelt and Hiram Johnson in 1917." *California Historical Society Quarterly* (September 1963).

Joint Army-Navy Technical Board

The Joint Army-Navy Technical Board (JANTB), also called the Joint Army-Navy Technical Aircraft Board, was established at the suggestion of the secretary of the navy a few weeks after the United States declared war. Its purpose was "to standardize, so far as possible, the designs and general specifications of aircraft, except Zeppelins." Originally, the board had three army and three navy members; BGen. Benjamin D. Foulois served as its first chairman. Lacking sufficient expertise, and with little information on the state of aviation at the front, the JANTB floundered for several weeks while it searched for direction.

The arrival in Washington of a cable from French Premier Alexandre Ribot in May 1917, resolved the board's initial dilemma. Ribot called for 4,500 aircraft and 2,000 aircraft for monthly replacements to achieve Allied air supremacy on the Western Front in 1918. Sent to the JANTB for consideration, the board endorsed the Ribot proposal within five days and forwarded it to the secretaries of war and navy for approval. The proposal then went to Congress, where it received speedy passage as part of a $640 million appropriation for aviation. Thus, the aircraft program to be implemented in the United States rested largely on the JANTB recommendation.

The Ribot cable had not, however, specified types of aircraft, and there was some confusion over what the 4,500 aircraft were to include. The JANTB, therefore, proposed a ratio of three observation aircraft to five fighters and one bomber. But the JANTB based its proposal on inadequate and misleading information. In August 1917, General Pershing attempted to override the JANTB proposal, arguing that the U.S. aircraft program should be based on the French experience that fighters and bombers were far more important than observation planes. The effect of Pershing's cable was to undermine the position of the JANTB. The board suffered an additional loss when Foulois departed for Europe in October 1917. Thereafter, the JANTB never regained its original prestige and it found itself struggling to have any say in the development of the U.S. aircraft program.

Furthermore, the JANTB came into constant conflict with the Bureau of Aircraft Production (BAP) over standards and designs. The dispute was one of priorities—quality versus quantity. From the BAP's perspective, maximum production could be achieved only when types of aircraft were established and design changes kept to a minimum. On its part, the JANTB maintained the position that only the most advanced models should be provided for American aviators. By spring 1918, the BAP emerged as the clear winner in this dispute. Civilians, who tended to represent the aircraft industry, subsequently replaced the military members of the JANTB. They were much more willing to incorporate the rapidly changing technical demands in aircraft design. By the latter months of the war, any influence the JANTB had on aircraft standards and design had all but ceased. The JANTB was abolished at war's end.

Jerold Brown

See also AIRCRAFT; UNITED STATES AIR SERVICE

Bibliography
Foulois, Benjamin D., with C.V. Glines. *From the Wright Brothers to the Astronauts:*

The Memoirs of Major General Benjamin D. Foulois. New York: McGraw-Hill, 1968.

Holley, I.B., Jr. *Ideas and Weapons: Exploitation of the Aerial Weapon by the United States during World War I: A Study in the Relationship of Technological Advance, Military Doctrine, and the Development of Weapons*. New Haven, CT: Yale University Press, 1953.

Judson, William Voorhees (1865–1923)

BGen. William Voorhees Judson was military attaché and chief of the United States Military Mission to Russia in Petrograd from July 9, 1917, to Jan. 23, 1918. Born in Indianapolis, Indiana, and graduated from the United States Military Academy in 1888, Judson spent most of his military career in engineering assignments. But in June 1917, he was ordered to Russia as military attaché to the Special Diplomatic Mission (Root Mission) sent to demonstrate American support for the Russian Provisional Government and to assess the condition of the Russian Army, which had been devastated by a series of defeats early in the war. Having concluded that the Russian Army, if properly supplied, could again become an effective fighting force, the mission requested that an American military officer be assigned permanently to Petrograd to coordinate Russian needs and American resources. Accordingly, General Judson remained in Petrograd as chief of the American military mission and military attaché to the American embassy.

Notwithstanding the Root Mission's optimistic appraisal of the fighting capacity of the Russian Army, Judson concluded that Russia's further military contribution to the war effort would be minimal. In this assessment, he was at odds with the American ambassador, David R. Francis, and the Department of State, who were convinced that the overthrow of absolutism in Russia would inspire Russian soldiers to fight in defense of democracy. Believing that only the restoration of discipline could make the Russian Army fight, Judson urged Francis to support measures to motivate the leaders of the Russian Provisional Government to impose military discipline upon the country's war-weary troops. Otherwise, Judson feared that the Russians would sue for peace and clear the way for the Central Powers to transfer all their forces to the Western Front.

Following the Bolshevik seizure of power in November 1917, Judson again found himself in opposition to official American policy in Russia. While following a "wait-and-see" approach toward the revolutionary government, the Wilson administration provided no guidance regarding the day-to-day activities of its representatives in Russia. Judson, hoping to prevent the Bolsheviks from making peace with Germany, wanted to establish regular channels of communication with the new regime. To that end, on Nov. 30, 1917, with Ambassador Francis's reluctant approval, Judson arranged a meeting between himself and Leon Trotsky, the Bolshevik commissar for war. Judson thus became the first American official to meet with a member of the Bolshevik regime. Because this conference was widely interpreted as tacit recognition of the Bolshevik government, the State Department disavowed the action and recalled Judson to Washington.

Until his death in 1923, Judson held Woodrow Wilson and the Department of State responsible for the failure of United States policy toward the Bolshevik regime and continued to believe that meaningful collaboration between Moscow and Washington could have been achieved if American policy had been based on practical rather than ideological considerations.

Jane Weyant

See also FRANCIS, DAVID ROWLAND; ROOT MISSION

Bibliography
Kennan, George F. *Soviet-American Relations, 1917–1920*. Vol. I: *Russia Leaves the War*. Princeton, NJ: Princeton University Press, 1956.

Jusserand, Jean Jules (1855–1932)

Jean Adrien Antoine Jules Jusserand, a French diplomat, scholar, and author, was the long-serving ambassador to the United States, whose tenure (1902–1925) included the crucial years before and during the First World War.

Jusserand was born at Lyons, France. After graduating from the University of Lyons and then Paris, he entered the French diplomatic service in 1876. His early assignments included work at the Quai d'Orsay, in Tunis, and as a counsellor to the French embassy in London. In 1898, he was appointed minister to Denmark, and in 1902, he began his long service as France's chief representative in Washington, where he succeeded Jules Cambon.

Jusserand brought important strengths to his Washington posting. He was married to an American, Elise Richards, who was herself French-born and whose arrival as the ambassador's wife in 1902 marked her first visit to her homeland. More importantly, in 1902, Jusserand was already known as a "literary diplomat," famous for his books in history and literary studies, such as *The English Novel in the Time of Shakespeare* and *A French Ambassador at the Court of Charles II*. In 1916, Jusserand won the first Pulitzer Prize in history for *With Americans of Past and Present Days*. After the Great War, he also served as president of the American Historical Association. When he served in London, his scholarly avocation gave him immediate access to Britain's literary and political elite; Lord Kitchener became one of his best friends. In the United States he quickly entered the circle of literary and scholarly brahmins so influential in the Gilded Age. He struck up an almost immediate and lifelong friendship with President Theodore Roosevelt; the two played tennis and shared a love of hiking. Jusserand also traveled widely during his tenure in Washington, and he came to know the United States better than perhaps any other foreign diplomat and, by all accounts, to gain an affection for America second only to his homeland.

Jusserand was extraordinarily well placed to represent France at the outbreak of the Great War. The reality of the German invasion gained much sympathy for France throughout the world. His country's resolute continental focus, which left the Atlantic blockade and the burden of the Allies' economic warfare efforts to Britain, also eased his diplomatic mission.

Jusserand appeared fitfully throughout the diplomatic accounts of the period, always conveying to Wilson and his cabinet France's unshakable resolve to fight on to victory. Presiden-

tial adviser Edward M. House termed him "the most forceful representative the Allies have here." Jusserand was unwilling to assist Wilson's efforts to mediate the conflict in the early years of the war. House even claimed that in 1915 the ambassador labeled Wilson pro-German for his restraint in the face of German submarine warfare, and his efforts to achieve a compromise peace. Revisionist accounts of America's entry into the war, not surprisingly, see him in unflattering terms. In his work *Why We Fought*, Hartley Grattan termed Jusserand "an emotional drunk for the duration of the war," whose views House took as mirroring French opinion at large and thus convinced the American of the uselessness of pursuing a negotiated settlement. More modern assessments do see Jusserand as helping to defeat Wilson's attempts in 1916 to call a peace conference.

Lionized after the war by the diplomatic and scholarly communities, from whom he received a spate of honorary degrees, Jusserand served on as the dean of Washington's diplomatic corps until 1925. Upon his retirement, he returned to France; when he died in 1932 he was still attempting to improve relations between the two countries. Jusserand completed only the first volume of his memoirs, *What Befell Me*, an account of his diplomatic service up to the presidency of Theodore Roosevelt.

Gary Cox

Bibliography

Daniels, Josephus. *The Wilson Era 1917–1923*. Chapel Hill: University of North Carolina Press, 1946.

Devlin, Patrick. *Too Proud to Fight: Woodrow Wilson's Neutrality*. New York: Oxford University Press, 1975.

Grattan, C. Hartley. *Why We Fought*, ed. by Keith L. Nelson. Indianapolis: Bobbs-Merrill, 1969.

Seymour, Charles. *The Intimate Papers of Colonel House*. Boston: Houghton Mifflin, 1926.

K

Kellogg, Frank Billings (1856–1937)

Frank Billings Kellogg was always a reasonable man. As United States senator from Minnesota in 1917–1923, he did his best to obtain passage of the Treaty of Versailles but found himself frustrated on the one side by the extremists led by Massachusetts Senator Henry Cabot Lodge, Sr., and on the other by the nonreservationists led by the President of the United States.

Kellogg had enjoyed a remarkable rise during the years after his birth in New York State. After the Civil War his family moved to Minnesota. As a farm youth, he nearly perished in the great blizzard of 1873. To escape the drudgery and penury of the farm he read law, passed the bar, and joined the law firm of a cousin in St. Paul. Soon he was representing railroad and mining firms and traveling to Washington. Friendship with Theodore Roosevelt brought an assignment to prosecute the Standard Oil Company, and in 1911, after several years of litigation, Kellogg won the case. The following year he became president of the American Bar Association.

Kellogg entered the Senate on March 4, 1917, and although a Republican, he ardently supported the Democratic president's program for war and peace. Early in 1919, Senator Lodge arranged a "round robin" in which more than one third of the Senate's membership in the forthcoming Congress, senators and senators-elect, who would have to pass on the peace treaty with Germany, announced that they did not favor the proposed League of Nations. Kellogg refused to sign the round robin. Shortly thereafter he asked Lodge to place him on the Foreign Relations Committee, and the Massachusetts senator refused him membership.

In 1919–1920, Kellogg led the moderate faction on the peace treaty in the Senate. On June 9, 1919, he telephoned President Nicholas Murray Butler of Columbia University and asked him to come to Washington and confer with a group of Republican senators. Two days later Butler arrived. Kellogg and Senator Frederick Hale of Maine met him at Union Station and took him to Kellogg's house, where a group of Republican senators had gathered for dinner—Charles L. McNary of Oregon, Walter E. Edge and Joseph Frelinghuysen of New Jersey, Arthur Capper of Kansas, William B. Kenyon and Albert B. Cummins of Iowa, Irvine L. Lenroot of Wisconsin, Selden P. Spender of Missouri, Henry W. Keyes of New Hampshire, and Warren G. Harding of Ohio. During dinner Kellogg asked Butler to give his views on the treaty. Butler suggested certain reservations, doubtless those Kellogg desired, such as exclusion of "matters of domestic policy," reservations concerning the effects on the Monroe Doctrine, and clarification of Article 10.

After writing out the reservations agreed to at the dinner, Kellogg apparently gave them to Ambassador Jules Jusserand of France. The ambassador cabled them to his government, which sent them to the British Foreign Office. After both governments agreed, Jusserand went to President Wilson and said that if Wilson would allow his supporters in the Senate to accept the proposed reservations, the treaty would pass.

By this time, the President had suffered the terrible stroke of Oct. 2, 1919. He was physically incapacitated and able only to concentrate on public issues for short periods—in no position to judge Jusserand's (that is, Kellogg's) proposal. To the ambassador's horror, the President replied in a stern voice, "Mr. Ambassador, I shall consent to nothing. The Senate must take its medicine."

After defeat for reelection in 1922, Kellogg became United States ambassador to London, and secretary of state during the administration of President Calvin Coolidge. In 1928, he was coauthor of the notable Kellogg-Briand Pact for the renunciation of war. Upon return to private life in 1929, he went back to his law practice in St. Paul. He died in 1937.

Robert H. Ferrell

See also PARIS PEACE CONFERENCE

Bibliography

Ferrell, Robert H. *Frank B. Kellogg and Henry L. Stimson.* New York: Cooper Square, 1963.

Kitchin, Claude (1869–1923)

Claude Kitchin was born near Scotland Neck, North Carolina. After graduating with honors from Wake Forest College in 1888, Kitchin studied law, and in 1890, he became an attorney in the small rural community of Scotland Neck.

As his legal practice prospered, Kitchin showed a growing interest in state and national politics. During the exciting presidential election campaign of 1896, he was an enthusiastic supporter of William Jennings Bryan and the agrarian wing of the Democratic Party. In 1900, Kitchin won election to the U.S. Congress. He served as a member of the House of Representatives from 1901 until his death in 1923.

Kitchin developed an impressive command of federal revenue policy and gained appointment to the powerful House Ways and Means Committee. In 1915, he became chairman of Ways and Means and majority leader of the House of Representatives. He was an intensely partisan Democrat who viewed the Republican Party as a conspiracy of the wealthy and privileged against ordinary Americans, especially farmers. As a friend and disciple of William Jennings Bryan, Kitchin served as an eloquent spokesman for the neopopulists and agrarian-progressives in Congress.

In 1912, Kitchin had welcomed the nomination and election of Woodrow Wilson to the presidency. During the first year and a half of the Wilson administration, he loyally supported the President's legislative program. However,

after the outbreak of war in Europe in August 1914, his relations with Wilson began to deteriorate. Troubled by what he considered the President's "unneutral neutrality," he worried that Wilson's anglophile bias and pro-Ally policies would eventually cause war between the United States and the Central Powers. Convinced that there was no compelling reason for the United States to intervene in Europe, Kitchin was appalled by the President's handling of the submarine dispute with Germany. He also opposed Wilson's preparedness campaign as unnecessary, expensive, and likely to lead to war. Working closely with a large number of anti-interventionist Democrats, Kitchin forced the Wilson administration to modify its preparedness program. During 1915 and 1916, he repeatedly urged the President to adhere to strict and impartial neutrality and pleaded with him to avoid entry into World War I.

In early April 1917, the President asked Congress to declare war on Germany. Kitchin was among the fifty members of the House of Representatives who voted against the war resolution. He asserted once again his belief "that we could and ought to have kept out of this war." Knowing that his negative vote would further antagonize a "yelping pack of defamers and revilers," Kitchin emphasized his willingness to support the war effort, even though he disagreed with Wilson's decision to go to war.

After the United States entered World War I, Kitchin usually backed the President's policies. Occasionally, however, he reverted to the role of critic. He vigorously opposed Wilson's plan to expand the armed forces through conscription, preferring that a volunteer system be tried before resorting to coercion. When Congress bowed to presidential pressure and authorized a military draft, Kitchin resolved that those who remained behind in safety and comfort should not reap excessive profits from the war while young draftees were fighting and dying in France. As House majority leader and head of the Ways and Means Committee, Kitchin favored substantial increases in taxation, especially on large incomes and wartime corporate profits. For him, sound fiscal policy required that much of the war's cost be paid for through taxation—and not solely by borrowing. Although he was forced to compromise with the White House, the Treasury Department, and the Senate, Kitchin's views helped shape the Revenue Acts of 1916, 1917, and

1918, each of which he steered through the House of Representatives.

His determination to tax large incomes and excess corporate profits triggered a storm of protest from business groups and others who wanted to pay for the war by borrowing and by taxes on consumption. Blaming Kitchin for high taxes and for other wartime irritants, spokesmen for the Republican Party made "Kitchinism" an issue in the off-year congressional elections of November 1918. Those elections produced a stinging defeat for the Democratic Party.

As House minority leader, Kitchin continued to resist those who wanted to reduce income tax rates on the wealthy and eliminate the excess profits tax. On April 9, 1920, after delivering a speech in the House of Representatives, he suffered a cerebral hemorrhage. He never fully recovered and thus was unable to resume his seat in Congress. He died on May 31, 1923, in Wilson, North Carolina.

Richard N. Chapman

Bibliography

Arnett, Alex W. *Claude Kitchin and the Wilson War Policies.* New York: Russell & Russell, 1971.

Kennedy, David. *Over Here: The First World War and American Society.* New York: Oxford University Press, 1980.

Link, Arthur S. *Wilson: Campaigns for Progressivism and Peace.* Princeton, NJ: Princeton University Press, 1965.

————. *Wilson: Confusions and Crises, 1915–1916.* Princeton, NJ: Princeton University Press, 1964.

Livermore, Seward W. *Politics Is Adjourned: Woodrow Wilson and the War Congress, 1916–1918.* Middletown, CT: Wesleyan University Press, 1966.

Knights of Columbus

Founded by Father Michael J. McGivney in New Haven, Connecticut, in 1882, the Knights of Columbus (K of C) is a Catholic fraternal insurance society that has 1.5 million members located in the United States, Canada, Mexico, the Philippines, and Puerto Rico. Its patron, Christopher Columbus, symbolizes the Catholic origins of the "New World" as a way of legitimating Catholic loyalties in a society given to periodic waves of anti-Catholicism and nativism. Hence, the Knights' self-understanding is rooted in its identity as a Catholic antidefamation society.

During World War I, the K of C was recognized as the preeminent lay Catholic organization. The story of its social service to soldiers begins not with World War I but rather with the U.S. Army's incursion into Mexico in retaliation for Gen. Francisco ("Pancho") Villa's March 9, 1916, attack upon Columbus, New Mexico. Nearly 250,000 National Guardsmen were encamped along the Mexican border during the year preceding the United States entrance into World War I. Several K of C councils in New Mexico, Arizona, and Texas spontaneously responded to the religious and social needs of the thousands of Catholic troops.

In April 1917, shortly after the United States entered the war, Supreme Knight James Flaherty of Philadelphia successfully sought permission to establish social centers not only for Catholics but for all servicemen. The Knights hoped that such a display of patriotism would dispel that form of anti-Catholicism that identified American Catholicism as an oxymoron.

By that summer the K of C had established its War Activities Committee under the chairmanship of Patrick H. Callahan of Kentucky. The Knights, along with other volunteer societies such as the YMCA, the Salvation Army, and the Jewish Welfare Board, were authorized to provide for the social needs of the armed forces. The Knights established service centers, or K of C huts, in training camps in the United States, rest and recovery hostels in England and Ireland, and huts behind the lines. After the war, they served in Allied-occupied areas in France, Germany, Italy, and even Siberia.

The Catholic bishops established a Catholic War Council that included representatives of the K of C. There were other Catholic organizations that also wished to sponsor service centers, but the K of C was the only society granted permission to work with the military. Alienated by the official status of a Catholic fraternal organization, several nondenominational fraternal societies unsuccessfully appealed to the government for such recognition.

Under the banner "Everyone Welcome, Everything Free," K of C secretaries provided servicemen with a wide range of social programs, including sports, music, and drama, while K of C chaplains ministered to their spiritual needs. The Knights raised several million dollars on their own and were allocated nearly $30 million from a combined fund drive.

K

In general, the K of C worked well with the other official social service organizations, but there were a few conflicts related to the K of C's policy not to charge for food, tobacco, and other materials. Subsequently, the War Department passed a resolution limiting free distribution to 10 percent of an agency's budget. The Supreme Board of Directors opposed the resolution on the rationale that such a policy would violate a public trust since the Knights had raised funds on the "everything-free" principle. Ultimately, a compromise was reached whereby the 10 percent limitation did not apply to stationery and periodicals. However, the policy was unenforceable as K of C secretaries continued to distribute everything free according to their traditional practice.

Immediately after the Armistice, K of C secretaries devised special postcards known as "Safe-and-Sound" cards by which soldiers notified their families that they had survived the war. Upon boarding a ship home, each soldier received a free K of C gift pack, with cigarettes, sweets, handkerchiefs, and shaving material.

After the war, the remaining funds were expended on a variety of K of C educational, vocational occupational, and employment programs for veterans. The K of C evening school program enrolled more than 50,000 students in its 100 schools in 1920. Its correspondence school, administered by the Supreme Office, enrolled 25,000 students and the Knights awarded more than 400 college scholarships to veterans.

The war and reconstruction work of the Knights of Columbus constituted a new era in the organization's history. During the 1920s, the leadership became conscious of the Knights' prestigious social and religious stature. The greatest tribute to the Knights war effort was the admiration demonstrated by the nearly 400,000 men who joined the K of C between 1917 and 1923.

Christopher J. Kauffman

Bibliography

Egan, Maurice Francis, and John B. Kennedy. *Knights of Columbus in Peace and War.* New Haven, CT: Knights of Columbus, 1920.

Kauffman, Christopher J. *Faith and Fraternalism: The History of the Knights of Columbus.* New York: Simon & Schuster, 1992.

Kuhn, Joseph Ernst (1864–1935)

Joseph Ernst Kuhn was born at Leavenworth, Kansas. He attended local schools and graduated first in his class from the United States Military Academy at West Point in 1885. Commissioned a second lieutenant in the Corps of Engineers, he held numerous engineer assignments over the next thirty years in the United States and the Philippines, while rising to the rank of colonel. He also taught at West Point from 1889 to 1894 and at the Army Service Schools at Fort Leavenworth, Kansas, from 1909 to 1912. He was an observer with the Japanese Army during the Russo-Japanese War (1904–1905).

Several months after World War I broke out in the summer of 1914, Kuhn went to Germany as a member of the American military mission, and in March 1915, he was named military attaché at the U.S. embassy in Berlin, with the added duty of observer at the German Army's headquarters. During the next twenty months, he frequently visited German units on both the Eastern and Western fronts, gaining an unmatched acquaintance with German military leaders and detailed knowledge about the organization, weapons, and methods of the German Army. Returning to the United States in December 1916, Kuhn was promoted to brigadier general and appointed chief of the War College Division of the War Department General Staff. In this post, he participated in planning the mobilization, organization, and training of the American Army and was able to apply the knowledge he had gained about the German Army to great advantage.

In August 1917, Kuhn was promoted to the temporary rank of major general and given command of the newly created 79th Division. A month later he was considered a possible replacement for the retiring chief of staff, Gen. Hugh L. Scott. However, Kuhn let it be known that he preferred duty in France as a combat commander, and he remained with his division. After months of training at Camp Meade, Maryland, Kuhn took the 79th Division to France in July 1918, where it continued to train until it entered the front line in September.

The high point of the war for Kuhn was his participation in the Meuse-Argonne offensive, which began on September 26 and lasted until the Armistice on Nov. 11, 1918. On the first day of the American attack, his essentially "green" division was assigned the difficult task of pushing four miles behind German lines to seize the formidable German position on Montfaucon, an imposing, heavily defended high spot which dominated the whole sector. In hindsight, it was clear that the American High Command was asking too much of Kuhn, for his division was too inexperienced and the German defenses were too strong for him to succeed. Very quickly Kuhn's attack stalled, and he was unable to achieve the "spectacular gain" on the first day that his orders prescribed, causing the whole American advance along the center of the front to be held back. On the second day of the offensive, Kuhn finally captured Montfaucon. But the delay had enabled the Germans to rush thousands of reinforcements and hundreds of artillery pieces to the Meuse-Argonne sector, effectively stopping the attack until the American Army could regroup. In early November, following a period out of the line so that its depleted ranks could be refilled with replacements, Kuhn's division captured the crucial height of La Borne de Cornouilles, east of the Meuse River, from which German observers had directed devastating artillery fire against the Americans for more than a month.

After briefly commanding IX Corps in early 1919, Kuhn returned to the United States with his division. He went on to command Camp Kearney, California, Schofield Barracks, Hawaii, Vancouver Barracks, Washington, and the 5th Infantry Brigade before retiring with the permanent rank of major general in 1925. Regarded as one of the most intelligent officers of his generation, Kuhn died in San Diego on Nov. 12, 1935.

John K. Ohl

See also UNITED STATES ARMY: 79TH DIVISION

Bibliography
Barber, J. Frank. *History of the Seventy-Ninth Division AEF during the World War, 1917–1919.* Lancaster, PA: N.p., n.d.
Coffman, Edward M. *The War to End All Wars: The American Military Experience in World War I.* New York: Oxford University Press, 1986.

L

Lafayette Escadrille

As a combat aviation squadron manned by American volunteers, the Lafayette Escadrille—officially the American Volunteer Squadron, French Air Service—became a symbol of principled sacrifice in France's struggle against German militarism. The unit operated from April 20, 1916, to Feb. 18, 1918, when it became the American Expeditionary Force's 103d Pursuit Squadron. A total of thirty-eight Americans and four Frenchmen flew over 3,000 combat sorties while assigned to the Lafayette Escadrille, which served in every sector of the Western Front. Squadron pilots absorbed a casualty rate of 30 percent, to include six pilots killed in aerial combat, while amassing thirty-nine confirmed victories and perhaps as many as 100 unconfirmed victories. These statistics, however, illustrate that the Lafayette Escadrille's combat record was not particularly impressive. The squadron's true significance derived from its role as a symbol. Large numbers of Europeans and Americans saw the members of the Lafayette Escadrille as self-sacrificing idealists who were prepared to serve "humanity" regardless of the niggling neutrality of the United States government. French propagandists and American interventionists championed the volunteers as crusading moralists dedicated to preserving the civilized world. They were men of honor who differentiated between right and wrong and who were prepared to fight the evil of German militarism. By lionizing the Lafayette Escadrille, the French government in particular hoped to shift public opinion in the United States away from neutrality and toward active support for France. Its technique, however, was almost to taunt American isolationists into emulating the "saviors of national honor" in the Lafayette Escadrille.

Norman Prince, a pioneer in American civil aviation, promoted the idea of a volunteer squadron assigned to the French Air Squadron as early as January 1915. The War Ministry failed to act on his proposal, and it took the involvement of Dr. Edmund Gros, a leader of the American ambulance service in France, to realize Prince's dream. Gros worked through Jarousse de Sillac, a senior official in the Department of Foreign Affairs who saw the propaganda value of a combat squadron manned by American volunteers. Sillac subsequently arranged a meeting between Gros and General Hirschauer, chief of French military aeronautics. Like his countrymen, Hirschauer hoped that the example of American volunteers selflessly helping France would erode neutralist sentiments in the United States. Therefore, he authorized the creation of the Lafayette Americaine (N-124), which began frontline service on April 20, 1916. The German ambassador to the United States, Count Johann von Bernstorff, complained about the unit's name, and the French, at Gros's behest, rechristened it the Lafayette Escadrille (Spa-124) in December 1916.

The Lafayette Escadrille began with seven Americans who had previously served with the French Foreign Legion: Victor Chapman, Norman Prince, Elliott Cowdin, William Thaw, Bert Hall, Kiffin Rockwell, and James McConnell. These airmen had unconventional backgrounds, as did those Americans who joined them later. For example, Bert Hall was a race car driver, Edward Hinkle was an artist studying at the École des Beaux Arts, Carl Dolan was an electrical engineer from MIT, and

Didier Masson had flown with Pancho Villa's forces in Mexico. These educated, high-spirited men were ostensibly under the command of Capt. Georges Thenault and the "recklessly brave" Lt. Alfred Laage de Meux, but Foreign Office and Ministry of War directives prohibited the Frenchmen from disciplining the Americans, who were mostly corporals and sergeants. As a result, the American airmen frequently flaunted Thenault's authority by performing individual (i.e., uncoordinated) air attacks in lieu of formation tactics. They claimed that individual attacks preserved their freedom of action, but the results were several needless deaths and lower combat effectiveness. Thenault's troubles were compounded by his lack of financial authority. The pro-interventionist American millionaire W.K. Vanderbilt contributed up to $10,000 a month to operate the Lafayette Escadrille and other French units manned by U.S. airmen.

Thenault and his subordinates began combat operations at Luxeuil-les-Bains, located in northeast France, forty miles from the front. Their first patrol occurred on May 13, 1916, after the Lafayette Escadrille finally received a consignment of Nieuport Bebes. The squadron subsequently participated in the Battle of Verdun, which included a murderous air zone located mostly over enemy territory. Within this zone, which was twenty miles long, five miles deep, and two miles high, the Americans flew two patrols a day. Specifically, they conducted search and destroy missions, protected French reconnaissance aircraft, and attacked German observation balloons. The Lafayette Escadrille spent 113 days at Verdun (May–September 1916) and amassed thirteen aerial victories, despite a series of mechanical problems and crash landings. The unit then returned north and acquired the Nieuport 17, a superior aircraft to the smaller Bebe, which it used to escort a force of British Sopwith "Strutters" and French Breguet-Michelin IVs in an unprecedentedly large strategic bombing raid against Germany. Forty bombers dropped almost five tons of explosives on the Mauser rifle factory in Oberndorf-am-Necker with seemingly good results. However, the death of Norman Prince, the co-founder of the Lafayette Escadrille, muted the propaganda value of an air attack conducted by the citizens of three nations. Subsequently, the Lafayette Escadrille joined the Group de Combat 13 and participated in the Somme and Nivelle

offensives. Bad weather hampered both operations, but in the Nivelle offensive, the Americans performed dangerous low-level aerial reconnaissance and identified troop positions and movements. As a result of this experience, the Lafayette Escadrille finally became a coordinated professional combat unit, as demonstrated in the Verdun offensive of 1917. In support of the French assault, the Americans were never busier. With their SPAD XIIIs, they escorted bombardment attacks against German rail centers, beat back enemy aerial observers while protecting their own, and supported the offensive thrusts near the Chemin des Dames. James Hall, the future author of *Mutiny on the Bounty*, secured the unit's final victory on Jan. 1, 1918, just prior to its disbandment.

Most members of the Lafayette Escadrille initially opposed their transfer to the U.S. Air Service. They questioned, for example, the qualifications of untested American airmen to command them. In contrast, Gen. William Kelney, chief of the Air Service, needed an experienced cadre of combat aviators and tried to waive all entry requirements that obstructed the transfer of the Lafayette Escadrille to his control. Kelney's successor, however, dithered over the issue. As a result, discharged members of the squadron continued to fly combat missions for the French Service Aeronautique as civilians. They eventually received commissions in the U.S. Air Service, but the process took most of January and February 1918. Only one volunteer, Edwin "Ted" Parsons, chose to remain with the French. Of those who transferred to the American air arm, seventeen joined the 103d Pursuit Squadron and six became unit commanders. Three became aces. Regardless of where they served, the alumni of the Lafayette Escadrille continued the tradition of honorable service first begun in 1916.

Peter R. Faber

See also UNITED STATES AIR SERVICE

Bibliography
Flammer, Philip M. *The Vivid Air*. Athens: University of Georgia Press, 1981.
Hall, James N., ed. *The Lafayette Flying Corps*. Boston: Houghton Mifflin, 1920.
Mason, Herbert Molloy. *The Lafayette Escadrille*. New York: Random House, 1964.

Lane, Franklin Knight (1864–1921)

Franklin Knight Lane embodied many traits of the Progressive Era. Born in Canada but raised in California, he practiced law and entered Democratic politics in San Francisco. Following unsuccessful races for governor and mayor, the gregarious Lane accepted an appointment from Republican President Theodore Roosevelt—whom Lane greatly admired—to the Interstate Commerce Commission in 1905. He was serving there in 1913 when Woodrow Wilson named him secretary of the interior.

As war issues pressed the administration, Lane, like Roosevelt, supported preparedness. In February 1917, he urged arming and convoying merchant ships. Wilson adamantly refused, but he abruptly relented when informed of the Zimmermann Telegram. In a crucial cabinet meeting in March, Lane joined the rest of the cabinet in arguing successfully for American intervention.

Lane had been appointed one year earlier to the Council of National Defense (CND). There, he urged cooperation and coordination between public and private spheres, a position compatible with his personal philosophy. With his support, the nation's railroad leaders voluntarily formed a Railroads War Board to meet the war emergency. Later, several railroad executives favored his heading the Railroad Administration.

Lane also helped resolve a touchy problem for the council. At Lane's suggestion, the CND formed a single Field Division, amalgamating the male-dominated state and local councils and the separate Woman's Committee. Lane then headed the division and its governing board of five men and five women.

An effective speaker, he addressed many audiences for the Committee on Public Information. His pamphlet *Why We Are Fighting Germany*, produced for the committee, was widely distributed, and his brief collection of addresses, *The American Spirit* (1918), was well received in wartime America.

Lane's love of conversation caused trouble in the Wilson administration. The President reportedly stopped discussing matters of importance at cabinet meetings because the secretary divulged confidential matters. This same quality, joined with his wit and brilliant letter-writing ability, however, makes his volume of candid letters and cabinet notes entertaining and informative reading.

Kevin B. Byrne

Bibliography

Lane, Anne Wintermute, and Louise Herrick Wall, eds. *The Letters of Franklin K. Lane: Personal and Political*. Boston: Houghton Mifflin, 1922.

Lansing, Robert (1864–1928)

Robert Lansing served in the United States Department of State throughout World War I. On April 1, 1914, after the Senate had approved his appointment, he succeeded John Bassett Moore as the department's counselor. A new opportunity opened for Lansing when William Jennings Bryan resigned as secretary of state on June 9, 1915. Wilson eventually chose Lansing to replace Bryan. In selecting him, the President followed his own inclination and also the advice of his close friend, Edward M. House, to have a weak secretary. Both Wilson and House wanted someone in that office who would accept their participation in shaping U.S. foreign policy outside the State Department. By the war's end in 1918, Lansing had lost whatever effectiveness he had once enjoyed in the conduct of U.S. diplomacy. His role at the Paris Peace Conference of 1919 was marginal. Wilson finally forced him to resign on Feb. 12, 1920.

Lansing's career before entering the State Department had prepared him to view world politics from the perspective of international law. His wife, Eleanor, was the eldest daughter of John Watson Foster, a distinguished international lawyer and former secretary of state. Foster had served as Lansing's mentor, promoting his career in international law. For more than two decades before World War I, Lansing represented the U.S. government at international tribunals and conferences as an attorney. He helped found the American Society of International Law. Prior to his appointment as counselor for the State Department, he established his reputation as one of the leading international lawyers in the United States.

Lansing thought that the United States, as an exceptional nation, should fulfill a special mission in the world. Like Wilson and Bryan, he was a devout Presbyterian. During his tenure at the State Department, he served as an elder in the Presbyterian Church that he regularly attended in Washington, D.C. His understanding of American interests combined elements of religious faith with legalism. He was convinced that the United States should not entangle itself in the Old World but should protect its sovereign rights under international law. This emphasis on legality distinguished Lansing's idealism from Wilson's, while they both believed that the United States was God's chosen nation.

Lansing contributed significantly to the establishment of U.S. neutrality during World War I. The proclamation of neutrality that Wilson issued on Aug. 4, 1914, was originally drafted by the counselor. With Wilson's and Bryan's support, Lansing attempted to secure the approval of the 1909 Declaration of London by all belligerents, but the British government continued to resist this new codification of international maritime and commercial rights. Within the framework of traditional international law, Lansing insisted upon the right of American merchants to sell munitions to belligerents. He saw no justification for an embargo on wartime trade in arms. Lansing also defended the right of Americans to extend loans and credits to belligerents. Although the inevitable consequence would be a stake in Allied victory over the Central Powers, he denied that these financial ties were unneutral. For him, any action that conformed to traditional international law, regardless of the practical implications, was consistent with U.S. neutrality.

More sympathetic toward the Allies than the Central Powers, Lansing interpreted international law in such a manner as to allow the British Navy much greater leeway than the German Navy. He saw no reason for the United States to resist the British government's restrictions on U.S. trade with the Central Powers that resulted from the November 1914 proclamation of the entire North Sea as a military area in which the British Navy would control neutral traffic. Even the tightening of these restrictions in March 1915 evoked no strong protest from Lansing. But when, in February 1915, the German government proclaimed a war zone around the British Isles, he recommended a policy of holding it strictly accountable for submarine attacks on U.S. ships or citizens.

Lansing expected German submarines to adhere to cruiser rules of warfare. He asserted the right of Americans to travel the high seas on belligerent vessels. This right created controversy in U.S.-German relations when a German submarine sank the British ship *Fabala* on March 28, 1915, killing an American citizen. The sinking of the *Lusitania* on May 7, which

cost 124 American lives, focused even more attention on this controversial question. Once Wilson strongly committed himself to Lansing's recommended policy, Bryan resigned from the cabinet on June 9, 1915, and was replaced by Lansing.

As the new secretary of state, Lansing wanted to protect U.S. neutral rights but did not seek to involve the United States in the war. He thought that the U.S. government should be patient and cautious while asserting its citizens' rights. The President expressed a similar reservation when he asserted that the United States was "too proud to fight." Both Wilson and Lansing desired to postpone U.S. belligerency.

Lansing placed the *Lusitania* affair in a larger ideological context as he concluded that Germany threatened Western civilization. He thought that the United States should help the Allies if they faced a real threat of military defeat. To that extent, he combined elements of a balance-of-power conception of international relations with a more traditional understanding of the American mission. The new secretary viewed Germany as a threat to both the nation's security and its principles. Anticipating Wilson's ideological rationale for U.S. intervention in the European war, Lansing favored a policy that emphasized the contrast between democracy and absolutism and that viewed a German victory in Europe as a threat to the United States.

When a German submarine sank the British freighter *Arabic* on Aug. 19, 1915, Lansing recommended a diplomatic break. Although he did not actually want war, he agreed with House that the United States could exert more influence as a belligerent. Wilson, however, avoided such provocative action. The *Arabic* crisis ended on September 1 when Ambassador Johann von Bernstorff promised that Germany would abide by the rules of cruiser warfare. German submarines, he assured Lansing, would warn before attacking and then rescue the passengers and crew. After another crisis, Germany's *Sussex* Pledge on May 4, 1916, reaffirmed this promise.

Although less inclined to press the British, Lansing sought to curtail their infringements on U.S. neutral rights. On Oct. 21, 1915, Wilson approved a note to Great Britain that the secretary had prepared. Lansing instructed the U.S. ambassador in London, Walter Hines Page, to deliver the note protesting the British off-shore blockade and definition of contraband. Affirming its rights in the spirit of impartial neutrality, the United States also revealed a reluctance to entangle itself in the Old World.

Lansing wanted to limit U.S. entanglement in East Asia as well as Europe. At the beginning of the war in 1914, at China's request and with Wilson's approval, when he was State Department counselor, Lansing endeavored to prevent Japan from attacking the German leasehold in China's Shantung Province. When this effort at neutralization failed, he sought to avoid any U.S. commitment to China that would alienate the Japanese. Like Wilson and Bryan, Lansing espoused the Open Door to equal economic opportunities for Americans in China and the potential independence and territorial integrity of China. In practice, however, he advised that the United States should acquiesce in Japan's special interests in East Asia, especially in northeastern China.

During the crisis that erupted in January 1915, when Japan made its Twenty-One Demands on China, the counselor drafted two notes for Bryan's signature, affirming the traditional principles of U.S. policy. The first note on March 13 sought to protect U.S. rights but acknowledged Japan's special interests. The second note on May 11 emphasized the Open Door and China's independence. When the Chinese conceded most of the Japanese demands, Lansing accepted this outcome. Concentrating on the particular interests of U.S. merchants, investors, and missionaries in China, he sought to avoid conflicts with Japan. This approach eventually culminated in the Lansing-Ishii Agreement on Nov. 2, 1917, which both affirmed the traditional principles of U.S. policy and recognized Japan's special interests in East Asia.

In early 1916, Wilson still hoped to insulate the Western Hemisphere from the Old World's problems. With Lansing's and House's assistance, he promoted Pan-Americanism. Throughout 1915, they had endeavored to convince the ABC countries—Argentina, Brazil, and Chile—to accept a Pan-American treaty that would link Latin America with the United States in partnership to uphold the Monroe Doctrine. The President publicized his proposal at the Pan-American Scientific Congress on Jan. 6, 1916. He appealed to the Latin American nations to join with the United States in a guarantee against both international revolution and external aggression.

Wilson's endorsement of Lansing's proposal for a modus vivendi clearly demonstrated his commitment to neutrality. On Jan. 18, 1916, the secretary proposed an agreement that would require the Allies to disarm their merchant ships in return for a pledge by the Central Powers to abide by cruiser warfare rules. Lansing and Wilson hoped that this modus vivendi would avert another submarine crisis in U.S.-German relations. Because British merchant ships attacked German submarines when they surfaced, the Germans argued that cruiser rules virtually prohibited their submarines from attacking Allied commerce. In effect, U.S. policy protected Allied shipping from this new weapon. Wilson and Lansing hoped to remove any cause for Germany to resort to indiscriminate submarine warfare that would involve the United States in the war.

Lansing's modus vivendi seriously antagonized the Allies and jeopardized House's peace mission to Europe. The British saw no reason to make any concession in return for a German pledge to abide by international law. Aware of intense British and also French reaction against the modus vivendi, House urged Wilson to drop the secretary's proposal before it resulted in the failure of his mission. Once Wilson agreed, Lansing announced the decision to the press. This cleared the way for House and British Foreign Secretary Sir Edward Grey to conclude a plan for possible American mediation of the European war, which they summarized in the so-called House-Grey Memorandum on February 22. Lansing, who never believed that House's efforts at mediation would succeed, regretted Wilson's sacrifice of the modus vivendi. The secretary had convinced himself that it would benefit the Allies and the Central Powers as well as the United States by upholding international law.

Wilson extended his idea of Pan-Americanism throughout the world in his vision for a postwar league of nations. At the League to Enforce Peace convention on May 27, he announced his commitment to collective security. Lansing, however, resisted the President's plans. He opposed any global guarantee involving force, preferring to rely on international conciliation and arbitration. He also feared that the extension of Pan-Americanism throughout the world would permit the European powers to violate the Monroe Doctrine.

While developing his liberal internationalism, Wilson still hoped to keep the United States out of the war. After winning reelection in November 1916, he decided to send a peace note to both the Allies and the Central Powers. He worked with Lansing in the preparation of this note. Wilson's peace note, which the State Department transmitted on Dec. 18, 1916, requested both sides to reveal their war aims. As Lansing had anticipated, neither set of belligerents welcomed the President's initiative.

Imperial Germany's decision in January 1917 to resort to unrestricted submarine warfare, ignoring its earlier *Sussex* Pledge to abide by cruiser warfare rules, came as welcome news to Lansing. Ambassador von Bernstorff informed him of this decision on January 31. The secretary immediately recommended to the President that he break diplomatic relations with Germany. Unlike Wilson and House, Lansing had never expected the American peace initiative to succeed. He hoped that Germany's action would force the United States into the war and guarantee the victory of democracy over absolutism.

Wilson hesitated to accept Lansing's advice. His conception of Western civilization, including white supremacy, made him reluctant to enter the war. Fearful of the "yellow peril" of Japan, he thought that the United States should possibly stay out of the war as a counter to the Japanese threat in Asia. This racist justification for inaction convinced none of Wilson's cabinet, which overwhelmingly shared Lansing's opinion that the United States should immediately break diplomatic relations with Germany. Wilson finally agreed and took this action.

Lansing used the revelation of the Zimmermann Telegram as another opportunity to shape American public opinion in favor of war. Arthur Zimmermann, Germany's foreign minister, had proposed an alliance with Mexico, and possibly Japan too, in the event of war with the United States. Bernstorff had relayed the telegram through the State Department to Mexico City on Jan. 19, 1917. The British had intercepted it and provided a decoded copy to the United States. Although the telegram totally failed to achieve its intended purpose, it provided useful propaganda for the United States. Lansing leaked it to the press on March 1 so that American newspapers could publish this evidence of a German plot. In his judgment, the telegram produced the desired impact on Congress.

Germany's submarine warfare pushed the United States toward war. News that German submarines had sunk three American merchant ships led Lansing to rejoice that "war is inevitable." Now he advised a declaration of war against Germany, urging Wilson to join the battle in defense of civilization. He explained that "the Entente Allies represent the principle of Democracy, and the Central Powers, the principle of Autocracy, and that it is for the welfare of mankind and for the establishment of peace in the world that Democracy should succeed." The President, however, still hoped to avoid war.

Other members of the cabinet, as well as House, agreed with Lansing that the United States should declare war against Germany. Wilson finally made the decision. At a special session of Congress on April 2, he recommended war, using Lansing's rationale that the European war was a struggle between democracy and absolutism. Four days later, Congress voted a declaration of war against Germany.

On April 6, 1917, the same day the United States entered the war, Wilson approved a message, which Lansing had drafted, to the new republican government in Russia that had replaced Tsar Nicholas II three weeks earlier. Lansing asserted that "the government and people of the United States rejoice that the great Russian people have joined the powerful democracies which were struggling against autocracy." He reiterated this message to Russia in June in connection with the special mission led by Elihu Root, a Republican elder statesman with whom Lansing had many common interests.

The Bolshevik Revolution in November 1917 evoked a different response from Lansing. He denounced the radicalism of Bolshevik leaders. He condemned their lack of respect and concern for international law and believed that their radical objectives would destroy civilization. On December 4, Lansing recommended, and Wilson agreed, that the United States should not recognize the new Bolshevik government, setting the policy of nonrecognition that would endure long after both men left office.

In response to the Russian Revolution, Wilson proclaimed his Fourteen Points on Jan. 8, 1918. Lansing remained skeptical about the President's emphasis on national self-determination. He expected difficulty in implementing this goal in the European and colonial settlements after the war. He thought, for example, that the German colonies could not govern themselves. Wilson's idea for a league of nations also lacked much appeal to Lansing, who believed that universal democracy would provide the best guarantee of permanent peace. For the present, he regarded a military victory over the Central Powers as the highest priority.

For the purpose of winning the war, Lansing eventually agreed that some U.S. and Allied troops should intervene in Siberia in the summer of 1918. Like Wilson, he had hesitated to condone this involvement in the Russian civil war. When the President finally acquiesced to Allied demands to restore the Eastern Front, and especially to rescue the Czechoslovak troops that were trapped in Russia, the secretary cooperated in the implementation of this decision. He did not, however, share Wilson's anti-Japanese orientation. Instead of justifying U.S. intervention as a counter to Japan's imperialism in East Asia, he emphasized its anti-Bolshevik purpose and continued to foster U.S.-Japanese cooperation within the framework of the Lansing-Ishii Agreement. With respect to Europe as well as East Asia, differences over the priorities of U.S. foreign policy increasingly alienated Wilson and Lansing from each other. Wilson's Fourteen Points provided the basis for the peace settlement with Germany after World War I. The secretary, despite his private reservations, notified the German government on November 5 that the Allies as well as the United States would conclude peace in accordance with Wilson's principles. The Armistice on Nov. 11, 1918, ended the war with this promise.

Despite their differences, Wilson included Lansing in the American delegation at the Paris Peace Conference of 1919. While favoring a league of democratic nations, Lansing opposed any guarantee of political independence and territorial integrity for all nations in the future League of Nations. Contrary to Wilson's desire, Lansing pursued his own approach to peace-making. He prepared a skeleton draft of a peace treaty, including an "association of nations" that would rely on arbitration rather than military force as the primary means of enforcement.

Wilson rejected Lansing's alternative, preferring his own idea for the League of Nations. He emphasized that its purpose was not only to resolve conflicts of the recent war, but also to achieve lasting peace. The secretary privately complained that the five great victorious powers—the United States, Great Britain, France, Italy, and Japan—were running the peace conference like the Congress of Vienna and would dominate this future league. Lansing himself played only a marginal role in the peace negotiations. Wilson selected House rather than Lansing to serve with him on the commission that drafted the League Covenant. House substituted for the President when he could not attend meetings in Paris.

Once the American and Allied leaders completed their work and submitted the peace treaty to Germany on May 7, 1919, they faced German requests for revision. Wilson and his colleagues in the U.S. delegation were generally reluctant to revise the Versailles Treaty. Lansing thought it required some substantial changes but kept his suggestions to himself. It appeared to him that the United States had not transformed the Old World but that European statesmen had instead overwhelmed Wilson. Lansing had applauded Wilson's stand against Italy's claim to Fiume and had opposed his compromise with Japan on Shantung Province of China, but the secretary exerted no real influence over events in Paris.

After returning to the United States, Lansing appeared at the Senate Foreign Relations Committee's hearings on August 6 and 11. He faced the impossible task of defending a treaty that he did not approve. He decided not to make a strong case for the League of Nations in his testimony, declining to answer questions about the Covenant's origins. Rather than press for unqualified ratification, Lansing urged the President to compromise with Republican senators, but he failed to persuade him. The secretary understood that the Senate would not approve the treaty unless Wilson accepted some Republican reservations. The failure of Wilson's western tour in September 1919 came as no surprise to Lansing.

Wilson adamantly refused to compromise with Republicans to save the Versailles Treaty. Lansing blamed both political parties for this impasse. At a cabinet meeting on Dec. 16, 1919, he recommended a modest concession without persuading his colleagues. Wilson's faithful cabinet refused to encourage him to take a conciliatory approach with Republican senators, and certainly not with their leader, Henry Cabot Lodge of Massachusetts.

Wilson's handling of Lansing's subsequent resignation discredited his own leadership. He accused the secretary of usurping presidential authority during his illness, especially by convening the cabinet. This charge of disloyalty did not provide a plausible justification for requiring Lansing to leave the State Department. Because it appeared mean and petty, Lansing

L

benefitted from favorable public reaction to his resignation on Feb. 12, 1920. There were, however, good reasons for Wilson to replace him. The two men had disagreed over fundamental aspects of U.S. foreign policy, notably during the Paris Peace Conference. Although Lansing had lost his effectiveness as secretary of state, he departed at least with some dignity.

Lloyd E. Ambrosius

See also LANSING-ISHII AGREEMENTS; ZIMMERMANN TELEGRAM

Bibliography

Ambrosius, Lloyd E. *Wilsonian Statecraft: Theory and Practice of Liberal Internationalism during World War I.* Wilmington, DE: Scholarly Resources, 1991.

——. *Woodrow Wilson and the American Diplomatic Tradition: The Treaty Fight in Perspective.* Cambridge, UK: Cambridge University Press, 1987.

Beers, Burton F. *Vain Endeavor: Robert Lansing's Attempts to End the American-Japanese Rivalry.* Durham, NC: Duke University Press, 1962.

Gilderhaus, Mark T. *Pan American Visions: Woodrow Wilson in the Western Hemisphere, 1913–1921.* Tucson: University of Arizona Press, 1986.

Smith, Daniel M. *Robert Lansing and American Neutrality, 1914–1917.* Berkeley: University of California Press, 1958.

Lansing-Ishii Agreement

The Lansing-Ishii Agreement, signed on Nov. 2, 1917, following talks in Washington from September to late October 1917, was an accord between the United States Secretary of State Robert Lansing, and Japan's special Ambassador Viscount Kikujiro Ishii.

Both countries, not just the United States, were prepared to recognize "that territorial propinquity creates special relations between countries." The government of the United States "recognized that Japan had special interests in China, particularly in the part to which her possessions are contiguous." The Japanese regarded this as an American recognition of Japanese dominance in areas such as southern Manchuria. However, both governments denied they had any purpose "to infringe in any way the independence or territorial integrity of China" and declared "they always adhere to the principle of the so-called 'open door' or equal opportunity for commerce and industry in China." The agreement also included a secret protocol (revealed in 1938), which stipulated that the governments of both countries "will not take advantage of the present [i.e., wartime] conditions to seek special rights or privileges in China which would abridge their rights of the subjects or citizens of other friendly states." It was, in part, Lansing's attempt to cancel out the Japanese advantages of the Twenty-One Demands on China in 1915, and it represented a Japanese concession.

Lansing also hoped to preserve American economic and political interests and to prevent China from playing off the Japanese against the United States, following U.S. Ambassador to China Paul Reinsch's success in persuading China to declare war on the Central Powers. Ishii requested formal recognition of Japan's special interests in any joint statement that was issued.

Some historians have suggested that it was the price America paid to keep Japan in the war following Ishii's revelation that Germany had three times appealed to Japan to desert the Allies. Others have seen it as a temporary expedient to deal with East Asia while the United States had the disadvantage of being engaged in the European war and as part of Wilson's as well as Lansing's strategy of containing Japanese expansionist drives in Asia.

The agreement began to fray almost immediately when Britain proposed that Japan serve as the Allies' manpower to control the Trans-Siberian Railroad. Secretary of State Lansing began to have misgivings almost immediately. In April 1923, Japan agreed to an annulment of the Lansing-Ishii Agreement, for it conflicted with the Nine-Power Treaty.

Frederick C. Drake

See also JAPANESE-AMERICAN RELATIONS; LANSING, ROBERT; TWENTY-ONE DEMANDS

Bibliography

Dennett, Tyler. *Americans in East Asia.* New York: Barnes & Noble, 1963.

Dulles, Foster Rhea. *Forty Years of American-Japanese Relations.* New York: Appleton-Century, 1937.

Gardner, Lloyd. *Safe for Democracy: The Anglo-American Response to Revolution, 1913–1927.* New York: Oxford University Press, 1984.

U.S. Department of State. *Foreign Relations of the United States, The Lansing Papers, 1914–1920.* 2 vols. Washington, DC: Government Printing Office, 1939–1940.

———. *Papers Relating to the Foreign Relations of the United States, 1917.* Washington, DC: Government Printing Office, 1919.

League of Nations

The League of Nations, established in 1920, was the first truly international peacekeeping organization in world history. Perhaps appropriately, its founding is most often associated with President Woodrow Wilson and his heroic, but abortive, crusade to persuade his fellow Americans to join the international partnership after the First World War. The Covenant of the League of Nations, incorporated as Article I into the Treaty of Versailles in April 1919, contained twenty-six articles, aimed essentially at three areas of concern. First, the League would require signatories to avoid hostilities and submit disputes between them to the process of arbitration; the emphasis thereon was on delay and publicity—in order to permit passions to cool and to expose the quarrel to the court of world opinion. Second, the League was to preside over a significant reduction of armaments among the Great Powers, so that no single nation posed an immediate military or naval threat to another. The final basic element was collective security, or the mutual obligation (as Article 10 of the Covenant states) "to respect and preserve as against external aggression the territorial integrity and political independence" of all the members. This meant that should a nation make war on a League member, the others would be bound to cease commercial and diplomatic intercourse with the aggressor; if that did not bring about a satisfactory result, then the League would unite in closing the frontiers of the offending nation, using any force necessary to accomplish that objective.

As for its administrative structure, the organization was composed of a Secretariat, a body of delegates (the Assembly), and an executive cabinet (the Council). Each state could send three representatives to the Assembly, with one vote per national delegation. The Council of the League was to consist of five permanent members from the Great Powers—the United States, Great Britain, France, Italy, and Japan—and four nonpermanent members selected by the Assembly. In deciding whether to employ economic and military sanctions, the Council was entrusted with ultimate authority, in which case unanimity was required.

Whereas he was surely the most dramatic and imposing figure to advance the plan, Wilson was by no means alone in his advocacy; nor was he the sole author of the Covenant. From the strictly Wilsonian standpoint, however, the President's ideas grew out of his efforts to keep the United States out of the European war. From August 1914 to April 1917, the government pursued an official policy of neutrality and, beginning in early 1915, tried to bring about a negotiated settlement of the war through American mediation. In private, Wilson had already sketched out a four-point program for a league. These proposals included agreements to eliminate the production of munitions by private enterprise, to settle disputes through the process of arbitration, and to protect the political independence and territorial integrity of the contracting parties. Also in 1914–1915, he made confidential overtures to Argentina, Brazil, and Chile about the possibilities for a regional collective security arrangement known as the Pan-American pact.

At roughly the same time, a new internationalist movement came into being in the United States. This movement was composed of two divergent aggregations of activists, which one historian has described as "progressive internationalists" and "conservative internationalists." Although his relationship with both groups was of fundamental importance, the progressive internationalists probably had a more decisive impact on Wilson and vice versa.

Feminists, liberals, pacifists, socialists, and social reformers filled the ranks of the progressive internationalists. Their organizations—for example, the Woman's Peace Party, the American Union Against Militarism, and various elements of both the Democratic Party and the Socialist Party of America—were at once the advance guard of the so-called "new diplomacy" in the United States and the impassioned proponents of an Americanized version of social democracy. For them, the search for a peaceful world order provided a logical common ground; because of the war's potential to set back the cause of liberal and socialist reform, foreign policy and domestic politics had suddenly become inextricably intertwined. Peace was essential to the survival of the labor movement and of their campaigns on behalf of women's rights, the abolition of child labor, and social justice legislation in general. Whether it was the "Program for Constructive Peace" of the Woman's Peace Party or the Socialist Party's "Manifesto . . . on Disarmament and World Peace," most progressive internationalist platforms looked upon both warring coalitions as equally blameworthy. Thus they advocated an immediate armistice, international agreements to limit armaments and nationalize their manufacture, a reduction of trade barriers, self-determination, machinery for arbitration, and, finally, a "Concert of Nations" to supersede the old balance-of-power system.

The program of the conservative internationalists was different in both subtle and conclusive ways. It was developed mainly by the organizers of the League to Enforce Peace (LEP), established in June 1915, in Philadelphia and led by former U.S. President William Howard Taft and many others prominent in the field of international law. In most respects, the LEP's recommendations closely resembled those of the Bryce Group, an influential roundtable of conservative internationalists in Great Britain. The LEP's platform was entitled "Warrant from History." It called for American participation in a league that would assemble periodically to make appropriate changes in international law and employ arbitration and conciliation procedures to settle, respectively, "Justiciable" and "non-justiciable" disputes. Unlike progressive internationalists, the LEP did not concern itself with issues such as self-determination or advocate disarmament or a military standoff in Europe. Significantly, the slogan "The LEP does *not* seek to end the present war" appeared on their letterhead in the autumn of 1916.

Initially, the differences between progressive and conservative internationalists were more apparent than real, but they became more pronounced as the presidential campaign of 1916 approached. Throughout that year, Wilson met and corresponded with representatives of both groups. For example, in May 1916, he held a lengthy White House colloquy with members of the American Union Against Militarism and for the first time articulated to persons other than his absolute confidants his ideas for a "family of nations." Later that month he delivered an extremely important address to the LEP, the occasion of his first public endorsement of American membership in some kind of postwar peacekeeping organization. Then, on the eve of his reelection campaign, Wilson's polestar moved somewhat to the left of the American center; in late summer, he pushed through Congress an impressive array of primarily social justice legislation that established the eight-hour day for railroad workers, restricted child labor, provided workmen's compensation for federal workers, and secured a progressive income tax weighted heavily against corporations and the wealthy. It was not entirely coincidental that progressive internationalists enthusiastically applauded these endeavors and endorsed his reelection, while leading conservative internationalists lined up as his chief domestic critics.

As the epiphenomenon of his advanced progressivism, Wilson made American membership in a league of nations one of the main themes of his campaign as well, a theme that complemented his campaign slogan "He Kept Us Out of War." Thus, the public gradually came to identify the league idea with Wilson and the Democrats. But the issue also acquired a vexatious partisan dimension because conservative internationalists had failed to secure even a vague endorsement of their position in the Republican Party platform. At any rate, the seeds of partisanship over the issue of a league of nations were planted as early as the campaign of 1916.

After his reelection, Wilson made a climactic attempt to end the war in his address "Peace Without Victory" to the Senate on Jan. 22, 1917. In this progressive internationalist manifesto, the President launched a critique of European imperialism, militarism, and balance-of-power politics and called for a new world order sustained by procedures for the arbitration of disputes between nations, general disarmament, self-determination, and collective security. The chief instrumentality of this sweeping program was to be, of course, a "League of Peace." So great was the impact of this address around the world that the creation of some kind of postwar league was a virtual certainty. Within days, however, Germany reinstituted unrestricted submarine warfare. By April 1917, the United States was at war.

Wilson never wavered in his fundamental aim. He referred to the future league in his war address to Congress and made it the capstone of his famous Fourteen Points address of Jan. 8, 1918. Nonetheless, his immediate priorities inexorably shifted toward the exigencies of mobilization. And, in part owing to stinging

Republican criticism of "Peace Without Victory" as the basis for the postwar settlement, he refused to discuss his plans in any detail throughout the entire period of American belligerency. He also neglected to lay essential political groundwork for the League of Nations at home. Ultimately, by the autumn of 1918, important segments among both conservative and progressive internationalists had grown disenchanted with Wilson, albeit for entirely different reasons.

This development would prove to be as unfortunate as the overt, partisan opposition to the idea led by Theodore Roosevelt and Henry Cabot Lodge, the President's nemesis. On one hand, Wilson repeatedly frustrated the wartime efforts of the conservative internationalists of the LEP, especially Taft, who wanted to make formal plans for a league in cooperation with the British government. On the other hand, he failed to nurture the left-of-center political coalition of 1916 that had elected him to a second term. If this dynamic political force had remained intact, Wilson might have prevailed in the critical midterm elections of 1918 which, in turn, might have made it possible for him to secure American leadership in a progressive peacekeeping organization. But he began to lose his grip on his former base of support as a tidal wave of superpatriotism known as "One Hundred Percent Americanism" swept over the country. Indeed, Wilson contributed to the breakdown of his coalition in his acquiescence in the suppression of civil liberties and the radical press. American participation in the Allied intervention in the Russian Revolution, reluctant though Wilson was about it, contributed to the unraveling as well.

The circumstances surrounding the congressional elections of November 1918 greatly compounded the larger problem. Against the Democrats and the Wilsonian peace plan, the Republicans launched a fiercely partisan and ultraconservative campaign. Wilson, most historians maintain, commited the worst blunder of his presidency by responding with an appeal to the public to return a Democratic Congress. When the Republicans won majorities of forty-five in the House of Representatives and two in the Senate, they could claim that the President had been repudiated. They also thereby gained control over congressional committees, including the Senate Foreign Relations Committee, which would be chaired by Lodge.

Even in the face of these setbacks, Wilson's arrival in Europe for the Paris Peace Conference was a triumphal event. In the streets of Paris, London, Rome, and Milan, millions of people turned out to hail "the Moses from Across the Atlantic." These unprecedented demonstrations on behalf of "the Savior of Humanity" strengthened his hand in the early stages of the peace conference and helped to insure the inclusion of the League of Nations as an integral part of the treaty of peace. In the ensuing negotiations, Wilson was ably assisted, as well, by Lord Robert Cecil of Great Britain and Gen. Jan Christiaan Smuts of the Union of South Africa. Yet, while he could not have prevailed without the massive outpouring of public support and the contributions of Cecil and Smuts, Wilson still paid a heavy price for the League. Fully aware of the Republican opposition in the Senate, the statesmen of Europe—David Lloyd George, Georges Clemenceau, and Vittorio Orlando—used their acceptance of the Covenant as a lever to gain concessions on other vital and contentious issues.

For example, Wilson was forced to swallow a less than satisfactory compromise on the disposition of captured enemy colonies, which the Allies such as South Africa and Australia coveted. On threat of withdrawal of their endorsement of the League, Clemenceau demanded for France military occupation of the Rhineland; Orlando claimed for Italy the Croatian port city of Fiume; and the Japanese insisted on retaining sweeping economic concessions in China's Shantung Province. On several occasions, Wilson, almost miraculously, was able to moderate the more extreme Allied demands and uphold the spirit of the Fourteen Points. But then, on the verge of physical exhaustion, he permitted the Allies to impose upon Germany a potentially huge reparation burden and, on top of everything else, to saddle that country with the legal and moral responsibility for having started the war. Wilson took comfort in the hope that once the "war psychosis" had receded, the League would be in a position to rectify the injustices contained in the peace treaty itself.

Had the question been the subject of a national referendum when Wilson returned home in the summer of 1919, the United States almost certainly would have joined the League. But it failed to do so for a number of reasons. To begin with, Wilson had already lost the active support of most left-wing progressives, not to mention that of the socialists. Many liberal supporters, too, turned their backs on him after reading the Treaty of Versailles. They believed, regardless of his motives, that he had forsaken the Fourteen Points, that he had conceded too much to the Allies in the territorial settlements, and that the League of Nations would be bound to uphold an unjust peace. Thus, Wilson's political base outside the Democratic Party had already seriously eroded.

As for the Senate itself, on one hand, sheer partisanship motivated much of the opposition. What would become of the Republican Party, a friend asked Senator Lodge, if Wilson got his League of Nations and the Democrats could boast of "the greatest constructive reform in history"? On the other hand, many of the senatorial objections were grounded in ideological principles. Simply put, Republicans believed that Wilson had consigned too many vital national interests to the will of an international authority. Although during the peace conference he had responded to early criticism and amended the original Covenant—to provide for withdrawal from the League and to exempt the Monroe Doctrine and domestic matters such as immigration from its jurisdiction—he had not done enough to assuage the anxieties of the majority of Republicans.

Then, too, a small but powerful cluster of Senators called the "Irreconcilables" flat-out opposed the League in any form. Not all of the fifteen or so Irreconcilables were partisans or reactionaries, however; many of them based their opposition on progressive convictions similar to those of many socialists and liberals. It should also be emphasized that, Irreconcilables or not, only a few of Wilson's opponents were isolationists, strictly speaking. As Gilbert M. Hitchcock of Nebraska, the Democratic leader in the Senate, aptly declared at the beginning of the parliamentary struggle, "Internationalism has come, and we must choose what form the internationalism is to take." And that, fundamentally, was what the great debate was all about.

By the end of the summer, the Senate Foreign Relations Committee, dominated by Republicans and Irreconcilables, had formulated forty-six amendments as the conditions for ratification; by autumn, these had evolved into fourteen formal reservations. The most controversial was Reservation 5, which concerned Article 10 of the Covenant: "The United States assumes no obligation to preserve the territorial integrity or political independence of any country . . . unless in any particular case the Congress . . . by act of joint resolution [shall] so provide." Reservation 5 addressed the corollary to the collective security provision—that is, the restrictions that League membership would also presumably impose against independent, unilateral coercive action by the United States. It also declared that the United States would not submit to arbitration any questions or disputes that related in any way to the Monroe Doctrine, without the express consent of the Congress. Other reservations raised doubts about compliance with disarmament, economic boycotts, membership in the International Labour Organization, and financial contributions to the League.

Meanwhile, Wilson held a series of White House meetings mainly with groups of Republicans called "Mild Reservationists" to try to persuade them to ratify the treaty as it was written. None of these conferences changed any senator's mind. Then, against the advice of his personal physician, Wilson decided that he must take his case directly to the American people. For three weeks, in September 1919, he traveled 10,000 miles throughout the Middle and Far West, making forty impassioned speeches to hundreds of thousands of people. Despite the importance he himself attached to Article 10, the President told his audiences that he did not believe that military sanctions would come into play very often—in part because of the deterrent manifest within the threat of collective force; in part because of the "cooling-off" provisions in the arbitration features of the League; and in part because disarmament would help eliminate most potential problems from the start.

But it was all or nothing, he said in essence, if the world was going to have a truly effective League. The United States could not go in grudgingly, under conditions of its own choosing. The "Lodge Reservations" would "change the entire meaning of the Treaty." Full-fledged, unqualified participation in the League, he declared, was the only way to avoid, "sometime, in the vengeful providence of God, another struggle in which, not a few hundred thousand fine men from America will have to die, but as many millions as are necessary to accomplish the final freedom of the peoples of the world."

As the crowds grew larger and the cheers louder, Wilson grew weaker and weaker. At last, his doctor called a halt to the tour and rushed him back to Washington. Two days later, on

October 2, the President suffered a catastrophic stroke that nearly killed him and permanently paralyzed the left side of his body. From that point onward, Wilson was but a fragile husk of his former self, a tragic recluse in the White House shielded by his wife and doctor. During the initial stage of his illness, the Senate roll was called. On November 19, the Irreconcilables joined the Democrats to reject the treaty with the fourteen reservations, by a vote of fifty-five to thirty-nine. On a motion to ratify unconditionally, the Irreconcilables then helped the Republicans defeat it by fifty-three nays to thirty-eight ayes. When, on March 8, 1920, the Lodge version of the treaty came up for a final ballot, twenty-one Democrats defied the President and voted with the Republicans; but, again, it failed, forty-nine to thirty-five, or seven votes short of a two-thirds majority. In the autumn of 1920, Warren G. Harding, the Republican presidential candidate, won a landslide victory over the Democrat James M. Cox. The Republicans were more than happy to view the returns as the "great and solemn referendum" Wilson had said he had wanted for his Covenant. "So far as the United States is concerned," Lodge now declared, "that League is dead."

In surveying the ruins, many historians have tended to emphasize Wilson's stroke as the primary factor behind the outcome. They argue that a healthy Wilson surely would have grasped the situation and arrived at a compromise on the question of reservations. Other historians have maintained that the President's refusal to compromise was characteristic of his personality throughout his life, that his personal psychology would never have permitted him to bend to the Republicans, regardless of the state of his health. Still other historians, while acknowledging both the stroke and Wilson's personality, have made the case that fundamental ideological differences and domestic political conditions that had taken shape in the months before the peace conference foreclosed a happier outcome. In this sense, the struggle over ratification represented no more and no less than a denouement to a sequence of events set in motion at the birth of the American internationalist movement in 1915–1916 and in the forging of Wilson's victory coalition of 1916. This plus the circumstances surrounding the dissolution of progressive internationalism—in particular, wartime political repression and Wilson's failure to rekindle the coalition just as

the showdown with the Senate was getting under way—at length sealed the fate of a Wilsonian league.

There is merit in all of these interpretations. Whatever the central cause of his historic failure, Wilson's more conservative and partisan adversaries earnestly believed that his was a dangerously radical vision of world order. His severest critics among progressives believed he had not done enough, particularly at Paris, to rally the people to his side and resist the forces of reaction. Wilson's own response was a cry of anguish. "What more could I have done?" he asked historian William E. Dodd shortly before leaving the presidency. "I had to negotiate with my back to the wall. Men thought I had all power. Would to God I had had such power." His voice choking, he added, "The 'great' people at home wrote and wired every day that they were against me." Dodd himself described the debacle as "one long wilderness of despair and betrayal, even by good men." Perhaps more perceptively than anyone, Ray Stannard Baker commented on Wilson's fate: "He can escape no responsibility and must go to his punishment not only for his own mistakes and weaknesses of temperament but for the greed and selfishness of the world."

Not until the Second World War did the significance of the legacy of the "stern covenanter" begin to be fully appreciated. In 1945, President Harry S. Truman stated that the Charter of the United Nations had at last vindicated Wilson. Historians and political scientists, both admirers and critics, subsequently would designate him the father of modern American "globalism."

Thomas J. Knock

See also AMERICAN UNION AGAINST MILITARISM; FOURTEEN POINTS; WOMAN'S PEACE PARTY

Bibliography

Ambrosius, Lloyd E. *Woodrow Wilson and the American Diplomatic Tradition: The Treaty Fight in Perspective.* Cambridge, UK: Cambridge University Press, 1987.

Bailey, Thomas A. *Woodrow Wilson and the Great Betrayal.* New York: Macmillan, 1945.

Baker, Ray Stannard. *Woodrow Wilson and World Settlement.* 3 vols. Garden City, NY: Doubleday, Page, 1922.

Knock, Thomas J. *To End All Wars: Woodrow Wilson and the Quest for a New World Order.* New York: Oxford University Press, 1992.

Link, Arthur S., et al. *The Papers of Woodrow Wilson.* 69 vols. Princeton, NJ: Princeton University Press, 1966–1993.

Lejeune, John Archer (1867–1942)

John Archer Lejeune was born in Pointe Coupee Parish, Louisiana, on January 10, 1867. He entered Louisiana State University in 1882 but left during the spring of 1884 to prepare for admission to the United States Naval Academy that summer. Lejeune was graduated with the class of 1888 and served as a passed midshipman aboard the USS *Vandalia,* which went down during the disastrous hurricane that struck Apia, Samoa, on March 16, 1889.

At the end of the two-year probationary period, the class reassembled at Annapolis for permanent assignment, and Lejeune secured a commission in the United States Marine Corps. During a distinguished career of nearly forty years, he served in a variety of assignments. He led the marine guard aboard the USS *Cincinnati* during the Spanish-American War, commanded marine troops in Panama in 1903–1904, saw duty in the Philippines, and participated in the U.S. landing at Veracruz in 1914.

In 1915, Lejeune was appointed assistant to the commandant, a key role in the hierarchy of the Marine Corps. He requested reassignment when the United States entered the war in April, 1917 and assumed command of the new marine barracks at Quantico, Virginia, on Sept. 15, 1917. On July 28, 1918, General Pershing took the unusual step of appointing Lejeune to command the U.S. Army 2d Division. He held this position through the actions at St. Mihiel, Blanc Mont Ridge, and the Meuse-Argonne campaign.

After the Armistice, the division moved into southern Belgium. On Dec. 13, 1918, as part of the Third Army, the 2d Division crossed the Rhine River into Germany. The division remained there, based at Coblenz, until its return to the United States in July 1919.

Lejeune again assumed command of the Quantico base until June 20, 1920, when he was appointed major general commandant of the Marine Corps, a post that he held for nine years. During that time he was responsible for maintaining a high degree of efficiency in the corps despite major cutbacks in appropriations and was an important influence in the expansion of the Marine Corps schools system. Upon retirement from the Marine Corps, he became superintendent of the Virginia Military Institute until 1937.

Lejeune died at Union Memorial Hospital in Baltimore on Nov. 20, 1942.

A.C. Venzon

Bibliography

Lejeune, John A. *Reminiscences of a Marine.* New York: Arno Press, 1979.

Lever Food and Fuel Act

During World War I, the Allied Powers generally suffered from considerable food shortages. This was the result of German occupation of much of Western Europe, a decreased flow of supplies from Eastern Europe, and reduced availability of shipping tonnage between Europe and other regions.

While the United States was an excellent potential source of food and other vital goods, war profiteering and supply-demand problems caused prices for these American items to climb drastically by 1917. Simultaneously, a fuel supply problem was developing within the United States, particularly affecting coal-based industries. Poor fuel transportation and storage facilities were the principal causes of this problem, which, in turn, reduced production of war materials.

Soon after America's declaration of war in April 1917, President Woodrow Wilson began to regulate various aspects of the food industry, a move that he based on his executive authority. To this end, he established the Council of National Defense. Subsequently, Wilson asked Congress for statutory authority for his actions. On Aug. 10, 1917, Congress passed the Lever Food and Fuel Act, also known as the Food and Fuel Control Act. This act passed despite opponents' claims that it would grant near dictatorial powers to the executive branch.

Its substantive provisions were designed to maximize the availability of congressionally defined "necessaries," a term including both foods and fuels. The act generally forbade the hoarding, destruction, monopolizing, or limiting of production of these items. The procedural provisions authorized the President to license production and distribution of necessaries, to regulate and requisition production and other facilities, to fix prices, and to make regulations and orders necessary to administer the act. Wilson immediately took steps to enforce the new law. Among other things, he created the Food and Fuel Administrations to execute the act's various provisions.

In passing the Lever Act, Congress gave the executive branch sweeping authority to regulate the nation's food and fuel resources based on the Constitution's war power. This was the first occasion in American history that Congress had done so. Without the implied power given to Congress to prosecute a war successfully, it would have had no legal basis for granting the President this authority. In the 1921 case of *United States v. Cohen Grocery Company*, the Supreme Court struck down Section Four of the act, but it never ruled upon the act's general validity or upon the extent of the war powers of Congress. The Lever Act thus became a model for later wartime regulation of the economy as the century of total war progressed.

Buckner F. Melton, Jr.

See also UNITED STATES FOOD ADMINISTRATION

Bibliography

Berdahl, Clarence A. "War Powers of the Executive in the United States." Ph.D. dissertation, University of Illinois, 1920.

Grundstein, Nathan. *Presidential Delegation of Authority in Wartime*. Pittsburgh: University of Pittsburgh Press, 1961.

Swisher, Carl B. "The Control of War Preparations in the United States." *American Political Science Review* (December 1940).

Willoughby, William F. *Government Organization in War Time and After*. New York: Appleton, 1919.

Liberty Engine

The Liberty aircraft engine was the main product of America's World War I aircraft production program, one of the most ambitious schemes ever undertaken by government and industry. Many Americans believed that the rapid supply of overwhelming airpower, mass-produced in accord with the new "Detroit methods" of assembly-line auto manufacture,

would be their nation's major contribution to Allied victory. So confident in America's manufacturing potential were congressmen, for example, that on July 14, 1917, they approved without dissent $640 million dollars for army aviation—the largest appropriation ever made by Congress to that point. With these funds and with their widely publicized expressions of confidence in the quick success of mass-produced airpower, Congress put aircraft at the center of the mobilization of industry and of popular war enthusiasm.

The hopes for American airpower were disappointed, however, mainly because complex wood and fabric airplanes and the rapidly changing technology of military aeronautics did not lend themselves to mass-production techniques in the way much simpler automobiles did. Huge sums were wasted in the attempt, and the only advanced American combat planes, which were produced outside the mass-production program, were constructed too late to see action. Large output was approached only for trainers, the obsolescent de Havilland-4 (DH-4) observation plane, and, most successfully, the Liberty engine, which was designed for mass production and standard military use.

Apart from its effects in mobilizing American public confidence, the Liberty engine had only an insignificant place in the Allied war effort. Air power itself played a minimal role in the war's outcome, and only a fraction of that role was filled by the Liberty engine. Among the most powerful engines in use by the belligerents, the Liberty had trouble finding a home as it proved too heavy for the key fighter type. According to Grover Loening, a pioneer aircraft designer, the problems with the Liberty program could be "boiled down to the great error of trying to fit an engine to a plane." The two were interdependent and had to be flexibly developed in tandem. The Liberty was put to work in a number of larger sea- and land-based bombers of British, Italian, and, later, American design, as well as in the DH-4. But these applications came close to war's end. For the most part, Liberty engines formed surplus stockpiles, filling a variety of military, government, and private uses at home and abroad during the interwar period.

The speedy genesis of the Liberty engine in the early summer of 1917 remains the stuff of legend, even though the idea that a standard engine for warplanes could be developed seems misguided, given the pace of improvement and the multiplicity of aircraft roles, types, and sizes. The design for the Liberty, which was initially called the U.S.A. Standardized Aircraft Engine, was produced in just six days by two young engineers, Jesse G. Vincent, vice president for engineering of Packard Motor Car Company and Elbert J. Hall of the Hall-Scott Motor Company in San Francisco. The two men were among the small number of Americans who had experience in aircraft engine design and had kept abreast of developments across the Atlantic where this field was considerably more advanced. Under the encouragement of the new Aircraft Production Board, Vincent and Hall collaborated in a marathon design session from May 29 to June 4, 1917, in a room at the Willard Hotel in Washington, D.C.

The Liberty, an in-line V water-cooled engine, drew much from European and British designers, especially Mercedes and Rolls Royce. However, a basic design that could be interchangeably produced in 4-, 6-, 8-, and 12-cylinder versions was generated by Vincent. He had been disturbed by reports that the Allies were producing some sixty different aircraft engines. The European approach violated Vincent's efficiency-mindedness. He argued that if the United States hoped to produce large-scale airpower rapidly, it had to avoid multiple engine models since such multiplicity meant low-volume production, minimal parts interchangeability, and complicated maintenance. It took little from Vincent to persuade the Aircraft Production Board of the desirability of a standard engine. Its chairman, Howard E. Coffin, was a leading figure in a movement among engineers that sought to standardize and rationalize metal-working manufacturing industries.

If the design of a standard aircraft engine and then a large commitment to its mass production can be faulted in hindsight, the technical achievement of the Liberty's co-designers should not be slighted. Aircraft engines were a complex specialty involving challenges fundamentally different from those in auto engine or electric motor design. In aircraft, the needs were high horsepower, extreme reliability, and low weight, as well as economical fuel consumption and maintenance. As the power-to-weight ratio was increased, the problems of design and precision manufacture grew geometrically. Vincent and Hall aimed high—the 400-horsepower range for the 12-cylinder model (the typical 1917 front-line fighter was powered at 160 horsepower). Within ten days of their first meet-

ing, prototypes of an 8-cylinder version were being built at the Packard works in Detroit. By June 15, numerous auto and engineering concerns had received preliminary drawings. By mid-August, the first Liberty-12 was on the test stand with impressive results. At the end of August, it was deemed a proven engine by the Bureau of Standards. At about the same time, the Liberty's first flight was made at Buffalo, New York.

The various planned models of the Liberty, from the 4- to 12-cylinder versions, were designed to use such parts as pistons, rods, and crankshafts interchangeably. Nevertheless, the trend of developments at the front seemed to call for concentration on the most powerful version, while requirements in the lower power ranges could be filled adequately by proven smaller engines already or soon to go into production, such as the Hall-Scott A-7, the Curtiss OX-5, and a Hispano-Suiza design being built in the United States under license. Only seventy versions of the Liberty were built apart from the 12-cylinder models. The "beefed-up" Liberty-12 was rated at 400 horsepower at 1,800 revolutions per minute. Its bore and stroke was five inches by seven inches, and its weight per horsepower was 2.1 pounds.

The Liberty was produced by auto firms under contract to the army, which also contracted Liberty production for the navy and for the Allies. The Engine Production Section of the Equipment Division, Signal Corps, was put under the charge of Lt. Harold H. Emmons, formerly a Detroit attorney close to auto firms. The government contracted for 56,000 Liberty-12s plus spare parts. Only 20,478 were built, 13,574 of these before the Armistice—6,500 Liberties were built by Packard, 6,500 by Lincoln Motor Company, 3,950 by Ford, 2,538 by the Cadillac and Buick divisions of General Motors, and 1,000 by the Nordyke and Marmon Company. The project involved twenty-three separate plants and seventy-nine parts factories, mainly near Detroit and in Ohio.

Liberty contracting was at cost plus a fixed profit. The initial price per Liberty was set at $6,087 plus a $913.05 profit, with an efficiency and cost-minimizing incentive known as a "bogey." This provided for a bonus to the manufacturer equal to 25 percent of any reductions in production costs. The price was continually revised downward. By late 1917, the figures were reduced to $5,000 and $625. In the end, the Liberty's average cost was about $4,000 apiece.

In sharp contrast to its rapid design, production of the Liberty was long delayed by a range of problems. Many of these were connected to the kinds of administrative confusions, competing demands, and shortages of materials, parts, and personnel that seem to be an inevitable part of a sudden shift to large-scale war production. Despite the high priority granted the Liberty program, numerous difficulties were encountered in securing tools, equipment, and supplies, as well as competent personnel who could build high-performance aircraft engines, monitor costs, and ensure quality production. With the draft and the high national demand for labor and supervision, the personnel bottleneck for aircraft engine production would have been severe under any circumstances. For the Liberty program, the difficulty was compounded by the strict insistence on standardization and interchangeability of manufacture among separate firms and across different factory-floor conditions. The precision tolerances required in machining aircraft engine parts, and then assembling them, were unprecedented in the auto industry's experience and required much greater use of skilled labor than had been anticipated when the mass-production, assembly-line scheme for the Liberty was conceived.

The standardized, high-quality requirements of Liberty production were formidable enough without the continual intervention in production by army agents seeking to incorporate any design change that might coax from the Liberty engine yet another increment in performance. The results were seemingly endless delays and rising overhead, as production lines were halted and rearranged to accommodate changes. By February 1918, overall production stood at just 70 Liberties per month. Output reached mass-production levels only in September, climbing to 3,878 per month by October. Even though organization for Liberty production at Ford had begun in October 1917, output in May 1918 was only 8 engines. The convertibility of Ford's equipment and workers to Liberty production proved to be much less than expected. In addition, constant changes were insisted upon by the military, thus disrupting efficient production. In March 1918, a frustrated Henry Ford, whose men had already coped with 950 changes, refused to entertain any more. "We are going to shut our eyes and produce as we stand equipped," he announced.

Ford output grew rapidly during the summer of 1918. The highest level of daily production was reached, ironically, on Armistice Day, when 11,200 workers produced 75 Liberties. Indeed, the main practical contributions of the Liberty were made during the postwar period. Production stopped in early 1919, but the army still had 11,871 Liberty engines on hand in October of that year. A dependable, powerful, but fuel-hungry engine, the Liberty propelled such famous craft as the Martin bomber and such milestone flights as the first Atlantic crossing in May 1919 and the aerial circumnavigation of the globe, completed in 1924 by the Douglas World Cruisers. Designers and manufacturers complained that the great surplus of Liberties dampened the market for new engines and constricted airframe design around this one power plant. But given the limits of peacetime federal funding for aviation and the weakness of commercial aviation, it seems that the Liberties contributed to a higher level of aviation activity than would have been possible otherwise.

Jacob Vander Meulen

See also AIRCRAFT

Bibliography
Dickey, P.S. "The Liberty Engine, 1918–1942." *Smithsonian Annals of Flight*. Washington, DC: Smithsonian Institution, 1968.
Sweetser, A. *The American Air Service*. New York: Appleton, 1919.

Liberty Loans

After April 1917, the Wilson administration was confronted with several options to finance the United States war effort—(1) to raise taxes, (2) to borrow, and (3) combinations of the first two. By the end of the war, the government had borrowed 20 percent of the $33 billion spent; the rest was paid by taxes. The former was achieved through a series of bond sales, four of which were known as Liberty Loans. The fifth, launched in the spring of 1919, was called a Victory Loan.

The first Liberty Loan was announced in April 1917. William Gibbs McAdoo, Wilson's secretary of the treasury, sold $3 billion of debt to the public at an interest rate of $3^1/_2$ percent. As an incentive to buy U.S. bonds, the Treasury

Department excluded interest income from all taxes except estate and inheritance taxes. The bonds could also be converted to subsequent notes of higher interest.

The first Liberty Loan proved a financial success. Secretary McAdoo observed, "We went direct to the people; that means to everybody—to businessmen, workmen, farmers, bankers, millionaires, school teachers, laborers. We capitalized the profound impulse called patriotism." Overall, some 30 percent of all bonds sold during the war were purchased by individuals earning less than $2,000 per year.

October 2, 1917 marked the beginning of the second Liberty Loan. In this campaign, the Treasury Department authorized a $3 billion loan offering at 4 percent interest. This time a surtax was applied to interest income in excess of $5,000 dollars.

On April 3, 1918, the Treasury Department borrowed $3 billion of bonds bearing an interest rate of $4^1/2$ percent—the third Liberty Loan drive. The tax provisions on interest income from this issue was similar to those of the second.

The fourth Liberty Loan, of September 1918, saw the Treasury selling $6 billion of bonds bearing an interest rate of $4^1/2$ percent. Individuals buying these bonds were given a postwar two-year tax moratorium. After that a surtax would apply to interest income exceeding $30,000.

In March 1919, the Treasury Department launched a post-Armistice bond drive, called the Victory Loan. Here the government borrowed $4.5 billion at an interest rate of $4^3/4$ percent. The bonds were exempt from all but estate and inheritance taxes.

The United States government, by encouraging individuals to save rather than spend, sought to dampen inflationary pressures during the war. Certainly that was one effect of the Liberty Loan drives. Some critics have alleged, however, that when the Treasury borrowed from commercial banks in anticipation of its public loan drives, the expansion of credit and money supply exacerbated rather than depressed inflationary pressures.

Manley R. Irwin

See also McAdoo, William Gibbs

Bibliography
Hardach, Gerd. *The First World War 1914–1918*. Berkeley: University of California Press, 1977.

Ratner, Sidney. *Taxation and Democracy in America*. New York: Wiley, 1942.
Studenski, Paul, and Herman E. Kroos. *Financial History of the United States*. New York: McGraw-Hill, 1963.

Liggett, Hunter (1857–1935)

Hunter Liggett was graduated from the United States Military Academy in 1879 and was commissioned in the infantry. He served for thirteen years in the 5th Infantry Regiment, commanding small units in the western states. He saw combat in several minor engagements against Indians and was promoted to first lieutenant in 1884 and to captain in 1897.

During the Spanish-American War, Liggett accepted a posting as a major of volunteers. He served with units training in the southeastern United States and was sent to Cuba in 1899. He was then stationed in the Philippines until 1902, when he was promoted to major and transferred first to Fort Snelling, then served for four years as adjutant general of the Department of the Lakes, headquartered in Chicago. In 1907, Liggett commanded an infantry battalion at Fort Leavenworth, Kansas. He attended the Army War College from 1909 to 1910.

After graduation, Liggett remained at the War College as a director of instruction. He served concurrently as a member of the army's General Staff, responsible for war planning. During this assignment, Liggett's scholarly and military capabilities were recognized at the highest levels of the army, and by 1913 he had been promoted to brigadier general. As president of the Army War College from 1913 to 1914, he infused the course with sessions on operations planning and staff procedures for modern war. He also prepared and updated War Department plans for possible interventions in Latin America and for upgrading defenses in the Philippines. From these high-level staff activities, Liggett gained a reputation as a sound and innovative military planner.

In 1916, Liggett was appointed commander of the Department of the Philippines. He was promoted to major general in March 1917, becoming one of only seven to hold that rank—the highest in the army at that time. Upon the United States entry into World War I, Liggett took command of the 41st Division composed largely of National Guard units from the western states. He took the 41st to France in October 1917. Upon arrival there, Liggett toured the major headquarters along the Western Front. This tour provoked negative comments by American and Allied leaders upon Liggett's fitness to command in war. He was fat; arthritis caused him to move with difficulty; he looked old and unimpressive. Nevertheless, his reputation as a leader caused the commander-in-chief of the American Expeditionary Force (AEF), Gen. John J. Pershing, to decide to retain Liggett in command of his division in France.

At the end of 1917, Pershing activated two corps headquarters. Liggett took command of I Corps on Jan. 20, 1918. Although the initial responsibilities of the corps headquarters involved mostly supervision of the training of the assigned divisions, command of the corps was a post of great honor; assigning such command to Liggett indicated Pershing's confidence in Liggett's leadership and judgment. However, it was in this phase of preparing his troops to fight that he took exception of Pershing's dictum that American troops be trained in "open-warfare" tactics. Liggett expressed his doubt as to the applicability of open warfare to attacking the well-defended entrenchment system that had caused an impacted battlefield on the Western Front. He went on to define appropriate tactics for the battlefield and to suggest that Pershing's emphasis in training was appropriate to a later phase of combat that would begin after breaking through the German defenses. In what amounted to defiance of Pershing's directives, Liggett had the courage to state what most experienced U.S. and Allied leaders were saying privately. Liggett announced and executed a modified version of Pershing's training program, and Pershing chose not to challenge him.

On July 4, 1918, I Corps entered the war. Liggett commanded this corps in its first action in the Château-Thierry sector against the German offensives of 1918. In this sector, the spirited defenses and counterattacks by elements of I Corps were vital to stopping the German spring and summer offensives. In the subsequent Aisne-Marne offensive, problems attributable to inexperienced unit leadership slowed I Corps' drive and caused unnecessarily high casualties; still, in hard fighting the corps achieved all its objectives, forcing the Germans back behind the Ourcq and Vesle rivers. I Corps then went over to the defensive in the Champagne and later the Lorraine sectors. Liggett strengthened his command structure, and used the time in defense to retrain his troops in

preparation for participation in the first campaign of the American First Army.

On Sept. 12, 1918, Liggett's I Corps, one of the four corps of the newly formed U.S. First Army, participated in the St. Mihiel offensive. Enemy resistance was slight since the Germans had initiated a withdrawal from the St. Mihiel salient as the Americans began their offensive. I Corps advanced well into its sector, taking objectives ahead of schedule and assisting in the capture of the remaining defenders. At the same time as he conducted this short campaign, Liggett was required to shift his command and support elements some sixty miles to the north, to be poised to launch his corps in the Meuse-Argonne campaign two weeks later.

The First Army launched its offensive in the Meuse-Argonne sector on Oct. 26, 1918, with I Corps on the army's left. I Corps' assault divisions were the 28th, 35th, and 77th, with the 92d Division in reserve. The area assigned to the corps was among the toughest in the American sector, with the tangled undergrowth of the Argonne Forest on the left and the open terrain of the Aire valley on the right. The entire sector was well defended, with bunkered machine gun emplacements providing for enfiladed fire throughout the Argonne. I Corps divisions fought forward against stiffening resistance, with the 77th struggling slowly through the Argonne Forest. To break the strong defenses opposing the 77th, Liggett showed unique initiative by launching the 82d Division, fresh from the army reserve, across his front to the west. This cross-compartment attack broke the German hold on the forest and allowed the entire corps line to move forward. The Argonne Forest was cleared by October 10, but the Germans had escaped Liggett's trap and had withdrawn to prepared defenses to the north. The heavy fighting had attrited the strength of I Corps, and that of the entire First Army, resulting in a stalled offensive all along the fighting line.

On October 12, Hunter Liggett relinquished command of I Corps to Gen. Joseph Dickman in order to take command of the First Army from General Pershing. Liggett took advantage of the period of the halt in the American advance to visit the units of the army that he would command. Upon taking command on October 16, he firmly resisted Pershing's pressure to attack; instead, he refitted and retrained his depleted army for the remainder of the month.

When the First Army, under Liggett, resumed the offensive on November 1, it was a rested and better-coordinated command, due mainly to the guidance and leadership of its new leader. Moving with professional competence against dwindling enemy resistance, the army used its support more effectively and seized objectives with little delay. Attacking all along its front, both day and night, the First Army closed on the heights south of Sedan as the Armistice was declared on Nov. 11, 1918. Liggett had been brevetted a lieutenant general upon taking command of the First Army; he was one of many commanders and staff of the AEF to be denied recognition of promotion by decision of the War Department to stop promotions after the Armistice.

Following the Armistice, Liggett continued to head the First Army until April 30, 1919, when he was appointed to command the Third Army, which was in occupation duty at Koblenz in the German Rhineland. In July, Liggett returned to the United States to again head the U.S. Army's Western Department.

Liggett retired on March 21, 1921, as a major general. In retirement, he wrote two books on his service in the war: *Commanding an American Army: Recollections of the World War* (1925) and *A.E.F.: Ten Years Ago in France* (1927). Liggett was advanced to the rank of lieutenant general in retirement in 1930. He died in San Francisco on Dec. 30, 1935.

Paul F. Braim

Bibliography

Braim, Paul F. *The Test of Battle: The A.E.F. in the Meuse-Argonne Campaign.* Newark: University of Delaware Press, 1987.

Coffman, Edward M. *The War to End All Wars: The American Military Experience in World War I.* New York: Oxford University Press, 1968.

Liggett, Hunter. *A.E.F.: Ten Years Ago in France.* New York: Dodd, Mead, 1927.

———. *Commanding an American Army: Recollections of the World War.* Boston: Houghton Mifflin, 1925.

Lippmann, Walter (1889–1974)

As an editor of the *New Republic*, Walter Lippmann became a significant political commentator and later an adviser on postwar European reconstruction. Lippmann advocated "The Case for Wilson" in the *New Republic*'s Oct. 14, 1916, edition praising his intelligence, experience, and leadership. During the next year, he and the *New Republic* were supportive of the administration's diplomacy and drew close to Col. Edward M. House; the two men discussed matters "perhaps once a fortnight."

When the United States entered the war, Lippmann served as a labor assistant in his friend Newton D. Baker's War Department. Subsequently, in September 1918, he was assigned as an army captain to work on political propaganda on Colonel House's staff in Paris. In 1917, Lippmann had been appointed as the secretary to The Inquiry, the research organization authorized by President Wilson to assemble the diffuse materials—ethnic, geographic, and political—on the tangled skein of issues that would confound the participants at the Paris Peace Conference. Among other issues, The Inquiry drafted memoranda on the territorial components of the Fourteen Points. Germany's acceptance of the Fourteen Points as terms of surrender meant that Wilson's general principles had to be rendered specific. Lippmann was assigned to draft the explanatory "official commentary" on the Fourteen Points. It was cabled to the President and received his endorsement. Lippmann left Paris in February 1919. Over the next several months the peace deliberations revealed what happens when extravagant expectations collide with intransigent geopolitical imperatives. Lippmann had profound misgivings about the Versailles Treaty and the League of Nations. Although Lippmann bore a share of the responsibility for the language of the treaty and the breathtaking expansiveness of its objectives, he recoiled from the Versailles negotiations and reassumed his *New Republic* post.

When the final text of the treaty, with its severe treatment of Germany was announced, it stunned liberals, and a revulsion against Wilson swept through their ranks. The *New Republic* led the anti-Wilson charge, imploring the Senate to reject the treaty. Lippmann did not resign from the magazine, nor did he dissent from its critique of results that his very own internationalist rhetoric had helped to create. In alliance with isolationists, the liberal internationalists defeated the treaty in the U.S. Senate and led to noninvolvement in the League of Nations.

The Great War left an indelible imprint upon Lippmann's social thought. Although an early adviser on the shape of the Committee on

Public Information (CPI), Lippmann concluded that its work had endangered fundamental American liberties. While the war had necessitated the creation of a unified public opinion, it had impeded and impaired vigorous democratic self-government. The problem of achieving a democratic public opinion remained a lifelong challenge for him.

Frank Annunziata

See also FOURTEEN POINTS; HOUSE, EDWARD MANDELL; INQUIRY, THE

Bibliography

Lippmann, Walter. *Early Writings*. New York: Liveright, 1970.
———. "Notes for a Biographer." *New Republic* (1930).
———. *The Public Philosophy*. New York: Mentor, 1955.
Seymour, Charles, ed. *The Intimate Papers of Colonel House*. Boston: Houghton Mifflin, 1938.
Steel, Ronald. *Walter Lippmann and the American Century*. New York: Random House, 1980.

Lloyd George, David (1863–1945)

The man whose destiny was to lead a weary British Empire to victory in the "War to End All Wars" arose from very humble beginnings. His father William was an elementary school headmaster in Manchester, and his mother, Elizabeth Lloyd, was the daughter of a Baptist minister. Poor health led his father to move to a farm in Pembrokeshire, Wales, where he died the next year when David was a year old. Elizabeth then moved in with her brother Richard, a shoemaker, a Baptist minister, and a radical. In this environment young David was brought up to believe in the idea of Welsh nationalism, the right of people to worship as they chose, the importance of temperance, and the need to work for the improvement of social conditions of the lower classes in the face of oppression from the aristocracy. When he was only sixteen, despite relative poverty, he started training as a lawyer and served an apprenticeship with the firm of Beese, Jones and Casson of Portmadoc. In 1884, he passed the bar and set up practice. In 1888, Margaret Owen of Criccieth agreed to marry Lloyd George. Despite his many notorious affairs, she stood by him for over half a century of marriage although in later years the couple spent much of their time apart.

Young Lloyd George took part in the local elections on behalf of the Liberal Party; the party leadership soon noticed his intelligence, enthusiasm, and speaking skills. In 1890, he defeated Ellis Nanney, the squire of Llanystumdwy, by eighteen votes on a recount and took his seat for Caernarvon Boroughs on April 17 in the House of Commons, where he continuously represented the Welsh borough for fifty-five years. After he entered the Commons, Lloyd George studied hard and became a master at parliamentary debate and maneuvers. In the beginning, he consistently championed those causes favorable to Wales and favored Ireland as well, seeing it as another oppressed nation within the British Empire. As he became more influential, however, he found that he had to tone down his Welsh interests so as not to jeopardize his national policies and ambitions. The fact that the various Welsh political groupings could not agree among themselves on home rule was also discouraging. The same held true for the quagmire in Ireland.

The death of Thomas Edward Ellis, who was a founder of the Wales of the Future movement in April 1899, pushed Lloyd George into the front ranks of Welsh political leaders. However, he gravely weakened his national standing and personal safety with his outspoken opposition to the Boer War.

When Sir Henry Campbell-Bannerman formed the first Liberal ministry in British history after the resignation of Arthur J. Balfour in December 1905, Lloyd George was appointed president of the Board of Trade, where he was responsible for such important legislation as the Merchant Shipping Act, the Patent and Designs Act, and the Port of London Act. This legislation led to fundamental changes in the way the country conducted business and was a sound framework with which to face future growth and challenges. Lloyd George was also heavily involved in labor relations and in improving the conditions of the workers.

When Herbert H. Asquith was appointed prime minister on April 5, 1908, Lloyd George was invited to take Asquith's place as chancellor of the exchequer. For many men this position had proved to be a stepping stone to greater responsibilities, and Lloyd George was eager to show what he could do with the office. His first "People's" budget of 1909, with its new taxes and development funds, created political gridlock with the conservative House of Lords, which was against using tax money to fund social programs with which they disagreed. They did agree with the government, however, on the necessity of increased funding for more battleships to meet the challenge posed by Germany's expanding high seas fleet. The gridlock forced a general election in January 1910. The Liberals won and the budget was passed basically unaltered.

The confrontation with the Lords led to a constitutional crisis, another election, and the eventual passage of the Parliament Act of 1911 that limited the Lords' ability to control legislation sent up by the lower house. Lloyd George's speeches supporting Asquith against the Lords infuriated many of the country's ruling class. But Lloyd George's interests were already beginning to stretch beyond the country's shores. In July 1911, it was he, not Prime Minister Asquith or Foreign Minister Sir Edward Grey, who during a speech at the traditional Bankers' Dinner publicly issued a warning to Germany that Whitehall would support France in the Agadir crisis in Morocco.

With the war clouds gathering over Europe in the summer of 1914, Lloyd George was at first against British involvement on the Continent. But the German invasion of neutral Belgium on August 4 awakened in him his natural tendency to side wholeheartedly with the underdog against the bully. His primary duty was to assure the monetary foundation of the country, which he did by directing the issuance of new bank notes, guaranteeing banks against bad debts, and imposing new taxes. However, as the war dragged on, he could do little to stop the mortgaging of British assets to finance the Allied war effort. Lloyd George also expended much effort to restrict the sale of alcohol, since he felt that drunken workers greatly affected the production of war materiel. However, he was never able to bring "the trade," an important and emotional part of British custom and everyday life, under total government supervision. Because of his speaking ability and appeal to the common man, Lloyd George was often called upon to help settle differences with a restive labor force over pay and working conditions.

As the war developed, Lloyd George quickly came to differ with the grand strategy of the Allies. He felt that it was a mistake to bet everything on huge offensives in France that gained little ground against strong German defenses but produced long casualty lists. Instead, he came to be identified with the "Easterners," those who felt that operations in Mesopotamia, Italy, and the Balkans would have significant negative influence in the capitals of the Central Powers. These really were "sideshows," as he called them, and they did little but divert Allied strength and attention from the main theater of war and cause immense discord with other Allied leaders. This latter group, the "Westerners," favored using brute force against the Western front to gain victory.

The incredible ferocity of the "modern" war led to a huge demand for artillery shells, which, like most of the combatants, the British armaments industry was ill prepared to meet in the early period of the conflict. At first everyone was predicting a short war, and therefore armies would not need huge supplies of war materiel; events soon proved this to be a false hope. The severe shortage of shells hampered British military operations, needlessly cost many young lives, and led to a serious political scandal at home. Lloyd George felt that the secretary of state for war, old Field Marshal Earl Horatio Herbert Kitchener of Khartoum fame, should take chief responsibility for the deplorable situation. In addition to the shell shortage, there was the stalemate at Gallipoli, which led to the resignation of First Lord of the Admiralty Adm. Sir John Fisher. Because of public and parliamentary disappointment with these important matters, Prime Minister Asquith reformed his ministry as a coalition government with the Conservative Party on May 25, 1915. Lloyd George was appointed as the first minister of the new Munitions Ministry. Here he was able to direct his energy to cut through bureaucratic red tape, increasing the production of vitally needed munitions. Changes in manufacturing procedures, collection of more resources, enrollment of new experts, expansion of factories, and the introduction of women into the workforce brought about greater production. By July 1916, thanks in part to the efforts of Lloyd George and his staff, the British had sufficient ammunition stocks to launch the terribly costly and inconclusive Somme offensive.

There is some dispute as to whether or not Lloyd George had intended to accompany Kitchener on his "semi-secret" trip to Russia in the summer of 1916, the purpose of which was to boost Russian spirits and to investigate the supply situation in that war theater. Kitchener rightly felt that the Russian front was far more important to the war effort than wasteful operations in the Balkans or Mesopotamia. The diversion of German resources to fight a well-organized, -supplied, and -led Russian army would have made things much easier for the Allies in the West. At the time, Lloyd George was busy in London with the aftereffects of the bloody Easter Rebellion in Ireland, to which he had been assigned by the prime minister, and he did not accompany Kitchener on the ill-fated Russian mission. Kitchener drowned when the cruiser H.M.S. *Hampshire* hit a mine off the Orkney Islands on June 5 on its way to Archangel; his death dealt a great blow to Allied morale at a critical time. Lloyd George then assumed Kitchener's position at the War Ministry despite some misgivings on the part of his colleagues.

Lloyd George had long felt that Asquith was entirely too weak to be leading the great commonwealth in the prolonged war. Many ranking members of the military, the government, the political parties, and the press shared that opinion. The public was also disheartened by the bloody stalemate on the Western Front. Although both sides were toying with tentative peace feelers, Lloyd George was still in favor of a "knock-out blow" against the Central Powers, which could only be delivered on the Western Front. After some complicated behind-the-scenes maneuvering, Prime Minister Asquith was forced out in December 1916 to be replaced by Lloyd George.

One of the new prime minister's first actions was to replace the cumbersome twenty-three-member cabinet with a five-man War Cabinet to meet at 5 P.M. every day. Sir Maurice Hankey headed up a secretariat to record cabinet decisions and minutes, a service that had been sorely lacking previously. Prime Minister Lloyd George worked with a close circle of trusted aides called "the Garden Suburb," consulted closely with organized labor, and, more importantly, sought the counsel of the various dominion leaders, notably Jan Christiaan Smuts of South Africa.

Of great urgency for Britain when Lloyd George assumed the prime ministry was the German undersea threat to its vital sea lanes. The resumption of unrestricted submarine warfare on Feb. 1, 1917, brought a United States declaration of war on April 6, but it would be months before the American presence would be felt on the Allied side. The achievement of the German U-boats in sinking ten ships a day in April was greatly aided by the Royal Navy's

incredibly obstinate refusal to institute the convoy system, despite its proven success with this method during the Napoleonic Wars. The British Empire was close to losing the war because it could not safely transport food and other necessities to the home islands. On April 30, an exasperated prime minister stormed into the Admiralty to demand answers. The new first sea lord, Adm. Sir John Jellicoe, under Lloyd George's constant pressure introduced convoying and guided the development of depth charges and underwater sound-detection equipment. Thereafter the losses of merchantmen declined, and more supplies flowed to Europe, although the rationing of food in Britain had to be undertaken the next year. Lloyd George also appointed a new director of shipping, shipowner Sir John Maclay, who was able to increase ship production.

By now it was too late for Lloyd George to change substantially the Allied strategy of prosecuting the war on the Western Front. The Russian tsar abdicated in March 1917, and the Russian Army was beginning to melt away. It was only with great reluctance and foreboding that Lloyd George agreed to Field Marshal Sir Douglas Haig's plan for a summer offensive near the coast to relieve pressure on the French lines after the disastrous Nivelle offensive of April and May, which had led to mutinies among the French troops. Unfortunately, the British Army's efforts turned out to be as unsuccessful as the French. The one bright spot was the introduction of British tanks at the Battle of Cambrai in November 1917. Lloyd George had a hand in their development while he was munitions minister. However, due to mechanical unreliability and poor deployment, these noisy monsters were not able to sustain the offensive, and their effect quickly wore off as the enemy figured out how to counter them.

Through all of this, Lloyd George had to deal with a multitude of strikes by disenchanted workers, along with the continuing problem of how to govern Ireland. The leaders of the Easter Rebellion were released from prison, but British troops sorely needed on the Continent were still kept in Eire to maintain control. A satisfactory arrangement was never achieved, so the muddled state of affairs continued. Foreign Secretary Arthur J. Balfour issued his famous declaration regarding the establishment of a Jewish state in Palestine with the prime minister's full support. Then the disaster that befell the tired Italian army at Caporetto in

October 1917 forced Lloyd George to deal with another crisis at the same time that the failed Passchendaele offensive was winding down. He met King Victor Emmanuel of Italy in November and agreed to send British divisions to bolster the Italian line along the Piave River.

A problem that frequently seems to bedevil democracies in wartime is the proper command relationship between the civilian and military leadership. Lloyd George was concerned on two fronts. The first was the lack of a formal method of coordination among the nations for grand strategy, each one preferring to go its own way. At Rapallo, Italy, in November 1917, after much negotiation and resistance among all parties, he was at last able to attain agreement for the establishment of a Supreme War Council. The second and much more difficult issue was how to achieve unified control over the forces in France. There was a temporary arrangement in 1917 when the British were placed under Gen. Robert Nivelle for his great offensive, but it ceased when the French assault collapsed. Lloyd George felt he could not just order unification of command due to the political power of the military and supposed popular feelings of not wanting to serve under foreign commanders. He kept pushing this idea, however; the serious internal dispute that this caused occupied much valuable time and energy of all concerned.

Disagreements with members of the uniformed services and their powerful supporter Lord Northcliffe, who owned *The Times*, over the proper involvement of the government in military operations, led Lloyd George seriously to consider resigning his office, but he was dissuaded from doing so. General Sir William Robertson resigned as chief of the Imperial General Staff, in February 1918 after many disputes with Lloyd George and was replaced by General Sir Henry Wilson. The prime minister still did not trust Haig as commander of the British field army and supposedly kept him short of troops so that Haig would not launch any more costly attacks. When Gen. Erich Ludendorff attacked in March 1918 in his all-out spring offensive, he almost split the British line. The British and French retreated but managed to hold their lines in desperate fighting with the help of the newly arrived Americans. It was this emergency that finally convinced Haig to agree to a unified command under General Foch. This new command setup lasted from April 1918 until the Allied offensives of the late summer and fall finally forced the German Supreme Command to give up hope of victory.

At the Paris Peace Conference, Lloyd George was intent upon securing Britain's security vis-à-vis Germany, but he was not as concerned as French Premier Georges Clemenceau or the British public with keeping the Hun down forever. The Germans had a moral obligation to pay reparations, he felt, but not to such an extent that they could do nothing else. For him, the best way to improve Europe's dismal economic and political situation was to get trade and industry in Europe up and running again; one way to do this was to let Germany rebuild its powerful industrial engine and that would pull the rest of the Continent along with it. The British prime minister found himself conducting a balancing act between the French desire for revenge and U.S. President Woodrow Wilson's idealistic intentions.

Immediately after the Armistice, Lloyd George had called an election to reaffirm popular support for his coalition with the Conservatives. He angered many in the Liberal Party by his awarding "coupons" of approval only to those who had supported him, which turned out to be mostly Tories. Asquith and a number of Liberals lost their seats. Finally, after controversies over the Irish Treaty and relations with Turkey, David Lloyd George relinquished power on Oct. 18, 1922. He had generated too much distrust among the press and politicians through the years to ever return to power, although he kept his seat in the Commons. He kept busy commenting on national political problems, fighting with colleagues in the Liberal Party, and proposing various plans for dealing with the economic situation. To fill his time, he wrote his *War Memoir,* in which he rarely admitted mistakes or the validity of the beliefs of others. He died at Ty Newydd, his small farm, on March 26, 1945.

Lloyd George was a complicated, woman-chasing, scheming politician. He was passionate in his love of Wales, the defense of the weak, and the improvement of social conditions for the underprivileged. He did not care if he stepped on the toes of the powerful. Perhaps of greatest significance in the long run was his establishment of national insurance for the British people and improving the economic foundation of the country. But it was his two years of service as a wartime prime minister that brought him fame and glory. His undying belief in victory and his energy in prosecuting the war stiffened the resolve of a dispirited country; almost by the sheer force of will did the country hold out until help came from the New World and its enemies collapsed. Until Churchill's magnificent performance in even more desperate times outshone everyone else, David Lloyd George was indeed the country's greatest political leader since the Napoleonic era.

Daniel Blewett

See also HAIG, DOUGLAS

Bibliography

Beaverbrook, Lord. *The Decline and Fall of Lloyd George, and Great Was the Fall Thereof.* London: Collins, 1963.

Hankey, Maurice. *The Supreme Command, 1914–1918.* London: Allen and Unwin, 1961.

Lloyd George, Richard. *Lloyd George.* London: Muller, 1960.

McCormick, Donald. *The Mask of Merlin: A Critical Study of David Lloyd George.* London: Macdonald, 1963.

Owen, Frank. *Tempestuous Journey: Lloyd George His Life and Times.* London: Hutchinson, 1954.

Lodge, Henry Cabot (1850–1924)

Normally, individual members of the U.S. Senate play only modest roles in shaping an administration's foreign policies. But the period following most major twentieth-century wars has been marked by a different pattern: the rise to prominence of senators of the opposing party who established a strong voice in forming U.S. foreign policy.

In the aftermath of World War I, Senator Henry Cabot Lodge of Massachusetts gained control of the terms by which the United States would be permitted to join the League of Nations; after World War II, Senator Arthur Vandenberg of Michigan played a key role in shaping the details of the Truman administration's aid and defense policies; and after Vietnam Senator Henry Jackson of Washington built a congressional majority that limited the Nixon and Ford administrations' efforts to strengthen detente with the Soviet Union. It is unlikely that Lodge would have agreed with everything that Vandenberg and Jackson stood for; but as a fervent believer in the Senate's

rights and responsibilities in foreign affairs, he almost certainly would have applauded their insistence on congressional influence in foreign policy.

Born into a wealthy and prominent Boston family in 1850, Lodge came to maturity believing that the Republican party (GOP) had saved the Union during the Civil War and that only the GOP could provide the far-sighted leadership the country needed to continue along the path to national greatness. He won election to the Massachusetts state legislature in 1879 and to the U.S. House of Representatives in 1886. After making a name for himself in that body, Lodge was appointed to a seat in the Senate in 1893, a position held until his death in 1924. Like his close friend Theodore Roosevelt, Lodge vigorously supported commercial and military expansion overseas. Believing that President Roosevelt had done a superb job of advancing American's interests abroad, Lodge became highly critical of the foreign policies of Roosevelt's two successors, Republican William Howard Taft and Democrat Woodrow Wilson.

In the words of biographer John A Garraty, the differences between Lodge and Wilson during the struggle over the League of Nations involved "principles, politics, and prejudices" so closely intertwined that it would be "both impossible and unprofitable" to try to "disentangle" them. Most of these differences developed during the passionate debates that occurred between 1914 and 1917 over U.S. policy toward the war in Europe; thus they emerged well before the fight over the League took center stage in early 1919.

Although Lodge distrusted all Democrats and regretted Wilson's victory in 1912, he was willing to give the new president an opportunity to prove himself in foreign policy. Thus Lodge largely withheld criticism on foreign affairs during Wilson's first year in office. In 1914, however, the senator accused the administration of incompetence and indecisiveness in its policies toward Mexico. He also agreed with Roosevelt that Wilson was misguided in trying to fashion an evenhanded policy of neutrality toward the European war when Germany—in Roosevelt's and Lodge's opinion, at least—was the clear aggressor. Believing that an Allied victory was required for lasting peace, Roosevelt and Lodge pushed hard for military preparedness from late 1914 through early 1917. They were disappointed by Wilson's lukewarm support for preparedness, and by his efforts to serve as a mediator in order to bring about a "peace without victory."

More than any other incident, a legislative fight in late 1914 and early 1915 triggered Lodge's lasting personal hatred of Wilson. Faced with a shortage of merchant shipping, the administration proposed a ship purchase bill that would permit the government to buy and operate foreign ships. Lodge and many other senators of both parties doubted the wisdom of this bill—especially when considering the possibility that under it Wilson might buy German-owned ships trapped in U.S. harbors and thus send money to Germany that could be used for military supplies. Wilson refused to make any compromises, and he pressured Senate Democrats to pass the measure unchanged. After a prolonged fight in which Lodge played a key role, the bill was finally defeated.

A bitter Lodge wrote to Roosevelt in February 1915 that, except for James Buchanan, Wilson was "the most dangerous man that ever sat in the White House" because of his "determination to have his way, no matter what it costs the country." In a subsequent letter he told Roosevelt that he "never expected to hate any one in politics with the hatred I feel towards Wilson." This hatred deepened in January 1917 when Wilson turned down an invitation to attend a non-political event in Washington after he learned that Lodge would be sharing the platform with him.

Despite his animosity toward Wilson, Lodge applauded one of the President's actions: his speech on April 2, 1917, asking Congress for a declaration of war against Germany. The senator strongly supported the war effort, but worried that Wilson might be tempted to seek a compromise peace with Germany. Thus in a speech in August 1918 Lodge urged the president to insist that Germany surrender unconditionally. Like other Republicans who believed that they had loyally supported the war effort, Lodge was angered by Wilson's appeal in October 1918 for the election of a Democratic Congress so that he could serve as the American people's "unembarrassed spokesman in affairs at home and abroad." On November 5 the voters rebuffed Wilson by electing a Republican Congress, and Germany agreed to an armistice six days later. The administration had managed the war, Lodge and other Republicans quickly concluded, but they were determined to put their stamp—and Congress's—on the peace.

A great debate over what conditions the United States should join the League of Nations began shortly after the 1918 election and continued until March 1920, when the Senate failed in its second and last effort to ratify the Versailles Treaty and thus bring America into the League. During the first six months of this debate—that is, roughly from December 1918 through June 1919—most of the public and the press supported U.S. entry into the League largely on President Wilson's terms. Thereafter, however, support grew for Senator Lodge's reservations, and Wilson increasingly was criticized for failing to make meaningful compromises. Lodge deserves a good share of the credit for this shift in the political winds.

As his biographer, William C. Widenor has emphasized, Lodge—like Wilson—was an internationalist; that is, the senator believed that the U.S. should be involved directly in shaping and ensuring peace in Europe. Lodge believed that these goals could best be achieved through an alliance (or league) of the victorious nations in World War I, which would work together ensuring that Germany did not rise up to power and to go war again. As he commented in April 1919, "I should like to see a League among the Nations with whom we have been associated in the war which would tend to promote and secure the future peace of the world, without impairing certain rights and policies of the United States which do not in the least concern or trouble Europe." Lodge feared that Wilson's more universal league would be too diffuse to focus on maintaining peace in Europe—as indeed proved to be true in the 1930s.

Even after becoming Senate Majority Leader and Chairman of the Senate Foreign Relations Committee in May 1919, Lodge lacked the power to create the league of victors that he desired. Only the President could finish negotiating the Versailles treaty and bring it home for the Senate's consideration. What Lodge could do, however, was to try to achieve his two main objectives: (1) keep the Republican party relatively united on the League issue so that it would not split in two during the 1920 election as it had in 1912; and (2) limit and clarify U.S. obligations as a member of the League, thereby protecting American's freedom of action and congressional influence in U.S. foreign policy. These objectives were tied together, if Lodge kept his party relatively united, Wilson would be forced to accept Republican reservations in order to achieve his goal of U.S.

entry into the League. A practical political reason also prompted insistence on Republican "improvements" in the treaty: Lodge and other GOP leaders did not want the Democrats to be able to run in 1920 on the claim that their party alone had brought about lasting peace.

Lodge did a superb job of orchestrating Republican strategy on the League. He persuaded Senator William Borah of Idaho and other "irreconcilable" opponents of U.S. membership in the League to agree to vote for Republican amendments or reservations, thus ensuring their passage over Democratic opposition. He worked closely with a GOP elder statesman, Elihu Root, and with other so-called "mild reservationists" to write reservations that would protect U.S. interests without destroying the League or requiring the U.S. to enter into new negotiations on the issue with its European allies. Thus, when Wilson tried in July and August to gain the support of the "mild reservationists," he found that, having drafted several of the key reservations, they were already firmly on Lodge's side. Finally, Lodge assured the so-called "strong reservationists" (whose views most closely reflected his own position) that he would never accept Wilson's position on Article 10 of the treaty, the article that most directly challenged U.S. freedom of action. By early September, when Wilson embarked on his ill-fated speaking tour on behalf of the League, Lodge and his fellow Republicans were firmly in control of the situation.

The severe stroke that Wilson suffered on September 25 and that cut short his speaking tour symbolized his declining fortunes. Inflation, labor unrest, race riots, and other domestic problems had eroded the President's popularity since the end of the war. Meanwhile, Irish-Americans, the backbone of the Democratic party in many northern states, denounced the League as a plot to maintain British sovereignty over Ireland; several other ethnic groups joined the chorus of dissent.

In November 1919 the Senate defeated the League both with and without the Republican reservations. After these votes the Democratic leader, Senator Gilbert M. Hitchcock of Nebraska, went to see the gravely-ill Wilson and urged him to compromise with Lodge. "Let Lodge hold out the olive branch," Wilson replied testily.

Wilson maintained his uncompromising, bitter stance through the final votes in March 1920. Aware that most American and Allied leaders of opinion wanted the U.S. to join the League, Lodge and other Republican senators tried to find a basis for compromise with Wilson's supporters throughout the winter. Ultimately, however, they discovered that the reservation that dealt with Article 10 could not be compromised: either the U.S. had an "obligation" under this article to respond to aggression, as Wilson insisted, or it had to be free to decide in each case, as the Republicans contended. As author Ronald N. Stromberg has observed, Lodge and other GOP leaders were convinced "that if the United States admitted an obligation that she subsequently refused to honor, she put herself in a false and potentially humiliating position." The American tradition of looking over legal documents very carefully before signing them thus worked against Senate ratification of the treaty.

On March 19, 1920, forty-nine senators—including many Democrats from the North and West—voted in favor of the treaty with the Republican reservations, and thirty-five senators—including the "irreconcilables" and Democrats loyal to Wilson, mostly from the South—voted against it. If treaties could be ratified by majority vote, the treaty with the reservations would have passed easily; but it was still seven votes shy of the two-thirds majority required by the Constitution. The struggle over the League having ended in stalemate, the Senate turned to other business.

In a letter written three days after the final vote, Lodge argued that the Republicans handled the situation "very well" and blamed the defeat entirely on Wilson:

> We have twice succeeded in creating a situation where Wilson either had to take the treaty with strong reservations which made it safe for the United States or else was obliged to defeat it. He had twice taken the latter alternative. His personal selfishness goes beyond what I have ever seen in any human being.

In the 1920 election the Republicans ran against "Wilson's league" and for a "return to normalcy." Their top leaders interpreted the GOP's overwhelming victory as a rejection of U.S. membership in the League, and the issue never again came to a vote in Congress. Although Lodge continued to blame Wilson for the defeat of the treaty, he wrote in 1924 that the outcome of the fight over the League "was not without its elements of tragedy." As the senator had come to recognize, the nation had swung away not only from Wilson's faith in the League, but also from Lodge's own balance-of-power internationalism. The result, Widenor rightly concludes, was an "insular nationalism" that rejected U.S. leadership in maintaining European stability and thus contributed to the complete collapse of the Versailles settlement in the 1930s.

If any one person deserved to be blamed for America's failure to enter the League, it was Wilson. The President injected partisanship into peacemaking with his call for the election of a Democratic Congress in 1918, and then tried for the next two years to ignore the outcome of the election. More specifically, Wilson refused to recognize that Elihu Root and other Republican "mild reservationists" supported U.S. entry into the League and sincerely sought to clarify American's obligations under the treaty, and that Lodge and other "strong reservationsits" were siding with the "mild reservationists" when the treaty itself was being voted on. Finally, the President, with his health seriously impaired, was unable or unwilling to see the Senate's defeat of amendments that would require renegotiation of the treaty as the tremendous victory for him that it in fact was. Instead, he insisted that the treaty be passed with meaningless reservations that he supplied to Democratic senators, or not at all.

It is much harder to criticize Lodge. He had legitimate reasons for wanting to keep the Republican party united and to reestablish the Senate's influence in U.S. foreign policy. Lodge also was right not to yield to his personal hatred of Wilson and totally oppose U.S. membership in the League, but rather to work with Root and others to clarify and limit American's obligations as a member of that body.

In short, the circumstances and the outcome were tragic in many ways, as contemporaries and more recent scholars have acknowledged, but it would be unfair and inaccurate to blame Lodge and Wilson equally. As biographer Arthur S. Link has noted, by late 1919 Wilson had come to live in a "world of unreality," and his "strategic errors" contributed the most to American's failure to enter the League.

Ralph B. Levering

Bibliography
Garraty, John A. *Henry Cabot Lodge: A Biography.* New York, 1953.
Link, Arthus S. *Woodrow Wilson: Revolution, War, and Peace.* Arlington Heights, IL, 1979.
Lodge, Henry Cabot. *The Senate and the League of Nations.* New York, 1925.
Stromberg, Roland. *Collective Security and American Foreign Policy.* New York, Praeger, 1963.
Widenor, William C. *Henry Cabot Lodge and the Search for an American Foreign Policy.* Berkeley, 1980.

Logan, James Addison, Jr. (1879–1930)

A military officer, diplomat, and banker, James Addison Logan, Jr., was born in Philadelphia. Logan entered the Army War College after spending a year at Haverford College but left to enlist as a private in the Pennsylvania Volunteers during the Spanish-American War. He eventually reached the rank of captain during the Philippine Insurrection and in 1901 transferred to the Regular Army.

When fighting erupted in the autumn of 1914, Logan was dispatched to Europe, where his expert knowledge of the French language and customs made him a logical choice to serve as chief of the American Military Mission to Paris. Following the U.S. entry into the war in April 1917, Logan worked closely with the French General Staff to draft plans for American participation. Woodrow Wilson incorporated some of these into his initial plans of May 14, 1917, for the American Expeditionary Force (AEF) and its cooperation with the French Army. When Gen. John J. Pershing arrived in Europe in June 1917, Logan became assistant chief of staff at AEF general headquarters.

Logan's participation in Europe did not end with the signing of the Armistice, for soon after the battlefields of Europe fell silent, he became Herbert Hoover's principal assistant in providing food relief to millions of the war's refugees. He then served as the coordinator of the technical advisers to the several new states of Eastern and Central Europe, as an American representative to the Supreme Economic Council, as an unofficial American delegate to the Reparations Committee, and as an adviser to the American Relief Administration responsible for Russian relief. Logan's retirement from the army in 1922 hardly interrupted his involvement in diplomatic circles, and his continued work with the Reparations Committee helped to shape the Dawes Plan of 1924.

Logan was associated with the banking firm of Dillon, Reed and Company from 1925 until his death in 1930.

Michael McCarthy

"Lost" Battalion

One of the more romantic episodes of the American involvement in the First World War is that of the so-called "Lost" Battalion. This sobriquet given it by the popular press at the time is, however, misleading at best. The units concerned—Companies A, B, C, E, G, and H of the 308th Infantry; Company K of the 307th Infantry; and Companies C and D of the 306th Machine Gun Battalion, all part of the 77th Division—constituted more than one battalion. Additionally, they were never lost, nor were they subsequently rescued. These facts in no way diminish the incredible feat of arms performed by this small force under the command of Maj. Charles W. Whittlesey, a soft-spoken graduate of Williams College who would eventually be awarded the Medal of Honor and receive world wide acclaim for his actions. Tragically, the memory of events would weigh heavily on his mind, and he disappeared from a ship while in mid-ocean, a presumed suicide.

During the American assault on the Argonne Forest, the 77th Division had fought for seven straight days until, on Oct. 2, 1918, they reached a standstill facing heavily defended German positions at the Ravine de Charlevaux, a deep rectangular ravine closed on all sides by steep slopes and dense woods. The objective of the American forces was to press forward along the line to reach the ridge on the far side of the ravine and eventually advance through the forest. Accordingly the 1st and 2d battalions of the 308th Infantry and elements of the 306th Machine Gun Battalion moved forward into the ravine.

Harassed by machine gun fire, they eventually succeeded in reaching the floor of the ravine and crossed a small stream. The command then proceeded part way up the slope, where it halted and proceeded to establish its position on the reverse slope where it would be protected from hostile artillery fire. The position held was approximately 300 yards long and 60 yards deep,

on a steep and rocky hillside. In addition to thick woods, the ground was covered with a tangle of undergrowth. A series of two-man runner posts had been left along the way to act as a link with the American rear. As day broke on October 3, the command sent out patrols, which reported German activity on both flanks and to the front. When the seventy-nine men of Company K, 307th Infantry arrived, they reported heavy enemy activity to the rear of the position and along the line of the runners posts. By 10:30 A.M., word was received that the runner post line had been broken and the position was encircled by strong enemy forces. Major Whittlesey deployed his forces, which totaled 550 men, in a square, with his nine machine guns on the flanks to sweep the valley and allow more men to the front and rear of his position.

As darkness fell, German voices were heard on the left, and all quarters reported seeing fleeting glimpses of Germans through the trees. The talking of the enemy grew louder and more excited all along the front, the left flank, and the rear of the position. As the talking reached an excited crescendo, a voice from the top of the hill called out *"Dritte Kompagnie alles zusammen!"* (Third Company all together!) and suddenly the position was enveloped in a rain of hand grenades. As the Germans again called to one another for a second attack, the American forces opened fire. This caught the Germans off guard and inflicted enough casualties to stop another grenade barrage. However, German machine guns began to rake the position.

With his small force ·thus invested, Whittlesey could do little but send out patrols to search for weak spots and dispatch runners to try and reestablish communications with his rear. This only added to the attrition in his ranks. When his force had moved out they had not carried rations for an extended period, on the presumption that they would be fed by their field kitchens. As this was no longer possible, they were reduced to the emergency rations they carried with them, and food almost at once became a problem. A system of rationing was set up within the companies, but matters were complicated by men who had none. In addition, there were no blankets, and the men had only the clothes on their backs, with no overcoats or rain coats. Ammunition was limited, as were grenades. There was no doctor with the command. The members of the medical detachment quickly exhausted their supplies of bandages and were reduced to taking them from the dead to put on the injuries of the newly wounded. As the water the men carried in their canteens ran out, they began to crawl to the bottom of the ravine to fill canteens in the stream. The Germans had sighted machine guns all along the stream, and casualties mounted so quickly from these water expeditions that orders were issued forbidding men to attempt them.

The position was continually under fire from German mortars, grenades, machine guns, and rifle fire. The only way to move during the day was to crawl, and soon the hungry and tired men stopped trying to bury the dead at night in the rocky ground, leaving them where they fell, often to be moved by constant shelling of the position. On October 4, a friendly artillery barrage descended behind the command on the Germans there. To the horror of the Americans, it slowly crept along the floor of the ravine and back up the slope to where they were already barely holding on. Amidst the fury of this barrage, Whittlesey sent the last pigeon, Cher Ami, with a message giving their position and telling the artillery to stop the shelling. After an anxious thirty minutes, the barrage lifted over the ridge and fell on the Germans who were massing for another attack.

At several points throughout the six-day ordeal, Allied planes were seen circling over the position. The men laid out signal panels and attempted to attract the pilots' attention, but to no avail. Finally, the pilots attempted to drop supplies from the planes, but these fell outside the American position and into German hands. Through the course of the action, the Germans were heard to call out false commands in English and to try to send rumors of a withdrawal in hopes of dislodging the Americans. As these ruses failed, they began to shout insults and challenges. These were answered in kind or, more simply, with a burst of rifle or machine gun fire.

On the afternoon of October 7, the enemy ceased fire, and a private of Company H was seen limping into the American position with a white handkerchief tied on a cane. He explained to his battalion commander that he and eight of his comrades had gone after a food basket dropped from a plane. They had stumbled across the German line, where five of them were killed, and the rest wounded and captured. He had been sent back with a message to Whittlesey, appealing in the name of humanity for him to surrender. It also praised him and his

men for putting up a good fight and asked him not to punish the private who delivered the message as he had been made to do so under duress. A legend has grown up that the major responded with the words "Go to Hell." The truth is that no reply was sent, and the private remained in the fighting lines. When it became clear that there was to be no surrender, the Germans renewed the attack with a fury. As evening fell on October 7, the command was down to only two working machine guns, and the men moved in a trancelike stupor as they settled down for another harrowing night. At about 7 P.M., a runner arrived with the news that an American officer and some men had arrived on the right flank. Major Whittlesey went to verify this and found that elements of the 307th Infantry were moving into the position with food and medical supplies for the beleaguered defenders. Through the course of the night, reinforcements filtered into the position and the Germans, aware of what was happening, pulled out leaving the area quiet for the first time in a week. On the morning of October 8, 1918, Major Whittlesey marched out the remains of his command—194 men. In all, 111 had been killed and 199 wounded. They had been 104 hours without food or medical attention.

In the course of the operation, Whittlesey and his men had reached their objective while other units had not. The salient they formed had been quickly surrounded, and it had taken days for the American forces to straighten the line and relieve them. In the course of this operation, two battalions had been practically eliminated trying to reach them, and numerous attempts to aid them by air had been attempted and failed. Following their relief, the American forces drove the Germans out of the Argonne, but the heroes of the Argonne were always to be the "Lost" Battalion. As the few who could walk away left what had been their home for the last few murderous days, an observer commented: "I couldn't say anything to them. There was nothing to say, anyway. It made your heart lump up in your throat just to look at them. Their faces told the whole story of their fight."

Michael J. Knapp

Bibliography
Seventy-Seventh Division. *History of the 77th Division.* New York: Crawford, 1919.
American Battle Monuments Commission. *Summary of Operations of the 77th Di-*

vision in the World War. Washington, DC: Government Printing Office, 1944.

Ludendorff, Erich (1865–1937)

"Like Atlas," said Field Marshal Hindenburg, "he carried a world on his shoulders." An apt description of the man who perhaps more than any in the First World War epitomized the strengths and weaknesses of the German General Staff corps officer: operational brilliance without strategic vision. Born in Kruszczewina (Posen), West Prussia, to a family of small businessmen, Erich Ludendorff chose a military career. He received his commission in 1882 at age seventeen, serving in the usual assignments and completing training as a general staff officer. In 1904 came the call to Berlin to serve on the supreme General Staff. He worked in Section II, responsible for deployment and mobilization plans. In 1908, he became head of the section, the most prestigious position after the chief of the General Staff.

Having an excitable and high-strung temperament, the strong-willed Ludendorff proved a difficult subordinate. Charged with refining and improving the Schlieffen Plan in the years before the First World War, he became convinced that Germany lacked the trained manpower to defeat the French in a rapid campaign. Ludendorff insisted that the government raise additional forces. When this suggestion met disapproval, he bypassed his superiors and initiated contact with politicians in an effort to influence the budget. That the German political system could not bear the cost of additional units was something he never considered. To him, it was a matter of will. The response was a transfer to a regiment in Dusseldorf, safely away from Berlin. A year later he was given a brigade in Strasbourg and promoted to general, but his mobilization orders as quartermaster general of the Second Army indicated he was still persona non grata in Berlin.

When war came in August 1914, fortune smiled on Ludendorff. In the confusion of the attack on Liège, he received the surrender of the city, and Germany had its first war hero. The kaiser personally decorated him with Prussia's highest award, the Pour le Merite, the second in the war. The situation in the east, where two Russian armies threatened to break through German defenses, demanded his brilliance and capability for superb staff work. As a counterweight to his volatility, the Supreme Command recalled from retirement Gen. Paul von Hindenburg, a phlegmatic, no-nonsense, even cautious officer, to command the Eighth Army. Ludendorff became chief of staff. The two generals met for the first time en route to East Prussia. The situation they confronted was threatening and risky, but by no means hopeless. With the able assistance of the Eighth Army's operations officer, Max Hoffman, the Germans routed the Russians at the Battles of Tannenberg (August 1914) and Masurian Lakes (September 1914). The impressive victories electrified Germany and cemented Ludendorff's reputation as the man of genius. The image of the invincible duo of Hindenburg and Ludendorff took root in the German mind. They became legends to a people demoralized by the bloody stalemate in the west. For Ludendorff, who grew increasingly critical of the western war effort, the lack of success reflected a lack of will. He called for "total war." Convinced of his own judgment, he campaigned endlessly against those who opposed his ideas of how to conduct the war, and his vocal criticism of the war effort mounted.

The apostle of total war got his chance when the kaiser, staggered by the losses at Verdun, sent Hindenburg and Ludendorff westward to assume command of the German war effort in France. Ludendorff took the title "quartermaster general" and received a promotion to lieutenant general, while Hindenburg, already a field marshal, became chief of the General Staff. Shocked by the materiel superiority of the Allies and convinced that the civilian leadership lacked the will to prosecute the war to the fullest, Ludendorff initiated the Hindenburg Program. Largely a military takeover of the economy, including compulsory labor, coupled with a ruthless exploitation of occupied territories, the unpopular program resulted in considerable production gains while sapping home-front morale. Convinced German defense operations were too static and hence too costly, Ludendorff introduced new tactics that emphasized an elastic defense in depth. To free divisions for reinforcements, he conducted a massive shortening of German lines by evacuating his forces to the Siegfried Line in early 1917. The evacuated area was left a wasteland.

Ludendorff recognized that the strategy of the war had become one of attrition. With inferior resources compounded by the strangling English naval blockade, Germany could not win with its current strategy. Consumed by fears that losing the war would cause the collapse of Germany, Ludendorff convinced Hindenburg that Germany had to husband resources for a knock-out blow on the Western Front. Shortening the lines to free units, stepping up the Hindenburg Program, and wrapping up the war in the east would make available resources needed for the decisive blow.

Convinced that only total effort could achieve victory, Ludendorff shrank from nothing. Accepting the navy's contention that a return to unrestricted submarine warfare would bring a halt to the delivery of vital American munitions to the Entente, Ludendorff urged its adoption despite the certainty that it would bring the United States into the war. He severely underestimated both the American military potential and the speed with which it could be brought to bear.

By now there were voices of opposition in Germany to Ludendorff's increasingly bullying manner and excessive authority. Hardly an area of German life remained outside his grasp by 1918. The kaiser loathed and feared him, but he could not stand up to him. Ludendorff contemptuously dismissed peace initiatives and war weariness as manifestations of a lack of will. He spared no one, including himself and his family. Two of his stepsons fell in combat, losses that made him harder. He relentlessly attacked those who opposed his measures, including Chancellor Theobald von Bethmann Hollweg, whom he forced from office by mid-1917.

The submarine campaign that he espoused served only to bring the United States into the war. American forces began arriving in Europe at a rate undreamed of by their foes. Only the collapse of Russia, to which Ludendorff had indirectly contributed by transporting Lenin from Switzerland to Russia, brightened the otherwise disastrous picture. Convinced any peace terms would be unacceptable, a belief fed indirectly by his own draconian demands upon the hapless Russians, he cobbled together German resources for one last great push, the spring offensive of 1918. By stripping units from the east, Ludendorff increased his strength in the west by 30 percent. Special units trained in new infiltration tactics used surprise and mobility to bypass enemy strong points and emerge behind enemy lines into the open. Traditional infantry units following along reduced the bypassed areas. A complete absence of the new weapon, the tank, constituted a major weakness to the oth-erwise formidable restructuring. Ludendorff had seen tanks, but he belittled their importance and dismissed his soldiers' concerns as a lack of will, a strange lapse in a man who usually incorporated his subordinates' suggestions.

Ludendorff's spring offensive called for a series of attacks rather than a single breakthrough. The quartermaster general planned a number of sharp blows to collapse the entire Allied Western Front. The first onslaught began on March 21. Although badly shaken, the Allies finally held, and Ludendorff called off the advance in early April. His next two operations followed the same pattern: extraordinary initial successes petering out owing to a lack of reserves and supplies. The end had come; the Germans could not make good their losses.

Ludendorff collapsed under the stress. He had lost his second son in the offensive, and on occasion his ravings against defeatists and incompetent civilians turned into uncontrollable tantrums. On September 28, he told Hindenburg and his staff that Germany must seek an immediate armistice. The kaiser and Chancellor Georg von Hertling heard this sad news the next day and agreed. When Ludendorff later publicly reversed his position about Germany's ability to continue the war, the kaiser demanded his resignation.

Ludendorff's postwar career tarnished his reputation. Fearing revenge, he fled temporarily to Sweden. He wrote his *Memoirs*, blaming Germany's defeat on his innumerable foes and their lack of will power. He railed at the new Weimar Republic and his new enemies—the Jews, Jesuits, and Freemasons—whom he blamed for stabbing Germany in the back. He became the darling of the extreme right, marching with Hitler during the Beer Hall Putsch. In 1925, he ran for *Reichspresident*, polling a mere 1 percent. His views and demons grew more extreme, and he fell to bickering with Hitler and his former comrades. One by one he broke relations with his staff and colleagues, even his wife, whom he suddenly left for Mathilde von Kemnitz. She encouraged his fantasies. In 1935, he published *The Total War*, reversing Clausewitz's dictum and arguing that politics must serve war. On Dec. 22, 1937, he died, shortly after declining Hitler's offer of promotion to field marshal with the remark, "A field marshal is born, not made."

Michael B. Barrett

See also HINDENBURG, PAUL VON

Bibliography

Asprey, Robert B. *The German High Command at War: Hindenburg and Ludendorff Conduct World War I.* New York: Morrow, 1991.

Kitchen, Martin. *The Silent Dictatorship: The Politics of the German High Command under Hindenburg and Ludendorff, 1916–1918.* New York: Holmes & Meier, 1977.

Ludendorff, Erich. *Ludendorff's Own Story, August 1917–November 1918.* New York: Harper, 1919.

Lusitania

The story of the British passenger ship *Lusitania* is still shrouded in mystery and intrigue. It rests in the legal arguments surrounding submarine warfare, naval blockades, selling military materiel to nations at war, and freedom of the seas for neutrals. Ultimately, these issues came to a head when the *Lusitania* was sunk on May 7, 1915, and the United States, which, up to this point, had been equally divided between sentiments for the British and the Germans, lurched toward an antisubmarine and thus anti-German stance that eventually resulted in U.S. intervention in the Great War.

The *Lusitania* was conceived, designed, and built in the era of the great naval arms race between Germany and Great Britain. At the same time the rapidly developing German Navy began to threaten British dominance on the high seas, the German liner *Kaiser Wilhelm II* captured the "Blue Riband," the much coveted symbol of naval prestige awarded to the liner making the fastest trans-Atlantic crossing. The *Lusitania* was one response the British offered to the German challenge.

The British Admiralty subsidized its construction by the Cunard shipping line. Designed by Leonard Peskett, the *Lusitania* was 760 feet long, had a beam of 87.5 feet, displaced 45,000 tons, was capable of achieving 25.88 knots at sea, and carried a crew of 900 to tend a possible 2,300 passengers. The ship was not only a technical marvel, but beautiful to behold as well. Peskett had been instructed to build the most luxurious ship in history, which he did. The *Lusitania* was launched at Clydebank on June 7, 1906. It was the biggest and fastest ship afloat, the pride of the Cunard Line, and the symbol of British maritime excellence. It made its first of many runs from Liverpool to New York on Sept. 7, 1907, immediately recapturing the Blue Riband from the German Empire.

Peskett had gambled on design innovations to improve speed and adhere to regulations imposed by the Admiralty. The 6,600 tons of coal required for one journey were stored in longitudinal bulkheads between the inner and outer hulls. Conventional theory considered the coal a shield to absorb gunfire in the event of hostilities. But later events demonstrated that it only made the ship more vulnerable. When coal is not stored in a warm, dry environment, it produces an invisible, odorless gas (coal damp), which is highly explosive. Also, bits of coal often clogged the watertight doors of the bulkheads, thus breaking their seal. In addition, Peskett had designed the *Lusitania* very tall in order to provide for the luxuries but stay within the dimensions set by the Admiralty. This, combined with a waterline-to-beam ratio that was not unlike a canoe, made the big ship amazingly unstable.

In an effort to protect its crucial sea lanes from a possible war with Germany, the British Admiralty began to arm merchant ships. In May 1913, the *Lusitania* was drydocked to be fitted with posts that could house artillery. The Great War began on Aug. 4, 1914, and on Sept. 14, 1914, the Admiralty informed Cunard that the *Lusitania* was to carry war materiel, a clear violation of the Cruiser Laws, the traditional laws of naval warfare established in 1512 by Henry VIII. Three days later the *Lusitania* was once again at sea, now registered as an auxiliary cruiser and boasting an impressive arsenal of twelve six-inch guns. Until the day it sank, the liner carried war materiel on all but its first wartime journey.

The United States government had decided early in the war that private individuals could trade with individuals abroad, a decision that allowed American businesses to cater to both sides of the conflict. From October 1914 until it entered the war, the government allowed over half a million tons of cordite, guncotton, nitrocellulose, fulminate of mercury, and other explosives to be sent to the Allies. However, the British naval blockade choked off American commerce with Germany while trade with the Allies blossomed. In a move to level the playing field, the German government, on Feb. 18, 1915, announced that the waters surrounding Great Britain were now considered a war zone and all shipping within it was subject to U-boat

L

attack. In effect, the Germans declared a counterblockade.

While the U-boat commanders had been instructed to observe the Cruiser Laws with regard to unarmed merchant vessels, the British merchant fleet had been instructed to violate them blatantly by attacking, even ramming, an enemy submarine. This forced the U-boats to rely on their stealth and attack without warning in an effort at self-preservation. Captain Schweiger, the commander of the U-20, was one of the many U-boat captains who made themselves infamous by sinking merchant ships without warning.

The German government, well aware that its policies on the high seas jeopardized the neutral position of the United States, wanted to print a public warning against American travel on British ships. They approached U.S. Secretary of State William Jennings Bryan on April 26, with the knowledge that the *Lusitania* was going to carry 6 million rounds of ammunition on her next voyage. Bryan cleared the publication of the famous warning to American travelers from the German Empire, and it appeared in the newspapers on May 1, 1915, the day *Lusitania* set sail.

The *Lusitania* embarked on the voyage that it would never finish with a host of contraband. She is known to have carried fifty-one tons of shrapnel shells, seventy-four barrels of fuel oil, ten and a half tons of .303-caliber rifle cartridges, a still unknown cargo on the lowest decks, and an undisclosed amount of guncotton, the explosive used in mines that detonate upon contact with sea water. The Cunard liner also picked up a little extra cargo from a mechanically troubled S.S. *Queen Margaret* that included 200 additional tons of ammunition and sixty-seven men from the Sixth Winnipeg Rifles.

A bizarre combination of bad weather and as yet unexplained poor handling by the Admiralty put the unescorted *Lusitania* off the coast of Ireland by the Old Head of Kinsale at the same time as *U-20*. Captain Schweiger had only one torpedo left, and although he knew one torpedo could not sink this huge vessel, he decided to see exactly how much damage one torpedo would cause. At 1:35 P.M., Greenwich Mean Time on May 7, 1915, one German G-type torpedo struck the *Lusitania* just forward of the bridge on the starboard side. The dull thud and water spout was followed by a much larger rumble that shook the ship from stem to stern. The plates along the entire bow bottom had been blown out. Eighteen minutes later the pride of Cunard shipping was under 300 feet of water, taking 1,198 lives with it, including 124 Americans.

Regardless of the legal questions of neutral rights and the law of the seas, the sinking of the *Lusitania* gave the European conflict an immediacy that it had lacked and enraged the American public. But while editors and pundits proclaimed their outrage, there was little clamor for war among the population. President Wilson, still determined to maintain American neutrality, issued the first "*Lusitania* note" on May 13, 1915, reaffirming the right of U.S. citizens to sail on the high seas, demanding reparation for losses to the United States, and calling for a disavowal of the sinking. Germany, while deploring the loss of life, insisted that, because of its contraband cargo, the *Lusitania* was not an unarmed merchant vessel and asserted that *U-20* was acting in self-defense.

Wilson sent another, substantially stronger note on June 9. Bryan was so shocked by its tone that he resigned from the cabinet, giving the impression that the government was divided on the issue and seriously weakening Wilson's position. As the correspondence continued between the governments, American interest waned. It was not until February 1916 that Germany accepted liability for the affair, and agreed to pay some reparation. However, the Wilson administration considered even this inadequate, and the controversy continued to smolder until the declaration of war on April 6, 1917, when it became a moot point.

Matthew Heiser

Bibliography

Link, Arthur S., et al. *The Papers of Woodrow Wilson.* Vol. 33. Princeton, NJ: Princeton University Press, 1980.

Simpson, Colin. *The Lusitania.* Boston: Little, Brown, 1972.

M

McAdoo, William Gibbs (1863–1941)

William Gibbs McAdoo played leading roles in formulating a financial policy for the United States during World War I and in overseeing federal control of the nation's extensive railroad network. Prior to the nation's entry into the war, McAdoo, as secretary of the treasury, was also busy stabilizing the country's economy during a period when international trade was seriously disrupted.

He was to play a pivotal role in establishing a financial framework to stabilize prices and trade during the war years. Starting in 1914, McAdoo's attention was drawn to the disruption in international trade. The German merchant fleet was either trapped in Germany or interned in foreign ports, and the American fleet was not particularly keen to sail into a war zone. Correspondingly, the United States economy faced critical dislocations. Almost immediately McAdoo established shipping boards to oversee marine insurance and thus encourage shippers to continue trading with Europe. He went one step further and attempted to push for a shipping bill that would give the government extraordinary powers to gain control over the nation's shipping industry. Fueling McAdoo's intentions was a progressive philosophy of government responsibility for the greater economy. His attempt was, however, blocked by shipping interests and their supporters in the Senate. The incident was a formative one and colored his actions during the war emergency years of 1917–1918.

Following American entry into the war, McAdoo's position as secretary of the treasury took on added importance. His principal responsibility was to finance the war effort both at home and abroad. Working closely with the House Ways and Means Committee, McAdoo submitted a draft bill to authorize government bonds of over $7 billion. A portion of the funds were to prop up the ailing finances of the Allied Powers in Europe, and the rest were to pay for the American war effort. The amount was unprecedented in its enormity. Congress passed the measure, but it was McAdoo's responsibility to convince the American people to participate in what was to become known as the Liberty Loans. As the loan drive progressed, McAdoo introduced other innovative measures to oversee the war effort. To streamline production, he established the Inter-Allied Purchasing Commission, which investigated the respective needs of the Allies, and thereby acted as purchasing agent. To oversee the new and vast responsibility of running the financial war effort, McAdoo surrounded himself with business and banking officers. The reason was simple and effective: it quieted opposition from these groups to the growing involvement of the government in the economic affairs of the country. By the end of the war, the Treasury Department had been transformed from one that McAdoo described as a "remote" and "gloomy institution" to one that epitomized "energy, vitality, and movement."

For all McAdoo's efforts at the Treasury Department, he is perhaps best remembered during the war years as director general of the railroads. By late 1917, the country's rail system of 240,000 miles had virtually ground to a standstill. Railroad owners refused to coordinate transportation of war materiel, and the result was congestion at eastern terminals. By November 1917, the rail network was in serious danger of collapsing. In response, President Woodrow Wilson, through proclamation, took control of the nation's railroads on December 26. To oversee their operation, McAdoo was appointed director-general of the newly formed U.S. Railroad Administration.

McAdoo faced a system that was on the verge of collapse and a disgruntled and strike-threatening labor force of over 2 million workers. He immediately embarked on a program to rationalize the system and to placate the restless workforce. To relieve congestion on the eastern seaboard, he instituted a policy of prioritizing freight movement. To assist him in his momentous assignment, McAdoo adroitly appointed railroad officials as his staff. To ease the reorganization, the country was divided into regions, and important railroad officials, generally presidents of lines, were named regional directors. A Division of Labor was also formed to investigate the wages and working conditions of the extensive workforce. By early 1918, the Division of Labor recommended wage increases that went far to satisfy the needs of the workers and at the same time ensure that many would not leave the employ of the railroads for better-paying jobs in war-related industries. McAdoo's efforts paid off. By mid-1918, the nation's rail system was again operating in an efficient manner, and the restless labor force had been pacified.

The wartime experiences, however, left McAdoo exhausted. His war had started in 1914 as secretary of the treasury and finished one day after the Armistice, when he handed in his resignation. McAdoo's energy and commitment during the war years certainly took their physical toll, but in his autobiography he expressed his satisfaction for a job well done. Moreover, McAdoo represented that progressive character of personal service to country, using the qualities of efficiency and good will as its signpost.

Colin Davis

See also UNITED STATES RAILROAD ADMINISTRATION

Bibliography

Broesamle, John J. *William Gibbs McAdoo: A Passion for Change.* Port Washington, NY: Kennikat Press, 1973.

Hines, Walker D. *War History of American Railroads.* New Haven, CT: Yale University Press, 1928.

Kerr, K. Austin. *American Railroad Politics, 1914–1920.* Pittsburgh: University of Pittsburgh Press, 1968.

———. "Decision for Federal Control: Wilson, McAdoo, and the Railroads, 1917." *Journal of American History* (December 1967).

McAdoo, William G. *Crowded Years: The Reminiscences of William G. McAdoo.* Boston: Houghton Mifflin, 1931.

McAlexander, Ulysses Grant (1864–1936)

Ulysses Grant McAlexander was born in Dundas, Minnesota. He graduated from the United States Military Academy at West Point in 1887 and was commissioned in the infantry. He served several tours as instructor in military science and tactics at both Iowa Wesleyan and Oregon State College during the late nineteenth and early twentieth centuries. As a captain of volunteers, he fought in the Santiago Campaign during the Spanish-American War and participated in the occupation of the Philippines and the Philippine Insurrection.

After a relatively undistinguished career in the army, he was ordered to France in June 1917. From July through December 1917, he commanded the 19th Infantry and in early 1918 he was a member of the inspector general's staff. McAlexander was then given command of the 38th Infantry of Gen. Joseph T. Dickman's 3d Division, with which McAlexander made a reputation as "The Rock of the Marne," a sobriquet also attached to his regiment, which stoutly defended its portion of the river.

When the great German offensive of July 15, 1918, began, the 38th Infantry and its commanding officer were on the western edge of the Marne River knob opposite Jaulgonne. With a fifty-mile front, German forces advanced four miles deep into the defenders' lines except at the "knob," where the 38th bore the brunt of the attack. They repelled every German assault, even though the regiments to their right (French) and left (30th U.S. Infantry) fell back, exposing the 38th's flanks. They held a small rise of ground for twenty-one hours even though enemy fire from both flanks continued to harass them all during that time. The 38th received the attention of the 5th and 6th Prussian Grenadiers and the 175th Infantry Regiment. From the beginning, McAlexander was right in the midst of the fighting. Captain Wooldridge, his intelligence officer, cautioned him, "'Colonel, don't you know that nothing can live in this place?' and [McAlexander] shrugged his oxlike shoulders, 'well, while anyone is left alive, let's give them hell.'" The 38th blunted the German assault in the nearly two days they were at the center of the action, causing the Germans grievous damage. For this action, the colors of the 38th were decorated with the Croix de Guerre with Palms. McAlexander was the hero of the hour.

McAlexander received the Distinguished Service Cross for his part in stopping the German advance and in August he was promoted to brigadier general and given command of the 180th Infantry Brigade in the 90th Division, which he led in the St. Mihiel and Meuse-Argonne operations. He served with the occupation forces in Germany until June 1919. Upon his return to the United States, he held a variety of positions, retiring as a major general in 1924. McAlexander died in Portland, Oregon, on Sept. 18, 1936.

George B. Clark

MacArthur, Douglas (1880–1964)

General Douglas MacArthur was born into a dedicated military family. His father, General Arthur MacArthur II, had a distinguished Civil War career followed by service in the Spanish-American War and the Philippine Insurrection; and his aristocratic, strong-willed mother, Mary P.H. MacArthur, became the driving force promoting her son's advancement until her death in 1935. His exceptional abilities, personal ambition, and family's influence combined to produce one of the twentieth century's most acclaimed military records.

MacArthur entered West Point in 1899, finishing first in the class of 1903, and was posted to the Philippines, Wisconsin, Kansas, Texas, and Panama. He served as an aide to his father in the Philippines and to President Theodore Roosevelt, and from 1913–1917 was a member of the War Department's General Staff. During the Veracruz incursion of 1914, in Mexico, he was an intelligence officer. Promoted to the rank of colonel after the American entry into World War I, he was appointed chief of staff to the 42d Infantry (Rainbow) Division. MacArthur served with distinction in France. Popular with superiors and ranks alike, he excelled at both staff work and combat command. Wounded twice, he received numerous decorations for bravery and leadership, including two Distinguished Service Crosses, the Distinguished Service Medal, and seven Silver Stars. Promoted to brigadier general in July 1918, he

performed brilliantly at the St. Mihiel salient in September 1918 and the Meuse-Argonne offensive in October–November 1918 before assuming command of the 42d Division.

As superintendent of West Point for the period 1919–1922, he instituted much needed academic reforms there. Following extended tours in the Philippines, he was appointed army chief of staff in 1930. Despite the effects of the Great Depression on the military establishment, he developed mobilization programs critical to the United States in the early days of World War II. Unfortunately, his otherwise positive tenure was marred when MacArthur, at the direction of President Hoover, evicted the Bonus Army from its tent city at Anacostia Flats in Washington, D.C., on July 28, 1932.

From 1935 to 1941, MacArthur held the rank of field marshal in the Philippine Army. He served as military adviser to the Philippine Commonwealth in preparation for its independence from the United States. Given the growing tensions in the Pacific, President Franklin Roosevelt named MacArthur commanding general of United States forces in the Far East in July 1941. As such, MacArthur organized the Philippine defenses but was forced to retreat before the invading Japanese. Roosevelt later named him Supreme Commander of the Southwest Pacific, and he led American forces across the western Pacific to accept the surrender of all Japanese armies in September 1945. He supervised the postwar occupation of Japan and then commanded United Nations forces in Korea in 1950.

In 1951, President Truman "fired" MacArthur because of his public statement calling for the invasion of China. Unsuccessful in his quest for the Republican presidential nomination in 1952, he retired from the public arena to live in semiseclusion until his death in 1964.

Fred Arthur Bailey

Bibliography

Hunt, Frazier. *The Untold Story of Douglas MacArthur*. New York: Devin-Adair, 1954.

James, D. Clayton. *The Years of MacArthur*. Boston: Houghton Mifflin, 1970.

MacArthur, Douglas. *Reminiscences*. New York: McGraw-Hill, 1964.

Manchester, William. *American Caesar: Douglas MacArthur, 1880–1964*. Boston: Little, Brown, 1974.

McCoy, Frank Ross (1874–1954)

Born on Oct. 29, 1874, McCoy grew up in Lewiston, Pennsylvania. He won an appointment to West Point, graduating in 1897 as a second lieutenant of cavalry.

During America's war with Spain, Frank Ross McCoy deployed to Cuba, where the young lieutenant saw action until wounded at Kettle Hill. Once recovered, he joined the staff of Gen. Leonard Wood, governor of Cuba, where he became a staunch admirer and receptive student of Wood's expansive vision of the army's role in the new era inaugurated by the events of 1898. In 1902, McCoy followed his mentor to the Philippines. McCoy emerged from this tour a seasoned hand in the business of policing empires. Furthermore, his intimacy with Wood brought him to the attention of Washington's reigning political elite. Acquaintances such as Theodore Roosevelt helped McCoy garner a succession of nontraditional appointments, among them a tour as military aide to the President, participation in the Taft-Bacon Mission of 1906, and a number of covert missions to China, Colombia, and Cuba. These experiences affirmed McCoy's reputation as an able and well-connected officer of unusually broad experience.

American entry into World War I found McCoy, just promoted to major, serving as military attaché in Mexico City. He now turned to influential friends to secure his reassignment and was soon en route to France.

McCoy joined Pershing's general headquarters (GHQ) at Chaumont and was appointed secretary of the General Staff. To serve at Chaumont during the months required to build the AEF was exhilarating and rewarding—promoted twice, McCoy became restive, even offering to give up his colonel's eagles for a chance to join the line. Pershing refused such entreaties: McCoy was critical to the functioning of GHQ.

Finally, in April 1918, Pershing relented, selecting McCoy to command the 165th Infantry, one of four regiments comprising the 42d Division. Better known as the "Fighting Sixty-Ninth," the Irish New Yorkers of the 165th were a rambunctious and unruly lot. Failure to control the regiment's rowdies had led to the relief of the previous two commanders. Joining his regiment in a quiet sector at Bacarat, McCoy lost no time in establishing himself as commander in fact as well as in name. Key to this effort was his success in winning the support

and friendship of the regimental chaplain, Father Francis P. Duffy.

In early July, McCoy led his regiment to new positions east of Rheims. Assigned to the French XXI Corps, the 42d Division received the task of holding part of the huge salient created by the German spring offensive. The 165th's first major action began on July 14, a sharp four-day fight in which the regiment repulsed a series of German attacks at the cost of 269 casualties. Once these final spasms of the enemy offensive subsided, the Allies counterattacked to eliminate the German salient. After a brief respite, the 165th joined this attack on July 25. McCoy's regiment led his division's advance and fought with particular valor in the bitterly contested struggle for crossings over the Ourcq River. Success did not come cheaply: by the time it withdrew from the line on August 3, the 165th had sustained nearly 2,000 additional casualties.

McCoy's cool effectiveness during this operation earned him promotion to brigadier general and command of the 63d Brigade, part of the 32d Division. Throughout the Allied offensives culminating in the Armistice, McCoy led his brigade with distinction.

Victory brought accolades. Marshal Pétain decorated McCoy with the Legion d'Honneur and the Croix de Guerre with Palm. McCoy was among the ten general officers to whom Pershing personally awarded the Distinguished Service Medal. But victory also generated fresh demands for McCoy's talents.

Within days of the Armistice, McCoy was reassigned as director of the Army Transport Service and subsequently as AEF director general of transportation. He spent months sorting out the transportation problems impeding redeployment. Just prior to his own return home, MajGen. James G. Harbord recruited McCoy as chief of staff for a military mission to Armenia.

The Harbord Mission spent six weeks crisscrossing Asia Minor from Constantinople to Baku, traveling over 5,400 miles by rail, automobile, and horseback. They discovered that while the plight of the Armenians had been exaggerated, the region as a whole suffered from crushing backwardness, inefficiency, and corruption. In the Harbord Report, they advocated an American military mandate to protect the entire region from predators and to assist in its recovery. However, President Wilson had no interest in such a mandate, so the report was shunted aside.

In January 1920, McCoy finally returned to the United States. His career prospered, continuing to alternate between traditional military duties and increasingly sensitive diplomatic assignments. His supervision of elections in Nicaragua in 1927–1928, for example, earned him promotion to major general and led to his subsequent designation as the American representative on the Lytton Commission, created by the League of Nations in 1931 to investigate the Manchurian crisis. Even after retiring from the army in 1938, McCoy remained active in public life. From 1939 to 1945, he served as president of the Foreign Policy Association. Finally, from 1945 to 1949, he served as chairman of the Far Eastern Commission, the body charged with devising Allied policy toward occupied Japan. Frank McCoy died on June 4, 1954.

Andrew J. Bacevich

Bibliography

Bacevich, Andrew J. *Diplomat in Khaki: Major General Frank Ross McCoy and American Foreign Policy, 1898–1949.* Lawrence: University Press of Kansas, 1989.

Machine Guns

World War I saw the arrival of the machine gun as a fixture of modern warfare. Drawing on the experiences of the Allies, the United States was no stranger to the machine gun, and the American Expeditionary Force (AEF) used several types of guns throughout the war.

Berthier Light Machine Gun

The Berthier light machine gun was designed by a French army officer, Andre Virgile Paul Marie Berthier, who, since 1905, had been experimenting with a design for a light weapon for the infantry that had the firepower of the heavier Hotchkiss machine gun. His design relied on the gas pressure from the escaping bullet to be funneled into a gas tube that ran parallel to the barrel. This pushed a piston down the gas tube until it compressed the spring, which ejected the spent shell and then placed the gun back in battery. Earlier guns were water cooled, but by 1916 Berthier had changed to a fluted barrel that would dissipate heat, thus allowing the surrounding air to cool the barrel and greatly reduce the overall weight of the gun. The 1917 model was the final evolution of Berthier's design. The gun consisted of a fluted barrel that

locked into a milled receiver. The magazine was mounted on the top of the receiver. There was a simple bipod located on the front of the barrel and the buttstock was a metal tube with a pad for the shoulder. A pistol grip and trigger assembly were located on the bottom of the receiver where the buttstock joined it. A gas cylinder ran beneath the barrel where it joined the receiver and the gas port at the bottom front of the barrel. The gun was fired from the shoulder or from the hip.

The U.S. Army and Marine Corps tested the gun in May and June 1917. Following some changes, the Berthier light machine gun was approved by both services, and the army ordered 5,000, with a further 2,000 for the navy and the marines. The contract was awarded to Hopkins & Allen Co. of Norwich, Connecticut, which controlled the Berthier manufacturing rights, with the provision that it not interfere with rifle production that was already planned. Financial problems arose, production of the gun was never started, and all contracts were canceled. Only a few trial models were ever produced in the United States.

Browning Machine Gun, Model 1917

On May 1, 1917, an army board held tests to investigate and recommend machine guns to be used by the U.S. Army. The water-cooled machine gun perfected by John Moses Browning proved, at the conclusion of the test, to be the most effective weapon of its type. Browning, a lifelong inventor and gunsmith, had been closely associated with the army's development of automatic weapons for many years and was familiar with the requirements of the services for a reliable and durable weapon. He had designed a heavy machine gun using the .30-caliber service round already in manufacture for the service rifle model of 1903. Similar to the German Maxim gun and the British Vickers, it was a water-cooled, belt-fed, recoil-operated gun. With a rate of fire of 500 rounds per minute, the Browning M1917 was an ideal weapon from the army's standpoint.

The weapon consisted of a rectangular milled receiver, at the rear of which was a metal pistol type grip and trigger. On the top of the receiver was an adjustable sight. The whole top was hinged to enable it to swing up and provide access to the mechanism. A charging handle was located on the right side of the receiver. A barrel was attached to the front of the receiver, and it, in turn, was surrounded by a cylindrical hollow jacket holding the water used to cool the weapon while firing. This jacket had a filling plug on the top and a drain plug at the bottom. A hose could be attached to this drain, and when heated by firing, the steam created could be vented into a water can and later added back to the jacket. The gun itself weighed thirty pounds when the water jacket was empty and thirty-six pounds, nine ounces when filled.

The weapon fired from a tripod, which could be adjusted to sit level on all terrain. It could also be adjusted to different heights, and the mechanism allowed the gun to be traversed and elevated to adjust its fire. The tripod weighed fifty pounds and was easily detached from the gun when required.

The gun was fed by means of a cloth belt holding 250 cartridges at a weight of fifteen pounds, seven ounces. This belt entered the gun on the left side of the receiver. A charging handle pulled toward the gunner and released several times until the first round in the belt was engaged. The bolt assembly caught the base of the round and extracted it from the cloth loop in the belt. It then carried the round beneath the belt and inserted it into the chamber, at the same time cocking the firing mechanism. When the trigger was squeezed, the firing pin moved forward and discharged the round. The recoil of the discharge caused the bolt assembly to move backward, carrying the spent casing out of the chamber. As the bolt assembly moved upward to engage another round, the spent casing was extracted and fell through an opening in the bottom of the receiver. The cycle was repeated as long as the trigger was depressed or until the belt ran out. Over 30,000 of these guns were ordered by the army in 1917 alone.

Browning Automatic Rifle

Another weapon brought to the 1917 army tests by J.M. Browning was his automatic rifle (BAR). Designed as a light machine gun to be used in assaults and fired from the hip or shoulder, it also performed extremely well. The BAR was gas operated and fed by a box magazine which held twenty rounds of service ammunition. The gun, with a loaded magazine, weighed seventeen pounds three ounces.

Its outward appearance was that of a slightly oversized rifle. It had a rectangular milled receiver to which fitted a wooden buttstock of typical shape. The bottom of the receiver had an opening for the magazine and behind that was an integral trigger guard and trigger assembly. There was an adjustable sight on the top of the receiver and a charging handle on the right side. There was also an opening on the right side for the ejection of spent shell casings. The barrel extended from the front of the receiver, and directly beneath it was the gas cylinder, which extended most of the length of the barrel. A wooden handgrip around the barrel assembly directly in front of the receiver covered half the length of the barrel.

To fire, a magazine was fitted into the opening and the charging handle pulled to the rear, thus cocking the firing mechanism. When the handle was released, it moved forward, and the bolt engaged a round and guided it out of the magazine and into the chamber, while locking the bolt securely. When the trigger was depressed, the firing pin struck the round, causing it to fire. As the round passed through the barrel, some of the propellent gas was siphoned off into the gas tube and pushed the piston inside to the rear. This in turn pushed back the bolt, which retracted the spent shell while also recocking the firing mechanism. As it traveled further back, it struck the ejector, which caused the spent shell to be thrown out the port, and as the bolt reached the limit of its travel, it again flew forward repeating the cycle. There was a selector switch that allowed the gun to fire single shots or to fire automatically as long as the trigger was held.

Chauchat Machine Gun

The Chauchat automatic rifle model of 1915 was the final evolution of a quest begun by the French military in 1903 for a light machine gun. It was an air-cooled gun that operated by means of recoil. It was developed by a commission of four men—Chauchat, Suterre, Ribeyrolle, and Gladiator—and was sometimes referred to as the CSRG. It was designed to be cheap and easy to manufacture, as is evidenced by the simplicity of its components, basic tube metal and crudely shaped wood.

It is perhaps the most readily recognizable machine gun of World War I. The receiver and barrel were both tubes of metal set in line with one another. Beneath this ran a sheet-metal support frame that had a square wooden pistol grip attaching to a metal rigger guard. Directly in front of this was a bulbous wooden handle intended to be used to steady the weapon while firing, and in front of this was the unique crescent-shaped magazine. A wooden buttstock sat at the rear. All of these were directly in line with one another making a very narrow weapon. There was a bipod constructed of two metal rods in front of the magazine. An adjustable rear sight on the top of the receiver tube completed the weapon. With a full magazine of twenty rounds, the weapon weighed twenty pounds thirteen ounces. Initially manufactured for the French 8mm ammunition, it was later made to use the American .30 caliber as well. It had the dubious honor of being the most unreliable machine gun of World War I, despite its use by the French and American forces as the light machine gun of choice.

The weapon could be set to fire single shots or to operate fully automatically. The mechanism was cocked by pulling the charging handle on the right side of the receiver. Depressing the trigger released the bolt, which traveled forward, picking up a cartridge from the magazine and guiding it into the chamber. As the bolt locked in place, the firing pin struck the cartridge, firing it. The recoil of the discharge caused the bolt to travel backward, removing the spent case from the chamber to the ejection port where it was expelled. The recoil continued to drive the mechanism rearward until it had again been cocked and the cycle repeated.

Colt Machine Gun, Model 1917

Another of John Browning's designs, the gas-operated Colt machine gun M1917, was originally patented in 1895 and built by Colt's Patent Fire Arms Manufacturing Company of Hartford, Connecticut. It went through several design refinements and was first adopted for use by the navy, which purchased it for landing parties. Its successful use in the Spanish-American War led the army to order some of its own.

The gun was designed to be fired from a tripod because of the mechanical action when the gun fired. The escaping gases from the firing of the round were funneled into a small port on the bottom of the barrel. This pressure caused an actuating arm to swing downward from the barrel expelling the used cartridge, recocking the mechanism, and chambering a new round. The gun was fed from a cloth belt containing 250 rounds. Its cumbersome early design required the gunner to insert the brass tab on the leading edge of the belt into the gun, while at the same time pulling the actuating arm downward by hand to cock the weapon and chamber the first round. This design did not allow the weapon to be fired from the prone position and required its constant elevation on its tripod.

The gun consisted of a rectangular receiver, on top of which was set the barrel running the entire length of the receiver. The front half of the barrel was fluted to help dissipate heat. At the rear of the receiver was a solid pistol grip with a trigger below. The adjustable sight was located on the barrel at the rear. Just visible at the front of the receiver and below the barrel was the end of the actuating arm, which opened and closed over the gas port. A mount on the left side accepted a box that held the cloth ammunition belt, which entered from that side. Both the empty belt and spent cases were thrown out on the right side. The entire actuating arm was visible when the gun was fired as it swung downward, often creating clouds of dust, and if set up improperly, striking the ground and digging a small furrow. For this reason, it was nicknamed the "Potato Digger."

The gun weighed thirty-five pounds and the tripod fifty-six pounds. The belt was an additional fifteen pounds. Even though hopelessly outdated, this first-generation heavy machine gun was ordered in large quantities by the army at the outbreak of the war. But all new orders were canceled almost at once, and it was relegated to training. Even so, 1,500 guns were delivered. It was purchased by many South American countries as well as Russia, and the Canadian Expeditionary Forces' first contingency to arrive in England was armed with these as well.

Hotchkiss Machine Gun, Model 1914

At the beginning of World War I the French suffered from a serious shortage of automatic weapons. Accordingly, they issued orders for thousands of machine guns, including the Hotchkiss gas-operated model 1914, based on an earlier design of 1897. The Hotchkiss M1914 proved to be a most reliable and effective weapon. One section of French troops, armed with two M1916s, resisted determined German attacks at Verdun for two days, each gun firing over 75,000 rounds without mishap.

A true heavy machine gun, the gun itself weighed fifty-four pounds, and the tripod that it used weighed another fifty-four pounds. It was fed with twenty-four round flat metallic strips or from an articulated metal belt, which held 250 rounds. A loaded strip weighed one pound, twelve ounces. It was designed to fire the French 8mm round; however, to alleviate supply problems, the Americans also had versions manufactured in .30 caliber.

The gun consisted of a rectangular receiver with an integral loop handle at the rear. A pistol grip that incorporated a trigger guard and trigger was placed at the bottom of the receiver. The barrel extended from the front of the receiver and had five parallel "rings" at the point where it joined. These provided extra surface to aid in the air cooling of the barrel. An adjustable sight sat on top of the receiver directly behind these rings. Below the barrel was the gas cylinder, joined to the barrel by a rather bulbous coupling allowing the escaping gas from the barrel to enter the gas cylinder.

As with other gas-operated weapons, the Hotchkiss was loaded with a strip of ammunition on its left side, and the charging handle was worked by hand to cock the mechanism and load the first round. When fired, the escaping gas entered the cylinder and forced the gas piston therein rearward. This piston was connected to the bolt, which in turn moved backward, ejecting the spent case, advancing the strip, and recocking the mechanism. It then traveled forward to reload the weapon and if the trigger was still depressed, allowed the firing pin to strike the cartridge, repeating the cycle. Until the adoption of the Browning M1917 and the Vickers, the Hotchkiss M1914 was the heavy machine gun used by the AEF. Twelve of the twenty-eight divisions in France were also armed with this weapon.

It is worth noting that a lighter (thirty-pound) version of this weapon, with similar appearance, but hand carried and using a bipod instead of the cumbersome tripod, was designed by an American, Lawrence Benet, in about 1900. It was known as the Light Hotchkiss in England and was used throughout the war by British tanks. In the United States it was called the Benet-Mercie and was adopted by the army in 1909. Although light, its inconsistent performance during Pancho Villa's raid on Columbus, New Mexico, in 1916, caused it to be discarded in favor of other less complicated types.

Lewis Machine Gun, Model 1917

First invented by Col. Isaac Newton Lewis of the United States Coast Artillery in 1896, the Lewis gun, as it came to be known, was an intriguing design that incorporated both a gas system with a piston and a clock spring mechanism in the same weapon. Weighing thirty-six pounds eight ounces, with a loaded "pan" of forty-seven rounds adding an additional one pound twelve ounces, the Lewis gun was de-

signed for mobility and could be used by one man rather than a crew of three. In 1911, Lewis had traveled to Washington to show prototypes of his weapon to the army staff, and on June 7, 1912, Capt. Charles D. Chandler became the first man successfully to fire an automatic weapon from an aircraft in flight, using a Lewis gun. None of this, however, convinced the army to adopt the weapon. Lewis then went to Europe, where he met with greater success. After showing the weapon in several cities, he founded the Armes Automatiques Lewis Company in Belgium. Initial production was in Liége; the gun's manufacture later moved to England and was taken up by the Birmingham Small Arms Company (BSA). The British enthusiastically adopted the weapon as the standard infantry light machine gun and also as an aircraft weapon. Lewis machine guns were considered prized trophies by the German troops whenever they were fortunate enough to capture them. Ironically, the United States Army used them solely as training weapons for the entire war.

The appearance of the Lewis gun is unique. It had a long narrow receiver, which appeared oval when viewed in cross section. Beneath this was a wooden pistol grip with an integral trigger guard and a trigger assembly and in front of that a circular protrusion that housed the clock spring. The gun had a traditional wooden buttstock. Early models had a cylindrical metal oil reservoir mounted in the stock, and in 1916, designers developed a spade grip, which saw extensive use in the aircraft version. At the rear of the receiver there was an adjustable sight mounted on top, and the distinctive ammunition drum or "pan" sat on the front of the receiver. The infantry version of the Lewis gun held forty-seven rounds, while the aircraft version held ninety-seven and had a higher profile. At first glance, the barrel appeared to be that of a cannon. However, it was actually a steel jacket surrounding an aluminum sleeve with numerous vanes that radiated outward from the center like spokes on a wheel. This sleeve surrounded the barrel and allowed for the passage of air to cool the barrel. Suspended from the front of the barrel jacket was a folding bipod, which swung up underneath when not in use.

The operation of the weapon was a mechanical feat. A drum of ammunition was placed on a fixed post on the top of the receiver. The gunner pulled the charging handle to the rear, which cocked the mechanism and at the same time rotated the drum slightly. This rotation allowed the first round to drop from the central core of the drum into the receiver. When the trigger was depressed, the bolt went forward by means of gears operated by the clock spring. This carried the round into the chamber and caused the firing pin to strike the cartridge. After the bullet passed down the barrel, the exhaust gases were vented off into the gas cylinder and pushed the gas piston to the rear. This forced the bolt backward, ejecting the spent casings, rotating the drum, loading another cartridge, and at the same time winding the clock spring. This process was continued until the trigger was released. There was no single shot option with the weapon, for it was designed only to fire fully automatically.

Marlin Machine Gun, Model 1918

In an effort to ease the dearth of machine guns in the American Army, the Marlin-Rockwell Corporation developed the Marlin machine gun. Essentially, it was a modification of the Colt M1917 that did away with the operating lever and its downward swing and replaced it with a straight-line gas piston. This hybrid was the Marlin aircraft machine gun.

Weighing twenty-four pounds, the gun had the same outward appearance as the Colt, with the addition of a large charging handle on the right side next to the pistol grip. To fire the weapon, one grabbed this handle and drew it to the rear. The internal mechanism worked the same way except that instead of forcing the lever below the barrel downward, the expelled gasses pushed a piston located below and parallel to the barrel to the rear. This in turn ejected the spent casing, cocked the weapon, and carried a new cartridge into the chamber. In 1918, trials were made with the Marlin machine gun as a tank machine gun by adding aluminum cooling fins to the barrel, a modification that worked well. The Marlin was not used as a ground gun after that. However, it was one of the better aircraft machine guns of the period. A total of 38,000 were manufactured by war's end.

Vickers Machine Gun, Model 1915

When the United States Army conducted its test of machine guns in 1914, the board unanimously found the Vickers gun to be superior to the other seven competitors. In December 1916, the army placed an order for 4,000 of these guns to be manufactured by the Colt Company.

By September 1918, over 12,000 had been made in the United States.

The gun was designed by Sir Hiram Maxim, a French Huguenot whose family moved to America, where he first learned the art of gunsmithing. He eventually was knighted by the British crown after revolutionizing the machine gun and changing forever the face of warfare. The Vickers M1915 was a modification, in conjunction with Messrs. Vickers and Sons of London, on the design of his highly successful model 1908 Maxim gun, the standard machine gun of the German Army throughout World War I. The Vickers was a recoil-operated, water-cooled heavy machine gun. With a weight of thirty-two and a half pounds for the gun with its water jacket empty, and a tripod weighing upward of forty pounds, it was able to deliver sustained accurate fire. It was belt fed from a 250-round cloth belt, which, when loaded, weighed sixteen pounds.

The Vickers had a rectangular milled receiver, with a recoil spring covered by a steel stamping located outside on the left side. There was a small charging handle on the right rear of the receiver. There was an adjustable sight on the top, rear of the receiver, along with a set of handles. Between these was a trigger, which was depressed with the thumb to fire the weapon, while at the same time pulling a safety to the rear with the index fingers. This rather awkward position did much to prevent accidental discharges of the weapon. An opening through the receiver from left to right accommodated the ammunition belt. The circular water jacket was fluted longitudinally. A filler plug sat at the front, offset from top dead center, with a drain port on the bottom, which also allowed a hose to be attached so that steam could be vented into a water can and reused when it condensed. The tip of the barrel protruded from the front of the water jacket several inches. It was located in the lower portion of the jacket and had one of several designs of flash suppressor attached.

To fire the weapon, an ammunition belt was inserted on the right side of the receiver. The gunner pulled the charging handle to the rear and released it until a round was seated in the mechanism and the weapon cocked. When the trigger was pressed, the firing pin struck the round, which traveled down the barrel. Excess gas pressure caused the recoil, which pushed the bolt to the rear, at the same time extracting the spent case from the chamber and extracting a new cartridge from the belt. As it traveled its full backward path, it recocked the mechanism and fully ejected the spent round. Then, it dropped the new round into place and seated it in the chamber with the mechanism ready to repeat the process as long as the trigger was held down.

The Vickers was the standard heavy machine gun of the British forces through the First World War and up to the 1960s. It was adopted and used by American troops along with the Browning M1917. The Vickers, in a lighter version, was the primary machine gun used in Allied airplanes during the war.

11mm Vickers Aircraft Machine Gun

At the United States entry into the war, tests were ordered to determine the feasibility of rechambering the Marlin machine gun to fire .433-caliber incendiary ammunition for aircraft use. It was found to be too difficult to rework the Marlin, so experiments were carried out on several Russian contract Vickers at the Colt plant. One of these guns was already bored for 11mm French ammunition. Some minor changes were made in the lock mechanism and the resulting tests were so successful, that the remaining 800 Russian guns were modified to the 11mm standard, thus saving considerable time and money.

World War I saw a proliferation in the design and use of machine guns. Those discussed above were the major weapons used by the United States, although numerous other designs and models were employed during the course of the hostilities.

Michael J. Knapp

Bibliography

Chinn, George M. *The Machine Gun.* Washington, DC: Government Printing Office, 1951.

Crowell, Benedict. *America's Munitions, 1917–1918.* Washington, DC: Government Printing Office, 1919.

U.S. Army Ordnance Department. *Handbook of Ordnance Data.* Washington, DC: Government Printing Office, 1919.

McIntyre, Frank (1865–1944)

Frank McIntyre was born in Montgomery, Alabama. A West Point classmate of General Pershing, upon graduation in 1886 he was assigned as a second lieutenant to the 19th Infantry in Texas. After duty at Fort Leavenworth, Kansas, and as an instructor at West Point, he was part of the first expedition to Puerto Rico in the Spanish-American War. McIntyre served briefly on the staff of the military governor of Puerto Rico and later participated in the fighting at Subig Bay in the Philippines. In 1902, he returned to the United States and was selected as a member of the first War Department General Staff. In 1908, McIntyre was assigned to the Bureau of Insular Affairs and soon became acting chief and then chief of the bureau.

During the First World War, as well as serving as chief of the Bureau of Insular Affairs, McIntyre was chief military censor from June 1917 to June 1918. He was then appointed executive assistant to Gen. Peyton C. March, chief of staff of the army.

In 1919, McIntyre was awarded the Distinguished Service Medal "For exceptionally meritorious and distinguished service as Executive Assistant to the Chief of Staff. His breadth of view and sound judgement have contributed materially to the formation and carrying out of policies essential to the operation of the military establishment."

After the war, Major General McIntyre rejoined the Bureau of Insular Affairs, where he remained as its head until his retirement in 1920. He died in Miami Beach, Florida on Feb. 16, 1944.

James L. Collins

Bibliography

Fredericks, Pierce G. *The Great Adventure.* New York: Dutton, 1960.

Pershing, John J. *My Experiences in the World War.* New York: Stokes, 1931.

McNair, Lesley James (1883–1944)

Lesley James McNair was born in Verndale, Minnesota. When he graduated from the United States Military Academy in 1904, he was eleventh in a class of 124 cadets. Assigned as a second lieutenant of artillery to Fort Douglas, Utah, he was promoted to first lieutenant in 1905 and detailed to the Ordnance Department. Back in the Field Artillery in 1908, he spent four years with the 4th Field Artillery Regiment at Fort D.A. Russell, Wyoming. In 1912, he went to France, where he served as an observer of the French artillery.

Upon his return to the United States in 1913, McNair was assigned to Fort Sill, Oklahoma, and served in the American expedition to Veracruz, Mexico, the following year. In 1916, he again went to Mexico with the Punitive Expedition led by Gen. John J. Pershing.

In 1917, Major McNair was appointed to the staff of the newly formed 1st Division, which sailed for France on June 14. As one of two assistant chiefs of staff (George C. Marshall was the other) of the division, he soon gained a reputation as an able trainer and artillery expert. In August 1917, McNair was transferred to the training section of the general headquarters of the American Expeditionary Force (AEF). He was soon promoted and became the youngest brigadier general in the AEF. He was the senior artillery officer in the Training Section and as his subsequent citation for the award of the Distinguished Service Medal stated, "He was largely responsible for impressing on the American Army sound principles for the use of artillery and for improving methods for the support of infantry. . . ."

Upon his return to the United States after the Armistice, he reverted to his permanent grade of major and held various assignments, mainly in the area of training. In World War II, he became the commander of the Army Ground Forces, responsible for training the millions of soldiers in the United States. As part of the deception plan for the Allied invasion of Normandy in 1944, Lieutenant General McNair went to England, ostensibly to command a fictitious army group to convince the Germans that the Pas de Calais region would be the area of the main attack. On a visit to France to observe frontline units near Saint-Lô, General McNair was killed on July 25, 1944, by a bomb from an Allied plane that fell short of its target.

James L. Collins

Bibliography

Greenfield, Kent Roberts, Robert R. Palmer, Bell Wiley, II. *The Organization of Ground Combat Troops: United States Army in World War II*. Washington, DC: Historical Division, United States Army, 1947.

Marshall, George C. *Memoirs of My Services in the World War 1917–1918*. Boston: Houghton Mifflin, 1976.

Weigley, Russell F. *History of the United States Army*. Bloomington: Indiana University Press, 1984.

March, Peyton Conway (1864–1955)

Brilliant, decisive, and caustic, Peyton Conway March's reputation as a soldier and administrator was well known among his fellow soldiers. For heroism at the Battle of Manila in the Spanish-American War, MajGen. Arthur MacArthur recommended March for the Medal of Honor and later paid tribute to his abilities: "No officer has rendered more efficient or brilliant field service than he to the Island of Luzon." George C. Marshall, on the other hand, acknowledged March as an able administrator but often saw him lacking in tact and sensitivity when dealing with others.

March's place in history was predicated upon his role as the army's chief of staff during World War I. Under his leadership and against strong opposition, he reorganized the General Staff and established himself and the staff system as the supreme governing body of the Army. His reorganization for "efficiency" helped the Army to send men and supplies quickly to France and plan the complicated process of demobilization. Although March was responsible for setting up the Army's current administrative system, he remains unknown to many Americans who often equate World War I with John J. Pershing and the AEF.

March was born to an upper-class family. His father, Francis Andrew March, was a renowned philologist, and his mother, Margaret Conway March, was related to many of the aristocratic Virginia families. March's family expected him to obtain an education and excel in some field of endeavor. Complying with parental expectations, after graduating from Lafayette College, he attended the United States Military Academy at West Point and graduated in 1888. For the next decade, he served as an artillery officer in an army governed by a cadre of Civil War veterans.

His chance to demonstrate his soldierly abilities came during the Spanish-American War and Philippine Insurrection. Following completion of a two-year course at the Artillery School in March 1898, he took command of the Astor Battery. Leading this motley group of Ivy Leaguers and seasoned veterans from the Canadian, British, and American armies, as well as the New York Police Force, which he and his officers recruited and trained, March led a successful charge against the enemy in what turned out to be a war that was already over. March later acknowledged privately that "it was only the abominable marksmanship of the Spaniards that saved our lives. . . ." Once the Astor Battery was dissolved, March returned to the Philippines as an aide to MajGen. Arthur MacArthur, first as a major, then a lieutenant colonel in the 33d Volunteer Infantry. During this time he received five more citations for gallantry.

Much of March's administrative talents were developed while serving in the Philippines and as a member of the first War Department General Staff. In the Philippines, he was the provincial governor of Abra Province and commissary general of prisoners. As a member of the General Staff, he became educated in the intricacies of army bureaucracy. His position gave him opportunities to make important personal contacts, including Newton D. Baker, who later became secretary of war.

In spite of administrative assignments, March still spent much of the period between 1903 and 1917 as a troop commander. On the eve of World War I, Col. March commanded the 8th Field Artillery and by the fall of 1917 was a major general in France in the American Expeditionary Force (AEF) and commander of its artillery. While in France, he spearheaded the development of the artillery program.

In February 1918, Secretary of War Newton D. Baker recalled him to Washington to assume the post of army chief of staff. Prior to March's appointment, Hugh L. Scott, Tasker H. Bliss, and John Biddle served as chief of staff and worked to mobilize, train, and deploy the military overseas. Poor organization coupled with the brief time necessary to shift the nation's economy from peace to war caused many errors and organizational failures. Baker believed that March had the right mix of boldness and simplicity to get the army on track.

On March 4, 1918, March became the acting chief of staff; in May, he was promoted to the temporary rank of full general and was appointed chief of staff. First on his agenda was to mobilize, train, and transport the necessary troops to France in order to break the stalemate and win the war. Upon assuming command, March streamlined the General Staff and coordinated efforts between it, the War Department, and the army. By the late spring of 1918, under his direction, the AEF grew to over 2 million members and the total size of the army doubled.

March was also instrumental in initiating a number of key reforms. In the War Department, he placed the supply functions under the assistant chief of staff and negated the power of the administrative bureau chiefs. Structural reform in the army included creating the new branches of the Air Corps, Chemical Warfare Service, Tank Corps, and Motor Transport Corps based upon their technical functions. Moreover, he eliminated the distinctions between the Regular Army, the National Army, and the National Guard. Other actions included shortening the course at West Point to one year and making army information more readily available to the public by scheduling regular press conferences. These changes helped solidify the new position of the chief of staff of the army, which March codified in General Order 80. He was now the "key" adviser to the secretary of war and the army's senior soldier.

These changes sent ripples up and down the army's chain of command. Most notably, the commander of the AEF, John J. Pershing, disliked March's disregard for tradition and his aggrandizement of power. Pershing felt that the chief of staff should subordinate himself to the commanding general. In time, March and Pershing openly fought over the future strength of the AEF. Pershing demanded a 100-division force; this overlooked the nation's ability to carry out such a program. March refused. Only the Armistice stopped the Pershing-March imbroglio from escalating into a major showdown.

Following the end of the war, March directed the demobilization and transition of the army to a peacetime footing. Pershing and others continued to harangue March over his actions. This opposition, along with congressional disapproval of a 500,000-member army and a universal training program, helped March opt for retirement on June 30, 1921.

During his retirement, March traveled, studied, and remained an advocate for a strong military. After his travels to Europe, he settled in Washington and began to work on his memoirs. Largely in response to Pershing's attacks on the War Department about administrative failures during the war, many officers, including Gen. Douglas MacArthur and Secretary of War Patrick J. Hurley, importuned March to "write the real story." In 1932, March published *The Nation at War*. More than just a vindication of the War Department's role in World War I, the work attacked Pershing's shortsightedness and opened old wounds. March continued to follow national events such as World War II and the Korean War. In 1953, President Dwight D. Eisenhower presented March with a

Congressional Resolution thanking him, not for his active service, but rather for "his selfless and patriotic interest in the United States Army since his retirement." March still did not receive the credit due him for his singular achievements as chief of staff.

Nevertheless, there were many who were aware of March's contributions and were not afraid to say so. Newton D. Baker described March's accomplishments to the chairman of the Senate Military Affairs committee in 1919 as the main sparkplug behind the War Department's effort. "He organized, expedited, and stimulated our mobilization at home," Baker explained, "and made effective that support and cooperation upon which, under modern war conditions, the success of the commander in the field belongs." "His driving power," Baker added, "his high professional equipment, and his burning zeal imparted to our whole machine an impetus which never slackened." A crusader for the army, March played a major role in bringing the military into the modern age. Tough, decisive, and strong-willed, Peyton C. March handled the "hilt of the sword" (the army administrative structure) with deftness and courage.

Mark R. Grandstaff

See also UNITED STATES ARMY GENERAL STAFF

Bibliography

Coffman, Edward M. *The Hilt of the Sword: The Career of Peyton C. March*. Madison: University of Wisconsin Press, 1966.
———. *The War to End All Wars: The American Military Experience in World War I*. New York: Oxford University Press, 1968.

Marine Corps, United States

See entries under UNITED STATES MARINE CORPS

Marne, Second Battle of the

The American Expeditionary Force (AEF) began its involvement in the Second Battle of the Marne (also known as the Aisne-Marne offensive), on May 31, 1918, and it terminated in late July 1918. Elements of nine U.S. divisions were engaged. The 1st, 2d, 3d, and 4th (Regular) divisions and the 26th National Guard—and to a lesser degree, the 28th, 32d, and 42d National Guard, plus the 77th Division, National Army, all participated.

The Second Battle of the Marne began when the German Army undertook its third major offensive of 1918, on May 27, with upward of fifty divisions in two armies, the First commanded by Gen. Otto von Below and the Seventh under Gen. Max von Boehn. The armies were concentrated in a period of eight days and nights, between Pontoise and Reims. They amassed twenty-eight divisions, of which twenty-three were those that pierced the British Fifth Army formation in March 1918. These two armies were considered by the German High Command as storm troops, trained in the relatively new tactics, sometimes called the "Hutier" tactics. The German Army was at its strongest in World War I at this point in time, having altered the situation in the East and having removed almost all the divisions once facing the now defunct Russian Army.

The two French armies facing this awesome German array, the Sixth commanded by Gen. Denis Duchêne and the Fifth under Gen. Alfred Micheler, had eight divisions between them, in four separate corps, one of which was the British IX. The Sixth Army, whose general was then in Paris visiting "the ladies," faced the major portion of the offensive where fifteen German divisions, each superior numerically to any French division, were opposite four French divisions. The first two days of the offensive brought the Germans close to Soissons on their right flank and within five miles of Reims on their left. By May 31, 1918, they were at Château-Thierry, the farthest point of their advance. And they were driving hard for Paris, the heart of France. If Paris should fall, France would probably fall with it. After arriving at the southern edge of the Château-Thierry bridgehead, the 7th Motorized Machine Gun Battalion of the 3d Division, U.S. Army, through sheer willpower, managed to keep the Germans on the north side of the Marne River. They maintained their position until the balance of the 3d Division began arriving on or about June 2, each unit of the division taking over positions in the line and restraining the German advance at the Marne. The Germans then pushed westward, north of the Marne River, which ran, at that point, almost directly east and west. The French forces in that pathway were unable to maintain formation, and even the elite French Alpine "Blue Devils" were forced to retreat.

Nothing of substance stood between the Germans and Paris.

Meanwhile, the 2d Division of the U.S. Army was hastily transported from its bivouac, about thirty-five miles north of Paris, to an area just north and west of Château-Thierry. By June 1, most of their units were finally assembled in the area after a ride in camions that would never be forgotten by the riders. The two infantry brigades were astride the Metz-Paris road, the 4th (U.S. Marines) in the north and the 3d (U.S. Army) on the south side of the road with no divisional artillery as yet. As with the 3d Division, the Germans were still trying to make progress forward on this front, but they were stopped from further encroachment by the 2d Division. The German Army made its furthest penetration, about thirty miles from Paris, at Les Mares Farm, where the 55th Company of U.S. Marines held the line. The rapidity and accuracy of the American rifle fire caused the Germans to retreat and re-form and then to go on the defensive.

Within a few days the French Sixth Army sent orders for the 4th Marine Brigade to assault the woods in front of their position on June 6, 1918. The marines did, and on that day incurred more casualties than any American unit had suffered since the Civil War. Over 1,000 marines were killed or wounded on that day alone. But the marines took some of Belleau Wood and held it until they were finally able to oust all Germans from it on June 25, 1918, when Belleau Wood was "all Marine." Even Gen. Robert L. Bullard, who was no friend of the marines, wrote: "The Marines didn't 'win the war' here [Belleau Wood]. But they saved the Allies from defeat."

The German Army tried its final offensive of the year and the war when they began, on July 15, the so called "Peace Offensive." The attack was launched between Château-Thierry on the German right flank and Massiges on their left, about fifty-five miles in distance. They had about thirty divisions in that area for the attack.

One of the American divisions on the line was the 3d Division. One of its regiments, the 38th Infantry, which was defending a massive loop in the river, earned the *nom de guerre* for which they still take great pride, "Rock of the Marne." No German unit was allowed to penetrate the 3d Division's designated position. The division beat back every German attempt at crossing, even guard divisions, and eventually the German Army gave up the unequal challenge.

After a few weeks rest and refit, the 2d Division, which had been in rest bivouac just behind the French lines, and the 1st Division, which had held the Germans at Cantigny a few weeks earlier, were hurriedly marched to the Bois de Retz, just south and west of Soissons. There they were combined with the 1st Moroccan Division of the French Army on the morning of July 18, and the three divisions, many without proper rest from their exertions in getting to the point of departure, advanced in line, the 1st being on the left flank, the Moroccans in the center, and the 2d on the right. Although stoutly resisted by the Germans, the three managed to overtake their assigned objectives easily on the first day. The second day was a bit more difficult, but again the regiments advanced across open fields under tremendous shell, machine gun, and rifle fire and overran the German defensive positions. The Moroccan division, which included the remnants of the French Foreign Legion as well as the native units from North Africa, were acknowledged as the best France could offer. By this date, every American soldier knew what could be expected from the two "race-horse" divisions, the 1st and 2d. The two were constantly struggling to outperform each other, and the same could be said of each brigade in each division as each contested its counterpart. This made for two outstanding divisions since each would only accept the concept that the other might be its only equal in the AEF.

Eventually, the Battle of Soissons was considered by both sides as the turning point of the war. Pershing called it "the Gettysburg of this war," and Chancellor Georg Hertling of Germany once wrote of the Second Marne and especially of the Battle of Soissons: "At the beginning of 1918 I was convinced that before the first of September our adversaries would send us peace proposals. We expected grave events in Paris for the end of July. That was on the 15th. On the 18th even the most optimistic of us knew that all was lost. The history of the world was played out in three days."

The 26th Division had replaced the 2d Division in the Château-Thierry sector in late June and on July 18, as part of I Corps, the division advanced through the ground that the Germans had held in June against the violent, continuous attacks of the two brigades of the 2d Division. Though the going was not too difficult during June 18, June 19 and 20 were an entirely different matter. The division reported severe fighting all the afternoon of June 19, and by the late afternoon of the next day they had advanced approximately two miles from their original jump-off positions. During the next five days of their advance, they encountered continued obstinate German resistance. On June 24, the town of Epieds was taken by the 26th Division and then retaken by the German 5th Guard Division and then retaken by the 26th that same day. By the end of the day, the division had achieved nearly a dozen miles and its objective. The retreating enemy had crossed the Ourcq River, just five miles to the division's front, shortly afterward. The 26th was relieved by the 42d Division on the morning of July 26.

In the meantime, the 4th Division also was part of Hunter Liggett's I Corps during the early part of July. During the action of July 18–22, the division did not function as a whole. Instead, units of the division were brigaded with French troops. The 7th Brigade, which included the 39th Infantry, was part of the French II Corps. The rest of the division was brigaded with the French VII Corps approximately four miles further south. The division was in large part composed of inexperienced draftees but was able to fight with distinction and courage in the troop's first engagement of the war. In spite of horrendous weather conditions, the weary troops of the divided division accomplished their mission, though not without suffering serious casualties. The men of the division went forward and seized the most important objective, the Soissons–Château-Thierry highway, but they paid too high a price for French mistakes and their own reckless behavior. French officers and men regarded the Americans with both admiration and regret, for while their actions were heroic, they were not the disciplined behavior of soldiers.

By early August, the Second Battle of the Marne had passed into history, but not before four more American divisions—the 42d, 28th, 32d, and 77th—had participated during the final days and also with great success. Never again would the Germans launch an offensive during World War I.

George Clark

See also Belleau Wood, Battle of; Cantigny; Château-Thierry Sector; Soissons

Bibliography
American Battle Monuments Commission. *26th Division Summary of Operations in the World War*. Washington, DC: Government Printing Office, 1944.
Bach, Christian. *The Fourth Division*. Garden City, NY: Garden City Press, 1920.
Bullard, Robert L. *American Soldiers Also Fought*. New York: Longmans, Green, 1936.
U.S. Army. *Order of Battle of the U.S. Land Forces in the World War*. Washington, DC: Government Printing Office, 1931.

M

Marshall, George Catlett (1880–1959)

In the annals of American military history, General of the Army George Catlett Marshall continues to stand as the most towering military-strategic leader of World War II. His efforts to prepare the U.S. Army for war during the period 1939–1941 are a remarkable example of effective strategic leadership. What is not widely understood, however, is the degree to which his approach was shaped by his experiences in World War I. Those events left a deep impression on him, particularly in regard to the unpreparedness of the United States. He was driven by the desire to enter the next war, if it came, at a much higher state of military readiness. This sense of mission drove his actions during the period between the two wars and sustained his efforts in the face of profoundly discouraging circumstances.

In 1901, Marshall graduated from the Virginia Military Institute. He received a commission as a second lieutenant in the U.S. Army in 1902 and served briefly in the Philippines. In 1903, he returned to the United States to study at the Army Staff College and the Army School of the Line at Fort Leavenworth, Kansas, from which he subsequently graduated first in his class. He then held a variety of posts in the United States and returned to the Philippines in 1913. During the course of training exercises on the islands, his genius for planning became obvious to everyone involved.

The dominant impression held by Marshall in 1917 was of his nation's complete unpreparedness for war. A full year was required after Congress had declared war in 1917 before even a crudely formed army could be deployed. Marshall sailed for France with the 1st Division, a hastily formed group of regiments thrown together at the port of embarkation to form a "division." Marshall, as G-3 (chief operations officer) met the other members of the division staff on board the *Tenadores* headed "over there." There was confusion not only about division organization, but also how the division was supposed to operate in war.

Until 1917, the U.S. Army had been, in essence, a constabulary force of companies and battalions; with entry into the First World War the troops were hastily thrown together to form regiments, brigades, and divisions without the experience of large-scale maneuvers to develop the doctrine, procedures, tactics, or techniques of large-unit operations. In point of fact, there was no American experience to draw upon beyond the Civil War. Fortunately, most of the initially deployed U.S. divisions had almost a year to get organized and trained behind the lines before being committed to battle *en masse*. Even so, Marshall observed that American casualties were excessive because of a lack of sustained training in both small- and large-unit operations.

Not only did the American Expeditionary Force (AEF) arrive in France disorganized and untrained, but it also arrived largely unequipped. U.S. war production never had time to gear up. As a result, the AEF fought primarily with French- or British-made guns, ammunition, rifles, airplanes, supplies, and equipment. While American factories eventually produced mountains of supplies and equipment, the public was generally unaware that very little of it ever got into the hands of our soldiers before the war ended—a situation that was not lost on Marshall.

The 1st Division set up shop in the area around Gondrecourt. Almost immediately Marshall was ordered to join Col. John M. Palmer, Pershing's chief of operations, in a survey of the entire Neufchâteau region in preparation for the arrival of three divisions later in the year. Back with the 1st Division, Marshall, as its chief of operations, concentrated on the most basic training of what he still viewed as raw recruits. Being close to General Pershing's General Headquarters (GHQ) at Chaumont, the general was a frequent visitor. Under tremendous pressure himself, those visits only added to the strains of the lower echelons. On Oct. 3, 1917, after a particularly difficult review and scathing criticism from Pershing, which Marshall found totally uncalled for, the captain stunned his colleagues by taking Pershing to task for his comments. The outburst apparently made a favorable impression

on the general and proved the beginning of a close association.

On Jan. 16, 1918, the 1st Division went into the line between St. Mihiel and Pont-à-Mousson. In March, Lieutenant Colonel Marshall was temporarily detached to lecture on 1st Division operations at the American General Staff College at Langres. He was unable to complete the series, for the Germans launched their last major offensive, and he was called back to his division at once. During this period Marshall honed his already outstanding skills, participating in the planning of the successful assault on Cantigny.

That was his final assignment with the 1st Division, for on July 13 he was ordered to duty at GHQ. There Marshall immediately began planning for the reduction of the St. Mihiel salient, scheduled for September 12. Planning for that operation proved far more complex than it might have because American troops were also committed to participate in the Meuse-Argonne offensive, slated to begin on September 26. That meant, first and foremost, that the initial attack at St. Mihiel had to succeed as planned. It also meant more than 400,000 troops and over 2,700 guns would have to move at night under blackout conditions—many across the rear of the attacking army. Working with Cols. Hugh Drum and Fox Conner, the maneuver was accomplished with surprisingly few setbacks, due in large part to Marshall's flexibility and willingness to improvise.

Despite the success of his staff work, Marshall was keenly aware that the lack of Allied unity of command, or even effective coordination before mid-1918, had greatly aided the Germans, prolonged the war, and caused needless casualties on a massive scale. He came away strongly believing in the need for Allied unity of effort both in the military-strategic direction and theater operations should there be another war.

From 1919 to 1924, Marshall was Pershing's senior aide. As executive officer of the 15th Infantry Regiment, Marshall served in China during the period 1924–1927. He returned to the United States in 1927 and assumed command of the Infantry School at Fort Benning, Georgia, a post he held until 1932. Later he worked with the Civilian Conservation Corps and served as senior instructor for the Illinois National Guard.

Marshall was promoted to brigadier general in 1936 and in 1938 was appointed chief of the War Plans Division of the War Department. Soon thereafter he became deputy chief of staff of the army. On Sept. 1, 1939, the day Germany invaded Poland, General Marshall became chief of staff of the U.S. Army. As such, he directed major strategic planning for the war in Europe and the Pacific.

Marshall retired in late 1945, but President Truman appointed him as a special envoy to China to attempt to mediate between Nationalist and Communist forces. In 1947, he returned to the United States to become secretary of state. During his tenure there he developed the European Recovery Program, better known as the Marshall Plan. His last governmental position was that of secretary of defense, an office he held from 1950 to 1951. Marshall died on Oct. 16, 1959.

John T. Nelson

See also CANTIGNY; MEUSE-ARGONNE CAMPAIGN; ST. MIHIEL

Bibliography

Marshall, George C. *Memoirs of My Service in the World War 1917–1918*, ed. by James L. Collins. Boston: Houghton Mifflin, 1976.

Pogue, Forrest C. *George C. Marshall: Education of a General*. New York: Viking Press, 1963.

Marshall, Thomas Riley (1854–1925)

Thomas Riley Marshall served as vice president of the United States from 1913 until 1921. A lawyer, Marshall had been governor of Indiana from 1909 to 1913. His administration of the state was competent and mildly progressive, if hardly outstanding. In 1912, he was Indiana's favorite-son candidate for president at the Democratic National Convention in Baltimore. Following the exhausting convention floor battle, which resulted in Woodrow Wilson's nomination for the presidency, Thomas Taggart, the Democratic Party boss of Indiana, was able to engineer Marshall's nomination for the vice presidency. Wilson, when told by his managers that Marshall was to be his running mate, is reported to have protested that the Indianian was "a very small-caliber man." However, when informed that Marshall's nomination was advisable to balance the ticket, Wilson agreed.

Wilson's offhand appraisal and acceptance of Marshall set the tone for the vice president's eight years in office. Marshall's basic problem was that no one took him seriously, perhaps not even Marshall himself. Though their formal relations were correct and outwardly cordial, Wilson in fact simply ignored the vice president. There is no record that the President ever consulted Marshall on any matter of consequence. Marshall had to content himself with his constitutional duty of presiding over the Senate, which he did with competence and humor, through the tumultuous years of the administration. A good public speaker and a very likeable person, Marshall was a loyal supporter of Wilson's domestic and foreign policies and spent much time defending them on the hustings and the lecture platform.

Marshall echoed Wilson's, and the nation's reluctance to become involved in World War I during the period of American neutrality. He also reflected the fervent patriotism of both after the decision for American belligerency had been made. He became a favorite speaker at rallies for the sale of war bonds and other patriotic events. When Wilson went to Europe in 1919 to attend the Paris Peace Conference, Marshall firmly rejected suggestions that he assume the duties of the presidency, a position that foreshadowed his stance following the onset of the President's catastrophic illness in September and October 1919. The vice president presided over cabinet meetings for a time during Wilson's absence in Europe but then characteristically decided that his presence was unnecessary.

Marshall's election for, and tenure in the vice presidency were all too typical of the incredibly casual and irresponsible way in which American political leaders have selected candidates for that office and treated them while in power. Woodrow Wilson's health was fragile at best and the assassination of William McKinley as recently as 1901 should have reminded Wilson and his advisers of the necessity of a carefully considered choice. If they really believed that Marshall was a total nonentity, they were grossly negligent in allowing his renomination in the critical year of 1916. However, there is no evidence that Wilson or anyone else seriously considered the possibility of replacing Marshall on the Democratic Party ticket that year. Thus the stage was set for the crisis in presidential leadership, which began with Wilson's crippling illness in late 1919.

John E. Little

Bibliography

Marshall, Thomas Riley. *Recollections of Thomas R. Marshall, Vice President and Hoosier Philosopher: A Hoosier Salad.* Indianapolis: Bobbs-Merrill, 1925.

Thomas, Charles Marion. *Thomas Riley Marshall, Hoosier Statesman.* Oxford, OH: Mississippi Valley Press, 1939.

Masaryk, Tomáš Garrigue (1850–1937)

The son of a Slovak father and a germanized Czech mother, Tomáš Garrigue Masaryk was the principal architect of the Czechoslovak state established in 1918. After training at Charles University in Vienna, Masaryk taught philosophy at Prague. He was active as a publicist for the Czech cause, criticizing the pro-German and anti-Slav policies of the Vienna government. He served in the Austrian Reichsrat from 1891 to 1893 and again from 1907 to 1914. Late in 1914, Masaryk left for western Europe, Russia, and the United States, where he organized support for the cause of Czech independence. In 1917, he established the Czechoslovak National Council (CNC) in Paris with Edvard Beneš and M.R. Stefanik. At the Pittsburgh convention of the CNC in 1918, Masaryk was instrumental in convincing the large Slovak community in the United States to support a future federated Czecho-Slovak state. Masaryk also championed the idea of a Czecho-Slovak exile army to oppose the Central Powers. Eventually, the Czech Legion was formed. A small force was raised for service in France and a considerably larger number was gathered from Czechs and Slovaks among the Austro-Hungarian POWs in Russia. The latter became embroiled in the Russian Civil War when they attempted to leave for France via Siberia. The existence of the so-called Czech Legion prompted Allied recognition, in 1918, of the Czechoslovak National Council as a virtual Provisional Government in exile. Masaryk returned to Prague in December 1918 as president of Czechoslovakia, a position he held until 1935.

Austere and single-minded, Masaryk had courage and integrity. His erudition and humanistic ideals caused many to apotheosize him the "philosopher-king." However, Masaryk's unwillingness to recognize the separate identity of the Slovaks foreshadowed continuing difficulties for Czechoslovakia. His principal contribution was his inspiring conviction of the historical and moral right of his people to independence.

M. B. Biskupski

Bibliography

Kovtun, George J., ed. *The Spirit of Thomas G. Masaryk, 1850–1937: An Anthology.* New York: St. Martin's Press, 1990.

Masaryk, Thomas G. *The Making of a State.* New York: Stokes, 1927.

Winters, Stanley B., Robert B. Pynsent, and Harry Hanak, eds. *T.G. Masaryk (1850–1937).* 3 vols. New York: St. Martin's Press, 1990.

Zeman, Zbynek. *The Masaryks.* London: Weidenfeld & Nicolson, 1976.

Masses, The

Founded in January 1911 as a magazine devoted to spreading the gospel of the cooperative commonwealth to the working class, *The Masses* underwent a critical transformation when Max Eastman was named editor in December 1912. Henceforth, *The Masses* distinguished itself as a conspicuously left-wing periodical of popular nondoctrinaire socialism and free artistic expression. Owned and published collectively by its editorial board—Eastman, Floyd Dell, John Reed, Art Young, Robert Minor, Louis Untermeyer, among others—it avoided commercial obligation to stockholders and advertisers.

With the outbreak of war in Europe, the magazine shifted its focus away from proletarian-revolutionary socialist goals toward an effort to keep America out of war, devoting an entire issue at the close of 1916 to antipreparedness. Faced with the Espionage Act's curtailment of First Amendment rights, Eastman and Dell decided that continuing to publish for the cause of peace took precedence over any confrontation with government censors. Before mailing the August 1917 issue, *The Masses'* business manager met with George Creel, chairman of the Committee on Public Information, who gave assurance that nothing in the issue violated the law. Yet the Espionage Act empowered Postmaster General Albert S. Burleson to withhold objectionable material from the mail, and after inspection, the August issue was deemed "unmailable." Eastman went so far as to offer to delete any offending material, but Burleson refused to specify which passages violated the law.

The Masses was the first major magazine to be halted by the Post Office, and the editors went to court to argue, successfully, for an injunction, issued by U.S. District Judge Learned Hand and to bring their case to public attention. At the trial the government was obliged to identify the treasonable material: the illustrations by Henry Glintenkamp as well as cartoons by Boardman Robinson and Art Young, a satire on the Root Mission to Russia, articles and a poem defending conscientious objection and expressing admiration for draft resistance. Upon appeal by the Post Office, the Circuit Court immediately overturned Hand's decision. When the September issue of *The Masses* was presented for mailing, the postmaster revoked its second-class mailing privileges claiming that it no longer qualified as a monthly periodical since it had missed its August issue. The postmaster's ruling was upheld on appeal, and the next three issues of *The Masses* were sold only on newsstands, economically crippling the magazine. The Post Office had dealt the fatal blow; *The Masses* ceased publication with its December 1917 issue.

While its editors survived two conspiracy trials, in August and November 1918, *The Masses* had been reorganized and revived under a distinctly more cautious guise, now called *The Liberator,* under the control of Eastman and his sister Crystal. The inaugural issue in March 1918 looked much like its predecessor, with art and literature printed alongside political commentary, but Eastman's deliberate efforts to avoid provoking the censors eventually led to Reed's resignation from the editorial board, although he continued to contribute articles. The impetus for the new publication was Reed's reports on the Bolshevik Revolution and Eastman's desire to spread news of Russia in America.

John Saltmarsh

Bibliography

Eastman, Max. *Love and Revolution: My Journey through an Epoch.* New York: Random House, 1964.

Fishbein, Leslie. *Rebels in Bohemia: The Radicals of the Masses, 1911–1917.* Chapel Hill: University of North Carolina Press, 1982.

Zurier, Rebecca. *Art for the Masses (1911–1917): A Radical Magazine and Its Graphics.* Los Angeles: University of California Press, 1985.

M

Mayo, Henry Thomas (1856–1937)

Commander of the Atlantic Fleet during World War I, Henry Thomas Mayo, like so many of his fellow officers in the post-Civil War navy, spent several decades of uneventful service in a variety of ship and shore billets. After graduating from the Naval Academy in 1876, Mayo saw duty in the Asiatic Squadron, spent considerable time with the Coast and Geodetic Survey in Puget Sound and off the coast of Maine, participated in the 1883 Greely Relief Expedition to the Arctic, and served on several small warships as well as on the battleship *Wisconsin*.

Mayo's first sea command came in 1907 aboard the protected cruiser *Albany* which was stationed on the West Coast and saw duty in Central American waters. Two years later, he became captain of the armored cruiser *California*, similarly stationed on the West Coast. In 1911, Mayo took command of the Navy Yard at Mare Island. While in command, he so impressed visiting Secretary of the Navy Josephus Daniels that Mayo was appointed aide for personnel at the Navy Department in April 1913, with a promotion to rear admiral. Thrust into the highest command levels of the navy, Mayo was able to obtain a coveted sea command with promise of substantial professional advancement: commander of the Fourth Division, Atlantic Fleet stationed in the Caribbean.

This too might have been a routine, albeit professionally important, assignment. But any routine ended in April 1914, when, in response to the arrest by Mexican authorities of some of his sailors who were securing oil and mail at Tampico, Mayo demanded not only their release but also a public apology. This precipitated a brief international crisis which almost led to war, though events in Veracruz later that month overshadowed the Tampico incident. Admiral Mayo emerged from the affair as a public hero and an officer assured of rapid advancement in the navy. By June 1916, he was both a full admiral and commander of the Atlantic Fleet.

During World War I, Admiral Mayo was commander of all American warships in Atlantic and European waters. Completing reports on the fleet's wartime activities dominated his postwar duties, but he was able to take the important step of incorporating aircraft into the fleet maneuvers held off Cuba. When the navy's fleet structure was reorganized in January 1919, Mayo became commander of the combined United States Fleet, a position he held until his June assignment to the General Board for his last months on active duty. He retired in December 1920 with the rank of rear admiral. Mayo died on February 23, 1937.

Donald A. Yerxa

Bibliography

Bradford, James C. "Henry T, Mayo: Last of the Independent Naval Diplomats." In *Admirals of the New Steel Navy: Makers of the American Naval Tradition*, ed. by James C. Bradford. Annapolis, MD: Naval Institute Press, 1990.

Reynolds, Clark G. *Famous American Admirals*. New York: Van Nostrand, 1978.

Merchant Marine

America's merchant marine played a central role in World War I. Attacks on U.S. merchant ships were the direct catalyst for American entry into the war. In the face of great losses of Allied tonnage to German submarines, American merchant ships were vital to the winning of the war, and the war radically changed the relationship between the merchant marine and the United States government.

The decades preceding the war had seen a great decrease in the American-flag merchant marine, even as its foreign trade increased. The merchant fleet of 1910 was only half the size of that of 1870, and instead of carrying 38 percent of America's exports, it only carried 9 percent. America's merchant marine was privately owned, and received very minimal subsidies from the government. Federal law had always required that American-flag ships be American-built, and U.S. shipyards could not compete with those of some other nations, especially since the transition from sail to steam and from wood to iron and steel.

During the Civil War, many shipowners in the North had transferred their ships to foreign registry to avoid the danger of Confederate attack and the certainty of high insurance rates, and this practice continued, for purely economic reasons, long after that war ended. The United States was embarrassed during the Spanish-American War, when foreign merchant ships were needed to transport U.S. troops and to refuel naval vessels, but the situation remained the same until 1914.

The outbreak of war in Europe created a novel and urgent situation. The United States was neutral, and most Americans assumed that the country would remain aloof from the conflict. America, now an industrial as well as an agricultural giant, suddenly had the opportunity to expand greatly its exports to Europe—and indeed to the rest of the world—but there was no way to get the goods across the ocean. Ships of both sides scurried to friendly or neutral ports to avoid capture. British and German ships were docked side by side in American harbors. Even those American shipowners who thought that their neutral flag would keep their vessels safe were prevented from sailing by a dramatic increase in insurance rates to prohibitive levels.

The Wilson administration and Congress were quick to respond to this emergency. In August 1914, the first month of the war, the government offered marine insurance to U.S. ships at reasonable rates and enacted the Ship Registry Law. This act allowed foreign-flag ships of any age to transfer to American registry and authorized the President to suspend the long-standing rule that all personnel on American ships be U.S. citizens. Since American ships were not being attacked at the time, many owners were induced to transfer their vessels to American registry. Half of all American-owned, foreign-flag ships "returned" in the first two months of the war.

While President Wilson insisted that it was our right and our duty as a neutral nation to trade with both sets of belligerents, naval realities dictated otherwise. The British Navy dominated the surface of the sea, preventing the German merchant marine from operating at all. German ships that had taken refuge in American ports at the outbreak of hostilities were destined to remain there until the United States entered the war, at which time those ships were seized by the American government as enemy property. Neutral ships were kept from trading with Germany by a British blockade.

Allied merchant vessels did operate, often convoyed by the Royal (British) Navy, but were vulnerable to attack by German submarines. Over the course of the war, Britain lost 7.8 million gross tons of merchant shipping to enemy action. This represented 44 percent of her prewar tonnage. Further tonnage was diverted for use as troop transports and cruisers. About 15 million tons of the world's merchant shipping was destroyed in World War I.

The reduced supply of shipping, combined with the increased demand for goods, drove freight rates up to astonishing levels. The wheat rate rose 1,250 percent; the cotton rate increased 2,100 percent. The private sector seized this opportunity for profit.

Besides transferring hundreds of thousands of tons of American-owned shipping from foreign registry, Americans began to buy foreign-owned ships to bring under the U.S. flag, until other governments prohibited such sales. American vessels were diverted from coastwise to foreign trade routes, and American shipyards were working to capacity to build privately ordered ships.

President Wilson was as anxious as anyone that the United States take full advantage of the world maritime crisis, but he felt that the rapid expansion of our merchant marine should be sponsored by the government. Private maritime interests, of course, were opposed to having the government as a commercial rival, and Wilson's proposal to have the government buy and operate merchant ships did not pass Congress at first. But the changing nature of the war, and American's changing attitudes concerning our possible involvement, especially after the sinking of the *Lusitania* in 1915, led to the passage of the Shipping Act of 1916.

While the Shipping Act was intended by its authors to influence the postwar international maritime situation in ways favorable to American interests, it won broad support as an aspect of military preparedness, and its chief impact came through its creation of the U.S. Shipping Board and of the Emergency Fleet Corporation (EFC) to purchase, construct, and operate merchant vessels in time of "national emergency."

As it turned out, the EFC only had a few months to start building a merchant marine before the United States entered the war. In early 1917, Germany took a desperate gamble. To ensure winning their planned spring offensive, they abandoned the humanitarian restraint that Wilson had insisted they observe and resumed "unrestricted submarine warfare" against both Allied and American merchant shipping carrying supplies to their enemies. Unless Wilson were to impose a Jeffersonian-style embargo on U.S. foreign trade—which was repugnant to him philosophically and economically suicidal—there was no choice. In spite of a filibuster by isolationist senators, Wilson ordered the arming of American merchant ships in February. This did not deter German attacks, and the United States declared war in April.

Since the EFC was preparing for war from its inception and since it achieved little before the United States entered the war, its career may be considered as one seamless unit. It must, however, be noted that the declaration of war was followed by legislation increasing the powers of the EFC and of the President over the maritime industry.

Precious months were lost as the heads of the Shipping Board, William Denman, and the Emergency Fleet Corporation, Gen. George Goethals, debated whether the fleet should be built of wood (Denman) or steel (Goethals). This question was not as absurd as it appears because the Navy had priority on the best steel shipyards and steel was in short supply. However, the United States had many idle shipyards suited to building wooden ships and people with the skills to build them. The concern was winning the war, and it was not critical that the Emergency Fleet be competitive in peacetime or even remain seaworthy for more than the three years or so that the war was expected to continue. In fact, so desperate was the government for tonnage, that the EFC did build over 600 small steamships with either wooden or concrete hulls, though the bulk of the production was steel.

The Shipping Board was placed under the EFC and with the resignations of both Denman and Goethals, Edward N. Hurley, former chairman of the Federal Trade Commission, was put in charge, given sweeping powers and a budget that eventually reached $4 billion. Because American participation in the war only lasted nineteen months, Hurley's chief contribution to victory was in commandeering, purchasing, and chartering huge quantities of existing ships or ships already under construction.

Expecting a long war, the EFC began an ambitious program to build huge new shipyards—most notably Hog Island on the Delaware River—and hired 300,000 workers to build a projected 3,000 vessels. Mass-production methods were adopted, with identical parts being manufactured all over the country. The time for building a ship was cut from about a year to as little as one month. The standardized ships—forever after called "Hog Islanders"—measured 535 feet long. They

M

were designed with few curves to speed construction and with silhouettes intended to confuse a U-boat as to which end was the bow and which the stern.

Hurley also negotiated agreements with the seamen's unions that raised wages, allowed a 50 percent bonus for service in a war zone, and compensated crewmen for lost personal effects in case of a sinking. In return, the unions relaxed their apprenticeship rules, allowing the recruitment of more men.

In 1918, Hurley was replaced by Charles Schwab, who moved to end waste and inefficiency in the shipbuilding program. Schwab ended the use of cost-plus contracts, which had encouraged waste at the taxpayers' expense. He had every ship inspected by three different authorities and gave his own money as bonuses to workers who exceeded their quotas.

The war ended rather abruptly, and Schwab had to decide whether to complete the hundreds of ships then under construction. Not only were they completed, but over 800 more keels were laid after the Armistice and those steel ships completed. Only the wooden and concrete ship orders were canceled.

Postwar realities proved this to be a great mistake. In spite of Schwab's economies, the ships built by the EFC cost $200 per ton, were relatively slow, and proved unable to compete in the postwar maritime economy. The EFC had built a total of 7 million tons, while the enemy had sunk a modest 339,000 tons of American shipping. The United States had the world's largest fleet in the 1920s—five times its prewar size—but there was much less demand for shipping, and what there was went to the modern ships built after the war by those nations whose ships had been sunk and not replaced during the war. When the government tried to sell its ships to private owners after the war, there were no buyers. Only when World War II began were these surplus ships again in demand, as, indeed, were the methods used to build a huge merchant fleet in a short time.

Allan A. Arnold

See also EMERGENCY FLEET CORPORATION; SHIPPING BOARD

Bibliography

Albion, Robert G., and Jennie B. Pope. *Sea Lanes in Wartime*. New York: Norton, 1942.

Allin, Lawrence C. "Ill-Timed Initiative: The Ship Purchase Bill of 1915." *American Neptune* (July 1973).

Lawrence, Samuel A. *United States Merchant Shipping Policies and Politics*. Washington, DC: Brookings Institution, 1966.

Safford, Jeffrey J. *Wilsonian Maritime Diplomacy, 1913–1921*. New Brunswick, NJ: Rutgers University Press, 1978.

Thurston, William N. "Management Leadership in the United States Shipping Board 1917–1918." *American Neptune* (July 1972).

Williams, William J. "The American Concrete Shipbuilding Program of World War I." *American Neptune* (Winter 1992).

Meuse-Argonne Campaign

This final and most important campaign was fought by the American Expeditionary Force (AEF) in World War I from Sept. 26, 1918, to Nov. 11, 1918. The area is located in southeastern France, twenty miles north of Verdun. The geography of the Meuse-Argonne sector, about eighteen miles east to west, is ideal for defense, deadly for the attacker.

The area is divided by three dominating features: the heights of the Meuse along the east bank of the unfordable Meuse River, the hills of Montfaucon in the center, with approaches from east and west, and the rising terrain of the heavily wooded Argonne Forest, a plateau in the west of the zone. The Germans had built a strong interlocking network of defenses in this area for three years. They had constructed a defensive zone from the line of contact. Three east-west belts of manned fortifications, to the north of the Allied (French) entrenchments, lay athwart the zone given the AEF.

The supreme commander of Allied forces, French Marshal Ferdinand Foch, assigned the AEF to an offensive in the Meuse-Argonne just as the Americans were beginning their offensive (by the newly created First Army) in the St. Mihiel region some sixty miles to the south. Reluctantly, Gen. John J. Pershing, the commander-in-chief of the American Expeditionary Force, accepted the task. This required the AEF to conduct one major offensive while moving many of its command and support organizations to take part in the "grand offensive" designed by Marshal Foch. The American First Army, in the act of organizing its forces and

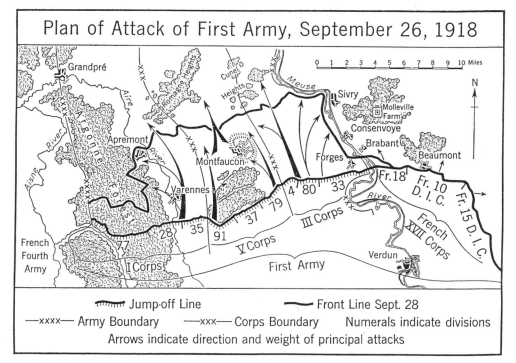

Plan of Attack of First Army, September 26, 1918

Jump-off Line   ▬ Front Line Sept. 28
—xxxx— Army Boundary   —xxx— Corps Boundary   Numerals indicate divisions
Arrows indicate direction and weight of principal attacks

Meuse-Argonne. Taken from American Armies and Battlefields in Europe, *American Battle Monuments Commission, Government Printing Office, 1938.*

conducting the St. Mihiel offensive, was given the task of seizing the Meuse-Argonne.

Three corps headquarters, fifteen divisions, Allied fire support, and a whole skein of logistical and communication units had to displace forward. The totals involved were approximately 600,000 men moving in, 220,000 moving out. Also moving into the sector were 3,980 artillery guns and 90,000 horses; these moved in a steady stream, forwarding personnel, equipment, and the great requirement of 900,000 tons of ammunition and supplies over three muddy farm roads and three single-track railroads. For secrecy, this huge and diverse agglomeration of men, animals, equipment, and materiel had to be moved only at night. Col. George C. Marshall, newly assigned to the staff of the First Army, planned and coordinated the move. It is to his great credit that the displacement succeeded in the time required.

The assemblage of logistical, communication, and administrative elements for the Meuse-Argonne campaign, mostly part of the Service of Supply (S.O.S.), was itself a complex arrangement, linking hundreds of agencies together by a fragile network of roads and rails. Ammunition depots were established at twenty-

four locations to store and send forward 40,000 tons of ammunition per day. Railheads at nineteen points provided automatic resupply to the army's twelve ordnance depots, which issued and retrofitted weapons and equipment; nine gas and oil depots provided fuel; nine furnished quartermaster supplies (food and forage); twelve, engineer supplies (bridging, road materials, lumber); eight, water supplies; six, chemical warfare supplies. Thirty-four evacuation hospitals were set up; 164 miles of light railway lines were constructed or rebuilt. Personnel replacement camps were built, and freight regulating stations were expanded. Aircraft gathered at forward fields. Of the 668,000 personnel assigned to the Service of Supply, 291,000 were engaged in direct logistical support of the First Army, including personnel of the three divisions used as laborers in the rear.

The American First Army headquarters moved to Souilly on Sept. 21, 1918. At midnight on September 22, Pershing, who had assumed command of the First Army while continuing to command the AEF, accepted the responsibility for the entire zone formerly held by the French Second Army. This zone included the entire sector from the Moselle River west to the juncture with the French Fourth Army on the west of the Argonne Forest. The First Army also assumed operational command of the French II Colonial Corps and XVII Corps, both corps, along with elements of the American III Corps, defending territory from the east bank of the Meuse to the Moselle. Because many American divisions had been shipped hurriedly to France, to offset the German buildup in the spring of 1918, most were without their supporting tanks, artillery, or aircraft. By prior agreement of the Allies, the bulk of these weapons systems were provided by the French. Approximately one-half of these weapons were manned by Americans.

The First Army planned to attack across the zone with three corps abreast, each with three attacking divisions. (An American division consisted of about 28,000 men, twice the number of that of Allied and German divisions.) The plan was for I Corps, commanded by MajGen. Hunter Liggett, to drive north along the Aire valley, also clearing the eastern portion of the Argonne Forest. V Corps, under the command of MajGen. George Cameron, was to advance to Montfaucon and to seize that commanding terrain after bypassing it on both flanks. III Corps, under the command of MajGen. Robert Bullard, on the right was to advance in "sector." A major mission of the two flank corps was to assist the advance of V Corps by outflanking Montfaucon. The corps was to come abreast at the corps objective line, running east-west north of Montfaucon, and then it was to guide the advance of V Corps along the high ground to seize objectives on the army's first-phase line— east and west from Cunel to Romagne. The First Army desired to reach the corps objective line in one day, the army's first-phase line the second day, a projected advance of ten miles. Further advances to link up with the French Fourth Army at Grandpré were to be directed as the battle progressed. Pershing was aware of the restrictive terrain and the extensive defenses that he planned to overcome in such a short time. However, he counted upon surprise to overwhelm the outnumbered defenders before reserve forces could be moved into the Meuse-Argonne to strengthen their positions.

A total of 2,775 artillery pieces, more than half of them manned by the French, were registered to support the attack. The density of artillery was one gun for approximately ten yards of front. The French had supplied 189 light tanks to attack in coordination with the advance of the infantry; 142 of these tanks were manned by Americans. Fuel had been stockpiled in the forward area by the commander of the tankers, LtCol. George S. Patton. Poised at support airfields were 821 aircraft, 604 of which were piloted by Americans. The attacking infantry were armed, primarily, with the British Lee-Enfield rifle. But the Americans had little or no experience in active combat; only four divisions had had any front-line duty. Over half of the troops were recent draftees; some had only received individual training. A few said later that they had never fired their rifles before. As "H Hour" approached, all of the 100,000 men in the first wave felt tension as they crouched in the night, waiting for the order to move out. The troops were tired from the hasty move forward; many were sick with Spanish Influenza, which was raging in Europe.

The "Yanks" had overwhelming superiority in fighting strength—on the order of eight to one, depending upon who and what is counted. They were far stronger in artillery, in aircraft, and in tanks—the Germans had no tanks in this campaign. The enemy, however, were in strong fortifications; the Argonne Forest was a maze of camouflaged, mutually supporting strong points. The front from Verdun to the Argonne Forest was the responsibility of German Army Group "von Gallwitz." Along this front were eighteen divisions, with twelve more in reserve, most of the reserve clustered around Metz. Five divisions were in defensive positions in the sector that the Americans would attack; these enemy were under the command of the German Fifth Army. It was estimated by the AEF that the Germans could reinforce with nine additional divisions within three days.

The enemy troops were of poor quality; a large number were Saxons and Austro-Hungarians, who were of doubtful dedication to the German cause. These enemy divisions were at one-third their authorized strength. However, the command structure was effective, and the German High Command had stressed the need for stubborn defense in Lorraine. The entire German Army was at risk, the High Command stated, if its southern flank were turned.

On Sept. 26, 1918, at 5:30 A.M., U.S. forces attacked in the Meuse-Argonne, moving behind a rolling barrage about 100 yards to their front. In a heavy fog mixed with cordite smoke, accompanied by the incessant roar of artillery, the "doughboys" climbed in and out of great shell holes, bunching up at the enemy barbed wire; someone cut some of the wire, some worked their way over and through it; whistles sounded in the mist and shouting. Then the enemy machine guns opened up, and their artillery and trench mortars joined in firing heavy defensive barrages. Crouched in their positions in the Argonne from La Harazee east to Vauquois was the 1st Prussian Guards Division. Behind them on the Kriemhilde Stellung (line) were the 5th Prussian Guards, both good units but low in strength. The other enemy units were reserve divisions; these were rated as "poor in morale and effectiveness." They, however, were fighting tenaciously. Among the advancing American troops, cries went up for aidmen and litters as the Germans attempted to stem their advance. Some men in the assaulting units became lost; others drifted into the low ground, where they gathered in groups. But Yankee spirit was up, and the pressure of those advancing from behind pushed the line of contact forward.

The initial German defenses were quickly overrun—the enemy had manned these lightly and would make his stand on the first prepared *stellung*. The tanks supporting the American attack came forward slowly, many breaking down a few hundred yards into the attack. Control of the supporting artillery was poor because it was difficult to ascertain the exact locations of the attackers. The artillery continued firing blindly their prearranged barrages. Some of the infantry insisted their own artillery was firing into them.

At 9:30 A.M., the sun broke through the mist. Whenever the doughboys burst into a patch of open terrain, they were hit by frontal and flanking fire from hidden machine guns. The "green" troops moved fast until they hit the first effective enemy fire; then, according to friendly and enemy observers, they tended to mill about, remaining in the killing zone, taking no action to silence the fire. This was clearly a failure in small-unit leadership and training.

On the east, III Corps made the best early advance, its forward elements moving abreast of Montfaucon. However, its 33d Division, along the Meuse, was pounded by heavy artillery fires and drenched with poison gases. In the center, V Corps was mostly pinned down on the approach ridges of Montfaucon. I Corps, on the left, was advancing slowly, with high casualties from the hidden defenses in the Argonne Forest. On the second day, in hard and bloody fighting, V Corps took Montfaucon, and the other corps came abreast. The First Army was only a day behind the optimistic time schedule,

but casualties were high, and the attacking units were lacking support. The American offensive had run out of steam.

To get the offensive moving again, the AEF moved the best of the veteran division from St. Mihiel into the fighting line, replacing the depleted attacking forces. Reconstituting the support forces was a more difficult problem. Rain continued to fall, and the roads and trails through no-man's-land turned into quagmires. Craters and shell holes from earlier fighting had limited the capacity of these routes at the beginning of the offensive. By this time they were virtually impassable. Long lines of traffic were stalled for days. Wounded could not be evacuated; food and ammunition could not get forward. By September 28, the First Army was literally dead in its tracks.

Overworked engineers struggled to shore up the roadbeds with any solid materials they could find. Reserve units, headquarters personnel, and even malingerers drifting rearward were pressed into service to move the traffic and shore up the roadway. By the evening of September 28, all artillery had been shifted forward. Divisions continued to report communication and supply problems through the end of the month. Many units were without food for days. Tank strength had been reduced to one-third of its original complement by breakdowns and by accurate enemy artillery fire. Frontline units conducted local attacks, repulsed counterattacks on September 29 and 30, and improved their defensive positions. Units belatedly received supplies and some replacements; patrols were sent forward, and the men gained some badly needed rest. The AEF had undergone its baptism of fire. It had met the challenge of the Meuse-Argonne and advanced. Badly mauled and mired in the mud in front of the main German defenses, the Kriemhilde Stellung, it was hardly a victorious army.

The German strength facing the Americans from the Moselle to the Argonne as estimated by AEF intelligence (G-2) on Oct. 4, 1918, increased to twenty-three divisions in line and in local reserve. In the next week, this strength increased to twenty-seven divisions, with eleven between the Meuse and the Argonne. Many of these divisions were very low in strength; however, they had orders to defend to the last man.

On October 4, the First Army resumed its offensive—with rested troops and wiser, somewhat more experienced leaders. These attacks were being made against the main German de-

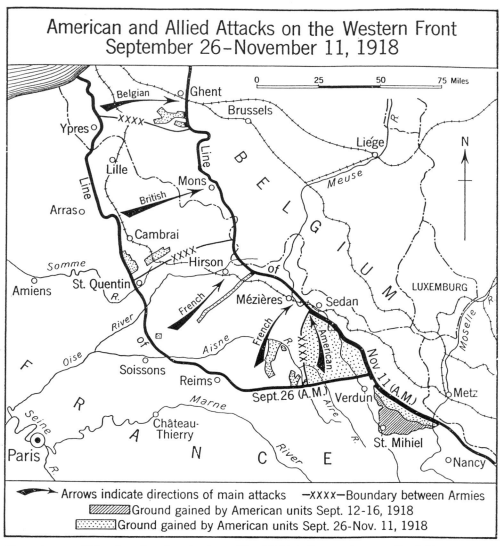

American and Allied Attacks on the Western Front September 26–November 11, 1918

0   25   50   75 Miles

Belgian — Ghent
Ypres — Brussels
Lille — Liège
Mons
Arras — British
Cambrai
B E L G I U M
Somme — Hirson
Amiens — St. Quentin
French — Mézières — Sedan
LUXEMBURG
Aisne — French
Oise — River of
Soissons
Reims — Sept. 26 (A.M.) — Verdun — Nov. 11 (A.M.) — Metz
Marne
Château-Thierry
Paris — F R A N C E — St. Mihiel — Nancy
Seine
N

→ Arrows indicate directions of main attacks —XXXX—Boundary between Armies
▨▨▨ Ground gained by American units Sept. 12-16, 1918
⬚⬚⬚ Ground gained by American units Sept. 26-Nov. 11, 1918

Meuse-Argonne. Taken from American Armies and Battlefields in Europe, *American Battle Monuments Commission, Government Printing Office, 1938.*

fenses of the Kriemhilde-Stellung. Key positions in this defensive complex were the heights of Cunel in III Corps' zone, Romagne (including the Côte Dame Marie) in V Corps' sector, and Hill 272, St. Juvin, and the Argonne ridges in I Corps' zone. These defenses were supported by interlocking direct fires, observed artillery fire from flanking promontories and from the heights east of the Meuse. The First Army directed all commanders to use more fire support, to use smoke on enemy observation points, and to maneuver so as to avoid flanking fire. III Corps and V Corps, acting in concert, were to seize both the Cunel heights and those on the east of Romagne. V Corps and I Corps were to

take the Romagne heights. All corps were to maximize counterbattery artillery fire, and to make maximum use of gas shells.

The infantry attack moved out at 5:30 A.M., Oct. 4, 1918, and immediately made heavy contact with the enemy all along the front. III Corps fought its way up the approaches of the Cunel heights but stalled under heavy fires from the hills. V Corps also moved forward on the low ground southwest of Cunel but was halted by bitter fighting. I Corps made the greatest advance on the left of the army, driving down the Aire valley with tanks leading behind rolling artillery barrages. The 77th Division on the left of I Corps was still struggling in the forest with minor gains. The offensive was stopped again, but heavy fighting continued as divisions consolidated their gains.

Galled by Allied demands for greater American progress, General Pershing decided to broaden his attacking zone and bring more U.S. forces into the offensive. He appointed Liggett commander of the First Army and created a Second Army, under command of Bullard. The First Army was to continue to attack to seize the heights of Cunel and Romagne and to take Grandpré without delay. On October 14, the weary and ill American troops drove into the teeth of the defensive fires. V Corps took the heights of Romagne quickly, and this broke the "crown" of the Kriemhilde defenses. Then III Corps took the Cunel defenses, while, in hand-to-hand fighting, I Corps drove the Germans out of Grandpré. The Americans now held the high ground, and their artillery could strike the vital German railroad through Sedan. But the army was nearing combat ineffectiveness. Casualties had reached 100,000, with half these losses due to the influenza epidemic. The Second Army also was stalled on the heights east of the Meuse. Despite demands from Pershing to continue the offensive, Liggett rested and refitted his army and visited his subordinate commands. The First Army prepared to continue the attack on November 1 to uncover the heights overlooking Sedan. The Second Army was to make a coordinated attack into the Woëvre plain. The AEF at this point was a far more professional fighting force than that which had begun the campaign. It was said that the Americans had "learned to fight by fighting."

At 3:30 A.M. on November 1, the black of night burst bright as day as the last barrage of the war struck the enemy positions like a million hammers. Gun barrels glowed as the artillery rained fire on enemy battery locations, reserve positions, crossroads, headquarters, bridges, and areas suspected of being occupied by reserve units. The infantry assault jumped off at 5:30 A.M., the American troops following the customary rolling barrage. This time, however, smoke and gas were adjusted along the flanks of the advancing forces. The artillery preparation had devastated the enemy's defenses. The attackers closed quickly on their objectives; active strong points were invested by direct-fire weapons, while the bulk of the troops swung around these and surged forward. The German defenses broke, the defenders fleeing north-ward, followed by the fast-moving Yanks. III Corps quickly took Andevaune, protecting V Corps' flank. V Corps stormed and seized the heights of Barricourt. After supporting V Corps' movement by fire, I Corps drove the Germans out of Buzancy on November 2, and the entire army line moved north. By November 4, the First Army had advanced twenty miles and the Germans began a general withdrawal to a new line north of the Meuse. The Americans continued their pursuit. On November 5, III Corps and V Corps crossed the Meuse and I Corps reached a point on the heights five miles south of Sedan.

On November 6, Pershing created an international furor by announcing his desire that American forces take Sedan. At Pershing's request, the First Army directed I Corps, assisted by V Corps, to bend all its energies to capturing Sedan, the site of the great French defeat in the Franco-Prussian War. Understandably, the French were determined to have the honor of liberating Sedan—but the Americans were on their way. Pershing halted his more aggressive commanders just before the 42d Division and the 1st Division became hopelessly entangled, partly in the zone of the French Fourth Army, on the heights overlooking Sedan.

The American Second Army moved east into the Woëvre plain on November 9 and continued its advance while the First Army secured the heights over Sedan. Both armies were planning further pursuits north and east when the Armistice was declared. At the eleventh hour on the eleventh day of the eleventh month of 1918, the fighting ceased. The Armistice came as a gradual realization of silence.

The Meuse-Argonne campaign lasted forty-seven days. A total of 1.2 million Americans were engaged in the campaign, of which 850,000 were combat troops. Twenty-two American divisions were engaged in the battle; 2,417 artillery pieces supported this fighting, firing a total of more than 4 million shells. The American ground battle was supported by 840 airplanes, most of these manufactured by the Allies. In addition, 324 tanks also supported the American campaign in the Meuse-Argonne; all of these tanks were of Allied manufacture, and many were manned by Allied troops. The AEF claimed to have drawn to the Meuse-Argonne a total of forty-four enemy divisions. This figure was disputed by the Allies and could hardly be proven. The First Army reported the capture of 26,000 prisoners of war in this campaign, though other statistics record only 16,000. They also listed the capture of 874 artillery pieces and over 3,000 machine guns. The First Army claimed to have inflicted 100,000 enemy casualties, at a cost of 117,000 American casualties. Clearly, the campaign was of vital importance to the Allied victory.

Paul F. Braim

Bibliography

Baldwin, Hanson. *World War I: An Outline History*. New York: Harper & Row, 1962.

Braim, Paul F. *The Test of Battle: The AEF in the Meuse-Argonne Campaign*. Newark: University of Delaware Press, 1983.

Toland, John. *No Man's Land: 1918, the Last Year of the Great War*. Garden City, NY: Doubleday, 1980.

Miller, David Hunter (1875–1961)

David Hunter Miller, lawyer, diplomat, and historian, was born in New York City. He was the partner of Gordon Auchincloss, son-in-law of Col. Edward M. House, President Wilson's friend, confidant, and adviser. On June 17, 1917, Miller joined the State Department as a special assistant at the salary of $1 per year.

Miller was one of the original members of The Inquiry and after January 1918 headed its international law section. His memoranda significantly influenced the definition of American war aims as articulated in the Fourteen Points, and he was recognized as an extraordinary legal draftsman. He wrote the legal defense of the President's personal attendance at the Paris Peace Conference and then accompanied House to Europe as technical adviser to the American Commission to Negotiate Peace.

Although confident that the bankruptcy of the Old World would lead eventually to unconditional acceptance of Wilson's peace program, Miller was shaken by the British and French attitudes that he encountered. He urged Wilson to prepare his own agenda before meeting with Allied leaders and played a central part in those preparations.

Once an uncompromising opponent of restoring German power, Miller became much more concerned with limiting French revanchism. He argued against war crimes trials, helped draft the international status of Danzig, and was the chief architect of the futile effort to retain German sovereignty over the Saarland. He also defended reparations by insisting that Germany's liability was narrowly limited.

Although not as alarmed as others by the Red Menace, Miller opposed William C. Bullitt's plan to establish normal relations with the Russian Bolsheviks. However, Miller supported the Hoover-Nansen relief effort because it entailed few formal contacts with the Soviet government and promised to end the suffering on which, he believed, Bolshevism fed.

Miller drafted Washington's rejection of a French plan to base the peace conference on inter-Allied agreements antedating the Fourteen Points, thereby rendering void Allied promises of Fiume and parts of the Dalmation coast to Italy (although he was sympathetic to Italian claims). House let Miller take the lead in negotiating with the Italians at Paris and endorsed his plan to give Italy nominal sovereignty over Fiume. But Yugoslavia, aware that Wilson would not agree, absolutely refused. The negotiations failed, the Italians left the conference, and House and Wilson never fully reconciled.

Miller's chief responsibility at Paris was in drafting the Covenant of the League of Nations. Miller and Sir Cecil Hurst wrote the draft that was the basis for deliberations of the Commission on the Covenant. Miller championed broadening the League Council beyond the Great Powers, the special protection of the Monroe Doctrine, and the provision that became Article XIX, by which the League could recommend revision of obsolete treaties. With Secretary of State Robert Lansing, he favored a "negative commitment" by member states not to violate provisions of the Covenant, as opposed to Wilson's call for a "positive commitment" to use force if necessary against violators, which Miller feared would unconstitutionally require the United States to declare war. He came to accept Wilson's language because he believed any future war would pit the League of Nations against its opponents, and the United States would retain the right to sever its connection with the League. By the same reasoning, he concluded that Wilson's concern for freedom of the seas was moot.

Miller's highest goal was the creation of a world league in which the influence of the United States would be paramount. He campaigned vigorously for the treaty, branding the arguments against it "an incredible farrago of balderdash."

Miller returned to private law practice but remained an unstinting advocate of American involvement in world affairs. He chaired William G. McAdoo's campaign for the 1924 Democratic presidential nomination in New York and helped write what became the Geneva Protocol in 1925. At substantial financial sacrifice, he became editor of treaties in the State Department in 1929 and from 1931 to 1938 served as historical adviser to the department as well. He retired from public life in 1944 and died in Washington on July 21, 1961.

Richard A. Harrison

Bibliography

Birdsall, Paul. *Versailles Twenty Years After.* New York, 1941.

House, Edward M., and Charles Seymour, eds. *What Really Happened at Paris: The Story of the Peace Conference, 1918–1919, by the American Delegation.* New York, 1921.

Miller, David H. *Drafting the Covenant.* New York: Putnam, 1928.

———. *My Diary at the Conference of Paris.* New York: Appeal Printing, 1924.

Tillman, Seth P. *Anglo-American Relations at the Paris Peace Conference.* Princeton, NJ: Princeton University Press, 1961.

Mines

Among the first advocates of the use of underwater explosives to destroy enemy shipping were David Bushnell and Robert Fulton during the Revolutionary War period. However, all they were able to accomplish was proof that explosives could be detonated under water and, if properly placed, could destroy a ship. How mines, then called torpedoes, could be delivered to a target defeated them. Although many of their mines were successfully tested, none ever received much support. It was not until the Civil War that sea mines were used on a relatively large scale by the Confederacy, which was credited with the first effective use of underwater mines with safety devices that protected those who assembled and planted them. It was the Battle of Mobile Bay, in which victorious Admiral David Farragut became famous for saying "Damn the torpedoes [mines], full speed ahead."

Modern mines were, and are designed for deployment against many different types of ships. Some of these mines are used against vessels of varying sizes, while others are intended primarily for use against submarines. Mines are classified into three categories, which are determined according to the position they assume in water. There are ground mines, moored mines, and drifting mines. Ground mines, commonly referred to as bottom mines, are most effective in shallow water. They have a large negative buoyancy (tendency to sink), which allows the mine to rest on the ocean floor. Drifting mines float free at or near the surface. They have no anchoring device, and their buoyancy is neutral. Additionally, because drifting mines are not controlled, they were restricted by the Hague Convention of 1907. Finally, moored mines are somewhat different from ground mines. They are deep-water mines and are most effective against submarine and surface ships. Their explosive charge and firing mechanism are stored in a positive buoyancy case and held at a predetermined depth below the surface by a cable that is attached to an anchor on the sea bottom. The method by which all these mines are delivered can further be categorized into three areas: aircraft-laid mines, submarine-laid mines, and surface-laid mines.

After the Civil War, the United States Navy did not perpetuate experimentation in the use of sea mines in naval warfare. It was not until World War I that underwater mine production rapidly increased. The German employment of torpedoes and mines, especially by their U-boats against Allied ships, was a great danger and hampered the shipping industry, which was Britain's life line. The British, however, quickly learned the value of the mine field (a term used to describe the area where mines are planted) against the German submarine. Naval mines emerged as the Allies' primary weapon against the German submarine. A course of action was developed by the English to deny the German subs ready access to the Atlantic. A mine barrage in the North Sea was proposed but suspended because of the enormity of the task. The plan included the use of British H.II mines (which used chemical horns copied from captured German weapons), but the amount of mines required for this task would have exceeded the manufacturing or laying capacity of Britain.

When the United States entered the war, the United States Navy revived the mine barrage scheme and went to work to develop a mine that would be effective against the submarine while keeping the mined area safe for surface vessels. Inventors and planners were solicited all over the country for their ideas and contributions in developing a device that would be effective against the German submarine. The schemes poured in. One design came from Ralph C. Brown, of Salem, Massachusetts, for an electrolytic-firing "K-device," which was part of a proposal for an underwater gun using the electrolytic firing device for target detection. Cmdr. Simon P. Fullenwider, a retired American naval officer, was recalled to duty in 1917 and sent to work for the Bureau of Ordnance, where he was responsible for design, development, and procurement of a mine system that could be used against submarines. He saw significant potential in Ralph Brown's proposals. He then redesigned and developed an antenna-type moored contact mine that would increase coverage in depth by use of an insulated (insulation prevents premature firing due to strong currents) copper wire attached to a float above the mine. An influence firing mechanism triggers a mine actuation when it receives a signal from its detector, which requires contact for the influence to occur. Upon receipt of the electrical signal from the detector, the firing mechanism analyzes the signal to determine its validity, i.e., enemy vessel, size, etc. This newly developed, relatively cheap mine, which could be mass-produced, required contact between the steel hull of a ship and the copper wire antenna that generated an electrical current that detonated the mine. The Bureau of Ordnance authorized the inventor to proceed with this idea and so launched the production of the Mark VI mine.

In August 1917, Adm. Henry T. Mayo, USN, commander-in-chief of the Atlantic Fleet, was briefed on the potentialities of this new mine and sent to London to confer with British planners. At the Allied Naval Conference in London, Mayo and Adm. Sir John Jellicoe, his British counterpart, agreed that this newly developed mine, called the Mark VI, would be an ideal solution for their capacity and management problems in producing H.II mines. The plan for its use in the North Sea was stupendous. The North Sea Mine Barrage, as it was called, was to stretch roughly 250 miles across the North Sea from Aberdeen to the Norwegian coast and to be fifteen to thirty-five miles wide. Under the plan, American Mark VIs would be mined in the deeper sections; the middle of the area and the outer skirts and shallow areas near the Orkney Islands and Norwegian coast would be mined with the British chemical horn mines.

Operations in laying mines for the North Sea Barrage began on June 7, 1918, and ended October 26. The mine-laying operation was a combined effort between the British and American squadrons. The squadrons planted more than 56,000 Mark VIs and 15,000 British mines, which were moored at depths ranging from 80 to 240 feet. The North Sea Mine Barrage was estimated to have cost the United States nearly $80 million, including $41 million for mine laying and $39 million for production of the Mark VIs. The Mark VIs cost approximately 400 dollars a piece to manufacture, and 125,000 were produced. The war ended as the barrage was on the verge of completion. There is doubt as to how successful the barrage could have been if it were completed earlier. Nonetheless, with the incomplete barrage the Allies did sink six German subs and damaged more. The German subs that risked the barrage and managed to reach the Atlantic wasted time, effort, and fuel in having to employ the necessary evasive tactics. Although the Germans were still using the North Sea exit by war's end, the effectiveness of the mine barrage really lies in its psychological effects as much as, if not more than, in the actual losses it inflicted.

After the war, the immediate problem was to find a home for the excess Mark VI mine material, as well as those mines to follow. On Aug. 7, 1918, by presidential proclamation, the Navy Mine Depot (now known as the Naval Weapons Station) was established at Yorktown, Virginia.

Michelle Jackson

See also NORTH SEA MINE BARRAGE

Bibliography
Cowie, J.S. *Mines, Minelayers and Minelaying.* Oxford, UK: Oxford University Press, 1949.

"Four Mining Campaigns." *Naval War College Review* 19 (June 1967).

Hartman, George K., and Scott C. Truver. *Weapons That Wait, Mine Warfare in the U.S. Navy.* Annapolis, MD: Naval Institute Press, 1991.

Hoffman, Roy F. "Offensive Mine Warfare: A Forgotten Strategy?" *U.S. Naval Institute Proceedings* (1977).

Melia, Tamara Moser. *"Damn the Torpedoes." A Short History of U.S. Naval Mine Countermeasures.* Washington, DC: Naval Historical Center, 1991.

Mitchell, William Lendrum (1879–1936)

William ("Billy") Lendrum Mitchell's place within the military history of the United States has been primarily defined by his dissent from orthodoxy during the early interwar period. His 1925 court-martial for conduct prejudicial to good order and discipline held the nation's attention for fifty-one days. Indeed, the tremendous public fascination with the trial and defendant suggests much about America's need for individualistic heroes in an age of mass society, and the airman's ability to meet that need.

The scion of a leading Wisconsin family, Mitchell was born in Nice, France, while his parents, Harriet and John, were taking a lengthy tour of Europe. Young "Willie" grew up in a secure, somewhat isolated pastoral setting where he developed a strong taste for outdoor adventure. His military life began during the Spanish-American War when he left George Washington University and enlisted as a private in the First Wisconsin Volunteer Regiment. His father, now a United States Senator, used his influence to obtain a second lieutenant's commission for his son in the Second Volunteer Signal Company of the same regiment. Mitchell's entry into the United States Army coincided with the initial transformation of that institution from an anachronistic frontier constabulary to a military organization with global responsibilities. Foreign adventure combined with the reform agitation from "Young Turks," who sought to create an officer corps cognizant of the importance of efficiency, proper organization, and professional expertise, to make the army at the turn of the century an exciting place for intelligent young officers.

In April 1901, Mitchell accepted a first lieutenant's commission in the Signal Corps of the Regular Army. At age twenty-four, he became the youngest captain in the army, a result of his pioneering work in land and wireless signal communication. A distinguished graduate of the School of the Line at Fort Leavenworth, Kansas, strong performance at the Army Staff College, and his continued success in Signal Corps operational assignments left Mitchell with a distinguished service record. In 1913, at thirty-four years of age, he became the youngest officer to serve on the General Staff.

The year 1916 proved pivotal for "Billy" Mitchell, as he now was known. Promoted to the rank of major after his three-year tour with the General Staff, he was made chief of the Signal Corps' new Aviation Section. Mitchell turned up in France only four days after the United States declared war on the Central Powers. In anticipation of the United States becoming a belligerent, he had been dispatched to Europe to review wartime aeronautical developments and make recommendations for the creation of an American Air Service. Once there, however, Mitchell concentrated on the operational nature of aerial warfare. He examined doctrinal concepts with Allied air leaders, becoming especially taken with MajGen. Hugh Trenchard's views and command of the Royal Flying Corps (RFC). During April and May 1917, Major Mitchell took advantage of every opportunity to observe combat missions, tour training facilities, and spend time with logistical experts. He also began to formulate his own ideas about the proper employment of aircraft in support of a ground campaign.

Energetic, knowledgeable, and expressing clearly his views on the future of American aviation at the front, Billy Mitchell came to the attention of Gen. John J. Pershing, commander of the American Expeditionary Force (AEF). In June 1917, Pershing made Mitchell a member of his staff, which also carried a promotion to the rank of lieutenant colonel. Mitchell spent the next year jockeying for position with other talented aviation officers in the expanding Air Service of the AEF. It was a period marked by often bitter organizational disputes, especially with Col. Benjamin Foulois, over areas of responsibility, control of resources, and command. Concerned by the growing intensity of this intramural conflict, and cognizant of the need to provide his aviators with strong leadership, Pershing reorganized the army air arm under the overall command of Col. Mason Patrick. Mitchell was placed in command of all American air units on the front line—euphemistically termed the "zone of advance."

Mitchell's wartime performance paralleled the remarkable progress of his early army career. In April 1917, he not only became the first United States officer to fly over the Western Front, but also received the French Croix de Guerre. Although he was volatile at times, his firm grasp of aerial warfare and his inspirational leadership held an inexperienced, as well as technologically inferior, American air brigade together during the crucial battle of Château-Thierry. By the time Pershing's First Army was prepared to eliminate German positions in the St. Mihiel salient, a prelude to a major thrust into the Meuse-Argonne region, Mitchell had become the accepted American air combat leader. At St. Mihiel he led a coalition force of more than 1,400 American, British, French, and Italian airmen. It was the single largest concentration of air power in World War I, and it marked Mitchell as one of the leading air commanders of the entire conflict. By the end of the war, Billy Mitchell had risen to the rank of brigadier general and was directing the operations of forty-five frontline squadrons.

After the war, Mitchell served as assistant chief of the U.S. Army Air Service. During his tenure, he wrote extensively on the capabilities of air power and advocated that the Air Service become an independent branch of the armed forces. He proved the value of the plane by sinking a total of six naval vessels in the course of two experiments.

Mitchell was bitter and argumentative in his struggle for an independent Air Service. His vigorous, at times outlandish, even violent, demands for a new national defense format based on air power led to Mitchell's court-martial for defiance of his superiors. His extraordinary army aviation career came to a close when court members reached a guilty verdict on December 17, 1925, ironically, the twenty-second anniversary of the first successful powered flight at Kitty Hawk, North Carolina. He resigned his commission rather than accept a five-year suspension.

Mitchell died of heart failure in New York on February 19, 1936.

Michael Grumelli

Bibliography

Hurley, Alfred. *Billy Mitchell: Crusader for Air Power.* Bloomington: Indiana University Press, 1975.

Levine, Isaac Don. *Mitchell: Pioneer of Air Power.* New York: Duell, Sloan & Pearce, 1958.

Mitchell, Ruth. *My Brother Bill.* New York: Harcourt, Brace, 1953.

Mitchell, William L. *Memoirs of World War I.* New York: Random House, 1960.

Morgenthau, Henry (1856–1946)

Henry Morgenthau served as United States ambassador to Turkey from 1913 to 1916. Morgenthau was born in Mannheim, Germany, and immigrated with his family to the United States in 1866. Trained as a lawyer, he made a fortune trading in real estate in New York City.

Active in the settlement house movement and other social reform activities, he became one of the largest contributors to Woodrow Wilson's presidential nomination and election campaigns and served as chairman of the finance committee of the Democratic National Committee in 1912. He retired from business in 1913 to devote himself to public service.

Morgenthau at first refused Wilson's offer of the ambassadorship to Turkey because the post had come to be considered as a token slot for a Jew. He had hoped to be appointed to Wilson's cabinet. However, he changed his mind while vacationing in France and accepted the appointment in August 1913. Following a brief return to the United States, he made the long journey to Constantinople where he arrived on November 27. Morgenthau immediately made it clear that he would be fully in charge of embassy business. He selected as his interpreter and personal adviser an Armenian, Arshag K. Schmavonian, who had long served as the legal adviser of the embassy. The Turkish discrimination against and persecution of minority groups within the empire, especially Armenians and Jews, was to be Morgenthau's principal concern during his tenure in Constantinople. He maintained close relations with American Protestant missionary organizations and Jewish assistance groups working in the empire. Zionist leaders in the United States and in Europe constantly urged Morgenthau to act on behalf of a Jewish Palestine, then a province of the Turkish empire. Morgenthau himself was not a Zionist and became increasingly opposed to that movement.

Following the outbreak of World War I in August 1914, the Turkish government's persecution of minority groups grew ever more oppressive. The Armenians, in particular, who were chiefly located in the border areas adjacent to Russia, were suspected of treason and were repeatedly subjected to genocidal massacres. Morgenthau protested these actions again and again, both in diplomatic contacts with Turkish authorities and in public statements. He even attempted to enlist the powerful German ambassador in joint protests against the persecution of Christian Armenians. However, he was ultimately forced to admit that his objections had had little impact beyond personally alienating Turkish officials. He returned to the United States on home leave in February 1916 and resigned the ambassadorship on March 23.

In May 1917, Morgenthau suggested to Secretary of State Robert Lansing that the Turkish government might be sufficiently war-weary to consider a separate peace with the Allies and that he, Morgenthau, should go abroad to feel out the Turkish officials on the subject. President Wilson showed interest in the project, and it was agreed that Morgenthau should proceed to Egypt with the ostensible objective of arranging relief for the Jews of Palestine. Morgenthau apparently never received any detailed instructions from either the State Department or the White House. He sailed from New York in June and stopped in Gibraltar to confer with British and French representatives in early July. The British government, as well as Zionist leaders, were opposed to the whole idea of a separate peace with Turkey. The British representative sent to Gibraltar, the strongly Zionist Chaim Weizmann, persuaded Morgenthau to postpone his mission. The latter proceeded to France to await further instructions and was soon distressed to find his mission repudiated by the United States government.

In June 1919, Wilson and Lansing selected Morgenthau to head a commission to visit Poland to investigate anti-Jewish atrocities. Though neither Morgenthau nor any of the other commissioners could speak either Polish or Yiddish, they did conduct a reasonably thorough investigation that confirmed many anti-Semitic outrages. Morgenthau's report, made in October 1919, pleased neither the Polish government nor Jewish and Zionist leaders. Atrocities had indeed occurred, he avowed, but both sides should make greater efforts to assimilate the Jewish population into Polish life and culture as a whole. The Polish mission proved to be Morgenthau's last important public service.
John E. Little

Bibliography
Morgenthau, Henry. *All in a Life-Time*. Garden City, NY: Doubleday, Page, 1922.
———. *Ambassador Morgenthau's Story*. Garden City, NY: Doubleday, Page, 1918.
Morgenthau, Henry III. *Mostly Morgenthau: A Family History*. New York: Ticknor & Fields, 1991.

Moseley, George Van Horn (1874–1960)
Born in Illinois, George Van Horn Moseley graduated from the United States Military Academy in 1899. Commissioned in the cavalry, he served in the Philippines both as a troop commander and as a staff officer. He joined the War Department General Staff after graduating from the Army War College in 1911. Thereafter, he worked in the War Department's Militia Division and oversaw all militia cavalry matters.

Moseley served with troops between 1912 and 1915, when he returned to Washington to work with the assistant chief of staff, MajGen. Tasker H. Bliss. With problems along the United States-Mexican border and relations with Germany strained, the army was preparing itself for war, and Moseley's duties focused on planning for universal military training. In 1916, however, he left Washington to join the 5th Field Artillery called to the Mexican border.

After the United States declared war on Germany, Moseley accompanied the 5th Field Artillery overseas as part of the 1st Division. Upon landing in France, he became a temporary colonel and took command of the regiment. In late August 1917, the regiment moved into a training area around the town of Le Valdahon, near the Swiss border. Here Moseley spent the next two months instructing his men in the basics of artillery operations, working out the last details of the unit's organization, and conducting target practice. In early November, Moseley left the 5th to join the American Expeditionary Force (AEF) General Staff, where he helped integrate the activities of the AEF's various supply and administrative agencies, both among themselves and with the combat units.

In April 1918, Moseley became the head of the supply section and, in June, a brigadier general. This new position placed Moseley in the senior leadership of the AEF and involved him in all top-level planning. During the summer of 1918, the American supply situation became critical. There were problems in transporting men and supplies and the Service of Supply suffered from severe organizational and personnel problems. Moseley played a key role in unraveling these difficulties, earning both the praise of the AEF commander John J. Pershing, and the Distinguished Service Medal.

Following the Armistice, Moseley continued to head the supply section until June 1919. Now, however, most of his problems concerned returning soldiers to the United States and disposing of equipment and supplies. He also briefly served as a diplomat when, in January 1919, he successfully conducted negotiations with the Netherlands to open the lower Rhine River to American military traffic.

Moseley returned to the United States in November 1919 after serving on the Harbord Mission to examine conditions in Armenia. After a brief tour on the War Department General Staff, he took command of the 2d Field Artillery Brigade. In 1921, he served as an assistant to Charles G. Dawes and helped organize the new Bureau of the Budget. Thereafter, he rotated through a number of troop and administrative commands, including deputy chief of staff of the army and commander of the Third Army. He retired in September 1938 and died in November 1960.

Richard Kehrberg

Bibliography

Pershing, John J. *My Experiences in the World War.* New York: Stokes, 1931.
Smythe, Donald. *Pershing: General of the Armies.* Bloomington: Indiana University Press, 1986.

Motion Pictures
See FILM IN THE FIRST WORLD WAR

Muir, Charles Henry (1860–1933)

Charles Henry Muir was born in Erie, Michigan, and graduated from the United States Military Academy in 1885. Commissioned a second lieutenant in the infantry, he served on the western frontier, graduated at the head of his class from the Infantry and Cavalry School at Fort Leavenworth, Kansas, and was an instructor in engineering at the Fort Leavenworth school from 1895 to 1898. During the Spanish-American War, Muir fought in Cuba and was awarded the Distinguished Service Cross for gallantry for his role as a sharpshooter in silencing a Spanish artillery piece in the Santiago campaign. In 1899, Muir was sent to the Philippines, where he saw considerable action against the insurgents, and in 1900, he was a member of the American contingent of the International Relief Expedition dispatched to China during the Boxer Rebellion. Between the turn of the century and American entry into World War I, Muir rose to the rank of colonel, serving on the War Department General Staff from 1903 to 1907, in the Philippines from 1907 to 1910, as an instructor with the Illinois National Guard from 1911 to 1915, and in the Panama Canal Zone and along the Mexican border from 1915 to 1917.

Soon after American entry into World War I, Muir was promoted to the temporary rank of brigadier general. In December 1917, he was promoted to the temporary rank of major general and given command of the 28th Division. During the early months of 1918, Muir directed the division through its final training in the United States and then took it to France for additional training with the British in Picardy. In July 1918, the 28th Division went into the line, and during the next months Muir led it through the difficult fighting in the Champagne-Marne defensive, in the Second Battle of the Marne, in the Fismes sector on the Vesle River, and in the early phase of the Meuse-Argonne offensive.

Although he was never popular with superiors or subordinates because of his abrasive personality and dour nature, Muir's hard driving style and tactical skills made him an effective, albeit not spectacular, combat commander. As a result, when Gen. John J. Pershing reshuffled his top field generals in October 1918 after the American Army stalled in the Meuse-Argonne offensive, he elevated Muir to the command of IV Corps, a post he held through the remainder of the war and the initial stage of the occupation of Germany. Muir resumed command of the 28th Division in April 1919, remaining with it until it was mustered out of service at Camp Dix, New Jersey, later that spring.

Thereafter, Muir commanded Camp Merritt, New Jersey, the General Service Schools at Fort Leavenworth, Camp Lewis, Washington, and the III Corps Area, his final assignment before retiring from the army in July 1924 with the permanent rank of major general. Muir's career, like those of his contemporaries, mirrored the transition of the American Army from a frontier and imperial constabulary to a modern fighting force in the international arena. Muir died in Baltimore on Dec. 8, 1933.

John K. Ohl

Bibliography

Martin, Edward. *The Twenty-eighth Division, Pennsylvania's Guard in the World War.* 5 vols. Pittsburgh: 28th Division Publishing Co., 1923–1924.
Millett, Allen R. *The General: Robert L. Bullard and Officership in the United*

States Army, 1881–1925. Westport, CT: Greenwood Press, 1975.

Proctor, H.G. *The Iron Division: The National Guard of Pennsylvania in the World War.* Philadelphia: Winston, 1919.

Stallings, Laurence. *The Doughboys: The Story of the AEF, 1917–1918.* New York: Harper & Row, 1963.

Music

Wartime cultural production, of which music is an integral part, is an important vehicle through which to analyze issues of consensus and democracy, as well as perceptions of the enemy and the national "self." During World War I, popular music often reflected shifting and even ambivalent sentiments about the conflict and this country's role in it. In the realm of high culture, much German or Prussian "kultur" was denigrated by arbiters of cultural Americanism as a product of a "barbarous race." At the same time, standard works of German, Austrian, and Hungarian composers were much valued as part of this country's "high culture" in the concert hall.

Prior to the spring of 1917, the critical challenge for the consensus builders in the Committee on Public Information (CPI) was to inspire patriotic enthusiasm for a war in which the nation was, at that moment, technically a neutral party. When Woodrow Wilson ran for reelection on the slogan "He kept us out of war," neutral and even pacifist positions coexisted with a preparedness doctrine that nevertheless stressed noninvolvement in the actual hostilities. Popular songs like "I Didn't Raise My Boy to be a Soldier" reflected a pacifist perspective that was not inconsistent with the tenor of the times. In the tradition of story-telling popular melodies that reached a broad public through the technology of sound recording: the male narrator overhears and relates a mother's lament about the horrors of war, concluding, "There'd be no war today, if mothers all would say, I didn't raise my boy to be a soldier."

After President Wilson's war message to Congress in April, neutral and pacifist ideas were less in tune with prevailing sentiments, and Irving Berlin's "Let's All Be Americans Now," first recorded by Morton Harvey and his studio orchestra in June 1917, expressed a spirit of consensus that was intended to cross the ethnic and class lines that George Creel and the CPI

considered to be major barriers to consensus building in the new wartime climate. Songs written specifically for the war effort were popular advertisements for the cause. George M. Cohan's "Over There" provides an example of Wilsonian rhetoric and high moral purpose (expressed in a popular style) that pervaded wartime propoganda. Written in 1917 and first recorded by Nora Bayes, "Over There" was the hit of the war period and remains the one song most commonly identified with the conflict.

The message of consensus and support for the war reached everyday Americans through the activities of the Four-Minute-Men, whose slides with lyrics to popular and patriotic tunes became common features of public events and movie house presentations. The speakers intoned about the purpose of the war and the need for sacrifice on the home front, often ending their presentations by leading the audience in singing such familiar tunes as "The Star Spangled Banner" (which was not yet the national anthem), "Columbia, Gem of the Ocean," and "Keep the Home Fires Burning."

In October 1917, American opera and orchestra audiences learned that they would soon be paying a 10 percent tax on tickets to their favorite performances. Mandated by Title VII of the federal "act to provide revenue to defray war expenses," this surcharge was no doubt regarded by most concert music patrons as a necessary nuisance for the war effort. The challenge of supporting the war effort in a climate of tension between patriotism and high art that was mainly European in origin pervaded concert halls, orchestra and opera company managements, and the musical press.

Standard repertoire in concert halls in the United States had long meant music by composers of German, Austrian, and Hungarian origin. Indeed, a season without Mozart, Beethoven, or even Wagner would seem unthinkable for many music lovers. But the wartime context called into question the appropriateness of the standard repertoire. While popular music, as exemplified by such tunes as "Pack Up Your Troubles in Your Old Kit Bag," could be an effective vehicle for encouraging wartime solidarity and participation, concert music could not so easily be converted into a tool for selling the war. Given the assumption of the superiority of the European, specifically German, musical product, 100 percent Americanism, or even 100 percent anti-Germanism, was a virtual impossibility from a management or perfor-

M

mance perspective. While women in New York were asked to knit quietly for the cause at Philharmonic concerts that featured some, if not all, of the standard Geman repertoire and orchestra managements fretted about whether music by dead German composers could be considered less detrimental to the American patriotic spirit than that of living Germans, Autrians, and Hungarians (music by long-departed "enemies" was deemed safe in most cities), German music and musicians, like all aspects of German culture, came under attack in violation of the presumed sanctity of the separation of art and politics.

A public furor over the refusal of the Boston Symphony Orchestra to perform the "Star Spangled Banner" at a concert in Providence, Rhode Island, led to the dismissal, internment, and eventual deportation of renowned conductor Karl Muck. The Metropolitan Opera chose to program no German operas during the 1917–1918 season, including instead works by American composers Charles Wakefield Cadman and Henry F.B. Gilbert. Civic leaders in Pittsburgh forced the cancellation of a concert by the Cincinnati Symphony Orchestra because of the presence of its German-born conductor, Dr. Ernest Kunwald. Washington, D.C., and several other cities prohibited aliens from entering their borders, thus making it nearly impossible for most orchestras, whose players generally included many German-born players, from getting the necessary permits to give tour concerts. The Philadelphia Orchestra dismissed eight German-born members who had not filed applications for American citizenship. More moderate gestures of 100 percent Americanism included the playing of "The Star Spangled Banner" prior to concert or opera performances, the occasional pro-gramming of pieces by American composers (along with a greater presence on many programs of works by French and Russian composers), and statements in concert programs declaring the patriotic sentiments of orchestra managements.

For a brief period during and immediately after World War I, musical nationalism played a major role in discussions about concert and opera programming. By 1920, although some American music was still heard in the concert hall and opera house, American composers were again bemoaning the absence of second performances of their new works as German music reverted to its near canonical position in this country. Audiences remained essentially traditional in their tastes, accepting some of the new French and Russian pieces but turning out enthusiastically for the all-Beethoven or all-Wagner programs of the prewar years. Despite the powerful political influence of 100 percent Americanism, audiences in this country were loath to give up the standard repertoire, even at the height of hostility to all things German. With the resurgence of traditional cultural patterns in concert programming after the war, efforts at 100 percent musical Americanism seem to have made very little difference.

Barbara L. Tischler

Bibliography

Tischler, Barbara L. *An American Music: The Search for an American Musical Identity.* Chapter 3. New York: Oxford University Press, 1986.

Mystery ships
See Q-SHIPS

National Advisory Committee for Aeronautics

Congress established the National Advisory Committee for Aeronautics (NACA) in 1915 to correct United States deficiencies in aviation and aeronautics. NACA represented the culmination of a long struggle to institutionalize aeronautical research in the nation.

Samuel P. Langley, the Wright brothers, and other Americans pioneered work in aviation and aeronautics, but the United States, by 1910, had fallen far behind Europe in the operation of heavier-than-air aircraft and the theoretical study of flight. Mounting international tensions and increasing prospects for war prompted European nations to arm themselves in the air as well as on the land and sea. Europeans recognized more readily than Americans that progress in aviation proceeded from aeronautical research, and they established government-financed research programs and aeronautical laboratories to assist in the design, development, and production of aircraft.

American aviation, in the meantime, sputtered along, remaining dependent largely on the haphazard efforts of independent inventors. The government had invested $50,000 in Langley's research, but the crash of his first "aerodrome" in 1903 and the subsequent public and press controversy discouraged further governmental forays into aviation. Private funds for aeronautics were also lacking. Most Americans discounted the Wrights and Langley and ignored their achievements; few possessed enough confidence in these pioneers to invest large sums in their revolutionary ideas. Only the Aerial Equipment Association, a short-lived and largely ineffective organization funded by Mrs. Alexander Graham Bell, provided any substantial financial support for aviation before 1914.

Many Americans saw the backwardness of the United States in aviation as a national disgrace and a threat to national security, and some took steps after 1910 to remedy the situation. Most of these efforts revolved around plans to institutionalize aeronautical research in a European-modeled, government-operated national aeronautics laboratory. Between 1911 and 1914, aviation enthusiasts submitted various plans for such an agency, but their efforts were frustrated by concerns over economy and efficiency and by petty squabbles between the Smithsonian Institution, universities, the National Bureau of Standards, and the U.S. Navy over the location and purpose of the facility.

The outbreak of war in Europe and disturbing reports of the disparity between European and American aviation revived attempts to strengthen American aeronautics. Efforts now centered on more modest proposals. In February 1915, Charles D. Walcott, secretary of the Smithsonian and a leading figure in attempts to establish a national aeronautics laboratory, requested that Congress establish an advisory body similar to the British Advisory Committee for Aeronautics to advise the government on aviation matters and to coordinate aeronautical work in governmental bureaus and private laboratories. Hoping to circumvent the interdepartmental conflict and concerns over economy and efficiency that had scuttled earlier efforts, Walcott purposely avoided references to an aeronautical laboratory and requests for large appropriations. On March 3, Congress authorized creation of an Advisory Committee for Aeronautics consisting of twelve nonpaid members drawn from government and the scientific community to "supervise and direct the scientific study of the problems of flight with a view to their practical solution." Congress appropriated the modest sum of $5,000 to support the committee's work for 1916–1917. In April, committee members affixed the prefix "National" to the title, creating the acronym NACA that came into popular and official use.

NACA concentrated its energies initially on surveying the nation's aeronautical research and educational facilities and subsidizing research at private institutions, but its activities and responsibilities multiplied once the United States entered World War I. NACA became an important policy-making body, advising the government on aeronautical research, aviation inventions, experimental airmail services, and various related matters. It also supervised the design and testing of propellers, engines, and aerofoils at Stanford, M.I.T., the National Bureau of Standards, and other institutions. NACA also coordinated American aviation efforts and worked to defuse disagreements threatening to disrupt the design and production of high-quality aircraft. Its greatest wartime achievement involved mediation of a dispute between Glenn A. Curtiss and the Wright-Martin Company over aircraft control techniques. The resulting cross-licensing agreement allowed for the sharing of technology and made volume production of aircraft possible during and after the war.

NACA's enabling legislation left open the possibility of an aeronautical laboratory, and Walcott and other NACA members revived efforts to establish such a facility. In August 1916, Congress appropriated $85,000 to NACA for that purpose. Construction began at a site just north of Hampton, Virginia, in early 1917. Poor weather conditions and the railroad car crisis delayed work; Langley Memorial Aeronautical Laboratory, NACA's first research facility, was not formally dedicated until June 1920. Langley's facilities made the systematic study of aviation problems possible, and NACA gradually abandoned its policy-making role to concentrate on technical research. It continued in that capacity until 1958, when it dissolved and its remnant was incorporated in the National Air and Space Administration (NASA).

Daniel E. Worthington

Bibliography

Anderson, Frank. *Orders of Magnitude: A History of the NACA and NASA, 1915–1976.* Washington, DC: NASA Scientific and Technical Information Office, 1976.

Bilstein, Roger E. *Orders of Magnitude; A History of the NACA and NASA, 1915–1990.* Washington, DC: NASA Scientific and Technical Information Office, 1989.

Emme, Eugene M. *Aeronautics and Astronautics: An American Chronology of Science and Technology in the Exploration of Space, 1915–1960.* Washington, DC: Government Printing Office, 1961.

Holley, Irving B. *Ideas and Weapons: The Aerial Weapon During World War I.* New Haven, CT: Yale University Press, 1953.

Roland, Alex. *Model Research: The National Advisory Committee for Aeronautics, 1915–1958.* Washington, DC: NASA Scientific and Technical Information Office, 1985.

National American Woman Suffrage Association

The National American Woman Suffrage Association (NAWSA) was created by the merger of the National Woman Suffrage Association and the American Woman Suffrage Association in 1890, but the organization languished from 1896 to 1910 largely because no new suffrage states were won and the federal suffrage amendment was ignored. "Paralysis" aptly described NAWSA under the leadership of Anna Howard Shaw, an outstanding orator but an inflexible and ineffectual administrator. The stagnation ended with the assumption of leadership at the December 1915 convention by Carrie Chapman Catt. Catt appointed a new board and sent officers to the states to investigate conditions. Based on their reports, she conceived a plan that gave every state and every group a role to play in achieving woman suffrage. Adopted by NAWSA at an emergency convention in September 1916, Catt's "Winning Plan" combined lobbying for the amendment on Capitol Hill with continuing efforts to expand the number of states in which women could vote. NAWSA leaders also carefully cultivated relations with President Woodrow Wilson, an effort that resulted in his somewhat ambiguous declaration of support for suffrage at the 1916 NAWSA convention.

NAWSA made an official organizational response to World War I following the American break in diplomatic relations with Germany on Feb. 3, 1917. Catt, who believed that wartime service would win more support for the woman suffrage cause than pacifism, called a meeting of the NAWSA executive council to decide upon its most effective course of action. At her urging, the council voted overwhelmingly to offer the services of its 2 million members to the government in the event of war and quickly organized a mass meeting in Washington to publicize the decision. With several members of the Wilson administration in attendance, Catt explained that NAWSA members planned to stand by their country and at the same time to continue their suffrage work.

Within weeks of the declaration of war on Germany on April 6, 1917, the government appointed a Woman's Committee of the Council of National Defense (WCCND) and asked Shaw to be its chair, and Catt and Katherine McCormick, a NAWSA vice president, to serve on the eleven-member committee. Shaw's own suffrage work went into abeyance, but Catt and other NAWSA leaders continued their suffrage activities along with their war work and urged all suffragists to do the same. NAWSA members cooperated with WCCND state divisions; in many states NAWSA suffragists held positions in the WCCND, and the WCCND functioned essentially through the NAWSA state network.

NAWSA leaders were not only eager to demonstrate the patriotism of their members, but also were anxious to distinguish their organization from the National Woman's Party White House pickets. They criticized the pickets, but never the injustices the pickets faced in being denied their freedom of speech through arrests and imprisonments. Despite such disavowals, Catt was herself the target of strident attacks by antisuffragists as unpatriotic for continuing her suffrage work.

Clearly a convergence of factors, in which the NAWSA Winning Plan and suffragists' war service were instrumental, contributed to the progress in Congress on the suffrage issue. In 1917, North Dakota, Ohio, Indiana, Rhode Island, Nebraska, Michigan, and Arkansas gave women varying degrees of suffrage—most importantly, in November 1917, New York passed a referendum for a state suffrage amendment. The New York victory, first in the Northeast, convinced many that all American women would soon have the vote. Wilson himself was undoubtedly impressed by the suffragists' war service and the crucial New York victory because he came out unambiguously for a federal

amendment just prior to the House vote in January 1918. NAWSA's "all fronts" strategy, which continued along with war service, was instrumental in the final suffrage victory.

On Jan. 10, 1918, the House of Representatives passed a bill that provided for a constitutional amendment to give women the right to vote. Wilson made a personal appearance before the Senate to urge the bill's passage the next fall, but the measure failed in October 1918 and again in February 1919. The House repassed the amendment in May 1919, and the Senate finally followed in June. It was finally ratified by the last state in August 1920. Rather than slowing progress toward the achievement of woman suffrage, the evidence indicates that the war may have speeded the attainment of votes for women.

Barbara J. Steinson

See also COUNCIL OF NATIONAL DEFENSE: WOMEN'S COMMITTEE

Bibliography
Flexner, Eleanor. *Century of Struggle, The Woman's Rights Movement in the United States.* New York: Atheneum, 1973.

Harper, Ida H., ed. *History of Woman Suffrage.* New York: National American Woman Suffrage Association, 1922.

Scott, Anne F., and Andrew M. Scott. *One Half the People, the Fight for Woman Suffrage.* Urbana: University of Illinois Press, 1982.

Steinson, Barbara J. *American Women's Activism in World War I.* New York: Garland, 1982.

National Association for the Advancement of Colored People

During American participation in World War I, the National Association for the Advancement of Colored People (NAACP) fought for an increase in the number of black Americans serving in the armed forces and opposed racial discrimination directed at black servicemen. When Germany and the United States declared war on one another in April 1917, the NAACP Board of Directors, most of whom were white and held antimilitary opinions, unanimously demanded that additional military units should be created to accept African Americans who would then have the same opportunity as white citi-

zens to serve their country. At NAACP instigation, a conference of 700 leaders representing
black interests was held in May 1917. There the
leaders decried the exploitation of black Americans. But the conference also encouraged black
Americans to join the army and to support the
war effort even though they would undoubtedly
continue to be the victims of discrimination.
Stress was placed on the right of black Americans to serve as combat soldiers, to act as leaders of other blacks in combat, and to receive
training preparing them for these service and
leadership roles.

Joel Spingarn, chairman of the NAACP
board, supported the establishment of an officers' training camp for blacks only. At first, the
board was reluctant to support its chairman because an exclusively black training camp would
only perpetuate segregation. Nonetheless,
Spingarn continued to support the effort because he believed it was the only realistic means
whereby qualified blacks could begin to assume
positions of leadership and authority in the U.S.
Army. He saw it as a temporary expedient that
would demonstrate that blacks were capable of
making a genuine contribution to the army. Finally, on May 14, 1917, with two dissenting
votes, the NAACP board supported the black
officers' training camp. It was opened at Des
Moines, Iowa, on June 17, 1917, and by October more than 600 men had been commissioned
as officers.

Perhaps the single most serious problem
in race relations involving the military during
the war occurred on Aug. 23, 1917, in Houston, when members of the 24th Infantry Regiment, an all-black unit, reacted violently to the
behavior of the civilian police toward black
soldiers. The result was a riot during which
over twenty people, both black and white,
were killed. Nineteen of sixty-three rioters
were hanged. The NAACP aided in the soldiers' defense.

Many other concerns were expressed by
the NAACP during American involvement in
the war. They included restricting black army
physicians to service in black regiments; the
ineligibility of black American nurses to serve
in the Red Cross; discrimination against black
soldiers by YMCAs in southern states and in
Detroit; and discrimination practiced by the
War Camp Community Service, a civilian
agency providing for the general welfare and
entertainment of soldiers in training camps.
Even a suggestion by the NAACP to appoint a

representative to the Community Service's national body and an offer to help raise money for
this effort were rejected. Other issues raised by
the NAACP were objection to the inclusion of
race identification on draft registration papers;
unwillingness to accept black volunteers in the
armed services in proportion to their numbers
in the general population; exclusion of blacks
from the artillery, air corps, and navy; possible
conscription of blacks for labor and menial
employment rather than regular military duty;
refusal to allow blacks to enter training camps
on the same terms as whites; delay in establishing the black officers' training camp; delay in
awarding commissions to black officer trainees;
uncertainty over the future of black National
Guard units; delay in calling up black draftees;
general treatment of black recruits; and the
forced early retirement from active service of
Col. Charles Young, one of the highest ranking
black officers in the army.

The recipient of most of these complaints
was Secretary of War Newton D. Baker, who
did not believe that it was his responsibility to
solve racial problems, even though the NAACP
implied that he was obliged to deal with issues
related to the training and employment of black
troops. Few of the issues were resolved to the
satisfaction of the NAACP. However, in spite of
its long list of grievances, the NAACP, including members such as W.E.B. Du Bois, believed
that the fight for the preservation of democracy
was more important than its own immediate
problems.

John Imholte

See also BLACK AMERICANS

Bibliography
Franklin, John Hope. *From Slavery to Free-
dom, A History of Negro Americans.*
New York: Alfred A. Knopf, 1967.
Hughes, Langston. *Fight for Freedom, the
Story of the NAACP.* New York: W.W.
Norton, 1962.
Kellogg, Charles F. *NAACP, A History of the
National Association for the Advance-
ment of Colored People.* Baltimore:
Johns Hopkins Press, 1967.
Nalty, Bernard C. *Strength for the Fight, A
History of Black Americans in the Mili-
tary.* New York: Free Press, 1986.
Scott, Emmett J. *The American Negro in the
World War.* Washington, DC: Home-
ward Press, 1919.

National Defense Act of 1916

The possibility that the United States might be drawn into conflict, whether with Mexico as the result of civil war there or with Germany in the war in Europe, led the War Department's General Staff to renew its studies of national preparedness after August 1914. The General Staff focused on the facts that the small United States Regular Army (100,000 officers and men in 1914) could not fight a major war without trained reserves drawn from the citizenry and that the country might not be granted sufficient time in which to train adequate forces after the outbreak of war. The General Staff had little faith in the organized state militias, collectively known as the National Guard, to serve as a reserve for the Regular Army, not only because the National Guard was hardly larger than the army, but also because the General Staff believed that, under the Constitution, guardsmen could not be compelled to serve outside the territorial United States. Rather than rely on the National Guard to volunteer for service abroad, the General Staff proposed the creation of a relatively large federal militia, one trained in peacetime and without any constitutional limit on its deployment.

In 1915, under the influence of the General Staff, Lindley M. Garrison, Wilson's secretary of war, rejected the National Guard as the country's primary reserve and sought the creation of a federal militia called the Continental Army, a force of nearly 400,000 volunteers, to be trained in increments of 133,000 men a year for three years. The junior officers for such an army could be commissioned from graduates of state military colleges, from the military training programs of land grant colleges established under the Morrill Act of 1862, and from college students, business and professional men who volunteered for summer camp training such as that provided by the Plattsburg Movement.

President Wilson formally endorsed the Continental Army Plan on Dec. 3, 1915, but the plan immediately encountered strong opposition from the politically influential National Guard Association. There was almost no support for it in the House of Representatives by early 1916. Instead, Congressman James Hay, the powerful chairman of the Military Affairs Committee, put his support behind a proposed federal pay bill for the National Guard that would encourage its expansion, establish higher standards for its officers, and impose an obligation of extended federal service as a condition of federal support. Hay also believed that constitutional remedies could be found for the compulsory service of the National Guard beyond the territory of the United States. Probably sensing that reform of the National Guard had a better chance of passage than adoption of the plan for a Continental Army, Wilson announced in early February that he was prepared to consider the National Guard as the nation's primary reserve land force.

Garrison was so incensed by Wilson's rejection of his plan for a federal militia that on Feb. 9, 1916, he submitted his resignation as secretary of war. Subsequently, Wilson appointed Newton D. Baker as Garrison's replacement at the War Department. In March, Congress passed a militia pay bill conforming to Hay's ideas, and in April, it approved a measure for a federal reserve system as a sop to the supporters of the Continental Army Plan. After House-Senate compromises in May, a bill was passed by Congress and sent to the President. On June 3, Wilson signed the National Defense Act into law.

The National Defense Act of 1916 specified that the principal components of the land forces of the United States would be the Regular Army, the Regular Army Reserve, composed of veterans of Regular Army service, and the National Guard (Organized Militia) of the states when in federal service. Officers and men of the National Guard were to take a dual oath, federal and state, and, when in federal service, they obligated themselves to serve wherever the President of the United States might direct. With federal financial assistance, the National Guard was to be increased from 100,000 to 400,000 troops, but, in order to qualify for federal assistance, higher federal standards had to be met. All guardsmen were required to attend a minimum of forty-eight paid drill meetings a year and to undergo fifteen days of training in the field annually under supervision of the Regular Army. The secretary of war was empowered to enforce standards on the Guard by withholding money from states that did not comply, while overall training of the Guard was supervised by a Militia Bureau of the General Staff headed by a Regular officer. The act also authorized the raising of a Volunteer Force in time of war as the Congress and President might direct.

The National Defense Act of 1916 authorized an expansion of the Regular Army to a peacetime strength of 175,000 men, and by accepting volunteers to increase its units to full strength in time of war, the Regular Army could reach an authorized strength of 286,000 men without further legal authority. Its enlisted reserves were to be veterans of tours with the Regular Army and recruited through a system of bounties. The act also established an Officers Reserve Corps, and a Reserve Officer Training Corps was to be established on university and college campuses across the nation to commission graduates after completing a prescribed course of instruction. Reserve officers could also be commissioned after completion of training in summer camps.

Finally, the National Defense Act delegated to the President powers for conducting economic mobilization in the event of war, including the placing of orders for war materials, federal seizure of industries that did not comply with such orders, and the setting of limits on prices charged the government and profits made by the war industries.

Soon after signing the act into law, Wilson began mustering National Guardsmen into federal service for the possibility of war with Mexico. When instead war came with Germany on April 6, 1918, of the 186,000 men in the Guard, 80,446 were on federal duty. However, with the Guard at less than half its authorized strength by that date, a Regular Army of 127,588 men, and a federal reserve of about 17,000 personnel, the men who constituted the land forces of the United States were entirely insufficient to the needs of a world war.

To meet the crisis, Congress modified the 1916 act. It suspended recruiting limits on both the army and the National Guard, enabling both organizations to accept hundreds of thousands of volunteers for wartime service. However, the greatest single source of manpower for the American armies of World War I was the Selective Service Act of May 18, 1917. It required all men between twenty-one and thirty years of age to register for the draft and later all men between eighteen and forty-five. Conscripts, or draftees, were collectively termed the National Army, and of the 4 million men who served in the American land forces at one time or another, 2,180,296 of them were soldiers of the National Army. Effectively, the National Army substituted for the Volunteer Force established by the 1916 National Defense Act. Nevertheless, the Regular Army, the federal reserves, and the National Guard played crucial roles in providing elements for both the American Expeditionary Force (AEF) and cadres to train troops in the United States for the AEF's expansion. The Plattsburg Movement of summer training camps provided a model for the short-term commissioning programs for junior officers—almost two out of three officers who served in the land forces graduated from them. It was therefore appropriate that in August 1918 General Peyton C. March, army chief of staff, ordered the amalgamation of all mobilized American land forces—Regular Army, Federal Reserves, National Guard, and National Army—into one United States Army.

Larry Addington

See also CONTINENTAL ARMY RESERVE PLAN; GARRISON, LINDLEY MILLER; PLATTSBURG MOVEMENT; SELECTIVE SERVICE ACT

Bibliography

Bernardo, C. Joseph, and Eugene H. Bacon. *American Military Policy: Its Development since 1775.* Harrisburg, PA: Military Service Publishing, 1955.

Dupuy, R. Ernest. *The Compact History of the United States Army.* New York: Hawthorne Books, 1956.

Millis, Walter. *Arms and Men: A Study of American Military History.* New York: Putnam, 1956.

Millett, Allan R., and Peter Maslowski. *For the Common Defense: A Military History of the United States of America.* New York: Free Press, 1984.

Weigley, Russell F. *History of the United States Army.* New York: Macmillan, 1967.

National Defense Act of 1920

With the demobilization of the American wartime land forces underway, Gen. Peyton C. March, chief of the General Staff of the War Department, proposed to Congress a plan for the postwar forces in January 1919. March's plan envisioned a Regular Army of 500,000 troops, or about four times as many as those serving in April 1917, and one that would be organized in skeleton units so that they could be rapidly expanded to wartime strength by the mobilization of a half million Federal Reserves trained in peacetime. March counted on compulsory military service to insure that sufficient numbers of men entered the reserve, and the Regular Army would dominate its organization and training.

March's proposals contradicted the terms of the 1916 National Defense Act, which had given the National Guard, the organized state militia, the role of being the country's primary reserve land force, and implied that only secondary importance was attached to any form of a federal reserve. The situation was further complicated by the fact that professional soldiers did not agree among themselves on a postwar policy. General of the Armies John J. Pershing, lately returned from France as head of the American Expeditionary Force (AEF), testified before Congress in the fall of 1919 in favor of a Regular Army of 300,000 officers and men but one with units maintained at full strength. For a reserve, he favored the plan of Col. John M. Palmer, which called for the army to be supplemented by a mobilizable federal militia of citizen-soldiers who would serve under their own officers. The Regular Army would provide training to this force in time of peace, but the federal militia would take the field to fight alongside, rather than as part of, an expanded Regular Army. Pershing agreed with March that some form of compulsory military service would be necessary for the creation of any kind of federal reserve.

The result of conflicting influences on Congress was eventually a compromise that amounted to a collection of amendments to the National Defense Act of 1916. The National Defense Act of 1920, signed into law on June 4, provided that the land forces of the United States would be known collectively as the Army of the United States (AUS), and the AUS would consist of the United States Army (the Regular Army) with an authorized strength of 297,000 officers and men, a National Guard of 435,000 troops, and a federal Organized Reserve of unstated numbers. However, all military service in the components of the AUS would be voluntary. The continental United States was divided into nine army corps areas, and each corps area was authorized one Regular, two National Guard, and up to three Organized Reserve divisions. In time of peace, the Regular Army would assist in the training of the divisions of the National Guard and Organized Reserve, while veteran reserve officers of the Great War and officers commissioned through the Reserve Officer Training Program (ROTC) were counted on to provide most of the citizen-officers.

The National Defense Act of 1920, and the related Army Reorganization Act of the same year, created an impressive organization on paper, but one never to be fully implemented in practice. After Pershing succeeded to the post of army chief of staff in 1921, he was frustrated by public indifference and by congressional parsimony with military budgets. By 1922, the Regular Army had been reduced to 137,000 troops, and instead of nine Regular divisions at full strength, it was left with the equivalent of three full-strength divisions. Lack of money and popular interest also hobbled the National Guard's recruitment. It possessed scarcely 200,000 officers and men throughout the interwar period, or fewer than half the number needed for eighteen full-strength divisions. The Organized Reserve had no divisions to offer as it hardly attracted any enlisted men and became chiefly a reserve of officers.

Pershing's successors and chiefs of staff in the interwar period had little better luck in meeting the goals of the 1920 act. In 1933, Congress made a modest improvement by amending the act to provide a dual status for the National Guard; under the militia clauses of the Constitution, the act recognized the Guard as the organized militia of the states; under the army clause of the Constitution, it recognized the Guard as a permanent reserve of the United States Army. Upon being summoned to federal duty, the National Guard of the states would assume the identity of the National Guard of the United States. Still, just prior to the outbreak of the Second World War in Europe in September 1939, the Regular Army numbered only 210,000 troops, the strength of the Guard was still about 200,000 men, and the Organized Reserve remained a pool of 100,000 officers. None of the components of the AUS was well-armed or furnished with much modern equipment.

The National Defense Act of 1920 addressed other matters of military importance. In recognition of the importance of air power in the Great War, the Army Air Service (AAS), which had emerged as a wartime improvisation from the prewar aviation section of the Army Signal Corps, was severed from its ties with its parent organization and established formally as a combat arm. But, whereas in World War I the AAS had a peak strength of nearly 200,000 personnel, the peacetime AAS was authorized a strength of 178,500 officers and enlisted men. The debate over the postwar organization of the army's aviation was contentious in part because some army airmen, especially BGen. William

Mitchell, assistant chief of the AAS, believed that American air power should be concentrated in a U.S. Air Force, an independent service coequal with the army and the navy. The National Defense Act of 1920 did not go nearly so far, but it did make the AAS unique among the combat arms of the army by allowing it to control its own research, development, and procurement. Moreover, in 1926, the act was amended to redesignate the AAS as the Army Air Corps and to create the post of assistant secretary of war for air.

Among the wartime arms, armor suffered the most from the terms of the 1920 act. The Army Tank Corps—like the AAS, a wartime improvisation—was abolished; its tanks transferred to the infantry branch and its armored cars to the cavalry branch. The cavalry's later experiments with tracked armored vehicles could only be conducted by officially calling them "combat cars." The organization imposed by the 1920 act thus helped to create confusion over the roles, missions, and proper organization of armor, and, along with lack of money, served to hobble experiments with armored forces for most of the interwar period. Moreover, by creating separate chiefs of arms responsible for developing doctrine for the infantry, cavalry, field and coast artilleries, respectively, the 1920 act encouraged branch isolation.

The National Defense Act of 1920 did have some positive effects. It created a single promotion list for the entire army in place of separate promotion lists for each branch; it established the Chemical Warfare Service, giving permanence to the wartime improvisation known as the Gas Warfare Service; it gave permanence to the wartime Finance Department; it created the Medical Administrative Corps; and it gave members of the Army Nurse Corps relative military rank. It also gave the War Department's General Staff an adequate complement of officers, including four assistant chiefs of staff and eighty-eight other officers in the rank of major or above. (Under the National Defense Act of 1916 only nineteen General Staff officers served in the War Department at one time.) Pershing was enabled to reform the General Staff of the War Department in line with his experience with the General Staff of the AEF, a more efficient organization, and his establishment of a War Plans Division was to be especially important for the future. The 1920 act also charged the assistant secretary of war with planning for industrial mobilization, thus preparing the way for the later Industrial War College, where officers might study the problems and techniques of wartime industrial mobilization.

Larry Addington

See also NATIONAL DEFENSE ACT OF 1916

Bibliography
Bernardo, C. Joseph, and Eugene H. Bacon. *American Military Policy: Its Development Since 1945.* Harrisburg, PA: Military Service Publishing, 1955.

Millis, Walter. *Arms and Men: A Study of American Military History.* New York: Putnam, 1956.

Vandiver, Frank E. *Black Jack: The Life and Times of John J. Pershing.* College Station: Texas A&M Press, 1977.

Weigley, Russell F. *The American Way of War: A History of United States Military Strategy and Policy.* New York: Macmillan, 1973.

National Guard

Efforts to define the National Guard's place in American military policy formed the background of its role in World War I. Congress resolved a fifteen-year struggle between the Regular Army and the Guard when it approved the National Defense Act of 1916. The act assured the Guard its traditional role as the first-line reserve, provided federal pay for weekly drills in state armories, and increased national spending substantially to equip the state forces.

At the same time, the new law obligated all guardsmen to take a dual oath, the traditional commitment to state service and an oath to respond to a presidential call for federal service. The latter permitted the President to use Guard forces outside the United States. The act prescribed strict standards for state officers and allowed the War Department to assign specific types of military units to state forces in order to create properly balanced National Guard divisions.

President Woodrow Wilson had barely signed the new law on June 3, 1916, when escalating conflict on the United States-Mexican border led him to federalize most of the National Guard. Mobilization came just as the state forces were responding to the new defense law, and many were not yet in compliance, leading to much confusion and hindering a prompt response. More significantly, the mobilization reinforced the Regular Army's perceptions that the Guard could never meet its obligations as a first-line reserve.

While the states mobilized their units fairly quickly, most Guard units were far under war strength, poorly equipped, and unfamiliar with the demands of routine military service. Guard forces lacked proper balance, being largely infantry units, and far short of cavalry, artillery, engineer, and other support organizations needed to create modern combined arms divisions. Finally, the Guard had always maintained it could recruit sufficient volunteers to bring its units up to strength, but it now proved unable to do so. Some historians contend that the Guard's woeful performance during the border mobilization and its inability to recruit volunteers was central to the army General Staff's decision to seek conscription when the United States entered World War I.

From late June 1916 through the end of February 1917, over 150,000 Guardsmen served for varying lengths of time along the Mexican border, largely in Texas or in state camps. The state soldiers did not march into Mexico but spent most of their time in training and on field maneuvers, many protesting vociferously that their energy and efforts were wasted. Inadvertently, however, the border experience served as a preliminary mobilization test for eventual American entry into World War I.

Some guardsmen were still in federal service when the United States severed diplomatic relations with Germany in early February 1917. Others had only been demobilized a short time when President Wilson issued a partial call for the National Guard in late March. The new call put federalized guardsmen on duty to protect vital transportation, utility, and industrial facilities from German sabotage. When Congress declared war on April 6, 1917, some 80,000 state soldiers were already on federal duty.

From the declaration of war in April until the end of August, that part of the Guard not on federal duty bided its time while the Wilson administration scrambled to organize for war. The delay in calling all of the state soldiers into federal service revealed the War Department's unpreparedness for war and suggested that many of the problems that accompanied the Mexican border call-up were not merely the National Guard's fault but were endemic to the American military system. Until August 5, when President Wilson "drafted" the Guard for war service, the states could do little but recruit volunteers and provide them with rudimentary military training.

The War Department waited until August to activate the National Guard because it lacked the arms and equipment to supply state units, and there were no military camps where guardsmen could be concentrated for organization into full divisions and given advanced training. The need to provide supplies and training facilities for the hundreds of thousands of drafted men due to report for service in early September further delayed mobilizing the National Guard. Furthermore, upon the recommendation of General Pershing and his staff following their arrival in France, army planners completely reorganized the table of organization for divisions, dropping the triangular organization built around nine infantry regiments and adopting the square division composed of four much larger infantry regiments. Until sufficient mobilization camps were built and divisional reorganization planning completed, there was little purpose in calling up the National Guard.

Wilson's "draft" of the Guard—based on a provision in the May 1917 Selective Service Act and not the National Defense Act of 1916—brought guardsmen to federal service as individuals, not as members of their units. The May draft law promised to retain "insofar as practicable the state designations" of National Guard units. Drafting the Guard and the necessity to comply with square divisional tables, however, led to major reorganization. The process cost many National Guard colonels and brigadier generals their regimental and brigade commands. In addition, the army deemed it necessary to adopt a systematic means of designating all military units, regardless of their origins. The new numbering system created uniformity in military terms, but it ended a long tradition of state units taking their names into combat. Many guardsmen resented both the drastic reorganization and the loss of state and local unit identities.

Some National Guard divisions, notably the 26th and 42d divisions, spent little time in training camps but moved directly to embarkation ports for transport to France. Others spent a cold and uncomfortable winter in the South, living in tents and attempting to train with limited arms and equipment. All the Guard divisions were filled to war strength with draftees and officers from officer training schools. It was impossible to maintain units composed entirely of men from the same state. Indeed the initial attempt to differentiate between Regular Army, National Guard, and National Army (selective service) divisions became impossible, and in August 1918 Army Chief of Staff Peyton C. March ordered an end to the practice.

Nearly 450,000 National Guardsmen, who voluntarily enlisted in state units, served during the war. The Guard provided the organizational foundation for eighteen divisions, 40 percent of the divisions in the AEF, the 26th through 42d and the 93d Division. Black Guardsmen formed the core of the 93d's four infantry regiments, the 369th through the 372d. The latter were initially assigned to the French Army and only belatedly organized into the 93d Division after the Armistice. Six National Guard divisions were broken up upon their arrival in France to provide replacements for understrength divisions soon to be committed to combat, but the remainder saw as much or more fighting as divisions committed to the Western Front.

The National Defense Act of 1916 ensured the National Guard a significant role in World War I. In the aftermath of war, however, many guardsmen expressed discontent with their wartime experience. Higher ranking Guard officers who lost their commands during reorganization often believed the army deliberately denied state soldiers the chance to play a significant part in the war. Some stressed the fact that only one guardsman, MajGen. John F. O'Ryan, 27th Division (New York National Guard) led his division throughout the war. What irked guardsmen the most was the fact that since President Wilson "drafted" the Guard under the Selective Service Act rather than "call" it as provided under the National Defense Act of 1916, the War Department demoralized guardsmen by discharging them as individuals. The process left the state forces in complete disarray in 1919 and 1920 and significantly delayed reorganization of the state forces. These lingering resentments contributed to the bitter political struggle surrounding passage of the National Defense Act of 1920.

Jerry Cooper

See also NATIONAL DEFENSE ACT OF 1916; NATIONAL DEFENSE ACT OF 1920; SELECTIVE SERVICE ACT

Bibliography

Hill, Jim Dan. *The Minuteman in Peace and War: A History of the National Guard.* Harrisburg, PA: Stackpole, 1964.

Kriedberg, Marvin A., and Merton G. Henry. *History of Military Mobilization in the United States Army, 1775–1945.* Washington, DC: Department of the Army, 1955.

Weigley, Russell F. *History of the United States Army.* New York: Macmillan, 1967.

White, Lonnie J. *Panthers to Arrowheads: the 36th (Texas-Oklahoma) Division in World War I.* Austin, TX: Presidial Press, 1984.

National League for Woman's Service

The National League for Woman's Service (NLWS) emerged from the relief and preparedness activities of the Woman's Department of the National Civil Federation (WDNCF). Founded by Grace Parker and chaired by Maude Wetmore, NLWS was based upon the British Women's Voluntary Aid Detachments. On Feb. 3, 1917, the NLWS presented Walter Gifford, director of the Council of National Defense (CND), with a recommendation for an official registration of women for volunteer war service and for the creation of a Woman Power Board. The NLWS expected to be the organization through which the government would accomplish these tasks. CND rejected the proposal, but NLWS began its own registration of women and implied it had government sanction. It put its members into uniform, used military terminology, and required military drills. Although the United States was still a nonbelligerent, the activities prescribed for the various divisions of the organization—social and welfare, home economics, agriculture, motor driving, general service, and signaling and map reading—were all geared to a nation at war.

By the time the United States entered the war, NLWS sections had been established in thirty-one states and 50,000 women had enrolled for service. The greatest accomplishment of the league in the spring and summer of 1917 was its work in connection with mobilization of working women for war needs in industry and agriculture. Financed by the NLWS, its Bureau of Registration secured lists of firms working on government contracts, examined contracts involving female laborers to ascertain where shortages existed, and when necessary, recruited women workers. In addition to the central bureau in Washington, the league established bureaus in fifteen states where female labor shortages existed. Five months after the United States entered the war, Secretary of Labor William B. Wilson decided that it was necessary to transfer NLWS's work to the Department of Labor, where its work was assumed by the Bureau of Labor Statistics and the Federal Employment Service.

Many NLWS members expected their organization to become the official arm of the government for women's war-related work, but the CND instead appointed a separate Woman's Committee (WCCND) to coordinate women's activities. Although Maud Wetmore was appointed to WCCND's executive committee, state WCCND divisions and league branches clashed repeatedly in the ensuing months. The most serious conflicts arose over registration of women for volunteer war service. Disappointed because they had originally publicized their drive as an official venture, NLWS encouraged women to continue to register for volunteer training and service with the league. The registration drives, in any case, had more symbolic than practical importance, for few of the millions who registered were ever called to serve.

The motor corps division of the NLWS served as the motor division of the Red Cross until June 1918, when the Red Cross decided to form its own motor fleet. Created to provide transportation for military officers and ambulance service for the sick and wounded, the league motor corps performed a wide range of services. Most NLWS motor corps women on the local level ignored league requests to remain independent and became integral parts of the Red Cross motor corps during the war.

Although the NLWS did not disband at the end of the war, only the larger branches planned to continue their activities. Determined to retain at least a skeleton organization, the NLWS became incorporated in April 1919. The organization, however, failed to establish a new program, and it continued to exist in name only. During the postwar period, some of its leaders became very active in promoting Americanism and opposing Bolshevism.

Barbara Steinson

See also COUNCIL OF NATIONAL DEFENSE

Bibliography

Finnegan, John P. *Against the Specter of a Dragon: The Campaign for American Military Preparedness.* Westport, CT: Greenwood Press, 1974.

National League for Woman's Service. *Annual Report for the Year 1918.* New York: NLWS, 1919.

National Security League. *Proceedings of the Congress of Constructive Patriotism held under the Auspices of the National Security League.* New York: NSL, 1917.

Steinson, Barbara J. *American Women's Activism in World War I.* New York: Garland, 1982.

National Security League

Of the organizations most active in fostering the preparedness movement that swept the United States shortly after the outbreak of the First World War, none attained the prominence of the National Security League (NSL). On Aug. 6, 1914, England declared war on Germany; that same day the future structure of the NSL was conceived by a prominent New York attorney, S. Stanwood Menken. While in London to facilitate the return to the United States of displaced Americans in Europe, Menken witnessed Parliament's first clumsy attempts at national mobilization. Back home, Menken quickly formed the nucleus of his association, which included such luminaries as international lawyer Frederic R. Coudert, former Secretary of War Henry L. Stimson, publishers George Haven Putnam and Lyman Abbott, and inventor Henry Alexander Wise Wood.

The NSL set about its preparedness campaign at once. Committees on the navy, army, militia, and the Congress were selected to investigate the conditions in America's national defenses. Tons of boilerplate revealing the horrors of enemy invasion and occupation flooded the country, while the NSL "flying squadrons" addressed hundreds of rallies. The year 1916 witnessed the formation of seventy branches across the United States despite the defection to the American Defense Society of its publicity committee led by Clarence Smedley Thompson. Overcoming internal friction, Menken's colleagues called for a program of compulsory military training, an issue soundly defeated in the National Defense Act of 1916.

Following America's intervention in Europe, the nation was receptive to Menken's preparedness views. Warmed by national acceptance, his associates began to define patriotism as a collective adoption of their own standards for correct thought and action. In an intensive campaign of education as to the causes of the war and how to win it, college and university professors, editors, and educators were mobilized under the NSL's Committee on Patriotism through Education. Under the direction of Princeton's Robert McNutt McElroy, professor of American history, this propaganda agency sought to aid the war effort through eradication of all alien influences in the United States, a reinterpretation of American history stressing the interdependence of the United States and the Allies, and, finally, the removal of all instructors of questionable loyalty. Operating under virtually autonomous leadership, and with objectives frequently at odds with the executive committee, McElroy continually clashed with Menken. This dilemma ended dramatically in June 1918 when Menken was forced to resign in favor of Charles E. Lydecker, a colorless, conservative Republican. Lydecker embroiled the league in the congressional elections of 1918 and ultimately in a disastrous congressional investigation, caused by NSL opposition to numerous candidates embittered by the league's meddling. A special committee of the House of Representatives found the National Security League in violation of the Corrupt Practices Act, which declared that organizations engaged in politics must file a report of expenditures with Congress.

The league continued to debate postwar military policy until its demise in 1942, although the association lost many old supporters as a result of the investigation. Once a proud society led by men knowledgeable in the requirements for a strong national defense, the league spent the next twenty-three years in pursuit of issues extraneous to the principles of its incorporation.

John C. Edwards

Bibliography
Edwards, John C. *Patriots in Pinstripe: Men of the National Security League.* Washington, DC: University Press of America, 1982.
——. "The Price of Political Innocence: The Role of the National Security League in the Congressional Election of 1918." *Military Affairs* (December 1981).
Ward, Robert D. "The Origin and Activities of the National Security League, 1914–1919." *Mississippi Valley Historical Review* (June 1960).

National War Labor Board

A year after the United States entered the war, President Woodrow Wilson created the National War Labor Board (NWLB) to serve as the "Supreme Court of Labor Relations" during the emergency. Wilson acted with the cooperation of the National Industrial Conference Board (NICB), an amalgam of employer associations, and the American Federation of Labor (AF of L) in an effort to end a growing number of strikes—3,500 between April 1917 and early 1918. By the fall of 1917, the NICB, the AF of L, and the President's Mediation Commission—which Wilson had appointed to suggest means to halt production losses—all recognized the need for effective national mediation machinery. In January 1918, Secretary of Labor William B. Wilson appointed the War Labor Conference Board (WLCB) to devise plans for a centralized board. Five of its members, selected by the NICB, represented employers; five, chosen by the AF of L, spoke for employees; and two joint chairmen, named by business and labor members themselves, were expected to represent their constituents and the public. By March, the WLCB had devised a set of principles and procedures to guide the proposed National War Labor Board. In April, the President appointed the members of the WLCB to serve on the NWLB. The NWLB greatly influenced the development of federal labor policies until the Armistice in November, and it officially existed until August 1919. The board considered approximately 1,250 cases, referred many to other agencies, and handed down almost 500 awards or findings. In most of the awards, the decision was favorable to labor.

The members of the NWLB included former President William Howard Taft and Frank P. Walsh, the former chairman of the United States Commission on Industrial Relations, who served as joint chairmen. Prewar critics of each other, the two men worked well together and generally led the board in reaching its most important decisions. The labor members, although they represented divergent factions within the AF of L, all supported the war effort and represented unions vital to war work: Frank J. Hayes, president of the United

Mine Workers; William L. Hutcheson, president of the United Brotherhood of Carpenters and Joiners; Thomas A. Rickert, president of the United Garment Workers; Thomas J. Savage, member of the executive council of the International Association of Machinists; and Victor Olander, secretary-treasurer of the Illinois State Federation of Labor and a vice president of the International Seamen's Union. The industrialists represented a cross section of the business community and stood behind the open shop: Loyall A. Osborne, vice president of Westinghouse Electric and Manufacturing Company and chairman of both the executive committee and the advisory committee of the NICB; William H. VanDervoort, a member of the NICB advisory committee and president of an engineering company, an automobile manufacturer and an ordnance firm in Illinois; Leonor F. Loree, president of the Delaware and Hudson Railroad and numerous coal and iron companies; B.L. Worden, president of the Lackawanna Bridge Company and the Submarine Boat Corporation; and C. Edwin Michael, a former vice president of the National Association of Manufacturers and president of the Virginia Bridge and Iron Company.

The NWLB's principles, which the WLCB members drafted and approved, reflected the contradictory objectives of businessmen and labor leaders. The WLCB first condemned strikes and lockouts and then became ambiguous about them. It sanctioned both open shops and union shops as "existing conditions" to be maintained, but also affirmed labor's right to organize and to bargain collectively "through chosen representatives." It forbade employers from discharging workers for union membership or for "legitimate" union activities but also forbade workers from using "coercive" means to build union power. The NWLB would consider prevailing local conditions in reaching settlements, but it would not be bound by them. It would award the basic eight-hour day when required by law and would otherwise adjust hours according to the needs of the workers and "governmental necessities." The principles called for a "living wage" to "insure the subsistence of the worker and his family in health and reasonable comfort." Finally, the board called for equal pay for equal work for women who did work "ordinarily performed by men."

Using these principles, the NWLB could attempt to resolve any controversy in a war-related industry if no other agency had jurisdiction or if another agency had violated an NWLB principle. The board could arbitrate a dispute only if both parties submitted to its jurisdiction and if the NWLB members could agree unanimously to an award. In practice, a two-man section of the board was generally assigned to propose an award that the full board could approve. If a section of the NWLB could not reach unanimity, an NWLB umpire, one of ten men initially selected by President Wilson, could make an award as sole arbiter. If either the employer or the employees in a dispute refused to accept the board's jurisdiction, the board could recommend a settlement by majority vote. Even when the board or an umpire had the initial cooperation of both parties, either could refuse to accept an award. The NWLB had no powers of enforcement. Officially, its ability to function depended on voluntary cooperation.

Not surprisingly, two employers openly defied the NWLB over the issues of union organization and collective bargaining, and in another case, employees went out on strike in protest against the wage decisions of an NWLB umpire. In these three cases, cooperation with the NWLB became involuntary. President Wilson nationalized the Western Union Company when it refused to follow an NWLB directive to permit workers to join the Commercial Telegraphers Union of America and then bargain collectively, and the War Department seized the Smith and Wesson Arms Company in a show of support for the NWLB when the firm rejected the NWLB's method of doing business in consultation with unionized employees in shop committees. In both of these cases, the defiant companies had reflected the sentiment of the business members of the NWLB, who tried unsuccessfully to protect yellow-dog contracts and the closed nonunion shop under the guise of "existing conditions." Similarly, when the machinists in Bridgeport, Connecticut, struck with the support of the machinists' union president because their new wages would remain below union standards, Wilson ordered them back to work and threatened to bar them from work in war-related industries and to lift their draft exemptions if they stayed out.

The awards and majority recommendations handed down before the Armistice in 1918, coupled with the administration's willingness to compel compliance with the NWLB, established the board's reputation as a proponent of social justice as well as full production.

In large measure, the board's decisions were made possible by Taft's continual willingness to check the employers on the board who had sat, as Walsh observed, "like hawks . . . [ready] to pounce down on any person making an effort to ameliorate the conditions of the workers any place." Equally important to its success, the board did nothing radical as it gradually set unofficial wage and hour standards. NWLB policies, furthermore, steered a mid-course between what John Fitch called "the employers' desire to smash the unions and the demand of the organized workers for . . . the closed shop."

A sampling of the board's wage decisions makes its moderate reformist position clear. The NWLB made headlines when it granted common laborers in Waynesboro, Pennsylvania, who earned twenty-two cents an hour a new rate of forty cents instead of the thirty cents the workers had requested. The public also took notice when the joint chairmen handed down twenty-two awards in street railway cases that month. Unlike some other industries, the street railway had no cost-plus contracts with the government, and throughout the country they were deeply in debt. In most cases, Taft and Walsh raised wages regardless of whether the railways stood to receive fare increases. Before the awards, experienced conductors on the lines under consideration received an average pay of thirty-four cents an hour. Their new wages, in general, were forty-eight cents in larger cities, forty-five cents in second-class cities, and forty-two cents in communities with recognizably low costs of living. By May 1919, the board handed down about 100 street railway awards, settled 40 strikes, diverted 98 threatened walkouts, and increased wages on 110 lines. The NWLB was unable to agree on a "living wage," however, and set men's wages well below the standard that Frank Walsh wanted adopted. (Walsh, supported by NWLB staff experts, argued that a common laborer needed to work 300 eight-hour days per annum—at seventy-three cents an hour, $5.85 a day—to support a wife and five children in minimum comfort.) The board usually awarded common laborers forty to forty-two cents. Yet in part because of NWLB awards, common laborers in 1918 earned an average hourly wage of thirty-nine and one-half cents; again, in part because of the NWLB, the real wages of street railway employees increased by 3 percent in 1918 and by another 11 percent

in 1919, which brought their purchasing power in that year to its highest level since 1905.

Adjusting hours under the NWLB's principle proved difficult for a variety of reasons. The federal eight-hour day law was complicated by the war. President Wilson had suspended the actual eight-hour day in favor of the basic eight-hour day, which provided for overtime after eight hours, by executive order; and many firms under contract to the government also had nongovernmental work. The NWLB's labor members considered the adoption of the basic day among their highest priorities. The employer members wanted to prevent widespread use of what they considered a means to raise wages and worried about setting precedents that would outlast the war. Furthermore, the War Labor Policies Board (WLPB), chaired by Felix Frankfurter, asked governmental labor relations boards to grant the basic eight-hour day only when specifically required by law until it could determine federal hours policy. The NWLB decided to act independently of the WLPB but, as in the matter of the living wage, was unable to reach a consensus on the easy application of its own principle, which had promised consideration of the needs of the workers and of the government as well as existing law. NWLB umpires Henry Fore and Justice Walter Clark of North Carolina made awards granting eight-hour days when a deadlocked board would not. The NWLB, nonetheless, earned a reputation as a strong proponent of the eight-hour day. It granted the eight-hour day, basic or actual, in 151 cases. The NWLB also sometimes refused to change hours, sometimes awarded a basic nine-hour day, and sometimes left the determination of hours to shop committees that it established.

The most controversial of the NWLB's policies concerned the rights of union members in open shops and the rights of all employees to representation in collective bargaining arrangements. Although the NWLB did not require employers to recognize unions, it ordered the reinstatement of employees who had been dismissed for joining unions regardless of whether or not they had legal individual employment contracts. The board's stand against yellow-dog contracts as set forth initially in an award for the General Electric Company in Pittsfield, Massachusetts, neatly sidestepped the U.S. Supreme Court's decision in *Hitchamn Coal and Coke Company v. Mitchell* and encouraged the growth of organized labor. So, too, did the NWLB's establishment of some eighty-six shop committees that permitted the election of union members to represent their fellow employees in open-shop companies. The elections and operations of the shop committees were overseen by the NWLB examiners in order to protect both workers' rights and emerging NWLB wage and hour standards. Because these kinds of awards forced employers to share some measure of power with employees, often unionized employees, and because NWLB shop committees seemed intent upon outlasting the war emergency, affected companies often became adversarial. Among them, Western Union and Smith and Wesson defied the NWLB and were nationalized; the Bethlehem Steel Company dragged its feet about implementing the NWLB's award, which threw out its bonus system and mandated shop committees, until the Armistice. Then, as Bethlehem president Eugene Grace told the NWLB examiner assigned to the case, the award "was dead."

In dealing with women workers, the NWLB left a checkered legacy. Its principle calling for equal pay for women who did men's work reflected twin desires to protect wage levels and to prevent an unnecessary flood of women into the workforce (1.5 million women had taken jobs in war-related industries). In forty-eight cases, sixteen of which involved women streetcar conductors, the board awarded equal pay. In fourteen of the forty-eight, it also set minimum wages for women as much as ten to twelve cents below the minimums it set for men in the same plants, giving women thirty to thirty-three cents an hour. The awards gave men about $21 a week and women about $15, a figure that Taft and Walsh considered a living wage for a woman in a small city and without dependents. The lower minimums resulted in part because women generally worked at lower paying jobs and in part because the NWLB found that equal work in jobs normally performed by men was difficult to determine. Even those minimums, however, were more generous than the standards set by states that regulated women's pay, where the average wage for adult experienced women in 1919 was just $10. Persistent confusion over the status of women, who were frequently subject to protective legislation, led the board to create two separate women's divisions within the NWLB staff, which was directed by W. Jett Lauck. When Lauck and the head of the women

examiners, Marie Obenhauer, disagreed over policy, he abolished her division. Meanwhile prominent supporters of women's rights launched an unsuccessful campaign to have two women appointed to the NWLB itself. Among NWLB members, only Walsh supported the idea. When the war ended, a different issue came before the board. Did women have the right to retain their new, higher paying jobs? Specifically, should they be retained as street railway conductors, where they did equal work and earned equal pay? Initially, the NWLB agreed with local unions and said "no"; then, in March 1919, it reversed itself at a time when its awards were generally being ignored. That month the New York State Department of Labor estimated that two-thirds of the women who had replaced men in jobs in the state received less than the $15 weekly wage that the NWLB often awarded.

William Howard Taft thought the NWLB "had nothing to live for" when the war ended, and Frank Walsh resigned on December 3 because he believed that thereafter the NWLB could only be a disappointment to working people who had believed in it. Taft stayed on the job, while Walsh went to work as an attorney before the NWLB for striking New York Harbor workers and women streetcar conductors who had lost their jobs. Walsh also worked closely with Basil M. Manly, his successor as joint chairman, to formulate plans for a permanent labor relations board with real power to bring social justice and with broader-minded employer members than their antiunion colleagues on the NWLB. After the Armistice, some of them had even advised fellow employers that the NWLB had no clout. Meanwhile, persistent problems with Eugene Grace and with Postmaster General Albert S. Burleson, whose antiunion policies and high-handed attitudes dominated his management of Western Union, demoralized the entire board. Finally, in August 1919, it dissolved itself.

Valerie Jean Conner

Bibliography

Conner, Valerie Jean. *The National War Labor Board: Stability, Social Justice, and the Voluntary State in World War I.* Chapel Hill: University of North Carolina Press, 1983.

Montgomery, David. *The Fall of the House of Labor.* New York: Cambridge University Press, 1987.

Wynn, Neil A. *From Progressivism to Prosperity: World War I and American Society.* New York: Holmes & Meier, 1986.

National Woman's Party

The National Woman's Party (NWP), founded by militant suffragist Alice Paul in 1916, was a single-issue pressure group dedicated to winning the vote for American women. As the organization's guiding spirit, Paul borrowed tactics from the British suffragette movement to bring the issue to the attention of the American people and to coerce Congress and the President into supporting the federal woman suffrage amendment. In January 1917, the NWP placed pickets before the gates of the White House with banners that asked: "Mr. President, How Long Must Women Wait For Liberty?" Woodrow Wilson remained unmoved by the pickets; he merely tipped his hat to the banner-bearing women as he drove back and forth through the gates.

With the advent of World War I, the NWP saw in Wilson's wartime proclamations on democracy abroad a wedge with which to pry support for woman suffrage from the preoccupied Wilson. New banners appeared bearing excerpts from Wilson's writings and speeches on democracy. Indignant bystanders gathered around the little band of pickets daily, and soon riots broke out. To quell the disturbances, District of Columbia police began to arrest the suffragists on the charge of obstructing the sidewalks. At first they were given fines and scoldings, but as the picketing continued, jail sentences were handed down. Since the press gave full coverage to the arrests and sentencings, Paul was convinced that her strategy was working. With each arrest, more Americans learned that there were women willing to risk a prison term for the right to vote. While some critics censured the NWP pickets for unpatriotic behavior, the newspaper photographs of gray-haired women being manhandled into jail for exercising their right to peaceful assembly won the sympathy and support of many. Moreover, the President's demands for democracy abroad seemed increasingly hollow while women were daily imprisoned for asking for democracy at home. Embarrassed by the hypocrisy of his position, Wilson pardoned eleven jailed militants in July 1917. To the President's dismay, Alice Paul immediately announced that the picketing would continue.

By August, the White House gates were the scenes of riots. Arrests began again, this time netting Paul herself. She received a lengthy prison term, but she continued to direct the pickets from her cell in the District of Columbia jail. Ironically, it was there that she devised a plan that at last convinced Wilson to support the federal suffrage amendment. Paul and other imprisoned suffragists began a hunger strike. After several days, prison officials began to force-feed the prisoners. Through smuggled notes, Paul alerted the press. NWP activists also hired a train, called the "Prison Special," that traveled across the nation publicizing the plight of the picketers.

By fall 1917, many Americans were alarmed by the administration's actions regarding the pickets, and by the President's apathetic attitude toward woman suffrage. In late November, Alice Paul received a late-night visitor who had close ties to the administration. Although denying that he represented the President, the visitor asked Paul if she would agree to abandon picketing if the administration guaranteed that the suffrage amendment would pass the House in early 1918 and the Senate in 1919. What Paul replied is unknown, but within days she was released. On Jan. 8, 1918, Woodrow Wilson announced his support of the federal woman suffrage amendment, and the next day, the Nineteenth Amendment passed the House of Representatives. As action on the amendment stalled in the Senate, the NWP briefly returned to militant tactics by burning an effigy of Wilson, but for the most part the suffragists concentrated on lobbying Senators to act on the Nineteenth Amendment. Senate approval came in June 1919, and the amendment was ratified in August 1920.

Sally Hunter Graham

Bibliography

Graham, Sally Hunter. "Woodrow Wilson, Alice Paul and the Woman Suffrage Movement." *Political Science Quarterly* (Winter 1983–1984).

Irwin, Inez Haynes. *The Story of the Woman's Party.* New York: Harcourt, Brace, 1921.

Lunardini, Christine A. *From Equal Suffrage to Equal Rights: Alice Paul and the National Woman's Party, 1910–1920.* New York: New York University Press, 1986.

Stevens, Doris. *Jailed For Freedom.* New York: Boni and Liveright, 1920.

Naval Consulting Board

The Naval Consulting Board was a civilian agency created to provide the United States Navy with technical advice during World War I. Staffed by prominent inventors, scientists, and businessmen, the board evaluated inventions submitted to the navy by the public. At the beginning of the war, the navy did not have an organization or procedure to develop and test new inventions. The problem had become acute by 1915, when it was clear that the navy lagged behind its European counterparts in the development of submarines and airplanes.

Navy Secretary Josephus Daniels responded to this challenge in July 1915, following the publication of an interview with Thomas Edison in which the inventor outlined a plan for military preparedness. Daniels, who was particularly interested in Edison's ideas for the creation of a permanent military research laboratory, asked the inventor to serve on an entity created to advise the navy on technical matters. Edison agreed, becoming the president of the Naval Consulting Board. Edison's chief engineer, Miller Reese Hutchinson, also became a member of the board.

The others members of the board were selected by eleven technical and scientific societies. The American Chemical Society elected William R. Whitney, research director at General Electric, and Leo H. Baekeland, a chemist who had invented a type of electrical insulation. The American Electro-Chemical Society nominated Joseph W. Richards, a professor of mineralogy at Lehigh University, and Lawrence Addicks, superintendent of the U.S. Metals Refining Company.

William L. Saunders and Benjamin B. Thayer represented the American Institute of Mining Engineers. Saunders, president of the Ingersoll-Rand Company, was an inventor of compressed air equipment, while Thayer was president of Anaconda Mining Company. The American Aeronautical Society picked Hudson Maxim, a well-known inventor of firearms and explosives, and Matthew B. Sellers, technical editor of *Aeronautics*.

Frank J. Sprague and Benjamin G. Lamme were selected by the American Institute of Electrical Engineers. Sprague was a General Electric consulting engineer and a pioneer inventor of electric traction equipment. Lamme was an engineer for the Westinghouse Electric Company and an inventor of alternating current generators. The American Society of Mechanical Engineers nominated William L. Emmett and Spencer Miller to the board. Emmett was a General Electric engineer and an inventor of a vertical shaft steam turbine. Miller was chief engineer of the cableway department of the Lidgewood Manufacturing Company and a specialist in the development of coaling ship cable systems.

Henry A. Wise Wood and Elmer A. Sperry represented the American Society of Aeronautical Engineers. Wood, an engineer and businessman interested in aeronautics, was noted for his work in printing technology. Sperry was an inventor and manufacturer of gyrostabilizing equipment for ships and airplanes. The American Society of Automobile Engineers selected Andrew L. Riker, an inventor of electric-powered automobiles and gasoline engines, and Howard E. Coffin, vice president of the Hudson Motor Car Company.

Alfred Craven and Andrew M. Hunt represented the American Society of Civil Engineers. Craven was chief engineer of the New York City Rapid Transit Commission, while Hunt was an engineer who specialized in the construction of hydroelectric plants. The American Mathematical Society selected two prominent university scientists, Robert S. Woodward and Arthur G. Webster. Woodward had been a professor of mathematics at Columbia University and president of the Carnegie Institution. Webster was a professor of physics at Clark University. The Inventor's Guild elected Peter Cooper Hewitt and Thomas Robins. Hewitt was an electrical inventor, while Robins, who served as the board's secretary, was president of the Robins Belt Conveyor Company.

Formally organized on Oct. 7, 1915, the board adopted a set of rules and created fifteen technical subcommittees. Organized according to subject, including submarines, ordnance and explosives, mines and torpedoes, and ship construction, these subcommittees tested inventions submitted by the public. The board received approximately 110,000 suggestions, most dealing with the submarine. Of these submissions, only 110 were considered worthy of referral to one of the subcommittees, while only one, the Ruggles orientator, was produced during the war. The orientator, a simulated pilot's seat mounted on a set of gimbals, allowed trainers to simulate aircraft motions for pilot trainees.

In February 1917, the board created a Special Problems Committee to address the submarine issue. This committee received thousands of suggestions from the public for shields and nets to protect surface vessels from submarine attack. Other ideas for camouflage and smoke reduction were also tested. None of these ideas were practical.

The technical work of board members was of more consequence. Elmer Sperry developed a number of improvements for airplanes and submarines, including a device to detect hydrogen in submarines, improved steel airplane propellers, and remote-control devices for aerial bombs. Hudson Maxim invented improved contact mines and torpedo fuel. Peter Cooper Hewitt conducted extensive experiments on helicopter design, while Frank Sprague developed depth charges, underwater fuses, and armor-piercing shells.

Leonard DeGraff

See also EDISON, THOMAS ALVA

Bibliography

Dupree, A. Hunter. *Science in the Federal Government.* Cambridge, MA: Belknap Press, 1957.

Hughes, Thomas P. *Elmer Sperry: Inventor and Engineer.* Baltimore: Johns Hopkins University Press, 1971.

Noble, David F. *America by Design: Science, Technology and the Rise of Corporate Capitalism.* New York: Knopf, 1977.

Scott, Lloyd N. *Naval Consulting Board of the United States.* Washington, DC: Government Printing Office, 1920.

Navy, United States

See entries under UNITED STATES NAVY

Navy League

The Navy League of the United States was a private civic organization dedicated to promoting support for a strong navy. The league was founded in New York City in 1902, but it remained small and had little apparent influence before 1910. It was a tiny shadow of the vast and powerful pro-navy organizations in Europe, especially in Germany and Great Britain. Whereas in 1912 the United States Navy League had an annual income of $15,000 and about 7,000 members, the German Navy League had over 1 million members and an annual budget of about $250,000. Membership in the U.S. Navy League peaked in 1917 at only 13,000. In addition, its Woman's Section had more than 15,000 members. The Woman's Section, founded in July 1915, was the first of many American preparedness organizations.

Despite the rapid expansion of the United States Navy in the first two decades of the twentieth century, the Navy League believed that more should be done. The league generally supported construction plans of the U.S. Navy's General Board, which were sometimes higher than the President requested and usually higher than what Congress ultimately approved. In 1912, the league helped convince the three major political parties to pledge support for a strong navy in their presidential campaign platforms. A Navy League committee actually drafted the defense plank of the Democratic Party in 1912. However, the league was disappointed in the first years of the Wilson administration when the President and Secretary of the Navy Josephus Daniels consistently slashed the building requests of the General Board. Not until July 1915 did President Wilson begin to advocate a really massive naval buildup that promised a navy second to none.

In addition to support of the navy's proposals for new ship construction, the league also lobbied for the promotion of naval officers by merit rather than seniority and called for the establishment of a Council of National Defense to coordinate a national strategy between Congress and the executive. The Navy League's influence peaked in 1916 when, after the great Anglo-German naval battle of Jutland, Congress approved President Woodrow Wilson's request for an unprecedented naval construction program to make the United States Navy second to none. Other league goals were also substantially adopted in that bill. Its influence declined thereafter, partly as a result of its very success in 1916, but especially because of a vituperative conflict between the league and Secretary Daniels. The league accused Daniels of suppressing information that indicated that radical elements of organized labor were responsible for the devastating Black Tom explosion. Daniels was livid at the charges, which were later proved totally false, and in August 1917, he officially banned navy cooperation with the organization.

Neither the league nor its various publications were ever on a firm financial footing. From its inception, its major benefactor was Col. Robert M. Thompson, chairman of the board of International Nickel. Thompson was also a director of the league and its president during the war years. Public critics of the league's militarism, including Henry Ford and publisher Oswald Garrison Villard, emphasized the business interests behind the league's call for a strong navy. Thompson's International Nickel, a monopoly in the United States, gained about $200,000 in sales for the armor of each 30,000-ton battleship built. Other league officers had big-business connections, including H.L. Satterlee, son-in-law of J.P. Morgan, Sr. Yet the Navy League never got anywhere near the amount of funds from business that went to the peace organizations. By July 1919, it had accumulated over $138,000 in debt. Thompson saved it from bankruptcy by assuming the debt himself. However, he was not prepared to finance singlehandedly the league, which languished through the isolationist 1920s and 1930s, reemerging as an active force for preparedness immediately before the outbreak of World War II.

James H. Nolt

See also NAVY LEAGUE: WOMAN'S SECTION

Bibliography

Navy League. *Addresses Before the Eleventh Annual Convention of the Navy League of the United States, Washington, D.C., April 10–13, 1916.* Washington, DC: Navy League, 1916.

———. *Sea Power.* Washington, DC: Navy League, 1916–1921.

———. *Seven Seas Magazine.* Washington, DC: Navy League, 1915–1916.

Rappaport, Armin. *The Navy League of the United States.* Detroit: Wayne State University Press, 1962.

Navy League: Woman's Section

The Woman's Section of the Navy League (WSNL), formed in July 1915, was the first national women's preparedness organization. Eager to capitalize on public outrage over the May 1915 sinking of the *Lusitania*, Navy League officials responded positively to the suggestion by two sisters, Elisabeth Ellicott Poe and Vylla Poe Wilson, that a woman's section be created. Although the rationale for the WSNL was to guard the country against the possibility of foreign invasion and to arouse patriotism among American women, organizers also sought to dispel the antimilitary image of women created by the feminist pacifists. They contended that the protective functions of women made it their duty to demand strong military defenses and that the country should listen to women's pleas for military protection of the homes and lives under their care. Attacking the idea that women did not want their sons to go to war, WSNL supporters argued that a strong navy was the best hope for keeping their sons and their country safe.

The WSNL received support from leaders of nine women's patriotic organizations and from the National Association Opposed to Woman Suffrage. Within three months of its founding, the WSNL claimed over 25,000 members. The WSNL sponsored a Women's National Defense Conference in Washington, D.C., in November 1915. This meeting attracted a large crowd and featured numerous prominent speakers who denounced pacifists and called for preparedness. Delegates passed resolutions urging Woodrow Wilson and Congress to do all that they could to provide the necessary defenses for the country.

The most novel activity of the WSNL, the establishment of women's service camps, demonstrated women's desire to participate fully in the nation's defense effort. The First National Service School opened at Chevy Chase, Maryland, on May 1, 1916, and served as the model for three other camps that year held at the Presidio in California, Lake Geneva, Wisconsin, and Narragansett Bay, Rhode Island. Most of the camps lasted a month, with two-week sessions that accommodated both resident and day students. They were modified versions of Plattsburg, the popular civilian training camps run by Gen. Leonard Wood in New York. Although course work in the camps emphasized domestic over martial arts, the domestic training was placed within the routine of a military camp with required military calisthenics, drilling, and marching. Testimonies by campers revealed that through the military camp environment and camp training, the women developed obedience, alertness, and a sense of unity. Some of the young women experienced a soldierly sisterhood and underwent a kind of patriotic conversion experience. Campers came to believe that trained and dedicated women were essential for the defense of the country. In addition to their profound impact on the campers themselves, the camps attracted valuable publicity for the defense cause.

In March 1917, the organization shifted to more traditional knitting relief work with the creation of the WSNL Comforts Committee. Although the WSNL sponsored two more camps for women after the United States entered the war—the second encampment of the First National Service School in Washington, D.C., and the Fifth National Service School at the New York State School of Agriculture on Long Island, knitting had a greater appeal for the WSNL membership as a form of activity that enabled women of all ages and classes to participate in the war effort. The plan of the Comforts Committee, headed by Elizabeth Van Rensselaer Frazer, was to supply every American warship in the European war zone and on active patrol duty with hand-knitted hoods, scarves, and wristlets. A dispute between the male leadership of the Navy League and Navy Secretary Josephus Daniels complicated distribution of Comforts Committee articles. The women declined the suggestion by Daniels that they form a Red Cross auxiliary and send articles in the name of Mildred Dewey, since the Navy League had been banned from entering ships or naval stations. Although considerable confusion ensued, with women around the country uncertain about how to get their knitted goods to the navy, the group ultimately distributed over 250,000 pieces to American sailors.

WSNL turned its attention to convalescing soldiers in September 1918, when it began taking patients at Walter Reed Army Hospital on excursions down the Potomac River to Mount Vernon. In 1919, the WSNL worked to secure funds and arrange adoptions for French war orphans, but in September, Frazer announced that, with the war over and tensions relaxed, the Comforts Committee was discontinuing its work. The WSNL had no interest in developing programs unrelated to the war emergency and revived only with the onset of World War II.

Barbara Steinson

See also NAVY LEAGUE

Bibliography

Navy League. *Sea Power*. Washington, DC: Navy League, 1916–1921.
———. *Seven Seas Magazine*. Washington, DC: Navy League, 1915–1916.
Rappaport, Armin. *The Navy League of the United States*. Detroit: Wayne State University Press, 1962.
Steinson, Barbara J. *American Women's Activism in World War I*. New York: Garland, 1982.

Nearing, Scott (1883–1983)

Scott Nearing was born in Norris Run, Pennsylvania in 1883. He graduated from the University of Pennsylvania with a degree in economics and then taught economics at Swarthmore College, his alma mater, and Toledo University. Embroiled in the domestic struggles of progressive reform, Nearing was caught off guard by the outbreak of war in Europe. He immediately took an antiwar position, but his thinking remained directed at a critique of the capitalist system, focusing on the exploitation of child labor, unequal distribution of wealth in the country, and the increasing class divisions in American society.

By the fall of 1915, he had stepped up his antiwar activities in response to President Wilson's attempts to sell his preparedness plan to the American people. Nearing accused the business class of promoting preparedness to protect investments and increase profits, and he denounced Wilson as a tool of the wealthy. Throughout 1916, Nearing maintained his pacifism and became more vocal in his critique of war as the result of an economic system that put enormous wealth and power in the hands of a small privileged class. In March 1917, he joined the American Union Against Militarism and found himself the target of those who condemned his beliefs as unpatriotic and disloyal. In April, shortly after the United States declared war on Germany, Nearing was fired from his teaching post at the University of Toledo.

Nearing then taught at the Rand School for Social Science in New York City under the auspices of the American Socialist Society, and he focused his efforts on the antiwar movement in the United States. In July, he joined the Socialist Party, the nation's only antiwar party, and sided with the radical wing of the American Union Against Militarism, the group associated with Roger Baldwin's Bureau of Conscientious Objectors, later to become the American Civil Liberties Union. Nearing also was prominent in the People's Council of America for Democracy and Peace, which drew its inspiration for postwar peace and democratic ideals from the February and October revolutions in Russia.

During July 1917, the Justice Department began surveillance of Nearing. On September 18, federal agents raided his home in the first domestic raid of the war in an attempt to find evidence of sedition in violation of the wartime Espionage Act. In March 1918, the United States government indicted Nearing under the Espionage Act for his 1917 antiwar pamphlet *The Great Madness: A Victory for American Plutocracy*. While under indictment, he ran as the Socialist Party candidate for the 14th Congressional District seat of New York City. Although he doubled the 1916 Socialist vote, he lost to a fusion ticket supporting the incumbent Fiorello LaGuardia. At his trial in February 1919, Nearing was acquitted for writing the pamphlet, but the American Socialist Society was found guilty for publishing it. The war had the effect of further radicalizing both Nearing's politics and his anticapitalist economic analyses. Nearing continued his reform and Socialist activities. After the Second World War, he became concerned with ecological issues, moving to a farm in Vermont and later in Maine. He continued lecturing and writing on economics and social issues until his death on August 24, 1983.

John Saltmarsh

Bibliography

Nearing, Scott. *The Making of a Radical: A Political Autobiography.* New York: Harper & Row, 1972.

Saltmarsh, John. *Scott Nearing: An Intellectual Biography.* Philadelphia: Temple University Press, 1991.

Whitfield, Stephen J. *Scott Nearing: Apostle of American Radicalism.* New York: Columbia University Press, 1974.

Neville, Wendell Cushing (1870–1930)

Wendel Cushing ("Buck") Neville was graduated from the United States Naval Academy in 1890. He spent an additional two years aboard ship as a passed midshipman and was then commissioned a second lieutenant in the Marine Corps. He served at Guantanamo Bay during the Spanish-American War, where he earned the Brevet Medal. Neville was then ordered to China with a battalion of marines for the relief of Peking, following which he was appointed military governor of Basilan Province in the Philippines. Later he served in Cuba, Nicaragua, Panama, and Hawaii. Neville landed at Veracruz, Mexico, in 1914, where he commanded the 2d Marine Regiment and for which action he was awarded the Medal of Honor. Afterward, he returned to China where he commanded the legation guard at Peking.

Colonel Neville arrived at St. Nazaire, France, on board the USS *De Kalb*, on Dec. 28, 1917. He reported for duty with the 4th Brigade on Jan. 1, 1918, and thereupon assumed command of the 5th Marine Regiment. Except for a short hospitalization after being wounded at Château-Thierry, he retained command of the regiment until July 29, 1918, when he was promoted to brigadier general and replaced by Gen. John A. Lejeune. General Neville led the 5th Marine Regiment, and subsequently the 4th Marine Brigade, with distinction through all the fighting those units experienced while in France, including actions at Belleau Wood, the Aisne-Marne offensive, St. Mihiel, Blanc Mont, and the Meuse-Argonne, and he participated in the occupation of Germany.

Neville returned home with his division in 1919 and was promoted to major general in March 1920. He first served as assistant to the commandant, and later as commanding general of the Department of the Pacific. He was appointed commandant of the Marine Corps in 1929, but he had little opportunity to put his personal imprint on the future of the corps. He died just over a year after his appointment.

George Clark

Bibliography

Metcalf, Clyde. *A History of the United States Marine Corps.* New York: Putnam, 1939.

Nicholas II (1868–1918)

Nicholas II came to the throne of Russia in 1894 determined to rule as an autocrat, but lacking the personal force, decisiveness, and insight to do so effectively. The erosion of his credibility as a leader began with his failure to show concern for people killed and injured at a coronation celebration and continued with his brutal repression of liberalizing movements, the murder of peaceful petitioners on Bloody Sunday in 1905, the disastrous Russo-Japanese War, and his betrayal of the South Slavs in the Bosnian crisis of 1908–1909. When he tolerated the presence in his court of the crude and licentious "holy man," Rasputin, whose hypnotic powers relieved the pain of the hemophiliac heir apparent, even conservatives began to contemplate alternatives to Nicholas.

Throughout the diplomatic crisis caused by the assassination of Archduke Franz Ferdinand, heir to the Austro-Hungarian throne, in 1914, Nicholas worked for a peaceful solution. Doubting that Russia could sustain the burden of a war with the Central Powers, but haunted by the humiliations of the Russo-Japanese War and the Bosnian crisis and realizing that further national disgrace could endanger his throne, he allowed himself to be persuaded to order a partial mobilization.

The outbreak of war generated an outburst of patriotism that temporarily strengthened the tsar. Yet the terrible defeats at Tannenberg and the Masurian Lakes in 1914 and the stunning German-Austrian successes on the Galician front in the summer of 1915 drastically altered public opinion. It was apparent that the army was ill-trained and ill-equipped, the casualties were enormous, and the economy was beginning to crack under the strain of wartime expenditure while the mobilization of peasants left the nation unable to feed itself. Public outcries against governmental corruption and calls for a new cabinet were the initial manifestations of growing and hardening hatred of the tsar and his family. After only a halfhearted attempt to deal with the political situation, Nicholas was persuaded by his wife, the Tsarina Alexandra, to sack the commander-in-chief of the Russian forces and assume supreme command of the armed forces himself.

At Stavka (the army headquarters at Mogilev), Nicholas could avoid the turmoil of a household unsettled by fears for his son's health and by the excesses of Rasputin, and he could avoid unwelcome political news. He played only a peripheral military role, seldom interfering with operational decisions and enjoying the camaraderie of military life. Isolated and out of touch, he was unable to assess the buildup of anticourt and antigovernment sentiments. Even the 1916 assassination of Rasputin by conservative members of the aristocracy did not open his eyes to the dangers facing him as a ruler. The February Revolution of 1917 in Petrograd caught him unaware, and he was unable to control the situation. When the government resigned, the Duma and the army called for his abdication. Within a week of the onset of rioting, Nicholas abdicated in favor of his brother, Michael, whose refusal of the crown ended the Romanov dynasty.

Nicholas had been at Pskov, foiled in an attempt to return to Petrograd, when he abdicated. The Provisional Government under Alexander Kerenskii brought him back to his palace at Tsarkoe Selo and detained him in comfort while discussing with the British ambassador the project of sending him to exile in England with his family. The British cooled to the idea, and a failed Russian offensive in the summer encouraged the Bolsheviks to riot, strike, and rise up against the Provisional Government. Nicholas and his family were moved to Tobolsk in Siberia to protect them from assassination. When the Bolsheviks came to power in October, they decided to put Nicholas on trial for crimes against the people, and in April 1918, the entire family was moved to Ekaterinburg (Sverdlosk). During the summer, anti-Bolshevik forces approached the city and local authorities, ordered by Lenin to forestall a rescue, shot Nicholas and his family early on the morning of July 17, burned the bodies, and threw them into a pit in the woods nearby.

Joseph M. McCarthy

Bibliography

Lincoln, W. Bruce. *The Romanovs*. New York: Dial Press, 1981.
Massie, Robert. *Nicholas and Alexandra*. New York: Atheneum, 1967.
Oldenburg, Sergei. *The Last Tsar*. Gulf Breeze, FL: Academic Informational Press, 1975–1978.
Pares, Bernard. *The Fall of the Russian Monarchy*. London: Cape, 1939.
Radzinsky, Edvard. *The Last Tsar: The Life and Death of Nicholas II*. New York: Doubleday, 1992.

Nolan, Dennis Edward (1872–1956)

When MajGen. Dennis Edward Nolan retired in 1936, he was the second ranking officer of that grade in the U.S. Army. Although his principal distinction was as the senior intelligence officer of the American Expeditionary Force (AEF) in World War I, General Nolan held many important posts during nearly forty years of active service. He participated in the preparation of the National Defense Act of 1916; led the War Department General Staff Intelligence Division (G-2) after World War I; commanded at the brigade, division, army corps, and army levels; and served as both the G-4 and deputy chief of staff of the army.

Born in Akron, New York, he graduated from West Point in 1896. On a subsequent assignment to the faculty at West Point, he taught history and military law, and in 1902, he was named head football coach. Following a brief stint as an "additional second lieutenant," Lieutenant Nolan joined the 1st Infantry Regiment in August 1896. In Cuba during the Spanish-American War, he was brevetted twice and won two Silver Stars for gallantry in action. During the Philippine Insurrection, Captain Nolan commanded a squadron of volunteer cavalry. Following the establishment of the War Department General Staff in 1903, Captain Nolan was one of very few officers of his grade assigned to it. After duty in the Philippines and Alaska, from 1906–1915, he returned to General Staff duty. General Pershing selected Nolan for his AEF staff in 1917.

During World War I, Colonel (later General) Nolan served as the assistant chief of staff, G-2, AEF, except for the ten days during the Meuse-Argonne campaign when he commanded the 55th Infantry Brigade of the 28th Division, during which time he won the Distinguished Service Cross for heroism in repulsing a German tank attack. As G-2, Nolan was the senior American intelligence officer in France. Part of his responsibilities was the supervision of journalists and the staff of the *Stars and Stripes*. He received the Distinguished Service Medal for his work as G-2, AEF.

His personal relationship with Ralph Van Deman and Marlborough Churchill made the coordination of intelligence matters with the War Department reasonably smooth, even though the bureaucratic organization of both agencies was not well developed. Nolan had the personal confidence of both General Pershing and General March, the army chief of staff.

General Nolan died in New York City on Feb. 26, 1956.

John Votaw

Bibliography
Bidwell, Bruce W. *History of the Military Intelligence Division, Department of the Army General Staff: 1775–1941*. Frederick, MD: University Publications of America, 1986.
Coffman, Edward M. *The War to End All Wars: The American Military Experience in World War I*. New York: Oxford University Press, 1968.
Van Deman, Ralph H. *The Final Memoranda*. ed. by Ralph E. Weber. Wilmington, DE: Scholarly Resources Books, 1988.

Nonpartisan League

Entry by the United States into the First World War raised crucial constitutional issues regarding the role of dissent within a nation at war. A number of organizations which attempted to continue the domestic reforms of the Progressive Era clashed with a host of state and federal statutes designed to curb criticism of the war effort. The Nonpartisan League (NPL), a midwestern-based farmers' organization, became an unintentional participant in this struggle to balance freedom of expression with national security.

The Nonpartisan League originated in North Dakota in 1915 and utilized founder Arthur Townley's idea of combining agrarian reform goals with the mechanics of the new state primary elections system. Grass-roots NPL caucuses supported a platform of economic programs and sponsored candidates in the dominant party primary in legislative districts and at the state level. With the aid of a strong organization and the weekly *Nonpartisan Leader*, the league swept to victory in the June 1916 primaries, winning every nomination it sought, primarily within the Republican Party. Success continued, and in the November general election, the league gained control of the North Dakota House of Representatives and every state constitutional office except that of treasurer.

This wave of successful political protest did not go unnoticed in neighboring Minnesota, and the farmers there rallied to the league's organizational efforts. However, they ran into considerable opposition from Republican Party stalwarts aided by the patriotic frenzy that accompanied United States entry into the war. In April 1917, the Minnesota legislature enacted a sedition law that made it illegal to print, circulate, or advocate the idea that one should resist military service. The legislature also established a functionally independent Commission of Public Safety (CPS) to coordinate wartime economic activities and to insure loyalty to wartime programs.

The commission issued a series of orders, enforced by its own corps of badge-toting officers empowered to protect private property and to make arrests without warrants. During its short life of less than two years, the commission answered 1,689 complaints involving issues such as alleged interference with Liberty Loan sales, the teaching of the German language, and violations of work or fight orders. There were 682 complaints involving charges of sedition—many directed against the Nonpartisan League. Although similar wartime statutes and programs existed in other states and Congress soon enacted espionage and sedition acts, the Minnesota attempt to use its wartime regulations to suppress the activities of the league was among the most serious instances of alleged interference with civil liberties.

As the league intensified its Minnesota membership campaign in the fall of 1917, CPS officials worked to discredit the farmers' organization. Commissioners interfered with NPL meetings and circulated literature claiming that leaguers were disloyal and pro-German, despite their friendly relations with the Wilson administration and support of Liberty Loan drives. By early 1918, twenty of Minnesota's eighty-seven counties had forbidden NPL meetings, and violence had erupted against the league. Incidents continued after the league's state convention in March when it nominated former Congressman Charles A. Lindbergh Sr. as their gubernatorial candidate in the Republican primary. As the June 1918 election neared, violence increased. Several times unruly crowds dragged Lindbergh from the speakers' platform, and on one occasion, a gunman fired on Lindbergh's automobile as he left a campaign appearance.

In the midst of the primary campaign, authorities also arrested a number of league organizers who eventually would face a total of seventeen indictments in Minnesota courts. The most celebrated of the league free-speech trials was that of organization manager Joseph Gilbert, which took place in Red Wing during May 1918, just one month before the primary election. On March 14, 1918, a grand jury indicted Gilbert for remarks made on Aug. 18, 1917, when he suggested that the United States conscript wealth as well as men, an idea Congress later enacted in the form of an excess profits tax. At the Red Wing trial, the state paraded numerous witnesses who all recited verbatim the words of Gilbert quoted in the indictment.

The charge of disloyalty proved to be too much for the league. Gilbert's conviction added fuel to the anti-NPL fire, and the farmers lost miserably in the Republican primary. During the summer of 1918, while war continued in Europe, the CPS held a series of loyalty meetings that often focused on questioning the patriotism of NPL members. The intimidation continued, even though President Wilson issued a statement commending the league for its wartime assistance to his administration.

Despite the disappointment of 1918, the Nonpartisan League continued as a force in North Dakota politics. Later in the year, the remnants of the Minnesota NPL regrouped to form the nucleus of the Farmer Labor Party, which became one of the strongest and most long-lived third parties in U.S. history.

Joseph Gilbert appealed his case all the way to the United States Supreme Court, which, in 1920, upheld his conviction as a valid exercise of state police powers. However, the dissent by Justice Louis Brandeis helped to establish an alternate line of reasoning that became a majority position five years later. Brandeis argued for the nationalization of the Bill of Rights, the idea that constitutional guarantees such as freedom of speech and press are protected from the encroachment of state legislatures as well as from Congress. Thus, a central thesis in twentieth-century civil liberties owes its genesis in part to the wartime struggles of the Nonpartisan League.

Carol E. Jenson

Bibliography

Chrislock, Carl H. *Watchdog of Loyalty: The Minnesota Commission of Public Safety During World War I*. St. Paul: Minnesota Historical Society Press, 1991.

Jenson, Carol E. *Agrarian Pioneer in Civil Liberties: The Nonpartisan League in Minnesota During World War I*. New York: Garland, 1986.

———. "Loyalty as a Political Weapon: The 1918 Campaign in Minnesota." *Minnesota History* (Summer 1972).

Morlan, Robert L. *Political Prairie Fire*. Minneapolis: University of Minnesota Press, 1955.

North Sea Mine Barrage

One of the pet projects of Admiral Reginald Bacon, commanding the Dover Patrol, was a North Sea Mine Barrage. Assistant Secretary of the Navy Franklin D. Roosevelt and officers in the U.S. Bureau of Ordnance began considering the project in 1916. Secretary of the Navy Josephus Daniels spoke to the General Board of the U.S. Navy and to others about it in October 1917. Daniels later called it "the most daring and original naval conception of the World War."

When VAdm. William S. Sims, commander, U.S. Naval Forces in European Waters, spoke with the British Admiralty about the project, the answer was, "If we haven't mines enough to build a successful barrage across the Straits of Dover, which is only twenty miles wide, how can we construct a barrage across the North Sea, which is 230?" Such was the vast extent of water and of its depth (from 360 to 900 feet, with an average depth of 600 feet) that many mines of an improved type would be needed. The 400,000 mines that were required would not be available until late 1918. The standard contact mine had "horns," glass vials that when broken served as primers to detonate its main charge. If a more efficient mine could be produced, fewer mines would be required and the barrage could be laid earlier. The answer came in the American "antenna" mine, designed by Reginald Belknap. Its advantage lay in a long, thin copper cable kept suspended just a few feet below the surface of the water by a small metal buoy. If a hull struck the antenna, it electrically fired the mine anchored below. Planners projected that only about 100,000 of these new mines would be needed, that it would take fewer minelayers to lay them, and that laying time would be reduced. Official approval for the project came on Nov. 2, 1917, with an estimated cost of $40 million, which ultimately ballooned to nearly $80 million.

After the mines were manufactured, they were sent to nearby Portsmouth, Virginia, where they were loaded on to cargo vessels. Starting in February 1918, two or three ships sailed every day for bases on the Scottish coast, where Americans had built warehouses for them. Protected by American and British naval units, a fleet of hastily converted minelayers sailed into the North Sea. The minelayers were fitted with little railroad tracks, and at appropriate intervals, the crews pushed the mines down the tracks and into the deep. Americans laid 56,571 of the antenna mines and the British 13,546.

Accounts of the number of U-boats lost to the barrage vary from four to eight, but its real value was psychological; it was a deterrent that helped break down German morale and defeat Germany.

Paolo E. Coletta

See also BELKNAP, REGINALD; MINES

Bibliography
Belknap, Reginald. "The Yankee Mining Squadron, or Laying the North Sea Mine Barrage." U.S. *Naval Institute Proceedings* (December 1919; January 1920; February 1920).

Cowie, John S. *Mines, Minelayers, and Minelaying.* New York: Oxford University Press, 1949.

Grant, Robert M. *U-Boats Destroyed: The Effect of Anti-Submarine Warfare, 1914–1918.* London: Putnam, 1964.

The Northern Barrage, Mine Force United States Atlantic Fleet, the North Sea. Annapolis, MD: Naval Institute Press, 1919.

U.S. Navy Department, Office of Naval Records. *The North Sea Mine Barrage and Other Mining Activities.* Washington, DC: Government Printing Office, 1920.

Orlando, Vittorio Emanuele (1860–1952)
Vittorio Emanuele Orlando was born in Palermo on May 19, 1860. He was an internationally recognized jurist, who held a chair at the University of Rome from 1901 to 1931 and was a member of the Chamber of Deputies from 1897 to 1925.

Before the First World War, he had served as minister of education from 1903 to 1905 and as minister of justice from 1907 to 1909 in the governments of Giovanni Giolitti. During the entire course of the war, Orlando participated in the governments of Italy first as minister of justice under Antonio Salandra (1914–1916), as minister of the interior under Paolo Boselli (1916–1917), and finally as prime minister from October 1917 to June 1919. In that final capacity, Orlando rallied Italy after the disastrous defeat at Caporetto, but his government fell as a result of the clash with President Woodrow Wilson and the Yugoslavs over Dalmatia and Fiume.

As a left Liberal, he had been allied with Giolitti, but Orlando broke with him to support Salandra's decision to join the Allied war effort in May 1915. Orlando and Sidney Sonnino were the most prominent members of Boselli's "National Coalition" government in 1916 and 1917. With Soninno, Orlando fruitlessly attempted to reconcile the internal opponents of the conflict, the Giolittians, the Socialists, and the Catholics, to the war effort. Orlando's efforts were sabotaged by General Luigi Cadorna, commander of the Italian Army, who had insulated himself from civilian government supervision and blamed the government for everything that went awry. Cadorna especially attacked Orlando, whom he accused of being too weak and too tolerant of subversive propaganda.

This, Cadorna claimed, had undermined the army's morale.

Orlando became Italy's third wartime prime minister on Oct. 29, 1917, in the wake of Caporetto. He succeeded in uniting the "democratic interventionists," the Liberals, and the Nationalists into a patriotic union ministry. He then had his revenge on Cadorna, whom he promptly sacked, and, in face-saving exactitude, "moved up" to the new "Supreme Inter-Allied Council."

In response to Woodrow Wilson's January 1918 Fourteen Points address, Orlando ambiguously lauded Wilson's idealism but simultaneously emphasized Italy's desire to complete the nation's unification and to provide for the security of its Adriatic coast. Orlando sympathized with the followers of Luigi Bissolati, who advocated territorial moderation in an effort to accommodate Yugoslavia, but he was unable to overcome the expansionism of Sonnino, the foreign minister. During the pre-Armistice discussions in November, Orlando acceded to Sonnino's unsuccessful attempt to insert a formal reservation that provided that the new frontiers of Italy would conform to historical considerations and to Italy's security interests. In December, Bissolati responded by withdrawing from the government.

As the Paris Peace Conference convened, Orlando was preoccupied with domestic political difficulties. Francesco Nitti, the finance minister and a political competitor of Orlando, resigned. Orlando reconstructed a weak cabinet, but his continuing concern over his personal political position divided his attention during his negotiations with Wilson. He had also been accused by Vincenzo Macchi di Cellere, the Italian ambassador to the United States and a partisan of Sonnino, of creating problems for Italy through his insistence on dominating the negotiations for Italy and because of his inconsistence and lack of firmness.

Orlando and Sonnino were not able to convince Wilson of Italy's right to Fiume and part of the Dalmatian coast. Due to Russian influence, Fiume had been denied to the Italians in the 1915 Treaty of London. Following the October Revolution, Russian opinion was no longer a factor, and Italy pressed for inclusion of the city, which, if its predominantly Slavic suburb of Susak were excluded, was principally Italian in population. Orlando apparently saw the acquisition of Italian Fiume as a concession that would placate Italian nationalists over the impending failure of Italy's claim to Dalmatia. Wilson, who steadfastly opposed Italy's acquisition of Dalmatia, was unwilling to offer Fiume as an alternative. The demand for Fiume then created new difficulties as Italian national sentiment became fixated upon the city.

Early in February 1919, Orlando accepted in principle the notion of arbitration by Wilson that had been proposed by Ante Trumbić, the representative of the Yugoslav National Council. He, however, balked at the American decision that Italy should be restricted to the Treaty of London line in the north and that eastern Istria, Dalmatia, and Fiume should all go to Yugoslavia. On April 3, when David Lloyd George and Georges Clemenceau agreed that Italy should not receive Fiume and that the Yugoslavs should be heard, Orlando refused to attend what he labeled the "Italian funeral."

Efforts to reach a compromise continued. Orlando was exclusively involved in the negotiations for Italy because Sonnino inflexibly demanded the line established by the Treaty of London. Compromise, however, was made problematic by a complexity of interests and antagonisms. Orlando continued to refuse to meet with the Yugoslavs, stating that his government was probably doomed, and that only a solution personally effected by Wilson could possible pacify the Italians. Simultaneously, the virulent anti-American and annexationist campaign in the Italian press angered the Americans, who believed that it had been engineered by the Italian government.

On April 19, Orlando, accompanied by Sonnino, met with the other three representatives of the Council of Four. Instead of basing Italy's claim upon the Treaty of London, to which the United States had not been a party,

Orlando argued Italy's claim to Fiume on the basis of the self-determination of its inhabitants and based demands for Dalmatia on the requirements of Italian security. He argued that Danzig was more crucial to Poland than Fiume to Yugoslavia, and yet it was denied to the Poles. Sonnino added that Wilson's intention to deprive Italy of part of Istria and Dalmatia would have given Italy less than Austria had been willing to concede in 1915 in return for Italian neutrality.

Clemenceau recognized that France was bound by the Treaty of London. However, he believed that Italy could not use the treaty to acquire Dalmatia and yet ignore its provisions to advance an Italian claim to Fiume. Lloyd George agreed that if Italy invoked the principle of self-determination, it should be applied to Trieste, Istria, and Dalmatia, as well as to Fiume. Orlando countered that if the Treaty of London were applied, he would agree to a separate solution of the Fiume question. Wilson was adamant in his opposition and announced his intention to make his opposition to the London frontiers public.

On April 20, Orlando threatened to leave the negotiations if Italy were not granted what had been promised to it by the Treaty of London. Late on April 22, he indicated some flexibility, but he held firm to his threat made earlier that day to refuse to sign the peace with Germany and depart the conference if Italy's frontier demands were not recognized. Col. Edward M. House, Wilson's confidant and a member of the U.S. peace delegation, doubted the Italian resolve and urged that their bluff be called. Fiume remained the principle stumbling block, and on that point Wilson remained inflexible. On April 23, the President's manifesto, which was his attempt to explain to the Italian people the "truth" of what was happening at the conference, appeared in *Le Temps* of Paris in which Wilson argued that with the disintegration of Austria-Hungary, the Treaty of London was outdated. Orlando and Sonnino looked upon this as an intrusion into domestic policy and withdrew from the conference.

On April 24, Orlando issued his reply to Wilson, but its real target was Italian public opinion. Though Orlando skillfully employed irony in pointing out the inconsistencies of Wilson's approach, his specific argument was weakened by the contradictory bases of his claims for the London Treaty territory and Fiume. Nevertheless, it was Orlando rather than Wilson who reached the Italian public. The Italians, who believed that they were being discriminated against and treated as a minor power, united in common hostility to Wilson. In an overwhelming outpouring of nationalism and injured pride, the American president was generally excoriated.

Orlando, whose government had been in trouble, was able to use Wilson's manifesto to his temporary advantage. Citing Wilson's direct appeal to the Italian people, Orlando, on April 29, asked for the Italian parliament to confirm his mandate before he returned to negotiate further. Though he was accorded this and praised as an Italian patriot, Wilson was unmoved.

During the absence of the Italian delegation, the council had distributed the former German colonies and had authorized a Greek landing at Smyrna, where Italy had been given a primacy of interest by the 1917 agreement of St. Jean de Maurienne. To bolster their position, the Italians had sent ships to Turkish waters and had occupied Marmaris, a coaling station on the Turkish coast. On May 7, Orlando declared "that if mandates were a burden, Italy was ready to accept them. If mandates had advantages, then Italy has a right to share in them."

Despite Wilson's inflexibility, Orlando and Sonnino hurriedly left Rome on May 5 and rejoined the conference the following day rather than risk the completion of both the German and the Austrian treaties in their absence. Clemenceau had suggested that the Italians had broken the Treaty of London by their departure and that if they did not return, any reference to Italy should be stricken from the treaty with Germany. Colonel House, who sympathized with Italy, attempted to soothe matters by offering Wilson an apology from Orlando and Sonnino for the vituperation to which the President had been subjected by the Italian press. House believed that taken as a whole the Italian demands were more moderate than those of the other Allies. House, with David H. Miller, legal counselor of the American delegation, proposed that the Italian frontier not abutting Yugoslavia be settled at once but that the Italo-Yugoslav frontier settlement be delayed for five years with the League of Nations controlling the disputed territories. Orlando accepted this as a basis for bargaining but was reluctant to commit himself in order to maintain the freedom to seize any opportunity that might be presented. He still insisted upon Fiume, a fixation that cost Italy dearly. Orlando exaggerated its value, and his concentration upon it rather than upon the settlement in general not only prevented a settlement at Paris, but also sacrificed the more favorable terms that Italy could have surely obtained. Macchi di Cellere believed that the compromise should have been accepted and could have been imposed upon Wilson if Orlando had only used the Treaty of London to compel the Allies to pressure Wilson.

Lloyd George proposed larger concessions to Italy in Anatolia in exchange for Italian concessions along the Adriatic, but Clemenceau saw this as a threat to French interests. House and Miller, who were sympathetic toward Italy, continued to seek a compromise favorable to Italy. They advocated direct negotiations between the Italians and the Yugoslavs, which they expected would lead to Yugoslav concessions. Wilson's opposition and the inflexibility of the Yugoslavs, who knew that they could rely upon the President, aborted these efforts. When the Americans finally placed Italian and Yugoslav negotiators in separate rooms and attempted to serve as go-betweens, they failed because neither side was willing to budge on the question of eastern Istria. Italian determination to have the territory as a bridge to an Italian or an independent Fiume was met by equal determination on the part of the Yugoslavs.

The Italians could not understand Wilson's rigidity. They believed that he was unfairly attempting to force concessions from them. Despite the efforts of House and Miller, Wilson's inflexibility destroyed the possibility of an agreement that, ironically, would not have been substantially different from the 1920 Treaty of Rapallo, which was directly negotiated between the Italians and the Yugoslavs. In that treaty, Italy retained most of Istria and four Dalmatian islands but surrendered the Dalmatian coast south of Fiume with the exception of Zara (Zadar). Fiume remained a free city until 1924, when another agreement assigned the port to Italy but the suburbs to Yugoslavia.

There was also concern that despite Italy's support for France in particulars involving the German Treaty, France was betraying Italian interests in the successor states to the Habsburg Empire in an attempt to prevent an Anschluss between Austria and Germany. The responsibility for these multiple failures fell upon Orlando. He and his ministry were taken to task in the Italian press.

Orlando met with the Council of Four on May 26, at which the conflicting positions were merely reiterated. The next day, Orlando appealed to André Tardieu, a member of the French delegation, to introduce a French proposal for the settlement of the Adriatic dispute. Previously, Tardieu had been approached by Silvio Crespi, a member of the Italian delegation, who had grown impatient over Orlando and Sonnino's stalling. That evening, Tardieu, with the approval of Clemenceau, presented to Crespi a draft proposal. On May 28, the Tardieu Plan, with its proposal for a Fiume buffer state, was brought before the Council of Four. Immediately, Wilson, and even Lloyd George, expressed reservations. Orlando, too, was hesitant, and the plan failed at this juncture.

The Italians won recognition of the Brenner frontier with Austria on May 29. Having gained that advantage, Orlando, on June 5, expressed his willingness to Clemenceau to accept the Tardieu Plan. Wilson now proposed a less generous counterproposal, which gave Italy only slightly more of Istria than the original line drawn by the Americans and cost Italy Sebenico and the island of Cherso assigned to it both by the Treaty of London and the Tardieu Plan.

Fiume had become an obsession in Italy, and Orlando's ministry was dependent upon its acquisition. The gains made by Italy were completely overshadowed by the failure to gain Fiume, and the failure to acquire the city doomed Orlando's government. He was upbraided for his vacillation and his self-defeating antagonizing of the Allies. When he returned to Rome to defend his conduct before parliament, the majority found his vague public statement on the Adriatic settlement unacceptable. Members repudiated his government by a vote of 262 to 78. Francesco Saverio Nitti formed a new government bent upon placating the Allies and appointed Tommaso Tittoni foreign minister. When Nitti and Tittoni replaced Orlando and Sonnino in Paris, the idea of a Fiume buffer state became the basis for an interim settlement. Without the interference of the Americans, Nitti was able to gain from Britain and France acceptance of an agreement that approximated the Tardieu Plan. Wilson, who by now had returned to the United States, vetoed this. The settlement eventually worked out by Giolitti and the Yugoslavs had to await the end of Wilson's presidency.

Though Orlando retained his seat in parliament, he was not at the center of political developments during the period of turmoil that preceded Benito Mussolini's rise to power. In November 1922, Orlando, hoping that the Fascists could be moderated through a coalition with the Liberals, joined in a vote of confidence for Mussolini's government. He also joined an anti-Socialist and anti-Popular Party electoral coalition with the Fascists in April 1924. However, following the murder of Giacomo Matteotti, Orlando urged the king to intervene against Mussolini. Disillusioned, Orlando resigned his seat in protest against Fascist violence in 1925 and resigned from his chair at the University of Rome in November 1931 rather than take an oath of loyalty to the Fascists. He continued to serve as an adviser to Victor Emmanuel, and supported his dismissal of Mussolini in 1943. In 1944, Orlando served as president of the Chamber of Deputies and was elected in 1946 to the Constituent Assembly. He denounced the Italian government's "lust for servility" when it agreed to the 1947 peace treaty, which imposed reparations and stripped Italy of Istria, Dalmatia, and Fiume. He was, nevertheless, appointed in 1948 to the Senate for life. Orlando died in Rome on Dec. 1, 1952.

Bernard A. Cook

See also CADORNA, LUIGI; CAPORETTO, BATTLE OF; PARIS PEACE CONFERENCE

Bibliography

Albrecht-Carrié, René. *Italy at the Paris Peace Conference.* Hamden, CT: Archon Books, 1966.

Mayer, Arno J. *Politics and Diplomacy of Peacemaking: Containment and Counterrevoltuion at Versailles 1918–1919.* New York: Knopf, 1967.

Orlando, V.E. *Memorie, 1915–1919,* ed. by Rodolfo Mosca. Milan: Rizzoli, 1960.

Salandino, Salvatore. "Orlando, Vittorio Emanuele." In *Historical Dictionary of Fascist Italy,* ed. by Philip V. Cannistraro. Westport, CT: Greenwood Press, 1982.

Salvatorelli, Luigi, and Giovanni Mira. *Storia d'Italia nel periodo fascista.* Turin: Einaudi, 1964.

O'Ryan, John Francis (1875–1961)

Educated at City College of New York and trained in the law at New York University, John Francis O'Ryan was admitted to the bar in

1898. Although he practiced law, O'Ryan had enlisted in the New York National Guard in 1897. He rose through the ranks to command the New York Division in 1912.

Having attained the rank of major general, O'Ryan forsook the law to concentrate on military service. He attended the Army War College in 1914, and commanded the 6th New York Division on the Mexican border in 1916. Following the outbreak of war in 1917, O'Ryan's division was mobilized as the 27th Division of the United States Army.

In May 1918, the 27th Division comprised of 24,000 officers and men sailed for France. At age forty-two, O'Ryan was not only the youngest general to command an American division for an extended period in World War I, but he was also the only National Guard officer to remain in such a post throughout the war. The 27th trained with the British in Flanders, seeing its first combat in the Ypres and Mont Kemmel sector in July 1918. As part of the British Fourth Army, the 27th Division subsequently participated in the bloody fighting required by the breach of the heavily defended Hindenburg Line, including the canal and tunnel near St. Quentin in late September and early October 1918.

Demobilized in April 1919, O'Ryan returned to New York City and his law practice. He subsequently served as police commissioner of New York City in 1934 and civilian defense director of New York State in 1941 after the United States entered World War II. Retiring from public service, O'Ryan, the epitome of the citizen soldier, practiced law again until his death in 1961. He was the author of *The Story of the 27th Division* (1921).

John Lindley

Bibliography

Coffman, Edward M. *The War To End All Wars*. New York: Oxford University Press, 1968.

Otranto Barrage

The Otranto Barrage was established by the Italian, French, and British navies to bottle up German and Austro-Hungarian submarines in the Adriatic Sea. The submarines' egress into the Mediterranean Sea where they could utilize their torpedoes against the congested sea lanes could cause grievous harm to the Allied seaborne traffic. The barrage consisted of three lines of ships across the Adriatic, extending from the island of Corfu westward to the Italian boot. At that point, the Adriatic was about twenty-four miles wide but at least 600 fathoms, which was far too deep to anchor mines. Mine fields did extend out from Italy's shore line, but from there ships were the main part of the barrier. The ships consisted of destroyers, Canadian fishing vessels, and the U.S. Navy's own development, the "Splinter Fleet." These wooden-hulled eighty-ton boats were mainly captained by young Ivy-league undergraduates who managed to learn seamanship and command in short order. The boats were sent to join the Otranto Barrage in May 1918 and were fully accredited by the end of July.

The one moment of glory came on Oct. 2, 1918, when eleven subchasers, under the command of Capt. Charles P. Nelson of the United States Navy, screened a force of Italian battleships and British cruisers and destroyers during the bombardment of Durazzo, Albania. Durazzo was the major Austrian base in the area and was considered almost impregnable. Austrian submarines were issuing from there faster than the ships of the barrage were able to destroy them. The only way to stop them was to destroy Durazzo. If the Austrians had managed to beat off the attack and annihilated the ships of the Italian Navy, Italy may have gone down to defeat. Italian morale was hanging by too slender a thread to have survived the blow. However, the Italian Navy, along with the British and U.S. forces, completely destroyed Durazzo. Just six men from the Allied fleet were killed and a few wounded. Victory was complete and crushing. The Otranto Barrage was the only general engagement the United States Navy participated in during the war.

Austria collapsed just nineteen days before the Armistice of Nov. 11, 1918. A message directed toward all ships in the barrage stated, "Sink no more enemy submarines." Ironically, while Germany did not recognize the Armistice, their submarines in the Adriatic took advantage of it, scrambling past the Allied ships and heading home on the surface with no interference. There was some consternation in the Allied fleet, but not one ship interfered in the exodus. The German subs finished off their race for home by sinking a British battleship on November 8. The sailors of the Splinter Fleet spent a peaceful Christmas in Malta and after a stopover in Spain and Portugal, sailed for home.

George B. Clark

See also SPLINTER FLEET

Bibliography

Knox, Dudley W. *A History of the United States Navy.* New York: Putnam, 1936.

Millholland, Ray. *The Splinter Fleet of the Otranto Barrage.* Indianapolis: Bobbs-Merrill, 1936.

Ottoman-American Relations

From the formal inception of relations in 1830 through the 1924 conclusion of the Treaty of Lausanne, United States involvement with the Ottoman Empire passed through three stages: political nonentanglement accompanied by a vigorous yet unofficial American presence, profound but brief American political participation in the postwar peace settlement under the leadership of President Woodrow Wilson, and withdrawal from the area with reversion to nonentanglement.

Until the outbreak of World War I in 1914, United States activities in the Ottoman Empire were confined largely to business, missionary, educational, and archeological undertakings. American missionaries were particularly active and influential, establishing such centers as the Syrian Protestant College, now the American University of Beirut, and working extensively with the Christian minorities of the empire. Business interests remained at a fairly low level. The United States imported about one-quarter of Turkey's exports, especially tobacco, but also licorice, rugs, hides, and opium, while Turkey took few American products. Nonetheless, certain U.S. corporations, among them Singer and Standard Oil, operated throughout the empire. Although in general the U.S. government declined to support these efforts officially, American representatives on the spot devoted most of their energies to the defense of such interests.

On the "Eastern Question"—the issue of the fate of the decaying Ottoman Empire that had occupied the Great Powers for more than a century—the United States pursued a policy of nonentanglement. Aside from the American tradition of political noninvolvement overseas, the State Department feared that U.S. intervention in an area so long a Great Power preserve would arouse resentment. Therefore, Washington made little comment on the 1908 "Young Turk" revolution nor, despite requests for mediation, did it participate in the various Balkan crises of 1908–1913 or the Italo-Turkish War of 1911–1912. On similar grounds, the United States also gave no support to Zionism, confining itself instead to protection of American Jews resident in Palestine. The great exception to the rule was American championing of the Armenians, who as Christians and the victims of brutal treatment at the hands of the Ottomans, elicited sympathy throughout the United States.

The nonentanglement policy began to change with the eruption of World War I. Initially, the United States declared its neutrality, and despite the Ottoman entry into the war on the side of the Central Powers, Constantinople worked to accommodate American desires. Nonetheless, Ottoman-American relations were strained by a number of incidents, among them the 1915 abolition of the "Capitulations," an act the United States refused to recognize. More serious were the infamous Armenian massacres of 1915, in the course of which much of the Armenian population of the empire—some of whom collaborated with Allied forces against Turkey—was either killed or dispersed. The suppression of the Armenians contributed to the movement for war with the empire that followed the American declaration in April 1917 of war on Germany. However, although diplomatic relations between Washington and Constantinople were severed in late April, President Wilson managed to resist pressure for a declaration of war that he felt would be strategically pointless and harmful to the efforts of American relief workers within the empire. Wilson may also have been motivated by hopes of achieving a separate Turkish peace through the efforts of former ambassador to the Ottoman Empire, Henry Morgenthau. Whatever the case, although the United States did not engage in hostilities against the empire, it was deeply interested in the Turkish peace that followed.

Many difficulties complicated the postwar disposition of the Ottoman Empire. Since Washington had never been at war with Constantinople, its grounds for participating in the peace were shaky. Yet as Wilson saw it, such participation was essential, for the resolution of destabilizing European rivalries in the empire would do much to preserve international peace. The President managed to use America's decisive role against Germany, as well as his essential role in the all-important Versailles negotiations, to insure his influence over the Turkish peace. Wilson set out his peace aims for Turkey in the twelfth of his Fourteen Points, which called for free navigation of the Straits (the passage between the Black and Mediterranean seas) and sovereignty for the Turkish portions of the Empire. The President's plans, however, ran up against such secret wartime agreements as the Sykes-Picot Treaty, by which the Allies divided the empire among themselves. In addition, the British had made conflicting promises to Jewish and Arab groups in the Middle East and both vigorously defended their rights, while other minorities jockeyed for position and worked for realization of the Wilsonian principle of self-determination. These conflicts made it difficult, if not impossible, for the conferees to agree on a settlement.

The major dispute concerned the subdivision of the Ottoman Empire. The Great Powers claimed the region; each sought to annex considerable territory. Wilson, however, forced a compromise that placed the former subject lands, as well as the colonies of the German Empire, in the hands of the League of Nations, which would mandate these areas (to be known as "mandates") to the powers so as to prepare them for eventual self-rule. The Great Powers accepted this half-loaf, which yet permitted them influence in the Middle East, and sought to tie the United States to the plan by urging American acceptance of mandates for Armenia and the Straits.

The arrangements, however, quickly broke down. The plans proved unacceptable to many of the Middle Eastern peoples, among them Arabs and Armenians, while Britain and France failed to agree on the assignment of the mandates. Meanwhile, war erupted in Turkey as Italy, impatient to gain territory, battled rival Greeks for control. Simultaneously began the rise of Turkish Nationalist Mustafa Kemal, who was eventually to seize power in Turkey, thus further destabilizing conditions. Any real possibility of American involvement in the area was destroyed when President Wilson suffered a debilitating stroke during the autumn 1919 campaign to win Senate acceptance of the Versailles peace. When the Senate rejected the treaty in November, America once again retreated from political involvement in the region. Although it sent observers, the United States did not participate officially in the negotiations of the Sèvres or Lausanne treaties, nor did Congress approve Wilson's request to accept an Armenian mandate. Later, the Senate rejected both the Treaty of Lausanne and the Turkish-American treaty of amity and commerce negotiated along with it. Not until after World War II would the United States emerge again as a player in the Middle East.

Elizabeth Steele

Bibliography

DeNovo, John. *American Interests and Policies in the Middle East, 1900–1939.* Minneapolis: University of Minnesota Press, 1963.

Evans, Laurence. *United States Policy and the Partition of Turkey, 1914–1924.* Baltimore: Johns Hopkins University Press, 1965.

Sachar, Howard. *The Emergence of the Middle East, 1914–1924.* New York: Knopf, 1969.

Trask, Roger. *The United States Response to Turkish Nationalism and Reform, 1914–1939.* Minneapolis: University of Minnesota Press, 1971.

Overman Act

Persuaded by President Woodrow Wilson, Senator Lee Overman, a conservative Democrat from North Carolina, proposed the legislation that bears his name. The Overman Act, which went into law on May 20, 1918, gave the President the authority to drop, add, or reorganize executive and administrative agencies without congressional approval for the duration of the war and for six months following. It provided the President with almost dictatorial powers. In fact, one wag suggested an amendment which stated that "if any power, constitutional or not, has been inadvertently omitted from this bill, it is hereby granted in full." The Overman Act transformed the six existing war agencies (shipping, fuel, food, railroads, war trade, and war industries) into a virtual war cabinet.

Sensitive to President Lincoln's difficulty in taming Congress during the American Civil War, Wilson had tried to obtain congressional approval for almost all of his initiatives, and thereby he appeared to be overly cautious and indecisive. Wilson's opponents castigated him as being incompetent to administer the government during time of war. The passage of the Overman Act was a reaction to Republican opposition, and some Democratic efforts, to seize control of the direction of the war. The legislation gave Wilson the authority to act decisively and to rebuff charges of inefficiency and incompetence leveled against him. Indeed, by the dramatic augmentation of his ability to act, the President made it embarrassingly difficult for his opponents to oppose the Overman Act, since the powers it provided would enable the President to do what his opponents had been demanding all along. From now on, the opposition would accuse Wilson of acting in an arbitrary manner more befitting a dictator. The ultimate irony is that Wilson used his expanded powers carefully and sparingly.

John Imholte

Bibliography

Kennedy, David M. *Over Here, the First World War and American Society.* New York: Oxford University Press, 1980.

P

Paderewski, Ignacy Jan (1860–1941)

Ignacy Jan Paderewski was born in Russian Poland. His brilliant concert career made him an international celebrity by the turn of the century. He was also increasingly active in a number of Polish charitable and patriotic activities. When the Great War broke out in 1914, Paderewski, living in Switzerland, supported the Entente because of his profound aversion to Germany. In January 1915, he joined the celebrated novelist Henryk Sienkiewicz in establishing the "General Commission for Polish Relief" in Vevy, Switzerland, to direct international succor for war-ravaged Poland. Paderewski's efforts on behalf of the Vevy Committee took him to Paris, London, and, in April 1915, the United States. His purpose was to organize relief efforts for Poland; associated goals included consolidating the Polish population of America into a powerful lobby and reaching influential circles in Washington.

Paderewski's celebrity status, his forceful oratory, and devoted patriotism won him immense admiration among the American populace, including that of President Woodrow Wilson and his closest adviser, Col. Edward M. House. By war's end, Paderewski had organized a Polish-American lobby, had spearheaded a recruiting campaign that caused more than 20,000 Poles living in the United States to join the Polish-American Army, and was part of a virtual Polish Provisional Government (the Polish National Committee) headquartered in Paris. In December 1918, Paderewski returned to Warsaw and became the prime minister of a re-created independent Poland. His influence in the United States and the devoted support of millions of Poles in America were the major source of his political authority. After a brief tenure as premier (and representative of Poland at the Paris Peace Conference), Paderewski retired to resume his musical career.

He reemerged in 1939 to join the Polish Government in Exile as the largely ceremonial president of the National Council. He died in 1941 and was buried at Arlington National Cemetery. In 1991, in accordance with his last wish, his body was returned to his beloved, and again free, Poland.

M. B. Biskupski

Bibliography

Archiwum Polityczne Ignacego Paderewskiego. 4 vols. Wroclaw: 1973–1976.

Biskupski, M.B. "Paderewski as a Leader of American Polonia, 1914–1918." *Polish American Studies* 43 (1986).

Drozdowski, Marian Marek. *Ignacy Jan Paderewski: A Political Biography*. Warsaw: Interpress, 1981.

Paderewski, Ignacy Jan, and Mary Lawton. *The Paderewski Memoirs*. New York: Scribner, 1938.

Zamoyski, Adam. *Paderewski*. New York: Atheneum, 1982.

Page, Thomas Nelson (1853–1922)

Thomas Nelson Page was a Virginia-born novelist and man of letters and United States ambassador to Italy, 1913–1919. Though trained as a lawyer, Page spent most of his life up to 1913 as the author of works of fiction and history that presented a highly romanticized view of the antebellum South. Page was proposed for an ambassadorship by the two influential United States senators from Virginia soon after the inauguration of President Woodrow Wilson in 1913. Wilson himself had only a casual acquaintance with the Virginia writer. He at first rejected the idea of appointing Page to any diplomatic post because of his alleged reactionary tendencies and associations but then, a few days later, suddenly reversed himself and agreed to Page's appointment to Rome.

As has been all too typical of American ambassadors and ministers both before and since, Page could not speak the language of the country to which he was appointed at the time of his selection. However, less typically, he set out to learn Italian and mastered it well enough eventually to make speeches in it. He came to be admired and respected by Norval Richardson, a career diplomat in the Rome embassy, and by Gino Speranza, the highly critical Italian-American adviser to the embassy.

Page's career as ambassador followed a pattern similar to that of most Wilsonian diplomats in Europe: a period of routine and ceremony up to the outbreak of the World War in August 1914; an interval of great confusion after the beginning of the conflict as American citizens stranded abroad sought assistance in returning home; a lengthy and often difficult effort to explain and defend American neutrality to uncomprehending and frequently unsympathetic government officials and citizens of the host country; and, finally, a long period of struggle to coordinate policies of war and peace with the host country after the entrance of the United States into the war in April 1917.

Page generally took a favorable view of the Italian people and their government, especially following Italy's entry into the war on May 24, 1915. He declared in a letter to President Wilson in 1917 that the king of Italy, Victor Emmanuel III, was a man of a high order of intellect and character, perhaps the best king in Europe, a view that many of his contemporaries would not have shared. However, Page was capable of an impartial, or even critical, view of the Italian scene when the occasion warranted. On November 4, 1917, immediately following the Battle of Caporetto in which Austrian and German forces had routed and virtually destroyed the Italian Second Army, Page wrote a lengthy letter to Wilson in which he set forth in unblinking clarity and detail the full dimensions of the disaster. Italy, he stressed, had suffered very heavy casualties and the loss of about one-third of its military materiel, and it remained to be seen whether the Italian people would rally in the wake of the massive defeat. He ventured the cautious prediction that they would do so, and his optimism was proved correct in the next two months as the Italian armies did in fact halt the enemy advance and stabilize their front. Page repeatedly urged the sending of an American military mission to Italy as a token of support for the Italian war effort; this was finally done in February 1918, and Page immediately reported that the gesture had had a most favorable impact on the Italian government.

After the Armistice of Nov. 11, 1918, Page's chief task became that of explaining to his government the role that Italy would play in the peace negotiations in Paris and, specifically, both the territorial demands that Italy would make and the support for those demands among Italian politicians, the press, and the public at large. With the arrival in Paris in mid-December 1918 of President Wilson and the American Commission to Negotiate Peace, Page began to send many letters and dispatches directly to that city. Wilson made a brief official visit to Italy between Jan. 3 and 6, 1919, but it is unclear how much Page was able to tell him of the Italian situation amidst the crowded schedule of the trip. As early as January 18, Page warned Wilson in a telegram that the Italian government and people were likely to stand firm on extensive territorial concessions on the east coast of the Adriatic Sea. Above all, he believed, Italy would not tolerate Yugoslav dominion over Italians living in that area.

Page, in a letter to Edward M. House dated April 17, 1919, attempted to alert Wilson to the recent popular upsurge of feeling in Italy demanding that the port city of Fiume (now Rijeka) on the Adriatic coast of Croatia should become a possession of Italy rather than of Yugoslavia. He warned that the existing Italian cabinet of Premier Vittorio Orlando could not survive unless the Paris Peace Conference granted control of Fiume to Italy. He also noted a rapid increase in anti-American feeling in Italy. Wilson certainly read Page's letter, but it did not alter his determination to keep Fiume out of Italian hands. On April 23, the President issued his famous statement appealing to the Italian government and people to accept a just peace settlement in which Fiume would fall under the control of Yugoslavia. This manifesto led to the temporary departure of Orlando and his foreign minister, Sidney Sonnino, from Paris for Rome and created a tremendous popular furor in Italy.

From this time onward, Page's dispatches to Paris were filled with reports of strongly anti-American newspaper editorials and popular demonstrations that denounced Wilson and demanded Italian sovereignty over Fiume. He made repeated efforts in interviews and letters to persuade Orlando, Sonnino, and other Italian leaders to attempt to cool down the anti-American agitation. He also began to urge Wilson and other American negotiators in Paris to reopen talks toward a settlement of the Fiume question acceptable to Italy. He realized that this might lead to the charge that he was too favorable to the Italian position, but he felt that the true situation in Italy was not realized in Paris and that amicable relations between the United States and Italy were in great peril.

On May 8, 1919, Page suddenly decided to go to Paris himself in order to impress his views of the Italian situation on Wilson and other American delegates to the peace conference. Wilson at first refused to see him. One observer noted that the President now appeared to detest Page. Edward M. House warned Wilson that Page might resign immediately if he were not granted an interview. Wilson responded angrily that it did not matter whether Page resigned then or later. The President finally saw Page briefly on May 10 and again on May 13. There is no record of what transpired at those meetings. However, back in Rome on May 29, Page once more wrote to Wilson in earnest advocacy of the Italian cause.

Page had written to Wilson about his possible retirement as ambassador to Italy in late January 1919. In July of that year he finally did submit his resignation.

Like his better-known, but unrelated, namesake, Walter Hines Page of the same period, Thomas Nelson Page made a creditable record as a diplomat, but lost much of his influence on American policy when he lost the confidence of Woodrow Wilson. In both cases the American diplomatic representative appeared to the President to have lost his objectivity and to have become an advocate of the causes and objectives of the country to which he was accredited.

John E. Little

Bibliography

Albrecht-Carrié, René. *Italy at the Paris Peace Conference.* Hamden, CT: Archon Books, 1966.

Gross, Theodore L. *Thomas Nelson Page.* New York: Twayne, 1967.

Page, Roswell. *Thomas Nelson Page: A Memoir of a Virginia Gentleman.* New York: Scribner, 1923.

Page, Thomas Nelson. *Italy and the World War.* New York; Scribner, 1920.

Page, Walter Hines (1855–1918)

Walter Hines Page's identity as a strongly opinionated American ambassador to Great Britain during 1913–1918 often has eclipsed the fact that he had a noteworthy earlier career. Born in North Carolina in 1855, educated at Trinity College (now Duke University), Randolph-Macon University, and Johns Hopkins University, he moved rapidly in the fields of journalism and publication. A writer of clear and moving prose, he left his mark largely as an editor, having directed such periodicals as *Forum* and *Atlantic Monthly*. His career in literature was topped off by helping to found, in 1900, the publishing firm of Doubleday, Page and Company, and in his editorship of a new periodical, the *World's Work*, from 1900 until his entry into government in 1913.

Page's participation in the New York publishing world drew him easily into politics of the Progressive Era of the early twentieth century. A conservative reformer who supported the vitality, and many of the goals, of Progressivism, he was one of the first individuals to identify Woodrow Wilson, president of Princeton University and later governor of New Jersey, as a potential Democratic presidential candidate. Page's association with Wilson and his friend Col. Edward M. House, his support in the presidential campaign of 1912, as well as the general understanding that he was a capable man placed him in line for a post in the Wilson administration that began in 1913. The fact that he became ambassador to Great Britain was more a matter of circumstances—Page was unassigned and the London post was open—than of an established competence in the field of foreign policy.

Page's reputation in American history grew largely out of his activity in London between 1914 and 1917, the so-called period of American neutrality, during the European war. Given his native Anglophilism and his close association with high British officials, notably Foreign Secretary Sir Edward Grey, Page argued from the beginning of the war that the American government should not quarrel with British efforts to keep American goods from going to Germany. The future of Western civilization, he insisted, depended upon a British victory. His complaints about pestering Britain with notes of protest vexed the White House and Department of State; his private assistance to Grey on handling of policy with the United States probably exceeded the bounds of diplomatic propriety. His identification in Washington as an extreme Anglophile lessened the impact of his advice on policy with Britain and on his urging, begun in 1915, that the United States should go to war with Germany. While Wilson came to ignore his outspoken ambassador (he even stopped reading his letters), the President's failure to replace Page revealed a hesitation to muddy the waters of Anglo-American relations possibly beyond his control. Thus, through a long and tortured course, Page received what he wanted. He stayed on as ambassador until virtually the end of the war, and his departure came partly because of failing health. He died on Dec. 21, 1918.

Page's experience in London stands not as an exercise in skillful and effective diplomacy, but as a forceful statement for an American policy: for going to war with Germany and cooperation between Britain and the United States, if not for an Anglo-American dominated world in the twentieth century. These positions, as well as some of the most moving descriptions of life in wartime London, were put forth in Page's eloquent letters published after the war in *The Life and Letters of Walter Hines Page.*

Ross Gregory

Bibliography
Cooper, John M. *Walter Hines Page: The Southerner as American, 1855–1918.* Chapel Hill: University of North Carolina Press, 1977.
Gregory, Ross. *Walter Hines Page: Ambassador to the Court of St. James.* Lexington: University Press of Kentucky, 1970.
Hendrick, Burton J. *The Life and Letters of Walter Hines Page.* 3 vols. Garden City, NY: Doubleday, Page, 1924–1926.

Palmer, Alexander Mitchell (1872–1936)

A. Mitchell Palmer was born in Moosehead, Pennsylvania, in 1872. In 1891, he graduated from Swarthmore College and was admitted to the Pennsylvania bar two years later. Palmer became active in local Democratic politics. In 1908, running as a "reformer," he was elected to the 61st Congress. He was subsequently reelected to the 62d and 63d Congresses.

During his first term in the House, Palmer won recognition for his speaking prowess when he opposed the Republican-sponsored Payne-Aldrich Tariff Act. When the Democrats won control of the House during the 62d Congress, Palmer was given a seat on the tax-writing Ways and Means Committee. He helped write the iron and steel section and the income tax section of the Underwood Tariff Act.

Palmer supported other progressive measures during his six years in Congress. He and Senator Robert L. Owen jointly sponsored the first child labor law, and through Palmer's efforts, Congress ultimately passed the nation's first child labor law, the Keating-Owen Act, which President Wilson signed in 1916.

Palmer was an ardent supporter of Woodrow Wilson. As chairman of Pennsylvania's delegation to the 1912 Democratic National Convention, he helped secure Wilson's presidential nomination, even though he was offered the vice-presidential spot on the ticket of opposing candidate Champ Clark if he would support Clark's candidacy.

Because of his loyalty to the New Jersey governor, Palmer was named to the Democratic campaign committee and became one of Wilson's trusted advisers and confidants. After Wilson defeated Taft and Roosevelt in the November general election, the President-elect offered Palmer the post of secretary of war. Palmer, a Quaker, declined the position because of his religious beliefs.

Rather than seek another House term, in 1914, Palmer acceded to Wilson's request that he run for the United States Senate. Although Palmer's senatorial bid was unsuccessful, Wilson rewarded his friend by appointing him to the U.S. Court of Claims. Palmer resigned his judgeship within a year because he disliked the sedentary lifestyle and was reluctant to abandon his extensive law practice to hold public office.

Despite his disdain for public office, in 1917 Palmer accepted President Wilson's appointment to the post of alien property custodian. This position, which was created by the Trading-with-the-Enemy Act of 1917, made Palmer the trustee of $600 million worth of property owned by or owed to enemy aliens. As legal trustee of this property, Palmer was authorized by Congress to sell it to American citizens.

Palmer held this post from October 1917 until March 1919.

In the spring of 1919, Attorney General Thomas W. Gregory resigned. Wilson's presidential secretary, Joseph Tumulty, led the campaign to get Palmer appointed to the cabinet. Tumulty described Palmer to the President as a young, militant, fearless leader who appealed to the young voters—a definite asset to the Democratic party. Wilson eventually took Tumulty's advice and named Palmer attorney general, a post that he held during the last two years of Wilson's administration.

Immediately upon assuming leadership of the Justice Department, Palmer faced a series of problems, beginning with profiteering. Palmer responded by establishing price-fixing committees throughout the nation. These committees were partially successful in preventing increases in the cost of necessities. In addition, a number of profiteers were prosecuted and punished. Palmer was also instrumental in ending a coal strike led by John L. Lewis in 1919 and succeeded in dissolving the "beef trust."

Palmer's greatest notoriety as attorney general resulted from his attack on alleged domestic radicalism during the "Red Scare" of 1919–1920. In April 1919, a few lunatic radicals created near-panic by mailing bombs to thirty-eight prominent citizens, including Justice Oliver Wendell Holmes and Palmer himself. Two months later, several direct bombings occurred. One exploded in front of Palmer's Washington home, killing his would-be assassin.

Although the April and June bombings were isolated criminal activities, anti-Communist sentiments were running high in the United States during this period; so with the help of the newly created Federal Bureau of Investigation, Palmer initiated a strenuous campaign against aliens and radicals. During the first raid, Palmer arrested 250 members of the Union of Russian Workmen, many of whom were beaten during the arrest. The Justice Department could find cause to deport only thirty-nine of them. In December 1919, another "Palmer raid" resulted in the deportation of 250 individuals, including Alexander Berkman and Emma Goldman.

On Jan. 2, 1920, Palmer ordered raids on Communist meetings throughout the country. More than 4,000 people were thrown into jail. Most were seized on suspicion only, arrested without warrants and held incommunicado. In all, 556 aliens were deported following this third raid. Palmer continued to warn the nation about Red plots. but when the violence he predicted for May Day 1920 failed to materialize, criticism of Palmer began to surface. The public grew weary of his unfounded alarms. By the summer of 1920, the Red Scare was largely over.

In 1920, Palmer reached the height of his political career as a leading contender for the Democratic presidential nomination along with William G. McAdoo and Governor James Cox of Ohio. After losing the nomination to Cox, Palmer retired from public service and resumed his law practice. Palmer died in Washington in December 1936.

Burton A. Boxerman

Bibliography

Coben, Stanley. *A. Mitchell Palmer: Politician*. New York: Columbia University Press, 1963.

Murray, Robert K. *Red Scare: A Study in National Hysteria*. Minneapolis: University of Minnesota Press, 1955.

Palmer, Frederick (1873–1958)

Frederick Palmer, a renowned newspaper correspondent, began his career with the *Morning Post* in Jamestown, Virginia, in 1888 at age fifteen. In 1893, he began working for the *New York Press*, sailing to Europe in 1895 as its correspondent. The first war he covered was the Greco-Turkish War of 1897. His next adventure was a trip through the Klondike during the gold rush. Following that period, he covered the Philippine Insurrection, returning to the United States aboard Admiral Dewey's flagship; next he covered the Allied Relief Expedition to Peking during the Boxer Rebellion, uprisings in Central America and Macedonia, the Russo-Japanese War, Teddy Roosevelt's cruise of the Great White Fleet, the Balkan Wars, and the Mexican Revolution.

Palmer was the only American war correspondent accredited to the British Army until 1917. His version of events, like so many other correspondents assigned to the British or French armies, was dictated exclusively by the British High Command. He was cited in Sir Gilbert Parker's *American Press Resume*, a weekly analysis of the range and influence of British propaganda in the United States, as producing "amongst the thoroughly satisfactory articles."

Palmer and Gen. John J. Pershing were friends of long standing. After the United States officially entered the war, Pershing offered, and Palmer accepted, a commission as a major in the U.S. Army to organize and direct the American correspondents. Palmer became more of an army officer and less a newspaperman as time went on, causing many other correspondents anguish as he provided them with nothing but laudatory reports about the American Army and its operations, mostly manufactured by the military and aided by Palmer's own censorship regulations.

One of the major problems encountered by the American Expeditionary Force (AEF) was the confusion and disorganization within the Service of Supply that had hampered the army from the first. Several of the more knowledgeable correspondents threatened to expose the mess, and Palmer introduced three of them to Pershing at a private meeting. They all agreed to write a less critical commentary but that was not an acceptable compromise to Newton D. Baker, secretary of war, who refused to allow any correspondent to break the story. When Heywood Broun, a thorn in Palmer's operation, returned to the United States and broke the story, abrogating his signed pledge not to, the scandal made headlines for weeks. Censorship was under heavy attack by many of the correspondents, and the Broun articles forced the army to make some adjustments to Palmer's stringent regulations.

Later, Palmer claimed to have eased the censorship "as much as I dared," also acknowledging "that nature did not intend me to be a censor." He was relieved of his burden by Capt. Gerald Morgan, AEF press chief, and returned to the United States with Col. Edward M. House's mission in December 1917. Back in the United States, Palmer lobbied senators who were outspokenly opposed to censorship, to give up their attempts to revoke, or modify, military control of news emanating from France. He returned to France in February 1918 with a memorandum "giving the correspondents at the front more freedom," and shortly afterward was assigned to accompany Secretary Baker on a tour of the front and then to London.

Back in France, Palmer assumed a new position. He was nominally in charge of the War Diary in an office at Chaumont, just down the hall from Pershing's office. From that point on, his major task seemed to embody being "public relations" officer for the commander-in-chief. According to his own biography, it was his job to make Pershing aware of what was going on between soldiers of the Regular Army and the citizen soldiers because Pershing was "so remote" and to make suggestions to him that Palmer thought were valuable.

After the war ended, Palmer looked about at the Peace Conference in Paris and came to the conclusion "that more wars are already in the making." Palmer wrote many books, most of them nonfiction, the last being a biography of Pershing. He died in 1958.

George B. Clark

Bibliography

Knightley, Phillip. *The First Casualty*. New York: Harcourt Brace Jovanovich, 1975.
Palmer, Frederick. *With My Own Eyes*. Indianapolis: Bobbs-Merrill, 1933.
Peterson, H.C. *Propaganda for War*. Norman: University of Oklahoma Press, 1939.

Palmer, John McAuley (1870–1955)

John McAuley Palmer was born in Springfield, Illinois. He graduated from the United States Military Academy in 1892, subsequently serving in Cuba, in China during the Boxer Rebellion, and in the Philippines, where, among other assignments, he was a district governor in the Moro Province. During a tour at the Command and General Staff School at Fort Leavenworth (where he worked with a junior officer named George C. Marshall), Palmer wrote an article urging a tactical organization for the U.S. Army. It caught the attention of Chief of Staff Leonard Wood and led to an assignment on the General Staff. After further duty in China and the Philippines, Palmer returned to the General Staff in 1916 where he was involved in planning for the Selective Service Act of 1917 upon the U.S. entry into World War I.

Although Gen. John J. Pershing had not previously met LtCol. John Palmer, Pershing selected him as chief of operations, American Expeditionary Force (AEF) on the basis of his reputation as a creative thinker. A brief visit to the British Army headquarters in London appalled Palmer and his fellow officers, who immediately saw how utterly inadequate was their tiny staff in contrast to the many hundreds manning the complex British staff supporting their war effort.

In Paris, Palmer and a handful of aides set to work preparing for the arrival of U.S. divisions as they hastily completed their training back home. Lacking experience with the technological advances in weaponry and equipment which had occurred between 1914 and 1917, Palmer and his men visited French and British units to learn all they could. While benefitting from Allied innovations, they had to resist being induced to accept French and British doctrine as well as their hardware. General Pershing was determined not to succumb to Allied attempts at amalgamation (using U.S. troops merely as replacements in the Allied armies). He wished to avoid the static siegelike character of trench warfare by keeping the AEF free to maneuver. To this end, Palmer negotiated with the French for a purely U.S. sector on the front. The British held the Channel end of the line close to their island base, and the French covered Paris, the symbolic heart of the nation, so the logical section for the AEF lay on the right.

One of the most pressing problems confronting the operations staff was to revise the structure of the AEF to suit the situation encountered in France. Given the lack of experienced senior officers to head the larger formations and to provide ample manpower to sustain action in the absence of a replacement system, Palmer and his colleagues decided upon a four-division corps to have two divisions in the line and two in reserve, thus permitting corps and their artillery to stay put while rotating divisions. Corresponding adjustments in the lesser formations resulted in a massive 28,000-man division and 250-man companies, all of which required an immense amount of detailed planning by the tiny operations staff. Especially vexing were the politically sensitive problems of effecting such changes in National Guard formations.

Overworked and overwhelmed, Palmer became ill, and to help him recuperate, General Pershing sent him on a quasi-diplomatic mission to Italy to help shore up Italian morale after the disastrous retreat at Caporetto. Following a rest in the United States, Palmer returned to France where, as a colonel, he was immediately given command of the 58th Brigade in the 29th Division, a National Guard organization. There he proved to be an effective combat commander; his brigade, though reduced from 10,000 to some 7,000 men, advanced aggressively, breaking through the layered German defenses of the Hindenburg Line. His promotion to brigadier general had been approved by General Pershing when the Armistice stopped all promotions.

Colonel Palmer returned to the United States as Pershing's special emissary to advise on postwar legislation for the peacetime army. In this capacity he served as a special adviser to the Senate subcommittee working on the measure. Palmer favored a small Regular Army, supplemented by a well-trained and organized reserve of citizen soldiers secured through a scheme of universal military training. In the National Defense Act of 1920, Congress rejected universal training but adopted many of the features Palmer advocated, providing for the effective utilization of citizen soldiers. After retiring in 1925, as a brigadier general, Palmer wrote a number of books expounding an army based upon citizen reservists. He was recalled to duty during World War II as a special adviser to the General Staff and General Marshall, the oldest officer on duty at age seventy-five. Palmer retired for a second time in 1946. He died in Washington, D.C., on Oct. 26, 1955.

I.B. Holley, Jr.

Bibliography

Holley, I.B., Jr. *General John M. Palmer, Citizen Soldiers and the Army of Democracy*. Westport, CT: Greenwood Press, 1982.

Palmer, John M. *America in Arms*. New York: Arno Press, 1979.

———. *Statesmanship or War*. Garden City, NY: Doubleday, Page, 1927.

———. *Washington, Lincoln, Wilson: Three War Statesmen*. Garden City, NY: Doubleday, Doran, 1930.

Paris Gun

At approximately 7:20 A.M. Saturday morning, March 23, 1918, an explosion took place on the cobblestone street in front of house No. 6 on the Quay de Seine in the southern section of Paris, creating a fifteen-foot-wide, five-foot-deep crater. Though no one was killed, shrapnel hit buildings and broke windows. Fifteen minutes later, a second explosion took place in the center of the Boulevard de Strasbourg, killing nine and injuring thirteen Parisians. The explosions continued at the rate of three to four an hour. By the end of the day, at least forty-five people were killed or injured by the more than twenty explosions that took place in and around Paris. The explosions were caused by shells fired from a newly developed piece of German ultra-long-range artillery. The Paris Gun, as it was eventually called (also known as the Kaiser Wilhelm Geschutz) was one of several German secret weapons used during World War I.

On March 29, a second Paris Gun opened fire. Though it fired only four shots that day, it caused the most casualties in any single shelling when a shell landed on the Church of Saint Gervais—more than 100 casualties resulted when part of the church's ceiling collapsed on the congregation. From March 23 to August 9, 1918, 303 shells landed in and around Paris, killing 256 people and injuring 620 more.

Before the fielding of the Paris Gun, the German physicist, Dr. Rauschenberger, developed a theory that if he could fire a projectile into the stratosphere, taking the minimum time required, he would have imparted to it the speed necessary for it to attain very long range without the friction encountered in the air near the earth's surface. To attain such velocity, an extraordinarily long barrel had to be used to afford the sustained push necessary for the shell. A large chamber capacity would be necessary. All of this would be obtained at the expense of significant erosion of the gun barrel. Further, such a weapon would be extremely heavy, or it would not attain any accuracy at the desired range. German tests concluded that a 210mm gun with a barrel length of 93.3 feet would be necessary to propel a 264-pound projectile to the distance desired. Calculations indicated that a projectile would reach a range of seventy-two miles if it had an initial flight velocity of approximately 5,250 feet per second and was fired at an elevation of fifty-five degrees.

In the spring of 1916, Gen. Erich Ludendorff approved a plan for the construction of an experimental gun capable of shelling Paris from behind German lines, then about fifty-five miles away. The German Admiralty and the Krupp ordnance works began work on the project. In February 1917, Ludendorff increased the weapon's requirement to 120 kilometers. The actual size of the weapon caused several problems. Without bracing, the 112-foot-long barrel would droop, thus making it useless, so braces were fitted to support the barrel and provide the proper alignment of the gun's muzzle and shell breech. Despite the bracing, the barrel would whip side to side for several minutes after firing.

The gun tube was rifled through three-quarters of its length with sixty-four grooves at constant right pitch of four degrees, and the pressure in the barrel of the gun would rise from normal to 67,000 pounds per square inch within a hundredth of a second. The projectile itself was three feet in height and weighed 264 pounds, of which only 18 pounds were explosives. Because of the size of the explosive charge, the shell did less damage than the conventional eight-inch artillery of the period.

The only evidence of the existence of the Paris Guns, besides the damage they caused, were their emplacements. In August 1918, when the Germans withdrew from the Soissons-Reims salient, the Allies came across the near completed gun emplacement near Château-Thierry. The emplacement consisted of a thirty-five-foot base and a rotating section. The railroad carriage gun mount would be rolled on to the emplacement. Once in place, the mount would be lifted by four jacks and the railroad trucks then removed. The three firing locations were seventy-five miles from Paris in a thick wood near Laon.

The Germans knew that the sound-ranging systems available at the time would locate the Paris Gun battery within a matter of days of the first shot. In addition to elaborate camouflage, eight-inch guns were placed every few kilometers along the front line. These guns would be fired at the same time as the Paris Gun in order to mask the location of the battery firing on the French capital. But, despite the concealment measures, the battery was located. French artillery fire was then directed against the Paris Gun. During the first two weeks of the French counterbattery fire, the Germans reported that more than 5,000 shells landed in and near their positions. In one ten-hour period, more than 700 French shells landed in and around the German battery. Though the bombardment caused no material damage, seven men were killed and thirteen wounded.

Under the terms of the Versailles Treaty, Germany was supposed to turn over one complete Paris Gun to the Allies, but none was ever delivered. After the war, the U.S. Ordnance Board at Westervelt Arsenal concluded that "such guns have no military value and their construction is not justified."

Vincent P. Grimes

Paris Peace Conference, 1919–1920

The Legacy of the War

When the representatives of the Allied and Associated Powers convened in Paris in January 1919 to work out the terms of a peace settlement with the defeated Central empires, they faced a task even more difficult and complex than that of the statesmen assembled at the last great peace congress held in Vienna a century earlier. Four years of unprecedented carnage and destruction had shattered the very foundations of the European concert of power and had struck deep at the roots of the social and economic life of the Continent. It had left millions dead and many more millions wounded, created famine and poverty, mortgaged the wealth of future generations, and led to severe dislocations in the societies of both the victorious and defeated nations.

Everywhere, it seemed, familiar boundaries were shifting or dissolving. The collapse of four empires had thrown Central and Eastern Europe into turmoil. In parts of the old Austro-Hungarian territories and on the rim of the late Russian Empire, hostilities among neighboring peoples continued to erupt, as long oppressed nationalities emerged as independent states, and old and new nations alike tried to seize as much as possible of the former Habsburg and Romanov lands. Revolutionary paroxysms were convulsing Berlin and other German cities, a bloody civil war was raging in Russia, and hardly a stable government could be found anywhere east of the Rhine. The Russian situation, in fact, contributed an additional layer of complexity to the business of the peace conference. With the Bolsheviks' revolutionary ideology vying for the allegiance of the masses of Europe's crisis-torn societies, the fear of widespread upheaval and anarchy was never far from the minds of the peacemakers.

Conflicting Visions of Peace

The legacy of the war would have made the task of peacemaking daunting enough, even if the five principals—the United States, Great Britain, France, Italy, and Japan—had shared a common vision as to the kind of settlement they hoped to establish and the type of Europe they sought to rebuild. During prearmistice negotiations, the European Allies had given in to American pressure and reluctantly agreed to accept, with two qualifications, Woodrow Wilson's Fourteen Points as the basis for peace.

However, many of Wilson's pronouncements were open to divergent interpretations when applied to complex postwar realities, and some of them openly conflicted with the war aims of the Allies and the terms of their secret wartime agreements.

Central to Wilson's idealism was the belief that hostilities among nations were the inevitable result of an international order that was founded on balance-of-power politics and dominated by secret alliances, militarism, imperialism, and economic nationalism. A durable peace, Wilson argued, could only be achieved by replacing this atavistic fabric with a policy of open diplomacy, universal disarmament, freedom of the seas, free trade, and self-determination of all peoples in a system based on international law and collective security. It was to be anchored in a League of Nations, which would mediate international disputes and guarantee the political independence and territorial integrity of great and small states alike. To integrate the chastened and newly democratized Central Powers into this new world order, and to keep their people from succumbing to the lure of revolutionary Bolshevism, the peace settlement was to be characterized by a sense of moderation and high-minded justice that promoted a spirit of reconciliation.

Wilson's call for a permanent role for the United States in a new world order through membership in the League of Nations was a radical departure from America's traditional isolationist policy, and the President's proposals did not meet with universal approval at home. Although most of Wilson's critics, including Republican leaders, were not irreconcilable isolationists, they feared that, by committing itself to a system of collective security, the United States would relinquish a large measure of its national sovereignty. It did not portend well for the ultimate fate of Wilson's design that the Democrats, in the elections on Nov. 5, 1918, lost control of both houses of Congress and thus of the crucial Senate Foreign Relations Committee. Since Wilson had appealed for a Democratic victory as a show of support for his leadership, Republicans could now claim with some justification that the President did not represent the American people at the peace conference. Thus, when Wilson arrived in Europe, he did so with enormous international prestige but a less than solid political base at home.

To the masses of the Allied nations, Wilson was the savior of civilization and the harbinger of a new and peaceful era. Yet, while millions of people enthusiastically welcomed the President during his triumphal tour of the Allied capitals prior to the peace conference, their adulation for him did not mean that they embraced all the principles of the American peace program. The impartial and high-minded justice that Wilson hoped would prevail at the conference was altogether different from the retributive justice that the majority of the Allied peoples expected to see meted out to the hated foe.

While the Allied statesmen had to consider domestic pressures, the need to retain American support made it imperative for them to show a degree of approval for Wilson's ideas and to turn them into an appropriate framework for the achievement of their principal war aims. They quickly learned to argue their cases on the grounds of "justice," "self-determination," "democracy," and other Wilsonian principles. Yet the substance of their demands remained rooted in political realism and old-style power politics.

The French, in particular, were wary of Wilson's lofty goals. For Georges Clemenceau, their seventy-seven-year-old prime minister who had begun his political career during the Franco-Prussian War of 1870–1871, victory over France's intrinsically more powerful neighbor must be exploited to guarantee French security against future German aggression. The loss of Russia as an ally could be somewhat offset by forming an anti-German coalition with the new states of Eastern Europe; but the only way to assure French security was to weaken Germany permanently. Although Clemenceau did not endorse the large-scale territorial dismemberment of Germany advocated by hardliners around Marshal Ferdinand Foch and President Raymond Poincaré, he insisted upon the recovery of Alsace-Lorraine, the disarmament of Germany, the establishment of autonomous republics under French control on the left bank of the Rhine, and possession of the Saar Valley. In addition, France badly needed money to finance its massive reconstruction and help alleviate its staggering national debt. With the refusal of the United States to forgive French war debts, German reparations assumed a high priority to France.

The British position alternated between support for American principles on some issues and endorsement of French claims on others, depending on which arrangement best served the particular interests of Great Britain. Generally, their concern for the traditional balance of power prompted Prime Minister David Lloyd George and his colleagues to promote the survival of a politically and economically viable German nation (minus its navy, of course) and to try to prevent the emergence of French predominance on the Continent. However, the British were most adamant on the question of German reparations. During the Coupon Election in December 1918, Lloyd George had essentially promised to make Germany pay for the entire cost of the war, not just the civilian damages stipulated in the prearmistice agreement, and the Conservative members of his coalition government were determined to hold the prime minister to his pledge. In addition, the British pursued openly imperialist policies in their economic and strategic designs for the Middle East and their attempts to secure for themselves and their dominions substantial pieces of the German colonial empire.

The remaining two Great Powers, Italy and Japan, were primarily interested in the territorial gains promised to their respective countries for their entry into the war. Thus, the Japanese, as part of a long-term plan for the penetration of China, laid claim to the German interests on the Shantung Province, as well as to all the German islands in the Pacific north of the equator. The Italians insisted, first and foremost, on the terms of the Treaty of London of 1915, by which they were to receive the Trentino, South Tyrol up to the Brenner Pass, Trieste, Istria, the islands along the Dalmatian coast, and the northern half of Dalmatia itself. However, victory over Austria had resulted in a nationalist frenzy among the Italian Right and put tremendous pressure on the government of Prime Minister Vittorio Emanuele Orlando to hold out for additional rewards. The target of all the impassioned agitation was the former Hungarian port city of Fiume, which the Treaty of London had specifically assigned to a possible Croatian state but whose possession now turned into a symbol of Italian honor.

Although Wilson was under no illusion as to the deep-seated differences between his own peace program and the demands of the European Allies, it was with high hopes and a supreme confidence in the ultimate victory of his ideals that he left for France in early December 1918. He realized that concessions and compromises would be unavoidable; but he vowed not to betray his principles. William C. Bullitt noted in his diary of the peace conference that Wilson instructed his advisers on the *George Washington* en route to Paris, "Tell me what is right, and I'll fight for it." The United States alone among the victorious powers did not seek material advantages from the settlement. Thus, in a speech to American servicemen on Christmas Day 1918 at Humes, Wilson hoped that he would be free to "make good in the establishment of peace upon the permanent foundations of right and justice."

Organization of the Conference

In the broadest sense, the Paris Peace Conference lasted from Jan. 18, 1919, until Aug. 10, 1920. It opened with great fanfare, high hopes, and intense publicity as a brilliant assemblage of the leading statesmen of the time and quietly closed thousands of meetings later in near obscurity, its routine business being conducted by the Allied ambassadors in France. The conference ultimately produced a total of five treaties with those nations who had earlier signed armistice agreements with the Allied and Associated Powers: the Treaty of Versailles with Germany (June 28, 1919); the Treaty of Saint-Germain with Austria (Sept. 10, 1919); the Treaty of Neuilly with Bulgaria (Nov. 27, 1919); the Treaty of Trianon with Hungary (June 4, 1920); and the Treaty of Sèvres with Turkey (Aug. 10, 1920). Its most important phase was the period up to the signing of the Treaty of Versailles. It was during those initial months that the leaders of the victorious powers discussed many of the crucial issues and took a number of far-reaching decisions that determined the fate of Europe and much of the world.

The French had worked out an elaborate program for the conference that emphasized the settlement of war-related issues over any efforts to establish a system of collective security through the League of Nations. The Americans, however, rejected this program as an attempt to perpetuate the "old order." As Wilson argued at London's Guildhall on Dec. 28, 1918, the individual provisions of the peace were "worthless unless there stood in back of them a permanent concert of power for their maintenance." Since no detailed alternative arrangements were ever made, many of the eventual structures and procedures of the conference were the result of haphazard decisions and accidental developments.

The Allied and Associated Powers appointed a total of seventy delegates to the conference. The Great Powers were represented by five plenipotentiaries each. They were assisted by huge staffs of historians, geographers, economists, financial and legal experts, military and naval specialists, and political and diplomatic advisers. As the host, Clemenceau presided over the plenary sessions, which were, however, few and far between. They did little more than ratify agreements that had been reached beforehand among the Great Powers. Initially, the main forum of the conference and the real seat of power was the Council of Ten, which was composed of the heads of government of the Great Powers and their foreign ministers. When this body proved too cumbersome for any real progress, it gave way in late March to informal meetings among Wilson, Clemenceau, Lloyd George, and Orlando, who took charge of the decision-making process in the so-called Council of Four. The foreign ministers continued to meet in a separate body, the Council of Five, to dispose of less important matters. The members of the principal councils were supported in their work by over fifty advisory committees and commissions, whose findings on a host of issues formed the basis for most of the provisions that found their way into the treaties. After the signature of the Germany treaty, the various heads of government left the conference. As a result, the Council of Four was superseded by the Council of the Heads of Delegations, which, in turn, was replaced in early 1920 by the Conference of Ambassadors.

In addition to the delegations of the Allied and Associated Powers, the emissaries of a number of neutral countries, as well as scores of missions and envoys representing nationalities and ethnic groups with a myriad of interests, made their way to Paris. All of them hoped to receive a hearing before the conference and expected the Great Powers to grant them the justice they had promised to the world. Much to their dismay, however, they played a very limited role and were consulted only when their specific interests happened to coincide with larger issues.

The League of Nations

For Wilson, the issue that took precedence over all other considerations at the conference was the establishment of the League of Nations, the backbone of his concept for a new order in international relations. To demonstrate that the new organization was the key to the entire settlement, Wilson insisted that the creation of the League be the first major item on the agenda and that, once approved, its constitution be incorporated into each of the peace treaties. He realized that, in return, he might be forced to make concessions on other questions, but he was convinced that any wrongs in the settlement would eventually be righted through the instrumentality of the League.

The task of drawing up the constitution, or Covenant, of the League of Nations, devolved upon a special commission with members from fourteen nations, chaired and dominated by Wilson. On the basis of an Anglo-American draft and in close cooperation with Lord Robert Cecil, the chief British delegate on the commission, Wilson steered the negotiations during ten often contentious meetings toward acceptance of a version that included all the principal provisions of his own earlier drafts. The main controversies centered on questions that involved the very character of the League. The French and, to a certain extent, the Italians, advocated an organization that would commit the United States and Great Britain to the defense of the postwar order through the creation of an international army with far-reaching supranational powers. The Americans and the British, on the other hand, viewed the League as a means of averting hostilities in the first place.

As it turned out, Wilson did have to retreat on other issues in order to secure universal consent for the Covenant. Except for the Japanese, who blatantly bartered their membership in the League of Nations into American acquiescence in their imperialist designs on Shantung, the other powers did not openly use their approval as a bargaining chip. But Wilson was constantly aware that the French and Italians, or even the British, might simply walk away from the conference and thus jeopardize the creation of the new organization if he did not meet them halfway on questions they considered vital. Moreover, domestic opposition to the League, and particularly the objections of Republican leaders in the Senate, seriously undermined the President's negotiating position in Paris. Thus, after his return in mid-March from a brief trip to Washington, Wilson was forced to ask his Allied colleagues for a set of amendments to the Covenant in order to try to assuage his critics at home. While the other powers eventually agreed to incorporate changes that, among other things, recognized the validity of the Monroe Doctrine, exempted purely internal matters from the purview of the League, and established a mechanism for withdrawal from the organization, they realized that Wilson was vulnerable and that a strong stand on their part might compel him to compromise on some of his principles.

As eventually adopted in the plenary session on April 28, the Covenant of the League of Nations provided for an Assembly of all members, an executive Council composed of the Great Powers and four smaller states, as well as an independent judiciary branch, the Permanent Court of International Justice. It outlined machinery for the arbitration of international disputes and stipulated a system of sanctions against aggressor states, emphasizing moral condemnation and economic boycotts over military measures. It also created a permanent Secretariat of the League and set up various commissions charged with executing or supervising specific terms of the peace settlement and with promoting international cooperation in economic and social areas.

While French commentators spurned the League of Nations as an inane debating society, and the Germans, excluded from the organization pending proof of peaceful intentions, vilified it as a league of victors and a new Holy Alliance, Wilson regarded it as the crowning achievement of the conference and the cornerstone of a new world order based on the ideals of progressive internationalism.

The Peace Settlement of Versailles
The Allies agreed early on that of all the issues resulting from the war, those pertaining to the settlement with Germany had the widest implications and were to receive priority in the proceedings. They included, among other things, the redrawing of Germany's eastern frontier and the extent of its territorial cessions to the resurrected Polish state, rectification of its Danish and Belgian borders, and new economic, financial, and commercial arrangements. To address the overriding French concern for security against German aggression, one of the first questions considered at the conference involved the military, naval, and aviation terms of the future treaty, and they were eventually agreed upon with relatively little controversy.

Still, to the French, German disarmament alone did not suffice; more important for the security of their country was a frontier that could be easily defended and that would deprive the Germans of the staging area for a possible invasion. And, as Marshal Foch pointed out: "Nature has provided a barrier on the road to invasion, but only one: the RHINE." Only the separation of the left bank of the Rhine from Germany and the creation of one or more buffer states, nominally independent but under French control, would guarantee the safety of France. While Foch presented the Rhineland scheme in purely military and strategic terms, André Tardieu, Clemenceau's chief adviser, sought to give it a Wilsonian veneer by claiming that it promoted the self-determination of the Rhenish people and their liberation from Prussian oppression.

Wilson and Lloyd George, however, were not convinced. While conceding the need for French security, they were unalterably opposed to the dismemberment of Germany in the west. Not only would it violate the Fourteen Points and the prearmistice agreement; the separation would sow the seeds of a new war. What followed, then, were four weeks of intense, often acrimonious debate, chiefly between Clemenceau and Wilson. Overlapping, as it did, an equally bitter Franco-American confrontation over the disposition of the Saar Basin, it resulted in the first great crisis of the conference. During this period, Clemenceau, grim-faced, accused the American president of being pro-German, while Wilson did not hide his aggravation with French intransigence. And both men threatened at various times to leave the conference. The impasse on the Rhineland question was finally resolved in mid-April when Clemenceau—over the strong objections of Foch, Poincaré, and the French parliament—abandoned the demand for autonomous buffer states in return for three guarantees: a temporary extension of the wartime coalition through separate treaties pledging the United States and Great Britain to come to the immediate assistance of France in the event of unprovoked German aggression, the demilitarization of a zone extending from the French border to fifty kilometers east of the Rhine, and Allied occupation of the left bank and four bridgeheads of the Rhine, to be divided into three zones and evacuated sequentially after five, ten, and fifteen years.

If the French policy in the Rhineland was based on strategic considerations, the annexation of the coal-rich Saar Basin was regarded as economic necessity. It was designed to compensate for the losses France had suffered from the wanton destruction of its coal mines in the

Nord by the retreating German forces. In the long run, however, it was intended to alleviate France's traditional dependence on German coal, boost the output of French heavy industry, and facilitate the industrial expansion made possible by the recovery of the iron ore mines of Lorraine. Again, Wilson, backed by Lloyd George, strongly resisted the transfer of territory that had been in German hands for more than a hundred years. In the end, Clemenceau dropped his demand for outright annexation and agreed to a compromise that gave France ownership of the Saar mines and assured an additional supply of coal from Germany. The area itself was placed under the administration of the League of Nations for a period of fifteen years, after which its permanent status would be determined by plebiscite.

The single most contentious issue pertaining to the German settlement and the subject of the most protracted, and ultimately fruitless, debates among the United States, Great Britain, and France was the question of German reparations. It was also a highly emotional and volatile issue that exposed Clemenceau and Lloyd George to enormous public pressure. The Americans had made it clear in the fall of 1918 that they would insist on repayment of the loans they had made to the European Allies during the war. They had also decided not to commit Treasury funds to European economic restoration, preferring to leave the matter to private American banks through commercial credit arrangements. Hence, the British and French came to rely increasingly on German reparation payments to put their countries back on a solid financial footing.

During the prearmistice talks, both Lloyd George and Clemenceau had accepted the American position that demands for compensation should be strictly limited to civilian damages and that Germany was not to be saddled with a huge indemnity. However, they had also repeatedly assured their people that they were determined to exact the "uttermost farthing" from Germany and would, in fact, make the Germans pay for the total cost of the war to England and France.

Soon after the opening of the conference, a special commission of financial experts set to work to evaluate the losses suffered by the Allies and to assess Germany's capacity to pay. After two months of tedious deliberations, however, the commission was unable to reach a consensus on either figures or the kind of damages for which Germany was responsible. Although the British and French eventually dropped their demand for reimbursement of war costs, they continued to demand much higher sums than the Americans thought it possible for Germany to pay. When the Council of Four took charge of the matter in late March, it, too, failed to agree on the fundamental principles. For political reasons, Lloyd George and Clemenceau were unwilling to admit openly that the amount of reparations would have to be limited, and they maintained that, in theory at least, Germany should be required to pay for everything it actually owed. Wilson, on the other hand, argued consistently for a realistic bill that should be based on Germany's capacity to pay and should not exceed $30 billion, while the payment period should be limited to a maximum of thirty years. But for Lloyd George and Clemenceau, politics took precedence over economics, and, in the end, the Council decided not to include any total amount in the treaty. Instead, it was agreed to postpone the entire problem and to appoint a permanent Reparations Commission, which would determine, by May 1, 1921, the amount, timing, and modality of the German payments. Until then, Germany was to remit $5 billion in gold or in kind to enable the Allies to proceed with the immediate restoration of their economic and industrial life.

Yet, the failure to specify a total sum or a limited period had far-reaching consequences. Lloyd George had earlier managed to persuade Wilson to disregard the prearmistice agreement and to include service pensions and separation allowances in the category of damages. This was simply a way to increase Britain's share in the reparations since the civilian damages they had suffered were minimal. Wilson had made this crucial concession, which effectively doubled Germany's liability, on the understanding that the conference would eventually fix the total amount of the reparation payments and that it would be based on Germany's capacity to pay. Thus, the inclusion of pensions and separation allowances would simply alter the apportionment of reparations among the victors, but it would not affect the amount. However, when neither a final sum nor a definite payment period were mentioned in the treaty, it had the result of forcing the Germans not only to sign an open account, but also to commit themselves to the reparation of vastly more than just the civilian damages they

had agreed to in the Armistice. Although the Reparations Commission finally fixed the amount at $33 billion in gold and in kind, later drastically reduced and ultimately converted into a small lump sum that was actually never paid, the reparation problem saddled the young democratic regime of the Weimar Republic with a heavy burden and remained a major irritant in international relations for more than a decade.

One of the most clear-cut controversies between Wilson's idealistic principles and the self-interests of his European and Japanese colleagues erupted over the disposition of the former German overseas empire. Both sides were in accord that the colonies, which had been seized by Allied forces, should not be returned to Germany, but that was as far as their understanding went. In his Fourteen Points, Wilson had called for an "absolutely impartial adjustment of all colonial claims," with due regard for the interests of the indigenous populations. He later elaborated that the former German colonies should become the common property of the League of Nations, to be governed by small nations under international mandate. The problem was that these territories were already spoken for: Britain, France, and Belgium had laid claim to some; others had been pledged to the British dominions; and Japan, too, had been promised its share. After a good deal of verbal sparring, the victors did get their spoils, though not as outright possessions but under mandates of the League of Nations. Britain took most of German East Africa and split the Cameroons and Togoland with France; Belgium gained Rwanda-Burundi, and South Africa received German South-West Africa; Australia acquired New Guinea; New Zealand obtained the German part of Samoa; and Japan secured the Mariana, Marshall, and Caroline islands.

Yet, for the Japanese, the award of the Pacific islands was a relatively minor victory compared to their ambitions in China. Under the terms of a treaty with Great Britain, the Japanese had entered the war in 1914, captured the German naval base at Kiaochow, and overran the entire German concession in Shantung Province. In the infamous Twenty-One Demands, they had subsequently forced China to recognize their rights as Germany's successor in Shantung and had won an endorsement of their vested interests in secret agreements with Britain and France in 1917. While the Japanese were in an impregnable legal position, their claims were a major violation of the principle of self-determination, giving the Chinese high hopes of recovering their lost provinces at the conference.

In his determined opposition to the Japanese demands, Wilson received no support from Lloyd George or Clemenceau, both of whom maintained that their hands were tied. In the fight for his principles, there was little Wilson could actually do other than resort to moral exhortations and plead with the Japanese delegates, at a meeting of the Council of Four in April 1919, to "concentrate less upon the rights that one or the other of us has and more upon the duties incumbent upon us." The controversy dragged on for several months, climaxing when the Japanese openly threatened to leave the conference and refuse to join the League of Nations unless their legitimate claims were honored. In the end, Wilson yielded; he regarded Japan's membership in the League as crucial for peace in the Far East and was hopeful that, through the intercession of the League, a just solution might ultimately be worked out. In the final agreement, the Japanese succeeded to the German concession in Shantung but pledged eventually to restore full sovereignty over the province to China. The Chinese had little faith in Japan's promise, felt betrayed by the Americans and Europeans, and was the only one among the Allied and Associated Powers that did not sign the treaty with Germany. Although Wilson came to believe that the Shantung settlement was the best that could be arranged, it was one of the few substantive clauses that generated strong resentment against the Versailles Treaty in the United States.

With the Shantung controversy out of the way, all the major differences on questions concerning the German treaty had been patched up. In a plenary session on May 7, a draft treaty of some 200 pages was handed to the German plenipotentiaries. They were given fifteen days, later prolonged by another week, to communicate their observations in writing. Stunned by the severity of the provisions, the Germans fired off a spate of memoranda with scores of objections and counterproposals, arguing that the exactions of the treaty were more than their people could bear and that, in many respects, they flagrantly contradicted the Fourteen Points. Implied in these protests was the dire warning that the German government would not sign the treaty in its present form.

German counterproposals, which were often skillfully and convincingly argued, eventually led to minor adjustments in some of the terms. Moreover, the full weight of the German rebuttals made the British increasingly anxious lest a German refusal to sign might precipitate an Allied invasion and prolonged occupation of Germany at immense cost. As a result, under heavy pressure from Liberal, Labor, and religious leaders at home, and moderate members of his delegation, Lloyd George, on June 2, confronted his colleagues in the Council of Four with an ultimatum, demanding a substantial softening of the treaty in return for the British signature. Clemenceau resisted any modifications, and Wilson, exasperated by Lloyd George's "chameleon mind," and his willingness to do whatever was politically expedient, maintained that he would agree to changes only in those provisions that were clearly unjust and not simply harsh. Lloyd George, nevertheless, won significant concessions, most of them at the expense of France and Poland. He secured, for example, a redrawing of the German-Polish border in Germany's favor, a plebiscite in Upper Silesia instead of its outright award to the Polish state, the establishment of a civilian commission to oversee the Allied occupation of the Rhineland, and an agreement that the costs of the occupation would be deducted from the reparation payments to France. He failed, however, to gain Germany's immediate admission into the League of Nations, and the reparations settlement remained a morass.

In their reply to the German counterproposals on June 16, the Allies gave the Germans five days, later extended to seven, to signify their intent to sign the treaty. In the meantime, considering the possibility that no German government could be found that would accept the peace terms, the Council of Four made hasty preparations for the Allied armies to drive to Berlin and they discussed a possible resumption of the naval blockade. In Germany, the treaty sparked outrage and passionate opposition; there was talk of armed resistance; and the first republican government resigned rather than accept responsibility for the "death plan." Finally, only hours before the deadline, a new coalition government of Majority Social Democratic and Catholic Center parties under Prime Minister Gustav Bauer, "yielding to overwhelming force, but without on that account abandoning its view in regard to the unheard of injustice of the conditions of peace," declared its willingness to sign the treaty. In the afternoon of June 28, 1919, the fifth anniversary to the day of the assassinations at Sarajevo, the German plenipotentiaries signed the treaty during a brief ceremony in the Hall of Mirrors at Versailles Palace and sealed the death of the German Empire in the very room that had witnessed its birth less than fifty years before.

The Treaty of Versailles was a formidable document of 440 articles. In addition to the terms discussed above, it included provisions that resulted in the loss by Germany of about one-eighth of its territory, an equal proportion of its economic and industrial capacity, and approximately one-tenth of its prewar population of 70 million people. Most of Germany's territorial losses were in the east, where it ceded Posen and West Prussia to the reconstituted Polish state in a settlement along roughly ethnic lines that honored the stipulation of the Fourteen Points for Polish access to the Baltic Sea but also created a corridor that separated East Prussia from the rest of Germany. As Poland's outlet to the sea, the overwhelmingly German port city of Danzig was constituted a free state and placed under the administration of the League of Nations. On the northeastern border of East Prussia, Germany gave up the port of Memel and its surrounding area, which ultimately passed to Lithuania. The fate of Upper Silesia and the East Prussian districts of Allenstein and Marienwerder were to be determined by plebiscite; but whereas the latter two reverted to Germany in 1920, the League of Nations disregarded the outcome of the popular vote in Upper Silesia in 1921 and partitioned the area in a way that gave Poland the smaller but highly industrialized section with its valuable coal mines. Although another small wedge of Upper Silesia was awarded to the new Czechoslovak state, Germany's borders with the former Austro-Hungarian Empire were generally maintained, resulting in a situation that left 3 million Sudeten Germans under the rule of Prague. A plebiscite was also prescribed for Schleswig on the Danish border to be held in two zones, of which the northern eventually went to Denmark and the southern to Germany. In the west, Germany returned Alsace Lorraine to France and ceded the small districts of Moresnet, Eupen, and Malmédy to Belgium.

Under the political provisions of the treaty, Germany denounced the treaties of Brest-Litovsk and Bucharest and recognized the independence and full sovereignty of Belgium, Poland, Czechoslovakia, and German Austria. The latter provision effectively deprived the Austrian people of their right to self-determination by prohibiting a political union of Germany and German Austria. In addition to the reparation clauses and the Saar settlement, other economic and commercial terms included the confiscation of all of Germany's foreign assets; the surrender of the bulk of its merchant marine, a quarter of its fishing fleet, and a substantial part of its rolling stock; and the delivery of large amounts of raw materials, particularly coal and lumber, to France, Belgium, and Italy.

The military, naval, and aviation terms sought to destroy the Prussian war machine by providing for Germany's radical disarmament. Conscription was abolished; the German army was limited to a mere 100,000 men, including a maximum of 4,000 officers, and was deprived of tanks and heavy artillery. To prevent the creation of a large reserve of trained recruits, enlisted men had to serve for twelve years, officers for twenty-four. Germany was to have no air force; its navy was restricted to a few small battleships, light cruisers, and torpedo boats; and no submarines were allowed. Virtually all production of war materiel was prohibited, and Germany agreed to destroy various fortifications and military installations. To ensure German compliance with these conditions, an Inter-Allied Commission of Control was set up in Berlin, authorized to conduct military inspections at its discretion.

The treaty also called for the arraignment of the former German emperor "for supreme offense against international morality and the sanctity of treaties" and his trial before a special tribunal of five judges named by the Great Powers. Wilson opposed this provision, which, he argued, would turn the kaiser into a political martyr. In the end, the Allies were spared possible embarrassment when the Dutch declined to extradite the emperor from his neutral asylum in the Netherlands. In a similar view, the treaty required the Germans to surrender for trial before the Allied military tribunals some 900 persons accused of war crimes and atrocities. In the end, only twelve of the accused were tried before the German Supreme Court at Leipzig; half were acquitted and the others received only light sentences.

No single provision in the treaty provoked as much vehement opposition and outrage in Germany as the so-called war-guilt clause of

Article 231, by which the Allies affirmed, and the German government accepted the responsibility of the Central Powers for "causing all the loss and damage to which the Allied and Associated Governments and their nationals have been subjected as a consequence of the war imposed upon them by the aggression of Germany and her allies." While to the Allies this statement merely acknowledged the truth, it was never meant to imply the sense of German responsibility that the German government, in its obsession with the war-guilt question, read into it. In fact, the article had slipped into the treaty rather inadvertently during the lengthy discussions of German reparations. Drafted by John Foster Dulles, then an adviser in the American delegation, it was designed to reconcile the Franco-British viewpoint on reparations with the American position by first establishing the potential extent of German liability, before then limiting it in the subsequent articles to Germany's capacity to pay. It was German propaganda against the treaty and the government's irate condemnation of the war-guilt clause as a defilement of Germany's national honor that invested the article with the sense of a moral verdict. Article 231 became the centerpiece of furious German attacks on the "peace of infamy" for years to come.

If the Germans were appalled at the treaty, the British and French were far from happy with it either. In Britain, the assault on the treaty was spearheaded by disillusioned Wilsonians such as the economist John Maynard Keynes, who depicted the peace conference as a "morass" that had witnessed the triumph of Clemenceau's "Carthaginian peace" over Wilson's Fourteen Points. In time, many Britons came to regard the Versailles settlement as too severe, believing that it would destroy Germany's economy and jeopardize its fragile democracy. Consequently, successive governments embarked upon a quasi-apologetic course toward Germany that lent an open ear to German demands for a revision of the treaty and culminated in the British appeasement policy of the 1930s. Many Frenchmen, on the other hand, argued that the treaty was not harsh enough and claimed that it did not contain sufficient guarantees for French security.

The United States, of course, dealt the biggest blow to the maintenance of the Versailles settlement by refusing to ratify the treaty. Although there was some criticism of its general terms, especially the Shantung arrangement, the major opposition centered on America's unreserved commitment to a system of collective security under the Covenant of the League of Nations. Except for a minority of die-hard isolationists, even Wilson's chief adversaries favored a continuing international role for the United States, but they strongly objected to the obligations to guarantee the political independence and territorial integrity of every member nation throughout the world imposed by Article X of the Covenant. Republican leaders in the Senate argued that such a sweeping commitment would of necessity embroil the United States in foreign conflicts and even violate the Constitution by placing the decision over questions of peace and war in the hands of an international agency. While the Senate Foreign Relations Committee, under the leadership of its Republican chairman, Henry Cabot Lodge, eventually proposed ratification of the treaty with fourteen reservations intended to preserve American freedom of action under the Covenant, Wilson insisted on unqualified acceptance of the treaty. Any substantive amendments, he claimed, would be a "nullification of the Treaty," and a reservation to Article X would cut "the very heart out of the Treaty." In early September, he embarked on a hastily arranged national tour designed to rally support for his position and, in early October, suffered a debilitating stroke. On Nov. 19, 1919, the Senate rejected both the original treaty and the treaty with reservations. By the time of the second and final vote on March 19, 1920, it had become clear that only a treaty with reservations had any chance of gaining the consent of the Senate. However, Wilson instructed the members of his own party to oppose the amended treaty. Although twenty-one Democrats defied the president and voted for the treaty with reservations, it failed by seven votes to receive the required two thirds majority. The Treaty of Versailles was lost, and the United States turned its back on Europe.

The failure of the Senate to consent to the ratification of the Versailles Treaty meant, of course, that the United States would not join the League of Nations and would leave the execution of the settlement to the European powers. Thus, the Senate did not even consider the proposed French security treaty, which Wilson had offered to Clemenceau in exchange for his agreement to the Rhineland compromise. This, in turn, released the British from their obligation, and they refused to honor the pledge of assistance. As a result, with the United States unwilling to assume definite international responsibilities and Britain increasingly appeasement-minded and ambiguous about its commitments on the Continent, the French felt they had to provide for their own security by establishing a system of alliances with the new states of Eastern Europe and pursuing a harsh policy intended to prevent the resurgence of German power.

The Russian Quagmire

While Russia was the only major belligerent conspicuously absent from the peace conference, events inside the country and along its borders cast a long shadow over the deliberations at Paris. Not only was the future of Russia and its integration into the new European order considered crucial for the overall settlement, but also anxieties over the spread of Bolshevism made a solution of the Russian situation appear all the more imperative to the Allies. However, as with many other issues, the Western powers found it exceedingly difficult to develop a common approach toward Russia. Their policies were confused, indecisive, and often contradictory, ranging from half-hearted attempts at a rapprochement with Moscow to grandiose plans for a grand crusade to overthrow the Bolsheviks. In the end, the Allies failed to exert any decisive influence on Russian affairs, and their indecisive diplomatic and military maneuvers only served to widen the gap between the Bolsheviks and the West.

Ever since Russia had left the war at Brest Litovsk in March 1918, the policies of the British and French governments had turned increasingly hostile toward the Bolsheviks, culminating in the Allied blockade and the military intervention in the summer and fall of that year in an effort to reestablish the Eastern Front and support the White armies in the civil war. While Wilson had strongly opposed any interference in internal Russian affairs for many months, he had eventually consented to a limited American cooperation with Allied plans. At the same time, however, he was still convinced of the deep desire of the Russian people for democracy, and he kept searching for ways to end the civil war and to find a modus vivendi with the Bolsheviks.

On the eve of the peace conference, the economic and military situation of the Bolsheviks was precarious, and they gave some indications that they were prepared to negotiate with the Allies. For example, in late October and early November 1918, Lenin's commissar of foreign affairs, Georgii V. Chicherin, addressed two long notes to Wilson protesting against the military intervention and offering a cease-fire in return for the evacuation of the Allied troops. The following month, Maksim M. Litvinov, the former Soviet "ambassador" in Great Britain, informed the Allied governments that he had been authorized to enter into "preliminary peace negotiations," and he appealed to Wilson on the principles of the Fourteen Points. Whether or not these approaches were genuine and presented a favorable opportunity for an early reconciliation between the Bolsheviks and the West has been a matter of considerable debate. In any event, the Allied leaders could not agree on a Bolshevik representation at Paris, and while Wilson and Lloyd George favored negotiations, Clemenceau demanded more forceful military intervention.

Shortly after the conference got underway, Wilson and Lloyd George did succeed, however, in directing an appeal to the rival factions in Russia, proposing a cease-fire and asking them to send representatives to the island of Prinkipo in the Sea of Marmara. The Bolsheviks accepted the invitation but ignored the call for a truce; the Whites, with the backing of the French, openly rejected both. Moreover, at about the same time, Lenin issued his long-delayed call to the European Socialists to form the Third (Communist) Internationale. Thus, it appeared that the Bolsheviks were playing a double game by ideologically undermining the very governments with which they professed to seek normal relations.

Still, behind the scenes, attempts to establish a basis for negotiations with the Bolsheviks continued. At the initiative of Colonel House, whom Wilson had put in charge of Russian matters, William C. Bullitt, a young State Department official and attaché to the American peace delegation, traveled to Petrograd and Moscow in early March 1919 for direct talks with Lenin and other Soviet leaders. Lenin offered an immediate cease-fire and declared his willingness to enter into peace negotiations and grant an amnesty to all Russians who had collaborated with the Allies. In return, he asked that the Allies agree to evacuate all their forces from Russian territory, stop supporting the Whites, and terminate the blockade. When an optimistic Bullitt returned to Paris at the end of the month, however, the conference had all but collapsed over the Rhineland question; Lloyd George was under enormous pressure from conservative MPs to avoid any accommodation with the Bolsheviks; and the declaration of a Soviet republic in Bavaria and Béla Kun's Communist coup in Hungary had added to the nervous anxiety of the Allied leaders. In addition, the large counterrevolutionary army of Admiral Aleksandr V. Kolchak had advanced west of the Urals from Omsk in Siberia, leading many to believe that he might soon reach Moscow or join the White armies around Archangel. As a result of those developments, the Allied leaders refused to consider the proposals Bullitt had brought back from Moscow and began increasingly to look for a military solution in Russia.

Even Wilson was gradually persuaded to give up on the Bolsheviks and throw his support behind Kolchak, whom the various White groups acknowledged as their supreme authority by the end of May. Although Wilson stopped short of extending official recognition to the Omsk government, he did join his colleagues in the Council of Four in pledging material aid to Kolchak's armies after the admiral had vaguely agreed to institute democratic reforms in Russia in the event of his victory.

Actually, the Allied move turned out to be too little too late. Over the summer and fall, the Red Army routed Kolchak's forces and turned back the advances of the other White armies. Only a large-scale Allied military intervention could have turned the tide, but there the Big Four drew the line. They realized that, despite the urgent pleas by Marshal Foch and Winston Churchill, the British secretary of state for war, they were not in a position to launch an anti-Bolshevik crusade. Not only did they lack the military forces and the financial resources to operate on such a large scale, but their war-weary populations and agitated labor unions would have also strongly opposed it. Instead, evacuation of Allied troops got underway in the fall, and the last American soldiers left Vladivostok in April 1920.

Although the Allies ultimately had to admit that Russia was "lost," they were determined not to let other parts of Eastern Europe fall to Communism. To contain the spread of Bolshevism, they constructed a *cordon sanitaire* by strengthening Russia's western neighbors as bulwarks against Communism and supporting their territorial aspirations even in violation of the principle of national self-determination. Thus, as a result of the Russo-Polish War of 1920–1921, the Bolsheviks were forced to give up large parts of Byelorussia and the Ukraine to Poland; they also lost Bessarabia to Rumania and had to recognize the independence of Finland and the Baltic states of Lithuania, Latvia, and Estonia.

The Reshaping of East-Central Europe

In their effort to settle the questions involving the historically troubled lands extending between Germany and Russia and stretching from the Mediterranean to the Baltic Sea, the peacemakers were called upon, above all, to perform what British Foreign Secretary Arthur Balfour aptly characterized as "the immense operation of liquidating the Austrian Empire." As the Allies went about parceling out the remains of the Dual Monarchy, they decreed far-reaching changes in sovereignty, drew and redrew dozens of boundaries, and tried to sort out the horrid jumble of conflicting claims and rival demands advanced by newly liberated nationalities and existing states alike. In the process, they treated the new republics of Austria and Hungary, which had replaced the monarchy in the last days of the war, as the heirs of the defeated dynasty; held them responsible for past Austro-Hungarian policies; and consistently supported the interests of wartime allies like Rumania and the so-called successor states of Poland, Czechoslovakia, and Yugoslavia (officially called the Kingdom of the Serbs, Croats and Slovenes until 1929) that had arisen on the ashes of the Habsburg Empire.

The new arrangements for east-central Europe were enshrined in the peace treaties with Austria, Bulgaria, and Hungary, signed at Saint-Germain (Sept. 10, 1919), Neuilly (Nov. 27, 1919), and Trianon (June 4, 1920), respectively. Their political, military, and economic provisions closely paralleled those of the Versailles Treaty. All three states had to acknowledge war guilt, agree to radical disarmament, and accept reparations obligations, although the latter were later forgiven when it became clear that they could not be collected. With regard to territorial renunciations, Bulgaria surrendered most of its gains from the Balkan Wars of 1912–1913, and all of its recent conquests, suffered some minor rectifications on its western borders in favor of Yugoslavia, and lost its access to the Aegean Sea by relinquishing most of Western Thrace to Greece.

By contrast, the new Austrian republic that emerged from the war bore little resemblance to the Austria of the Habsburgs. Its territory was limited to the German-speaking parts of the old empire, and it was turned into a small landlocked country, deprived of its major resources. It was partly out of concern over the economic viability of their country as a separate state and partly out of nationalistic impulses that the Austrians had exercised what they understood to be their right of self-determination by specifically constituting their republic as "a component part of the German Republic" in November 1918. However, the treaties of Versailles and Saint-Germain contained identical articles prohibiting the union between the two German-speaking nations. It is easy to understand why the Allies refused to sanction the enormous addition to German territory and power that would have ensued from *Anschluss*. Nevertheless, it left both the Germans and Austrians with a sense of injustice that could appeal to the Wilsonian principle of self-determination in driving home the moral weakness of the Allied position. Its denouement would become starkly evident in less than twenty years.

Although Hungary eventually sustained even more extensive losses than Austria, the Hungarians were not willing simply to submit to the fiat from Paris. In light of the hostile treatment by the Allies and the threatened dismemberment of the ancient Magyar kingdom, the moderate government of Count Mihály Károly, an opponent of Austria-Hungary's participation in the war and a sincere believer in Wilsonian principles and Western constitutional democracy, resigned in March 1919. For the next five months, Hungary was a Communist republic under the leadership of Béla Kun, who initially enjoyed the support of the old aristocracy, former Habsburg military officers, and large parts of the bourgeoisie when he turned to Bolshevik Russia for help in resisting Allied pressures. It was not until Rumanian troops, backed by the Allies, advanced toward Budapest and made it obvious that even the Bolsheviks could not save the territorial integrity of Hungary that a counterrevolution drove Kun from power, and a new government of Magyar royalists and agrarian reactionaries capitulated to Allied demands. In the end, Hungary was stripped of its non-Magyar lands, and it ceded almost three quarters of its former territory, with two-thirds of its prewar population to its old and new neighbors.

The disposition of the former Habsburg lands created a new system of states in east-central Europe, and the resultant map looked startlingly different from the prewar one. The largest of the new creations was Poland, resurrected to national existence for the first time since 1795. It received or appropriated substantial territories from all three of its former partitioners, including the Habsburg province of Galicia. Czechoslovakia was formed out of Bohemia, Moravia, Slovakia, and Sub-Carpathian Ruthenia. While this arrangement provided the new republic with a defensible western border, as well as a riverine outlet on the Danube and a source of important raw materials, it also added 3.5 million Sudeten Germans and 1 million Magyars to its already diverse ethnic composition. Prewar Serbia constituted the nucleus of the new Yugoslav kingdom, an alliance of convenience of several national groups with different cultures, traditions, and religions that included Croatia, Slovenia, Bosnia, Herzegovina, and parts of the Banat and later also absorbed Montenegro. Of the states that had already existed in 1914, perhaps none benefitted as handsomely from the settlement as did Rumania. In light of its rather questionable wartime loyalty to the Allied cause, Rumania did well indeed, being awarded Transylvania, parts of the Banat, and Bukovina from Hungary and wresting Bessarabia from Russia.

Ideally, the territorial settlements of east-central Europe were to be based strictly on the Wilsonian principle of national self-determination. However, in this ethnically heterogeneous region, people were so hopelessly intermixed that even plebiscites would not have provided any clear answers. Moreover, time and again, the self-rule of a people had to be balanced against equally important political, economic, geographic, strategic, or historic considerations, and the territorial pledges that the European Allies had made to each other during the war added further complications.

For example, while in Carinthia and the Burgenland Austria's borders with Yugoslavia and Hungary were determined by plebiscites in Austria's favor, the 2 million German-speaking inhabitants of South Tyrol were not consulted when their province was awarded to Italy for military reasons and in fulfillment of British and French wartime promises. Ignorant of the facts of the matter, Wilson had agreed to this violation of his own principles even before the peace conference had convened. Yet, when the Italians went on to press not only their extensive claims on the Dalmatian coast, but, in addition, demanded the former Hungarian port city of Fiume, which the Treaty of London had assigned to Yugoslavia as its only good outlet to the sea, Wilson dug in his heels.

Wilson's categorical refusal to countenance any further violations of the principle of self-determination and Orlando's truculent insistence on Italy's maximum demands precipitated the most acrimonious controversy and the most drawn-out dispute of the entire peace conference. For both sides, the issue of Fiume assumed a crucial symbolic significance that transcended its intrinsic importance. To the Italians, the question was one of national honor and pride; to Wilson, it was a clear case of right versus wrong, of new diplomacy versus old. With the British and French standing on the sidelines, Wilson, on April 23, vented his frustration in a public appeal to the Italian people—a breach of diplomatic etiquette that caused Orlando and his colleagues to bolt the conference and seek confirmation of their mandate from their parliament. While they eventually returned, no progress whatsoever was made on the issue, and it was actually never resolved at Paris. In June, Orlando's government fell over the question; in August, Fiume was declared a free city; and in September, a band of Italian nationalists, led by the fiery poet Gabriele D'Annunzio, occupied the city. In the end, the matter was decided through direct negotiations between Italy and Yugoslavia. To the Italians, however, the quarrel over Fiume became emblematic for what they considered their "mutilated victory," stirring up fierce nationalistic passions that contributed to the rise of Mussolini's Fascists only a few years later.

While the settlements in east-central Europe constituted a sincere attempt to solve the long-standing problems by applying the principle of nationality, the peacemakers, and particularly Wilson, were later severely reproached for what was called the "Balkanization" of the region that replaced one large multinational empire with several small multinational states. Yet, while it is true that, in some cases, frontiers might have been drawn closer along lines of nationality, given the ethnic composition of the region, it would have been virtually impossible to satisfy each and every claim and still create viable states without displacing any populations. Of course, whether such a concept as a Yugoslav or a Czechoslovak nationality could, in fact, be developed or

whether these states would forever remain hybrid and artificial creations, only time would tell. But overall, the new map of east-central Europe corresponded much more closely to ethnic boundaries than ever before, the national aspirations of millions of people were fulfilled, and the number of minorities under alien rule was drastically reduced.

The Demise of the Ottoman Empire and the Reorganization of the Middle East

The long and contentious debate over the conclusion of peace with the Ottoman Empire cast into sharp relief the imperialist ambitions of the major European powers in the Middle East and their longtime political and economic rivalry in the region. The United States, on the other hand, tried to act as a mediator among the Allies and refused to assume any direct responsibility in the Turkish settlement. For months on end, Great Britain, France, Italy, and Greece engaged in protracted negotiations, angry altercations, and some military and naval posturing over the spoils of victory in the Middle East. There was never a question that, in its general outlines, the settlement was to be based on the various secret wartime treaties that the European Allies had concluded among each other. Although many of the details of the settlement had to be reconsidered due to the elimination of Russia as a claimant to Constantinople and the Straits and the intrusion of fanciful demands by the Greek government, the Treaty of Sèvres on Aug. 10, 1920, along with accompanying informal understandings among the Allies, effectively dismembered the Ottoman Empire.

In accordance with this settlement, Turkey renounced its claims to all Arab territories as well as its suzerainty over Egypt and Cyprus. To avoid the charge of blatant imperialism, the European powers assumed control over their coveted areas under mandates from the League of Nations: Great Britain received Palestine, Transjordan, and Iraq; France acquired Syria and Lebanon, and Cilicia, just north of the French mandate, was recognized as a French sphere of influence; southern Anatolia was reserved as a zone for the Italians, who also won full ownership of the Dodecanese Islands. To hold Italian ambitions in check, the Greeks were awarded Smyrna and its hinterland. Since the United States refused to assume a proposed mandate for either Armenia or Constantinople and the Straits, the former gained its independence, while the latter was demilitarized and

P

placed under an international commission. All that remained of the former empire was a small state in Asia Minor burdened with heavy reparations and subjected to foreign control over its economic affairs.

As it turned out, however, the Treaty of Sèvres was not worth the paper on which it was printed. Although the weak government of the sultan at Constantinople signed the treaty, the Turkish National Assembly, under the leadership of the war hero Mustafa Kemal, refused to ratify it. Kemal set up a Nationalist countergovernment in Ankara, rallied his armies in the interior, obliterated the new Armenian republic, and set about to drive all foreign influence from Asia Minor. The task of enforcing the treaty fell on the Greeks, who eagerly seized the opportunity to extend their influence in Asia Minor. In the ensuing Turko-Greek war of 1920–1922, the brilliant military leadership of Kemal and sharp rivalries and jealousies among the European Allies led to a complete defeat of the Greek armies. In return for economic concessions, the Italians and French were persuaded as early as the spring of 1921 to give up their spheres of influence in Asia Minor and work for a revision of the Treaty of Sèvres. At the same time, Turkey signed a treaty of friendship with the new Soviet Union. In the end, even the British, the most ardent supporters of Greek ambitions, had to agree to new negotiations, which resulted in the Treaty of Lausanne of July 24, 1923.

Idealism and Power: The Imperfect Compromise

Looking back at the achievements of the Paris Peace Conference, contemporary observers and historians alike easily concluded that the peacemakers had fallen far short of the promises they had made in the fall of 1918. After months of painstaking labor, the new European order that had emerged from Paris was, if anything, more volatile and unstable than the pre-1914 world. To be sure, the various settlements had liberated millions of long oppressed nationalities and eliminated many age-old injustices, but, in turn, they had created different problems and given rise to fresh grievances. Their central weakness lay in the fact that they afforded the defeated powers the opportunity to cast themselves in the role of victims of discrimination in the application of the principle of self-determination, the war-guilt clause, and the reparations provisions. If the League of Nations had ever developed

into more than a bold and noble experiment, if the notion of collective security had indeed triumphed over narrow nationalistic interests, many of the imperfections of the settlements might have been subsequently overcome more easily.

While the so-called political realists resented and ridiculed the intrusions of Wilsonian moralism, liberals on both sides of the Atlantic felt that the American president had betrayed their trust in him by compromising his own ideals. As Harold Nicolson pointed out: "We had hoped to call a new world into existence; we ended only by fouling the old." While this observation is neither accurate nor entirely fair, it shows the tremendous disappointments that many people felt with the settlements. However, given the various visions and conflicting interests of the peacemakers, a purely Wilsonian peace was never possible, and the final settlement could not be anything but an imperfect compromise between idealism and power politics.

Manfred F. Boemke

See also CLEMENCEAU, GEORGES; LEAGUE OF NATIONS; LLOYD GEORGE, DAVID; ORLANDO, VITTORIO; WILSON, WOODROW

Bibliography
Link, Arthur S., et al., eds. *The Papers of Woodrow Wilson.* 69 vols. Princeton, NJ: Princeton University Press, 1966–1993.
Mantoux, Paul. *The Deliberations of the Council of Four (March 24–June 28, 1919),* ed. and trans. by Arthur S. Link and Manfred F. Boemke. 2 vols. Princeton, NJ: Princeton University Press, 1992.
Mayer, Arno J. *Politics and Diplomacy of Peacemaking: Containment and Counterrevolution at Versailles, 1918–1919.* New York: Knopf, 1967.
Nicolson, Harold. *Peacemaking, 1919.* Leeds, UK: University of Leeds, 1946.
U.S. State Department. *Papers Relating to the Foreign Relations of the United States, the Paris Peace Conference, 1919.* 13 vols. Washington, DC: Government Printing Office, 1942–1947.

Parker, Frank (1872–1947)

MajGen. Frank Parker was born in Georgetown, South Carolina, and was graduated from the United States Military Academy in 1894. Following service at Tampa during the Spanish-American War, he was military attaché in Venezuela and Argentina and became an instructor of cavalry for the Cuban Army from 1904 to 1908. High-spirited and ambitious, Parker became fluent in both Spanish and French, and studied at the École Superieure de Guerre in France. When World War I broke out, he was serving as an observer with the French Army. During the war, he commanded the 18th Infantry Regiment and the 1st Infantry Brigade of the 1st Division, and took command of the division in October 1918. Parker succeeded his close friend and mentor, MajGen. Charles P. Summerall, who had moved up to command V Corps. Like Summerall, Parker was an aggressive and hard-driving leader who exercised a strong hold on those who served under him. In the opinion of several of his superior officers, however, he was also too self-centered, too impulsive, and too interested in his own prospects to consider matters from the viewpoint of his superiors.

Parker played a prominent part in the "Sedan incident," when, in early November 1918, he marched his division toward the German-occupied city of Sedan through elements of the 77th and 42d divisions of I Corps, which lay between the 1st Division and the city. In the resulting confusion, phone lines were snarled, traffic piled up, and Americans fired on each other. On orders from First Army headquarters and Summerall, Parker withdrew his division, and order was restored before further damage occurred. The order to take Sedan had been less than precise, and Summerall interpreted it to mean that his corps and the 1st Division, in particular, were in a "race" with I Corps and the French to capture Sedan. Parker, moreover, apparently expected to encounter only Germans and had no idea that both the 42d and 77th divisions were between him and Sedan.

Summerall and Parker have been criticized for their actions before Sedan. Historian Edward M. Coffman faults both for putting the quest for glory and honor for the 1st Division, and for themselves, before what should have been a greater regard for the interest of the entire army. Gen. Hunter Liggett, who commanded the First Army, later said that he would never trust Summerall where sentiment was concerned and that Parker should never have a command larger than a regiment. For their part, Parker and Summerall believed they had been unfairly blamed for the "snafu" at Sedan. When his promotion to brigadier general was delayed for six years, Parker attributed this to opposition from those who held him responsible for the Sedan incident.

After the war, Parker remained in France to study and teach at the École Superieure de Guerre and returned to the United States in 1923 as a student-teacher at the Command and Staff School at Fort Leavenworth. From 1927 until 1929, during Summerall's term as United States Army chief of staff, Parker served as the assistant chief of staff. He went on to command VI Corps and the Second Army, the Philippine Department, and VIII Corps. Parker retired from the army in 1936. From 1942 until 1945, he was executive director of the Illinois War Council in Chicago, where he actively promoted army and reserve training activities. He died in Chicago in March 1947.

Gary Nichols

Bibliography

Coffman, Edward M. *The War to End All Wars: The American Military Experience in World War I*. New York: Oxford University Press, 1968.
Dickman, Joseph T. *The Great Crusade: A Narrative of the World War*. New York: Appleton, 1927.
Harbord, James G. *The American Army in France, 1917–1919*. Boston: Little, Brown, 1936.
Liggett, Hunter. *Commanding an American Army: Recollections of the World War*. Boston: Houghton Mifflin, 1925.
Smythe, Donald. "A.E.F. Snafu at Sedan." *Prologue* (Fall 1973).

Patrick, Mason Mathews (1863–1942)

Mason Mathews Patrick was the son of a Confederate veteran. He graduated second in the class of 1886 at the United States Military Academy, a classmate of John J. Pershing. Commissioned into the Corps of Engineers, Patrick served at numerous posts and rose to the rank of colonel by 1916. When the United States declared war, Patrick was commanding the 1st Engineers. The regiment embarked for France aboard the U.S. Army transport *Finland* on Aug. 7, 1917. Upon arrival in France, Patrick learned that he had been breveted brigadier general. Pershing employed Patrick in various positions in general headquarters of the American Expeditionary Force (AEF), including commanding general of the Line of Communications (later Service of Supply) and director of the Construction and Forestry Division. In May 1918, Pershing asked Patrick, now with the rank of major general, to take command of the AEF Air Service, which at that time was in considerable disarray. Although he was not an aviator, Patrick accepted the assignment, reorganized the service, ended the feuding between Billy Mitchell and Benjamin Foulois, and created an efficient and functional air force. In March 1919, Patrick was appointed to the aeronautics commission of the Supreme War Council.

Upon returning to the United States, Patrick reverted to his permanent rank of colonel and returned to duties in the Corps of Engineers. In August 1919, before a subcommittee of the congressional committee investigating waste in the War Department, he defended the AEF Air Service policy of burning obsolete aircraft. In October 1921, he accepted the position of chief of the Air Service (CAS), again with the rank of major general. As CAS, he learned to fly at age 60, then steered the Air Service through a critical period of its development, including the Mitchell court-martial and the 1926 legislation that transformed the Air Service into the Air Corps. After retiring from the army in December 1927, he served as chairman of the Public Utilities Commission of the District of Columbia from 1929 to 1933. Patrick died in Washington, D.C., on Jan. 29, 1942.

Jerold Brown

Bibliography

Goldberg, Alfred, ed. *A History of the United States Air Force, 1907–1957*. Princeton, NJ: Princeton University Press, 1957.

Maurer, Maurer, ed. *The United States Air Service in World War I*. Vol. 1, *The Final Report and a Tactical History*. Washington, DC: Government Printing Office, 1978.

Patrick, Mason M. *The United States in the Air*. Garden City, NY: Doubleday, Doran, 1928.

Patton, George Smith, Jr. (1885–1945)

A cavalry officer and 1909 graduate of the United States Military Academy, George S. Patton, Jr. became the first American assigned to duty with tanks and was the architect of the U.S. light-tank training program at Bourg, France.

Patton had earned distinction after serving as Gen. John J. Pershing's aide-de-camp during the Punitive Expedition to Mexico in 1916. He was in the first group of American Expeditionary Force (AEF) officers to reach France in April 1917. Assigned as the adjutant and headquarters commandant at Chaumont, the aggressive Patton quickly tired of his job and sought duty with a combat unit. When word of the AEF commander's decision to create a tank corps reached Patton's ear, the young cavalry captain volunteered for assignment to the fledgling combat arm.

Patton was ordered to the AEF schools at Langres in November 1917 and instructed to establish a light-tank training center. During the remainder of 1917 and the first half of 1918, Patton observed British and French training and operations, devised a training program, recruited and trained two battalions' worth of light-tank crews, and worked with the AEF Tank Corps staff, led by BGen. Samuel D. Rockenbach, to devise tactics and organizations compatible with U.S. Army doctrine.

As spring turned to summer in 1918, Patton, by then a lieutenant colonel, honed his two light-tank battalions, the 326th and 327th (redesignated the 344th and 345th on September 12) to fighting pitch. As commander of the newly organized 1st Tank Brigade (redesignated the 304th on November 6), Patton led the only U.S. tank brigade to see action during the war.

The brigade's first operation was in support of the First Army's IV Corps in the St. Mihiel offensive, which kicked off on September 12. Throughout the three-day battle, Patton ignored instructions to maintain communications with Rockenbach's headquarters and instead traversed the battlefield on foot, keeping up initially with the lead elements of Capt. Ranulf Compton's 345th Tank Battalion in the 42d Division sector, then Maj. Sereno Brett's 344th Tank Battalion in the 1st Division zone. Patton's infrequent reports via messenger and pigeon were not nearly enough to satisfy Rockenbach's desire for information, and the Tank Corps commander was in a dither.

Although the 1st Tank Brigade was praised by the units it supported, Patton was the target of Rockenbach's wrath. The Tank Corps commander nearly relieved Patton but let him off with a sharp rebuke—and specific instructions to position himself in brigade headquarters during future operations—when laudatory reports of Patton's and his subordinates' battlefield performance continued to flood the headquarters.

The reprimand had little effect on Patton. He remained in his headquarters for less than an hour after the First Army's doughboys went over the top in the Meuse-Argonne on September 26. Shortly before noon, while leading a small group of 35th Division stragglers in an assault on Cheppy, Patton was severely wounded by machine gun fire. The wound ended Patton's participation in the campaign. But the brigade, inspired by Patton's earlier exhortations and personal example on the battlefield, which earned him the Distinguished Service Cross, performed yeoman service in the following weeks.

After the Armistice, Patton, then a colonel, remained on occupation duty in Germany until early 1919, when he returned to Camp Meade, Maryland, the Tank Corps' home in the United States. There he met LtCol. Dwight D. Eisenhower, and the two became leading voices in the effort to preserve the Tank Corps as an independent combat arm. Their efforts failed with the passage of the June 1920, National Defense Act, which allocated tanks to the infantry. In the ensuing force reduction, Patton reverted to his permanent grade of captain and sought to return to the cavalry—a request that was granted later that summer.

For Patton, command in the Tank Corps proved to be a harbinger of the future. It provided him with the opportunity to develop and hone the unique leadership style that characterized his subsequent career. It also exposed him to armored warfare, and the lessons he learned on the battlefields of France in World War I laid the groundwork for his future success as commander of the Third Army in its dash across Europe a generation later.

Dale E. Wilson

See also EISENHOWER, DWIGHT DAVID; TANKS; UNITED STATES ARMY TANK CORPS

Bibliography

Blumenson, Martin, ed. *The Patton Papers, 1885–1940*. Boston: Houghton Mifflin, 1972.

Eisenhower, Dwight D. *At Ease: Stories I Tell to Friends*. Garden City, NY: Doubleday, Doran, 1967.

Paul, Alice (1885–1977)

P

Born to Quaker parents in 1885 in Moorestown, New Jersey, Alice Paul spent most of her adult life working to secure equality for women. Educated as an undergraduate at Swarthmore College, Paul later earned a PhD. at the University of Pennsylvania. Interest in the women's movement for Paul emerged during a visit to England in 1907. There she participated in marches for women's suffrage, was imprisoned, and force-fed during hunger strikes until her return home in 1910.

Initially, Paul worked with the National American Woman Suffrage Association (NAWSA) to obtain the vote for women, but she broke with that organization over the direction of the struggle. NAWSA focused on state legislation, while Paul believed that success had to be achieved at the federal level. To accomplish that goal, Paul worked within the Congressional Union, which, in 1916, became the core of the National Woman's Party (NWP). In the 1914 and 1916 elections, Paul organized her followers to work for the defeat of the Democratic candidates. As the party in power, Paul held them responsible for the failure to include an amendment for suffrage in the party platform. Under her leadership, the NWP advocated a militant, although non-violent approach to winning the vote.

When it seemed clear that the United States would enter the war against Germany in 1917, the NWP voted to continue its struggle despite an unsympathetic public reaction. Throughout the war, Paul and other members of the NWP picketed the White House to attract the attention and support of President Woodrow Wilson. Although arrested and imprisoned, the protesters challenged the quest for democracy abroad, while the United States denied the vote for women at home.

Early in the process of working for suffrage for women, Paul recognized the necessity of extending the scope of the NWP to include equality for women. Therefore, after the ratification of the Nineteenth Amendment in 1920, Paul spent the rest of her life working for the passage of a federal Equal Rights Amendment. Committed to that cause, Paul remained a leading spokesperson in the women's rights movement until her death in 1977.

Judith Johnson

See also NATIONAL AMERICAN WOMAN SUF-FRAGE ASSOCIATION; NATIONAL WOMAN'S PARTY

Bibliography

Gillmore, Inez Haynes. *The Story of Alice Paul and the National Woman's Party.* Fairfax, VA: Denlinger's, 1977.

Lunardini, Christine A. *From Equal Suffrage to Equal Rights: Alice Paul and the National Woman's Party, 1910–1920.* New York: New York University Press, 1986.

People's Council for Democracy and Peace

The People's Council for Democracy and Peace (PC) was an antiwar coalition publicly announced at the First American Conference for Democracy and Terms of Peace held in New York City on May 30–31, 1917. With the American declaration of war on April 6, 1917, the vast majority of participants in the World War I peace movement retreated from antiwar activism. The PC evolved from discussions in New York City among some remaining peace activists, antiwar socialists, radical labor leaders, single-taxers, and disaffected intellectuals. Louis Lochner, Lella F. Secor, and Rebecca Shelly, who had been involved in the Ford Peace Ship, the American Neutral Conference Committee, and the Emergency Peace Federation, directed the organization.

Envisioned as a popular front that would represent the common people, the PC drew its inspiration from the Russian Revolution and its plan of organization from the newly created Council of Workmen's and Soldiers' Delegates in Russia. Plans were set to establish the PC at a constituent assembly to be held in the Midwest in September. Although not successful with farmers' organizations, the PC initially received significant support from organized labor. Most American Federation of Labor trade union leaders opposed it, but leaders of the three major garment unions and other immigrant-dominated unions in New York City endorsed the PC. Late in June, a Workmen's Council was created as the radical labor component of the PC. Emphasizing that the new organization represented all the people, PC leaders downplayed the role of pacifists and socialists who comprised the core of their leadership.

Despite initial optimism, support for the PC began to erode even before the formal constituent assembly as groups and individuals began to question the wisdom of continuing opposition to war in a climate of official and unofficial repression. The history of the PC over the next few months is one marked by official harassment, dwindling support, and disintegration. The constituent assembly was to be held beginning Sept. 1, 1917, in Minneapolis, but the Minnesota governor banned the group from the state, as did the governors of Wisconsin and North Dakota. A last-minute invitation by Chicago Mayor William Thompson to meet in his city with police protection meant that the assembly could be held as scheduled, but the Illinois governor opposed Thompson's actions and in his absence ordered police to disperse the first meeting. Thompson returned and provided police protection, but a second session was truncated when news arrived that the National Guard was on its way. The PC executive committee worked out a platform at a nearby hotel, but a majority then voted not to present it to the entire group of delegates.

After the Chicago debacle, the PC reorganized and both the leadership and program changed. Scott Nearing, a young Socialist, became the dominant figure in the group; Shelly and Secor were eased out of their leadership roles, and the influence of pacifists waned. Under Nearing's leadership, the idea of the people's congress was abandoned. Groups and individuals drifted away from the PC. The most serious defections were the labor unions, which, by the spring of 1918, had taken a prowar stance for reasons of economic expediency. Nearing himself gave up all peace work except through the Socialist Party, and by mid-1918, the most radical of the new peace organizations had ceased to function.

Barbara Steinson

Bibliography

Florence, Barbara M., ed. *Lella Secor, a Diary in Letters, 1915–1922.* New York: Franklin, 1978.

Grubbs, Frank L., Jr. *The Struggle for Labor Loyalty: Gompers, the A.F.L. and the Pacifists.* Durham, NC: Duke University Press, 1968.

Marchand, C. Roland. *The American Peace Movement and Social Reform.* Princeton, NJ: Princeton University Press, 1972.

Steinson, Barbara J. *American Women's Activism in World War I.* New York: Garland, 1982.

Pershing, John Joseph (1860–1948)

General of the Armies of the United States, commander of the American Expeditionary Force (AEF) in the First World War, John Joseph Pershing was born in Laclede, Missouri, on Sept. 13, 1860. Son of a small storekeeper and railroad worker, he compensated for poor education by self-instruction and finally became a schoolteacher in Laclede's public school system. Chance reading of a newspaper notice led him to try for admission to the United States Military Academy, and he matriculated in January 1882.

John, known to friends as "Jack," struggled with the first year's curriculum; French proved especially elusive, and most academic subjects tested his weak background. But in "military art" he ranked high from the start, and in his last year he was selected first captain of the Corps of Cadets—an honor reserved to one most respected by both faculty and peers.

High standing overall (he ranked thirtieth in the graduating class of 1886) won a choice of service branch. He picked the mounted arm and soon joined the Sixth Cavalry in New Mexico. The late 1880s marked the last days for most of the Plains Indians. Pershing's regiment helped round up scattered tribal remnants, worked at establishing heliograph stations between frontier forts, made maps, and chased stragglers across stretches of desert. He spent time at Fort Bayard and Fort Stanton at the end of an era, but he served long enough never to lose the mystique of the U.S. Cavalry in the West.

An appointment as professor of military science and tactics at the University of Nebraska took Pershing to Lincoln in September 1891, an unexpectedly cultured center on the prairie frontier. Teaching math, pursuing a law degree, and winning national drill team honors occupied the young officer's time. His classes boasted such members as Willa Cather and Dorothy Canfield, daughter of the university's chancellor, James H. Canfield; his circle of friends included Ezra Pound, Charles Dawes, and William Jennings Bryan. His three years in Lincoln, extended by dispensation to four, polished his manners and opened his mind in unexpected ways. He hated leaving, but he went back to the cavalry.

Hard campaigning, terrible weather, the roughness of a small and active army, all shaped Pershing into a tough and seasoned soldier. Picked to herd stray elements of Cree Indians back to Canada in the summer of 1896, he learned more of the resilience, the cunning, the bravery of native forces. Those lessons, combined with those in bravery, loyalty, and devotion taught by black troopers in the Tenth Cavalry (Pershing's new regiment), were not lost on his questing mind. It was service with black troopers that earned him the nickname "Black Jack."

Indian service offered freedom, independence, authority beyond rank, and these got First Lieutenant Pershing into some trouble when he returned to more cloistered duty. Happily he returned to West Point on June 15, 1897 as a "tac," short for tactical officer, one who harassed cadets about such mundane matters as room decorum and appearance. Someone as familiar with field conditions should have been far more understanding than Pershing. Return to the academy apparently released old habits of harshness, and he became the most unpopular "tac" in recent memory, so bad, in fact, that he earned the infamous "silence," that awesome void of sound when he entered the dining hall. From first captain to "last tac" signaled a martinet's beginning. Luckily for him, approaching trouble with Spain took him to Washington for a stint as an aide to General in Chief of the Army Nelson A. Miles, the old Indian fighter. The heady duty of squiring congressional and generals' daughters to capitol functions charmed a handsome bachelor.

In the realm of Washington politics, Pershing showed promise and soon won approving notice from presidents. William McKinley noted his efficiency, largely because Miles pointed the way, and Elihu Root, secretary of war, found Pershing a man of his own worldly vision. Pershing's law degree made him the logical choice to head the innovative War Department's Bureau of Insular Affairs—an agency charged with making policies to govern such colonial areas as might fall to the United States as a result of expansionism. Facing vital issues of international economics and constitutional law, Pershing built an efficient bureau that handled new territories through turbulent years. Although aware of the importance and recognition conferred by his job, he yearned for a combat assignment as war with Spain broke out in 1898. A few pulled strings propelled Pershing to the Tenth Cavalry in Cuba. There he participated in fighting around Kettle and San Juan hills, became a skilled supply man, and served with an old acquaintance, Col. Theodore

Roosevelt of the Rough Riders. When fighting ended in Cuba, Pershing received orders to the Philippines, where he fought against Emilio Aguinaldo's insurgents on Luzon, then against the Moros on Mindanao and Jolo.

Moros, the easternmost outpost of Islam, had stubbornly resisted conquest by Spaniards and Filipinos, and their alliance with Aguinaldo was tenuous. Pershing, now a captain, undertook a march to subdue Moro dissidents in strongholds ringing hostile Lake Lanao. With a relatively small force of Regulars, Philippine Scouts and Constabulary, plus some mountain artillery, he attacked the lofty bastions of hereditary chiefs, or "dattos," and completed his victorious march around Lake Lanao on May 13, 1903. His exploits were written up in the press back home, and victory brought Pershing notoriety both in the army and in Washington.

Captain Pershing had commanded an independent force worthy of a colonel and led it in battle with skill and energy. He tempered war with diplomacy, for wherever he went, he made friends of old enemies. Praise from prominent dattos and sultans surprised old Philippine hands and caught the notice of now-President Theodore Roosevelt. The President wanted to reward Pershing by promoting him to brigadier general, but regulations made that almost impossible. Rigid seniority stifled army development, and Roosevelt longed to change the system.

Selected for the new General Staff Corps in 1903, Pershing returned to Washington. There he met and married Frances Warren, daughter of Republican Senator Francis Warren of Wyoming. The Roosevelts attended the wedding and entertained the newlyweds at the White House—which further entrenched Pershing in the President's mind. When war erupted between Japan and Russia, Pershing won a coveted place as a U.S. observer at Japanese field headquarters in Manchuria. It was there that he learned much about such modern tools of war as machine guns and long-range artillery.

Pershing quit Manchuria for Japan in 1905, rejoining his wife in Tokyo. In mid-September of the following year, Roosevelt, helped by Senator Warren (who sat on the Armed Services Committee), nominated Pershing for promotion to brigadier general. Although clouded by scandalous rumors for a while, the promotion did win approval, and the new general left his growing family (his daughter Helen was born on Sept. 8, 1906, in Tokyo) to travel to San Francisco for assignment. Posted back to the Philippines, he took command of Fort McKinley near Manila. The family went back to San Francisco in 1908. The worries about promotion, long foreign and field service had sapped Pershing's energy. A stay at the army hospital in Hot Springs, Arkansas, in November 1908, restored his customary good health. On Oct. 5, 1909, he and wife Frances, and the Pershing clan again sailed for the Philippines.

In November 1909, he became military governor and commander of Moro Province, with headquarters in Zamboanga. The governor's duties were difficult: he had to keep his vast province peaceful, guide its economic development, and create conditions and regulations for transition to civil government as soon as feasible.

Following his usual procedure, Pershing visited all important dattos and sultans, villages and towns; he went, usually alone or with one officer, to show that the U.S. government had no fear and wanted peace and progress. When authorities in Manila decided that Moros should be disarmed, Pershing pushed a careful program of persuasion and reward. But all trouble could not be avoided, and he met it firmly. He took the field against recalcitrants, fought them fiercely and successfully at Bud Dajo, a volcanic crater on Jolo Island in December 1911, and earned the respect of important Moro leaders. Slowly calm descended on Moroland—and proud, touchy people grew bored. A large outbreak against American rule rocked Jolo Island in 1913.

Worried that progress toward civil administration might be damaged, Pershing swiftly led a strong force to Jolo and fought the major battle of Bagsak Mountain (Bud Bagsak) on June 11–15, 1913. Heavy fighting brought U.S. victory and high Moro casualties; but, again, came respect from the vanquished.

His work in Moroland won Pershing the admiration of those who had opposed his promotion. He had risen to every challenge. In recognition, the general was posted to take command of the 8th Brigade at the Presidio, and the family was thrilled at being "home."

Pershing thought a brigade command seemed small but settled into making the 8th the best brigade in the army. Rigorous training again became his hallmark, as did close attention to details of appearance, discipline, and supply. Because of his work with the 8th Brigade, he was chosen in April 1914 to command

Fort Bliss, an important post in El Paso, Texas. While he was arranging family quarters at Fort Bliss, tragedy struck at the Presidio. Early on the morning of August 27, 1915, fire swept through the Pershing house, killing Frances and their daughters Helen, Annie, and Mary Margaret. Warren alone survived.

In Texas, Pershing fought loneliness and heartache with work. Fortunately for him, Texas-Mexico border problems filled his time. Revolution had long riddled Mexico, and in the northern area the renegade leader Francisco "Pancho" Villa vied with Venustiano Carranza's government for political and military power. On the night of March 8–9, 1916, Villa's men raided Columbus, New Mexico, killed nine civilians and eight troopers of the 13th Cavalry, then plundered the town and escaped. A reluctant President Woodrow Wilson ordered retaliation.

Responsibility fell on Pershing since his command was closest to Columbus. Swiftly pulling together various cavalry, infantry, and artillery units, along with such new elements as field radio transmitters, machine guns, and motor truck companies, even the 1st Aero Squadron, he led some 11,000 men into Chihuahua on March 15, 1916. Just as Pershing left Fort Bliss an eager young lieutenant— George Patton—talked his way onto the general's staff.

American forces had invaded Mexico before; this time Wilson insisted that United States troops were engaged in a "Punitive Expedition" on President Carranza's invitation, to punish Villa. That invitation left much to be desired. Conditions were made for Pershing's actions. His troops could not enter Mexican towns without the mayor's approval, could not use east-west railways or main roads, and were to cooperate with government forces whenever possible. These restrictions were harsher than any imposed on an American expeditionary commander before—but Pershing obeyed them. This made direct pursuit of Villa's band difficult; Villa loomed an almost Robin Hood-like figure in Chihuahua, especially since the North Americans chased him. Refuge opened to him everywhere; information of his whereabouts came to Pershing's men in bits and dribbles. Skirmishes and occasional battles with Villa's men won little but increased enmity between the two nations.

In winter quarters near Colonia Dublán in northern Chihuahua, Pershing created a large tent city, replete with medical facilities, airplane repair shops, drilling grounds, storage facilities, even approved brothels. Training focused not only on cavalry tactics, but also on trench warfare methods. Pershing kept a close eye on the sprawling trench lines in France and realized that his command had most of America's supply of the latest military tools. He worked to familiarize his men with the newer ways of war.

On Sept. 25, 1916, Pershing became a major general in the relatively small United States Army. Recommendations for his promotion had come from many superiors, not just from Senator Warren: careful management of difficult situations in Mexico plus wide and distinguished foreign service earned him the new star. When he led his expedition back into Texas on Feb. 5, 1917, he ranked as one of America's most experienced commanders.

The sudden death of his immediate superior, MajGen. Frederick Funston, commander of the Southern Department, on Feb. 19, 1917, offered new opportunities, and the assignment went to Pershing. He handled department command with customary ease. He gathered around him a skilled, efficient staff (still including Patton), kept a close eye on details, and began to prepare for America's entry into the European war.

In April 1917, President Wilson asked Congress to declare war on Germany. Pershing was summoned to Washington to speak with Secretary of War Newton D. Baker. The President and the secretary, after careful consideration of available generals, had selected Pershing to lead a symbolic division to Europe as America's Expeditionary Force (AEF). Republican Senator Warren basked in his son-in-law's assignment and was relieved that his party affiliation had not interfered. Pershing plunged into his job by building a staff and designating units for the division. Almost immediately he heard that America would send more than a division; he would lead a United States Army to France. What was an army? How many divisions comprised it? These basic questions Pershing addressed with the War Department as he worked on his weak French and on rounding out his staff.

Everyone wanted to join him. Theodore Roosevelt offered himself, then his sons; old friends claimed preference; but Pershing held a rigid standard and took only the vigorous and adaptable. On May 28, 1917, he and a staff of about 180 sailed for France on the SS *Baltic*. En route, Pershing and his staff designed the outlines of an army and devised a schedule for development of the AEF.

Liverpool, London, and Boulogne offered loud welcomes in early June, but Paris exploded in a paroxysm of joy on the thirteenth when the U.S. forces rode through the city. Pershing's limousine sagged under the weight of flag-waving, war-weary Parisians thrilled that the "Yanks" had arrived—no matter they were so few. Toasted, feted, and adored, Pershing did things right. He visited Marshal Joseph Joffre, France's doughty first commander; at Napoleon's tomb, he found the emperor's sword thrust in his hand—and instinctively he kissed it. Word of the gesture thrilled Frenchmen everywhere. Modest, businesslike, serious, the old Indian fighter charmed and impressed everyone.

Nonetheless, Pershing saw clearly that Germany was likely to break the trench stalemate in the wake of French Marshal Robert Nivelle's failed offensive on the Chemin des Dames the previous winter. British efforts to divert pressure resulted in small changes in the front but cost nearly a million Allied soldiers. There seemed to be no end to trench warfare. Allies and Germans alike were squandering thousands of troops. By summer 1917, the Allies faced a serious shortage of men. The Americans were more than welcome; they were fresh fodder. Without them, the war might be lost in 1918.

Pershing knew that the British wanted his American troops to fill their thinning ranks; he knew too that the French coveted his men for the same replacement scheme. Armed with almost total authority from Wilson and Baker to direct the U.S. effort in France, Pershing resisted the siphoning of his men to Allied armies. He resolutely sought to build a separate American Army of 1 million men—a goal that frustrated Field Marshal Sir Douglas Haig, commander of the British armies in France, and dismayed both Gen. Henri-Philippe Pétain, who had replaced Nivelle in command of French forces, and Gen. Ferdinand Foch, French chief of staff.

Pershing's stout protection of America's position ranks as an outstanding accomplishment. Fearing that piecemeal distribution of his "doughboys" would result only in waste and defeat, he argued that a strong U.S. Army could shoulder the main effort by 1919. He yielded only in moments of crisis. During the great German drive toward the English Channel, which began on March 21, 1918, he let American divisions help the French and British and offered total cooperation to the newly selected Allied supreme commander, General Foch, when the Germans launched their "final push" in the spring of 1918. Still, he kept building his own force.

On Sept. 12, 1918, the U.S. First Army, Pershing in command, attacked the St. Mihiel salient, which thrust into Allied lines behind Verdun. Planned, staffed, and organized entirely by American officers—especially by George Marshall—the drive smashed old German defenses and cleared the salient by September 13. American confidence soared. Allies carped at the creaking liaison, the awkward schedules, the random artillery blankets—but veteran German observers were dismayed by the fresh valor of Pershing's men. "They charged into their own artillery," one noted, and lamented that German troops had not done that since 1914. Americans were rated as potential shock troops.

Pershing's staff planned a rapid extraction of some of the St. Mihiel divisions, their move some thirty miles north and their reinsertion into the front line in time to attack heavy German defenses in the Argonne near Verdun. Again, Marshall headed the planning group. Allied experts doubted so complicated a move could be made—even by veteran planners and troops—but Pershing began the First Army's major attack in the Meuse-Argonne sector on Sept. 26, 1918, right on schedule.

Initial objectives were the heights of Montfaucon and the blocking of the attacker's right flank against the west side of the Meuse. The Yanks took Montfaucon in a day and a half, blocked the flank at the same time, and probed on against Barricourt ridge. Progress stalled after the first few days. Pershing stepped up to Army Group command, and turned the First Army over to LtGen. Hunter Liggett in mid-October.

Fighting intensified across the Meuse, where the Bourne Cornouiller ("Corned Willy Hill") harbored long-range German guns. In the Aire valley, American troops struggled in dense forestland and hard ground to wrest villages from the enemy in hand-to-hand combat. One unit—the Lost Battalion—was cut off for five days. By October 11, the Americans had broken out of the Argonne at Sommerance, and by the first week of November were pushing the enemy rapidly toward the Meuse.

Confusion at the end of the war marred the occupation of Sedan, but in the excitement of victory few cared—among them, Pershing. Even he did not press an issue possibly embarrassing to the whole American command. He went to Paris for peace talks and joined in the wild celebration of the Armistice on November 11.

Jealous always of the reputation of his men and his armies (he had formed the U.S. Second and Third armies toward the war's end), he resented Allied hints that Americans had not really contributed to victory, that success came in spite of amateurish U.S. efforts. He knew better. Clearly, American fighting in Belleau Wood, along the Marne, and at Château-Thierry had helped blunt the giant German Marne onslaught in June and July 1918. Clearly, too, American cooperation with Gen. Charles Mangin's French Tenth Army in attacking the Marne salient on July 18, 1918, had helped shatter this last German drive of the war. British Field Marshal Haig freely admitted that American participation in the St. Quentin and Hindenburg Line operations had been crucial and generally praised Pershing's efforts.

Most troubles came from Foch. Quirky, officious, and not a little condescending, Foch had ridden Pershing hard through the Meuse-Argonne campaign and even threatened to remove him from command. Pershing pushed back, fought for himself and his men, and recognized that insecurity sparked Foch's truculence.

Too professional to claim perfection, Pershing knew that much of the American effort lacked British and French, and even German, polish. But he also knew that much American error and awkwardness stemmed from inexperience and noted that his men were quick studies; had the war continued into 1919, as many expected, he boasted that the U.S. Army would have dominated the war. It was American courage, ingenuity, and perseverance that made the difference in 1918. Pershing remained convinced that victory would not have come without his armies in the line. His *Final Report*, published in 1920, dealt fairly with the Allies but made clear his admiration for his command.

He had a model partnership with Secretary Baker, who only once thought of removing his Missouri general—and that idea passed almost as soon as it came. Pershing's overall conduct of planning, training, and operations, Baker rated as outstanding; his handling of delicate diplomatic relations with Allied and neutral leaders had been beyond expectations. How could such service be rewarded?

When the fighting was formally over, Pershing's duties continued as the Allies organized partial occupation of areas along the Rhine and as the U.S. Army shrunk because of forces returning home. Staying in Europe until September 1919, Pershing enjoyed the trappings of fame, as well as some special female companionship. He traveled to Italy and England, where he received a hero's welcome. On Sept. 1, 1919, Marshal Foch went to the docks at Brest to bid a fond farewell to his stubborn friend.

Some intrigue muddied his return. During the war, he had fought with Gen. Peyton C. March, the army chief of staff, over preferences for the AEF. March, stiff, formal, and punctilious, maintained he had concerns beyond the AEF—a position Pershing found arch, if not false. March's elevation to full general put him on a par with Pershing and Tasker H. Bliss, U.S. representative to the Supreme Allied War Council, and apparently reduced the importance of the AEF leadership. More than that, March opposed the use of Sam Browne belts, a hallmark of Pershing's officers, and ordered the belts removed on return to the United States. This apparently trivial matter smoldered as Pershing traveled home. Would he have to take that badge of honor off when he docked? He felt hurt and somewhat unappreciated.

But his spirits were lifted when, on September 5, the message came that the President recommended, and Congress approved Pershing's promotion to be General of the Armies—a rank only held before by George Washington.

Wilson could not meet him when his ship docked, for he was traveling in support of the League of Nations. Secretary of War Baker waited at the gangplank, and so did a vast outpouring of affection from the country. A ticker-tape parade in New York on September 10, 1919, when he led the AEF in triumphal parade, a speech to a Joint Session of Congress—he talked of his men and their deeds—welcomed home an authentic American hero.

Between his triumphant return and May 13, 1921, when he became the army chief of staff, he made an inspection tour of forts and stations. He testified before Congress concerning the National Defense Act of 1920, an act designed to construct the peacetime U.S. forces. Pershing warned against rash economies of size and scope; troubles might rise again. But a heady return of isolationist sentiment made his warnings trite, and he knew his stint as chief of staff would not be easy.

As chief of staff, Pershing concentrated on making the best of smaller numbers and on maintaining the efficiency of the officer corps by keeping an eye on such rising stars as George Marshall, George Patton, and Dwight D. Eisenhower and on a small cadre of possible future leaders known as "Pershing's Men."

Retirement from the active army on Sept. 13, 1924, brought more time for such friends as Bernard Baruch and the Fox Conners and for his son Warren, who had been raised with aunts and relatives and felt estranged from his father. In the 1920s and 1930s the "old man" became a friend of Warren's—to mutual enjoyment. Pershing survived the Depression without mishap, helped by the wisdom of Baruch and others. Winters were passed in Arizona, summers in New York, sometimes in Europe.

The possibility of running for the presidency intrigued him, and he permitted his name to circulate for the Republican nomination in 1924. Nothing came of it, and he never tried again. Instead, he turned to ceremonial duties and to service on the American Battle Monuments Commission, which had charge of marking the AEF's fields. He supervised a highly competent staff, including Major Eisenhower, in preparing a superior *Guide to American Battlefields in Europe*, published in 1927.

Much of his time between 1924 and 1931 he spent writing his memoirs. With the help of old comrades, such as George Marshall, and the young aides permitted to the General of the Armies, he wrote several drafts of his monument to the AEF. Published in 1931, *My Experiences in the World War* reflected Pershing's unadorned judgments of men and events and spoke his admiration for his armies. It won the Pulitzer Prize for history in 1932. He compiled recollections of his whole career but never published them.

During the 1930s and 1940s, heart trouble plagued him—the residue of long and hard campaigning and a long and active life. While war was building again in Europe, he moved to an apartment in Walter Reed Army Hospital in Washington to be near his favorite doctor, Dr. Shelly Marietta.

When the United States entered the war in 1941, he offered his services to another President Roosevelt, who refused him but said, "You are magnificent." One more time he offered the advice of years and suggested to FDR that George Marshall was the only man capable of running a two-front war as chief of staff.

Roosevelt listened. As "Pershing's men" went to war again, they stopped to pay their respects to an aging soldier whose eyes still flashed when he urged a final march to Berlin. Near war's end, President Truman sent Pershing the following birthday message:

September 13, 1945

Dear General Pershing:

This should be one of the happiest of your many birthdays as you remember that this time we went all the way through to Berlin, as you counseled in 1918. I hail a great soldier who happily exemplified also the vision of the statesman.

Very sincerely yours,

Harry S. Truman

Pershing lived to see the end—to see some of "his" men return. He died at Walter Reed Hospital on July 15, 1948.

His had been a fascinating life filled with opportunity, excitement, chaos, tragedy, and shining success. His career paced the history of his times, and he helped create the army that sustained a global power. More than that, his life lent luster to West Point's motto of "Duty, Honor, Country."

Frank E. Vandiver

Bibliography

O'Connor, Richard. *Black Jack Pershing*. Garden City, NY: Doubleday, 1961.

Palmer, Frederick. *John J. Pershing, General of the Armies: A Biography*. Harrisburg, PA: Military Service Publishing, 1948.

Smythe, Donald. *Guerilla Warrior: The Early Life of John J. Pershing*. New York: Scribner, 1973.

———. *Pershing, General of the Armies*. Bloomington: Indiana University Press, 1986.

Vandiver, Frank E. *Black Jack—The Life and Time of John J. Pershing*. 2 vols. College Station: Texas A&M University Press, 1977.

Pétain, Henri-Philippe (1856–1951)

In 1914, Henri-Philippe Pétain was an obscure, fifty-eight-year-old colonel of infantry in the French Army. By 1919, he had risen to the rank of marshal, becoming commander-in-chief of the largest army in French history and a member of the military coalition that defeated the Central Powers in World War I. The story of his rise chronicles the failures and victories of the French High Command's struggle to defeat the Imperial German Army and expel it from French soil.

Henri-Philippe Pétain was born in 1856 at Cauchy-la-Tour in the Artois region of northern France. His parents were peasants of middling circumstances. Although reared in a Catholic family, Pétain was indifferent to religion in later life. In 1876, the young Pétain gained admission to the French military academy, Saint Cyr, and graduated two years later with the rank of second lieutenant of infantry. His subsequent military career prior to the outbreak of World War I was characterized by solid performance rather than spectacular achievement. Unlike many of his more ambitious and adventurous colleagues, he eschewed service in France's colonial army, preferring duty within metropolitan France. In 1888, he attended the École de Guerre, the French war college that was established in 1878 as part of the military reforms undertaken in the army after the defeat by Prussia in 1870. In 1901, he returned to the École de Guerre as an instructor in tactics. It was here that Pétain's ideas about the lethality of modern warfare took shape. His study of military history since the age of Napoleon convinced him that firepower had gained an ascendancy over maneuver in warfare and that the next war would be one requiring overwhelming artillery support to augment the most carefully controlled and conservative infantry attacks. Pétain's advocacy of tactical caution put him at odds with the advocates of the offensive, led by Ferdinand Foch (also a lecturer at the École de Guerre at that time) and Louis Loyzeau de Grandmaison, who would become the author of Plan XVII, France's military blueprint for war in 1914. Pétain's failure to win the doctrinal argument, though influenced by a number of factors, rested in part upon the aloof, cold manner in which he delivered his lectures. His detached manner stood in stark contrast to the charismatic and flamboyant Foch, who was the darling of the school.

At the outbreak of the war, Pétain was serving in what had been planned to be his last assignment before his retirement—commander of the 4th Infantry Brigade. At the crucial First Battle of the Marne in September 1914, Pétain demonstrated exceptional cool under fire as well as methodical use of artillery fire to repulse the German attacks in his sector. For his performance at the Marne, he was promoted to brigadier general and installed as commander of the 6th Infantry Division. In the first few months of the war, the French commander-in-chief, Gen. Joseph Joffre, "cashiered" more than fifty generals for incompetence and promised more would fall if performance did not improve. These mass dismissals afforded the opportunity for capable officers such as Pétain to move up rapidly in rank and responsibility.

By the end of 1914, the stalemate on the Western Front had coalesced. Following their failure at the Marne in September, the Germans attempted to outflank the Allied line in northern France without success and finally decided to dig in along a line that snaked from Switzerland in the south to Flanders in the north. In January 1915, Joffre selected Pétain to command XXXIII Corps and ordered him to prepare for a spring offensive designed to break through the German lines and restore a war of movement. As usual, Pétain prepared carefully for the offensive, taking special care in assembling and organizing a powerful collection of artillery to smother the German line before his infantry assaulted. Pétain's corps took its initial objective, the crest of Vimy Ridge, in the first day of the offensive, May 9, 1915, after a six-day bombardment of the German defenders. Although the attack subsequently bogged down and the Germans regained the heights, Pétain's performance again received the notice of the High Command, and he was again selected for promotion, this time to become commander of the Second Army.

Following the failure of the May attack, Joffre planned to launch another offensive, this time attacking in both the Artois and Champagne. Pétain again demonstrated careful leadership and organization by creating balloon observer units and a network of target acquisition spotters to increase the effectiveness of artillery. He also encouraged his subordinates to innovate, an attitude that resulted in Robert Nivelle's development of the rolling barrage to move at a measured pace ahead of advancing infantry. Once again, however, the initial offensive broke down, and the casualty lists mounted as Joffre attempted to "nibble away" at the German defenses in subsequent attacks against alerted positions.

The German attack at Verdun in February 1916 caught the French High Command by surprise and in a difficult position. The forts of the city had been largely evacuated of their garrisons and heavy weapons in order to reinforce other sectors of the front. The east bank of the Meuse, with all the important forts such as Douaumont, Vaux, and Souville, was defended by only two understrength reserve divisions that were decimated by the initial attack. To stem the German advance, Joffre sent for Pétain and gave him orders to hold the east bank at all costs. With reinforcements streaming in from Bar-le-Duc to the south, Pétain set about reorganizing French defenses by centralizing artillery support under his command and rotating divisions through tours at the front. By March, the German attacks on the east bank had been stopped at the cost of great numbers of casualties, and in April, the attack shifted to the west bank of the Meuse, where the struggle took on a new ferocity. By the end of the month, Pétain's forces had subdued these attacks too, but in the process he had incurred the displeasure of General Joffre, who opposed Pétain's requests for more divisions and heavier artillery to fortify Verdun. Joffre wanted these forces to take part in the great Allied offensive that he was planning to undertake with the British on the Somme River in June 1916. In May, Joffre elevated Pétain to command of Army Group Center and placed his more pliable subordinate, Robert Nivelle, in charge of the Second Army at Verdun. The start of the offensive on the Somme on July 1, 1916, finally led the Germans to break off their attacks at Verdun. In the following months, Pétain and Nivelle cooperated to retake all the ground lost to the Germans since the start of the campaign. In October 1916, Gen. Charles Mangin led the successful attack to retake Douaumont, the key fort of the Verdun system. On November 2, a similar attack retook Fort Vaux. By mid-December, all ground lost to the Germans was recovered.

Casualties at Verdun were heavy, however, for both the troops and the generals. The French Army suffered more than half a million casualties in the eleven-month period, and the first signs of mutiny appeared among units returning for another tour in the trenches. After a parliamentary inquiry, Joffre was promoted out of his position as commander-in-chief and replaced by Nivelle. Pétain had been considered for commander-in-chief but apparently was rejected after he sarcastically commented to Raymond Poincaré, president of the French Republic, that France was being neither governed nor led in the present conflict. Unlike Pétain, Nivelle was smooth in presentation, confident about prospects for the next offensive, and fluent in English—which impressed Britain's Prime Minister David Lloyd George when the two met in London in January 1917. Nivelle unveiled for the British ambitious plans to break through the German lines in Champagne using the methods he had developed at Verdun, confidently declaring, "We have the solution!"

After Verdun, however, much of the political leadership in Paris had tired of overconfident generals. When the government of Aristide Briand fell on March 17, the new premier, Alexandre Ribot, appointed Pétain as chief of staff of the army and convened a conference at Compiègne on April 6 to discuss the plan of attack. At this meeting, Pétain raised many doubts about the ability of the French to break through and win the war at a single blow, which greatly angered Nivelle. Nevertheless, Nivelle got his offensive, promising that if it did not succeed, he would break off the attack after forty-eight hours and avoid the heavy casualties of past offensives. By the time the attack commenced on April 16–17, 1917, the German High Command had a complete copy of the French plan and had completed a series of new defensive positions far to the rear of the French zone of attack. When the attack came, it was immediately driven back with heavy French losses. Despite his promise, Nivelle continued the attacks until May 9, when Premier Painlevé forced him from office.

Pétain was at last appointed commander-in-chief of the French Army, but his hour of success was one of great despair for the army. Grievances had built up within the ranks over the empty promises of the High Command. Food was poor, leave nonexistent, and mail from home was incredibly slow. Officers took too little interest in training and in the morale of the men and promised more than they could deliver on the battlefield. From April to August, the army experienced a wave of protest strikes and in some cases outright mutiny. Though the French military archives remain closed on the period, it seems likely that two-thirds of the divisions in the army were affected, essentially rendering the French incapable of combat for the rest of 1917. Pétain quelled the unrest with a remarkable balance of firmness and reform. He tried a number of the most egregious mutineers but executed fewer than two dozen. He visited every division in the army, demanding better treatment for soldiers and promising that offensives would be strictly limited in the future. He also increased the number of tanks, heavy guns, and airplanes available for future offensives. In his directives to his subordinate generals, Pétain stressed the need for careful preparation of attacks with plentiful artillery and an end to the quest for a decision through attrition. Along with his defense of Verdun, Pétain's handling of this painful episode ranks as his greatest achievement—and one that was vital to keeping France in the war.

By 1918, the French Army had begun to recover confidence in itself and its commander. French factory production was peaking with weapons that would inundate the Germans on the Western Front before year's end. Pétain finally became convinced that the French would win the war by 1919, if they could simply hold on until the growing American Army could make its way to France and be trained for trench warfare. Like Sir Douglas Haig, commander of the British Expeditionary Force, Pétain looked upon Gen. John J. Pershing's American Expeditionary Force (AEF) with longing and suspicion. Pétain favored the direct incorporation of American infantry regiments into French divisions, arguing that the Americans possessed neither the trained staffs nor the heavy weapons to run an army on their own. He felt that this incorporation, or "amalgamation" as it was known, was the fastest way to train American manpower and get it fighting against the Germans. When Pershing resisted, however, Pétain relented and offered to let the Americans use the military schools and weapons ranges that the French had established. Without that assistance, it is difficult to imagine how the Americans could have had any impact on the war in 1918, given their unfamiliarity with the fighting on the Western Front.

In the fighting of 1918, Pétain's caution of the previous four years got the better of him. When Ludendorff unleashed the *Friedensturm* offensives beginning in March, Pétain was extremely concerned about covering the approaches to Paris, which he believed to be the likely objective, and refused to release any reserves to assist the British, upon whom the first German blows fell at the Somme. At the Doullens Conference on March 26, 1918, he displayed much greater pessimism than General Foch about the Allied ability to prevent the development of a breach between the British and French lines. His pessimism undoubtedly influenced the naming of the eternally optimistic Foch to supreme commander. Nevertheless, in the defensive fighting that stemmed the final German offensives and the counterattacks that led to the November Armistice, Pétain's efforts to repair the damage of the 1917 mutinies were evident. Everywhere that French troops attacked, they were accompanied by new masses of artillery, tanks, and airplanes.

Pétain's role in the French Army after the war has remained a subject of the bitterest and most intractable controversy within France. In 1919, Pétain was elevated to the rank of marshal and spent much of the 1920s on the Supreme Defense Council advocating the defensive reinforcement of France's eastern frontiers, which finally resulted in the construction of the Maginot Line. In the 1930s, he lapsed into semiretirement until appointed ambassador to Franco's Spain just before World War II. With the defeat of France in 1940, Pétain became head of the Vichy government, a position for which he was imminently unsuited, given his health and advanced age. With the Nazi occupation of Vichy in November 1942, he was eventually taken into German captivity, where he spent the remainder of the war. Tried after the liberation for collaboration with the Germans in various war crimes, he was sentenced to death by the government of Charles de Gaulle, who had, ironically, been a subaltern in Pétain's regiment before World War I and his protégé in the interwar years. His sentence was commuted to life, and he served out his remaining years, a solitary prisoner on the Isle de Yeu in the Bay of Biscay. Pétain died in July 1951 at the age of ninety-five.

James Hogue

Bibliography

Horne, Alistair. *The Price of Glory: Verdun.* London: Macmillan, 1962.
Pedroncini, Guy. *Pétain, General en chef, 1917–1918.* Paris: Presse Université de France, 1974.
Pétain, Henri-Philippe. *La Battaille de Verdun.* France: Les Editions Lorraines, 1932.

Ryan, Stephen. *Pétain the Soldier.* New York: Barnes, 1969.

Serrigny, Bernard. *Trente Ans avec Pétain.* Paris: Plon, 1959.

Plattsburg Movement

The Plattsburg Movement came about largely through the efforts of two men, Grenville Clark, a New York attorney and prominent social figure, and Leonard Wood, commanding general of the Department of the East and former chief of staff of the United States Army. The former was the originator, while the latter was the primary motivator and proponent of the movement. Concerned about and spurred on by the *Lusitania* disaster, Clark and ninety-nine others of like mind, set up a reserve military training organization at Plattsburg, New York, in the summer of 1915, in order to learn the rudiments of war. Included in this group were Richard Derby and Philip Carroll, both of whom had been ambulance drivers for the Allies in France during the early days of the First World War. Another early supporter, and one who brought prestige to the movement, was former President of the United States Theodore Roosevelt.

When the movement found difficulty raising federal subsidies, its members sought private funds. Those in attendance received training and instruction not only in the nomenclature and function of specific weapons but also in basic infantry tactics. In a short period of time, the idea caught on, and by the late summer of 1915, the organization finally received recognition as well as funding for some of its ventures by the War Department. Even so, this reserve corps, as it began to be called, never overcame public suspicion altogether. For one thing, it appeared to be an attempt to garner officer slots in the Regular Army for its members, many of whom were members of privileged northeastern families from the section's economically and socially elite class. In some ways, the muster roll read like a page torn from *Who's Who.*

There were other reasons why the public's suspicions were aroused. In time, the camp became something of an instrument of propaganda for Wood's particular views on preparedness and military organization. As such, it earned the wrath of the Democrats in general and the Wilson administration specifically, particularly after Roosevelt gave an intemperate speech condemning Wilson's foreign policy and lack of military preparation. Despite Roosevelt's apologies and attempt to distance his views from those of the Plattsburgers, the movement remained under something of a cloud. Withal, the movement grew and in time additional camps met at other sites. Originally, the plan called for the enrollment of men between the ages of the late twenties and early thirties, but as time went on, college-aged men were included as well, for it became evident that only younger men would fill commissions for platoon leaders and company commanders.

The Plattsburg Movement was dealt a severe blow with the passage of the National Defense Act of 1916. The act was the result of a union of three elements. One was the National Guard; another was the House Military Affairs Committee led by its formidable chairman, James Hay of Virginia, a long-time supporter of the Guard. The last was Gen. Frederick Ainsworth, who had been adjutant general and nursed a bitter grudge against Wood, who, he believed, had ruined his career. Neither was Hay fond of Wood. These elements also defeated Secretary of War Lindley M. Garrison's Continental Army Plan, which was endorsed by Wood, for they were opposed to any measure that would replace or even question the National Guard's jealously protected military authority and preeminence as the nation's first line of defense behind the Regular Army. Accordingly, the National Defense Act effectively restricted reserve officer recruitment from any source not already in existence. Passage of the legislation effectively destroyed the Continental Army Plan, forced Garrison's resignation, and succeeded in reducing Wood's earlier accomplishments.

Although the Plattsburg Movement itself did not die, it was injured; but in testimony to its resilience, years after its inception its ideals and concepts continued to survive and even prosper. The 1920s, 1930s, and 1940s saw its influence continue through the Military Training Corps Association (MTCA). The legacy of the Plattsburg Movement and the MTCA persists to this day through the ideas of preparation for war in time of peace and the military education of heretofore untrained young men as junior officers in time of war.

James W. Pohl

See also PREPAREDNESS

Bibliography

Clifford, John Garry. *The Citizen Soldiers.* Lexington: University Press of Kentucky, 1972.

Derthick, Martha. *The National Guard in Politics.* Cambridge: Harvard University Press, 1965.

Hill, Jim Dan. *The Minute Man in Peace and War.* Harrisburg, PA: Stackpole, 1964.

Poincaré, Raymond (1860–1934)

Raymond Poincaré was an indefatigable French statesman who is remembered as the apostle of military and diplomatic preparedness prior to the outbreak of World War I, as chief of state during and immediately after the conflict, and as enforcer of the Treaty of Versailles in the Ruhr crisis of 1923.

Much, perhaps too much, has been made of Poincaré's Lorraine origins. He was born at Bar-le-Duc in 1860, and as an impressionable ten-year-old, he experienced France's humiliation at the hands of Bismarck's Prussia in 1870–1871. Without question the occupation of his native land inculcated a deep mistrust of Germany and a fervent sense of national pride. But he was too cautious and conservative a politician to be a crusading advocate of revenge. He had experienced the chaos and destruction of war at firsthand, and this shaped his determination to avoid further war and defeat through an emphasis on military and diplomatic preparedness.

A brilliant student, Poincaré was educated at lycées in Bar-le-Duc and at the prestigious Louis le Grand in Paris. He studied law at the Sorbonne and was admitted to the bar in 1882. His political career began when he was elected to the Chamber of Deputies for the Meuse in 1887. He remained active in governmental affairs for over a decade, serving in several ministries and as vice president of the Chamber of Deputies. From 1899–1912, however, he refused to join any government except for a brief period as minister of finance in the Sarrien cabinet from March to October 1906. During this period, he won a seat in the Senate and devoted himself to law practice, becoming one of the wealthiest and most successful lawyers in France. His literary ambitions, expressed largely through newspaper and journal articles, were also crowned by election to l'Academie Française in 1909. Poincaré became known as a disciplined administrator with an enormous capacity for work and with a reputation for personal honesty and probity. These same characteristics marked him as legalistic and cold in his relationships with colleagues.

In January 1912, in the wake of the second Moroccan crisis, Poincaré was designated to form his first ministry. His appointment coincided with a nationalistic revival in France, which resulted in raising the level of tension between France and Germany. Critics of Poincaré have accused him of using his position to pursue war with Germany as an act of revenge for the latter's seizure of Alsace-Lorraine in 1871. This view considerably exaggerates the prime minister's genuine concern to discourage potential German aggressiveness by invigorating France's military and diplomatic posture. That foreign affairs were to be a hallmark of his government became apparent when he took for himself the foreign ministry portfolio. Concerned with maintaining France's security and prestige, Poincaré worked to strengthen the alliance with Russia and to clarify both military and naval understandings with Great Britain. In the case of Russia, it was a matter of closing fissures in the alliance that successive Radical Party ministries had allowed to open. The Radicals did not entirely trust France's autocratic ally. At the same time, however, Poincaré carefully avoided offering Russia a free hand in the Balkans for fear of becoming involved in a war in southeastern Europe where French interests were slight. With Great Britain, he aimed to transform the Dual Entente into an alliance. Whereas that objective proved impossible to achieve, he did succeed in reaching an understanding with Sir Edward Grey, the British foreign secretary, to the effect that the two governments would consult during periods of international crisis and, if necessary, bring into effect military and naval plans that had been developed by their respective general staffs.

These efforts brought Poincaré's popularity to a peak at a time when presidential elections were scheduled for January 1913. Seeing an opportunity to maintain long-term continuity in the handling of France's foreign policy and intrigued by a tendency in popular opinion to favor more vigorous executive leadership, Poincaré declared his candidacy for the presidency of the Third Republic. Although opposed by a candidate championed by radical leader Georges Clemenceau, Poincaré triumphed in a close contest with support from conservatives who admired his patriotism. Unlike a number of his predecessors, Poincaré was determined that his new position would not be merely decorative. He intended to use the latitude provided to the president by the constitution in the area of foreign policy and in the choice of new governments. His first two appointees as prime minister, Aristide Briand and Louis Barthou, put together cabinets that were virtual mirror images of Poincaré's first ministry.

The new president made it clear that he intended to pursue the theme of military and diplomatic preparedness. To that end, he vigorously supported the Three Years' Law, extending French military service from two to three years, thus ensuring that the number of French soldiers in the field paralleled German troop strength. His activism in this matter led to further enmity with Clemenceau and the left wing of the French political spectrum. In diplomacy he continued policies he had initiated as premier. He supported the appointment of a strong ambassador to Russia, Théophile Delcassé, and worked to preserve peace by ensuring that the Entente powers remained strong and unified. His personal diplomacy took him on official state visits to Great Britain in June 1913 and to Russia in July 1914. He was en route home from Russia, accompanied by his premier and foreign minister and the director of the French Foreign Ministry when Austria-Hungary delivered its ultimatum to Serbia on July 23, 1914. Thus, in the final weeks leading to the outbreak of World War I, France's political and diplomatic leaders were effectively isolated from the fateful events taking place in Europe. Poincaré and his entourage returned to Paris only five days after Germany's declaration of war on France on Aug. 3, 1914.

Poincaré continued his activist presidency throughout the war and into the immediate postwar period. Following Germany's declaration of war, he made his famous appeal to the French parliament for a national coalition (union sacrée) to close political ranks for the duration of the conflict. He rallied French determination by visiting military hospitals, training camps, and the front lines. A major test of his plea to put the country above politics came in November 1917, when he appointed his long-time political rival, Georges Clemenceau, to be prime minister. Although the two men's initial cooperation played an important role in the victory over Germany, their underlying antipathy surfaced again in bitter disagreements over the nature of the peace treaty. Poincaré backed Marshal Ferdinand Foch in the latter's

effort to secure a separate Rhineland state as a buffer between France and Germany. He also supported a firm stance on Germany's obligation to pay heavy reparations. Ultimately, however, given the constitutional limits on his presidential powers, Poincaré saw no alternative but to resign himself to the Versailles Treaty. He had been the strongest president in the history of the Third Republic. But his strength lay principally in the force of his personality; he made no basic alteration in the structure of the office itself. His term came to an end on Feb. 18, 1920.

Reelected to the Senate in 1920, in the wake of the failure of a promised Anglo-American military guarantee treaty, Poincaré rejected the conciliatory policies of Aristide Briand and insisted on the vigorous enforcement of the Versailles Treaty as France's only sure means of preserving national security. Such a stance ensured his recall to the premiership and to the foreign ministry in January 1922. Convinced that Germany was insincere in its commitment to pay reparations, he persuaded Italian and Belgian delegates on the Reparations Commission to join France in finding Germany in default in January 1923. The occupation of the Ruhr valley, one of Germany's richest industrial areas along the frontier with France, began immediately. After nine months of passive resistance and rekindled wartime bitterness, Germany capitulated. In return for France's withdrawal from the Ruhr, Germany agreed to revisit the question of reparations. Poincaré's effort to enforce the treaty by military action was successful in the short run, but the protracted Ruhr crisis engendered tensions with Great Britain and the United States. Fundamentally a moderate statesman, he returned to negotiations with his World War I partners. The result was the adoption by the Reparations Commission of the Dawes Plan of 1924, which led to the resumption of German reparation payments on a relatively substantial scale.

An alliance among the Socialist and Radical parties over taxation policy forced Poincaré from office in June 1924. The *cartel des gauches,* however, failed to deal effectively with the crisis. Poincaré was recalled to the prime ministry on July 23, 1926, and—this time with public opinion behind him—was able to initiate new taxes and enforce a number of other financial stringencies sufficient to stabilize the franc and maintain its buoyancy for much of the rest of the decade. His achievement earned him the popular sobriquet, Poincaré-le-franc.

He remained in office, with one brief interruption, until 1929, his governments laying the foundation for the Young Plan, a final effort to resolve the reparations/war debts dilemma before the onset of the Great Depression. Ill health drove Poincaré into private life, where he devoted much of his remaining energy to writing his memoirs, ten volumes of which appeared between 1926 and 1931. He died on Oct. 15, 1934.

William Shorrock

Bibliography

Keiger, John F.V. *France and the Origins of the First World War*. New York: St. Martin's Press, 1983.

Miquel, P. *Poincaré*. Paris: A. Fayard, 1961.

Payen, F. *Raymond Poincaré: L'Homme, le parlementaire, l'avocat*. Paris: Grasset, 1936.

Poincaré, Raymond. *The Memoirs of Raymond Poincaré*. Garden City, NY: Doubleday, Page, 1926–1931.

Wright, Gordon. *Raymond Poincaré and the French Presidency*. Stanford, CA: Stanford University Press, 1942.

Polish-American Army

The powers that had partitioned Poland at the close of the eighteenth century were ranged against each other at the outbreak of war in 1914. Poles everywhere realized that a great power conflict could place the so-called "Polish Question"—i.e., the possibility of re-creating an independent Poland—on the international diplomatic agenda. Many Poles became captivated by the idea of Polish military units playing some role in the war and thereby gaining attention for Polish national aspirations. Early in the war small Polish units were formed within the Russian and French armies and more numerous Polish Legions fought under Austrian command. In the United States, repeated efforts by resident Poles to create discrete units in foreign armies had proven abortive, but wide-spread drilling and preparatory work had been organized by the Polish Falcons (Zwiazek Sokolow Polskich). With the American declaration of war in April 1917, the Falcons announced plans to raise a large contingent of American Poles; an effort championed by Ignacy Jan Paderewski, the world-famous Polish pianist and composer, an emerging leader of the Polish Provisional Government. At first, the role of this Polish-American force was unclear, but on June 4, 1917, the French announced their sponsorship of an official Polish Army. Therefore, recruiting in America began, with War Department approval, in October.

Volunteers were sent for training to Ontario and Quebec and later to Lewistown, New York. Thus France, Canada, and the United States—which indirectly provided financial assistance—were involved in the project. The Polish National Department, a Polish-American organization led by Paderewski, directed recruitment. A total of 38,108 enlisted, of which 20,720 eventually sailed for France in several contingents. There they were joined by former German and Austrian POWs who were of Polish nationality and volunteers from Polish settlements worldwide. The army, commanded by Gen. Józef Haller and under the direction of the Polish National Committee in Paris, saw action on the Western Front in 1918 under overall French command. After the war, the army was sent to Poland and played a significant role in defending the renascent state. Many of the Polish-American volunteers later returned to the United States. The contingent also is known as the "Haller Army," the "Blue Army" (after the color of their uniforms), and, most frequently, the Polish Army in France.

M. B. Biskupski

Bibliography

Gasiorowski, Waclaw. *Historia Armii Polskiej we Francji*. 2 vols. Lodz: N.p., 1931, 1939.

Pliska, Stanley R. "The Polish-American Army, 1917–1921." *Polish Review* 10 (1965).

Sierocinski, Jozef. *Armia Polska we Francji. Dzieje wojsk generala Hallera na obczynie*. Warsaw: N.p., 1929.

Skarzynski, Wincenty. *Armia Polska we Francji w swietle faktow*. Warsaw: N.p., 1929.

Trawinski, Witold H. *Odyseja Polskiej Armii Blekitnej*. Wroclaw: N.p., 1989.

Polk, Frank Lyons (1871–1943)

Frank Lyons Polk, a great-nephew of President James K. Polk, was born in New York City. After graduating from Yale University in 1894 and Columbia Law School in 1897, he joined a distinguished New York law firm and became active in Democratic Party politics. Polk suc-

P

ceeded Robert Lansing as counselor (chief legal adviser) of the State Department in 1915, when the latter replaced William Jennings Bryan as Woodrow Wilson's secretary of state. During the period of American neutrality in the First World War, Polk shared the pro-Allied sentiments of his chief at the State Department. When the United States intervened in the war against Germany in the spring of 1917, Polk played an important behind-the-scenes role as a supporter of Wilson's efforts to secure a negotiated settlement of the conflict.

When Lansing accompanied President Wilson to the Paris Peace Conference after the Armistice of Nov. 11, 1918, Frank Polk remained in Washington as acting secretary of state. During this phase of the peace conference, Polk kept Wilson and Lansing informed, via cable, of political developments at home, candidly reporting the widespread disillusionment with the project for a League of Nations that Wilson had persuaded the Allied chiefs of state in Paris to endorse. Polk managed the affairs of the department until July 1919, when President Wilson asked him to replace Lansing as the United States representative at the peace conference. At this time, the U.S. Congress also changed his official title at the State Department from counselor to under secretary.

Polk assumed leadership of the American delegation in Paris on July 28, 1919, taking over the offices that had been vacated by Wilson's personal representative, Col. Edward M. House. His principal duties concerned the preparation of the peace treaties with Germany's allies—Austria, Hungary, Bulgaria, and Turkey. In December 1919, following the United States Senate's refusal to approve the Versailles Treaty and the Covenant of the League of Nations, President Wilson ordered Polk to return to the United States. When Wilson dismissed Lansing in February 1920 for insubordination, Polk again served as acting secretary of state. He faced the difficult task of dealing with the exasperated representatives of the Allied governments in Washington as they attempted in vain to promote a compromise between the Senate and the reclusive, invalid president during the winter of 1919–1920. When Wilson passed over the experienced acting secretary of state and named attorney Bainbridge Colby as Lansing's successor, Polk retired from government service and returned to his law practice in New York City.

William Keylor

Pontoon Bridges

The armies of World War I made use of two distinct classes of bridges: heavy and light equipage. The heavy pontoon bridge was designed to cross the heaviest elements of the marching army with a roadway of approximately ten feet wide and a floor system capable of carrying the soldiers with their trains. In addition, the heavy pontoons were designed to ferry soldiers to the far shore until it was safe enough to construct the bridge. The light pontoon bridge was of the same general configuration except that its components were designed to handle smaller loads such as light infantry and cavalry.

The elements of design for these bridges were governed by the following factors: (1) The bridge equipage had to be sufficiently mobile to accompany the movements of the column in which it was traveling. (2) The equipage must provide the capability to ferry infantry soldiers rapidly across rivers under enemy fire. (3) The bridge train had to provide the means to cross an army with its trains over the largest and most rapid rivers in the area of operations.

The basic components of the pontoon bridge were the pontoon boat, trestle, transom, balk, side rail, and chess. The boats and trestles formed the piers or the main supports of the bridge. The transom was the horizontal beam that was placed upon the pontoon boat or the trestle if on land. The balks were the wooden stringers that connected the separated pontoon boats/trestles. The side rails were the wheel guards that prevented carriages from sliding off of the bridge platform. And the chess, or deck planking, was the basic roadway floor upon which all traffic crosses.

There were four basic methods of construction for pontoon bridges during World War I—by successive pontoons, by parts, by rafts, and by conversion. Although the descriptive terms may have varied among the belligerent armies, the methods of construction remained the same.

Construction by successive pontoons was the most common technique. In this case, all of the bridge equipage was stored near the abutments. To start the construction, an abutment sill was laid perpendicular to the bridge axis and secured by pickets. Depending upon the shore approaches to the river, one or more trestle spans were then placed on the bank, and the first pontoon boat was brought adjacent to the bank. Next, a set of balks was brought up and the cleats emplaced on the saddle of the pontoon boat and lightly lashed in place. Once the shore end of the balks were secured, the pontoon boat connections were firmly lashed together and the chess laid. The pontoon sections were then rowed into position one at a time and the operation repeated until the far shore was reached. The bridge was thus constructed in succession either from one or both abutments.

In the method by parts, the bridge equipage was stored on one or both shores upstream from the crossing site. Bridge sections consisting of two bays were constructed at these bridge sites and later rowed into place to construct the bridge successively by parts.

The raft method was quite similar to the method by parts. In this case, rafts were constructed to ferry troops and equipment across the river prior to bridging operations. Once it was decided to construct a bridge, the rafts were lashed together with end boats in place to form the bridge platform. This method enabled rapid disassembly in the event of an enemy attack or if the bridge was liable to damage from floating objects.

In the method by conversion, the bridge equipage was stored along one shore upstream from the crossing site. From this position, the entire bridge was constructed parallel with, and adjacent to, the shore. Once completed, the bridge was floated downstream and swung into position, normally by pivoting about one of the abutments.

To resist the forces of current and wind, World War I pontoon bridges were sometimes anchored in place. The number of anchors required depended upon the strength of the current. It was generally sufficient to cast an anchor upstream for every alternate pontoon and approximately 50 percent of that number downstream. In situations when the current was rapid, it became necessary to anchor every boat upstream. A corresponding percentage of downstream anchors were also needed to prevent the horizontal oscillation of the bridge when soldiers marched over it.

The distance of the anchor from the bridge needed to be at least ten times the depth of the stream. With distances less than that ratio, the bow of the pontoon tended to sink too deeply into the water. The direction of the cable fastened to the bridge also needed to match the direction of the current. Hence, the pontoon needed to have the same position that it would assume if riding freely at the anchor. In general, the weight of anchors required per foot run of pontoon bridge was roughly from four to ten pounds; cask and raft bridges gave a heavier stress on cables than pontoons.

A wide variety of materials was used to build the pontoons for bridge flotation. Frequently, European armies employed standard pontoon boats made of steel plating. The U.S. Army employed wooden pontoon boats that provided greater buoyancy than its steel counterparts. When standard pontoons were not available, armies also employed ordinary boats, log rafts, or wooden casks to provide the desired buoyancy. To adjust to these nonstandard designs, the transoms were either spiked or lashed to their points of junction with the pontoons.

Michael Toguchi

Bibliography
Bond, Paul S. *The Engineer in War*. New York: McGraw-Hill, 1916.
Fiebeger, Gustave J. *Military Engineering*. West Point, NY: War Department, 1920.
Great Britain. War Office. *Military Engineering. Part IIIb. Military Bridging*. London: H.M. Stationery Office, 1914.

Preparedness

Between August 1914 and April 1917, the United States maintained official neutrality in the war in Europe. However, by the first months of 1916, President Woodrow Wilson's policies had evolved from strict neutrality to overt sympathy for the Entente powers, if not outright support. This change of policy reflected Wilson's concern for the course of the war itself, domestic political considerations, and his own views of the necessity for American intervention. Still Wilson refused to press Congress to authorize military preparations. Opposing authorization for increased military appropriations in December 1914, calling America the "champion of peace" as late as February 1917, only five weeks before his war message to Congress, the President informed the nation, "I am not now preparing or contemplating war or any steps that need lead to it."

Nevertheless, preparations for American military mobilization had progressed significantly during the thirty-three months between the beginning of the conflict and American intervention. The so-called "preparedness" movement was from its inception a crusade by largely Republican interventionists—individuals such

P

as former President Theodore Roosevelt, former Secretary of War Henry Stimson, financier J.P. Morgan, and powerful Senator Henry Cabot Lodge—and such partisan organizations as the National Security League, the National Civic Foundation, and the Navy League to ready the country for what they believed was the inevitable entrance of the United States into the war in Europe.

At its best, the preparedness campaign reflected a realistic assessment of America's obligations as a world power and the dangers of isolationism. At its worst it was a frenzied crusade to evoke war hysteria, to instill rabid patriotism, or 100 percent Americanism, and to incite anti-German hatred. The movement placed the Wilson administration on the defensive, forcing it to justify remaining out of the great struggle for democracy and justice. Politically, Wilson and progressives feared the campaign would jeopardize liberal reforms at home. Still, Democrats could not simply ignore preparedness advocates, and favoring intervention himself, the President cautiously, and then openly, courted the prowar faction while attempting to distance himself from alarmists in his own party. Thus preparedness in the United States was never a single-issue movement—nor was its focus ever entirely military.

The sinking of the *Lusitania* on May 7, 1915, increased pressure on the administration and gave greater credence to the proponents of preparedness. On Aug. 10, 1915, Gen. Leonard Wood, acting on the urging of Grenville Clark, Roosevelt, and other interventionists, opened the first "businessmen's" military training camp at Plattsburg, New York. Secretary of War Newton D. Baker authorized Regular Army officers and noncommissioned officers to staff these camps, which, by the summer of 1916, "unofficially" provided 40,000 men with basic military training, six months before the enactment of the Selective Service Act. While Wilson had been publicly opposed to these activities, events gradually caused a shift in his opinions until October 1916, when, in the course of the presidential election campaign, Wilson strongly endorsed prowar activists in spite of the fact that his actions caused a deep split within the cabinet and among liberal progressives and angered peace groups, many of which had taken his support as a given.

Although disavowing America's preparation for "aggression" or "attack," the President, nevertheless, accelerated the transformation of American institutions and the mobilization of the nation's energies for war. In adopting war as the litmus test of Americanism, Wilson thus lent powerful support to those calling for intervention. As the President confided in late 1916, "We do not covet peace at the cost of honor."

While much of the nation focused on the European conflict, worsening relations between the United States and Mexico between 1914 and 1916, culminating with a raid by Francisco "Pancho" Villa on Columbus, New Mexico, convinced Wilson of the necessity of a punitive military intervention in that country's civil war. On March 15, 1916, Gen. John J. Pershing led 6,000 troops across the border in pursuit of Villa's forces. Despite their best efforts, the Americans never caught up with the bandit. However, the Punitive Expedition and the subsequent mobilization of National Guard units highlighted some major weaknesses in the American military establishment. In response to this situation, Congress enacted a sweeping military authorization—the National Defense Act of 1916, on June 18, 1916. The act provided for substantial increases in the Regular Army, created a federal National Guard, a federal reserve, and Reserve Officer Training Corps (ROTC), and on Aug. 29, 1916, the Naval Act authorized construction of a "Navy second to none," to include twenty-six battleships and battle cruisers, fifty destroyers, and other support craft. This commitment to massive increases in the nation's military establishment proved a desperately needed head start to full national mobilization after April 1917.

Preparedness advocates were also aggressively calling for psychological mobilization and a moral crusade. In the battle to win the hearts and minds of a deeply divided public, President Wilson authorized an active propaganda campaign. The Committee on Public Information (CPI, or Creel Bureau, named for George Creel) and private and quasi-governmental groups, such as the National Security League, National Board for Historical Service, and the Committee on Patriotism Through Education, were among the most prominent and efficient of hundreds of national and state organizations.

To prepare the nation for war and the inevitable productive and financial dislocations, Wilson dramatically expanded the number of emergency federal agencies, creating the Council of National Defense, the Civilian Advisory Commission, and the Shipping Board. These were augmented after intervention by the War

Industries Board, the War Labor Board, and dozens of other wartime administrative bodies.

Thus, in the months before the United States entered the war in Europe, Americans were submitted to a barrage of anti-German propaganda and patriotic exhortation to support the forces of democracy and liberalism against tyranny and were driven to war by charges of disloyalty against those who hesitated.

Jonathan M. Nielson

See also PLATTSBURG MOVEMENT

Bibliography

Clifford, John Garry. *The Citizen Soldiers: The Plattsburg Training Camp Movement, 1913–1920.* Lexington: University Press of Kentucky, 1972.

Gruber, Carol S. *Mars and Minerva: World War I and the Uses of the Higher Learning in America.* Baton Rouge: Louisiana State University, 1975.

Mooney, Chace C., and Martha E. Lyman. "Some Phases of the Compulsory Training Movement, 1914–1922." *Mississippi Valley Historical Review* 38 (1952).

Peterson, H.C. *Propaganda for War: The Campaign Against American Neutrality, 1914–1917.* Norman: University of Oklahoma Press, 1939.

Prisoners of War

When the First World War shattered the peace of Europe in the summer of 1914, most Europeans were caught by surprise. Even the generals who had spent their professional lives preparing for war were shocked by its arrival. What surprised them even more were the nature and duration of the conflict that the diplomats had unleashed. For a century, most of Europe's wars had been short and decisive. The generals had assumed that the next would be like those past. But they miscalculated. With the failure of Germany's Schlieffen Plan, the short decisive war of movement that they had anticipated bogged down into one of attrition. This had a decided impact on the fate of prisoners. The machine guns and artillery churned out by Europe's factories, combined with the deadlock on the front lines, produced a quantum leap in casualties above anything known to Europeans in the preceding century. The same conditions that produced mass casualties produced prisoners in unprecedented numbers.

Just as the generals were unprepared for modern industrialized warfare, the governments they served were unprepared to accommodate the hordes of prisoners their armies captured. Expecting a short war, none of the belligerent powers had made any serious plans for the long-term detention of large numbers of prisoners. Yet within six months there were between 1.3 and 1.4 million men in captivity throughout Europe. Never before in European history had so many prisoners been detained. By the end of the war, at least 6.5 million and perhaps as many as 8.5 million prisoners were held in camps dispersed throughout the continents of Europe, Asia, Africa, and North America. Of these, Germany held some 2.5 million and Russia 2.24 million—roughly 70 percent of the total. Since Germany captured most of its prisoners early in the war while it was on the offensive, it also held them much longer than the French, British, and the Americans, who captured the majority of their prisoners in the last year of the war as Germany finally collapsed.

No nation was even remotely prepared to deal with this huge influx of unexpected guests. Consequently, each scrambled and often failed to find suitable housing for prisoners. At the war's outset, the "host" countries set up tent camps and used all sorts of vacant buildings, ranging from breweries and stables to convents, castles, military barracks, steamboats, and warehouses. Some of these facilities were adequate and some were not, but by and large, the belligerent powers attempted to improve conditions, when time and resources permitted them to do so. Furthermore, they tried to live up to their obligations under international law. In this respect, the conditions of military captivity during the First World War were decidedly superior to those that prevailed across wide theaters of conflict during the Second World War.

During the half century preceding the outbreak of the war, European statesmen had made a major effort to regulate the conduct of warfare. Beginning in Brussels in 1874, a number of conferences drafted codes of conduct designed to humanize military conflict. This diplomatic trend culminated in a pair of "peace conferences" that took place in The Hague in 1899 and 1907. Each of these conferences drafted conventions regulating the conduct of warfare. An entire section of each convention was devoted to the care and treatment of prisoners. Thus, only seven years prior to the outbreak of the war, Europe's diplomats had agreed upon and codified an unprecedented statement about how they would treat prisoners in the event of another war. Yet, comprehensive as these agreements were, they proved deficient.

The major purpose of the prisoner sections of these agreements was to insure uniformly humane treatment of those incarcerated. This, however, proved extraordinarily difficult for a number of reasons inherent in both the treaties and the circumstances of the war. First, the 1907 agreement was technically not in effect at the outbreak of the war because it had not been ratified by all parties to the conflict. This was not as great an obstacle to implementation of its terms as it might have been. The 1899 convention, which was very similar, had been ratified by all concerned and therefore was in effect; furthermore, most of the major belligerents declared their intention to honor the terms of the 1907 agreement notwithstanding its nonbinding status as long as the enemy did so on a reciprocal basis. Reciprocity thus became the key to uniformity of treatment.

Reciprocity, however, depended upon the exchange of accurate information about how the enemy was treating prisoners. Given wartime conditions and animosities, such information was difficult to obtain. As a consequence, rumors of mistreatment spread widely and rapidly, spurring public demands for retaliation. If left unchecked, this situation could have escalated out of control. Fortunately for Europe and its prisoners, however, a number of neutral nations, the United States most prominent among them, intervened through the use of their good offices as protecting powers to supply the necessary information. The United States served as protecting power for German prisoners captured by Britain, France, and Russia. It likewise served as protecting power for British prisoners captured by Germany. As a consequence, American embassies and consulates in these nations and their dependencies served as bases from which American diplomats fanned out to visit and inspect prison camps throughout the nation to which they were accredited. Copies of the reports they filed were sent back to those governments whose soldiers were interned abroad, thus providing them with an accurate picture of prevailing prison conditions. Typically, these reports indicated that the detaining powers were making a reasonable, good-faith effort to abide by the Hague regulations. This

information thus replaced the rumors and misinformation that circulated prominently in the press and made it possible for governments to resist the common demands for harsh retaliatory treatment. The neutral inspection program, which was also carried out by Spanish, Swedish, and eventually Swiss diplomats, thus short-circuited the retaliatory spiral that might otherwise have developed. In this way, neutral inspection, which was pioneered quite early in the war, made it possible for the belligerent powers to attempt to adhere to the Hague rules. They did not always succeed, but this was seldom due to malice. More often than not, it was the result of incompetence, disorganization, and the sheer inability to deal with the huge numbers of prisoners whom they had captured.

Despite the availability of accurate information, there were other obstacles to uniformly humane treatment of prisoners. One of the most persistent problems was that the applicable terms of the conventions were subject to conflicting interpretations. Each convention, for example, called for the detaining power to house, clothe, and feed prisoners in the same way it housed, clothed, and fed its own troops. Since these conditions varied from one army to another, strict adherence to these standards meant that some prisoners would be treated better than others. German prisoners of the Russians, or British prisoners of the Germans, would not fare as well as they were accustomed to, even if the host power lived up to its obligations under the 1907 convention because lower standards existed in those countries.

Although the delegates to the Hague conferences had attempted to anticipate all the problems that would arise, they failed. They had drafted conventions that might have worked during the short conflicts of the nineteenth century when prisoners were exchanged or repatriated quickly. But given the extended duration of captivity that prevailed during the First World War, all sorts of unexpected issues arose to complicate the administration and diplomacy of captivity. Pay scales, for example, varied from nation to nation and led to constant disputes between the belligerents about how much to pay prisoners (enlisted men were paid for their labor, while officers were paid even though they could not be required to work). Dietary habits, likewise, differed and led to acrimonious disputes not covered by the terms of the agreements. British prisoners did not like German food; German prisoners did not like

French or Russian food. What is more, different ration quantities were in effect in each army, thus leading to disagreements about both quantity and the menu. Disagreements of this sort broke out among the belligerents about virtually every aspect of the confinement of prisoners. Disagreements included, but were not limited to, the quality of their housing, the nature and extent of mail privileges, the number of blankets issued, the number of baths permitted, and the nature and hours of labor demanded of them. To their great credit, the belligerent powers more or less successfully negotiated agreements during the war resolving most of these disputes. The conferences that took place and the agreements that they reached were notable diplomatic achievements of the war.

An early example of the manner in which the belligerents cooperated to overcome the harsh realities of internment was a program run by the Swiss permitting the internment in Switzerland of invalid prisoners of several nationalities. What began as an experiment in January 1916 with the internment of 100 German and 100 French prisoners quickly expanded until about 26,000 French, British, and German invalids were interned by the year's end. Although there was regular turnover among these prisoners as they were mutually repatriated, their overall numbers remained about the same through the remainder of the war. The internment of sick and wounded prisoners in a neutral country was a humanitarian experiment unique to the First World War. Not only did it help preserve the lives and health of tens of thousands of prisoners, but it also served as a "confidence-building measure" that led to the negotiation of comprehensive bilateral agreements among the British, French, Americans, and Germans regulating the treatment of war prisoners.

In May 1917, the French and the Germans met in Berne, Switzerland, in order to negotiate a comprehensive prisoner-of-war agreement to supplement the Hague conventions. Shortly after they reached agreement, the British met the Germans in The Hague for the same purpose. Like the French, they too drafted a convention that attempted to fill in the gaps in the Hague arrangements. A year later, the Germans and British met again to expand upon their first agreement. Finally, on Nov. 11, 1918, as the Armistice went into effect on the Western Front, the Germans and the Americans signed an extraordinarily comprehensive agreement regulating the treatment of prisoners in exquisite detail. This series of agreements thus addressed and overcame many of the shortcomings of the Hague conventions.

There was, however, another type of obstacle to uniformly humane treatment of prisoners. This difficulty was grounded in inadequate infrastructure, disorganization, incompetence, and sheer inability to handle large numbers of prisoners. Problems of this sort were most apparent in Russia, the state least able to withstand the economic, social, and political pressures engendered by the conflict. In Russia, organizational and logistical problems were compounded by severe weather, which contributed heavily to the relatively high mortality rate among prisoners held there. There are no reliable statistics regarding the death of prisoners in Russian custody, but it is clear that somewhere between 400,000 and 600,000 died. This is a mortality rate of between 17 and 25 percent—roughly four to five times the 4.8 percent mortality rate in German prison camps.

Although inclement weather took its toll in Germany as well, poor conditions, overcrowding, and shortages caused by the overwhelming number of prisoners and the British blockade, which materially affected the health of the civilian population, clearly had an effect on prisoners. Other problems in German camps were caused in significant measure by a highly decentralized military structure that administered the camps. This administrative arrangement made it difficult for Germany to maintain uniformity of treatment from camp to camp because it gave a great deal of independence to individual camp commanders. Some of these were competent, well-disposed officers who did their best to make captivity tolerable if not pleasant for their charges. Others were harsh disciplinarians who believed it their duty to make life miserable for the prisoners in their custody, often in retaliation for the rumored mistreatment of their own countrymen held abroad. Such difficulties were particularly common early in the war not only in Germany but also across Europe. But as international accords were reached, the powers began to replace the overly harsh and incompetent commanders with more just and efficient ones. They likewise began to replace the tent camps that sprang up in 1914–1915 with more permanent barracks that provided better housing. While conditions did improve as the war progressed, particularly in the West, this was not the case in Russia, which underwent economic, political, and military collapse under the pressure of war and revolution.

Throughout Europe, as men poured into the armed forces, labor shortages developed. In part, women filled the gap, but prisoners were also put to work in increasing numbers as the war went on. The Hague conventions made it illegal to compel officers to work, but there was in international law no impediment to the labor of enlisted prisoners.

France and Germany each began to employ prisoners early in 1915. Britain did not begin to do so in significant numbers until over a year later. Initially in France there was a good deal of public opposition to the use of prisoner labor, but eventually the Ministry of War insisted that various government agencies employ prisoners on a trial basis. The experiment was an overwhelming success and quickly spread throughout the economy. In January 1915, barely 10 percent of the prisoners in France were employed; by July, roughly 75 percent were. By the end of the year, the government could not meet the demand for prisoner labor.

The picture was much the same in Germany. The employment of prisoners began on a small scale early in 1915, but by the end of 1916, over 1.1 million prisoners were at work in Germany. Of these, about 340,000 worked in industry, while the remainder labored in agriculture. The Russians also employed prisoners in large numbers. Shortly before the collapse of the monarchy at the beginning of 1917, the government estimated that approximately 1,077,000 prisoners were employed. Of these, some 43 percent were involved in agriculture, while 27 percent worked in mines and factories. Most of the remainder worked in the timber industry or on railroads and canals.

The employment of prisoners in British custody was relatively late to develop and was never complete. As noted, British employment of prisoners did not even begin until mid-1916 and then only on a very limited basis. British use of prisoners on the Continent began with the employment of a mere 3,000 and had only reached 12,300 German prisoners by October. By March 1917, there were only about 7,000 German prisoners at work in Britain proper; by the end of the war, that number had grown to only 67,000, fewer than half of those in custody and available to work in the United Kingdom. The United States was much more efficient in its use of prisoners. The American Expeditionary Force captured some 48,280 enemy sol-

diers. Almost all of these were held in camps in France, and almost all were put to work.

The Hague conventions stipulated that "the tasks [at which prisoners were employed] must have nothing to do with military operations." At first, the belligerents attempted to honor this restriction, employing the bulk of prisoners well behind the lines in agriculture, forestry, and other pursuits with but a tangential relationship to the war effort. But as the war went on, prisoners were increasingly employed in occupations with a more direct relationship to the war if not to specific operations. In France, for example, many were engaged in manufacturing military equipment, while others repaired rails and roads in the "zone of military operations." The French initially hesitated to employ prisoners in this way, but by October 1915, they became convinced that the Germans were doing so. With that they dropped their inhibitions and retaliated in kind. Work with a fairly direct relationship to military activities accordingly became a common feature of the prisoner's experience regardless of which nation held him in detention. The labor of war prisoners eventually became vital to the economies of most of the European belligerents.

During preceding centuries, it had been the practice to exchange prisoners during hostilities, usually "man for man, rank for rank," in accordance with an elaborate plan worked out either between battlefield commanders or diplomats. This relatively humane practice was a casualty of the American Civil War and was not revived during the First World War. As a result, most prisoners, once captured, remained in custody until they died, escaped, were interned, or were repatriated at the conclusion of hostilities. The vast majority had to await the end of the war.

On the Eastern Front, the repatriation of German, Austro-Hungarian, and Russian prisoners was nominally governed by the terms of the Treaty of Brest Litovsk, which superseded those of the Hague conventions. The treaty required the prompt repatriation of prisoners, but neither side made much effort to comply with this provision. Russian prisoners had become a vital source of agricultural labor in Germany, which could spare no soldiers from the front to replace them. As a consequence, the Germans delayed the repatriation of prisoners as long as possible.

The Treaty of Brest Litovsk was only in force between March and November 1918, when it was superseded by the terms of the Armistice. During that time, the Germans and the Austro-Hungarians were able to compel the repatriation of roughly 1 million prisoners held in Russia. Nevertheless, well over 1 million remained in Russia by November. Of these, the Bolsheviks recruited at least 50,000 and perhaps as many as 200,000 Hungarians, Germans, and Austrians into the Red Army's International Brigades, which fought during the Civil War. Others, such as Kolchak's famous Czech Legion, joined the counterrevolutionaries and fought on the other side in Russia's internal conflict. Tens of thousands of others who were repatriated both before and after the November Armistice had been infected with revolutionary propaganda, and they returned to Germany and especially Austria and Hungary as dedicated revolutionaries.

With the German collapse in November 1918, tens of thousands of ragged German and Austro-Hungarian prisoners who had not been swept up in the Russian Civil War began the long trek home on foot. Simultaneously, as civil order began to break down in Germany, tens of thousands of equally ragged Russian prisoners in Germany began the trek eastward. The Russian prisoners were unwelcome wherever they went. Poles regarded them with deep hostility. In Russia itself, the returning prisoners were suspect. Whites regarded the enlisted men as potential Bolshevik recruits, while the latter regarded the officers as counterrevolutionaries. Returning Russian prisoners often faced the choice of execution or recruitment into a combat unit. Whether they traveled east or west, thousands perished as a result of hunger, disease, and violence during this long, cold march home. In short, a chaotic process of repatriation was underway east of the Elbe.

In the west meanwhile, the triumphant Allied powers insisted upon the rapid return of their own nationals from Germany. Just as in the east, many British, French, and American prisoners began to walk overland across Germany. But the Allies quickly established a Subcommission on Prisoners of War of the Permanent International Armistice Commission to coordinate the repatriation of war prisoners. Accordingly, reception units were created within the Allied armies to process returning prisoners. The large majority of Western prisoners were repatriated in accord with the plans made by the commission. Over 576,000 had arrived in France by the end of the year, and by the beginning of February, virtually all 937,000 non-Russian prisoners in German custody had been returned. Meanwhile, the chaotic flow of prisoners on the Eastern Front continued as did the Soviet Civil War. Close to 100,000 German and Austro-Hungarian prisoners remained in the Soviet Union in mid-1920. As late as 1924, between 6,000 and 7,000 had not returned home.

The repatriation of German prisoners in Allied custody was also subject to considerable delay; although when it finally did get underway, it was well organized and efficient. The Allies refused to repatriate German prisoners until the conclusion of the peace conference in June 1919 at the earliest. But even then, the French in particular, who wanted to exploit prisoner labor as long as possible, tried to delay their return until after the ratification of the treaty. But the British and Americans who had little use for prisoner labor found their maintenance burdensome and insisted on repatriating their prisoners as soon as possible. Accordingly, the British repatriated all German prisoners in their custody during September and October 1919. The Americans repatriated all of their German prisoners in late September. Upon the completion of the Anglo-American repatriation effort, the French finally returned German prisoners to their homeland. For prisoners, the war was over at last.

The First World War marked a watershed in the treatment of military prisoners. For the first time in modern European history, huge numbers of prisoners were seized and held in captivity for years. Several hundred thousand, especially in Russia, perished as a result of hunger and disease. Millions probably suffered and survived the ravages of both. Yet most lived lives of spartan simplicity and returned from the camps with their health intact. Most prisoners, especially west of the Elbe, were better off spending four years in an enemy prison camp than in a trench on the Western Front. The scale of suffering was unprecedented by the standards of the nineteenth century; yet it was modest in comparison to the catastrophic experience of prisoners during the Second World War.

In stark contrast to the calculated cruelties and deliberate genocide of the Second World War, most of the suffering during the First World War was caused by incompetence, disorganization, and the collapse of the military and political institutions responsible for the custody of prisoners. It was a tragic consequence of total war waged by nations unprepared to do so. It was not the result of policy. Indeed, Europe's diplomats made extraordinary and unprecedented efforts to expand and elaborate upon the protections granted prisoners in the Hague conventions.

Richard B. Speed

Bibliography

Brandstrom, Elsa. *Among Prisoners of War in Russia and Siberia*. London: Hutchinson, n.d.

Dennett, Carl P. *Prisoners of the Great War*. Boston: Houghton Mifflin, 1984.

McCarthy, Daniel J. *The Prisoner of War in Germany: The Care and Treatment of the Prisoner of War with a History of the Development of the Principle of Neutral Inspection and Control*. New York: Moffat, Yard, 1918.

Speed, Richard B. *Prisoners, Diplomats and the Great War: A Study in the Diplomacy of Captivity*. Westport, CT: Greenwood Press, 1990.

Williamson, Samuel R., Jr., and Peter Pastor, eds. *Essays on World War I: Origins and Prisoners of War*. New York: Columbia University Press, 1983.

Propaganda

British Propaganda in the United States

British propaganda rightly could be stated to have begun on Aug. 5, 1914, when Britain cut the cables between Germany and the United States. From that date forward, neither the Imperial German nor the American governments could rapidly communicate with the other. The news from Britain became the only war news received in the United States. It was not until later in the year that German dispatches to the United States via trans-Atlantic wireless resumed. Transmission was limited and slower than the British communications; consequently, it failed to have an immediate impact on the American public.

At about this same time, the British government inaugurated censorship of its own news media under the Defense of the Realm Act and in effect curtailed, even more than before, the war news received by the American public. From that point onward, the news became entirely controlled. News in Britain was issued through the military and naval censors under a government body entitled the Press Censorship Committee until 1916, when its name was changed to Press Bureau. All news coming out of Europe flowed through Britain and filtered through its censors. American newspaper editors, not able to circulate their own correspondents in the war zone because of French and British restrictions and not able to obtain more than "advance sheets" from their opposites in Great Britain, had to rely upon French and British official communiques, which were nothing more than propaganda handouts. The next step for the British government was to establish a postal censorship on Aug. 29, 1914, which, by early 1916, had 2,000 employees doing the censoring and by 1917 had increased to over 5,000. In addition to managing what news was going out of Britain by reading mail, the censors managed to keep tabs on potential as well as genuine enemies.

In September 1914, the British government, through its Foreign Office, established a War Propaganda Bureau and installed it at Wellington House, London. Sir Gilbert Parker was assigned the task of heading that section of the bureau that directed its product to the United States. Its name became the American Ministry of Information. As his assistants, Parker selected Macneile Dixon of Glasgow University and A.J. Toynbee of Oxford University. They soon established a mailing list of approximately 260,000 influential Americans. It was not long before they were sending position papers, books, pamphlets, and the like to libraries, universities, and colleges and to every organization where their releases would gain the attention of trendsetters in U.S. public opinion. Among those well-known British writers who were induced to write opinions and essays for the Americans were G.K. Chesterton, Arthur Conan Doyle, E.J. Trevelyan, and Hilaire Belloc as well as many others less well known. All-in-all, Wellington House was the organization from which the British government controlled what American citizens were allowed to know and think about the war going on on the European continent.

Other, mostly volunteer, groups were organized to spread British propaganda. One of them, the Central Committee for National Patriotic Organizations, located in London, started its efforts in November 1914 and soon organized many subcommittees throughout the empire and the rest of the world. Their task was to preach the British line wherever they were located. Members spoke before social clubs, working men's clubs, unions, national and international societies, and wherever they were invited. In their presentations they gave the Allied version of the facts about the war as proclaimed by the War Propaganda Bureau in Britain.

In order for British propaganda to be successful in the United States, the American citizen had to be educated rapidly and made aware of what sort of "monsters" the Allies were up against. It was not long after the war started that British propaganda agents were garnering strong support from pro-British groups and individuals in the United States. They were helped by some propaganda groups in Britain, such as the Pilgrim's Society, and in France by the Alliance France. Several American organizations also assumed the mantle of dispensers of Allied propaganda, for example, the British-American League and the Allies Aid Association. Also religious leaders (even from the pulpit), politicians, teachers, and, of course, journalists soon joined in.

From the very beginning, the British decided to make the issue one of Good versus Evil. They almost went so far as to charge that the war was a holy one. Unfortunately for the Germans, through ignorance and heavy-handedness, their actions gave credence to certain Allied postures. The invasion of Belgium set the tone. That blunder played right into the hands of the Allied propagandists. The world was horrified. Britain, which only two years before had refused to guarantee Belgium's neutrality, now conveniently had a cause to bring its own people into the war. "Poor little Belgium" was the standard cry. No less an Anglophile than Walter H. Page, the American ambassador to Great Britain, admitted that Britain would have gone to war with Germany even if France had violated Belgium. George Bernard Shaw reflected that "if our own military success were at stake, we would violate the neutrality of heaven itself." Yet the "Rape of Belgium" became the single most influential issue British propagandists used to invoke the wrath of the noncommitted world.

Certain Americans, however, were not unaware of British efforts. Col. Edward M. House, friend and confidant of President Wilson, noted in his diary on Sept. 25, 1916, "We resented some of the cant and hypocrisy indulged in by the British; for instance, as to Belgium." And Arthur Styron remarked in *The Cast Iron Man*, "Britain adopted the attitude of self-righteousness even while engaged in practices which they utterly condemn in any other nation."

The attitude put forth most frequently was that Britain was fighting the battle for democracy and for the United States and it was time for the Americans to do their part. The British continued to point to the interests and ideals of both nations as one and the same. Wellington House produced a mass of reading materials identifying goodness with "British Ideals" and any negatives as "German Ideals." Sometimes the publication titles would include the United States' "ideals and responsibilities in this war." It soon was made clear that Americans should be pro-Ally and that would make them patriotic. To be pro-German was to be anti-American. It did not take long for the average person in the United States to be convinced that to defend oneself, one had to support the Allied cause and prepare for German aggression against Americans.

The fact that the British and Americans had a common language made it easier for the propagandists to imply that Germans and their language as well as their attitudes were foreign and therefore a cause for concern. Soon, hostility toward people of Central European origins, especially Germans and Austrians, became common in the United States. Those persons, many of whom were not German, were badgered and later severely harassed by "patriotic" Americans in spite of the fact that most were American citizens.

In doing their job, the staff of Wellington House followed certain well-developed techniques. Some of those were to tell part of the truth, only that part that would benefit the Allies; to use material that implied situations for which there was not hard evidence but which put the enemy in the worst possible light; and, finally, to repeat constantly even dubious charges.

By using the semblance of accuracy in their stories, the British managed to make their propaganda more readily accepted as fact. They found that using the names of authorities to support their position lent credence to the reports. The use of writings and statements of Germans critical of Germany, albeit prepared months or years before the war, was a very successful ploy. Those tomes were reprinted many times. The British continued to appeal to every segment of the population by addressing issues as seen by every class. Constant usage of such rallying cries as "to make the world safe for democracy" or to "defend poor little Belgium" and to curb "the Hun" were among the most commonly used platitudes. Additionally, the sinking of the *Lusitania* and the execution of nurse Edith Cavell [who in fact *was* a spy], the development of heroes such as Albert, King of the Belgians, and Pétain and Haig of the British and French armies were all exploited to show how magnificent the Allies were. Conversely, the kaiser and his foolish utterances made him a perfect, ready-made villain. The fact that he was not much different in his tactless statements than Theodore Roosevelt was not fully appreciated at the time. Very easily he was portrayed to be the principal person responsible for the war. While he was pictured as a monster, his son, the crown prince, was portrayed as a weak, contemptible wretch.

British propagandists confidently predicted the eventual victory for Allied arms. Without an expectation of victory, the Americans might have reconsidered their growing desire to aid the Allies, so the imminent defeat of Germany was proclaimed as "guaranteed." Once the United States actually entered the war, American leaders were advised that victory was not certain and defeat faced the Allies if the United States did not quickly move troops to France and the firing lines.

The stories that abounded about the behavior of the German soldier in occupied Belgium and France are legion. Tales of gross demeanor—the violation of young mothers, murder of infants, destruction of homes and farms—were rampant. The worse the story, the more adherents it seemed to have. The use of implication rather than fact was a strong weapon in the British propaganda war. News about the destruction of a village would be made to seem like a willful act on the part of the enemy rather than as a regrettable act of war. The stories of German cruelty toward civilians became part of the standard package and were not corrected until after the war.

Britain also developed the "report" to a higher degree than the other belligerents. Most famous was the Bryce Report, a conglomeration of distortions, innuendo, and blatant lies. Most people that read it believed most, if not every, word in it. Later, Frederick Palmer, a pro-British American newspaperman, in his book *With My Own Eyes* said, "One could forgive Lord Bryce, so simple, so benign and ingenuous—this great liberal—for believing the evidence of extreme instances [of atrocities] which was shown him." There were many other exposés of the same type; most have the imprint of His Majesty's Stationery Office to lend further credibility to the production. There were Grey Books, Black Books, and many other color-coded titles, each offering exposés to satisfy even the most jaded reader. Of great interest was the story told by Gertrude Atherton, a well-known novelist of the time, describing the Germans inoculating prisoners with tuberculosis germs. It was not true.

To a large degree, British propaganda efforts worked. By early 1917, exposed to a steady stream of Allied stories even in their own newspapers, pulpits, social clubs, movies, and books, the American public was ready to intervene when President Wilson made his call for war to Congress on April 2, 1917.

George B. Clark

Bibliography

Kennedy, David M. *Over Here: The First World War and American Society*. New York: Oxford University Press, 1980.

Knightley, Phillip. *The First Casualty, from Crimea to Vietnam: The War Correspondent as Hero, Propagandist, and Myth Maker*. New York: Harcourt Brace Jovanovich, 1975.

Millis, Walter. *Road to War: America 1914–1917*. Boston: Houghton Mifflin, 1935.

Palmer, Frederick. *With My Own Eyes*. Indianapolis: Bobbs-Merrill, 1933.

Peterson, H.C. *Propaganda for War: The Campaign Against American Neutrality, 1914–1917*. Norman: University of Oklahoma Press, 1939.

German Propaganda in the United States

The United States remained neutral during the first thirty-two months of the war, but that status provided no protection from the barrage of propaganda that the belligerents hurled at the American public. The Germans, for example, lost no time in launching a comprehensive propaganda campaign designed to capture the sympathy of the civilian population in the United States in this most important of the uncommitted powers.

The German ambassador, Count Johann Heinrich von Bernstorff, returned to the United States in late August 1914, accompanied by German Privy Counselor Heinrich F. Albert, an agent of the Ministry of the Interior, and by Bernhard Dernburg, former chief of the German Colonial Office, who came as a representative of the German Red Cross. Within a year, Albert was designated commercial attaché by the ambassador, probably to give him diplomatic immunity. As an envoy of the Central Purchasing Agency, he soon exercised control over all German financial operations in the United States, including purchasing and shipping supplies to Germany, underwriting espionage and sabotage activities, and floating war loans.

Early in September 1914, Bernstorff established the German Information Service, a propaganda bureau, in New York City, under the immediate direction of Dernburg. Here, too, Albert would come to exercise broad leadership in all matters of propaganda. Indeed, he would eventually carry on all his activities from these offices on Broadway. Assisting him was a small staff from the idled Hamburg-American Line, German diplomatic officials from the Far East stranded in New York, and a few German-American and American sympathizers. Among these were Matthew B. Claussen, press agent; Julius P. Meyer, vice-director; and Alfred Cronemeyer, passenger agent of the Hamburg-American Line. In addition, there were Karl A. Fuehr, formerly in the German consulate in Yokohama, two other consular officials from the Far East—Karl Mechlenburg and Wilhelm H. Plage—and Privy Counselor Anton M. Gerhard, who came from the Colonial Office with Dernburg.

Significantly, George Sylvester Viereck, German-American poet, journalist, and flamboyant publicist, was asked to join the bureau at the outset. Within weeks of the outbreak of the war in Europe, he launched the weekly journal, the *Fatherland*, devoted to placing the "German side of this unhappy quarrel fairly and squarely before the American people." Weekly circulation quickly reached more than 100,000 copies, and it remained more popular than any other pro-German journal prior to American entry into the war. Viereck's success soon brought him financial rewards from the German Foreign Office and the propaganda bureau for this and other journalistic endeavors. Another major contributor was the well-known author and journalist with the Hearst News Syndicate, William Bayard Hale.

The necessity of reaching the American public as soon as possible with the German interpretation of events was immediately apparent to the propagandists in New York. The quickest way to catch the eye of the American reader was through the daily newspaper. Thus, it was decided to circulate a daily news bulletin. The first issue, which was published by the American Press Association, appeared late in October 1914 and was circulated to a large number of newspapers from coast to coast. The sheet carried the message that the material included was offered for "publication without charge" and was "released for use upon receipt." The topics in each issue varied widely. A typical issue in the spring of 1915 carried columns on munitions shipments to the Allies, the threat of Russian conquest in the Balkans, German occupation of the French industrial areas, British difficulties in obtaining recruits, Russian atrocities against Jews and Catholics, the cruel treatment of refugees by the French, and the humane treatment of prisoners by the Germans. The majority of articles were designed to favor the Central Powers; nevertheless, there were a sufficient number of purely informational items that might appeal to an American press surfeited with news of the Allied side of the war. Many important papers accepted the bulletins. The *New York Evening Post*, for one, announced in August 1915 that it had regularly received and made use of the news sheets.

By the fall of 1915, the Information Service was under the editorial direction of Hale, and its activities had expanded to include the publication and circulation of scores of pamphlets and books. The service opened two more offices, and meetings were also held at New York's Ritz-Carlton Hotel and the offices of the Hamburg-American Line.

Dernburg's connection had been terminated with his recall to Germany after, in a speech in Cleveland, he had offered a strident defense of the sinking of the *Lusitania*. The service, meanwhile, in conjunction with Viereck's *Fatherland* had established the Jackson Press, from which poured an increasing flow of pro-German or anti-Ally literature. With German assistance, Viereck also organized or revived several journals, such as the *International Monthly, Current Opinion, Vital Issue,* the *American Independent,* and the *National Courier*, all of whose columns were heavily weighted with stories on the German side of the conflict.

While the bureau was still under Dernburg's direction, the members began experimenting with motion pictures as a propaganda device. The American Correspondent Film Corporation was established under approval of the Foreign Office in the spring of 1915. Scores of German war films and pro-German films made on the home front were circulated, particularly in the middle and western states. The operation was headed by Karl A. Fuehr, Matthew Claussen, and Felix Malitz. They managed to secure the cooperation of the Hearst newspaper syndicate in sharing films and also obtaining the services of American commentators to supplement the films with lectures. Although German officials supported the enterprise, German commercial film companies were not cooperative, and the potential of this form of disseminating news and opinion were never fully realized. Even so, the film corporation continued in operation until after the United States entered the war.

The propagandists did not confine their activities to issuing bulletins and press releases nor even to circulating pro-German films or a host of materials that flowed in directly from Germany. Dernburg traveled widely, speaking on every side of the German cause and writing articles for journals such as the *New York Times, Current History*, the *Independent, North American Review,* and *World's Work* among others. Topics such as "The Case of Belgium," "England—Traitor to the Whole Race," "When Germany Wins," and "The Ties That Bind America and Germany" drew much response and helped keep the German side ever before the American public. Fuehr's *The Neutrality of Belgium . . . Under Its Aspects in Political History and International Law* was a detailed analysis of the Belgian case based in part on documents from the Belgian Foreign Office archives and received several favorable reviews in the American press. Hale offered, among other works, "American Rights and British Pretensions on the Seas," "Peace or War: The Great Debate in Congress on the Submarine and the Merchantman," and "Thou Shalt Not Kill: The Exportation of Arms and Munitions." The latter was a severe indictment of the munitions trade written for the Organization of American Women for Strict Neutrality, in whose origin and operation Hale played an important role.

The German Information Service also circulated spontaneous defenses of the German side by American professors who had studied in Germany, such as John W. Burgess, James Harvey Robinson, William R. Shepherd, George Stuart Fullerton, and others. Joining these American professors was a number of prominent German professors who were teaching in the United States; Hugo Munsterberg and Edmund von Mach of Harvard and Kuno Francke of Boston wrote extensively and frequently, gaining respectful attention in the press for such works as "The Peace and America," "Germany's Point of View," "Why Germany Is at War," and many articles on German culture and its people.

Fuehr and his associates did not fail to see the advantages of working through American minorities. From the first, the Irish Americans were valuable allies. They were frequently willing to combine their anti-British campaigns with German efforts. The propaganda bureau with the approval of Bernstorff also extended help to American Jewish groups who were vocal in their opposition to an entente in which Russia held a partnership. Aid went as well to Hindu factions in the United States who hoped to foster a rebellion in India. Some of this kind of activity bordered on sabotage, and, indeed, some German consular officials who were leading these efforts were apprehended by American authorities and imprisoned.

Thus these varied activities and agencies helped to create a German propaganda machine of many cogs. One essential cog, however, was missing from the apparatus at the beginning. Important though the information bulletins were, there could be little certainty as to their use. The Germans needed not only to supply news, but also to control an outlet with broad public contact. The importance of owning a reputable daily journal was recognized by German officials at the outset. By the end of 1914, the search had settled on the *New York Evening Mail,* which was available and recommended by Edward A. Rumley, a friend of Dernburg. After months of exchanges with the Foreign Office, the latter agreed to the purchase of the newspaper for an eventual sum of approximately $2 million, the bulk of which reportedly came from the sale of German Treasury notes in the United States.

As a weapon of propaganda, the *Evening Mail's* impact was lessened by the necessity to obscure its ownership and effect at least a semblance of neutrality. On the other hand, the newspaper's usefulness to the Germans should not be underestimated. They were now assured of open channels for news from Central Europe and afforded a direct line to the American public. But the opportunities provided by the acquisition of the *Evening Mail* came late in the game. No doubt, as Viereck later claimed, because of the lack of early and vigorous support from the home office, the propagandists lost the opportunity to acquire several strong newspapers with an open mind to the causes of the war and that might have stiffened the resistance of those numerous Americans opposed to the war.

Even a partial survey of their activities reveals that Germany's spokesmen succeeded in a whole host of campaigns to place the German interpretation of the war and its causes before the American people. The Germans were not cut off in America as the British claimed. There was a constant flow of information and materials via the mails and open shipping lines and the wireless from the Continent. As a matter of fact, the British never succeeded in isolating the Germans in America.

Of course, the propagandists never entertained any realistic hope that the United States would enter the war on the side of the Central Powers. The strong Anglo-American cultural bonds were never underestimated. But a presentation of the facts as the Germans saw them was not to be enough in the face of the course of events. Beginning with the sinking of the *Lusitania* in May 1915, the horror of the submarine seemed ever on the horizon reminding Americans of the ruthlessness of the German military. Most military incidents on the land seemed deliberately planned to intensify the difficulties of the propagandists. The work of German agents and saboteurs was constantly being exposed until Americans began to see German spies behind every tree. The usually astute Albert added to the troubles when, in July 1915, he absentmindedly left his briefcase on the New York elevated train. It was quickly seized by a United States Secret Service agent, and subsequently much of the contents were published in the *New York World*. His papers revealed that Albert was head not only of a vast system of propaganda, but more importantly of an intricate system of espionage. The exposures were a severe blow to the work of the German propagandists. But that work by no means came to an end. The circulation of news, articles, and books continued apace, though the tone of articles became perhaps more informative and less assertive. The ambassador made special efforts to cultivate the press, and there was an increasing flow of statements from leaders of the German government appealing for understanding of the German position and their reasons for the coming of war. Also a steady and impressive flow of eloquent messages came from the academic and religious leaders of Germany and were given special attention in the press by their American counterparts.

In time, both the British and the Americans were to express admiration of the quality and vigor of the German campaign to influence neutral America. The United States took thirty-two months to reach the decision to put aside its neutral stance. The constant insistence by the German spokesmen in America that there were two sides to the whole issue of the war may have had more influence on that long decision than usually acknowledged.

David W. Hirst

Bibliography

Bernstorff, Johann von. *My Three Years in America*. New York: Scribner, 1920.

Doerries, Reinhard R. *Imperial Challenge: Ambassador Count Bernstorff and German-American Relations, 1908–1917*. Chapel Hill: University of North Carolina Press, 1989.

Hirst, David W. "German Propaganda in the United States, 1914–1917." Ph.D. dissertation, Northwestern University, 1962.

Viereck, George Sylvester. *Spreading Germs of Hate*. New York: Liveright, 1930.

Pruden, Alfred Adino (1866–1942)

Alfred Adino Pruden was born in Virginia and was educated at the Suffolk Military Academy of Virginia. After graduating from the Theological Seminary of Virginia in 1894, Pruden was ordained an Episcopal minister and served as chaplain to the First North Carolina Volunteer Infantry in the Spanish-American War. After the war, Pruden returned to civilian life, but in 1901, he was sworn in as a chaplain in the Regular Army with the rank of captain. In 1909, Pruden served as one of a six-member board of senior chaplains that met at Fort Leavenworth, Kansas, to make recommendations to the War Department for a more effective chaplaincy. Of the twelve points proposed by the board, six were approved and two, including an increase in the number of chaplains, were postponed. However, Pruden's most important contribution to the chaplaincy came during World War I when he planned and organized the first army training school for chaplains.

With the entrance of the United States into World War I in April 1917, the nation was immediately faced with the necessity of building up its small army to a size not seen since the Civil War. This expansion meant a large increase in the number of chaplains in order to serve these new forces. The central problem faced by the Army was how to introduce large numbers of priests, ministers, and rabbis, with little or no military background, into the service. The answer was obviously a school for these newly chosen chaplains. The next challenge to be met was how this new school was to be structured. In the fall of 1917, the General Committee on Army and Navy Chaplains, a government agency that oversaw applications for service as chaplains, presented a plan to the War Department for the establishment of a training school for candidates. The department approved this initiative and turned it over to Chaplain Pruden to develop the details. Under Pruden's plan, the school to be located at Fort Monroe, would provide a curriculum to introduce the new chaplain to military life. The General Committee accepted the plan and recommended its adoption by the War Department. The latter concurred with the recommendation, and on Feb. 9, 1918, the Secretary of War approved Pruden's design with only a few minor changes. Chaplain Pruden, known as the "Father of the U.S. Army Chaplain School," was appointed as the school's first commandant, also in February, and remained commandant while the school was located at Fort Monroe. After the facility was transferred to Camp Zachary Taylor, Kentucky. Pruden was reassigned in September 1918. He was later promoted to the rank of lieutenant colonel, and retired from the army in 1920.

William J. Hourihan

Bibliography

Honeywell, Roy J. *Chaplains of the United States Army.* Washington, DC: Office of the Chief of Chaplains, 1958.

Stover, Earl F. *Up From Handymen: The United States Army Chaplaincy, 1865–1920.* Washington, DC: Office of the Chief of Chaplains, 1977.

Psychological Testing

Mass psychological testing technology emerged in World War I as psychologists helped U.S. Army officers rationalize personnel selection. The assessments known as Army Alpha and the Trade Tests, which were prototypes of modern "aptitude" and "achievement" tests, took shape as the products of a series of accommodations. The compromises that wartime exigencies induced—within and between psychology and the military and between the diverse interests of positivist research, the division of labor, upper-class elitism, middle-class bureaucracy, and meritocracy—formed the pervasive technology of modern social control that is mass mental testing.

Army Alpha, the first nationally standardized mental test that was given to large groups simultaneously, emerged with a new purpose for testing "general intelligence," also known as "g." Prior to the war, the most prominent American intelligence testers, Robert M. Yerkes and Lewis M. Terman, developed rival scales (series of tests) to diagnose mental abnormality (deficiency and genius). Yerkes and Terman both believed their research would distinguish theoretical from practical abilities as the most important development in mental evolution. Both also believed their research presented the rational next step in social progress, although they differed regarding the social purposes to which "g" testing should be put.

Yerkes developed the "point scale" examination method. The scale would pinpoint the range of "g" amounts that defined, for him, the quantitative continuum between primate and human mentality. Based on his presumption of a linear evolutionary hierarchy, Yerkes planned to design one scale for all humans age three and older. A single scale would make a "pure" objectification of evolutionary reality, which would be very useful in discerning the degrees of "g" Yerkes expected to find differentiated by racial, class, and gender groupings.

Much less than "pure," in Yerkes's opinion, was Terman's Stanford Revision of Alfred Binet's "age scale(s)," a collection of test series designed for each pre-adult age group. While the point scale bolstered the traditional social supremacy of upper-class white males, the age scale bolstered the nineteenth-century liberal ascendancy of middle-class white males by facilitating the public school system's division of students into age grades.

Yerkes and Terman competed for Rockefeller Foundation funding of a national experimental program, but neither was successful and neither was willing to accept the foundation's advice to combine their research projects. American entry into World War I inspired Yerkes to renew his funding application with a proposal that addressed wartime needs, at least as Yerkes conceived them, and ignored Terman's research.

As president of the American Psychological Association (APA) in 1917, Yerkes was the first to bring psychology to the military's attention. Working through the new National Research Council (NRC), Yerkes gained the support of Army Surgeon General William Gorgas (an NRC member) for a plan to eliminate the mentally deficient with the use of the point scale. After psychiatric members of the Army Medical Corps objected to the plan as an intrusion on their own clinical mission and quashed the renewed application by Yerkes for Rockefeller funds, the method of "g" testing began shifting away from clinical diagnosis.

The shift originated in the prewar research of lesser-known psychologists, some of whom were colleagues and students of "g" testers concerned with superior levels of mentality. Walter V. Bingham, a "pure" intelligence tester who reluctantly accepted the opportunity to found the first American department of applied psychology, oversaw the experimentation of Louis Leon Thurstone and Walter D. Scott with group testing devices. Three weeks after America entered the war, Bingham asked Terman if he would consider the development of a mass administration format. Terman responded that his student, Arthur Otis, was working on a stencil system for rapid grading of answers to multiple-choice questions. Bingham relayed this information to Yerkes, who, following the latest Rockefeller rejection, invited Terman to a national conference on intelligence examining at the Vineland, N.J., Training School for the Feeble-minded. On the first day of the meeting, which followed the enactment of the first U.S. conscription law (May 18, 1917) by ten days, Bingham and Terman convinced Yerkes to direct psychological activities toward the construction and administration of a group intelligence test. Otis was then summoned to the conference, which in six weeks developed and conducted a preliminary trial of group mental test questions (in ten categories, including analogies, general information, and mathematical ability).

The conference ended with a new testing format in hand but without consensus on how to validate it. As test "validation" at this time was synonymous with test reliability (consistency of results after repeated administrations of the same test), Yerkes and Terman again competed over whose clinical scale of "g" would be used as the basis for corroborating the group test. Whoever's scales were used for this purpose stood to receive greater "legitimacy," or at least greater publicity. Not much thought was given to the idea of what the military might consider valid or valuable.

Bingham and Terman realized that army approval of intelligence testing depended on its ability to make a positive contribution to mobilization, but they did not know how the group test would be implemented to benefit the military. From his work with Thurstone and Scott, Bingham believed that the group test of general intelligence might somehow identify recruits with special talents. This practical purpose, however, existed as a vision since professional consensus was lacking for such an illogical commensuration. Indicative of the psychologists' blind faith in the determinism of "g" inheritance and resulting lack of preparation for dealing with the broad number of recruits who could not read, but who otherwise demonstrated high levels of intelligence, adjustment here led to the creation of a test for illiterates, called "Beta," which led to the naming of the original test as "Alpha."

In order to mediate his differences with Terman, Yerkes called upon another prominent intelligence tester to decide between the point and age scale validations—Edward L. Thorndike, a recent APA president whose research in animal psychology had inspired Yerkes's early career and whose development of intelligence tests for public school use was better known than Terman's. Thorndike's testing research emphasized "mediocre" human mentality, however, which led him to reject "g" theory. He conceived intelligence as a diverse mix of inherited ability complexes that the social (i.e., vocational) environment selected for survival. While refining curricula for school administrators and teachers' education at Columbia Teachers College, Thorndike developed assessments of socially useful mental abilities, such as handwriting. Between 1912 and 1917, Thorndike provided businesses with scales to rate clerical skills in employees that complemented the student evaluation process. He inspired Scott, who had the most experience of any psychologist in working with business clients, to develop a Rating Scale for Selecting Salesmen. Scott tailored the qualities to accommodate the personal criteria employers desired in their salesmen or, in wartime, the qualities that majors sought in prospective captains.

After Yerkes dismissed Scott's research as crudely utilitarian early in the war, Scott approached the army separately, though with the assistance of Thorndike. Scott found numerous open doors. Meeting the staff officers who oversaw general manpower mobilization policy, Scott discovered that the army lacked a coherent system of promoting officers. Due to the inchoate professional development of the military, Scott's plan for rationalizing the promotion judgments of senior officers caught the attention of leaders of three interest groups who were contending for control over officer selection in the coming million-man army and who recognized that scientific personnel evaluation methods might legitimate the criteria of officer promotion they favored. In July 1917, Maj. Grenville Clark, Adjutant General Henry P. McCain, and War College Director Joseph E. Kuhn—leaders of the elite Plattsburg (officer training) Movement, the traditional bureaucracy, and the new professional General Staff, respectively—met the psychologist who was most skilled in demonstrating the social usefulness of his then little-recognized profession.

Walter D. Scott, the leading applied psychologist in America, jumped at the chance to adapt his own pliable style of research to the social tastes of Clark, McCain, Kuhn, and numerous other officers in staff and line. His amenability and "unideological" ideology sped his success in gaining approval for the establishment of a civilian psychological committee. His better-known and more purely scientific colleagues, whose less-compromising experimental style led them to test "IQ" and "g" (and usually to scoff at Scott), immediately joined the committee to pursue their own research.

The oldest social influence on the selection of U.S. Army officers dates from the colonists' experience with the British standing army. The ensuing legacy of voluntarism gave local social elites the power to select militia officers from their own kind, by their own criteria. After the Civil War, a professional middle class emerged among certain West Point graduates. While

advancing the study of warfare as a science, they developed leadership criteria reflecting the merits of academic training and prudent expertise. The Army War College and modern General Staff, which centralized military command amidst U.S. imperial expansion, originated in the scientific planning vision of West Pointer Emory Upton, but it was realized through the patrician political leadership of Elihu Root and Theodore Roosevelt. Opposing the centralization of the military and the patrician-professional alliance that instigated it, the traditional bureau chiefs and their congressional allies struggled to defend their turf, seniority, and patronage from the intruder. However, pressure from the world stage drove Congress to create a Reserve Officer Corps to train elite volunteers on college campuses.

The model for these training centers was the voluntary preparedness project that Gen. Leonard Wood and Theodore Roosevelt helped promote at Plattsburg, New York, during the European phase of the war. When the United States entered the war, the military had to rely initially on this pool of elite officers, which led to the reservist commissioning of Clark, the Plattsburg Movement's key organizer, in the adjutant general's office.

Even though patrician preparedness was helpful in the early stages of mobilization, President Wilson's War Department did not intend to allow upper-class social status to become the key to a commission. While Roosevelt had helped sway public opinion about the need for a national draft, Secretary of War Newton D. Baker denied Roosevelt's request to raise a national volunteer Rough-Rider division early in the war; General Kuhn helped Baker deny an overseas command for Wood. Republican congressional assistance in passing the Selective Service Act (May 18, 1917) had produced a system that allowed local elites to staff the draft boards that enlisted or deferred men. But the War Department made the draft more democratically appealing on June 4, when McCain announced that candidates for later officer training camps would be selected exclusively from the ranks of conscripted men with military experience. War College Director Kuhn, who was a West Point graduate, planned a system of officer promotion based on merit rather than on seniority or upper-class background. While upper-class interests had helped institute the War College and General Staff, Kuhn's meritocratic interests reflected the Wilson administration's antipathy to Republican elitism. Despite high-level support, however, Kuhn lacked staff and a constituency among line officers and congressmen.

In order to circumvent the democratic officer promotion policy, Clark devised a method of evaluating soldiers that awarded high scores to those with prep school and college education, business experience, and membership in social clubs. Clark modeled his method on a psychological rating scale that Assistant Secretary of War Frederick P. Keppel (formerly dean of Columbia Teachers College) had brought to his attention. After the method failed to impress McCain, Clark asked that the author of the original rating scale be interviewed at the adjutant general's office. Keppel had received the scale prepared by Scott from a long-time neighbor and Columbia University colleague, E.L. Thorndike.

Scott came to Washington and began rewriting his scale to suit not only Clark, but also the traditional interest of line officers, whose approval McCain required for further War Department consideration. After a whirlwind tour of several officer training camps in mid-July, during which time Scott continually rewrote the qualitative criteria to gain widespread support, he met with Secretary Baker, who requested that Scott gain approval from the remainder of the bureau chiefs and leaders of the General Staff.

Before he met the "top brass," Scott was persuaded by a colleague to combine other psychological activities in the new committee he was proposing. Bingham had been helping develop a more sophisticated "psychological test" of inherited intelligence with the president of the American Psychological Association, Yerkes. Under Thorndike's direction, Bingham began collecting data from the officers who rated soldiers according to Scott's scale and from the new mass intelligence test. Correlation of subjective scale judgments with objective intelligence scores could demonstrate the value of the latter as a more efficient selection device.

The only objection to the psychological establishment that Scott confronted during his tour of the top military leaders was Kuhn's. The War College director reacted with outrage to the visionary plans of "college professors" but then reconsidered. Kuhn discovered the managerial potential for psychological evaluations as a whole, particularly as they might reveal recruit "aptitude." Kuhn intended to establish the new psychological committee under War College oversight, but General McCain and Major Clark made certain that the committee would be in the adjutant general's office. The Committee on the Classification of Personnel in the Army was created on Aug. 5, 1917, under the leadership of Scott, Thorndike, and Bingham.

Richard T. von Mayrhauser

Bibliography

Clifford, John Garry. *The Citizen Soldiers: The Plattsburg Training Camp Movement, 1913–1920.* Lexington: University Press of Kentucky, 1972.

Kevles, Daniel J. "Testing the Army's Intelligence: Psychologists and the Military in World War I." *Journal of American History* (1968).

Von Mayrhauser, Richard T. "Making Intelligence Functional: Walter Dill Scott and Applied Psychological Testing in World War I." *Journal of the History of the Behavioral Sciences* (1989).

———. "The Manager, the Medic, and the Mediator: The Clash of Professional Psychological Styles and the Wartime Origins of Group Mental Testing." In *Psychological Testing and American Society: 1890–1930,* ed. by Michael M. Sokal. New Brunswick, NJ: Rutgers University Press, 1987.

Pullen, Daniel D. (1885–1923)

Daniel D. Pullen spent his first two years as an officer following graduation from West Point in 1910 learning the engineering trade in Panama and on the Ohio and Willamette rivers in the United States. From August 1913 through August 1917, he was assigned as an instructor and assistant professor of military engineering at the United States Military Academy.

After a brief stint with the 7th Engineer Regiment as a staff officer and battalion commander at Fort Leavenworth, Kansas, in late 1917, Pullen, by then a major, was ordered to France in January 1918. Upon arrival there, he was assigned to the American Expeditionary Force (AEF) Tank Corps headquarters and ordered to spend time with French and British tank units learning as much as possible about the mechanical capabilities of their vehicles and how they were employed tactically.

In early June 1918, shortly after being promoted to lieutenant colonel, Pullen became chief of staff of the AEF Tank Corps, a post he held until the eve of the St. Mihiel offensive. Concerned that he might miss out on combat action, Pullen asked for and received a transfer to the 2d Engineer Regiment on August 15. Five days later he was called back to command the 3d Tank Brigade.

The 3d Tank Brigade was a headquarters and liaison organization only. BGen. Samuel D. Rockenbach, commander of the AEF Tank Corps, had made arrangements with the French to equip the two tank battalions in LtCol. George S. Patton, Jr.'s 1st (later 304th) Tank Brigade with Renault light tanks. In addition, the French agreed to supply the 1st Assault Artillery Brigade with two companies of Schneider and St. Chamont heavy tanks and three battalions of light tanks to support the American effort to reduce the St. Mihiel salient. These units operated under Pullen's tactical control. During the battle, Pullen, after personally directing a tank attack on the Bois de Cuisy, went back and rallied a force of disorganized doughboys. He led the infantry forward through a hail of machine gun fire to the ground his tanks had occupied. He was awarded the Distinguished Service Cross for his actions.

The French tank units remained in support of the U.S. First Army for the Meuse-Argonne offensive, and Pullen continued to lead them until they were withdrawn on October 10. His headquarters returned to Langres, where it picked up two light tank battalions and a heavy tank battalion and began training in preparation for relieving Patton's 1st Tank Brigade. No additional tanks were made available, and on November 9, Pullen's brigade, minus the heavy tank battalion, took over the vehicles being used by Patton's tankers. The war ended before Pullen could get his troops back into action.

Pullen remained on occupation duty in Germany with engineer units until the summer of 1919, when he was transferred to Panama. He served there as the department engineer until June 1922, when he became district engineer in Norfolk, Virginia. Pullen became ill in the summer of 1923 and died on September 22 in Walter Reed Army Hospital.

Dale E. Wilson

Bibliography

Blumenson, Martin, ed. *The Patton Papers, 1885–1940*. Boston: Houghton Mifflin, 1972.

Wilson, Dale E. *Treat 'Em Rough! The Birth of American Armor, 1917–1920*. Novato, CA: Presidio Press, 1989.

Q

Q-Ships

Q-ships, or mystery ships, were armed merchant ships manned by naval crews but disguised as unarmed civilian vessels in order to trap U-boats.

In the early years of the war, before depth charges, sound detection, and patrol aircraft, submarines were all but immune to detection or attack while submerged. However, German submarines coming upon a lone merchantman would usually conserve their limited store of torpedoes and pay lip service to international law by approaching on the surface, allowing the crew to abandon ship, and then sinking the ship with gunfire. The British Royal Navy conceived a way of exploiting this habit by sending out armed decoys disguised as merchant vessels. The Q-ship, packed with buoyant material to keep it afloat if torpedoed, would straggle behind a convoy or sail alone, hoping to entice a U-boat into approaching on the surface. If the U-boat seemed hesitant, a "panic party" of Q-ship sailors would take to the lifeboats while other crewmen remained hidden on board. Once the U-boat was within range, the Q-ship would raise its true colors, uncover its concealed guns, and destroy the U-boat before it could submerge.

The Royal Navy employed almost 200 of these ships with some success, while German U-boats continued to sink small targets with surface gunfire rather than precious torpedoes. After Germany adopted unrestricted submarine warfare in January 1917, sinking ships on sight without surfacing, the Q-ships' effectiveness dropped dramatically. In 1917, they sank only six U-boats at a cost of twenty-seven Q-ships, prompting the Royal Navy to abandon the effort. The Q-ships' contribution to the Allied war effort was small in proportion to the risks involved, accounting for only 11 of the 178 enemy submarines sunk during the war, but they probably had some deterrent effect on U-boat attacks. They also created an impressive legend, recalling the revered buccaneer roots the British and American navies shared, and produced a number of genuine heroes, such as Royal Navy Q-ship Captain Gordon Campbell, VC.

Although the Q-ships' day had passed by the time the United States entered the war in 1917, RAdm. William S. Sims, commander of the U.S. naval forces in Europe, was sufficiently impressed to ask the Royal Navy for the loan of a Q-ship, to be manned by an American crew. This American Q-ship, USS *Santee*, was torpedoed on its maiden voyage in December 1917. Its buoyant packing kept it afloat, and the crew waited eagerly for their attacker to surface to finish the job with gunfire, but the Germans wisely departed without chancing a surface appearance. The *Santee* returned to port and was retired without ever firing a shot.

Despite their modest record, both the Royal Navy and the United States Navy revived the Q-ships in the Second World War and lost several ships without sinking a single U-boat before abandoning the program once again.

David MacGregor

Bibliography

Marder, Arthur J. *From the Dreadnought to Scapa Flow*. London: Oxford University Press, 1978.

Sims, William S. *The Victory at Sea*. New York: Doubleday, Page, 1920.

Trask, David F. *Captains and Cabinets: Anglo-American Naval Relations 1917–1918*. Columbia: University of Missouri Press, 1972.

R

Railroad Administration

See UNITED STATES RAILROAD ADMINISTRATION

Railroad Transportation Services

Critical to the war effort was the smooth functioning of the nation's railroad system. Ever since railroads became sufficiently interconnected to open national markets in the 1870s, both they and an increasingly specialized and interdependent business economy evolved in mutual dependence. As railroads improved, the scope of business increased, and as business increased, traffic pressures caused the railroads to improve further. By 1917, almost 200 major private railroad corporations employed 1.7 million workers to operate over 200,000 miles of track. Although new forms of transportation were becoming significant, America's by then sophisticated industrial economy could not function without the railroads.

Such dependency posed problems for the United States government because in 1917 the country's railroads were in a depressed condition. For years shippers resented the powerful railroad corporations on whom they depended. About 1906, their political power began to overtake that of the previously invincible railroad corporations. With the passage of the Hepburn Act of 1906 and the Mann-Elkins Act of 1910, shippers controlled the policy of the Interstate Commerce Commission. They then held down railroad rates during an inflationary period, and through Congress and state legislatures, they sponsored vast tax-supported public works intended to make water and road competition to the railroads viable.

These actions depressed railroad earnings and alarmed railroad investors. After 1907, capital improvements in the railroad industry failed to keep up with traffic growth, which quadrupled between the end of the depression in 1897 and 1917. Despite the unprecedented traffic growth, railroad managers not only slowed the pace of improvements after 1907, but they also increasingly deferred maintenance and refused wage increases to their skilled employees, whose pay lagged behind that in comparable industries. By 1916 an under-maintained U.S. rail system was running at near capacity with endemic car shortages and congested terminals. About a fifth of U.S. railroad mileage operated in receivership. Various employee organizations threatened nationwide strikes. Most worrisome for all the roads was that skilled railroad workers were quitting in droves for better-paying jobs in other industries. The prospects of the railroads handling added wartime traffic looked grim.

In the Army Appropriation Act of 1916, Congress granted the President the right to take control of the private railroad system in time of war. The European belligerents either already had nationalized railroad systems before the war or had seized control of their private railroads upon the outbreak of hostilities. When Congress declared war in April 1917, however, President Wilson, despite the dire predicament of the railroad industry, chose not to follow this path. Instead, he relied on the initiatives of railroad managements to handle the emergency.

To meet the war challenge, presidents of the nation's railroads met in Washington five days after the declaration of war. Additional wartime traffic obviously would overwhelm the railroad system as it was currently operated.

What the railroad presidents wanted to do was create a mechanism by which they could enhance capacity by jointly using each others' facilities. At the same time, they wanted to ration use of the railroads. To accomplish the first objective, they formed a five-member council known as the Railroads' War Board, which would coordinate the operations of the private railroads. To accomplish the second objective, they hoped that government agencies would ration demand through traffic prioritization.

At first the dual strategy of capacity enhancement and traffic rationing met with some success. By transferring empty cars from railroads having surpluses to those with car shortages, the Railroads' War Board reduced the national car shortage by 75 percent by the end of the summer of 1917. It also persuaded the eastern railroads to discontinue passenger trains, which totaled about 20 million train miles. This was about as much service as that offered by one modestly large railroad. Cars and locomotives thus freed up could move war traffic. Such measures enabled the railroads to carry 14 percent more traffic during the summer of 1917 compared to 1916, with much less congestion.

Success was short-lived. As traffic built up, inadequate facilities increasingly plagued the railroad system. Terminal tracks too few in number and too short caused traffic to back up, as did insufficient passing and double tracks on the main lines. As an unusually severe winter gripped the country in November 1917, outmoded shops and roundhouses emerged as the most critical investment problem. For several years prior to World War I, railroads had bought progressively larger steam locomotives to pull longer and heavier trains, but the huge locomotives could not fit inside many of the old engine houses. Because of the shortage of improvement funds, many railroads tried to repair the modern machines in make-shift outdoor facilities. Under the severe traffic pressures and the bitter winter weather, such inadequate facilities could not keep the engines running.

A shortage of skilled labor, including mechanics to repair the engines, posed another problem. Rising wages and better conditions in manufacturing industries had lured many away, and those who remained became increasingly bitter. In December 1917, railroad labor was poised to call a national general strike.

To fund direly needed improvements and increased wages, railroad managements tried again to raise rates in 1917. Shippers again blocked them. By late 1917, railroad management had lost all hope for solving either the capital or the labor problem.

The Railroads' War Board also exercised insufficient authority to coordinate operations. Until the eleventh hour, it limited its efforts primarily to moving empty cars from one railroad to another. Other forms of coordination, such as joint use of terminals or arrangements for sharing traffic among competing railroads, violated the Sherman Antitrust Act. In addition, the board's limited efforts in these areas were often ignored by railroads that feared loss of competitive advantage. Only when the congestion crisis rose to alarming levels in December 1917 did the board choose to make a more concerted effort to use facilities jointly. The Justice Department then announced that it would prosecute railroads for violating the Sherman Antitrust Act.

Efforts at traffic rationing also failed dismally. Because each government department defined its traffic as having priority, the majority of rail freight traffic moved under priority designations. In August 1917, Congress created a priorities director to sort out the problem, but Judge Robert Lovett from the Union Pacific Railroad, who filled the position, chose not to act decisively. Claiming insufficient powers, he would not cancel priorities that already had been issued, nor would he determine relative priorities of freight movements that occurred after he became director.

Compounding this problem, shippers used freight cars as warehouses. After arriving at their destinations, cars sat for days or weeks before being unloaded. Railroads had indulged the shippers in this practice for years, but under the heavy demands of the fall of 1917, the practice choked yards with cars awaiting unloading.

The cumulative effects of these problems took their toll by late 1917. Augmented by a bountiful fall harvest and heavy traffic demand for heating coal, the railroads' already heavy and war-laden freight traffic surged upward in October and November. Much of the traffic moved toward eastern terminals unable to accommodate it. By November, tens of thousands of loaded cars sat awaiting their eventual unloading at factories or onto ships, leaving no room for arriving trains. Eastbound trains began backing up in passing tracks and intermediate yards for as far as 1,000 miles inland. Coal could not reach people freezing in their homes or ships waiting to sail, and unless the loaded ships departed and empty ones arrived, many of the loaded cars in the terminals could not be unloaded. The swelling numbers of loaded cars that were tied up in terminals also quickly depleted the empty-car supply, keeping shippers from getting empty cars in which to load critical goods. There also were no spare locomotives, a general strike was about to be called, and the Justice Department was on the verge of instituting an antitrust suit.

This combination of calamities compelled President Wilson to take control of the nation's railroads on Dec. 26, 1917. Congress ratified the takeover with the Federal Control Act of March 1918, under which the railroads operated until March 1, 1920. Ownership remained in private hands. In most cases the same management teams continued to direct the affairs of individual roads, but ultimate authority for directing operations resided in the director general of the United States Railroad Administration (USRA). Wilson appointed his son-in-law, Secretary of the Treasury William Gibbs McAdoo, to this position.

Under the terms of the federal takeover, the USRA was to pay the private railroad companies an annual rent equal to the average of their net income over the preceding three years. It also was to return the railroads to the private owners within twenty-one months of the cessation of war in a physical condition no worse than at the time of the takeover. If roads were returned in better condition, private owners would owe the government nothing; if roads were returned in worse condition, USRA would have to compensate the railroads for the amount of deferred maintenance.

The USRA's objectives differed little from those of the Railroads' War Board. Its most important task was to move war-related traffic where it needed to go, while reasonably serving the civilian economy. McAdoo intended to do this by increasing capacity through coordination among railroads while rationing railroad use. He also resolved to carry out these objectives with little drain on the U.S. Treasury. Railroad revenues were to pay most, if not all, railroad expenses, including the annual rents to the owners. McAdoo would make needed investments for the war effort, but he resolved not to have the government make up for years of investment and maintenance neglect prior to the war.

Unlike the Railroads' War Board, the USRA had significant powers to carry out its job. After passage of the March 1918 Federal Control Act, the USRA could ignore the Interstate Commerce Commission, state regulatory commissions, and the dictates of shippers. It could ignore antitrust laws in allocating traffic to the shortest routes or to roads with spare capacity. It could dictate traffic priorities to government departments or private shippers. It could raise rates at will. Further, it could raise capital for investment in needed facilities and rolling stock, and it could grant wage increases to retain skilled labor.

In its first year of operation, the USRA readily used all of these powers. Within days of taking power, McAdoo issued the first USRA general order directing railroad managers to develop and implement plans for eliminating competitive services, for jointly using tracks and terminals, and for eliminating unneeded passenger service. Within weeks, managers under USRA direction were routing freight over the shortest route with available capacity, regardless of railroad ownership. They used terminals with spare capacity, while they routed locomotives to roundhouses and shops with available space, regardless of shop or locomotive ownership. Where one railroad paralleled another on a crowded route, the USRA had them jointly operated as a double-track railroad. On uncrowded routes it sometimes designated one road as a main line and downgraded the other to secondary status.

The USRA greatly changed passenger operations. Where competitive passenger service existed, managers were directed to favor the service with the shortest route. In complying, railroad managers reduced the frequency of local trains while eliminating extra-fare limiteds and competitive service. By June, discontinued service equaled about 67 million annual passenger train miles. Such large-scale cutbacks provided locomotives and cars for troop trains, which operated over 12 million train miles in 1918, with each train an average of 12 cars long. This policy also provided additional locomotives for freight service and freed scarce track space for freight movement.

As an example of the types of passenger changes that occurred, the Santa Fe eliminated much of its local service in California, as well as its transcontinental service between Chicago and San Francisco, in both cases in deference to the Southern Pacific. One the other hand, both the Southern Pacific and the Salt Lake route eliminated through service between Los Angeles and Chicago in deference to the Santa Fe. Some of these changes occurred as early as January 1918; most were completed by June 1918.

Under USRA orders, railroads consolidated competing city ticket offices; in cities where track configurations and capacity permitted, they also consolidated their passenger operations into one terminal. They reduced the number of Pullman sleeping cars available for public use and reduced the assignments of observation, lounge, and dining cars. Remaining dining-car runs offered table d'hôte rather than à la carte menus. An ardent prohibitionist, McAdoo, with one day's notice, terminated the sale of alcohol in all dining cars and railroad restaurants in August 1918.

To solve the labor problem, McAdoo announced in early January 1918 that he would substantially raise wages as soon as Congress gave him authority to do so, and he would make the increases retroactive to Jan. 1, 1918. The retroactive wage increases, which were implemented in May 1918, boosted hourly rates and gave all railroad employees the eight-hour day that engine and train men had won from Congress in the Adamson Act of 1916. Most employees continued working long hours; they merely started receiving time-and-a-half pay for working more than eight hours. However, this provision required the railroads to hire about 101,000 new employees on top of their 1.73 million-person labor force of 1917. Overall, these provisions increased the costs of railroad labor by about $875 million per year. These steps were consistent with the labor market and the need to keep the railroads operating without strikes.

To pay for these provisions, the USRA raised rates as soon as the Federal Control Act gave it authority to do so. In May 1918, freight and passenger rates were hiked by 25 and 20 percent, respectively. Neither shippers nor the Interstate Commerce Commission (ICC) had a say in or recourse to USRA decisions. Because of their lack of voice, both became implacable foes of federal control.

Shippers felt USRA's power in other ways as well. The government body abolished shippers' privileges for storing goods in freight cars, and it instituted a centralized permit system by which it rationed traffic. USRA representatives in government departments and in different regions of the country funneled requests to the agency's Traffic Department, which then issued traffic permits in accordance with priorities that it established. No traffic moved without a permit.

The USRA also set up a centralized Division of Capital Expenditures for setting investment priorities. The division solicited capital improvement requests from the railroads for what they considered to be their most urgently needed projects. It then set priorities based on the importance of the project for the war effort. The planning work took several months; ultimately, the division approved $1.2 billion in projects evenly split between road improvements and new rolling stock. Only about $550 million of this amount was spent in 1918, but the USRA brought the program to completion in 1919 and early 1920, despite the fact that the war had ended. Roundhouses and shops received the highest priority, followed by passing and yard tracks, signals, and fuel stations. In addition, 2,130 new locomotives and 100,000 new freight cars built to standardized drawings were also purchased. In most cases, USRA financed the projects, but the railroads receiving them ultimately became financially responsible.

Just as the USRA was getting started, the war unexpectedly ended in November 1918. Rail labor lobbied for permanent nationalization of the railroads, and McAdoo wanted to extend federal control for five years, but most other interest groups did not. Congress soon made clear that it intended to return the railroads to their private owners, and as it debated the means for doing so over the next sixteen months, the USRA continued to run the railroads as a highly criticized caretaker organization. McAdoo resigned as director general in January 1919, and Walker D. Hines, chairman of the board of the Atchison, Topeka and Santa Fe Railway and McAdoo's assistant during most of 1918, stepped into his shoes.

During World War I, few groups criticized the manner in which the USRA managed the railroads, but shippers attacked federal control as soon as hostilities ended. They objected to the dictatorial powers of an organization vitally important to them, but over which they exerted no control. Railroad executives attacked the organization somewhat later and for other reasons, including allegations of insufficient maintenance, returning the railroads to private owners in a deficit position, and executing national agreements with labor. Of these, only the labor complaint carried weight.

The USRA returned the railroads to private owners in a run-down state in 1920, but it had legitimate reasons for doing so, and it was prepared to compensate owners for any deferred maintenance that it caused. Part of the reason that the railroads were in such condition is that they had been run down in 1917. The government had no obligation to improve them. In general, however, the railroads were in worse shape in 1920 than in 1917 because Hines, although a railroad official, was loyal to the government and did not want to give the railroads a gift in the form of enhanced maintenance. He chose to err on the side of undermaintenance and compensate the owners for the difference. Hines exacerbated this decision when he canceled the 1919 maintenance program because Congress delayed giving USRA a grant in early 1919. Although Hines later reinstated the program, it could not be carried out in its entirety during the remaining weeks of good weather. The USRA ultimately paid the railroads $204 million for deferred maintenance.

The USRA also increased the American railroad capital deficiency because of its legitimate policy of investing only in the barest essentials needed for the war effort. Its capital program was not intended to make up for the deficient capital expenditures of the prewar years. When adjusted for inflation, the annual USRA capital improvement expenditures fell below those of the private railroads in the decade before World War I.

Hines also was criticized for returning the railroads in a deficit position. The major rate increase of May 1918 failed to compensate completely for the added labor, materials, and fuel costs in 1918, partly because the labor settlement was retroactive to the first of the year, while the rate increase took place in June. Labor settlements in 1919 of almost $200 million and additional price increases for materials and fuel resulted in higher deficits for 1919. Additional rate increases were needed, but fearing the wrath of shippers, Hines refused to implement them. He believed that a reconstituted ICC, reflecting the interest of both private railroads and shippers, should deal with this issue, which it did after March 1920. Consequently, during federal control rail revenues covered expenses, but they fell short by $642 million of paying the rents that Congress guaranteed the private owners. Including the de-

ferred maintenance payments, six months of net revenue guarantees made after March 1920, and other expenses not related to railroads, the USRA cost taxpayers about $1.2 billion. Had the railroads remained private, this expenditure could have been avoided only if the private owners would have accepted greatly reduced net income from what they received under federal control.

Finally, Hines was criticized for his labor decisions. When the war ended, he could have abrogated the various USRA general orders that gave workers the eight-hour day, that classified their work, that specified work rules, and that raised their wages. Although private industry rescinded many of the benefits it gave workers during the war, Hines chose not to follow this course. Instead, he institutionalized the general orders in the form of national agreements between the nation's railroads and the various brotherhoods representing its workers. He reasoned that he had to give the workers something. They supported a permanently nationalized railroad system and turned sullen when McAdoo resigned. Still higher wages would have placated them, but Hines refused to saddle the railroad industry with such an expense. Instead, he institutionalized what the workers already had while giving them a small wage boost of about $200 million. This short-sighted decision proved to be the most negative legacy of federal control, or, more accurately, the transition from federal to private control. It hamstrung railroad management in the following decades as technological change made increasingly obsolete the rigid work rules that it institutionalized.

Although the USRA barely started its mission when the war abruptly ended, it accomplished what it was supposed to do. Traffic congestion and car shortages began to lessen in March 1918 and largely ended by May. They did not return during the rest of the year. Only 4 percent more traffic moved in 1918 compared to 1917, but it moved with little delay. War industries and the military received what they needed, where they needed it, and when they needed it. Civilians received at a minimum essential goods and services, and usually much more. Recognizing the benefits achieved from joint use of facilities and traffic agreements between railroads, Congress in the Transportation Act of 1920 allowed railroads to continue these practices under private control.

Gregory L. Thompson

R

See also HINES, WALKER DOWNER; MCADOO, WILLIAM GIBBS

Bibliography

Cunningham, William J. *American Railroads: Government Control and Reconstruction Policies.* Chicago: Shaw, 1922.

Godfrey, Aaron A. *Government Operation of the Railroads: Its Necessity, Success and Consequences 1918–1920.* Austin, TX: San Felipe Press, 1974.

Hines, Walker D. *War History of American Railroads.* New Haven, CT: Yale University Press, 1928.

Klein, Maury. *Union Pacific: The Rebirth 1894–1969.* New York: Doubleday, 1989.

Rainbow Division

See UNITED STATES ARMY: 42D DIVISION

Randolph, Asa Philip (1889–1979)

Asa Philip Randolph was one of the early leaders of the modern civil rights movement. His political activism spanned over five decades beginning in 1917.

Although as an adult he considered himself an atheist, Randolph had been born into a religious family on April 15, 1889. His father was a preacher in segregated Jacksonville, Florida, where Randolph grew up. He attended Cookman Institute, later known as Bethune-Cookman College, in nearby Daytona Beach. In 1911, he became part of the Great Migration as many southern blacks moved north in search of better living and working conditions. He attended night classes at the City College of New York while working manual jobs during the day.

Randolph's political involvement began with labor concerns. He was keenly influenced by prominent spokesmen of the labor movement, such as Eugene Debs and Bill Haywood, and the political theories of Karl Marx.

In 1917, A. Philip Randolph, with Chandler Owens, founded the *Messenger,* the first black radical journal with a major following. Through the journal he advanced his beliefs of socialism and labor unionism. The *Messenger* argued strongly that World War I was created to benefit the capitalists and, therefore, had little relevance for the working class. In 1918, Randolph was jailed for his antiwar sentiments.

He continued his political involvement, but his efforts to include blacks in the major labor movements were largely unsuccessful. Recognizing that the vast majority of working blacks were unskilled laborers, he began to involve himself in organizing black laborers into their own unions.

One of his major accomplishments was the formation of the Brotherhood of Sleeping Car Porters, which was finally acknowledged by the Pullman Company in 1937. Randolph continued his involvement in the civil rights movement throughout his life. He died on May 16, 1979.

Donna Gates Thomas

Bibliography

Anderson, Jervis. *A. Philip Randolph: A Biographical Portrait.* New York: Harcourt Brace Jovanovich, 1973.

Pfeffer, Paula F. *A. Philip Randolph, Pioneer of the Civil Rights Movement.* Baton Rouge: Louisiana State University Press, 1990.

Rankin, Jeannette Pickering (1880–1973)

Born near Missoula, Montana, Jeannette Pickering Rankin graduated from the University of Montana in 1902 and taught briefly in public schools. She then worked as a social worker for a short period in Montana and Washington State, but this proved unsatisfying for her, so in 1909 Rankin entered the University of Washington to pursue other studies. There she joined the suffragist movement and became an activist.

After helping gain the vote for women in Washington in 1910, Rankin returned to Montana, where she launched her own political career. As field secretary for the National American Woman Suffrage Association from 1913 to 1915, Rankin played a crucial role in gaining the vote for women in Montana in 1914. Her efforts had made her known throughout the state and helped her win election as the first woman to serve in the United States House of Representatives.

During her campaign, Rankin ran on a progressive platform, but it was as a pacifist that she left her mark on American history. On April 6, 1917, just four days after she had taken the oath of office, Rankin joined fifty-six other members of Congress in voting against entry into World War I. Although at the time she asserted that an overwhelming majority of Montanans were against the war, she later explained that she had voted against the war because it was "a commercial war" and because she knew "that none of the idealistic hopes would be carried out." Whatever the case may be, as the war continued, public opinion in her home state turned against her pacifist stance, causing her to lose her campaign for the U.S. Senate in 1918.

After completing her term in the House of Representatives, Rankin continued to work for world peace and progressive legislation. In 1919, she served as a delegate to the Second International Congress of Women. She was a field secretary for the National Consumer's League and in 1928 established the Georgia Peace Society. From 1929 to 1939, Rankin worked as a lobbyist in Washington for the National Council for the Prevention of War. Her outspoken opposition to Franklin Delano Roosevelt's foreign policy led her to run for Congress from Montana in 1940. Elected on an isolationist platform, Rankin voted against Lend-Lease, the draft, the repeal of the neutrality acts, and military expenditures. Most important, she cast the only vote against American entry into World War II.

In 1968, the eighty-eight-year-old Rankin decided to seek a third term in Congress. Although she was forced to drop out of the race because of poor health, she continued to travel and speak out against war. She suffered a fatal heart attack on May 18, 1973.

Justin Murphy

Bibliography

Josephson, Hannah. *Jeannette Rankin: First Lady in Congress.* Indianapolis: Bobbs-Merrill, 1974.

Read, George Windle (1860–1934)

George Windle Read was born in Indianaola, Iowa. He excelled at the United States Military Academy, being appointed first captain of the corps of cadets his senior year. Upon graduation in 1883, Read received an infantry commission but soon transferred to the 5th Cavalry and served in Wyoming and the Indian Territory. In 1889, he became professor of military science and tactics at the State University of Iowa; four years later, Read returned to duty with his former unit. During the Spanish-American War, he served as an ordnance officer, remaining in Cuba until 1899, when he was promoted to captain and transferred to New Mexico. After returning to Cuba in 1906, and then serving a tour on the General Staff, Read was appointed to the rank of major in 1910 and sent to the Philippines as inspector general of Mindanao. Recalled to the United States two years later, Read served along the Mexican border, and then attended the Army War College, graduating in 1914. Newly promoted to lieutenant colonel, he was assigned as adjutant general of the 2d Division and later sent to the adjutant general's office at the War Department.

In April 1917, when the United States entered the First World War, Colonel Read was given the challenging command of army recruiting. Promoted to brigadier general in August, Read took control of the 15th Cavalry and was promoted to major general three months later. In April 1918, he secured command of the 30th ("Old Hickory) Division, which immediately proceeded to France to begin training with the British. Once in Europe, Gen. John J. Pershing chose Read to lead II Corps, which consisted of five American divisions, all serving along the British front. From June to August, General Read's command diminished as three divisions were transferred in preparation for the St. Mihiel offensive. Read's two remaining divisions, the 27th and 30th, were ordered to operate as a corps in the British Army, and they actively participated in operations along the Ypres sector. These units were used to spearhead a major offensive near St. Quentin in August 1918; they performed well against stiff German resistance. The corps continued to see action on the front lines until late October. With the Armistice, Read was given command of the embarkation center at Le Mans. He returned to the United States commanding the 42d ("Rainbow") Division, then took control of V Corps at Camp Jackson, South Carolina, until retiring in 1924. Read died in Washington, D.C., in November 1934.

Eric W. Knapp

Bibliography

Coffman, Edward M. *The War to End All Wars.* New York: Oxford University Press, 1968.

Pershing, John J. *My Experiences in the World War.* 2 vols. New York: Stokes, 1931.

Requa, Mark (1865–1937)

Director of the Oil Division of the U.S. Fuel Administration in World War I, Mark Requa was a prominent mining engineer. He was born in Virginia City, Nevada, the only son of Isaac Lawrence Requa and Sarah Jane Requa. He was educated at home by tutors and attended a private school. Although admitted to Yale University, he could not attend because of his poor eyesight.

Instead, he entered the world of business. The younger Requa joined his father in a succession of profitable joint ventures, developing new mines and building small railroads, drilling wells in the Coalinga fields, and founding the mining engineering consulting firm of Requa, Bradley, and MacKenzie in San Francisco.

In many ways, Requa's career paralleled that of Herbert Hoover during these same years. The two men first met in 1905 and became lifelong friends. Both were successful mining engineers, prosperous entrepreneurs, and technocrats with a conscience. When President Woodrow Wilson appointed Hoover as director of the U.S. Food Administration in June 1917, Hoover immediately invited Requa to become a member of his staff. Late in 1917, the President established a new Oil Division within the U.S. Fuel Administration to deal with a shortage of oil for the navy and appointed Requa to head it.

During the next eighteen months, Requa sought to coordinate production and marketing policies and to direct the oil industry to serve the nation's military needs. Although he had extraordinary wartime powers under the Lever Act of 1917, wherever possible Requa preferred to rely on voluntary cooperation and persuasion. With the end of the war the U.S. Fuel Administration was dissolved on June 30, 1919. Requa returned to private life and again focused attention on his extensive business ventures.

While he did not hold public office during Hoover's presidency, Requa became one of his chief spokespersons in advocating conservation of oil and other natural resources. During the last decade of his life, he lived in Santa Barbara, California. He died in 1937. Requa should be credited as the chief architect of federal oil programs in World War I.

Gerald D. Nash

See also LEVER FOOD AND FUEL ACT

Bibliography

Nash, Gerald D. *United States Oil Policy, 1890–1964.* Pittsburgh: University of Pittsburgh Press, 1968.

Revenue Act of 1917

From the beginning of World War I until one year after its end, military spending by the United States was an estimated $26 billion, an amount almost equal to all federal expenditures between 1791 and 1917. That figure actually tells only part of the story, for a 1970 congressional report estimated that the total long-term costs for World War I, including veterans' benefits and interest payments on war loans, which were still being made at that time, would reach $112 billion.

While the war was going on, the debate over how the nation should pay for the conflict became a major political issue, dividing Congress along regional and ideological as well as party lines. Few Americans contended that taxes alone could or should pay for the war, but just how much of the total should come from income, inheritance, and excess profits taxes and how much from consumption taxes and borrowing sparked bitter battles.

In his war message to Congress on April 2, 1917, President Wilson declared that he intended to keep government borrowing to a minimum by increasing taxes and revising the tax code, changes that were certain to rekindle a controversy that had ignited the previous year. In 1916, the Wilson administration had attempted to finance a modest buildup of the nation's military forces by revising the tax laws. Congressional progressives, mainly legislators from the West and South, seized the opportunity to make the existing, very marginally progressive tax structure more egalitarian by increasing taxes on the more affluent. Many of the same congressmen, such as the chair of the House Ways and Means Committee, Claude Kitchin, and Wisconsin Senator Robert La Follette, also opposed American involvement in the European war and reasoned that if people had to pay higher taxes, their enthusiasm for military spending would diminish. The progressives successfully changed the tax code in 1916 to shift more than 95 percent of the federal income tax onto those whose annual incomes exceeded $20,000 annually. By capitalizing on Wilson's war message, they hoped to expand progressive tax principles even further in 1917.

Initially, Secretary of the Treasury William Gibbs McAdoo, Wilson's son-in-law, believed that 50 percent of the war costs could be financed by taxes, but as expenditures mounted, he revised the figure to 35 percent. Even more discouraging for those favoring a more progressive tax structure, after his war message, Wilson seemed to lose interest in financial policy.

The 1917 war revenue bill was introduced in April, almost in tandem with a Liberty Loan bill calling for a $2 billion bond issue bearing interest at 3.5 percent but exempting the interest from all federal income taxes and allowing the bonds to be converted into any future issue that offered a higher interest rate. Congress passed the bond measure within three weeks but battled over the controversial tax bill for almost six months. The original tax bill reported out of the House Ways and Means Committee in May proposed to raise $800 million by increasing the income and excess profits tax rates, by lowering exemptions, and by levying new excise taxes on luxury items such as automobiles. The measure brought a quick and sharp response from those who would pay the bulk of the additional taxes. In particular, corporate spokesmen zeroed in on the excess profits provision, which called for a graduated tax on all profits greater than 8 percent on the nebulously defined "invested capital." Opponents argued instead for a war-profits tax based on the difference between earnings during wartime and average earnings in the immediate prewar years. Southern congressmen retorted that a war-profits tax discriminated against industries such as southern textiles, which had experienced low profits prior to the war, and favored northern firms with more consistent profits.

Despite opposition, the bill passed the House easily with few substantive changes but ran into much stiffer criticism in the Senate. By mid-summer, the administration's estimates of the war's costs had more than doubled. Desperate for money to fight the conflict, Secretary McAdoo agreed to rely significantly more on loans than taxes. Senate progressives bitterly opposed McAdoo's concession. However, many of those, such as Senator La Follette, who argued for higher taxes, had voted against entering the war. Their adversaries discredited the progressives' arguments by charging that they were trying to use the tax issue to hamstring the war effort, and the antiwar taint cost the progressives the votes of some senators sympathetic to the plea for increased taxes.

After weeks of bitter debate, the Senate passed the bill in September by a comfortable margin, and Wilson signed the Revenue Act of 1917 the following month. In its final form, the measure promised to raise an estimated $2.5 billion, about $600 million more than the bill initiated by the House Ways and Means Committee. The money was to come from a variety of changes in the tax law. The normal income tax on individuals jumped from 2 to 4 percent, and the surtax increased with brackets up to 63 percent. Thus, in the highest bracket, the combined normal and surtax reached 67 percent. Tax exemptions were cut from $4,000 to $2,000 for married persons and from $3,000 to $1,000 for singles. Congress also voted to remove the highly unpopular pay-as-you-go, tax-at-the-source arrangement introduced with the first individual income tax in 1913.

By no means did the tax increase ignore business. The corporate income tax increased to 6 percent, and an excess profits tax was enacted. Differences over the latter resulted in a compromise between the concept of a tax based on profits above a set percentage on invested capital and an arrangement with war profits based on the differences between wartime earnings and average prewar earnings. The tax, which applied to corporations, partnerships, and individuals, used average profits in 1911, 1912, and 1913, to determine the taxpayer's profit level eligible for exemption from the excess profits tax but set the exemption at not less than 7 percent nor more than 9 percent of the invested capital for the taxable years. The excess profits tax was graduated from 20 to 60 percent, and a special penalty tax was imposed upon undistributed corporate earnings.

James Heath

See also LIBERTY LOANS; McADOO, WILLIAM GIBBS

Bibliography

Gilbert, Charles. *American Financing of World War I*. Westport, CT: Greenwood Press, 1970.

Kennedy, David M. *Over Here: The First World War and American Society*. New York: Oxford University Press, 1980.

Livermore, Seward W. *Politics is Adjourned: Woodrow Wilson and the War Congress,*

1916–1918. Middletown, CT: Wesleyan University Press, 1966.

Paul, Randolph. *Taxation for Prosperity*. Indianapolis: Bobbs-Merrill, 1947.

Revenue Act of 1918

Congressional progressives professed disappointment that the Revenue Act of 1917, enacted in October, had not gone further in making the nation's tax structure more egalitarian. Yet most progressive legislators reacted coolly to Secretary of the Treasury William Gibbs McAdoo's call in early May 1918 for a new tax bill to raise $6 billion to $7 billion to finance World War I. Many congressmen emphasized that the congressional session was almost over and that members were anxious to return home to prepare for the year's primary and general elections. Most ignored or rejected McAdoo's claim that the Treasury Department's records documented extensive war profiteering during the past year and that congressmen who remained in Washington and supported a new tax bill could benefit politically. Although the desire to tend to reelection chores was clearly the key factor in the legislators' cool response, many also maintained that any higher business taxes would be passed along to the public anyway by increased prices; hence, the congressmen argued, the Wilson administration should concentrate for the time being on raising the needed funds by selling Liberty bonds.

McAdoo did succeed in convincing President Wilson that new taxes were essential, and the Chief Executive delivered a stirring speech before a joint session of Congress in late May hoping to convince the legislators not to go home. Capitalizing on the wartime spirit of sacrifice, Wilson declared that "politics is adjourned" and challenged Congress to do its duty and raise new taxes, which, he emphasized, should fall mainly on excess profits and luxury consumption. The public responded so favorably and enthusiastically to the President's appeal that Congress had no choice but to stay in session and address his tax requests. Ironically, many of Wilson's fellow Democrats were angry with his pressure tactics and not inclined to cooperate with the administration. Others, such as Senator Robert La Follette, praised the President's message and jumped at the chance to pass progressive tax legislation.

A make-shift arrangement by which members of Congress took short summer electioneering vacations on a rotating basis while Congress remained technically in session eased some of the legislators' concerns about getting reelected but failed to produce a new revenue act. When the Armistice was signed on November 11 ending the war, the Senate Finance Committee was still considering a revenue bill of over $8 billion passed by the House in late September.

In the November elections, the Republicans won control of both chambers of Congress and looked expectantly toward winning the presidency in 1920. Perhaps reasoning that with the war over higher taxes would spark public anger at the Wilson administration, Republican enthusiasm for raising taxes grew significantly. Businessmen, characteristically fearful of uncertainty and anxious to know what their future tax obligations would be, softened their opposition to the revenue bill. With the fighting ended, McAdoo reduced his estimated revenue needs, and Congress cut the total amount of revenue to be raised from $8 billion to $6 billion while dropping or diluting many of the more progressive features in the bill.

The lengthy and complex Revenue Act of 1918, finally signed into law on Feb. 24, 1919, applied retroactively to the previous year and placed an estimated 80 percent of the total federal tax load on large incomes, profits, and estates. The measure left exemptions unchanged but increased the normal tax for 1918 from 4 percent to 6 percent on individual net incomes up to $4,000 and to 12 percent on incomes above $4,000. The surtax began at $5,000 and reached 65 percent in the top bracket. Thus, an individual in the highest bracket in 1918 paid 77 percent. For subsequent years, the normal tax rate dropped to 4 percent on incomes up to $4,000, 8 percent on incomes above $4,000, and 9 percent for the surtax. Corporate taxes were set at 12 percent for 1918 and 10 percent for subsequent years, while the maximum rate for the graduated excess profits tax climbed to 65 percent.

The higher tax rates would be relatively short-lived. Congress repealed the excess profits tax in 1921 and over the course of the postwar decade substantially reduced other tax rates as well. Nevertheless, the principle of progressive taxation on incomes, profits, and estates became, during World War I, a basic part of the American tax consciousness.

James Heath

Bibliography

Gilbert, Charles. *American Financing of World War I.* Westport, CT: Greenwood Press, 1970.

Kennedy, David M. *Over Here: The First World War and American Society.* New York: Oxford University Press, 1980.

Livermore, Seward W. *Politics is Adjourned: Woodrow Wilson and the War Congress, 1916–1918.* Middletown, CT: Wesleyan University Press, 1966.

Paul, Randolph. *Taxation for Prosperity.* Indianapolis: Bobbs-Merrill, 1947.

Rickenbacker, Edward Vernon (1890–1973)

Born in Columbus, Ohio, in 1890, Edward Vernon ("Eddie") Rickenbacker supported his seven brothers and sisters after his father's early death. He held a variety of jobs before becoming fascinated with combustion engines while working at a car company in 1906. He completed a mechanical engineering course from a correspondence school and took a job as an engineer with the Columbus Buggy Company, where he experimented with automobiles. Automobile racing soon dominated Rickenbacker's life, and he worked to find a way to keep water from boiling out of engines in hot weather. He participated in the first 500-mile race held at Indianapolis and set the auto speed record at 134 miles per hour at Daytona Beach, Florida. By 1916, Rickenbacker ranked third among U.S. speed champions.

With America's entry into World War I, Rickenbacker urged the creation of an American flying corps composed of auto racers and mechanics. He enlisted in the army on May 25, 1917, and went to France as a sergeant on General Pershing's Motor Car Staff; he often drove the car of Col. William ("Billy") Mitchell, a leading proponent of air power. On August 25, he was assigned to flight school at Issoudun. Upon completion of flying and gunnery schools and after serving briefly as chief sergeant at the main training base, Rickenbacker went to the 94th ("Hat-in-the-Ring") Squadron in March 1918. On March 29, he scored his first victory, downing a German Albatross near St. Baussant, the fourth enemy plane to be downed by an American airman serving for the United States. By the spring of 1918, Rickenbacker commanded Flight One of the squadron and scored his first victories against Manfred von Richtofen's (the Red Baron) Flying Circus along the Toul sector. On May 30, he shot down his fifth plane, and he was promoted to captain and squadron commander. He scored his most spectacular victory on September 25 when he attacked seven German planes and downed two; for this action, he was awarded the Medal of Honor.

His last overseas duty included taking his squadron to the American occupation headquarters at Coblenz. In 1919, he published his war memoirs, *Fighting the Flying Circus.*

After the war, Rickenbacker returned to the automobile industry, but by 1938, he had become president, general manager, and director of Eastern Airlines. During the Second World War Rickenbacker's technical knowledge prompted Secretary of War Henry Stimson to send him on an inspection tour of U.S. bases abroad. He and seven companions survived twenty-three days in small rafts after their plane was forced to ditch in the Pacific. He returned to Eastern Airlines after the war and oversaw its greatest period of growth. Rickenbacker died in 1973.

Laura Matysek Wood

Bibliography

Adamson, Hans C. *Eddie Rickenbacker.* New York: Macmillan, 1946.

Rickenbacker, Edward V. *Fighting the Flying Circus.* 1919.

———. *Rickenbacker.* Englewood Cliffs, NJ: Prentice-Hall, 1967.

———. *Seven Came Through.* Garden City, NY: Doubleday, 1943.

Robins, Raymond (1873–1954)

Raymond Robins led the American National Red Cross Mission to Russia during World War I. During the summer and fall of 1917, he tried to help stabilize the Russian Provisional Government so that it would continue the war effort. Following the Bolshevik Revolution in November 1917, Robins served as the United States liaison to the Soviet government. His position was of major significance after the U.S. embassy staff fled the advancing Germans. Robins moved to Moscow with the Soviet government and tried to obtain American military assistance for the Red Army in exchange for a Bolshevik recommitment to the war effort.

Robins was born into a poor family in New York City. As a teenager, he was an itinerant worker. However, he managed to keep up his education, earned a law degree, and began a practice in California. Robins went to Alaska during the Gold Rush and was one of the fortunate few who did discover gold. He then moved to Chicago, where he became involved in social work and Progressive politics. In 1916, Robins was selected chair of the Progressive National Convention. The Progressive Party under Robins supported United States participation in World War I as a war against militarism and in defense of liberty, democracy, peace, and internationalism. Robins also believed that the March Revolution in Russia was a major event because it advanced the strength of democratic forces.

Theodore Roosevelt suggested that President Wilson include Robins in the American National Red Cross Mission to Russia during World War I. The mission's task was to alleviate illness and hunger. Shortly after the mission's arrival in Russia in July 1917, Robins realized that the Red Cross had to work with the revolutionary Soviets as well as the Provisional Government in St. Petersburg. The local Soviets had substantial influence over transportation systems in some areas, and their cooperation was essential to distribute food and medicine. Thus, Robins initiated a relationship with Soviet leaders, including Lenin and Trotsky.

At the same time, Robins joined the American-Russian Educational Committee and the Committee on Civic Education. Through these committees he sought to educate Russian peasants about the benefits of democracy and their responsibility to support the war effort. His work and travels highlighted to him the extreme discontent and chaos in Russia. Robins realized the Provisional Government needed substantial economic aid to reestablish domestic order and military aid to continue the war effort. When the Provisional Government fell to the Bolsheviks in November 1917, Robins was not surprised.

Once the Bolsheviks seized power, Robins's liaison with them became extremely significant because the United States did not want an official relationship between the ambassador and a revolutionary organization. Yet, Robins continued to petition Washington to assist the Bolsheviks in exchange for their support for the war effort. Following the Soviet ratification of the separate Brest Litovsk Peace Treaty, Robins urged the United States to pursue peaceful coexistence and trade with Soviet Russia.

Robins, like Wilson, saw Russia as a litmus test of the Versailles Peace Treaty. He argued that cooperation was necessary to create lasting peace with the Bolsheviks and throughout Europe. He contended that United States-Soviet economic cooperation would be mutually beneficial. American industry would gain access to Russian raw materials and profit from investments. The American presence also might counter German influence.

The American National Red Cross Mission would continue, but Robins's political role had become controversial. In particular, the American consul general in Moscow, Maddin Summers, complained to the State Department about Robins's contacts with the Bolsheviks after they ratified the Brest Litovsk Treaty. Summers also may have resented the importance Ambassador David R. Francis attached to Robins's unofficial advisory role. The controversial nature of his position is highlighted by the fact that although Robins was recalled from Russia on May 7, 1919, the State Department rescinded the recall in order for him to negotiate the details of cooperation with the Bolsheviks. Robins departed Moscow, however, before the rescind order arrived.

Robins did present Lenin's plan for economic cooperation to Secretary of State Lansing after he returned to the United States. In response to recommendations by Robins, President Wilson stated, "I differ from them only in practical details." Allied wartime demands, however, led to delays in cooperation.

After World War I, Robins continued to push for United States-Soviet cooperation. He believed the United States could positively impact socialism in the Soviet Union. In 1933, when the United States finally recognized the Soviet government, Robins briefly was considered for the ambassadorial post. Robins remained active in the movement to outlaw war and in various conservation and agricultural movements. However, ill health curtailed his official activities after 1935.

Joan Davison

See also AMERICAN NATIONAL RED CROSS: IN RUSSIA

Bibliography

Davison, Henry P. *The American Red Cross in the Great War, 1917–1919.* New York: Macmillan, 1943.

Francis, David R. *Russia from the American Embassy.* New York: Scribner, 1921.

Hard, William. *Raymond Robins' Own Story.* New York: Harper, 1920.

Libby, James K. *Alexander Gumberg and Soviet-American Relations, 1917–1933.* Lexington: The University Press of Kentucky, 1977.

Lockhart, Bruce. *British Agent.* New York, Putnam, 1933.

Rockenbach, Samuel Dickerson (1869–1952)

An 1889 graduate of the Virginia Military Institute commissioned in the cavalry, Samuel Dickerson Rockenbach, who was fluent in German, was assigned as an observer with the German Army shortly after war broke out in Europe in 1914. Deteriorating diplomatic relations forced his recall to the United States in the spring of 1915, and he was promoted to major, detailed to duty with the Quartermaster Corps and assigned to BGen. John J. Pershing's staff as quartermaster for the 1916 Punitive Expedition in Mexico.

General Pershing, impressed with Rockenbach's performance in Mexico, retained him on his staff when he was selected to command the American Expeditionary Force (AEF) during the early spring of 1917. In France, Rockenbach, who had recently been promoted to lieutenant colonel, presided over quartermaster functions at Base Section 1 in St. Nazaire until General Pershing selected him to assume command of the newly organized AEF Tank Corps on Dec. 22, 1917.

The job as Pershing's principal tank adviser, U.S. representative to the Inter-Allied Tank Commission, and commander of the AEF Tank Corps was a natural for Colonel Rockenbach, who had demonstrated exceptional administrative skills, a talent for improvisation, and an ability to cooperate with the Allies. He had the added benefit of experience working with motor vehicles during the Punitive Expedition.

Upon reporting for duty at AEF headquarters at Chaumont, Rockenbach found only two other officers—Capt. George S. Patton, Jr., and 1st Lt. Elgin Braine—assigned to assist him with the development of a force that would number more than 12,000 men less than a year later. The trio worked through the remainder of the winter of 1917–1918 to establish schools, create tables of organization and equipment for both heavy and light tank units, procure vehicles for the force, and recruit men. Rockenbach allowed Patton a free rein with doctrinal, tactical, and training matters and sent Braine back to the United States in late February 1918 to act as the AEF Tank Corps' liaison with the Ordnance Department and civilian manufacturers contracted to build French Renault light tanks for the U.S. Army.

By the mid-summer of 1918, the AEF Tank Corps had two light tank battalions fully trained at Patton's Light Tank School in France and a heavy tank battalion fully trained at the British Heavy Tank School in England. Unfortunately, efforts to mass-produce tanks for the AEF had so far come to naught, and Rockenbach was forced to enlist Pershing's support to get the French to supply 144 Renaults to equip the units in Patton's 1st Tank Brigade and the British to provide the forty-seven Mark IV or V heavy tanks needed by the 301st Tank Battalion in England. Both Allies agreed, although the British insisted that the heavy tanks be used in support of American divisions fighting in the British Fourth Army sector.

Rockenbach was promoted to brigadier general on July 11, 1918, and commanded a force of 419 tanks (consisting of Patton's 1st Tank Brigade and the French 1st Assault Artillery Brigade) in support of U.S. First Army operations in the St. Mihiel offensive in mid-September and the Meuse-Argonne campaign from September 26 until the Armistice. The units performed with distinction, earning praise from commanders of the divisions and corps they supported.

Rockenbach returned to Fort Meade, Maryland, in June 1919, replacing Col. Ira C. Welborn as Tank Corps director in the United States. He spent the next year waging a losing battle with conservative army leaders and penurious congressmen who sought to reduce the Tank Corps' size and terminate it as a separate combat arm. He reverted to his permanent grade of colonel and was forced to transfer to the infantry branch in order to remain in command of the Tank School at Fort Meade when the National Defense Act of 1920 was passed in June.

With control of tanks passing to the infantry, many of Rockenbach's subordinate officers, disgruntled by his failure to preserve a separate tank force and fearful of their own career opportunities, began an exodus back to their original branches. Rockenbach remained at the Tank School until he was promoted back to brigadier general in January 1924. He retired in 1933 after serving as commander of the Military District of Washington, the 2d Cavalry Brigade, the 2d Artillery Brigade, and the 2d Division. He died in 1952.

Dale E. Wilson

See also PATTON, GEORGE SMITH, JR.; TANKS; UNITED STATES ARMY TANK CORPS; WELBORN, IRA C.

Bibliography

Blumenson, Martin, ed. *The Patton Papers, 1885–1940.* Boston: Houghton Mifflin, 1972.

Gunsberg, Jeffrey A. "Samuel Dickerson Rockenbach: Father of the Tank Corps." *Virginia Cavalcade* (Summer 1976).

Wilson, Dale E. *Treat 'Em Rough! The Birth of American Armor, 1917–1920.* Novato, CA: Presidio Press, 1989.

Roosevelt, Franklin Delano (1882–1945)

Franklin Delano Roosevelt (FDR) was born in Hyde Park, New York. His father James was a member of the Hudson River valley aristocracy. Tutored privately at home, Roosevelt grew up in the company of his parents, enjoying their holidays in Europe, and boating and sailing at Campobello Island, between Maine and New Brunswick, Canada. At fourteen he was enrolled at Groton. It was there, under the tutelage of Headmaster Peabody, that the young Roosevelt decided to follow a career of public service. He next went to Harvard, where he was the editor of the college newspaper. Roosevelt entered Columbia University Law School in 1904. He married his fifth cousin, Eleanor Roosevelt, on March 17, 1905.

In 1910, seeking new challenges within public service, he ran successfully for the New York State Senate. In 1912, he bucked the Democratic Party establishment by supporting Woodrow Wilson for the presidential nomination. On the eve of World War I, FDR became the assistant secretary of the navy in the Wilson administration, where he served for over seven years. His love of the sea and ships made FDR an ideal man for the job. FDR advocated preparedness, a two-ocean navy, and active foreign policy involvement through a strong Wilson presidency. A yachtsman himself, FDR spoke the nautical terms of the sailor, mixed readily with the admirals, appreciated the seventeen-gun salute, and was so dedicated to his job that he had a special flag designed to be flown when he was aboard a ship.

He administered an enormous budget and dispersed contracts and supplies to shipyards with consummate skill and diplomacy. Although they contrasted sharply in their styles, backgrounds and often in their policies, Secretary of the Navy Josephus Daniels authorized Roosevelt to handle labor relations, personnel, and procurement. FDR oversaw between 50,000 and 100,000 civilian employees, and there was never a strike in the navy shipyards.

Roosevelt understood the shipbuilding business and was not afraid to build, secure, or maintain whatever was essential to the overall navy program. He loved inspections and visited sites from San Diego to Bremerton and Kittery to Pensacola. Although he toyed with the idea of introducing the Taylor system of scientific management in the naval yards, he would not risk the wrath of the unions to adopt it.

FDR was able to balance the war fitness of the fleet with the demands for economy and businesslike management. For the benefit of U.S. seamen, he encouraged that each ship be assigned a home yard for port repairs. He was careful about the work schedules and government contracts so as to keep shipyard employees on the payroll without layoffs. He authorized the installation of safety devices on machines and encouraged recreation rooms for employees. Responding to a plea from the Brooklyn Navy Yard, FDR also fixed the wage scale each year for shipyard workers, and through judicious raises, he secured their loyalty. During World War I, when tremendous numbers of additional workers joined the shipbuilding industry, they were integrated with the minimum of disruption and friction thanks to the good will created by Roosevelt.

Under FDR, it was mandatory that the assistant chiefs of the Bureau of Construction and Repair of Yards and Docks be naval officers rather than chief clerks and that supervision of all industrial work be carried out by competent trained engineers who knew ship mechanics thoroughly. The strengths of the secretary and his assistant complimented each other: Daniels worked the politicians at the Capitol and Roosevelt the admirals at the clubs. Both Daniels and Roosevelt supported a big navy policy. But while Roosevelt was eager to use it on the eve of World War I, Daniels was the last member of Wilson's cabinet to vote for a declaration of war in April 1917.

After the Germans declared their intention to resume unrestricted submarine warfare on Feb. 2, 1917, FDR asked President Wilson if he could bring the U.S. fleet at Guantanamo, Cuba, north to their home berths on the East Coast to ensure combat readiness, but Wilson and Daniels denied his request. However, FDR participated in the circle of decision makers who determined to arm merchantmen, and he supported Wilson's message to Congress asking for a declaration of war.

His full attention now turned to winning the war. Everywhere FDR could, he endeavored to speed mobilization, encouraged the calling up of the naval militia and reserve, and authorized vast purchases of naval stores. His greatest task was to bring the German submarines under control. To that end, FDR had a hand in running the Atlantic convoy system, increasing the number of destroyers and subchasers under construction in American shipyards. He also supported the North Sea Mine Barrage, which was laid with newly developed mines in the spring of 1918. At war's end, Roosevelt went to Europe and effectively negotiated the disposal of surplus property and an end to the naval contracts and agreements with the Allied forces.

In 1920, after resigning his post in the administration, FDR was selected to be the Democratic Party's nominee for vice president, running with James M. Cox. Failing to win election he returned to New York, where he established a law firm. Despite being stricken with polio in 1921, he continued to participate in politics, winning the governorship of New York in 1928. In 1932, in the depths of the Great Depression, he was elected President of the United States, based largely on his successful track record in fighting economic difficulties in New York. But not only did he face economic challenges as president, he was now faced with the struggle against Fascism and Nazism. His apprenticeship while assistant secretary of the navy during World War I helped him to shoulder ever greater burdens with aplomb during World War II, bringing America to superpower stature by the time of his death in his fourth term as president in April 1945.

Barbara Bennett Peterson

Bibliography
Burns, James MacGregor. *Roosevelt: The Lion and the Fox*. New York: Harcourt, Brace, 1956.
Daniels, Jonathan. *The End of Innocence*. Philadelphia: Lippincott, 1954.
Freidel, Frank B. *Franklin D. Roosevelt: The Apprenticeship*. Boston: Little, Brown, 1952.
Rollins, Alfred B., Jr. *Roosevelt and Howe*. New York: Knopf, 1962.
Tugwell, Rexford G. *The Democratic Roosevelt: A Biography of Franklin D. Roosevelt*. Garden City, NY: Doubleday, 1957.

R

Roosevelt, Theodore (1858–1919)

A hero of the Spanish-American War, a popular and effective president, and the most successful third-party candidate for president in American history, Theodore Roosevelt (TR) did little during World War I to enhance his historical reputation. Motivated by an excessive nationalism and by what historian Henry Pringle has called an "almost psychopathic" hatred of President Wilson, Roosevelt's criticism of the Wilson administration attracted limited support at the time, and years later it seemed unfair and excessive. Yet Roosevelt's protests were usually sincere and frequently courageous, and by the time of his death in January 1919, the ex-Rough Rider had emerged as a leading contender for the Republican presidential nomination of 1920.

Before the outbreak of World War I, Roosevelt had attacked the Wilson administration for failing to protect United States interests in Mexico during the Mexican Revolution, for attempting to preserve world peace through a series of arbitration treaties, and for proposing to pay Colombia $25 million in damages for American support of Panama when that country broke away from Colombian rule in 1903. When war erupted in Europe in August 1914 and German armies invaded Belgium in order to attack France, the violation of Belgian neutrality disturbed Roosevelt, but he hesitated to condemn Germany. Writing in *Outlook* magazine on August 22, the former president suggested that "when giants are engaged in a death wrestle, as they reel to and fro, they are certain to trample on whoever gets in the way of either of the huge straining combatants." In the first weeks of the war, despite his earlier differences with the White House, TR deferred to Wilson's call for American neutrality. Roosevelt's position as titular leader of the Progressive Party gave him a reason to avoid any warlike comments likely to embarrass his party's candidates, most of whom opposed American entry into the European conflict, in the state and congressional elections of 1914.

After the November vote, Roosevelt began to speak out more freely, criticizing Wilson for not protesting the German invasion of Belgium and calling for a stronger national defense, including a program of military training for all healthy young men. Even Roosevelt, however, recognized that the vast majority of Americans supported Wilson's efforts to maintain American neutrality and that many people regarded the former president as a reckless militarist. After a German U-boat sank the *Lusitania* in May 1915, with a loss of 124 American lives, he complained to his son Archibald that Wilson and Secretary of State William Jennings Bryan were "abject creatures" who "won't go to war unless they are kicked into it." At the same time, Roosevelt began to move back into the Republican Party, in part because he believed the Republicans were more sympathetic to his foreign policy views and in part because he believed the GOP offered the better vehicle for defeating Wilson in 1916. TR hoped to be the Republican candidate, but his outspoken views on the war and opposition from party conservatives, who believed he was too liberal on domestic issues, made that impossible. The eventual Republican nominee, Charles Evans Hughes, failed to excite Roosevelt; nevertheless, he campaigned hard against Wilson's reelection.

Speaking at Cooper Union in New York on Nov. 3, 1916, Roosevelt referred to Wilson's former summer home Shadow Lawn, in Long Branch, New Jersey, and delivered his most bitter attack yet on his Democratic foe: "There should be shadows now at Shadow Lawn; the shadows of men, women and children who have risen from the ooze of the ocean bottom and from graves in foreign lands; the shadows of the helpless whom Mr. Wilson did not dare protest lest he might have to face danger; the shadows of babies grasping pitifully as they sank under the waves; the shadows of women outraged and slain by bandits."

Wilson's victory disgusted Roosevelt, but he briefly muted his public criticism of the President when Wilson asked Congress in April 1917 for a declaration of war against Germany.

Pleased that the United States had finally come to the aid of the Allies, Roosevelt also needed Wilson's cooperation. Since the 1880s Roosevelt had tried to raise volunteer military units to respond to various national crises. He succeeded once—with the Rough Riders in 1898. As early as the summer of 1915, Roosevelt had begun plans to organize a volunteer cavalry division to fight Germany once the United States entered the war. Of course, Roosevelt was to be their commander. Even before Congress declared war, he began writing to Secretary of War Newton D. Baker for permission to proceed. On April 10, 1917, Roosevelt met with Wilson at the White House and renewed his request. Thousands of men seemed ready to heed Roosevelt's call for volunteers, and French leader Georges Clemenceau believed that Roosevelt's presence at the front would give the sagging morale of the Allied troops a much needed boost. The administration, however, never gave the proposal serious consideration. Roosevelt blamed his rebuff on Wilson's fear of giving a political rival an opportunity to earn military honors, but a host of other factors were against him. Almost sixty, Roosevelt suffered from a variety of physical ailments, including a chronic infection from a leg injury suffered on an expedition to Brazil. Military leaders believed that Roosevelt's volunteer division would siphon off experienced officers needed by the Regular Army. Brash, boisterous, and accustomed to being in command, the former president would have had difficulty functioning as a loyal and cooperative subordinate. No one questioned his personal courage. As he wrote Baker, in "two victorious aggressive fights" during the Spanish-American War, the Rough Riders "lost a third of the officers and a fifth of the enlisted men, all within a little over fifty days." Those figures may suggest the administration's single most important reason for denying a military command to Roosevelt: concern that a division led by a daring commander with little training in modern warfare would suffer enormous casualties. As French Marshal Joseph Joffre reportedly advised Baker, educating a major general could cost 10,000 to 15,000 lives.

Denied an opportunity to join the fighting, Roosevelt busied himself mobilizing support for an efficient, aggressive war effort. Probably no one had done more to prepare public opinion for the conflict. In the fall of 1917, Roosevelt launched a widely syndicated newspaper column in the *Kansas City Star*. His writings and speeches ridiculed the administration's delay in equipping an army and getting troops to the front. He called for American involvement in every theater of the war, including the Balkans and the eastern Mediterranean, and he supported military intervention in Russia to suppress the Bolshevik Revolution. During the war, a wave of paranoia and xenophobia swept the country; Roosevelt helped fan the flames of intolerance. Demanding "100 percent Americanism," he condemned conscientious objectors and what he called "hyphenated Americans"—recent immigrants and their descendants who maintained close ties to their native lands and cultures. He proposed deporting immigrants who failed to learn English. The old Rough Rider wanted to ban German-language newspapers and the teaching of German in the schools. He advocated loyalty oaths for school teachers. Roosevelt did, however, oppose a provision in the 1918 Sedition Act forbidding criticism of the President. Given his contempt for Wilson, he suggested he himself might become a test case for the law.

As his efforts to raise a volunteer division demonstrated, Roosevelt did not hesitate to put his convictions into practice. He was an early supporter of the Plattsburg Movement to ready a volunteer unit for overseas service, but later he distanced himself from the movement. He aided his four sons in their efforts to join the fighting, even though he was "quite prepared that none of them should come back." He used his influence to help son Kermit obtain a commission in the British Army. After fighting in Mesopotamia, Kermit served as a captain of field artillery with the American Expeditionary Force (AEF). Sons Archibald and Theodore, Jr., also fought with the AEF. Archibald was badly wounded by shrapnel in the leg and arm and later was decorated for his service by the French government. Young Ted was gassed and afterward shot in the leg. The youngest son, twenty-year-old Quentin, served as a pilot. After downing a German plane, Quentin was killed in combat in July 1918.

In the eyes of many Americans, the nation's eventual entry into the First World War had vindicated Theodore Roosevelt. At the same time, the war years had produced no strong candidate for the 1920 Republican presidential nomination, and Roosevelt seemed a likely choice. In rejecting a proposal by party leaders that he run for governor of New York in 1918,

Roosevelt explained, "I think I should reserve my strength in case I am needed in 1920." His strength was indeed ebbing. On Nov. 11, 1918, the day of the Armistice, he entered a hospital for treatment of inflammatory rheumatism. By Christmas Eve, he had returned to his home at Oyster Bay, New York, and resumed writing his newspaper column, including one endorsing the League of Nations, with certain reservations. Early on the morning of Jan. 6, 1919, Theodore Roosevelt died at Oyster Bay of a coronary embolism.

Jeffrey Broadwater

See also PLATTSBURG MOVEMENT

Bibliography

Cadenhead, I.E. *Theodore Roosevelt: The Paradox of Progressivism*. Woodbury, NY: Barron's Educational Series, 1974.

Cooper, John Milton, Jr. *The Warrior and the Priest: Woodrow Wilson and Theodore Roosevelt*. Cambridge: Harvard University Press, 1983.

Gardner, Joseph L. *Departing Glory: Theodore Roosevelt as Ex-President*. New York: Scribner, 1973.

Harbaugh, William H. *The Life and Times of Theodore Roosevelt*. New York: Oxford University Press, 1961.

Pringle, Henry F. *Theodore Roosevelt A Biography*. New York: Harcourt, Brace, 1931.

Root, Elihu (1845–1937)

Born in to a family that traced its roots in America to 1639, Elihu Root became a lawyer and rose in Republican political and business circles defending the Sugar Trust and other monopolies. In 1899, President McKinley chose him as his secretary of war. Root established America's neocolonial system in Cuba, Puerto Rico, and the Philippines. At the same time, he reformed the army, establishing the General Staff and the Army War College to professionalize military leadership and education. Root resigned from the War Department in 1904 but became Theodore Roosevelt's secretary of state the next year.

During his stewardship of the State Department, Root directed American diplomatic delegations at the Algeciras Conference (1906) and the Second Hague Conference (1907). He convinced Japan to accept a "gentleman's agreement" ending Japanese immigration into the United States and to negotiate the Root-Takahira Agreement of 1908, which supported the Open Door in China and the status quo in the Pacific. For his many services to international law and arbitration, he was awarded the Nobel Peace Prize in 1912.

In 1909, Root retired as secretary of state and was elected to the U.S. Senate from New York. He presided over the 1912 Republican National Convention that rejected Theodore Roosevelt and renominated William H. Taft—thus alienating his former patron. By the time he retired from the Senate in 1915, Root's party was divided and out of power.

Root spent most of the period of American neutrality in the Great War as a bystander. Although he felt that Germany desired to dominate Europe, he felt it unpatriotic and divisive to criticize Woodrow Wilson's policies publicly until 1916. By then thoroughly disgusted with Wilson's equivocations, he joined the National Security League and demanded military preparedness and a hard line against German unrestricted submarine warfare. In March 1917, Root claimed that Germany was already at war with the United States and asserted that its autocracy and militarism were a threat to American institutions. In April, he hailed Wilson's war message and urged Republicans to support Wilson wholeheartedly. He also called for an end to partisan obstructionism, demanded universal military service, and urged the administration to send an American Expeditionary Force to France. At the President's request, he headed the Root Mission to Russia to express the nation's sympathy toward the new Provisional Government.

After the war, Root supported the Treaty of Versailles and the League of Nations with only minor reservations, breaking with his friend Senator Henry Cabot Lodge over the issue. Although he served on the committee of jurists that framed the Permanent Court of International Justice, he was unable to convince one U.S. administration after another to join the court. In 1921, he was appointed as an American delegate to the Washington arms-limitation conference, and he served as the director of the Carnegie Endowment for International Peace from 1910 to 1925. Consistent with his commitment to international peace and justice, he denounced the Nazi regime in Germany for its attacks on civil liberties. He died in 1937.

David Esposito

See also ROOT MISSION

Bibliography
Jessup, Philip C. *Elihu Root*. Hamden, CT: Archon Books, 1964.
Leopold, Richard W. *Elihu Root and the Conservative Tradition*. Boston: Little, Brown, 1954.

Root Mission

President Woodrow Wilson viewed the February 1917 Revolution in Russia, which toppled the tsar and put Russian liberals in power, as evidence of the resurgent power of democracy over autocratic governments. In his speech asking Congress to declare war on Imperial Germany just three weeks later, Wilson called the Provisional Government "a fit partner in a league of honor." However, after hearing disturbing reports about deteriorating conditions within Russia, Wilson decided to send a discreet American mission under an elder statesman to stem radicalism by showing America's sympathy with the new government and to encourage Russia to stay in the war. Wilson's options for a leader for the expedition were limited. His usual emissary, Col. Edward M. House, simply refused to go, and the Democratic Party was otherwise short of prominent statesmen. House and Secretary of State Robert Lansing recommended Elihu Root, whose international stature and recent calls for nonpartisan support for the President's war policies made him an attractive candidate. Root accepted the assignment, but he faced a firestorm of criticism from liberal circles due to his "reactionary" past.

Other important members of the mission included Army Chief of Staff Hugh L. Scott; businessmen Charles R. Crane and Cyrus McCormick; banker and Democrat Samuel Berton; John R. Mott of the YMCA; James Duncan, a vice president of the American Federation of Labor; and prowar Socialist Charles E. Russell. All together twenty-six men, including translators and secretaries, participated in the mission.

The Root Mission set out across the Pacific for Vladivostok aboard the aged cruiser USS *Buffalo*. One ominous sign military members of the mission noticed was the fact that no Russian officials met them at the dock; indeed, no one challenged them entering the harbor. For a warship to enter a belligerent port in wartime without so much as being hailed was eloquent evidence of the disintegration of the Provisional Government.

The commissioners traveled overland in the ex-tsar's private train on the Trans-Siberian Railroad, arriving in Petrograd eleven days later on June 13. During their trip, they saw mounting evidence of the apathy and confusion that was undermining the Provisional Government: few troop trains going to the front, apparent insubordination, supplies rotting on railway sidings. Root and his colleagues spent four weeks in the capital with occasional side trips. Mission members extended America's regards to the new government, delivered speeches, which were soon forgotten, and collected information, which was soon outdated. Root could do little more than discuss the international situation in pious platitudes—he had been directed by Wilson specifically not to discuss war aims. Nevertheless, he discovered that Soviet radicals had seized on the President's earlier idea of "Peace Without Victory" and recast it in their slogan "No Annexations, No Indemnities."

Root met with then Minister of War Aleksandr Kerenskii and reported being impressed with his determination to continue the war. When General Scott, on a trip to the front, asked Kerenskii if there was any subject he should avoid in speaking to the troops, Kerenskii replied, "Politics." On July 1, Scott witnessed the beginning of General Brusilov's offensive into Galicia, and it completely changed his opinion of Russian soldiers and the willingness of the new government to fight. Despite his rank, Scott had never before observed modern combat operations, and the ferocity of the attack led him to overestimate Russia's willingness to fight. Scott was unable to remain long enough to witness the successful German counterattack a few weeks later.

The only foreign aid Root and his party were able to secure for the provisional regime was an emergency $74 million loan to pay disgruntled Russian troops in Finland. The Root Mission left Petrograd on July 9 and returned across the Pacific, arriving in Washington on August 8. After a few brief meetings with Wilson and State Department officials, Root and his colleagues were never again consulted about the Russian situation. The purpose of the mission was almost entirely symbolic—to convey the best wishes of the Wilson administration and the American people. However, Root and his colleagues were not able to discourage Rus-

sian radicals or keep Russia in the war—a task almost certainly beyond the powers of any foreign statesman.

David Esposito

Bibliography

America's Message to the Russian People. Boston: Marshall Jones, 1918.
Lash, Christopher. *American Liberals and the Russian Revolution.* New York: Columbia University Press, 1962.
Root, Elihu. *The United States and the War, the Mission to Russia.* Cambridge: Harvard University Press, 1918.

Rosenwald, Julius (1862–1932)

Julius Rosenwald was born and educated in Springfield, Illinois. Rosenwald, with his brother-in-law, Aaron Nussbaum, bought a half interest in a mail-order firm called Sears, Roebuck & Company. Rosenwald served as vice president and treasurer of the firm from 1895 to 1910, as president from 1910 to 1925, and as chairman of the board of directors until his death in 1932.

Rosenwald, however, is best remembered as a philanthropist and humanitarian. Most of his gifts were made through the Julius Rosenwald Fund, which he created in 1917 for the "well-being of mankind." Although the bulk of its donations were designated for "Negro welfare," gifts were also made to health and medical facilities, to library extension, and to rural education. Other recipients were the Hebrew Union College in Cincinnati, the University of Chicago, the Hoover German Children's Relief fund, and Jewish colonization work in Russia. While not a Zionist, Rosenwald gave generously to the Hebrew University of Jerusalem, to other cultural agencies in Palestine, and to the relief of Jews in that region.

Although opposed to war, Rosenwald supported President Wilson during World War I with both his money and his time. In 1915, Wilson appointed Rosenwald, Bernard Baruch, and Samuel Gompers to serve on the Council of National Defense. Rosenwald also served as chairman of the Committee on Supplies. In 1918, he went on a special mission to France to tell American soldiers that their country was proud of them. He visited hospitals, where he was introduced as "General Merchandise" and distributed Sears, Roebuck catalogues. Military officials agreed that nothing gave the patients more comfort than those reminders of home.

Burton A. Boxerman

Bibliography

Werner, M.R. *Julius Rosenwald: The Life of a Practical Humanitarian*. New York: Harper, 1939.

Russia

October 1917 Revolution

The October Revolution which toppled the Provisional Government of Aleksandr Kerenskii on Oct. 25 (Nov. 6, according to the Gregorian calendar instituted in Russia in February 1918), 1917, came about because Vladimir Ilyich Lenin, the leader of the Bolsheviks, a Russian Marxist party, believed that the situation in Russia after the fall of Tsar Nicholas II could be turned into a socialist revolution. Such a revolution, Lenin felt, would pull Russia out of the World War and thus inspire the workers of Europe to rebel and sweep away the capitalist system that had caused the war, creating a new socialist world. At the time of the February (1917) Revolution, Lenin lived in exile in Switzerland, unable to put his ideas into practice. The German government, interested in Lenin as a revolutionary who would subvert Russia's war effort, agreed to let him cross its territory into Russia. Germany later subsidized his movement in the hopes of knocking Russia out of the war in order to concentrate Germany's strength on the western front.

When Lenin arrived in Russia in April 1917, he found the country laboring under an incredibly inefficient government. After the ouster of Nicholas II, two bodies established themselves as competing governments. The liberal parties of the wartime Duma (parliament) had formed a Provisional Government, under Aleksandr Kerenskii, but they spoke for only a small part of Russia's population. The socialist parties—the Mensheviks and the Socialist Revolutionaries (SRs)—who claimed to speak for the workers, soldiers, and peasants, refused to join a "bourgeois" government. Instead, they formed the Petrograd Soviet, a council of socialist representatives for the workers and soldiers of Petrograd that claimed to speak for the lower classes of Russia. In fact, a network of Soviets appeared in the major cities of the empire. The Petrograd Soviet used its influence to hamper the workings of the Provisional Government when the latter appeared too conservative, but it would not advance its own socialist agenda, believing that this would be premature. Effective government quickly became impossible.

Russia in 1917 had no time for governmental paralysis. Issues of great importance demanded speedy answers. The continuation of the war posed many problems. Would Russia insist on territorial gains if the Allies won? Would it continue to fight a defensive war? How could discipline be maintained in the army after the Petrograd Soviet had urged the troops to form Soviets of their own? To these and so many other pressing questions, both the Provisional Government and the Petrograd Soviet had the same answer—wait. A Constituent Assembly, they promised, would be elected soon, and that body would address these questions. As 1917 dragged on, and the elections for the Constituent Assembly were postponed again and again, Lenin began to stand out as a decisive figure against this background of inertia and indecision by promising simple solutions to complex questions.

Lenin's "April Theses," which demanded an immediate end to the war and the transfer of all power to the Soviets, initially attracted few supporters, even among the Bolsheviks. Russia's future appeared to lay in the hands of its energetic minister of war, the 36-year-old Aleksandr Kerenskii. A socialist who had defied party discipline to join the Provisional Government, Kerenskii used his gift of oratory to persuade himself and Russia that the army would fight better after the fall of the autocracy. In mid-June, the Russians opened an offensive against the Austro-Hungarians, but the Kerenskii-inspired enthusiasm of the troops soon wilted, and a German counteroffensive rolled the Russians back. Discipline in the ranks soon broke, and desertions swelled ominously.

Military defeat provoked a political crisis when the Provisional Government proposed sending troops from the swollen Petrograd garrison to the front. In early July, Bolshevik-influenced soldiers and sailors rioted in the streets of the capital, demanding that the Petrograd Soviet take power. The crisis of the so-called "July Days" sputtered out when the leaders of the Soviet refused to act and the government published information linking Lenin and the Germans. Bolshevik popularity plummeted, and Lenin fled to Finland to escape arrest.

Nevertheless, the continued failure of the non-Bolsheviks to address the issues facing Russia meant that the July Days would be only a temporary setback for the Bolsheviks. They promised a quick end of the war to the soldiers, land to the peasants, bread to the cities, and self-determination to the non-Russians. Their membership grew from 40,000 in April to 200,000 in August. The most important of these new members was the shrewd and able Leon Trotsky, who had finally ended his feud with Lenin. Trotsky's oratorical skill and his gift for organization proved decisive in the October Revolution and civil war.

Ironically, Kerenskii himself gave vital support to the Bolsheviks through his botched handling of the "Kornilov Affair." After becoming premier, he appointed the popular war hero General Lavr Kornilov as commander of the Russian Army. Kornilov viewed socialists with contempt and began declaring that Russia needed order. The general's popularity alarmed Kerenskii, who viewed a troop movement to Petrograd in August as the opening move of a coup against the revolution. In order to mobilize society against the bewildered Kornilov, Kerenskii freed imprisoned Bolshevik leaders and let them form the Red Guards, a workers' militia, to defend Petrograd. Kornilov quickly resigned, protesting his innocence, but the Red Guards remained.

Worried that the November election of the Constituent Assembly would end the chance for a socialist revolution, Lenin now urged the Bolsheviks to seize power. The Bolsheviks resisted this policy until October 10, when Lenin convinced them that they must act at once. Trotsky modified Lenin's plan so that the Bolsheviks would seize power on the eve of the Second Congress of Soviets, which would then approve the deed. Two major Bolsheviks, Grigorii Zinov'ev and Lev Kamenev, still opposed the plan and went public with their opposition to an armed uprising.

Despite this warning, the Provisional Government conducted business as usual in the Winter Palace. Meanwhile, the Bolsheviks took control of the Petrograd Soviet's Military Revolutionary Committee, housed in the Smolny Institute, and used it to plan the takeover of the capital. They propagandized among the 160,000-man garrison, claiming that Kerenskii was preparing to move against the Soviet to become dictator and the Bolsheviks were merely responding to this threat. Soon Kerenskii could only rely on several hundred Cossacks, and a few units of teenaged military cadets and women soldiers to defend his government.

On the evening of October 24–25, the Red Guards began occupying the important railroad stations, telegraph and telephone exchanges, bridges and intersections of Petrograd in accordance with Trotsky's plans. The city fell into their hands with so little violence that Petrograd's night life continued as usual. At 9 A.M. on October 25, Kerenskii fled the Winter Palace dressed as a Serbian officer in a car borrowed from the American embassy. He hoped to rally support for his cause among the troops outside Petrograd, only to discover that the army despised him for his treatment of Kornilov. By nightfall, the defenders of the Winter Palace began to desert, and the triumphant Red Guards took possession of the building. The unfortunate Provisional Government had fallen, and only a handful of people had perished.

The Second Congress of Soviets had begun to meet in Petrograd even before the Red Guards entered the Winter Palace. The Bolsheviks enjoyed a commanding position in the congress, with 390 out of 650 delegates, and their strength increased when their moderate socialist opponents walked out in protest over the seizure of power. This enabled the Bolsheviks and their Left SR allies to create a new government, the Council of People's Commissars. Lenin agreed to serve as chairman and announced his intention of removing Russia from the war.

The Bolsheviks, however, did not control all of Russia yet, and on October 30, a force of about 600 Cossacks loyal to Kerenskii attempted to retake Petrograd. They encountered several thousand Red Guards and sailors at Pulkovo, a suburb of the capital, and although a number of Red Guards fled, the Cossacks could make no progress against the sailors and retreated at the end of the day. Kerenskii went into exile. In Moscow, the Bolsheviks fought for a week to take possession of the traditional capital of Russia, but by early November, the major cities of Russia had fallen into their hands.

The Bolsheviks now began to break up the old institutions of government and create a new social order. One exception to this was the decision to let the elections to the Constituent Assembly take place as scheduled. Apparently, the Bolsheviks hoped that their Decree on Land, which gave the land to those who worked it, would win them substantial peasant support. However, the Bolshevik gamble failed. All men and women over the age of twenty could vote, and more than 44 million did so. The Bolsheviks received only 24 percent of the total, for 175 of the Constituent Assembly's 715 seats.

Lenin then began taking steps against the Constituent Assembly. First, the Bolsheviks postponed its first meeting until January and claimed that its electoral ballots did not reflect the actual political situation. When the Constituent Assembly finally met on Jan. 5, 1918, soldiers loyal to the Bolsheviks surrounded it in the Tauride Palace and suppressed pro-Assembly demonstrations outside. Inside the Tauride, the delegates debated until 5 A.M. the next morning when the soldiers asked them to leave. The Bolsheviks then declared the Constituent Assembly dissolved. Its end marked the close of Russia's experiment with parliamentary government.

The October Revolution had begun the process of turning Russia into a one-party dictatorship.

Michael Samerdyke

Bibliography

Chamberlin, William H. *The Russian Revolution.* 2 vols. New York: Macmillan, 1952.
Daniels, Robert V. *Red October.* New York: Scribner, 1967.
Keep, John L.H. *The Russian Revolution.* New York: Norton, 1976.
Pipes, Richard. *The Russian Revolution.* New York: Knopf, 1990.
Sukhanov, N.N. *The Russian Revolution, 1917,* trans and ed. by Joel Carmichael. New York: Oxford University Press, 1955.

United States Intervention in North Russia
American intervention in North Russia (comprising the Archangel and Murmansk regions) was undertaken by the United States in mid-1918 at the urgent request of its World War I allies, Great Britain, France, and Italy. Motivated by his cobelligerents' deep concern about the impact of the Russian Revolution of 1917 on their ongoing war efforts, President Wilson conceived of intervention as a sharply restricted operation with essentially limited objectives. In practice, however, his policy soon became enmeshed in inter-Allied military strategy and the

emerging Russian civil war with consequences that far exceeded the modest intentions of the United States. As a result, from its inception in mid-July 1918 to its termination just over one year later, American intervention in North Russia was characterized by confusion, controversy, and disaffection.

On July 17, 1918, in response to almost six months of persistent Allied supplication culminating in a direct appeal from the Supreme War Council in Paris, President Wilson issued a famous aide-mémoire authorizing the dispatch to North Russia of three battalions of American infantry together with appropriate ordnance and auxiliary forces. In taking this action, however, the President specifically stipulated that these troops were only to be used "to help the Czecho-Slovaks," an embattled pro-Allied force, part of which was then attempting to leave Russia via the north, and, more ambiguously, "to steady any efforts at self-government or self-defense in which the Russians themselves may be willing to accept assistance." Under no circumstances, insisted Wilson, were American troops to be employed for military intervention in Russia, which, he emphasized, the United States rejected "in principle." In effect, it was the imprecision of these instruction that led to much of the subsequent confusion surrounding American intervention in North Russia.

On July 22, acting on the President's orders, the War Department directed Gen. John J. Pershing to detach from his command in France the necessary American troops for service in North Russia. As selected by Pershing, these forces included the 339th Infantry Regiment (three battalions), the 1st Battalion, 310th Engineers (two companies), the 337th Field Hospital, and the 337th Ambulance Company. Under the overall command of Col. George E. Stewart, these units, totaling 4,487 officers and men, formed the nucleus of the so-called American Expeditionary Force, North Russia (AEFNR). Hastily trained and equipped in England, the Americans, more than half of whom were conscripts from Michigan and Wisconsin, embarked for North Russia on Aug. 27, 1918.

In fact, while the AEFNR was still in the course of preparation, developments in North Russia had already taken a turn sharply at odds with American intentions. This situation was largely attributable to the aggressive activities of British MajGen. Frederick C. Poole, who had recently been appointed Allied commander-in-chief in the area. Operating from headquarters at Murmansk, Poole, an ardent interventionist, at once began to implement an extremely ambitious plan of proposed operations in the region that called, in effect, for the virtual invasion of northern European Russia with a projected army of 5,000 Allied troops supplemented by an expected volunteer force of some 100,000 anti-Bolshevik Russians. On August 2, as the first stage of this plan, Poole carried out the occupation of Archangel employing a polyglot force of just 1,500 Allied troops, including 54 sailors from the previously dispatched USS *Olympia*. Thereupon, despite his lack of any significant reserves, the British commander launched an energetic offensive to the south with the cities of Kotlas and Vologda, deep in the interior, as his ultimate objectives.

In these circumstances, on September 4, General Poole greeted the arrival of the AEFNR at Archangel with great enthusiasm and, on the very next day, issued orders directing two of the three battalions of the 339th Infantry to take up positions on the fighting fronts. These orders, which were in direct violation of President Wilson's aide-mémoire, placed Colonel Stewart on the horns of a dilemma. Convinced that Poole's directives were not in accord with Washington's intentions but unable to secure any countervailing support from American Ambassador David R. Francis, Stewart retired to his headquarters and thereafter refused to take any part in the strategic disposition of his troops. As a result, within days of their arrival in North Russia, American soldiers, in direct violation of their government's instructions, found themselves engaged in numerous small-scale combats with units of the Bolshevik Sixth Red Army.

Among the first Americans to become involved in the hostilities were the members of the 1st Battalion of the 339th Infantry. They had been transshipped directly from their transports in Archangel, some 175 miles upstream to the so-called Northern Dvina River front. There, after several sharp skirmishes, an Allied line was finally established at Tulgas, a little less than halfway down the river to General Poole's ultimate objective at Kotlas. Then, beginning on September 27, three of the battalion's four companies were transferred westward to bolster the Allied position on the Vaga River front, located on a swift-flowing tributary of the Northern Dvina. Headquartered at Shenkursk, the region's second largest city, these Americans alternated in occupying several villages situated some twenty miles below Shenkursk at the southern-most point ever occupied by Allied troops in North Russia.

Simultaneous with the battalion's dispatch down the Northern Dvina, the 3d Battalion of the 339th, together with Company B of the 310th Engineers, was packed off to the Vologda Railroad front, whose terminus, some 400 miles to the south, was General Poole's other chief objective. Here again, after several sharp clashes, as well as the stabilization of a subsidiary so-called "Seletskoe Column" to the east, a front line was established just above Emtsa, not even one quarter of the way to Vologda. Finally, in order to protect the flanks of the invading forces, small contingents of American troops were also detailed to create the Pinega and Onega river fronts located, respectively, to the far east and west of the main lines of Allied advance. Thus, within two months of their arrival, American troops, despite strict orders to the contrary, were in sporadic contact with enemy forces on five widely dispersed fronts in North Russia fanned out over a vast territory extending southward some 150–200 miles from Archangel.

In early September, as if their military misuse was not sufficient violation of Washington's wishes, American troops were also drawn into the trammels of local Russian domestic politics in the wake of an unsuccessful coup d'etat in Archangel. So sharp was the American reaction to this development that General Poole was relieved of his command in mid-October and was replaced by a new, British chief, MajGen. W. Edmund Ironside. Ironically, although he had arrived in Archangel with a contingent of 503 American replacement troops, the new commander was immediately confronted by a general memorandum circulated by the United States to all its major allies that bluntly demanded that "all military effort in northern Russia be given up except the guarding of the ports and as much of the country round them as may develop threatening conditions." In these circumstances, General Ironside at once abandoned his predecessor's offensive strategy in favor of a new scheme emphasizing the consolidation of a strong defensive position in the region. Whatever its intention, this new plan failed to address the problem of Ironside's American troops, who continued, in spite of their renewed orders to the contrary, to constitute the majority of the actual combat forces on virtually all of the far-flung fronts of North Russia.

R

Coming in early November, the conclusion of the World War left unresolved the American military dilemma in North Russia. In fact, on the very same day as the war's termination on the Western Front, American soldiers on the Northern Dvina River were engaged in a savage clash with the enemy at Tulgas, which its participants later sarcastically labeled "the Battle of Armistice Day." By the same token, at year's end, American forces with the Seletskoe Column fought gallantly at Kodysh, about 100 miles south of Archangel, in a failed attempt to capture Emtsa, which General Ironside considered essential to the consolidation of a strong position on the Vologda Railroad.

For his part, President Wilson, whose dissatisfaction with the policy had long been evident, believed that the Armistice in Europe had effectively removed all of the original justifications for intervention in Russia and therefore desired to withdraw American forces "by the first boat." Confronted, however, by British and French objections to any precipitate resolution of the Russian problem, the Chief Executive was finally prevailed upon to retain his troops in the region until their ultimate disposition could receive inter-Allied consideration at the impending Paris Peace Conference.

At Versailles in January 1919, it soon became apparent, President Wilson's fond hopes notwithstanding, that the Allies were utterly unable to reach any mutual agreement with regard to intervention in Russia. On the contrary, in spite of at least two determined American efforts to resolve the problem, it gradually became clear that Britain and France were adamantly opposed to any solution of the Russian situation that left in power the hated Bolsheviks, whose treacherous withdrawal of Russia from the war in early 1918 had left the Allies in so precarious a position on the Western Front.

In mid-January, already dismayed by Allied intransigence in Paris, President Wilson was still further distressed by the consequences of a sudden and unexpected Soviet counteroffensive in North Russia. Directed initially against the exposed Allied salient around Ust' Padenga at the southernmost extension of the Vaga River front, the brunt of this overwhelming assault, which pitted some 3,000 Soviet attackers against a few hundred Allied defenders, was borne primarily by American troops. In spite of a spirited Allied defense, this so-called Shenkursk operation, which entailed the highest American casualties

of any single engagement in the entire North Russian campaign, resulted in the surrender of the region's second largest city and a forced retreat of some fifty miles to the north.

The Shenkursk debacle, which coincided with a rising tide of domestic opposition to any further American intervention in Russia as well as the continuing inability of the Allies to reach any satisfactory resolution of the Russian problem at Versailles, finally convinced President Wilson to evacuate U.S. troops unilaterally. Thus, on February 18, responding to a British request for the dispatch of two additional companies of American transportation troops to the Murmansk Railroad front 200 miles west of Archangel, the President gave his agreement, but only on the strict condition that all American and Allied troops be withdrawn from North Russia "at the earliest possible moment that weather conditions will permit in the spring."

As it turned out, the need to delay American evacuation until the thawing of the harbor at Archangel had some unfortunate consequences. To begin with, having endured a long Arctic winter with few amenities and no clear sense of purpose, American troops experienced a wave of disaffection in the late winter of 1919 that produced several incidents and at least one brief episode of insubordination. By the same token, in late March and early April, the inability to effect an earlier departure from the North caused American soldiers to be drawn into the defense of Bolshie Ozerki, a village situated some twenty miles west of the Vologda Railroad. There, at some additional cost, they contributed to the successful containment of the final phase of the Bolsheviks' midwinter counteroffensive.

The battle at Bolshie Ozerki was the last gasp of American intervention in North Russia. On April 17, 1919, BGen. Wilds P. Richardson, having been briefed personally by President Wilson, arrived at Archangel to direct the final evacuation of the AEFNR. Within weeks, the new commander completed a phased withdrawal of American troops from each of the various fronts to bases in and around Archangel. Thereupon, commencing in early June, all of the American forces at Archangel, followed by those units more recently disembarked at Murmansk, were gradually shipped out. As a result, on July 28, 1919, the unintentional American war in North Russia, which had exacted a toll of just over 500 Americans killed, captured, or wounded in action, came officially to an end.

John W. Long

Bibliography
Gordon, Denis. *Quartered in Hell: The Story of the American North Russian Expeditionary Force, 1918–1919.* Missoula, MT: G.O.S, 1982.
Halliday, E.M. *The Ignorant Armies: The Anglo-American Archangel Expedition, 1918–1919.* New York: Harper, 1958.
Kennan, George F. *The Decision to Intervene.* Princeton, NJ: Princeton University Press, 1958.
Long, John W. "American Intervention in Russia: The North Russian Expedition, 1918–1919." *Diplomatic History* (1982).
Rhodes, Benjamin D. *The Anglo-American Winter War with Russia, 1918–1919: A Diplomatic and Military Tragicomedy.* Westport, CT: Greenwood Press, 1988.

United States Intervention in Siberia

As the Wilson administration committed military forces to North Russia, it also ensnared itself in more complex and dangerous events 5,000 miles to the east in Siberia. President Wilson's decision to join with Japan and other Entente forces in this questionable venture was one of his most controversial decisions of the war.

Throughout 1918, Soviet-Allied relations were in a state of flux. After assuming power, Lenin was willing to risk cooperation with the Allies because he considered Germany the greater danger. The Petrograd government and the Narkomindel (Soviet Foreign Commissariat) during the six months before the signing of the Treaty of Brest Litovsk, credited as accurate rumors of impending Allied intervention. Lenin's policy of "caution, discretion, and restraint" reflected this appraisal of Allied intentions and Soviet military weakness.

The Allies also adopted cautious policies toward Lenin's government, hoping above all to convince him of the necessity for continuing Russia's participation in the war on the Eastern Front. However, as Russia's intentions to leave the war gained more certainty, the Entente, in some desperation, sought to shape events to its own interests. In response to the October Revolution, the Japanese government informed the British Foreign Office that as provided for in the Anglo-Japanese Treaty, Japan was prepared to send an army into Siberia, but it would not do so without the approval of the American government. At this point in the war, the British government was not prepared to press Washington for a military commitment in a distant secondary theater, especially when the situation on the Western Front was precarious.

However, concern over American intentions led the Japanese government to send a diplomatic mission to Washington in October 1917 led by Viscount Kikujiro Ishii, ostensibly to discuss Japanese-American cooperation in the war. Secretary of State Robert Lansing and Ishii negotiated in secret and agreed to the Lansing-Ishii Agreement of Oct. 31, 1917, confirming Japan's "special interests" in China and pledging both nations not to take advantage of the war to "seek special privileges in China that would abridge the rights of the subjects or citizens of other friendly states." The intended ambiguity served the interests of both nations at the expense of China and positioned Japan for its intervention in Russian Siberia.

On Jan. 26, 1918, Lord Balfour, British foreign secretary, cabled notes to the Allied and American governments, requesting that they accept Japan as their mandatory in Siberia to protect war supplies stockpiled at Vladivostok as well as the vital Trans-Siberian Railroad (the TSRR linked the Amur Province port city of Vladivostok through Manchuria via Harbin to Lake Baikal, west to Samara on the Volga, to Moscow).

During the three critical months between December 1917 and March 1918, the Supreme War Council (SWC) and Allied General Staffs debated and reached decisions regarding Russia. In a series of notes issued beginning on December 23, the Entente powers, and reluctantly the United States, moved toward intervention in North Russia and Siberia. In Note 16 of Feb. 19, 1918, the SWC first approved military intervention by Japan at Vladivostok. From this point on, the Wilson administration came under increasing pressure from Japan, Britain, and France for cooperative joint action. Even after committing the United States to the interventions at Murmansk and Archangel in April 1918, President Wilson continued to oppose the Siberian intervention and expressly Japanese machinations. As much as he disliked the Bolshevik regime, he balked at American military entanglement and subversion of a government in violation of the principle of self-determination.

However, Wilson himself sent conflicting signals. On March 1, he had decided not to oppose the Siberian intervention, in the name of Allied solidarity, but he was persuaded by Col. Edward M. House and Ambassador David R. Francis to reverse himself. Thus, on March 4, Washington expressed its opposition in a note to all governments concerned. From Petrograd, Lenin assured Allied representatives that despite Russia's surrender to Germany, it would continue to resist German imperialism and assist in their war effort to defeat Germany, short of war, but he also warned against intervention in Russia's internal affairs. Commissar for Foreign Affairs Leon Trotsky explicitly cautioned against Japanese military adventurism in the Far East, insisting that this could only drive Russia into the arms of Germany as protector. While ignorant of much of these developments, Wilson attempted to influence the Russian government's ratification of the Brest Litovsk Treaty in an address to the All-Russian Congress of Soviets. The President assured the Russian people of American friendship but indicated that the United States could offer no help against Germany should Russia continue the war. Predictably, the effect of this message was to assure ratification of the treaty and make Allied intervention more likely, but events were not Wilson's to control. A somewhat conciliatory "Message to the American People" from Lenin was ignored by the expressly anti-Bolshevik State Department.

With Germany's renewed offensives on the Western Front in March 1918, Lenin's and Trotsky's opposition to Allied intervention softened somewhat. On March 25, Georgii Chicherin informed British representative Robert Lockhart that Russia would be glad to accept Allied help, including the "Japanese Corps," provided there were guarantees for the "inviolability of Soviet territory" and nonintervention in its political affairs. With the collapse of Finland and German advances toward Petrograd, the French government, through its ambassador Joseph Noulens, began a campaign from Vologda to subvert the Bolsheviks. Failed conferences between Trotsky and Allied representatives between April 3 and April 5 marked the end of attempts to reconcile mutual antagonisms and suspicions. On April 6, Trotsky warned that Russia would declare war on Japan, perhaps with German support, if the Allies did not make their intentions clear. While there apparently was some consideration in

Petrograd of simply abandoning Siberia in exchange for Allied military help against Germany, any possibility of that ended with the crisis of April 25.

On that day, Chicherin denounced all Allied governments for complicity in an "anti-Soviet conspiracy," and the following week Lenin authorized Trotsky to negotiate with the German government for military assistance. However, even at this late date, Lenin held out the prospect of cooperation if for no other reason than to exploit Allied disagreements and indecision. This policy might have continued if not for two developments.

First, and most important, was the presence of the Czech Corps, better known as the Czech Legion, a full army corps of two divisions, which was stranded in Russia after the Revolution. Deployed in the Ukraine near Kursk, the Czech Legion declared its neutrality in the ensuing civil war, and the National Government negotiated its repatriation to France via the northern ports, or Vladivostok. In March, sixty trains began carrying the Czechs from Kursk eastward on the Trans-Siberian Railroad when German forces overran the Ukraine. Lenin and Trotsky were concerned about this armed force, and Trotsky, who hoped to use the Czechs as the nucleus of the new Red Army, delayed their progress.

By early April, only a few thousand Czechs had reached the Volga, and by that time the Allied governments had recognized counterrevolutionary possibilities for the Czech Legion. On April 25, the SWC, after receiving Trotsky's conditional approval of evacuation of the legion, ordered Czech troops east of Minsk to proceed to Murmansk, with the remainder proceeding on to Vladivostok. This agreement was not immediately communicated to the Czechs, whose trains were halted. On May 2, the increasingly anti-Bolshevik and suspicious Czechs refused orders to disarm, following a shooting incident at Chilyabinsk. There, on May 14, their leaders proclaimed the Czech Legion in revolt, and Allied governments on June 4 informed the Russian government that any attempt to interfere with the legion would be considered a hostile act. At Vologda, Allied representatives now began openly supporting anti-Bolshevik elements.

The Soviet hard-line response by Lenin on June 6 ended all further hope of accommodation, and that same day President Wilson gave in to Allied diplomatic pressure. Fearful of unchecked Japanese action in the Far East, he agreed to joint Japanese-American military intervention at Vladivostok to "rescue the Czechs." Indeed, Japan was prepared to act unilaterally but preferred British and American agreement.

In his aide-mémoire of July 6, Wilson established the guidelines for American intervention. The United States was acting only to help "the Czechs consolidate their forces" and would refrain from interfering "in any way with the political sovereignty of Russia" or impairing its territorial integrity." On August 8, Secretary of War Newton D. Baker ordered MajGen. William S. Graves, commander of the 8th Infantry Division, to assume command of a 7,000-man American Expeditionary Force in Siberia. Between August 14 and 16, the 27th and 31st Infantry regiments left their base in Manila aboard the troopships *Warren, Merritt,* and *Crook.* They landed in Vladivostok to establish America's first military presence in Russia. These forces were soon joined by other elements of the division and by the protected cruiser *Albany,* its sailors, marines, and other support personnel.

Given the policy split within the administration and the anti-Bolshevik animus of Ambassador Francis, the ambiguity of the orders to Graves could have ensnared the United States more deeply in counterrevolutionary (also known as White) factional politics than subsequently occurred. Although General Graves proved a cautious and skilled commander who resisted all attempts by the State Department and by Allied governments to deepen American involvement, his and other Allied forces were, by agreement, under Japanese command, and the Japanese had by far the most aggressive agenda. Still, whatever the intention and stated justification, the very nature of American policy between August 1918 and April 1920 betrayed any pretense of neutrality. General Graves had no misgivings about his dilemma. "There could be no unity of action," he recalled after the war, "because the representatives of Britain, France, and Japan were partisans in the Russian conflict and I was not."

Vladivostok, as all of Siberia, was in political and military chaos by the summer of 1918. Several factions struggled for power, and by the time of American intervention, a Moderate Socialist "Directory" based at Omsk, nominally controlled the region. Stockpiled in huge warehouses were thousands of tons of Allied stores. The harbor bustled with military and civilian shipping, and a volatile, multiethnic, multinational population, gave Vladivostok a rough frontier mentality.

Japan had first landed troops briefly on Dec. 30, 1917, and it did so again in April 1918 after the murder of Japanese nationals. Indeed, this event provided the pretext for Japan's major intervention. Now, in August 1919, the Japanese 12th Division joined American, Canadian, British, and French contingents, and by November Japanese strength exceeded 75,000.

While General Graves deployed units 300 miles north to Khabarovsk, Japanese commanders claimed the Czech Legion was threatening the TSRR along the Ussuri River, a pretext for further Japanese penetration. In the so-called "Ussuri campaign," several clashes with dissident White factions flared, killing and wounding several Americans. In protecting the strategic Suchen mines west of Vladivostok, American units fought dozens of small guerrilla actions—even against Japanese-supported rival Cossack bands.

On November 18, only a week after the Armistice, the Directory at Omsk was overthrown by the anti-Bolshevik forces and government of Adm. Aleksandr V. Kolchak, and with escalation of the counterrevolution, Allied forces became more dangerously entangled in Siberia. In early March, Allied military representatives and the Kolchak government signed a Railway Agreement, which changed the status and objectives of the intervention. By its terms, a six-mile-wide security zone along the TSRR was to be protected by American and Japanese troops, keeping the route open for the Czechs, but also freeing thousands of White forces for combat against advancing Red troops. On June 25, Wilson received Senate approval of this new commitment.

Two battalions of the 27th Infantry guarded sections in the Lake Baikal region and they quickly became involved in numerous small encounters and serious inter-Allied friction. Japanese duplicity nearly provoked open warfare with Cossack forces under Ivan Kalmikov. However, it was at the town of Romanovka that the most serious military action occurred. There twenty-five men of the 31st Infantry were killed or wounded in a predawn attack by local partisans, before being rescued by an armored train. This was only the bloodiest of dozens of clashes between Americans and rival White factions. Further, General

Graves's difficulties were compounded when he was given the task of delivering 50,000 rifles from the United States to Kolchak's forces, transporting them safely but only after American troops averted a tense standoff at Chita with Gregorii Semenov, another Cossack, and his forces. Continued clashes with Semenov, Kalmikov, and other partisans kept American forces in constant danger.

The Allied misadventure in Siberia, ill-conceived and unproductive, became untenable with the decline of White fortunes by January 1919 and with the failure of the Paris Peace Conference to fashion any coherent Allied policy toward Russia. Red Army counterattacks took Kazan and Simbirsk and recaptured Ekaterinburg. Kolchak's spring offensive failed, Omsk fell, and the admiral himself was captured and executed in February 1920. American and Czech forces barely escaped being cut off in the retreat, and the White government reestablished itself at Irkutsk. With the fall of Odessa in the south, however, Allied governments ended their involvement in the Russian civil war.

General Graves informed Washington that the counterrevolution was doomed and advised that American troops be withdrawn. A pro-Soviet coup in Vladivostok at the end of January was only defeated by superior Japanese forces. President Wilson's stroke in October 1919, had left American policy in Russia even further adrift, and its occupation continued by its own momentum. Clearly with the end of the Czech crisis, and the collapse of White military efforts to overthrow the Bolshevik regime, any pretext for continued American involvement no longer existed. Moreover, failure of the Prinkipo conference and the Bullitt Mission to Russia ended any hope of a diplomatic solution.

The War Department ordered the evacuation of Graves's command as soon as practical, and the first United States forces began leaving Vladivostok on Jan. 26, 1920. On April 1, Headquarters, AEF, and supporting units departed on army transports and the American intervention had ended. Other Allied forces also withdrew albeit more reluctantly. However, Japanese troops remained until Oct. 25, 1922, ending its support of the Far Eastern Republic, the buffer state agreed to by the Bolshevik government until it had consolidated its power. In November, Siberia was formally annexed into the Soviet Union.

In all, 165 Americans died in Russia in a commitment few Americans, or the troops themselves, understood. Whatever Wilson's motivations—cooperation with the Allies, fear of Japanese hegemony, help for the Czechs, or a combination of these—in the end his policy made the United States complicit in the ill-considered and poorly executed attempt to overthrow the Bolshevik regime and illustrated the futility of intervention in the internal affairs of Russia.

Jonathan Nielson

See also CZECH LEGION; GRAVES, WILLIAM SIDNEY; LANSING-ISHII AGREEMENT; TWENTY-ONE DEMANDS

Bibliography

Graves, William S. *America's Siberian Adventure*. New York: Jonathan Cape and Harrison Smith, 1931.

Unterberger, Betty Miller. *America's Siberian Expedition, 1918–1920: A Study of National Policy*. Durham, NC: Duke University Press, 1956.

White, John Albert. *The Siberian Intervention*. Princeton, NJ: Princeton University Press, 1950.

Russian-American Relations

Prior to the United States entering World War I, the attitude of the American government toward Russia was ambivalent. Early in the war, President Woodrow Wilson expressed sympathy for the Russians' need for a warm water port for year-round access to the seas of the world and endorsed Russian acquisition of Constantinople in a peace settlement. At the same time, he feared the ascendancy of tsarist despotism in Europe if Germany were defeated. The overthrow of the tsar in 1917 was seen by some American experts as relieving a difficult situation. It would facilitate Russian participation in World War I by sweeping away internal discontents and streamlining the inefficient bureaucracy. The disappearance of tsarist autocracy would also lend more credibility to President Wilson's justification for America's entry into what he called a "fight to make the world safe for democracy." Yet Wilson foresaw that the Russians might prefer to make peace so as to concentrate on domestic affairs.

When the Provisional Government began to encounter political opposition to the war from the Petrograd Soviet and other soviets throughout Russia, therefore, the American government quickly attempted to support the Provisional Government by sending missions to investigate ways in which the United States could assist the Russian war effort and by committing $450 million in aid on assurance of Russia's intention to pursue hostilities against the Central Powers. After the overthrow of the Provisional Government by the Bolsheviks, the United States and its allies rejected the alternatives of recognizing the new government diplomatically and/or colluding in peace negotiations between Russia and Germany. Instead, Wilson flirted with projects for channeling financial aid for the Whites in Russia through the British and French and for intervening militarily in Siberia. He also accepted back-channel diplomatic contacts with the Bolsheviks in the hope of stiffening their spines in negotiations with the Germans and enunciated his Fourteen Points as a means of providing a formulation that stressed areas of agreement with Bolshevik foreign policy (e.g., self-determination of nations, open diplomacy, a peace without annexations or indemnities), inducing the Bolsheviks to closer cooperation with the Allied Powers. None of these strategies made much of a difference. The Bolsheviks were committed to a peace agreement for internal political purposes; they were clear-sighted about their inability to counter the renewed German military offensive of February 1918 and cynical about the possibility of receiving effective assistance from the West. The Bolshevik government left the war via the Treaty of Brest Litovsk on March 3, 1918, bartering huge quantities of territory, population, and industry for the opportunity to consolidate its power.

The prospect of German divisions from the Eastern Front being freed up to participate in massive offensives on the Western Front daunted the Allies, as did the possibility of military supplies that had been sent to Murmansk, Archangel, and Vladivostok falling into German hands. In June 1918, President Wilson, though skeptical of the virtues of military intervention, succumbed to British pressure and sent the 339th Infantry Regiment (about 5,000 men) to North Russia to serve in a combined British-French-American force under British command. Some fantasists hoped that, in addition to guarding the military supplies, this force could fight its way to the Urals, link up with the Czech Legion, some 70,000 Austro-Hungarian prisoners of war who had been fighting on the Russian side and were now cutting their way out of Russia, and together support White counter-revolutionaries. In fact, Murmansk and Archangel were each over 700 miles from Petrograd or Moscow. The dense forests, impassable swamps, and weather made military operations extremely difficult, and the only transport linkage available was a completely inadequate railway line connecting Murmansk to Petrograd. The American regiment spent the winter fighting sporadic small-scale engagements, losing 139 killed and 266 wounded in defense of a perimeter around Archangel whose most extended point was 150 miles to the south of the town. It was withdrawn in August 1919 when the expedition was deemed a failure. In August 1918, Wilson sent MajGen. William S. Graves with the 27th and 31st infantry regiments (about 9,000 men) to Vladivostok to facilitate the evacuation of the Czech Legion, which was withdrawing across Siberia via the Trans-Siberian Railroad. The Japanese had been proposing to occupy Vladivostok, ostensibly to prevent it and its warehouses from being used to the detriment of the Allied war effort. Wilson resolved to join them as a means of limiting their advance into Siberia, then expanded the joint effort to include British, French, Chinese, Canadian, and Italian troops. The American contingent resisted pressures from the other Allies to intervene in the Russian Civil War on the side of Adm. Aleksandr V. Kolchak's White forces beyond carrying out orders to protect shipments of rifles to them. Instead, it guarded the Trans-Siberian Railroad tracks from Lake Baikal to Vladivostok until the arrival and evacuation of the Czech Legion, and itself withdrew in April 1920, having suffered 35 killed and 52 wounded.

These military fiascoes were undertaken during the final phase of hostilities with Germany and continued after Germany's defeat removed their ostensible rationale of keeping Russia in the war. The Allies became entrapped in the Russian Civil War with confusion as to goals and muddle as to means. The diplomatic brokering of the Russian Civil War was always at the mercy of the desire to bring an end to the Bolshevik regime, always frustrated by the divergence of interests of the various Allies. Wilson and British Prime Minister Lloyd George sought to deal with the situation by floating in January 1919 the project of a meeting of all the Russian factions on the Prinkipo Islands in the Sea of Marmara. Though the Bolsheviks accepted, the French encouraged Admiral Kolchak's Whites to torpedo the proposal by refusing to participate. In March 1919, William C. Bullitt, head of an unofficial American diplomatic mission to scout means for resolving the Civil War, brought back from Lenin a proposal to pay off Russian debts, renounce territorial claims, and declare a general amnesty in exchange for a cease-fire and withdrawal of Allied troops. Lloyd George and Wilson, preoccupied with drawing up the Versailles Treaty and fearful of French reactions, brushed the proposal aside. In the same month, Herbert Hoover advanced a Russian relief scheme whose hidden agenda was the erosion of Bolshevik power through Allied control of the transportation system. His suggestions was summarily rejected by Lenin. Though there were some Allied leaders, most notably Marshal Foch, who advocated a large-scale attack on Russia from bases in eastern Europe, such a project was obviously impossible to sell to the citizens of Britain and the United States, and the Allies found themselves unable to influence events in Russia.

Joseph M. McCarthy

See also RUSSIA

Bibliography
Kennan, George F. *Russia and the West under Lenin and Stalin.* Boston: Little, Brown, 1961.
———. *Russia Leaves the War.* Princeton, NJ: Princeton University Press, 1956.
Maddox, Robert J. *The Unknown War with Russia: Wilson's Siberian Intervention.* San Rafael, CA: Presidio Press, 1977.
Rhodes, Benjamin D. *The Anglo-American Winter War with Russia, 1918–1919: A Diplomatic and Military Tragicomedy.* Westport, CT: Greenwood Press, 1988.
Unterberger, Betty Miller. *America's Siberian Expedition, 1918–1920: A Study in National Policy.* Durham, NC: Duke University Press, 1956.

Russian Railway Service Corps

In February 1917, the first Russian revolution succeeded in overthrowing the government of Tsar Nicholas II and establishing a provisional democratic government in its place. Soon afterward, American journalist Stanley Washburn contacted the Advisory Commission of the U.S. Council of National Defense.

Washburn told the commission chairman that, in his opinion, the 5,000-mile Trans-Siberian Railroad (TSRR) had almost ceased to function. Consequently, the vast war stores that the tsarist government had purchased from the United States for use on the Eastern Front were stalled in the Pacific port of Vladivostok. Washburn argued that the only way to move these supplies to the Eastern Front was to reorganize the operation of the railroad in Siberia. The council approached President Woodrow Wilson with the problem.

Wilson's solution was to ask permission from the new Russian government to dispatch a team of American railroad experts to survey the TSRR and to offer suggestions for reorganization. With the consent of the Provisional Government, Wilson created the Advisory Commission of Railway Experts and appointed John F. Stevens as its head. By July 1917, the commission had completed its inspection, and in its report to the Russian government it recommended sweeping changes in the railroad's operation.

In September 1917, the Russian government asked the United States to provide, in exchange for payment, a corps of American railway engineers to oversee the railroad's reorganization and instruct its personnel in more efficient means of management. In response, Secretary of War Newton D. Baker, authorized Stevens to recruit a Special Russian Railway Service Corps. This corps was under the supervision of Stevens and was to function under the direct command of Col. George H. Emerson, the general manager of the Great Northern Railroad. Emerson was assigned to recruit officers for service in Siberia. On Nov. 19, 1917, the 215 members of the corps, together with more than 70 machinists and a number of interpreters left San Francisco for Vladivostok.

When the corps arrived in mid-December, it found Vladivostok in chaos as a result of the Bolshevik Revolution. Stevens decided to send the corps to Japan until conditions in Siberia stabilized enough for the Americans to begin their work. By the end of the following month, the U.S. consul in Vladivostok informed Stevens that the corps could enter Siberia safely.

Stevens and Emerson's first action was to convince Russian officials operating the Chinese Eastern Railway in northern Manchuria to allow an American contingent to operate that railroad. By March 1918, the corps began inspection of the tracks, supervision of repairs of rolling stock, and elimination of inefficiency along the line.

In April 1918, Emerson led a part of the corps on a trip to meet with the American ambassador David R. Francis, at Vologda, in northern Russia. This journey proved slow and arduous and filled with delays. By late May, the group had traveled no farther inland than Irkutsk.

There Emerson and his men tried to bring an end to the fighting that had erupted between the local Bolshevik government and Czechoslovak troops who had deserted from the German Army. These troops were en route eastward on a round-the-world trip to serve with the Allies on the Western Front when the local government attempted to disarm them. By early June, the uprising had spread, and local anti-Bolshevik groups were joining the Czechs and establishing counterrevolutionary governments along the Trans-Siberian Railway. The Russian civil war had begun; from Irkutsk, Emerson reported that the Allies had probably instigated the anti-Bolshevik uprising. Finally, the American consul there halted Emerson's efforts at mediation. In the aftermath of the Czech uprising, however, President Wilson announced his decision to join other Allies and dispatch an American Expeditionary Force to Siberia.

By August 1918, the Russian Railway Service Corps, which had been unable to land in Siberia, finally arrived and began work. In early 1919, the Inter-Allied Railway Committee was established to supervise the operations of the railroad in regions where Allied military forces were active. Stevens headed this committee's Technical Board from March 1918 to November 1922. His task was to administer not only the vast stretches of the Trans-Siberian Railroad not under Bolshevik control, but the entire Chinese Eastern Railroad as well. His efforts were largely hampered by collusion among the Allies, the expansionist designs of the Japanese Army, the inefficiency and corruption of the counterrevolutionary Kolchak government, the banditry of the Cossacks, and sabotage by Red partisans.

The greatest asset for Stevens was the assistance of the Russian Railway Service Corps. He assigned the corps to oversee the TSSR's main line from Vladivostok to Omsk; here the corps made substantial improvements in the line's efficiency.

In December 1919, Benjamin O. Johnson replaced Emerson as commander of the corps, and in June 1920 the corps received orders to return to the United States. A handful of officers, however, chose to remain with Johnson and Stevens, and for another two and one-half years this group continued to work on the rehabilitation of the railroads.

Wilson's sole purpose in creating the Russian Railway Service Corps had been to help the Russian people operate their vital rail system. During its stay, the corps found its mission frustrated by civil war. Politics frequently intruded on what Wilson had intended to be a humanitarian mission. Since the Corps' area of operations was limited to the portion of Siberia that was under counterrevolutionary control, the Bolshevik government and succeeding Soviet historians viewed it with suspicion and hostility. In the United States, on the other hand, the corps' work remained largely unrecognized.

Carol Kingsland Willcox Melton

See also STEVENS, JOHN FRANK

Bibliography

Graves, William S. *America's Siberian Adventure, 1918–1920.* New York: Peter Smith, 1941.

Link, Arthur S., ed. *The Papers of Woodrow Wilson.* 69 vols. Princeton, NJ: Princeton University Press, 1966–1993.

Unterberger, Betty Miller. *America's Siberian Expedition, 1918–1920: A Study in National Policy.* Durham, NC: Duke University Press, 1956.

———. *The United States, Revolutionary Russia, and the Rise of Czechoslovakia.* Chapel Hill: University of North Carolina Press, 1989.

Ryan, John Dennis (1864–1933)

The son of a prosperous mining engineer and prospector, John Dennis Ryan chose to make his own way as a young man. For a time, he worked in his uncle's general store in Michigan, then took a job as a traveling salesman. While selling lubricating oils to miners in Montana, he established contacts with a number of influential bankers and miners, including Marcus Daly, one of the directors of the Anaconda Copper Mining Company. After marrying his childhood sweetheart, Nettie Gardner, Ryan began purchasing stock in Daly's bank. This led Ryan, in the years after Daly's death, to become a successful and influential businessman in Montana. He rose to president of Amalgamated Copper Company and merged it with Anaconda, creating one of the world's largest industrial corporations. His business interests eventually expanded into electric power and railroads in the United States and extensive mining properties in Mexico and South America.

Like many of the nation's business leaders in 1917, Ryan was anxious to serve his country when the United States declared war. He resigned as president of Anaconda to become vice-chairman of the War Council of the American National Red Cross and advised the War Industries Board. Although President Wilson had refused Ryan appointments earlier because of his staunch Republican affiliations, he named Ryan to succeed Howard Coffin as director of aircraft production in April 1918. Ryan immediately set about reorganizing aircraft production facilities, asking Congress for $100 million and the creation of a public corporation to accomplish that task. In August, Secretary of War Newton D. Baker nominated Ryan to be second assistant secretary of war, with virtually total control over acquisition and plans for U.S. air assets in the final months of the war.

Less than two weeks after the war ended, Ryan resigned his wartime position and returned to private business. Soon Ryan, the Aircraft Production Board, and the Spruce Board (which Ryan had also controlled) came under increasing criticism from the House committee investigating aviation expenditures during the war. Allegations and charges abounded, including questions of impropriety and conflict of interest against Ryan for excessive costs expended to build a spur for the Chicago, Milwaukee, and St. Paul Railroad (on whose executive board Ryan had sat before the war). Although Congress brought no formal charges against Ryan, the furor did not leave him untouched. When he died suddenly in 1933 of a heart attack at age 69, he was once again under subpoena to appear before Congress regarding his business affairs.

Jerold Brown

Bibliography

Cuff, Robert D. *The War Industries Board: Business-Government Relations during World War I.* Baltimore: Johns Hopkins University Press, 1973.

S

Sabotage

Sabotage deals with the underworld of spies and saboteurs and relies upon destruction, terror, and treachery as major weapons in its war against an enemy. It is the deliberate destruction or tampering actions taken by enemy agents or sympathizers in time of war.

It is not a new device in war. The use of arson, explosives, and assassinations to strike at the enemy's home front has been common to all modern wars. Until the Second World War, when it became state policy of the Nazi regime, it was regarded as an auxiliary weapon. Even during the Great War, the German High Command never gave more than lukewarm support to Franz von Papen's sabotage ring in the United States.

Modern sabotage is directed at industry, agriculture, transportation, the press, finance, labor, the armed forces, and politics, striking at the very core and mind of the opposing people. It can function successfully only as a secret weapon. Understanding it is the first step toward nullifying its potency.

The Central Powers considered the actions of the United States in delivering war materiel to the Entente a breach of neutrality that justified the use of illegal methods to prevent arms shipments reaching the enemy. While both the German and Austrian governments repeatedly stated their willingness to be bound by international law, mounting evidence of German espionage and sabotage in the United States unfolded long before the United States officially became a belligerent on April 6, 1917.

In January 1915, Section IIIB (Intelligence and Counter-Espionage) of the German General Staff—not the Ministry of War—authorized acts of sabotage in the United States. The case

that aroused the most public interest at the time concerned Capt. Franz von Rintelen, professionally a banker, now a naval officer, who spoke perfect English. He was sent to the United States as an agent in April 1915, to carry out acts of sabotage by organizing strikes among longshoremen, delaying the loading of war materiel, or placing bombs on board those ships to damage or sink them en route to Europe. However, the German Admiralty recalled him immediately, fearing that relations with the United States would be on a collision course if Rintelen carried out any part of his plans. Traveling with a false passport, he was taken off his ship in the English Channel by the British in July 1915 and sent back to the United States. Subsequently, he was tried and did receive a jail term. The American government commuted his sentence at the end of the war.

Evidence of German espionage and planned sabotage in the United States was further clarified when a Secret Service agent picked up Heinrich Albert's briefcase, which he had forgotten on the New York City El, and the damaging documents it contained were exposed in the *New York World*. The damaging evidence was reinforced when the British confiscated documents carried by James F.J. Archibald, an unofficial courier for the Central Powers, and forwarded them to Washington. Both seizures revealed developing networks aimed at spreading propaganda, causing work stoppages in munitions plants, and damage to America's chemical and metallurgical industry.

At the same time, Joseph Goricar deserted the Austrian espionage service and published information documenting a 3,000-man network directed by Franz von Nubar, the Austrian consul general in New York. The German military and naval attachés Capts. Franz von Papen and Karl Boy-Ed directed a similar network for their government.

The American public was aroused by the Black Tom case, in which a major munitions plant in New Jersey was leveled by a mysterious explosion, later proved to be perpetrated by German saboteurs. Unaccountable explosions in factories and a series of explosions in marshaling yards belonging to the Lehigh Valley Railroad, rumors of bomb plots, and the attempt of Eric Munther to assassinate financier J.P. Morgan fueled the growing sense of uneasiness among the American public toward the Central Powers. Finally, the British provided the United States government with irrefutable evidence of German machinations with hostile Mexican leaders in the form of the Zimmermann Telegram. Sabotage and conspiracy only added to the difficulties caused by Germany's resort to unrestricted submarine warfare, and Congress declared war on April 6, 1917.

Albert Dorley

Bibliography
Papen, Franz von. *Memoirs*. London: Deutsch, 1952.
Rintelen, Franz von. *The Dark Invader*. London: Dickson, 1933.
Sayers, Michael, and Albert E. Kahn. *Sabotage*. New York: Harper, 1942.

Sabotage Act

At the start of the First World War, the United States government possessed statutory authority to prosecute sabotage only on military bases and facilities. Attorney General Thomas W. Gregory's request for additional federal legislation to deal with the "intrigues" of foreign agents went unheeded because many members of Congress were concerned that the proposals would curtail political rights and freedom of expression. Just days after war was declared on Germany, the Senate approved a sabotage bill, but the House again balked. It was not until a year later, in April 1918, that President Woodrow Wilson signed a sabotage measure acceptable to conferees from both houses. The law prescribed maximum prison sentences of thirty years and fines of $10,000 for an individual convicted of damaging military stores or facilities or willfully producing defective war material.

Gregory regarded the Sabotage Act as the most effective and sweeping of all the wartime measures aimed at enemy agents and disloyal dissenters. The American Protective League, an organization that investigated "unfriendly aliens" and German Americans, joined the Justice Department in supporting the measure. And yet, unlike the Espionage Act of the previous year and the Sedition Act passed in May 1918, the Sabotage Act was only sporadically and capriciously enforced. The most notable cases involved the "raincoat conspirators," twenty manufacturers indicted for producing defective military raincoats. The law was similarly employed to convict two Ohio union men of conspiring to tamper with machinery in an effort to gain a closed shop. The little-used Sabotage Act led to more prosecutions of American businessmen and workers than enemy saboteurs.

Willard C. Klunder

Bibliography
Vaughn, Stephen. *Holding Fast the Inner Lines: Democracy, Nationalism, and the Committee on Public Information*. Chapel Hill: University of North Carolina Press, 1980.
Jensen, Joan M. *The Price of Vigilance*. Chicago: Rand-McNally, 1968.

St. Mihiel Campaign

As the lines became stabilized along the Western Front in September 1914, a salient formed around the French city of St. Mihiel. Jutting over fifteen miles into Allied territory, the salient formed a rough triangle with Verdun, St. Mihiel, and Pont-à-Mousson as its vertices. It cut the railroad from Verdun to Toul and allowed German artillery fire to range on the rail line from Paris to Nancy. More importantly, the salient flanked any Allied offensive in the strategic Meuse-Argonne area. The St. Mihiel area had to be neutralized for the Allies to carry the war to Germany.

The French had attacked the salient in the years up to 1916 but were never successful at dispelling the German threat to the region or securing the flank of the Meuse-Argonne. The German defense consisted of three lines of barbed-wire entanglements, concrete bunkers and dugouts, and a well-constructed network of machine guns. However, many of the German defenses had fallen into disrepair as the war

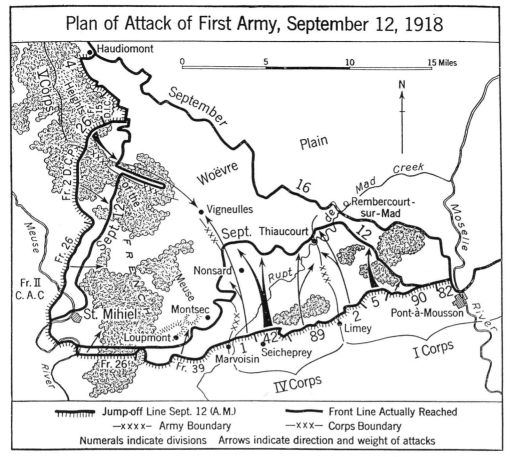

Plan of Attack of First Army, September 12, 1918

St. Mihiel. Taken from American Armies and Battlefields in Europe, *American Battle Monuments Commission, Government Printing Office, 1938.*

stagnated. On July 24, 1918, the Allied commanders agreed on a strategic plan of offensive operations in France that immediately called for the reduction of any salient in the lines that would disrupt the buildup of Allied logistics and manpower. Foremost in the minds of the planners was an attack on the St. Mihiel salient. The Allies agreed this attack would be made primarily by American forces.

This was the mission for which Gen. John J. Pershing had been planning. Since American combat units landed in France, he had directed that an American Army be organized under American command. The German spring offensives of 1918 prevented that formation until Aug. 10, 1918, when the American First Army was given the mission of eliminating the St. Mihiel salient.

As this was the first "all-American" operation, the Allies as well as the Germans would be watching the success or failure of the attack with great interest, particularly since Pershing was withdrawing American divisions from French and British sectors. The morale of the American public was also of prime importance in the thinking of General Pershing. The offensive must succeed.

The initial intent of the Americans was to pierce all three lines of the salient and eliminate the German defenses entirely, but by early September, the American First Army was given the larger mission of attacking the Meuse-Argonne region. Despite this, the St. Mihiel salient attack was not scaled back to an operation designed only to support the larger attack by securing the flank of the Argonne offensive. For the St. Mihiel operation, 550,000 American and 110,000 French troops were assembled.

Three coordinated attacks were planned to reduce the salient. The main attack by I Corps, commanded by MajGen. Hunter Liggett, and IV Corps, commanded by MajGen. Joseph T.

Dickman, would strike the southern "face" of the salient. The open plains in front of IV Corps were the chief target of the attack, as the assaults in the rest of the salient would be against ranges of high ground. The second attack would be made by V Corps, commanded by MajGen. George H. Cameron, against the western "face." A third attack by the French II Colonial Corps would strike the tip of the salient to hold the Germans in place while the two primary attacks broke the salient apart. Nine German divisions, or almost 90,000 men, defended the area, but six of the divisions were made up of reserve and Landwehr units, which were less than dependable. However, the defense was designed to hold until reinforcements could reach the salient from Metz.

Successful coordination and supply of the American Army was critical to the success of the offensive. Two of the three American corps headquarters and four of the nine divisions in the attack had yet to experience offensive combat. Preparations were massive. At least 3.3 million artillery shells were needed for the planned minimum of five days of combat as well as engineer and communications equipment, construction of airfields, hospitals, railroad depots, supply depots, and, most importantly, concealment of all preparations so as not to alert the German defenders of the coming attack. Most of the troop movement was conducted at night. Finally, the largest aviation force yet assembled in the war, composed of over 1,400 aircraft, supported the operations.

A heavy rainfall began in the evening of September 11 and continued into the early morning hours of September 12. At 1:00 A.M. on that morning, 2,900 Allied artillery pieces began the preattack bombardment. It lasted only four hours, enough time to damage the German defenses but still maintain the element of surprise. At 5:00 A.M., the American southern attack began, followed by the French supporting attack an hour later. Each assault moved quickly across no-man's-land, following a rolling barrage. The French diversionary raids against the tip of the salient also began at 6:00 A.M. The western attack began at 8:00 A.M., assisted by an additional three hours of daylight bombardment. It was closely followed by another supporting French attack at 9:00 A.M.

The assault on the southern face proved highly effective. Much of the German wire entanglements were old and rusted and were easily crossed, while others were quickly cut

through. The Americans were so successful in crossing the barbed wire that French officers were sent to study the operation after the battle. The first trench line encountered contained only scattered patrols and was easily captured. The main German trenches were then attacked, but again only scattered resistance was encountered. Many Germans simply surrendered to the advancing Americans.

Typical of the offensive was the experience of the 2d Division, commanded by Gen. John A. Lejeune, USMC. The unit advanced six miles over rough terrain in a little over eight hours, capturing the town of Thiacourt at 11:00 A.M., and then assaulted the high ground just north of the town. The heights soon fell, giving the Americans command of the primary German supply route to the salient. By the end of the first day's fighting on the south face, most of the objectives planned for the second day had already been captured.

The west face attack, however, bogged down against heavy resistance and failed to achieve the first day's objectives. The attacks were hit from strong German defensive positions on either flank. Supporting French attacks on each face had achieved their objectives, but the raids on the tip of the salient were less than successful. Yet the German resistance seemed to be crumbling. Reports from both ground troops and aircraft reconnaissance reached First Army headquarters informing General Pershing that the roads to the rear of the salient were packed with fleeing German troops and vehicles.

Accordingly, the offensive timetable was advanced, and units of IV and V Corps attacked toward the town of Vigneulles. General Pershing himself used the phone to direct units on both sides of the salient to advance and link together at Vigneulles. Elements of the 26th Division from the west face attacked under the cover of night and after moving six miles reached the town at 2:15 A.M., September 13. At dawn, the lead troops in the 1st Division from the south face assault linked up with the men of the "Yankee" Division. The St. Mihiel salient was a salient no more, having been cut in two.

Unknown to the American planners, the Germans intended to withdraw from the salient on September 11 and actually had begun the withdrawal of some heavy artillery. When the American and French attack occurred, the German High Command ordered the lines to be held while the evacuation continued, but the rapid Allied advance prevented any real lines to be formed. The Germans withdrew as fast as they could to form a more permanent line across the base of the salient.

The First Army continued to advance during the day, pushing forward to establish a new defensive line set along the ground established as the final objective point for the attack. German counterattacks on the left of I Corps were defeated, and only small operations continued through September 16. The American commanders were sorely tempted to continue the advance, but they stopped operations to support the planned Meuse-Argonne offensive.

The St. Mihiel offensive proved to be a textbook-type successful offensive operation. Allied casualties for the operations totaled approximately 7,000, while the Germans alone lost over 15,000 soldiers captured as well as 450 artillery pieces. The First Army recaptured over 200 square miles of French territory and directly threatened the German stronghold of Metz. Moreover, the quick victory boosted Allied morale while demonstrating to the Germans what they could expect from the growing American forces in Europe. Pershing's firm belief in an American army commanded by Americans was proven to be correct.

J. Michael Miller

See also MEUSE-ARGONNE OFFENSIVE

Bibliography

American Battle Monuments Commission. *American Armies and Battlefields in Europe.* Washington, DC: Government Printing Office, 1938.

McClellan, Edwin N. *The United States Marine Corps in the World War.* Washington, DC: Headquarters, U.S. Marine Corps, 1920.

Pershing, John J. *My Experiences in the World War.* 2 vols. New York: Stokes, 1931.

Smythe, Donald. *Pershing: General of the Armies.* Bloomington: Indiana University Press, 1986.

St. Quentin Canal Attack

On Sept. 29, 1918, the 27th and 30th American divisions lead a massive assault to break the Hindenburg Line on the front from Cambrai to St. Quentin in northern France. The St. Quentin Canal sector, where the Americans attacked, was thought by many to be the strongest por-

tion of the Hindenburg Line. The elaborate defensive complex along the St. Quentin Line was made up of three trenches that incorporated the St. Quentin Canal and Tunnel. The canal was about forty feet wide and over thirty feet deep in most places, making it impassable to an attacking ground force. In addition, most of the canal ran through a four-mile tunnel along the length of the St. Quentin front. The Germans used the tunnel to shelter their troops and supplies. Intertwined throughout the defensive system were barbed-wire entanglements, machine gun emplacements, and artillery fire zones. The Germans had hoped to hold the Hindenburg Line until winter and then sue for a favorable peace settlement in spring 1919.

In mid-September 1918, the Fourth Army of the British Expeditionary Force (BEF) reached the St. Quentin Canal sector and initiated several assaults, attempting to capture the outpost positions of the Hindenburg Line. Though only partly successful, plans to attack the main German trench complex on September 29 went unchanged. The American II Corps (composed of the 27th and 30th divisions) was ordered to lead the offensive. The 30th Division moved into the trenches on the night of September 23. The 27th Division went into the line on the left of the 30th Division the following night. Each division placed one infantry regiment in the front trenches, one in immediate support, and the other two regiments in division reserve.

The position held by the 30th Division included the former German outpost line, recently taken by the Australian Corps. The 27th Division took the line previously occupied by the British III Corps. The British had failed to capture their portion of the outpost line after several costly attacks. Since it was critical to secure the outpost line before the September 29 assault, the 27th Division's 106th Infantry Regiment was then ordered to capture the ground. In addition, the 30th Division's 118th Infantry Regiment was ordered to attack to better secure its line. On September 26, a preliminary artillery bombardment began against the German positions, lasting two days. On the morning of September 27, the 106th and 118th Infantry regiments attacked the German outpost line. At day's end, the 118th Infantry had captured its objectives. The 106th Infantry had a more difficult time. Three key objectives for the 106th were the Guillemont farm, the Quennemont farm, and a hill called the Knoll. Elements of the 106th Infantry, supported by two companies of the 105th Infantry, managed to capture these positions, only to be forced back by severe German counterattacks. The Knoll exchanged hands at least three times in heavy fighting. By nightfall, the 106th Infantry held positions in and around its objectives, but the battle line was fragmented—the Americans holding some sections, the Germans other sections. The 106th Infantry lost 1,119 officers and men out of 2,000 it took into battle. Every officer but one was killed or wounded. The two companies of the 105th Infantry suffered 259 casualties.

On September 28, the 27th and 30th divisions sent two new infantry regiments into the front lines to prepare for the main assault scheduled for the following day. In the 30th Division, the 119th and 120th Infantry regiments replaced the 118th Infantry. In the 27th Division, the 106th Infantry was isolated and still fighting to hold the enemy outpost line along the division front, so it could not be relieved. Enemy fire forced back all units sent to support the 106th. The 107th and 108th Infantry regiments could only move into line well behind the 106th and wait for the next morning's attack. To support the infantry, seventy-four tanks were sent for the assault: forty from the American 301st Battalion were assigned to the 27th Division, and thirty-four from the British 4th Brigade were assigned to the 30th Division.

At 5:50 A.M., September 29, the St. Quentin Canal attack began when the artillery bombardment changed to a rolling barrage and the infantry went "over the top." At the start, the 30th Division's infantry moved rapidly forward from the jumping-off tape along the German outpost line but soon lost all sense of organization. The battlefield was covered with water-filled shell holes, tangled wire, debris, and bottomless mud. A heavy fog and the smoke from shellfire limited visibility. Officers leading the advance managed to keep direction only by compass readings. Tanks helped clear some of the wire entanglements but drew enemy fire that endangered the infantry following close behind. German counterfire soon destroyed most of the tanks and tore holes in the advancing waves of infantry.

Despite confusion and casualties, the 30th Division's 119th and 120th Infantry regiments broke through the Hindenburg Line by 7:30 A.M. Two hours later, the 120th Infantry captured Bellicourt and by midday had taken Nauroy, its final objective. Meanwhile, the 117th Infantry moved to the right flank and linked up with advancing British troops. To the north, the 119th Infantry was stopped after only partially crossing the Hindenburg Line. Enemy fire on the regiment's left flank prevented further advance, even after reinforcement by two battalions, one from the 117th and the other from the 118th Infantry regiments.

The 27th Division did not experience the same success. Its infantry could not begin the advance from the jumping-off point because it could not reach the 106th Infantry's line, where the barrage started. This placed the advancing troops 1,000 yards behind the rolling barrage of artillery fire meant to cover their attack. German machine gun and shellfire cut into the advancing soldiers as soon as they left the protection of their trenches. Shortly thereafter, thirty-eight of the forty tanks with the 27th Division were knocked out of action.

Eventually, portions of the 108th Infantry managed to reach the Hindenburg Line, but most of the regiment was stopped when trying to pass the Guillemont farm defensive. Directly opposite the farm, the 107th Infantry suffered heavy casualties in several unsuccessful attacks. The regiment captured the Knoll but could not advance much further. The 105th Infantry came up in support, and the two regiments had to fight off numerous German counterattacks the rest of the day. Under such adverse conditions, the 27th Division troops could not continue any foreward movement. It was all they could do to hold the positions already captured.

By midday, the Australian divisions came up and passed through the American lines to press the attack. On the 30th Division front they were able to drive the Germans even further. But when the Australians moved up to the firing line established by the 27th Division, they too met with a storm of shot and shell. It took the next four days for the Australians to win the objectives first assigned to the 27th Division. On the night of September 30, the 27th Division was pulled out of the battle and sent to the rear for rest and reorganization. The 30th Division was sent back on the night of October 1.

Both American divisions suffered heavy casualties in the St. Quentin Canal attack. In the 27th Division, 4,641 men were killed or wounded in the five days on the front. The 30th Division lost almost 3,000 men in seven days. Most casualties in both divisions came during the September 29 attack that broke the Hindenburg Line. Although the 30th Division troops were credited with being the first to break the famous defensive line, the 27th Division shared in the accomplishment of forcing through what the Germans believed no army could break. The victory the two American divisions won in the St. Quentin Canal attack influenced Germany's decision to sue for the cease-fire that ended the war on Nov. 11, 1918.

R.J. Marshall

See also UNITED STATES ARMY: 27TH DIVISION; UNITED STATES ARMY: 30TH DIVISION

Bibliography

Murphy, Elmer A., and Robert S. Thomas. *The Thirtieth Division in the World War.* Lepanto, AK: N.p., 1936.

O'Ryan, John F. *The Story of the 27th Division.* 2 vols. New York: Wynkoop Hallenbeck Crawford, 1921.

U.S. Army. *Operations of the 2d American Corps in the Somme Offensive.* Washington, DC: Government Printing Office, 1921.

Salvation Army

The Salvation Army had no detailed plan in April 1917 for support activities for American military personnel. Undeterred, the army's American commander, Evangeline Cory Booth, offered as much of her organization's personnel and resources as could be spared from ongoing activities. Salvationist war work was under the direction of Col. Edward J. Parker; the contingent in France was commanded by LtCol. William S. Barker. Overall policy was determined by Booth herself, who laid down three general principles based upon the Salvation Army's traditional domestic ministry. Details were left to field operatives, who were expected to be brave, adaptable, and frugal. The principles were: (1) the Salvation Army, as the church of the working man, aimed its activities at enlisted men (officers were welcome but were to receive no special treatment); (2) the army's evangelistic Christian Gospel was not to be diluted, although attendance at religious services was not to be a condition for any form of service; and (3) Salvationists on overseas duty were to carry as much of their work as possible "to the Front," where the needs of American service personnel would be greatest.

The Salvation Army divided its wartime activities between training camps and mobilization depots in the United States and the AEF in France. It was one of the "Seven Sisters" that made up the Commission on Training Camp Activities. The Salvation Army operated a total of ninety-one canteens and clubs during the years 1917–1919. Activities included the provision of snack items, stationery, personal "kit" items, reading rooms, musical activities, voluntary religious services, and writing letters for wounded personnel. Facilities for these activities varied. In a few central camps, the Salvation Army built its own large "huts" to house activities and provide accommodations for visitors to the camp. Acting upon information supplied by their colleagues in France, Salvation Army officers in the United States paid reassuring, or consoling visits to the homes of American service personnel. The Salvation Army also sponsored several small-scale vacant-lot "farming" schemes to support the war effort.

Its most famous wartime activities took place in France. The first contingent of Salvation Army war workers arrived there in August 1917. Eventually, 250 Salvationists of both genders, all of them volunteers, served in twenty-four locations. In addition, the Salvation Army, recognized by the U.S. Army judge advocate general in September 1917 as a denomination, provided five commissioned military chaplains.

Salvation Army activities in France were the same as those provided in the stateside training camp canteens, with the difference that these activities were appreciated by the American service personnel overseas, and publicized by them on a scale out of proportion to volume. Soldiers unused to the military caste system appreciated the democratic treatment in Salvation Army canteens. Many were grateful for the honest tone of Salvationist religious services—the army's traditional street-corner tunes such as "Brighten the Corner Where You Are" were constant favorites in France. The willingness of Salvationists to carry their ministry to the front lines especially endeared them to American service personnel.

The most famous Salvation Army activity in France—and the one for which the army became and remained famous among servicemen—was the production of doughnuts. Salvationist women operatives (called "lassies" like their stateside comrades) were ordered by Booth to "mother" American soldiers. Determined to provide fresh baked goods for the troops, they hit upon the doughnut as the easiest item to produce under conditions of haste, limited materials, and primitive cooking facilities. Thousands of these tasty items were produced and conveyed to grateful troops, often within sight and sound of combat. The doughnut became to the AEF as much a symbol of the Salvation Army as its brass bands and Christmas kettles. As a result of its wartime activities in France, the Salvation Army achieved great popularity among American service personnel, which continued into the postwar era.

Edward H. McKinley

See also COMMITTEE ON TRAINING CAMP ACTIVITIES

Bibliography

Booth, Evangeline, and Grace L. Hill. *The War Romance of the Salvation Army.* Philadelphia: Lippincott, 1919.

Durham, Weldon B. "'Big Brother' and the 'Seven Sisters': Camp Life Reforms in World War I." *Military Affairs* 42 (April 1978).

McKinley, Edward H. *Marching to Glory: The History of the Salvation Army in the USA, 1880–1980.* San Francisco: Harper & Row, 1980.

Piper, John F., Jr. *The American Churches in World War.* Athens: Ohio University Press, 1985.

Sasse, Ralph I. (1889–1954)

Ralph I. Sasse was commissioned a second lieutenant in the cavalry following graduation from the United States Military Academy in 1916 and promoted to first lieutenant just sixteen days later with the rest of his classmates. Initially assigned to the 2d Cavalry at Ft. Ethan Allen, Vermont, he deployed to France in August 1917, where he joined the 1st Infantry Division and earned promotion to captain.

Shortly after making major in June 1918, Sasse, dissatisfied with his current assignment, wrote to Maj. George S. Patton, Jr., commander of the Light Tank School at Langres, requesting duty with tanks. Patton was able to obtain Sasse's transfer to the Tank Corps, and he was sent to Bovington, England, where the 301st Heavy Tank Battalion was training at the British Tank Center. Sasse became the battalion tactical officer and took command of the heavy tank unit on Sept. 9, 1918, when LtCol. Henry E. Mitchell was promoted to command of the 2d Tank Brigade.

The 301st, because it had trained in England and was equipped with heavy tanks provided by the British, was tasked with supporting the advance of the U.S. II Corps as part of the British Fourth Army's assault on the Hindenburg Line in the vicinity of St. Quentin on September 29.

Sasse commanded the battalion for the remainder of the war, participating in major attacks on September 29–30 near Le Catelet, on October 8 near Brancourt, the Selle River crossing on October 17, and Catillon on the night of October 23–24. He was awarded the British Distinguished Service Order for the personal heroism he displayed while leading his battalion and for rallying a large group of leaderless 27th Infantry Division doughboys and leading them to their objective during the assault on the Hindenburg Line on September 29.

The 301st was the only American heavy tank unit to see action. It lost six officers and eighteen enlisted men, eighteen officers and ninety-one enlisted men wounded, and seven enlisted men missing. In addition, of the forty-seven tanks with which the battalion went into battle, thirty-five were destroyed or damaged by artillery fire or mines. The battalion had only twelve operational vehicles when it was finally pulled from the line.

Following the war, Sasse returned to Fort Meade, Maryland, where he remained in the Tank Corps until mid-1920. Like many Tank Corps officers, Sasse, who reverted to his permanent rank of captain in June of that year, was concerned about the future of tanks in the army. The National Defense Act of 1920 disbanded the Tank Corps as a separate arm of the service and made it subordinate to the infantry branch. Shortly after that action, Sasse volunteered to return to the cavalry. During the next two decades he served in various cavalry assignments and became West Point's most successful football coach, leading the Black Knights to a 30–9–4 record in four seasons. He retired from the army as a lieutenant colonel in November 1940.

Recalled to active duty on July 8, 1942, Sasse was promoted to colonel in October and commanded an armored group at Fort Knox in 1942–1943 and the 7th Armored Regiment at Fort Meade and Camp Adair, Oregon, in 1945. He retired again in 1946 and died in Lewis, Delaware, on Oct. 15, 1954.

Dale E. Wilson

Bibliography

Blumenson, Martin, ed., *The Patton Papers, 1885–1940*. Boston: Houghton Mifflin, 1972.

Wilson, Dale E. *Treat 'Em Rough! The Birth of American Armor, 1917–1920*. Novato, CA: Presidio Press, 1989.

Schlieffen Plan

The Schlieffen Plan—the German plan for war against France and Russia—was named for its author, Alfred Graf von Schlieffen, chief of the German General Staff, 1891–1905. It called for a vast wheeling movement by the bulk of the German Army through neutral Belgium, letting the last man on the right "brush the Channel with his sleeve," as Schlieffen allegedly urged, outflanking the French armies, skirting Paris to the south, and driving the French against their own fortress line to encirclement and destruction in a giant battle of annihilation.

Before Schlieffen's tenure as chief of staff, German war plans, in considering the theoretical possibility of a two-front war, had envisioned dividing the German Army into two nearly equal parts: one part to conduct a holding operation against France, while the rest of the army joined with their Austro-Hungarian allies to defeat Russian forces deployed in central Poland, then a province of the Russian Empire. There was no real expectation of decisive victory; as late as 1888, the Germans expected to fight an offensive defense in the west against France while fighting Russian armies to a standstill in the East.

The appointment of Alfred von Schlieffen as chief of the General Staff brought about a fundamental change in this war plan. By all accounts Schlieffen was a taciturn, single-minded soldier utterly devoted to his profession. Reputedly, he often sent complex military problems to his most promising subordinates to solve over their Christmas holidays, and his oft-quoted evaluation of a beautiful lake bathed in East Prussian moonlight—"an unimportant military obstacle!"—complete the image of a monocled martinet narrowly focused on military operations. There is certainly truth in this portrait, but added to it must be the adulation and loyalty many younger general staff officers felt for their chief. These feelings help explain the exalted reputation he has enjoyed since the end of the Great War.

During Schlieffen's tenure as chief of staff, the specter of a two-front war became a reality with the signing of the Franco-Russian Entente in 1894. What had been to some degree at least a staff exercise now assumed the greatest importance: planning to fight a war simultaneously against France and Russia. Schlieffen worked out a highly original solution to Germany's strategic dilemma. Like most students of war in this period, he had been imbued with the importance of gaining the decisive battle, and he was convinced that winning such a battle was dependent on turning the enemy flanks, since frontal assault, always costly, allowed the enemy to retreat along his own line of communications, drawing supplies and reinforcements to the army and enabling it to pick another position from which to continue resistance.

Schlieffen's solution to this two-front dilemma was to use Germany's interior lines and superior railway system in an attempt to hold off one adversary with minimum forces, while the bulk of the German Army sought decisive victory in the other theater of operations. Once that victory was secured, the victorious forces would be transferred to deal with the remaining foe. Schlieffen chose to attack France first because France's railroad network and smaller geographical size indicated that it would mobilize more quickly than Russia, threatening Germany with an invasion from across the Rhine. From the German perspective, however, France's ability to mobilize quickly also provided an opportunity. If properly conducted, a German offensive might "bag" most of the French Army, driving that country from the war. In Schlieffen's eyes, Russia's very massive mobilization would take many weeks to complete, and until the Russian Army was mobilized and concentrated, western Russia offered few, if any, decisive objectives for the German Army to attack. Always there remained grave concern about the immense spaces of the Russian interior and its ability to swallow up an invading army.

As early as 1892, Schlieffen seems to have concluded that he must seek decisive victory in the west. Beginning in that year, he initiated planning for a quick victory over France. Early versions of his plan called for the bulk of the German armies to stop an anticipated French offensive toward the Rhine, while strong reserves struck the French left wing in the vicinity of Verdun. Yet, the chief of the Great General Staff remained fearful that the French might delay the German offensive, and each day's delay made the intervention of the Russian "steamroller" against Germany's eastern frontier that much nearer. Ultimately, he decided that Germany simply could not afford to await the French attack. Russia, humiliated by its performance in the Russo-Japanese War, had embarked on a crash course to improve its military capabilities. Each improvement cut into the advantages of Germany's quicker, more streamlined mobilization that Schlieffen counted upon to wage a two-front war successfully. Germany, he decided, had to attack in order to ensure a rapid defeat of France and the quick redeployment of the army eastward. By the end of 1905, about the time he retired, a series of staff rides, war games, and constant study had convinced him that Germany's best hope lay in an offensive of breathtaking boldness. Rather than a narrow enveloping counterattack near Verdun, Schlieffen now opted for a massive wheeling movement through central Belgium. Elements of the right wing would violate the neutrality of Luxembourg and, via the "Maastricht appendix," Holland as well.

The allocation of forces further indicated the plan's boldness. Schlieffen proposed leaving only ten divisions with supporting local troops to face the Russians, while sixty-eight total divisions marched west. Of those committed to the great offensive, fifty-nine would deploy with the right-wing armies; the remaining nine divisions would guard the common frontier between France and Germany, perhaps even retreating before French forces to entice them further and further east, away from the decisive right wing.

This campaign plan, as amended by Schlieffen's successor, Helmuth von Moltke (the Younger), was utilized by the German Empire in the opening campaign of the First World War. Since the war's end, scholars and soldiers have endlessly debated Schlieffen's great plan. Two principal threads of criticism have emerged. At the operational level, critics charge that the plan simply was not practical; the German Army lacked the forces, and more importantly, the logistical "tail" to support so vast and rapid a movement. There also seems to be no notion in the plan of the Clausewitzian concept of "friction," the technical military equivalent of "Murphy's Law." In allocating only six weeks to defeat France, Schlieffen tacitly expected a campaign that ran like clockwork. Mistakes, breakdowns, bad weather, or just bad luck were not considered in his timetable. Criticism of the plan at the strategic level focuses on three closely interrelated points. By invading neutral Belgium, Schlieffen virtually assured Great Britain's entry into the war, since Britain, along with Prussia, was a guarantor of Belgium's neutrality and had shown a long-standing opposition toward any great land power controlling the Low Countries. Perhaps more importantly, Schlieffen's critics charge that his plan, with its emphasis on speed and on running grave risks to obtain victory, put Germany's soldiers and statesmen under the intense and ultimately unbearable pressure once the crisis of 1914 broke out: the imperatives of time, the absolute requirement to win quickly—these acted as accelerators, pushing Germany's decision makers to opt for war lest they lose their carefully crafted and crucial advantage in speed of mobilization. Most importantly, Schlieffen's critics underscore that in the very homeland of Clausewitz, Schlieffen put together his war plan without any apparent consultation or influence from Germany's government. Rather than policy directing war, the ultimate negation of Clausewitz's famous dictum had occurred—war was now driving policy.

Schlieffen's defenders generally claim that, operationally, the plan came very close to success, despite being drastically modified and then haltingly implemented by Schlieffen's successor. Had the old general himself been in charge, they assert, things might well have gone differently. The issue of bringing Britain into the war is answered by the general belief, shared by Schlieffen, that the next European war would be short: a great battle would decide its outcome. In this scenario, Britain's fleet and economic power would not be an important part of the equation. Finally, there is no record that Germany's statesmen ever protested or in any way tried to alter the Schlieffen Plan.

In retirement, Schlieffen continued to study and tinker with his great work. He died in 1913, at age eighty. His oft quoted last words, "It must come to a fight. Keep the right wing strong!" even if apocryphal, fittingly capture his obsession with the plan, which was to have such fateful consequences for Germany and the world.

Gary Cox

Bibliography

Miller, Steven E., Sean M. Lynn-Jones, and
    Stephen Van Evera, eds. *Military Strat-*

egy and the Origins of the First World War. Princeton, NJ: Princeton University Press, 1991.

Ritter, Gerhard. *The Schlieffen Plan: Critique of a Myth*. New York: Praeger, 1958.

———. *The Sword and the Scepter*. Vols. 2 and 3. Coral Gables, FL: University of Miami Press, 1972.

Van Creveld, Martin. *Supplying War: Logistics From Wallenstein to Patton*. Cambridge, UK: Cambridge University Press, 1980.

Schwab, Charles M. (1862–1939)

Charles M. Schwab was born in Pennsylvania. He left home at age seventeen to take a dollar-a-day job in one of Andrew Carnegie's steel mills. His cheerful personality and hard work brought him to Carnegie's attention. The magnate took an immediate liking to the young man, and under Carnegie's sponsorship Schwab rose rapidly: at age twenty-seven he was supervising the firm's largest mill; eight years later he was company president. When Carnegie sold his firm in 1901 to the newly organized United States Steel Corporation, Schwab became president there as well. Leaving U.S. Steel in 1903, he acquired the Bethlehem Steel Company and developed it into one of the world's largest steel producers, with a substantial shipbuilding subsidiary. A key reason for Schwab's impressive business success was his remarkable personality; he combined business acumen with infectious enthusiasm and optimism.

In the spring of 1918, when the United States Shipping Board came under political attack for not producing merchant tonnage quickly enough, the board's chairman, Edward Nash Hurley, invited Schwab to become director general of the government-owned Emergency Fleet Corporation. Hurley recognized that Schwab's reputation as a great industrialist and shipbuilder would significantly boost the corporation's public image. Schwab accepted the position, patriotically donating his services to the government for a dollar a year.

He did not, however, take an active role in the day-to-day supervision of the shipbuilding program, a task he left mostly to the corporation's vice president, Charles Piez. Schwab focused instead on what he called "human engineering," by which he meant instilling in shipyard management and labor enthusiasm for greater output. To this end, he visited doz-

ens of yards on speaking tours and encouraged competitions that pitted one plant against another to see which could build ships faster. When the production of tonnage increased significantly in the summer and fall of 1918, the public gave Schwab much of the credit; in truth, though, this output was primarily the result of groundwork that had been laid by Hurley and Piez before Schwab joined the corporation. Three weeks after the Armistice, Schwab resigned his government position and returned to Bethlehem Steel. He died in 1939.

William Williams

Bibliography

Hessen, Robert. *Steel Titan: The Life of Charles M. Schwab*. New York: Oxford University Press, 1975.

Hurley, Edward N. *The Bridge to France*. Philadelphia: Lippincott, 1927.

Mattox, W.C. *Building the Emergency Fleet*. Cleveland: Penton Publishing, 1920.

Wall, Joseph F. *Andrew Carnegie*. New York: Oxford University Press, 1970.

Scott, Emmett Jay (1873–1957)

Emmett Jay Scott was born in Houston, Texas. He attended Wiley University at Marshall, Texas, from 1887 to 1890 and worked as a reporter for the *Houston Post* from 1891 to 1897. From 1894 to 1897, he was also the editor of a small black newspaper, the *Texas Freeman*. Under his guidance, this was to become one of the most influential black newspapers in the state of Texas. In 1897, Scott met Booker T. Washington and was invited to become Washington's personal secretary at Tuskegee Institute. He was to remain there until 1919, serving from 1912 on as the secretary of the Institute.

During World War I, Scott was chosen by Secretary of War Newton D. Baker to be special assistant for Negro affairs to the secretary of war. This position, the highest government position held by a black American up to 1918, was created in response to the increasing racial tensions of the time and the ongoing exodus of rural southern blacks to northern cities. It was in this capacity that Scott wrote a report for the Carnegie Endowment for International Peace on the migration of 400,000 southern blacks. As Baker's assistant, he was able to oversee training and camp life of black troops and was privy to documents that were restricted to other writers outside the War Department. In 1919, he wrote *Scott's Official History of the American Negro in the World War,* which covered all aspects of black participation both in Europe and at home during the war.

Following the war, Scott was secretary-treasurer of Howard University in Washington, D.C., until 1938. He was director of personnel for Sun Ship Co., in Chester, Pennsylvania, during World War II and served as assistant director of the Republican National Committee from 1939–1942. He published several works on blacks and Booker T. Washington. He died on Dec. 11, 1957.

Michael J. Knapp

Scott, Frank A. (1873–1949)

Frank A. Scott was a successful, forty-four-year-old Cleveland businessman when Secretary of War Newton D. Baker tapped him to head the Munitions Standards Board in March 1917. Scott went on to chair the General Munitions Board in April and the War Industries Board in July. His task in these agencies essentially was to facilitate the equipping and arming of the military services through a rational distribution of contracts and resources.

An avid student of military history, Scott was unusual among top civilian mobilization officials in his sympathetic relationship with the army. While many businessmen who served in the wartime government considered soldiers inept in industrial mobilization, Scott's deep interest in military institutions led him to value officers' expertise as essential to successful production of munitions. He strived to mediate between the officers and the commercial men, but he underestimated the depth of the gulf separating the two groups. Conciliation could not effect the necessary reforms of overly autonomous military supply bureaus. Civilian-military conflict seriously weakened the General Munitions Board and the War Industries Board, neither of which enjoyed a sufficient grant of power from the Wilson administration during Scott's tenure.

More than half a year of crushing work and constant stress in the uphill battle of industrial mobilization sapped Scott's strength. His prodigious strivings largely frustrated, he suffered a nervous breakdown and resigned as War Industries Board chairman on Oct. 25, 1917. A modest man, he, nonetheless, resented the eclipse of his efforts in the shadow of the highly touted accomplishments of his eventual successor at the War Industries Board, Bernard Baruch.

Terrence J. Gough

Bibliography

Cuff, Robert D. "Newton D. Baker, Frank Scott, and 'The American Reinforcements in the World War.'" *Military Affairs* 34 (February 1970).

———. *The War Industries Board: Business-Government Relations during World War I.* Baltimore: Johns Hopkins University Press, 1973.

U.S. Congress. Senate. Special Committee Investigating the Munitions Industry. *Munitions Industry: Minutes of the General Munitions Board from April 4 to August 9, 1917.* 74th Cong., 2d Sess., 1936.

———. Special Committee Investigating the Munitions Industry. *Munitions Industry: Minutes of the War Industries Board from August 1, 1917, to December 19, 1918.* 74th Cong., 1st Sess., 1935.

Scott, Hugh Lennox (1853–1934)

Hugh Lennox Scott served as U.S. Army chief of staff from 1914 to 1917, and during that time he worked to prepare the nation for war. After the United States entered the First World War, he was a member of the Root Mission to Russia in 1917 and later commanded Camp Dix, New Jersey.

Born in Kentucky and raised in New Jersey, Scott graduated from the United States Military Academy in 1876. He spent most of the next two decades on the Great Plains with the cavalry and became an expert on Native American culture and sign language. Following the Spanish-American War, he served as the governor of Sulu Island in the Philippines. These early assignments not only allowed Scott to develop his military skills, but also highlighted his talent as a negotiator. He returned to the United States in 1906 to become superintendent of the U.S. Military Academy, holding that position until 1910.

Scott's career developed a dual focus in the years immediately before the First World War. In addition to his military duties, he became deeply involved as a diplomat, both with various Indian tribes in the United States and, following the revolution of 1910, with Mexico.

Between 1913 and 1917, Scott often served as a "diplomatic fireman" settling local disputes along the United States-Mexican border. He first became involved in the situation while commanding troops along the border. Afterward, his familiarity with Mexican leaders, fluency in Spanish, and negotiating skills made him a frequent choice to handle cross-border disagreements.

The most important dispute Scott managed came in 1916 after Francisco "Pancho" Villa's raid on Columbus, New Mexico. In response to the invasion, President Woodrow Wilson ordered a Punitive Expedition into Mexico. War between the United States and Mexico appeared close at hand just as U.S. relations with Germany were deteriorating. In order to avert a war, Scott held a series of talks with the Mexican minister of war, Alvaro Obregón. Although not a complete solution to United States-Mexican problems, the talks temporarily eased tensions along the border and allowed the Wilson administration to focus its attention on European affairs.

In addition to his diplomatic involvements, Scott became U.S. Army chief of staff in 1914. While his diplomatic duties were often a distraction, as chief of staff he worked to solidify the position of the General Staff within the War Department and to protect it from a hostile Congress eager to make personnel cuts. He also strove to prepare the nation for war. His quiet style and commitment to working within the system, however, often irritated the more vocal proponents of reform and preparedness within the army, especially MajGen. Leonard Wood. Moreover, "preparedness" quickly became a highly charged political issue. President Wilson combined a traditional Democratic aversion to the military with a strong desire to remain neutral in the European war. Therefore, he viewed almost any attempt to prepare the nation for war as not only politically distasteful, but also provocative to the Europeans. While the advocates of preparedness, such as Scott's friends Theodore Roosevelt and Wood, were interested in improving the military, they were also Wilson's political opponents and generally not as interested in neutrality. Thus, whatever actions he took, Scott was likely to offend either his superior or his friends.

Despite these problems, Scott worked to improve the army, especially the military manpower system. With his encouragement, Secretary of War Lindley M. Garrison proposed the Continental Army Plan in 1915. This controversial plan called for an increased Regular Army as well as the creation of a large, federally controlled reserve system. The measure failed in Congress in 1916 after a bitter fight, but Scott remained supportive of the plan even after Wilson withdrew his backing. While Garrison and his assistant resigned in protest after the plan's defeat, Scott was able to remain.

The partial mobilization of the army and National Guard during the Punitive Expedition that same year further convinced Scott that the military needed major reforms. The mobilization was chaotic, and units arrived without the proper equipment, indifferently trained, and understrength. Scott immediately directed a revision of the army's mobilization plans and sought to further federal control over the states' National Guards. Additionally, he ordered the General Staff to prepare a plan for universal military training.

After the United States declared war on Germany in April 1917, Scott oversaw the army's initial mobilization. New camps had to be built, equipment ordered, and new weapons developed and manufactured. Scott worked closely with the new Secretary of War Newton D. Baker to expedite matters. The pair issued orders and spent funds even before Congress had met to appropriate the money. Most importantly, manpower had to be mobilized, and Scott submitted the universal military training plan he had ordered the previous year. After some modifications, it became the basis for the Selective Service Act of 1917.

The qualities that had allowed Scott to work well within the Wilson administration in peacetime—his quiet demeanor, his preference to work within the bureaucracy, and his loyalty to subordinates and friends—did not necessarily suit a wartime chief of staff. Furthermore, his age, he was nearly sixty-four, complicated matters. He was simply neither ruthless enough nor aggressive enough for the job.

In May 1917, President Wilson ordered Scott to accompany the Root Mission to Russia. In his absence, his assistant, Tasker H. Bliss, would assume the duties of chief of staff. The Root Mission's purpose was to express American support for the Provisional Government established after the overthrow of the tsar in February. Scott enjoyed the trip, especially seeing Siberia. He was also able to witness the fighting on the Eastern Front. The mission, however, accomplished nothing of importance since the Provisional Government fell to the Bolsheviks that autumn.

Upon returning to the United States, Scott resumed his office, but he was retired for age in only a few weeks. Baker instantly recalled him to active duty and gave him command of the 78th Division at Camp Dix, New Jersey. Nevertheless, Scott toured the front in France and met with the American Expeditionary Force commander, John J. Pershing, before reporting to the division. Scott took command of Camp Dix and the 78th in January 1918 and intensified the division's training regime. As the division readied to go overseas, however, he found that Pershing considered him too old to lead the 78th in combat. In addition to his age, Scott also believed that Pershing did not want any of his former superiors in France. Disappointed at being left in the United States, he continued to command Camp Dix for the remainder of the war.

Following the war, Scott again retired from the army. In retirement, he continued his lifelong interest in the Plains Indians. He wrote extensively on Native American culture and compiled a dictionary of sign language. From 1919 until 1929, he served on the Board of Indian Commissioners. Beginning in 1923, he also served for ten years on the New Jersey State Highway Commission. Hugh L. Scott died at Walter Reed Army Hospital in April 1934.

Richard Kehrberg

See also ROOT MISSION

Bibliography
Scott, Hugh L. *Some Memories of a Soldier.* New York: Century, 1928.

Sedan Incident

The "Sedan Incident" occurred a few days before the Armistice, as American and French forces were driving the Germans from the Meuse-Argonne region of eastern France. Elements of I and V Corps of the American First Army ran into each other around Sedan in an extraordinary snafu that involved several outstanding figures on the American side and that became one of the great controversies of the American Expeditionary Force (AEF) in World War I.

Located about eighty miles east-northeast of Paris, Sedan was an important rail center and had great sentimental value for the French, for it was here that Emperor Napoleon III and his army of 80,000 were captured in a humiliating defeat at the close of the Franco-Prussian War of 1870. Sedan had been taken again by the Germans in their initial push in 1914.

As the Allied offensive advanced late in September 1918, the American First Army west of the Meuse began to move faster toward Sedan than the French Fourth Army, which was driving west of the Argonne Forest toward the city. Aware of the significance of Sedan to the French, the Americans had agreed to a change in its sector's boundaries so that Sedan would be in the zone of advance of the French force. When, however, Gen. John J. Pershing, commanding the American Army Group, consisting of the First and Second Armies, noted the faster advance of the First Army, he decided that American soldiers should take Sedan.

In early November, therefore, he met with his counterpart, Gen. Paul Maistre, commander of the French Group of Armies of the Center, and they agreed that the Americans should capture Sedan if they arrived first before the city. Pershing was pleased and excited, for he felt the capture of Sedan could be the final great action of the war and would definitely bring to an end a string of "modest communiques" about American accomplishments, thus winning for his forces the glory he knew they deserved. Perhaps he also believed that it would confirm the superiority of his army to that of the French.

On November 5, Pershing visited MajGen. Joseph T. Dickman, whose I Corps lay along the right flank of the French and was the closest corps to Sedan. Pershing told Dickman that he "would like to see his Corps have the honor of taking Sedan." Dickman promised to do everything in his power to succeed.

That same day, BGen. Fox Conner, AEF operations chief, arrived at First Army headquarters and told the operations chief, Col. George C. Marshall, Jr., of Pershing's desire that the First Army capture Sedan. Both the commanding general, Hunter Liggett, and his chief of staff, BGen. Hugh Drum, were not present as Conner dictated a message from Pershing to the commanding generals of I and V Corps. Drum returned shortly after Conner had left, and together with Marshall drafted a memo based on Conner's message and sent it to Dickman and MajGen. Charles P. Summerall, who commanded V Corps on Dickman's right flank. Surprisingly, they did not bother to inform First Army commander Liggett about the order, even though they issued it in his name. They also neglected to provide instructions for coordinating the movements of the two corps. The memo read as follows:

Subject: Message from the Commander-in-Chief [Pershing]

1. General Pershing desires that the honor of entering Sedan should fall to the 1st American Army. He has every confidence that the troops of the 1st Corps, assisted on their right by the 5th Corps, will enable him to realize his desire.

2. In transmitting the foregoing message, your attention is invited to the favorable opportunity now existing for pressing our advance throughout the night. Boundaries will not be considered binding.

Dickman, realizing that Pershing and the French had reached an understanding, directed the 42d Division, next to the French on his left, to move onto Sedan. The 77th, which was on his right, he ordered to continue toward the Meuse. If he needed assistance from Summerall and his V Corps, which he doubted, he could always call on him for help.

Summerall, however, apparently interpreted the statement—"Boundaries will not be considered binding"—to mean not only that boundaries between American and French forces were relaxed, but also that those between Dickman's corps and his own no longer applied. On November 6, therefore, he went to the headquarters of the 1st Division, under BGen. Frank Parker, and ordered him to move as fast as possible on Sedan and capture the city. Surprisingly, Summerall issued this order without contacting or consulting with Dickman—and without knowing the exact location or plans of I Corps.

The 1st Division had just settled in along the right flank of the 42d and 77th divisions, about two and one-half miles west of the Meuse, after an exhausting all-night march on November 5 through rain and mud. Tired and disgruntled, the division deployed into five columns and started out after dark on November 6 in a northwesterly direction toward Sedan.

Parker had not informed either the 42d or the 77th of his march, and apparently expected to encounter only Germans. Everyone was surprised and confused, therefore, when 1st Division columns began to run into men from the 42d Division already marching toward Sedan and others from the 77th Division advancing toward the Meuse. In the confusion, phone lines were snarled, traffic piled up, and Americans fired at each other. Elements of the 1st also mixed with French forces moving toward Sedan, thus compounding a dangerous, disorganized, and confused situation.

The French quickly and loudly complained over the telephone, and MajGen. Charles T. Menoher, commanding the 42d Division, was irate. At I Corps headquarters, Dickman flew into a rage and told Menoher to take command of all troops in his sector. Then he ordered Col. Henry J. Reilly, commanding a brigade of the division, to locate Parker and tell him to get his men out of the area. In the meantime, however, Summerall had arrived at Parker's advanced headquarters before Reilly and ordered Parker to withdraw his division.

At First Army headquarters, Liggett learned about the situation on the seventh and lost his temper completely. Rushing to I Corps headquarters, he was able to regain his composure and tried to calm Dickman. He missed Summerall at V Corps headquarters, but informed the chief of staff that the action of the 1st Division was "a military atrocity." On the eighth, boundaries were adjusted to insure that the French would take Sedan. On November 11, however, the fighting stopped before French forces could reach the city. Ironically, no one ever recaptured Sedan.

On November 8, Liggett ordered Summerall and Parker to make written statements explaining their actions. In their reports, both asserted that they were merely obeying orders. Summerall added that he thought that the order of November 5 had lifted all boundaries between his corps and Sedan; for his part, Parker stressed that his purpose was "to cooperate fully . . . with . . . the 42d and 77th Divisions." Liggett was dissatisfied, but since a disaster had not occurred and the Germans were beaten, he let the matter drop. The next day Pershing visited Liggett and agreed that there was no reason to pursue the matter further.

Something, however, had gone wrong on the road to Sedan. Personal feelings had overridden professionalism and good sense. In addition, Drum and Marshall, who had served previously under Pershing while he commanded the First Army, failed to inform their present commander, Hunter Liggett, about a major change in the mission until after all the trouble started, an oversight that could be attributed to a lapse of professional judgment and to the closer personal relationship which existed between Pershing and Conner on the one hand and Drum and Marshall on the other.

Although the Sedan incident had no real effect on the war, it affected relationships among the U.S. Army High Command for years to come. Dickman and Summerall became bitter enemies. Dickman resented Summerall's success and reputation as Pershing's favorite commander, and Summerall became his implacable foe, to the point of later accusing Dickman of being an agent for the Germans. For the rest of their lives, any friend or close associate of one became the enemy of the other. Frank Parker, for example, believed that Dickman was responsible for delaying for five years his permanent promotion to brigadier general. Later, in his position as army chief of staff, Summerall attributed any criticism or resistance he encountered to the entrenched influence of Dickman's supporters. It became impossible to criticize him without incurring his wrath and rejection. Perhaps the Sedan incident revealed a dangerous tendency among officers of high command in any army: namely, that in the approach of victory and triumph the race for fame and glory can become the most important goal.

Gary Nichols

See also DICKMAN, JOSEPH THEODORE; DRUM, HUGH ALOYSIUS; LIGGETT, HUNTER; MARSHALL, GEORGE CATTLET; SUMMERALL, CHARLES PELOT

Bibliography

Coffman, Edward M. *The War to End All Wars: The American Military Experience in World War I.* New York: Oxford University Press, 1968.

Dickman, Joseph T. *The Great Crusade: A Narrative of the World War.* New York: Appleton, 1927.

Harbord, James G. *The American Army in France, 1917–1919.* Boston: Little, Brown, 1936.

Liggett, Hunter. *Commanding an American Army: Recollections of the World War.* Boston: Houghton Mifflin, 1925.

Smythe, Donald. "A.E.F. Snafu at Sedan." *Prologue* (Fall 1973).

Sedition Act of 1918

The passage of the Sedition Act of 1918 during World War I marked one of the greatest restrictions on civil liberties in American history. Propelled by the overwhelming current of patriotism that swept through the United States following its entry into the war, both private citizens and their government praised the ideals of "Americanism" and demanded conformity to the war effort. While the Committee on Public Information, under George Creel, organized patriotism through propaganda, the federal government took coercive measures in the name of "national security." Having already at its disposal the Alien Enemies Act of 1798, which authorized the President to imprison dangerous enemy aliens without trial, Congress enacted more stringent legislation after the United States entered the war. The Trading with the Enemy Act, the Alien Act of 1918, and the Espionage Act of 1917 were specific in their attempt to protect national security. The Sedition Act, however, was vague in its scope and abused civil liberties in its application.

Passed in 1918 as a comprehensive amendment to the Espionage Act, the Sedition Act made it a crime to "utter, print, or publish disloyal, profane, scurrilous, or abusive language about the form of government, the Constitution, soldiers and sailors, flag, or uniform of the armed forces" with the intent to bring scorn, contempt, and disrepute upon them. Even more stringent was the provision that made it illegal for anyone "by word or act [to] support or favor the cause of the [enemy] in the present war, or by word or act [to] oppose the cause of the United States." With the force of this act behind it, the federal government launched a wide-ranging attack on civil liberties, especially targeting the Socialist Party and other radical groups—a precursor to the Red Scare of 1919–1920.

More than 1,500 prosecutions resulted in over 100 convictions under the various wartime acts, with most of them falling under the Sedition Act. Some of the cases were ludicrous. One film producer was sentenced to ten years in jail for producing a film on the American Revolution because the government feared it might cause anti-British sentiments. A Vermont minister was sentenced to fifteen years for citing Jesus as an authority on pacifism. Serious action was also taken against socialists and other radical groups. Socialist Congressman Victor Berger, who also edited the *Milwaukee Leader*, was sentenced to twenty years in prison for writing editorials that denounced the war as a "capitalist conspiracy." Eugene V. Debs, the perennial presidential candidate of the Socialist Party, received a twenty-year sentence for giving a speech in which he said Americans should oppose militarism.

Since prosecutions under these acts involved First Amendment rights, they were challenged before the courts and resulted in many landmark Supreme Court decisions. In upholding *Schenck v. United States* (1919), Justice Oliver Wendell Holmes, Jr., established the famous "clear and present danger" standard. Holmes declared "the question in every case is whether the words used are used in such circumstances and are of such a nature as to create a clear and present danger that they will bring about the substantive evils that Congress has a right to prevent."

Although the Sedition Act paled in comparison to wartime restrictions in Great Britain, France, and Germany, it, nonetheless, departed from American tradition. As the war hysteria ebbed, however, most Americans recognized the need for "eternal [vigilance] against attempts to check expression of opinions that we loath" dangers that Holmes had expressed in his dissent to *Abrams v. United States*. As a result, organizations such as the American Civil Liberties Union were founded to challenge any infringement upon civil liberties in the future.

Justin D. Murphy

Bibliography

Barker, Lucius J., and Twiley W. Barker, Jr. *Civil Liberties and the Constitution: Cases and Commentaries*. Englewood Cliffs, NJ: Prentice-Hall, 1986.

Ferrell, Robert H. *Woodrow Wilson and World War I, 1917–1921*. New York: Harper & Row, 1985.

Murphy, Paul L. *The Constitution in Crisis Times, 1918–1969*. New York: Harper & Row, 1972.

Seicheprey

Seicheprey, a village on the southeast face of the St. Mihiel salient below Verdun gave its name to a day-long fight between doughboys of the U.S. 26th ("Yankee") Division and a 3,000-man enemy raiding party on April 20, 1918.

Judged against the standard of the time, the conflict was merely a good-sized skirmish, involving little more than a battalion of Americans. However, as the first fight of any real size between United States and German troops, it gained considerable publicity and attention, particularly as United States and Allied officers sought to evaluate the fighting abilities of American troops in their combat debut.

The action took place along the St. Mihiel salient, a sixteen-mile wedge in the Allied lines created in 1914 as part of a failed German pincer movement on the French fortifications at Verdun. Twenty-five miles across the base, the salient was shaped roughly like a triangle with points near Pont-à-Mousson, St. Mihiel, and Verdun.

St. Mihiel was considered a quiet sector in early 1918. American Expeditionary Force (AEF) commander Gen. John J. Pershing used the "hernia," as the French called it, to acclimate his green troops to combat, with the idea that the sector would provide him with a more extensive area of operations in the future.

Elements of the U.S. 1st Division went into the line on the southeastern face of the salient near the village of Seicheprey in early February, followed by the 2d Division, which went into the trenches on the opposite face of the salient in mid-March.

On March 28, troops from the 26th Division relieved U.S. doughboys of the 1st Division in the trenches on the lower face of the salient. The Yankees took over 20,000 yards of front, relieving a brigade of the U.S. 1st Division, a French division, and a regiment of infantry. Control passed to the 26th Division's commanding officer, Gen. Clarence Edwards, on April 3.

The experience of the 1st Division in the sector had consisted of fairly routine shellings and raids. The enemy raids were not mere pinpricks—one cost the 18th Infantry twenty dead—but neither were they major actions. During its stint in the sector the 1st Division lost eighty-three officers and men killed, wounded, or captured.

While still novices, the 26th Division was not completely without experience, having undergone its first training period in the Chemin des Dames sector earlier in the year, where it learned about enemy artillery fire and patrol actions.

Arriving in the Toul sector, as the Seicheprey area came to be known, the units went into position in the mucky trenches. Infantry regiments on the line from left to right were the 104th in the Bois Brule subsector, the 101st in and around Xivray and Rambucourt, the 102d in Seicheprey and Remières Wood, and the 103d Infantry in reserve. On the division's left was a regiment of the 10th Colonial Division (French). On the right was the French 162d Regiment.

Dominated by German-held high ground, the 26th Division troops found their positions less than ideal from a defensive standpoint. The forward lines were composed of short sections of trench organized as resistance centers. In reality, these were sacrifice positions and could expect no reinforcement from the principal line of resistance further to the rear. Mud and the poor condition of the defense works would hamper resistance to any German attack.

Though officially a "quiet sector," the doughboys were under constant pressure at St. Mihiel, harassed by enemy artillery fire and raiding parties. On April 10 the Germans raided the 104th Infantry, without much success. That raid was followed by a more forceful effort on April 12. The Yankees acquitted themselves well, losing one prisoner, while capturing forty Germans. The French were so impressed that they decorated 117 officers and men.

Stung, the Germans planned a still more powerful effort to be directed at the 102d Infantry holding the 3,300 yards of front from Seicheprey to Remières Wood.

A special assault unit—a *Sturmbataillon*—suddenly appeared in the German sector. Known to the Allies as Hindenburg's Traveling Circus, the *Stosstruppen* were the cream of assault troops, culled from units throughout the German Army. Their intelligence was flawless: captured doughboys were later told that Germans wearing U.S. uniforms had penetrated the lines, mingled with units, and even eaten from company kitchens, picking up mess-line gossip.

On the Seicheprey front, the 102d Infantry was organized into two main points of resistance, each manned by one company. One was located in and about the village of Seicheprey itself and the other was located in Remières Wood just east of the village. The other companies of the front-line battalion were echeloned a thousand yards in the rear in the forward trenches of the main position in front of Beaumont village. Headquarters for the 102d Infantry was located in Beaumont.

A single trench, very lightly held, ran between Seicheprey and Remières Wood. A few shell-proofs had been constructed in the village cellars. The wire entanglements were in good condition.

In front of Seicheprey and Remières Wood the terrain rose in a gentle slope, unsuitable for effective defense. The main trench of this system was Sibille trench. The Remières trench connected the garrison of Seicheprey with the strong points in the wood. From Remières Wood, the Jury *boyau* (communicating trench) connected with Jury Wood, held by the 162d French Infantry, on the right. To the west of Seicheprey, a ravine curved into U.S. lines from the north.

The night of April 19, the 1st Battalion, under the command of Maj. George Rau, relieved the 3d Battalion which had been holding the line since March 31. C Company took over Remières Wood, D Company went in and about Seicheprey (where the battalion headquarters was also located), and A and B companies occupied the support trenches in the main line of resistance further to the rear.

The relief was completed at 1 A.M. At 3:05 A.M., the Germans opened with a massive artillery bombardment, using guns of all calibers up to 210 millimeters. The entire sector received thorough attention. Within eight minutes, all wire communications out of Beaumont were cut with the exception of a single line to the artillery.

Gas, mixed with high-explosive shells, broke the front-line defenders into isolated groups. One platoon was reduced from fifty to eight men. Regimental headquarters was temporarily put out of action. Adding to the confusion, daybreak revealed a heavy ground fog, which helped conceal German intentions.

At 5 A.M., the German artillery threw box barrages around Seicheprey and Remières Wood with a rolling barrage across the front to precede the attacking enemy infantry. Soon doughboy observers spotted German assault troops plunging out of the mist in the wake of the barrage.

The attack was spearheaded by about 600 men of a *Sturmbataillon*. Their support troops were the 259th Regiment, two companies of the 258th Regiment, and one battalion of the 250th Regiment, giving the attack a total strength of approximately 3,000 men. Facing them, the Americans had two lone rifle companies—about 400 men—in the front lines.

They came in three columns: one up the wide draw to the west and south of Seicheprey; another party flanked Remières Wood from the east; and the third drove straight against the thinly held front. The *Sturmbataillon* led the attack, supported on the flanks by two battalions of infantry, with detachments of signal men and pioneers.

The enemy swept into Seicheprey from the flank and rear, capturing the battalion aid station with most of its personnel. Many doughboy survivors of the outpost lines were also snatched up.

The raiders quickly linked up with the group that came through Remières Wood. Seizing Sibille trench, they began organizing it against counterattack. In Seicheprey itself, the raiders methodically set contact mines and laid communications wire.

Rau's first revelation that a ground attack was under way arrived in the form of a lieutenant who dashed up to his headquarters with a group of German raiders in hot pursuit. Rau scraped together a hasty defense force of orderlies, clerks, and runners at battalion headquarters. They were joined by about twenty U.S. 1st Division personnel who had been left behind on work details for disciplinary punishments. The scratch force—about 50 men all told—drove the Germans out of Seicheprey proper and back to the village cemetery and Sibille trench. The village was cleared by 6 A.M., but fighting continued in Remières Wood.

Meanwhile, confusion reigned at the regimental and divisional levels. Not until 6:30 A.M. was word received at regimental headquarters that Seicheprey was under attack. Officers and scouts sent forward from Beaumont could learn nothing due to the intensity of the fire. U.S. artillery began shelling the town, endangering doughboys still in possession. As of 1 P.M., regimental headquarters was under the impression that the front line had crumbled away.

Meanwhile, the French regiment on the right had also come under attack, losing four machine gun posts and a number of prisoners. Fearing the worst, the French corps commander arrived at U.S. brigade headquarters and took charge, reducing the commanding brigadier, Peter Traub, to an ornamental role.

In fact, the situation was not as grim as either the French or Americans thought, though the Yankees had been hit hard. Small groups of doughboys continued to resist and even battle back along the shattered front. By early afternoon, the enemy retained possession of Sibille trench and part of Remières Wood in force, but was scarcely in a position to overrun the main line of resistance.

Nevertheless, that is just what American and French officers feared. In an effort to thwart exploitation of the attack on the main line of resistance, the 102d Infantry brought up the 3d Battalion to man the trenches, while two companies of the 101st Infantry were also rushed in. By nightfall, these arrangements were completed and the regiment felt more confident about its ability to hold its main line of resistance.

Other preparations were also under way. Late in the afternoon, brigade headquarters sent down a memorandum to the 102d Infantry, outlining a counterattack should the Germans remain within the outpost line the morning of April 21. The attack would be made by four companies of the 102d in conjunction with two French companies on the right. The objectives were to be Sibille trench and Remières Wood if patrol reports indicated any portion of the U.S. line was still in enemy hands.

Plans were made, changed, and amended throughout the evening until about 11:30 P.M. final instructions were issued. Briefly, the order contemplated a thirty-minute artillery preparation followed by the advance of the four companies—along with the French on the right—at 4:30 A.M.

Meanwhile, the situation remained unclear as patrols sent out to reconnoiter had failed to return, including a last patrol sent out at 2 A.M.

With only thirty minutes to go before jump-off, the battalion commander in charge of the morning counterattack took it upon himself to call off the assault. This officer, a Regular Army major, based his decision upon a variety of circumstances, including a delay in the arrival of his troops at the jump-off line, absence of information from the front, and what he considered incomplete equipment for his troops. The officer was subsequently relieved of his command and sent home in disgrace.

As it happened, by the time the planned counterattack broke down, the Germans had already withdrawn under the cover of darkness. Relief parties coming up to Seicheprey found the American survivors still in possession of the battlefield.

Nevertheless, the Germans had inflicted a heavy blow to the Yankees. They took about 130 prisoners, including several officers. Total casualties were 634, including the prisoners and 80 dead. Two infantry companies and a machine gun company were reduced by more than 50 percent and the organized defense of the sector was temporarily thrown into confusion. As a raid, the operation succeeded handsomely.

From the U.S. standpoint, the troops had also inflicted their share of damage on the enemy. Certainly, the raid had been no walkover. Upward of 150 German dead were left on the field; the German official report later admitted close to 600 casualties.

Back in the United States, Seicheprey was heralded as victory. In fact, as professional soldiers were well aware, this action did not reflect entirely well on the 26th Division. The Yankees had lost prisoners quite out of proportion to the number of casualties. The failure in communications, the lack of coordination between the troops, and the failure to respond smoothly to the attack were symptomatic of inexperienced troops and staffs.

The key problem was experience. As a German report noted, the Americans made a good military impression and had much potential. "As soon as the American soldier, after more thorough training and greater experience, gains greater confidence in himself and his officers, he is sure to prove an opponent not to be underestimated in trench warfare."

James Hallas

See also UNITED STATES ARMY: 26TH DIVISION

Bibliography

Sibley, Frank P. *With the Yankee Division in France.* Boston: Little, Brown, 1919.

Strickland, Daniel W. *Connecticut Fights, the Story of the 102d Regiment.* New Haven, CT: N.p., 1930.

Taylor, Emerson G. *New England in France.* Boston: Houghton Mifflin, 1920.

Selective Service

"Selective Service" was the name given to the modern military draft—selective national conscription—when it was first established in the United States during World War I. It differed significantly from America's earlier experiment with national conscription during the Civil War and was, in part, designed to avoid many of the problems of that experience. In the middle of the Civil War, both the North and the South had adopted forms of selective national conscription to prod enlistments and to help keep veteran soldiers in the field. But the draft was administered directly by the army, and there were gross inequities in those draft laws, including provisions that allowed draftees to hire substitutes. There was widespread evasion and active resistance to it in both regions, and major draft riots in many northern cities. As in most American wars prior to the twentieth century, the Civil War was fought mainly by volunteers; draftees and substitutes made up only 8 percent of the Union Army and 21 percent of the Confederate Army. In contrast, the draft obtained 72 percent of the 4 million men in the wartime American Army in World War I.

Adoption of national conscription in the United States in World War I was influenced in large part by a movement between 1915 and 1917 to revise American military institutions. One of the primary goals of the so-called "preparedness" movement was the elimination of reliance on the state militia (the National Guard) and the old system of wartime U.S. Volunteers (ad hoc units that were locally raised and officered and federally funded and commanded). In its place, "preparedness" leaders such as former President Theodore Roosevelt and former Army Chief of Staff General Leonard Wood, sought a wholly national reserve force based upon a permanent system of short-term universal military training and service. The "preparedness" movement, composed particularly of northern business and professional leaders, failed to achieve this goal. But its campaign, and the decision by Great Britain in 1916 to adopt selective conscription, helped convince many Americans of the efficacy of a selective national draft over a purely volunteer system for raising a mass wartime army equitably and with minimal disruption of an industrial economy.

Although Woodrow Wilson accepted the concept of wartime selective conscription, opposition from the agrarian South and West and from many anti-British and anti-Russian ethnic groups led the President during the planning stage in February and early March 1917 to advocate a trial of the traditional volunteer system before any resort to conscription. His view changed, however, when at the end of March 1917 his old political nemesis, former President Roosevelt, insisted on being allowed to raise and command one or two divisions of U.S. Volunteers and take them to France. It was at least in part this potential challenge to Wilson's wartime leadership by Roosevelt that led the president to eliminate the U.S. Volunteers and turn directly and immediately to conscription.

Volunteering would be permitted only into the Regular Army and the National Guard. The bulk of the wartime army would be raised through national conscription. In addition, substitution was specifically prohibited and draftees were to serve in person for the duration of the war. A system of industrial and agricultural deferments was provided for those whose skills were deemed essential to the war effort; and men could also be deferred if they were the sole support of needy dependents who could not be maintained on a serviceman's pay and dependency allotments.

There was much opposition to the draft in Congress. Democratic House Speaker James Beauchamp ("Champ") Clark announced that to Missourians "there is precious little difference between a conscript and a convict." Nevertheless, after several votes that split largely along urban-rural lines on various alternatives, Congress finally adopted the President's conscription plan by a vote of 397 to 24 in the House and 81 to 8 in the Senate. Wilson signed the Selective Draft Act into law on May 18, 1917.

The organization of the draft agency, the Selective Service System, was devised primarily by the army's chief legal officer, BGen. Enoch H. Crowder, and his key aide, Maj. Hugh S. Johnson, and modified somewhat by Congress. Under Crowder's concept of "supervised decentralization," some 4,000 local draft boards composed of civilian members of the community decided on the induction or deferment of particular individuals within overall guidelines established by Congress, the administration, and the military officials in Crowder's office, Selective Service headquarters in Washington, D.C.

During the war, Selective Service effectively registered 23.9 million Americans and drafted 2.8 million men, most of them between 21 and 30 years of age. Another 2 million Americans volunteered for service, mainly in the navy (which also accepted 11,000 women as clerks, typists, and nurses; the army refused to accept women except in the Army Nurse Corps). In an era of increased racial discrimination and segregation, African Americans were drafted disproportionately. Draft boards composed exclusively of whites proved more liberal in granting deferments to whites than to blacks, a result of whites' prejudice and of blacks' poverty and lack of industrial jobs that might qualify for deferment. The Selective Service drafted one in three black registrants but only one in four whites.

Because of the widespread opposition in America to U.S. entry into the war, many feared a repetition of the bloody draft riots of the Civil War. There were no such disruptions, however. Authorities broke up antidraft meetings and arrested and imprisoned antiwar activists such as Emma Goldman. Aside from socialist newspapers, most of the daily press endorsed wartime conscription, and in the *Arver* case (1917), the Supreme Court unanimously upheld the constitutionality of the national draft. Draft protests were limited to isolated rural areas, where some two dozen persons were killed in gun battles between draft resisters and local police. The largest protest, the so-called Green Corn Rebellion in eastern Oklahoma in the summer of 1917, was bloodless as a local posse arrested more than 500 impoverished tenant farmers and migrant workers who gathered to stage a protest march.

Overt draft evasion proved more characteristic. Officials estimated privately that perhaps 3 million men successfully avoided draft registration. Most were never discovered. In addition, 338,000 (12 percent of those actually drafted) failed to report or deserted after arrival at training camp. About half of these were caught, some in the controversial "slacker" raids in which service people and local and federal law enforcement officers stopped men of military age in major cities and demanded to see their draft registration cards.

A number of war opponents became conscientious objectors (COs). The draft law allowed traditional religious pacifists, such as Quakers and Mennonites, to serve in noncombatant roles in the armed forces, but many other objectors applied for CO status on religious, humanitarian, or, in the case of socialists and anarchists, political grounds. Some 64,693 draft registrants claimed CO status, but of the 20,000 COs drafted, 80 percent were persuaded or coerced at training camp into abandoning their objections. Some 4,000 draftees, however, continued to refuse to bear arms. Of these, 1,300 ultimately accepted duty in the medical corps or other noncombatant branches, but 2,700 "absolutists" refused to cooperate with the military in any manner. By the end of the war, most of these had been furloughed for agricultural work. However, 540 were court-martialed and incarcerated in military prisons, where perhaps as many as seventeen died of pneumonia or other ailments resulting from deprivation and physical abuse. The persecution of COs and other draft opponents in World War I helped to make civil liberties a national issue and led to the creation of the American Civil Liberties Bureau.

Despite such problems, the concept of the national draft was widely accepted in the United States in World War I. By the end of the war, Selective Service was hailed by the press as one of the most efficient of the government's wartime mobilization agencies. In the concept of temporary selective wartime military obligation and an administrative operation based on "supervised decentralization" of national headquarters and local draft boards, policymakers had found an effective and largely acceptable political-military mechanisms for raising mass armies in an urban, industrial nation and for projecting American military power overseas, at least in time of major war or threat of one. The Selective Service model was used again in World War II and during the Cold War, until the consensus behind it broke down during America's ill-fated expeditionary war in Vietnam.

John Whiteclay Chambers II

See also Conscientious Objectors; Crowder, Enoch Herbert; Preparedness

Bibliography

Chambers, John Whiteclay II. *To Raise an Army: The Draft Comes to Modern America*. New York: Free Press, 1987.

Lockmiller, David A. *Enoch H. Crowder: Soldier, Lawyer, Statesman*. Columbia: University of Missouri Studies, 1955.

Murphy, Paul L. *World War I and the Origin of Civil Liberties in the United States*. New York: Norton, 1979.

Peterson, Horace C., and Gilbert C. Fite. *Opponents of War, 1917–1918*. Madison: University of Wisconsin Press, 1957

Service of Supply
See United States Army Service of Supply

Sharp, William Graves (1859–1922)

William Graves Sharp served as United States ambassador to France from 1914 until 1919. Though trained as a lawyer, Sharp made a fortune as a manufacturer specializing in pig iron, chemicals, and charcoal. He served as a Demo-

cratic congressman from the district including his home town of Elyria, Ohio, from 1909 to 1914. He was a member of the House Committee on Foreign Affairs during his terms in Congress.

Woodrow Wilson and his advisers showed little urgency in the selection of an ambassador to France. Wilson first offered the post to his presidential campaign manager, William Frank McCombs, about March 1, 1913. The erratic McCombs, after changing his mind several times, finally rejected the position sometime in May. After that, Wilson, Edward M. House, and Secretary of State William Jennings Bryan occasionally discussed various candidates for the ambassadorship in desultory fashion but did nothing more until June 1914, when Wilson named Sharp to the post.

Sharp resigned from Congress on July 23, 1914. However, owing to the illness of his wife, he did not sail for France until August 26, over three weeks after France had declared war on Germany. He arrived in Paris on September 3, on the eve of the First Battle of the Marne. Myron Timothy Herrick, appointed ambassador to France by President William Howard Taft in 1912, was still the incumbent and was to remain so for three months due to indecision in the State Department as to just when Sharp should replace him. Sharp finally took over as ambassador on Dec. 1, 1914.

Several scholars have asserted that Sharp had only a minor role in Franco-American relations during World War I. Most important negotiations, they believe, took place in Washington, where Jean Jules Jusserand, the French ambassador to the United States from 1902 to 1925, presided as the dean of the diplomatic corps. However, Sharp, though totally devoid of diplomatic experience, proved to be a figure of considerable importance in the wartime American foreign service. His business and industrial experience proved to be a major asset. He took the initiative, for example, at the time of the German submarine attack on the French channel steamer *Sussex* on March 24, 1916, in securing physical evidence, which, in addition to eye-witness reports from Americans on board the vessel, proved beyond reasonable doubt that the ship had been damaged by a torpedo rather than by a mine as the German government claimed. This evidence served as the basis for President Wilson's ultimatum to Berlin on April 18, 1916, which secured from the German authorities a pledge to refrain from sinking merchant vessels without warning, a concession that kept the United States out of the conflict for nearly another year.

Shortly after the United States entered the war, Sharp began to provide careful evaluations of France's needs for military and economic assistance. He reported on one occasion, for example, that it was necessary to improve French seaport and railroad facilities so that vitally needed supplies might reach the fighting fronts. Sharp's military interests ranged widely. Long concerned with the potentialities of airplanes, he became an early advocate of military airpower, arguing that the use of many more and better aircraft offered the only hope of breaking the stalemate of trench warfare in Europe.

Sharp's estimates of the French political and social scene were sometimes a bit rose-tinted, but he could and often did provide shrewd opinions of persons and trends. For instance, Sharp declared Georges Clemenceau to be vigorous, forceful, cynical, skeptical of high ideals as applied to European politics and a man of intense prejudices but unquestionably the dominant figure in his government. Perhaps most importantly, Sharp repeatedly provided much needed assurance to the American government that the war-weary French, despite their enormous problems, would persevere to final victory against Germany. Sharp occasionally took surprisingly advanced and even courageous views on European politics. On the eve of his departure for the United States in April 1919, he wrote a farewell letter to President Wilson stating that, while deploring the atrocities of the Bolshevik regime in Russia, he believed that the United States and its allies must find some way to open negotiations with Lenin and the other Soviet leaders.

Sharp's efforts and his wisdom were not unappreciated. Gen. John J. Pershing, who had extensive dealings with Sharp, declared him to be high-minded, conscientious, and efficient. Woodrow Wilson, in March 1918, told Colonel House that he considered Sharp the most satisfactory ambassadorial appointment he had made. House, in November of that year, suggested Sharp's name to Wilson as a possible American plenipotentiary delegate to the Paris Peace Conference. As it turned out, nothing came of that suggestion. Sharp submitted his resignation as ambassador to Wilson in Paris on Dec. 19, 1918, but agreed to stay on until his successor should be appointed and arrive in France. His service came to an end on April 14, 1919.

John E. Little

S

Bibliography
Sharp, William Graves. *The War Memoirs of William Graves Sharp: American Ambassador to France, 1914–1919*, ed. by W. Dawson. London: Constable, 1931.

Sharpe, Henry Granville (1858–1947)

Henry Granville Sharpe was born in Kingston, New York, in 1858. He was educated at Phillips-Andover Academy, Rutgers University, and the United States Military Academy at West Point, from which he graduated in 1880. He served for two years as a lieutenant of infantry and then resigned from the army. In 1883, he returned to the army from the railroad construction he had been engaged in and was commissioned a captain in the Subsistence Department. He was promoted to major in 1895, lieutenant colonel in 1898, and colonel in 1902. In 1897, he coordinated flood relief in the upper Mississippi Valley, served with the army in Puerto Rico in 1898, and then was made chief commissary at the army camp at Chickamauga Park, Georgia, until January 1899.

After the United States entry into World War I, the Quartermaster Corps under Brigadier General Sharpe, now quartermaster general, organized twenty-eight different types of units for service both overseas and in the United States. Sharpe was responsible for the creation of a quartermaster training school at Camp Joseph E. Johnson, where 82,000 men prepared to serve in 405 special technical units, 360 of which were sent to France. He organized schools for bakers and cooks at several army camps, where a total of 16,000 mess sergeants, 50,000 cooks, 1,200 instructor cooks, and 9,000 bakers were trained. His early experiments with different types of retained heat cookers led to the development of the rolling field kitchen, which was used extensively in France by the American Expeditionary Force.

Under his control, the Quartermaster Corps clothed and equipped 1,582,014 men by January 1918, and beginning in September 1917, all troops sent overseas were fully equipped and provided with reserve supplies for six months.

Sharpe was also responsible for the establishment of a remount division and service that was to have charge of the purchase and transport of horses and mules overseas. Over 9,400 men were employed in this establishment. The creation of graves registration units in 1917 also fell under the purview of the Quartermaster Corps, and it was Sharpe who decreed that no remains of soldiers killed in Europe should be returned until the cessation of hostilities. This policy led to the creation of the permanent American military cemeteries in Europe.

Sharpe was a member of the War Council of the secretary of war, and in June 1918 he was assigned to the command of the Department of the Southeast. He held this post until May 1, 1920, when he retired. He wrote several books dealing with the supply of armies in wartime, as well as *The Quartermaster Corps in the Year 1917 in the World War* (1921) which provides a history of the measures taken to get the U.S. Army into the field. He died on July 13, 1947.

Michael J. Knapp

Shaw, Anna Howard (1847–1919)

An ordained minister and a medical doctor, Anna Howard Shaw gave up both vocations to become a lecturer for temperance and suffrage. Singled out by Susan B. Anthony for her oratorical skills, Shaw received an appointment as national lecturer of the National American Woman Suffrage Association (NAWSA) in 1891. She served as vice president of the organization from 1892 until 1904 and president from 1904 to 1915. Her eloquence was not matched by administrative skills, nor an ability to work with people, nor flexibility, and NAWSA as an organization languished under her leadership.

Shortly after the United States entered World War I in April 1917, Shaw was appointed chairman of the Woman's Committee of the Council of National Defense (WCCND). NAWSA had pledged the services of its 2 million members to the government shortly after the break in diplomatic relations with Germany, and Shaw believed her appointment and those of two other leading suffragists—Carrie Chapman Catt and Katherine McCormick—would benefit the suffrage movement. Shaw's own suffrage work went into abeyance because she believed that a successful handling of the WCCND job would do more to help the cause than anything else she could do.

Shaw, however, soon faced frustration in the WCCND. Lacking a clear mandate, she and her committee decided that the WCCND should serve as a clearing house for women's organizations involved in war service activities, function as the official channel between the government and women, and organize state divisions. The male bureaucracy envisioned a more circumscribed role, so conflict were inevitable.

Although Shaw maintained a positive front in public, she was a persistent critic within the wartime bureaucracy of the "pettiness of public officials." For example, the WCCND cooperated fully with the food conservation campaign launched by Food Administrator Herbert Hoover, but Shaw discovered that men in government thought that women ought to obey without question.

Shaw came close to resigning in the summer of 1917 because she was angered by the lack of support for the WCCND from either the state CND councils or the national CND. She believed that the male state councils were jealous of the WCCND and did not want women to do anything on their own initiative. Shaw deserves credit for keeping the committee from becoming another vehicle of wartime hysteria and intolerance. She refused to attack others like Jane Addams who were being condemned as unpatriotic, and she opposed universal military training and lowering the draft age. She did, however, urge the conscription of women for war service once they had received the vote. A woman's army was necessary, Shaw claimed, because they were being used so inefficiently. Her proposal was never taken seriously by the Wilson administration and was probably only made as a way of drawing attention to the continuing problems of the WCCND. Only months before the Armistice the government created a Field Division to merge the functions of the WCCND state divisions and CND state councils and to give the women joint authority in the states. With the end of the war, the Field Division was asked to help find jobs for returning servicemen. Shaw requested that the state divisions be continued in order to aid women workers in the conversion to a peacetime economy, but her suggestion was not heeded. She hoped for continuing responsibilities for women in the reconstruction process, but with no official authorization, Shaw and the other members of the WCCND resigned. In May 1919, she received the Distinguished Service Medal for her efforts.

Rather than returning to suffrage work as planned, she joined former President William Howard Taft and Harvard President A. Lawrence Lowell on a speaking tour to promote Woodrow Wilson's plan for the League of Nations. While on the tour, she contracted pneumonia and died in July 1919.

Barbara Steinson

See also COUNCIL OF NATIONAL DEFENSE: WOMAN'S COMMITTEE

Bibliography

Blair, Emily Newell. *The Woman's Committee, United States Council of National Defense, An Interpretive Report.* Washington, DC: N.p., 1920.

Breen, William J. *Uncle Sam at Home: Civilian Mobilization, Wartime Federalism, and the Council of National Defense, 1917–1919.* Westport, CT: Greenwood Press, 1984.

Linkugel, William A., and Martha Sullivan. *Anna Howard Shaw: Suffrage Orator and Social Reformer.* Westport, CT: Greenwood Press, 1991.

O'Neill, William L. *Everyone Was Brave, The Rise and Fall of Feminism in America.* Chicago: Quadrangle Books, 1969.

Shaw, Anna Howard. *The Story of a Pioneer.* New York: Harper, 1915.

Shell Shock

In the autumn of 1914, newspaper reports began circulating among the European combatants of a strange new malady, which in England was labeled "shell shock" and which eventually was designated everywhere as "war neurosis." What was initially a curiosity for newspaper readers soon became an obsession for the military and governments of all the warring powers. For as the war of movement bogged down and the Western Front solidified, there were ever increasing numbers of "mental" casualties among both officers and men. Soldiers were invalided home from the front suffering from hallucinations, panic and anxiety attacks, delusions, hysterical deafness, blindness, and paralysis. What was both astonishing and disturbing was that the causes of their afflictions were overwhelmingly nonorganic. By 1916, as the number of such cases mounted, one may speak of a genuine crisis of war neurosis, which became the business of everyone from medical officers to the General Staff. The sheer volume of mental casualties raised significant problems of evacuation, housing, and treatment and eventually the question of postwar rehabilitation and pensions. Of more immediate importance for the European General Staffs were a wide range of issues stemming from the shell-shock crisis having to do with morale and discipline. In a life-and-death struggle that tested not only every soldier but every nation to the utmost, leaders asked how they could send men home from the front who had no visible wounds, men who, indeed, were often acting in what traditionally would be considered a cowardly fashion. Such questions raised profound moral issues about character and what one could expect from a soldier.

What had caused the massive numbers of breakdowns on the Western Front? A brief summary of the conditions to be found in the nightmare world of the trenches may indicate why in this war for the first time mental illness became a significant factor among casualties. Concussion from exploding shells was the earliest remarked factor, hence the name "shell shock." Of far greater consequence, however, was the strain of serving in the inhuman conditions of trench warfare and the exhaustion that followed from the soldier's inability to sleep in the line. The witnessing of the mutilation or annihilation of a comrade often produced cases of severe shock. This was compounded by the lingering survivors' guilt syndrome, which years after the war continued to plague veterans. Too many such sights in conditions of static warfare could produce feelings of futility and despair. Such factors could be enhanced or mitigated by unit morale, which varied from battalion to battalion. For officers especially, a crushing sense of responsibility and the fear of showing fear were additional factors that might lead to mental collapse. For all ranks, the very nature of battle on the Western Front, a static struggle dominated by machines where the individual counted for little, contributed greatly to widespread mental illness after November 1914, when the stalemate began.

World War I was a great revolution in all spheres of national life, including the perception and treatment of mental illness. In Europe and America before the war, a somatic (physically based) theory of neuroses and hysteria was still a powerful force in the medical community. Coupled with the view was a tendency to judge such cases in moralistic terms. An ancient conception of character, already enunciated in Aristotle's *Ethics*, was widely shared in pre-1914 Europe. Indeed, a central task of elite education, whether in the German gymnasium, the French lycée, or the English public school, was to promote the values of fortitude and courage. Furthermore, "character training" was an integral aspect of the pan-European "Cult of the Offensive," which shaped all military planning before the war.

It was views such as these which greeted the first shell-shock casualties of the war. These attitudes were reinforced initially because medical officers, like the General Staff, were caught up in the voluntaristic vision that decreed that success in battle depended upon a soldier's *élan vitale*, that is, vital spirit or energy. The Great War after all, in the opinion of many observers, was supposed to demonstrate the power of character, of will power, of spiritual forces over modern materialism. Thus shell-shock cases were regarded with particular distaste in light of these widely shared ideas about how war ought to be conducted and the goals it was expected to achieve. By 1915–1916, steadily rising mental casualty statistics had severely challenged these widely held assumptions.

Initially, as we have seen, "shell shock" was attributed by medical officers of all armies to the effects of high explosives. By 1915, however, General Staffs had begun to accept that some of their best soldiers were breaking down in the war not from concussion but from mysterious "mental" factors. Yet so much was invested in the pre-1914 ideals of courage, character, and *élan vitale* that, unless evidence of an organic wound was present, those who collapsed were often punished, sent back to the front, or even executed.

In each country, medical men had to find quick cures for the thousands of cases of hysteria, "neurasthenia," and traumatic neuroses sent back from the front. In each country experimentation went on in the early years of the war. Too often treatment was determined by class prejudices. The English tended to encourage rest, recuperation, and occupational therapy for their officers. Cold douches, forcible movements, and, to a lesser extent, electric-shock treatment were employed for "Other Ranks." At the basis of all treatment was the lingering fear that so-called shell-shock victims were in reality malingerers trying to escape their duty.

In Austria and Germany, there was a tendency to employ a brutal, rapid "treatment"—a mixture of punishment, torture, and "cure"—to drive the patient back to duty. One of the most notorious of the "quick" treatments was the "Kaufmann" cure. Denounced by the French and the English (who themselves had occasion to employ variations on it), the Kaufmann method combined powerful electrical shocks with shouted commands to perform certain exercises.

One alternative to these mechanistic/punitive cures was the Freudian psychoanalysis, or the "talking cure." Yet such was the hostility toward a psychogenic explanation of war neuroses, especially one coupled with a sexual etiology of neuroses, that medical officers only grudgingly accepted the insights of psychoanalysis. Austria-Hungary, the birthplace of psychoanalysis, was among the most hostile toward treatment based on Freud's theories. Having exhausted other avenues of cure, however, the Central Powers, by September 1918 were actively considering employing psychoanalysts such as Simmel, Abraham, and Ferenczi in new military mental hospitals. Indeed, they sent observers to the 5th International Psychoanalytic Congress held in Budapest in September 1918. The collapse of the Central Powers shortly thereafter prevented the official utilization of Freudian psychoanalysis on a wide scale. In England, therapists such as W.H.R. Rivers employed such psychoanalytic insights as dream analysis in their treatment of mentally afflicted officers. The English governmental and military authorities, however, strongly resisted enlisting the talents of Freudian psychoanalysts; such men as M.D. Eder and Ernest Jones never played a significant role in the treatment of war neuroses in England.

Whatever treatment was used by medical authorities, it was soon obvious that war-neurosis casualties must be segregated from those suffering from physical wounds and provided with special evacuation and treatment facilities. This was done both to enable medical officers to scrutinize suspect cases for malingering and to preserve morale by separating mental casualties from the rest of the army. The British Army demonstrated growing sophistication in treating mental casualties with the establishment, by 1916, of a tightly run closed system for the observation, evaluation, and evacuation of mental cases via a series of carefully regulated medical stages ranging from the battalion aide station at the front to the base hospital in the rear and, if necessary, to a hospital at home. The latter was always a last resort, for it was universally recognized that once invalided home, a mental causality would almost certainly never return to the front. During the Great War, the British Army developed a famous formula, in use to this day by medical officers in all Western armies, i.e., that of "immediacy, proximity, and expectancy." That is, a mental casualty should be examined, treated, and evaluated for futher service as soon as possible and as close to the line as feasible.

The American government profited from what European governments had so painfully learned through three and a half years of experience in the treatment of war neurosis. Indeed, already before the war American cultural and medical attitudes toward the mentally ill were being transformed by such "progressive" organizations as the National Committee for Mental Hygiene, which propagandized in favor of better care and treatment of the insane. It followed naturally that in the spring of 1917, as the United States moved toward war, this committee and its medical director, Thomas W. Salmon, would be deputized by the Surgeon General's Office to prepare the American official response to expected high rates of war neurosis among the American Expeditionary Force. In May–June 1917, Salmon visited British hospitals and consulted with leading experts in the treatment of war neurosis. Based on these observations, Salmon and Pierce Bailey established field hospitals for treatment of war neuroses and ensured that psychiatrists accompanied the American Expeditionary Force to France in 1918. One lesson gleaned from European experience was that in 1914–1915 many volunteers had been accepted who were likely to break down under the stress of total war. The result was that the United States undertook a vast effort to screen recruits via psychological testing under the direction of the famous psychologist Robert M. Yerkes.

After the Armistice, there was much questioning among former combatants of the methods used to treat shell shock and of the punishment and even execution of mental casualties in the early stages of the war. In Austria and in England, this tide of criticism led to full-scale government investigations. Behind both investigations were charges leveled by critics that the military authorities were callous and brutal in the handling of shell-shock victims. English public opinion, especially, was concerned with the possibility that among those executed for cowardice and desertion in the early stages of the war were victims of war neurosis who were not responsible for their actions. The English investigation conducted by the War Office Committee of Enquiry into "Shell-Shock" (1920–1922) was also motivated by the larger question of how to prepare soldiers to better withstand the strain of another world war, which, with the addition of airpower and mobile armor, was likely to be fought on a still more terrible scale.

Whereas the English investigation was specifically focused on shell shock, the Austrian Commission for the Investigation of Derelictions of Military Duty (1919–1920) was concerned with many other military matters connected with the lost war. One of these matters was the alleged medical abuse of war-neurosis victims. In October 1920, the commission heard evidence regarding the case of a former Jewish Austrian officer who claimed that he had been "tortured" by the distinguished psychiatrist Julios von Wagner-Jauregg, who had employed electric-shock apparatus as part of therapy. During the proceedings an expert in the field of psychiatry was brought in to testify, no less a figure than Sigmund Freud. Eventually, Wagner-Jauregg was exonerated by the commission of all wrongdoing.

The English Committee of Enquiry tended to regard victims of war neurosis with far more sympathy and understanding than its Austrian counterpart. After much soul-searching, the English committee came close to the Freudian view that there are only gradations of mental health. In spite of testimony that Jews, Welshmen, city-bred people, and the degenerate lower classes generally were more liable to break down in war, the committee specifically declared that anyone might collapse on the front. Furthermore, the War Office Committee of Enquiry came to the extraordinary conclusion that cowardice could no longer be differentiated with certainty from shell shock, and thus, by implication, execution for such acts must be abolished. Ultimately, this would lead in 1930 to the abandonment of the military death penalty for cowardice altogether. Thus the English committee had removed some of the stigma from those who broke down.

Attitudes toward Freudian psychoanalysis also differed markedly. The English Committee of Enquiry specifically declared that Freudian psychotherapy was of no use in curing war neurosis: intense hostility was displayed toward Freud's "sexual" theories throughout the committee hearings. In the Austrian official investigation, in contrast, Freud was treated with respect and called in as an expert to testify before the commission. Perhaps the Austrians better understood what Ernest Jones had declared in 1918: however unwieldy psychoanalysis as a therapy might be in time of war, its insights into the mechanisms of repression and the psychical origins of hysteria were invaluable in the treatment of war neurosis.

What had been learned by governmental and medical authorities as a result of the "shell-shock" crisis in the Great War? First, that it was necessary to screen recruits carefully for susceptibility to mental breakdown under the stress of war. Second, that all men feel fear in combat, and everyone is liable to break down if stress is severe enough. Third, high morale and unit cohesion are good prophylactics against war neurosis. Fourth, realistic rigorous training helps lower mental casualties. These were some of the lessons that would be incorporated by Western nations into future military planning. In a sense, perhaps the most profound lesson learned was a new comprehension of the limits of the human mind and a new understanding and tolerance for those who, during the war, had broken down and been condemned as malingerers or cowards.

Theodore Bogacz

Bibliography

Babington, Anthony. *For the Sake of Example.* New York: St. Martin's Press, 1983.

Bogacz, Theodore. "War Neurosis and Cultural Change in England, 1914–1922: The Work of the War Office Committee of Enquiry into 'Shell-Shock.'" *Journal of Contemporary History* 24 (1989).

Eissler, Kurt. *Freud as an Expert Witness.* New York: International Universities Press, 1986.

Ferenczi, S., Karl Abraham, Ernst Simmel, and Ernest Jones. *Psycho-Analysis and the War Neurosis.* London: Hogarth Press, 1921.

Hoffman, Louise E. "War, Revolution and Psychoanalysis: Freudian Thought Begins to Grapple with Social Reality." *Journal of the History of Behavioral Sciences* 17 (1981).

Shipping Act of 1916

The outbreak of war in August 1914 led to a severe disruption of shipping that threatened the welfare of American exporters. To deal with the economic emergency Secretary of the Treasury William G. McAdoo had a ship purchase bill prepared shortly after the start of hostilities. This legislation called for the creation of a government-owned corporation to purchase and operate vessels on overseas trade routes. President Wilson firmly backed McAdoo's proposal, but in Congress many condemned the idea of a government-operated merchant fleet as socialistic, expensive, and likely to involve the United States in diplomatic disputes over wartime commerce. In September 1914, Congress adjourned without taking action on the bill. Undaunted, the Wilson administration reintroduced the legislation, and on Feb. 17, 1915, the House of Representatives passed an amended version. In the Senate, though, the measure was killed by a filibuster.

Despite this defeat, McAdoo and Wilson did not give up the fight, for they both believed a strong merchant marine was essential not only to American prosperity, but also to military preparedness since merchant ships could serve as naval auxiliaries. McAdoo reworked the administration's shipping bill and had it introduced in the House in January 1916. He and Wilson showed a willingness to compromise on this legislation and accepted amendments limiting the power of the agency the bill established, the United States Shipping Board. The most important of these amendments required the board to stop operating merchant ships five years after the end of the war (limiting the "socialistic" time frame of the legislation and also emphasizing its emergency nature) and prohibited the board from purchasing ships belonging to belligerent nations (reducing the possibility of diplomatic complications arising out of American neutrality). The bill quietly and steadily worked its way through a Congress preoccupied with debates over army and navy preparedness, passing the House on May 20, 1916, and the Senate on August 18. The vote in both chambers generally followed party lines.

In its final form, the act provided for the establishment of an independent Shipping Board made up of five commissioners, appointed by the President and confirmed by the Senate. The board had the authority to rule on proposed transfers of American vessels to foreign registry, to establish freight rates, and to determine U.S. shipping routes—powers comparable to those exercised by the Interstate Commerce Commission over railroads. Most importantly, during the "national emergency" the board was authorized to form a subsidiary corporation, with a capital stock of $50 million, for the "purchase, construction, equipment, lease, charter, maintenance, and operation of merchant vessels in the commerce of the United States." Five years after the end of the war, however, any corporation formed would automatically be dissolved and government operation of merchant shipping cease. President Wilson signed the Shipping Act into law on Sept. 7, 1916.

William Williams

See also EMERGENCY FLEET CORPORATION; SHIPPING BOARD.

Bibliography

Allin, Lawrence. "Ill-Timed Initiative: The Ship Purchase Bill of 1915." *American Neptune* 33 (July 1973).

Broesamle, John J. *William Gibbs McAdoo: A Passion for Change, 1863–1917.* Port Washington, NY: N.p., 1973.

Link, Arthur S. *Wilson: The Struggle for Neutrality, 1914–1915.* Princeton, NJ: Princeton University Press, 1960.

Safford, Jeffrey J. *Wilsonian Maritime Diplomacy, 1913–1921.* New Brunswick, NJ: Rutgers University Press, 1978.

Smith, Darrell H., and Paul V. Betters. *The United States Shipping Board: Its History, Activities and Organization.* Washington, DC: N.p., 1931.

Shipping Board

The Shipping Board was responsible for overseeing the construction and operation of American merchant vessels during U.S. participation in World War I. This was a truly massive task, for when the United States entered the conflict, its small merchant marine was incapable of transporting a large army to France and keeping it supplied or of providing the Allies with the war materiel and foodstuffs they so desperately needed. German submarines, moreover, were sinking hundreds of thousands of tons of merchant shipping every month, and the output of American shipyards amounted to only a fraction of these losses. Not even British yards, the world's most prolific prior to the war, could begin to make good the tonnage sunk by U-boats. Great Britain, and its allies, thus counted on the newly formed Shipping Board to expand American merchant vessel construction quickly and dramatically.

The board, however, got off to a rocky start. The initial commissioners were William Denman, a lawyer from California who served as chairman; Bernard N. Baker, a shipping executive from Maryland; John A. Donald, a shipowner from New York; John B. White, a retired lumberman from Missouri; and Theodore Brent, a business executive from Louisiana. Unfortunately, there was an immediate controversy: Baker resigned before the board held its first meeting, upset over the fact that he would not be chairman, and that Denman—who would be—seemed to know nothing about shipping. Baker's harsh opinion proved valid, for Denman soon decided to embark on an impractical scheme to mass-produce a thousand small wooden steamers. This plan was developed by an amateur yachtsman from Massachusetts, Frederic A. Eustis, who believed American wooden shipyards could turn out standardized steamers faster than German submarines could sink them. Denman and Eustis convinced President Wilson that one of the nation's best-known civil engineers would be willing to head their ambitious program—MajGen. George W. Goethals, the famed builder of the Panama Canal. The White House announced to the press that Goethals would take the job, which caught Goethals completely by surprise, for although he had discussed shipbuilding with Denman and Eustis in several informal settings, he had never agreed to take charge of the wooden ship program. A forceful man with strong opinions, Goethals was enraged over the conspiratorial manner in which the Shipping Board conscripted him. He tried to talk the President into finding someone else to take the position, but Wilson, realizing the general's quick resignation would be a public relations disaster, insisted that Goethals stay.

The general reluctantly accepted the President's decision but in a stormy meeting with Denman made it clear he did not like the way he had been drafted into service. He did not like Denman or Eustis, and he did not like the plan for building wooden ships. Although Goethals was not a shipbuilder, he quickly recognized the problems that wooden vessels would face—they were small, slow, and obsolete; in addition, they could not be efficiently mass-produced since wood cut into standardized sections at mills would not retain its precise shape due to shrinkage, checking, and rot. Goethals saw that steel tonnage would have to be produced to solve the shipping crisis, and he took steps to put more emphasis on steel construction. Specifically, he encouraged shipbuilders to look into the mass production of steel vessels by fabricating standardized parts at factories across the country and then transporting these to specially designed yards that would assemble the fabricated shapes into vessels, a plan that would eventually be adopted. Baker's replacement on the board, Raymond B. Stevens, an ex-congressman from New Hampshire, supported Goethals's ideas, as did, eventually, Commissioner Donald, while Commissioners White and Brent backed Denman, giving the chairman a three-to-two majority. Goethals was not a member of the board itself; he served as general manager of the Emergency Fleet Corporation, the organization the board formed, in accordance with the provisions of the Shipping Act of 1916, to build and operate vessels.

Denman, meanwhile, served as both president of the corporation and chairman of the Shipping Board. The bitter dispute between Denman and Goethals severely hampered the progress of America's shipbuilding program. Although Denman eventually came to realize the importance of producing steel tonnage, and Goethals ultimately agreed to place orders for scores of wooden ships, the animosity between the two men was so great that they could not work together. Goethals finally became so frustrated that he submitted a letter of resignation to the President on July 20, 1917. Wilson decided to make a clean sweep and on July 24 asked Denman to resign, which the chairman did. Commissioners White and Brent also resigned, leading to a reorganization of the board.

The new chairman was Edward Nash Hurley, a Chicago businessman who had previously served Wilson as chairman of the Federal Trade Commission. Replacing White and Brent were Bainbridge Colby, a New York attorney, and Charles R. Page, an insurance executive from California. Hurley, Donald, Stevens, Colby, and Page would all stay until after the Armistice, thus stabilizing the Shipping Board for the remainder of the war. But the nature of the board would change under Hurley. During Denman's tenure, the organization of the Shipping Board and Emergency Fleet Corporation had been very informal, consisting essentially of groups that centered on Denman and Goethals, and lines of authority had been confused. Under Hurley, the Shipping Board became, in effect, a board of directors that oversaw the work performed by the Emergency Fleet Corporation, which directly supervised both the building and operation of America's merchant marine for the rest of the war.

William Williams

See also EMERGENCY FLEET CORPORATION; SHIPPING ACT OF 1916; SHIPPING CONTROL COMMITTEE

Bibliography

Bishop, Joseph B., and Farnham Bishop. *Goethals, Genius of the Panama Canal.* New York: Harper, 1930.

Hurley, Edward N. *The Bridge to France.* Philadelphia: Lippincott, 1927.

Mattox, W.C. *Building the Emergency Fleet.* Cleveland: Denton, 1920.

Safford, Jeffrey J. *Wilsonian Maritime Diplomacy, 1913–1921.* New Brunswick, NJ: Rutgers University Press, 1987.

Smith, Darrell H., and Paul V. Betters. *The United States Shipping Board: Its History, Activities and Organization.* Washington, DC: 1931.

Shipping Control Committee
The Shipping Control Committee, an agency of the Shipping Board, was established in New York on Feb. 11, 1918. The United States was desperately short of merchant ships, and it was vital that more efficient use be made of existing tonnage. To make matters worse at this critical juncture, the War Department, the U.S. Navy, and the Shipping Board were all operating separate merchant fleets.

In February 1918, Shipping Board Chairman Edward N. Hurley appointed P.A.S. Franklin of the International Mercantile Marine, one of the leading shipping experts in the nation, to head this new committee. Franklin, who was already active in the war effort, accepted this new responsibility on the condition that he have total authority to control the allocation of tonnage. He went so far as to have his own lawyer draft the resolution whereby the Shipping Board conferred this authority on him.

Hurley also named H.H. Raymond of the Clyde and Mallory Steamship Company and Sir Connor Guthrie, the British Ministry of Shipping's representative in New York, to the committee.

Franklin soon brought a much greater sense of order to the allocation of tonnage. He placed all American shipping in what Hurley called "liquid" form. All government departments requested the tonnage they needed, and Franklin's committee provided it on the basis of priority need. Franklin drastically cut the turn-around time for merchant ships from a high of thirty-eight days in France and thirty-four in the United States to nineteen and twenty-three days, respectively. At the same time, the committee increased the amount of tonnage carried by 400 percent. In his memoir, *The Bridge to France*, Edward Hurley lavishly praised Franklin for saving the United States "the equivalent of hundreds of ships."

Assisting Franklin were J. Parker Kirlin, who served as general counsel to the committee, J.H. Thomas and Joseph T. Lilly, who directed the U.S. Army's cargo fleet, W.J. Love, who controlled the nonmilitary fleet, and W.F. Gibbs, a naval architect and statistician who worked out elaborate timetables for ship sailings. Harold W. Amberg, a Chicago lawyer served as liaison between the Shipping Control Committee and all the government agencies.

A separate agency of the Shipping Board, the Division of Planning and Statistics was also organized in February 1918 to provide the factual data that the Shipping Control Committee needed to allocate its tonnage intelligently. Chairman Hurley appointed Edwin Gay, the distinguished dean of Harvard's Graduate School of Business Administration as its director. Every Wednesday Franklin journeyed to Washington to meet with Gay, Hurley, Charles Schwab, director of the Emergency Fleet Corporation, and representatives of the army to discuss the tonnage situation.

From the beginning, Gay and Franklin clashed openly. Gay insisted that Franklin remove ships from the South American trade for military use. Chairman Hurley, who also found Franklin a very difficult man to work with, tried to act as peacemaker. The showdown came at the weekly meeting of the Tonnage Committee on Oct. 4, 1918. In a dramatic four-hour session, the army sided with Gay, and Franklin was forced to take all suitable vessels off the Latin American trade routes at once. The army threatened to remove all of its ships from Franklin's control unless the Shipping Control Committee followed Gay's recommendations on tonnage allocation. In early November, the Shipping Board passed a resolution reasserting its authority over the operation of ships. Under the new arrangement, Gay was to report to the Shipping Board, not Franklin. The board, in turn, would oversee decisions on tonnage allocations. Franklin's defeat soon became a moot point as the war ended a few weeks later and Franklin resigned on Dec. 11, 1918.

Charles Tull

See also MERCHANT MARINE; SHIPPING BOARD

Bibliography

Hurley, Edward N. *The Bridge to France.* Philadelphia: J.B. Lippincott, 1927.
Heaton, Herbert. *A Scholar in Action: Edwin F. Gay.* Cambridge: Harvard University Press, 1952.

Sibert, William Luther (1860–1935)

William Luther Sibert was born in Gadsden, Alabama, to William J. and Marietta Ward Sibert. Educated in rural schools, Sibert at the age of fourteen returned to the family farm to help run it. In 1878, he entered the University of Alabama. He entered the United States Military Academy in 1880 and graduated seventh in a class of thirty-seven in 1884.

Second lieutenant Sibert received his commission in the Corps of Engineers on June 15, 1884, and reported to the Battalion of Engineers at Willets Point, New York, in September. From July 1887 until September 1898, he served in engineering posts in Ohio, Kentucky, Michigan, and Arkansas. Following a teaching assignment at the Engineer School of Application at Willets Point in July 1899, he was posted to the Philippine Islands for a number of assignments, including duty as chief engineer and general manager of the Manila and Dagupan Railroad. Captain Sibert returned to the United States in June 1900 to take up duty as officer in charge of the Louisville, Kentucky, River and Harbor District. In December 1901, he took over the Pittsburgh, Pennsylvania, River and Harbor District. While assigned in Pittsburgh, he served on a number of boards and commissions dealing with improvements to river and canal waterways. Having come to the attention of President Theodore Roosevelt because of his experience with lock and dam construction, Major Sibert served briefly with the (Panama) Isthmian Canal Commission from March 10 to March 16, 1907. In June 1907, he took up duties as the officer in charge of designing and building the locks and dams connected with the Isthmian Canal, later assuming the post of division engineer, Atlantic Division, Isthmian Canal, a post he held until April 1914. On that date Lieutenant Colonel Sibert became the officer in charge of the Cincinnati, Ohio, Engineer District. From June to October 1914, he served as chairman of a board of engineers that studied flood prevention problems in China.

On March 4, 1915, Sibert was promoted to the grade of brigadier general and assumed command of the Pacific Coast Artillery District at San Francisco. In May 1917, General Sibert reported for duty at the War Department for eventual assignment to the American Expeditionary Force (AEF).

On June 8, 1917, the date the 1st Division was officially organized, Major General Sibert took command, then shipped out on June 14 for France. For the next six months he concentrated on organizing, equipping, and training the 1st Division for combat. During his period of command, the 1st Division underwent rigorous training with French and British instructors and incurred its first casualties in action. On Dec. 14, 1917, General Sibert was replaced in command by MajGen. Robert L. Bullard.

Upon returning to the United States, General Sibert commanded the Southeastern Department at Charleston, South Carolina, from January to May 1918, then took up duty as the director of the army's Chemical Warfare Service in Washington, D.C., a post he held until February 1920. He was awarded the Distinguished Service Medal for his work in organizing and administering the Chemical Warfare Service. The French government awarded him the Legion of Honor. In March and April 1920, he served as commanding general, 5th Division at Camp Gordon, Georgia. He made his home, following retirement on April 4, 1920, on his farm near Bowling Green, Kentucky, where he died on Oct. 16, 1935.

John F. Votaw

See also UNITED STATES ARMY: 1ST DIVISION

Bibliography
"William Luther Sibert." *Annual Report.* Association of Graduates, United States Military Academy, 1937.

Signal Corps
See UNITED STATES ARMY SIGNAL CORPS

Sims, William Sowden (1858–1936)
On Jan. 31, 1917, Germany announced that unrestricted U-boat warfare would begin the next day. In response to this action, President Woodrow Wilson broke diplomatic relations with Germany on February 3. Clinging to the dim hope that he could serve as an impartial mediator in the Great War, Wilson waited to see if American ships and lives were lost prior to asking Congress for authority to protect them. The die was cast when he learned that eight American vessels had been torpedoed in the North Sea during the first two weeks in March, with lives lost from three of them.

Given this situation, on March 24, Wilson asked Secretary of the Navy Josephus Daniels to establish confidential liaison immediately with the British. Daniels selected Canadian-born RAdm. William Sowden Sims, president of the Naval War College, for he knew Sims would be well received in Britain and that he had extensive experience with destroyers, the best ships for antisubmarine warfare (ASW). Sims was told to aid the British to counter the U-boat and, at President Wilson's direction, nudge them to adopt convoying.

On April 6, while Sims was at sea, Wilson approved a congressional resolution calling for war against Germany. On that very day the British notified Washington that the chief needs of the Allies were for shipping and financial aid for war purchases. No American battleships were needed, "but all craft from destroyers downward capable of dealing with submarines would be absolutely invaluable." On April 13, Wilson approved sending across six destroyers, with twenty-six more to follow. On April 28, Daniels authorized Sims to command the American ships in European waters.

Meanwhile, on April 10, Sims had spoken in London with Ambassador Walter H. Page, who took him to see First Sea Lord Adm. Sir John R. Jellicoe, and on the twelfth Page introduced him to Prime Minister David Lloyd George. Jellicoe described the seriousness of the

ASW campaign and concluded that Britain could not hold out beyond November as things stood. Sims saw that much of the Admiralty's problem lay with its using ships to patrol suspected U-boat areas rather than using convoys. On April 14, he sent home the first of many cables describing his most critical needs. Since victory could be won only where the sea lanes converged in the western approaches to Britain, the greatest aid the United States could give its new ally was to "send maximum number of destroyers accompanied by small antisubmarine craft" and provide merchant tonnage. Further, the United States should provide its own floating repair facilities and thus aid the Allies in a combined effort. Two battleship divisions sent to France would serve for morale purposes.

Sims noted that the British Grand Fleet was secure because it was escorted by numerous destroyers but that the British were doing little, as President Wilson put it, to "destroy the hornets [U-boats] in their nests." Why, Daniels and Benson asked Sims, could the British not keep a close blockade of the German and Belgian coasts and prevent the sortie of U-boats? Sims replied that the British could not overcome the land defenses of German ports or bottle up the U-boats with nets and mines. Why did the British not use convoys? Sims replied that they lacked sufficient escort ships. However, the Admiralty was studying the matter, and if the United States provided enough ships, he would nudge the British to adopt the convoy system.

Sims worked under many serious handicaps. He was denied an independent command; Washington was often slow in responding to his messages or misinterpreted them; he was not given sufficient trained staff until early 1918; and the Navy Department often did not let him select his own officers. He was given only 21 percent of America's ASW vessels, and Washington never tired of trying to direct the war effort by correspondence.

On May 2, the British and French agreed that Sims should command all ASW craft in European waters and coordinate the work of the three navies. Jellicoe insisted that the only remedy for overcoming the U-boat was for the United States to provide ASW vessels for patrol duty. Sims and Lloyd George succeeded in having Jellicoe order studies of it. Finally, when pressed to do so also by the commander of the Grand Fleet, Adm. Sir David Beatty, Jellicoe authorized the use of experimental convoys. A convoy of seventeen ships with a mere two escorts left Gibraltar on May 10 and arrived safely in Britain on the twenty-second. To Sims, that exploit "marked one of the great turning points of the war," and he was pleased when the Admiralty adopted the convoy system for all incoming ships. A second experimental convoy, this time from Hampton Roads, Virginia, also arrived safely. Losses on the Gibraltar-Britain route had been up to 33 percent. Of the 333 ships that sailed under escort during the last two weeks of May, losses fell to 1.5 percent.

After Daniels and Chief of Naval Operations Adm. William S. Benson belatedly agreed to adopt the convoy system, results were spectacular. The 870,000 tons of shipping losses of April fell to 600,000 tons in May and finally leveled off to about 350,000 per month by August. In August, meanwhile, ships *outbound* from Britain also left in convoy.

Sims could wish for no fuller cooperation from the British and French. He placed his ships in British waters under British operational command, thus providing unity of command, but kept his vessels in French waters under his own control. American destroyers that operated from Queenstown, Ireland, were larger and faster and had much greater range than their British counterparts. The commander at Queenstown, Adm. Sir Lewis Bayly, was so friendly that he used Sims's chief of staff as his own chief and during a leave period insisted that Sims fly the American flag while commanding during the Briton's absence. Moreover, the British Admiralty, with which he sat daily when in London, kept no secrets from Sims, and his fairly fluent French enabled him to get along well with French naval leaders and thus still further maximize Allied cooperation. On the other hand, Sims felt that he lacked cooperation from Washington.

Benson viewed Sims as merely "a transmitter of information" who was subordinate to him and to the commander of the Atlantic Fleet, RAdm. Henry Thomas Mayo. Daniels believed Sims was "an assistant abroad to Benson." Further, because the Navy Department obtained information from many sources other than Sims, officials there believed they could better determine wartime and postwar policies than he could from London. Benson and Daniels believed he was so pro-British that he was incapable of independent judgment and since Britons directed his ships' operations, they felt that Sims did not warrant a large staff. Neither Daniels nor Benson believed that the U-boat crisis was a bad as Sims depicted it, and they felt that American troops in Europe would be the determining factor in the war. They overlooked the fact that troop transports had to be escorted. Further, President Wilson told Sims that the British were not using their great naval superiority in an effective way. He wanted offensive action. What did Sims think needed to be done?

As he told Daniels and Benson, Sims replied to the President that the British were using all the small craft they could spare from the Grand Fleet to escort convoys. They could not attack German ports because of the latter's concealed guns. If he had his way, he would have all American ASW craft sent over, postpone the building of heavy ships in favor of ASW and merchant craft, lend all possible support to the convoy system, and have an American representative sit with the British War Council. He argued that he could send better information if Naval War College graduates were on his staff. The naval policies Daniels finally sent Sims on July 7, 1917, stated that the United States would cooperate with the Allies against the U-boat to the degree "compatible with maintaining an adequate defense of home waters." It would join the Allies in any offensive operations they undertook and gladly discuss future plans for Allied operations.

Sims disagreed with Washington on the vital point of escorts for troop transports. Because the sinking of a transport would create serious public relations problems, President Wilson, Daniels, and Benson held that they should be escorted. American transports were sent to Brest and several Biscay ports. When Daniels directed Sims to escort these ships, Sims objected because he lacked enough destroyers to escort both the supply ships that brought the materials upon which Britain depended for survival and the troopships that followed a more southerly course to France. The key question, said Daniels in early 1918, was, "Could America land enough soldiers in France in time to check the German offensive?" It was a difficult question to answer. How did one balance the demands for men for the Western Front with those for food and supplies that the Allies, and those very troops, required from the United States? As Sims saw it, the sinking of a transport carrying 5,000 men would be horrible, but that number merely equated with the daily carnage on the Western Front. Moreover, the more men were sent to Europe, the greater the strain on

the logistical supply line. And since allied victory depended upon American logistic support, every merchant ship lost denied the Allies vitally needed foods and war materiel. Fortunately for the Allies, in the spring of 1918, the Germans underestimated the number of men the United States could send across and thought they could stop supply ships. When they tried to shift U-boat attacks from cargo ships to troop ships, they failed.

In speaking to the officers of the Atlantic Fleet on Aug. 11, 1917, President Wilson had reiterated his demand for aggressive action against the U-boat. He was willing to sacrifice half the Anglo-American navies in order to "crush that nest, because if we crush it, the war is won." Sims took Wilson's request for antisubmarine warfare ideas from anyone, regardless of his rank, as a slap in the face. Sims was also displeased with Wilson's refusal to send representatives to inter-Allied war conferences. He disapproved of the President's prohibition against discussing strategy with the Allies, and Wilson's depiction of Sims as "hopelessly pro-British." Sims, therefore, invited the Navy Department to send observers to witness conditions in the Allied countries and see the need for inter-Allied councils that would direct the war effort. Wanting aggressive action taken against U-boats and their bases, Wilson sent Admiral Mayo to Europe. While the British gave Mayo full information on their needs, procedures, policies, and future plans, they had no plans to "crush the hornets in their nest" that were worth the cost. Mayo agreed that trying to block all German ports in the North Sea and Baltic by sinking old battleships and cruisers would be useless but that laying a mine barrage across the North Sea might prove fruitful. Few saw, as Sims did, that although a North Sea mine barrage might help, the remedy for the U-boat had already been found in the convoy.

Sims was pleased when Mayo supported his demands for a Planning Section in his headquarters and for far greater inter-Allied cooperation. Finally, in September, Gen. Ferdinand Foch suggested holding a conference in which Allied military and naval leaders would discuss which Allies would build merchant ships, transport American troops to Europe, pay for facilities built in Europe for American forces, and control neutral trade. Sims agreed that such a conference was needed and applauded Lloyd George's underscoring to President Wilson the need to "create some kind of Allied joint council, with permanent military and probably naval and economic staffs, to work out plans for the Allies, for submission to the several Governments concerned." Moreover, Wilson should send a mission to study European conditions at first hand. Prodded to do so by Sims, Gen. John J. Pershing, and several cabinet members, among others, Wilson sent a mission headed by his closest adviser, Col. Edward M. House. House was merely to clear up financial and logistic matters; he must not commit the United States to support any British or French war aims nor express any opinion on strategy until the United States had an army in the field. The naval adviser to the mission, Admiral Benson, would seek to arrange for the laying of the North Sea Mine Barrage and the undertaking of more aggressive steps against Germany.

After the British told Benson basically what they had told Mayo, it was suggested that an Allied Naval Council (ANC) be established with the members being the ministers of marine and chiefs of the naval staffs of the Allies and of the United States. On Nov. 20 Benson told the British War Cabinet that he approved a Planning Section for Sims's office and the pooling of tonnage regardless of nationality, as well as offensive operations against U-boat bases in Belgium, the laying of the North Sea Mine Barrage, and the creation of an ANC. The last was approved by the British and American governments in late November. Sims would serve as the United States representative.

By November 1917, Sims had a staff adequate to supervise the operations of 370 American ships, 5,000 regular and reserve officers, 70,000 men, and 45 bases stretching from Murmansk through Scotland, Ireland, and England to Malta and Corfu in the Mediterranean and to the Azores in the Atlantic. With his staff handling details, he had time for his most important duties: his daily conferences with Allied officers and attendance at the ANC. Therein the most obstreperous member was the Italian admiral, Paolo Thaon di Revel, who subordinated Italian naval operations to political considerations. He would not agree to foreign command of Italian forces or engage in offensive operations against the Austrian Navy that would weaken his fleet. Nor would he permit any but Italian domination of the Adriatic Sea or its Dalmatian coast.

Sims also faced an ugly interservice problem when the head of the AEF's Aviation Service, MajGen. Benjamin D. Foulois, told him that land planes were army weapons and that the navy had no business attacking land targets. Moreover, Foulois wished to command all American aircraft in a unified air force. However, General Pershing ruled that navy and marine aircraft could attack U-boat bases and enemy supply installations and airfields. Meanwhile, Sims supported the attempts of retired RAdm. Bradley A. Fiske to produce an effective torpedo plane that, unlike Allied ships, could attack the German High Seas Fleet in its harbors.

Lacking an officer with suitable rank to do so, Sims himself attended an ANC meeting held in Rome in February 1918. He held that ANC decisions took precedence over those from home and shifted decision making to Europe. He was also pleased when several estimates of the situation made by his Planning Section were approved at SWC and ANC meetings held in March.

During the summer of 1918, the tide of war on both land and sea swung to the Allied side. Sinkings of ships in convoy fell to .41 percent, and small craft and aircraft made it very dangerous for U-boats to operate in coastal waters. In addition to the blockade of its ports, Germany was hurt by rigid American control of exports to its neutral neighbors. Moreover, the German big push on the Western Front between March 2 and April 18 seriously weakened its manpower and economic stability and lowered the will of its people to continue the war. Meanwhile, President Wilson agreed to the creation of a supreme commander who would decide when and where the Allies would attack or defend. In September, General Pershing disregarded advice from Sims and others to merge his troops with British forces and launched his own offensives. However, Sims was greatly pleased when, finally, both President Wilson and Benson fully approved of his work. On September 18, Austria sued for peace, and on October 3, Germany asked Wilson for an armistice. Wilson replied that peace could be restored on the basis of his Fourteen Points. Naval peace terms written by Admiral di Revel were accepted for Austria and those written by the ANC by Germany.

With the war over, Sims sought neither a fleet command nor the billet of CNO, but a return to the presidency of the Naval War College. He would seek a reorganization of his navy on the basis of wartime lessons and leave political questions to politicians. He opposed the

Wilson-Daniels policy of completing the 1916 shipbuilding program in order to achieve "a navy second to none."

The chance for Sims to reorganize his navy on the basis of wartime lessons came early in 1920 when he told Congress that on January 7 he had written Secretary Daniels a letter on "Certain Naval Lessons of the Great War." In it he charged that the Navy Department "failed for at least six months to throw full weight against the enemy." During the critical months of the U-boat campaign, from April to October, 1917, he said, the department violated the strategic principle of concentration of maximum force in the critical area of the conflict—the western approaches to the British Isles. The result was that for the first six months of American involvement in the war, the department had "cost the Allied cause 2,500,000 tons of shipping, 500,000 lives, and $15 billion." Daniels rebutted that what counted was "results." In the end, if he established that there was room for improvement, Sims failed to prove that shortcomings in the department stemmed from Daniels's administration.

Paolo E. Coletta

See also Allied Naval Council

Bibliography

Daniels, Josephus. *The Wilson Era: Years of War—1917–1923*. Chapel Hill: University of North Carolina Press, 1946.

Morison, Elting E. *Admiral Sims and the Modern American Navy*. Boston: Houghton Mifflin, 1942.

Lloyd George, David. *War Memoirs of Lloyd George*. 6 vols. London: Nicholson & Watson, 1933–1936.

Sims, William Sowden, and Burton J. Hendrick. *The Victory at Sea*. Annapolis, MD: Naval Institute Press, 1984.

Trask, David F. *Captains and Cabinets: Anglo-American Naval Relations, 1917–1918*. Columbia: University of Missouri Press, 1972.

Sino-American Relations

See Chinese-American Relations

Slacker Raids

The passage of the Espionage and Sedition acts enabled "extralegal" and ultranationalistic organizations to retaliate against individuals and groups not thoroughly supporting the war effort. Reprisals ranged from individual beatings to group lynchings. By the spring of 1918, the Wilson administration denounced this trend toward mob violence and pleaded that such action provided negative propaganda for critics of America's involvement in the war. Attorney General Thomas W. Gregory warned the American Protective League (APL) and the Council of National Defense that only the Justice Department could legally suppress sedition, but his efforts proved ineffective.

Thereupon Gregory decided that these organizations' zealousness would actually benefit the government if it were used against groups of men who violated the 1917 Selective Service Law. Gregory believed that this would quell the public's displeasure toward such organizations, but, more importantly, it would assist the War Department in tightening control of draft resisters of "slackers." "To attempt to apprehend so great a number of offenders by running down individual cases obviously would have been futile," Gregory wrote to Wilson. "Some form of dragnet process . . . was absolutely essential."

By March 1918, Justice Department officials had enlisted the support of these "extralegal" organizations to round up draft-age men in selected cities at varying times and conduct "swift" investigations of their draft status. The first "slacker raid" occurred in Pittsburgh in early spring and spread to Minneapolis, Boston, Chicago, Cleveland, Atlantic City, and, by early September, to "slacker heaven," New York City. The tactics used during these seven months consisted of raiding theaters, hotels, ballparks, restaurants, union halls, train stations, and even some residences; forceably taking draft-age-looking men; and herding them into detention centers, where, with the aid of the local draft board, their registration or classification status was determined. Sometimes weeks passed before the draft board completed its investigation and released the suspect. Ironically, while innocent men were incarcerated without legal authority, the government was equally unsure what to do with legitimate draft evaders because the regulations remained so vague.

Gregory accepted full responsibility for adopting and implementing the "slacker raids." When asked by Wilson for a full accounting, Gregory replied that "the great body of our people will cheerfully submit to minor inconveniences which the execution of any such plan of necessity entails." Gregory's prediction proved incorrect, for regardless of the victorious spirit resounding throughout America in the fall of 1918, numerous men, not subject to the Selective Service law opposed this incursion on their civil liberties.

By the end of the war, the Justice Department's "slacker raids" netted 40,000 draft evaders. While Wilson voiced concern during the September raid in New York City, it never appeared again in his correspondence.

Steven Wright

Bibliography

Chafee, Zechariah, Jr. *Free Speech in the United States.* Cambridge: Harvard University Press, 1941.

Jensen, Joan M. *The Price of Vigilance.* Chicago: Rand McNally, 1968.

Murphy, Paul L. *World War I and the Origins of Civil Liberties in the United States.* New York: Norton, 1979.

Peterson, H.C., and Gilbert Fite. *Opponents of War, 1917–1918.* Seattle: University of Washington Press, 1957.

Scheiber, Harry. *The Wilson Administration and Civil Liberties, 1917–1921.* Ithaca, NY: Cornell University Press, 1960.

Small Arms

The United States entered World War I with insufficient amounts of many items upon which an army depends. One of these was small arms—rifles and pistols. Most of the members of the small Regular Army carried the very fine U.S. Magazine Rifle, Caliber .30, Model 1903, commonly referred to as the Springfield '03, but there were not enough of these to outfit the tremendous numbers of volunteers and draftees that were expected. Nor were there enough Colt Model 1911 automatic pistols. Army ordnance officers were faced with three possibilities. They could (1) seek increased production of the current weapons, (2) issue obsolete rifles from storage until the increased production was sufficient to meet the demand, or (3) obtain rifles from the Allies. All three expedients were adopted with regard to rifles and the first two with regard to pistols.

Springfield Rifle

The Springfield rifle was a direct outgrowth of the Spanish-American War. American ordnance experts recognized the superiority of the German-made Mauser rifles with which the Spaniards were armed and studied them carefully. After a short period of trial and error design the new rifle, the Model 1903, began to be issued to American troops in 1904.

This new rifle had a 24-inch barrel, which was six inches shorter than that of the Model 1898 Krag that it superseded. This presented a problem when it came to designing a bayonet for the new weapon because military thinkers had come to regard the Krag, with its ten-inch bayonet, as being of optimum length. The problem was solved by the introduction of the Model 1905 bayonet with a sixteen-inch blade.

By the spring of 1917 there were 600,000 Springfield rifles on hand, all of which had been manufactured by the two government armories at Springfield, Massachusetts, and Rock Island, Illinois.

An obvious improvement over the Krag was the method by which the Springfield was loaded. Rather than dropping five loose rounds into the magazine, the soldier armed with a Springfield was equipped with five-round stripper clips with which he could quickly charge the magazine. The ammunition itself, however, was soon modified. Upon the German introduction of the spitzer—or pointed—bullet, American designers quickly decided that the round-nosed 220-grain bullet of the Model 1903 was inefficient. The new round, adopted in 1906, was lighter at 150 grains and became known—by its caliber and date of adoption—as the .30-'06. This ammunition remained standard in the U.S. Army through the Korean War.

Paralleling the introduction of the Springfield rifle was the beginning of powered flight, and it was not long until military men saw the advantages of merging both technologies. Within a very few years of the Wright brothers' historic 1903 flight, 910 Springfield rifles had been modified for use from the air. Armorers fitted these Air Service rifles with shorter stocks, modified rear sights, and 25-round detachable box magazines. As early as 1910, 2d Lt. Jacob E. Rickel demonstrated the practicality of the weapon when, flying as a passenger, he fired at targets on the ground from an altitude of approximately 300 feet. In spite of Lieutenant Rickel's demonstration, however, there is no indication that these rifles saw action in World War I. Several of them, however, may be seen in the Springfield Armory Museum.

The realities of trench warfare sparked more modifications of the 1903 Springfield. One of the greatest difficulties facing soldiers in the trenches was the fact that they had to expose their heads and shoulders in order to fire their rifles. To counter this problem, two Cleveland inventors, J.L. Cameron and L.E. Yazzy, came up with a means to fire over the trench parapet without exposing any part of the body to enemy return fire. Their device consisted of a metal frame into which the soldier locked his rifle. The frame had a built-in periscope, remote bolt operator and trigger, and the same detachable 25-round magazine that had been used on the U.S. Air Service rifle. In use, only the rifle would be above the parapet, with the soldier completely safe in the trench below. These contrivances were bulky, however, and Cameron and Yazzy were still trying to improve their invention when the war ended.

A similar device was that of a Los Angeles inventor named Guiberson. This method did not employ any external frameworks. Instead, the stock of the rile itself was hinged and had a built-in periscope. In use, the soldier opened the hinge, adjusted the periscope, and fired. While the Guiberson device was much more compact than that of Cameron and Yazzy, it had major drawbacks. It did not make use of the standard Model 1903 Springfield but required a specially built stock, and, since there was no remote bolt, the soldier had to bring the rifle back down into the trench after every shot to cock it for the next one. Guiberson's invention remained in the development stages until the Armistice and was never issued to the troops.

The nature of trench warfare also fostered the search for improved grenades, and some of the accompanying development was in the area of rifle-fired grenades. The U.S. Army had adopted the Babbitt-type rifle grenade in 1911. This grenade was attached to a hollow rod that was inserted into the rifle barrel. A special blank cartridge was then fired to propel the grenade and arm it to explode upon impact. Under ideal conditions a soldier could reach a target 300 yards away with a Babbitt grenade.

During the war, the United States began experimenting with the French grenade VB Mark I, designed by Jean Viven and Gustave Bessière in 1916. This grenade fit on the end of the rifle and did not require the long rod or the special blank cartridge. Instead the grenade had a hole through its center. The soldier then fired a regular cartridge, the muzzle gases projected the grenade, and the bullet ignited the primer as it passed through the body of the grenade. Production problems were encountered when trying to adapt this system to the American rifles—both the Model 1903 Springfield and the Model 1917 Enfield—and they were not completely overcome in time to be of use in France. Nevertheless, American troops did receive 50,000 French-made rifle grenades, and by the end of the war, such American firms as Westinghouse, Briggs and Stratton, American Radiator Company, and Stewart Warner Speedometer Corporation were manufacturing 250,000 grenades per day.

Although the Model 1903 Springfield rifle was a very accurate weapon as manufactured, this accuracy was greatly enhanced by the fitting of special telescopic sights. Such specially equipped rifles were not a product of the twentieth century but had long been recognized as useful tools for snipers. As early as 1904, American ordnance officers had begun testing telescopic sights on the new rifles. By World War I, the Warner and Swasey models of 1908 and 1913 had been adopted. Originally these were hand-fitted to specific rifles, but during the war this practice was discontinued and 4,000 six-power Model 1913 sights were delivered to the army.

The Winchester Repeating Arms Company was another manufacturer of telescopic sights. First produced in 1907, the Winchester Five-Power Style A5 was an improvement over the Warner and Swasey model, but the army was slow to break its connection with that firm.

Shortly after America's entry into the war, firearms designer J.D. Pedersen approached the chief of ordnance with a novel invention that he thought could turn the tide of battle on the Western Front. Pedersen had come up with a modification that would, in effect, turn the Springfield rifle into a semiautomatic assault rifle in a matter of a few seconds. It consisted of a replacement bolt and chamber, which a soldier could install as needed, and a detachable box magazine that held forty rounds of .30-caliber pistol cartridges.

The Pedersen device was demonstrated for General Pershing and other interested officers in France in December 1917. The tests were so successful that an order was issued to Remington Arms-Union Metallic Cartridge Company for 100,000 devices and 500 million rounds of ammunition. In order to protect the secrecy of this invention, however, they were only to be issued in minimum amounts of 50,000. To further enhance security, the official name for this modification was to be "automatic pistol, caliber .30, Model 1918." In September 1918, before any deliveries had been made, the order was increased to 500,000 devices and 800 million rounds to be ready for the planned 1919 Allied spring offensive.

By the Armistice, some 65,000 devices had been completed, but none had been issued to troops in the field. Even with the war over, however, extreme secrecy surrounded this revolutionary modification, and field testing continued both in the United States and among occupation troops in France.

Out from under the immediate pressures of war, the Pedersen device did not fare so well under the scrutiny of ordnance officers and others. Critics began to find fault with the extra weight of the device and its ammunition. The replacement bolt itself weighed just over two pounds in its metal scabbard. The recommended 400 rounds of ammunition added another ten pounds to the already heavily laden infantryman. Another perceived shortcoming had to do with the potency of the Pedersen cartridges. The bullets themselves only weighed about half as much as those of the standard rifle round, and they left the barrel at only about half the speed of the .30–'06. Critics also found fault with the fact that effective range was much less than the rifle cartridge. Finally, it was feared that in the heat of battle a soldier attempting to swap the rifle bolt for the Pedersen device would inadvertently lose the rifle bolt, thus denying himself the use of a powerful, long-range weapon when next he needed one.

After formal rejection, the 65,000 Pedersen devices were put into government storage in 1920. Over the next decade Pedersen and others continued to work on designs of semiautomatic rifles, further ensuring the obsolescence of the Pedersen modification of the Springfield rifle. In April 1931, virtually all of the Pedersen devices, along with 60 million rounds of ammunition, were destroyed. A few devices were saved for exhibition at various army museums, and today these rare items can be seen at the West Point Museum and the Ordnance Museum at Aberdeen, Maryland.

Enfield Rifle
American ordnance officials did not believe that production rates could be increased enough for the Model 1903 rifle to meet the needs of the rapidly expanding army, so they looked to commercial arms manufacturers for other solutions. The obvious answer to the shortage was to contract with these firms to build Springfields. The problem with this, however, was the lead time required to retool the factories and the fact that the major American arms makers were already swamped with orders from the Allies, particularly Great Britain, to build rifles for their armies.

Both Remington and Winchester were building Enfield Pattern 14 (1914) Rifles for Britain. Each factory had had difficulties meeting the required quality standards; the British government had bought out the factories for some $20 million. America's entrance into the war prompted Great Britain to sell its interest in these plants to the United States. For $900,000, the American government got all of the tools, dies, jigs, fixtures, gauges, cutters, and raw material on hand.

The bargain was tempered somewhat by the fact that the 1914 Enfield was chambered for different ammunition than was used by the United States. Retooling was hastened, however, and the changes were not major, so that by late summer of 1917 the modified rifles—now called the Model 1917 Enfields—were being produced by both Winchester and Remington.

Actual production of the 1917 Enfield got off to a rapid start due to the availability of large amounts of parts already manufactured under the British contracts. Problems soon arose that hampered ongoing production. There were periodic shortages of properly seasoned walnut for the rifle stocks, and there were difficulties in obtaining high-quality steel for the barrels. Even when these logistical and technical problems were overcome, there seemed to be a constant shortage of competent workmen. This, of course, was due to the simple laws of supply and demand. Workers with arms-making experience were in great demand by both government-run facilities and companies such as Remington and Winchester. Workers found it very easy to go from one employer to another as often as a higher salary was offered. The turnover in the workforce was so severe at the Remington plant at Ilion, New York, that during the first six months of 1918, 30,000 men were hired for 6,000 jobs.

Whether all of the production problems were actually solved or whether they were just tolerated, production of the Model 1917

S

Enfield did reach 10,000 per day by the end of the war. (The Enfield, like the Springfield, remained in U.S. arsenals until World War II when 275,000 of them were shipped to our Allies under the provisions of the Lend-Lease Act.)

Toward the end of the war, the Winchester Company, along with Springfield Armory, began work on a special sniper rifle—the United States telescopic rifle, Model 1918. This weapon was, in fact, a modified Model 1917 Enfield with a Winchester 2.7-power telescopic sight, but the war ended before more than a few prototype models could be completed.

Model 1898 Krag Rifle

Even though Model 1903 Springfields and Model 1917 Enfields were rushed to the troops in Europe as fast as they could be turned out, there was still a shortage of weapons with which to train the soldiers before they went overseas. It was this shortage that led to the issue of obsolete Model 1898 Krag rifles to stateside training facilities. Although the troops would not take these rifles overseas with them, they could at least learn such things as how to march with a rifle, proper marksmanship traits, and how to keep their weapon clean and in working order.

The Model 1898 rifle, known familiarly as the Krag after one of its inventors, had been the first magazine-fed, bolt-action rifle adopted by the U.S. Army back in the early 1890s. Minor changes throughout the last decade of the nineteenth century had resulted in the Model 1898. It was the rifle, in a slightly earlier form, with which the Regular Army had been equipped to fight in Cuba, Puerto Rico, and the Philippines.

The Krag was not considered a first-class weapon, but it was a bolt-action, .30-caliber rifle whose weight and overall length were not significantly different from those of its descendents. For these reasons and, as noted, due to the lack of adequate numbers of Springfields and Enfields, numbers of Krags were issued for training purposes and for routine guard duty within the United States.

Foreign Weapons

As American soldiers began reaching Europe in ever increasing numbers, some of them found themselves being issued foreign-made rifles. This occurred primarily among those units assigned to British or French commands. It made sense to issue the same weapons to the Ameri-

cans that their host armies were using so there would be fewer problems with keeping American troops well supplied with ammunition and spare parts.

Short-Magazine Lee-Enfield

The standard British rifle of World War I was known as the Short-Magazine Lee-Enfield (SMLE). This rifle, first adopted into British service in 1895, went through several design modifications prior to the war. As issued during the war, its physical dimensions placed it between America's main-line rifles. It was slightly longer than the Springfield but shorter than the Enfield. The SMLE fired a .303-caliber bullet with a lower muzzle velocity than the American rifles, but it was a robust weapon able to stand rough treatment in the trenches. The 27th and 78th divisions were among the American units supplied with the SMLE.

Fusil d'Infanterie Modèle 1907 Transforme (Mle 07/15) and Fusil d'Infanterie Modèle 1916

When black American combat troops of the incomplete 93d Division arrived in France, they were assigned to a sector of the line controlled by the French Army. Although they retained their American regimental organizations, these troops were under the command of French officers. Therefore, in order to minimize logistical problems, these men received complete outfits of French field gear—including their rifles.

This weapon is often mistakenly referred to as a Lebel, but Andre Berthier was actually its main designer. The French government first adopted this rifle in 1890, but improvements followed and by the second year of the war French infantrymen carried the Model 1907 infantry rifle as modified in 1915. This was the Fusil d'Infanterie Modele 1907 Transforme (Mle 07/15), which was issued to the black American troops upon their arrival in France. The weight of this rifle was about the same as that of the American weapons, but at slightly over fifty-one inches in length, it was five inches longer than the Model 1917 Enfield and eight inches longer than the Model 1903 Springfield.

Extra length was not the only drawback to the French rifle. Although it, too, used a bolt-action mechanism, it only had a three-round magazine capacity. This might be enough for a hunting trip, but was not enough for warfare. The Mauser rifles with which the Germans were equipped had five-round magazines, and the

British fighting alongside the French were able to fire their Enfields ten times before reloading. In the face of this firepower deficiency, French authorities again modified the original design in 1916 to accept a five-round magazine. This became the Fusil d'Infanterie Modèle 1916. It still is not clear whether the Americans armed with the earlier model received these.

Model 1891 Mosin-Nagant Rifle

After the withdrawal of Russia from World War I following the Treaty of Brest Litovsk, officials in the United States and Great Britain grew anxious over the safety from German troops of Allied war supplies stockpiled at Archangel in North Russia, near that country's only year-round port of Murmansk. Allied leaders dispatched troops, including the Michigan and Wisconsin National Guardsmen of the 339th Infantry Regiment to this potential trouble spot in the fall of 1918.

In order to make use of ordnance supplies on hand, the American troops involved used Russian rifles and ammunition. These rifles were the 3-Lineyaya Vintovka Obr 1891, or 3-line rifle, Model 1891. A "line" was a unit of measurement used in tsarist Russia and equal to about a tenth of an inch. The 3-line rifle, therefore, had a bore of three lines, or approximately .30 caliber. In the Western world these rifles are known by the name of their designers and are simply referred to as the Model 1891 Mosin-Nagant rifles. In fact, large numbers were manufactured in France, Switzerland, and Austria until Russian factories could take over in the mid-1890s. After the start of World War I, the American firms of Remington Arms-Union Metallic Cartridge Company and New England Westinghouse both received large contracts for these rifles.

This weapon combined features designed by Sergei Ivanovich Mosin, an officer in the Imperial Russian Army, and Emile and Leon Nagant of Belgium. It was a rugged .30-caliber bolt-action rifle with a five-round magazine capacity. It was five inches longer than the Model 1917 Enfield and eight inches longer than the Model 1903 Springfield, and at slightly over nine and one-half pounds it was heavier than either of them. The bayonet for this rifle differed from those on American service rifles in that it was of the old socket pattern. Rather than being attached along the underside of the barrel, its sleeve, or socket, slipped over the end of the barrel and then locked in place. The multisided blade tapered to a screwdriver point, allowing the soldier to use his bayonet to take his rifle apart for cleaning or other maintenance.

This rifle underwent periodic modifications, but the Russian Army used it until the end of World War II.

Model 1918 Browning Automatic Rifle (BAR)

During World War I, firearms designers constantly sought the ultimate infantry weapon. The nature of trench warfare imposed certain requirements on any such weapon. Before an army could send its infantry forward to attack enemy positions, its artillery would pound those positions heavily. The artillery must necessarily, however, lift its fire as the foot soldiers swept forward across the intervening space to minimize the possibility of killing its own. This often gave the defenders enough time to scramble up out of their bunkers to receive the attack. The assault force needed a weapon that would allow it to continue to advance even after the enemy had returned to his fighting positions.

A decision was reached that the best solution would be to provide American infantrymen with weapons with which they could sweep the enemy trench lines with automatic fire as they moved across no-man's-land. If they could thus keep the Germans pinned down as they advanced, they would have a greater likelihood of reaching their objectives. Prolific American firearms inventor John M. Browning developed such a weapon with the U.S. Automatic Rifle, Caliber .30, known more familiarly as the Browning Automatic Rifle, or simply the BAR.

Browning's design was based around the standard .30-'06 cartridge used in America's infantry rifles. It came with a twenty-round detachable box magazine and had a selector switch that would allow the soldier to fire it either as a machine gun or only one shot at a time. It was considerably heavier than the regular rifle so after initial manufacture it began to be furnished with a bipod to help the soldier steady the weapon when firing from a prone position.

The BAR seemed like the ideal solution to a vexing problem, but it had several shortcomings. Its weight, over eighteen pounds with the bipod, made it too heavy to shoot comfortably from the shoulder. On the other hand, it was too light to absorb all the vibrations when it was being fired at a rate of 500 rounds per minute and was therefore difficult to keep on target. Added to this, its magazine capacity was rapidly expended when firing fully automatic, and this meant frequent reloading.

Despite its limitations, the firms of Colt, Winchester, and Marlin-Rockwell produced 85,000 BARs by war's end. After the war, slight modifications were made, and the BAR remained as America's squad automatic weapon through World War II and the Korean War.

Shotguns

As the war along the Western Front approached a stalemate, both sides sought some sort of weaponry advantage that would ensure victory. This search led to such developments as the Browning Automatic Rifle, the use of poison gas, and the tank. In one instance, however, American military men merely turned to a weapon that had been around for some time—the pump shotgun. They believed that a rapid-firing, short-barreled shotgun would be ideal for the close fighting of the trenches.

Having made the decision to adopt a shotgun, army authorities did not have far to look to find a suitable model. The Winchester Company had introduced a shortened version of its Model 1897 twelve-gauge pump shotgun in 1898. This "riot gun," designed by the famous John M. Browning, found immediate favor among urban police departments across the country, and the army used it during the Philippine War. Winchester later introduced its Model 12, which did away with the exposed hammer of the earlier version. After specifying certain modifications, the government ultimately bought 19,196 of these guns from Winchester and perhaps as many as 5,000 more on the open market. The military modifications consisted of adding a carrying sling and the installation of a bayonet attachment on the underside of the barrel that would accept the Model 1917 Enfield rifle bayonet. As adopted, these trench guns had twenty-inch, cylinder bore barrels and were slightly over thirty-nine inches long without the bayonet. Their tubular magazines held five shots, and the soldier could carry a sixth round in the chamber.

Another large American arms producer, Remington, also provided such weapons. Remington, too, had begun offering a riot gun version of its twelve-gauge Model 1908 repeating shotgun within a year of its initial appearance. Designed by another famous arms inventor, John D. Pedersen, this shotgun also featured a twenty-inch-cylinder bore barrel and, like Winchester's Model 12, had a concealed hammer. After the onset of World War I, Remington ceased production of this weapon in order to fill the huge orders for military rifles coming from England and Russia. With American entry into the war, Remington quickly resumed production. The Remington trench guns, which had been redesignated as the Model 10, had a slightly longer barrel, at twenty-one and one-half inches, than the Winchester. About the only other difference between the two was the fact that a soldier firing the Remington had to release the trigger between each shot, but the Winchester user could simply hold the trigger down and fire as fast as he could work the slide.

The Germans repeatedly protested the American's use of shotguns as inhumane and contrary to established usages of war as codified by the Hague Conference of 1899. They even threatened to execute any American soldier or marine captured with a shotgun or with shotgun ammunition. Upon receiving this threat, the judge advocate general of the U.S. Army gave it as his opinion that the German interpretation of the Hague Convention was faulty and that if any Americans were executed as a consequence, the United States would retaliate in kind.

Shotguns were well suited to guarding captured prisoners, and doughboys found them to be quite handy when raiding German trenches and when repelling such raids. Soldiers with particular bird-hunting skills from civilian life were also reported to have used the trench guns to down German message-carrying pigeons as well as for deflecting incoming hand grenades.

Due to the high humidity often encountered in France, the paper-hulled shotgun shells issued with these weapons sometimes softened and swelled, causing the guns to jam and become inoperable. If this occurred, the soldier would find himself carrying a weapon that was little better than a club. Brass shells would alleviate this condition, but none arrived in France until after the Armistice. The field solution was for the men to jack all of their shells through the weapon periodically to make sure they would all work properly.

After the war, the trench guns went into government storage until World War II when they were again issued to troops. The World

War I trench guns and their more modern descendants have been in American military arsenals in every war since then.

Handguns

Handguns were issued to officers and noncommissioned officers, perhaps as much as a badge of authority as a weapon, and to mounted troops. As the war proceeded, however, soldiers found them quite useful when trying to clear enemy trenches. (Soldiers in Vietnam would apply the same logic to their use in tunnel-clearing operations.) As America entered the war, the standard military handgun was the Model 1911 Colt automatic, although stocks of older revolvers were still on hand. Wartime needs and the inability of American industry to keep up with the demand for the automatics caused the War Department to have considerable quantities of new revolvers manufactured as well.

U.S. Pistol, Automatic, Caliber .45, Model 1911

The use of the term "automatic pistol" is, in most cases, a misnomer. A truly automatic firearm continues to fire as long as the trigger is held down. Most automatic pistols are actually "semiautomatic" in that they require a separate pull of the trigger for each round fired. What is automatic about them is that each time they fire they automatically eject the spent cartridge case and feed another round into the firing chamber. Such automation had long been sought by weapons designers, and by the time of World War I several versions were in production.

The automatic pistol approved by the U.S. Army in 1907 tests was a design by the prolific arms inventor John M. Browning. Browning had a long string of firearms designs to his credit, including several rifles and shotguns, before his automatic pistol design was selected by the army. As tested in 1907, it proved superior to most other entries, but some minor changes were required before adoption in 1911.

The Model 1911 pistol was eight and one-half inches long and weighed two and one-half pounds empty. A seven-round detachable box magazine located in the handle fed the five-inch barrel with 230-grain .45-caliber bullets.

These weapons are usually referred to as Colt automatics; in fact, most of them were built by Colt before and during the war. When the

United States entered the war, it became apparent that more of these pistols would be needed than were on hand. Moreover, by early 1918, it appeared that the Colt factory, which until this time had made most of these weapons, would not be able to keep up with the increased demands alone; therefore, other sources were sought.

The government armory at Springfield, Massachusetts, had turned out the Model 1911 pistols until switching its entire workforce to the production of Model 1903 rifles in 1916. Nevertheless, during the first six months of 1918 a shortage of spare rifle parts caused this facility temporarily to discontinue rifle production. As the spare parts inventory was built back up, excess manpower was turned again to producing automatic pistols. Working around the clock, the Springfield Armory eventually shipped 45,000 pistols before resuming full rifle production at the end of June 1918.

In February 1918, at about the same time that Springfield got back into pistol production, the Remington Arms-Union Metallic Cartridge Company signed a contract to produce 150,000 pistols. It was hoped that retooling could be completed and production under way by June, with deliveries to begin in August. Overcoming various technical difficulties, Remington had just begun to ship finished pistols when a labor strike disrupted production. Deliveries resumed in September, but the war ended soon thereafter. Even though Remington was allowed to keep assembling guns from parts already on hand until June of 1919, less than 22,000 were produced.

Ordnance officers approached Winchester and New England Westinghouse, but both of these firms were already working at capacity to fill their existing contracts for rifles and machine guns for the United States, Great Britain, Canada, France, and Russia. Contracts were then issued to seven other firms, including two in Canada, for a total of just over 2.5 million pieces. Among these contractors were established firearms manufacturers, such as Savage Arms Company of Utica, New York, and the Dominion Rifle Plant in Quebec. The Burroughs Adding Machine Company and the National Cash Register Company also received contracts. By the time the war ended, fewer than 200 pistols had been completed, and the rest of the contracts were canceled.

In spite of the disappointing results in securing additional manufacturers, Colt turned out a half million Model 1911 pistols between 1917 and 1919.

U.S. Revolver, Model 1917
Colt

Just as the shortage of Model 1903 rifles in 1917 led to the adoption of the modified Model 1914 British Enfield, the lack of Model 1911 automatic pistols caused ordnance experts to look for a substitute. Since both the Colt and Smith and Wesson companies had large-frame, heavy-duty, double-action revolvers in current production, both were selected to furnish a military version using the same cartridge as the automatic.

The basis of Colt's military revolver was the New Service Model, first introduced to the civilian market in 1897 in a wide variety of calibers and manufactured in .455 caliber for the British early in the war. The U.S. military had adopted an earlier version, the Model 1909, but with the introduction of the Model 1911 automatic pistol, relatively few of the revolvers were purchased. Nevertheless, ordnance officials remembered the rugged Model 1909, and although it was chambered for a slightly different cartridge than was now called for, only relatively minor alterations would be necessary to bring it up to specifications.

The Model 1909 pistol was also .45 caliber, but the cartridge for which it was designed was longer than the one used in the Model 1911 automatic and there was a pronounced rim on the base of the shell. The .45 ACP (Automatic Colt Pistol) rounds, on the other hand, were rimless and could not engage the ejector mechanism on the weapon's swing-out cylinder. Instead of ejecting all six fired cases at once, a soldier would have to carry a short stick with which to push each empty shell manually out of the cylinder. One solution, developed before the end of the war, was a slightly modified cartridge, the .45 auto-rim. This was virtually the same as the .45 ACP but with the addition of a rim on the base. The ejector could then engage this rim. Another solution was a small metal clip in the shape of a half-moon that would grasp three .45 ACP rounds at once and would provide a surface for the ejector to engage. Not only could a soldier now eject all of his spent casings at once, but loading was speeded up considerably since he could now load three shells at once instead of having to insert cartridges individually.

Dubbed the U.S. Revolver, Caliber .45, this weapon weighed two and one-half pounds, was ten and three-quarter inches long, and featured a barrel of five and one-half inches. Its six round capacity put it at a slight disadvantage against the Model 1911 automatic pistol and, even with the convenience of the half-moon clips, reloading was also slower. Nevertheless, Colt produced 150,000 of these handguns. They proved to be reliable second-line weapons, while production of the automatic remained less than the demand. They were still in limited use in the U.S. Army during World War II.

Smith and Wesson

Like Colt, Smith and Wesson produced handguns for Great Britain early in World War I so when the U.S. government began looking for a substitute for the Model 1911 automatic pistol it did not have far to look. Smith and Wesson designated their large-frame revolver the "hand ejector model," and by the end of 1916 it had produced almost 75,000 for the British in .455 caliber. As the war in Europe continued to drag on, Smith and Wesson engineers developed a version of this big revolver by 1916 that would fire the same cartridges as the Model 1911 automatic pistol. Thus, when the United States entered the war, Smith and Wesson was ready.

Although company officials had planned to build a new factory building in which to produce their revolver for the government, construction had barely begun when a government contract for revolvers was issued. By September 1917, the first of these weapons was completed and production soon reached 5,000 per month. This number tripled after the new building was finished; by the end of the war, Smith and Wesson had furnished over 153,000 Model 1917 revolvers.

In outward appearance these handguns were almost identical to those being built by Colt. Mechanically, the main difference is in the cylinder release button. One must push forward on the Smith and Wesson button to open the cylinder and pull back on the Colt.

After the war, Smith and Wesson manufactured a commercial version of the Model 1917 revolver which enjoyed steady sales success through the 1930s. The Brazilian government bought 5,000 Model 1917s in 1938, and the factory finally ceased producing this model in 1949.

James McCaffrey

Bibliography

Dooly, William G., Jr. *Great Weapons of World War I*. New York: Walker, 1969.

Hogg, Ivan V., and John Weeks. *Military Small Arms of the 20th Century*. London: Arms and Armour Press, 1985.

Smith, Joseph E. *Small Arms of the World*. Harrisburg, PA: Stackpole Books, 1969.

Soissons

In the summer of 1918, when the fields of Picardy were garbed in red poppies, blue and yellow flowers, and endless acres of wheat, the men of the 1st Division endured extreme hardship in their squalid trenches, punctuated by occasional raids into the German positions. The division moved on July 12 to help counter the German offensive launched on May 27, which had created a large salient between the Aisne and Marne rivers, with its "shoulders" stretching from a point just west of Soissons to the southeast near Reims and its "nose" at Château-Thierry. In June, the American 2d Division, with its famous brigade of U.S. Marines, had fought a bloody action west of Château-Thierry at Belleau Wood.

In July, as the Germans were preparing for offensive action along the eastern face of the salient, the French were planning a major counteroffensive against the western face of the salient near Soissons. The main attack to seize the heights south of Soissons was assigned to the French XX Corps (French Tenth Army), which included the French 1st Moroccan Division and the U.S. 1st and 2d divisions. This main attack, which would be supported all along the salient by the coordinated action of more than twenty more divisions, was scheduled for the morning of July 18. The two American divisions had just received new commanders—MajGen. Charles P. Summerall in the 1st and MajGen. James G. Harbord in the 2d. Both divisions had redeployed with great difficulty, moving by truck convoy at night and hiding in woods during the day to avoid detection from the air, arriving near Compiègne and Villers-Cotterêts on the night of July 15–16. At this same time, the American 3d Division was earning its nickname, "Marne Division," in heavy fighting along the Marne River east of Château-Thierry. Although only the 1st, 2d, and 3d divisions are mentioned here, 310,000 Americans took part in the Aisne-Marne campaign and 67,000 were casualties.

A heavy rain on the night of July 17 turned the fields and roads into a sea of mud. Mustard gas from previous German artillery bombardments laced the pools of water at the bottom of most of the ravines of that criss-crossed the terrain within the salient. The 42d French Aero Reconnaissance Squadron, which had supported the 1st Division at Cantigny, was again attached, along with French tanks, artillery, and balloons. On the seventeenth, pressed to complete their preparations, the American units abandoned their earlier attempts at secrecy and struggled to get all the artillery into position to support the attack, scheduled for 4:35 A.M. the next morning.

Montefontaine, immediately in the rear of the American positions, was a huge traffic bottleneck, with endless columns of horses, trucks, and artillery competing for road space with the infantry, engineers, and machine gunners. No artillery registration or preliminary bombardment was permitted prior to H-hour. Senior staff officers of the 1st Division were astonished that the Germans, with their airplanes, failed to anticipate this attack.

At the moment of the attack, a defensive barrage from the German artillery landed in the American assembly positions, but there was no return fire to give away the imminent attack. Many of the troops in both American divisions had barely reached the line of departure before H-hour, and they ran forward to stay in position behind the rolling barrage. The attack zone from west to east was a plateau covered with waist-high wheat. The 1st Division on the left (north) was immediately on the plateau, but the 1st Moroccans in the center, who had pulled in both flanks to make room for the Americans, and the 2d Division on the south had to fight for the high ground first in order to eliminate a strong German position in the northeastern tip of the Retz Forest. The attacking divisions later would encounter deep ravines traversing their front as they advanced eastward.

The artillery fire plan called for a rolling barrage, mostly from the divisional 75-mm guns, to advance at a rate of 100 meters in two minutes with the infantry following close behind. At the first objective line about 2,000 meters away, the barrage was to halt for twenty minutes, then move forward again to the second objective line near Missy-aux-Bois ravine in the 1st Division's sector.

Although the German artillery and machine gun positions had not been silenced in the barrage and counter-battery fire, the 1st Division reached its first objective line by 5:30 A.M. The Missy-aux-Bois ravine was about 1,000 meters wide with steep banks. A marshy swamp about 600 meters wide lay at the bottom. The Germans had registered their artillery on the ravine and, using corduroy roads, had even placed batteries at the bottom to fire directly into the advancing American infantry. They had an extremely strong position at the village of Breuil from which they could enfilade the 1st Division's infantry formations. Five of the French tanks were destroyed at the western edge of the ravine. As the men of Cantigny struggled to gain control of the Missy ravine, the Moroccans were falling behind the pace of the American attack, leaving the flanks of those two divisions exposed to attack. The 2d Division, which had to begin its attack with a complicated change of direction to face northeast, were about three miles into their zone when they encountered the Vierzy ravine.

The normal confusion of battle, poor map reading, bad weather, and heavy casualties among battalion officers (the 2d Battalion, 28th Infantry lost every officer except its commander, Maj. C.J. Huebner) eroded effective control of operations. However, junior officers and noncommissioned officers stepped forward to reorganize their units and continue the attack. Across the lines, German units depleted by "grippe" did their best to stem the attack.

At the end of the first day's fighting, the 1st Division held the eastern edge of Missy ravine and the 2d Division had moved east of Vierzy, about two and one-half miles from the line of departure. In World War I, nightfall brought relief and terror. After a full day of fighting, soldiers discovered their exhaustion, thirst, and hunger. Then enemy artillery and mortar crews began their methodical harassment of the infantry trying to find cover.

In the 2d Division sector, orders had arrived very early on the morning of the nineteenth directing the division to continue the attack at 4 A.M. The only available troops anywhere near combat ready were the 6th Marines. They were able to move and launch their attack at 8:25 A.M., then advance about 2,000 meters, but had to dig in about 800 meters short of the Soissons-Château-Thierry road, having suffered more than 50 percent casualties. The division was entirely spent; General Harbord requested relief for his unit, which mercifully came just after midnight on July 20 by a French division.

In the north, the 1st Division fared better. General Summerall managed to get his division moving at the designated H-hour of 4 A.M. toward an objective line from Berzy-le-Sec to Buzancy on the far side of the Soissons-Château-Thierry road. At the end of the day on July 19, the division had secured a hold on the Ploisy ravine in the north of their zone and had cleared to the east side of the Chazelle ravine in the south. Casualties were mounting, however—nearly twice that of the 18th.

The Moroccans did better on the second day of fighting and managed to keep up, but the French units on the north of the 1st and the south of the 2d divisions again fell behind, leaving open flanks to be dealt with.

The German Ninth Army command group knew that further advances by the wildly aggressive Americans would jeopardize their communications laterally across the salient and eliminate the Germans' chance to withdraw their forces from the Château-Thierry sector. They stiffened their defenses near Berzy-le-Sec, the new objective for the 1st Division on July 20 and 21. The village commanded the heights on a plateau above the Crise ravine, through which ran the Soissons-Paris railroad and the Soissons-Château-Thierry road.

By mid-morning on the twenty-first, the 1st Division was in control of the Berzy-le-Sec and the heights above Buzancy. On the twenty-second, the division straightened its front lines and endured harassing fire from the German artillery. More than 7,300 officers and men of the 1st Division had been killed or wounded in the five days of fighting across six and one-half miles of fiercely contested terrain. Combined casualties in the 1st and 2d divisions were 11,259.

The Germans lost about 3,500 prisoners and ninety guns to the 1st Division. The 2d Division had taken about 2,900 prisoners, excluding additional wounded taken to the rear.

The Moroccan Division had been relieved on the night of the twentieth by the French 87th Division, but the Americans had to wait for relief by the 15th Scottish Division, which came on the night of July 22. The French XX Corps finally was in control of the major lines of communication from Soissons to the south and west.

The 1st Division had met its initial test at Cantigny, the 2d at Belleau Wood, and the 3d at Château-Thierry. The Marne salient was eliminated by August 6. It was clear to the Germans that in addition to the ever increasing numbers of Americans in France, the fighting quality of those Yankee units was improving with every action. Sixteen months after the United States had entered the war as a belligerent, more than 1 million American troops were in France; 812,000 were serving in twenty-nine combat divisions, with the rest training or supporting operations.

Although the operations to reduce the St. Mihiel salient in September 1918 included the debut of the American First Army, doughboys already had fought effectively in both French and American army corps prior to that time. For the 1st and 2d divisions at least, the fighting at Soissons put temper in their steel.

John F. Votaw

Bibliography

American Battle Monuments Commission. *American Armies and Battlefields in Europe: A History, Guide, and Reference Book*. Washington, DC: Government Printing Office, 1938.

Coffman, Edward M. *The War to End All Wars: The American Military Experience in World War I*. New York: Oxford University Press, 1968.

History of the Third Division United States Army in The World War for the Period December 1, 1917 to January 1, 1919. Andernach-on-the-Rhine, Ger.: 3d Division, 1919.

Society of the 1st Division. *History of The 1st Division During the World War, 1917–1919*. Philadelphia: Winston, 1922.

Spaulding, Oliver Lyman, and John W. Wright. *The 2d Division American Expeditionary Force in France, 1917–1919*. New York: Hillman, 1937.

Somme Offensive

By July 17, 1918, the German offensive drives designed to win the war had spent their force. Although the Germans had inflicted enormous casualties and had taken ground at a rate unheard of since the summer of 1914, they had failed their objective and had suffered 1 million casualties in the process.

Even while the Germans were in the last hours of their desperate attacks, Gen. Sir Douglas Haig was planning a major counterattack east of Amiens with his reorganized and reinforced British Fourth Army. The Allied offensive of British and French forces was launched on August 8. It was designed to end the German threat to the Paris-Amiens railroad and reduce the salient caused by the German "Michael" offensive. Its brilliant success and the evidence it provided of collapsing German capabilities marked it as the first of a series of virtually continuous attacks against the enemy that lasted until the Armistice. In its later stages, the offensive on an Amiens-Aulnoye axis was to inflict mounting casualties, break through the major German defenses of the Hindenburg Line, and seize the strategic rail junction at Aulnoye on the Sambre River. In Allied hands this junction would cripple the German transportation network and doom the possibility of supply, reinforcement, or withdrawal.

During the desperate days of German success, the American Expeditionary Force (AEF) continued to grow but played a small part in the defense of the Somme sector. Elements of the U.S. 33d Infantry Division, however, did participate in an attack on July 4 and became embroiled in the debate over the use of American forces. Original plans called for ten companies of the division's 131st and 132d Infantry to gain some supervised battle experience by joining the Australian 4th Division assault on Le Hamel, south of the Somme and twelve miles east of Amiens. On July 2, General Pershing objected to the parceling out of American troops in a "nonemergency" and demanded that they be withdrawn from the attack. Gen. Sir John Monash, the Australian Corps Commander, argued that the entire plan would have to be scrapped if the integrated American units were withdrawn and further warned that Australian-American cooperation would be irreparably damaged. Ultimately, General Haig permitted C and E companies of the 131st and A and G companies of the 132d to participate. Despite their small numbers, the Americans were appreciated by the Australians, and a good working relationship began. Pershing was irritated that his express orders had been ignored by the British, the Australians, and his own subordinates. Henceforth, Americans attached to British formations were allowed to fight with them, but only if attached to the British force solely for that purpose.

The succession of probing attacks along the Somme throughout the spring and summer culminated in the Second Battle of the Somme that began on August 8. To execute it, the British marshaled, in great secrecy, 440,000 men with eighteen divisions organized into five corps: the Canadians with their four divisions and the British 32d Division; the Australian with their five divisions; the British III Corps with four British divisions and the American 33d Division; the Cavalry Corps with three cavalry divisions; and IX Corps headquarters. On the right flank the French First Army had ten divisions. To support their force, the British had over 2,000 guns, 500 tanks, and 800 planes. Combined with the French, Allied aircraft numbered 1,900 against 365 German planes.

The blow fell at 4:20 A.M. when the first of 450,000 British shells crashed down on the five German divisions to the Allied front, and eight British, Australian, and Canadian divisions attacked. When the fog lifted at midmorning the enormity of the German disaster became apparent. Whole divisions had disappeared. The Canadian and Australian troops advanced up to eight miles on a broad front and in the process overran the German gun line. Most ominous for the German High Command was the fact that over 15,000 German troops surrendered. It was, in General Ludendorff's words, "The Black Day of the German Army," but it was only the first of many to come.

Despite the great success, the Allies suffered setbacks on the first day. In III Corps area, the British 58th Division had taken heavy casualties in recent fighting and was unable to advance. As a result, the Australian 3d Division came under heavy enfilading machine gun and artillery fire from the Chipilly Spru, a bare ridge that projected into a large horseshoe bend north of the Somme. The U.S. 131st Infantry of the 33d Division was attached to the British 58th Division and ordered to seize the ridge. The 131st conducted a night march and, after double-timing part of the last four miles to the line of departure, attacked at 5:30 A.M. on August 9. Supported by the Australian 4th Division across the river, the Americans took the high ground and supporting German positions, then under the operational control of the Australians joined the attack on Etinehem on August 13 and remained in the line until August 19.

Allied offensive operations now became almost continuous. Though infantry casualties had been 22,000 on August 8 alone, they were relatively light by the standards of the time. However, 25 percent of the aircraft had been lost on August 8, and by August 12 only six tanks were still fit for action. The general attack was taken up again along a thirty-five-mile front. The German High Command insisted on fighting for every foot, even though their front-line commanders realized that time was quickly running out. The penetration of the Drocourt-Quéant Switch (the Wotan Stellung) by the Canadians and the capture of Mont St. Quentin by the Australians on September 2, led the Germans to begin a general retreat into the Hindenburg Line while fighting a rear-guard action primarily with machine gun units.

The Hindenburg Line, first occupied by the Germans in March 1917, included some of the strongest defenses of the Western Front. Although its extensive wire entanglements produced the appearance of a "line" from the air, it was in fact a series of interlocking and mutually supporting strong points. The system, with many variations to conform to the terrain and other variables, was generally 6,000 to 8,000 yards deep, and consisted of a forward battle zone (formerly known as the outpost line), a main battle zone, a support zone, and a reserve zone. These zones had been so thoroughly developed that they had such mass-produced, prefabricated components as pill boxes and shelters. Only the forward battle zone and the main battle zone had been completed, but they provided a formidable obstacle. The forward battle zone, sited on high ground, included a maze of trenches 600 to 1,000 yards deep protected by as many as three belts of wire each ten to fifteen yards wide. Although originally designed as an outpost line, the Hindenburg Line had been strengthened to the point that it was as strong as the main battle zone a mile to the rear. In the sector confronting the British Fourth Army, the main German position was on lower ground but positioned behind the St. Quentin Canal. This barge canal joining the Somme and Scheldt rivers was a veritable moat, thirty-five feet wide at the base with 50- to 100-foot banks rising at a fifty-degree angle. The bottom was filled with water or mud. At one point, however, the canal passed through a tunnel that began just south of Bellicourt and continued 6,000 yards to the Scheldt thus forming a land bridge across the canal. In this sector, the Germans had placed their main position in front of the subterranean canal and had compensated for the lack of a moat with reinforced defenses. The tunnel itself had been converted into an elaborate shelter and integrated into the defensive positions with service galleries. This land bridge was in the

Australian zone of operations when the British Fourth Army closed on the Hindenburg Line on September 18.

During the extensive planning that followed, General Monash made it clear that his corps needed fresh troops to continue the attack. The American II Corps, consisting of the U.S. 27th and 30th divisions less their artillery and many combat support elements, was placed under Australian Corps operational control.

The Australian plan assumed that the German forward battle position, the outpost line, would be in friendly hands. The two American divisions would use it as a line of departure on September 29 to attack the German main battle and support positions—a distance of about 4,400 yards. The Australian 3d and 5th divisions would pass through the Americans and proceed an additional 4,000 yards through the reserve line, thus breaching the entire German defensive position in a single day.

From the American perspective, the plan went wrong from the very beginning. In the northern part of the American sector held by the 27th Division, the British III Corps in a week of hard fighting had failed to seize the outpost line by the time they were relieved on September 25. This line of departure was integrated into an elaborate artillery preparation to be fired by over 1,600 guns. Rather than make changes in this intricate plan, the Fourth Army ordered the 27th Division to seize their own line of departure on September 27. The 27th's front was 4,000 yards wide and marked by three strong points: Quennemont farm, Guillemont farm, and the Knoll (running in a straight line from south to north and between 500 and 1,000 yards to the division's front). All three battalions of the 106th Infantry Regiment attacked at 5:30 A.M., supported by twelve tanks and K and M companies of the 105th Infantry. The 106th went into the attack with approximately 2,000 rifles, but with only eighteen officers in the twelve rifle companies. Although small parties made their way to the objectives through mist and a smoke screen, the Germans, past masters of this type of defense, inflicted a bloody repulse. By day's end, the regiment was back at the start line. Only one company officer had escaped unscathed, and the next morning the regiment could muster only 9 officers and 252 men. Later reports revealed that the 27th Division had suffered 1,537 casualties, practically all from the 106th, and it was not known at the time how many Americans were still holding their positions in the German trenches or were in no-man's-land. It was decided, therefore, to carry out the general attack on September 29, as originally planned. The line of departure was still to be the rear trenches of the outpost line, now held by the 30th Division in its sector but still 1,000 yards in front of the 27th sector. It was hoped that the division could "steal" this ground at H-1 and coming abreast of the 30th Division on the right at H-Hour proceed to its objective. Furthermore to avoid killing missing members of the 106th Infantry, the barrage was to start as planned 1,000 yards behind the Germans still dug in from Quennemont farm to the Knoll.

The attack began at 5:50 A.M. on September 29. Along the entire front, British artillery provided a powerful barrage, which before the day was out amounted to 427,000 rounds. It was of little comfort to troops of the 27th Division that the barrage was falling harmlessly behind the German defenders, who immediately sprayed them with heavy machine gun fire. The division attacked with two battalions of the 107th Infantry on the left and two battalions of the 108th Infantry on the right, each with a battalion in support. The 107th was also supported by a provisional battalion of 350 men of the 106th, all that was left of the regiment, and was followed by the 105th Infantry in division reserve. On the extreme right, small groups of the 108th Infantry seized portions of the Hindenburg Line south of Bony and were later joined by troops of the Australian 3d Division. In the center and left, the assault elements had been joined by all support elements. They engaged in desperate fighting, particularly around the Knoll. At midday, units of the 10th Australian Brigade of the 3d Division joined the attack. By day's end, the German outpost line had been seized, but the Allies were still two miles from their objective. The 107th Infantry suffered 337 men killed and 658 wounded, the highest one-day total of any American regiment of the war. Losses in the 108th Infantry were almost as great and included all the officers of the assault companies. From September 21 until October 2, the 27th Division had 4,642 casualties.

In the 30th Division sector, the attack went forward on schedule. Attacking at 5:50 A.M. from the German outpost line with four battalions of the 119th and 120th Infantry abreast from north to south, the Americans advanced steadily through mist and heavy smoke. The

S

119th was through the main German position by 7:30, but it took heavy casualties on its exposed left flank where it had left the 27th Division far behind. The 120th Infantry reached Bellicourt, behind the Hindenburg Line, immediately on top of the St. Quentin Tunnel and reached the German support line at Nauroy by 11:00 A.M. Even this complete success was not without cost. Division losses for September 29 to October 2, almost all of which were suffered on September 29, amounted to 505 killed and dead of wounds and 1,989 wounded.

To the south of the Americans, British 46th Division troops, armed with rifles and life jackets, crossed the canal and by nightfall had overrun the main and support positions to a depth of over 6,000 yards. The German main line of resistance had been breached on a six-mile front, but at a terrible cost to the 27th Division.

While the attack continued, the 27th and 30th divisions were withdrawn from the line beginning on September 30; for those intermingled with Australian units still in combat, the process took several days. After a few days of rest, the American II Corps was ordered to relieve the Australian Corps. The 30th Division carried out the relief on the night of October 5–6 between Beaurevoir and Montfrehain about four miles east of where they had broken through the Hindenburg Line. The 27th Division was in reserve.

The issue was no longer in doubt, and the Germans could no longer hold for extended periods against determined Allied attacks. Nevertheless, their units maintained cohesion and could put up a stout defense and even launch limited counterattacks. Their continued ability to deliver punishment became evident on the morning of October 7 when the 117th Infantry carried out a "line-straightening attack" preliminary to the general attack planned for October 8. After advancing only a few hundred yards, the regiment came under murderous fire and was driven to ground. It, nevertheless, joined in the general British Fourth Army attack on the following day, and the 30th Division advanced ten miles to the Selle River in three days of fighting. In the process, the division suffered 2,600 casualties, of which the 117th Infantry accounted for over 1,000. While pausing at the river line, the 27th Division came up on the 30th's right flank. On October 17, both divisions crossed the Selle and for the next three days fought their way toward the Sambre Canal against a beaten but still dangerous enemy.

The Allied attack continued right up to the Armistice, but on the night of October 19–20, the 30th Division was relieved as was the 27th Division the following night, thus ending American participation in the Somme offensive.

Charles Endress

See also ST. QUENTIN CANAL ATTACK

Bibliography

American Battle Monuments Commission. *27th Division Summary of Operations in the World War.* Washington, DC: Government Printing Office, 1944.

———. *30th Division Summary of Operations in the World War.* Washington, DC: Government Printing Office, 1944.

Bean, C.E.W. *The Australian Imperial Force in France During the Allied Offensive, 1918.* The Official History of Australia in the War of 1914–1918. Vol. VI. Sydney: Angus and Robertson, 1942.

U.S. Army Center of Military History. *Military Operations of the American Expeditionary Force.* United States Army in the World War 1917–1918. Vol. 7. Washington, DC: Government Printing Office, 1990.

Sonnino, Sidney (1847–1922)

Sidney Sonnino was born in Pisa. From 1880 to 1919, he sat as an independent Liberal on the center-right of the Italian Chamber of Deputies. He was a consistent proponent of universal suffrage, equity in taxation, labor legislation, and governmental and administrative freedom.

Sonnino served as the undersecretary of the treasury in 1889 and as the minister of the treasury from 1893 to 1896 in Francesco Crispi's government. Though Sonnino twice served as prime minister, neither ministry was successful nor prolonged. The first lasted only from February to May 1906 and the second from December 1909 to March 1910. In both instances his brief ministries collapsed because of parliamentary opposition to his proposed reforms.

At the beginning of the First World War, Sonnino argued that Italy should remain loyal to the Triple Alliance that tied it to Germany and Austria. By the time he became foreign minister in the new Salandra government, his opinion had changed, and he and Salandra were primarily responsible for the entry of Italy into the war on the side of the Entente. One of the few consistent points of Italian foreign policy was to remain on good terms with Great Britain. Sonnino, in addition, feared that a neutral Italy might be spurned by the victors, whoever they might be, that the monarchy and liberal institutions could not survive a peace that brought Italy nothing, and that a victorious Austria might increase its influence in the Balkans at the expense of Italy.

On April 26, 1915, Italy signed the Treaty of London with Britain, France, and Russia. Italy agreed to enter the war on the Allied side within a month. In return the Allies promised that at the end of the war Italy would receive Trentino, Alto Adige, Istria, and, despite reluctance on the part of Russia, part of Dalmatia. France and Britain recognized Italian sovereignty over the Dodecanese and Libya. They also promised Italy a just share of Turkey, if it were partitioned, and equitable compensation in Africa, if there were any French or British gains there. The Italian demand for Dalmatia was made on the basis of security, but, in reality, Sonnino and Salandra wished to transform the Adriatic as much as they could into a closed Italian sea. According to the treaty, Italy was also to receive a large war loan and was assured that the Vatican would not be allowed to participate in the postwar peace conference. Italy, which had withdrawn from the Triple Alliance on May 3, declared war on Austria-Hungary on May 23. To the consternation of its new allies, however, Italy did not declare war on Germany until Aug. 27, 1916.

In June 1917, Sonnino attempted to lay the groundwork for Italy's postwar dominance in Albania by declaring it an Italian protectorate. In August 1917, he successfully sabotaged any hopes for a separate Allied peace with Austria by holding firm to the commitments which the Allies had made to his country in 1915. His expansionist position, however, was rendered questionable by Italy's defeat at Caporetto. He was able to retain the foreign ministry in Vittorio Emanuele Orlando's government, but faced opposition from democrats in Italy who opposed Sonnino's demands for South Slav territory. He, nevertheless, responded to Woodrow Wilson's Fourteen Points by emphasizing Italy's needs for security and the necessity of territorial compensation in the eastern Mediterranean to preserve the balance of power.

Sonnino continued to affirm tenaciously the Treaty of London. The bargaining power, however, which he had possessed in 1915 had disappeared with the defeat of Germany and the dissolution of Austria-Hungary. Italy was now no more than the weakest of the Great Powers. At the time of the Versailles Conference, Sonnino not only had to defend his demands for Yugoslav territory against opponents in Italy, but also against President Wilson. To prevent Wilson from undercutting Italy's demands through a direct appeal to the Italians, Sonnino successfully insulated the President from the Italian people during his preconference trip to Italy.

At Versailles, Sonnino and Orlando demanded everything assigned to Italy by the Treaty of London. In fact, the line set by the Oct. 31, 1918, Armistice with Austria, had exactly corresponded to the concessions to Italy in the Treaty of London. Sonnino had also, without success, attempted to insert a formal reservation during the pre-Armistice discussions that the new frontiers of Italy had to conform to historical considerations and Italy's security concerns. Wilson, despite qualms about the violation of the principle of neutrality, generally acceded to Italy's demands but balked over Dalmatia.

The new demand advanced by the Italian government for Fiume did not improve matters. Fiume, due to Russian influence, had been denied to the Italians in 1915. With Russian opinion no longer of any import, Italy pressed for the city, which, if its predominantly Slavic suburb of Susak were excluded, was principally Italian in population. Sonnino, in fact, only used it as a bargaining chip to employ in his quest for Dalmatia. A contradiction, however, immediately arose among the Italians. While Sonnino was willing to sacrifice Fiume to gain the fruits of the secret treaty, the democratic interventionists, supported by Gen. Armando Diaz, the commander of the Italian Army, asserted the principle of nationality and were willing to sacrifice Dalmatia for Fiume. Sonnino, unwilling to forsake the strategically important Dalmatian coast, was compelled to hold firm for both.

Wilson publicly expressed his opposition to the acquisition by Italy of either the Dalmatian coast or Fiume. On January 27, Sonnino had a stormy session with Wilson. He told Wilson not to meddle in European affairs, and Wilson responded in kind. On February 17, Sonnino repudiated the notion that any of the goals for which Italy had fought a long war should be subjected to arbitration by Wilson or that commitments made to Italy in the Treaty of London should be subjected to revision by a committee. He insisted that the peace with Austria proceed simultaneously with that for Germany, lest Italy be isolated after the completion of the peace with which the French and British were primarily concerned. Sonnino also demanded that Yugoslavia not be accorded an equal voice in the determination of issues of interest to Italy. He attempted to draw a parallel between French interests with regard to Germany. He argued that the frontier in question was a dispute between Italy and Austria, an enemy state, but his argument faltered due to the fact that Yugoslavia, albeit a new entity, had not been an enemy. Wilson was repelled by the fact that the Italian case was based upon legal rights rather than justice, and Robert Lansing, the American secretary of state, went so far as to propose that neither Italy nor Yugoslavia should participate in the discussions.

On April 19, Orlando, accompanied by Sonnino, met with the other three representatives of the Council of Four. Instead of basing Italy's claim upon the Treaty of London, to which the United States had not been a party, Orlando argued Italy's claim to Fiume on the basis of the self-determination of its inhabitants and to Dalmatia on the basis of Italian security. Sonnino argued that Wilson's intention to deprive Italy of part of Istria and Dalmatia would give Italy less than Austria had been willing to concede in 1915 for Italian neutrality. To protest against Wilson's direct appeal to the Italian people on April 23, 1919, Sonnino and Orlando withdrew from the conference. In Italy they were treated as heroes. The Italians excoriated Wilson, the Allies in general, and the Italian democratic interventionists. Though Wilson did not budge, Orlando and Sonnino hurriedly left Rome on May 5. They rejoined the conference on May 6 rather than risk the completion of both the German and Austrian treaties in their absence.

Sonnino exasperated Wilson further by insisting that the Trieste to Vienna rail line passing through Assling and Klagenfurt be retained by Austria rather than transferred to the new Yugoslavian state. Col. Edward M. House attempted to soothe matters by offering Wilson an apology from Orlando and Sonnino for the vituperation to which the President had been subjected by the Italian press. House, along with David Hunter Miller and George Beer, members of the American Committee to Ne-

gotiate Peace (ACNP) who were sympathetic toward Italy, continued to seek a compromise favorable to Italy. House and Beer believed that, taken as a whole, the Italian demands were more moderate than those of the other Allies, and Beer believed that the Italians deserved consideration because of their moderation on questions of African territory. He believed that, with American and British pressure, the Yugoslavs would agree to a settlement acceptable to the Italians. The opposition of Wilson and the inflexibility of the Yugoslavs who knew that they could rely on the American president, aborted their efforts.

The Italians pointed out the inconsistencies between Wilson's flexibility with regard to others and his rigidity toward them. They believed that he was unfairly attempting to force concessions from them. Sonnino quipped that "he provoked among the Italians the impression that he wanted to retrieve his virginity at our expense." Given this situation, Sonnino argued that it would be best to leave the whole issue unsettled and continue the military occupation by Italy of all the territory assigned to it by the Treaty of London.

After gaining the Brenner Pass in the Austrian treaty, Orlando and Sonnino returned to Rome, and Orlando, on June 19, defended their actions before the parliament. Resentment against the Americans and the Allies and the "mutilated victory" cost the Orlando government its parliamentary support. When the majority found his vague public statement on the Adriatic settlement unacceptable, Orlando chose the procedural issue of a public debate as the question upon which his ministry would stake its continued existence. By a vote of 262 to 78, his government was repudiated. Francesco Saverio Nitti formed a new government bent upon placating the Allies and appointed Tommaso Tittoni as foreign minister. Tittoni replaced Sonnino at Paris, where he was condemned to preside over the completion of Italy's disappointment.

Sonnino, whose expansionist expectations had been thwarted, gave up politics. He was appointed to the Senate by his old nemesis Giolitti but never attended. He died in Rome on Nov. 24, 1922.

Bernard A. Cook

See also PARIS PEACE CONFERENCE

Bibliography

Albrecht-Carrié, René. *Italy at the Paris Peace Conference*. Hamden, CT: Archon Books, 1966.

Mayer, Arno J. *Politics and Diplomacy of Peacemaking: Containment and Counterrevolution at Versailles, 1918–1919*. New York: Knopf, 1969.

Renzi, William A. *In the Shadow of the Sword: Italy's Neutrality and Entry into the Great War, 1914–1915*. New York: Lang, 1987.

Sonnino, Sidney. *Opera omnia di Sidney Sonnino*, ed. by Benjamin F. Brown and Pietro Pastorelli. 7 vols. Rome: N.p., 1972–1975.

Thayer, John A. *Italy and the Great War: Politics and Culture, 1870–1915*. Madison: University of Wisconsin Press, 1964.

Spanish Influenza

Spanish Influenza was a virulent strain of influenza that first appeared in the spring of 1918 and eventually spread to every part of the globe. The disease was far more debilitating than typical cases of the flu, with victims reporting high fevers, sore throats, headaches, severe muscle cramps, and disorientation. The mortality rate among an infected population was high, with many of the victims dying only twelve to forty-eight hours after the rapid onset of symptoms. In addition to the disease itself, pneumonia and other secondary infections also took a high toll, making the Spanish Influenza pandemic the deadliest attack of influenza yet known in history. Between March 1918 and August 1919 the Spanish Flu claimed an estimated 20 to 30 million lives worldwide. By comparison, the death toll from the First World War was approximately 8.5 million in four and a half years of fighting.

Despite its name, it is quite apparent that the Spanish Influenza did not originate in Spain. Speculation at the time also blamed the disease on the Chinese, Indians, and even the French. One popular wartime rumor had the disease originating in German laboratories and being released into the Allied countries by secret agents or by U-boats operating off the coasts. In reality, the disease was probably a strain of swine influenza with its origins in the central United States.

The first known outbreak of Spanish Influenza was at Camp Funston, Kansas, in March 1918. The disease rate was high, and the appearance of symptoms was both rapid and debilitating. The flu disappeared from Camp Funston after only five weeks but left in its wake 233 soldiers with pneumonia, of whom 8 died. Similar outbreaks soon occurred at many training camps across the nation. There were outbreaks of influenza that spring among the civilian population as well, most notably among auto workers in Detroit and prisoners in San Quentin. In most instances, however, the symptoms were generally mild, and the mortality rate was low.

In late spring 1918, when tens of thousands of American troops sailed for Europe, outbreaks of influenza on the troop ships were common, and many a soldier was ill when he first stepped on French soil. The first reported European outbreak was on April 15 at an American Expeditionary Force (AEF) base near Bordeaux. By May, the virus was firmly established on the Continent, and was making its impact felt on the war. The British Grand Fleet had 10 percent of its ships' crews ill, and the British Army reported 31,000 cases among the ranks in June 1918 alone. At Belleau Wood, the Americans had to contend with influenza as well as the German Army.

The disease was gripping armies on both sides of the trenches. Gen. Erich Ludendorff blamed the flu in part for the eventual failure of his Meuse-Argonne offensives that summer. No belligerent would admit that its armies were sick, and because of wartime censorship, neither side knew the extent of the illness in its enemy's lines.

Neutrals were also affected. By June influenza was ravaging Spain, where over 8 million people, roughly 40 percent of the population, contracted it. Unlike the belligerent powers, Spain had no censorship, so its newspapers reported on the epidemic. To the less-informed population in the warring nations, it appeared as though the disease had originated in the Iberian Peninsula. Thus, it quickly became known as the Spanish Influenza.

Though influenza impeded the war efforts of both the Allied and the Central Powers in the late spring and summer of 1918, it had virtually disappeared from the United States. But in late August, it reappeared in Boston and in a much deadlier form. By the end of September, severe outbreaks of Spanish Influenza with very high mortality rates were reported in Boston, Philadelphia, New York, and Seattle. By the end of

October, the disease was epidemic throughout the United States. Similar outbreaks were occurring on every continent making the influenza a pandemic, or a global, epidemic.

Several factors crippled the ability of health authorities in the United States in their fight against the epidemic. To begin with, the medical community did not even know what was causing the disease. The existence of something as small as a virus had yet to be proved. Most bacteriologists instead believed that Pfieffer's Bacillus, a companion infection often found in flu victims, was the causative agent. As a result, most of the various vaccines and serums produced in an effort to control the disease were based on Pfieffer's Bacillus and were therefore totally useless. Even had those drugs proved effective, most communities were short of trained medical personnel since sizable numbers of doctors and nurses were away on war duty.

Lacking any real medical ability to combat influenza, state and local health authorities instead relied on various methods of population control in an effort to slow or stop the spread of the virus. In many cities, such as New York, Cincinnati, and Pittsburgh, the authorities resorted to closing most public gathering places, schools, churches, and restaurants and banning public gatherings. Some, like San Francisco, even required the wearing of gauze surgical masks in public. Many others quarantined the homes of the infected. None of these methods worked, and they proved to be a poor substitute for any real medical solution to the epidemic. In most places where closing orders were in effect, business offices and factories remained open, especially those connected to the war effort, allowing ample opportunity for a sick but patriotic worker to pass on the disease. Most municipalities held scheduled war bond parades and drives in spite of the flu and in some cases even canvassed flu victims for additional subscriptions.

In addition, health authorities' attempts to enforce the bans and closings were hampered by the fact that initially, at least, many people did not take the epidemic seriously. Since influenza is usually a mild infection and the closings appeared to be haphazard and random, most people found it easier to ignore them than to obey them.

The Spanish Influenza "crested," or reached its peak morbidity and mortality rates, at various dates depending largely upon geographic location. The epidemic crested in Boston and Philadelphia in early October, but most regions reported a peak in both flu cases and deaths in either late November or early December. Sporadic outbreaks continued for months, but by late spring 1919, Spanish Influenza had again all but vanished from the United States, leaving behind an estimated half million influenza-related deaths. Though there were occasional reports of Spanish Influenza cases over the next few years, the disease never again reached epidemic proportions. By 1923, it had disappeared entirely from the human population, quite possibly remaining only to plague its original hosts—swine.

James E. Westheider

Bibliography

Crosby, Alfred W. *America's Forgotten Pandemic: The Influenza of 1918.* Austin: University of Texas Press.
———. *Epidemic and Peace, 1918.* Westport, CT: Greenwood Press, 1976.
Hoehling, A.A. *The Great Epidemic.* Boston: Little, Brown, 1961.
Luckingham, Bradford. *Epidemic in the Southwest 1918–1919.* El Paso: Texas Western Press, 1984.
Pettigrew, Eileen. *The Silent Enemy: Canada and the Flu of 1918.* Saskatoon, Canada: Western Producer Prairie Books, 1983.

Splinter Fleet

The Splinter Fleet, wooden-hulled submarine chasers, were part of the major effort launched by the British and United States navies to control submarine egress into both the North Sea and the Mediterranean. The American sailors of those 80-ton ships were mainly newcomers to the United States Navy. Few old salts would deign to serve on noniron ships of that class. Many of the officers were recent graduates of naval training programs and, just prior to that, students at Ivy League colleges. The enlisted crews were mainly from the large body of patriotic volunteers attracted to the sea as their forthcoming battlefield. With little or no seagoing experience, the newly created sailors sailed their little ships, often in midwinter. They proceeded to Europe by way of Bermuda and then to the Azores. In May 1918, the first six ships were transferred from the Azores to Portsmouth, England. Another thirty ships, under the command of Commander (later captain) Charles P. Nelson, USN, arrived at Gibraltar on

May 13, 1918, for service in the Mediterranean. A third group, under Capt. Arthur J. Hepburn, operated from Queenstown, Ireland, after Aug. 21, 1918. In June, 1918, an additional dozen ships were sent to England, and all the chasers in England were placed under the command of Comdr. Lyman A. Cotten and based at Plymouth.

Antisubmarine warfare was still in its infancy when the United States entered the World War in April 1917, and most of the service of the Splinter Fleet was in the North Sea and at the Otranto Barrage, under the overall command of Adm. William S. Sims, although many were destined to spend some, if not all, of their service just off the East Coast of the United States, hunting German submarines.

The Strait of Otranto was located between the very southeastern tip of the boot of Italy and the island of Corfu, just off the western coast of Greece. Those chasers destined for Otranto mainly patroled the area bounded by the island of Malta on the west and the southern tip of Greece on the far eastern flank. The mine barrage and splinter boats were there to prevent the Austro-Hungarian Navy, especially its submarine fleet, from doing irreparable damage to both the Italian and British ships in the Mediterranean and to protect British troop convoys headed for the Mideast from German as well as Austro-Hungarian submarines.

The technology the Splinter Fleet used to locate undersea craft was mainly hydrophones, generally the "S.C. tube." This tube consisted of two rubber ears mounted on the ends of an inverted "T" pipe lowered under the vessel's hull. The rubber ears were hollow balls, each with a copper tube inserted into it. The tubes, protected by a bronze pipe, were extended up and inside the chaser. The two ears, substituting for human ears, could detect vibrations from submarines when in motion through the water. The listener could rotate the device and determine direction and location by using a physician's stethoscope connected to the copper tubes. The strategy was to deploy three chasers in a triangular formation to detect the presence of a submarine. This proved to be a reasonably accurate method of tracking a submerged sub.

Weaponry on a splinter boat was rather limited. A new device, called the "Y-gun," was the main armament against submarines. The Y-gun was able to launch two depth charges of 400 pounds each from either the starboard or port barrel at a nearby submarine, causing grievous harm to the U-boat even when not making a direct hit. As its name implies, it had two barrels, each at a ninety-degree angle from the other. Every chaser was also equipped with a three-inch gun as its main battery (used as either an antiaircraft or antiship weapon), and two Lewis guns of thirty caliber.

The operations out of Portsmouth were greatly hampered by sound interference from the enormous amount of shipping in those waters. In addition, enemy submarines did desist from active work in the area until the chasers were diverted to Brest, France, in late August 1918.

All told, 120 American sub chasers were employed overseas before the war's end, all engaged in offensive operations against the enemy, both German and Austro-Hungarian. Their assistance insured that German submarines, dominating the lifelines about Europe, would not strangle the Allies before the overwhelming industrial strength and manpower of the United States could be brought to bear and turn the tide.

George B. Clark

See also NORTH SEA MINE BARRAGE; OTRANTO MINE BARRAGE

Bibliography
Knox, Dudley W. *A History of the United States Navy*. New York: Putnam, 1936.
Millholland, Ray. *The Splinter Fleet of the Otranto Barrage*. Indianapolis: Bobbs-Merrill, 1936.
Sims, William S. *Victory at Sea*. Annapolis, MD: Naval Institute Press, 1984.

Spring-Rice, Cecil Arthur (1859–1918)

Sir Cecil Arthur Spring-Rice was a British career diplomat whose service culminated with his appointment as ambassador to the United States. He held this highly prestigious position from 1913 to 1918, retiring several months before the end of the First World War. Educated at Eton and Oxford, he entered the Foreign Office in 1882. At the beginning of his career Spring-Rice had the added good fortune to work directly under Lord Granville and Lord Rosebery when each was foreign secretary. With such a start, and with considerable natural ability, his rise in the service was assured.

In 1886, he received his first posting abroad, as third secretary to the British Embassy in Washington. This marked the beginning of unusually close ties with the United States which he maintained for the rest of his life. Soon he numbered among his friends such prominent Republicans as John Hay, Henry Cabot Lodge, and, most important of all, Theodore Roosevelt. In fact, Spring-Rice was best man at Roosevelt's wedding. For much of the next decade, save for a brief interlude in Tokyo, he remained in Washington, where both his knowledge of American affairs and his circle of friends widened steadily.

From 1895 to 1913, Spring-Rice's duties took him from one world capital to another, including Berlin, Constantinople, Teheran, Cairo, and St. Petersburg. Then his prospects changed for the better. Britain's ambassador in Washington, the famous scholar James Bryce, wished to retire. Spring-Rice's knowledge of the United States made him an obvious candidate—indeed, he had been seriously considered for the post before Bryce accepted it. It came as no surprise when his appointment to Washington was announced in late 1912. Only later did it become apparent that Spring-Rice was an unfortunate choice at this time. His friendships with leading Republicans were a liability at a moment when the Democrat Woodrow Wilson, whom he did not know, had just become President. And if a general European war broke out, Britain would need a tougher personality in Washington than this sensitive and highly strung career diplomat.

When Spring-Rice arrived in the United States in early 1913 he immediately faced two thorny problems. One concerned the Panama Canal tolls, a matter ultimately resolved by President Wilson. More serious was the tangled state of affairs in Mexico, where the United States favored one faction and most European nations favored another. Britain had important commercial interests in Mexico, but the Monroe Doctrine ruled out direct intervention. Fortunately, the Mexican imbroglio did not cause a serious rift between Britain and the United States, but it left Spring-Rice with a poor opinion of the competence of the Wilson administration. Illness curtailed his activities in the latter part of 1913, and he was home on leave when the European war began in August 1914.

An intimidating task awaited him on his return to Washington, and the pressures on him mounted steadily over the next three years. Faced with a president who was determined to observe the strictest neutrality, while at the same time German-Americans and Irish-Americans spoke and acted vehemently against the Allied cause, Spring-Rice had to walk a tightrope while virtually gagged. As Britain's ambassador, he had to observe the utmost discretion lest he alienate President Wilson and antagonize that large section of American opinion eager to think the worst of Britain. The fact that his friends in Republican ranks, chief among them Theodore Roosevelt, adopted a strongly pro-Ally stance made matters even more difficult. In consequence, the constraints under which Spring-Rice labored drove him to write unduly alarmist reports to his superiors in London. Nor was his position helped by Wilson's grey eminence, Col. Edward M. House, who came to regard Spring-Rice as a mere cipher and therefore not worthy of any meaningful access to the White House.

Friction soon developed between the United States and the Allies, Britain in particular. Traditional British strategy when fighting a European war was to establish a tight naval blockade. This ran directly counter to American interests and American principles. As Britain tightened its grip on contraband, which included such important American exports as copper and cotton, Spring-Rice labored hard and with considerable success to minimize the damage to Anglo-American relations despite the resentment caused in many quarters by the interference with American ships, goods, and mails.

It was a thankless task and one that won him few friends on either side of the Atlantic. In Woodrow Wilson's opinion, Spring-Rice had become a "highly excitable invalid" whom he did not wish to meet. Yet there can be no doubt that Spring-Rice's approach to wartime diplomacy was the right one. He never abandoned the conviction that it would be a disastrous mistake to try to push the Americans into war with Germany. Only the pressure of events, such as unrestricted submarine warfare, would have the desired result. Spring-Rice's nerves suffered severely from the strain, and in early 1917 during an interview with Secretary of State Robert Lansing, the ambassador almost broke down. By this time Britain had a new prime minister, David Lloyd George, who had fresh ideas on dealing with Washington.

Immediately after American entry into the war, London announced that the new foreign secretary, Arthur James Balfour, a former prime minister, would go to the United States "to concert policy and action." In effect, Spring-Rice had been superseded, though he remained at his post in Washington. A few weeks later another famous personage arrived to head what was called the British War Mission in America—the famous newspaper magnate Lord Northcliffe, in the past a frequent critic of Spring-Rice. Friction between the two men was inevitable, especially since Northcliffe's status and powers were not clearly defined in advance. Spring-Rice's ability to act effectively was damaged beyond hope of recovery by Northcliffe's presence.

By August 1917, matters had reached the point where Lord Robert Cecil, Balfour's right-hand man, was asking Colonel House frankly if Spring-Rice should be replaced. House replied that the ambassador was "temperamentally unfit" to cope with the situation. Shortly afterwards Lord Reading, lord chief justice of England and an intimate of Lloyd George's, arrived in Washington to take charge of British affairs. Spring-Rice, deeply hurt, recognized the finality of this and prepared to go quietly. In January 1918, he proceeded to make his way back to England via Ottawa, only to die suddenly in the Canadian capital.

On the eve of leaving Washington, he sent a farewell letter to William Jennings Bryan and enclosed some verses that he termed "a sort of spontaneous outpouring." They began with the words: "I vow to thee my country . . . the service of my love . . ." and ended, "and her ways are ways of gentleness and all her paths are Peace." After Spring-Rice's death these lines were set to some well-known music of Gustav Holst, and even today are to be found in hymn books in parts of the Anglican communion. It was a fitting legacy from the man known as the "silent ambassador."

John McEwen

Bibliography

Gwynn, Stephen, ed. *The Letters and Friendships of Sir Cecil Spring Rice. A Record.* 2 vols. Boston: Houghton Mifflin, 1929.

Spruce Production Division

Keeping the wartime economy functioning smoothly was as important to the nation's war effort as successfully conscripting millions of men into the wartime army. To prevent workers from striking, the government appointed conservative labor leaders to the War Industries Board, which, in turn, adopted generous wage

and hour guidelines. High wages helped keep civilians on the job in most key wartime industries, though in the spruce lumber industry the workforce remained transient. In these Pacific Northwest lumber enterprises, the turnover rate was over 600 percent a year, as mills engaged in a constant bidding war to lure experienced workers away from competitors. Poor working conditions also encouraged lumbermen to move from mill to mill in search of a better environment. Exasperated with their horrendous working conditions, lumber workers went on strike in the summer of 1917.

The War Industries Board could do little to stem unrest in the industry because the government refused to recognize the region's predominant union, the Industrial Workers of the World (IWW), as a legitimate representative of lumber workers. The Wobblies, as IWW members were called, proposed a radical redistribution of wealth and power in American society, pronouncements that the wartime government labeled as seditious. Under the guise of wartime censorship laws, the government mounted an aggressive, nationwide campaign to suppress the Wobblies and succeeded in weakening them so severely that the movement never regained its prewar momentum.

The decision to organize approximately 30,000 wartime troops into the Spruce Production Division reflected these multiple concerns. By giving Col. Brice P. Disque the power to send soldiers into approximately 234 lumber mills and forests to work alongside civilian lumbermen throughout Oregon and Washington, the government hoped both to stabilize the lumber industry and to root out IWW organizers in the region. Soldiers in this division were assigned to mills operating under government contracts and were the only noncombatants in the whole army to be paid civilian-scale wages for civilian-type work. Disque used his troops as the basis for a new, conservative lumber union called the Loyal Legion of Loggers and Lumbermen and eventually enlisted close to 120,000 civilians in the company union. Members pledged to work diligently to produce the spruce lumber used in the construction of army planes and signed a no-strike pledge. Soldiers were available to take the jobs of all "disloyal" lumbermen who refused to join the union or stay at one mill. To reward those who professed loyalty to the government and the war effort, Disque set about improving the deplorable working conditions which had been responsible for much of the instability within the spruce industry. Negotiations with mill owners resulted in the region's first eight-hour day, a maximum wage to prevent bidding wars, and better living facilities in the lumber camps. The Spruce Production Division was part of the government's overall effort to use a combination of accommodative and repressive tactics to keep the wartime economy functioning smoothly.

Jennifer Keene

See also INDUSTRIAL WORKERS OF THE WORLD

Bibliography

Hyman, Harold L. *Soldiers and Spruce: Origins of the Loyal Legion of Loggers and Lumbermen.* Los Angeles: University of California Press, 1963.

Jenson, Vernon. *Lumber and Labor.* New York: Farrar & Rinehart, 1945.

Kennedy, David M. *Over Here: The First World War and American Society.* New York: Oxford University Press, 1980.

Tyler, Robert L. "The United States Government as Union Organizer: The Loyal Loggers and Lumbermen." *Mississippi Valley Historical Review* 47 (1960).

U.S. Spruce Production Corporation. *History of Spruce Production Division.* Portland, OR: Kilham Stationery and Printing, 1919.

Starrett, William Aiken (1877–1932)

Born in Lawrence, Kansas, William Aiken Starrett received a B.S. in civil engineering from the University of Michigan in 1895. He was the founder and vice president of Thompson-Starrett Construction Company. After war broke out in Europe, Starrett became involved in the preparedness movement and attended the Plattsburg training camp in New York in 1916. When World War I was declared, Starrett, who was already serving as a captain in the Corps of Engineers, was appointed a member, and later chairman, of the Committee on Emergency Construction, formed in May 1917 to develop plans for construction of army facilities needed for the war. The Starrett Committee, as it came to be known, successfully created a mammoth building program requiring incredible speed and enormous sums of money. The committee developed a cost-plus contract method, pressed for a centralized construction agency, insisted on employing the best men and organizations

in the construction industry and oversaw the rapid building of emergency army camps, cantonments, flying fields, and enlarged munitions factories.

The committee's accomplishments, the cost-plus contract in particular, often drew heavy criticism. After the war, Congress examined charges against Starrett and some members of his committee of profiteering, favoritism, conspiracy, and fraud. Starrett was later named as co-defendant in an indictment against former Secretary of War Newton D. Baker for conspiracy to defraud the government. Since the controversies were largely politically motivated, Starrett subsequently answered the accusations satisfactorily, leading to the dismissal of the indictments.

After Starrett received an honorable discharge from the army in 1919, he applied his executive abilities to the building of skyscrapers in Tokyo and the United States. He also wrote and spoke extensively, primarily about skyscrapers and the art of building. He died in Madison, New Jersey, in 1932.

Dora Alford

Bibliography

Clarkson, Grosvenor B. *Industrial America in the World War, The Strategy Behind the Line, 1917–1918.* Boston: Houghton Mifflin, 1923.

Fine, Lenore, and Jesse A. Remington. *The Corps of Engineers: Construction in the United States.* Washington, DC: Government Printing Office, 1972.

Stars and Stripes

The *Stars and Stripes*, perhaps the best-known army newspaper of all time, originated at general headquarters of the American Expeditionary Force (AEF) at Chaumont, France, in late 1917. It was launched on Feb. 8, 1918, and appeared every Friday until June 13, 1919, a run of seventy-one weeks. Its clientele were the officers and men of the American Army in Europe, eventually over 2 million strong. The paper began with a circulation of less than 30,000 copies; it eventually reached more than 526,000, produced by a staff of over 300 men. Under the direction of the Press Section of the Censorship and Press Division of the Intelligence Branch (G-2) of the General Staff, AEF, the paper was printed in Paris at the offices of the *London Daily Mail*'s continental edition. It was later produced on the presses of the French paper, *Le Journal*.

The *Stars and Stripes* was established primarily to improve troop morale. It sought to encourage and inspire the uncertain, fearful, though eager, soldiers recently arrived in Europe; to evoke a grin in the face of the horrors of battle; to stimulate the patriotism that was already present; and, in general, to call forth enthusiasm and obedience in doing the many dirty, often boring, jobs associated with the waging of war. The paper assisted Gen. John J. Pershing, the AEF's commander-in-chief, in managing the anomaly of a democratic army.

A remarkable collection of newspapermen, most of whom had experience on American newspapers prior to their entering the army, published *Stars and Stripes*. Essentially civilians in uniform, and enlisted men for the most part, they clung to their civilian newspapermen ways—naturally, having, on occasion, to take into account military constraints. Men who would be well known after the war wrote for the paper, such as Harold Ross, later founder of the *New Yorker* magazine; Alexander Woollcott, the theater critic; Grantland Rice, the sports writer; and the columnist, Franklin Pierce Adams. John Tracy Winterich and Hudson Hawley were also on the editorial staff. The original officer in charge was Lt. Guy T. Viskinski. In November 1918, Maj. Mark S. Watson, who later won a Pulitzer Prize for reporting for the *Baltimore Sun* papers, took over. One of the assistant officers in charge was Capt. Stephen T. Early, later FDR's press secretary.

The paper was famous for its cartoons, especially the creation of Pvt. Abian "Wally" Wallgren, of the U.S. Marine Corps, who specialized in cartoons of lighter relief. Those of Pvt. Cyrus LeRoy Baldridge, an infantryman, focused on more serious topics. The staff also published much doughboy verse, and the paper's editorial page included lively comment and commentary, not only by the staff but also its readers, which added to the paper's interest. Letters from troops were published, thus serving as a safety valve for much discontent. Articles often stressed athletics, though the sports page was temporarily suspended to protest the determination of sports stars at home to carry on business as usual while bending every rule to stay out of the military services or by seeking cushy jobs in the shipyards. However, some celebrated athletes did do their patriotic duty by joining the armed forces or permitted themselves to be drafted, much to the paper's gratification.

The *Stars and Stripes* included advertising, which was regarded as unnecessary for revenue purposes, but highly desirable for the sense of familiarity that the ads created. The paper was rather expensive, costing fifty centimes (about ten cents) and was circulated and paid for in rather ingenious ways. The man in charge of distribution was Capt. Richard H. Waldo, who had been with the *New York Times* and *Good Housekeeping* magazine.

The paper prided itself on its relative independence and the fact that it was largely in the hands of an enlisted staff. However, it was kept under control by the High Command, though it did operate on a rather long leash. To be sure, some skillful propaganda found its way onto its pages, and it had to publish certain articles that the High Command desired. Nevertheless, the paper did remain, to a remarkable degree, a publication for the doughboy rank and file. Also, its tone and content corresponded closely to what the men felt, which accounts in part for its vast popularity.

Among the paper's legacies were the World War II editions of the *Stars and Stripes*, as well as its revealing to a considerable degree what life was like in the American Army in Europe during World War I. The paper informed its readers as to social, cultural, and intellectual matters, what the AEF was reading, what movies it was viewing, what songs it was singing, what its religious convictions were, and what sports it played. In addition, for historians of World War I and others interested in the period, details as to uniforms, decorations, chow, medical care, discipline, morale, and dozens of other aspects of the general mode of military life, so difficult to ascertain from official documents and other accounts, are clearly revealed in the paper's pages.

Alfred E. Cornebise

Bibliography

Cornebise, Alfred E. *The Stars and Stripes. Doughboy Journalism in World War I.* Westport, CT: Greenwood Press, 1984.

Katz, Harry L. *The History of the Stars and Stripes.* Washington, DC: Columbia Publishing, 1921.

Winterich, John Tracy. *Squads Write! A Selection of the Best Things in Prose, Verse and Cartoon from the Stars and Stripes,*

Official Newspaper of the A.E.F. New York: Harper, 1931.

Woollcott, Alexander. *The Command is Forward. Tales of the A.E.F. Battlefields as They Appeared in* The Stars and Stripes. New York: Century, 1919.

Stevens, John Frank (1853–1943)

John Frank Stevens, a noted civil engineer, was born in West Gardiner, Maine. He attended Maine State Normal School and with no additional formal education began his engineering career in 1874 as assistant city engineer in Minneapolis. From 1876 to 1903, he worked for a variety of railroads in the West and Midwest, achieving positions of increasing responsibility and a reputation as one of America's premier railway civil engineers.

In 1905, Secretary of War William H. Taft appointed Stevens as chief engineer of the Isthmian Canal Commission. Stevens drafted the plans for most of the Panama Canal, organized the work force, supervised the rebuilding of the Panama Railroad, and began digging the Culebra Cut. In 1907, he was appointed chairman of the Canal Commission but resigned a month later when the project was placed under the jurisdiction of George W. Goethals and the United States War Department.

Stevens then became vice president of the New York, New Haven and Hartford Railroad and later served as president of a group of James J. Hill's rail lines. From 1911 to 1917, he was a consultant in private practice. In 1915 he became chairman of a committee to alleviate the congestion in the Port of New York caused by the war in Europe.

After the United States entered the war, President Woodrow Wilson sent Stevens to Russia as chairman of a commission of railway experts. The Kerenskii government asked the commission to assist in correcting the problems besetting the Trans-Siberian Railroad. In June 1917, the commission made its recommendations and returned to the United States. Stevens, however, remained in Russia as special adviser to the Russian Ministry of Ways and Communications.

At Stevens's suggestion, the Provisional Government asked the United States to send over 200 American engineers to reorganize the railways and agreed to finance the operation. In spring 1918, these engineers were commissioned by the secretary of war as officers in the Russian Railway Service Corps, under the command of Col. George H. Emerson. The engineers worked in fourteen-man units along the Chinese Eastern Railway and the Trans-Siberian Railway as far west as Omsk. Stevens and Emerson faced many problems, including deterioration of rolling stock and a shortage of spare parts. Stevens also had to deal with the antiquated Russian Railway Technical Board.

When Japan dispatched troops to Siberia in 1918, it wanted to control the railroads. The Japanese, however, feared the effect of removing the American engineers who had kept the roads running despite the outbreak of civil war in Russia. By early 1919, Stevens proposed the formation of an Inter-Allied Railway Committee composed of representatives of the United States and those Allied Powers intervening in Siberia. Its major function was to divide the railroads into zones that were to be guarded by military detachments of the various powers in Siberia. The Railway Service Corps withdrew from Siberia in 1920 after evacuating 45,000 Czech troops who had been there since 1918. Stevens, as president of the Inter-Allied Technical Board, remained in Siberia until the last foreign forces left in 1922. For his services, his appreciative government awarded him the Distinguished Service Medal.

From 1923 until his retirement, Stevens lived in Baltimore, where he was a private consultant as well as a member of the board of the Baltimore and Ohio Railroad Company. He died in Southern Pines, North Carolina, on June 2, 1943.

Carol Kingsland Willcox Melton

See also RUSSIAN RAILWAY SERVICE CORPS

Bibliography

Goldhurst, Richard. *The Midnight War: The American Intervention in Russia, 1918–1920.* New York: McGraw-Hill, 1978.

Unterberger, Betty Miller. *The United States, Revolutionary Russia, and the Rise of Czechoslovakia.* Chapel Hill: University of North Carolina Press, 1989.

Stone, William Joel (1848–1918)

In March 1914, William Joel Stone, senior senator from Missouri and one of the senators most active in supporting the major items of President Woodrow Wilson's reform program, assumed the chairmanship of the Senate's Committee on Foreign Relations. With the outbreak of war in Europe, Stone, like the President and a majority of the American people, initially stressed the necessity for neutrality on the part of the United States. As time passed, however, it seemed that his interpretation of neutrality was not always the same as that of the President, despite the chairman's careful support of important Wilson pronouncements.

Since Missouri was one of the states with the highest percentage of German Americans in its population, Stone soon was accused by much of the urban press of having pro-German leanings, despite the fact that the German Americans were largely Republican and thus not Stone's supporters. While not a true Anglophobe, Stone did harbor suspicions of British seapower and trade aspirations. In the spring of 1916, Stone found it increasingly difficult to support Wilson's position on the submarine issue. Stone did not accept the distinction between the Allied blockade, which followed the dictates of international law, and the German use of submarine warfare, which violated those canons. Although Wilson endeavored to explain to him the significance of upholding international law, Stone remained concerned even though publicly supportive of the President's position.

The Senator did, however, espouse former President William Howard Taft's noble idea of a league to enforce peace. When Wilson decided that the Democratic platform of 1916 should contain a plank endorsing the league, he chose Stone to serve as chairman of the platform committee to see that the provision was included.

Following his reelection, Wilson held several conferences with the foreign relations chairman in which the President shared his plans to bring the warring powers to the peace table and mediate what he termed a "peace without victory." Stone became enthusiastic about the possibility. He envisioned a ringing statement in Wilson's unequaled prose that would electrify the peoples of the world, belligerents as well as neutrals. Then, with the economic might of the United States as a weapon to force both sides to accept his terms, Wilson could largely dictate a peace settlement. Stone ignored the fact that this scenario rested to a great extent on wishful thinking.

The announcement by Germany on Jan. 31, 1917, that it would adopt unrestricted submarine warfare in violation of the *Sussex* Pledge caught both Wilson and Stone by surprise. The President had already committed himself to the severance of diplomatic relations in the event Germany resorted again to submarine warfare. Stone accepted that decision, but he angrily opposed Wilson's request for congressional authorization to arm American merchant vessels. Stone regarded this proposal as a congressional relinquishment of the war power to the President. When Wilson attempted to rush the resolution through Congress in the last three days of the Sixty-fourth Congress, Stone refused to handle the resolution. After voting against it in his committee, he handed it to the ranking Democrat, Gilbert M. Hitchcock, to sponsor while Stone led the fight on the floor against the resolution.

Stone made a masterful four-hour address in which he cited numerous constitutional and legal authorities and precedents and uttered solemn warnings of the implications for the future if Congress surrendered its control over the war power. Although Stone's speech did not diverge from the issue, he was included by the press in the "little group of willful men," as Wilson angrily characterized opponents of the armed ship bill. Wilson was particularly angered that one who had been so loyal and faithful would refuse to accept his judgment that this bill was necessary.

Therefore, it was not surprising that Wilson did not even consult the chairman of the Senate Foreign Relations Committee when drafting the address calling for a declaration of war, and turned to Thomas S. Martin, Senate majority leader, to introduce the war resolution. In a brief speech delivered with great emotion, Stone spoke against the war resolution. His was one of six votes cast in the upper chamber against war.

Although Stone had been known in Missouri politics for his political expediency and compromising tactics, he did not play politics with the war issue. In fact, he believed that he jeopardized his political future by his opposition, and well he might as a chorus of denunciation followed in which "traitor" was one of the milder terms of opprobrium hurled at him. He was satirically awarded the Iron Cross for service to Germany and hung in effigy on a Washington lamp post.

Once the Congress, the body empowered by the Constitution to make the decision for war, had so declared, Stone became again a loyal supporter of the administration. Although he continued to believe that this war was a needless one, he supported the Selective Service Act, endorsed the Liberty Loan drive, and took charge of the resolution calling for a declaration of war against Austria-Hungary in December 1917. More significant was his expression of admiration for the Fourteen Points that Wilson presented to Congress on Jan. 8, 1918. In a kind of reconciliation between the President and his onetime ally and friend, Stone headed the committee chosen to welcome the President and escort him to the rostrum. When Stone observed the normal courtesy of proferring his arm to the Chief Executive, Wilson with equal politeness accepted, and friends of both cheered with enthusiasm as the two walked up the aisle. Following the President's address, Stone expressed his adherence to the principles that the President had so nobly outlined.

On April 10, 1918, Stone suffered a cerebral hemorrhage on a street car while on his way to the Senate chamber where he was scheduled to speak in connection with the Sedition Act. He died on April 14.

Ruth M. Towne

Bibliography

Baker, Ray Stannard. *Woodrow Wilson: Life and Letters*. Garden City, NY: Doubleday, Page, 1935–1937.

Link, Arthur S. *Wilson: Campaign for Progressivism and Peace, 1916–1917*. Princeton, NJ: Princeton University Press, 1965.

Notter, Harley G. *The Origins of the Foreign Policy of Woodrow Wilson*. Baltimore: Johns Hopkins University Press, 1937.

Ryley, Thomas A. *A Little Group of Willful Men*. Port Washington, NY: Kennikat Press, 1975.

Towne, Ruth Warner. *Senator William J. Stone and the Politics of Compromise*. Port Washington, NY: Kennikat Press, 1979.

Submarines

See ANTISUBMARINE WARFARE

Sugar Equalization Board

The Sugar Equalization Board was an agency of the United States Food Administration established during World War I for the purpose of purchasing and distributing the Cuban and United States sugar crops among American consumers and the Allied nations during the years 1918–1919.

Prior to the outbreak of World War I, Europe depended upon sugar produced in France, Germany, and Austria. As the war raged in Europe, destroying most of the local sugar industry, Europeans began looking to Cuba and the United States for their supply of sugar. Allied demand soon overwhelmed the United States and Cuban suppliers. The failure of a voluntary sugar control committee, established in 1917, to oversee distribution, prompted President Wilson to approve the formation of the Sugar Equalization Board, which was incorporated on July 11, 1918, with George Rolph as president. The board was responsible for stabilizing the cost of sugar and securing the equitable distribution of sugar domestically and abroad.

After prices were negotiated for Cuban and domestically grown sugar, the board, acting as middleman, purchased the sugar and contracted to sell it to refiners. In the spring of 1918, new regulations restricted manufacturers of products containing sugar to 80 percent of their preceding year's consumption. States were allocated sugar based on population, and their allotments were then distributed to retail outlets and restaurants by state food administrators. Certificates of different value were issued by the board to grocers, who were then responsible for allotting sugar to their customers. (The certificate plan was abandoned in December 1918 after the signing of the Armistice.) From Aug. 1 to Nov. 1, 1918, the allocation was two pounds of sugar per month per person. In November, individual allocations were increased by another pound. Overall, domestic sugar consumption in 1918 decreased more than 1.3 billion pounds, thus making more sugar available to the Allied countries.

The board also entered into an agreement with the British royal commission on sugar supplies, which acted on behalf of all the Allied nations, to allocate to them one-third of the total 1918 Cuban sugar crop. To relieve the labor shortage abroad, sugar was refined in the United States.

The Sugar Equalization Board was reorganized in January 1919 for the purpose of returning the market to normal conditions, and in February 1919, the board began releasing sugar for export, ceasing operation shortly thereafter.

Betsy Nash

Bibliography

Berhnardt, Joshua. *Government Control of the Sugar Industry in the United States: An Account of the Work of the United States Food Administration and the United States Sugar Equalization Board, Inc.* New York: Macmillan, 1920.

———. "Government Control of Sugar During the War." *Quarterly Journal of Economics* 33 (August 1919).

Surface, Frank M., and Raymond L. Bland. *American Food in the World War and Reconstruction Period: Operations of the Organizations Under the Direction of Herbert Hoover 1914 to 1924.* Stanford, CA: Stanford University Press, 1931.

Suicide Fleet

The Brittany Patrol, sometimes called the Suicide Fleet by its members, was the naval organization composed of French and American ships of many types that from the spring of 1917 until the Armistice operated in the Bay of Biscay. The patrol covered an area from Brest, south to the Pyrenees and westward, halfway to the Azores. American ships participated in the patrol for a year and a half, and their main responsibility was escorting U.S. troop and supply ships. Although some merchant vessels were sunk by submarines in the first part of the period, no troopships were victims, and by March 1918, no ships succumbed to the Germans in the area patroled.

At first, the American "fleet" consisted mainly of yachts donated by wealthy Americans, but later, U.S. Navy destroyers became an integral part of the organization. The first yachts to reach Brest with the first convoy in June 1917 were the *Corsair* and *Aphrodite*. Two days later, July 4, 1917, thirteen more privately owned yachts arrived. They all had been owned by famous, wealthy Americans, whose names appeared on the then current "Who's Who."

Brest became the major U.S. naval base in France. Although the private yachts were the first contribution to the patrol, regular navy destroyers, subchasers, minesweepers, tenders, tugs, and other vessels were added as time went on. RAdm. Henry B. Wilson, USN, served as the American chief of the Brittany Patrol.

Most of the ships carried five-inch guns, fore and aft, as well as depth charges and some Y-guns. Of course, the regular navy ships were equipped as their class would normally be.

During the patrol period, many exchanges occurred between the American ships and German submarines, some of which ended successfully for the U-boats but most of which were victories for the Allies. One of the most unusual was the capture of the only U.S. naval officer by a German submarine. On the morning of May 31, 1918, the *President Lincoln* was attacked and, after the crew was removed, sunk. Lt. E.V. Isaacs, unfortunately, had not concealed his coat and hat, bearing the insignia of a naval officer, and he was immediately ordered from the life boats and into the submarine as a prisoner of war. Although the submarine, the *U-90,* was attacked by the American destroyer *Smith*, it managed to avoid destruction and Isaac ended up at the German naval base at Kiel. He managed to escape four times but was recaptured. Finally, on the fifth attempt, he made it to Switzerland, where he managed to avoid internment and returned to naval headquarters in Paris.

Most of the period was consistently hectic, with many ships attacked. Although some submarines were successful in their quest, most were not. While no troop transports were sunk en route to France, on the return voyage, after leaving the escorts, some vessels did become casualties of preying U-boats. Several of the ships of the patrol were also lost while defending their charges.

When the war was over, some of the Suicide Fleet were ordered to the North Sea, others to the Baltic. Some ended up in England and Ireland, others in Germany, the Mediterranean, and the Black Sea. The private yachts, those that survived, were sent home as soon after the war as was practical, beginning on Dec. 5, 1918. Most were sold off by the navy, but one in particular had an interesting career. The *Kanawa II,* formerly owned by John Borden of Chicago, was transferred back to him on July 1, 1919. He in turn sold the yacht to a John M. Briggs, who then sold it to Marcus Garvey. Garvey included the ship in his *Black Star Line*, running between New York and Jamaica and thence to Liberia. It was ultimately wrecked on the Jamaican shores.

George B. Clark

Summerall, Charles Pelot (1867–1955)

Charles Pelot Summerall graduated from the United States Military Academy in June 1892. Commissioned an infantry second lieutenant, Summerall transferred to the artillery on March 6, 1893, for a tour of duty with Heavy Battery, 5th Artillery at the Presidio of San Francisco. During the Spanish-American War, he served as aide-de-camp to two generals, then returned to the 5th Artillery in December 1898. In July 1900, he served with Light Battery F (Reilly's Battery), 5th Artillery, participating in the China Relief Expedition. He then held a number of line and teaching posts until September 1914 when he reported for duty at the War Department.

Now a General Staff officer, Major (later Colonel) Summerall served with the Militia Bureau, the Field Artillery of the National Guard, and the military mission to study the British and French armies from May to July 1917. In September 1917, newly promoted Brigadier General Summerall was in command of the 67th Field Artillery Brigade of the 42d (Rainbow) Division at Camp Mills, New York. He shipped out for France with his brigade in October. In France Summerall took command of the 1st Field Artillery Brigade of the 1st Division on Dec. 23, 1917.

The division's artillery underwent intensive training under French and British gunners at Le Valdahon in southeastern France. MajGen. Robert L. Bullard, then commanding the 1st Division, had known Summerall since 1899 in the Philippines. Together the two officers had fought the Filipino insurgents from exposed positions in the front lines, Summerall "strutting up and down in the open" completely exposed to enemy fire. This led to a lifelong professional association that was renewed on the battlefields of France.

The action at Cantigny proved to be the baptism of fire for Summerall's artillery—consisting of the 5th Field Artillery (155-mm guns), the 6th and 7th Field Artillery (75-mm guns), and the 1st Trench Mortar Battery. It was reinforced by French field and fortress artillery units.

When Bullard was promoted to command an army corps, Summerall was promoted to the grade of major general on June 26, 1918, and took command of the 1st Division on July 15, 1918. His immediate challenge was the division's attack at Soissons, for which he was decorated with the Distinguished Service Cross.

He continued in command of the division through the St. Mihiel operation when he was promoted to command the U.S. V Corps, which he led until the Armistice on November 11. For his distinguished accomplishments in positions of great responsibility General Summerall received the Distinguished Service Medal in 1919. During the war he also was decorated with the Silver Star for valor four times.

General Summerall commanded the U.S. IX Corps in France, then the U.S. IV Corps in Germany following the end of the war. He again commanded the 1st Division in Kentucky and New Jersey from September 1919 until June 1921. He served as chief of staff of the army from November 1926 until November 1930, when he and his wife, Laura Mordecai Summerall, briefly retired to Florida. He was appointed president of the Citadel, the military college of South Carolina, in September 1931, remaining in that post until June 30, 1953. He died on May 14, 1955.

The only episode to mar an otherwise outstanding performance in the Great War came just days before the Armistice, when Summerall and MajGen. Joseph T. Dickman both joined in the race to liberate Sedan. Orders were misinterpreted, troops intermixed and became confused, and the Sedan Incident led to lifelong animosities among the senior officers involved.

John F. Votaw

See also SEDAN INCIDENT

Bibliography

Addington, Larry H. "Charles Pelot Summerall." In *Dictionary of American Military Biography,* ed. by Roger J. Spiller. Westport, CT: Greenwood Press, 1984.

Anger, Charles L. "Charles Pelot Summerall." In *Dictionary of American Biography.* New York: Scribner, 1977.

Bullard, Robert Lee. *Personalities and Reminiscences of the War.* Garden City, NY: Doubleday, Page, 1925.

Supreme War Council

The Allied Powers of World War I did not create an organization to coordinate policy and strategy for over three years, one reason why they were unable to force a decision on the Western Front despite extraordinary expenditures of blood and money. The establishment of the Supreme War Council in November 1917 came only after a series of disasters during that year. These included the abject failure of French and British offensives in France, the huge losses of shipping exacted by the German U-boats, the Italian defeat at Caporetto, and the collapse of Russia. The only favorable portent in the midst of otherwise unrelieved defeat was the American intervention in April, but it seemed possible that the Central Powers would prevail before the United States, unprepared for serious warfare in Eurasia, could generate sufficient power to tip the balance toward the Entente.

Despite the evident need for an inter-Allied body to provide higher direction, the immediate circumstances that led to the founding of the Supreme War Council was a conflict within the British government. Prime Minister David Lloyd George, appalled by the tremendous casualty lists of 1917, had lost confidence in his principal military advisers, the chief of the British General Staff, Gen. Sir William Robertson, and the commander-in-chief of the British Expeditionary Force, Field Marshal Sir Douglas Haig, who were exponents of the "western strategy," the idea of concentrating all available strength in France to seek a decision against the German Army on the Western Front. Victory there would mean victory everywhere else, but it also meant terrible losses. Lloyd George leaned toward an "eastern strategy," an approach preferred among those in Britain who wanted to minimize losses and others who were particularly interested in the preservation of the empire. Devotees of this idea wanted to attack the lesser Central Powers—Turkey, Bulgaria, and Austria-Hungary—who were much weaker than Germany. Their defeat would set the stage for a victory on the Western Front and guarantee British influence east of Suez.

To prepare the way for a shift in inter-Allied strategy, Lloyd George urged the establishment of a "joint council" that could foster "effective unity in the direction of the war." Seeking support from President Woodrow Wilson, he noted the need for "an Allied Body which had knowledge of the resources of all the Allies, which could prepare a single coordinated plan for utilizing those resources in the most decisive manner, and at the most decisive points, looking at the front of the Central Powers as a whole and taking into account their political, economic, and diplomatic as well as their military weaknesses."

President Wilson favored a unified direction of the war, but he supported the western strategy, deferring to the views of his military advisers. The War College Division of the General Staff reported: "The Western Front is nearest to us; it can be most readily reached and with the least danger; we there fight with England and France with whom we have the greatest natural interests; and we can make our power felt on that front quicker and stronger than anywhere else; and we are there opposed by Germany, who is our only real enemy." MajGen. John J. Pershing, the commander-in-chief of the American Expeditionary Force, was also a dedicated westerner.

Lloyd George approached French Premier Paul Painlevé, in search of support for a joint council. The French favored unity of command, which would mean appointment of a French "generalissimo" to direct the armies in France, an expedient that found little favor in Great Britain. Also, the French were strong proponents of the western strategy. Nevertheless, Painlevé decided to support Lloyd George's scheme for unity of control through a joint council because it might lead to a unified command.

The Italian defeat at Caporetto gave Lloyd George an opportunity to force the creation of the joint council. He met the French and Italian leaders at Rapallo in northern Italy, and on Nov. 7, 1917, he gained acceptance of a "Scheme of Organization of a Supreme War Council." This organ would include the head of government and a member of the government of Britain, France, the United States, and Italy. Its mission was "to watch over the general conduct of the war. It prepares recommendations for the decision of the Governments, and keeps itself informed of their execution and reports thereon to the respective Governments." To provide expert analysis, the Rapallo Agreement created a group of permanent military representatives (PMRs), one from each member nation. They were to observe "the situation of the forces, and the means of all kinds of which the Allied armies and the enemy armies dispose." Independent of their nations' general staffs, they were made responsible to the council, although they received instructions from their governments. The council was to meet at Versailles each month to consider measures required to assure effective coordination of the inter-Allied effort.

The Supreme War Council held its second session in Paris on December 1, during a major conference of the Allied and Associated Powers. An American delegation headed by Col. Edward M. House was present. It also included the American chief of staff, MajGen. Tasker H. Bliss, and the chief of naval operations, Adm. William S. Benson. The United States favored unity of control but wished to prevent inter-Allied political arrangements that might compromise the nation's freedom of action after the war. President Wilson had in mind a peace settlement that diverged in various ways from the intentions of the Entente Powers. He, therefore, condoned the appointment of a permanent military representative, General Bliss, but declined to send a political representative to sit on the council itself.

The Paris Conference led to the establishment of additional inter-Allied agencies to manage specific aspects of the war effort. Among them were the Allied Naval Council, the Inter-Allied [Land] Transportation Council, the Allied Blockade Council, the Allied Food Council, the Allied Munitions Council, and the Allied Council on War Purchases and Finance. These made important contributions to the Allied war effort during the final year of the war. The Supreme War Council on occasion coordinated their efforts.

The Supreme War Council met eight times during 1918. Its procedure was to consider items of agenda proposed by members or "joint notes" prepared by the PMRs. They met fifty-five times to consider joint notes. If these documents were unanimously accepted, they went to the council.

The first task of the PMRs was to consider strategy for 1918. At this juncture it had become obvious that Germany planned an end-of-the-war offensive on the Western Front to force a decision before the American reinforcement could turn the tide to the Allies. Joint Note No. 1 called for a defensive posture on the Western Front while the Allies awaited American reinforcements sufficient to permit resumption of the offensive. A more detailed exposition followed, Joint Note No. 12, entitled "1918 Campaign." It maintained that France and Britain could hold their lines in France provided American divisions arrived at the rate of two per month. Meanwhile, it proposed to annihilate the Turkish Army, a reflection of the British preoccupation with secondary theaters. The French and Americans inserted a proviso that no action should occur that would divert men and materials required in France.

To deal with the impending German offensive, which became feasible because of the transfer of forty veteran divisions from the Eastern Front after Russia left the war, the PMRs developed Joint Note No. 14, entitled "General Reserve." Thirty divisions were to be stationed at appropriate locations behind the lines from which they could maneuver to reinforce areas attacked by the Germans. On January 30, an Executive War Board was set up with Gen. Ferdinand Foch, the French chief of staff, as its president. It decided upon a reserve of fourteen French, ten British, and seven Italian divisions. Unfortunately, Field Marshal Haig and the French commander-in-chief, Gen. Henri Philippe Pétain, sabotaged the arrangement by refusing to contribute divisions. Instead, they agreed to support each other if in need.

The Haig-Pétain agreement did not survive the initial German attack, which began on March 21. Gen. Erich Ludendorff forced a breakthrough and threatened the vital communications center of Amiens. This grave crisis forced the Supreme War Council to move from unity of control to unity of command. Foch became the overall commander of the armies in France, including the American Army, with the power to give strategic direction. This authority was extended to the Italian front in May. The national commanders retained direct tactical control of their forces.

Foch's command at first appeared to undermine the Supreme War Council, but soon it shifted its emphasis from general direction of the armies to strategy in secondary theaters and to specific issues of great military and political significance. Among these the most important were the utilization of American manpower, proposed interventions in Russia, and operations in secondary theaters. After Foch defeated the German Army, the council decided the terms of armistice and the political basis for postwar peace negotiations.

When the United States entered the war, President Wilson and his military advisers decided to mobilize a huge independent army that would fight under its own flag with its own commanders and staff following its own doctrine in its own sector of the Western Front with separate services of supply. Given the nation's unpreparedness, the creation of this force would require at least two years, postponing significant American contributions to the battle until

1919 or perhaps even 1920. The decision to field an independent army meant that only four divisions of American troops reached Europe by the beginning of 1918. The threat of a great German attack in 1918 led Britain and France to urge what became known as "amalgamation," the insertion of small units of American combat troops into their armies as replacements to counter the manpower superiority that Germany had gained in France by transferring forty divisions from the Eastern Front. General Pershing opposed all forms of amalgamation intransigently, seeking to preserve the integrity of his forces. The Wilson administration supported its field commander, recognizing that the public and the army desired an independent force and that the presence of a victorious independent army in the field after the war would strengthen the American position during the postwar peace negotiations.

When the German offensive began in March, it stimulated constant inter-Allied discussion of the utilization of American troops, most of it within the Supreme War Council. The crisis finally forced Pershing to agree to temporary amalgamation of a few American divisions primarily for training. They would soon be withdrawn to form independent American corps and field armies. In return, Great Britain promised to provide sufficient shipping to transport the American army to Europe. General Bliss privately came to support the Entente position on amalgamation, but he remained loyal to Pershing's views in deliberations of the PMRs. During an acrimonious meeting of the Supreme War Council at Abbeville on May 1–2, Pershing was forced to make a further concession. He agreed to the shipment of infantrymen and machine gunners only at the rate of 120,000 troops per month from May to July. Other types of personnel, such as artillerymen and engineers needed to conduct independent operations, would follow. In return, Pershing gained a firm commitment from the Allies to allow him to form an independent force when possible. The Abbeville agreement was modified during the next meeting of the Supreme War Council to provide for the shipment of 500,000 troops in June–July, 310,000 of them combat troops. After that period, the issue of American manpower declined in importance as the influx of reinforcements provided Foch with sufficient manpower to assume the offensive and force a decision by November.

During 1918, the Supreme War Council gave considerable attention to a political event of great military significance, the Bolshevik Revolution in Russia. To counter it and to establish a military presence in Russia, the Allies contemplated various schemes of intervention. Most were aimed at the North Russian ports of Murmansk and Archangel and at Vladivostok in eastern Siberia. Proponents of the western strategy, among them the Americans, opposed such interventions as diversions of resources needed on the Western Front. The United States also resisted such projects because they appeared likely to violate the fundamental democratic premise of national self-determination. The Americans also opposed Japanese involvement in Siberia. Wilson hoped that the Bolshevik phenomenon would fade as the Central Powers met defeat.

These conflicting views greatly affected the discussion of projects for intervention. On February 16, the PMRs, including General Bliss, approved Joint Note No. 16, "Japanese Intervention in Siberia," but President Wilson decided to oppose any such measure, making his opposition known to Japan in a powerful diplomatic note of March 5. The PMRs then formulated Joint Note No. 20, "The Situation in the Eastern Theatre," which offered a strong rationale for intervention, but on this occasion Bliss refused to sign, following his guidance from Washington. Then a new element led to further propositions of intervention. Large numbers of Czech prisoners of war were located in camps along the route of the Trans-Siberian Railroad. In Joint Note No. 25, "Transportation of Czech Troops from Siberia," the PMRs proposed to concentrate the Czechs at Vladivostok and Murmansk and then relocate them to the Western Front as reinforcements. The Supreme War Council approved this project at Abbeville on May 1–2. Pressure to act increased when the Czechs revolted and seized large sections of the Trans-Siberian Railroad. Joint Note No. 31, "Allied Intervention at Russian Allied Ports," provided for the occupation of Murmansk and Archangel. The United States sent the cruiser *Olympia* and a small force to the region as part of an inter-Allied expedition. It was assumed that this operation was intended principally to protect war materiel stockpiled at the White Sea ports.

The Russian question came to a head at the seventh meeting of the Supreme War Council on July 2. The British, French, and Italian prime ministers sent a note to Wilson seeking his agreement to send an expedition to Vladivostok in which Japan would participate. Its mission would be to help the Czechs. This initiative led to a major policy review in Washington. The result was an aide-mémoire of July 17 that contained powerful arguments against extensive intervention in Russia. The United States agreed only to a modest venture that would protect military stores at Vladivostok and support the departure of the Czech troops. In return for this concession the United States demanded assurances that the operation would not compromise Russia's territorial integrity, internal affairs, and political sovereignty.

This tepid response threw cold water on extensive plans for intervention. A small expedition was dispatched, in which the United States participated. Japan violated the terms of the agreement and sent far more troops than expected. In any event, the issue of intervention declined in priority as Foch conducted his operations on the Western Front during July–October that led to the defeat of Germany. Russian questions, of course, again assumed great importance during the postwar peace conference.

Foch's successes promoted a period of general inactivity at the Supreme War Council. It did not hold regular meetings in August and September. Some attempts were made to promote various projects of intervention in secondary theaters, especially in Macedonia where an inter-Allied force at Salonika faced the Bulgarian Army. Local victories in Macedonia and in Palestine eliminated the need to divert resources to the region.

The last major activity of the Supreme War Council was to consider the terms of armistice for Germany and the separate question of the basis of postwar peace negotiations. In October, Germany approached President Wilson with a proposal to end the war. Bilateral negotiations led, by October 26, to an agreement to negotiate peace based on Wilson's Fourteen Points address of January 1918 and associated pronouncements. To consider this arrangement, the Supreme War Council met in Paris in late October. Col. Edward M. House was sent to represent the United States. The council first de-

cided upon the military, naval, and air terms of armistice, which were sufficiently stringent to preclude Germany from resuming the conflict. General Pershing opposed conditions of any nature. He sent an unauthorized letter to the Supreme War Council in which he advocated unconditional surrender. An angry President Wilson wanted to reprimand Pershing, but Colonel House arranged the withdrawal of the letter.

The council then turned to the terms of peace. Significant opposition to various aspects of the American peace program existed among the Entente Powers. House then intimated that the United States would withdraw its troops if the council rejected Wilson's agreement with Germany, an act that cleared the way for its acceptance. The pre-armistice agreement of November 4 provided for peace negotiations based on Wilson's program with two exceptions. The French obtained agreement on the right of the Allies to demand war reparations and the British reserved their views on the issue of freedom of the seas. The pre-armistice agreement was perhaps the most important accomplishment of the Supreme War Council.

The Supreme War Council lived on during the Versailles Peace Conference as the Council of Four. It prefigured many inter-Allied arrangements made during World War II. After World War II, its main features found expression in the Council of the North Atlantic Treaty Organization.

The history of the Supreme War Council reveals the usefulness of institutions designed to coordinate the political goals and strategic designs of alliances. It also exposes the difficulties posed by conflicting national interests.

David F. Trask

See also ABBEVILLE CONFERENCE

Bibliography

Trask, David F. *The United States in the Supreme War Council: American War Aims and Inter-Allied Strategy, 1917–1918.* Middletown, CT: Wesleyan University Press, 1961.

T

Taft, William Howard (1857–1930)

Until elected President as a conservative Republican, William Howard Taft had held only appointive judicial and executive offices. In the former he earned a reputation for safeguarding the rights of private property rather than those of labor and issued so many injunctions against strikes that he became known as "the Father of Injunctions." He also served as the first civilian governor of the Philippines (1901–1904), directing a number of surprisingly progressive programs for that country's development. From 1904 to 1908, he served as Theodore Roosevelt's secretary of war. He not only directed the department, but also served as an unofficial troubleshooter for the President. As President himself (1909–1913), Taft continued and expanded a number of the Progressive initiatives of his predecessor, particularly in the areas of trust and tariffs. In foreign affairs, the administration pursued a policy of "dollar diplomacy" and negotiated a series of arbitration treaties with Great Britain and France.

In 1913, Taft returned to his alma mater, Yale University, to teach constitutional law. In 1917, at the request of President Woodrow Wilson, he took leave from Yale and served for fourteen months as chairman of the National War Labor Board, which arbitrated disputes between employees and management involved in vital war industries. He confounded friends and enemies alike by softening his former hard line on labor rights as he learned more about the working conditions and wage levels of labor. He helped to support existing agreements on the open or closed shop and advanced labor's cause by applying the eight-hour workday policy, the principle of equal pay for women and men for equal work, and the general right to a "living wage." He also sought recognition for the right to organize unions free from employers' interference and the right of collective bargaining by "chosen representatives."

Taft's work was rewarded by the incidence of fewer strikes, the quick settlement of those that occurred, diminution of the radical labor movement, and the growth of the organized labor force from 3 to 4 million members.

Originally opposed to the United States entering the Great War, Taft supported President Wilson's wartime measures. However, the two differed on the type of peace settlement desired. Unlike the Wilsonian approach, Taft held it necessary, in cases in which nations refused to submit their disputes to arbitration, to "fight fire with fire" and would use both economic and military force to curb errant parties.

Although unhappy that Wilson did not name him a member of the American delegation to the Versailles Conference, he supported the creation of a League of Nations. Taft was president of the League to Enforce Peace from its inception on June 17, 1915, until 1921, when he became chief justice of the Supreme Court, where he served with distinction until two months before his death in 1930.

Paolo Coletta

Bibliography

Anderson, Judith I. *William Howard Taft: An Intimate History*. New York: Norton, 1981.

Bartlett, Ruhl J. *The League to Enforce Peace*. Chapel Hill: University of North Carolina Press, 1944.

Conner, Valerie J. *The National Labor Board: Stability, Justice, and the Voluntary State in World War I.* Chapel Hill: University of North Carolina Press, 1985.

Cuff, Robert D. "The Politics of Labor Administration during World War I." *Labor History* 21 (Fall 1980).

Pringle, Henry F. *The Life and Times of William Howard Taft.* 2 vols. New York: Farrar & Rinehart, 1939.

Tanks

Crawling slowly across the mangled, ruptured earth, through the mist and smoke, a strange iron creature roared into view. Giving the illusion of enormous speed to its crew, the steel box nonetheless moved deliberately at about two and one-half miles per hour. Carefully, the crew zig-zagged their war engine across no-man's-land, partly to avoid the deep, water-filled craters, but also to avoid the destructive fire of enemy field guns. Many of those "prehistoric beasts" carried bundles of sticks on top of their hulls so that when an unspanable trench was encountered, "fascines" would be thrown in to create a bridge over the gap. Some of the monsters were "males" with cannon armament, and others were "females" with machine guns. World War I had spawned another technological change in the conduct of war.

American soldiers fought in tanks in World War I, but not in American-made tanks. The first two American-made Renault seven-ton tanks arrived in Bourg on Nov. 20, 1918. The country that provided the technological innovation in the caterpillar tractor did not field the first fully tracked operational fighting machines. The United States exhibited in 1917 the same lengthy process of fielding new equipment that is typical even today. So the history of American experience with tanks in the First World War is an amalgam of Yankee organizational and tactical innovation with French, and sometimes British, tanks and equipment.

Despite the often passionate arguments of the tanks corps officers, the machine was usually considered by the General Staff as an infantry support weapon to be distributed along the line with every possible unit receiving a few. With the exception of the attack at Cambrai in 1917, the tactics of massed formations of armored vehicles lay in the future beyond the Great War.

The tank was one of the great mystery innovations of World War I, although the possibility of such a battlefield device was anticipated by H.G. Wells and a few others in their imaginative writings. Its identity and purpose were concealed by active disinformation and the descriptive term "tank." A British military engineer, LtCol. Ernest D. Swinton, learned about Benjamin Holt's caterpillar tractor and its potential for military use in July 1914 from a South African friend who had seen one in Antwerp. It was not until October that Swinton seized on the caterpillar tractor as the solution to the tank's mobility problem in swampy, shell-pocked terrain. On October 26, a small number of Holt tractors had arrived in England for military tests. It took the creative energy of a small group of British officers and inventors to make the technological leap from armored scout cars, used to recover downed aviators from no-man's-land, to fully tracked combat machines. The early auditions for the tractor in 1914 and 1915 by the British War Office were unsuccessful, but the idea of an armored "land cruiser" caught the attention of First Lord of the Admiralty Winston Churchill. By mid-1915, the Holt tractor already was in use in the British Army as a prime mover for heavy artillery pieces.

Under the guidance of the Admiralty's Landship Committee, "Little Willie" gave way to "Mother," the first of the "Big Willie" series of true tanks, whose caterpillar tracts ran up over the top of the machine encircling it like a pair of giant elastic bands. Two six-pounder guns were mounted in "sponsons" jutting from the sides of "Big Willie." The tendency toward naval terminology stuck as the tank reached mature development—it had a "hull" and a "bow" as well.

Following a successful trial in February 1916, the War Office ordered 100 tanks for use on the Western Front in France. These first machines were produced in Great Britain in six months under a veil of complete secrecy. LtCol. Swinton had been struggling to find the solution to the German soldier's skillful use of wire entanglements protected by hails of accurately placed machine gun fire. He envisioned some type of armored vehicle that was, as he described it in his personal account, *Eyewitness*, powerful enough to negotiate no-man's-land with its shell holes and trenches, impervious to machine gun bullets, and able to roll over barbed-wire entanglements.

The idea of a moving pillbox that both protected its crew and carried the withering fire of automatic and large-caliber weapons forward with the infantry was not new, but a practical solution in the available time seemed remote. Working logically and sequentially through the various parts of the mechanical problems, Swinton and his colleagues also had to lobby continually to keep the idea of the tank alive among the senior staff whose priorities seemed to be elsewhere.

The American divisions arriving in France after June 1917 did not have their own tanks; therefore, they relied on support from French and British tank units. The U.S. Tank Corps was created in December 1917 under the command of BGen. Samuel D. Rockenbach. Capt. George S. Patton was one of two other officers in the unit; his initial assignment was to organize a school of light tank tactics. The Renault light tank was well suited to American theories of "open" warfare, where maneuverability commanded a premium.

Cantigny—a rural village in the Picardy region of France about fifty miles north of Paris—was the scene of the first American battle in World War I. Supporting the Yanks were twelve Schneider CA.1 heavy tanks from the French Army. They accompanied the 2d Battalion, 28th Infantry, which was assigned to attack and seize the village. The Schneider was a huge cheesebox on tracks with one 75-mm gun protruding from a turret on the right side and two Hotchkiss 8-mm machine guns. The Americans had not trained extensively with tanks but did rehearse for several days prior to the battle, which was conducted with speed and violence on May 28. The village was taken in thirty-five minutes with very light casualties.

French Schneiders and two other models— the St. Chamond with its 75-mm cannon protruding like a giant snout from the front of the vehicle and four machine guns guarding each side, front and rear and the toylike Renault two-man, seven-ton tank with only a single 37-mm gun or 8-mm machine gun in a turret on top— effectively supported the Americans at Soissons in July 1918. Up to that point, the Germans had underestimated the worth of tanks.

American tank units made their first appearance at St. Mihiel in September 1918, along with French tank units. At St. Mihiel, the American Tank Corps, comprising two brigades: Patton's 1st consisting of Renaults (144 tanks) and Schneiders (24 tanks) in the attached French IV Groupement, and Lt Col. Daniel D. Pullen's 3d, consisting of 216 Renaults in the attached French 505th Regiment and 35 St.

Chamonds and Schneiders in the French XI Groupement. The promised 150 British heavy tanks were withdrawn before the battle. The Americans were to support the attack of the U.S. IV Corps against the south face of the triangular salient on September 12 after five days of steady rain. "General Mud" commanded the battlefield that day. In many cases the tanks had become separated from the infantry units they were supporting. The value of tanks in the attack still was to be demonstrated, but the reduction of the salient facilitated the next operation—Meuse-Argonne.

The 1st Tank Brigade was in action from October 4–14 when it was withdrawn to Exermont for major refitting and repairs. On October 29, the 3d Tank Brigade moved to Varennes and relieved the 1st Brigade. The U.S. First Army resumed the offensive on November 1, but the American tank units had not completed their relief in place—only fifteen tanks were available to support the start of the attack. A new tactic was used in the U.S. 2d Division zone where the tanks were supporting units. As the signal was given to begin the attack, the infantrymen withdrew 500 yards from their forward trenches while a ten-minute artillery barrage pounded the area just ahead of the front lines. German machine gunners traditionally "hugged" the forward positions to avoid the artillery preparations; this time they were destroyed. When the tanks surged forward ahead of the infantry, they met little machine gun resistance.

On November 6, the American tank brigades were redesignated as the 304th, 305th, 306th, and 307th Tank brigades. The 304th Tank Brigade (formerly Patton's 1st Tank Brigade) had 171 men killed and wounded in the Meuse-Argonne fighting, with eighteen tanks destroyed by enemy fire.

The U.S. 301st Heavy Tank Battalion had a separate battle history with the British Army. Equipped with British Mark V and Mark V Star tanks, the Americans were committed in late September 1918 to support the U.S. 27th Division's attack near Gouy in the British Fourth Army's zone. The open terrain favored the use of heavy tanks, but the Germans prepared their defenses accordingly. Some coordination failures between infantry and tanks left many of the tanks exposed in the fog and smoke. With that less than satisfactory outcome behind them, the American tankers prepared in early October to support MajGen.

T

George W. Read's U.S. II Corps to keep the pressure on the Germans, who were falling back on their prepared works dubbed the Hindenburg Line. The outcome of the fighting through October 23 was more satisfactory, but the analysis, like that of the performance of light tank units, produced mixed conclusions. The tank-infantry team had considerable potential, but it was largely unrealized in World War I.

By and large, American tank units performed admirably, but best in those areas where the infantry divisions had prior experience with tanks, such as the 1st and 2d divisions. The presence of the tank on the battlefield had a nerve-piercing effect on the German soldier's morale, perhaps out of proportion to the tank's actual lethality. In World War II, the tank reached the zenith of its potential.

John F. Votaw

See also UNITED STATES ARMY TANK CORPS

Bibliography

Dooly, William G., Jr. *Great Weapons of World War I.* New York: Bonanza Books, 1969.

Liddell Hart, Basil H. *The Tanks: The History of the Royal Tank Regiment and Its Predecessors Heavy Branch Machine-Gun Corps, Tank Corps and Royal Tank Corps 1914–1945.* 2 vols. London: Cassell, 1959.

Macksey, Kenneth, and John H. Batchelor. *Tank: A History of the Armoured Fighting Vehicle.* New York: Scribner, 1970.

Swinton, MajGen. Sir Ernest D. *Eyewitness.* Garden City, NY: Doubleday, Doran, 1933.

Wilson, Dale E. *Treat 'Em Rough! The Birth of American Armor, 1917–1920.* Novato, CA: Presidio Press, 1989.

Tardieu, André Pierre Gabriel Amédée (1876–1945)

Born to an upper-middle-class Parisian family, André Pierre Gabriel Amédée Tardieu's career as a prolific journalist and renowned politician spanned the first third of the twentieth century. Elected to the French Chamber of Deputies in 1914, he maintained his seat until 1924, and again from 1926 to 1936. During the interwar years, Tardieu held many portfolios in various cabinets of the Third Republic and served as prime minister on three occasions between 1929 and 1932.

Even before the outbreak of World War I, Tardieu had made a mark in public life, first as political secretary to Prime Minister René Waldeck-Rousseau (1899–1902) when he had a hand in drafting legislation that led to the separation of church and state and as a journalist. Although Tardieu championed a policy of reconciliation with Germany before 1911, the Agadir crisis of that year convinced him that firm measures of military security vis-à-vis Germany were essential. He became a supporter of Raymond Poincaré's efforts to invigorate France's military and diplomatic posture; his outspoken advocacy of the Three Years' Law, a measure to increase the length of military service, accelerated his move toward the political right.

On the eve of war, Tardieu held simultaneously a position at the Ministry of Interior, two professorships of diplomatic history, and was foreign affairs editor of both *Le Temps* and *Le Petit Parisien.* His political influence was summed up by German Chancellor von Bulow: "There are the six great powers, and then there is André Tardieu."

When the war broke out, Tardieu insisted on active duty, serving on the General Staff of both General Joffre and General Foch and then at the front, where he was wounded. On the day the United States declared war on Germany in April 1917, Tardieu published a proposal for complete cooperation among the Western allies and the United States. He envisioned the pooling of all resources, including men, weapons, money, and food.

On the basis of such proposals, President Poincaré appointed Tardieu to the position of High Commissioner for France in the United States. He remained in Washington until the end of the war, departing for Paris on Armistice Day, Nov. 11, 1918, to join Premier Georges Clemenceau in organizing the peace. In his eighteen months in Washington, he had helped the United States send 1.6 million tons of grain, 300,000 tons of sugar, 2.8 million tons of steel, 170 million tons of 75-millimeter shells, 430,000 tons of fuel, and 2 million soldiers to France—virtually guaranteeing victory over the Central Powers.

Tardieu and Clemenceau were determined to forge a victor's peace, and it was the former who articulated France's initial hard-line stance with regard to the Franco-German border—restoration to France of Rhenish territory lost in 1815, ownership of the Saar basin, an independent Rhineland state, and inter-Allied occupation of the Rhine bridges. But whereas Clemenceau remained obdurate, Tardieu used his good relations with American officials (especially President Wilson's confidant, Col. Edward M. House) to effect the compromises necessary to conclude the Treaty of Versailles in 1919. For example, in lieu of France's maximum program of demands against Germany, which violated Wilsonian principles of national self-determination, Tardieu persuaded Clemenceau to accept the promise of an Anglo-American military guarantee of French security.

Much of what Tardieu tried to accomplish in the era of the First World War fell short of his aspirations. Before the war, his policy of practical reconciliation with Germany came to nothing. His vision of total cooperation among the Allied and Associated Powers did not survive the victory. And his efforts to guarantee French security by achieving a victor's peace gradually melted away—first, in the failure of the Anglo-American guarantee and, finally, in Germany's piecemeal escape from the restrictive clauses of the Versailles Treaty during the 1930s. Tardieu, a disillusioned man, retired from active political life in 1936; he suffered a debilitating stroke in 1939 and died in Menton in 1945.

William Shorrock

Bibliography

André Tardieu, par Louis Aubert, Ivan Martin, Michel Missoffe, Francois Pietri, Alfred Pose; introduction par Gabriel Puaux; hommages de Bernard Baruch, Lord Vansittart, Paul van Zeeland. Paris: Librairie Plon, 1957.

Binion, Rudolph. *Defeated Leaders: The Political Fate of Caillaux, Jouvenal, and Tardieu.* New York: Columbia University Press, 1960.

Tardieu, André. *France and America.* Boston: Houghton Mifflin, 1927.

———. *The Truth About the Treaty.* Indianapolis: Bobbs-Merrill, 1921.

Taussig, Joseph Knefler (1877–1947)

Joseph Knefler Taussig, born in Germany, was the son of a U.S. naval officer stationed in Europe. He graduated from the United States Naval Academy in 1899 and served in China as a passed midshipman during the Boxer Rebellion of 1900. While in the hospital recovering from wounds received during the International Relief Expedition, he made the acquaintance of a wounded Royal Navy captain, John R. Jellicoe, who would remember Taussig warmly seventeen years later when Jellicoe was first sea lord of the Royal Navy.

When the United States entered the war in April 1917, the German submarine blockade had Britain on the verge of starvation and the Royal Navy desperately needed American reinforcements for its hard-pressed escort force. In May 1917, Taussig led Destroyer Division Eight in a stormy Atlantic crossing to join the British antisubmarine forces in Ireland. When British Vice Admiral Lewis Bayly asked how soon his six destroyers would be ready to go to sea, Taussig replied, "We are ready now"—as soon as they could be refueled—to the British admiral's delight. Taussig's warm relationship with his British colleagues was vital to the smooth functioning of an unprecedented naval alliance and contributed crucially to the early success of the American destroyers.

After the war, Taussig served at the Naval War College through most of the 1920s, a seminal era during which many of the successful strategies and tactics of the Second World War were developed. In the 1930s, he commanded a battleship, served first as chief of staff to the commander-in-chief, U.S. Fleet, and then as assistant chief of naval operations. In 1940, Taussig warned a congressional committee that war with Japan was imminent, for which he received an official reprimand. The following year his son, Ensign Joseph K. Taussig, Jr., was severely wounded as officer of the deck of the battleship *Nevada* during the Japanese attack on Pearl Harbor. Taussig commanded the 5th Naval District in Norfolk, Virginia, before retiring as a rear admiral in 1941. He was recalled to active duty in 1943, serving as chairman of the Naval Clemency Board until 1946. He died in 1947.

Taussig was a courageous and forceful individual, often outspoken but also capable of self-effacing humor. When asked about his confident reply to Bayly, for instance, Taussig joked that he had thought Bayly asked when he would be ready to go to eat.

David MacGregor

Bibliography

Sims, William S. *The Victory at Sea*. Garden City, NY: Doubleday, Page, 1920.

Trask, David F. *Captains and Cabinets: Anglo-American Naval Relations 1917–1918*. Columbia: University of Missouri Press, 1972.

Taxation

See INCOME TAX; REVENUE ACT OF 1917; REVENUE ACT OF 1918

Trading with the Enemy Act

In the summer of 1917, President Woodrow Wilson submitted to Congress a series of legislative proposals to aid the nation's war effort. The topics ranged from draft regulations to seditious conduct to penalties against espionage. Concerned that speeches, periodicals, or newspapers might ignite a debate as to the merits of U.S. intervention, the administration formulated the Trading with the Enemy Act. Passed by both houses of Congress, President Wilson signed the legislation into law on Oct. 6, 1917.

The act empowered the postmaster general to regulate war-related information that appeared in magazines, pamphlets, letters, and newspapers—particularly U.S. foreign-language newspapers. Postmaster General Albert Sidney Burleson required that all articles be cleared by his office prior to publication.

At the outset, Burleson's censorship standard was explicit. As he put it: "There is a limit. And that limit is reached when it begins to say this Government got in the war wrong, that is, in for wrong purposes or anything that will impugn the motives of the government for going to war."

Burleson, for example, banned one article suggesting that the U.S. war effort be financed through higher taxes rather then selling bonds. Another publication was enjoined from printing Thomas Jefferson's essay on the merits of permitting Ireland to establish a republic—ostensibly to avoid upsetting the British.

Beyond the broad powers of censorship, the postmaster general could withdraw second-class mailing privileges from suspected publications—especially those with socialist leanings. Burleson rescinded second-class privileges from several periodicals, perhaps most notable from the leftist *The Masses*, and, as a result, a number of those publications went out of business.

The Trading with the Enemy Act also empowered the government to seize the properties and assets (gold, silver, bonds, etc.) of individuals classified as "enemies." Under this mandate a new agency—the Alien Property Custodian—was formed under the direction of A. Mitchell Palmer. Individual and corporate assets, largely German, were confiscated and sold on the open market. The proceeds from such sales were not insignificant. The largest buyer of U.S. Liberty Bonds in the fall of 1917 was none other than an arm of the federal government—the Alien Property Custodian.

Manley R. Irwin

See also ALIEN PROPERTY CUSTODIAN; BURLESON, ALBERT SIDNEY

Bibliography

Johnson, Donald. "Wilson, Burleson and Censorship in the First World War." *Journal of Southern History* (1961).

Kennedy, David. *Over Here: The First World War and America*. New York: Oxford University Press, 1980.

Traub, Peter Edward (1864–1956)

Peter Edward Traub was born in New York City. He graduated from the United States Military Academy in 1886 and was commissioned as a second lieutenant of cavalry. In 1887, he served in campaigns against the Crow Indians, and from 1890 to 1891, he participated in campaigns against the Sioux in South Dakota. During the years 1892 to 1898, he was a member of the languages department at the United States Military Academy. During the Spanish-American War, he commanded the 1st platoon, Troop G, 1st Cavalry in the Battle of Las Guasimas, Cuba, on June 24, 1918, for which he was subsequently recommended for a brevet captaincy for "gallantry in action." He was further breveted to major at the Battle of San Juan, July 1–3, and the siege of Santiago. Traub served in the Philippines as the assistant adjutant general of the Department of Luzon from 1900 to 1901 and in April 1902 secured the written agreement of surrender from General Guevara.

Traub returned to the United States and became head of the department of languages at the Army Signal School, Army Staff College from 1904–1907; between 1904 and 1905 he was a member of several foreign missions. By invitation of the kaiser, he witnessed German army maneuvers in Breslau in 1906. Traub returned to West Point and served as a professor of modern languages in 1907. He was a member of a mission to the isthmus of Panama in 1908 to oversee the election of a president and served again in the Philippines from 1911 to 1917.

On Aug. 16, 1917, Colonel Traub was appointed commander of the 51st Infantry Brigade, and he served in France from 1917 to 1919. From July 20 to December 26, 1918, he commanded the 35th Division, which had gone into the line at a quiet sector in the Vosges Mountains near Wesserling. The division conducted large-scale raids against German posts until September, when it was assigned to I Corps in preparation for the St. Mihiel offensive scheduled for September 12. The assault was so successful that the 35th was not needed, giving the division time to prepare for the next offensive and begin its move to the Meuse-Argonne front. In this campaign the division was to advance up the Aire valley to take the ridge southeast of Charpentry. Despite the division's relative inexperience, it carried out its orders efficiently and achieved its objectives at 12:30 P.M. September 26. Confusion and failures of communication resulted in a near hopeless intermingling of units as the advance continued, now against the German 1st Guard Division, a crack enemy unit. The fog of war and an experienced, determined opponent resulted in thousands of American casualties by the time the division was relieved on September 29. The shattered division was moved to an inactive sector. After the Armistice, the 35th engaged in salvage operations.

Traub again received a citation for gallantry in action, and was wounded in action twice. He was awarded the French Croix de Guerre with Palm, and made a commander of the Legion of Honor.

Following the war, Traub commanded several Army posts and performed a variety of staff and line duties until his retirement on Oct. 15, 1928. He died in September 1956.

Michael Knapp

Treat, Charles G. (1859–1941)

Charles G. Treat attended the United States Military Academy, where he graduated thirteenth in the class of 1882. After being commissioned in the field artillery, Treat served from 1889–1894 as aide-de-camp to Gen. Oliver O.

Howard, well known for his Civil War record and his later service as commissioner of the Freedmen's Bureau.

During the Spanish-American War, Treat served as adjutant of the Light Artillery Brigade in action at Santiago, Cuba, then as assistant adjutant general for the military governor of Cuba until 1900. From 1901 to 1905, he was the commandant of cadets at West Point.

Following graduation from the Army War College in 1911 and command of the 3d Field Artillery Regiment at Fort Sam Houston, Texas, Treat served on the War Department General Staff from 1914–1916. After briefly commanding the Hawaiian Brigade in 1916, he assumed command of the 37th Infantry Division, Ohio National Guard, at Camp Sheridan, Alabama, on Sept. 3, 1917. In the fall of 1917, he visited the American Expeditionary Force (AEF) in France on an inspection tour as part of a group of generals. On May 8, 1917, he relinquished command of his division to MajGen. Charles S. Farnsworth, who led the division overseas. Treat was assigned to command the Western Department with headquarters at San Francisco and later saw service overseas.

In June 1918, the War Department assigned General Treat to Italy as the chief of the American Military Mission, with command of the AEF troops in Italy. After the Armistice, he briefly served on a committee appointed by the Supreme War Council to investigate incidents at Laibach, Yugoslavia, before returning to the United States in 1919. General Treat was recognized for his military service in World War I with the Distinguished Service Medal as well as several foreign decorations.

At the time of his retirement in 1922, he commanded Fort Stotsenburg in the Philippines. Treat was well known for his advocacy of polo as an army and intercollegiate sport. He died in Washington, D.C., on Oct. 11, 1941.

John F. Votaw

Bibliography
The National Cyclopedia of American Biography. Vol. 42. James T. White, 1958.

Assembly. (July 1942).

Order of Battle of the United States Land Forces in the World War: American Expeditionary Force: Divisions. Washington, DC: Historical Section, Army War College, 1931.

Cole, Ralph D., and W.C. Howells. *The Thirty-Seventh Division in the World*

War, 1917–1918. 2 vols. Columbus, OH: 37th Division Veterans Association, 1926.

Treaty of Versailles
See Paris Peace Conference

Trenches and Trench Warfare

While not all the combat of the Great War involved trenches, their ubiquitous presence, the style of warfare they and the available weaponry dictated, and the special horrors associated with life and death in these "open graves" have indelibly linked World War I with trench warfare. The massive trench systems, dug by all the combatants, scarred not only the landscape but the psyche of generations of Europeans.

Of course, trenches were in no sense a new invention in 1914. Roman soldiers dug trenches to fortify their campsites at the conclusion of each day's march. In the Middle Ages, trenches were used to enhance fortifications. Generally, a trench, if filled with water termed a moat, surrounded most bastions. As fortifications became lower and thicker to withstand bombardment in the early modern period of warfare, attackers themselves utilized trenches, called parallels, to protect their troops and artillery as they besieged a position. The great French engineer Sébastien Le Prestre de Vauban perfected these methods, and his tactics, employing trenches to bring assault forces closer and closer to an enemy's fortifications, were so successful that they evolved into the stylized forms of siege warfare that dominated the late seventeenth and eighteenth centuries.

Trenches returned to the battlefield proper during the American Civil War, when both sides learned to dig in if their units were stationary for any length of time. Observers credited this tendency, which became habit, as an important factor in the ability of Sherman's western federal troops to blunt repeated Confederate attacks—most notably Hood's great counterattack around Atlanta. The final months of the war in Virginia were spent in the trenches around Petersburg. Combat there proved very similar to the warfare of the Western Front in the First World War. While rifle pits were used in the Franco-Prussian War, especially by the French Imperial Army, and at the siege of Plevna (1877) in the Russo-Turkish War, it was in the Russo-Japanese War of 1904–1905 that trenches first played a major role in land combat. The fighting in Manchuria was a clear precursor of what was to come a decade later, with trenches, barbed wire, and machine guns emerging as key technologies in land warfare. The major European armies scrutinized this conflict intensely, but they disregarded the importance of trenches because the Japanese Army, despite dreadful losses, successfully conducted offensive operations against the entrenched Russians.

The apparent ineffectiveness of entrenchments in Manchuria was only one reason why such fieldworks were not an integral part of the planning and training of pre-Great War armies. Since all the major powers, with the exception of Great Britain, began the war with plans that were entirely, or at least essentially, offensive, entrenchments were seen as unnecessary and even as undermining the intense offensive spirit needed for success on the modern battlefield. Again, the "lesson" of the Russo-Japanese War had been that determined infantry with sufficient élan could carry any defensive position, provided that it was willing to accept the inevitable heavy losses. Thus the opening battles on the Eastern and Western Fronts of the First World War did not feature elaborate field fortifications; very quickly, however, defenders found that "digging in" significantly enhanced their survivability and defensive power. After the First Battle of the Marne, both sides used entrenchments to free reserve units in an attempt to turn the other side's open flank—the so-called "race to the sea." After the failure of the last German offensive in the west in 1914, the famous *Kindermoerde* ("massacre of the innocents") at the First Battle of Ypres, the Western Front became fixed over the first winter of the war. By the spring of 1915, a more or less continuous line of entrenchments stretched from the North Sea to Switzerland. No such continuous line ever existed in the east, whose vast spaces dwarfed the available manpower of Imperial Russia, Germany, and Austria-Hungary.

Trench warfare soon imposed its own rhythms and requirements on all the armies. Of chief concern, particularly to the French, was devising effective tactics to break the trench deadlock and regain territory occupied by the Germans. The French Army, with some assistance from the expanding British Expeditionary Force (BEF), spent much of 1915 attempting what might be termed the "Japanese solution," mass attack, to break through ever strengthening German defenses. The result was massacre, with over 310,000 French dead in this year, the heaviest toll paid by France during any year of the war.

There were three fundamental obstacles that plagued attacking forces on both sides: the difficulty of getting a sufficiently powerful attacking force across no-man's-land and taking the enemy frontline trench; directing unprecedentedly large forces in extended tactical operations without adequate communications; and perhaps the most crippling problem, attempting to sustain and reinforce offensive operations once underway.

This last problem proved the most difficult to solve. Generally, it proved possible to seize an opponent's front line, especially as more sophisticated tactical means, such as the creeping barrage and poison gas, were introduced to aid the attacker. Communications failures were circumvented by adopting rigid attack schedules, thus attempting to minimize the need for tactical direction—even as this tactical rigidity often caused additional problems and losses for the attacking forces. But sustaining offensive operations, particularly in the face of the inevitable enemy counterattack, proved a task that stymied all the armies until the last year of the war. Not only did primitive communications make it extremely difficult to reinforce and thus expand successful operations, but massive bombardment almost inevitably turned the soil of northern France and Belgium, with its extremely high water table, into a peat bog, through which all reinforcements, supplies, and supporting artillery had to pass in order to sustain operations.

The defender's task was much easier, even if his conditions were equally terrifying and miserable. Although the Germans on the Western Front developed the most sophisticated trenches, complete with multiple defensive lines and deep bunkers to protect troops from bombardment, all the armies dug elaborate trench systems that included frontline and supporting trenches, often dug hundreds of yards apart to protect defensive reserves, as well as communication trenches used to move men and supplies up to the front. The vagaries of terrain, the need to avoid straight lines that made the defenders too vulnerable, and continual bombardment all dictated that the trench line not be a precisely dug surveyor's product but a jagged

system that crisscrossed hundreds of square miles.

Protected by barbed-wire entanglements yards thick, laid out in depth over hundreds, even thousands of yards, these massive fortifications required extensive maintenance. Indeed, a major part of the soldier's time "in the line" was spent in keeping the trenches in good repair. Trenches were widened, deepened, and drained; sandbags were filled; barbed wire entanglements were thickened and repaired. Days of tedium and backbreaking labor thus were interspersed with the terror of battle.

A day in the trenches began and ended with a "stand-to": at dawn and dusk all personnel manned defensive positions in anticipation of an enemy attack. If the enemy attack did not materialize, the day became one of routine. Food and supplies were brought up through communications trenches; weapons were cleaned and inspected, and such repairs and maintenance that could be effected in daylight were completed. At night this activity continued, albeit at a somewhat slower pace. Certain work, like repairing or strengthening the barbed wire, could only be carried out in darkness. Reinforcement or relief of frontline troops was usually a nocturnal activity as well. In addition to these strictly defensive pursuits, both sides used the night to stage raids on the enemy's trenches in order to gather intelligence, keep the enemy on edge, and maintain the "pluck" and fighting spirit of their own troops. These raids grew in size and violence as the war continued and often featured brutal and bloody fighting at very close quarters.

In the best of circumstances, conditions in the trenches could only be classified as miserable. Besides the ever present fear of sudden and violent death, the soldiers on the Western Front were continually at the mercy of the elements. Mud and standing water were always a problem. New maladies, such as "trenchfoot," caused by prolonged submersion of boot-shod feet in water, plagued frontline troops. The armies collectively proved unable to handle the problem of interment, especially since many men died in no-man's-land between the opposing trenches. Thousands of corpses were left to putrefy and rot; often those given hasty burial were disinterred by both side's artillery when it periodically churned up the ground. Veterans recalled with disgust the pervading stench, the clouds of flies, and the rats. Lice tormented all personnel, and coming out of the line always required delousing the soldier and his clothing.

Given this violent, wretched, and at times frankly disgusting environment, it is not surprising that some soldiers, confronted daily with horrific scenes of death, sometimes buried alive in massive bombardments, suffered mental breakdowns in the trenches—what came to be known as "shell shock." There were also incidents of cowardice and desertion, as well as the famous mutinies of 1917 in the French Army, when French soldiers refused to attack German lines, although promising to hold the line against attack. What is perhaps surprising is how steadfast the soldiers of all nations were in facing this ordeal.

Efforts to minimize the impact of this brutal warfare on the soldiers achieved at best mixed success. Since all the powers anticipated a short war, many months elapsed before a systematic rotation policy was developed. Units routinely cycled through the various trench positions, from deep reserve to frontline duty, spending several days in each position. Ultimately, the armies organized leave policies that allowed the soldiers to return home. While these visits home were certainly welcome, they also served to emphasize the tremendous gap between the average soldier's experience and the perception of that experience by the home front. Civilians, nurtured by generations of history and literature that portrayed war usually in the most heroic terms, and sustained by a press that, when not censored, tended fully to support the war, had great difficulty talking about the fighting with soldiers on leave. The returned men generally seem to have been reluctant to discuss the full horrors of the war in the trenches. The tremendous disparity between the soldiers' and the civilians' war explains the oft repeated assertion that the frontline soldiers felt more respect and kinship for the enemy than for the mass of their own civilians. In the postwar decades, the full revelation of what had occurred in the trenches doubtlessly contributed to the strong antiwar, antimilitary feeling that characterized the 1920s and early 1930s.

Ultimately, two ways were found to break the trench deadlock. The German solution, successfully implemented in March 1918, was based on new tactics. Following a short, ultra-violent "hurricane" bombardment, small bodies of elite storm troops, specially trained assault forces, would attack the enemy front line. Once these positions were carried, the storm troops continued to move forward, avoiding strong points, seeking the path of least resistance, attempting to advance at all cost. The Germans achieved outstanding tactical success. Fronts that typically were moved thousands or even hundreds of yards at the cost of massive casualties suddenly were ruptured. Before the first great German drive of March 21, 1918, was finally stopped, the British were forced to retreat some forty miles.

But if the Germans had found a tactical solution to the trench deadlock, those new tactics led to operational and strategic failure. While the Germans were able to break completely through the Allied defenses, they still had not solved the problem of sustaining their operations. The defenders were able to build up their forces more quickly than the attackers could bring up reinforcements to sustain their assault. The idea that attacking forces should bypass defensive strong points and "infiltrate" through defensive lines into weakly held areas in the rear, while successful tactically, frequently led attacking forces away from operational and strategic objectives. At the same time, the use of storm troops resulted in the best, fittest soldiers in the German Army absorbing the bulk of the casualties. The four great drives of 1918 cost Germany an estimated half million soldiers.

The Allies used technology, in the form of the tank, to break the German defensive system. Developed by the British at the behest of the always active and innovative Winston Churchill, tanks were first used on the Somme in 1916, then attained a spectacular, if momentary, success at Cambrai in 1917. By 1918, the Allies could mass hundreds of tanks. While these were rickety, mechanically unreliable machines, slow and vulnerable to artillery fire, the Allied armies used the weight of their effort to grind down the German defenses methodically. The tanks' greatest impact was on German morale. The great British victory of Amiens in August 1918 cost the victors most of their tank force. Still, German commander Erich Ludendorff termed it "the black day of the German Army" because of the shattering impact this mass tank attack had on army morale and discipline. Clearly, the tank proved to be the key to breaking the trench stalemate. Expectations of renewed trench warfare in World War II, even attempts to fight that conflict according to the defense-dominated tactics of the Great War, foundered on the ability of properly supported tank forces to pierce static defenses.

The American experience with trench warfare was of necessity a limited one. The Yanks entered the war too late to participate in the great battles of Verdun, the Somme, and Passchendaele. The year 1917 was one of mobilization and deployment for American forces, with a few divisions gaining experience by rotating through the trenches. Although American units were thrown into the line to help stem the great German spring offensives of 1918, the bulk of the American combat experience was in the Allied counteroffensives that steadily pushed the German lines back toward their homeland. American units performed bravely with superb élan, but tactically their lack of training often resulted in heavy casualties.

While the suffering and bloodshed of the other fronts certainly approximated the experience of the Western Front, the great trench systems of France and Flanders exerted an unusually depressing aura on all who saw them. Even Ludendorff and Hindenburg, on their first tour of the Western Front after assuming supreme command of Germany's forces, were repelled by what they saw. The scale and graphic horror of the experience combined to shape powerful opinions about war and foreign policy. The brutalization of European life and thought experienced in the trenches acted as no small step toward totalitarianism, genocide, and the Second World War. Ideas and movements as disparate as pacifism, strategic bombing, and existentialism were rooted in the four years European civilization spent living and dying in this—the words are Paul Fussell's—"troglodyte world."

Gary P. Cox

See also SHELL SHOCK

Bibliography

Ellis, John. *Eye-Deep in Hell: Trench Warfare in World War I.* New York: Pantheon Books, 1976.

Horne, Alistair. *The Price of Glory: Verdun 1916.* New York: Penguin Books, 1964.

Pitt, Barrie. *1918: The Last Act.* New York: Ballantine Books, 1963.

Winter, J.M. *The Experience of World War I.* New York: Oxford University Press, 1989.

Wolff, Leon. *In Flanders Fields. The 1917 Campaign.* New York: Time, 1963.

Truman, Harry S. (1884–1972)

Harry S. Truman was born in Lamar County, Missouri. Most of his childhood was spent in the small town of Independence, Missouri, where he developed an affinity for books as a small, shy child. After completing his high school education, Truman received an appointment to the United States Military Academy at West Point, but he was rejected because of his poor eyesight. Instead, he spent the next years working for the Santa Fe Railroad Company and with the National Bank of Commerce in Kansas City. He served briefly as the road overseer for the southern half of Washington County and as the postmaster of Grandview.

In 1905, Truman joined the National Guard and was honorably discharged at the end of his second enlistment in 1911. He immediately reenlisted after the United States entered World War I and was sworn in as a first lieutenant, having received help to pass the eye examination. Truman attended the Field Artillery School at Fort Sill, Oklahoma, and then helped organize the Second Missouri Field Artillery, which later became the 129th. In March 1918, he went overseas with the 35th Division as a captain and adjutant of the 2d Battalion. After further training, he received command of Battery D of the 129th Field Artillery, a battery known as "hard-boiled Kansas City Irish." Although the unit had worn out five previous captains, Truman won their respect and affection as he led them through the St. Mihiel and Meuse-Argonne offensives. Once during battle, when the panicky battery was on the verge of a disorderly retreat, he bawled them out in no-man's-land and restored order. The unit fired its last shot only fifteen minutes before the signing of the Armistice.

Truman returned to the United States shortly after the war and was discharged with a reserve commission. He became a founder of the Officers Reserve Corps Number 1 in Kansas City and in 1927 became a colonel in the Reserves. He remained active in the American Legion and lobbied for American preparedness.

Truman turned to politics in 1921 and gradually climbed the ladder of Missouri's Democratic politics. In 1934, he ran successfully for the U.S. Senate, and was narrowly reelected in 1940. His ability to get along with the various factions in the Democratic Party and his continuing support of President Roosevelt's policies made him a logical candidate for the vice presidency during Roosevelt's fourth election campaign. Truman succeeded to the presidency on April 12, 1945, after the death of Franklin D. Roosevelt.

Laura Matysek Wood

Bibliography
Goodman, Mark, ed. *Give 'Em Hell, Harry.* New York: Award Books, 1975.
Miller, Merle. *Plain Speaking.* New York: Putnam, 1974.
Steinberg, Alfred. *The Man from Missouri.* New York: Putnam, 1962.

Tumulty, Joseph Patrick (1879–1954)

Joseph Patrick Tumulty, secretary to Woodrow Wilson during his two terms in the White House, was an influential adviser to the President on domestic and foreign policy throughout the First World War. Born to an Irish Catholic family in Jersey City, New Jersey, Tumulty remained in his native state as an adult. He was elected to the state legislature and became an early supporter of and campaign strategist for Wilson in his successful gubernatorial campaign of 1910. After Wilson's election to the presidency in 1912, Tumulty gradually assumed more responsibility and acquired greater power until he became the de facto assistant president. He supervised patronage, handled relations with the press, and served as liaison between the aloof Wilson and Democratic officials and activists.

Though a staunch supporter of Irish independence, Tumulty defended his chief against the angry accusations of Irish-American groups that Wilson was pursuing a pro-British policy during the period of American neutrality in World War I. Tumulty became a vigorous advocate of preparedness and rearmament in response to German submarine attacks on Atlantic shipping, particularly after the sinking of the *Sussex* in March 1916. Upon the United States declaration of war against Germany in April 1917, Tumulty turned over his function as Wilson's public relations agent to George Creel, director of the newly created Committee on Public Information, in order to concentrate on serving as a buffer between the President and the various public officials and politicians who sought entrée to the Oval Office. Tumulty worked diligently to prepare for the congressional campaign of November 1918, in which, despite his efforts, the Democrats suffered a major electoral setback.

After the elections that gave the Republicans control of both houses of Congress and the end of the war in November 1918, Tumulty attempted and failed to persuade Wilson to appoint a distinguished Republican statesman such as Elihu Root to the U.S. delegation to the Paris Peace Conference in order to facilitate legislative ratification of the peace agreements. While the President remained in Europe from December 1918 through June 1919—except for a brief visit to the United States in the spring—Tumulty stayed in Washington to act as Wilson's intermediary with Congress, the party, and the public. During the Paris Peace Conference, Tumulty periodically warned his chief by cable of the growing disenchantment with some of his policies. On the President's return, his secretary convinced him to undertake a nationwide tour to counteract isolationist criticism of the Versailles Treaty and the Covenant of the League of Nations. Tumulty planned the President's itinerary and was at Wilson's side throughout the trip, which was cut short in late September 1919 by the President's stroke.

As Wilson served out the remainder of his term as an invalid suffering from the effects of a debilitating second stroke, Tumulty attempted to regain his old place as intermediary between the President and the outside world. But Edith Bolling Galt Wilson, the protective, suspicious second wife of the disabled chief executive, fended off his loyal secretary and took charge of his affairs. The former President broke with Tumulty in 1922 over a trivial incident involving a public statement at a Jefferson Day dinner made by Tumulty in Wilson's name. Tumulty then returned to the practice of law in New Jersey. He died on April 8, 1954.

William Keylor

Bibliography
Tumulty, Joseph P. *Woodrow Wilson As I Know Him.* Garden City, NY: Doubleday, Page, 1921.

Turkish-American Relations

See OTTOMAN-AMERICAN RELATIONS

Twenty-One Demands

The onset of the war in Europe exacerbated international rivalries in the Far East. There, the clash of Japanese and German imperial interests had serious consequences for the regional balance of power and for American-Japanese relations. Despite the fact that China had declared its neutrality at the onset of the Great War, on Aug. 15, 1914, the Okuma government issued an ultimatum to Germany, demanding withdrawal of the German fleet from the Far East and termination of the German leasehold in China. When Germany ignored the deadline for this ultimatum, Japan declared war eight days later. While Japan thus honored the Anglo-Japanese Treaty of 1902 as renewed in 1911, the action clearly served Japanese interests.

Japanese naval forces and marines seized the German-occupied Marianas (except for Guam) and the Marshall, Palau, and Caroline islands, and besieged the German fortress of Tsingtao in September 1915. Supported by a small British force, the Japanese were victorious and German defenses collapsed on October 7. By December, Kiaochow, the Chinese Eastern Railroad, and the entire Shantung Peninsula were under Japanese control.

With its historic economic and political interests in China, Japan's goals were clear: to take advantage of Allied commitments and preoccupation in Europe to expand its own sphere of influence at the expense of the feeble Peking government. Both Germany and Japan, to a greater extent, now violated Chinese neutrality and past pledges to respect the American Open Door policy for China. The Peking government appealed directly to President Wilson for military intervention.

Still neutral in 1915, militarily entangled in Mexico, and preoccupied with the *Lusitania* crisis, the Wilson administration informed the Chinese that the United States did not wish to become involved. On Jan. 18, 1915, Japan presented its Twenty-One Demands to the Yuan Shih-K'ai government. The demands, divided into five groups, required that China: (1) recognize Japanese rights in Shantung; (2) extend Japanese commercial rights and leases in Manchuria to ninety-nine years; (3) cede half-interests in coal facilities at Ta-yeh and iron and steel plants at Han-yang to Japan; (4) declare Chinese coastal regions exempt from lease or cession to any other power; and (5) allow greater Japanese political, financial, and military influence in the Yangtze River valley. In sum, acquiescence to these demands would have made China a virtual protectorate of Japan and slammed shut the Open Door.

Ignoring warnings to keep the demands secret, the Chinese government communicated their substance to Washington, D.C., viewing the United States as the only power capable of, or concerned with deterring Japanese imperialism. Secretary of State William Jennings Bryan issued a mild official protest, but in substance the United States position was conciliatory toward Japan and appeared to accommodate Japanese interests. While objecting to the demands, specifically the fifth group, which most directly affected American interests, Bryan acknowledged that the United States recognized the "special relations that territorial contiguity" created between Japan and China.

Only when Japan threatened to use force did President Wilson, on April 14, 1915, signal a change of policy, informing Bryan that the United States "should be as active as the circumstances permit in showing ourselves to be the champions of the sovereign state of China." Faced with American and British reservations, notwithstanding their inability to enforce threats against Japan, the Okuma government abandoned its least important fifth group of demands but continued to mobilize its forces.

Increasingly impatient and emboldened by secret Allied pledges (then unknown to the Wilson administration) to support Japanese military conquests and legitimacy in any postwar settlement, following Allied victory, Japan issued an ultimatum on May 7, confident that the United States would not act. The following day China acceded to Japan's ultimatum and officially recognized Japan's special and legitimate interests in China, signing two separate treaties and notes on May 25, 1915.

On May 11, the United States had responded to the Japanese ultimatum as Japan had expected, Bryan informing the Japanese and Chinese governments that it would not recognize any agreement that would impair the treaty rights of the United States, endanger its citizens, or threaten the "political or territorial integrity of the People's Republic of China, . . . or the Open Door." Beyond that, however, the United States would not and could not intervene.

American nonrecognition and moral condemnation had no practical affect except to erode further Japanese-American relations. As a result of the Twenty-One Demands, Japan's power in China, in the Pacific, and throughout the Far East generally was enhanced. For the remainder of the war, the Wilson administration attempted to use international economic leverage to contain Japanese imperial designs without success, especially in Manchuria. Indeed, on Nov. 2, 1917, Secretary of State Robert Lansing and Viscount Kikujiro Ishii, signed an agreement recognizing that "territory propinquity" accorded Japan "special interests in China." Thereafter Japan moved aggressively in the postwar decades to advance further its position in China, initiated by its Twenty-One Demands of 1915.

Jonathan M. Nielson

See also LANSING-ISHII AGREEMENT

Bibliography

U.S. Department of State. *Papers Relating to the Foreign Relations of the United States, 1915, 1916, 1917.* Washington, DC: U.S. Department of State, 1916, 1917, 1918.

U

Uniforms

See UNITED STATES ARMY UNIFORMS

United States Air Service

At the time of America's entry into the First World War on April 6, 1917, the United States possessed no viable air strength. This woeful situation meant that the United States Air Service was started virtually from scratch, from the small nucleus of aviators attached to the Aviation Section of the U.S. Army's Signal Corps.

The Aviation Section was comprised of just 55 aircraft, virtually all of them obsolete, 131 officers, and 1,087 enlisted men. By Nov. 11, 1918, the Air Service had several thousand aircraft, 20,000 officers and 175,000 enlisted men. In that year and a half, the United States had established a viable aircraft industry, trained, with the aid of its allies, large numbers of aviators and mechanics, and managed to field an effective fighting force of observation, bombing, and pursuit, or fighter squadrons. That was a considerable achievement, but it was not accomplished without numerous problems, delays, and miscalculations.

When the United States entered the war, LtCol. William "Billy" Mitchell of the Signal Corps had just arrived in Europe as an official observer. Mitchell was an especially capable officer who possessed unusual foresight at a time when most army officers lacked a full appreciation of the nature, capabilities, and requirements of an air force. Mitchell set to work at once organizing the affairs of the Air Service in Paris and making recommendations to Washington.

Mitchell's proposals went unanswered at first, but a cablegram from French Premier Alexandre Ribot to President Wilson on May 24, 1917, prompted action. Ribot proposed that the United States undertake a program to supply 4,500 airplanes, 5,000 pilots, and 50,000 mechanics to the war zone by the spring of 1918. The United States responded by sending an exploratory mission headed by Maj. Raynal C. Bolling to England, France, and Italy. After landing in Liverpool on June 26, the Bolling Mission made a thirty-day tour to lay the groundwork for the purchase and production of aircraft and overseas training of American personnel. The group recognized that it would be unwise to rely upon American designs for combat aircraft because of the rapid advances in aircraft design and America's great distance from the fighting front. Instead, the Americans took the advice of the Allies and evaluated new and existing aircraft used by them to select one primary type for production in the United States, while recognizing that the United States Air Service would purchase other types from its Allies. The Bolling group selected the British de Havilland D.H. 4, a two-seated bombing and observation plane, for U.S. production and also urged production of a new aircraft engine, an effort that culminated in the design and production of the Liberty V-12.

In the summer of 1917, army planners in both Washington and France were wrestling with the question of the ultimate size of the air service and its requirements of men and materiel. The first comprehensive plan, later known as Program Number One, was adopted on Sept. 18, 1917. It called for a total of 260 aero squadrons: 120 pursuit, 80 observation, and 60 bombing. Considering the vast requirements of manning and equipping such a large number of units and America's lack of trained aviation officers at the time, such plans were wholly unrealistic.

To field such an air armada would require a large training effort, and the army responded by increasing the number of its own training schools, as well as arranging for personnel to receive training in Canada, England, France, and Italy. However, there were considerable obstacles to achieving the training goals. At home, there was an acute shortage of skilled and experienced instructors and a lack of proper training aircraft. Overseas, the Allied air services had to accommodate the American trainees in their programs in addition to their native sons. Despite the additional burden, the Allied nations did a surprisingly good job, for their training programs were already fully operational. By the time of the Armistice, the Allies had trained over 1,300 American flying personnel—more than 400 in France, 500 in England, and 400 in Italy. In addition, thousands of mechanics received training in English and French schools as well as at American schools set up in France.

Shortly after the United States declared war, the team of Col. John B. Bennett, Maj. Benjamin D. Foulois, and a small staff went to Canada to study the Canadian method of training, which was subsequently adopted by the U.S. Air Service. It was a program with three phases: ground, primary, and advanced training.

The ground schools were set up in the United States at eight universities. In eight to twelve weeks, cadets studied the theory of flight, the use of codes, radio work, photography, meteorology, the operation and maintenance of engines and machine guns, and means of cooperation with the infantry and artillery. They also were schooled in military discipline and drill as part of their basic training.

After ground school, successful cadets went on to primary training, a six- to eight-week course, which included forty to fifty hours of flight training, usually in Curtis JN-4 "Jenny" aircraft. Of the more than 10,000 American pilots trained during the war, more than 8,000 took their primary training at one of the twenty-seven flying fields established in the southern and southwestern United States, while approximately 2,000 earned their wings at one of the sixteen flying fields used by the Americans in Europe.

Advanced training was generally accomplished in France. The main Aviation Instruction Centers (AIC) were in Paris, Tours, Issoudon, Avord, Bron, Pau, and Clermont-Ferrand, with one center in Italy and another in Great Britain. Though some of these schools used existing French facilities, several required large amounts of construction at a time when labor was in short supply. At Issoudon, the first aviation cadets found themselves involved in construction before they could fly!

Several of the schools provided specialized advanced training. Pursuit pilots learned aerobatics and air fighting in Nieuport single-seaters at Issoudon. Observers studied artillery observation, photography, and infantry cooperation at Tours and five other schools. Bomber pilots studied bombing at Clermont-Ferrand. Gunnery training was conducted at Cazaux and Saint Jean-de-Monts.

At the same time as it was building a force of airplanes, the service was also establishing a Balloon Corps, which, by the end of the war, maintained thirty-five balloon companies in France. For training purposes, the Balloon Corps used four schools in the United States and one in France. Balloon training consisted of five weeks of ground school and four weeks of balloon maneuvering. Observers were trained in general observation and artillery spotting.

The first American combat squadrons began to move to the front in the spring of 1918. In addition, the American personnel of the Lafayette Escadrille were redesignated as the 103d Aero Squadron, though their official transfer became mired in bureaucratic delays.

Though the uncertainties of supply and combat made it difficult to establish and maintain units at full strength, the pursuit squadrons were organized with a complement of twenty-five planes each, with a similar number of assigned pilots. Bomber and observation squadrons were organized with a complement of eighteen two-seater aircraft and a similar number of both pilots and observers. Most units actually operated at much less than full strength due to losses and the delays in receiving replacement aircraft and personnel.

Once sufficient units became available, they were organized in "groups" of four squadrons. The first such unit, the 1st Pursuit Group, was formed from the first four American fighter squadrons to be assigned to the front: the 94th, 95th, 27th, and 147th Aero squadrons. The 94th and 95th squadrons were operational in early April 1918, and the 27th and 147th joined them at the end of May to bring the 1st Pursuit Group to full strength.

The long-term goal for American air units was to support the growing American army. In its initial operations, however, the U.S. Air Service worked in cooperation with the French. The first squadrons were stationed on the relatively quiet Toul sector, west of the city of Nancy. This gave the units the opportunity to orient themselves to combat operations where enemy resistance was less formidable.

The American squadrons at Toul faced continuing difficulties in obtaining supplies and aircraft. The 94th and 95th Pursuit squadrons were equipped with a fast, maneuverable biplane, the French Nieuport 28. A lack of machine guns for the planes and the need for half the pilots of the 95th to take gunnery training added several weeks to the units' preparation.

The first American observation squadrons at Toul also were handicapped by second-line and obsolescent two-seater aircraft. The 1st Observation Squadron was equipped with a mix of Dorand AR.2s and SPAD XIs, while the 12th employed Dorands and the 88th used Sopwith 1–1/2 Strutters, all more or less outmoded models. Not until the summer would they be reequipped with more up-to-date aircraft.

The first success for the fledgling Air Service came on April 14, 1918. Two pilots of the 94th, Lts. Douglas Campbell and Alan Winslow, were on standby duty at their airfield at Gengoult, northeast of Toul. When word reached the 94th that two German planes were approaching, they took off to intercept them. A quick dogfight ensued right in view of the airfield, and both German planes were shot down. Winslow and Campbell became instant celebrities, and their double victory was heralded as the sign that the United States Air Service had "arrived." These were the first two victories credited to the 94th Aero Squadron, which was to be credited with the greatest number of enemy aircraft destroyed by any American pursuit squadron (a total of seventy in all).

Despite Winslow and Campbell's successes, the U.S. Air Service faced pressing problems. The requirements of training—adequate time, enough skilled instructors, reasonable flying weather—were considerable, and producing and maintaining sufficient numbers of suitable aircraft was difficult. In addition, ocean transport was a limiting factor, and when the German offensives in the spring of 1918 stretched the Allies perilously thin on the Western Front, the service saw much of its ocean transport diverted to carry infantry units and materiel to the beleaguered Allies. It was far short of its goals of having large numbers of squadrons in the war zone by the spring of 1918. This, coupled with morale problems caused by disorganization, led to the appointment of a new commander, MajGen. Mason M. Patrick, on May 29, 1918. He replaced BGen. Benjamin Foulois, who had presided over the service's initial buildup and deployment.

After gaining experience in the Toul sector, American air units were pressed into service assisting the French and American ground units involved in the battles at Château-Thierry in July 1918. The last of the great German offensives was occurring there in the Battle of the Aisne-Marne, and the 1st Pursuit Group, made up of the 94th, 95th, 27th, and 147th squadrons, and the 1st Corps Observation Group, comprised of the 1st, 12th, and 88th squadrons, were dispatched to that sector under the command of Col. William Mitchell.

The air fighting over the Aisne-Marne sector was fierce, and the relatively inexperienced Americans suffered losses. But they gave an excellent account of themselves and emerged from the campaign as battle-tested veterans. When the French and Americans launched their counteroffensive on July 18 through August 6, the air fighting reached its climax. In that period, the American pursuit pilots destroyed sixteen enemy aircraft against losses of fifteen of their own pilots killed or captured. The U.S. Air Service, though small in numbers, had established itself as equal in fighting ability to its enemy.

But the service was continuing to grow, as additional squadrons were deployed in the war zone. Two of the new American pursuit squadrons, the 17th and 148th, which had trained in England, were equipped with British Sopwith Camels and attached to the Royal Air Force in the British sector, near the North Sea. These two distinguished units, operating alongside their RAF allies from July 13 through October 28, accounted for 103 victories and produced several noteworthy aces. Among them were George A. Vaughn of the 17th and Field E. Kindley and Elliott Springs of the 148th.

As the summer wore on, additional American squadrons reached the war zone while many of the existing units reequipped with up-to-date aircraft that had at last become available. The Pursuit Group received French-built SPAD XIII single-seaters in July and August to replace its

Nieuport 28s. The two-seater squadrons replaced their obsolescent planes in June, July, and August with the much superior Breuget 14 and Salmson 2 A2. In August, the first unit to employ the American-built de Havilland DH-4 (DH-4 the American designation of the British D.H. 4) with Liberty engine, the 135th Observation Squadron, began operations. The new American-built planes arrived with a host of problems that required numerous field modifications, but over a dozen bombing and observation squadrons eventually flew them.

The St. Mihiel offensive in September was preceded by a buildup of air units. Two additional pursuit groups were formed from the new SPAD-equipped squadrons arriving at the front: the 2d Pursuit Group (13th, 22d, 49th, and 139th squadrons) and the 3d Pursuit Group (13th, 22d, 49th, and 139th squadrons). These were joined with the First Pursuit Group and the newly formed First Day Bombardment Group (11th, 20th, and 96th squadrons, later to include the 166th Squadron) to form the 1st Pursuit Wing. The First Army Observation Group (9th, 24th, and 91st squadrons) performed reconnaissance deep behind German lines for the entire American First Army. Three Corps Observation Groups, utilizing either Salmsons or American DH-4s were organized to work directly with their respectively numbered army corps closer to the front lines: I Corps Observation Group (1st, 12th, 50th squadrons) and V Corps Observation Group (99th and 104th squadrons). Each group also included at least one similar French escadrille.

These units were combined with dozens of French squadrons, forming the largest air armada yet assembled to support a ground offensive, and the whole was under the command of Colonel Mitchell. Elaborate plans to support the opening of the attack on September 12 were frustrated by foul weather, which made flying difficult during the first two days. The American aircrews carried out much of their work in spite of the inclement conditions. Better weather prevailed for the last two days of the offensive, and American units were fully engaged in all types of missions. Pursuit squadrons performed offensive patrols and ground attack duties, while the two-seater squadrons did high-level bombing, artillery spotting, photographic reconnaissance, and infantry contact patrols. The work was a resounding success, and Mitchell and his commanders were commended by the

commander of the AEF, Gen. John J. Pershing, for the success of the air operations.

After the quick conclusion of the St. Mihiel offensive, the American Army and Air Service began preparations for what would prove to be the final push of the war, the Meuse-Argonne offensive. The attack began on September 26 in the area northwest of Verdun, and this time Mitchell had just over 800 aircraft at his disposal, three-fourths of them American. Though many of the French air units had been withdrawn, most of the same American units saw action in the Meuse-Argonne offensive as at St. Mihiel. During October, three new aero squadrons began combat operations in support of the offensive: the 168th Observation and 166th Bombing squadrons with American DH-4s and the SPAD-equipped 141st Pursuit Squadron. Several other units started or were about to begin combat operations just as the war came to an end.

Despite extended periods of poor weather that made operations difficult, the U.S. Air Service performed well in the final offensive. The day bombing squadrons in particular suffered considerable losses but carried out effective operations against supply and transportation targets deep behind German lines. In one of the battle's most celebrated incidents, the 50th Observation Squadron made a series of extremely hazardous low-level missions on October 5–7 in attempts to locate and supply the "Lost Battalion," an element of the 77th Division that had become cut off and surrounded in the advance.

When the Armistice came on November 11, increasing numbers of additional air personnel were approaching readiness. The American training schools were at last producing larger numbers of trained airmen, but despite increasing production in the United States, the aircraft supply remained tight. The U.S. Air Service had, on August 17, 1918, adopted a revised plan for 202 squadrons at the front by July 1, 1919, but it is doubtful that it could have equipped half that number because of insufficient aircraft.

Though its organization and deployment had taken much longer than originally hoped, much had been accomplished by the new American air arm. When the war ended, there were forty-five squadrons and twenty-three balloon companies in combat service, which represented approximately 10 percent of the total Allied air strength at that time. The U.S. Air Service had lost 290 planes and 47 balloons to enemy action and had suffered the loss of 569 airmen in battle and 319 killed in accidents. The service credited its airmen with the destruction of 781 enemy aircraft and 73 balloons, though those numbers are no doubt unrealistically high.

Michael Carr

See also AERIAL WARFARE; AIRCRAFT; BOLLING, RAYNAL CAWTHORNE; BOLLING MISSION; FOULOIS, BENJAMIN DELAHAUF; MITCHELL, WILLIAM LENDRUM

Bibliography

Frank, Sam H. "Organizing the U.S. Air Service" (9 parts). *Cross and Cockade Journal*, 6, No. 2–8, No. 2 (1965–1967).

Hudson, James J. *Hostile Skies*. Syracuse, NY: Syracuse University Press, 1968.

Maurer, Maurer, ed. *The U.S. Air Service in World War I*. 4 vols. Washington, DC: Government Printing Office, 1978.

Thayer, Lucien B. *America's First Eagles*. San Jose, CA: Bender Publishing, 1983.

Toulmin, H.A., Jr. *Air Service, American Expeditionary Force 1918*. New York: Van Nostrand, 1972.

United States Army: American Expeditionary Force (AEF)

United States Army and Marine forces on the Western Front in France in World War I, known as the AEF, were created by a letter from Secretary of War Newton D. Baker, dated May 27, 1917, to MajGen. John J. Pershing, who was authorized to form, train, and commit to battle the military forces of the United States assigned to him in France.

On June 14, 1917, General Pershing and his small, hand-picked staff arrived in France, beginning the American commitment to the war on the Western Front. Charged by the War Department with recommending an organization to fight the war in Europe, Pershing quickly shook off the enthusiastic welcoming and introductory celebrations, settled into his temporary headquarters in Paris, and put his staff to work. Units of the U.S. 1st Division began arriving on June 26, 1917, and moved to Gondrecourt to begin training.

When General Pershing departed for France, the War Department had formed no definite plans for the American Expeditionary Force. After the AEF planning staff studied the military situation, and conferred with the War Department, a plan for American forces was formed. Known as the General Organization Project, the report, dated July 10, 1917, called for a balanced U.S. force of combat troops and support in France, totaling 3 million men—to be established in two years.

AEF headquarters also recommended an increase in the size, firepower, and staying power (ability to absorb casualties) of an American division. The War Department melded all recommendations into a divisional organization called the "square division"—a unit larger than most corps of contemporary British, French, and German divisions. It was composed of two infantry brigades (each with 8,500 infantrymen), one artillery brigade (one heavy and two light artillery regiments with a total of seventy-two guns), a combat engineer regiment, three machine gun battalions, plus signal and administrative units. Totaling 28,000 men, the division was strong (260 machine guns) but unwieldy and slow in reaction, maneuver, and movement by foot. It was found necessary to equip the soldiers of these divisions with the British Lee-Enfield rifle, as the U.S. armories, which had been providing the army's standard weapon, the 1903 Springfield, were unable to manufacture quickly the quantity of rifles that the wartime army required. After these huge divisions were organized into encampments, it was discovered that the great number of personnel in each unit caused problems in command and control for their inexperienced leaders. Furthermore, reorganizing the National Guard and Regular Army divisions according to this new table of organization and equipment created extreme turbulence at the very time that most organizations were being called to the colors.

It was obvious to Secretary Baker and to Army Chief of Staff Gen. Peyton C. March that AEF headquarters did not appreciate the problems with which the War Department was wrestling in matching limited resources to increasing demands. It was equally obvious to General Pershing that the War Department was failing to comprehend the enormity of his task—to organize a million-man theater of operations while receiving, training, equipping, and sustaining those early arrivals who were to flesh out the basic organizational structure itself.

Immediately after its arrival in France, the small AEF staff examined the organization of the British and French headquarters. Pershing approved a functional staff system for the AEF, modeled primarily upon that of the French,

U

with some attachments and sophistications based upon the fact that the American organization had to interact with the British and French forces, as well as French civil departments and agencies. Initially, the AEF planning staff was divided into three sections: operations, intelligence, and administration. Upon moving to their permanent headquarters at Chaumont, a more operationally oriented staff organization was effected. This AEF headquarters organization was based on a chief of staff and a four-way division of staff responsibilities among assistant chiefs, according to functions: that is, one staff agency was assigned responsibility for all matters having to do with personnel (G-1); one dealt with intelligence (G-2); one with operations and training (G-3)—training was later separated into its own staff function; and a final staff function dealt with supply and sustenance (G-4). Technical organizations and staffs, such as engineering and medical agencies abounded in association with these four, later five, primary staff functions. As the AEF staffs grew and their procedures became relatively standardized, the management of the war began to take on the appearance of a large business operation, as it had been for the Allies for the past three-and-a-half years.

Keeping uppermost in his mind that the United States desired to field a separate military force on the Western Front, General Pershing gained the approval of the Allies for the Americans to develop that force and support in the Lorraine sector of France, generally the area southeast of Verdun to the Swiss border. After the AEF opened its headquarters at Chaumont, the staff worked to establish the organizational and structural foundations of the American Expeditionary Force in France. The American sector was a relatively quiet portion of the front. However, because of its flanking location, close to German communication complexes and resource areas, it could pose a tremendous threat to the entire German front (a great salient into France north and west of the American area) if an American offensive were launched from there. It was also an excellent region for the establishment of the infrastructure necessary to support the AEF in the field from the ports and bases in the rear. While the British were generally established in the north of France, close to the English Channel ports for their support, and the French were established across the center of the fighting line, their location protecting the bulk of their vital installations and the capital

city of Paris, the area south of that of the French was relatively unencumbered by active Allied military installations. With improvements in the ports and throughput systems, it could function as an American operational area, based on the southwestern ports of France. It was upon this skein that Pershing and his growing staff built the complex organization of the American Expeditionary Force in France.

Out of the supply activities an organization grew to manage the "Line of Communications" functions from the ports to the rear boundaries of the combat forces. This was initially called the "Services of the Rear." It was divided into nine Base Sections for the receipt of supplies, each with one or more port complexes, an Intermediate Section in the center of the U.S. region for storage, classification, and transshipment of supplies, and an Advance Section for the distribution of supplies to the combat forces in the "Zone of Operations." Later this agency was called the "Service of Supply" (S.O.S.). Organizing these logistical activities while coordinating the shipment of supplies and personnel with the French, created many problems and bottlenecks. The organization became so large and its functions so complex as American forces arrived in the country that proposals were made to the secretary of war on several occasions, and ultimately to the President, that this agency be taken from General Pershing's personal supervision and made a separate organization, coequal with the AEF. Pershing rejected all these proposals, insisting that good management required that the theater commander be in command of all agencies in the theater.

With respect to training for battle, Pershing and most of the regular officers of the "Old Army," believed in the efficiency of the well-trained soldier using his rifle and bayonet. The "Regulars" were certain that the mass citizen army, formed by conscription with little professional leavening, would require extensive training and experience prior to undertaking combat operations. The AEF saw this training requirement as being largely the responsibility of the War Department and of the continental training establishment in the United States.

While Pershing expected the War Department to provide training guidance and doctrine appropriate to the battlefields of World War I, the department was unprepared for developing this doctrine, and clearly deferred to the AEF to provide recommendations in this regard. Pershing and his staff responded to their requests for guidance with a strong statement, the essence of which was that "the rifle and the bayonet remain the supreme weapons of the infantry soldier, and the success of the Army depends upon their proper use in open warfare." The AEF believed that the three years of trench warfare on the Western Front had established a "mind set" among the Allied commanders that was defensive in nature and accepted attrition in attack without seeking alternatives that would accomplish the same military objectives with fewer casualties. AEF leaders held that a self-confident individual soldier, skilled by training in bold maneuvers, could operate in open warfare on the Western Front. As the Americans gained direct combat experience in 1918, the AEF staff gradually formed tactics for the offensive, which muted their open warfare ideal with an appreciation of the realities of the power of defensive weaponry.

A greater problem than that caused by uncertain tactics was the extreme personnel upheaval taking place within army units in the United States. Divisions forming and training were frequently stripped of thousands of their troops to fill units deploying to France according to an accelerating schedule. Such drawdowns disrupted training—and required refilling of units with draftees and return to primary training. These moves gutted unit integrity and limited the time for commanders to get to know their men or to gain experience in leading their troops. Senior commanders and staff officers were absent, often on trips, attending boards, and busy with school details.

In the buildup of the AEF, which increased in geometric progression to a 2-million-man force, insufficient attention was given to the need for establishing supporting organizations, staffs, housekeeping, and labor elements. Thus, when the base support requirements became imperative, combat units were further stripped of civil specialists and technically qualified personnel to perform such functions—functions necessary to the equipping, sustaining, and processing of the combat units overseas and toward the front. The personnel chaos was compounded by an uneven flow of recruits from the draft levies. Adding to all this turmoil was the inadequacy of training facilities and the scarcity of weapons, equipment, and ammunition for training.

A major task for the new AEF headquarters was the training of American forces in France. It was recognized that the divisions shipped to the combat zone would require area training and acclimatization to the theater of war and to the nature of combat there. It was agreed between the AEF and the Allied headquarters that American divisions, on their arrival, would be placed in association with "veteran" French divisions—to be trained and to receive orientation and subsequently to take their place in the line as the final phase of their training.

To supplement this division-level training, the AEF established a large and sophisticated system of schools at corps and army level for training of men and officers as specialists in military skills and staff and command leadership—from horseshoeing to a General Staff College. The personnel requirements for staffing these schools, and the quotas for attendance, severely depleted the leadership of the first divisions arriving in France. After the early sessions of these schools, the quality of the students attending declined rapidly. Busy and harassed commanders preparing their units for combat, quite naturally, sent officers and men whom they could most afford to lose. A good man sent to school was lost at a critical time—and maybe lost forever—assigned to the school faculty or to a higher staff job. The AEF school system continued throughout the war, despite the intensity of combat. These schools graduated a total of 15,916 officers and 21,330 noncommissioned officers. All the courses were entirely too short for the nature of the training, and these were shortened again and canceled in the later rush to battle. Under the circumstances, they constituted a reasonable compromise between the demand for haste and the equally compelling demand for the preparation of soldiers for battle.

With respect to the organizational training of the deployed divisions, only the 1st Division (the first into France) went through the entire three-phase program, as prescribed by the AEF. The training of the next three American divisions to arrive was conducted according to the model of the 1st Division's training. The great German drive beginning on March 21, 1918, however, eliminated the third phase of the training of these divisions. Under the pressure of the circumstances that prevailed in April 1918, which demanded the early combat commitment of arriving divisions, the AEF shortened the division training to a four-week "first-phase" program of individual and small-unit training.

The peril that all the Allies recognized in 1918 was the growing reinforcement of German divisions on the Western Front, these divisions having been released from the Eastern Front by the surrender of Russia. The fear was that Germany would be able to launch the full weight of the Central Powers against the Western Front before the Americans arrived to balance the Central Powers' forces. On the other side of the line, the Central Powers were equally concerned with heavy losses. But their military leaders were confident that, by the rapid shifting of forces to the west, they could gain a final victory before the Americans could arrive in sufficient numbers. With this confidence, Gen. Erich Ludendorff, commander of the forces of the Central Powers, prepared his "spring offensive."

The Allies pressed the query: Where are the American reinforcements? The 1st Division had completed its training in the rear and had assumed a defensive position in the Vosges, a quiet sector of the line, on Oct. 21, 1917. On November 3, a German raid caught them unprepared; three American soldiers were killed, five were wounded, and twelve captured—the first American casualties in the war. By the end of 1917, four American divisions were in France. Two more were on the way. A total of 9,804 officers and 165,080 men were assigned to the AEF. The AEF continued to emphasize training, and the organization of a balanced, self-sustaining force, including a sizable administrative and logistical support complex. The small number of American combat forces compared to support forces was very disappointing to the Allies. Their entreaties for assignment of individuals and small units of American infantrymen as "fillers" in their armies now took on more strident tones.

In January 1918, Pershing made two positive responses to this continuing pressure. Agreeing with the Allies that the program for moving American divisions into the line should be expedited, Pershing also agreed to a British plan to expedite the shipment of American riflemen and machine gun units to France for training and service with the British, using British ships. Pershing insisted that the units involved would be trained for major independent operations and that they be returned to the American command when called for. The agreement, concluded on January 30, involved six American divisions; it was called the "Six-Division Plan." The British agreed on the ultimate return of American divisions, but their later complaints showed that they expected to employ these di-

visions indefinitely. As German power increased on the Western Front, so did the Allied demands for more American troops in France. On Jan. 19, 1918, the U.S. 1st Division took over a sector of the fighting line north of Toul. This sector was to be expanded to include an American corps, then an American army. The U.S. 26th Division ended its training and entered the line the Chemin des Dames sector on February 8; on February 21, the 42d Division entered the French line near Luneville. The 2d Division was brigaded with the French in the Verdun area on March 18.

The Germans, having trained their troops to attack closely following a rolling barrage of artillery, struck on the morning of March 21, after a short but intensive artillery barrage that was heavy in gas and smoke. Aided also by a thick fog, small groups of highly trained "shock troops" rushed forward; bypassing centers of Allied resistance, they seized vital terrain.

On April 9, the Germans struck again, this time along the Lys River in the British sector of Flanders, north of the Amiens salient. A third German offensive struck the French Fifth and Sixth armies in the Aisne region, south of the first penetration. This drive broke through the defenses on the Chemin des Dames on May 27 and gained twenty miles the first day. Three days later, the German forces stood on the banks of the Marne River at Château-Thierry, less than fifty miles from Paris—a position that they had not been able to reach since the early days of 1914.

In this crisis, the Allies renewed their pressures on Pershing, and even on President Wilson, for American infantry replacements for their forces. Pershing reluctantly concurred with Allied demands, which, by June 1, urged the shipment of 300,000 U.S. troops per month—to a total of 100 U.S. divisions. The War Department staff broke all precedent and plans to ship riflemen and machine gunners, the shipments reaching the tremendous total of 30,000 per day. The War Department staff tried to show that such shipments wrecked training and equipping schedules. They also tried to reason with AEF headquarters to the effect that 100 U.S. divisions in France would equal the strength of the entire force of the Central Powers on the Western Front. But the circumstances of the hour were urgent. The Allies promised to provide artillery and other support for these "light" divisions coming into the theater and again agreed, in principle, to return these for the creation of an American Army—as soon as the crisis was over. They also agreed that excess Allied shipping would be used to bring over personnel for the AEF's support structure.

The AEF's commitment of the American divisions in France to the Western Front at the Marne River helped sustain the fragile Allied defenses. By the night of May 31, 1918, the 3d Division was dug in at Château-Thierry on the Marne. On June 1, the 2d Division took positions north of the Marne, west of Château-Thierry, protecting the main route to Paris. Ludendorff, convinced that he was on the brink of a breakthrough, threw his reserves against the hastily deployed Americans. For the first days in June, the issue was in doubt at the highest headquarters—but not on the line. The Americans had stiffened the Allied defenses; their aggressiveness had inspired the weary French. Together, they stopped the German offensive cold.

Meanwhile, the 1st Division, in the first American offensive operation of the war, had attacked on May 28 and seized Cantigny and commanding ground at the tip of the Amiens salient. Holding on desperately, despite furious counterattacks, it lost more than 1,600 men but maintained its positions. On June 6, the 2d Division counterattacked. The fighting was fierce in Belleau Wood, Bouresches, and Vaux, but the Americans moved forward. These counterattacks stopped the German offensive all along the line. Total casualties for the American debut were 11,384. While the United States contribution resulted in only modest gains, it did provide bloody affirmations of American combat capability both to skeptical Allies and scornful enemy.

At the time, U.S. organizational and logistical problems were under tenuous control, but the problem of shipping more and more men became a nightmare of changes in schedules, commitments, and drawdowns on reserves for the War Department. The personnel and equipment shipping schedules reached their peak during the summer of 1918. The rapid changes in plans and programs were not fully coordinated with the military supply agencies and throughput facilities. Not only were there considerable problems within the continental United States (problems that saw the shipment to Europe of troops in a relatively untrained state, lacking uniforms, weapons, and equipment), but there were also tremendous backlogs of supplies at the ports in southern France

and at the various support installations within the Service of Supply. The War Department again tried to bring the S.O.S. under its direct control in order to improve the flow of troops and supplies, but the AEF again rejected this proposal.

On the Western Front, the German forces, although physically close to Paris, were fading rapidly in strength as June turned into July. Marshal Ferdinand Foch, supreme Allied commander, reported that the Germans still outnumbered the Allies—but the weight of numbers was fast swinging to the Allies. Foch was even preparing a counteroffensive when the Germans launched a drive in the Champagne-Marne region—their final offensive of the war. On the Marne River, a French division was outflanked and folded rearward, leaving the American 3d Division beset on three sides. Their steadfast defenses earned the division the title "The Rock of the Marne." Going around the Americans, the driving Germans "forced" the Marne and established a sizable bridgehead southwest of Reims; British divisions moved in and stopped the advance. French resistance around the Marne bridgehead anchored on the American 3d Division. Even as the Germans were attacking in the Champagne-Marne area, Foch launched a limited counterattack on July 18, in the Soissons region, to cut the German supply route from Soissons to Château-Thierry. The U.S. 1st and 2d divisions led this attack, under the French Tenth and Sixth armies, respectively. Some American units reached their attack positions on the run at "H hour" (the time for beginning the attack). Preceded by a short, heavy bombardment of artillery, in a rainstorm, the units jumped off at 4:30 A.M. The attack hit "trench" (second-rate) German divisions; it was a complete surprise. Assisted by French tanks, American and French divisions made gains of up to five miles the first day. This success caused the offensive to be extended to the east. When notified of the Allied gains, Ludendorff shifted reserves to Soissons, canceled the attack on Reims, and, later, abandoned the planning for an offensive in Flanders.

The American 3d, 4th, 26th, and 28th divisions took part in the Allied drive east and northeast; the American I and III Corps began actively directing the advance in their sectors, joined by the U.S. 32d, 42d, and 77th divisions. On July 19, the German resistance stiffened; then Ludendorff directed a phased withdrawal from the Marne salient to the line of the Aisne and Vesle rivers, covered by "stay-behind" machine gun teams and artillery barrages. The Allied counteroffensive halted at the new German positions on August 6. Eight American divisions had performed credibly in the offensive.

With the denouement of fighting along the Aisne-Vesle line, Pershing requested, on August 9, that the American forces be concentrated in one army in the Woëvre, with an offensive against the St. Mihiel salient their first responsibility. Foch agreed. Accordingly, with the cooperation of Marshal Henri Pétain, commander of the French forces, Pershing activated the American First Army in Lorraine on August 10 and placed it under the operational control of Pétain. By that time, a total of 1,275,000 Americans were in France, including thirty-five divisions. Most did not have their authorized complement of artillery, the result of the expedited shipment of infantry units. American corps artillery was nonexistent. Initially, Pershing assigned fourteen divisions to the First Army. He requested a tremendous level of Allied support for the upcoming St. Mihiel offensive, including 266 batteries of artillery, 450 tanks, and 21 aircraft squadrons. Nearly all of this requested support, or its equivalent, was provided by the French.

The St. Mihiel salient had existed as a threatening bulge into the French lines, fifteen to twenty-six miles south of Verdun, since its seizure by the Germans in September 1914. In 1915, the French had conducted many unsuccessful assaults to eliminate this salient. The St. Mihiel region had been selected for the offensive to "christen" the American First Army since it appeared to present a relatively easy task for that strong force. It was also likely to provide an early success, more symbolic than important to the Allied cause. It would give the American forces, and their people at home, a long-awaited victory for American arms. From a logistical standpoint, it was the focal point of most of the American lines of supply and communication from their ports in the south and southwest of France.

In organizing the forces for the First Army's attack on the salient, a tremendous reshuffling was necessary to gather American divisions that were scattered in training camps or serving with the Allies. Marshal Pétain was agreeable to releasing those requested by Pershing; the AEF was taking over a portion of his area of responsibility. As Pershing had

feared, British Marshal Sir Douglas Haig was disturbed at having to honor an agreement he had made when the Six-Division Plan was executed. The British were planning, and hoping, for an American army in their zone to be based at Dunkerque. Pershing reluctantly agreed to British retention of the American II Corps, with the U.S. 27th and 30th divisions, for the upcoming fall campaign.

This experience with the British highlighted the continuing pressure being exerted by all the Allies to use American troops to spare their own men and to forward their plans. Even the Italians were pressing for an American front in Italy. Foch also recommended the greater integration of American and French logistical support. The great blow to the independence of the American military effort came on Aug. 3, 1918, the same day General Pershing assumed command of the United States First Army (while retaining command of the AEF). General Foch visited Pershing's headquarters at Ligny-en-Barrois. After the usual pleasantries, Foch presented an entirely new plan for the employment of American forces. Pointing out the great success of the ongoing Allied offensives, especially in the north, and the relative disarray of the German forces, Foch then presented his concept for exploiting that continuing success and preventing German reorganization. The British, supported by the left of the French armies, would continue to attack in the general direction of Cambrai-St. Quentin. The center of the French armies would continue their "energetic" actions to throw the enemy behind the Aisne. The AEF's St. Mihiel operation should begin by September 10; the attack should be limited to reaching the Vignuelles-Regneville line, eliminating the salient only. Four to six American divisions should be turned over to the French Second Army for attack between the Meuse River and the Argonne Forest; an American army of eight to ten American divisions should be employed immediately west of the Argonne on both sides of the Aisne River to attack in conjunction with the French Fourth Army. The attacks on either side of the Argonne were to be made between September 10 and 20. To assist Pershing in planning and in directing the offensive west of the Argonne, two French generals should be assigned to the commander-in-chief of the American Army.

Pershing immediately objected to this late change in plans, and especially to dismembering the American Army. He made several offers for alternative employment of the First Army—all of which were rejected by Foch. After a second meeting in Foch's headquarters, it was agreed that the AEF would carry out a limited attack at St. Mihiel; then, the AEF was to move its forces to conduct a major offensive in the Meuse-Argonne region two weeks later. These changes in the AEF mission tended to overshadow the upcoming attack on the St. Mihiel salient. Downgraded to a limited offensive by a total of fourteen divisions (only six of which would make the initial assault), the preparations for the attack continued amid a veritable whirlwind of planning and movement for the Meuse-Argonne offensive to follow.

As railway and motor transport became available, the divisions for St. Mihiel, and their support, were shifted into position, and 3,000 artillery pieces, half of them manned by Americans, were moved into support positions. Ammunition totaling 40,000 tons was moved into forward dumps. A network of telephone, telegraph, wireless (radio), and pigeon communications systems was installed. Railheads were established in nineteen locations to break out daily supplies to the combat units. As many as 2,000 French trucks assisted in moving the men and material. The revised and final order for the St. Mihiel offensive directed an attack by I Corps, with five divisions, and IV Corps, with four divisions, against the south flank of the salient, with the objective of sealing it off from Vigneulles to Regneville. V Corps, with three divisions, was to attack along the line of Les Éparges-Vigneulles. The attack was to be conducted in two phases, linking up on the second day. The French II Colonial Corps, with three divisions around the southwest ring of the salient, was to advance after the American attacks had cleared the areas on the flanks.

After considering a number of offensive and defensive alternatives, German General Ludendorff ordered withdrawal from the salient to the "Michel-Stellung" defenses at the northern base of the salient—choosing that option in view of the Allied advances in Flanders and the tremendous American buildup. Execution of the withdrawal began on September 11; the American attack jumped off at 5 A.M. on September 12. Preceded by an intensive four-hour barrage by 3,000 artillery pieces and accompanied by 267 light tanks under the command of LtCol. George Patton, the infantry troops slogged forward in the rain. They struck and quickly overran the German rear guards. A "combined aviation element" of 1,500 American, French, British, Italian, and Portuguese planes, 600 under Col. William "Billy" Mitchell, gained and maintained air superiority and supported the attack. Air and artillery interdicted enemy columns attempting to move north out of the pocket.

The advance was rapid and coordination was good. Most of the tanks fell victim to mechanical failure or ran out of fuel, but the infantry moved rapidly. Both American and Allied leaders had worried about the U.S. infantry crossing the barbed wire because artillery had failed to cut gaps, and "bangalore torpedoes" to blow the wire and wire cutters were limited in supply. Some of the troops used chicken wire to breach the obstacles. Others stepped on the wire and just walked over it. The French were amazed and claimed it was possible only because the Americans had big feet.

By nightfall of the first day, the converging American divisions on the south and west were only ten miles from juncture. By the next morning U.S. forces had met and closed the gap on the salient. Strong U.S. patrols probed the Michel-Stellung, and the AEF headquarters was planning to attack Metz. But, according to prior agreement with the Allies, the operation was declared to be successfully over. Congratulations came from Allied forces and headquarters and from President Wilson. Critics, however, pointed out that the enemy had presented no great challenge. The Americans "merely relieved the Germans." Whatever the case, it is inarguable that 200 square miles of territory had been returned to France, and a dangerous salient had been removed. Over 1,500 prisoners of war were taken; also captured were 450 artillery pieces. American casualties were about 7,000.

The AEF was committed to an offensive in the Meuse-Argonne (twenty miles north of Verdun) as the Americans were beginning the first offensive in the St. Mihiel region some sixty miles to the south. Three corps headquarters, fifteen divisions, Allied fire support, and a whole skein of logistical and communication units had to displace forward. The totals involved were approximately 600,000 Americans moving in; 220,000 French moving out. Also moving into the sector were 3,980 artillery guns and 90,000 horses; these moved in a steady stream, forwarding personnel, equipment, and the great requirement of 900,000 tons of ammunition and supplies over three muddy farm roads and three single-track railroads. For secrecy, this huge and diverse agglomeration of men, animals, equipment, and materiel had to be moved only at night.

The assembly of logistical, communication, and administrative elements for the Meuse-Argonne campaign, mostly by the Service of Supply, was itself a complex undertaking, linking hundreds of agencies together by a fragile network of roads and rails. Ammunition depots were established at twenty-four locations to store and send forward 40,000 tons of ammunition per day. Railheads at nineteen points provided automatic resupply to the army. Aviation personnel and equipment gathered at forward fields. Of the 668,000 personnel assigned to the Service of Supply, 291,000 were engaged in direct logistical support of the First Army, including the personnel of the three divisions used as laborers in the rear.

The American First Army headquarters moved to Souilly on September 21. At midnight on September 22, Pershing accepted the responsibility for the entire zone formerly held by the French Second Army. This zone included the entire sector from the Moselle River west to the juncture with the French Fourth Army in the west of the Argonne Forest. The First Army also assumed operational command of the French II Colonial Corps and XVII Corps, both corps, along with elements of the American III Corps, defending territory from the east bank of the Meuse to the Moselle. By prior agreement of the Allies, the bulk of the supporting weapons systems continued to be provided by the French. Approximately one-half of these weapons were manned by Americans.

The First Army planned to attack across the zone with three corps abreast, each with three attacking divisions. A total of 2,775 artillery pieces, more than half of them manned by the French, were to support the attack. Poised at support airfields were 821 aircraft, 604 of which were manned by Americans. But the U.S. soldiers in the attacking divisions had little or no experience in active combat; only four divisions had had any front-line duty. The "Yanks" had overwhelming superiority in fighting strength—on the order of eight to one, depending upon who and what is counted. They were far stronger in artillery, in aircraft, and in tanks—the Germans had no tanks in this campaign. The enemy, however, were in strong fortifications. Three lines of fortified defenses faced the Americans. Montfaucon, in the center of the

sector, was the key position in the defense. On the right, the heights along the Meuse dominated the east of the zone; on the army's left, the Argonne Forest was a maze of camouflaged, mutually supporting strong points. Along the front in the sector were eighteen divisions, with twelve more in reserve. Five divisions were in defense in the immediate zone into which the Americans would attack. The enemy troops were of poor quality; a large number were Saxons and Austro-Hungarians, who had doubtful dedication to the German cause. Their High Command ordered a "stubborn defense in Lorraine."

On September 26, at 5:30 A.M., U.S. infantry attacked in the Meuse-Argonne, moving behind a rolling artillery barrage about 100 yards to the front. In a heavy fog mixed with cordite smoke, accompanied by the incessant roar of artillery, the doughboys climbed in and out of great shell holes, bunching up at the enemy barbed wire. Some men in the lead assault became lost; others drifted into the low ground, where they gathered in groups. But Yankee spirit was up, and the pressure of those advancing from behind pushed the line of contact forward. The initial German defenses were quickly overrun—the enemy had manned these lightly and would make his stand on the first prepared *stellung*. The tanks supporting the American attack came forward slowly, many breaking down a few hundred yards into the attack. Control of the supporting artillery was poor because it was difficult to ascertain the exact location of the attackers. The artillery continued firing their prearranged barrages blindly.

At 9:30 A.M., the sun broke through the mist. At the same time, some of the American mystique evaporated too. Whenever the Americans burst into a patch of open terrain, they were hit by frontal and flanking fire from hidden machine guns. The "green" troops moved well until they hit the first effective enemy fire; then, according to friendly and enemy observers, they tended to "mill about," remaining in the killing zone, taking no action to engage the enemy. This was, clearly, a failure in small-unit leadership and training.

On the east, III Corps made the best early advance, its forward elements moving abreast of Montfaucon. In the center, V Corps was mostly pinned down on the approach bridges of Montfaucon. Advancing slowly on the left was I Corps, with high casualties from the hidden defenses in the Argonne Forest. On the second day, in hard and bloody fighting, V Corps took Montfaucon, and the other corps came abreast. First Army was only a day behind their optimistic time schedule, but casualties were high, and the attacking units were lacking support. The American offensive had run out of steam.

To get the offensive moving again, the AEF moved the best of the veteran divisions from St. Mihiel into the fighting line, replacing the depleted attacking forces. Reconstituting the support forces was a more difficult problem. Rain continued to fall, and the roads and trails through no-man's-land turned into quagmires. Craters and shell holes from earlier fighting had limited the capacity of these routes at the beginning of the offensive; by this time, they were virtually impassable. Long lines of traffic were stalled for days. Wounded could not be evacuated; food and ammunition could not get forward. By September 28, the First Army was literally dead in its tracks.

Overworked engineers struggled to shore up the roadbeds with any solid material they could find. Reserve units, headquarters personnel, and even malingerers drifting rearward were pressed into service to move the traffic and shore up the roadway. By the evening of September 28, all artillery had been shifted forward. But divisions continued to report communication and supply problems through the end of the month. Many units were without food for days. Tank strength had been reduced to one-third by breakdowns and by accurate enemy artillery fire. The AEF had undergone its baptism of fire. It had met the challenge of the Meuse-Argonne and advanced. Badly mauled and mired in the mud in front of the main German defenses, the Kriemhilde-Stellung, it was hardly a victorious army.

In the next week, enemy strength increased to twenty-seven divisions, with eleven between the Meuse and the Argonne. Many of these divisions were very low in strength. However, they had orders to defend to the last man. On October 4, the U.S. First Army resumed its offensive—with rested troops and wiser, somewhat more experienced leaders. These attacks were being made against the main German defenses of the Kriemhilde-Stellung. Key positions in this defensive complex were the heights of Cunel in III Corps' zone, Romagne and the Argonne ridges in I Corps' zone. These defenses were supported by interlocking direct fires and observed artillery fire from flanking promonto-

ries and from the heights east of the Meuse. The First Army directed all commanders to use more air support, use smoke on enemy observation points, and maneuver so as to avoid flanking fire. Acting in concert, III Corps and V Corps were to seize both the Cunel heights and those on the east of Romagne. The remainder of V Corps, together with I Corps, were to take the Romagne heights.

The infantry attack moved out at 5:30 A.M., October 4, and immediately made heavy contact with the enemy all along the front. III Corps fought its way up the approaches of the Cunel heights, but the troops stalled under heavy fire from the hills. V Corps also moved forward on the low ground southwest of Cunel, but it too was halted in bitter fighting. I Corps made the greatest advance on the left of the First Army, driving down the Aire valley with tanks leading behind rolling barrages. The 77th Division on the left of I Corps was still struggling in the Argonne, with minor gains. The offensive was stopped again, but heavy fighting continued as divisions consolidated their gains.

Galled by Allied demands for greater American progress, General Pershing decided to broaden his attacking zone and bring more U.S. forces into the offensive. He appointed MajGen. Hunter Liggett (I Corps commander) commander of the First Army and created a Second Army, under the command of MajGen. Robert Bullard (who had commanded III Corps). First Army was to seize the heights of Cunel and Romagne and to take Grandpré without delay. On October 14, the weary and ill American troops drove into the teeth of the defensive fires. V Corps took the heights of Romagne quickly, and this broke the "crown" of the Kriemhilde defenses. III Corps then took the Cunel defenses, while, in hand-to-hand fighting, I Corps drove the Germans out of Grandpré. The Americans now held the high ground, and their artillery could strike the vital German railroad through Sedan. But the army was nearing combat ineffectiveness; casualties had reached 100,000 with half these losses due to the Spanish influenza epidemic. The Second Army also was stalled on the heights east of the Meuse. Despite demands from Pershing to continue the offensive, Liggett rested and refitted his army and visited his subordinate commands.

The First Army was ordered to prepare to attack to uncover the heights overlooking Sedan. Second Army was to make a coordinated

U

attack into the Woëvre plain. The AEF was now a far more professional fighting force than that which had begun the campaign. It was said that the Americans had "learned to fight by fighting."

At 3:30 A.M. on November 1, the black of night burst bright as day, as the last barrage of the war struck the enemy positions "like millions of hammers." The infantry assault jumped off at 5:30 A.M., the doughboys following the customary rolling barrage. This time, however, smoke and gas were adjusted along the flanks of the advancing forces. The artillery preparations devastated the enemy's defenses. The attackers closed quickly on their objectives; active strong points were invested by direct fire weapons, while the bulk of the troops swung around these and surged forward. The German defenses broke, the defenders fleeing northward, followed by the fast-moving Yanks. By November 4, First Army had advanced twenty miles.

The Germans began a general withdrawal to a new line north of the Meuse. The Americans continued their pursuit. On November 5, III Corps and V Corps crossed the Meuse, and I Corps reached a point on the heights five miles south of Sedan. The American Second Army moved east into the Woëvre plain on November 9 and continued their advance while First Army secured the heights over Sedan. Both armies were planning further pursuits north and east when the Armistice was declared. At the eleventh hour on the eleventh day of the eleventh month of 1918, the fighting ceased.

The AEF had fought through the Argonne, uncovered the Meuse, and secured control of the heights south of Sedan. The Meuse-Argonne campaign lasted forty-seven days. A total of 1.2 million Americans were engaged in the campaign, of which 850,000 were combat troops. Twenty-two American divisions were engaged in the battle; 2,417 artillery pieces supported this fighting, firing a total of more than 4 million shells. The American ground battle was supported by 840 airplanes, nearly all of these manufactured by the Allies. In addition, 324 tanks also supported the American campaign in the Meuse-Argonne; all of these tanks were manufactured by Allied industries, and many were manned by Allied troops. The AEF claimed to have drawn to the Meuse-Argonne a total of forty-four enemy divisions. AEF headquarters reported the capture of 26,000 prisoners of war. It also listed the capture of 874 artillery pieces and over 3,000 machine guns and claimed to have inflicted 100,000 enemy casualties at a cost of 117,000 American casualties.

After congratulations, came Allied criticisms, and efforts to downplay the importance of the U.S. contribution to the victory on the Western Front. The U.S. victory in the Meuse-Argonne was, by any measure, an important part of the Allied victory.

Paul F. Braim

Bibliography

Baldwin, Hanson. *World War I: An Outline History*. New York: Harper & Row, 1962.

Braim, Paul F. *The Test of Battle: The AEF in the Meuse Argonne Campaign*. Newark: University of Delaware Press, 1983.

Pershing, John J. *My Experiences in the World War*. 2 vols. New York: Stokes, 1931.

Smythe, Donald. *Pershing: General of the Armies*. Bloomington: Indiana University Press, 1986.

Toland, John. *No Man's Land: 1918, the Last Year of the Great War*. New York: Ballantine, 1985.

United States Army: 1st Division

In early May 1917, MajGen. John J. Pershing received a telegram from army Chief of Staff MajGen. Hugh L. Scott, who directed him to select four infantry regiments and one artillery regiment from his Southern Department to form a provisional division for service in France. Pershing picked the 16th, 18th, 26th, and 28th Infantry regiments and the 6th Field Artillery Regiment. When "Black Jack" Pershing arrived in Washington, D.C., on May 10, Scott informed him that he had been advanced over other senior officers and would command a division in France. Later the 5th and 7th Field Artillery regiments were added, along with a number of "necessary auxiliary units" to form the "expeditionary division" at a strength of 14,000 men.

Beyond selecting the infantry and artillery units for the new division, no model existed to fill out its "interior organization." Within days, as Pershing was pondering this problem of shaping his new command, Secretary of War Newton D. Baker, a self-confident former Cleveland lawyer, notified Pershing that he was to be commander-in-chief of all American forces in France. Instead of a nonexistent division, he now had to form an entire field army. The command of the 1st Division fell to MajGen. William J. Sibert, an engineer with Panama Canal experience. Pershing knew two of the division's brigade commanders well—BGens. Robert L. Bullard and Omar Bundy—but he had only a casual professional acquaintance with Sibert.

In order for the very large new division of the Regular Army—it had already begun to grow beyond the anticipated strength of 14,000 men by the addition of machine gun units and other supplements—to become an efficient combat organization, a rigorous training curriculum was needed. In this regard, the division was fortunate to have men like Bullard and a young operations officer named George C. Marshall.

After arrival in France on June 26, the 2d Battalion of the 16th Infantry Regiment paraded in Paris on July 4. The battalion was joined a few days later by the other units for a bumpy ride in French "40 and 8" boxcars to Gondrecourt. The artillery regiments began their voyage from Hoboken, New Jersey, to France in late July. Other units of the division arrived at Gondrecourt by early September, although a few support units did not join for another six months. Training began almost immediately there for most of the division and at Le Valdahon for the division's artillery units. The seasoned veterans of the French 47th Division, Chasseurs Alpins (the "Blue Devils") were the teachers for the green but eager Americans. Eventually, as the basic skills of marksmanship and survival were acquired, the Americans were sent to the front for some battle experience with French units. Despite Pershing's consistent refusal to let his units be used as fillers in depleted Allied formations and his rejection of trench warfare in favor of "open" warfare, he understood that training was best administered by those who knew its realities.

The division and the American Expeditionary Force (AEF) lost their first three soldiers, killed in action, on Nov. 3, 1917, during a German trench raid on the 16th Infantry positions along the Lorraine front. Cpl. James B. Gresham and Pvts. Thomas F. Enright and Merle D. Hay took their positions at the top of the division's honor roll, which would number more than 5,300 names by the end of the war.

Command of the division passed from MajGen. William J. Sibert to MajGen. Robert L. Bullard on Dec. 14, 1917. In recalling his assumption of command in a book published in 1925, Bullard noted that Pershing valued him most as a field commander. Bullard brought with him six months of practical experience in training American units in France in the AEF schools. Under his leadership, the 1st Division pointed toward certain commitment to combat operations in the near future by applying the lessons Bullard had learned from the French and British. Throughout the spring of 1918, the division sent staff and line officers to the front to study operations and procedures. For Bullard and Pershing, the task was to make the transition from trench warfare to open warfare, where marksmanship and maneuver by infantry units would restore the initiative to the attacking force.

The American infantry division had grown into a very large, formidable fighting unit consisting of two brigades of two infantry regiments each, an artillery brigade of three or four regiments, a support "train" of supply, transport, and service units, and many miscellaneous smaller specialized units to care for the more than 28,000 men and nearly 8,000 draft animals.

Having completed their initial indoctrination to trench warfare in the Toul sector by early April, the entire division was put in motion for transfer to the Cantigny sector about fifty miles north of Paris. The French 45th and 162d Colonial divisions moved left and right on the line to make room for the 1st Division. The commander of the French VI Corps, to which the 1st Division was now assigned, greeted his new fighting Yanks with General Order No. 32, published on April 20, 1918, noting that his corps was "particularly proud to gather to its side, before the enemy, the troops of the noble American nation and to wish them a cordial welcome." Pershing's wish for American fighting men to be in the line, under their own commanders and responsible for their own sector, had been fulfilled. Before the men of the 1st Division lay the fight at Cantigny, May 28–31.

As LtCol. George C. Marshall recalled in his memoirs of World War I service, Cantigny was a very small incident in a very large drama that was unfolding farther south. But for the Americans it was the fight at hand. It was their first battle. Marshall knew that success was essential because all the eyes of the Allied armies were on them, and morale needed a boost everywhere.

The 28th Infantry Regiment was given the principal attack assignment and was withdrawn several days before the attack to conduct rehearsals. It would be supported by the rest of the division and French tanks, artillery, flame throwers, and a few aircraft. Attacking the small rural village of several hundred people, most of whom had fled or were hiding in cellars, the Americans rushed forward on May 28 at 6:40 A.M. and seized the objective by 7:20 A.M. They waited for the inevitable German counterattacks, which soon came with the expected ferocity. For the next two and one-half days, the divisions shuddered under the weight of artillery and mortar fire, followed by counterattacks from the German 82d Reserve Division, which had been holding the village. On May 28, General Pershing wrote to General Bullard and told him that his division had made an important contribution, even though the action was a small one. As the division regrouped on May 31, they counted 1,067 of their number as casualties, with fewer than 100 of those incurred in the assault of May 28.

After some badly needed rest and refitting in Picardy, despite the hardship of short rations and the abominable conditions in the trenches, the 1st Division was alerted on July 4 for participation in the reduction of the Marne salient. As they departed Picardy, General Vandenburg, commander of the French X Corps, commended the American doughboys and proclaimed them "The Men of Cantigny." On July 15, 1918, MajGen. Charles P. Summerall, formerly commander of the division's artillery brigade, took over command of the 1st Division from General Bullard.

In the Marne salient, near Soissons, the division fought a series of engagements from July 18 to July 23. Places with names such as Missy, Ploisy, and Chazelle ravines and the villages of Berzy-le-Sec and Buzancy lay within the French XX Corps' sector at the base of the salient, to which the victors of Cantigny were assigned.

BGen. Beaumont B. Buck, who commanded the division's 2d Brigade, wrote in his memoirs that after Soissons battalions had been reduced to companies in size and companies might have only several dozen men in them. Every infantry battalion commander was a casualty; the division had suffered 7,317 casualties (killed, wounded, missing, and prisoners) but remained intact as an effective fighting unit. General Mangin, commander of the French Tenth Army, commended his "American Comrades! I am grateful to you for the blood so generously spilled on the soil of my country. I am proud to have commanded you during such days."

A brief tour of duty in the Saizerais sector preceded the next major battle of the division. The men of Cantigny had returned to the Gondrecourt area, where they had begun their training more than a year previously. The order of the day was more training. Even though the division was battle-hardened, there were always the new replacements to be indoctrinated. On Sept. 1, 1918, the rumble of artillery at St. Mihiel drew the attention of the veterans.

The heights of the Meuse River near St. Mihiel formed a deep pocket in the terrain held by the French. Mont Sec towered above all who tried to maneuver in the low marshes below. The St. Mihiel salient had been a thorn in the side of the Allies since 1915. The attack on the salient from the south between Mont Sec and the Moselle River was made by the U.S. IV Corps, with the 1st Division holding the left of the line. The division's front extended from Xivray to Seicheprey, a distance of about 2,700 yards. This was familiar ground to the experienced members of the division. They had occupied the same sector from January through March.

As with all deliberate attacks, much attention was given to artillery preparations and engineering. At 1:00 A.M. on September 12, the darkness was shattered by the blinding light of the artillery barrage; the attack was underway. Two days later, the 1st Division was "pinched out" by other advancing units and was regrouped in reserve. The offensive was a great Allied victory.

The final offensive for the 1st Division was the Meuse-Argonne. Initially in army reserve as part of the U.S. III Corps, which was commanded by General Bullard, the division was transferred to the U.S. I Corps on September 29 and ordered to relieve the U.S. 35th Division by daylight on October 1. The Argonne Forest was a nightmare—a tangle of shell holes, shattered trees, and elaborate fortifications and pillboxes sprouting machine guns. When passersby warned the men of Cantigny what lay ahead, someone retorted from the ranks, "We are the boys who can do it."

In the path of the division was the village of Fleville, which, like Soissons before it, would be revisited by the men of the "Big Red One" twenty-six years later. The battle began on October 4 with the crash of a barrage 220 yards in front of the division's front lines. Eight days later, on the evening of October 11–12, the 1st Division was relieved. General Summerall was promoted to command of the U.S. V Corps. The 1st Division had advanced 5 miles and defeated elements of eight enemy divisions. More than 7,500 men of the division were casualties. Each regiment left 100 men to finish burying their dead.

After a brief respite, the division again entered the line on November 5. German resistance was rapidly disintegrating as the Allied armies rushed forward toward Sedan, but pockets of bypassed and isolated German soldiers fought fiercely. When the guns finally fell silent on November 11, the 1st Division could at last catch its breath. BGens. Frank E. Bamford and Frank Parker, who had ably commanded the division successively as acting commanders, were followed by MajGen. Edward F. McGlachlin, Jr., who assumed command on November 21.

General Pershing issued his famous commendation for the men of the 1st Division on November 19 in paragraph 4 of General Order No. 201: "The Commander-in-Chief has noted in this Division a special pride of service and a high state of morale, never broken by hardship nor battle."

The 1st Division entered Coblenz, Germany, on December 12 and crossed the Rhine River on December 13 with the 3d Battalion, 18th Infantry in the van. The division headquarters was established at Montabaur. Life in the Coblenz bridgehead included special events, such as the all-soldier-produced circus and athletic competition with other units. The division newspaper, the *Bridgehead Sentinel*, published its first issue on Feb. 24, 1919, following the formation of the Society of the 1st Division on February 11. The society held its first celebration at Montabaur on June 6, a tradition that continues unbroken to this date.

Field Marshal Henri Pétain visited Coblenz on July 18 and decorated the colors of each of the division's regiments with the Croix de Guerre. As other American units were relieved and returned to the United States, the 1st Division took over the entire American bridgehead. In August, the division began its long road home, leaving behind a few units to serve with the American forces in Germany. Five soldiers of the division had received the Medal of Honor

for their gallantry and heroism in combat. Distinguished Service Crosses and French decorations too numerous to list hung on the tunics of many 1st Division veterans.

The famous patch consisting of a red numeral "1" on an olive-drab shield was fashioned, probably by a soldier using common materials found in the war zone—bits of uniform cloth. At a later time the division would adopt the motto that is its hallmark today—"No mission too difficult, no sacrifice too great, duty first!" The official motto of this historic division simply states—VICTORY.

John F. Votaw

Bibliography

Butler, Albert B., Jr. *"HAPPY DAYS!": A Humorous Narrative in Drawings of the Progress of American Arms, 1917–1919.* Washington, DC: Society of the First Division, 1928.

Coffman, Edward M. *The War to End All Wars: The American Military Experience in World War I.* New York: Oxford University Press, 1968.

Marshall, George C. *Memoirs of My Services in the World War, 1917–1918.* Boston: Houghton Mifflin, 1976.

Patch, MajGen. Joseph D. *A Soldier's War: The First Infantry Division, AEF (1917–1918).* Corpus Christi, TX: Mission Press, 1966.

Society of the 1st Division. *History of the 1st Division During the World War, 1917–1919.* Philadelphia: Winston, 1922.

United States Army: 2d Division

By any measure, the 2d Division established a World War I combat record that is, as proclaimed in its motto, "Second to None." In the vanguard of AEF divisions ready for combat, "The Indianheads" (from their shoulder patch) fought early in the critical defense of the Marne above Paris in June 1918, under the French XX Corps at Soissons in mid-July, and under Pershing's newly formed United States First Army in the few days of St. Mihiel. They were loaned back to the French Fourth Army for the ordeal of Blanc Mont in early October, and came back to the First Army for the final phase of the Meuse-Argonne campaign beginning November 1. The division remained with the Army of Occupation of the Rhineland until August 1919.

An AEF division, at 28,000 men about twice the size of a French or British division, was organized with, as its basic combat elements, four regiments formed into two brigades. The 2d Division, however, was unique in having its 3d Brigade consist of the army's historic 9th and 23d Infantry units, while the 4th Brigade was formed from the U.S. Marine Corps' 5th and 6th regiments. As a further historic distinction, the "Marine Brigade" was commanded by the Army's BGen. James G. Harbord in the Belleau Wood action, and Marine Corps MajGen. John A. Lejeune commanded the entire division from late July until the end of the war and through the occupation.

The United States declared war on April 6, 1917, and Franklin D. Roosevelt, then assistant secretary of the navy, was instrumental in insuring that marine combat units were represented in the ground war in France. When the army's 1st Division was hastily formed and sent to France as a token for faltering Allies, the 5th Marine Regiment was dispatched at the same time and initially trained with the 1st Division. After the 2d Division's headquarters was formed in October, the 5th joined the army's two infantry regiments, and filler units, including successive elements of the 6th Marines, arrived until the division was complete in February. For the coming months, during the time when the Germans launched their spring 1918 offensives to win before effective American intervention, the division under MajGen. Omar Bundy trained behind the lines and went to the Verdun sector for frontline experience in a quiet sector.

In May, Col. Charles Doyen, USMC, commanding the 4th Marine Brigade, became ill and AEF commander Gen. John J. Pershing shocked everyone by giving the command to his own army chief of staff, BGen. James G. Harbord. Pershing's charge to Harbord: "I'm giving you the best brigade in France, and if things don't work out, I'll know who to blame." Harbord took on the coloration of the marines and commanded that brigade through the bloody action known as Belleau Wood (June 6–26). The army regiments concluded the action by capturing Vaux on July 4. The tactical action, actually a limited counterattack, carried great significance in announcing American fighting capability to doubting Allies. It caught the special attention of the American public and generated some lasting army-marine resentments because a censorship judgment allowed the marine units to be widely publicized, with no unit identification for the army.

Pershing soon thereafter found Omar Bundy deficient as a division commander and replaced him with Harbord, promoted to major general, on July 15. Three days later, after frantic movement and a minimum of planning and preparation, the division attacked east against Germans in the Marne salient below Soissons. Under the French XX Corps, the American 1st and 2d divisions, with the French 1st Moroccan Division between, moved east on July 18. Attacking at first light and again in late afternoon, the 2d Division's two army regiments and 5th Marines went far ahead of adjacent units to penetrate five miles. On the next day, the 6th Marine Regiment came up from reserve and, with both flanks exposed, made another one and a half miles to come within gunshot of the critical Soissons-Château-Thierry road. Harbord obtained relief for his battered regiments that night. Veterans of the battle recalled it as two days in hell. The remnants of the 1st Division, constantly slowed by an open flank in the French sector to the north, secured the critical high ground just south of Soissons on the fifth day. Historians note this battle as pivotal because thereafter the Germans never again were on the offensive.

Soon after Soissons, Pershing dispatched Harbord to bring order to the ever growing logistics snarls in Service of Supply, and command of the division was given to MajGen. John A. Lejeune, USMC. For the reduction of the St. Mihiel salient beginning September 12, the division, again filled with replacements, was under the tactical command of Hunter Liggett's I Corps in the newly formed American First Army. The division attacked in columns of brigades, 3d Brigade leading, regiments abreast. Inconsequential after the experience of Soissons, little resistance was met as the 9th and 23d Infantry forces made a huge haul of prisoners and materiel at Thiaucourt.

For the coordinated Allied attack beginning September 26, the American First Army was assigned the area between the Meuse River and, to the west, the mass of the Argonne Forest, where it adjoined the French Fourth Army. There were then twenty-nine American divisions ready for action. Fifteen were marked for Meuse-Argonne, seven were left in St. Mihiel area, two were with the British, and three were still preparing in quiet sectors. The other two were the 2d and the new 36th, less its artillery.

Pershing later wrote, "It was a matter of keen regret that the veteran 2d Division was not at hand at the time, but at Marshal Foch's request it had been sent to assist the French Fourth Army." The French had not been able to advance north from Somme Py against Blanc Mont Ridge, which the Germans had made a dense defensive fortification. Starting October 3, all elements of the 2d Division fought to take the ridge and resisted furious counterattacks. The 36th Division relieved 2d Division elements by October 7. Pershing recorded the action as a brilliant success enabling the French to keep up their advance, and division commander John Lejeune wrote to his men: "To be able to say when the war is over, 'I belonged to the 2d Division: I fought at Blanc Mont Ridge,' will be the highest honor that can come to any man." This outstanding military passage is sometimes overlooked by historians because the division was not in the highly publicized opening phase of American First Army's Meuse-Argonne drive.

Before the November 1 phase of the Meuse-Argonne campaign, the 2d Division was restored to the American First Army and assigned to MajGen. Charles P. Summerall's V Corps. With the 89th Division alongside in a spearhead role, the Indianheads, with brigades abreast, ruptured the German lines and beat the Germans back five miles, moving through Barricourt; the 9th Infantry then made its spectacular penetration to Beaumont.

By November 7, the Germans were seeking an end, but there was no letup in Allied pressure. On the night of November 10, with an Armistice expected, elements of the 5th Marines and 9th Infantry made a valorous and costly crossing to the east bank of the Meuse and were pursuing Germans at 11 A.M. on November 11.

Of the 2 million American soldiers in France, about 240,000 made the initial advance into Germany for the Allied occupation of the Rhineland. The 2d Division spread its regiments within the American Third Army bridgehead at Coblenz and carried out routine duties until it was relieved on July 5, 1918, and sailed home to a New York City homecoming parade on August 8. The last elements of the division to return were in the ceremonial composite regiment formed in May 1919 to represent the AEF in the many ceremonies in France and England in the summer of 1919. With the 2d Division's Infantry Brigade and the Marine Brigade each contributing one handpicked company, the regi-

ment was featured in Paris, London, and at the homecoming parade for Pershing in New York City and again in Washington, D.C., on September 17.

Statistics in final reports of the AEF tell that the 2d Division led all in capturing prisoners, in number of awards for valor (7 Medals of Honor, 673 Distinguished Service Crosses) and, unfortunately, in aggregate division casualties at 25,232, just ahead of the 1st Division at 23,495 and 3d Division at 18,468. In total days in line, the division was behind three divisions and in distance advanced against fire, in second place.

Rolfe Hillman

Bibliography
American Battle Monuments Commission. *American Armies and Battlefields in Europe*. Washington, DC: Government Printing Office, 1938.
———. *2d Division Summary of Operations in the World War*. Washington, DC: Government Printing Office, 1944.
Harbord, James G. *Leaves from a War Diary*. New York: Dodd, Mead, 1925.
Lejeune, John A. *Reminiscences of a Marine*. Philadelphia: Dorrance, 1930.
Spaulding, Oliver L. *The Second Division American Expeditionary Force in France, 1917–1919*. New York: Hillman Press, 1937.

United States Army: 3d Division

Although the 3d Division played a significant role in two major campaigns and earned the sobriquet "The Marne Division" for its efforts on one desperate day of the war, its experience was that of a typical American division. It was raised at Camp Greene, North Carolina, on Nov. 21, 1917, under the command of MajGen. Joseph Dickman. It was a standard "square" division, with over 27,000 men, organized around two infantry brigades of two regiments each.

The 3d Division was composed of the 5th and 6th Infantry brigades with 8,324 men and 6,459 rifles each. The 5th Brigade consisted of the 4th and 7th Infantry regiments and the 8th Machine Gun Battalion; the 6th Brigade commanded the 30th and 38th Infantry regiments and the 9th Machine Gun Battalion. The 3,770-man regiments contained a headquarters, three battalions of four companies each, a machine gun company, and a supply company.

Divisional troops consisted of the 7th Motorized Machine Gun Battalion, the 5th Signal Battalion, and the 6th Engineer Regiment. Division artillery included the 3d Artillery Brigade composed of the 10th and 76th Field Artillery regiments armed with 75mm guns, the 18th Field Artillery Regiment with 155mm guns, and the 3d Trench Mortar Battery. Logistics units far surpassed anything seen before in the American Army. Division trains consisted of headquarters and military police, the 6th Engineers, and the 3d Ammunition and Supply trains. In addition, the 3d Sanitary Train consisted of the 5th, 7th, 26th, and 27th Field Hospitals, each with ambulance companies.

Although designated a Regular Army division, the 3d contained Regular officers only in the command and staffs at battalion and above and one Regular officer in each of the division's forty-eight infantry companies; thus it differed little from the other forty-three divisions shipped to France. The Regulars were joined by 10,000 draftees in December and January. Training began in December, but by then the 6th Engineers had already sailed from Hoboken, New Jersey, followed in February by the 5th Signal Battalion. The bulk of the division shipped out in March 1918 and completed its deployment by April, except for its artillery units.

In Europe, each American division was to go through a training cycle including a tour in a quiet sector supervised by seasoned troops. Twenty-nine U.S. divisions served in the front lines; the 3d Division was one of nine that received no frontline training. In addition, from the time it was raised in November 1917 until the middle of June 1918, when it took over a defensive sector, it never functioned as a complete unit.

Subordinate elements were, however, committed to combat during the German spring offensives. On March 21, while the bulk of the division was still in the United States, the 6th Engineers were supporting the British Fifth Army when the German "Michael" offensive ruptured the British line. Having no reserves, the Fifth Army created the ad hoc "Carey Force" composed of 2,200 Royal Engineers, school troops, and the 6th Engineers and committed the force as infantry to defend eight miles of front before Amiens. The 6th Engineers went into the line south of the Somme at Warfusee-Abancourt on March 27 and defended its sector until relieved on April 3.

In a similar crisis, the division's motorized 7th Machine Gun Battalion went into action on May 31 at the end of a 100-mile, 24-hour road march to support the French 10th Colonial Division at Château-Thierry. For two days, the battalions helped block German attempts to cross the Marne.

The 7th Infantry relieved the U.S. 2d Division's 5th and 6th Marine Brigades on June 15 in Belleau Wood. In a week of hard fighting, the 7th Infantry's freshness failed to compensate for its lack of training and experience. Fighting at night, in tangled terrain, the regiment suffered high casualties and achieved meager results. Its 1st Battalion made three attacks in seven days but was unable to make headway while suffering 237 casualties—25 percent of its strength.

The 7th Machine Gun Battalion and the 7th Infantry had been committed to help stop the third German offensive. This attack, codenamed "Blucher-Yorck," had been launched from the Chemin des Dames on May 27 and had reached the Marne in only four days. When the river crossing failed, the Germans shifted their attacks west of Soissons while they planned a new assault. During this respite, the remainder of the 3d Division closed on the Marne River.

The 3d Division was placed under the control of the French Sixth Army's XXXIII Corps. The division's subordinate units were placed under the command of French divisions and constantly moved about as the Allies attempted to stabilize the front.

On July 3, the division was finally reunited in its own sector. It took over the defense of the south bank of the Marne extending from just east of Château-Thierry to just west of Courtement-Varennes deploying the 4th, 7th, 30th, and 38th Infantry regiments on line from west to east. Anticipating a renewal of German attacks, the division followed XXXIII Corps directives, and in the time available, each regiment began organizing its positions in depth. The 4th and 7th regiments placed outposts along a railroad embankment where the ridges descended directly to the river and a main line of resistance along the Paris aqueduct approximately a mile to the rear. The 30th and 38th regiments, on the other hand, each occupied a more gently sloping ridge from the flood plain running south perpendicular to the river and separated from each other by the Surmelin Creek. These regiments organized four defense zones by beginning with outposts at the water's edge and half platoons at the railroad embankment several hundred yards back. A mile behind these forward positions was the Aqueduct Line, the main line of resistance and two miles from the river was the supporting Wood Line. The 38th regiment shared its ridge with the French 125th Infantry Division; consequently, much of the sector on its western slopes faced west and northwest overlooking the Surmelin Creek, with the back of their defenses protected by the French.

The division did not have long to prepare their defense. The Germans were almost ready to launch their Champagne-Marne offensive. This was to be a double envelopment on an eighty-five-mile front that would pinch off Reims and force the Allies to commit the last of their strategic reserves.

The 3d Division faced the German Seventh Army's XVIII Reserve Corps, which formed the western pincer. The 4th and 7th Infantry faced the 377th Regiment of the 10th Lanswher Division. The attack itself would be carried out by three regiments of the German 10th Division against the 30th Infantry and by three regiments of the German 36th Division against the 38th.

German preparations had not been concealed well, and the Allies had discovered both the time and general location of the intended attack. At midnight July 14–15, French and American artillery began a preattack barrage against assembled German artillery and infantry thirty minutes before the Germans were scheduled to begin their offensive.

Both sides suffered greatly in the ensuing artillery duel, which was maintained at a high level for almost four hours and continued with diminishing intensity until mid-morning. The Germans fired approximately 100,000 rounds into the 3d Division sector from eighty-four batteries. The barrage consisted of approximately one-half high explosives and shrapnel and one-half Blue Cross and Green Cross gas. For reasons never explained, the 7th and 30th Infantry troops were conducting a battalion relief of frontline units at the very time the expected German fire arrived. They suffered heavily. A battery of the division's 18th Field Artillery Battalion was also still moving into position and was destroyed.

German units assembling for the attack took commensurate losses from thirty-one Allied batteries. Battalions of both the German 10th Division's 398th and 47th Infantry disin-

tegrated under the bombardment, greatly reducing the effectiveness of the division attacks.

As the German 10th Division's 6th Grenadiers crossed the river on the railroad embankment and those of F and H companies pressed forward on the ridge line farther back, Allied guns swept the area, inflicting horrible casualties. After being driven back across the river by fire and counterattacks, the German 6th Grenadiers, having taken 844 casualties, could rally only 112 men. These losses, combined with those of the 398th and 47th regiments, wrecked the division; it never again saw frontline action.

The 5th Grenadiers of the German 36th Division crossed the river after taking heavy artillery casualties and also met strong resistance on their right flank where they expected the 6th Grenadier support. Instead, 100 yards into the American position they ran headlong into a counterattack by B and D companies of the U.S. 3d Division's 38th Infantry, which, rising from concealment in a wheat field, annihilated two German infantry companies in a point-blank firefight.

Throughout this fight the American 38th Infantry faced not only frontal assaults but was threatened on both flanks. By 5:00 A.M. the French 125th Division collapsed, exposing the American right flank. Meanwhile, the 30th Infantry had been forced from its outposts and later in the day had been ordered back from the Aqueduct positions to the Wood Line, leaving the 38th exposed on the left.

This withdrawal, coming as it did after the 6th Grenadier attack had spent its force, was the first of several controversial events involving the 30th Infantry. Its units had been badly punished by both the German artillery preparation and the subsequent attack. On the morning of July 16, they were relieved by the 28th Division's 111th Infantry and withdrawn for decontamination. Gas casualties were notoriously difficult to assess. Of the 2,000 self-reported cases in the 3d Division during the week from July 14 to 21, the division gas officer estimated that in fact there were only about 600. There was only one gas fatality during the week. Although the regimental commander claimed that his forces had suffered over 1,400 casualties, hospital admission figures indicate that the unit had taken 469 casualties, of whom 72 had been gassed. Nevertheless, the entire 30th Infantry was out of the line until July 21. These events attest to the disruptive effects of the dreaded new weapon—gas—on inexperienced troops already subjected to the stress of the battlefield.

By mid-morning of July 16, the German attack in the 3d Division sector had broken down, and on the next day, the German High Command called off the offensive. In the 3d Division sector the Germans had been stopped cold. The German decision to withdraw was hastened by a powerful French counterattack, which struck the western face of the salient on July 18.

The 3d Division restored its original front and then joined the Aisne-Marne offensive, crossing the Marne on July 21. From July 21 to July 29, they inched their way forward against a tenacious and methodical German defense that used a maze of well-placed machine gun positions covered by artillery concentrations to frustrate the Allied pursuit. With each passing day, the 3d's front narrowed, and its offensive power diminished. By July 24, the 6th Brigade could go no farther. On July 27, the 5th Brigade's 4th Infantry was carrying on the attack alone, and by July 29, only a single battalion was driven to ground after going only 200 yards. All told, the division had advanced seven and a half miles north of the Marne. The division participated in one last action of the Aisne-Marne offensive when the 6th Brigade, attached to the French III Corps, failed in heavy fighting to establish a bridgehead across the Vesle River from August 7–10. In twenty-six days, from the time of the German attack on July 15 until it was withdrawn on August 10 for rest and reorganization, the 3d Division had suffered 6,700 casualties, of which 1,440 had been killed in action or died of wounds.

The 3d Division was in the U.S. First Army, IV Corps reserve during the St. Mihiel offensive. The 10th Field Artillery Brigade participated in the preattack bombardment, and other units saw some detached service. The bulk of the division meanwhile rested, refitted, and reorganized behind the front. It was soon assigned to participate in the last and largest American operation of the war.

The Meuse-Argonne offensive was part of the coordinated Allied strategic drive to break through the German defenses, cut their communications and supply networks, and end the war. The American First Army area of operations ran north-northwest from Verdun to the key rail line running through Sedan. On the left flank, I Corps was to seal off the Argonne Forest and prevent observation and fire from its forward slopes; III Corps was to move forward with its right flank blocking on the Meuse River and its left flank supporting the general assault. In the center, V Corps would attack with three divisions to penetrate the main German positions.

German troops in the sector were a mixture of first rate units and worn out elements. They manned three major and one supplementary defensive belts, with many intermediate positions, to a depth of almost twelve miles. Eight miles behind the front, the Kriemhilde-Stellung, the local section of the Hindenburg Line, formed the third and strongest position. It was the main initial objective. Terrain favored the defense. The Argonne Forest's heavily wooded, broken ground was a major obstacle, and even the rolling, open terrain to the east of the Aire River contained steep, tangled ravines and many isolated thickets atop the successive ridge lines that dominated the area.

The general attack made good progress when it jumped off on September 26; in four days against mounting resistance, the troops drove the Germans back to the outposts of the Kriemhilde-Stellung. Before renewing the attack three fresh U.S. divisions were rotated into the line, including the 3d Division, now commanded by MajGen. Beaumont Buck. It began relieving the 79th on V Corps' right flank on September 30.

The First Army renewed the attack on October 4. What followed for the 3d Division was a three-week slugging match. The division led with the 7th Infantry on the left and the 4th Infantry on the right; each had a battalion on line and a battalion in support. This two-battalion front was typical of the assault formations used throughout the campaign. The 6th Brigade followed in support.

In the first week the division pressed forward a mile and a half from the Nantillois/Cierges road to the south edge of the Bois de Cunel, slowly driving back a desperate and entrenched German defense anchored by interlocking machine gun fire and heavy artillery support. On October 9, the 30th and 38th Infantry took up the attack and for five days unsuccessfully attempted to pound their way through the main German defenses just south of the Romagne-sous-Montfaucon/Cunel road.

On October 14, the 3d Division passed to the control of the U.S. III Corps and shifted its direction of attack north and east of Cunel into the Bois de la Pultière, Bois de Forêt, and Hill

299. On October 13, the 30th Infantry with the strength of less than a prewar battalion reorganized itself into four provisional companies, and on October 14, the 4th Infantry reorganized into two provisional battalions.

The division mounted one final operation on October 20–21. On October 20, it cleared the Clairs Chêne Wood with a force consisting of two battalions of the 7th Infantry organized as a 300-man provisional company, two companies of the 6th Engineers and a company of the 4th Infantry. On October 21, the division launched a final effort with every one of its available units. The attacking force consisted of what was left of the 7th Infantry, E Company/4th Infantry, a "provisional battalion" of the 38th Infantry, three companies of the 6th Engineers, and the 7th Machine Gun Battalion. They took Hill 299.

The 3d Division was finally taken out of the line on the night of October 26–27. It had gone into action on September 30 with 16,615 infantry and machine gun troops and on October 31 withdrew with a strength of 9,666. During the Meuse-Argonne offensive it took 7,775 casualties, of whom 1,781 were killed or died of wounds.

The 3d Infantry Division served eighty-six days in the frontline sector, more times than all but two other U.S. divisions and was in combat for fifty days, more than any other division but one. In the process the division suffered a total of 15,030 casualties.

Charles A. Endress

Bibliography

American Battle Monuments Commission. *3d Division, Summary of Operations in the World War*. Washington, DC: Government Printing Office, 1944.

Center of Military History, U.S. Army. *Order of Battle of the United States Land Forces in the World War*. Vol. 2. *American Expeditionary Forces: Divisions*. Washington, DC: Government Printing Office, 1988.

———. *Military Operations of the American Expeditionary Forces*. United States Army in the World War, 1917–1919. Vol. 9. Washington, DC: Government Printing Office, 1990.

Cochrane, Raymond C. *The Third Division at Château-Thierry; July 1918*. Washington, DC: Government Printing Office, 1959.

History of the Third Division United States Army in the World War; For the Period December 1, 1917 to January 1, 1919. Andernach-on-the-Rhine: N.p., 1919.

U

United States Army: 4th Division

On Nov. 19, 1917, the War Department ordered the formation of the 4th Division in the Regular Army at Camp Greene, near Charlotte, North Carolina. The division was to be comprised of Regular Army units stationed at Camp Greene and from Vancouver Barracks in Washington, as well as units at Monterey, California, and other smaller stations. The command of the division was given to MajGen. George H. Cameron. The official activation date of the division was listed as December 10, the date that Cameron arrived.

The principal units of the division were the 7th Infantry Brigade under the command of BGen. Benjamin A. Poore, which was comprised of the 39th and 47th Infantry regiments and the 11th Machine Gun Battalion. The 39th Infantry was a newly formed regiment created by transferring men from the 30th Infantry Regiment. The 47th Infantry, another newly formed regiment, was created by a cadre from the 9th Infantry. The other infantry brigade, the 8th, under the command of BGen. Samuel W. Miller, was made up of the 58th and 59th Infantry regiments and the 12th Machine Gun Battalion. The 58th and 59th were created by cadres from the 4th Infantry Regiment. The artillery was formed into the 4th Field Artillery Brigade comprised of the 13th, 16th, and 77th Field Artillery regiments and the 4th Trench Mortar Artillery Battery. The 13th and 16th Field Artillery were newly created units, but the 77th Field Artillery was initially organized as the 19th Cavalry Regiment. It was converted to field artillery and redesignated as the 77th Field Artillery on November 1. Other divisional units included the 10th Machine Gun Battalion, 4th Engineer Regiment, 8th Field Signal Battalion, and divisional trains. Most of the Regular Army units at the time were under strength or had been used to provide cadres for newly organized units and volunteers and draftees were used to bring the units up to full strength.

From December 10, the organization of the division proceeded as the various units arrived at Camp Greene. The arrival of fillers continued right up to the time the division was shipped overseas. The winter of 1917 was particularly severe, resulting in miserable living conditions for troops, who thought that the southern location would mean a more temperate climate. The cold, damp weather and the resulting mud was a prelude to the conditions along the Western Front.

The weather limited the amount of outdoor training. Space was another problem since the division was sharing the camp with the 3d Division. The British and French provided instructors for a variety of schools to familiarize the troops with the weapons and tactics that they would use in the line overseas. Schools for machine guns, grenades, bayonets, and trench mortars were organized.

Between March 10 and 21, over 10,000 troops arrived at Camp Greene as replacements and by April the division reached its authorized strength. The 3d Division left Camp Greene in the middle of March. This resulted in more housing for the 4th Division. As the weather improved, the amount of time dedicated to outdoor training increased. Special attention was given to road marches and handling of transport. On April 6, it paraded through Charlotte to inaugurate the Third Liberty Loan drive.

The German spring offensive created pressure on the Allied High Command to increase the number of Americans at the front. In response to that call, both the 3d and 4th divisions were ordered overseas. On April 15, orders were received to proceed to Camp Mills, New York, and Camp Merritt, New Jersey, for embarkation. Before leaving Camp Greene, General Cameron designated the insignia for the 4th Division—four ivy leaves in the form of a Roman numeral "IV."

The 4th Engineers became the first divisional unit to go overseas, leaving New York on April 29 and arriving in Bordeaux on May 12. The overseas trip was not without casualties. The transport *Moldavia,* on which the 4th Engineers sailed, was torpedoed and sunk, resulting in a loss of fifty-six men of the 58th Infantry. Troops aboard the transport *Olympia* also had their share of excitement when the transport rammed and sunk a German submarine en route to France. By June 5, the entire division of 29,180 was either in France or England.

Upon arrival in France, the division was subject to a German air attack on its first night while it camped about a mile outside Calais. The division—less its artillery brigade, field signal battalion, and elements of the 58th Infan-

try—moved to a training area in Picardy, where it was attached to the British 16th Irish Division for training and supply. Since it was expected that the 4th Division was going to remain with the British, it traded in its Springfield 1903 rifles for British Lee-Enfields. Another facet of being assigned to the British was the adoption of the British Army ration, which may have simplified supply considerations but was not at all popular with the troops. The British initiated an intensive training program to indoctrinate the newly arrived Americans to the conditions and weapons of the western Front. Again schools were organized to assist the newly arrived Americans to adjust to British ways and to the harsh realities of the trenches. The 4th Artillery Brigade moved to Camp de Souge near Bordeaux, where gunners set out to master the newly issued French 75mm and 115mm guns and the array of fuses used.

While the division was settling into training and adjusting to the British ways of doing things, the pressures on the Allied front caused by the German offensive that had broken through the French lines near Berry-au-Bac and had advanced to the Marne River caused the Allied High Command to readjust the distribution of American troops. The 4th Division's assignment was changed, and it was sent to bolster the French lines. The French reserves had been badly depleted by this offensive. On June 11, the 4th Division moved to the Meaux, about twenty-four miles west of Château-Thierry, the rear area of the French Sixth Army. The 7th Infantry Brigade was attached to the French 4th Division near Rosoy-en-Multien for training. The balance of the division was attached to the French 164th Division near La Ferte-sous-Jouarre. The division's signal battalion rejoined it on June 16. The process of reissuing some of the American equipment, particularly the Springfield rifle, was especially appreciated by the division. Training continued with the French until the Aisne-Marne offensive.

On the night of July 14–15, the Germans initiated their last major offensive of the war. The German advances were met with fierce resistance and the French Sixth Army, on July 16, initiated the Aisne-Marne offensive. The 4th Division, minus the 7th Infantry and 4th Artillery brigades, was attached to the French 164th Division and was ordered to attack the German main line of resistance between Rivière de Cligon and Ruisseau d'Alland. The units of the division entered the front lines and saw action for the first time. The 2d Battalion, 58th Infantry on July 18, assisted in the assault on and capture of Chevillon. Units of the 7th Infantry Brigade attached to the French 33d Division moved into the front lines on the night of July 16–17 and took Buisson de Cresnes and Noroy.

During the night of July 20–21, orders were received to withdraw the 4th Division, less the 10th Machine Gun Battalion, from the line. The 10th Machine Gun Battalion was relieved on July 23. The division's initial experience in combat had been costly. Fifteen officers and 382 enlisted personnel were killed in action, and 63 officers and 1,805 enlisted men were wounded. In addition, 67 were missing or captured. By the evening of July 23, the division's headquarters had been moved and established at Bourneville with the rest of the division billeted nearby.

On July 28, orders were received placing the division under American command for the first time, when it was assigned to the American I Corps. Headquarters was moved to Beuvarde. The division was assigned to assist the American 42d Division. The 4th Artillery Brigade rejoined the division on July 30 for the first time since it arrived in France. Then, during the night of August 2–3, the division relieved the American 42d Division on the front lines. On August 3, the division attacked toward the Vesle River. After bitter fighting, the 4th slowly advanced to St. Thibault. German observation points on high ground directed both machine gun and artillery fire, as well as gas, on to any movement. In the course of the afternoon of August 4, in spite of the heavy German bombardment of American positions and after heavy fighting, the division established and held the first bridgehead across the Vesle River. The Aisne-Marne offensive ended on August 6. During the advance, division losses were 53 officers and 1,357 enlisted men killed in action and 179 officers and 5,296 enlisted men wounded in action. The American 77th Division relieved the 4th on August 12.

The division moved first to Forêt de Fere then to the Reynel Training Area about twenty miles northeast of Chaumont, the location of the American general headquarters. While at Reynel, personnel replacements were received and equipment repaired or replaced. Also while at Reynel, General Cameron was transferred to command the American V Corps. MajGen. John L. Hines became the division's commander

on August 27, and the division was assigned to the V Corps, which was part of the American First Army.

On September 1, the 4th Division moved to Vavincourt for intensive training in anticipation of the St. Mihiel offensive. It was to be the first independent American operation carried out by the American Expeditionary Force (AEF). On the night of September 5–6, troops of the 59th Infantry began to occupy the front-line trenches in the Toul sector. This sector had been extremely quiet and held by the French since 1914. It was the first time that the Americans had occupied a trench system similar to one that they had trained in.

The St. Mihiel salient was the last one on the Western Front. The American First Army was given the order to reduce it. On the night of September 12, the artillery opened the offensive with one of the greatest barrages to date. The next afternoon, troops of the 8th Infantry Brigade advanced toward the German lines. The attacks were a tactical surprise, and the advance was so rapid that escaping Germans left hot food in their kitchens. The 7th Infantry Brigade was ordered to march to the junction of Grand Tranchée de Calonne and the Mouilly-Les Éparges road to serve as a reserve for the American V Corps. The American offensive was a complete success, and by the end of the afternoon of September 13, the assigned objectives of the offensive had been met. The Germans had lost 16,000 prisoners and 443 guns plus large stores of materiel and supplies. The St. Mihiel salient had been eliminated, and the Germans had been pushed back to their strong defensive positions.

The Americans were now assigned to the Meuse-Argonne front, where German lines were particularly dense and the terrain added a natural strength to the defensive positions that faced the twenty-mile-long American sector. The German positions (the Hindenburg Line) were up to twelve miles deep and had not seen action since the French offensives in 1915 and 1916. A breakthrough here would prevent the Germans retreating across the Rhine; consequently, it was expected that resistance would be fierce. The U.S. First Army assembled fifteen divisions, including the 4th, into this sector.

The 4th Division on September 19–20 moved to the vicinity of Lemmes, approximately six miles southwest of Verdun, and was assigned to the U.S. III Corps. On September 20, the First Army issued its orders to start the

U

Meuse-Argonne offensive. The III Corps orders were to protect the right and organize the line of the Meuse for defense. It was also assigned the capture of Montfaucon. The 4th Division was to attack the German positions along the Trieste and Tolomino trenches. The division organized the attack to be made by the 7th Infantry Brigade and supported by the 8th Infantry Brigade. The 7th Infantry Brigade arranged its front lines with the 47th Infantry on the right and the 39th on the left, side by side. Each regiment placed one battalion in the assaulting line and one in support. Two battalions were in brigade reserve. The division's 4th Artillery Brigade would support the division's operations with the assistance of both British and other American artillery units.

At 2:30 A.M., September 26, the opening barrages of the offensive started, and by 5:30 that morning, the assault troops began their advance. The morning fog was both an advantage, in that it covered the advance, and a hindrance, since it made it more difficult to maintain a cohesive advance. The 7th Infantry Brigade's objectives were met by 12:30 P.M., and the advance stopped to allow the adjoining 80th and 79th divisions to move forward. The 7th Brigade troops had advanced two and a half miles. At 5:30 P.M., the division received orders to continue the advance regardless of the progress made by adjoining divisions, and so the advance was resumed without artillery support. The four-hour delay had allowed the Germans to reorganize their defenses. The 7th Brigade advanced slowly until relieved by the 8th Brigade on the morning of September 29. Little progress was made for the next four days since the Germans were firmly entrenched. The American difficulties were compounded by rain, which turned roads into a sea of mud, making supply problems urgent.

The first phase of the Meuse-Argonne offensive, from September 26 through October 3, had swept through the first two lines of the German defenses. The second phase of the battle was to penetrate the German main defensive position, the Kriemhilde-Stellung. The objective assigned to the 4th Division was to hold the northern edge of the Bois de Brieulles, and then advance through Bois de Fays and Bois de Malaumont, and then turn east and sweep the Bois de Forêt to the Meuse River.

On the morning of October 4, troops of the 58th Infantry began to advance and established themselves by late afternoon in Bois de Fays. The advance was marked by intense fighting and counterattacks plus heavy bombardment including the use of gas shells. By the evening of October 4–5, the division had advanced to the eastern edge of Bois de Fays. From October 6–8, the situation remained unchanged. On October 9, Pershing decided on another major push, and III Corps ordered the 4th and 80th divisions to advance. The 4th Division was spearheaded by the 39th Infantry. After a day of heavy fighting, the advancing troops had cleared Bois de Fays and had taken a small section of the trenches at the southwest corner of the Bois de Forêt. It was during this period that MajGen. Cameron took command of the division again, when General Hines was transferred to command III Corps.

The advance continued again, and by the evening of October 11, the lines had advanced to the northern edge of Bois de Forêt where they essentially remained until the 3d Division relieved them on the morning of October 13. The 4th Division was ordered to hold the front lines on the northern edge of Bois de Brieulles. The 47th Infantry was given the front positions, and the division stayed where assigned until October 19, when it was relieved by the 3d Division and ordered to march to Forêt de Hesse for refitting.

The division's accomplishments in the Meuse-Argonne offensive had been significant. It had advanced approximately eight miles, captured 2,731 prisoners and fifty-seven artillery pieces. The advance had not been without costs: 45 officers and 1,120 enlisted men had been killed in action, and 6,219 officers and men were wounded or missing in action. It had been continuous action for twenty-one days, the longest fighting of any American division during the war. The Meuse-Argonne offensive had been a sweeping victory for the Americans and Allied front as the Germans had been pushed from east of the Meuse River and the Metz-Lille railroad vital to German movement was placed under Allied artillery fire.

On October 20, the 4th Division was assigned to the American Second Army and it moved to the Toul area, just north of Commercy. Divisional headquarters was established at Vignot, and the division was designated as Army Reserve, Second Army. On October 31, MajGen. Mark L. Hersey assumed its command. On November 3, orders were received assigning the division back to the First Army. It was ordered to move to Blercourt and assigned to III Corps. Before the move could be completed, however, orders were received revoking the division assignment to III Corps, and it was again assigned to the Second Army in anticipation of the offensive planned for the Lorraine front. On November 11, division headquarters was established at Bourcq. That night the front erupted into a display of fireworks and lights to celebrate the Armistice.

On November 20, the 4th Division as part of the Army of Occupation was assigned to an area west of Coblenz in Germany. On July 9, 1919, it moved to Brest for embarkation back to the United States. On August 10, 1919, the division's last unit arrived home and the division was sent to Camp Dodge, Iowa, where it was demobilized.

James Controvich

Bibliography

American Battle Monuments Commission. *4th Division: Summary of Operations in the World War*. Washington, DC: Government Printing Office, 1944.

Bach, Christian A., and Henry N. Hall. *The Fourth Division: Its Services and Achievements in the World War*. N.p.: 1920.

United States Army: 5th Division

On Nov. 17, 1917, the War Department directed that another Regular Army division, the 5th, be organized. Unlike National Army and National Guard divisions which were mustered at one location, the 5th Division was organized around the nucleus of existing Regular Army units at several camps throughout the United States. To fill the unit to strength, recruits, along with draftees, arrived in early 1918. The division never gathered at one location prior to its movement to France.

Organization of the 5th Division began on December 1 with the establishment of division headquarters at Camp Logan, Texas, south of Houston. MajGen. Charles H. Muir assumed command on December 11, for a day prior to departing to command the 28th Division. Col. William M. Morrow, designated commander of the 5th Train, assumed temporary command of the division. During December, units began forming throughout the country. The 5th Training headquarters, along with the 5th Ammunition Train and the 5th Sanitary Train, were raised at Camp Logan. At Camp Greene, North

Carolina, the 9th Infantry Brigade was created with the 60th and 61st Infantry regiments, both formed from the Regular 7th Infantry Regiment, and with the 14th Machine Gun Battalion. BGen. James H. McRae assumed command of the 9th Infantry Brigade on Jan. 2, 1918. On Dec. 12, 1917, the 5th Field Artillery Brigade had begun forming north of San Antonio, at Camp Stanley, Texas. It consisted of the 19th and 20th Field Artillery regiments, formed from the Regular 7th Field Artillery Regiment, and the 21st Field Artillery Regiment, formed from the Regular 3d Field Artillery Regiment. BGen. A.F. Flager took command of the 5th Field Artillery Brigade on December 31.

The 10th Infantry Brigade, commanded by BGen. Walter H. Gordon, formed at Camp Forrest, Georgia, on the Chickamauga battlefield. It was made up of the Regular 6th and 11th Infantry regiments and the 15th Machine Gun Battalion. At the same time, at Fort Leavenworth, Kansas, the 7th Engineer Regiment was formed from the Regular 1st Engineers. The 5th Supply Train was formed at Camp Johnston, Florida. BGen. John E. McMahon assumed command of the 5th Division on Jan. 1, 1918, followed by his promotion to major general on February 6.

Training of all units of the 5th Division began in December 1917 and continued until each unit shipped out. Because of significant equipment shortages, training was basic, focusing on marksmanship, bayonet exercises, gas drills, and field fortifications.

When organization was completed, the 5th Division consisted of the 9th Infantry Brigade with the 60th and 61st Infantry regiments and the 14th Machine Gun Battalion; the 10th Infantry Brigade with the 6th and 11th Infantry regiments and the 15th Machine Gun Battalion; and the 5th Field Artillery Brigade with the 19th and 20th Field Artillery (75mm), the 21st Field Artillery (155mm) regiments, and the 5th Trench Mortar Battery. Divisional troops were the 7th Engineer Regiment, the 13th Machine Gun Battalion, the 9th Field Signal Battalion, and Headquarters Troop. To support the division, the 5th Train consisted of its headquarters and military police, the 5th Ammunition Train, the 5th Supply Train, the 7th Engineer Train, and the 5th Sanitary Train with Field Hospitals 17, 25, 29, 30, and ambulance companies.

Movement overseas began for the 5th Division on Feb. 25, 1918, when the 7th Engineer Regiment moved from Fort Leavenworth to

U

Camp Merritt to Hoboken, New Jersey. Sailing on March 6, the engineers reached Le Havre via Liverpool on March 23. By March 29, the 7th Engineers were working for the Service of Supply (S.O.S.) at Gièvres, a key supply depot in central France. The remainder of the division moved after April 2, with the last elements reaching France on June 19. Units passed from home stations through Camps Merritt and Upton to one of three ports of embarkation: Hoboken, Montreal, or New York. The division infantry units sailed between April 9 and 30, followed by the trains and the 5th Artillery Brigade from May 27 through June 10. Arrival overseas was through several ports of debarkation: Le Havre, Brest, St. Nazaire, or Bordeaux in France and Liverpool in Great Britain.

On April 25, infantry units of the 5th Division moved to the 13th Training Area near Bar-sur-Aube in Lorraine to begin preparations for combat. This was the first time that the brigades from Camp Greene and Camp Forrest joined the division headquarters for a brief shakedown period. On June 1 the units moved east of Épinal near the Vosges to begin a two-week training period with divisions from XXXIII Corps of the French Seventh Army. The French 70th Division trained with the 5th Division headquarters, 9th Infantry Brigade headquarters, and the 61st Infantry Regiment. The French 62d Division worked with the 60th Infantry Regiment. The 10th Infantry Brigade headquarters and the 11th Infantry Regiment were affiliated with the French 77th Division. The 6th Infantry Regiment, which had arrived first and had completed several weeks of additional training in France, went into reserve for the 26th Division from June 2 to 14. While the infantry units were training with the French in the Vosges, the 5th Field Artillery Brigade, newly arrived, along with the 5th trains, moved to Le Valdahon to begin training.

On June 14–15, the 5th Division headquarters began working with the French 21st Division which occupied a portion of the front on June 16. Between June 14 and July 16, rotating units into the front provided the 5th Division its first taste of the war. The Americans occupied the trenches, patrolled, and staged several raids. Moving forward to the front trenches, the division suffered its first losses on June 14. Three days later, forward combat detachments underwent a heavy bombardment, laced with phosgene and mustard gas, but they easily repulsed a German raid. On June 30, the 7th Engineer

Regiment and Train rejoined the division from the Service of Supply. This phase of trench training under French supervision ended when the division moved to a sector near St. Dié on July 15.

On July 19, the 5th Division assumed command of a sector of the front with the 9th Infantry Brigade on the left and the 10th Infantry Brigade on the right. Both brigades immediately set out to establish dominance over "no-man's-land" through aggressive patrolling. By July 20, the 5th Supply Train had arrived, followed on June 28 by the 5th Field Artillery Brigade and the 5th Ammunition Train. For the first time since its organization, the entire division was located at one place. MajGen. McMahon, occupying an active sector of the front, now could try to create a team from units that had organized separately, moved separately, and trained separately. This would take time. The division conducted its first real combat operation on August 17. BGen. Walter H. Gordon, 10th Brigade, chose the 3d Battalion of the 6th Infantry Regiment, under the command of LtCol. E.M. Norton to capture the village of Frapelle and Hill 451 to its north. The Germans responded to the divisional artillery bombardment, catching three waves of supporting troops in its path. Casualties were heavy—16 percent of the troops engaged—but the objectives were taken quickly. On August 23, the 5th Division was relieved and moved into the Arches Training Area to regroup and retrain after two strenuous months in the trenches.

Almost immediately the division was ordered to move to the First Army to join I Corps along the eastern face of the St. Mihiel salient. On September 10, the 5th Division occupied a portion of the Villers-en-Haye sector in preparation for an attack. At 5:00 A.M. on September 12, after a four-hour artillery preparation, the 10th Infantry Brigade, commanded by Col. Paul B. Malone since August 27, attacked, advancing through the Bois de la Rappe about 6:15 A.M. and moving forward almost three miles by nightfall with the 2d Division on its left and the 90th Division on its right. The 9th Infantry Brigade followed in support. Losses were heavy: 150 killed and 468 wounded, but the division had advanced to the army objective line. On September 13, the division beat off a strong German counterattack. The next day, the 5th Division advanced about a mile against stiff resistance to include stopping another counterattack. Limited combat operations were conducted during September 15–16. Total losses for the 5th Division during the St. Mihiel operation were roughly 1,500. On September 17, the 78th Division relieved the 5th Division, which moved back for rest, rehabilitation, and retraining. The 5th Field Artillery Brigade remained in support of the 78th Division until October 3. Thereafter, it served with other divisions in the St. Mihiel sector, not rejoining the 5th Division until after the Armistice.

After a brief period of rest, the 5th Division, minus the 5th Field Artillery Brigade, moved to the Bois de Hesse on the night of October 5–6 as III Corps reserve to begin its service in the Meuse-Argonne offensive. During the nights of October 9–10 and 10–11, 5th Division units moved forward to the vicinity of Nantillois. During the night of October 11–12, the 9th Infantry Brigade, commanded by BGen. Joseph C. Castner, relieved the 80th Division near Cunel. On the morning of October 12, the 5th Division attacked toward the Bois de la Pultière. Lt. Samuel Woodfill, Company M, 60th Infantry Regiment, performed one of the most heroic exploits of the war, personally destroying four machine gun nests, killing over a dozen Germans, and capturing several more. At times, this required hand-to-hand combat. Woodfill, a former Regular Army noncommissioned officer, was awarded the Medal of Honor, one of only two earned by the 5th Division. After this short fight, the 3d Division relieved the 9th Infantry Brigade which reorganized with the division south of the Bois de Cunel.

During the night of October 13–14, the 5th Division formed to attack along the Mamelle trench west of Cunel with both brigades abreast, the 9th (60th Infantry) on the right and the 10th (with the 6th, 11th, and 61st Infantry) on the left. The 59th Infantry Regiment from the 4th Division served as division reserve. The infantry attacked on October 14 at 8:30 A.M. despite a heavy and effective German artillery barrage from 6:00–8:00 A.M., followed by a brief, deadly barrage once the advance began. Despite heavy losses and mixing of units, the advance continued. Cunel was captured. On October 15, confused fighting in the Bois des Rappes led Major General McMahon to act on incorrect information. The result was the unfortunate withdrawal of forces from the northern edge of the wood. Two days later, MajGen. Hanson E. Ely relieved McMahon as commander of the 5th Division. Two regimental

commanders were also relieved during this battle. Fierce fighting continued in the Bois des Rappes until it was finally occupied on October 21. The next day, the 90th Division relieved the 5th Division, which reconstituted in the vicinity of Montfaucon. During ten days of battle, the division suffered 4,100 casualties, not counting those evacuated for sickness. Officer casualties were high, with one battalion of the 60th Infantry loosing twenty of the twenty-four officers assigned prior to the attack.

After a brief rest in wet, muddy conditions under sporadic German artillery fire, the 5th Division relieved the 3d Division during the night of October 26–27. As the division prepared for the next attack, pressure was kept on German forward units by aggressive patrolling resulting, on October 30, in the capture of the village of Aincreville. On November 1, the final attack began. As the right flank division of III Corps, the division attacked along the Meuse River. The 5th Division captured Clery-le-Grand and Brieulles-sur-Meuse, followed on November 2 by Clery-le-Petit and Doulon on November 3. By then, the division was along the Meuse River, preparing for a difficult crossing of the rain-swollen river and its adjacent canal. The German positions were weakly held but were located on high ground that dominated the 5th Division's crossing sites west of the river.

On the night of November 4–5, bridgeheads were established across the Meuse and its canal near Brieulles-sur-Meuse and Clery-le-Petit. Infantry units rushed across footbridges under a hail of German fire, with resulting heavy losses. When one of the bridges was damaged and his men across the river appeared cut off, Capt. Edward O. Allworth, 60th Infantry Regiment, rallied the men, plunged into the ten-foot-deep, forty-foot-wide canal, and led the men up the slopes of Hill 260 to secure the crossing site. For his heroic action, Captain Allworth earned the Medal of Honor. Until the high ground east of the river and the canal could be secured, pontoon bridges could not be built to speed up the crossing. Gen. John J. Pershing commended the division when he wrote: "The feat of arms which marks especially the Division's ability as a fighting unit was the crossing of the Meuse River and the establishment of a bridgehead on the eastern bank. This operation was one of the most brilliant military feats in the history of the American Army in France."

U

After moving forces into the bridgeheads and seizing Dun-sur-Meuse, the division attacked to the northeast on November 6 with astonishing results. Ely pushed the division, taking advantage of weak German forces in the direction of his advance, assisting the French XVII Corps attacking the heights of the Meuse north of Verdun. The advance continued relentlessly until the Armistice on November 11. The 5th Division advanced further and faster than any other First Army unit from November 6 to 11. During this final phase of the war, the 5th Division lost over 2,000 men. Twenty-seven of the thirty days prior to the Armistice, the 5th Division was in the line conducting active operations.

After a few weeks spent manning the Armistice lines, training, and salvage work, the division was selected to serve with the Service of Supply for the Third Army, which occupied a bridgehead over the Rhine River at Coblenz. Initially, the 5th Division performed supply functions only in the southern part of the Grand Duchy of Luxembourg. However, as divisions returned to the United States, the 5th Division relieved the 33d Division on April 12, 1918, thus assuming all supply duties for the Army of Occupation and control of the Grand Duchy border with Germany.

By the summer of 1919, it was time for the 5th Division to return to America. On July 4, the division began arriving at Brest for transport home. From July 9 to 31, the division sailed for Hoboken. At Camps Merritt and Mills, the non-Regulars were released. On July 24, the division was moved to Camp Gordon, Georgia, while the 5th Artillery Brigade moved to Camp Bragg, North Carolina.

Robert D. Ramsey III

Bibliography

American Battle Monuments Commission. *American Armies and Battlefields in Europe.* Washington, DC: Government Printing Office, 1938.

———. *5th Division: Summary of Operations in the World War.* Washington, DC: Government Printing Office, 1944.

Center of Military History, U.S. Army. *Order of Battle of the United States Land Forces in the World War.* Vol. 2. *American Expeditionary Forces: Divisions.* Washington, DC: Government Printing Office, 1988.

Society of the Fifth Division. *The Official History of the Fifth Division, U.S.A.* New York: Wynkoop Hallenbeck Crawford, 1919.

United States Army: 26th Division

On August 14, 1917, advanced authority to organize the 26th Division was received by BGen. Clarence Edwards in Boston. Establishing his headquarters in Boston, Edwards took full advantage of the early notification, advising all the governors of the New England states of the situation and obtaining their support and cooperation. He was fortunate in that prior to assuming command of the division, he commanded the Northeast Department, the area from which his troops were to be derived. Edwards had worked well with the National Guard officers and soldiers, which separated him from many of his Regular Army peers who tended to dismiss the National Guard as a group of dilettantes.

The formal order mobilizing the 26th Division came on August 22. The new division would be the size of a Civil War Corps, totaling over 27,000 men. The first unit organized was the division headquarters, which was formed from Troop B, Massachusetts Cavalry. The primary combat power would be found in the two infantry brigades and the field artillery brigade. Each brigade would be comprised of two regiments. The 51st Infantry Brigade under the command of BGen. Peter E. Traub, consisted of the 101st and 102d Infantry regiments. The 101st was derived from the 6th and 9th Massachusetts Infantry, plus troops from the 5th Massachusetts Infantry. The 102d came from the 1st Connecticut Infantry and 1st Vermont Infantry, plus troops from the 2d Connecticut and 6th Massachusetts Infantry. BGen. Charles H. Cole assumed command of the 52d Infantry Brigade, composed of the 103d and 104th Infantry regiments. The 103d was from the 1st Maine and 1st New Hampshire Infantry units, with additional troops from the 8th Massachusetts Infantry. The 104th Infantry was formed from the 2d and 6th Massachusetts Infantry, with additional troops from the 8th Massachusetts Infantry. Artillery support was provided by the 51st Artillery Brigade under the command of BGen. William Lassiter. It was comprised of three field artillery regiments, the 101st, 102d, and 103d. The 101st came from the 1st Massachusetts Field Artillery and troops from the New England Coast Artillery; the 102d from the 2d Massachusetts Field Artillery and some New England Coast Artillery troops; the 103d primarily from Battery A, New Hampshire Field Artillery, along with three batteries of Rhode Island and two batteries of Connecticut artillery, and men from the New England Coast Artillery. Although the Selective Service Act of 1917 indicated that National Guard units should retain their identities to the extent practical, many historic units were being absorbed into the massive army being mobilized. Every state in New England contributed units to the 26th Division, and many were resentful of losing their historic designations in the widespread consolidations.

The assembly, reorganization, and training of the division was originally to be at Camp Greene in North Carolina, but units began assembling at Boxford, Framingham, and Westfield, Massachusetts; New Haven and Niantic, Connecticut; and Quonset Point, Rhode Island. The age-old duties of an army assembling were carried on: inspections, medical checks, issuance of uniforms and equipment, paperwork, drilling. An advance party went to Camp Greene to prepare for the arrival of the full division.

In a move that created some hard feelings later, General Edwards ordered Capt. A.L. Pendleton to Hoboken, New Jersey, to secure transports for shipment of the division to France. Pendleton was informed that no transport was available since the Regular Army and units of the 42d Division had priority. As the 26th Division units completed their mobilization and organization, they were sent overseas as space became available. The first National Guard unit to go overseas, the 101st Infantry was shipped out on September 6. General Edwards and the division headquarters sailed on September 25, on the commercial liner *New York*. The last of the division's units arrived overseas on November 8.

With the arrival of its last battalion, the 26th Division became the first complete American division overseas. Division headquarters was established on October 31 at Neufchâteau with the rest of the division's units billeted within a fifteen-mile radius. A comprehensive training and indoctrination program was organized. General Edwards was detached to observe British forces and tactics for a month. Schools were set up with the French Military Mission providing thirty-six hours of drill and

instruction a week to the troops. Artillery units were sent to Camp Coëtquidan in Brittany, not far from the French artillery center at Rennes.

The situation that first winter was one of intense training and organization. The movement of personnel exceeded the ability of logistics systems, and shortage of transport, food, clothing, shelter, and fuel were common. It was not until the end of November that supplies began to arrive in quantity. The French supplied many items, including artillery, machine guns, and hand grenades. The British supplied gas masks, known as "box respirators."

On Feb. 1, 1918, divisional artillery units began moving into an area under the command of the French Sixth Army north of Soissons at Chemin des Dames, followed by the rest of the division four days later. Each battalion and battery was to rotate under the control and guidance of the French through the trenches in what was known as a quiet sector to accustom the troops and officers to the duties of maintaining and administering a frontline trench system. Battery A, 101st Field Artillery fired the first shot by a National Guard unit at 3:45 P.M. on February 5. Infantry units from the 101st Infantry entered the line during the night of February 7–8. The division remained with the French until March 18, at which time it was ordered to Bar-sur-Aube for further training with the 42d Division.

The great German spring offensive of 1918, which started on March 21, caused a change in plans. The division was ordered to relieve the 1st Division in the Toul sector. By April 1, the 26th occupied an eleven-mile front from Apremont to Bussons, the first time that a complete American division occupied part of the trench system under the command of its own officers. The sector was primarily a marsh dominated on the German side by Mont Sec. For the next thirty days, a series of battalion and regimental clashes occurred between divisional units and the Germans. The spirit of the fresh American troops was tested repeatedly by the Germans, who used crack storm troops to attempt to break through the American lines. German assaults culminated with the major German assault at Seicheprey on April 20–21. The French troops were much impressed with the courage of the New Englanders, honoring them with a number of awards including decorating the colors of the 104th Infantry Regiment for its actions at Apremont, the first American units so honored during the war. The sector

U

turned quiet again in May with no activities mentioned in the daily operations reports other than the customary patrolling activity. Casualties during April amounted to 148 dead and 816 wounded and missing, including 250 gas casualties. Although listed as a quiet sector, the bulletins sent to the War Department are interesting in their description. For instance: "Twenty-Sixth Division, June 21st to June 22d, noon to noon; the day was quiet except for a rather heavy harassing executed by the hostile batteries. A total of 1,450 rounds, mostly small caliber including a little gas, were used by the enemy. The fire was distributed over most of the sector." Casualties in May amounted to 601 and in June to 1,226, including 89 dead and 875 wounded by gas. On June 28, the division was relieved and ordered to concentrate in the area of Toul.

Within twelve hours of its relief, the 26th Division received orders for a secret destination. On July 2 it was assigned first to the French III Corps and later to the American I Corps, Sixth French Army, to relieve the American 2d Division in the Pas Fini sector, at the tip of the Marne salient northwest of Château-Thierry. The Germans were still controlling the strategic moves of the war and were known to be preparing for a major drive to end the war. The division began relieving the 2d Division on July 4, and by July 9 the relief was complete. German attacks were expected to begin no later than July 15. On that day, the Champagne-Marne defensive began. The Germans began their long-awaited offensive by attempting to break through the lines in the Champagne sector, penetrating a little over six miles during the next two days to the southwest of Reims. As the German offensive moved, the Allies made plans for a counteroffensive. On the morning of July 18, American I Corps ordered the 26th Division to attack. The assault was described in *Stars and Stripes*: "By the terms of the general offensive the division was to act as a pivot until the bulge in the allied front running northwest toward the Forest [sic] de Villers-Cotterêts should be hammered in. This required the rest of the division to attack northward and northeastward, pivoting on Bouresches and guiding on the 167th French Division to its left, never getting ahead of the latter, but sweeping gradually to the northeast until the whole front to its left should have been straightened." The Germans, caught by surprise, gave ground, and the 51st

Infantry Brigade reached its objectives. Complying with the terms of I Corps orders, it waited for the troops of the French 167th Division, which were having a more difficult time reaching their objectives. On July 23, in compliance with orders from the French Sixth Army, the division was ordered to penetrate the German line on a regimental front. The 101st Infantry attacked that morning, advanced, but had to fall back to its line of departure. The attack was renewed by units of the 56th Infantry Brigade from the 28th Division, which temporarily attached to the 26th. Advancing troops the next day found that the Germans had withdrawn. Headquarters ordered the troops to continue the advance until they came into contact with the withdrawing Germans. The advance proceeded until nightfall, at which time they came under artillery and gas barrage. The division had advanced about nine and one-half miles. The 26th, less its artillery and engineers, was then ordered into reserve at Etrepilly. The time spent in reserve was used in absorbing replacements and acclimating officers to their new commands.

The Champagne-Marne defense had stopped the German offensive. It also changed the strategic balance of the war. American influence on the Western Front was beginning to be felt. The American command was successful in convincing Allied leadership to allow U.S. troops to take control of a section of the front. An American Army was formed before the St. Mihiel salient—the United States First Army, organized on August 10 under the command of Gen. John J. Pershing. Its mission was to reduce the salient, which was approximately twenty-six miles at its base and extended about fifteen miles into Allied lines.

On August 27, the division received orders to move to the St. Mihiel area and subsequently to occupy the Rupt sector of the line. The division assumed command of this sector on September 8, under the command of the American V Corps. The weather during the assembly had been a combination of rain and mist, which served to mask the American preparations from the Germans. The division launched its attack on September 12. Initially, the Americans encountered stiff resistance, primarily from machine guns, but after those were neutralized, troops began to advance rapidly. On the evening of September 12, orders were received from V Corps headquarters indicating a change in plans. The division was ordered to move on until it reached Vigeulles, an important transportation hub approximately seven miles behind crumbling German lines. It was to be a race with the U.S. 1st Division coming from the south to see which would reach it first. The 102d Infantry reached the village at about 3:00 A.M. the following morning. Contact was made with the advancing 1st Division at 6:00 A.M., closing the salient. A tragic incident occurred just before noon when Allied aircraft, believing the village still to be in German hands, bombed it, wounding thirty Americans. The 26th Division settled down to occupy the line between Fresnes and Thillot-sous-les-Côtes, a quiet sector except for the daily German harassing fire and occasional raid.

On September 22, General Edwards was told of the Meuse-Argonne offensive being planned. As its role, the division was to stage a raid against the Germans for the purpose of deceiving them as to where the main attack would occur. The 102d and 103d Infantry regiments supported by other elements of the division were assigned the task. On the morning of September 26, the 102d advanced toward Marcheville without difficulty due to the heavy fog that covered the entire area. German reaction became intense after aerial surveillance observed the American concentrations. The German counterattack inflicted heavy casualties, and heavy artillery fire often severed American communications. The order to withdraw was issued by 7:30 P.M. and completed by midnight. The raid accomplished its mission. The Germans concluded that it was the prelude to a larger attack. The division's sector was relatively quiet for the next few days. Then the 101st Infantry conducted another raid on October 2, resulting in the capture of 49 prisoners.

The 26th Division was relieved from its sector on October 8, moving to the area around Verdun in anticipation of its involvement in the Meuse-Argonne offensive. This offensive was designed to cut the principal supply line, the Carignan-Sedan-Mézière railroad, which was about thirty-three miles behind the front. To protect this line, the Germans had built four lines of strong field fortifications. The fortifications, when combined with the natural advantages of the terrain, were a challenge to any attacking force.

On October 13–14, the 26th moved into the area of the French XVII Corps, and by October 18 took command of a portion of the line near Flabas. The first unit into the line was the 104th Infantry. It was during this period that the divisional insignia the "YD" was adopted. Conditions along the line were poor, and in the continual rain and cold, disease became rampant. In an extremely controversial move, General Edwards was removed and replaced by BGen. Frank E. Bamford, a Regular Army brigade commander from the 1st Division. The troops resented the replacement, and it stirred deep emotions, even long after the war. Bamford's subsequent replacements, the day after he arrived, of Colonel Logan of the 101st Infantry, Colonel Hume of the 103d, and Brigadier General Cole of the 51st Infantry Brigade intensified the resentment toward the Regulars. The three officers were later reinstated by special order of General Pershing.

Between October 23 and 24, the division was ordered to consolidate the lines, and on October 26, an attack was ordered toward Carrefour de la Croix Antoine and Bois de Belleau (Belleau Wood). The division was ordered to engage in a series of raids on the German positions for the purpose of taking prisoners until November 8. Germans were seen leaving the line toward the rear, and corps headquarters had information concerning a general withdrawal. On November 9, the infantry was ordered to move forward to maintain contact with the retreating Germans. The advance was halted by fire from strong machine gun positions. The following morning, attacks continued, and the 26th again ran into strong resistance, advancing only 275 yards before being stopped. On the morning of November 11, slow advances were still being reported until stopped at 11 A.M.

Following the Armistice, the 26th was relieved and moved to the Benoitevaus and Nicey areas. The division's artillery moved to Bar-le-Duc. On November 17, the entire division began to assemble at Montigny-le-Roi. On Jan. 19, 1919, it moved again to the port of embarkation center at Le Mans to prepare for the return to the United States. The first units sailed from Brest on March 19, and the last unit arrived in Boston on April 22.

The division had spent 148 days in quiet lines and 45 in active sector trenches, suffered 13,000 wounded in action and 2,168 killed in action, captured 3,148 prisoners, and advanced against resistance 33 miles.

James Controvich

Bibliography

American Battle Monuments Commission. *26th Division, Summary of Operations in the World War*. Washington, DC: Government Printing Office, 1944.

Benwell, Harry A. *History of the Yankee Division*. Boston: Cornhill, 1919.

Taylor, Emerson G. *New England in France, 1917–1919. A History of the Twenty-sixth Division, U.S.A.* Boston: Houghton Mifflin, 1920.

United States Army: 27th Division

The 27th Division was one of the oldest organized divisions in the United States Army, only the 28th Division from Pennsylvania being older. It was organized as the New York division in the New York National Guard in February 1898 at Albany, New York. Mustered into service and redesignated as the 6th Division during the Punitive Expedition in Mexico, it served for six months during 1916. In February 1917, it was mobilized to guard vital installations and public utilities in the face of a mounting threat of war. On July 16, 1917, the division was mustered into federal service at Camp Whitman, New York, and redesignated the 27th Division.

While the division was mobilizing, orders were received to reorganize from a three-infantry brigade, each with three regiments, to a two-infantry brigade, each with two regiments, known as a "square" division. Although the Selective Service Act of 1917 indicated that National Guard units should retain their identities to the extent practical, many historic units were absorbed into the massive army being mobilized. The 27th division was under the command of MajGen. John F. O'Ryan. O'Ryan was unique among his fellow National Guard officers since he retained command of the division from its mobilization until its demobilization, the only National Guard division commander to do so during the war.

General O'Ryan was given the authority to reorganize his division and decide which units to retain. The 53d Infantry Brigade under the command of BGen. Robert E.L. Michie, a Regular Army officer, consisted of the 105th and 106th Infantry regiments. The 105th was derived from the 2d New York Infantry, the 106th from the 14th New York Infantry. BGen. James W. Lester, who commanded the brigade of the division during the Punitive Expedition,

assumed command of the 55th Infantry Brigade, composed of the 107th and 108th Infantry regiments. The 107th was the 7th New York Infantry. The 108th Infantry was formed from the 3d New York Infantry. Artillery support was provided by the 52d Artillery Brigade, which was made up of three field artillery regiments: the 104th from the 1st New York Field Artillery, the 105th from the 2d New York Field Artillery, and the 106th, which was originally the 65th New York Infantry.

National Guard troops were sent to camps rather than cantonments since it was expected that they would be shipped overseas before winter set in, and so on August 23, the division was ordered to proceed to Camp Walsworth, South Carolina. Upon arriving there, divisional troops worked on the construction of the camp. To assist the men in learning the intricacies of trench warfare, a trench system was constructed with 700 yards of trenches complete in every detail to those found in France. Schools were organized to teach the various weapons systems and tactics employed on the Western Front.

On September 18, General O'Ryan and a select number of headquarters officers were invited to observe the British and French armies. They arrived in France on October 7, and the party was assigned to the British 29th Division for orientation.

On May 1, 1918, an advanced detachment of the division left Hoboken, New Jersey, for France, arriving there on May 10. It was quickly followed by other units of the division, which were shipped out both from Hoboken and Newport News. On arrival in France, the division was assigned to the British Fourth Army for further training and indoctrination. To ease the integration into the line, the division was issued British weapons and equipment. While 200,000 American troops were received by the British, most were eventually sent to other fronts. Only the 27th and 30th divisions stayed with the British for the duration. Following its arrival in France, the 27th Division, less its artillery, was sent to the Rue-Buigny training area, about twelve and one-half miles north of Abbeville. The 52d Field Artillery Brigade went to Camp de Souge for training. It did not rejoin the division until after the war had ended, spending most of the time in support of the 33d Division.

The 27th Division began learning British tactics and procedures under the guidance of experienced British officers and noncommissioned officers. The American troops were almost completely dependent on British supply sources for clothing, rations, and munitions, since the American supply system did not start regular support of the division until after the Armistice. As a result, the division developed a mutual understanding and comradeship with their British counterparts.

On June 16, orders were received to proceed to the St. Valéry area south of the Somme. Division headquarters was established at Escarbotin, but its stay in the area was only to be for a few days since the division was to proceed to Beauval to support the British Third Army. But on July 2, it was ordered to the Flanders area, this time to support the British Second Army. The division began to move out on July 3, and its first casualties occurred during a night bombing attack on Nieurlet, where the 106th Machine Gun Battalion was billeted. One man was killed and twenty were wounded.

Division headquarters was established at Oudezeele in the Flanders sector on July 7. Along with troops of the U.S. 30th Division, the 27th began to organize and defend the positions of the East Poperinghe Line, which stretched from Scherpenberg hill on the south in a northeasterly direction to the villages of La Clytte and Dickerbusch. This line was the third but most important of the defensive positions of the British XIX Corps. The two divisions were ordered to further prepare the line and to hold it in the event of an attack. Plans called for the troops to study and familiarize themselves with the topographical features of the ground and the approaches to their sectors. To provide additional training so that the line would be held, small detachments were rotated into the frontline trenches held by the British divisions and troops were sent to a finishing course at the British ranges in the Tilques area. The first battle casualty due to ground combat occurred on July 13, when a soldier of the 102d Engineers was killed by enemy artillery fire. From July 25 through August 18, machine gun and infantry units of the 27th Division as large as battalions served with the British 6th and 41st divisions in the front lines stretching northwest of Kemmel to the vicinity of Elzenwalle. The troops were responsible for holding sections of the frontline trenches along with the British troops.

On August 15, the division was ordered to relieve the British 6th Division in the front lines, beginning on the night of August 21. Command of the sector passed to the 27th on August 23. The occupation of this sector was unusual for an American division since it was considered an active sector and the first deployment for most American divisions was in quiet sectors.

Information was received from British XIX Corps that the Germans were retreating, and the division was to send out patrols to locate the enemy. On August 31, the 53d Infantry Brigade led an advance southeast to the road from Neuve-Eglise to Ypres. Advancing battalions of the 105th and 106th Infantry regiments reported light resistance from the Germans, and the brigade was ordered to continue the advance on the Vierstraat ridge. It advanced through Vierstraat about one-third mile south of Voormezeele. The advance was ordered to continue the next day. The Americans encountered stiff resistance, and the command realized that the Germans had stopped their retreat and were attempting to hold the lines. The advance, however, continued on the night of September 1 and pushed ahead over 820 yards before being forced back by a heavy German counterattack.

The division was relieved by the British 41st Division during the night of September 2–3 and ordered to assemble near Doullens in the British Third Army area as part of the British general headquarters reserve. The actions at Dickerbusch Lake-Scherpenberg sector and the Ypres-Lys offensive had caused the division a total of 1,336 casualties including 185 killed in action.

The buildup of American troops had enabled the Allied forces to begin a series of offensive actions. The American First Army had reduced the St. Mihiel salient; the British Somme offensive had reduced the Amiens salient. Now the Allied armies confronted the Hindenburg Line, made up of a series of strong defensive positions between three and three-quarters and five and one-half miles in depth. The St. Quentin Canal was incorporated into the positions and the great tunnel at Bellicourt was used by the Germans as barracks for their troops, stables, and aide stations. The tunnel was nearly four miles long and passages led up to the defensive trench systems. In mid-September, British and Australian forces began to attack outposts of the Hindenburg Line with the intent of capturing jumping-off points for a general attack. The maneuvers were not entirely successful as the British were unable to secure the outer works positions before turning the sector over to the 27th Division.

U

During the night of September 24–25, the 27th Division moved into the line to relieve the British 18th and 74th divisions. It was under the command of the American II Corps, which also included the American 30th Division. II Corps' mission was to penetrate the Hindenburg Line over the St. Quentin Tunnel between Vendhuile and Ville Noire. The American troops were being used as assault troops to penetrate the strong German positions, and upon gaining the objectives, the Australian 3d and 5th Divisions would exploit the assault. The main attack was scheduled for September 29. The 106th Infantry of the 53d Infantry Brigade, which was holding the entire divisional front, was ordered to secure the outer defense line on September 27, while the rest of the division would carry out the main attack on the day scheduled. Earlier British troops had been unable to secure these positions. The attack was made on September 27 to capture outlying posts and although the regiment managed to take the German positions after intense fighting, it was unable to consolidate its positions and hold them against German counterattacks. The troops of the 106th were forced back with little or no gains. The battlefield situation was complicated since pockets of isolated survivors and wounded were behind the German lines holding fragments of trenches, shell holes, etc. The heroism of the Americans can be illustrated by the number of awards that were issued. There was criticism of the 106th since the troops failed to mop up overrun positions. But this criticism was muted after reviewing the size of the front and the number of troops that would have been necessary to accomplish the mop up. The 106th simply did not have enough men to conduct both an assault and a mop up. It took a full division of Australian troops, supported by part of the 27th Division, two days to accomplish that mission. Although the attack failed in securing the outer positions, it did succeed in inflicting heavy casualties on the Germans and disrupting their communications lines.

The mission of the U.S. II Corps was to secure Nauroy-Gouy, the main defensive line of the Hindenburg Line. Gouy was approximately 2,000 yards behind the Hindenburg Line in the 27th Division's sector. The division attacked at 5:30 A.M. on September 29 with the 54th Brigade, comprised of the 107th and 108th Infantry regiments, leading the attack supported by tanks and British artillery. The artillery was British since the division's own artillery had

been detached. Strong resistance was encountered. By midmorning, the outer works had been taken, and troops were advancing slowly through the main defensive positions. The Australian 3d Division was ordered to assist the attacking troops, and the command of the sector passed to the Australian 3d Division. Because of the intertwining of American and Australian troops, elements of the 27th Division were still in the lines and continued to support the Australians. The Hindenburg Line was penetrated on September 29 by the American 30th Division, and by the combined American-Australian forces on October 1. The U.S. II Corps had accomplished the tasks assigned to it. The British were quick to exploit the break in the German lines, and the Germans were forced to withdraw.

On October 1, the 27th was ordered to the Peronne area for rehabilitation. Troops still in the lines were allowed to stay until such time as they could be relieved. The division was assigned to the American II Corps reserve. Pursuant to orders of II Corps, it was ordered to relieve the American 30th Division on the line at St. Benin to Vaux Andigny during the night of October 11–12. The 54th Brigade occupied the line between the British 6th on the right and the British 50th Division to its left. There was constant patrolling, shelling, and raids to keep the German troops occupied. On October 17, the division was ordered along with the American 30th Division, to advance and cross the Le Selle River. The 102d Engineer Regiment was to provide support and repair bridges to allow tanks and artillery to cross. The attack was crossing the river and moved steadily ahead. The advance was so rapid, since troops were now advancing over open country, that large quantities of German supplies were captured, including a locomotive and fifteen cars. When relieved by the British 1st Division on October 20, the 27th Division had advanced about six and a half miles to the southern edge of Basuel.

The division was ordered into II Corps reserve at Corbie for a rest since it had been on the line for the better part of the preceding month. The area was in poor shape due to artillery fire. Divisional troops immediately began to make repairs and improvements. The area was devoid of civilians when the troops first arrived, but within days former inhabitants began to return. The division organized both an education and training program for officers to review the lessons of the preceding actions and an active entertainment program for the troops. Passes were granted in order to improve morale and to allow the troops to see some of the local sights. Replacements began to arrive toward the end of October, most of which went to the 106th Infantry.

News of the end of the war was greeted quietly without any great celebration. At the time of the Armistice, over 5,000 men were in hospitals as a result of wounds suffered in battle.

On November 23, the division, still less its artillery, moved to the American embarkation center at Le Mans for return to the United States. On December 13–14, the divisional artillery rejoined the 27th there. Divisional units began to ship out of Le Harve for New York on February 17, the last one arriving in New York in March 1919. On April 1, at Camp Upton, New York, the division was demobilized and reverted back to state control.

The division had served 57 days in active sector trenches, suffered 7,201 wounded in action, 1,785 killed in action, captured 2,358 prisoners, and advanced against resistance about seven miles.

James Controvich

Bibliography

American Battle Monuments Commission. *27th Division, Summary of Operations in the World War*. Washington, DC: Government Printing Office, 1944.

O'Ryan, John F. *The Story of the 27th Division*. New York: Wynkoop Hallenbeck Crawford, 1921.

United States Army: 28th Division

Organized around the Pennsylvania National Guard and unofficially known as the "Keystone Division," the 28th Division, previously designated the 7th Division, was mobilized on July 15, 1917, although individual units had already been called into service in April to guard bridges, dams, tunnels, munitions plants, and other war-related facilities throughout Pennsylvania. On August 5, the division was drafted into federal service, and during August and September, it moved to Camp Hancock near Augusta, Georgia, where it trained for eight months in such military matters as trench construction, rifle and bayonet practice, and tactics. At Camp Hancock, thousands of new recruits and draftees were added to the division to bring

its units up to authorized strength; so before long, only one-half of the division's men were Pennsylvanians. Moreover, the division was reorganized in line with the newly developed Table of Organization laid down by the War Department General Staff. As a result, its nine infantry regiments were consolidated into four regiments—the 109th, 110th, 111th, and 112th U.S. Infantry regiments—grouped into two brigades. At the same time, many of the division's general and field-grade officers either resigned or were discharged because they did not measure up to the Regular Army's physical and performance standards. Among those discharged was the division commander, MajGen. Charles M. Clement, who was relieved in December 1917, for physical reasons. He was replaced by MajGen. Charles H. Muir, a Regular Army officer.

These organizational and personnel changes bred much resentment among many Pennsylvania guardsmen. They were convinced that in choosing which Guard regiments to maintain as base units for the new regiments and which to eliminate, the War Department had not adequately considered the identity and historical records of regiments that deserved to be preserved and overlooked questions of community pride. Consequently, after much protest from guardsmen and political figures from the Pittsburgh area, the War Department revised its original plan for consolidating regiments and agreed to substitute the 18th Pennsylvania Infantry, a Pittsburgh regiment, for the 3d Pennsylvania Infantry, a Philadelphia unit, as the base regiment for the 111th Regiment. Guardsmen were also angered that Guard officers with long years of service were being replaced by Regular Army officers, who, in the opinion of the guardsmen, were prejudiced against the National Guard. This sentiment carried over to the division's service in France and was reinforced in July 1918, when BGen. Thomas W. Darrah, a Regular Army officer commanding the 55th Infantry Brigade, relieved the Guard colonels commanding the 109th and 110th regiments on grounds of "inefficiency." To guardsmen, the relief of the two colonels was not justified and was just another example of Regular Army hostility toward the National Guard.

In April 1918, the 28th Division broke camp, and in May, with its units divided among several convoys departing from New York City and Hoboken, New Jersey, sailed to England. From there the divisions quickly moved to

U

France, where it was brigaded with two British divisions while training in Picardy. During the second week of June, the division was transferred to the French front, and by the end of the month, now attached to the French Sixth Army, the division, minus its artillery brigade (which was in training in Belgium), went into a reserve position in the Château-Thierry sector of the line on the south face of the Marne salient and within German artillery range. The division suffered its first battle casualties on June 28, when four engineers were killed by shell fire.

The 28th Division, albeit with its two infantry brigades operating independently of each other, engaged in its first major combat actions in early July when units from the 56th Infantry Brigade fought alongside the French in sharp battles in the vicinity of Vaux and Hill 204. In mid-July, units from the 55th Infantry Brigade participated in the Champagne-Marne phase of the Second Battle of the Marne. The most notable were two companies, each from the 109th and 110th regiments, that were integrated into the French 125th Division, which was holding a section of the south bank of the Marne River east of Château-Thierry at the time the Germans launched an offensive on July 15 to cross the river. Under the weight of a shattering artillery barrage, the French withdrew without telling the Keystoners they were retreating, leaving four companies to be decimated by the swarming German infantry pouring across the river. Only a handful of survivors made it safely to the second line several miles to the rear, where supporting units from the 28th Division and other American and French divisions finally halted the German advance.

During the last days of July, the 55th Infantry Brigade participated in the Franco-American offensive down the spine of the Marne salient in the Aisne-Marne phase of the Second Battle of the Marne and was a leading unit in the assault across the Orucq River. From the outset, things went badly in the river crossing, largely because of mishandling by the French corps and army headquarters that were directing the offensive. Inadequate artillery support from French batteries and delays in receiving orders from French staff officers compelled the Keystoners to attack with minimal artillery preparation and almost no coordination with flanking units. As a result, the 28th had a tough time cracking the German position, and only after six assaults were the troops able to seize and hold part of the Bois

des Grimpettes on the far side of the river. While successful, the crossing was expensive, for in three days of fighting the brigade sustained 1,400 casualties, 300 of whom were killed or died of wounds.

At last together as a complete unit, the 28th Division spent a month from the first week in August to early September along the Vesle River in the vicinity of Fismes, maintaining a front line along the river in full view of the Germans and holding a precarious bridgehead across the river at Fismette. For the Keystoners, the Vesle became "Death Valley" as German artillery, machine gun, and sniper fire cost the bloodied division nearly 200 casualties each day. Convinced that the bridgehead at Fismette could not be defended against a concerted German attack, General Muir decided to abandon it on August 26. But he was overruled by Gen. Jean Degoutte, commander of the French Sixth Army. Soon afterward tragedy struck when a crack German assault battalion attacked the bridgehead and in vicious house-to-house fighting wiped out the two companies from the 112th Regiment holding the town. The Fismette debacle was a bitter pill for the American High Command to swallow, coming as it did after the previous instance of French sloppiness with American lives, and helped give the lie to the specious argument put forth by British and French leaders during the amalgamation controversy that American soldiers would be better served if they were led by battle-wise Allied commanders rather than American generals. By early September, as the Allies advanced beyond the Vesle toward the Aisne River in pursuit of the retreating Germans, the division was exhausted and was pulled out of the line for some desperately needed rest and refitting.

In late September, the 28th Division, recently assigned to the American First Army and with its depleted ranks brought back up to strength with thousands of replacements, took part in the initial American assault in the Meuse-Argonne offensive. It was charged with driving a wedge into the German line along the eastern edge of the Argonne Forest, which dominated the left of the Meuse-Argonne sector, and pushing forward through the valley of the Aire River. Like the divisions on its flanks, the 28th Division advanced slowly in the face of savage German resistance and the natural defensive features of the forest and the surrounding areas. For nearly two weeks, it inched its way ahead, and at one point, when the division seemed stalled, First Army headquarters sent two brigadiers from its staff and two new colonels in the hope that fresh leadership would enable the division to move faster. But the new combat leaders were little more successful than their predecessors in gaining ground in the rugged Argonne Forest and the fire-swept Aire valley, and the two brigadiers, wiser for the experience, soon returned to their staff posts. By October 7, when it was pulled out of the line, the division had suffered 6,200 casualties in the struggle, with another 1,200 evacuated because of influenza or pneumonia. After another period of rest and refitting, the still worn 28th Division, now commanded by MajGen. William H. Hay after Muir's elevation to the command of IV Corps, finished the war with the American Second Army in operations in the Thiacourt sector.

Following the Armistice on Nov. 11, 1918, the 28th Division remained in France until April 1919. It then returned to the United States and was mustered out of service at Camp Dix, New Jersey, after a giant homecoming parade in Philadelphia. Although the division was in action for little more than four months, it, nevertheless, acquired an outstanding record in some of the fiercest fighting for Americans in the war and played a role in several of the decisive battles of the Western Front. Evidence of the division's extensive combat experience was its casualties: 2,874 dead and 11,265 wounded, the fifth highest of total casualties among American divisions and second only to the 42d Division among National Guard Divisions.

John K. Ohl

Bibliography

American Battle Monuments Commission. *28th Division, Summary of Operations in the World War.* Washington, DC: Government Printing Office, 1944.

Martin, Edward. *The Twenty-eighth Division: Pennsylvania's Guard in the World War.* 5 vols. Pittsburgh: 28th Division Publishing Co., 1923–1924.

Murrin, James A. *With the 112th in France: A Doughboy's Story of the War.* Philadelphia: Lippincott, 1919.

Ohl, John K. "The Keystone Division in the Great War." *Prologue* X (Summer 1978).

United States Army: 30th Division

The 30th Division was initially comprised of National Guard units from North Carolina, South Carolina, and Tennessee. Its name, "Old Hickory Division," honored U.S. Army general and seventh president Andrew Jackson, who had connections with all three states. The division garnered several distinctions in the war: it was the first to break the German Hindenburg Line on the Cambrai-St. Quentin front, and its soldiers were awarded more Medals of Honor than soldiers in any American division. Also notable of the division, 95 percent of its original members came from American-born parents, rare when compared to other American divisions.

On July 18, 1917, War Department General Order No. 95 ordered the formation of the 30th Division. Many of its units had recently served on the United States-Mexican border during the dispute with bandit Pancho Villa. Most of the soldiers had just returned from the border and some were still there on duty when the War Department called the division into federal service on July 25, 1917. Beginning in July, the three states sent their guard units to Camp Sevier, near Greenville, South Carolina.

On Aug. 28, 1917, MajGen. J.F. Morrison took command of the division. On September 12, under the authority of the War Department, he ordered the complete reorganization of the division. Various state distinctions were eliminated; each state's unit was given a new designation; some units were split up to form new ones. In October, a contingent of draftees arrived from several other camps to fill the division's ranks. Many draftees were natives of the division's "home" states; others came from Kentucky, Indiana, Illinois, Iowa, Minnesota, and North Dakota. This increase brought the division to full wartime strength of about 27,000 men.

Training and reorganization for war service proved difficult through the fall and winter of 1917–1918. In November, the first outbreaks of disease, including measles, pneumonia, and spinal meningitis, broke out among the troops. Often entire companies of men were placed in quarantine, and many of the recruits died. These epidemics greatly compromised training efforts. During the same time, the division command structure was disrupted when General Morrison was replaced by BGen. Winfield S. Scott, who was then replaced by MajGen. C.P. Townsley. The lack of equipment also slowed combat instruction. Gun crews in the artillery brigade used pine logs to learn firing procedures.

In April 1918, the 30th Division was ordered to prepare for transfer to Europe. On May 1, troops began traveling north to embarkation points at Camp Mills, New York, or Camp Merritt, New Jersey. By May 7, the first soldiers left for Europe; others followed in the next weeks. On departure, MajGen. George W. Read assumed division command. After about a two-week voyage, most of the division units paused at Liverpool, England, before departing for Calais, France. By mid-June, all division personnel arrived in France. On arrival there, the 55th Field Artillery Brigade was detached from the division and was sent into training at Camp Coëtquidan. It was not returned to the division but was assigned to other American Expeditionary Force (AEF) divisions.

The bulk of the 30th Division joined the American II Corps, which was attached to the British Army in northern France. In June 1918, the division underwent extensive combat training under British supervision, and American equipment and firearms were exchanged for British-made weaponry. In mid-June, General Read was promoted to American II Corps commander; he was replaced by MajGen. E.M. Lewis, who commanded the division until the end of the war.

On July 2, 1918, the 30th Division was sent to the British Second Army in Belgium, where it received additional training for combat. On a rotating schedule different units of the division spent limited time on the frontline trenches. This arrangement changed on August 16 when the entire division was sent to the front. Here it replaced the British troops in the canal sector trenches between Ypres and Voormezeele. On August 19, the British Ypres-Lys offensive officially began.

On the canal sector the division engaged in battle for the first time. On August 31, the 60th Infantry Brigade (119th and 120th Infantry Regiments) sent combat patrols to learn if the Germans were abandoning their lines as reported. After meeting stiff resistance, most patrols were forced to withdraw to their own lines. On September 1, following a British artillery barrage, both regiments went forward again. During the next two days of fighting, they captured all of their objectives, including Lock No. 8 on the Ypres Canal, Lankhof Farm, and the village of Voormezeele. Some 300 enemy casualties were inflicted in the 1,500-yard advance. The two regiments' casualties were 37 dead and 128 wounded.

On September 3, the division was replaced and sent to the St. Pol area for rest. On September 15, it went to the Puchevillers area for additional training for its role in the Somme offensive. On September 20, the American II Corps (composed of the 27th and 30th divisions) was called to the Gouy-Nauroy sector and transferred to the British Fourth Army. By September 25, the American divisions were in position opposite the Hindenburg Line's St. Quentin trench complex. In the 30th Division, the 59th Infantry Brigade took position in line; the 118th Infantry Regiment held the frontline trench with 117th in direct support. The 60th Infantry Brigade was held in division reserve.

On the night of September 26, the American divisions each sent a regiment forward to capture the German outpost line. Securing the outpost line was critical to the assault planned against the main Hindenburg Line. The 30th Division occupied part of the line at the start; the 118th Infantry was successful in seizing the remainder of the line. The 27th Division was unable to capture its portion of the line due to stiff enemy resistance.

The British prepared for the massive assault with a two-day artillery bombardment on the German lines. On September 27, 30,000 mustard gas shells were fired on German positions, followed by high explosives and shrapnel. During this preliminary artillery bombardment, the 30th Division prepared for the attack. For several nights the 105th Engineers went out into no-man's-land to run barbed wire and to prepare paths through the wire for the attacking infantry. On the night of September 27, the 118th Infantry Regiment was replaced by the 119th and 120th Infantry regiments, the former on the left, the latter on the right.

At 5:50 A.M., September 29, the 119th and 120th Infantry regiments went over the top against the enemy lines. The 117th Infantry followed in support. In addition, thirty-four Mark V tanks were assigned to the attacking troops—twelve each for the 117th and 119th Infantry regiments, ten for the 120th Infantry. Due to high casualties, barbed-wire entanglements, and smoke from shell fire, the advancing lines lost all sense of organization.

Despite the confusion and losses, elements of the 30th Division broke through the Hindenburg Line by 7:30 A.M. Two hours later the 120th Infantry entered Bellicourt and then pushed on to Nauroy, its ultimate objective, which was won by midday. On the left, the 119th Infantry Regiment had difficulties. It crossed the Hindenburg Line well ahead of schedule but soon found its left flank unsupported by the 27th Division and exposed to enemy fire. The 27th Division was not there because it had been stopped by very stiff enemy opposition about a half mile behind the 119th advanced line. This left the 119th Infantry open to enfilading fire. The 119th held the ground it had won but was unable to advance further.

By 3:00 that afternoon, Australian troops passed through the 30th Division as planned and carried on the attack. The next day, September 30, the Americans were pulled out of the battle and sent to the rear. The attack made by the 30th Division was a tremendous success. The division was later credited as the first to break the Hindenburg Line. In addition to the large cache of enemy arms and equipment captured, about 47 German officers and 1,432 soldiers were taken prisoner. For these spoils and the 3,000-yard advance made against enemy lines, the division suffered about 3,000 casualties.

After only two days of rest behind the battle lines, the 30th Division was called back to the front. On the night of October 5, the 117th and 118th Infantry regiments went into the line, replacing the Australians. In the first two days of fighting, the division advanced over six miles, often leaving behind the British troops on both flanks. On October 10, the 119th and 120th regiments replaced the other two regiments and continued attacking the German rear guard positions. This advance was stopped by the enemy at Vaux-Andigny, near the La Selle River. On the night of October 11, the 27th Division replaced the 30th Division on the front line. In the five days of combat, the 30th Division lost another 1,108 men.

The division was again sent to the rear for rest and reorganization. Once more the respite was not long. On the night of October 15, the division was moved back into almost the same position near Vaux-Andigny that it had departed from days earlier. The British spent October 16 bombarding the German lines. The 59th Infantry Brigade of the division attacked and captured the town the next day and crossed the La Selle River. On the night of October 17, the 60th Brigade moved to the front and continued the attack until the night of October 19, when it was ordered to stop its advance. The

division was pulled out of combat and sent to the rear. This marked an end to its combat service. From July to October, the division's casualties were 1,641 killed or dead from wounds and 6,774 wounded (for a total of 8,415 losses), 198 missing, and 77 prisoners.

For the remainder of October and until the cease-fire on November 11, the 30th Division was being reorganized in the Querrieu area. On November 16, the division was transferred to the AEF. It remained in camp in the Le Mans area in France and was not part of the Army of Occupation. In February 1919, the artillery brigade rejoined the division, and in March, the division sailed home from St. Nazaire. Most of the division units landed in Charleston, South Carolina others disembarked at Newport News, Virginia. After the units took part in parades throughout North Carolina, South Carolina, and Tennessee, the men were discharged from either Camp Jackson or Fort Oglethorpe. Demobilization was completed by the end of April 1919.

R.J. Marshall

Bibliography
Conway, C.B., and G.A. Shuford. *History of the 119th Infantry, 60th Brigade, 30th Division, U.S.A.* N.p., n.d.
Murphy, Elmer A., and Robert S. Thomas. *The Thirtieth Division in the World War.* Lepanto, AR: N.p., 1936.
Royall, Sam J. *History of the 118th Infantry, American Expeditionary Force, France.* Columbia, SC: N.p., 1919.
Sullivan, Willard P., and Harry Tucker. *The History of the 105th Regiment of Engineers.* New York: Doran, 1919.
Walker, John O. *Official History of the 120th Infantry, "3d North Carolina," 30th Division.* N.p., n.d.

United States Army: 32d Division
The 32d Division fought in the Aisne-Marne, Oise-Aisne, and Meuse-Argonne offensives and, following the Armistice, participated in the occupation of Germany.

After the United States declared war on Germany, the War Department decided to use the troops of the Wisconsin and Michigan National Guards to form the 32d Division. In August 1917, soldiers from these two states began arriving at Camp MacArthur, Texas. Michigan troops formed the division's 63d Infantry Brigade and part of the 57th Field Artillery Brigade, while troopers from Wisconsin made up the remainder of the 57th Field Artillery, the 64th Infantry Brigade, and the bulk of the division's special troops. Despite shortages of equipment, weapons, and a constant turnover in personnel, military training of the forces moved forward, albeit on a basic level.

In January 1918, the 32d Division sailed for France. When it arrived, the American Expeditionary Force (AEF) designated it a replacement division and began transferring its men to other units. In March, 7,000 men left the 32d as replacements. The German spring offensive and the protests of the division commander, MajGen. William G. Haan, saved the division from complete dismemberment. By April, the Allies' need for new units had become critical, and the 32d Division regained its combat status and moved to a quiet sector in Alsace for further training.

In late July, the division moved into the Aisne-Marne region northeast of Paris and joined the French XXXVIII Corps. In June, the Germans had driven a huge bulge into the Allied line in the region; in July, the French and Americans had begun to reduce it. The Allied offensive was already underway when the 32d's 64th Infantry Brigade relieved the U.S. 3d Division in the front line during the night of July 29–30. That afternoon the 64th, along with the U.S. 28th Division on its left, attacked the German entrenchments in the trees of the Bois des Grimpettes. The division's artillery brigade had not yet arrived, so the 3d Division's artillery remained to provide fire support for the operation. After a short but intense artillery preparation, the infantry assault pushed back the German line and cleared the woods.

During the night of July 30–31, the 32d Division's other infantry brigade, the 63d, moved forward and took over the 28th Division's area. As the 63d Brigade moved into position, the French informed Haan that the Germans were pulling back toward the Vesle River, and Haan ordered an immediate pursuit. The division pushed forward and captured the village of Cierges, but faltered in the face of stubborn resistance from the German strongpoints along the forward slope of Hill 230 in the Bois de Jomblets and at Bellevue Farm. The guardsmen continued their attacks into the night, but the "retreating" Germans held.

The following morning, Haan renewed the attack on Hill 230. A predawn assault on the hill failed, but later in the morning the 64th Brigade was able to swing one of its regiments around the German eastern flank. In the early afternoon, the brigade attacked and captured Bellevue Farm. Simultaneously, the 63d Brigade fought its way into the Bois de Jomblets. By nightfall, the 32d had knocked out the last major German strongpoints south of the Vesle, and the Germans were in genuine retreat.

Early on the morning of August 2, Haan began his pursuit. Resistance was light and the division advanced over three-mile aisles through rolling farmland and a soaking rain. The next day, the men moved forward another four miles, but German opposition stiffened as the 32d approached the Vesle River. On August 4, the division pushed into the village of Fismes and on to the south bank of the Vesle. Fighting continued in Fismes the following day, and the division made several unsuccessful attempts to cross the river.

The U.S. III Corps, which had taken control of the 32d Division on August 4, decided that a fresh force should make the crossing of the Vesle and so pulled the 32d out of the line on August 7. In its first offensive action, the division had fought elements of three German divisions, with 777 guardsmen killed and another 3,162 wounded. Both the French and the American High Command were pleased with the division's performance. The commander of the French Tenth Army, Gen. Charles Mangin, referred to the 32d's troopers as les *soldats terribles*. Thereafter, the division's nickname was "*Les Terribles*."

After a two-week rest, during which time the 57th Field Artillery Brigade finally rejoined the division, AEF headquarters sent the 32d Division west to join in the Oise-Aisne offensive. Here the French Tenth Army was attempting to turn the German line along the Aisne and Vesle rivers by an attack toward the city of Laon. For its part, the 32d was to seize the heavily defended town of Juvigny. During the night of August 27–28, the division's 63d Brigade replaced the French 127th Division in the Allied positions a mile west of the town. Juvigny sat at the head of a wooded ravine, but the terrain to the west, north, and east of the town was open.

On August 28, the 63d seized a small ridge in front of its position and defeated a German counterattack, but the main assault did not begin until the following day. At 5:25 A.M., after a twenty-five-minute artillery barrage and accompanied by French tanks, the 63d Brigade began its attack. It had moved only a few hundred yards, however, before heavy German artillery and machine gun fire halted it. The French XXX Corps ordered another attempt, but Haan persuaded the corps commander to postpone it until he could make adequate preparations. That night, while the division staff made plans for a new assault, Haan withdrew the battered 63d and replaced it with the 64th Brigade. In just a few hours fighting, the 63d Brigade had lost 166 killed and 739 wounded.

Throughout the next two days, the 32d kept the German positions under constant shell fire. At 1:00 P.M. on August 30, XXX Corps notified Haan that the French had broken through the German positions south of his division. Without any increase in artillery fire, Haan ordered the 64th's two regiments to attack. One regiment advanced into the open ground in front of Juvigny in order to attract the defender's attention, while the other regiment rushed into the wooded ravine south of the town and then struck north into Juvigny itself. The audacious attack completely surprised the Germans, and by nightfall the Americans had captured the town and 156 prisoners.

The following morning the entire French Tenth Army moved forward again after a four-hour artillery bombardment. Haan added his own touch to the preparations by ordering a walking barrage in front of his division. German machine gunners usually remained in their shelters until the Allied artillery attack had passed over their positions. Then, they would dash out to their weapons and fire on the infantry following the barrage. Haan hoped that by shelling these positions twice after the initial barrage had passed he would catch the Germans unprotected. Despite Haan's precautions, casualties remained high during the division's mile-and-one-half advance.

During the night of September 2, the French Moroccan Division relieved the 32d in the line. Over five days, the 32d Division had fought parts of five German divisions and captured 937 prisoners. In the process, though, the division lost 4,885 men killed and 1,850 wounded. General Mangin praised the 32d's capture of Juvigny. Moreover, he took the unusual step of decorating all of the division's infantry regiments and machine guns battalions, as well as dozens of the officers with the Croix de Guerre.

After nearly twenty days training its 5,000 replacements, the 32d Division marched to join the U.S. First Army. On September 26, the First Army began a massive campaign in the Meuse-Argonne region. Initially in reserve, the 32d joined the U.S. V Corps' attack on September 30. The division attacked north along Andon Creek in an open valley. Dominating the terrain was the wooded face of Hill 287, or Côte Dame Marie, a high, steep ridge that blocked the division's path. Rain, fog, mud, and skillful German delaying actions hindered the division as it butted its way down the Andon valley.

On October 10, the 32d Division ran into the main German defensive line, the Kriemhilde-Stellung, which ran along the southern face of Côte Dame Marie and through the town of Romagne. Haan decided against a direct assault on the hill; instead, he decided to seize Romagne and then strike Côte Dame Marie from its eastern flank. After scouting out the German positions for two days, the division attacked on October 14. One regiment captured Romagne, while another actually slipped through the German barbed wire and secured a small portion of the ridge. The next day, the division renewed the assault and pushed the Germans off the ridge.

The Germans retreated to their next defensive line in the Bois de Bantheville. The 32d Division pounded the woods with artillery and machine gun fire. As the American fire subsided, strong patrols entered the woods and found that the Germans were offering only light resistance. Faced with sporadic opposition, the division waded into the woods and quickly pressed the enemy back. Soon the division had surged ahead of the American divisions on either side of it. Battered and tired from weeks of fighting, the 32d division was pulled out of the front line by V Corps for a rest on October 20.

After twenty days of continuous combat, the division had advanced nearly four miles against some of the strongest and best-organized opposition in the campaign. In the process, it fought elements of eleven German divisions and captured 1,095 prisoners. The division's 1,179 dead and 4,327 wounded reflected the tough going. Compared to its nearly 4,000 casualties in the nine days of the Aisne-Marne, the figures for the first phase of the Meuse-Argonne illustrated how much the division had improved since July.

The 32d Division joined the U.S. III Corps east of the Meuse River on October 27. Initially in reserve, the division took over the sector of the French 15th Colonial Division during the night of November 9–10. III Corps reported that the Germans were withdrawing, but Haan and the division staff were skeptical and ordered strong patrols to feel out the enemy's defenses. The division's 64th Brigade began its advance that morning enveloped in a thick fog. Against light opposition one regiment gained over a mile, but when the fog cleared at 9:00 A.M., it found itself behind a strong enemy position and surrounded by Germans. The regiment fought its way out, but losses were heavy and many of the wounded had to be abandoned. The division prepared a formal attack for the following morning. But as the troops prepared to leave their positions, Haan received word of the Armistice and stopped the operation.

With the end of the fighting, the 32d Division joined the U.S. Third Army for the march into Germany. In recognition of its war record, the AEF selected the division to lead one of the Americans columns into the Rhineland. For the next four months, the 32d Division occupied the area around Coblenz. Life in the Army of Occupation was not difficult, but the guardsmen were anxious to go home. In April 1919, the division returned to the United States and demobilized.

Richard Kehrberg

Bibliography

American Battle Monuments Commission. *32d Division, Summary of Operations in the World War.* Washington, DC: Government Printing Office, 1943.

Garlock, Glenn W. *Tales of the Thirty-Second.* West Salem, WI: Badger Publishing, 1927.

Joint War History Commission of Michigan and Wisconsin. *The 32d Division in the World War.* Milwaukee, WI: Wisconsin Printing, 1920.

United States Army: 33d Division

On July 18, 1917, the War Department authorized the National Guard troops of Illinois to form the 33d Division. The units were called into federal service on July 25, and on August 3, they were ordered to assemble at Camp Logan in Houston, Texas. MajGen. George Bell, Jr., assumed command on August 25 and retained command until June 1919. By August 24, the 65th Brigade was organized. It included the Illinois 3d and 4th Infantry regiments, later the 129th and 130th Infantry regiments, respectively, and the 123d Machine Gun Battalion. On September 10, the 58th Field Artillery (FA) Brigade was formed, including the 2d and 3d FA regiments and the 6th Infantry, all from Illinois, later the 122d, 123d, and 124th FA, respectively. On September 11, the 66th Brigade was organized to include the Illinois infantry regiments, 1st and 2d Infantry, and elements of the 5th and 7th, later 131st and 132d Infantry regiments and the 124th Machine Gun Battalion. Beginning October 1 with all these troops at Camp Logan, systematic training began. Between October 25 and November 13, an additional 5,600 National Army men arrived from the 86th Division, as did 1,000 from the 88th Division. The following April, 7,000 National Army men were transferred from the 84th, 86th and 88th divisions to complete the manpower requirements of the division.

Divisional units began their transfers to the East Coast for transport to France on April 23, 1918. The 108th Engineers and Train arrived at Camp Merritt, New Jersey, and the rest of the division went to Camp Upton, New York. By May 8, 1918, several units, as part of the advance group, sailed from Hoboken, New Jersey, and arrived at Brest, France, ten days later. On May 10, the infantry and several other units left from Hoboken, some arriving at Brest and some at Bordeaux from May 23 to May 30. The 58th Field Artillery Brigade and remaining units sailed on or about May 26 and June 5 and arrived at Liverpool, England, between June 8 and 15.

Though under administrative control of II Corps, the division began training with the British Army in Picardy. The infantry troops were based at the training areas at Martainneville and Huppy, while the 58th Field Artillery Brigade was assigned to training areas at Valdahon and Ornans. By June 21, the division less the 58th Field Artillery Brigade, 108th Engineers and trains, were moved to the Long and Martainneville areas near Amiens. Contrary to the promises made to General Pershing, the British commander in the area assigned elements of the 131st and 132d Infantry regiments to the 4th Australian Division to take part in an attack that captured Hamel and the high ground beyond. The attack took place on July 4, and by the next day was over. Gen. Henry Rawlinson, commanding the British Fourth

Army, sent a telegram congratulating General Bell on the performance of the American units, adding, "My only regret is that I was not permitted to employ a larger portion of your fine division." The British commander-in-chief, Field Marshal Sir Douglas Haig, subsequently assured Pershing that the British would not use American troops without permission again.

On July 5, the division was reviewed by British Prime Minister David Lloyd George, and on the following day the four companies of the 131st and 132d Infantry were relieved from the trenches and returned to their respective organizations. For the next four weeks, the division was again in training while II Corps was determining if the men were fit for active service. In the meantime, the British had determined to take Chipilly Ridge, directly opposite Hamel. The British line was seriously enfiladed by fire from that ridge, and since it and Bois de Gressaire were the key to the entire sector, Haig elected to make a supreme effort to eliminate the problem once and for all.

On Aug. 8, 1918, orders were received by Col. Joseph B. Sanborn of the 131st Infantry transferring the regiment to the command of Major General Ramsay, commanding the British 58th Division as reserve for the British III Corps. After arriving at the designated rendezvous, additional instructions were issued to regimental commanders directing them to assemble at a point on the Bray-Corbie road, about 3,000 yards south of Heilly. Upon arrival they were expected to attack at 1:00 A.M. the next morning. Because the troops had been marching most of the night and were without support and food, and had no idea what the terrain was like, Ramsay decided to postpone the attack. The 131st Infantry was sent forward to a position between Vaux-sur-Somme and Sailly-le-Sec. The regimental machine gun company was detached and shifted to Vaux and there to await orders. At 1:30 P.M. on August 9, Colonel Sanborn was advised that his regiment would be going forward to an attack zone, but first he must reconnoiter in the direction of Bois de Gressaire. But the party soon returned and informed Sanborn that the enemy held the entire region in force and that it was impossible for them to effect the reconnaissance.

At 3:30 P.M., General Ramsay came to the 131st personally to deliver the attack order for the regiment, but when it was realized that the regiment could not possibly reach the jumping-off line at the designated time, 5:00 P.M., the time was advanced to 5:30 P.M. The colonel and his regiment literally ran the four miles in order to make the attack on time. The battalions in line were as follows: 1st on the right, 2d at the left, and 3d in reserve. The regiment jumped off on time, led by their sixty-two-year-old colonel and a line of skirmishers, through a heavy barrage of enemy fire. Sanborn, being knocked down by a shell blast, returned to the rear and collected runners from the reserve battalion and established his command post in a ravine between Les Celestins and Bois de Malard.

The 131st could not be beaten back, and the Germans scattered. By 7:00 P.M., even the machine guns were unable to check the American advance and the 2d Battalion reported having reached its objective. Its left flank was unprotected since the 175th British Brigade was unable to keep up with the Americans and did not arrive until the following day. Unfortunately the 1st Battalion on the right flank along with its flank support, the 10th London Battalion, were held up by heavy machine gun fire from the woods northwest of Chipilly Ridge. The commander of the London Battalion called for help, and a company from the 3d Battalion, 131st, was dispatched to its aid. The enemy was thereupon driven out of the woods. Because of the heavy concentration of machine guns and enemy troops on the ridge, further advance was deemed impossible. That night a British detachment took the town of Chipilly, then advanced to the ridge, and captured all the machine guns along the ridge as well as the German commander. In the meantime, the 1st Battalion line extended from a point southwest of Bois de Gressaire east to the northern end of Chipilly Ridge and then south along the Somme to the road leading to the town of Chipilly. The 2d Battalion had both flanks unprotected until the following morning, August 10. Before that, it had been joined by the 1st Battalion at about 6:00 A.M. and a little later by the 3d Battalion.

Despite heavy, concentrated, artillery and machine gun fire, plus gas attacks, the regiment held its position. The ranks consolidated, and at 9:00 P.M. of August 10, the 13th Australian Brigade passed through their lines and set up positions opposite Bray-sur-Somme and the bend of the Somme River. During the night, the 131st changed front and occupied a line running from the crossroads at the eastern edge of the wood north of the Bray-Corbie road, south

U

to the Somme, then along the right bank to a point south of Chipilly Ridge. The attack by the 131st gave the British a much needed victory as well as the attainment of their objective. From then until August 16, the 131st Regiment was subjected to heavy and incessant fire and gas attacks. The losses sustained by the regiment for the entire period numbered more than 750. But the losses were not in vain, for the penetration of the German lines at Bois de Gressaire gave the British the initiative for their next and final advance.

For the next two weeks, the 33d Division trained behind the British lines, though frequently shelled by the enemy. On August 12, King George V arrived at division headquarters to honor the troops. After decorating Generals Pershing and Bliss, who had arrived the day before, the king proceeded to a place where 300 men of the 33d Division were drawn up. He then pinned decorations ranging from the Military Cross, the Distinguished Service Medal, to the Military Medal on twelve officers and men for gallantry while attached to British forces. Seven others singled out were unfortunately in a hospital and unable to participate in the awards ceremony.

The division commander received many written accolades from officers of the various British units to which the division had been assigned during the training and combat period. The division was also visited by Assistant Secretary of the Navy Franklin D. Roosevelt, who delivered a speech to the assembled 65th Infantry Brigade thanking them for the stirring deeds and telling them he had learned of their prowess from King George himself. On the night of August 23–24, the division began entraining for transfer to the U.S. First Army at Toul. New division headquarters were opened in the chateau at Tronville-en-Barrois on August 25, and by early next morning all units had detrained and occupied billets in the same vicinity. The following week was spent in further training. On September 5, the division received orders placing it "at the disposal of the Second French Army for tactical control, administration, and supply." That night, the division, being subsequently transferred to control by the French XVII Corps, entrained for the Blercourt area, southwest of Verdun.

By September 8, the entire division had reassembled at Blercourt. Division commanders received orders from XVII Corps headquarters directing the division to relieve the French 157th Division in the sector of Hill 304 as well as elements of the French 120th Division located in the Cumières-le-Morte-Homme sector. During the nights of September 7–9, the relief was accomplished. Command was transferred to the 33d Division the morning of September 10 at their new headquarters in Fromereville. The 52d Artillery Brigade, moved into the Bois de Sartelles on the night of September 11–12 to participate in a diversion to cover the American attack at St. Mihiel.

Another change then occurred. The division passed to the control of the American III Corps, commanded by MajGen. Robert L. Bullard, on September 14. The 33d modified and made adjustments in its original positions through September 17 and finally was in a position that satisfied corps headquarters. During this period, many division soldiers and officers attended various schools. In addition, the U.S. 4th Division spent time under guidance from the 33d, participating in trench duties and generally getting the feeling of what the front lines were all about.

Under plans for the impending Meuse-Argonne offensive, III Corps, part of the American First Army, was to attack in the direction of Buzancy and Stonne. The corps position was to be on the right flank, next to the Meuse River and to maintain liaison with the French XVII Corps to its right. The mission would require III Corps to break through the enemy positions between Ruisseau de Forges and the Bois de Forêt and to exploit its success by advancing northward from the Bois to Buzancy and Stonne. In addition, they were also required to organize the west bank of the Meuse for defense as the attack progressed. The attack was to include the 33d Division on the east, its right flank along the left bank of the Meuse, the 80th Division in the center, and the 4th Division on the west of the corps. The French 18th Division was to the east of the 33d Division, and the U.S. 79th Division maintained liaison with the U.S. 4th Division. The first objective for III Corps was the Hagen-Stellung Nord and the second objective, the American Army objective, was the Volker-Stellung. Both were to be reached during "D" day.

On September 26, the great attack began. The 66th Brigade jumped off from trenches north of Regneville and south of Forges. The 131st and 132d Infantry regiments were abreast, with the latter on the right and the former on the left. Their objective was to capture all the villages between them and the northern edge of the Bois de Forêt. The 65th Brigade was divisional reserve. The assault was made under cover of a rolling barrage. The terrain over which the attack was launched was considered a natural fortress of extraordinary strength. The German positions opposite the 33d Division rested at its western extremity upon a line of ridges running northward from Sivary-la-Perche through the Malancourt woods to the walled town of Montfaucon. It was connected with the huge forest of Forges by a series of ridges running east to the Meuse River. From these ridges, spurs jut to the northeast or southeast. The soil was chalky and mostly solid. Valleys alternated between the ridges and were mainly marshy and averaged about seventeen feet in width as they pointed toward the Meuse. The American position faced a brook called Forges. It was, in wet weather, a formidable obstacle.

To make matters worse, the German positions were organized in three lines in depth. The first obstacle, beside the brook, were the Hagen-Stellung, Nord and Sud. Each was organized into two trenches, Sud being mainly a covering line heavy with machine guns and Nord being the major position of the two.

Beyond the Hagen-Stellung was the second line of resistance, the Volker-Stellung. It was between one and two miles distant behind the trenches of Nord. Its head was in the Argonne Forest southwest of Montblainville and its tail at Dannevoux. Though much of this line had been recently strengthened, some of it was in deplorable condition. The third, or final withdrawal position was named the Kriemhilde-Stellung. It constituted part of the Hindenburg Line. Though begun nearly a year before, the Hindenburg system of trenches was only partly completed, but in the area east of the Meuse, it was nearly finished and was particularly strong.

At 11:30 P.M., September 25, all corps artillery began their preparation fire. The fire continued all night, joined by army and division artillery later on. The troops assembled at their appointed places. In the 33d Division, all was in readiness. The 108th Engineers began constructing nine passageways over the Forges Brook, building the approaches and laying the duckboards and the ropes leading to them. Despite enemy artillery and machine gun fire, the engineers managed to accomplish their mission before zero hour. At 5:30 A.M., the attack began. It was covered by a fog, machine gun fire, and a smoke screen. The 66th Brigade and the 131st and 132d Infantry side by side, led off, using the nine passages across the Forges Brook prepared by the engineers. They quickly re-formed on the northern bank of the Meuse. Because the 319th U.S. Infantry failed to arrive at its position, west of the 131st Infantry, at zero hour, the 131st had to detach the 1st Battalion to clean up a portion of the sector assigned to the 319th, thereby slowing down the 33d Division somewhat. But all units reassembled on the opposite bank by 6:25 A.M.

At 6:27 A.M., the rolling barrage commenced again, and the re-formed troops proceeded toward their targets. But it was more difficult on the northern side of the river. Well-placed machine guns and an immense amount of enemy fire slowed down the advance. Efforts to tie in with the 80th Division on their western flank again proved fruitless. For this reason, the left flank of the regiment remained exposed throughout the attack and until long after its mission was achieved. The 131st Infantry maintained a swift pace and attained the regimental objective by 10:00 A.M., about four miles from the point of departure. By arriving so unexpectedly, 8 German officers, including a colonel, and 138 soldiers were taken by surprise in their dugouts. This made a total of 406 prisoners taken by the 1st Battalion that morning. Upon arrival, the 1st Battalion had taken up positions along the Verdun-Sedan highway and railroad, over a mile in length, and since no other American troops were in evidence, held a very thin line. In early afternoon, the mission battalions and their missing companies reassembled, and the entire regiment was together in its assigned objective by 12:30 P.M.

The 132d Infantry was equally successful in its attack. Its proximity to the Meuse River made it the pivot for all operations west of the river. The 132d also crossed the Forges Brook in the same manner as did the 131st. It ran into considerable machine gun fire at the southern edge of the Bois de Forges just after jumping off, but its advance was not halted. Company D of the 1st Battalion was given a special mission to take the village of Forges on its eastern front, reduce all opposition, and to mop up all the trenches in that vicinity. They did so and then rushed to rejoin their battalion.

As the batallion approached Bois de Forges, the troops were forced to break up into small units in order to advance through the wood without undue delay. They did so while mopping up the machine gun nests in their path along with bringing down the many German snipers who took refuge in the trees. As they approached the Ravin du Rapilleaux, they encountered stiff machine gun fire from a commanding German position on the opposite bank. This was quickly silenced by the battalion. At the same time, the left company of the battalion closed in on German battalion headquarters situated at the eastern edge of the woods between the mouth of the ravine and the Ravin Pimpanel. There the company surprised the defending Germans and captured a considerable number of prisoners and many machine guns.

The 66th Infantry Brigade of the 33d Division also covered itself with glory on September 26. On that day, the brigade had broken through an enemy position that had beaten back every attempt to take it during the previous four years, had taken the Bois de Forges, a formidable barrier, and had established itself on the west bank of the Meuse. The casualties suffered by the brigade amounted to 241 officers and men, of which only 36 had been killed. Its spoils included 1,400 prisoners, 26 artillery pieces, and over 100 machine guns. And in four hours, the brigade had advanced about four miles from its starting point.

For the next dozen days, the division dug in in the positions occupied, with modifications, and the men were subjected to heavy and incessant artillery and gas attacks. There was constant patrolling and training with the usual effects for front-line units. From September 26 to October 15, the division's 58th Field Artillery Brigade and 108th Ammunition Train supported the 91st and later the 32d Division in the Meuse-Argonne operation. On October 7 the 33d Division passed to the tactical control of the French XVII Corps, except for the 3d Battalion and machine gun company of the 132d Infantry, both of which remained under control of the U.S. 4th Division.

Two battalions of the 132d Infantry crossed the Meuse at Brabant-sur-Meuse on October 8 and moved in a northwesterly direction while maintaining contact with the French 18th Division. The regiment had reached a line including the northern outskirts of Consenvoye. One battalion from the 131st crossed the river to support the 132d as did one battalion of the 129th Infantry on October 9. On the night of October 9–10, the remaining infantry units crossed to the east bank and came to the sup-

port of the 66th Brigade. On October 10, the 33d Division continued to attack and reached a point east of Vanne on Highway No. 64. On October 12 and 13, a new line of resistance was formed south of the then front line and occupied by the division. The new position ran east and west through the Bois de Plat-Chêne and to the north of Hill 316. The battalion assigned to the 4th Division rejoined its parent there.

From October 18 through the night of October 20–21, the division was relieved by the French 15th Colonial Division. After a two-day rest period, the division relieved the U.S. 79th Division from Doncourt-aux-Templiers to Fresnes-en-Woëvre. While this was going on, the 58th Field Artillery Brigade was reassigned to support the 89th Division in the Meuse-Argonne operation.

From that date on, the 33d Division remained in the relatively quiet sector in which it found itself. It was, on November 11, at the village of Marcheville, about one mile beyond Fresnes-en-Woëvre, that it again saw action.

The division served with the Army of Occupation from November 12 until April 25, 1919. Between April 25 and May 5, the division moved to Brest, France, and within a few days was on its way home. By May 27, the last of the units had arrived in the United States, and final demobilization took place at Camp Grant.

During the war the 33d Division performed extremely well, usually under adverse conditions, even when thrown into the lines to attack along with seasoned Australian troops so very soon after arriving in France. Its part in the early stages of the Meuse-Argonne offensive helped to set the stage for the eventual success of the operation. Before this offensive, the men had ably assisted the British III Corps between the Somme and Ancre rivers and on the heights of Chilpilly Ridge and the Bois de Gressaire. The division was frequently detached for service with the French XVII Corps in September and early October, lending valuable assistance to whatever attacks they were engaged in. From the records it appears that the 58th Field Artillery Brigade never served as a component of its own division, but rather it was always attached to other divisions in a support function.

During its service in France, the 33d suffered 7,255 casualties, of which 993 were battle deaths. It was in the front lines a total of 98 days and advanced about twenty-two miles, capturing nearly 4,000 prisoners. The 33d Division had the distinction of being the only U.S. division that served under American, British, and French commands.

Charles Johnson

Bibliography

Center of Military History, U.S. Army. *Order of Battle of the United States Forces in the World War*. Vol. 2. *American Expeditionary Force: Divisions*. Washington, DC: Government Printing Office, 1988.

Huidekoper, Frederick L. *The History of the 33d Division A.E.F. Illinois in the World War*. Vol. 1. Springfield, IL: N.p., 1921.

United States Army: 35th Division

The War Department authorized the 35th Division on July 18, 1917. It was to be formed from the National Guard troops of Kansas and Missouri. Concentration of the division began at Camp Doniphan, Fort Sill, Oklahoma, on August 23. The troops trained there until April 1918. On April 16, the 35th began embarking for Europe from Brooklyn, Hoboken, New York, and Philadelphia. Some units went directly to Brest, France; others proceeded first to England and then on to France.

The division adopted the Santa Fe Cross as its insignia since the Santa Fe Trail originated from Camp Doniphan. Thus, it was sometimes referred to as the "Santa Fe" Division.

Upon its arrival in France, the division was attached to the British 30th Division for training in the Gamaches Training Area near Eu. The artillery brigade, field signal battalion and other such units were separated for specialized training.

While in France, the division was to undergo several changes of command. First named to command the division was MajGen. William M. Wright (Oct. 1, 1917, to June 16, 1918), followed by BGen. Nathaniel F. McClure (June 16 to July 20, 1918), and finally by MajGen. Peter Traub, a West Point classmate of General Pershing. Traub, who was highly regarded, would command the division through the end of the war, including the bulk of its combat experience.

The division left Gamaches in early June for the Arches Training Area near Épinal. From June 11 to September 2, it was assigned to the French XXXIII Corps (French Seventh Army) for training in the front lines.

On June 18, elements of the division moved into the Wesserling sector in the Vosges Mountains southeast of Épinal. Units of its 69th Infantry Brigade entered the front lines on June 20, the honor of being the first going to the 2d Battalion, 138th Infantry Regiment. Wesserling was considered a quiet sector, suitable for training new troops and resting tired units. The eager Americans found the French exhausted and anxious to keep the sector quiet. A few weeks later, however, the French withdrew, leaving the sector to the 35th Division.

During July, the doughboys conducted two fairly large-scale raids against German positions. A few men on both sides were killed and wounded, and several enemy prisoners were taken. By the time the division left the sector, it had suffered nearly 100 dead, the majority from accident and disease.

On September 2, the 35th Division was assigned to I Corps, which was stationed as part of the front near Pont-à-Mousson in preparation for the St. Mihiel offensive scheduled to jump off September 12. The 35th, with its artillery brigade, which had rejoined the division in August, moved into a position about twelve and one-half miles south of Pont-à-Mousson as the First Army reserve for the St. Mihiel operation. However, the attack was so successful that the 35th Division was not needed. On September 15, it began the move to the Meuse-Argonne front for the next offensive, which was to be the biggest American operation of the war.

During the night of September 20–21, the 35th Division relieved the French 73d Division near Vauquois, taking its place as one of the assault divisions for the Meuse-Argonne attack scheduled for September 26. Command of the sector passed to the 35th Division on the morning of September 21, though French troops remained in the outposts as a screen until the night of September 25–26.

The 35th was assigned to the right of I Corps (First Army), attacking alongside the 28th Division on its left. To its right was the 91st Division, assigned to V Corps. According to the First Army plan, I Corps was to drive down the Aire valley east of the Argonne Forest, flanking enemy positions in the forest.

The 35th Division field orders were issued at 5:00 P.M. September 24. According to those orders, the 69th Infantry Brigade would lead, while the 70th Brigade followed in division reserve. No frontal attack was to be made against Vauquois Hill and the wood to the northeast. Assault and support battalions were directed to drift to the east and west of these positions, which would then be mopped up by a battalion from division reserve.

The 35th Division's objective would be the ridge southeast of Charpentry. The attack would jump off at 5:30 A.M. under artillery and machine gun barrages. Smoke and gas would be placed on Vauquois Hill in an effort to mask this dominant terrain feature.

The division's objective was a tough one, and questions would later be raised as to why such an inexperienced organization was trusted with so much responsibility. The heights at Vauquois had repulsed all attack by the French in 1915, and the ground was torn by mines and countermining operations conducted during those assaults. The Aire valley where the 35th Division doughboys would have to advance was also zeroed in by enemy artillery and completely visible to enemy observers on the heights above.

Meanwhile, the division had suffered an organizational blow in the days just preceding the attack. Friction between National Guardsmen and Regular Army officers was common to virtually all of the National Guard organizations fielded in France. In mid-September, the friction in the 35th came to a head when the division was purged of many of its Guard officers. The commanders of both infantry brigades, three of the division's four infantry regiments, and one artillery regiment and the division chief of staff were replaced with Regular Army officers. As a result, the division was entering the Meuse-Argonne battle with considerable internal dissension, lack of familiarity between units and their commanders, and much mistrust and bitterness.

The division attacked on schedule at 5:30 A.M., September 26. The initial advance went well. On the right, elements of the division advanced east of Vauquois, and elements of two battalions were in front of the enemy main line of resistance in Cheppy by 8:30 A.M. The strongpoint fell about 12:30 P.M. under U.S. attack assisted by tanks. It was in the fighting around Cheppy that the first of two Medals of Honor earned by the division was won by Capt. Alexander R. Skinker, a company commander with the 138th Infantry. Unwilling to sacrifice his men when his company was held up by relentless machine gun fire from pillboxes at Cheppy, Skinker personally led an automatic rifleman and carrier in an attack on the guns. The carrier was killed instantly, but Skinker

seized the ammunition and continued through an opening in the barbed wire, feeding the automatic rifle until he too was killed.

It was in the same vicinity that Pvt. Nels Wold, also of the 138th Infantry, won the other Medal of Honor that same day. Wold attacked and silenced machine gun after machine gun. Later that day, while attempting to rush a fifth machine gun nest, he was killed.

On the left, elements of the division pushed forward to Hill 202 south of Charpentry. Varennes was also seized, mopped up in house-to-house fighting, which the doughboys learned the hard way, having no training in such techniques.

At 2:45 P.M., I Corps directed the 35th Division to continue the advance to the army objective (a generally northeast-southwest line from Exermont to Apremont). At 6:35 P.M., division headquarters tried to pass that order along, directing the 69th Infantry Brigade to attack. In what was to become an all too common occurrence in the days ahead, communication between headquarters broke down and the order was never received by the frontline battalions. As a result, the division did not advance during the night.

The error was compounded the following day. I Corps issued field orders at 1:00 A.M., September 27, directing that the attack be resumed at 5:30 A.M. toward the combined army objective—a point about three miles north of Fleville. Through a misunderstanding, the 35th Division issued two orders for the attack. The final orders set the hour of attack at 6:30 A.M., one hour after the time designated by corps.

The 140th Infantry on the right passed through the 138th Infantry at 5:30 A.M. and advanced at 6:30 A.M. with very weak artillery support. On the left, the 139th Infantry vainly waited for its artillery support until 9:00 A.M., then finally attacked without it. Both regiments were stopped by enemy fire after advancing only a short distance.

Another attempt to advance, assisted by tanks, was made about noon. The 139th managed to scratch out about 330 yards when artillery fire put the tanks out of action and ended the advance. The 140th received its tanks later in the afternoon and made no progress.

At 5:30 P.M., after more tanks and better artillery support was supplied, the 140th Infantry pushed forward to a line on the ridge northeast of Charpentry and dug in for the night. The 137th and 139th Infantry regiments also advanced at about dark. Despite much mixing of units and lack of cohesion, they managed to take Charpentry and Baulny.

Field orders from I Corps, issued at 11:00 P.M. September 27, directed a renewal of the attack at 5:30 A.M. the next morning. The objective remained the same: the combined army first objective. The advance was to proceed with no regard to troops on the right or left. The division command verbally ordered the frontline regiments to press the attack.

The 140th Infantry, on the right, attacked at 5:30 A.M. as directed but made little progress. On the left, intermingled units of the 137th and 139th Infantry regiments did not attack, but they did beat off an enemy counterattack from Bois de Montrebeau at 6:30 A.M.

At 7:30 A.M., elements of the 137th Infantry attacked; a battalion of the 139th Infantry attacked soon afterward. The 140th Infantry, assisted by tanks and elements of the 138th Infantry, attacked at about 9:45 A.M. These attacks resulted in the capture of Bois de Montrebeau and the open terrain to the east.

By now, the units of the division were hopelessly intermingled. Indicative of the lack of cohesion, on the night of September 27, the commander of the 139th Infantry Regiment went forward and got lost, roaming around the battlefield for twenty-four hours before finally stumbling into the positions of the adjacent 28th Division. While he was missing, his replacement could not find the regimental command post—or even the regiment itself—and the position of the 139th Infantry Regiment was unknown to both brigades and division headquarters.

The inexperienced 35th Division troops also had the misfortune of facing the crack German 1st Guard Division, the best enemy troops on the Meuse-Argonne front. The 1st Guards defended their positions with great tenacity and the 35th, which was supposed to advance rapidly, continued to bog down after its gains of the first day.

Losses in the 35th Division were horrendous—specific figures from day to day are unobtainable—but hundreds and soon thousands of men were being killed and wounded in the daily assaults. Many of these casualties were officers and noncoms, which contributed to the breakdown of the organization.

Lack of open warfare training, heavy combat, and internal dissension were all contributing to the breakdown of the division. The First Army chief of staff would later report that after September 27, the 35th was a division in name only; as of that date, maneuvering power with intact units, except the engineers, ceased to exist.

When at 11:00 P.M. September 28, I Corps issued orders for resumption of the attack at 5:30 A.M. September 29, the division ordered the attack to be made in the general direction of Exermont and Bois de Boyon. Due to the mixed condition of the units and poor liaison, the frontline units did not receive the orders until nearly daylight, when it was impossible to execute them in detail.

Despite poorly coordinated artillery support, about 135 men of the 137th Infantry advanced from the northern edge of Bois de Montrebeau and reached a point immediately south and west of Exermont at 6:10 A.M. There they were enveloped by German infantry and subjected to heavy artillery and machine gun fire. Unsupported, the doughboys were forced to withdraw to the northern edge of Bois de Montrebeau about 8:00 A.M.

On the right, the 138th Infantry failed to receive its orders on time. In an effort to keep the attack moving, the 140th Infantry was ordered to take its place, and at 6:30 A.M. the 140th attacked. Supported by tanks, it advanced in the direction of Exermont, reaching the town and nearby objectives between 8:00 and 10:00 A.M. Heavy artillery was directed at the U.S. troops that had crossed the creek beyond the village. About noon, the Germans launched a strong counterattack against the outlying doughboys. They drove elements of all four U.S. infantry regiments south of the stream and gained a foothold in Bois de Montrebeau.

Hammered by this counterattack, the 35th Division had clearly reached the end of its combat effectiveness. Virtually all units of the 35th withdrew by dark—as ordered—to prepared positions along the ridge northeast of Baulny. Field orders issued at 1:00 A.M. September 30 directed the division to maintain defensive positions and maintain contact with the enemy by deep patrolling. A counterattack at 9:00 A.M. by German troops in Bois de Montrebeau was repulsed.

No effort was apparently made by the division to push the divisional line of resistance forward. In fact, the 35th was probably incapable of any significant contribution by this time. Units were badly disorganized and tactical chains of command virtually nonexistent. The 35th Division had been shattered. That same day, General Traub asked that his division be withdrawn from the line for reorganization.

The relief of the division by the U.S. 1st Division was ordered by First Army at 4:30 P.M. September 29. Command of the sector was to pass to the 1st Division at 3:00 A.M. October 1. Upon relief, the 35th Division assembled in the vicinity of Very and Cheppy. On October 3, it was designated First Army reserve.

On October 4, the division moved to the vicinity of St. Mihiel; on October 11, it was assigned to the French XXXIII Corps. The night of October 14–15, the division relieved the French 15th Colonial Division near Fresnes-en-Woëvre and Haudimont in the St. Mihiel area. The division remained in this nonactive sector until November 7, when it was relieved by the 81st Division. It was out of the line but slated to participate in the Second Army's offensive in the St. Mihiel sector when the Armistice was declared November 11.

After the Armistice, the 35th Division was assigned to salvage materiel. In early December, it moved to Commercy, and in early March, it entrained for the American embarkation center at Le Mans. On March 29, the division moved to Brest and St. Nazaire for transport to the United States. The first units sailed from St. Nazaire on April 6 and the last elements arrived at Philadelphia on April 20. The division was subsequently demobilized, the bulk of the men at Camp Funston, Kansas.

While overseas, the 35th Division had served ninety-two days in quiet sectors and only five days in active sectors. But those five days in the Meuse-Argonne campaign had cost the division over 6,000 of the nearly 6,800 casualties it suffered in service, including over 1,000 battle deaths. It is credited with having advanced twelve and one-half miles, but the campaign virtually destroyed the division.

An army investigator later blamed the virtual destruction of the division in the Meuse-Argonne on poor discipline, lack of leadership, and "probably poor preparation." The Kansans and Missourians fought well as individuals— surprisingly well under the circumstances—but their unit structure let them down, thanks in some part to higher command that left the division in the line too long, contributing to its fragmentation.

James Hallas

Bibliography
American Battle Monuments Commission. *35th Division, Summary of Operations in the World War.* Washington, DC: Government Printing Office, 1944.
Hoyt, Charles B. *Heroes of the Argonne.* Kansas City, MO: Franklin Hudson, 1919.
Kenamore, Clair. *From Vaquois Hill to Exermont.* St. Louis: Guard Publishing, 1919.

United States Army: 36th Division

The Texas and Oklahoma National Guards no sooner returned from the Rio Grande where they were stationed during General John J. Pershing's Punitive Expedition into Mexico in 1916 than they were called to arms in World War I. During the summer of 1917, they were increased about threefold in strength and collected at numerous mobilization points. Several units, especially the 1st Oklahoma Infantry Regiment at Fort Sill and the veteran Texas infantry regiments sent once more to the border, underwent rudimentary training. Simultaneously, Camp Bowie, one of sixteen tent camps authorized for the training of the National Guard, was established on the southwestern outskirts of Forth Worth, Texas, for use by the Texas and Oklahoma militias. The campsite was sedulously solicited by the city, which benefited economically from the construction of facilities and the military trade.

From the numerals 26 through 75 reserved for the National Guard, the War Department selected 36 for the Texas-Oklahoma division. MajGen. Edwin St. John Greble, a West Point graduate and Regular Army veteran, was appointed commanding general. He arrived at Camp Bowie on Aug. 25, 1917, ahead of most Guard organizations, whose arrivals were staggered so as to avoid confusion. The opposition of many guardsmen to the abolition of the old Guard designations in favor of the new unit designations was mitigated by the placement of whole Guard organizations in the larger divisional units. For example, the 1st Oklahoma and 7th Texas Infantry regiments were merged to form the 142d Infantry Regiment. Understrength organizations were filled by 5,000 Texas and Oklahoma conscripts from Camp Travis, Texas, the training installation of the 36th's draftee counterpart, the 90th Division. Although the 36th was comprised largely of white members, it did contain a large Hispanic population and more Native Americans than any other American division with the possible exception of the 90th. The preponderance of Texas officers reflected the predominantly Texas composition of the division. Vacancies in the junior ranks were filled principally by Texas and Oklahoma graduates of the officer training camps at Leon Springs and Camp Bowie, the latter conducted by the 36th Division, and by reserve officers commissioned in Illinois.

The veteran guardsmen, though they numbered less than one-third of the total personnel, together with a sprinkling of Regular Army officers and veteran foreign advisers, constituted a valuable cadre in the training of the division. The long training period and divisional schools were particularly beneficial to the Guard officers and noncoms with no previous military background. Much of the 36th's basic instruction was directed by BGen. George Blakely, the Regular Army chief of the 61st Field Artillery Brigade, who commanded the division while Greble was away during the fall on a tour of the Western Front. Upon his return, Greble stressed discipline in contrast to the informal tendencies of the guardsmen and open warfare over trench fighting in tactical exercises in compliance with the wishes of the rigid, offensive-minded commander of the American Expeditionary Force (AEF), General Pershing. Training was impeded by the incomplete camp construction, a flu-measles-pneumonia epidemic, equipment and ordnance shortages, and transfers of skilled personnel to understrength units overseas or en route thereto. Losses were replenished largely by Texas and Oklahoma draftees, who were interspersed among the veteran trainees.

One of the division's greatest assets was its high morale. At Camp Bowie, the guardsmen responded positively to the adulation heaped upon them not only by the citizens of Fort Worth, who regarded the 36th as their own, but also by Texas and Oklahoma, which also claimed it as their own. Social needs were gratified by a recreational program conducted under the aegis of the Commission on Training Camp Activities, whose primary goal was, for moral and physical reasons, to keep the American servicemen busy. The commission supervised athletic and entertainment events run by social welfare organizations such as the YMCA, the Red Cross, and the Salvation Army and enlisted the services of city leaders, local churches, private organizations, and business groups in providing leisure activities. It was also responsible for a town and camp crusade against the nefarious operations of bootleggers and bordellos. The sports program stimulated pride more than any other activity. In football, the 111th Engineers defeated the 142d Infantry for the camp championship. Esprit de corps was also promoted by the adoption of a divisional motto, song, crest, flag, and sobriquet. The 36th was called the "Panther Division" in honor of Fort Worth, the Panther City.

With the exception of the 143d Infantry, which embarked for France at Newport News, Virginia, the 36th was transported by rail in July 1918 to the New York Port of Embarkation. The southwesterners were processed for overseas duty at Camp Mills on Long Island. They were joined at the port by their new commanding general, MajGen. William R. Smith, a West Point graduate and former commander of the 62d Field Artillery. His predecessor was one of several major generals rejected for service abroad by General Pershing, who favored younger divisional combat commanders.

The 36th sailed from Hoboken, New Jersey, in five convoys, one of which sustained a U-boat attack, and landed in France at three ports, mainly Brest, to become the twenty-ninth American division in France. With the exception of the 61st Brigade, which was sent to the artillery training center at Coëtquidan, where it remained for the duration, the 36th was conveyed in French boxcars to the 13th (Bar-sur-Aube) Training Area southeast of Paris. The arduous drill decreed by the AEF corrected defects in the 36th's instructions and revealed that the division had not been diligent enough in eliminating unfit officers. Forty-five officers including BGen. Henry Hutchings, commander of the 71st Infantry Brigade and former Texas adjutant general, were sent to Blois for reclassification or discharge. Their posts together with other posts vacated due to routine officer transfers were filled by veterans from other divisions, especially the 42d. Few of the 2,000 enlisted men of the division shipped out, however, were replaced. The 36th also lost the services of its engineers, who were sent first to St. Mihiel and after to the Meuse-Argonne.

Although understrength, short of supplies and equipment, and without the customary adjustment in a quiet sector, the 36th Division on Oct. 3, 1918, following its transport to the Marne for service with the French, was assigned

U

to the French Fourth Army, whose drive in the Champagne region in support of the American First Army in the grand Meuse-Argonne offensive, had stalled at Blanc Mont. Placed at the front ahead of the 36th was the famed army and marine 2d Division under MajGen. John A. Lejeune. Fresh from St. Mihiel, the 2d suffered exhaustion in achieving a near breakthrough in the sector. On October 8, one day after relieving the 3d and 4th brigades of the 2d Division near St. Étienne, the 71st Brigade of the 36th Division under BGen. Pegram Whitworth, a West Point alumnus, with two 2d Division battalions covering its flanks, went over the top as part of an all-out attack in the Champagne sector. The green troops behaved splendidly and advanced nearly six hundred yards in the face of heavy shelling, gas attacks, relentless machine gun fire, and strafing by airplanes. French tanks with the 71st were ineffective. The price of success was high, however; there were nearly 1,300 casualties.

The next day the 71st Brigade undertook local actions to straighten its line. On October 10, General Smith assumed command of the sector and passed the 72d Infantry Brigade, commanded by BGen. John A. Hulen, Texas National Guard, through the 71st Brigade. The 2d Division's artillery and engineers remained in support of the 36th Division. The 72d Brigade dogged the Germans as they withdrew northward to the Aisne River and drove their rear guard from Moscou Farm and the Ardennes Canal on the south bank. The French Fourth Army halted at the Aisne to wait for supplies and for Pershing to come abreast on the right. The 36th zone was extended, and the 71st Brigade placed on the right of the 72d. Local clashes and German fire from across the river caused a number of casualties. A French division had been unable to clear the loop of the Aisne, the last major German fortification on the south bank. The battle-hardened 141st and 142d Infantry regiments of the 71st Brigade was given the job, and it overran the strongpoint in less than an hour on October 27. The "Forest Farm" operation, as it was called after an abandoned farm inside the bend, was carefully planned and almost flawlessly executed. The Native Americans, mainly Choctaws, who transmitted messages in their native languages, made a unique contribution to the triumph. The relief of the division for its return to American control was completed amid a German shelling early on October 29.

The total losses of the 36th Division, which saw no further action, came to 2,584, of which 591 were battle deaths. Although the division was officially credited with 548 prisoners, it actually took 813. Its advance of over 13 miles entitled it to seventeenth place among the twenty-nine American divisions in the war zone for distance gained against the enemy. It was highly commended by the French for its performances at St. Étienne and Forest Farm. Two Medals of Honor, 39 Distinguished Service Crosses, 7 French Military Medals, and approximately 400 French War Crosses were awarded to its more heroic members.

Shortly after its relief, the 36th Division received an official insignia composed of a khaki T on a cobalt-blue arrowhead known in World War II as the "T-Patch." In World War I, however, it was purely a T-arrowhead emblem symbolic of Texas and Oklahoma. The 36th was called the "Arrowhead Division" and the troops were nicknamed "Arrowheads."

The 36th was in the Triaucourt-Bar-le-Duc area when the Armistice was announced. Several divisions were ordered to Germany while others including the 36th were withdrawn to better training grounds to await developments. The division including the 111th Engineers and 3,600 replacements occupied billets in the Tonnerre Training Area on Thanksgiving Day 1918. Homesickness notwithstanding, troop spirits did not languish appreciably thanks to the elaborate educational and recreational programs and generous leave policy implemented by the AEF with the cooperation of the omnipresent welfare organizations and the relaxation of drill. The 36th football squad won the First Army championship but was defeated by the 89th Division for the AEF title at Paris on March 29, 1919. The divisional newspaper the Arrowhead was also an important factor in fostering the division's good morale.

In February 1919, the AEF published a timetable for its exodus from Europe. By June 1 well over one-half of Pershing's command, including the 36th Division, had sailed. The 61st Brigade in western France was sent to Texas via St. Nazaire and Newport News some two months ahead of the bulk of the 36th, which left Tonnerre early in May. The veterans were deloused at Le Mans, embarked at Brest, and debarked at Hoboken and Newport News. They were demobilized in June and early July at those stations nearest their homes, principally Camps Bowie and Travis. Their homecoming was marked by parades and enthusiastic receptions. The 36th as a divisional designation subsequently became the valued property of the Texas National Guard.

Lonnie White

Bibliography

American Battle Monuments Commission. *36th Division, Summary of Operations in the World War*. Washington, DC: Government Printing Office, 1944.

Chastaine, Ben H. *Story of the 36th: The Experiences of the 36th Division in the World War*. Oklahoma City: Harlow, 1920.

Jary, William E., Jr., ed. *Camp Bowie, Fort Worth, 1917–1918: An Illustrated History of the 36th Division in the First World War*. Fort Worth, TX: N.p., 1975.

Otto, Ernest. *The Battle at Blanc Mont*. Annapolis, MD: Naval Institute Press, 1930.

White, Lonnie. *Panthers to Arrowheads: The 36th (Texas-Oklahoma) Division in World War I*. Austin, TX: N.p., 1984.

United States Army: 37th Division

On July 18, 1917, the War Department directed that National Guard units from Ohio and West Virginia become the 37th Division to be formed at Camp Sheridan, near Montgomery, Alabama. On August 5, the Ohio National Guard, recently returned from nine months of federal service along the Mexican border, was drafted into federal service, permitting it to serve overseas. By August 26, when BGen. William R. Smith assumed temporary command, units from the Ohio National Guard were arriving at Camp Sheridan amidst construction of the camp. MajGen. Charles G. Treat arrived to command the division on September 3. Initially, the division was organized into the 73d Infantry Brigade from the 5th and 8th Ohio National Guard Infantry regiments, with elements from the 1st, 2d, 7th, and 10th Ohio regiments; and into the 62d Field Artillery Brigade from the 1st, 2d, and 3d Ohio National Guard Field Artillery regiments with elements from the 7th and 10th Ohio regiments.

On September 15, the division was reorganized according to the War Department's Aug. 8, 1917, Table of Organization. This caused confusion and frustration as regiments lost state identity and many officers found themselves without a job. In its final organization the 37th Division consisted of the 73d Infantry Brigade with the 145th and 146th Infantry regiments and the 135th Machine Gun Battalion; the 74th Infantry Brigade with the 147th and 148th Infantry regiments and the 136th Machine Gun Battalion; and the 62d Field Artillery Brigade with the 134th and 135th Field Artillery regiments (75mm), the 136th Field Artillery Regiment (155mm), and the 112th Trench Regiment, the 134th Machine Gun Battalion, the 112th Field Signal Battalion, and a headquarters troop. To support the division, the trains consisted of the 112th Train Headquarters and Military Police, the 112th Ammunition Train, the 112th Supply Train, the 112th Engineer Train, and the 112th Sanitary Train with Field Hospitals 145, 146, 147, and 148 with ambulance companies. By September 30, the division had 21,700 men assigned. Additional drafts totaling 1,000 men arrived in October. Losses through the winter reached 3,000.

On October 29, training began, despite equipment and personnel shortages. For the next six months, training focused on discipline, physical training, marksmanship, and trench warfare exercises. The War Department training program had to be modified because of personnel and equipment shortages. Individual training received greater emphasis than unit training. On May 8, 1918, MajGen. Charles S. Farnsworth, who would lead the division in France, took command. His training priorities became marksmanship, gas drills, marching, and physical training. Unfortunately, time for training was limited.

When the 37th Division left Camp Sheridan for overseas, no one knew that it would never be reunited as a combat division in France. Deployment for Europe began with the May 20–25 movement to Camp Lee, Virginia, of the division headquarters, the infantry brigades, the engineer regiments, and the divisional machine gun battalion and with the July 14–17 movement of the 62d Field Artillery Brigade and the trains to Camp Upton, New York. Units were brought to full strength with draftees, who required additional training. The 37th Division used seven ports of debarkation: Baltimore, Philadelphia, Brooklyn, Hoboken, New York, Newport News, and Montreal. From June 6 to June 15, the division headquarters and the 73d Infantry Brigade sailed to Brest, arriving between June 18 and June 27. On June 22, the 74th Infantry Brigade, 112th Engineer Regiment and Train, and 112th Field Signal Battalion sailed, arriving at Brest on July 5. On June 27 and 28 the 62d Field Artillery Brigade and the remaining divisional units sailed to Great Britain, arriving between July 10 and 18 at Liverpool, Birkenhead, and Glasgow. After a brief stay in rest camps, these units proceeded to France via either Le Havre or Cherbourg. By the third week in July, the 37th Division had reached France.

Initial combat training for the 37th Division's infantry units began on June 25 when they moved to the 3d Training Area near Bourmont. Training focused on rigid discipline, prompt obedience to orders, physical fitness, precision in drill, and marksmanship. Personal appearance and military courtesy were stressed. After less than a month, the division moved to the Baccarat sector in Lorraine for training with the 77th Division from July 28 to August 4. The 62d Field Artillery Brigade arrived in France and began its training on July 15 at Camp de Sourge near Revigny. It would see limited service with other divisions late in the war.

From August 4 to September 16, the 37th Division, minus its artillery brigade, occupied a portion of the Baccarat sector. Trench warfare and patrolling, day and night, were emphasized as the division sought to dominate no-man's-land. Units not in the front conducted intensive training in the rear. On August 6, the division suffered its first fatality. Of the thirteen initial casualties for the division, nine were accidental. During this time the division did conduct several small raids.

After this brief, incomplete training period, the 37th Division on September 23–25 moved by rail, truck, and foot to occupy a portion of the Avocourt sector in preparation for the Meuse-Argonne offensive. The division, supported by the 55th Field Artillery Brigade of the 30th Division, attacked at 5:30 A.M. on September 26 as the center division of V Corps. The 79th Division was on its right and the 91st on its left. Farnsworth attacked with the 73d Brigade, commanded by BGen. Charles X. Zimerman, on the right and with the 74th Brigade, commanded by BGen. William P. Jackson, on the left. Forward units of both brigades reached the northern edge of the Bois de Montfaucon by nightfall, well short of the objective for the day. The next day, in a rainstorm, the attack resumed. Progress was slow but steady. By evening, the troops halted along the road from Ivoiry to Montfaucon. Near Ivoiry

on September 27, 2d Lt. Albert E. Baesel, 148th Infantry Regiment, fearlessly moved forward to rescue a wounded squad leader, isolated forward of his unit. German machine gun and artillery fire were severe. Just as Baesel reached the wounded soldier and got him on his shoulders, both were killed by machine gun fire. For his actions, Lieutenant Baesel received posthumously the only Medal of Honor awarded during the war for the 37th Division. By September 28, the division had taken the village of Cierges but soon lost it to a German counterattack. Two attempts on September 29, one supported by tanks, failed to recapture Cierges. After five days of heavy fighting with limited gains, the division, disorganized and exhausted, was relieved by the 32d Division on the night of September 30. During its first major battle, the 37th Division had over 3,100 killed and wounded.

The 37th Division, minus artillery, moved to Pagny-sur-Meuse on October 3 for refitting. On October 7, it replaced the 89th Division in the Pannes sector east of Verdun. After a brief stint at the front, the 28th Division relieved the 37th on October 16. At this time, Marshal Ferdinand Foch requested that General Pershing provide two divisions for service in Belgium. He chose the 37th and the 91st divisions to join the French Army of Belgium, a part of the Group of Armies of Flanders under the command of Belgian King Albert I.

On October 18, the 37th Division, minus artillery, moved north to the Hjooglede area near Roulers in Flanders. On October 26, it moved into Belgium to join the French XXX Corps, French Sixth Army. During the night of October 29–30 the 37th Division relieved the French 132d Division along the Courtrai-Ghent railroad. Supported by French artillery units, at 5:30 A.M. on October 31, the 37th Division attacked eastward toward the Escaut (Scheldt) River. Against stiff artillery and machine gun fire, the troops advanced about two and one-half miles and dug in for the night. The attack resumed on November 1, catching the Germans in a withdrawal. An advance of about five miles captured the villages of Cruyshautem and Eyne and brought the division to the Escaut River. Early on November 2, against heavy fire, the 37th Division secured a crossing over the Escaut by improvising a bridge from trees felled near the river. Between November 2 and 4, forces across the Escaut advanced about one-half mile. At 5:00 P.M. on

November 4, the division repulsed a German counterattack. Then, on the night of November 4–5, the 37th was relieved by the French 12th Division. During its five-day fight, the 37th suffered almost 1,500 casualties.

Upon relief, the division moved to the Thielt area for rest and preparation to continue the battle. On November 8, it moved forward to support the French XXXIV Corps in its attack. On November 10, the 37th Division relieved the French 11th and 12th divisions along the Escaut River, north of its previous fighting. A French attempt to cross on November 9 had been repulsed. On November 10, the 37th Division again fought across the Escaut, remaining firmly on the far bank by evening. German forces began a general withdrawal. By 11:00 A.M. on November 11, when the Armistice went into effect, the division had advanced almost two and one-half miles, practically with no opposition. During the last two days of the war, the 37th Division suffered another 200 casualties.

After the Armistice, the 37th Division moved to several training areas in northern France. After a short wait, the division began to concentrate at the American embarkation center at Le Mans for the return to the United States. On Feb. 3, 1919, the 112th Engineer Regiment moved to Le Mans, followed on February 9 by the 62d Field Artillery Brigade, rejoining the division for the first time since landing in France. On February 17, the 37th Division moved to the embarkation center. Ten days later, it moved to Brest. On March 10, the first units sailed for home, followed quickly by the remainder of the division. The last unit returned to the United States on April 30, 1919.

Upon arrival at Camp Sherman, Ohio, the demobilization of individuals and units began. From April 8 to 11, the infantry and artillery brigades were disbanded. After completing the mustering out of the soldiers, the 37th Division finally disbanded on June 23, 1919. This National Guard division had been Ohio's major contribution, other than individual draftees, to the fighting forces in France.

Robert D. Ramsey III

Bibliography

American Battle Monuments Commission. *American Armies and Battlefields in Europe.* Washington, DC: Government Printing Office, 1938.

————. *37th Division: Summary of Operations in the World War.* Washington, DC: Government Printing Office, 1944.

Center of Military History, U.S. Army. *Order of Battle of the United States Land Forces in the World War. Vol. 2, American Expeditionary Force: Divisions.* Washington, DC: Government Printing Office, 1988.

Cole, Ralph D., and W.C. Howells. *The Thirty-Seventh Division in the World War, 1917–1919.* 2 vols. Columbus, OH: Heer Printing, 1929.

United States Army: 42d Division

On Aug. 1, 1917, the War Department directed that a National Guard division be formed of composite units and personnel. It was drawn from twenty-six states and the District of Columbia and was the only Guard division so constructed. The Table of Organization, drawn up on August 8, was implemented on August 14, and by August 21 the 83d Brigade, which included the 69th New York (later 165th Infantry), the 4th Ohio (166th Infantry), and Companies B, C, and F of the 2d Wisconsin (150th Machine Gun Battalion) regiments of infantry was organized. On September 1, the 84th Brigade, which included the 4th Alabama (167th Infantry), 3d Iowa (168th Infantry), and Companies B, C, and F of the 2d Georgia (151st Machine Gun Battalion) regiments of infantry was completed. And thus the 42d Division, known as the "Rainbow Division," came into being. Gen. Douglas MacArthur in later years related the story of how the division received its nickname. He stated that when the decision to form the 42d Division was made by the War Department, he advised representatives of the press, saying that "in the makeup and promise of the future of this division it resembles a rainbow." One of the correspondents spoke up and said, "Rainbow—there's the name for the division—I shall call it the Rainbow in my dispatch."

On September 5, the 67th Field Artillery Brigade, which included the 1st Illinois (149th Field Artillery), the 1st Indiana (150th Field Artillery), and the 1st Minnesota (151st Field Artillery) regiments of field artillery was formed along with a Trench Mortar Battery made up from Maryland (3d Company Coast Artillery) National Guard units. Engineers came from North Carolina, South Carolina, and California. Missouri provided a signal battalion and several companies of the Virginia Coast Artillery were formed into the 117th Train Headquarters and Military Police. The composition of the Sanitary Train itself was to include National Guardmen from New Jersey, Oklahoma, Michigan, Tennessee, Oregon, Colorado, and Nebraska. Kansas sent National Guard units with which to form the 117th Ammunition Train. The 117th Supply Train was organized in Texas. The Louisiana National Guard became the headquarters troop. Most of the National Guard units had seen active service, some as recently as the Punitive Expedition against Pancho Villa in 1916.

On September 5, MajGen. William A. Mann, USA, assumed command of the division. On September 10, formal training began. By September 13, the command was completed, and by October 18, the main body of the division moved to Hoboken, New Jersey, for embarkation to France. Earlier, on September 23, an advanced party left the division to go to France, arriving at St. Nazaire on October 6. By this date, the division numbered approximately 27,000 officers and men. The movement overseas took place between October 18 and December 8, with some units leaving from Montreal, others from New York, and the balance from Hoboken. Many of the units arrived at Liverpool, England, and after a short stay proceeded to Le Harve, France. On Dec. 19, 1917, MajGen. Charles T. Menoher assumed command of the division.

Serious training for the division began when some of the earlier arrivals were sent to the 5th Training Area at Valcouleurs. They were subsequently transferred to the 4th Training Area at Rimaucourt and then, on December 26, relocated to the 7th Training Area at Rolampont. Training with the French, in Lorraine, began on Feb. 17, 1918, and lasted until June 21. On February 21, the leading elements of the division entered the line of the French VII Corps in the Lunéville sector and from then until July 21 remained on active service with the French.

With the French VII Corps, the division was active in the Baccarat sector from March 31 to June 21. The four French divisions comprising the corps were, from left to right on the line, the 41st in the Dolmbasle sector, the 164th in the Lunéville sector, the 14th in the St. Clement sector, and the 128th in the Baccarat sector. Headquarters of the 42d Division was established at Lunéville, which was alongside the 67th Field Artillery Brigade and was VII Corps headquarters as well. The 83d Infantry Brigade headquarters was placed with headquarters of the French 14th Infantry Division in Benamenill. The 84th Infantry Brigade headquarters was assigned to Baccarat with the headquarters of the French 128th Division.

The infantry units of the division were dispersed for combat training with the regiments assigned as follows: the 165th Infantry and one battalion each of the 149th and 150th Field Artillery were allocated to the French 164th; the 166th Infantry and the remainder of the 149th Field Artillery were allocated to the French 14th; the entire 84th Brigade along with the 151st Field Artillery and the 117th Trench Mortar Battery and one battalion of the 150th Field Artillery were assigned to help cover the ten miles already manned by the 128th French Division. Interestingly, both the 84th Brigade and the French division infantry units were numbered 167th and 168th.

The 42d learned the common activities of trench life during this period—nightly patrols, methods of relieving units in the lines, and becoming familiar with no-man's-land. The division engaged in raids on German trenches and learned to defend against them, suffering from huge concentrations of German artillery when the enemy made large raids against the division newcomers. Supporting units, such as ambulances and field hospitals, also learned their jobs "on the line" because of the casualties absorbed by the infantry and artillery. Engineers had on-the-job training also, primarily in repairing wire and trenches after enemy raids and shelling. During this phase, Col. Douglas MacArthur, the division chief of staff, came to be considered "a character" by the men in the line when he would appear wearing a turtleneck sweater and a cap, disdaining the standard steel helmet. Not realizing his rank, men would address him as "Hey, buddy" or "Say, you," or with other impertinent comments, which, according to his biographer, he ignored.

French officers, including the general commanding the 128th division, praised the Americans' dash and competence during the division's service with VII Corps. The 42d's casualties, killed and wounded during the various raids on German trenches, were not heavy, but they were sufficient to make it a seasoned division in fairly short order.

After the German offensive of March 1918, General Pershing assigned all American divisions then in France that were not otherwise engaged to replace French divisions in prepared positions so that the French might counterattack. The 42d was back in the Baccarat sector during this time, and it was assigned to the trenches. Trench service quickly became monotonous and remained so for the men for the three months they were so occupied. When the "Rainbow" Division was finally relieved from this duty on the night of June 20–21, it had suffered a total of 1,076 casualties, of which 105 were killed or later died of their wounds, and 971 wounded. The division reassembled near Châtel-sur-Moselle as part of the reserve of the French Eighth Army. The following day it moved to St. Germain-la-Ville, where it was placed at the disposal of the French armies of the north as a reserve. After five months in the lines, the 42d was rated a first-class division.

On June 28, the division moved to Camp de Châlons and to the south of the Esperance and Souain sectors, twenty-five miles east of Reims, where it remained from July 5 until July 18. While in the zone of the French XXI Corps, the 42d was affiliated with the French 13th and 170th divisions and assumed the second position in the defense of a front extending from Tahure to Vaudesincourt. Five battalions of the division served with both French divisions in the intermediate position, the most heavily defended of the sector and which extended north of the towns of St. Hilaire-sur-Suippes, Souain, and Perthes-les-Hurlus.

A plan, devised by Gen. Henri Philippe Pétain, was very successful in the impending Champagne-Marne defensive. It made the first line insignificant, to be vacated almost as soon as the enemy arrived at that line; the second was to be the one most heavily defended; and the third was to be the last line of defense to which the remaining defenders would fall back upon in case of disaster. German commanders of the forces facing XXI Corps were quite careless about displaying their troops, which appeared to be massing for an attack, enabling the Allied artillery to register. The defensive began when Allied artillery opened up on the German lines at 11:30 P.M. the night of July 14. Four hours later the second line was warned by the first line that the Germans were overwhelming their position. Substantial losses were sustained by the division at this time. When the Germans arrived between lines one and two, American and French artillery "descended like an avalanche" upon them, as described by Douglas MacArthur, who was with the troops in the intermediate line. The most savage fighting took place on July 15 north of Souain, where the enemy penetrated the lines of the 167th Infantry, but they were soon dislodged in a bloody counterattack. The Germans, who had expected to be in Châlons by the morning of July 16, were unable to break through the intermediate position for three days. By July 18, their advance had been checked. The 42d Division withdrew and assembled at Châlons. After this engagement ended on July 21, the 42d was reunited with I Corps, AEF, near Épieds and Verdilly.

Between July 25 and August 6, the division participated in the Aisne-Marne offensive, which had begun at Soissons on July 18. The 26th Division had taken over the lines held by the 2d U.S. Division near Château-Thierry and made a successful advance to a point near the Croix Rouge Farm, about ten miles in all. During the night of July 25–26, the 84th Infantry Brigade passed through the 26th Division, AEF, alongside the 56th Infantry Brigade of the 28th Division. Both were defending the Bois de Fère between La Logette Maison west, to just beyond the Croix Rouge Farm. The French 167th Division was on their left and the French 39th Division was to their right. On July 26, cooperating with the 39th Division, the two brigades captured the farm. On the night of July 26–27, the 83d Infantry Brigade relieved the French 167th Division, on the left flank. The 42d Division now held the entire corps front, and the enemy retired toward the Orucq River. The division commanders at first believed that the Germans were in full flight but soon learned that very day, July 27, that they were wrong. The Germans had established themselves on the heights above the Orucq River. The "Irish" 165th Infantry during the afternoon was subjected to heavy shelling when it occupied the village of Villars-sur-Fère, which was located on the south bank of the Orucq. The troops were also inundated with gas shells, and low-flying German planes strafed the infantry in the open ground. About midnight, General Menoher received orders from the French Sixth Army to cross the swollen Orucq before dawn to take the heights; if the Germans did not stand fast, his men were to advance to the Vesle River, about fifteen miles ahead. An hour before sunrise the division advanced, the 83d Brigade on the right and the 84th on the left. Although the Americans did take the town of Sergy, just across the river, the Germans eventually retook it. The town changed hands seven times, but the Germans retained control at the end of the day.

The following day, July 28, the division's four infantry regiments were finally in line—from right to left: 168th Iowa, 167th Alabama, 165th New York, and 166th Ohio—in a sector of their own without detachments to any other division. Following Order No. 26, the division forced a crossing of the Orucq and the next day two battalions of the 47th Infantry, 4th U.S. Division, were attached. The joint force resumed the attack and captured Sergy and Seringes-et-Nesles by July 30. It was on that day that the 42d division's most famous sergeant, Joyce Kilmer of the 165th Infantry, was killed in action while on a reconnaissance patrol. The division continued its advance until August 2–3, when the 4th Division passed through and took up the advance positions. The 42d supported the 4th until August 10, when it was withdrawn to the La Ferté-sous-Jouarre area and then on August 16 to the 3d Training Area.

On August 18, the division was ordered to join the U.S. First Army. Between August 28 and September 11, the 42d moved, less divisional artillery, to the 2d Training Area and then to the 6th Training Area. Eventually, it moved to the Forêt de la Reine, where it occupied assembly positions behind the U.S. 89th Division the night of September 9–10. The following day the division occupied a portion of the Lucey sector between Flirey and Seicheprey, relieving elements of the 89th Division on the night of September 11–12.

During the period September 12–16, the division participated in the St. Mihiel offensive with the 84th Infantry Brigade on the right and the 83d Brigade on the left, advancing abreast, with the U.S. 1st Division to their left and the 89th to their right. The advance began on September 12, and the division had successfully completed its assigned task by the next day, reaching the Woëvre River and so, other than local actions, consolidated its position for the next three days. The 84th Brigade, now led by Brigadier General MacArthur, with the 167th Infantry on the brigade's left and the 168th on the far right, pressed forward. Its advance exceeded expectation even though a squadron of tanks led by Col. George S. Patton, Jr., were mired in muck and unable to support the brigade. The two infantry regiments were also

soon bogged down in the mud. Though stubbornly resisted in the Sonnard Woods, the 168th Infantry soon pushed through and pursued the Germans. The 167th outflanked and overcame the German positions to its front. By 3:30 P.M., the regiment was abreast of the crossroad town of Pannes, where it refused its right in order to connect up with the U.S. 89th Division. When the 167th came up on line, about one hour later, the 168th moved to the east of Pannes.

Meanwhile, the 1st Battalion, 165th Infantry of the 83d Brigade reached the edge of the Thiacourt Woods at about 2:00 P.M., the 2d Battalion dug in near Pannes and the 3d Battalion was held in reserve. The 166th Infantry was on the extreme left wing, with the 3d Battalion in the lead, arriving at their second-phase line by 1:00 P.M. Although the regiment was ordered to provide two battalions to make contact with the 26th Division, which was approaching the town of Vigneulles, the 1st Division made a rapid advance and the transfer was unnecessary. The 83d Brigade set up headquarters in Essey, while the regiment occupied Pannes. The day had been a "wild gallop" with intermittent German resistance. But patrols of the 165th had reached further north than any other unit of the 42d Division, reaching the northern edge of Bois de Beney.

The following day, September 13, the division jumped off at 6:10 A.M., the 165th Infantry with the 1st Battalion in the lead and the 2d Battalion in support. The regiment pushed on to Bois de Beney, just beyond Thiacourt Woods and then to the Sebastopol Farm, where the leaders were advised that the Germans were in retreat just ahead of the brigade. On the division's right, the 167th Infantry, 84th Brigade, in advance, pushed forward reaching the outskirts of the town of Haumont. There the troops were forced to withdraw due to heavy German fire from Michel Stellung, the outer fortifications of the Hindenburg Line. Further efforts by the division put it, at 9:30 A.M., in the town of St. Benoît and at the château of the same name. Upon arrival at the château, the troops found that the headquarters of the German XIX Corps had recently vacated the premises, leaving a fully prepared meal in the dining room. The 83d Brigade, commanded by BGen. Michael J. Lenihan, in the meanwhile encountered light resistance, passed through the Bois de Vignotte and captured the village of Hassavant. The division remained in the area, consolidating its position, until relieved by the 89th Division on September 30, whereupon the 42d moved to the vicinity of Souilly in the Meuse-Argonne region, where it joined the reserves of the First Army.

On October 4, the division removed to the Recicourt area, where it went into corps reserve. The following day the division moved to Montfaucon Woods. The 67th Field Artillery Brigade and the 117th Ammunition Train were moved to the vicinity of Romagne-sous-Montfaucon, where they supported the 32d Division in the Meuse-Argonne offensive during the period of October 7–12. The rest of the division spent a miserable time during a damp, cold interval in a forest that had been torn to pieces by shellfire of the recent past and just shattered trunks of what once were magnificent trees.

The division, less the artillery and train, was moved to the vicinity of Cierges and the Emont Woods, and then to the woods south of Exermont on October 10. The following day the 42d began its relief of the 1st Division at the northern edge of the Bois de Romagne and the northwestern slope of Maldah Hill north of Exermont. Two days later the division, still without its artillery, extended its lines to include Sommerance on the left, with the 82d Division on that flank. The right of the line ended in the Bois de Romagne, with the 32d division as its right flank. The next day, October 13, the division artillery and train returned to the fold while the division extended its right to include those elements of the 32d west of the Transvaal Farm in the Genses Woods.

The following day, October 14, the division attacked toward the town of Landres-et-St.-Georges after a rather heavy artillery preparation beginning at 8:30 A.M. It made little progress against the German Kriemhilde-Stellung position, the second and most important line in the Hindenburg system. For the next few days, the Germans retained control of the area. References in the history of the 89th Division indicate that it was believed that the 42d had been "thrown back," which, not surprisingly, Brigadier General MacArthur refuted. In a summary provided by Colonel Judah, of division intelligence, dated noon to noon, October 16–17, he stated "The 84th Brigade . . . succeeded in penetrating the Kriemhilde Stellung at its apex on Côte de Chatillon." In the following day's report Judah claimed that prisoners were taken from twenty-three different enemy divisions including a railway and

agricultural battalion. Regardless of Judah's reports, the facts are that the division advanced no more than 1,000 yards between October 14 and 31 and about halfway to Landres-et-St.-Georges, their objective.

The division was relieved by the 2d Division on November 2, and until midnight November 4–5, it was more or less at rest. On November 5, the division passed through the 78th U.S. Division and pursued the retreating enemy until the troops arrived at a point about one-half mile southwest of Stonne, along the height of La Grange du Mont. The 77th Division was on the division's right and the French 40th Division on its left. The division was about ten miles south of Sedan, at this time.

On November 6, the 42d advanced toward Sedan, and the next day it reached the heights of the Meuse River on a front extending from west of Remilly-sur-Meuse to Cheveuges, and within two to three miles of Sedan. General Pershing wanted desperately to have American troops take Sedan, and a lot of energy was expended toward that goal. The division boundary was reduced to a zone encompassing Chemery, Bulson, Thelonne, and Bazeilles. The 77th Division began the relief of the 42d Division on November 9 and on November 10 command passed to the 77th Division. The 42d Division moved to the vicinity of Buzancy on November 11.

Between November 14 and 19, the division assembled in an area east of the Meuse and prepared for the advance into Germany. On November 20, the 42d began its advance, moving as a reserve division through Belgium, Luxembourg, and then into Germany, crossing at Welschbilling, then on to its designated station at Kreis uf Ahrweiler, at which the division arrived on December 14. Between December 15 and April 4, 1919, the division formed part of the Army of Occupation.

The division was returned to the United States beginning on April 5 and ending with the arrival of the 117th Ammunition Train at Newport News, Virginia, on May 1. Demobilization began on May 5 at Camp Upton for the 83d Brigade; on May 9, at Camp Dix for the Divisional Headquarters; on May 12, for the 84th Brigade at Camp Dodge; and the same day for the 67th Field Artillery Brigade at Camp Grant.

The 42d Division, National Guard, was the second National Guard division considered ready for overseas and followed the 26th National Guard Division to France. Almost from the beginning, the division was sent to train in trenches, spending nearly six months at that task before being seriously considered, by AEF headquarters, as ready for combat. When its men entered the "arena," they were not found wanting. Only once was the 42d unable to solve a problem quickly with the attainment of an assigned objective. And it was not the only division that had difficulty penetrating the Hindenburg Line. The 42d served in France and Germany from Nov. 1, 1917, until the division left France on April 5, 1919. During that time the 42d suffered 14,700 casualties, of which 2,800 were battle deaths.

Charles A. Endress

Bibliography

Center of Military History, U.S. Army. *Order of Battle of the United States Land Forces in the World War. Vol. 2, American Expeditionary Force: Divisions.* Washington, DC: Government Printing Office, 1988.

Duffy, Francis P. *Father Duffy's Story.* New York: Doran, 1919.

James, D. Clayton. *The Years of MacArthur, 1880–1941.* Vol. 1. Boston: Houghton Mifflin, 1970.

Reiley, Henry J. *Americans All, The Rainbow at War.* Columbus, OH: Heer Printing, 1936.

United States Army: 77th Division

The 77th Infantry Division, National Army, was created on Aug. 5, 1917, and MajGen. J. Franklin Bell assumed command at Camp Upton, New York, on August 18. As a National Army division it was composed of draftees from the New York area, a fact later reflected by its Statue of Liberty shoulder patch. The unit was leavened by a small number of Regular Army officers and NCOs and members of the Officer Reserve Corps, but most of its officers were newly inducted from civilian life and had been trained in the officers training program at Plattsburg, New York. As a result of its composition, the division typified the American experience of World War I in which a newly created army of several million citizen soldiers was created, transported to Europe, and sent into battle with very limited training or experience. Evaluations of the American experience must be made with this in mind.

The division was the standard "square" type of over 27,000 men built around two infantry brigades of two infantry regiments each for a total rifle strength of approximately 13,000. The 153d Brigade included the 305th and 306th Infantry regiments and the 305th Machine Gun Battalion, and the 154th Brigade consisted of the 307th and 308th Infantry regiments and the 306th Machine Gun Battalion. The 152d Field Artillery (FA) Brigade included the 304th and 305th FA battalions fielding 75mm guns and the 306th with 155mm howitzers and the 302d Trench Mortar Battery. Divisional troops consisted of the 304th Machine Gun Battalion, 302d Engineers, 302d Field Signal Battalion, and a headquarters troop. These large American divisions required considerable logistic support. The 77th Division's train included the 302d Headquarters and Military Police, the 302d Ammunition, Engineer, and Supply trains, as well as the 302d Sanitary Train, including the 305th, 306th, 307th, and 308th Field Hospitals, each with their own ambulance companies.

The first group of draftees arrived at Camp Upton on September 10, and training began. Throughout the fall and winter, there was extensive shifting of personnel including a 4,500-man levy against the division in January and February 1918. New recruits continued to pour into the division right up until the division moved out in March. The infantry regiments embarked between March 29 and April 16 from Boston, Brooklyn, New York, and Hoboken; they were followed at the end of April by the artillery brigade and division trains. General Bell, having been found medically unfit for field service, was relieved, and BGen. Evan Johnson was given interim command and took the division to Europe.

Proceeding to northwestern France via Liverpool and Dover, England, and Calais, France, the division was attached to the 39th (British) Division for training, which was conducted from April 15 to June 5. The artillery brigade went into training at Camp de Souge, south of Bordeaux, where it completed its training on July 4.

On June 21, the 77th Division arrived in the Vosges Mountains and went into the line northeast of the division's headquarters at Baccarat on the Meurthe River. It was the first National Army division to enter the line. From June 21 to July 15, the division's four regiments were deployed on line under the tutelage of the 61st (French)

Division, which introduced them to the intricacies of trench warfare. From the perspective of divisional history, this was rather a quiet time, but for the individuals involved, night patrols, trench raids, and shelling were a frightening introduction to the real war. The French withdrew after three weeks, and from July 16 until August 4, the 77th served as the first National Army division independently to hold a sector of the Western Front. The division was withdrawn from Lorraine beginning on August 1 and was transferred to the Champagne region, where it was assigned to III Corps as part of the Sixth (French) Army. The 77th relieved the 4th Division on the Vesle River on August 12.

As the Germans grudgingly backed out of the Marne salient during the Allied counteroffensive that began on July 18, they used the Aisne River and the Vesle, its tributary, to block the Allied advance. The Vesle, a sluggish river averaging less than thirty feet wide and six to eight feet deep, meandered through marshy bottomland about a third of a mile wide; its banks were a tangle of low undergrowth and German-laid wire. The river was flanked on both sides by steep and open ridges to the north and south. The Germans dug in on high ground north of the river and maintained observation and deadly fires over the whole sector including the American bridgeheads in the river bottom and their support positions on the bare forward slopes south of the river. The 4th Division, 164th (French) Division, and the 6th Brigade, 3d Division had taken heavy casualties while gaining a tenuous foothold north of the river, but they had not been able to advance or even to construct adequate defenses before being relieved.

Orders from Gen. Jean Degoutte, Sixth Army commander, were for III Corps to consolidate a strong defense on the south bank of the Vesle, but also to expand the bridgeheads north of the river and to maintain pressure through heavy patrolling. On the night of August 12–13, III Corps undertook this task with the 77th Division on the left and the 28th Division on the right. The American commanders felt they were in an impossible position. They were not allowed to draw back into a strong defensive position on high ground well south of the river, nor could their limited attacks expand their bridgeheads to the high ground north of the river. Company-size attacks, particularly in the week of August 22–27 around Bazoches and Château Diable, were met by strong German

machine gun fire and battalion-sized counterattacks supported by accurate artillery. During this fighting, MajGen. George B. Duncan was relieved of command for medical disability, and division command passed to MajGen. Robert Alexander. The unhappy stalemate lasted until attacks north of Soissons made the German position on the Vesle untenable. On the morning of September 4, 77th Division patrols found the north bank of the Vesle abandoned except for rear-guard machine gun positions, and the division began a pursuit across the plateau between the Vesle and the Aisne rivers. The division advanced with the 153d on the left and 154th on the right. By September 6, the 153d stood at Villers-en-Prayeres with its patrols on the Aisne Canal, but the 154th had been slowed by the failure of divisions on their right to keep pace. The 154th was able to make only limited progress between September 6 and 16 when the division was pulled out of the line.

The division had only a brief respite, for it was moved immediately to the Argonne Forest. It was assigned to I Corps' left flank for the upcoming Meuse-Argonne offensive. Two days before the attack the division received over 4,000 replacements from the 40th and 41st divisions, which brought its strength up to just under 26,000. The replacements were draftees from western states who had entered the service in July and August and had spent most of their time in the army moving toward the front. They were dispersed among the infantry units. The regimental histories testify that many had never seen a grenade or fired a rifle. Nevertheless, they were welcomed as having strong backs and with a lack of experience no bad habits. The 305th Infantry received 900 of the new men; M Company alone, 150. The 307th added 72 men a company, or over 850. The 308th Infantry got 1,250 men and "I" Company, which had come out of the line on the Vesle with only 80 men remaining, got 110. In addition, infantry units were issued new types of grenades and flares, whose utility, consequently, ranged from useless to ineffective. The 77th Division's area of operations was to be completely within the Argonne Forest, an area approximately seven and one-half miles wide and nineteen miles along the axis of attack (half of whose length was in American hands at the time of the offensive). It was the largest wooded area in Europe west of the Rhine, and those who fought in its tangled ravines often referred to it as a "jungle" or compared it to the "Wilderness" of the Civil War.

U

The division's mission was to fix German forces in the forest to prevent them from intervening with either fire or movement against the 28th Division, which was to screen the forest on the east while V Corps carried the major offensive mission breaking through the German defenses in more open country to the east. The 77th Division faced the German 2d Landswehr Division along a four-mile front. General Alexander deployed all four regiments on line (308th, 307th, 306th, and 305th from west to east), each battalion column with a two company front. At 5:30 A.M., September 26, the division moved out into a dense fog. Men groped their way forward in small packets, and even after the fog lifted around noon, unit coordination was impossible. Unit cohesion was completely lost, and all gains made were on the basis of individual and small-group initiatives. The Germans had generally abandoned their frontline positions. Though sharp opposition was encountered at Barricade Pavillion and St. Hubert's Pavillion, the main difficulties encountered came from the deep ravines, dense underbrush, fog, masses of wire, and felled trees. In the face of these difficulties, the 305th advanced two and one-half miles on the right flank and the 308th about one mile on the left, with the average advance for the day about a mile and a quarter along the line.

This advance brought the division against the first major German defensive position. The whole of September 27 was spent attempting to find and sort out units, reorganizing the attack, and trying to locate and penetrate the German defenses by trial and error. Early on September 28, the Germans fell back about a mile to a second prepared zone, with which the Americans made contact in the afternoon. The 153d Brigade on the right had heavy going the next day as the 154th advanced almost two miles. In the process, the Americans overran the famous German rest area of Abri de Crochet and Champ Mahaut with its theater, bowling alley, library, and deep concrete shelters.

Having penetrated the German positions to a depth of about four and one-third miles by October 1, the Americans hit another heavily defended zone held by the 76th (German) Reserve Division. At this juncture occurred one of the most popularly celebrated events of American arms during the war. Early on October 2, the division carried out a general attack, but only three companies of the 1st Battalion, 308th Infantry, commanded by Maj. Charles S.

Whittlesey, intermingled with three companies of the 2d Battalion, commanded by Capt. George McMurtry, were able to find their way through a gap in the German lines. Under orders to continue without regard to their flanks, the "battalion" advanced a little over a half mile to the division objective—the east/west Apremont-Binarville road, which bisects the forest. They dug in on a slope below the road just to the east of Moulin Charlevaux. That evening the Germans reestablished positions where the 308th had passed through their lines, effectively cutting off and surrounding the battalion.

The precarious situation was discovered on the morning of October 3 when Company E failed in its attempts to make contact with Companies D and F. Only one platoon returned from the foray with the news that the command was surrounded. Around 7:00 A.M. on October 3, Whittlesey's command, consisting of Companies A, B, C, E, G, and H, 308th Infantry; two machine gun sections of Companies C and D, 306th Machine Gun Battalion, was somehow joined by 82 men of Company K, 307th Infantry. The total force of 670 men defended the position along 400 yards of wooded slope for five days while the division mounted repeated, though often uncoordinated, attempts to break through to what now became known to the American public as the "Lost" Battalion. During this period, the command was subjected to infantry attacks as well as continual machine gun and mortar fire. Efforts to resupply the position from the air failed with the loss of two planes and all supplies. The last indignity came on the morning of October 7 when French artillery, certain that the Americans must have surrendered, shelled the entire position. By the time the 307th Infantry broke through to Major Whittlesey's force at 9:00 P.M. October 7, he had fewer than 200 effective troops.

This relief marked the end of major German resistance in the Argonne Forest. Pressured in the Aire valley to the east by attacks on the 82d Division, the Germans in the Argonne were in danger of being encircled. In fact, they may have delayed their withdrawal in hopes of bagging the surrounded force. The dogged 77th Division attacks from September 26 until October 7 turned into a pursuit on October 8.

Despite snipers and rear-guard machine gunners, the division advanced about six and a quarter miles on October 10 and 11 and stood just south of the Aire River before Grandpré, the gate to open country.

The division was ordered to cross the Aire River by seizing St. Juvin to the east of Grandpré. General Alexander planned to take the city with a frontal demonstration accompanied by an envelopment through the 82d Division zone of operations. His concept was not properly communicated to the attacking units. The lead battalion of the 306th Infantry instead carried out a frontal assault with the Aire River between it and the objective. In the midst of a bloody repulse in front of the town, the regimental commander, acting on his own initiative, maneuvered his battalions to the east in conformity with what in fact had been the original concept. St. Juvin fell before nightfall. The division subsequently attacked and seized Grandpré on the night of October 14–15.

Having entered Grandpré, the division was relieved by the 78th Division during the night of October 15–16. For the next two weeks, it rested in corps reserve until it returned to the front just north of St. Juvin on October 31 in preparation for the renewal of the attack. The general offensive was renewed at dawn on November 1. The 77th Division, in the center of I Corps, participated in a three-division attack and broke through the Brunhilde-Stellung during heavy fighting around and to the east of Champigeulle. In the days that followed, the Germans fell back rapidly all along the line before the inexorable torrent. By November 6, the 77th pursuit had covered twenty-five miles and had reached Remilly-sur-Meuse, four miles southeast of Sedan. Bridging was begun, and patrols were sent east of the Meuse, but the Armistice intervened before offensive operations were renewed.

The 77th Division was almost immediately withdrawn from active duty. During its operations in France, it had served 117 days in the line and had more days in combat, 63, than any other division. During its service, the division suffered 9,673 casualties. It began embarkation from Brest on Feb. 9, 1919, with the bulk of the division boarding ships on April 17. The last of the division entered New York harbor on May 6 and received a tumultuous welcome. The division was demobilized at Camp Upton on May 9, 1919.

Charles A. Endress

See also "Lost" Battalion

Bibliography

Alexander, Robert. *Memories of the World War, 1917–1918.* New York: Macmillan, 1931.

History of the Seventy-Seventh Division; August 25, 1917–November 11, 1918. New York: N.p., 1919.

Miles, L. Wardlaw. *History of the 308th Infantry, 1917–1919.* New York: Putnam, 1927.

Rainsford, W. Kerr. *From Upton to the Meuse with the Three Hundred and Seventy Infantry.* New York: Appleton, 1920.

Tiebout, Frank B. *A History of the 305th Infantry.* New York: The 305th Auxiliary, 1919.

United States Army: 78th Division

The 78th Division ("Lightning Division") was activated on Aug. 29, 1917, at the country's newest army base, Camp Dix, New Jersey, which was named for MajGen. John Adams Dix, commander of volunteers in the Civil War. MajGen. Chase Kennedy commanded the division, followed briefly by BGens. John S. Mallory and James T. Dean. On Jan. 7, 1918, MajGen. Hugh L. Scott, former chief of staff of the army, took command, until he was relieved by MajGen. James H. McRae on April 20, just one month before the Lightning Division began its march to war. General McRae led the 78th into battle and eventually brought the division home in 1919.

The first arrivals to this new division were a select group of men mobilized from New Jersey, New York, and Delaware. The first assignments placed men from New York in the 309th and 310th Infantry and the 307th and 309th Artillery. Recruits from New Jersey manned the 311th and 312th Infantry and 308th Artillery. The Divisional Machine Gun Battalion came from Delaware. The 1st Battalion, 303d Engineers were from New Jersey and the 2d Battalion, 303d Engineers hailed from New York. This attempt at localization in assignment soon showed many defects, and the system of assigning men according to their qualifications rather than their homes was adopted. By the time the division went overseas, it had became quite cosmopolitan in character, since large numbers of men from other states had joined it.

U

When men of the 78th first arrived at Camp Dix, they were heavily outnumbered by the civilian construction crews, but by the end of September, the camp had gradually become a military base. Early that month, contingents from Regular Army regiments, noncommissioned officers, and new appointees arrived to form training cadres for the various divisional units. By early November, most units, except certain special services such as the Ammunition and Supply trains, were up to 70 percent of their authorized strength. Intensive training began. It included much pick-and-shovel work, apparently to prepare the troops for trench warfare, which was soon to come. The 78th trained virtually, round the clock, and in just under three months the division had attained a reasonable level of preparedness. The soldiers were alert, hard, well disciplined, and ready to go "over there." For diversion during off hours, they visited the YMCA or Knights of Columbus huts where entertainment and recreation programs were scheduled. The nearby town of Wrightstown was booming, and the men thronged to local stores and theaters. Morale and pride in their division was high until a series of events tore sections of units apart.

A large transfer of men to other outfits occurred in early November. Some of these men were immediately sent overseas, while others joined different divisions. Similar transfers were made in December and January, which reduced company ranks from 175 to 50. This left the 78th considerably below strength in March 1918 with the major units lacking up to 50 percent of their authorized strength. In April, the wholesale transfers of trained men ceased, and a high-speed influx of new inductees brought the 78th back up to proper strength. It became apparent that the 78th Infantry was about to head for France. On May 6, an advance party of officers quietly slipped out of Camp Dix. On May 18 and 19, the soldiers left camp for embarkation at Boston, New York, or Philadelphia.

Between May 23 and May 27, seventeen transports jammed with men of the 78th assembled in Halifax Harbor, Nova Scotia, and soon were on the high seas; some units left from other ports. In the first week of June, the division, less its artillery, passed through England to Calais. In Calais, the 78th went into the "rest camps." A welcoming committee from Germany, whose air arm greeted the division soon after its arrival, dropping several bombs some distance from their encampment, provided the troops with their first glimpse of a night sky streaked with searchlight beams and sundry pyrotechnics. It was here that the soldiers exchanged their Springfield rifles for British Enfields. Meanwhile, the 78th Division's artillery regiment had crossed the English Channel and landed at Le Havre, from which it proceeded to Camp de Meucon, near the city of Vannes. There for eight weeks they studied the intricacies of the famous *Soixante Quinze* (French 75mm guns) and other artillery pieces.

Early in June, the division moved to its training area near Ypres, where it was attached to the British Second Army. Training cadres were the Northumberland Fusiliers, the 14th Highland Infantry, and the 15th Royal Scots. During this period of training, the 78th acted as a reserve unit for the British in the Hasbrouck sector, with the understanding that in the event of an enemy drive, it might be employed to stop the Bosche. A number of picked men were detached to observe front line and trench warfare tactics, and it was during one of these four-day battleground tours that the 78th Division suffered its first battle casualties: Corporal Smith of the 310th Infantry was killed, and Majors Abernathy and Cossman were wounded.

On July 4, the division moved to a staging area in the St. Pol area near Arras. Moonlight bombing attacks on the railhead at Tincques, the British ammunition dump, and 78th Division headquarters at Roellecourt made the attachment to the British First Army a far from pleasant assignment. On August 8, King George V of England visited division headquarters at Roellecourt. Two weeks later, the Division parted company with the British and started for the American sector. This pleased the enlisted men as it meant a return to more ample rations. A two-day journey to Bourbonne-les-Bains allowed the men to get a glimpse of the outskirts of Paris, the Marne battlefield, and the battered town of Château-Thierry.

On September 14, the U.S. Army I Corps issued the following order: "Upon arrival of the attacking divisions on the Army Objective, the position now held by the 2d and 5th Divisions and the left Brigade of the 90th Division on the Corps Front will become the 'Army Line.' The 78th Division will be charged with the defense of this position." Division headquarters was established at Loge Mangin, and the various units proceeded to their designated areas amidst harassing artillery fire; a battalion of the 312th

Infantry had to fight through an ongoing German counterattack in order to take up its position. The front that the division took over was called the "Limey" sector. It was about four and a half miles wide with hilly and rolling ground broken up with ravines and stretches of dense woods. Aggressive patrolling of enemy territory was a nightly duty, and in one instance the 309th Infantry pulled off a startling patrol in broad daylight through Rembercourt, in German-controlled territory. Four such powerful raids were carried out, including an offensive operation against Mon Plaisir Farm on September 22, where several prisoners were taken and valuable information was gathered. The 78th suffered several casualties in the attack.

The 78th began a full-scale diversionary action on September 25 to cover a major First Army attack west of the Meuse. The 3d Battalion of the 309th Infantry, aided by a six-hour artillery bombardment of the enemy lines, managed to attain its objective with a minimum of losses. The last offensive operation in this sector was a daylight attack by the 312th Infantry on a machine gun nest at La Saucisse, which was taken with few casualties. During its operation in the Limey sector, the 78th Division had performed well under the most difficult circumstances, and though suffering many casualties because of the very nature of its mission, it had displayed great valor on the field and intelligence of direction.

On October 3 and 4, elements of the 89th and 90th divisions relieved the 78th. The tired and depressed men were in hopes of getting a well-earned rest, only to find that they were ordered to march about twenty-one miles from St. Mihiel to the Argonne Forest. Though thoroughly exhausted, they continued on, even trying to catch a few "winks" while walking. They moved on through Mecrin, Campigny, and Menil to Pierrefitte and Nicey where they slept in heavy rain until French trucks manned by Chinese drivers took them to some temporary barracks on the outskirts of the Argonne area, where they got some much needed rest. There the 78th's Artillery Brigade and Ammunition Train rejoined the division after service with the 90th Division.

The 78th moved north into the Argonne on October 10, and on October 14 over 1,400 replacements were received from the 86th Division, who were immediately assigned to various units and were given a crash course in attack deployment since their lack of training and experience was obvious. Orders were received to relieve the 77th Division in the Grandpré-St. Juvin sector on a three-and-one-half-mile front. The relief was ordered to be completed by 6 A.M. on October 16. There were two enemy strongholds against which operations had to be directed—Hill 204 on Talma Hill and the so-called Citadel. The Citadel was the key to Grandpré. Without its capture, Grandpré was a death trap for division forces. The 77th, when relieved, held a line south of the Aire River extending through Chevieres, St. Juvin, and the ridge north of Sommerance. When the 2d Battalion of the 312th Infantry advanced to relieve the 77th units in Grandpré, the enemy was found to occupy the Citadel and all the northern and eastern parts of the town. It took five days of house-to-house fighting to complete the capture of the town. The 310th engaged in furious fighting in its attack on the Bois des Loges in the early hours of October 18. Companies A and C of the 310th were held up by a line of machine gun nests midway through the woods, and every officer of these companies was a casualty. The attack continued on with unabated fury, but enemy forces remained determined to hold their positions, cutting down the attackers on every hand. The medics carried on their work in the face of a constant storm of machine gun bullets and artillery fire. On October 25 a new attack, supported by heavy artillery fire, was begun. A foothold was gained by the Americans in the Bois des Bourgogne; Talma Hill was taken; Bellejoyeuse Ferme attained. The troops of the 312th Infantry had their advance broken up once again by incessant machine gun and artillery fire, but during this battle, the Citadel in Grandpré fell, and on October 27 and 28, the defenders were overwhelmed.

While these battles were underway, preparations were being made for a major attack across the Aire River to take place on November 1. The artillery opened up at 3:30 A.M. and at 5:30 A.M. that day the infantry jumped off, having been standing in their positions since 1:00 A.M. Initial resistance was formidable, and casualties were again severe, particularly when the attackers encountered murderous machine gun fire from countless German Maxims echeloned in depth on the front and on the heights to the northwest. By the end of November 2, Bois des Loges, Le Morthomme, Briguenay, and Bois de Thenorgues had been taken, the division having penetrated over three and one-half miles beyond the German lines. By the next evening, the division had advanced some six miles and had captured Boult aux Bois, Germont, Belleville, Châtillon-sur-Bar, Authe, Brieulles, Autruche, and Verriers. On November 4, the towns of Armoisses, Tannay, and Bois de Sy fell as the Americans advanced another two and one-half miles. On November 5, after the capture of Sy, the fighting career of the 78th Infantry Division came to an end.

During the course of the fighting in the Argonne, division casualties numbered over 4,900 killed, wounded, or missing. Two men were awarded the Congressional Medal of Honor posthumously—Sgt. William Sawelson of Company M, 312th Infantry, and Parker Dunn of the 1st Battalion, 312th Infantry. More than 140 Distinguished Service Crosses, 34 Croix de Guerres, and 5 Distinguished Service Medals were awarded to the men of the 78th Division.

After the postbattle assembly at Germont, the troops began their march back to several encampments. On November 16 and 17, the division moved by rail to the 21st Training Area around Semur en Auxois, where it remained until April 6, when it was released to the U.S. Service of Supply for return home. Embarking from Marseilles and Bordeaux, most of the 78th Division returned to Camp Dix, although several companies of the 310th and all of the 311th were sent to Camp Merritt, New Jersey, because of overcrowding at Camp Dix. On June 15, 1919, the 78th Infantry Division was officially demobilized.

Walter T. Morse

Bibliography

American Battle Monuments Commission. *78th Division, Summary of Operations in the World War*. Washington, DC: Government Printing Office, 1944.

Meehan, Thomas F. *History of the Seventy-eighth Division in the World War, 1917–1919*. New York: Dodd Mead, 1921.

United States Army: 79th Division

On Aug. 5, 1917, the War Department established the 79th Division, National Army, at Camp Meade, Maryland. In the last week of August, a cadre of officers and men from the Regular Army and the first Officers Training Camp at Fort Niagara arrived, and over the next eight months, draftees from Pennsylvania, Maryland, and Washington, D.C., filled the ranks. During June 1918, the division was completed with the addition of drafts from New York, Ohio, Rhode Island, and West Virginia and from transfers. On June 30, the advanced detachment sailed from Hoboken, New Jersey, for France and was followed by the division's main body from July 6 to 10. The first elements landed in Brest on July 12; by July 21, the majority of the division was in place in France.

Although the division's authorized strength fluctuated under changes in the American Expeditionary Force's (AEF) Table of Organization, its maximum authorized strength was 991 officers and 27,114 men. The division's primary armament was 24 155mm howitzers, 48 75mm guns, 12 6-inch trench mortars, 260 machine guns, and 16,193 rifles. The 79th Division was composed of the 157th and 158th Infantry brigades, the 154th Field Artillery Brigade, and the 310th Machine Gun Battalion, the 304th Engineers, the 304th Field Signal Battalion, and division headquarters and trains.

For roughly the next two months the 79th Division received intensive final training before entering into the battle line. Between July 19 and 29, the division moved to the 10th Training Area at Prauthoy. However, the 154th Field Infantry moved separately to Montmorillon on August 5. It would not rejoin the 79th until after the Armistice. The division's artillery support during the war came from attached French and other American artillery units. In Prauthoy, the Americans were taught individual soldier skills by British and French instructors. They were instructed in marksmanship, attack, defense, and the skills necessary to survive in the trenches. Furthermore, on the insistence of AEF commander Gen. John J. Pershing, all American units received considerable instruction in open-warfare tactics. It was the belief of the American military leadership that the stalemate on the Western Front was the result of the Allied obsession with trench warfare, an obsession that caused them to neglect training their soldiers in open-warfare tactics and doctrine. The men of the 79th Division would take this emphasis on open maneuver with them when they went into combat in September as part of the Meuse-Argonne offensive.

The plan of the Meuse-Argonne offensive was for an American army under American command to launch a major attack in conjunction with a great Allied convergent offensive. The Americans would attack between the

Meuse River and the Argonne Forest, with a French army in support on their left between the Argonne and the Suippes River. Simultaneously, the British and French would attack between the Oise and Scarpe rivers and east of Ypres in Flanders.

The American attack in the Meuse-Argonne would be directed at the primary German lateral supply line, the Carignan-Sedan-Mézières railroad, centered at Sedan, about thirty-two miles from the front. If this vital supply line were cut, the German positions west and northwest would become untenable, and the necessary withdrawal could lead to a rupture in the entire German front. However, the Germans were well aware of the strategic importance of the region and had spent the last four years constructing a strong defensive system arranged in four main belts. The first was located just behind the front lines. The second transversed the Argonne on a line of Autry-Montblainville-Montfaucon. The third was a component of the great defensive Hindenburg Line. This position extended across the heights of Cunel and Romagne. The fourth position was located along yet another high ground called the Barricourt Heights. Aside from the field fortifications, the Argonne Forest possessed exceptional natural defensive characteristics, as it was very rugged, dense, and steep with few roads or paths that could be used by an attacker.

On September 13, the 79th Division began relieving the French 157th Division in the Avocourt sector. The next day, the 79th was assigned to the American III Corps, which assumed command of a portion of the French XVII Corps' front. The relief was completed on September 16, and at 8 A.M., command of the sector passed to the 79th Division. The next week was spent in preparation for the offensive as the American First Army got itself into battle positions. On September 21, the 79th Division was assigned to the American V Corps, which assumed the section of front from Malancourt to Vauquois. That same day the American First Army received its field orders for the opening of the Meuse-Argonne offensive.

V Corps was positioned between the American III Corps on its right and the American I Corps on its left. Within V Corps' sector, the 79th Division was on the extreme right, flanked on the left by the 37th Division. The attack would begin on the morning of September 26 with the corps objective for that day

being Nantillois, about six miles from the start position. The 79th Division's mission was to advance rapidly to the corps objective (which lay in its zone), seizing the village of Malancourt and the strongpoint Montfaucon along the way.

At 5:30 A.M. on September 26, the 79th Division jumped off, preceded by a barrage of smoke, artillery, and poison gas. Its advance was slow: the infantry had trouble getting through the wire, and the barrage had felled trees and cratered the few roads, thus adding to the existing obstacles. Furthermore, the inexperienced soldiers often lost their way in the limited visibility caused by the smoke, gas, and heavy morning fog. Malancourt was reached about 8:00 A.M., but the advance bogged down further as the division advanced toward Montfaucon. The leading infantry units had not kept up with their supporting rolling barrage, and the 79th soon found itself without artillery support and pinned down by heavy machine gun fire both to the front and the rear.

The 79th Division pressed onward. The advance was slow and steady, and the strains of the battle showed. Casualties were high, and ammunition supplies ran low. Units became hopelessly intertwined. Communications between headquarters and subordinate units were intermittent at best, and the division found itself unable accurately to track or control the battle. By 4:00 P.M., the division's leading elements had secured the woods, the Bois de Cuisy, before Montfaucon. Division headquarters ordered the 157th Brigade to seize Montfaucon and committed a detachment of French tanks to assist, but without artillery support the assault bogged down and the men retreated to the Bois de Cuisy for the night. As a result, the Germans were able to strengthen and reinforce Montfaucon during the night. The 79th resumed the attack on September 27. After bitter fighting all morning, it succeeded in taking the village early in the afternoon but could advance no further.

The delay in taking Montfaucon is bitterly ironic. On the right flank of the 79th, the experienced 4th Division made considerable progress on September 26. Keeping together in the fog and smoke, the 4th found itself more than a mile forward and east of Montfaucon when the weather cleared. The division easily could have taken the strongpoint that afternoon, but the rigid American operational doctrine forbade the crossing of divisional and corps boundaries. The 4th Division's orders were to stay in even contact with their flanking units, so they dug in and waited for the 79th to catch up. It is estimated that the failure to take Montfaucon on September 26 gave the Germans thirty precious hours to regroup, and contributed significantly to the American offensive slowing to a halt.

The 79th Division continued its attack on September 28, capturing Nantillois after much bitter fighting. However, after four days of constant engagement, the division was spent. Casualties were very high, particularly among the infantry officers, and the remnants of infantry battalions had to be amalgamated to form provisional battalions. Ammunition, food, and medical supplies were critically short, and the transportation problems, which plagued the entire American First Army, prevented effective resupply. On September 30, the 79th Division was relieved in the line by the 3d Division and assembled in III Corps area near Malancourt.

The 79th Division remained at rest in that area until October 3, when it was moved north of St. Mihiel and assigned to the French II Colonial Corps. The division reentered the line on October 8 when, together with elements of two French divisions, it relieved the 26th Division in the Troyon sector. The division remained in the line until October 26, when it was relieved and assigned to the French XVII Corps reserve near Dieu-sur-Meuse. Rested and reorganized, the 79th Division again entered the line on October 30, relieving the 29th Division northeast of Consenvoye. There the division prepared for the last push of the war.

On November 4 and 5, elements of the 79th Division, in conjunction with the French, attacked the heights known as La Borne de Cornouiller. The attacks succeeded, and by November 7, the Germans had been pushed back about a mile and one-quarter. On November 8, the division successfully completed a complicated pivot to the east, and soon occupied the villages of Bois de Wavrille, Bois de la Grande Matagne, Bois d'Ecurey, Etraye, and Reville on a five-mile front. The division continued making limited, but highly successful, attacks in the next two days, rapidly seizing the villages of Creipon, Wavrille, Chaumont-devant-Damillers, and Buisson Chaumont and capturing large numbers of prisoners. On November 11, the division assaulted the Côte de Romagne and the Côte de Mortimont, and was attacking right up until the 11:00 A.M. Armistice deadline.

Under the terms of the Armistice, the 79th Division spent the next month examining posts along the Armistice line, enforcing the terms of the Armistice, salvaging war materiel, and training. On December 26, the division moved to the Souilly area for training, where it stayed until March 28, 1919, when it moved to the Rimaucourt Training Area. Then, on April 21, the 79th moved to the Nantes Training Area before finally assembling at the port of St. Nazaire on May 11 to be shipped home. The first units sailed on May 13, and the last elements of the 79th Division arrived in New York on June 11, 1919. From there they proceeded to the demobilization site at Camp Dix, New Jersey.

Although committed to combat relatively late, the 79th Division was an active and competent American division. The difficulties it encountered in the opening phases of the Meuse-Argonne offensive were not unique; they were typical of all of the American divisions when they first entered the line, especially during that operation. A by-product of General Pershing's insistence on maintaining an independent American Army, the American units suffered acutely from inexperience in logistical and operational planning and execution. Furthermore, part of the blame for the high American casualty lists can be placed on the American Army's tactical doctrine. The emphasis on open-warfare maneuver during training resulted in the American infantry using costly wave-type assaults that the Europeans had discovered to be suicidal back in 1914. The Americans did learn by their bloody mistakes, however, and the veteran units such as the 1st and 2d divisions and, by November 11 the 79th, successfully integrated their energy and aggressiveness with the realities of modern warfare.

The 79th Division's solid contributions to the American war effort are reflected in *The War With Germany: A Statistical Summary* by Leonard P. Ayres. During the four months of the war the 79th served in France, it spent forty-five days in the line, seventeen of them in active sectors. It advanced over twelve miles against the enemy, and captured 1,077 enemy prisoners. The division suffered 7,590 combat casualties, of which 1,396 were battle deaths. It is estimated that an equal number died of disease, most succumbing to the Spanish Influenza epidemic before embarking for France. While statistically the 79th Division could not compare with such Regular Army units as the 1st or 2d divisions, the natives of eastern Pennsylvania, Maryland, and Washington, D.C., wrote a proud page in the history of the American Expeditionary Force.

Jeffrey D. Schnakenberg

Bibliography

American Battle Monuments Commission. *American Armies and Battlefields in Europe: A History, Guide, and Reference Book.* Washington, DC: Government Printing Office, 1938.

————. *The Summary of Operations in the World War, 79th Division.* Washington, DC: Government Printing Office, 1944.

Center of Military History, U.S. Army. *Order of Battle of the United States Land Forces in the World War.* Vol. 2. *American Expeditionary Force: Divisions.* Washington, DC: Government Printing Office, 1988.

Paschall, Rod. *The Defeat of Imperial Germany, 1917–1918.* Chapel Hill, NC: Algonquin Books, 1989.

United States Army: 80th Division

The first official mention of the 80th Infantry Division appears in War Department General Order No. 95 of July 18, 1917. One section of the order directed that the cantonment authorized at Petersburg, Virginia, would be the home of the 80th Infantry Division, which was made up of men from New Jersey, Virginia, Maryland, Delaware, and the District of Columbia. The cantonment was to be known as Camp Lee, in honor of Robert E. Lee.

This mention of the 80th Division was merely a convenience, for not until August 3, in General Order No. 101, did the War Department actually establish the division as an organization. It was to include the 313th Machine Gun Battalion, the 155th, 159th, and 160th Infantry brigades, the 305th Engineers, headquarters, and support trains.

On August 5, the War Department realigned the geographical area from which men for the 80th would be drawn. It now encompassed Virginia, West Virginia, and western Pennsylvania, including Pittsburgh. MajGen. Adelbert Cronkhite, who as brigadier general had been military governor of the Panama Canal Department, was assigned to command the 80th Division and Camp Lee.

Thousands of young men who, in most cases, had never seen a Regular Army soldier were called up under the Selective Service Act to form the division. Only a few uniforms were available for the new soldiers, and improvised wooden rifles were common equipment for them. For several weeks, companies drilled and worked in a weird mixture of civilian and military attire. But once initial perplexity and bewilderment had been supplanted by the eagerness to learn, the men swiftly acquired martial skills.

General Cronkhite decided that the 80th was to be known officially as the "Blue Ridge" Division, for the three states from which the men were drawn all shared the mountain beauty of the Blue Ridge chain. The slogan selected, "*Vis Montium,*" translates from the Latin as "Strength of the Mountains."

On May 12, 1918, all leaves and passes were summarily terminated, and men were quarantined. It was clear to all that the long-awaited order for movement overseas had been issued. Formal departure of units was led by the 319th Infantry on May 17 from Newport News and continued until the last troops were boarded on ships on May 25. The 80th made the crossing without a casualty and landed at St. Nazaire, France, the last of the transports landing on June 8.

Debarkation completed, the troops remained in "rest camps" at Brest, St. Nazaire, or Bordeaux for two to seven days before being sent by rail to training areas. The inadequate French railroads were already overburdened, and it was several weeks before all of the units of the division were reunited.

Elements of the 80th Division proceeded to the Imbroune and Fruges areas for training by the 16th Irish Division. On May 29, British headquarters directed the 80th to proceed to Calais for equipment with British arms before moving to its appointed training areas. While at Calais, several units experienced their first air raids and saw air service units in action. The training by the decimated Irish division ended when the Irish troops were directed to return to England for restoration to battle strength. Another depleted unit, the 34th Division, took its place to train the 80th.

The division's training consisted principally of instruction in gas defense, musketry, use of the machine gun and a Lewis gun, bombing, bayonet fighting, signaling, and physical training. Then on June 14, elements of the 80th, composed of the division's officers and noncom-

U

missioned officers of the intelligence sections, were attached to divisions of the British First and Second Armies. As July neared, it was apparent that the initial phase of training was approaching completion. Campaign hats were discarded in favor of the overseas service cap of the American Expeditionary Force. The prospect of more active duty with the British stirred the men of the 80th. They had observed the U.S. 4th, 28th, and 77th divisions hurrying southward to join the Franco-American forces on the Marne, and now perhaps they were to see action with the British Third Army along the Ancre River and in the Somme region. It was in that direction that the division was headed.

The entire division, with the exception of the artillery brigade and several lesser units, was about to experience the front. To the 317th Infantry went the distinction of furnishing the first platoons. Total casualties suffered by the 317th between July 25 and August 6 were nine killed, forty wounded, and two missing, both of whom were captured by the enemy after being severely wounded while engaged on a raid in no-man's-land. Sgt. Fred B. Stultz, of Company B, killed in action on July 27, was the regiment's first battle loss.

Beginning on July 27 and continuing through August 12, platoons of the 318th Infantry were attached to frontline battalions of British units along the Ancre River, between Martinsart and Bouzincourt, in front of Thiepaval Ridge and the small town of Albert. During this tour, the regiment lost one killed and thirteen wounded. Units of the 319th Infantry did trench duty from July 27 through August 5. During its frontline service, the regiment sustained losses of five killed and fifteen wounded. The 320th Infantry's attachment to the British VI Corps began on July 28, when platoons of the 3d Battalion went into line, remaining until August 1. They were succeeded by the 2d Battalion August 1–5, and by the 1st Battalion August 5–9. In the thirteen-day tour by the 320th Infantry, nine men were either wounded or died of wounds. Due to their late arrival, the machine gun units did not enter the lines until August. The 313th Machine Gun Battalion had one platoon of each company enter the line in the southwest sector of Gommecourt and Hebuterne on August 1 for a four-day period. Two elements of the 314th Machine Gun Battalion entered the trenches for a two-day observation tour on August 3. Both battalions of the 318th Machine Gun

Company were attached to the 38th Machine Gun Battalion, 17th British Division, then holding a sector of V Corps' front between Martinsart and Bouzincourt and opposite the town of Albert. Since its arrival in the Harponville area in mid-July, the 305th Engineers had been living under war conditions, building and repairing the British trench system.

Upon relief from the front, the regiments of the 80th Division returned to their former billeting areas for a brief rest and resumed their usual training. The 80th Division's frontline training was to take place with the British Third Army as that army prepared to guard the British Fourth Army's left flank. An attack on August 8 on the right of the 80th found elements of the division in the middle of their frontline training, thus involving the division in the Somme offensive.

On August 14, General Pershing directed the 80th Division to join the American First Army, which he was assembling in the Lorraine sector of France. The division entrained at four points—Bouquemaison, Bernaville, and Prouville East and West—with the movement to be made at the rate of eighteen trains in twenty-four hours. The division's destination, Stainville, was only announced after entrainment. From Stainville, the 80th went into reserve at St. Mihiel. On the night of August 25, shortly after the division's deployment was complete, the 80th struck its first blow against the Germans, only to receive word that it would no longer be needed.

The 80th Division's greatest accomplishment of World War I was the role it played in the Meuse-Argonne when an American-French attack cut the vital Sedan-Mézières railroad supply line. The offensive, destined to break the back of the German armies, began on Sept. 26, 1918. Three times the spearheading 80th was called upon; three times it took its objective. By November 8, when the 80th was relieved by the 1st Division, the Blue Ridge infantrymen, along with other Allied divisions, had shattered German defenses.

At the end of the war, the Blue Ridge Division was rated first of all National Army divisions by the War Department. The artillery of the division boasted more days of continuous combat firing than the batteries of any other American division and it is of interest to note that the 80th captured two Germans and one machine gun for every man wounded and one piece of artillery with the gun crew for every ten men wounded.

Thirty-seven officers and 553 men of the 80th were laid to rest in France, and 5,463 men of the division who returned home had been gassed in action.

Robert T. Murrell

Bibliography

American Battle Monuments Commission. *80th Division, Summary of Operations in the World War*. Washington, DC: Government Printing Office, 1944.

United States Army: 81st Division

War Department General Order No. 101, effective Aug. 5, 1917, ordered the formation of the 81st National Army Division—a division of draftees. Initially, the men were drawn from North Carolina, South Carolina, and Florida. Later, additional draftees, especially from Alabama and New York, were sent to complete the division.

Although named the "Stonewall Division" in honor of Confederate Gen. Thomas J. ("Stonewall") Jackson, it was known primarily as the "Wildcat Division," in recognition of an irascible creature that inhabited southern states and from Wildcat Creek, a creek that ran near Camp Jackson, South Carolina, the home base of the 81st. A wildcat silhouette was adopted as a shoulder patch for the division, the first insignia worn by troops in the American Expeditionary Force (AEF). At first, Gen. John J. Pershing disapproved of the use of an insignia in the 81st Division, but later permitted all American divisions to adopt their own distinctive symbols.

Organized at Camp Jackson in September 1917, the 81st was placed under the temporary command of BGen. Charles H. Barth until October, when MajGen. Charles J. Bailey assumed command.

Training the 81st Division in the fall and winter of 1917–1918 was difficult. When the first draftees arrived at Camp Jackson, they found only thickly wooded sand hills. Their first duties were to clear the site and to construct all of the drill fields, roads, and buildings. Then in October, 50 percent of the men were taken from the division and transferred to other divisions being sent overseas. This depletion delayed training of the remaining soldiers and required a complete reorganization of the division when new draftees were sent to fill the empty ranks.

As a result, the 81st Division was delayed from entering combat in France even though it was one of the first National Army divisions organized.

The division was ordered to Camp Sevier, near Greenville, South Carolina, in May 1918 for two months of intensive training. In July, it was ordered to Camp Upton, New York, to prepare for transfer overseas. The first units sailed for Europe on July 31 and arrived at Liverpool, England, on August 11. By the end of August, all personnel were in the Tonnerre Training Area in France. There the 156th Field Artillery Brigade was detached and transferred to Valdahon for training.

After a month of additional combat instruction, the 81st Division was sent to the front in mid-September 1918 and arrived in the St. Die sector in the Vosges Mountains region on September 19. Assigned to the XXXIII Corps and later to the X Corps, French Seventh Army, the division held what was considered a quiet front, though it often had to fight off German trench raids and endure enemy artillery bombardments, during which it suffered 116 casualties. On October 19, the division was relieved and sent to the rear to await transfer to the American First Army, which was fighting in the Meuse-Argonne offensive.

In early November, the 81st Division proceeded to the Sommedieve sector south of Verdun to join the French XVII Corps in reserve. On November 6, all four of the division's infantry regiments entered the front line east of Verdun, replacing units of the American 35th Division. Since its own artillery was detached, the 81st Division was supported by the 60th Artillery Brigade of the 35th Division. This deployment to Verdun placed the 81st on the far right flank of the American First Army, on the east side of the Meuse River. Here the division was attached to the French II Colonial Corps, which was serving with the AEF.

All along the Western Front, German forces were being slowly beaten back by the Allied armies. To push the Germans even farther, all available Allied divisions were sent into battle. On November 8, the 81st Division was ordered to attack east of Verdun.

The division front, however, was too long for an assault to be effective; all four infantry regiments were on the front line, leaving no reserve units to support any successful advance. Also, in the middle ground opposing the division was a densely wooded area that was heavily defended by the Germans. Because of the extended front and the unfavorable terrain, 81st Division commanders were determined to bypass the forest and to attack German positions on either side of the wooded tract. Accordingly, the 161st Infantry Brigade was ordered to attack on the north side, and the 162d Infantry Brigade was sent forward on the south side. Each brigade was supported by a machine gun battalion and by two companies of the 306th Engineers Regiment.

On the morning of November 9, both infantry brigades attacked the enemy lines. The terrain was low and marshy, in some places flooded, and broken with belts of thick woods. The Germans had placed barbed-wire entanglements with numerous concrete machine gun emplacements throughout the area. All ruined farms and villages were strongly organized as defenses. Heavy fog and smoke hindered visibility, but these conditions probably saved American lives in the attack.

When the assault was ordered, American commanders believed that the Germans were withdrawing from the front and would offer only limited resistance. They were wrong. From the outset, the 81st Division's troops of the 322d and 324th Infantry regiments met heavy German machine gun and artillery fire. Enemy aircraft commanded the sky; they called in artillery strikes on the advancing soldiers and even strafed the Americans with their machine guns. Artillery fire from the Allied lines was largely ineffective because of a shortage of shells and because it was outranged by the German counterfire, which harassed the American battery positions. For the most part, the infantry was alone in its attack on a determined enemy.

By midday, the 322d Infantry Regiment had advanced to the outskirts of Moranville, which it finally captured by late afternoon. On the south side of the forest, the 324th Infantry Regiment slowly pushed the Germans back and captured Noir-Haies and Claires-Chenes. Attempts to advance farther were stopped because the American 33d Division on the left did not move forward and because of intense enemy machine gun and artillery fire. By late afternoon, much of the ground gained by the 324th Infantry Regiment was abandoned when its soldiers were withdrawn to safer positions. One company in a wooded area did not learn of the withdrawal and was soon cut off and decimated by German counterattacks. The end of the day's fighting, therefore, brought mixed results, suc-

cess north of the woods and frustration to the south.

The following day, the 324th Infantry Regiment spent much of its time repositioning its troops along the Fresnes road. Little if any forward movement was attempted, and by late afternoon and evening the regiment was replaced by the 323d Infantry Regiment. To the north, the 322d Infantry Regiment continued its attack, capturing the ruins of Grimaucourt early in the morning and positions to the east of the village throughout the afternoon. During the evening, just as the regiment reached the main German trench lines, intense enemy artillery fire forced a withdrawal to the west of Grimaucourt. On the night of November 10, the 321st Infantry Regiment relieved the 322d on the battle line.

During the night, rumors reached 81st Division commanders that an armistice might be signed the following day, November 11. Because no official word was received about a cessation of hostilities, plans were made for an early morning attack. The 321st Infantry Regiment was ordered forward at daylight to attack the main German trench line. The 323d Infantry Regiment was ordered to attack along its front but not until supported by 33d Division troops on its right flank. It was hoped that on November 11, the German lines would be captured or there would be an armistice, whichever came first.

At daybreak, the 321st Infantry Regiment soldiers went "over the top" for the first time and attacked the German trench positions north of the forest. After passing Grimaucourt, part of the regiment was stopped along another wooded area, Bois de Petite Cognon. After pushing past these woods, the troops re-formed and slowly advanced through the heavy fog and German shell and machine gun fire. At 10:30 A.M., the 323d Infantry Regiment began its attack to the south of the woods. By 10:45 A.M., the 321st Infantry Regiment reached the barbed-wire entanglements along the German main trench line. Soldiers fought their way into and through the wire; some of the Americans entered the German trenches. Then, at 11:00 A.M. the firing abruptly stopped. The war was over!

Following the Armistice on November 11, the 81st Division marched 175 miles to the Chatillion-sur-Seine area, where it remained over five months. Here its artillery brigade rejoined the division after detached service. The division was not part of the Army of Occupation in Germany. In France, the 81st Division left 1,104 casualties—248 killed or dead from wounds and 856 wounded—for the short time it was in combat. In mid-May 1919, the division was ordered to the Le Mans area and then to Brest and St. Nazaire in early June to be shipped back to the United States. By the end of the month, division troops landed in either Charleston, South Carolina, or Newport News, Virginia, and were discharged from service.

R.J. Marshall

Bibliography

Johnson, C. Walton. *Wildcats, History of the 321st Infantry, 81st Division*. Columbia, SC: N.p., n.d.

Roster and History of the 306th Engineers and 306th Engineers Train. Columbia, SC: N.p., n.d.

White, Charles H. *Memories of Ambulance Company No. 321, 81st Division AEF*. Greensboro, SC: N.p., 1929.

Workman, John H. *Company K, 324th Infantry, 81st Division*. N.p., n.d.

United States Army: 82d Division

On Aug. 25, 1917, the 82d Division, which became known as the "All-American Division," was organized in the National Army of the United States. National Army units were to be composed entirely of draftees as compared to the Regular Army and National Guard troops. The organization started in Camp Gordon, Georgia, under the command of MajGen. Eben Swift. The first week was spent organizing officers, only a third of whom were Regular Army, most of whom came from the First Officers Training camp at Fort McPherson, also in Georgia.

The division's organizational structure primarily included three brigades, two infantry and one artillery, supported by the 307th Engineer Regiment, 307th Field Signal Battalion, 307th Ammunition, Sanitary, Engineer, and Supply trains, plus the 319th Machine Gun Battalion. The 163d Infantry Brigade under the command of BGen. Marcus D. Cronin was comprised of the 325th and 326th Infantry regiments and the 320th Machine Gun Battalion; the 164th Infantry Brigade commanded by Col. (later brigadier general) William P. Burnham of the 327th and 328th Infantry regiments and the 321st Machine Gun Battalion. The 157th Field Artillery Brigade commanded by Col. Earle d'A.

Pearce was made up of the 319th, 320th, and 321st Field Artillery regiments. The 320th and 321st were armed with 75mm guns and the 319th with 155mm guns.

Initially, troops came from southern states, particularly Alabama, Georgia, and Tennessee and a training cadre of noncommissioned officers mostly from the 6th and 17th Infantry. The expansion from peacetime to wartime footing created havoc with training, and six weeks after the first troops arrived, all enlisted personnel were transferred to various southern National Guard units, leaving only draftees to fill the division.

By Nov. 1, 1917, approximately 28,000 men from across the country had entered Camp Gordon. Training was hampered by the fact that approximately 20 percent of the draftees were of foreign birth and a number of them could neither read nor write English. As a matter of fact, a few could hardly speak English, so an English-language school was created to assist non-English speakers. A number of men were discharged since they came from enemy countries. Another 3,000 were transferred out after it was determined that they had occupational specialties that were needed elsewhere. In March 1918, another 5,000 replacements arrived.

The mobilization of large numbers of troops exceeded the ability of the nation to equip them. Troops were forced to train with wooden rifles and machine guns. When the first rifles finally arrived, they were missing web equipment. Heavy equipment such as artillery was very limited right up until the division was shipped overseas. Stokes mortar platoons never saw a Stokes mortar while in the United States. Other equipment was either nonexistent or found in very limited quantities. General Swift placed great emphasis on road marching and organizational singing and gave considerable attention to marksmanship, bayonet training, and military courtesies. French and British officers supervised special unit training and offensive tactics.

On Nov. 24, 1917, Swift was ordered overseas. BGen. James B. Erwin assumed command of the division, but he stayed with it only a month before being transferred to command the 6th Division. He was replaced by the 164th Brigade commander, BGen. William R. Burnham, on December 26.

The division was inspected by the War Department in February and March and

U

deemed ready to be shipped overseas. On April 10, division headquarters moved to Camp Upton, New York, for embarkation, and the division began overseas shipment from New York City on April 25. The last unit left the United States on May 3. The division arrived at Liverpool, England, and after a short stay at various English rest camps, embarked at Southhampton for transport to Le Harve, France.

On the way to Southhampton, the 325th Infantry Regiment marched through the streets of London and was reviewed by King George and the royal family. The parade was the first that offered the English a glimpse of American troops. The London Times commented: "The War has given London many scenes—some gay, some grave—but few have surpassed yesterday's, when three thousand soldiers of the Republican America marched through the capital to parade before the Sovereign Ruler of the British Empire. . . . Every state in the Union had its representative, for these were not men of the Regular Army, such as had 'come across' twelve months ago with General Pershing: they were the vanguard of the new American Army, that almost numberless force which America is raising to crush for ever the evil spirit of Prussian militarism."

After arriving at Le Harve, troops moved to the St. Valéry-sur-Somme Training Area with headquarters at Escarbotin, and the 82d was assigned to train with the British 667th Division. Since it was training with the British, it reequipped with British rifles, machine guns, and other materiel. An intensive training program was initiated to indoctrinate and familiarize the recent arrivals with the British approach and methods, and headquarters instituted a program of rotating each battalion up to a frontline British unit to acclimate the men to trench warfare.

On June 15, orders were received to move the division to the Toul area, where it would be under the French Eighth Army. On June 24, it moved to the Woëvre from where, with the French 154th Division, it participated in the occupation of the Lagney sector on the southern face of the St. Mihiel salient from June 25 to July 17. On July 18, the 82d Division assumed control of the Lucey sector, where it remained until its relief by the 89th Division on August 10.

The Allied command ordered the formation of an American front, and General Pershing concentrated American forces in the Lorraine sector. The American First Army, made up of three American and one French corps, was organized on August 10 and given the mission of reducing the St. Mihiel salient, a roughly triangular-shaped area with its corners near Pont-à-Mousson, St. Mihiel, and Verdun. It was approximately twenty-six miles across the base and extended about sixteen miles into the Allied lines. Strategically, the salient was important since it cut the Verdun-Toul railroad and had allowed German artillery to interrupt traffic on the Paris-Nancy line.

On August 20, the 82d was assigned to the American I Corps in the Marbache sector. This area had been used as a rest area for both Allied and German units. It was here that the 157th Field Artillery Brigade rejoined the division having completed its training at La Courtine. The mission assigned by I Corps headquarters to the division on September 6 was to maintain pressure and contact with the enemy.

The St. Mihiel offensive started on September 12. The 82d was ordered to execute a holding mission in order to prevent German flanking actions against the right lines of the U.S. First Army. The division sent strong patrols to locate German lines and strong points. Since orders did not entail a general attack but continual probing, little ground was captured. The 328th Infantry captured Norry on September 13 and was subjected to strong German artillery reactions and counterattacks on September 14 and 15. The 164th Infantry Brigade ordered the 328th to maintain close contact with the 90th Division and advance with it. The 90th was unable to advance, so there was no change in the 328th position. The rest of the line was basically unchanged. The American efforts to reduce the salient were successful, and the offensive actions were replaced by sector occupations activities.

French units relieved the 82d on September 21, and divisional headquarters moved to Liverdun. The division's stay lasted only three days before it was ordered to the area of Clermont as part of the U.S. First Army reserve. Division headquarters was located at Grange-le-Comte. The weather had turned miserable, and troops suffered from the rain, mud, and colder temperatures of the new area. The Meuse-Argonne offensive was beginning. It was designed to cut the Germans' principal supply line, the Carignan-Sedan-Mézières railroad, which was thirty-three miles behind the front. To protect this line, the Germans had built four lines of strong field fortifications. The fortifications, when combined with the natural advantages of the terrain, were a challenge to any attacking force. The troops were ordered to be ready to move out on two hours' notice. I Corps ordered the 327th Infantry detached from the division and sent to Varennes to report to the 28th Division. The 327th occupied a section of the trenches between the 28th and 35th divisions near Baulny and returned to the 82d on October 3. The 307th Engineers were ordered to Clermont-en-Argonne, where they were placed under the command of the First Army Engineers to assist in general road repairs.

On the night of October 6–7, the 164th Infantry Brigade, under the command of BGen. Julian R. Lindsey, relieved the troops of the 28th Division, which held the line in the area of Fleville to La Forge, along the eastern bank of the Aire River. The balance of the division, less the 163d Infantry Brigade, which was kept in corps reserve, on October 7, was ordered to attack the northeastern edge of the Argonne Forest. The following night, the 163d was released from corps reserve and ordered to join the division. On October 8, Corporal Alvin C. York of the 328th Infantry won the Medal of Honor near Châtel Chehery. The official report concerning the incident read: "Practically unassisted, he captured 132 Germans (three of whom were officers), took about 35 machine guns and killed no less than 25 of the enemy, later found by others on the scene of York's extraordinary exploit." The actions of the 328th Infantry had a far-reaching effect in insuring American success in the Argonne Forest. The quantities of prisoners and materiel captured was impressive—300 prisoners, approximately 200 dead, four 77mm guns, 1 trench mortar battery, 1 signal unit, and 123 machine guns.

The 82d Division then advanced to capture Cornay and Marcq. On October 11, it continued its advance and occupied Sommerance. On October 14 and 15, the division passed through the Hindenburg Line and reached the road connecting St. Georges and St. Juvin. From October 22 to 27, it consolidated its positions. Then, on October 28, the 82d, less its artillery, was relieved by the 77th and 80th divisions.

The division then moved back through the Argonne Forest during the night of October 31–November 1, with division headquarters transferred to Champ Mahaut. The division continued to move south for the next three days until arriving at Bourmont, where it was when the Armistice was signed on November 11. Five days later, the division was again on the move to the 10th Training Area with headquarters at Prauthoy. On arriving there, the 82d began improving the physical accommodations and embarked upon a training schedule. During December, the division's artillery rejoined the 82d. In February 1919, the division received instructions to return to the United States. On February 9, the 307th Trench Mortar Battery was the first divisional unit to leave. On February 26, the rest of the division moved to Bordeaux to await shipment home. On April 22, the advance divisional headquarters sailed from France and arrived in New York on May 5. A detachment of the 326th Infantry was the last unit to reach New York on June 6.

Immediately after arriving home, units were shipped to demobilization areas and deactivated. The divisional headquarters was demobilized on May 27, 1919, at Camp Mills, New York.

The 82d Division had spent 70 days in quiet lines, 27 in active sector trenches, suffered 6,248 wounded in action, 1,298 killed in action, captured 845 prisoners, and advanced 10.5 miles against resistance.

James Controvich

Bibliography

American Battle Monuments Commission. *82d Division, Summary of Operations in the World War*. Washington, DC: Government Printing Office, 1944.

Official History of the 82d Division, American Expeditionary Force, "All American Division," 1917–1919. Indianapolis: N.p., 1919.

United States Army: 89th Division

The War Department established the 89th Division on Aug. 5, 1917, to be organized at Camp Funston, Fort Riley, Kansas, and staffed by draftees from Arizona, Colorado, Kansas, Missouri, New Mexico, and South Dakota. MajGen. Leonard Wood was named commander.

The initial drafts of 2,200 men arrived between September 5 and 10; an additional 18,600 men arrived September 19 to 24; 17,300 arrived October 3 to 8, and final drafts and transfers completed the division in May 1918. On May 21, the division moved to the embarkation ports of Boston, Brooklyn, Montreal, and New York. General Wood was relieved at this time, and BGen. Frank L. Winn assumed command. Advance detachments sailed from New York for Liverpool, England, on June 4. The last unit landed in England on July 8 and then all proceeded to Le Havre and Cherbourg, France.

Upon arrival in France, the troops went by rail to the Reynel Training Area located in the Haute-Marne between Chaumont and Neufchâteau about thirty-seven miles from the front. Troops were scattered throughout the area—some being billeted among the French populace, others being assigned to barracks.

Training emphasized infantry fundamentals and new formations for attack against machine guns. For the first time at Reynel, the men were given live grenades, and they practiced camouflage, trench raids, and sniping. The doughboys also learned the rudiments of trench warfare, occupying a network of practice trenches in the training area. Meanwhile, the division artillery was undergoing training at Camp de Souge near Bordeaux. It was during this training period that the division insignia, the letter "W" enclosed in a circle, was adopted. The official explanation of its meaning was that it designated the "Middle West Division" as the central letter could be read as an "M" in one aspect or a "W" in another.

On August 3 and 4, 1918, the 89th Division (less its artillery) loaded into trucks and started for a frontline sector north of Toul, taking over a section of the line between the towns of Remenauville and Bouconville on the south face of the St. Mihiel salient. This sector, which had previously been occupied by the U.S. 1st and 26th divisions, was considered a quiet one where green troops could be sent to gain experience and where exhausted divisions rested while still holding down part of the line. The 89th relieved the 82d Division.

Soon after relieving the frontline battalions of the 82d, the 89th Division received its first taste of real war. On the night of August 7–8, the units near the wrecked village of Flirey were bombarded with mustard and phosgene gas shells for nearly four hours. There were 556 casualties—most of them light, though at least 42 officers and men died of gas poisoning. The 82d Division, on its way out, suffered another 150 casualties. It was later determined that many of the 89th casualties occurred because the men did not know, or failed to observe, proper gas discipline. This failing was soon corrected by further training, and subsequent gas attacks on the division had far less impact.

The division immediately began patrolling its front. On the night of August 13–14, a twenty-six-man patrol from the 356th Infantry beat off two German patrols trying to penetrate the lines and captured four prisoners, the first to be taken by the division. On August 19, the Germans attempted a raid near Flirey but again were beaten off. The enemy attempted other probes through late August and early September with little effect on the high-spirited Middle West division.

In September, the 89th Division was assigned to IV Corps, one of three American corps assigned to lop off the St. Mihiel salient. The attack was scheduled for September 12. The 89th remained in place on the south face of the salient, masking the influx of other troops until the last moment. The division's mission in the assault was to drive from Flirey directly across the salient to Xammes and Beney. It would attack with the U.S. 2d Division on its right and the U.S. 42d Division on its left.

The division jumped off at 5:00 A.M. after a four-hour artillery preparation. The enemy had been preparing to pull out before the assault and resistance was spotty. Here and there German machine guns held up the advance and inflicted casualties, but progress was better than expected. The 89th's advance went so well that the division was ordered past its first-day objectives, ultimately capturing its second-day objective directly in front of the Hindenburg Line late that same evening. Hundreds of prisoners were taken.

The division earned its first Medal of Honor on September 12, awarded posthumously to Lt. J. Hunter Wickersham of Denver, Colorado. Severely wounded by a bursting shell, Wickersham dressed the wounds of his orderly, then ordered and accompanied the advance of his platoon though weakened by the loss of blood. He continued to fire his revolver with his good hand until he fell and died from his wounds.

Over the next few days, the 89th Division consolidated its positions, digging in under a galling German artillery fire. The division's artillery joined it, relieving French artillery support at this time. The division remained in the sector, expanding to take over the sector occupied by the 42d Division on the left and then part of the sector previously occupied by the 2d Division on the right.

Finally, on the nights of October 7–8 and 8–9, the division was relieved by the U.S. 37th Division and assembled in the vicinity of Commercy. It had been in the line or in battle continuously for two months and a day.

The division had performed well at St. Mihiel. Losses during the attack totaled nearly 200 officers and men killed, over 900 wounded, and 69 listed as missing in action. The division claimed capture of 2,287 prisoners, most from the German 10th and 77th Reserve divisions. Enemy killed were estimated at 300. The division captured 72 artillery pieces of various calibers, 95 machine guns, 1,000 rifles, enormous quantities of ammunition, and even several locomotives and railroad cars.

On October 9, the division moved via French camions to the rear area in the Meuse-Argonne sector where a huge Franco-American attack had been underway since September 26. Assigned to an area just east of the central part of the Argonne Forest, the 89th began to clean up, refit, and train, receiving replacements for its losses at St. Mihiel.

On October 12, the division was assigned to V Corps (which then included the 32d and 42d divisions in the front lines) and was ordered to move to the vicinity of Eclisefontaine and Epinonville in support. By October 14, the men were again under shell fire while acting as reserve of the V Corps behind the 32d Division. The division relieved the 32d Division the night of October 19–20.

The 32d Division was considerably disorganized by the hard fighting it had just undergone taking fortified positions forming the Kriemhilde-Stellung. Organizations were greatly depleted and much intermingled. Despite these difficulties, the relief was completed and the 89th Division was directed to seize Bois de Bantheville to its front. Contrary to expectations, this proved to be a difficult task and instead of requiring two platoons as first planned, ultimately saw three battalions engaged at one time or another.

Seizure of Bois de Bantheville on October 22 was followed by a period of waiting as the latest phase of the Meuse-Argonne offensive was readied. From October 21 through November 1, the 89th Division remained in position, patrolling its front and preparing for the general offensive scheduled for November 1.

Bois de Bantheville formed a small salient in the enemy line, and the Germans harassed the American troops with continuous shelling, airplane raids, and gas bombardment. On October 26 and 27 alone, several thousand gas and high explosive shells were hurled at two different parts of the division sector. Fortunately, tight gas discipline kept casualties to a minimum.

On October 31, two 89th Division men, Pfc. Charles D. Barger and Pfc. Jesse N. Funk, earned the Medal of Honor for voluntarily going forward under heavy fire to rescue two wounded officers left behind by a patrol.

The following day, November 1, the division jumped off as part of the general assault in the Meuse-Argonne—the last phase of the offensive which would end the war. The 89th's avenue of attack would take it over a series of ridges, its ultimate objective being seizure of the heights of Barricourt, which dominated the terrain as far as the Meuse River. The U.S. 2d Division would attack on the left, and the 90th was to advance on the right.

The division jumped off at 5:30 A.M. behind a rolling artillery barrage. Enemy lines were held by the German 88th Division, a comparatively fresh organization, having come into the line only a few days earlier. The 89th encountered heavy resistance from machine guns and enemy artillery.

When elements of the 353d Infantry were held up by withering machine gun fire from the woods just north of Bois de Bantheville, 1st Lt. Harold A. Furlong took a rifle, crossed an open space several hundred yards wide, and made his way to the enemy's flank where he silenced the guns one by one, killing the gunners and driving the survivors into friendly lines as prisoners. For this act, he was later awarded the Medal of Honor.

Also awarded the Medal of Honor for his actions on November 1 was Sgt. Arthur J. Forest, who singlehandedly assaulted a nest of six enemy machine guns, saving his platoon from possible annihilation.

The doughboys seized Remonville and pushed forward against stubborn resistance in Bois de Barricourt and the heights to the north. The dense forest contained trenches and dugouts. Snipers fired on the doughboys from the tree tops, and field guns continued to fire on the Americans until the gun positions were literally surrounded. Despite this resistance, the 89th was in possession of the heights by 4:00 P.M.

They dug hasty entrenchments in case of counterattack.

The night of November 1–2 was spent reorganizing and bringing up artillery and supplies, evacuating the wounded, and preparing for a resumption of the attack the following day. The 177th Infantry Brigade, which had led the previous day's attack, would continue the assault supported by the 178th Brigade.

The inability to bring up sufficient artillery during the night made the supporting barrage at 5:30 A.M. on November 2 wholly inadequate. Only twenty-two light guns were able to go into action on the whole division front of about two and a half miles. Meanwhile, the doughboys were under intense machine gun and artillery fire from German positions on the slopes beyond Barricourt.

It was late in the afternoon before the doughboys were able to make any real progress. The right of the line entered Tailly, its objective for the day at about 9:00 P.M. On the left, the troops were unable to seize Barricourt, but they did practically encircle the town and did enter Nouart.

The division commander decided to push the attack the following day with the fresh 178th Infantry Brigade. The objective was to attack and carry the heights overlooking Le Champ Haut and Beauclair and push strong reconnaissances toward Stenay.

The attack November 3 got off satisfactorily, and the 178th Brigade pushed forward to Beauclair. During the evening, V Corps directed the 89th to stand by to be relieved by the 1st Division. Gen. William M. Wright, commander of the 89th, contacted the corps command to ask permission to remain and continue the advance, saying his troops were in fine condition and would make better progress the following day. He particularly wanted to gain possession of the Forêt Dieulet, which would provide artillery positions for big guns to interdict the enemy rail net beyond Stenay. Corps granted the request.

November 4 began inauspiciously as the U.S. infantry showed little vigor. Beyond the river, convoys of Germans could be seen leaving Stenay. U.S. artillery was practically silent in the face of this target. Troops north of Beaufort were under fire and not advancing. The division commander finally got the units moving, and they reached the objective along the river shortly before dark. Lack of initiative, however, allowed large numbers of Germans to escape practically unhindered.

That night V Corps again directed the division to prepare to be relieved, and again General Wright persuaded corps commanders to allow the 89th to remain in the line. The division's mission was now to drive the enemy across the Meuse River and seize and hold the bridges to the front.

Early morning reconnaissance on November 5 revealed most of the bridges in the sector had been destroyed. However, Pouilly bridge, though badly damaged, was reportedly still passable for men on foot. Over the next four days, the division prepared to force a crossing.

On the morning of November 8, the division received orders from V Corps to push strong patrols across the Meuse River and maintain contact with the enemy. Elements of the 178th Brigade were directed to force a crossing at Pouilly that night, November 8–9, but this assault was delayed by request of the brigade commander. Several patrols attempted to swim the river that night, despite the low temperature of the water. Two crossings were effected, but no information was gained other than that the enemy continued to hold the east bank of the river all along the front. At the same time, U.S. troops were suffering from shortages of supplies and equipment due to inadequate transportation and road conditions behind the front.

The following day, November 9, the 178th Brigade commander was relieved and the 89th Division was directed by Corps HQ to cross the Meuse and seize the heights east and northeast of Inor. The operation was to begin at 4:00 P.M., November 10. The division commander decided to attempt the crossing at Pouilly.

Under cover of artillery fire, the doughboys effected a crossing by boat, footbridge, and catamaran ferry at 9:30 P.M. Casualties were minimal, the enemy garrisons apparently believing they were under artillery barrage only and not recognizing the ground attack in time to offer heavy resistance. Pouilly was encircled, then mopped up. Autreville was taken after daylight.

At 8:30 A.M. November 11, the division received word from corps that an armistice would go into effect at 11:00 A.M. and firing should cease at that time. Division promptly ordered the frontline troops to seize Stenay. Troops entered the town and occupied the northern portion about 10:00 A.M., meeting practically no resistance. The division commander then ordered the troops to push on until the enemy was actually encountered. This occurred at Inor and in Cervisy.

The German High Command subsequently made an official complaint that the U.S. troops on the Stenay-Beaumont front had not ceased attacking at 11:00 A.M. but continued their advance. The division commander excused his actions by claiming some frontline units had not received word of the pending armistice in time.

The operation closed with seven battalions of infantry east of the Meuse. During its twenty-three days in the line, the 89th Division had advanced about fifteen miles, taken over 2,000 prisoners, captured 360 machine guns, 24 77mm guns, and a great deal of other materiel. In exchange, the division suffered 800 officers and men killed, 87 officers and 2,399 men wounded, over 550 men gassed, and 201 missing.

The 89th remained headquartered in Stenay until November 24, when it began its march into Germany as part of the Army of Occupation. By December 10, the division had arrived in its area near Prum and Saarburg.

The division remained in Germany until May 1919, when it was directed to return home. The men were transported to Brest by train and the first elements embarked upon the *Leviathan* May 15, the remainder leaving over the next four days. Upon arrival at New York, the men were sent to Camp Upton, where many were discharged. The division was subsequently demobilized at Camps Funston and Taylor.

During its service overseas, the 89th Division received nine Medals of Honor, second only to the number won by the 30th Division. During its eighty-three days in the line (fifty-five in quiet sectors, twenty-eight active), the division captured over 5,000 prisoners—more than 8 percent of all prisoners taken by American forces (and surpassed only by the 1st and 2d divisions). The division advanced thirty miles, but had suffered heavy casualties in exchange for its accomplishments—a total of 7,047, including 1,516 officers and men killed in action.

James Hallas

Bibliography

English, George H. *History of the 89th Division*. Denver: Smith Brooks, 1920.

Masseck, C.J. *Official Brief History of the 89th Division, U.S.A.* N.p., 1919.

U.S. Battle Monuments Commission. *89th Division, Summary of Operations in the World War*. Washington, DC: Government Printing Office, 1944.

United States Army: 90th Division

Shortly after the United States entered the First World War on April 6, 1917, a National Army composed of draftees was created to augment the Regular Army and National Guard. The conscripts from Texas and Oklahoma formed the 90th Division, which was organized at Camp Travis, San Antonio, Texas, in the autumn of 1917. An old army town located in a moderate climate, the Alamo city was a logical choice for the campsite. Nevertheless, the city fathers were compelled to undertake a crusade against the illegal sale of liquor and sex as a condition of San Antonio's selection; later, they were required to continue the cleanup or lose the lucrative, if not vital, military trade of all the local army stations. Established on the grounds of an earlier Texas National Guard facility named Camp Wilson, Camp Travis adjoined Fort Sam Houston on its northeastern boundary. The Texas and Oklahoma men were called and processed for service while the new wooden installation was under construction.

A substantial cadre of Regular Army noncoms and senior officers, including the commanding general, MajGen. Henry T. Allen (a West Pointer, a veteran of the Spanish-American War and the Philippine Insurrection, and a recent subordinate of Gen. John J. Pershing in Mexico), were on hand to greet the draftees as they arrived. BGens. Joseph P. O'Neil and William Johnston commanded the 179th and 180th Infantry brigades, respectively, which became known as the Oklahoma and Texas brigades in recognition of the majority composition of their membership. The division in its entirety, however, contained more Texans than Oklahomans. The junior officers were principally Texans who were August 1917 graduates of the officer training class at nearby Camp Funston. Subsequent positions were filled mainly by Texas and Oklahoma graduates of Camp Stanley, formerly Funston, and a 90th Division officer training camp.

The relative stability of the officer personnel at Camp Travis, some transfers notwithstanding, was a plus for the division in training. General Allen was absent on a visit to the Western Front during the winter, but he was present for the early and final months of drill. During his absence, the training program was ably administered by General Johnston, who would eventually command his own division. In accordance with the wishes of General Pershing, the commander-in-chief of the American Expeditionary Force (AEF), Allen stressed open warfare over trench fighting in training. The Caucasians, Texas Hispanics, and Oklahoma Indians of the 90th possessed a positive attitude and responded to military instruction as readily as Regular Army or National Guard men. Training was hindered, however, by insufficient supplies of arms, equipment, and hardware; a flu-measles-pneumonia epidemic; and the transfer of thousands of men to understrength units at home and abroad. Vacancies at Camp Travis were filled by new draftees, including about 5,000 men from the upper Mississippi valley. When the 90th left for overseas in June 1918, only slightly more than one-third of the enlisted personnel had received more than about one month of formal training.

Thanks largely to the desire of the Wilson administration to keep the young men morally "clean," the U.S. armed forces of World War I enjoyed more recreation and entertainment than those of any previous conflict. The War Department's Commission on Training Camp Activities, the city of San Antonio, and several national welfare agencies, directly or otherwise, provided facilities, equipment, and services for the use and amusement of the trainees at Camp Travis. No other organization was more active than the YMCA, which built huts, showed movies, hosted civilian and military theatrical troupes, staged athletic contests, and maintained reading and writing rooms.

The 90th Division left for England from New York during the height of the overseas troop movement. Most units debarked at Liverpool, rode the train to Southhampton, and crossed the channel by boat to Le Havre or Cherbourg, France. The 165th Field Artillery Brigade went by rail to a training center south of Bordeaux. The infantry and other units were sent to the Aignay-le-Duc Training Area southeast of Paris for much-needed AEF prescribed exercises. On Aug. 20, 1918, some six weeks after its arrival in France, the 90th, less its artillery, which saw no action in the war, relieved the 1st Division at Villers-en-Haye southeast of St. Mihiel in accordance with Pershing's policy of placing "green" divisions in a calm sector as part of their preparation for active combat. Measured by the standards of later wars, the 90th's instruction may have been inadequate, but in the technologically and tactically less sophisticated World War I, it was satisfactory; certainly, it was more than sufficient when compared to the training provided in America's past struggles.

Propitiously located for participation in the St. Mihiel operation, the first predominately American campaign on the Western Front, the 90th served as the pivot in the northeastward sweep of the American First Army's I and IV Corps on the southern face of the triangularly shaped St. Mihiel salient. The operation, which began on September 12 and ended four days later, was successful and removed the salient as a rear threat to the projected American push in the Meuse-Argonne region. With the 360th Infantry as the anchor regiment on the right and the 357th at the opposite end of the divisional line on the left, looking northward, the 90th Division accomplished its swing without undue difficulty. Numerous acts of heroism and overall good leadership hastened the division's advance, although several officers were summarily relieved by General Allen for substandard performance. For some three weeks afterward, the 90th organized and stabilized its position, known officially as the Puvenelle sector. Local firefights, German artillery shellings, and gas attacks caused nearly as many casualties as the St. Mihiel offensive. On September 26, the day of the Meuse-Argonne attack, the 90th conducted a major diversionary raid into the Hindenburg Line on its front.

On October 21, the 90th relieved the 5th Division near Romagne and Cunel. At St. Mihiel both of the division's infantry brigades held the front line, but in the Meuse-Argonne offensive, one occupied the forward area, the other the rear. O'Neil's 179th Brigade straightened the line in the Bantheville zone to complete the American occupation of the Kriemhilde-Stellung and to prepare for an all-out assault on the next German defense system called the Freya Stellung. The 180th Brigade, commanded by BGen. Ulysses G. Alexander, in a well-executed attack marked by individual grit and fine leadership at all levels, pierced the Freya Stellung on November 1–2. The 179th once again took the lead and pursued the Germans northeastward across the Meuse River. The 179th was completing the capture of Stenay and Baalon when the fighting ended on November 11.

Casualties of the 90th Division for the Meuse-Argonne campaign totaled 3,596 men including 730 battle deaths. Aggregate losses for both the Meuse-Argonne and St. Mihiel fronts numbered 7,539, of which 1,488 were killed or mortally wounded. The 90th captured vast quantities of war materiel and took 1,876 prisoners, 975 in the Meuse-Argonne. Its average advance at St. Mihiel and in the Meuse-Argonne was about three and one-half and thirteen and one-half miles, respectively, for a total of approximately seventeen miles. Fourteen of the twenty-nine American divisions that saw combat gained more ground, but the 90th's place in the line on both fronts did not require greater advances. Its proven reliability during its seventy-five days under fire caused Pershing's headquarters to rate it as one of the top divisions in the AEF. Its operations were studied as a model in the AEF General Staff College and later in the General Service Schools at Forth Leavenworth, Kansas.

Soon after the Armistice, the 90th, including its artillery brigade, was ordered to Germany for service as part of the Third American Army, known also as the Army of Occupation. Since General Allen had been elevated to a corps command, the march to its new station on the Moselle River was led by General O'Neill, who remained in charge until the arrival of MajGen. Charles H. Martin in December 1918. Worn proudly by the Texans and Oklahomans in Germany was the new official division insignia, a red "TO" (for Texas and Oklahoma), designed by General Allen. Although the 90th was afterward often referred to as the "TO Division," it remained to many contemporaries the Alamo Division, the unofficial nickname applied to Camp Travis. Similarly, its members were sometimes called TOs or Alamos.

The division accepted its assignment to the Army of Occupation as an honor in recognition of its fine field performance.

The 90th Division left Germany in May 1919, and sailed for home from St. Nazaire. It was one of the last non-Regular divisions to leave Europe. The Third Army was dissolved on July 2, in favor of the small American units in Germany commanded by General Allen. The men from the 90th landed in Boston, Newport News, and New York and were then sent by rail to camps nearest their homes, mainly Camp Pike, Arkansas, and Camps Bowie and Travis, Texas.

Lonnie White

Bibliography

American Battle Monuments Commission. *90th Division, Summary of Operations in the World War.* Washington, DC: Government Printing Office, 1944.
Strickland, Riley. *Adventures of the AEF Soldier.* Austin, TX: N.p., 1920.
Twichell, Heath, Jr. *Allen: The Biography of an Army Officer, 1859–1930.* New Brunswick, NJ: Rutgers University Press, 1974.
Wythe, George. *A History of the 90th Division.* New York: The 90th Division Association, 1920.

U

United States Army: 91st Division

On Aug. 5, 1917, the War Department directed that the 91st Division, National Army, be established at Camp Lewis, American Lake, Washington. As a National Army division, the soldiers were drawn from draftees from adjoining states. Initial quotas by state were California, 23,060; Montana, 7,872; Washington, 7,296; Utah, 2,370; Idaho, 2,287; Nevada, 1,051; Wyoming, 810; and Oregon, 717. A cadre, established in August from Regular Army officers and men from the first Officers Training camps, formed skeleton units that the draftees eventually filled. On August 26, MajGen. Henry A. Greene assumed command and organized the division.

The 91st was organized into the 181st Infantry Brigade with the 361st and 362d Infantry regiments and the 347th Machine Gun Battalion; the 182d Infantry Brigade with the 363d and 364th Infantry regiments and the 348th Machine Battalion; and the 166th Field Artillery Brigade with the 346th Field Artillery Regiment (77mm), the 347th Field Artillery Regiment (4.7 inch), the 348th Field Artillery Regiment (155mm), and the 316th Trench Mortar Battery. Divisional troops included the 316th Engineer Regiment, the 346th Machine Gun Battalion, the 316th Field Signal Battalion, and a headquarters troop. Logistical support was provided by the trains: the 316th Train headquarters and Military Police, the 316th Ammunition Train, the 316th Supply Train, the 316th Engineer Train, and the 316th Sanitary Train with Field Hospitals 361, 362, 363, and 364 with ambulance companies.

Draftees arrived quickly. From September 5 to 10, an initial 2,300 reported, followed on September 19 through 24 by 18,000 more. After sorting through the replacements, basic training began in September. A final 1917 draft of 18,000 arrived between October 3 and 8. By the end of October, the 91st Division had 26,000 men assigned from 38,300 who had arrived. From then until movement overseas, the strength of the division fluctuated to meet the demands of other units deploying overseas. For example, from January 1918 through June of that year, the division received over 30,000 new draftees but lost, during the same period, over 25,000. By the end of March, the 91st Division was less than 20,000 men strong but increased in May and June to 23,000 for shipment overseas. These personnel fluctuations, compounded by extreme shortages of equipment, made progress in any training program beyond individual skills problematic.

Deployment overseas began on June 21 with movement to Camp Merritt, New Jersey, and Camp Mills, New York. The division sailed from Brooklyn, Manhattan, and Philadelphia. The advance party sailed on June 28, followed between July 6 and 12 by the rest of the division, minus the artillery and trains. The advance party arrived in Liverpool on July 10, with most of the division arriving in Great Britain between July 17 and 23. The 166th Field Artillery Brigade arrived in England on July 26. After a brief stay in rest camps in England, units moved to France via Cherbourg and Le Havre.

Training in France was curtailed by the division's arrival just prior to the final offensives of 1918. On July 21, the 91st Division, minus its artillery, moved to the 8th Training Area near Nogent-en-Bassigny for its initial training in France, which lasted about a month. The 166th Field Artillery Brigade began its training with the 348th Field Artillery Regiment near Clermont-Ferrand and the 346th and 347th Field Artillery regiments south of Bordeaux. Artillery training continued into November. The 166th Brigade did not rejoin the division for combat operations, nor did it support any other divisions in combat.

After joining the American First Army in early September, the 91st Division, despite its limited training in France and its lack of service in a quiet sector, was held in reserve to assist either IV Corps or French II Colonial Corps during the St. Mihiel operation. Not being needed, the division then moved to the Bois de Hesse. On September 20, it relieved the French 73d Division, minus outposts. Three days later, the 37th Division relieved the 91st Division, which assembled for final preparations for the Meuse-Argonne offensive. On the night of September 25–26, the 91st Division occupied the left of V Corps sector, prepared to attack.

Supported by the 58th Field Artillery Brigade of the 33d Division, at 5:30 A.M. on Sep-

tember 26, the 91st Division attacked with the 181st Infantry Brigade, commanded by BGen. John B. McDonald, on the right and the 182d Infantry Brigade, commanded by BGen. Frederick S. Foltz, on the left. Initially meeting little opposition, despite some confusion and intermingling of units as they made their way through the Bois de Cheppy in heavy fog, the attacking units met strong resistance from German machine guns in the open ground north of the Bois de Cheppy. The fighting was fierce, but the 91st Division made an advance of about five miles, capturing the villages of Very and Epinonville, which later was retaken by the Germans.

On September 27, in heavy rain, the attack continued. The 181st Infantry Brigade attacked the village of Epinonville three times, without success. With the assistance of French tanks, Eclisefontaine on the left was captured about 4:30 P.M. Again, on September 28, the advance continued against stiffening German resistance. During the day, Eclisefontaine was recaptured, along with Tronsol and Serieux farms. On September 29, Gesnes was temporarily captured, but the 91st Division occupied a salient caused by the divisions on its left and right not advancing. As a result of exposing flanks, the forward units were ordered to withdraw to the northern edge of the Bois Communal de Cierges to organize defensive positions, which were held until relieved by the 32d Division on October 4. The soldiers received their first warm food since September 25 in the Bois Communal de Cierges. Many soldiers suffered from diarrhea after four days without food and constant exposure to rain with few overcoats and blankets.

During its eight days of battle, the 91st Division lost almost 4,600 men, about 25 percent of its strength, not including those evacuated for illness. Most casualties were in the infantry units. On September 30, only 500 men of 3,000 authorized were forward with the 362d Infantry Regiment. Infantry officer losses were high—over 135. Units behind the front were not exempt from attack. In less than an hour, from aerial bombardment and artillery fire, the 91st Division headquarters lost 35 killed and 115 wounded. The splendid advance of the 91st Division had been made at a significant cost.

Lack of training was overcome by extraordinary enthusiasm and heroism by the inexperienced troops. Between September 26 and 29, 1st Lt. Deming Bronson, Sgt. Phillip C. Katz, 1st

Sgt. Chester H. West, Sgt. Lloyd M. Seibert, and Maj. Oscar F. Miller, all of the 91st Division, earned the Medals of Honor. In addition, many members of the division earned the Distinguished Service Cross for heroic actions under enemy fire.

Although the 91st Division moved into the U.S. V Corps reserve on October 4, the 181st Infantry Brigade, soon went into the line. On October 7, the 363d Infantry Regiment was attached to the 32d Division. The next day, the entire 181st Infantry Brigade was attached to the 1st Division. It took part in that division's attacks on October 10 and 11, capturing Hill 255. On October 12, the 181st Brigade was relieved by troops of the 32d.

Marshal Ferdinand Foch requested that General Pershing provide two divisions for service in Belgium. The 91st and 37th divisions were chosen to join the French Army of Belgium, a part of the Group of Armies of Flanders under the command of Belgian King Albert I. On October 16, the 91st Division, with the 53d Field Artillery Brigade from the 28th Division, moved north to the Ypres-St. Jean area.

On October 30, the 91st Division relieved the French 164th Division to join the French VII Corps attack toward the Escaut (Scheldt) River at 5:30 A.M. on October 31. On the first day, the division captured Spitaals Bosschen, a large wooded area near the jump-off positions. Flanking fire from its right, caused by the lack of progress by a French division, hampered progress. On November 1, the Germans withdrew, permitting an advance of five miles. Fighting for the town of Audenarde along the Escaut River lasted from November 1 to 3. As the 91st Division prepared to cross the river, it was relieved on November 4 by the French 41st Division. After a brief rest, the 91st division on November 10 joined the French XXX Corps in pursuit of the retiring Germans. On November 11, the advance prior to 11:00 A.M. (when the Armistice became official) was virtually unopposed. During its fighting in Belgium, the division lost almost 1,000 men.

After a week's rest near Audenarde, the 91st Division patrolled a portion of the Franco-Belgian border. On December 27, it moved to the American embarkation center at Le Mans. On March 16, 1919, the 91st Division, less artillery, moved to St. Nazaire, where it embarked for the United States beginning on March 21. The last elements arrived in the

United States on April 29. After crossing the United States, units demobilized on the West Coast: the 181st Infantry Brigade and the 16th Field Artillery at Camp Kearny, California, on April 19; the 182d Infantry Brigade at Camp Lewis, Washington, on April 28; and the 91st Division headquarters at the Presidio of San Francisco on May 13.

Robert D. Ramsey III

Bibliography

American Battle Monuments Commission. *American Armies and Battlefields in Europe*. Washington, DC: Government Printing Office, 1938.

————. *91st Division, Summary of Operations in the World War*. Washington, DC: Government Printing Office, 1944.

Center of Military History, U.S. Army. *Order of Battle of the United States Land Forces in the World War*. Vol. 2. *American Expeditionary Force: Divisions*. Washington, DC: Government Printing Office, 1988.

The Story of the 91st Division. San Francisco: Crocker, 1919.

United States Army: 92d Division

During the nineteenth century, the United States War Department segregated African-American troops into separate army regiments in response to the separatist sentiments that were so endemic in North America. By the 1890s, many of the key members of the army's High Command were white southerners who staunchly advocated the precept that black troopers were inherently incapable of performing ably in combat. They had to be placed in segregated units where their inefficient habits would not adversely affect their white counterparts. Thus, African-American outfits were assigned to combat support roles under the command of white officers.

However, some black regiments, including the 24th Infantry, had served with distinction in combat in both Cuba and the Philippines. Various high-ranking army general officers, such as LtGen. Henry C. Corbin, called for a major shift in army policy. Although no one seriously advocated racial integration of the armed forces, Corbin and his associates believed that trained black infantry troops would be needed for combat in Europe. It was decided that new all-black regiments would be created out of existing units;

moreover, most of the regimental officers under the rank of captain were to be black.

In October 1917, the War Department established the 92d Division, National Army, under the command of BGen. Charles C. Ballou. The division was divided into three brigades, including the 184th Infantry Brigade. Within this brigade was the 367th Infantry Regiment, which came to be called the "Buffalo Regiment."

The sobriquet "Buffalo Soldier" had been accorded initially to black cavalrymen involved in the frontier wars with the Great Plains Indian tribes in the 1880s. The Cheyennes invented the nickname because the African-American units, when charging, rode in close formation that reminded the braves of stampeding buffalo. By the early twentieth century that term was commonly applied to all black soldiers.

A career officer, Col. James A. Moss, who had led black troops in both the Spanish-American War and the Philippine Insurrection, commanded the Buffalo Regiment. Although a native of Louisiana, Moss had long advocated that black regiments be given extensive combat role. He announced, "I am glad that I am to command colored soldiers in this my third campaign . . . the greatest war the world has ever seen." Moss made these remarks in May 1918 as a forward to an article on the Buffalo Regiment in the *Outlook*. Interestingly, the author of this work, entitled "The Buffaloes," was an African-American staff officer, Lt. Osceloa E. McKaine of Sumter, South Carolina.

The majority of the new black noncommissioned officers of the Buffaloes rose from the ranks of regiments that had recently been involved in the American invasion of Mexico in 1916. After returning to the United States, those candidates were assigned to officer training at the Army Service School, Fort Leavenworth. In late October, they were dispatched to the headquarters of the 92d Division at Fort Riley, Kansas. Within a month, the officers of the Buffalo Regiment were sojourning eastward to Camp Upton, New York. This post served as headquarters to the 184th Infantry Brigade in the months prior to embarkation for France.

The War Department prudently arranged to have a solid nucleus of seasoned veterans among the ranks of the Buffaloes; however, most of the troopers were recent draftees drawn from all regions of the nation. Although many of these conscripts had already completed basic training, no one questioned Colonel Moss's belief that the 367th Infantry Regiment needed far more combat preparation. Accordingly, Moss instituted an intensive training program for his command that lasted throughout the early months of 1918. By May, Lieutenant McKaine could state, "The regiment has had a higher average on the target range than any other regiment ever stationed at Camp Upton."

Quite early on, Colonel Moss perceived that many of his troops who had been raised in warm climates would suffer during the winter months. Clearly, a large indoor facility was needed for the men to conduct their regular training drills. But no such building existed at Camp Upton; therefore, Moss proposed to his men that they erect a large auditorium that would also be an ideal recreation center for the regiment when off duty.

The officers and men of the regiment internally raised over $14,000 to cover the heavy construction costs. Furthermore, through various bond issues they secured an additional $26,000 from outside sources. Of course, most of the building labor was provided by the Buffaloes. But the "Buffalo Auditorium" was utilized by all the troops, white and black, stationed at Camp Upton. At any gathering held in this facility, the practice of race separation was simply not allowed, and by most accurate accounts, this experiment in integration was quite successful.

As planned, the auditorium served as a drill area in severe and inclement weather. All the preliminary bayonet instruction for the black soldiers, as well as the white regiments, occurred in that building. Also, Bennie Leonard, the noted welterweight champion, conducted boxing classes in the auditorium. Regimental lectures, special classes, choral practices, and many other activities that could not be held outdoors took place there.

By May 1918, all the component regiments of the 92d Division had arrived at Camp Upton, where the troops remained until embarkation. On June 10, the 367th Regiment sailed from Hoboken, New Jersey, on a nine-day voyage to Brest, France. The regiments of the 184th Infantry Brigade were then transported by rail to the Allied 11th Training Area, near Bourbonne-les-Bains, for "seasoning." At that locale, the troops experienced the rigors of camp life near the front. They also began to associate with the various French Army units stationed nearby. Numbers of the men felt those early months in the field were the most tedious experienced while overseas. Quite often, the Buffaloes were restricted to camp; therefore, they had to improvise their amusements. Most soldiers passed the time playing endless games of checkers, as well as many hands of poker and other games of chance. There was little access to current reading material, including several popular African-American newspapers or periodicals.

On August 22, the Buffalo Regiment participated in the Allied offensive into Lorraine. The 92d Division was assigned the task of securing the St. Die sector. Although the 367th Infantry Regiment participated in a series of fierce local skirmishes, its main duty was repairing the roads in that vicinity. By September 20, most units of the division, including the Buffaloes, were transferred to the Argonne Forest northwest of Clermont.

Initially, the 367th Infantry served in the reserve, but by October 3, the Allied command decided that the regiment should be included in the Meuse-Argonne offensive. It was during the next few days that the regiment really received its first major "trial by fire." On October 10, however, it was among the four American regiments abruptly transferred to the Marbache sector, south of the city of Metz.

For many months, the military strategists of the Allies had been planning a major drive on the great German fortress at Metz. The capture of this bastion was to be the prelude to a final invasion into Germany. This campaign was launched on schedule, despite clear reports that a general armistice was about to be signed. Certainly, the fierce fighting around Metz belied all the talk about peace.

On Nov. 9, 1918, Allied forces began a direct assault on the strongly fortified German installation. According to plan, the U.S. 56th Division was on the left flank, the 92d held the center, and the French Eighth Army was deployed on the right. The Buffalo Regiment led the advance and cleared resistance ahead of the flanking units. For the first time in World War I, black regiments in battle received direct fire support from African-American artillerymen. The Buffaloes and their counterparts were ably covered by batteries of the all-black 167th Field Artillery Brigade.

Although the German troops suffered heavy losses, they made the Allies battle for every foot of ground. Consequently, the Buffalo Regiment experienced two days of intensive fighting in wide-open terrain. By the evening of November 10, the 367th Infantry occupied a forward position on the west side of the Moselle River, just southwest of the strong fortifications of Metz. During the twilight, the troops repulsed a series of German sorties. With the darkness came a cessation of intensive action. The Buffaloes thus had the opportunity to reorganize for a renewal of the attack at dawn.

At one point during the morning fighting, the U.S. 56th Infantry Regiment of the 7th Division, while advancing, encountered a heavy barbed-wire entanglement that had not been cleared by artillery. Unable to advance further, the 56th began to receive a withering machine gun fire from the defenders. Maj. Charles L. Appleton of the Buffalo Regiment, observing the 56th's desperate plight, placed several platoons at a position where they could flank attack the Germans and cover the retreat of the 56th. Certainly, Major Appleton and his men saved the 56th from complete destruction.

When the bugle sounded the call to cease firing at 11:00 A.M. on November 11, Company H of the Buffalo Regiment held 800 yards of the battleground directly behind the German fortifications. The troops had held their position against heavy odds under intense shell and machine gun fire. The men of the 367th were the nearest Allied troops to Metz when the Armistice was formally announced.

With the conclusion of hostilities, the Buffalo Regiment was withdrawn with the 92d Division to the village of Mayenne. Many of the Buffaloes were issued furlough passes to visit Paris for the first time. They found the French (both civilians and military) quite friendly and without racial prejudice. However, most white American soldiers shunned them socially. Unfortunately, the cordial interracial friendships forged on the battlefield could not overcome the racism so strong among white Americans.

By late December 1918, the entire 92d Division was moved to the American embarkation center at Le Mans. By February, the Buffalo Regiment sailed from Brest to New York City. After a triumphant, though segregated, march up Fifth Avenue, the regiment headed for Camp Upton, New York, for demobilization. Within two months, most of the regiment was discharged to resume their civilian lives throughout the United States. They had helped make the world "safe for democracy," but found quickly that democratic rights would not always be extended to them.

Miles S. Richards

Bibliography:

Center of Military History, U.S. Army. *Order of Battle of the United States Land Forces in the World War. Vol. 2. American Expeditionary Force: Divisions.* Washington, DC: Government Printing Office, 1988.

Du Bois, W.E.B. "The History of the Black Man in the Great War." *Crisis* (June 1919).

McKaine, Osceola E. "The Buffaloes." *Outlook* (May 1918).

————. "With the Buffaloes in France." *The Independent* (Jan. 11, 1919).

United States Army: 93d Division

The 93d Division was a unit that never existed except on paper. It consisted of four odd infantry regiments, the 369th, 370th, 371st, and 372d Infantry. All were black troops. No supporting units were ever created, although a divisional staff existed for a brief time. The divisional infantry never served together.

Black soldiers had served in all previous American wars. In the Civil War, they served in segregated regiments under white officers. Four permanent regiments were created for service on the frontier. Black troops fought in the Spanish-American War and in the Philippine Insurrection. Their most recent service was when the 8th Illinois (National Guard) served in the Punitive Expedition against Pancho Villa.

The 368th Infantry originated as the 15th New York National Guard. William Hayward, a white New York Public Service commissioner, was authorized to create the unit in the fall of 1916, and he became its colonel. With five exceptions, all of its officers were white. When National Guard units were mobilized, the 15th was sent to Spartanburg, South Carolina, for training with other New York Guard units. The 15th was rejected as part of the Rainbow Division ("Black was not a color of the rainbow").

After twelve days of training in Spartanburg, several racial incidents presaged additional trouble. Lt. Napoleon Marshall, a graduate of Harvard University, was literally kicked from a street car. Noble Sissle, drum major (a noted composer and arranger), was assaulted and driven from a local hotel where he tried to buy a newspaper. Members of the regiment marched to the police station with loaded weapons when they heard some of their members had been arrested. Hastily, the 15th

was sent north for transport to France. In December 1917, the unit sailed, still under state colors.

After arrival in France, the unit was officially redesignated as the 369th Infantry but assigned to labor duties in various parts of France. Meanwhile, its excellent regimental band, under Lt. James R. Europe (a composer and arranger), introduced France to jazz as they played in many rest areas during a 2,000-mile tour.

Gen. John J. Pershing, commander of the American Expeditionary Force (AEF), was in a quandary over what to do with his orphan infantry regiment. His nickname "Black Jack" dated from his early service with black regulars. In conversations with the War Department, it was thought that the 369th, and the other infantry regiments of the 93d Division, might be used as replacements for casualties in the 92d Division ("Colored"). In the meantime, Pershing agreed to lend these unattached regiments to the French Army to fill out its decimated divisions. Colonel Hayward dubbed his troops "*les enfants perdu*."

The 369th became part of the 16th Division, French Fourth Army, in May 1918. When it took over its own section of front in April, this 1 percent of American combat troops constituted 20 percent of American troops in the line. After training in quiet sectors, the 369th had its baptism of fire in the Argonne, went over the top at Château-Thierry, and fought in Belleau Wood. Their valor at Butte de Mesnil, earned the men of the 369th congratulations from General Gouraud. Later they were engaged in the reduction of the Marne bulge. In all, the 369th was in combat for 191 days, longer than any other American unit; their casualties exceeded 1,500. The regiment was awarded a unit Croix de Guerre for the taking of Sechault; 170 individual Croix de Guerres were awarded also.

The 370th Infantry was originally the 8th Illinois National Guard from Chicago. It was mobilized for federal service in March 1917 under Col. Franklin A. Dennison and was the only black unit with a full complement of black officers. With other Illinois Guard units, it was detailed to Camp Logan, Texas, for training, and its advance company was there during the "mutiny" of the black 24th Infantry (Regular Army). There was some consternation in the Houston area when the 8th Illinois belatedly arrived in October 1917. In December, it was officially designated the 370th Infantry and sailed for France from Virginia in April 1918.

After arriving in France, the regiment began to lose its black officers. Colonel Dennison was relieved of duties for "reasons of health" and replaced by Col. T.A. Roberts, a white officer. His presence was resented by the men who chanted, "Blue eyes ain't our colonel, [LtCol. Otis] Duncan is." By the end of the war, there were several other white officers in the regiment; there were plans to transfer all black officers to other units.

The 370th saw its first action as part of the 73d French Division in the Argonne area in July. In the August drive against the German lines, the 370th took almost 1,900 prisoners and captured four cannon and other military equipment. In those two months, the regiment served with the 10th, 34th, and 36th French divisions in addition to the 73d. In September, it was with the French 59th Division on the Soissons front. After a rest in October, the regiment returned to the line in the final weeks of the war and was advancing into Belgium at the time of the Armistice.

The service of the 370th was far more controversial than that of the 369th. It was caught in the double bind of racism and of changing officers during combat, as well as prejudice on the part of some white inspecting officers. During its campaign, it suffered about 500 casualties. Company C was awarded a unit Croix de Guerre with Palm; there were seventy-one individual awards of that medal and twenty-one Distinguished Service Crosses were presented to members of the regiment.

For labor duties, the commander of Camp Jackson created a provisional regiment of black draftees from the Carolinas. All of the officers were white. This regiment was later designated the 371st Infantry and attached to the 93d Division. Sailing for France in April 1918, the 371st Infantry was assigned to the 157th French Division (the famous "Red Hand" Division) at Rembercourt, near Verdun. Regiment commander Col. Perry L. Miles was given no advance notification of this assignment. The troops trained at and behind the front until the major offensive of September 1918. There were some morale problems as white officers maintained a strict color line with their black troops and resented the equality those troops were granted by French civilians.

In the advance in Champagne, the 371st captured Trières Farm. Relieved in early October, the 157th Division went to a quiet area in the Vosges, remaining there until the Armistice. In all, 126 officers and men were killed or died of wounds, 914 were wounded. The regiment was awarded the Croix de Guerre with Palm; 60 officers and 124 men received individual awards.

The 372d Infantry was composed of smaller black National Guard units from various states and the District of Columbia. The First Separate Battalion of the District of Columbia Guard was the first Guard unit called into service, assigned to guard government buildings, the water supply, and transportation links in the nation's capitol. War Department planners feared possible sabotage from hyphenated Americans in white Guard units. There was no such fear with black troopers. Despite numerous racial complaints by southern members of Congress, the battalion carried outs its duties with efficiency.

Until early 1918, these unattached black Guard units trained at a number of camps. Eventually, the 372d's first battalion was created from the District of Columbia troops; Ohio guardsmen comprised the 2d battalion; and companies from Maryland, Tennessee, Massachusetts, and Connecticut (with some draftees) made up the third battalion. Col. Glendie B. Young was the commander. The rifle companies had black officers; staff officers were surplus officers from white Guard units. The regiment sailed for overseas duty in late March 1918.

Shortly after arrival in France, Young was replaced as colonel by Herschel Tupes. He immediately asked for the transfer of all his black officers. When that request was denied, he asked for efficiency boards to examine all black officers, and requested that no new ones be sent to the regiment. When the all-white efficiency boards condemned almost all of the black officers, serious demoralization resulted, though the board decisions were not implemented.

During this period, the regiment trained as it advanced toward the front in Champagne and was assigned to the 157th French Division. In the September offensive, the 372d aided in capturing Bussy Farm, advanced toward Ripont and helped take Sechault. They then relieved the 371st at Trières Farm and cleared the area toward Monthois. In early October, the regiment was transferred to a quiet area in Alsace.

In its combat service, the regiment suffered such heavy losses that the first and third battalions were combined into a single battalion. The regiment was awarded the unit Croix de Guerre with Palm: 41 officers and 111 men received that individual award; 4 others were given *medailles militaires*. In addition, 21 Distinguished Service Crosses were awarded. Cpt. Clarence Van Allen earned the Croix de Guerre with Palm, *medaille militarie,* and the Distinguished Service Cross.

In all, the 93d Division suffered 3,100 casualties during the service of its four regiments in France. This was a casualty rate of about 32 percent. All four regiments received unit citations ranging from company to regimental honors.

While the services of the units of the 93d Division were obviously appreciated more by the French than they were by the American Army, there were difficulties associated with this service. Compared to the Springfield, the French Lebel rifle was especially inaccurate, primarily serving to hold the bayonet. Firepower in a French unit was provided by machine guns; the American Army used one machine gun company per regiment.

The French ration was totally different from that of the Americans, consisting of starches, vegetables, and less meat and was based on soups. It also included a daily ration of two liters of wine that was not issued to the black troops. French soldiers carried an overcoat and blanket roll, while Americans used the knapsack. In all these regards, the black soldiers had to adapt to the French system. The only change they liked was that the French gas mask did not rely on the nose clip as the American one did.

Following the Armistice, the 369th established military governments as it was moved through territory formerly occupied by Germany. It was the first Allied unit to reach the Rhine River. On December 10, it left the Rhine to rejoin the AEF, where staff officers set up a training program for a regiment that had seen 191 days under fire. The 371st also moved up to the Rhine with French troops but almost immediately was recalled. All four regiments faced considerable prejudice and discrimination after their return to American command.

Black combat troops were among the earliest American troops to return to the United States in the early months of 1919. The 369th was the first New York unit to return and was given a victory parade up Fifth Avenue, marching in the solid phalanx formation they had learned from the French. Lieutenant Reese's band played only French marches, not the jazz that the band had made famous in France. Their welcome home dinner at the 71st New York's armory was the first time the entire regiment had been under one roof. The other regiments of the division were demobilized with less fanfare.

Arthur Barbeau

Bibliography

Barbeau, Arthur, and Florette Henri. *Unknown Soldiers*. Philadelphia: Temple University Press, 1974.

Bradden, William S. *Under Fire with the 370th Infantry, A.E.F.* Chicago: N.p., n.d.

Heywood, Chester D. *Negro Combat Troops in the Great War*. New York: AMS Press, 1969.

Little, Arthur. *From Harlem to the Rhine.* New York: Covici, Friede, 1936.

Scott, Emmett J. *The American Negro in the World War*. Chicago: Homewood Press, 1919.

United States Army: Chemical Warfare Service

The Chemical Warfare Service (CWS) was established by the War Department in June 1918 to centralize and better coordinate America's chemical warfare activities. The CWS unified research, development, testing, production, and supply of chemical weapons under one administrative agency.

Modern chemical warfare began in April 1915 when Germany employed chlorine-filled shells at Ypres. The success of these crude projectiles deflated traditional skepticism of chemical weapons, and European belligerents organized special units to investigate the military uses of noxious gases. Although not a belligerent, the United States took an early interest in chemical warfare. In late 1915, the War Department took steps to protect troops against toxic materials, authorizing the Medical Department to design, develop, and procure gas masks and other protective apparatus. Concern over chemical weapons subsided, however, once defensive measures employed by Europeans made gas attacks less effective. Between 1915 and 1917, neither the army nor navy made efforts to procure an adequate supply of protective equipment or to inaugurate scientific investigations on chemical weapons.

The United States foray into chemical warfare came not through the army or navy but through the Bureau of Mines. Since its inception in 1910, the bureau had retained on its staff a number of investigators to study poisonous and explosive gases found in mines, so it seemed natural that the bureau take a leading role in chemical weapons research. In February 1917, with war almost a certainty, Van H. Manning, director of the Bureau of Mines, wrote to Charles D. Walcott, chairman of the Military Committee of the National Research Council (NRC), offering the bureau's assistance in investigating war gases, gas masks, and rescue apparatus for the army and navy. Walcott presented the offer to his committee, which formally approved the suggestion on April 3. The NRC created a Sub-Committee on Noxious Gases consisting of representatives from the Bureau of Mines, the Bureau of Chemistry, the NRC Chemistry Committee, and the U.S. Army and Navy to coordinate investigation into noxious gases for war purposes. On April 4, the War Department approved this arrangement at a joint conference attended by representatives from the Bureau of Mines, the War College, and various army bureaus.

Manning appointed George A. Burrell, a Pittsburgh chemist formerly employed at the bureau, director of the bureau's chemical warfare work. Manning, Burrell, and others directed their attention to tracing out lines of research, developing and producing an adequate gas mask, and securing laboratory facilities. Lacking sufficient space and manpower to handle chemical warfare research, Manning and the bureau accepted, as an emergency measure, offers of assistance from college and university laboratories, government bureaus, and industrial concerns. By May 1917, 118 chemists in twenty-one college and university laboratories, three industrial laboratories, and three government bureaus were involved. This decentralized structure proved very inefficient, however, and Manning and the bureau initiated plans to build a large central laboratory to coordinate work being done in university and industrial laboratories and to undertake secret projects for the army and navy. After considering several potential sites, Manning and Burrell decided to construct the laboratory at the American University in Washington, D.C. In June 1917, the army and navy appropriated $175,000 to convert the university's classrooms for the bureau's use and to construct a temporary laboratory. Workers completed the temporary building in September, and chemical work began the same month.

Meanwhile, various U.S. Army departments took responsibility for other aspects of chemical warfare. The Trench Warfare Section of the Ordnance Department assumed authority over procuring toxic gasses and filling and proving gas shells. The Sanitary Corps of the Medical Department established a Field Training Section in September 1917 to train troops on how to employ chemical weapons and how to defend against gas attacks. The medical department also assumed responsibility for procuring and distributing gas masks. The Signal Corps took over developing and supplying gas alarms.

American forces in Europe followed the lead of the Bureau of Mines and the stateside army bureaus and established their own chemical warfare units. In August 1917, General Pershing recommended that the War Department unite all aspects of chemical warfare under a separate, independent AEF (American Expeditionary Force) agency. In September, the War Department established the Gas Service of the AEF to meet Pershing's specifications. Pershing appointed Col. Amos F. Fries chief of this service. In November, the War Department created the Chemical Warfare Section in compliance with Pershing's requests for a chemical laboratory to study war gases and powders, to which Pershing appointed LtCol. William H. Walker, professor of chemical engineering at M.I.T., as director. Walker recruited Mellon Institute Director Raymond F. Bacon and his assistant William A. Hanor to convert an old chemical laboratory near Paris into a chemical warfare facility. The Paris laboratory, opened in January 1918, investigated a variety of chemical and physical problems related to toxic substances and served as a consultant for the nonchemical branches of the AEF. Gilbert N. Lewis, Frederick Keyes, and other scientists in uniform continued this work until the Armistice.

In April 1918, the Bureau of Mines, the Ordnance Department, the Medical Department, the Signal Corps, and the AEF shared responsibility for chemical warfare. These agencies needed guidance, and the War Department created the Gas Service of the army to provide direction. Established in October 1917, under the command of Col. Charles C. Potter, the service served as a clearinghouse for information on chemical warfare. Potter was also authorized to coordinate the work of various agencies involved in chemical warfare, but he lacked the authority to direct or influence policy, research, and production. The service failed, therefore, to provide the kind of teamwork the War Department desired.

As the size and importance of chemical warfare grew, the need for centralized control and better coordination became apparent. Proposals surfaced demanding the unification of all chemical warfare activity under one strong administrative organization. Pershing, Fries, Walker, and other AEF officers were the first to request such an arrangement; university scientists and industrial chemists soon took up the refrain. Bowing to intense pressure and military considerations, the War Department finally took action in May 1918. On May 11, the department appointed MajGen. William Sibert, one of the architects of the Panama Canal, head of the Gas Service and instructed him to devise plans to make chemical warfare work more efficient. After due consideration, Sibert recommended to President Wilson that the service control all chemical warfare activity. The War Department immediately transferred to the Gas Service all Medical Department, Ordnance Department, and Signal Corps personnel engaged in war gas work.

Sibert also recommended that the Gas Service assume authority over war gas investigations, but Manning and the Bureau of Mines, the nominal sponsor of the work at American University and cooperating university and industrial laboratories, vigorously opposed this move. Despite written and verbal protests from Manning, Secretary of Interior Franklin K. Lane, and the NRC Sub-Committee on Noxious Gases, the army officers demanding military control won the day; President Wilson authorized transfer of research work to the War Department on June 25. Three days later, President Wilson and Congress authorized creation of the Chemical Warfare Service (CWS) to unite the Bureau of Mines organization, the stateside chemical warfare units, and the AEF Gas Service. General Sibert, the new chief of the CWS, organized work under nine divisions: overseas, research, administration, gas defense production, gas offense production, medical, proving, and testing. Of these divisions, six had originally formed part of the Bureau of Mines' organization.

In August 1918, the NRC's Sub-Committee on Noxious Gases dissolved, leaving the CWS in complete control of chemical warfare. Throughout the summer and fall, the CWS continued to strengthen and expand its organization. By October, over 1,600 officers and 18,000 enlisted men were serving under CWS auspices. The War Department moved rapidly to dismantle the CWS, however, once the war ended. CWS personnel were demobilized quickly, so quickly in fact that by June 1919, 97 percent of the wartime force had been mustered out of service. A small, skeletal force of technicians and chemists remained at American University to complete projects already in progress, but new projects were abandoned. University and industrial laboratories dropped wartime contracts and returned to peacetime pursuits. The War Department disposed of most of its contracts, returned expropriated facilities at American University and other institutions to their governing boards, and converted the chemical warfare production and testing facilities at the Edgewood Arsenal and the Lakehurst (New Jersey) Proving Ground to peacetime purposes.

Under the congressional general order authorizing the CWS, the agency was scheduled to continue operations for six months beyond the cessation of hostilities or until Congress either modified, revised, or rescinded its order. In July 1919, with peace talks progressing slowly and the CWS scheduled to dissolve shortly, Congress extended the life of the agency until June 30, 1920. Expectations for the CWS remained limited, however. In November, the War Department defined its peacetime mission as merely "the maintenance of a competent body of chemical warfare specialists with facilities for continuous research and experimentation." The department called on the CWS to keep in contact with civilian agencies interested in chemical weapons research, to train soldiers in the use of toxic substances, and to cooperate with industries capable of producing noxious chemicals. Congress provided little funding for continued research, however, and the War Department itself doubted the effectiveness and importance of chemical weapons.

Congress meanwhile began to study military reforms needed in light of the war. Representatives on the House and Senate Committees on Military Affairs faced a serious question: what should be done with the CWS? The military had added no new technical services since establishing the Signal Corps in

1860, and many questioned whether the CWS should be retained. War Department officials offered conflicting advice on the issue. Secretary of War Newton D. Baker recommended that the CWS be abolished and its work divided among the Corps of Engineers and other bureaus. Army Chief of Staff Peyton C. March, morally and philosophically opposed to chemical weapons, favored a similar arrangement. General Pershing, while uncomfortable with the use of noxious gases, leaned toward retaining the CWS as an independent body. Assistant Secretary of War Benedict Crowell became a vocal proponent of the CWS, and Sibert, Fries, and other former CWS officers joined in the chorus. Sibert, Fries, and others began a fierce lobbying campaign to save the CWS. They were joined in this crusade by many who believed that chemical weapons offered a strong deterrent to war and who hoped the CWS would heighten the importance of chemistry in society.

Fries proved particularly effective in the lobbying campaign. Obtaining General Pershing's endorsement, Fries used his wide military contacts and close friendships with Representative Julius Kahn, chairman of the House Committee on Military Affairs, and Senator George E. Chamberlain, chairman of the Senate Military Affairs Committee, to sway Congress toward his point of view. His efforts and the vocal support of the scientific community undoubtedly played a significant role in the decision by Congress to establish permanently the CWS as a separate agency of the army under the provisions of the National Defense Act of 1920.

Daniel E. Worthington

Bibliography

Brophy, Leo P. "Origins of the Chemical Corps." *Military Affairs* (Winter 1956).

Brophy, Leo P., and George J.B. Fisher. *The Chemical Warfare Service: Organizing for War.* Washington, DC: Office of the Chief of Military History, 1959.

———. *The Chemical Warfare Service: From Laboratory to Field.* Washington, DC: Office of the Chief of Military History, 1959.

Haber, L.F. *The Poisonous Cloud: Chemical Warfare in the First World War.* Oxford: Clarendon Press, 1986.

Manning, Van H. *War Gas Investigations: Bureau of Mines Bulletin 178–A.* Washington, DC: Government Printing Office, 1919.

United States Army: Command and General Staff College

Today's United States Army Command and General Staff College did not exist at the time of World War I. Instead, prior to 1922 when the School of the Line and the Staff School merged to form the Command and General Staff School, the educational organizations at Fort Leavenworth, Kansas, were the army's "middle-management" training facilities for officers. The Leavenworth schools often have been praised as the salvation of the American Expeditionary Force (AEF) in World War I and occasionally criticized as the source of a clique that infested the War Department and AEF staffs alike. In truth, it was mostly the former and very little of the latter.

After the Civil War, schools of practice (first an artillery school at Fort Monroe, Virginia, in 1868, then the infantry and cavalry school of application at Fort Leavenworth in 1881) were established to provide a classroom for the study of warfare and a laboratory for teaching tactics to line units. Both Gens. William T. Sherman and Philip H. Sheridan believed that theoretical inquiry must be supported by practical application.

In the years of growth and change in the U.S. Army prior to the Spanish-American War, officers learned both as students and as faculty members at Fort Leavenworth. Arthur L. Wagner, who had a formative influence on the army's intelligence agency, developed textbooks and nurtured many classes of students, some later called upon during World War I to exercise command and staff responsibilities at the highest levels. John F. Morrison served on the faculty from 1906 to 1912, then later commanded an infantry brigade in the Philippines (1916) and the 13th Division (National Guard) as a major general (1917). Morrison's prowess as a training director was noted by the American Expeditionary Force commander, Gen. John J. Pershing, but Morrison never made it to France as a combat commander. Arthur L. Conger made a mark as a first-class educator, then served on the staff of the 2d Division in France. Lt. Joseph T. Dickman lectured in 1896 at Leavenworth and commanded a division, an army corps, and a field army in France. The list of graduates of Leavenworth who served with distinction during the Great War is too long to repeat here. Students became teachers, then became commanders of their former students. The process of military education had been effectively formalized at Fort Leavenworth in the three decades before America's participation in World War I.

The U.S. Army prior to 1903, however, was not a coherent whole. There were regiments, army posts, staff bureaus, and then schools, but no permanent general staff existed to coordinate and manage the whole institution. From 1901 to 1903, Secretary of War Elihu Root, with the help of a former Fort Leavenworth faculty member, Maj. William Harding Carter, corrected that shortcoming. However, the passage of the General Staff Act in 1903 did not eliminate the hostility of the entrenched staff bureaus. In particular, the adjutant general, MajGen. Fred C. Ainsworth, fought the new general staff concept up to the eve of the First World War.

The Spanish-American War illuminated many targets for reform within the U.S. Army. As Graham Cosmas has shown in his book *An Army for Empire*, the performance of the army in 1898 was not nearly as bad as it was made out in the press. One of the challenges was to provide military education and training for an officer corps that might have to expand rapidly to command and control a mass army. In 1901, in addition to founding the Army War College, Root laid the foundation for the modern staff college at Fort Leavenworth. The Infantry and Cavalry School gave way to the General Service and Staff School (GS&SS). Root's intent clearly was to establish a coordinated hierarchy of military education opportunities for officers.

Form and substance often do not proceed at the same pace. The curriculum at the turn of the century at the GS&SS had not been improved beyond that which it had replaced. The new commandant in 1903, BGen. J. Franklin Bell, began to move the curriculum from remedial work in basic military skills to a genuine postgraduate experience. In 1904 the GS&SS became two schools: the Infantry and Cavalry School and the Staff College. In 1907, the former became the Army School of the Line. The sequence of military education now extended from the schools at the various army posts through the School of the Line, the Staff College and the War College—a chain of progressive educational development was experienced as an officer matured professionally.

In the period after the Spanish-American War, General Bell and his staff broadened the horizons of the curriculum to include the study of international law, military government, the relationship between strategy and logistics, mobilization and the movement of troops to distant theaters of operations, field sanitation, and a host of subjects not previously dealt with by officers in the classroom. However, the central experience at the Leavenworth schools remained tactics.

The realities of vastly improved military technology filtered back from Manchuria to Fort Leavenworth in the first decade of the twentieth century. American and European observers of the Russo-Japanese War had seen firsthand the lethality of massed fire from machine guns and rapid-firing artillery. The new conditions imposed on infantry tactics were debated by students and faculty alike, but they did not alter the curriculum emphasis on frontal assaults.

Despite firsthand knowledge of these new weapons by a handful of officers, the reports of military attachés (such as John J. Pershing, Peyton C. March, and John F. Morrison) had little effect on American doctrine and regulations. Curiously, knowledge of specific capabilities of new techniques and weapons did not lead the Leavenworth intelligentsia to challenge the assumptions underpinning tactical schemes of maneuver and modify them other than to open up the formations. The peculiar attitude of American soldiers was to suspect any non-American experience and treat it as irrelevant. Individual rifle marksmanship, verified reliable in previous combat, remained the hallmark of American tactics. Moreover, the unwieldy and often undependable machine guns were difficult to move forward in the attack, an essential feature of "open" warfare that dominated American operational concepts prior to World War I.

A major feature of the Leavenworth experience was the staff "ride," an aspect of military education adopted from the German Army. Student officers would study a particular campaign, often from the American Civil War, be assigned roles of the major participants in the campaign, then adjourn to the battlefield to replay the action and evaluate the decisions taken. All of the staff functions would be assigned and evaluated in this dynamic learning process. Capt. Eben Swift, a faculty member of the Staff College in the decade before World

War I, believed that both the staff rides conducted by Staff College students and the terrain rides conducted by Infantry and Cavalry School students strengthened an appreciation of the use of terrain and the limitations of maps.

The efficacy of instruction was tested in field maneuvers, a sort of graduation exercise for the students. Differing from terrain and staff rides, the field exercises involved actual troop units and stressed troop leading as well as staff estimation processes. The Leavenworth schools were the epitome of schools of application where formal textbook learning reinforced practical exercises.

In 1905, the Leavenworth process of education and training officers was codified in the first *Field Service Regulations* published by the United States Army. The architect of this important publication was Capt. Joseph T. Dickman, a former Leavenworth faculty member and later an important commander in France. The faculty at Leavenworth, under General Bell's supervision, revised the 1905 document in 1910, which, with minor changes, served as the source of doctrinal guidance for the AEF.

In the decade before American participation in World War I, the Leavenworth school system developed an outreach program to update officers of the National Guard and the Regular Army who had not attended the formal schools. A "short course" of six weeks was developed for senior field officers who had missed the experience.

The payoff in France came in two ways. First, a system of schools was established within the AEF, nominally under MajGen. Robert L. Bullard's direction as the commandant of the Infantry Officer's School. Cols. James W. McAndrew (later chief of staff, AEF), Paul B. Malone, and Harold B. Fiske served respectively as the chief of the AEF Staff College at Langres, G-5 AEF, and assistant G-5 AEF. Although there was overlap and confusion between the War Department General Staff and the AEF staff, a great deal of essential precombat individual and unit training was conducted in France. Second, almost all the principal staff members within the AEF were Leavenworth trained, although there were only about 400 of these officers available in mid-1917.

The Fort Leavenworth schools closed for two years during the American participation in World War I, but reopened in 1919. It was clear by 1922 that the School of the Line and the Staff School should be combined to create the Command and General Staff School.

John F. Votaw

Bibliography

Coffman, Edward M. *The War to End All Wars: The American Military Experience in World War I*. New York: Oxford University Press, 1968.

Cosmas, Graham A. *An Army for Empire: The United States Army in the Spanish-American War*. Columbia, MO: University of Missouri Press, 1971.

Dastrup, Boyd L. *The U.S. Army Command and General Staff College: A Centennial History*. Leavenworth, KS: J.H. Johnston III; Manhattan, KS: Sunflower University Press, both 1982.

Nenninger, Timothy K. *The Leavenworth Schools and the Old Army: Education, Professionalism, and the Officer Corps of the United States Army, 1881–1918*. Westport, CT: Greenwood Press, 1978.

———. "American Military Effectiveness in the First World War." In *Military Effectiveness*: Vol. I, *The First World War*, ed. by Allan R. Millett and Williamson Murray. Boston: Unwin Hyman, 1989 [1988].

United States Army: Corps of Engineers

During World War I, The United States Army Corps of Engineers was called upon to provide a very diverse range of military services. Not only did the engineers supply American combat divisions with the officers and men to staff their 1,600-man engineer regiments, but they also built the port facilities, roads, and railroads needed to bring essential war materiel to the divisions at the front. The engineers also harvested timber for military construction, employed searchlights in anti-aircraft defense, organized the first U.S. Army tank units, and developed chemical warfare munitions and defensive equipment. So important were armored and chemical warfare that the army, in 1918, created a separate Tank Corps and a Chemical Warfare Service, the latter headed in France by a career engineer officer, BGen. Amos F. Fries.

The U.S. Army engineers who served in the First World War brought with them varied amounts of military experience. Most senior engineer officers were graduates of the United States Military Academy. These Regular Army engineers had devoted the bulk of their careers to supervising domestic river and harbor improvements, although many had also served with U.S. Army units abroad, primarily in Cuba or the Philippines. Other engineer commanders had been civilian engineers who were members of National Guard or Officers Reserve Corps engineer units organized a few years before the United States entry into the war. But most of the 240,000 engineers who served in Europe during the war had no prior record of military service. Some 40,000 of them were African Americans.

After the United States declared war on April 6, 1917, the British and French governments asked the United States to give top priority to the deployment of American engineers to France. By the end of August 1917, nine newly organized engineer railway regiments and the combat engineer regiment of the 1st Division had arrived in France. Several of the railway regiments were assigned to British or French military formations pending the arrival of larger numbers of American combat troops in the summer and autumn of 1918.

While serving with the British Third Army near the village of Gouzeaucourt in northern France, Sgt. Matthew Calderwood and Pvt. William Branigan of the 11th Engineers were wounded by German artillery fire on Sept. 5, 1917, and so became the first casualties in any U.S. Army unit serving at the front. In late November 1917, the men of the 11th Engineers abandoned their railway work and helped the British construct new defensive positions that stopped a German effort to regain territory near Cambrai, which had just been lost to the British.

U.S. Army engineers made their most visible contributions to ultimate victory well behind the front lines. The nearly 2 million fresh American troops, who joined a larger Entente force drawn from various nations and territories around the world, could fight successfully only if provided with adequate logistical support. Career engineer officer and chief builder of the Panama Canal, MajGen. George W. Goethals, headed the War Department's logistical efforts in the United States. Engineer officers and troops, led among others by the AEF's chief engineer, MajGen William Langfitt, and by BGen. Edgar Jadwin, the AEF's director of construction and forestry, dominated a construction effort in France that was essential to the movement and supply of the American Expeditionary Force.

Timber was the most basic raw material for the engineers in World War I. The soldiers of the 20th Engineers, the U.S. Army's largest regiment, and other AEF forestry troops produced roughly 200 million board feet of lumber in France, as well as 4 million railroad ties and thousands of timber piles. LtCol. Henry Graves, on leave as the U.S. Forest Service's chief forester, helped organize the effort. By October 1918, American forestry engineers were operating 107 sawmills, primarily in southern and central France.

American soldiers, under the technical supervision of army engineers, used substantial amounts of these timber products in the construction of new and expanded port facilities for American troop and supply ships. Because British vessels clogged French ports on the English Channel, American ships had to dock at Atlantic ports from Brest to Bordeaux or at the Mediterranean port of Marseilles. Engineer officers commanded mixed crews of engineer, cavalry, marine, and labor troops, prisoners of war, and Spanish and Chinese civilians, who built a ten-berth pile dock at Bassens below Bordeaux. A three-berth pier that the engineers built at Montoir on the Loire River, together with its rail connection to shore, required 6.8 million board feet of lumber. Dredging by French contractors made the docks at Montoir and Brest built by American engineers available to vessels with 25-foot drafts.

France's intercity rail lines were basically adequate for the transportation of American military supplies to the battlefront, but the use of American engines and rolling stock and the construction of rail yards and repair facilities was required. A majority of the 1.5 million tons of engineer equipment the Americans brought to France related to railway construction and operation. The U.S. Army engineers built 937 miles of standard-gauge railroad tracks in France before the Armistice, primarily at docks and storage facilities. A notable addition to France's rail net was a five-mile cutoff the American engineers built to avoid a bottleneck in the French city of Nevers; the cutoff included a 2,190-foot bridge over the Loire River, the longest bridge built by the Americans in France.

As American military materiel moved to the front, it was stored in some 15 million square feet of covered storage space erected by the engineers. They constructed most depot buildings with wooden frames and corrugated-iron roofs and walls. Noteworthy among the storage facilities was the Romorantin Air Service Depot, which boasted 1.3 million square feet of shops and 765,000 square feet of storehouses and hangars.

American foodstuffs had to be imported to feed the AEF. U.S. Army engineers assured that the food would be well preserved en route. They used 100,000 cubic feet of locally obtained cork to insulate a 4,000-ton-capacity refrigeration plant at the port of Bassens. The beef storage warehouse that engineer Col. Ernest Graves built at the Gièvres Depot in central France had a capacity of 5,200 tons. It was cooled by ammonia circulating through thirty-five miles of two-inch pipe. A nearby ice-making plant could produce up to 500 tons of ice daily. Closer to the front lines, the engineers built at Is-sur-Tille Depot an electrically operated bakery that could bake up to 400 tons of bread daily. American troops would not go hungry.

The engineers assured that American troops would be well supported all around. The Pontanezen barracks they built at Brest could house 55,000 men. U.S. Army engineer officers oversaw construction of hospital facilities for 141,000 men, including a 6,000-bed hospital at Bazoilles and a 5,000-bed hospital at Rimaucourt. A switchyard at the Montoir Depot on the Loire River could repair eighteen large locomotives simultaneously. Four large gasoline storage tanks at Gievres Depot could together hold 2 million gallons. Having just completed the Panama Canal, the Americans knew how to think big.

American engineers also provided a variety of special services to the AEF. The engineers' Camouflage Section opened a workshop in an old dance hall in Paris in September 1917 and commissioned a number of American artists resident in that city. One of the senior camouflage officers was Capt. Homer Saint-Gaudens, son of the great American sculptor Augustus Saint-Gaudens. Employing a work force of up to 900 women garment workers, the section produced more than 3 million square yards of camouflage materials, including airplane hangar covers, fish nets, painted burlap, and sniper suits. The camouflage products were used most effectively to move artillery forward unobtrusively.

The U.S. Army's 56th Engineers operated thirty-six- to sixty-inch searchlights to assist American artillery units in protecting American troops from night air raids. U.S. engineers also provided searchlight service for the French First and Tenth armies, since the French did not develop this specialty.

Engineer Col. Roger Alexander led the Topographical Division of the AEF's General Staff's Intelligence Section. He coordinated the use of aerial photographs to obtain information on German trenches and troop dispositions and the production of army maps. The U.S. Army base printing plant at Langres printed some 22 million maps in 1918. Colonel Alexander also oversaw the use of sound and flash ranging to locate enemy artillery positions.

Eight engineer regiments built narrow-gauge railroads between the railheads of standard-gauge lines and the front. American-operated light railroads hauled 860,000 tons of materiel and personnel. Road construction tasks employed even larger numbers of forward troops, but pioneer infantry regiments provided more of the labor than did participating engineer units. A quarry operated by the 28th Engineers supported the road-building effort by producing more than 10,000 cubic yards of crushed stone in 1918.

During 1918, U.S. Army engineer units also engaged in combat from the Vosges Mountains near the Swiss border to Oudenaarde, Belgium. One battalion of the 310th Engineers, 85th Division, even served in the Archangel area of northern Russia.

Noteworthy among engineer combat service was the action of two companies of the 6th Engineers who stopped their construction of heavy steel bridges to join British and Canadian forces in frontline trenches before Amiens, where together they successfully defended that historic city from a heavy German assault in March and April 1918. These two companies suffered a total of seventy-seven casualties. During June and July 1918, troops of the 2d Engineers fought as infantry in their division's bitterly contested capture of the Belleau Wood and the hamlet of Vaux in the Aisne-Marne campaign. This regiment had a nearly 13 percent casualty rate, the highest for an engineer unit of its size.

American forces assaulting Hill 269 in the Romagne Heights along the Hindenburg Line on Oct. 8, 1918, were joined by a battalion of the 1st Engineers fighting as infantry. Engineer Sgt. Wilbur E. Colyer of South Ozone, New York, received the Medal of Honor for his services in this action. Colyer volunteered to locate a group of German machine gun nests that was blocking the American advance. He used a captured German grenade to kill one enemy machine gunner, turned his machine gun against the other enemy nests, and silenced each of them.

Other U.S. Army engineers won personal recognition for their actions in bridging the Meuse River. Maj. William Hoge, Jr., a June 1916 graduate of West Point who was serving with the 7th Engineers, 5th Division, won a Distinguished Service Cross for his heroism in reconnoitering a site for a pontoon bridge across that well-defended waterway north of Brieulles. Hoge selected that bridge site during the daylight hours of Nov. 4, 1918, while under enemy observation and artillery fire, and he directed the construction of the bridge that night. After German artillery destroyed three pontoon boats supporting the bridge, engineer Sgt. Eugene Walker, Cpl. Robert Crawford, and Pvts. Noah Gump, John Hoggle, and Stanley Murnane jumped into the icy river and held up the deck of the bridge until replacement pontoons could be launched and installed. These men also received the Distinguished Service Cross. This bridge was one of thirty-eight constructed by U.S. Army engineers during the critical Meuse-Argonne offensive.

The U.S. Army Corps of Engineers during World War I quickly redirected its primary efforts from improving the rivers and harbors of the United States to building the structures needed to supply, transport, and facilitate the battlefield movement of more than a million American combat troops in France. Engineer officers quickly developed a diverse group of troop units able to provide the AEF with a broad range of construction and other technical support services. The engineers combined courage on the battlefield, where they sometimes fought as infantry, with critically needed technical skills to provide services essential to the military successes achieved by the U.S. Army in World War I.

Charles Hendricks

See also CAMOUFLAGE; PONTOON BRIDGES

Bibliography

Graves, Ernest. *Construction in War: Lessons Taught by the World War, 1917–1919.* Washington, DC: Government Printing Office, 1921.

Parsons, William B. *The American Engineers in France.* New York: Appleton, 1920.

U.S. Army. American Expeditionary Force, 1917–1920. *Historical Report of the Chief Engineer, Including all Operations of the Engineer Department, American Expeditionary Force, 1917–1919.* Washington, DC: Government Printing Office, 1919.

U.S. Army. First Army. *Report of the Chief Engineer, First Army, American Expeditionary Force on the Engineer Operations in the St. Mihiel and Meuse-Argonne Offensives, 1918.* Washington, DC: Government Printing Office, 1929.

United States Army: Dental Corps

In World War I, for the first time in the history of the United States, dentists served in a war as official members of the United States military forces. Congress had created the Army Dental Corps in 1911 and the Naval Dental Corps in 1912.

On June 12, 1917, Gen. John J. Pershing, commander of the American Expeditionary Force (AEF) in France, asked Washington to establish dental units in France. In response, headquarters dispatched in August the first fully equipped dental unit in France. In compliance with Statute No. 1621, U.S. Army and U.S. Navy dentists served together under the Army Medical Corps overseas. Under that statute, all naval medical personnel were transferred to the army during World War I as part of the AEF.

The Army Dental Corps operated under a law of Oct. 6, 1917, that recognized the corps. Under that act, the senior dental surgeon served under the new chief surgeon of the AEF and administered dental operations out of Chaumont from September 1917 to March 1918, when the office moved to Tours. The dental corps in France installed complete field outfits and a laboratory, and each AEF hospital contained dental staff and appropriate equipment. Each combat division also established a headquarters dental clinic complete with laboratories and essential dental equipment. In the field each regiment included at least three dental surgeons, with one serving as the senior dental officer.

Before crossing the Atlantic, dental officers took training courses at Camp Greenleaf, a temporary medical training facility in Fort Oglethorpe, Georgia. The dental officers also received instruction in oral and plastic surgery in schools throughout the United States. Overseas, dental officers under jurisdiction of the medical corps worked together in the field with their British and French colleagues. Supervising all AEF dental activities overseas, Col. Robert T. Oliver served as chief dental surgeon in the AEF from July 1917 to July 1919. His deputy for the same period was LtCol. William S. Rice.

A total of 1,876 officers served in the AEF Dental Corps. Of this number, 79 came from the Army Dental Corps, 12 from the Navy, about 225 from the National Guard, and the remainder from the Dental Reserve Corps. The Army Reserve Corps contained 5,372 dentists by June 1918. In addition, slightly more than 2,000 enlisted men, many of them undergraduates in dentistry, served as dental assistants or as dental mechanics in the AEF Dental Corps. The federal government had authorized dental personnel at a rate of 1 to 1,000, but that number was never filled because of a shortage of over 300 dental officers by the time the Armistice was signed.

During the United States participation in the war, the majority of dental officers in the AEF served in France. Others, however, drew duty either temporarily or permanently in hospitals, aviation camps, and instructional centers in England, and a few went to Italy and northern Russia.

Handling facial and jaw wounds posed special difficulties during the war. Initially, the AEF Dental Corps encountered equipment problems for maxillofacial surgery and for prosthetic and reconstruction procedures because the equipment shipped from the United States did not arrive during the war. The AEF dentists managed by purchasing what equipment they could find in France and by learning about treatments of facial and jaw wounds from British and French dentists in the field. In May 1918, forty AEF specialists in general and dental surgery arrived in France for duty in the maxillofacial service. The chief surgeon in charge of the service sent some of these specialists to special treatment centers in England and Belgium. Base Hospital No. 115 at Vichy served as the main hospital for treating facial and jaw wounds. Out of approximately 2 million Americans serving in France between 2,000 and 2,500 suffered facial and jaw injuries. About two-thirds of these were successfully treated in France, and about 700 with more severe injuries requiring reconstruction were returned to the United States for care.

Other equipment deficiencies hampered the AEF dentists throughout the war, especially the lack of dental ambulances. The ambulances served as mobile dental clinics for outlying stations, but the dental officers received only two during the war. Two American dentists donated one through the American Red Cross hospital at Neuilly, and the other came from the American Red Cross through its medical director in Paris.

The dental service rendered overseas depended on local conditions. Generally during training the dentists could deliver first-rate tooth conservation service, so then men could participate in campaigns. In combat areas, however, the dental units would give only emergency treatment to relieve pain and could conduct only such simple procedures as extractions, minor surgery, and plastic fillings. Combat dentistry did enable soldiers to return to the battlefield. After the Armistice, the AEF dentists attempted to give optimal dental care to the servicemen before their return to the United States.

Ruth Harris

Bibliography

Ashburn, P.M. *A History of the Medical Department of the United States Army.* Boston: Houghton Mifflin, 1929.

Ford, Joseph H. *The Medical Department of the United States Army in the World War.* Vol. 2, Washington, DC: Government Printing Office, 1927.

U.S. Navy. *The Medical Department of the United States Navy with the Army and Marine Corps in France in World War I. Its Functions and Employment.* Washington, DC: U.S. Navy Department, 1947.

United States Army: General Staff

When continued criticism of the War Department for its inept management of the Spanish-American War forced the resignation in 1899 of Secretary of War Russell A. Alger, President William McKinley replaced him with Elihu Root. Ironically, it was a lawyer who knew nothing about the army who provided the spark that resulted in the formation of the General Staff. Root sought to create a coordinating body to solve some of the deficiencies made obvious by the "Splendid Little War." His first step was to create a War College with the power to digest and disseminate military data and information, develop military education and training, further the higher instruction of the army, and coordinate military administration. Following an intense legislative battle, Root's War College became a reality in an act of Feb. 3, 1901.

Buoyed by his initial success, Root submitted a measure to the 57th Congress that would create a General Staff charged with the consideration of military policy and the formation of comprehensive plans for national defense. The legislative battle again was difficult, with Gen. Nelson A. Miles, the commanding general of the U.S. Army, arguing that a General Staff would threaten the initiative of military commanders. Despite tenacious opposition, the bill was enacted on Feb. 14, 1903.

The General Staff consisted of a chief of staff, two general officers, and forty-two junior officers. It was divided into three divisions: the first dealt with administrative matters, the second oversaw military information and attachés, and the third directed military planning and training. The Army War College was now charged with assisting the General Staff in defense planning.

When MajGen. Leonard Wood became chief of staff in 1910, he reorganized the General Staff into three divisions: the Mobile Army, the Coast Artillery, and the War College, merging the General Staff planners and the Army War College into one unit which resulted in more integrated planning. The General Staff's work on a comprehensive military policy came to fruition in 1912 with Secretary of War Henry L. Stimson's report, "The Organization of the Land Forces of the United States." This plan recommended that the United States Army be organized into three distinct groups: a Regular Army ready for immediate deployment, a National Army of citizen soldiers to fill out the ranks of the Regular Army, and an army of volunteers to be organized if greater forces were needed. Woodrow Wilson's election in 1912, however, resulted in the shelving of the Stimson Plan. Respect waned for the General Staff, and by 1913, it had shrunk from forty-five to thirty-six members.

The outbreak of the First World War revealed the inadequacy of the American military. In response to a request from Secretary of War Lindley M. Garrison, the General Staff devoted much of 1915 to preparing the "Statement of a Proper Military Policy for the United States," which recommended increasing the size of the Regular Army from 100,000 to 230,000 men, continuing support for the organized militia, and establishing a reserve of trained citizens, officers, and supplies. Garrison adopted much of the "Statement" in his Continental Army Plan, which sought to establish a force of 500,000 men ready for instant call up.

The Continental Army Plan was opposed both by those who thought it went too far and by those who found it insufficient. President Wilson eventually withdrew his support, and on Feb. 10, 1916, Secretary Garrison and Assistant Secretary Henry Breckinridge resigned in protest.

Faced with an absence of executive guidance and the country's serious military shortcomings revealed during the American intervention in Mexico, Congress seized the initiative in 1916. After extensive hearings, the National Defense Act of 1916 finally became law on June 3. Based in part on the 1915 "Statement," the Act provided that the United States Army would consist of the Regular Army, the Volunteer Army, the Officers' Reserve Corps, the Enlisted Reserve Corps, the National Guard, and any other forces that might be authorized by law. While it recognized the General Staff's work and planning, provisions deep within the National Defense Act boded ill for the General Staff. The staff was limited to three general officers and fifty-two junior officers, no more than half of whom could be on duty in or around Washington, D.C., at one time. The Mobile Army and Coastal Artillery divisions within the General Staff were abolished, and the jurisdiction of the organization was limited to nonadministrative matters, calling into question whether it still had supervisory control over the bureaus. Only the perception that the United States was rapidly drifting into the European conflict and the arrival of a new secretary of war saved the General Staff.

If anyone was a less likely candidate for the position of secretary of war than Elihu Root had been, it was Newton D. Baker. Apart from a short stint as private secretary to the postmaster general and two terms as mayor of Cleveland, Ohio, Baker had little administrative experience. Even more worrisome, Baker was an avowed pacifist. Nonetheless, he proved as strong a supporter of the General Staff as had Root.

Baker sought to resolve the question of the General Staff's relationship with the various bureaus. On September 13, he rendered his verdict. Basing his decision on the intent behind both Root's reforms and the act of 1903, Baker ruled that the chief of staff, acting in the name of the secretary of war, would coordinate and supervise the various bureaus and offices of the War Department. Thus, less than seven months before the United States declared war, a clear-cut decision on the General Staff's supervisory role was finally made. In spite of this favorable decision, the General Staff was still not prepared for the demands of the coming conflict.

When diplomatic relations between the United States and Germany broke down after the German resumption of unrestricted U-boat warfare, the United States found itself marching quickly down the road to war with no strategic plan to offer guidance. The task of formulating a global strategy for the nation thus fell to the shoulders of the nineteen members of the General Staff then stationed in Washington. Compared with the sizes of the General Staffs of Great Britain, France, and Germany at the outbreak of the war—232, 644, and 650, respectively—this number was absurdly small.

The demands of war spurred Congress to raise the number of General Staff officers to ninety-one, with fifty of those serving in the War College Division. Many of these officers, especially within the War College Division, soon grew anxious for duty in some of the newly forming units. Consequently, by September 1917, the War College had shrunk to twenty-four. In spite of its small size, the General Staff bore much of the burden of preparing the nation for battle.

The General Staff was charged with two main tasks during the war. First, the War College Division was responsible for devising the strategic plans for United States involvement, but the nature of that involvement had yet to be determined. Arguing that training a separate American force would prove time-consuming and fruitless, the British and French commanders-in-chief, Gen. Sir Douglas Haig and Gen. Robert Nivelle, suggested that the best way to incorporate the United States into the fight was through a policy of amalgamation—the direct assimilation of small units into the existing British and French lines under European command. American military leaders at all levels quickly rejected this idea, and all subsequent plans were based on the assumption that an autonomous American army would be created.

The United States also faced the choice of raising and training a complete fighting force on its own shores before sending it abroad or of sending a small force to Europe immediately. Members of the War College Division adamantly objected to the latter. Trained soldiers and officers were scarce in the United States, and organizing most of them into a single unit would hamstring future efforts at raising an independent army. Yet the immediate dispatch of an untrained force to Europe might mean the slaughter of the novice American soldiers.

President Wilson's desire to play a large role in shaping the postwar settlement required that the United States endure a significant share of the fighting and dying. Since the Allies would owe little to a country that wasted much time in training its army before it sent it abroad, Wilson decided that a force was needed in France immediately to show the flag. So, despite the General Staff's recommendation, a single division left for Europe under the command of Gen. John J. Pershing on May 19, 1917.

Timing was only one question facing the General Staff. During the second half of 1917, many political leaders in the United States questioned the wisdom of sending troops to the Western Front. Almost three years of relentless fighting there had left the terrain scarred with trenches and graves but had accomplished little else. In September 1917, Wilson submitted to Baker an "Eastern Plan," which he had received from Maj. Herbert H. Sargeant, advocating holding the line with the minimum possible force while concentrating American efforts against Turkey or Bulgaria. Since the plan came from the President himself, it demanded a detailed response.

The War College Division found several weaknesses in the Eastern Plan. Shipping for an Eastern campaign would require an additional 45 to 62 percent of the time required to send a comparable force to France. And the supply question was insurmountable at this point, since the American Army was already forced to rely on France for its artillery needs in the West. Other alternatives to servicing the Western Front, including an attack through Russia, fared just as poorly.

In dismissing these alternative strategies, the War College Division explained its reasons for concentrating on the Western Front. The United States hardly had adequate shipping to send a force to Western Europe; trying to go any farther would have proven logistical folly. Also, a common bond facilitated a degree of understanding with the French and British that would not have been the case with the Russians or any other group. Most importantly, American military planners saw the Western Front as the decisive theater of the war. They argued that American participation would break the deadlock in favor of the Entente Powers. The war would be won or lost in the West, and if the United States wished to earn a seat at the postwar settlement, it would have to stand side by side with the British and French in the trenches of the Western Front. It was this last argument that was probably decisive in the eyes of the President. The United States would fight in the West.

The General Staff then faced the task of filling the nation's ranks. From the outset, planners rejected the idea of a volunteer system to recruit troops. Though such was the traditional method of enlisting soldiers, and despite the problems associated with the draft during the Civil War, it was clear that nothing except conscription could provide adequate numbers of men. Citing the problems faced by the British, who had avoided a draft until 1916, Chief of Staff Hugh L. Scott convinced Baker in mid-February 1917 that conscription was necessary. Baker then persuaded Wilson, who instructed the secretary of war to draft the necessary legislation.

The War College Division submitted a plan for raising and training 4 million soldiers. This plan not only supported the general idea of conscription, it also provided for sixteen divisional training areas, which were to become indispensable in the coming months. The draft of 1917–1918 differed significantly from the one instituted during the American Civil War. Most importantly, it was administered by civilians rather than army officers. Wilson signed the bill on May 18, 1917, and then proclaimed June 5 as registration day. On that day, over 9.5 million American men between the ages of twenty-one and thirty signed up for the "great national lottery." In August 1918, the War Department asked Congress to broaden the age limits of 18–45 and to halt volunteering for all services. By the end of the war, the 4,648 local boards had registered 23.9 million men and furnished more than 2.8 million to the armed forces.

All did not go smoothly as America girded for war. Since many of the War Department bureaus were still reluctant to share responsibil-ity, mobilization suffered from a dangerous lack of coordination. While the General Staff raised the requisite manpower, the Quartermaster Corps provided for their supply. The extraordinary lack of communication between these two agencies led to gaps between the number of soldiers the former could muster and the number the latter could outfit. By the end of 1917, although the War Department had requested 687,000 troops, it could equip only 516,000. Transportation also was a serious problem, for until 1918, when the General Staff took over motor transportation and moved toward standardization, the competitive buying of the various bureaus resulted in such an assortment of vehicles that supplying spare parts was a nightmare. Yet in spite of this embarrassing confusion, the War Department in 1917 recruited, clothed, armed, equipped, began to train, and even started to ship to France a force five times the strength of the Regular Army on the day Wilson asked Congress for the declaration of war.

Problems within the War Department continued during the winter of 1917. Stories flourished of men clad in civilian clothes drilling with wooden sticks instead of rifles. Scott and his assistant chief of staff, Gen. Tasker H. Bliss, competent though they were, were both sixty-three years old. In this respect, they illustrated the War Department's problem of thinking in terms of an older, smaller army. In mid-December 1917, Congress launched an investigation of the War Department. Much criticism focused on the secretary of war, who considered resigning until the President publicly declared his support for the department. In response, Baker restructured the General Staff and appointed a new chief of staff.

General Order No. 14 of Feb. 5, 1918, reorganized the General Staff into five groups: Executive, War Plans, Purchase and Supply, Storage and Traffic, and Operations. The chief of staff would plan the development of the army program. The chief of the Purchase and Supply Division was to supervise the purchase and production of all munitions and other supplies and to direct all purchases, procurement, and production activities of the several bureaus and other agencies. The General Staff now had recognized authority over the entire War Department.

The plan of February 1918 gave much authority to the General Staff, but for the reorganization to be effective, Baker needed a strong chief of staff. Scott, Bliss, and MajGen. John Biddle had rotated in and out of that office six times in the previous eleven months, but Baker's new chief was to bring "that lifeless institution to life with the rudeness and suddenness characteristic of an electric shock." That man was Peyton C. March.

March's thirty-year military career was filled with distinction. After graduating Phi Beta Kappa from Lafayette College, he had entered the United States Military Academy in 1884. He received several citations for gallantry during both the Spanish-American War and the Philippine Insurrection. As a member of the first General Staff, he served as an observer with the Japanese Army during the Russo-Japanese War. A period with the Adjutant General's Office during 1916 complimented his experience in the line. Because of his excellent record, Pershing selected him as chief of the American Expeditionary Force (AEF) artillery. He returned from France in early 1918 and on March 4, took over as acting chief of staff.

March's first task was to exert control over the bureau chiefs by limiting their access to the secretary of war. He replaced the quartermaster general and the chief of ordnance with men of his own choosing, Robert E. Wood and Clarence Williams. He also consolidated Purchasing and Supply and Storage and Traffic, into a single division of Purchase, Storage, and Traffic. March named his old friend and builder of the Panama Canal, MajGen. George W. Goethals, as its chief. In contrast to its nineteen members at the time of the United States declaration of war, the General Staff under March swelled to over a thousand by the time of the Armistice.

On Aug. 26, 1918, General Order No. 80 provided that the chief of the General Staff would be the immediate adviser of the Secretary of War on all matters relating to the military establishment. March now increased the logistical power of the General Staff, permitting it to take authority over most of the supply function, making the Quartermaster Corps a subsidiary of the Purchase, Storage, and Traffic Division of the General Staff. As its head, Goethals now became an executive rather than merely a supervisor with advisory authority. At last, less than three months before the end of the war, the General Staff had a centralized supply agency.

Just as problematic as the lack of cooperation with the various bureaus was the General Staff's poor relationship with the general head-quarters of the American Expeditionary Force (GHQ AEF). March's forceful personality was matched if not exceeded by General Pershing's, and there was a severe lack of communication between Washington and Chaumont. Much of the misunderstanding surrounded the size of the AEF. Pershing's plan for the American role included a force of 100 divisions. Pershing believed that because of shortages among the Allies, only an army of this size could ensure victory in 1919. His request was based on little information about conditions in the United States, and when it arrived in Washington, the General Staff undertook an investigation of the nation's capacity for meeting these demands. Planners studied the availability of men and raw materials, the rate of industrial production, training, procurement of supplies, and the transportation of men and materiel to Europe.

The General Staff's first hurdle was to determine how many soldiers would be involved in Pershing's plans. On this, Pershing's request was vague, and although he thought in terms of 5 million men, the War Department considered anywhere between 3,375,000 to 4,260,000 men. Such confusion between the plans of the General Staff and the GHQ AEF, unfortunately, were not rare.

On July 18, March made his recommendation to Baker. He dismissed the 100-division proposal as impossible; merely clothing an army of such size would require nearly all the wood in the country! He argued that within the given time limit the United States could raise only 60 divisions for certain, but he compromised on a figure of 80 divisions—3,360,000 soldiers. The GHQ AEF, however, to the end of the war, had its own definition of an 80-division plan which included not only 80 combat divisions but also 16 depot divisions for a total of 4,585,000 soldiers.

March tried to eliminate some of the confusion between the War Department and the AEF by suggesting an exchange of officers between the two groups. Although there is no evidence that the plan was anything except innocent, Pershing's chief of staff, Gen. James G. Harbord, saw it as a thinly veiled attempt by March to supplant the commander of the AEF. Pershing sent the requested officers, but only three of the thirty were found fit for General Staff work, and thus the attempt failed.

Although they shared the goal of the defeat of the kaiser's war machine, Pershing and March lacked a mutual understanding of the

U

manner in which to achieve that end. The force of these two personalities combined with the lack of communication between the GHQ AEF and the General Staff created a chasm in war planning seemingly as wide as the Atlantic Ocean itself. Although much of the rumor of the "Pershing-March Feud" comes from their memoirs written during the 1930s, Baker was forced to deal with the constant tension these two military leaders generated in addition to his normal duties as secretary of war.

In the wake of the November 1918 Armistice, the General Staff was given the task of preparing recommendations on army organization that could be submitted to Congress. The plan granted great authority to the General Staff. Had it been adopted, the General Staff would have exercised direct authority over all the bureaus and offices of the War Department. The mood of Congress after the war, however, doomed the plan. The bureaus had not lost all of their political influence, and the legislature seems to have feared a powerful General Staff, which they saw as being answerable only to the secretary of war and the President.

The National Defense Act finally enacted by Congress on June 4, 1920, met with opposition both from the supporters and the opponents of the General Staff concept. While its provisions fell short of those desired by the War Department, the law recognized the General Staff as the main body for the creation of military policy, including all aspects of the mobilization of the nation's citizens and materials that might be necessary.

Michael McCarthy

See also BAKER, NEWTON DIEHL; CONTINENTAL ARMY RESERVE PLAN; GARRISON, LINDLEY MILLER; MARCH, PEYTON CONWAY; PERSHING, JOHN JOSEPH

Bibliography
Beaver, Daniel R. *Newton D. Baker and the American War Effort, 1917–1919.* Lincoln: University of Nebraska Press, 1966.

Coffman, Edward M. *The Hilt of the Sword: The Career of Peyton C. March.* Madison: University of Wisconsin Press, 1966.

Hewes, James A. *From Root to McNamara: Army Organization and Administration, 1900–1963.* Washington, DC: Center of Military History, 1975.

Kreidberg, Marvin A., and Morton G. Henry. *History of Military Mobilization in the United States Army, 1775–1945.* Washington, DC: Department of the Army, 1955.

Nelson, Otto L., Jr. *National Security and the General Staff.* Washington, DC: Infantry Journal Press, 1946.

United States Army: Infantry Organization and Doctrine

American infantry doctrine emphasized fighting a war of movement, or open warfare, and stressed the importance of the offensive and the individual riflemen. In seeking to adapt elements of this doctrine to the conditions on the Western Front, however, the United States Army borrowed heavily from French and British experience and manuals that emphasized the primacy of trench warfare and massive artillery firepower. The result was a doctrine with a confusing mix of contradictory views. While the army maintained its beliefs in open warfare, it also adopted techniques and tactics to fight in the trenches that were inconsistent with open warfare. Moreover, the American Expeditionary Force (AEF) designed its basic fighting unit, the division, to be a large, cumbersome organization more attuned to the demands of the war of attrition on the Western Front than the requirements of fighting a mobile battle.

Based on the experience of the American Civil War and flavored by subsequent campaigns against irregulars, both in North America and in the Philippines, the U.S. Army had developed a theory of combat based on maneuver and infantry firepower. Codified in the army's *Infantry Drill Regulations* (for brigades and smaller units) and *Field Service Regulations* (for divisions and larger units), this could only be achieved on the offensive and required that infantry formed under this theory—and all other elements of the army, especially the artillery—work closely together to bring the infantry within effective rifle range of the enemy. Artillery and machine gun fire remained the determining factor in any battle. Based on these assumptions, the 1914 *Field Service Regulations* emphasized the necessity of achieving fire superiority over the enemy and asserted that the defensive was only a temporary expedient; aggressiveness won battles. The 1911 Infantry Drill Regulations had applied these themes to the mechanics of conducting infantry operations.

The organization of the army's prewar division reflected this emphasis on rifle power. The division's combat power centered on its three infantry brigades, each of which contained three regiments. These regiments, in turn, consisted of a headquarters company, a machine gun company, and three four-company battalions. To support these troops, the division had a three-regiment field artillery brigade with forty-eight 3-inch field guns and twenty-four 3.8-inch howitzers, a regiment of cavalry, a regiment of engineers, a field signal battalion, an aero squadron with twelve planes, and supply units. At full strength, the division totaled 28,256 officers and men, with its twenty-seven infantry battalions fielding 10,476 riflemen. Although large by European standards, American officers were confidant that such a division could undertake the mobile, semi-independent missions envisioned for it in the 1917 *Field Service Regulations*.

Shortly after the United States declared war on Germany, French and British military missions arrived in Washington, D.C., to advise the United States Army on the appropriate organization and training for troops bound for the Western Front. The Allies believed that trench fighting had largely rendered training for open warfare obsolete. The labyrinthine nature of the trench system in Europe meant that the rival infantrymen fought one another at short ranges with little or no room to maneuver. Therefore, the British and French considered instruction in the use of hand grenades, trench mortars, and hand-to-hand fighting more important in infantry training than marksmanship. In their minds, trench fighting had nearly eliminated the role of the individual rifleman and the doctrine of open warfare that stressed aggressive attacks to drive the enemy out of its positions.

The French and British military missions' critique of fighting on the Western Front impressed the War Department. Based on this advice, and preliminary reports from American officers in France, it issued instructions emphasizing the primacy of trench warfare and advocating French and British training schemes. Moreover, in July, 1917, the War Department reorganized the American division to bring it more in line with those of the Allies.

Both the Allies and the Germans began the war with twelve-battalion divisions but subsequently reduced them to nine battalions in order to gain more flexibility and better control. Based on this experience, the War Department dropped one infantry brigade from its division and reduced the remaining two from three to two regiments each. Additionally, each of the remaining twelve infantry battalions converted one of its rifle companies into a machine gun company. While the field artillery brigade retained its three regiments and seventy-two guns, it added a battery of twelve trench mortars. The cavalry regiment, however, disappeared. With these reductions, the new division numbered 19,492 officers and men, of whom 7,344 were riflemen.

While the War Department restructured the division and began issuing directives on trench warfare, Gen. John J. Pershing led the first elements of the American Expeditionary Force (AEF) to France. Throughout the summer of 1917, Pershing and his staff observed the Allied armies in combat and studied their training in order to improve the efficiency of the AEF. The Allies' use of new weapons, particularly trench mortars, the small, handy 37-mm cannon, and tanks, impressed these officers, as did the ability of the individual Allied soldier to adapt to life in the squalid conditions of the frontline trenches. Nevertheless, the Americans came away convinced that three years of trench warfare had seriously eroded the offensive spirit of the Allied armies. Moreover, they believed that this diminished spirit promoted a defensive attitude that, in turn, produced the indecisive war of attrition then characterizing the Western Front.

Based on this analysis, Pershing concluded that if the Americans adopted the trench warfare tactics of the Allies, they too would succumb to the defensive mentality of the British and French armies. With the general agreement of his officers, Pershing directed that American training should be based on the fundamentals of open warfare envisioned in the 1917 *Field Service Regulations* and the 1911 *Infantry Drill Regulations*. Only open warfare training, Pershing believed, could instill the characteristics of aggressiveness, initiative, and leadership that the United States Army wanted in its soldiers. Pershing did not ignore the special demands of trench warfare, but felt that they could easily be learned in a short period of additional instruction after the fundamental infantry skills of open warfare had been mastered. While soldiers trained in open warfare could quickly adjust to trench warfare, most American officers believed that the reverse was not true. Moreover, when an attack did cross the trenches, they thought that soldiers trained in trench warfare would be unable to exploit the breakthrough because of their defensive mind-set; bewildered by his success, the trench-warfare-trained soldier would simply stop, dig in, and thereby continue the deadlock.

In addition to the psychological dimensions of open-warfare training, Pershing concluded that aggressive offensive action was the only way to break the deadlock on the Western Front. This point had strategic implications as well. Only by dramatically influencing the course of the war could the United States hope to gain the leverage on the peace settlement that President Woodrow Wilson desired. Furthermore, by asserting a separate mission for the AEF, Pershing could resist Allied calls for the amalgamation of American troops into the Allied armies. If the United States Army was to play a decisive, and independent, role in the war, Pershing reasoned, it had to force a return to open warfare.

Upon learning that the War Department had issued training instructions that reflected Allied doctrine, Pershing protested and forcefully stated his case for training the Army under the prewar doctrine. Again Pershing stressed that the sequence of training was critical. Open-warfare training, especially for small units, had to come first. More specialized instructions in the techniques of trench warfare could wait until the American divisions arrived in France. Influenced by Pershing's protest and a second stream of observer reports from Europe, the War Department reorganized military training in the United States under the prewar open-warfare doctrine.

While Pershing and his staff succeeded in directing American military training toward open warfare, they also restructured the division. Despite the pronouncements about a war of movement, the new AEF division was a compromise between Allied advice on trench fighting and the AEF's desire for open warfare. The AEF criticized the War Department's July 1917 division as being too weak in rifle power and worried that the heavy attrition of trench warfare would quickly exhaust the smaller division. Furthermore, Pershing and his staff fretted about the army's ability to produce a sufficient number of qualified commanders and staff officers to run a smaller, more numerous division. Therefore, the AEF decided it needed fewer,

larger divisions, with tremendous infantry and artillery firepower, capable of hammering their way through the trenches and into the open.

The new AEF division, approved in August 1917, maintained the idea of two infantry brigades with two regiments each but altered the infantry regiments. The new regiments increased its firepower with the addition of three 37-mm cannons, six 3-inch mortars to its headquarters company, and a machine gun company with sixteen heavy machine guns. Moreover, the regiment's three infantry battalions returned to a four-company organization, but they lost their machine gun companies. More importantly, the strength of the individual rifle companies expanded from 103 to 256 officers and men each.

In an attempt to assimilate the new weapons of trench warfare with its own emphasis on the rifleman, the AEF reorganized the rifle company into four platoons of four sections each. The first section, twelve men, served as "hand bombers," or grenadiers, while the nine men of the second section acted as rifle grenadiers. The seventeen men in the third section were riflemen, and the fourth section's fifteen men manned four French Chauchat automatic rifles. While the new company sported hand and rifle grenades and sixteen automatic rifles, the rifle sections and the rifle-armed ammunition bearers in the others gave it 216 riflemen. Thus, the new company incorporated the new weapons of trench fighting, while continuing to maintain the substantial rifle power that American officers felt necessary.

While the reorganization sought to accommodate new infantry weapons within the old doctrine, it did not overlook the importance of the machine gun. The AEF arranged the surplus battalion machine gun companies into two four-company machine gun battalions with sixty-four heavy machine guns each. One of these battalions served in each of the infantry brigades. Additionally, AEF planners created a third, motorized machine gun battalion of two companies (a total of thirty-two machine guns) to serve directly under divisional control.

Very little changed outside the infantry and machine gun units. The division maintained its field signal battalion, engineer regiment, and supply units with only minor changes. The field artillery brigade also remained at three regiments. In keeping with open warfare theories, two of these regiments were armed with light, quick-firing artillery pieces, either the American 3-inch or the French 75-mm guns. The AEF, however, rejected attempts to keep the third regiment equipped with light howitzers. Instead, it opted for the heavy French 155-mm gun, arguing that these guns were readily available from the French and that, although less mobile, they could provide the heavy firepower need for trench warfare. As finally organized, the AEF division contained 28,059 officers and men, of whom 12,000 were infantrymen, 224 heavy machine guns, 48 77-mm guns, and 24 155-mm guns. By contrast, the typical Allied or German division in 1918 numbered only about 10,000 men with 90 to 120 machine guns and 30 to 40 guns. Despite its inflexibility and cumbersome size, AEF planners believed the division had the infantry firepower and sheer weight of numbers it needed for sustained combat in France.

While the organization of the AEF division showed concessions to the problems of trench warfare, most notably the inclusion of mass units and heavy artillery, American training did as well. Pershing and his staff hoped to blend the best elements of Allied experience in trench warfare with their own open-warfare doctrine. Therefore, in the fall of 1917, the AEF began publishing British and French literature on trench fighting and modern weapons. Soon Allied, principally French, material supplemented the *Infantry Drill Regulations* on the conduct of offensive and defensive combat in trench warfare and even some aspects of open warfare. These changes reflected the increased flexibility of the reorganized infantry company and its new weapons and incorporated information on organizing and building trench systems. On the subject of trench warfare by large units (divisions and larger), French doctrine virtually supplanted the Field Service Regulations. In contrast to the *Field Service Regulations'* emphasis on a strong front line, the new instructions stressed defense in depth and created detailed guidelines for conducting large-scale trench warfare. Only in the area of open warfare by large units, the AEF's self-described area of expertise, did American doctrine remain unaltered. In effect, for large units, the AEF maintained two doctrines: one, based on French and British experience, for trench warfare and another, based on the 1914 *Field Service Regulations*, for open warfare.

While the AEF's dual doctrine befuddled commanders, the circulation of Allied training literature created confusion as well. Allied manuals contained valuable information on the conditions on the Western Front, but they also espoused ideas that were contrary to official American doctrine. The French and the British, for example, operated under the premise that the machine gun had replaced the rifle as the infantry's principle weapon, a notion that ran counter to the United States Army's stated faith in the importance of the individual rifleman. Moreover, Allied trench fighting techniques stressed deliberate planning, meticulously drafted operational orders, and centralized control of the battle, characteristics antithetical to those set forth in the *Field Service Regulations*. The practice of having American units train under French or British tutelage in France further complicated the situation. This meant that the instruction of American units was torn between two sometimes contradictory visions. The end result was confusion among American infantry officers and the failure of a coherent training scheme to emerge during the war.

Other factors also complicated the problem of implementing the official doctrine. After the German spring offensive of 1918, the need to rush troops to France meant that many units received only an abbreviated training program. Thus, while the U.S. Army stressed the importance of rifle fire, many men arrived at the front with little or no instruction in marksmanship. Small-unit leadership suffered too. The need to officer the rapidly expanding army meant that junior officers and noncommissioned officers received only rudimentary training and often lacked the leadership abilities and tactical skills needed to handle their units. While the AEF's troops often displayed the aggressiveness Pershing so desired in his soldiers, their training generally failed to develop the initiative and leadership necessary to carry out the type of war AEF planners had envisioned.

Additionally, the *Field Service Regulations* failed to take into account technologies such as airplanes, gas, and tanks and underemphasized others, especially machine guns. Trench warfare and the uneven quality of American infantry increased the importance of artillery during the war. Coordinating the infantry and artillery attacks, however, was difficult. After arriving in Europe, American infantry and artillery units often trained separately and thus had little opportunity to establish the close cooperation needed to develop a successful combined attack. Furthermore, poor communications meant that artillery fire could rarely be adjusted during an attack.

Pershing and most American officers envisioned the AEF fighting a mobile war on the offensive. Therefore, their open-warfare doctrine stressed that commanders were to press aggressive attacks making the best use of the terrain, flexible formations, and their supporting arms to bring their infantrymen within striking distance of the enemy. At that point, infantry fire superiority, combined with a frontal assault over a narrow front, would drive the enemy from his positions. In practice, however, the AEF fought set-piece battles. Because of their troops' limited abilities and the need to integrate artillery and other supporting arms into the attack, commanders issued rigid, highly detailed attack plans. Typically, the infantry moved forward in close formation over open ground with little regard to terrain, fire, or movement in order to overwhelm the enemy's trenches.

American infantry doctrine in the First World War reflected an attempt to blend traditional American military beliefs in the importance of maneuver and infantry fire power with the realities of trench warfare. Pershing and the AEF hoped to reintroduce maneuver to the Western Front and thereby break the stalemate and force an end to the war. Concerned that the British and French had lost their aggressive spirit due to trench fighting, the Americans looked to their own prewar open-warfare doctrine for guidance. Nevertheless, the AEF recognized that trench warfare posed some important changes and sought to mix the best elements of Allied trench-warfare tactics and techniques with American open-warfare doctrine. The inconsistencies inherent in this arrangement and problems in training and communications meant that the AEF's performance in battle never fully matched intentions.

American infantry organization also mirrored this attempt to integrate open-warfare beliefs with the conditions of trench warfare. In concession to prewar attitudes on the importance of infantry fire, the division was rich in riflemen. Based on the realities of the Western Front, however, the division included heavy artillery and substantially increased short-range firepower with more machine guns and supporting weapons, such as automatic rifles, 37mm cannons, grenades, and mortars. The division also bowed to the attritional nature of the fighting by adopting mass formations, despite their costs in mobility and flexibility. Like the attempt to modify its doctrine, the AEF division was only partially successful. It provided the manpower required to force a decision, but the difficulties experienced in keeping it supplied and its unwieldy size made it a blunt instrument rather than the quick cutting rapier American officers had envisioned before the war.

Richard Kehrberg

See also TRENCHES AND TRENCH WARFARE

Bibliography
Millett, Allan R. "Cantigny, 28–31 May, 1918." In *America's First Battles, 1776–1965*, ed. by Charles E. Heller and William A. Stofft. Lawrence: University Press of Kansas, 1986.

Rainey, James W. "Ambivalent Warfare: The Tactical Doctrine of the A.E.F. in World War I." *Parameters* (September 1983).

Spaulding, Oliver L. "The Tactics of the War with Germany." *Infantry Journal* (September 1920).

U.S. War Department. *Field Service Regulations: 1914: Corrected to July 31, 1918.* Washington, DC: Government Printing Office, 1918.

———. *United States Army in the World War, 1917–1919. Organization of the American Expeditionary Force.* Washington, DC: Government Printing Office, 1948.

United States Army: Medical Department
When the United States entered World War I, the Army Medical Department was a small organization struggling as it always had to provide adequate care for a peacetime army. MajGen. William C. Gorgas, a physician internationally acclaimed for his success in dealing with tropical diseases in both Cuba and the Panama Canal Zone, served as surgeon general until Oct. 30, 1918, when MajGen. Merritte Ireland succeeded him. The surgeon general was responsible both for the management of the department and for advising the secretary of war and the chief of staff on matters relating to the work of the department. He served on a committee of military and civilian physicians that assisted the medical members of the advisory commission of the Council of National Defense and functioned as a link between the Medical Department and other medical organizations both within and outside the military.

In addition to the surgeon general himself and his chief assistant, 5 other medical officers and 147 civilians worked in the Surgeon General's Office as part of the Supply, Sanitation, Personnel, and Library and Medical Museum Division, each component of which was headed by a medical officer. A chief clerk headed the Record, Correspondence, and Examining Division. The surgeon general was directly responsible for the Army Medical School, which trained young physicians in military medicine, and for the army's four general hospitals—Walter Reed in Washington, D.C., Letterman in San Francisco, Army and Navy in Hot Springs, Arkansas, and Fort Bayard Hospital for the victims of tuberculosis in New Mexico. He also assigned medical personnel to post hospitals in the United States and its overseas possessions and supervised their professional work.

When Congress declared war in April 1917, the commissioned personnel of the Medical Department were divided into a Medical Corps of fewer than 500 regular medical officers, a Medical Reserve Corps of less than 1,800 physicians of whom approximately 20 percent were on active duty, a Dental Corps of 86 dental surgeons, a Nurse Corps of 233 nurses supplemented by reserve nurses supplied through the Red Cross Nursing Service, and a Veterinary Corps of 62 officers. Nine contract surgeons handled responsibilities for which it was not feasible to detail medical officers. The department's enlisted force was limited to 5 percent of the army's enlisted strength and served in many capacities, from hospital corpsman to mechanic.

Regular medical officers and a few from the National Guard had been trained by the Army Medical School, which gave courses in tropical and military medicine, emphasized preventive medicine, and familiarized those new to the army with military routines. Regular medical officers serving as inspector-instructors had trained many National Guard physicians in their duties as medical officers, while a small number of Regular and National Guard physicians had taken courses offered by the Army's Command and Staff College at Fort Leavenworth, Kansas. A few Medical Reserve Corps officers had received training at summer camps organized for physicians, and many medical officers in all categories had had experience in the field while assigned to units serving near the Mexican border during the Punitive Expedition in 1916.

Recognizing the possibility of war, the Surgeon General's Office and the American Red Cross had already begun to cooperate in the formation of 500-bed base hospital units modeled on the army's base hospitals. The staffs of these units were provided by some of the nation's major hospitals and medical schools. The Medical Department had detailed Maj. Jefferson R. Kean to head the military division of the Red Cross.

Despite the previous experience and training of its personnel, the Army Medical Department, like the rest of the nation's military, was not prepared to meet the rapidly escalating demands imposed by the nation's entry into World War I. Because of the small size of the peacetime department, relatively few experienced medical officers were available to form the basis of a greatly expanded organization or to train thousands of civilian physicians responding to wartime needs. Supply presented additional problems; medical instruments had traditionally been bought in Europe, an adequate stockpile of medicine had not been created, and U.S. firms were not prepared to meet the need. A shortage of transportation further complicated attempts to meet the demands of the conflict in Europe.

Not long after the U.S. entry into the war, two new organizations for officers without medical, dental, or veterinary degrees were created. Sanitary engineers, chemists, psychologists, epidemiologists, laboratory technicians, experts in office management, and those with similar specialties formed the new Sanitary Corps. Their numbers had reached almost 3,000 by November 1918. The United States Army Ambulance Corps, which was headed by two regular medical officers, was also established in June 1917 to assist in field ambulance work on the French front.

Before the war ended, the Medical Department had grown to include a total of almost 1,000 regular medical officers, 229 regular dental surgeons, and 115 veterinarians. The National Guard contributed another 1,600 officers, physicians, dentists, and veterinarians to the wartime army, while 30,000 newly signed reservists and 1,000 contract physicians, of whom 55 were women assigned to work as anesthetists, laboratory technicians, and dispensary physicians, also served. Over 21,000 army nurses served at hospitals and other facilities, and more than 281,000 men served in the department's enlisted force.

To manage the work of the wartime Medical Department, the organization of the Surgeon General's Office became increasingly complex, employing as many as 200 medical officers and 1,600 civilians. As it expanded in size, sections of some existing divisions became divisions themselves. The former Record, Correspondence, and Examining Division became the Administrative Division, which, by June 1918, had been subdivided into seven sections. The appointment, assignment, and promotion of both enlisted and commissioned medical personnel, Regular, Reserve, and National Guard, was managed through the Personnel Division. The former Supply Division became the Finance and Supply Division and assumed the responsibility for examining accounts submitted by Medical Department officers previously exercised by the Record, Correspondence, and Examining Division. It was eventually subdivided into separate branches for finance, supply, property, and disbursing as well as for supply depots and units serving in Europe. The division for the medical museum and library was retained.

The Sanitation Division also grew significantly in size and complexity as the army grew. To meet its responsibilities, by June 1918, it had been subdivided into sections handling communicable diseases, sanitary inspections, sanitary engineering, current vital statistics, and medical records. July 1918 saw the creation of the Miscellaneous Section, which included a subsection that dealt with lice infestation.

Some new organizations within the Medical Department, among them the Veterinary Division, the Dental Corps Division, and the Army School of Nursing, represented an attempt to deal effectively with the demand for trained personnel. Shortly after war was declared, the creation of a Division of Medical Department Training to be responsible for medical officers' training camps demonstrated concern for the problems involved in preparing so many civilians for their military duties. Concern for the importance of the soldier's ration to his health led to a Division of Food and Nutrition in October 1917.

Other new divisions demonstrated the increasing complexity of modern medicine and the resulting growing tendency toward specialization within the medical profession as well as the need to deal more effectively and efficiently with the sick and wounded. In this category fell the Divisions of Infectious Diseases and Laboratories, Internal Medicine, Neurology and Psychiatry, Psychology, Roentgenology (the use of X-ray equipment), General Surgery, Military Orthopedic Surgery, and Surgery of the Head. The surgeon general ordered that at base and general hospitals these specialties be grouped into medical, surgical, and laboratory services.

Two new divisions, Air Service and Gas Defense, reflected new developments in warfare. Until the creation of the Chemical Warfare Service under the Corps of Engineers in 1918, the Medical Department was responsible not only for treating the victims of poison gas, but also for protecting soldiers from the effects of gas, which included obtaining and distributing masks for soldiers and horses and training soldiers to meet gas attacks. The creation of the Board of Publications and the General Publicity Board involved the department more deeply in the censorship of official publications and of those published by department personnel. The success of the department's history of the Civil War led to the organization of a division responsible for the research and writing for a similar study for World War I.

A Hospital Division was created to bear the responsibility for all such facilities, both abroad and within the United States. Its Overseas Section was one of the direct links between the Surgeon General's Office and the American Expeditionary Force in Europe. Through this section, base, evacuation, and field hospitals, ambulance trains, and hospital trains and ships were organized and staffed. Its activities eventually became so demanding that it was given division status with responsibility for the organization of all medical units intended for overseas service, handling liaison with the Navy's Bureau of Medicine and Surgery and supplying administrative personnel for overseas units. The need to prepare disabled soldiers for their return to civilian life through such means as occupational and physical therapy led to the formation of a separate Division of Special Hospitals and Physical Reconstruction in the summer of 1917.

During the war, the Army Medical Department received aid from many volunteer civilian organizations, chief among them the American Red Cross, which provided nurses, base hospitals, ambulance companies, sanitary training, surgical dressings, hospital clothing, and many other items and services. Physicians in these base hospital units who had not yet joined the reserves received reserve commissions, while the enlisted personnel became part of the regular army and the nurses were enrolled in the Army Nurse Corps. The Red Star organization assisted the army's veterinary services. The Medical Department also worked with various committees named by the Council of National Defense to add the efforts of the civilian medical world to that of the military.

Within the United States, the Medical Department's principal efforts were directed at preparing those new to the department for the responsibilities that would be placed on them—giving physical examinations to recruits, maintaining the health of those who had already joined the army, and preparing to receive the sick and wounded from overseas. To train new members of the Medical Department, a multitude of programs and schools were established. Although the Red Cross reserve provided enough nurses to meet the immediate demand, an Army Nurse School was established to meet possible future needs. Much training was conducted at medical officers' training camps, three for white and one for black medical officers, the largest of which was established at Camp Greenleaf, Chickamauga, Georgia. Sanitary and Dental Corps officers also attended classes there, while much of the training of enlisted personnel took place at a second medical officer's training camp set up at Fort Riley, Kansas. Programs to train physicians in the various specialties were established in connection with a number of medical schools across the country and at Camp Greenleaf.

The medical officers' training camps sent each divisional camp a field hospital, an ambulance company, and regimental medical detachments prepared to train other units for the divisional medical service. Because the base facilities were used for training, every effort was exerted to assign at least one Regular Army medical officer and two or three of the department's Regular Army enlisted men to each. Medical officers administered the large base hospitals at the divisional camps and conducted physical examinations of new recruits at these camps, in the process immunizing them against smallpox, typhoid, and paratyphoid. The number of enlisted men serving in the Medical Department was inadequate throughout the war, however, and a shortage of medical officers forced many to leave training programs before completing their courses. The management of health care provided at the camps occasionally suffered in the early months of the war as a result of inadequate training.

Furthermore, those planning camp facilities initially underestimated the sick rate among new recruits, although the problem of too few beds and inadequate operating and laboratory equipment was resolved with time. By the end of the war, some base hospitals held as many as 2,000 beds, but, even so, the demand placed on the division facilities by the influenza epidemic in the fall of 1918 overwhelmed some of them. The shortage of medical officers was exacerbated by the need to staff embarkation hospitals established near New York City and Newport News, Virginia, for soldiers who had to be left behind because they fell ill while waiting to embark.

Planning hospitals for patients returning from Europe was based on the assumption that 5 percent of the wounded and 2 percent of the sick from the American Expeditionary Force (AEF) would have to be sent home for treatment. At least one such hospital was established in each of the sixty-one draft districts. Plans to rely on civilian facilities for this purpose were soon abandoned as impractical, and available buildings in appropriate locations were remodeled to serve as hospitals. A majority of these facilities were general hospitals, under the direct control of the surgeon general rather than that of the line officer in command in the area. Many took in patients with a variety of illnesses, but limits were placed on the types of patients a few hospitals could take in so that the services of certain types of specialists could be more efficiently utilized.

Meeting Medical Department needs for personnel and supplies overseas became a significant challenge because of the difficulties involved in obtaining them and in finding space on transports to move them to France. The Overseas Hospital Division had no control over shipping priorities outside the Medical Department. Although successful efforts to obtain some of the needed items in Europe and a modification of the priorities that guided the loading of the transports in the summer of 1918 alleviated this situation, many of the nurses urgently needed by the AEF were still awaiting transportation when the Armistice was signed.

General Pershing had a strong influence on the organization and selection of Army Medical Department personnel in Europe. Under him, the medical organization of the AEF functioned in semi-independence of the Surgeon General's Office in Washington, D.C. The selection of Col. A.E. Bradley as chief surgeon of the

U

AEF and his subsequent promotion to brigadier general represented a compromise between Surgeon General Ireland's wishes and those of General Pershing, who preferred to have Ireland named to that position. When Bradley was invalided home in April 1918, Ireland succeeded him and in August received the rank of major general. Vacancies above the lowest commissioned rank were generally filled on Pershing's recommendation without the involvement of the Surgeon General's Office.

When the AEF arrived in Europe, the Medical Department became one of its supply departments, and thus part of the Service of Supply, headquartered at Tours and controlling most AEF activity outside the Zone of the Armies (the battle zone). The organization of Bradley's office resembled that of the Surgeon General's Office, with separate divisions for personnel, supply, sanitation, hospitals, finance, transportation, and veterinary activities. A superintendent of nurses was appointed for the AEF at Pershing's request.

The area to which the AEF was assigned in France was divided in sections, with the chief surgeon of each reporting to the chief surgeon of the AEF. When U.S. Army divisions began arriving in France, 300-bed camp hospitals served the sick and injured of the training camps where they were initially assigned. When the American First Army was created, its chief surgeon, Col. Alexander Stark, became responsible for the work of the Medical Department at the front, a responsibility he shared with Col. C.R. Reynolds after the American Second Army was formed. Although the surgeon general sent inspectors to visit all camps in France, the decentralization of Medical Department work in France isolated him from direct contact with the situation in Europe.

The chain of evacuation for both American armies called for battle casualties to be taken first to a battalion or regimental aid station, from which they were moved by litter to ambulance or dressing stations. Here motor ambulances took them back to two field hospitals of the four accompanying each division—the two remaining field hospitals were kept ready to move forward and take in the casualties of future action. In field hospitals emergency treatment was administered and triage performed. Some patients might then be sent to special hospitals staffed and equipped for the victims of gas or of certain specific types of wounds. A corps sanitary (ambulance) train moved most casualties in need of further treatment back either to a mobile hospital or to an evacuation hospital, located as a railhead. Plans had called for each division to have evacuation hospitals, but in practice it proved difficult to staff and supply even one. At the evacuation hospital more surgery could be performed if necessary before one of the AEF's twenty-one hospital trains hurried all wounded who could be moved out of the battle zone to base hospitals, which, unlike the field hospitals, were fixed units under the control of the Service of Supply.

Under normal circumstances, base hospitals, originally intended to hold 500 beds, held 1,000 beds, but in the event of emergency, their capacity could be doubled. The total number of beds to be available in them was 15 percent of the total number of soldiers in France, a figure that, in an emergency, might have to be raised to 25 percent. Great difficulties were experienced in finding adequate housing for these facilities, many of which had to be set up in existing buildings of marginal suitability. A new concept, the hospital center, was soon activated to group several base hospitals and a convalescent center under a common administration. Supplementing these units in Europe were four mobile surgical units, their equipment mounted on trucks so that urgently needed surgery need not be delayed by a shortage of equipment or personnel. Both mobile and stationary laboratories were available if requested by a chief surgeon. The staffs of all of these institutions were advised by teams of eminent specialists known as consultants who circulated among the medical facilities of the AEF.

A majority of the army's patients in Europe were the victims of war injuries, a change from previous wars when disease took a higher toll than the enemy. Of all the battle casualties treated in U.S. military hospitals in France, 31.4 percent had been gassed. Respiratory diseases formed the greatest threat other than battle injuries. Intestinal diseases such as typhoid and dysentery were present, but they did not present a serious problem. Venereal diseases caused great concern, but rates were generally lower than had been feared.

Demobilization in the Medical Department of the AEF began when the Armistice was signed. The basis of hospitalization was brought from 15 percent to 7.5 percent as rapidly as possible. Orders for future construction were canceled, and some new construction was halted. As patients were returned to the United

States and no more wounded were brought in, base hospitals were closed. By May 31, 1919, only 1,233 patients remained in Europe, cared for in the five base hospitals still in operation.

The chief surgeon of the American Third Army, which had been created to occupy Germany in the wake of the Armistice on Nov. 11, 1918, encountered a different challenge from that faced by his counterparts in the First and Second armies. Base hospitals were not moved to accommodate patients from the new army, and until mid-December, when evacuation hospitals could be moved and set up to serve as base hospitals and order restored to railroads, only field hospitals were available to care for Third Army sick and injured.

Demobilization brought reorganization to the Surgeon General's Office before the official end of the war. The number of divisions was reduced to eleven by December 1918. The Divisions of Personnel and Finance and Supply were retained, as was the Division of Sanitation. Many other divisions were promptly consolidated as sections of the Divisions of Surgery or Medicine, while a new Laboratory Division was created to contain both the Epidemiology Section of the former Division of Infectious Diseases and Laboratories and the Army Medical Museum. The remaining divisions included the Veterinary Division, and Division of Physical Reconstruction, a Library Division, and the Air Service Division. The Air Service Division came to an end in March 1919, and the Division of Reconstruction followed in June, shortly before the signing of the Versailles Peace Treaty.

Mary Gillett

Bibliography

Ashburn, P.M. *A History of the Medical Department of the United States Army.* Boston: Houghton Mifflin, 1929.

U.S. Army. Surgeon General's Office. *Medical Department of the United States Army in the World War.* Washington, DC: Government Printing Office, 1921.

United States Army: Nurse Corps

In 1901 the army created the U.S. Army Nurse Corps (ANC) realizing that women nurses were invaluable in modern war. In the Spanish-American War, women had served as "contract" nurses. Now the army nurtured its own; 125 women were on duty within the decade. Jane Delano, the second superintendent of the ANC and long-time leader of the American Red Cross, created the American Red Cross "reserve list" so that thousands of nurses could be mobilized quickly in the event of a war. Delano's foresight helped the U.S. Army. By December 1917, 424 regular nurses and 3,600 reserve nurses were serving the British and French armies and the American Expeditionary Force (AEF). By the Armistice, over 21,000 army nurses had served, including 3,500 regular and 18,000 reserve nurses. About half had served abroad, the rest in 174 U.S. sites. Much of the time there was nothing for them to do but combat boredom. When the casualties started arriving, the nurses proved their worth. With no antibiotics, patient nursing services were vital to the survival of many wounded, especially the victims of poison gas. Gas casualties were a gruesome new challenge.

The load ratio in overcrowded hospitals soared to as high as fifty patients per nurse. Nurses worked fourteen- to eighteen-hour days for weeks at a time; they were often short of food, heat, baths, and sleep. As Julia C. Stimson, head of nursing in France (and the postwar superintendent of the ANC) wrote in her diary, "I don't mind for myself, but it breaks my heart to see my children get hollow-eyed and white and see them one by one succumb, at least temporarily and have to be sent to bed."

Heroic nurses volunteered for surgical teams or emergency groups consisting of a surgeon, assistant surgeon, an anesthetist, two nurses, and several orderlies. These teams worked as close as possible to the front lines, often a few miles from the action, to treat the wounded too serious to remove to base hospitals. These teams were shelled and could themselves become war casualties. Nurses remembered spending "most of the night jumping out of bed into our trench coats and snatching our helmets and gas masks . . . not knowing just when a bomb would come crashing down on us." In all, 101 ANC nurses died overseas, 3 were wounded but not killed by enemy action, and 134 died in the United States, many from pneumonia or other illnesses related to the influenza epidemic. Over 200 nurses were decorated for bravery under fire; they received medals from the British, the French, and the AEF.

As soldiers continued to be wounded in record numbers, a nursing shortage soon developed. Before the war was over, Catholic sisters who were graduate nurses served in Red Cross and ANC units and even nurses aides were recruited. Fifty nurses'-aides trained at Smith College and reported directly to the chief surgeon at Château-Thierry as unpaid volunteers. Estimates are as high as 25,000 American women who served in some capacity overseas during the Great War, often as unpaid volunteers sent by local organizations. When the war broke out, over 1,000 black graduate nurses registered for the American Red Cross reserves. Despite the critical shortage, none of them were accepted until after the Armistice was signed. When the influenza epidemic hit and killed more soldiers than were killed during the war, 9 black nurses did serve at Camp Sherman, Ohio, and Camp Grant, Illinois, where large numbers of African-American soldiers were stationed.

Treatment of nurses varied from base hospital to base hospital and among the host countries. The chief surgeon ran each hospital with no interference or supervision from the ANC. Some encouraged the nurses and treated them with respect; others saw nurses as only capable of performing menial tasks and kept them assigned at this low level. Still others may have preferred no women in their hospital. Nurses serving with the British Expeditionary Force (BEF) often reported better treatment than those serving with the AEF. The ANC was under Superintendent Dora Thompson; her term began in 1914 and lasted until the end of the war. She fought and finally obtained a clause in the army regulations to state that after the medical personnel (the doctors), the nurses were the next in the chain of command. The problem, however, continued, in part because of tradition, in part because of contradictory regulations. The ward master's regulations stated that he was in charge of the patients and the enlisted staff. Nurses resented having to ask the ward master for the key to the linen closet or the medicine cabinet. Who outranked whom? In addition, the hospital surgeon was the commander of the nurses working in his hospital. That left little chance for communication or supervision from the superintendent of the ANC. Indeed, nurses had to obtain permission from the head surgeon before they could contact her. Thus, the ANC women had the worst of both worlds. They could not associate with the enlisted personnel nor were they taken seriously in terms of authority by the officers, the medical doctors. The probable reason the nurses were better treated by the BEF than the AEF lies in the rank structure. The British and Canadians had given their nurses "relative rank." That meant that the women were called lieutenant or captain, and they were respected by officers and enlisted men alike, although they did not get the same pay and privileges of men of the same rank and were not given command authority over men. The ANC did not receive relative rank until after World War I and after a major lobbying effort on the part of all nursing organizations teaming up with women's colleges and associations. By 1920, women had the right to vote in the United States and the nurses had "relative rank." In part, both were awards for the special roles women had played during the war. The ANC kept relative rank until the middle of World War II even though other women serving in the U.S. Army (WAC) and U.S. Navy (WAVES) were getting the same pay as the men. Nurses were not given permanent commissions with full benefits and privileges of rank until 1947.

Most American nurses during the Great War were registered and processed by the Red Cross. They then served with the army, navy, or the Red Cross in overseas hospitals organized and financed by the Red Cross. Some nurses frankly did not know if they were army, navy, or Red Cross nurses. The largest difference was that military nurse reservists were eligible for disability benefits if they were wounded or injured while in Europe; Red Cross nurses were not. The navy had about the same number of regular and reservist nurses, 1,400 regular, 1,100 reservists; but the army had only 3,000 regulars and 18,000 reservists. The differences between regulars and reservists were not significant during wartime. Many of the patients referred to all nurses as Red Cross nurses. Nurses had made a difference in the lives of thousands of soldiers, sailors, and Marines. A fitting tribute to these dedicated courageous nurses of the Great War was the British song which labeled them "The Rose of No Man's Land."

D'Ann Campbell

Bibliography

Kernodle, Portia B. *The Red Cross Nurse in Action.* New York: Harper, 1949.

Piemonte, Robert V., and Cindy Gurney, eds. *Highlights in the History of the Army Nurse Corps.* Washington, DC: Center of Military History, 1987.

Schneider, Dorothy, and Carl J. *Into the Breach: American Women Overseas in*

World War I. New York: Viking Penguin, 1992.

Shields, Elizabeth A. "A History of the United States Army Nurse Corps (Female): 1901–1973." Ed.D. dissertation, Columbia University Teachers College, 1980.

Stimson, Julia C. *Finding Themselves—The Letters of an American Army Chief Nurse in a British Hospital in France*. New York: Macmillan, 1919.

United States Army: Officer Acquisition

Shortly after the Armistice in 1918, a French officer commented to an American: "You had no officers' reserve to start with [but], you somehow found 200,000 new officers, most of them competent. This is what is astonishing and what was impossible. Tell me how that was done." The American could describe how it was done because he himself had earned his commission at one of the "ninety-day" Officer Training Camps in 1917.

Secretary Newton D. Baker later noted that "one of the most serious problems confronting the War Department in April, 1917, was the procurement of sufficient officers." Only 18,000 Regular Army and National Guard officers were available at the outset. Since the wartime army eventually numbered about 4 million men, including some 200,000 officers, the War Department had to recruit and train 182,000 officers within nineteen months. The Medical Department and other specialized branches offered commissions to 70,000 civilians. By commissioning qualified men from the ranks, the army added another 16,000 officers. Shortening the four-year course at West Point to one year produced a few hundred more. Nearly half (96,000) of the officers who served in the war, however, including some two-thirds of the line officers of the National Army, were graduates of the Officer Training Camps.

These officer camps grew out of the prewar training camp program of the Plattsburg Movement. The most imaginative of Gen. Leonard Wood's myriad schemes for military preparedness, the famous Business Men's Camp at Plattsburg, New York, had attracted some 1,200 of the nation's elite to undergo four weeks of voluntary military training along the shore of Lake Champlain in August 1915. The well-publicized trainees—among them the mayor and police commissioner of New York,

the Harvard football coach, a former secretary of state, and three sons of Theodore Roosevelt—formally organized themselves as the Military Training Camps Association (MTCA) and lobbied successfully for similar Plattsburg camps under Regular Army supervision in the National Defense Act of 1916. Headed by the indefatigable New York attorney Grenville Clark, the MTCA recruited more than 16,000 volunteers for Plattsburg and other camps in 1916. On April 5, 1917, just three days after Woodrow Wilson's war message, MTCA officials suggested that Plattsburg camps scheduled for the next summer should be converted to officer training camps. The War Department jumped at the idea and proposed sixteen camps, which could train 2,500 officers each in a three-month program of instruction beginning in mid-May. Since the army had neither the organization nor the personnel to handle the thousands of applications for the camps, Secretary Baker gladly accepted the MTCA's offer to act as recruiting agent.

Within three weeks the Plattsburgers set up volunteer-staffed offices in major cities throughout the country. The college alumni lists that the MTCA had circulated for the 1916 camps were used again, as was the MTCA roster of more than 20,000 persons who had attended federal training camps. The MTCA hurriedly printed hundreds of thousands of application forms, using its own funds for bulk mail, telephones, and telegraph. The full cost amounted to $350,000, none of it reimbursed. In New York City, some forty volunteer physicians examined applicants in groups of five in three-hour shifts from 8 A.M. to midnight. In all, the MTCA screened, examined, and certified to the Army 40,000 out of more than 150,000 applicants; of these, 27,341 eventually earned commissions.

The first sixteen camps were held at the following sites: two camps each at Plattsburg, Fort Benjamin Harrison (Indiana), and Fort Sheridan (Illinois), one at Fort Niagara (New York), Madison Barracks (New York), Fort Myer, (Virginia), Fort McPherson (Georgia), Fort Oglethorpe (Georgia), Fort Logan H. Roots (Arkansas), Fort Riley (Kansas), Fort Snelling (Minnesota), Leon Springs (Texas), and the Presidio of San Francisco. Each camp had fourteen regular companies—nine infantry, three artillery, one cavalry, and one engineering company—to provide instruction, with at least one regular officer who had experience at earlier civilian training camps. When the three-

U

month course ended on August 15, the successful graduates were commissioned: 18,929 as second lieutenants, 4,452 as first lieutenants, 3,722 as captains, 235 as majors, 1 as a lieutenant colonel, and 2 as colonels. Some graduates went into the Regular Army, some into the National Guard, and some were kept as instructors for the second series of officers camps in September. The army also held a special officers' camp for African Americans at Fort Des Moines, Iowa, from June to October, enrolling 1,250 and eventually commissioning 639 lieutenants and captains. Most of the new officers were ordered to the new camps under construction to train the first call-up of draftees beginning in September. They became, in effect, the officers and instructors of the new National Army.

The course of instruction in the first officer camps, while extended to three months and continually modified in light of overseas experience, essentially followed the same intensive and progressive training instituted by General Wood in the prewar training camps. Nevertheless, because of the greater urgency of 1917 and the need to coordinate officer training with the larger task of creating a National Army, unforeseen obstacles inevitably arose. The haste in assembling the camps ran afoul of equipment shortages and inadequate housing. Nor were there enough officers/instructors experienced in dealing with civilian elites, and the result in some cases was that officer training too closely resembled recruit training, without sufficient attention to developing leadership qualities. Some instructors had to work extra hard to keep ahead of their students. "It was a case of the blind leading the blind," recalled Lt. (later Gen.) Charles L. Bolte. Another complaint came when the War Department announced early in the training course that only 671 men from each camp would receive commissions, a number sufficient to officer only a single division and an additional cavalry regiment. The army's expanding manpower demands eventually reversed this policy, but not before causing damage to trainee morale.

Given the general state of unpreparedness in spring 1917, the snarls and confusions of the first officer camps were unavoidable. Red tape, shortages, complaints, sudden changes in policy—all were the inevitable consequences of having to improvise. If some in the army were slow and unimaginative, there always seemed to be officers ready to take the initiative—men like

Capt. George C. Marshall, who in May 1917 disregarded all normal procedures by purchasing "blankets, mattresses, and things of that sort" and shipping them express to Plattsburg without informing the quartermaster. Far outweighing the drawbacks to the camps was the very fact that they existed. "To send untrained troops into the field is manslaughter," the MTCA emphasized, "but to dispatch troops with untrained leaders is murder in the first degree." The first 180,000 draftees who arrived at the cantonments in September 1917 would have had no leaders at all if it had not been for the officer camps. The War Department's official history of the personnel system in World War I admitted that "in many ways, the Army [in 1917] faced a more difficult problem in securing officers than in securing men." Without the officer camps, the army could not have begun to solve either problem.

Although a second series of officers camps in the autumn of 1917 commissioned 22,000 more officers, the War Department decided to change the system. Beginning in January 1918, new officer training "schools" were attached to each of the twenty-odd divisions of the National Army. By training officers alongside draftees in each cantonment, there would be no dilution of Regular Army discipline, and Regular officers attached to the divisions could be used more effectively as instructors. Such procedures gave the army greater control than before. In addition, complaints about aristocratic bias in the first two series of officer camps made the War Department receptive to more egalitarian methods of officer procurement. The army thus obtained 90 percent of the officer candidates by selecting the top 1.7 percent of the enlisted men of each unit within the division as determined by a new scientific rating scale. The other 10 percent were chosen from college Reserve Officer Training Corps (ROTC) units in the area. Unlike the first camps, none of the would-be officers came directly from civilian life. The new training schools yielded only 11,657 officers in April 1918, all of them commissioned as second lieutenants.

The movement of divisions to France, escalating manpower needs, the declining educational qualifications of officer candidates, and pressure from the MTCA soon prompted a return to Plattsburg methods. Throughout the war, the MTCA insisted on four principal points: that commissions should come only after a prescribed training course and observation by regular officers; that candidates should be recruited from civilian life as well as from the ranks; that training should occur in advance of the mobilization of draftees; and that planning should be sufficient to provide for a maximum force. Plattsburg organizer Grenville Clark, now a colonel in the Adjutant General's Office, was instrumental in formulating policy regarding officers. Beginning in June 1918, the division schools were replaced by Central Officers' Training Schools, with capacities ranging from 1,000 to 5,000 trainees: five infantry schools at various sites around the country; a cavalry school at Leon Springs, Texas; a machine gunners' school at Camp Hancock, Georgia; and a school for field artillery at Camp Zachary Taylor, Kentucky. The four-month (later reduced to three) course of instruction was continuous, with classes graduating and new classes added at monthly intervals. As with the first two series of officer camps, the new schools were open to civilians, and the MTCA assisted in recruiting qualified applicants. The army's most ambitious plan, announced in late October, called for a new infantry school at Camp Fremont, California, open to civilians, with a capacity of 20,000 trainees, and with the course of instruction reduced to two months. The war ended before the camp opened.

The Armistice also cut short another notable experiment in officer procurement, the Students' Army Training Corps (SATC). With Clark chairing the planning committee, the War Department established the SATC in August 1918, comprising some 135,000 students in 518 of the nation's colleges and universities. To provide the necessary instructors, special camps that summer at Plattsburg, Fort Sheridan, and the Presidio offered selected students, faculty, and civilian volunteers a crash program in military education. In essence, institutions of higher education became army posts. All able-bodied students over eighteen were placed on active duty, with housing, uniforms, pay, and subsistence provided by the government through the colleges. Admission to the SATC remained the responsibility of the various colleges until October 1, after which time the War Department's Committee of Education and Special Training would select replacements from young men already in the National Army training centers. Students remained in school to follow a course of instruction organized to provide officer candidates according to the needs of the various services and then be subject to transfer when-

ever and wherever the army needed them. Its organizers optimistically envisaged the SATC as a "genuine national university—the university of Uncle Sam, in which every boy had an opportunity with every other boy to render his utmost service to the nation." Before the war ended, some 8,000 students had been transferred to the appropriate officers' schools. The War Department estimated that at least 20 percent of all future officer candidates would have been drawn from the SATC.

In contrast to earlier American wars, general officers (except for the National Guard) were not appointed from among civilian and political elites but were nominated through the Regular Army by committees of the General Staff, approved by the President, and confirmed by Congress. By replacing the volunteer system with conscription in 1917—indeed, Theodore Roosevelt's request to raise a division of "Rough Riders" helped to persuade President Wilson that selective service was the proper military format—the country no longer needed "political generals" to stimulate enlistments and inspire citizen soldiers. Only at the junior-officer level did voluntarism still predominate in World War I.

Notwithstanding the obvious military success achieved in World War I, the system of officer procurement did not receive universal approbation. Because the army that fought at the Argonne and Belleau Wood was raised primarily through the draft, the criticism arose, not without foundation, that officers of the AEF were drawn almost exclusively from the upper classes. These aristocratic officers may have been patriotic volunteers, but many owed their initial appointments to the officers' camps to personal connections. Because so many Plattsburg officers later graduated to high positions in financial and government circles—most notably, Henry L. Stimson, Robert P. Patterson, William J. Donovan, John J. McCloy, and Lewis Douglas—it has even been argued that they constituted a nascent "power elite" that always advocated martial solutions and an imperialist foreign policy. It should be noted, however, that future secretaries of war Stimson and Patterson served as officers in New York City's 77th Division and always believed that their shared military bond with immigrant Americans in the so-called Melting Pot Division exemplified "the national idea carried into practice." West Point graduates also resented the many temporary officers who remained in the

Regular Army after the war and delayed promotions in the 1920s and 1930s.

Whatever the merits of such criticism, the War Department made a special effort between the world wars to build up the country's reserve officer personnel through the National Guard, ROTC, Officers' Reserve Corps, and Citizens' Military Training Camps. When World War II came, the General Staff refused to accept potential officers directly from civilian life, insisting that the only avenue to Officer Candidate School should be through the ranks after basic training. This stand was prompted not only by the need to condition future officers physically and psychologically by service on the enlisted level, but also by a determination, in the words of the official historians, "to substitute a competitive and democratic system of procurement for the rather haphazard selection of young officers from a social and intellectual elite which had appeared necessary, for lack of a better means, in World War I." Even Secretary Stimson, whose military service in 1917–1918 marked a high point in his distinguished public career, reluctantly concluded that the Officer Candidate Schools of World War II represented "the fair and democratic war." When it had been needed, however, the Plattsburg system worked well.

J. Garry Clifford

See also PLATTSBURG MOVEMENT

Bibliography
Clifford, J. Garry. *The Citizen Soldier: The Plattsburg Training Camp Movement, 1913–1920.* Lexington: University of Kentucky Press, 1972.
Finnegan, John P. *Against the Specter of a Dragon.* Westport, CT: Greenwood Press, 1974.

United States Army: Pioneer Infantry Regiments
The advent of trench warfare placed a premium on an army's ability to construct field fortifications—trenches, machine gun emplacements, and bombproof shelters—as well as to maintain roads, bridges, and base facilities. The high losses the British and French armies had suffered among their highly trained engineer troops forced them to organize units of semiskilled men to supplement the engineers and in some less technical tasks to replace them entirely. Since British and French infantry regiments had traditionally contained a pioneer platoon or company to perform light engineering chores, these new units were called "pioneers." In the German army, however, *Pionier* refers to all engineer troops.

After the United States entered the First World War, the War Department sought to create its own pioneer units. Unlike the British and French pioneer battalions which were often assigned to individual divisions, the U.S. Army organized its "pioneer infantry" into regiments and planned to assign them to higher headquarters, such as an army corps or field army. These new pioneer infantry regiments were to be more skilled in simple field construction than the infantry but not as technically sophisticated as the engineers. Furthermore, these regiments were to be fully capable of fighting in the front lines if the situation demanded it. Therefore, their organization was similar to that of a regular infantry regiment with three battalions of four rifle companies each, as well as a headquarters and supply company. Unlike the infantrymen, however, the pioneers lacked a machine gun company and a 37-mm cannon section. Instead, the pioneers enjoyed an increased allotment of basic tools, such as axes, picks, and shovels. At full strength, a pioneer infantry regiment contained 3,351 officers and men as compared to 3,832 officers and men in an infantry regiment.

The War Department formed seven pioneer infantry regiments at Camp Wadsworth, South Carolina, and another at Camp Dix, New Jersey, in January 1918. The manpower for these regiments came from men made surplus by the reorganization of the National Guard the preceding fall. Nevertheless, all of the regiments needed a substantial number of draftees in order to approach their authorized strength. Before the end of the war, the government raised thirty-seven pioneer infantry regiments. White officers and black enlisted men composed twenty of these, while white officers and enlisted men made up the other seventeen.

Shortages of equipment, uniforms, and weapons hindered the schooling of pioneer units throughout the war. Moreover, the constant transfer of trained and semitrained men out of these units and their replacement with untrained men meant that overall instruction was never very advanced. An additional problem was the lack of specific War Department directives on the types of missions the pioneers were to perform. Therefore, frustrated commanders focused their training on basic infantry skills and physical fitness in the hope that more detailed information and instruction would be available in France.

In June 1918, the first pioneer infantry regiment joined Gen. John J. Pershing's American Expeditionary Force (AEF) in France, and over the next four months another twenty-five regiments followed. Despite their officers' hopes for further training, Pershing's headquarters put most of these regiments to work immediately. Although intended for use in the combat zone, Pershing assigned several regiments to the Service of Supply (S.O.S.), the AEF's logistical organization. Indeed, over 16,000 pioneers were laboring in the S.O.S. by the war's end. Split into work details ranging in size from a few men to a battalion, the pioneers built warehouses and transit camps, built and maintained railroad rights-of-way and pipelines, and repaired roads and bridges. Additionally, these men often formed labor parties to work in the Service of Supply's numerous ordnance and quartermaster depots. On these backbreaking details, pioneers loaded and unloaded ships and rail cars, shuttled supplies within the depots, and salvaged broken and discarded war materiel.

Pioneer infantry regiments assigned to army corps and field armies also found themselves routinely split into a number of work details and assigned to a wide variety of missions. Road repair predominated, but pioneers at the front also erected camouflage screens, built barbed-wire entanglements, repaired buildings, scoured the battlefields for salvageable equipment, and collected and guarded captured munitions and supplies. Additionally, they often had the grisly job of burying the dead. Unlike their comrades in the S.O.S., however, the pioneers generally worked close to the fighting and often came under fire. In fact, some companies briefly served on the front lines as combat troops.

The experience of the 1st Pioneer Infantry Regiment during the Meuse-Argonne offensive was typical for a pioneer regiment in the combat zone. Assigned to the U.S. Army's III Corps, the regiment provided platoon-sized detachments to accompany each of the corps' three assault divisions as well as the tank brigade supporting them. Another company went to supplement the engineer regiment responsible for clearing the German obstacles in the corps' path. The remainder of the regiment divided into two columns and followed the corps forward.

During the advance, the regiment periodically dropped off companies to repair the shell-torn muddy roads. German shell fire claimed a growing list of casualties among the pioneers, but the important road work continued. Within a few days, the regiment was scattered in company-sized work parties all along the roads in the corps area. Nevertheless, the corps headquarters continued to call on the pioneers to provide detachments for the frontline divisions. It also placed other demands on the pioneers by detaching companies for salvage work and guard duty. And, as the road repair crisis lessened, five of the regiment's companies shifted to railroad repair work.

Following the Armistice, the pioneer infantry regiments continued to perform many of these same duties, especially those with the S.O.S. Almost immediately, however, the Army began shipping home and disbanding units. By the end of November 1919, all of the pioneer infantry regiments had been demobilized.

Richard Kehrberg

Bibliography
Bliss, Paul S. *Victory. History of the 805th Pioneer Infantry Regiment, American Expeditionary Force.* Minneapolis: Augsburg, 1919.
Davis, Chester W. *The Story of the First Pioneer Infantry, U.S.A.* Utica, NY: Kirkland Press, 1917.
Thisted, Moses N. *Pershing's Pioneer Infantry of World War I.* Hemet, CA: Alphabet Printers, 1982.

United States Army: Service of Supply

The Service of Supply (S.O.S.) was the final name accorded the units involved in transportation, supply, service, and repair operations in the rear areas of the American Expeditionary Force (AEF). The boundaries of the Service of Supply ran from France's Atlantic and later Mediterranean ports almost to the front.

Tactical and logistical considerations led the French to assign the Americans to the St. Mihiel sector of the Western Front. Since the first year of the war, that sector had been relatively quiet, thus its choice afforded the untested Americans a chance to assemble and train their units in relative quiet. The English monopolized the English Channel ports, an arrangement that permitted them the shortest lines of communications from their home bases to their sector of

U

the front in northwest France and Belgium. With Paris perilously close to the front, the French naturally controlled that sector, reserving for themselves the enormous Paris rail hub. The Americans could not join the front in any of these areas without disrupting or taxing existing arrangements. On the other hand, men and supplies could move from seaports on the west coast of France to the northeastern front near Toul via the rail network that ran south of Paris.

The few words outlining organization for operations overseas contained in *Field Service Regulations*, the army's guide on how to conduct war, called for establishing a zone of the interior (essentially the United States) and a theater of operations, the latter being subdivided into a zone of operations and a zone of the line of communications. The line of communications contained three zones. The base zone received and stored supplies and equipment, while the advanced zone straddled the forward area of the line of communications and the rear of the zone of operations. Owing to the distance between the advanced and the base zones, and a determination to attain a ninety-day stock of all classes of supply and equipment, largely dictated by the concern over the German submarine threat, Pershing established an intermediate zone between the rear and advanced zones.

The Line of Communications, headquartered at Paris and initially commanded by BGen. R.M. Blatchford, began operations in August 1917. Blatchford proved unequal to the task, and at the end of November, MajGen. Francis Kernan took over. In January 1918, Kernan moved his headquarters to the city of Tours. He had hardly settled in when Pershing ordered sweeping organizational changes based on recommendations from a commission led by Col. Johnson Hagood, Line of Communications chief of staff. In February, Pershing sent all but the coordinating staff sections (G-1, G-2, etc.) from his staff at Chaumont to Tours. Prior to this reorganization, the efforts of Kernan's and Pershing's staffs often duplicated one another, adding confusion and delay to every transaction. This transfer brought all supply and service functions under the control and responsibility of the commander of the Line of Communications. The one exception was rail transportation, a condition later rectified. In addition, the Line of Communications was redesignated the Service of the Rear and later the Service of Supply. Pershing's General Headquar-

ters now provided quantities, locations, and arrival times to the S.O.S. commander; it was up to him how to accomplish these tasks.

Pershing decided to purchase not only what was unavailable in America, but anything that could be bought in Europe, for such buying freed shipping critically short owing to the submarine campaign. Prominent businessman (and later vice president) Charles G. Dawes was placed in charge of this program. The AEF actually purchased more supplies and equipment (10 of 18 million tons) in Europe than it shipped from the United States. Nonetheless, men and much of their equipment had to come from the United States.

The French initially provided three major ports for permanent American use: St. Nazaire, La Pallice, and Bassens (Bordeaux). St. Nazaire became the AEF's main port for receipt of supplies and returning wounded to the United States. La Pallice was the primary fuel center. Smaller ports were later added, and Brest became the major port for debarkation of troops. La Havre was used for U.S. troops arriving via England. Later, use of Marseilles and Toulon eased port crowding, while coal purchased from England came through the Channel ports. Eventually, the base zone of the S.O.S. had nine sectors, including one in England, each centered on a major port such as Bordeaux, St. Nazaire, La Pallice, Brest, etc.

Each sector within the base zone received and stored all classes of supply. Schools, hospitals, and repair facilities likewise were located in base sectors. From the base sectors, materiel moved to the intermediate zone, whose headquarters was located at Nevers. The intermediate zone's largest depot was at Gievres where 20,000 men ran an enormous complex containing virtually every category of supply and repair facility needed by the AEF. In the advanced zone, smaller depots fed supplies to troops stationed within the zone as well as to the vital regulating points. Here trainloads of all categories of supplies for the divisions engaged in combat and training were formed and sent forward to each division's railhead. A division required twenty-five boxcar loads of supplies daily. Repair facilities, personnel replacement centers, and hospitals dominated the advanced zone.

By the summer of 1918, troops and supplies began pouring into France. The United States buildup finally had reached its stride, and alarmed by the German successes in the spring, the English had provided extra shipping. American forces began arriving at a rate of 10,000 per day. The ports quickly became flooded, and mountains of supplies threatened to block further reception. Turn-around time for shipping (United States to France to United States) was 72 days. The inefficiencies of the convoy system did cause some of the delay, but Pershing wanted to instill a sense of urgency throughout the S.O.S. He replaced General Kernan at the end of July with MajGen. James G. Harbord, the former AEF chief of staff, then commanding the 2d Division. An additional consideration factored into this decision. Word of the congestion in the ports had reached Washington, and Army Chief of Staff Peyton C. March suggested sending Gen. William W. Goethals of Panama Canal fame to France as S.O.S. commander. Goethals, however, would be responsible to the War Department with authority equal to Pershing's. The AEF commander would have none of this, and his transfer of the able Harbord resolved this problem. Harbord revitalized the S.O.S. by establishing interport and interdepot competition with a promise that the best units would be the first home after the armistice. Efficiency rose, and in spite of ruthless "combing" of the S.O.S. for replacements during the St. Mihiel and Meuse-Argonne offensives, S.O.S. troops pushed supplies forward.

Transportation became the Achilles heel of the AEF. At first, it was shipping; there was not enough. As the submarine threat declined, the problem shifted to rail and motor transport. French lines and rolling stock were worn out, and motor transport was critically short. The United States shipped over large amounts of rolling stock and vehicles, but at the war's end, motor transport units only had 50 percent of their authorized vehicles, being short some 55,000 vehicles.

At its peak, soldiers assigned to the S.O.S. numbered 552,000, representing virtually all fields of support, supply, and service. The operating units, generally organized as companies, came under battalions or regiments as appropriate and finally under service or staff corps, the latter regarded as an independent branch. Under the S.O.S. were the following: Quartermaster Corps (84,000); Medical Corps (65,000); Engineer Corps (114,000); Ordnance Department (7,000); Signal Corps (4,000); Air Service (56,000); Engineer Corps (114,000); Motor Transport Corps (44,000); Transportation Corps (65,000); Chemical Warfare Service (2,000); Military Police Corps (7,000), and the Army Service Corps (104,000). For the most part, the senior officers in the S.O.S. came from the Regular Army. In a very few instances, specialists from industry were given appropriate rank and placed in charge of technical operations. For example, William W. Atterbury of the Pennsylvania Railroad and William Wilgus of the New York Central ran the army's rail network in France, while financier Charles Dawes headed the AEF's purchasing board. Atterbury and Dawes held temporary commissions as brigadier generals.

With the Armistice, the S.O.S. faced the task of returning to the United States the 2 million Americans serving in the theater along with their equipment and supplies and disposing of the numerous installations built in France. Thousands of contracts were canceled or curtailed. The U.S. Liquidation Commission handled the financial and accounting aspects, selling most supplies and equipment abroad, but the S.O.S. had to move soldiers and unit equipment back to the United States, not completing its functions until August 1919.

Michael J. McCarthy

Bibliography

Harbord, James G. *The American Army in France, 1917–1919*. Boston: Little, Brown, 1936.

Hagood, Johnson. *The Service of Supply. A Memoir of the Great War*. Boston: Houghton Mifflin, 1927.

Pershing, John J. *My Experiences in the World War*. New York: Stokes, 1931.

U.S. War Department. *United States Army in the World War, 1917–1919: Organization of the American Expeditionary Force*. Washington, DC: Government Printing Office, 1948.

United States Army: Signal Corps

Although poorly organized, trained, and equipped at the beginning, the Signal Corps met the challenges of World War I. During the conflict, Chief Signal Officer MajGen. George Owen Squier's office expanded from a staff of 124 to 3,547 people. The Corps' Land Section grew from 55 officers and 1,570 enlisted men to 2,712 officers and 53,277 men. At the beginning of the war, the Aviation Section included 52 officers and 1,100 men. By the time the section was removed from the Signal Corps on

May 20, 1918, it had grown to 16,084 officers and 147,932 men. When the Armistice was signed, the corps' American Expeditionary Force (AEF) comprised fifty field signal battalions and nineteen service companies totaling 1,452 officers and 33,038 enlisted men.

To train the sudden and ongoing influx of signalmen, training and mobilization camps were established in 1917 at Camp Alfred Vail, New Jersey, at Camp Samuel F.B. Morse, Fort Leavenworth, Kansas, and at Monterey, California. Special schools followed, such as the Signal Corps Radio School at College Park, Maryland, and the Signal Corps Buzzer School at Fort Leavenworth. In addition, special technical courses, radio communications courses, and classes in topics such as telephony, telegraphy, photography, and meteorology were offered at civilian colleges and technical schools. By the end of the war, more than 2,400 soldiers had graduated from these courses and some 3,300 were in training.

World War I was a trench war fought at close range, making visual signaling of limited use in the combat zone. Field wireless sets were inadequate. The open spark-gap radio and the crystal receiver could not be fine tuned in the transmission-glutted combat zone. As a result, Col. Edgar Russel, chief signal officer of the AEF, was forced to install and operate a network of telegraph and telephone wires. The Signal Corps had until July 1919 to complete this massive wire system extending from the seacoast to the American battle zone. The corps constructed a total of 2,000 miles of pole lines using 28,000 miles of wire and 32,000 miles of French poles; installed about 40,000 miles of combat lines; leased 22,000 miles of French wire; and established 134 permanent telegraph offices and two 273 telephone exchanges, excluding combat zone stations. Multiplex printing telegraph equipment linked Tours, Chaumont, Paris, and London.

While laying the extensive telegraph and telephone network, the Signal Corps experimented with radio. Before America entered the war, radio transmission for the most part was limited to Morse code, either by means of spark transmitters, which were heavy and cumbersome, or by continuous wave oscillations generated by triode tubes. When the United States entered the war, the Signal Corps provided two types of field radios. They were large high-powered quenched-spark transmitters. The SCR-49 pack radio set could be disassembled into several components and transported by two or three army mules. The SCR-50 was an even larger motor truck or tractor set. In combat since 1914, the European Allies were replacing their spark equipment with radiotelegraph equipment using tubes. The radiotelegraph transmitted in dots and dashes.

Some in the Signal Corps were convinced, even before the United States entered the war, that tubes were the key to superior military radio. Among them were Major General Squier, whose doctorate was in electrical engineering. As chief signal officer, Squier led the Signal Corps in cooperating with the communications industry to perfect radio tubes. Six months after the military radio tube program began, American factories were producing standardized, interchangeable, and rugged tubes. Striving for even better equipment, Squier established a major laboratory at Camp Alfred Vail and increased the corps' radio program from a few personnel (including radio pioneer LtCol. Joseph O. Mauborgne) in 1917 to several hundred by 1918. This research and development effort reached across the ocean in the form of the Signal Corps' Research and Inspection Division, AEF. In 1917, the Signal Corps developed small aircraft radiotelephones. These voice- or telephone-operated sets were freed from the limitations of telegraph. Two early sets were the SCR-68, an airborne radiotelephone, and the ground set, the SCR-67. By the middle of 1918, these sets were in France. Although not without their problems, the new American voice radios marked a revolution in radio communications.

The Signal Corps' earlier work in the development of aviation also paid significant dividends during World War I. Beginning with first Chief Signal Officer Albert J. Myer's abortive attempt to transport an observation balloon to the first battle of Manassas, during the Civil War, the Signal Corps' experimentation continued off and on in the years leading up to the Great War.

Chief Signal Officer Adolphus Greely formed a balloon section in 1892 with the first balloon appropriately named the *General Myer* in honor of the Signal Corps' founder. Early zeal waned. By the Spanish-American War the corps had only one balloon, which was used in the attack on San Juan Hill. Balloon activity was almost static until the branch purchased a new balloon in 1907. A year later, Chief Signal Officer BGen. James Allen directed the establishment of a balloon house and hydrogen plant at Fort Omaha, Nebraska, but once again ballooning activities became almost dormant.

Although the United States entered World War I with the army possessing only a total of five balloons (three functional and two captive), two balloon companies were in operation by mid-1918. That number had increased by Armistice Day to eighty-nine companies. However, it was the advent of the airplane that diminished the usefulness of balloons as well as the dirigible.

The Signal Corps' adventures with airplanes reached historic proportions when Chief Signal Officer Allen introduced them to the army. After the army awarded a contract to construct its first dirigible in 1907, an Aeronautical Division, led by Capt. Charles deForest Chandler, was established within the office of the chief signal officer. In December, the Signal Corps called for bids on a military airplane. On Dec. 23, 1907, Allen issued Specification No. 486 and called for bids for a flying machine with a speed of forty miles per hour capable of carrying two people a distance of 125 miles. It had to be managed in flight from any direction, stay aloft for a one-hour endurance demonstration, and land at the takeoff point undamaged. It must be easily disassembled and transportable. Although the army received forty-one bids by Feb. 1, 1908, only three met the specifications. Of those three, the Wright brothers' bid was the only one under which an airplane was delivered. On Feb. 10, 1908, the Wright brothers and the government entered a formal contract that provided for the delivery of "One (1) heavier-than-air flying machine, in accordance with Specification No. 486." The date scheduled for delivery of the machine at Fort Meyer was August 1908.

On Aug. 20, 1908, Orville Wright delivered the plane. The army's review board consisted of Majs. George O. Squier and Charles S. Wallace and Lts. Frank Lahm, Benjamin D. Foulois, and Thomas E. Selfridge. Test flights began on September 3 and continued successfully until tragedy struck. On September 17, Lieutenant Selfridge became the first airplane crash fatality. Flights were not resumed until June 1909.

The Wrights made minor modifications to their 1909 flyer. After more test flights, the official tests began on July 27. On that day, Orville Wright flew for one hour and twelve minutes, thereby fulfilling the endurance specifications.

On July 30, the speed requirement was surpassed. Three days later, on August 2, the army accepted the Wrights' airplane at a cost of $30,000, designating it Signal Corps No. 1. The Signal Corps retained control of the army's military aircraft until the Air Service was created on May 20, 1918. In World War I, the army deployed thirty-nine air squadrons in combat.

World War I developments in radio included the master-oscillator power amplifier circuit (MOPA), and Capt. E.H. Armstrong's superheterodyne circuit. The latter came too late for use in World War I but made a pivotal contribution to radio in the postwar period.

The Signal Corps expanded into other areas. On the orders of Gen. John J. Pershing, Colonel Russel established four new organizations within the corps' Land Section. They were combat photography, pigeons, meteorology, and radio intelligence. Although photography had been a Signal Corps responsibility since 1881, Pershing's orders made both ground and aerial photography an official mission. Ground photography, comprised of still and motion pictures, was assigned to the corps in August 1917, and Pershing's directive for combat motion pictures was a first. Aerial photography was of paramount importance to the Intelligence Service. A total of 54 officers and 418 enlisted men constituted the photographic personnel in France. Following the war, all aerial photography and ground photography relating to aviation activities were transferred to the Air Corps. The Signal Corps' remaining function was to maintain the historical files of still and motion pictures, produce training films, and manage ground photography not already under another service's control.

The Pigeon Service's main mission was to create and maintain a frontline communications system. By November 1917, two detachments of pigeoneers were in France. Pigeons were used in several engagements, including the St. Mihiel and Meuse-Argonne offensives. During the later campaign, the pigeon Cher Ami earned the Distinguished Service Cross by delivering a message to the 77th Division concerning the location of the "Lost Battalion." Pigeons successfully delivered some 95 percent of the messages assigned them. After World War I, the Pigeon Service was demobilized, but it remained a unit of the Signal Corps until dissolved in 1957.

The Meteorological Service, established with training and equipment assistance from the U.S. Weather Bureau, was responsible for providing meteorological and aerological support for aviation representatives of the Coast Artillery, Ordnance Proving Grounds, Gas Warfare Service, and the AEF. Maj. W.R. Blair, a former member of the Weather Bureau, traveled to France in September 1917 to organize the AEF Meteorological Service. In May 1918, the first American meteorological station was established in France. By October, twenty-two stations were operating. Among other activities, they supported aviation and artillery training stations, combat units, railway guns, a French Army corps, propaganda ballooning, and depots. Frontline stations transmitted radio reports of weather conditions opportune for gas attacks and supplied information critical to aerial and artillery warfare. The service also provided weather information to the U.S. Navy. The AEF Meteorological Service was the first to "apply the laws of dynamics of gases to upper-air data with the objective of serious forecasting." By the war's end, the AEF Meteorological Service was unequaled in providing military meteorological assistance. Many signalmen were relocated to the Air Corps. However, the Signal Corps continued providing for the development, procurement, supply, and maintenance of the meteorological equipment.

The Radio Intelligence Service was responsible for locating enemy transmitters, monitoring Allied transmissions, intercepting and decoding enemy transmissions, and breaking the enemy's codes.

The number of casualties suffered by signalmen was second only to those of the Infantry. Among the citations earned by Signal Corps members were fifty-five Distinguished Service Crosses and forty Distinguished Service Medals in addition to numerous foreign decorations. Pershing commended the Signal Corps when he remarked, "I desire to congratulate the officers and men of the Signal Corps in France and their work, which stands out as one of the great accomplishments of the American Expeditionary Force."

Carol E. Stokes and *Katherine R. Coker*

Bibliography

Clark, Paul Wilson. "Major General George Owen Squier." PhD. dissertation, Case Western University, 1974.

Marshall, Mac L. *The Story of the U.S. Signal Corps.* New York: Franklin Watts, Inc., 1965.

U.S. Air Force. *The U.S. Air Service in World War I.* Vol. 1. Washington, DC: Office of Air Force History, 1978.

U.S. Army. *Historical Sketch of the Signal Corps (1860–1941).* Fort Monmouth, NJ: Eastern Signal Corps Schools, 1942.

U.S. Army. Signal Corps. *Annual Report of the Chief Signal Officer.* Washington, DC: Government Printing Office, 1919.

United States Army: Tank Corps

The Tank Corps was created in the autumn of 1917 when Gen. John J. Pershing, responding to recommendations by members of his American Expeditionary Force (AEF) staff who had studied the employment of tanks by the British and French armies on the Western Front, directed that a separate Tank Corps be organized for the AEF.

In what might now be considered a prophetic move, the AEF headquarters commandant, Capt. George S. Patton, Jr. (whose name became synonymous with mobile mechanized warfare a generation later) was ordered to report to Langres on Nov. 10, 1917, to establish a light tank school. Patton thus became the first soldier in the American army formally assigned to duty with tanks.

The Tank Corps became a functional (at least on paper) part of the AEF on Dec. 22, 1917, when Col. Samuel D. Rockenbach, a cavalry officer who had been detailed to the Quartermaster Corps to help set up the AEF supply base at the port of St. Nazaire, reported to general headquarters to assume command of the AEF's armored arm.

During the first half of 1918, AEF Tank Corps officers busied themselves with recruiting and training tank crewmen for the First Army. Two light tank battalions, the 326th and 327th, were created at Patton's light tank school, and the 301st Tank Battalion was organized at Camp Meade, Maryland, and shipped from the United States to the British Tank School at Bovington, England, to train with Mark IV and V heavy tanks.

Many of the officers and men who joined the first light tank companies were recruited from AEF coast and field artillery units. They were to be equipped with American-made copies of the French Renault Car FT six-ton vehicle. 1st Lt. Elgin Braine, who had helped Patton establish the light tank school, was sent back to the United States in February 1918 to serve as the AEF Tank Corps' liaison with the War Department's Engineering Bureau to ensure the project moved smoothly.

Unfortunately, even after Col. Ira C. Welborn's appointment on March 5 as director of the Tank Corps in the United States, the light tank production program became bogged down in bureaucratic minutiae and political infighting within the armaments industry. Instead of waves of light tanks pouring out of American factories, only a dozen U.S. M1917 6.5-ton light tanks reached France before the Armistice. Poor Braine, unable to communicate directly with his superiors in France, spent a frustrating nine months before wangling his way back overseas.

Efforts to obtain heavy tanks were just as frustrating. The Allies entered into an agreement to produce a jointly designed and manufactured vehicle called the Mark VIII Liberty tank. The British agreed to provide armor plate, structural members, track shoes, guns and mounts, and ammunition. The Americans would provide automotive parts and twelve-cylinder Liberty aircraft engines. A huge assembly plant, in which 1,500 of the behemoths were to be built, was constructed at Neuvy-Pailloux. But the U.S. Army Air Service was siphoning off Liberty engines—considered one of the best aircraft powerplants produced up to that time—as fast as they came off the assembly lines. Furthermore, it was decided that a number of modifications were needed to adapt the engine for use in tanks. After nearly a year of delays, the British and French opted out of the program and Pershing was forced to terminate it on Nov. 27, 1918—more than two weeks after the Armistice—without a single vehicle to show for it.

Blissfully unaware of the burgeoning production problems in the United States, Rockenbach and his AEF tank officers set about preparing their crews for battle—the light tankers in Bourg using twenty-five Renault tanks borrowed from the French and the heavy tankers at the Royal Tank Corps' training center in England.

Once the ranks of Patton's two light tank battalions in France had been filled, the responsibility for recruiting and training additional tank battalions was given to Colonel Welborn in the United States. The plan called for building a corps consisting of ten heavy and twenty light tank battalions to support AEF operations in France by 1919.

One of the chief architects of this ambitious force was a young infantry captain,

Dwight D. Eisenhower, who so impressed Colonel Welborn with his organizational skills while helping the 301st Tank Battalion deploy to England, that the Tank Corps' stateside commander ordered Eisenhower to Gettysburg, Pennsylvania, with a force of 200 men to establish a tank training center. By the time the war ended, Eisenhower was a lieutenant colonel running a major installation with more than 10,000 officers and men under his command.

After the German Army had spent itself in a series of brutal assaults all along the Western Front in the spring of 1918, Allied planners developed a plan for a coordinated offensive set to kick off in late September. The American First Army was assigned the difficult terrain between the Meuse River and the French Fourth Army on the west side of the Argonne Forest.

In late July Pershing asked for and received permission to commit the First Army to battle in the lightly held St. Mihiel salient two weeks before the main offensive. Still without tanks, Rockenbach, by then a brigadier general, pleaded with the French and British for sufficient vehicles to outfit his three tank battalions. The French readily agreed, promising 144 Renaults for Patton's two light tank battalions, but the British were less generous. The Royal Tank Corps' leaders finally decided they could spare 47 of the 35-ton behemoths for the 301st Tank Battalion—but only if they were employed in support of the U.S. II Corps, which was operating under British Fourth Army control in the St. Quentin region. Pershing and Rockenbach reluctantly agreed.

This decision left Lieutenant Colonel Patton and his 1st Tank Brigade in a doctrinal quandary, however. How could he support the entire First Army with just two light tank battalions? Once again, the French willingly provided the solution: in addition to the 144 light tanks to be manned by Patton's two battalions, the French would send the XI Groupement with two Groupes (the equivalent of companies) of Schneider and Saint Chamond assault artillery vehicles to serve in the heavy tank role. The French also agreed to send the entire 1st Assault Artillery Brigade—consisting of the IV Groupement, with two more Groupes of Schneiders and Saint Chamonds, and the 505th Assault Artillery Regiment, with three battalions of Renaults.

This shot in the arm meant the First Army would go into battle with a force of 419 tanks in support of its two assaulting corps. To handle this sudden wealth of tanks and men, Rockenbach ordered LtCol. Daniel D. Pullen, the Tank Corps chief of staff, to create the 3d Tank Brigade headquarters to serve as liaison between I Corps and the French tankers. Patton and his 1st Tank Brigade would support the IV Corps attack.

At H-hour on Sept. 12, 1918, the first American-led and -manned tanks rolled into action. They battled little more than mud and fuel shortages, however, as the Germans had already begun withdrawing from their positions. Spurred on by the aggressive Patton, the tanks pushed far ahead of the infantry they were supposed to be supporting, especially the 1st Division sector, where elements of Maj. Sereno E. Brett's 326th Tank Battalion found themselves operating behind German lines in the vicinity of Jonville in the early afternoon on September 14.

Tank Corps casualties were light at St. Mihiel, most of them occurring on the first day of the offensive. Patton's battalions suffered four officers wounded, five enlisted men killed, and fifteen wounded. The attached French units lost five officers to wounds, six enlisted men killed, and twenty-three wounded. Patton's brigade lost only three tanks—all to artillery fire.

Following the St. Mihiel offensive the entire First Army shifted to the Meuse-Argonne sector. All of the tanks, with the exception of fifteen Renaults from the 327th Tank Battalion left behind to conduct a demonstration near Pont-à-Mousson, were moved by rail to the new First Army zone.

Patton's 1st Brigade, with the recently redesignated 344th and 345th Tank battalions (which had been the 326th and 327th, respectively), was assigned to support I Corps in the Aire River valley. Pullen's 3d Brigade headquarters again served as liaison for the French tankers, who were tasked with supporting V Corps on the First Army's right. Their force was augmented by the addition of the French 17th Light Tank Battalion, giving the 505th Regiment a total of four Renault-equipped battalions.

The German defenses in the Meuse-Argonne sector employed all of the tactical innovations developed by the German Army in 1917 in a massive belt five layers deep. The offensive, set to kick off the series of coordinated Allied assaults all along the Western Front on September 26, promised to be every bit as difficult as the St. Mihiel affair had been easy.

Bitter fighting raged throughout the remainder of the month before the First Army was forced to stop and regroup for a renewed assault on the so-called Hindenburg Line on October 4. Colonel Patton, seriously wounded less than half a day into the operation, had imbued his troops with an indomitable sense of duty and an aggressive spirit that permeated not only the officer ranks, but the entire organization. Furthermore, the experience gained at St. Mihiel and from training sessions conducted jointly right up to the eve of the Meuse-Argonne offensive led to excellent tank-infantry cooperation during the assault.

But success did not come cheaply. As the First Army prepared to renew the offensive on the morning of October 4, General Rockenbach could report that only half of the 1st Brigade's tanks were operational. Casualties of the fleet were nearly as bad, with 53 percent of the brigade's officers and 25 percent of its enlisted men either killed or wounded. The situation was nearly as grim in the French tank units supporting V Corps.

The second assault quickly ran out of steam as exhausted First Army troops made a dent in, but failed to crack, the vaunted Hindenburg Line. It was a good thing for the tank crews in the 1st Brigade that it did, for their tanks, which had been operating steadily for more than a month, were in terrible condition. By the morning of October 6, had the operation continued in force, the entire brigade could have mustered only seventeen operational vehicles. Despite their best efforts, mechanics were unable to keep pace, and the number of operative tanks in the 1st Brigade dropped to just eight by October 7. No 1st Brigade tanks participated in operations from October 8–10 as maintenance crews worked around the clock to get as many vehicles as possible back into the fight.

By the night of October 10, forty-eight tanks were reported operational. A call for a platoon of five tanks to support an attack by the 82d Division's 164th Brigade the following morning led to twenty-three vehicles being dispatched in order to ensure the required five survived the trek from Varennes to Fleville. The plan failed, however, as only four reached the front line—two of which broke down shortly after the attack began.

That operation was the last for the 1st Brigade's two light tank battalions, although the brigade continued to be represented by a provisional company left behind to support I Corps operations until replacements from Bourg could be brought forward. The French tankers supporting V Corps were withdrawn on October 10 after a week of disappointing results.

When the First Army went over the top on October 14, only ten of the twenty-four tanks Major Brett had sent forward the night before to join the 42d Division were able to participate in the attack, Pershing's last as an army commander. The AEF commander, realizing his force had grown to a size too large for one field commander, ordered the creation of the Second Army on October 12, and passed the First Army guidon to LtGen. Hunter Liggett. Liggett, determined to crack the Hindenburg Line once and for all, asked for and got a two-week breather for his troops. During that period elements of the rejuvenated 3d Tank Brigade, including the newly arrived 331st Light and 306th Heavy Tank battalions and a rested 345th Tank Battalion, began moving into place. They were unable to complete the relief of the 1st Provisional Tank Company, as Brett's remaining force was known, before the final phase of the campaign began.

All up and down the line, First Army doughboys charged forward on the morning of Nov. 1, 1918. The only tanks supporting them were fifteen Renaults in the 2d Division sector. The division secured its first objective within four hours. Of the fifteen tanks that started out with it, only four were still operational—the remainder succumbing to mechanical failure or "ditching," and these were placed at the disposal of the marine regiment commander for the rest of the day.

Unlike on the first day of the campaign more than a month before, this time the troops took most of their objectives. So stunning was their success that the Germans were forced into a general withdrawal to the Meuse River. The speed of the advance picked up so quickly that even trucks had a hard time keeping up. The war-weary Renaults remained behind, marking the end of Tank Corps' participation in the campaign.

The casualty toll in the 1st Brigade during the Meuse-Argonne offensive was three officers and sixteen enlisted men killed and twenty-one officers and 131 enlisted men wounded. Vehicle losses amounted to more than 123 percent. The fact that mechanics were able continually to recover, repair, and return tanks to action at the rate they did reflects well on their efforts. In all, eighteen tanks were destroyed by German fire.

On November 6, the AEF Tank Corps' brigades were designated to bring them in line with the system in use in the United States. The 1st Brigade became the 304th, the 3d became the 306th, and the newly organized 2d and 4th Brigades became the 305th and 307th respectively.

The only other Tank Corps unit to see action was the 301st Tank Battalion, commanded by Maj. Ralph I. Sasse. The 301st supported the U.S. II Corps' 27th and 30th divisions in the British Fourth Army assault on the Hindenburg Line in the vicinity of the St. Quentin Canal beginning on September 29. The men of the 301st battled the enemy and mechanical problems heroically until they were pulled from the line on October 23 in the vicinity of the Sambre Canal.

Like their light tank counterparts in the First Army sector, the heavy tankers acquitted themselves well. And, just as it had been in the Meuse-Argonne, the cost was high: four officers and twenty enlisted men killed, eighteen officers and ninety-one enlisted men wounded, and seven enlisted men missing. Twenty-seven of the battalion's forty-seven Mark IV and V heavy tanks were destroyed by enemy fire or mines.

Two Medals of Honor were awarded to Tank Corps soldiers—both Renault crewmen in Patton's brigade—as were thirty-nine Distinguished Service Crosses, a British Distinguished Service Order, eight British Military Crosses, nine British Military Medals, six British Distinguished Conduct Medals, two British Meritorious Service Medals, and four British Distinguished Service Cards.

In the wake of the Armistice, several Tank Corps battalions participated in the occupation of Germany before being returned to the United States in 1919. As with other branches, the size of the Tank Corps, which had grown to 1,235 officers and 18,977 enlisted men, was drastically reduced in the immediate postwar period. Stateside tank training centers were closed down and all of the tankers remaining on active duty were consolidated at Camp Meade, Maryland.

By the spring of 1920, it was clear that the doctrinal debate over how best to use tanks had been lost by Tank Corps officers, who had sought the status of a separate combat arm. The corps was formally disbanded after passage of the National Defense Act of 1920, which assigned all tank units to the infantry—where they would remain until the creation of the Armored Force in 1940.

Dale E. Wilson

See also PATTON, GEORGE SMITH, JR.; ROCKENBACH, SAMUEL DICKERSON; TANKS

Bibliography

Blumenson, Martin, ed. *The Patton Papers, 1885–1940.* Boston: Houghton Mifflin, 1972.

Coffman, Edward M. *The War to End All Wars: The American Military Experience in World War I.* New York: Oxford University Press, 1968.

Nenninger, Timothy K. "The Tank Corps Reorganized." *Armor* (March–April 1969).

Rogge, Robert E. "The 304th Tank Brigade: Its Formation and First Two Actions." *Armor* (July–August 1988).

Wilson, Dale E. *Treat 'Em Rough! The Birth of American Armor, 1917–1920.* Novato, CA: Presidio Press, 1989.

United States Army: Training

Prior to World War I, the *Infantry Drill Regulations* (IDR) covered most of what there was to know about training from the school of the soldier to the regiment. Linear warfare concepts dominated the drill, and only after 1911 was there a conscious move away from considerations of the effects of black-powder weapons on combat.

Training management also existed in outline only. When a soldier was recruited, he went to a recruit depot, where he was examined physically, given a uniform, and sent off to his unit. Training in the units was left up to the faithful noncommissioned officers. Only after the Spanish-American War and the Philippine Insurrection did recruit depots begin training soldiers before shipping them out.

Training tended to be fragmented, haphazard, and incomplete unless someone like Col. James Parker, U.S. Cavalry, and a premier trainer, took a direct interest in it. But even Parker's efforts were personalized and essentially without reference to higher guidance. Thus, as the United States Army approached its first major modern war, its training system continued to reflect the needs of a minor power with an internal foe.

There had been so little thought given to preparations for American participation in the war in France that while no draftees reported for training before September 1917, the training system was unready even then. The problem really began at the top. The chief of staff was nominally responsible for training and acted through a committee of the Army War College Division of the War Department General Staff. Actually, department commanders were officially charged with training responsibilities in which they were aided by the Inspector General's Office. Prewar training was conducted in two phases, six months of garrison training and six months of field training. For a few years, the Regular Army had conducted summer maneuvers with the National Guards of the various states, but for the most part the Guard remained ill-trained.

When the United States entered the war, only one plan for training the expanded army existed and that was an Army War College memorandum dated Feb. 3, 1917, which recommended gathering all the Regular Army and National Guard forces together to become the training base for whatever expeditionary force was required. The study recognized that even this approach would strain the existing army. The memorandum also contained the recommendation that each new division be formed on a base of some 900 Regular Army soldiers, but it failed to address in detail how this concept would limit the total number of divisions that could be raised.

That limited plan aside, President Woodrow Wilson was prevailed upon to send at least one token unit to France as quickly as possible after the United States entered the war. That unit was the 1st Infantry Division (provisional) consisting of a collection of units selected by General Pershing and raised to full strength with large numbers of recruits. In another variation, the 2d Infantry Division was raised by combining two army infantry regiments with two Marine Corps regiments cobbled together from Marine Corps units from around the globe.

The War Department, on April 14, 1917, published the *Manual for Noncommissioned Officers and Privates of Infantry of the Army of the United States, 1917,* which, while an excellent supplement to the standard IDR, failed to recognize the realities of fighting in France. Like the IDR, it did not address the problems of barbed-wire entanglements fifty yards deep, covered by dozens of machine guns and backed by hundreds of indirect fire artillery pieces, observed from balloons and airplanes. Almost all American training literature reflected the experiences of the Civil War or the Indian wars. The chaos of modern combat, even though faithfully reported by numerous sources, seemed beyond institutional comprehension.

In order to give some direction to the commanders of the newly formed divisions, on Aug. 27, 1917, the War Department published War Department Directive No. 656, *Infantry Training* (WDD 656). This document was intended to be the guiding directive for all training in the United States. It prescribed a sixteen-week course and emphasized the necessity for trench-warfare training, which included conduct of the attack from entrenched positions. It laid heavy emphasis on the traditional qualities of American soldiers, especially individual marksmanship. WDD 656 included the new skills demanded by modern warfare: grenades, gas, camouflage, entrenching, liaison, trench mortars, and automatic weapons of several varieties. It was an adequate document for the moment. In addition, the department published a large number of French and British documents addressing aspects of military operations in France. While all of these documents were "for information," the absence of American publications on some of the subjects gave the foreign documents some weight. Toward the middle of 1918, a new provisional Infantry Training Document was circulated for comment. One perceptive response was a plea to the War Department to state simply which existing documents were authoritative and which were not. There was an evident lack of authoritative direction of the training process.

Several issues made a training program based upon WDD 656 a problem. The first was that the structure of the infantry company did not initially provide for the new weapons systems. Then, once the company strength was raised from 150 to 250 men, partly to accommodate the inclusion of these weapons, the training plans gave no guidance as to how the company was to work together as a new unit. This deficiency was compensated for in part by the detail of numerous foreign officer specialists assigned to the American training camps to act as instructors. While this was an adequate stopgap, it quickly became apparent that each instructor taught his own national or unit system—again offering no standardization. Then came the greatest shock.

In December 1917, General Pershing read WDD 656 and vehemently objected to its trench-warfare focus. In its place he demanded strict emphasis on open-warfare training and insisted that that be the sole object of instruction in the United States. In March 1918, training in the United States shifted gears to accommodate General Pershing's demands, although exactly what was meant by open warfare was never defined.

Once in France, General Pershing devised his own training scheme. Under this plan, units arriving in France would undergo a three-phase program. For the first month, they would be tutored in the techniques of the war in France by an Allied unit, at least until enough Americans had learned those skills and could instruct their own. The second phase would see battalions and brigades fed into quiet sectors of the line under the command of senior Allied headquarters. The third phase would see entire American divisions in the line under Allied command. After this phased approach was completed and problems resolved, it was Pershing's objective eventually to field an entire American Army.

While the different styles of warfare noted above were difficult to resolve, other factors interposed themselves to further vitiate training effectiveness. In the United States, each division was responsible for the entirety of its training and expected to accomplish it within sixteen weeks. In reality, some units spent an entire year in training, although it seldom equaled a year of training.

There was never enough equipment to allow all the soldiers to handle or fire all the weapons with which they would have to fight. Each division had to create its own specialist schools and do so with its own resources. The cadres for these schools may have mastered their skills, but seldom had they learned others. Because there were so many new specialties, men with apparent aptitude were arbitrarily detailed to these schools. Mother Nature added to the man-made difficulties as thousands of men from around the country were brought together in close quarters and stressful conditions during the terrible winter of 1917–1918. At some of the northern camps, the weather was so severe that soldiers had to spend days digging out; then when the spring thaw arrived, the camps sank into muddy immobility. In addition, there were occasional epidemics, some of such severity as to bring training to a halt. The worst case was in the 1918 Spanish Influenza epidemic, which halted almost all training in the United States.

Personnel management practices were the most serious detriment to training. As units neared their departure date, reassignments were made to bring them up to full strength. In many cases the losses suffered in training, from sickness, to special skill reassignments, to earlier drafts and countless other causes amounted to 30 percent of the combat units. The result was that other units would be raided for replacements, often gutting relatively well-trained units and requiring them to begin again. Possibly the worst single case was the 86th Infantry Division, which saw 187,000 soldiers pass through its gates before it deployed. Obviously, training under these conditions was uneven or nonexistent and General Pershing began to rail about its inadequacy.

Upon arriving in France, Pershing realized that he would be required to create his own infrastructure and immediately demanded that thousands of men be shipped to perform the tasks of building port, rail, storage, and communications facilities. This task gave birth to an entire new command, the Service of Supply (S.O.S.), and drained off thousands of men in early stages of training.

In addition to facilities, General Pershing created an entire school system for staff and commanders in France. This step gave rise to a demand that units send forward one-third of their officers and noncommissioned officers early enough to attend the AEF schools and be ready to meet their units upon arrival. This demand was never met. However, the practice developed that when a unit arrived in France, many of its key personnel were immediately detached to attend the schools. It did not matter that the unit might have to enter combat before the schools were completed.

While the AEF school system was developing, American units were trained by the Allies. The British, in particular, had developed a thorough system of schools. These schools, as opposed to those of the French, laid heavy emphasis upon practical exercises. These were more congenial to the American way of training than French schools, which contained a high proportion of theoretical work that most Americans found boring and useless.

One of Pershing's principles was that accurate rifle fire and the bayonet would determine which infantry ultimately won the battle. Because firing ranges were scarce in France, he wanted every infantryman to arrive in France fully schooled in marksmanship and musketry (the controlled fire of many individuals against selected targets under the centralized control of the commander). Investigations by the newly created staff section for training, G-5, inspected arriving units to determine their levels of proficiency and were often appalled to find that only 30 percent of the soldiers had fired their weapons beyond the first few stages of the individual marksmanship course. Few officers understood what musketry was all about in the first place, and it appeared questionable whether it had any place at all in trench warfare. It was not unusual for American units training with the British to give up their Springfields for British Enfields, some to receive their Springfields back when reassigned to the American Army. All machine gun and artillery training was on Allied weapons, and the same held for airplanes and mortars.

At the root of the U.S. Army's problems in training was the absence of time. There had not been enough time to think through a system that had to be radically different from what had served before, and there was an inability to think on the scale required by the war. Not even Pershing was able to grasp the immensity of the task at hand or realize the speed with which events could change.

One example of these problems was the provision of replacements. As noted, divisions were initially expected to train themselves. Only after Gen. Peyton C. March was installed as chief of staff in March 1918 was coherent thought given to training centers for replacements. And at March's insistence combat-disqualified draftees were sent to development battalions to be trained for one of the thousands of noncombat duties. March also made successful efforts to maximize the contribution of the many non-English speaking draftees who dutifully reported to the induction stations. Many of them learned rudimentary English and contributed in various ways. One soldier, a German-speaking noncitizen, spent his time in France in an AEF intelligence platoon, much of the time between the lines, for which he was awarded several Silver Stars, Purple Hearts, and a Distinguished Service Medal.

American soldiers went to France in varying states of preparedness. Throughout, their training was uncoordinated, based on inadequate information, repeatedly disrupted by thoughtless personnel management practices and a lack of careful planning and forethought. The training they received in France from the Allies was enough to make them effective. Then, as the German spring offensives of 1918 crashed upon the Allies, every available soldier was rushed into combat to stem the tide. Once the German effort was halted, the Allies immediately went over to the offensive themselves, and the demand for manpower accelerated. By the end of the war, American soldiers were being sent into combat with little more than three weeks' training, some with more, many with less.

American soldiers did, indeed, turn the tide of the war, but they did so more by virtue of their valor and impetuous drive to get the job done than by their training.

James Victory

See also PREPAREDNESS

Bibliography

Pershing, John J. *My Experiences in the World War.* New York, 1931.
Coffman, Edward M. *The War to End All Wars: The American Military Experience in World War I.* New York: Oxford University Press, 1968.
Kreidberg, Marvin A., and Merton G. Henry. *History of Military Mobilization in the United States Army, 1775–1945.* Washington, DC: Department of the Army, 1955.
U.S. War Department. *U.S. Army in the World War, 1917–1919.* Washington, DC: Government Printing Office, 1948.

United States Army Uniforms

Experiences in the first years of the twentieth century had shown the United States Army that it was impractical to maintain the dark blue uniform it had worn since the American Revolution while campaigning in the field. In 1902, the army adopted a field service uniform, which was issued starting in 1903. It consisted of a khaki cotton sack coat and breeches for the summer and warmer climates and an olive drab woolen coat and breeches for more temperate weather. This basic pattern was slightly revised over the years, and on August 15, 1917, the War Department issued Special Regulations No. 42 describing the uniform worn in Europe by the American Expeditionary Force (AEF).

The officers' uniform consisted of a visored garrison or service cap in khaki with a broad leather visor and chin strap and a light khaki mohair braid cap band. The emblem worn with this was a bronze American eagle taken from the Great Seal of the United States. Officers also wore the felt campaign hat with its distinctive Montana peak. A hat cord of braided gold bullion was worn around the hat by general officers; officers below general rank wore one of gold bullion and black silk intertwined. As this hat was found too cumbersome to be worn in the field, it was replaced in France with the overseas cap, which was a soft side cap that would fold flat (the name, "overseas cap," was derived from the fact that it initially was only issued to those troops who landed in Europe). The edge of the officers cap was piped in the color of the arm of service to which the officer belonged. Insignia of rank was worn on the left front of the cap.

The coat worn by officers was a single-breasted sack coat slightly tapered at the waist with a stand collar that was closed with a hook and eye. The body of the coat was held closed with five bronzed buttons bearing the seal of the United States. The coat had four patch pockets with pointed flaps held closed by small buttons of the same pattern as the larger coat buttons. There were also pointed shoulder straps. These fastened at the base of the collar with a small button. Insignia of rank was worn on the shoulder straps above where the sleeve joined to the body. A one-half-inch-wide khaki (black for the General Staff Corps) mohair braid was worn around each sleeve, three inches from the end of the sleeve. Matching breeches were worn with brown boots. These were either riding style or front-lacing high boots or were ankle boots with leather or canvas leggings or spiral-wrapped cloth puttees. Bronzed metal letters "U.S." and insignia showing the arm of service were worn on each side of the coat collar.

Officers were issued khaki shirts with detachable collars, as well as the enlisted pullover shirt with attached collar. The uniform of the enlisted men was of the same general pattern; however, the wool was a rougher texture. The enlisted garrison cap lacked the mohair braid band, and the insignia was a bronzed disk with the eagle superimposed in the center. The hat band for the enlisted campaign hat was made of worsted wool in colors of the arm of service of the individual's unit. Enlisted overseas caps did not have the piping, and they had a small bronze disk with the letters "U.S." on the left front.

The enlisted coat was of the same cut as that of the officers but less tailored. It used the same buttons but lacked the mohair braid around the sleeve. Worsted rank chevrons were worn on both sleeves above the elbow; on the right collar a bronze disk with the letters "U.S." was worn, while on the left collar another disk with the symbol of the arm of service was worn. Enlisted men also wore breeches, cavalry troops having a double-thick reinforced area in the seat and inside the thighs. All enlisted men were issued brown ankle boots and wore either canvas leggings or wool spiral-wrapped puttees. They were issued a khaki wool pullover shirt with a three-button placket and double thick elbow patches. The shirt had an attached collar.

Both officers and enlisted men were issued overcoats. They were double-breasted with a stand-and-fall collar, two slash pockets, and a belted back, which could be loosened or tightened to accommodate the soldier. The enlisted model had two rows of four bronze buttons, while the officer model had horn buttons. Officer rank was indicated by a series of Hungarian knots on the sleeve cuffs; enlisted men wore rank chevrons on the sleeves above the elbow.

Officers could purchase the gabardine trenchcoat for inclement weather, but enlisted men were issued a raincoat made from waterproof canvas with wide stand-or-fall collar and overshoe-type buckles. There were also short mackinaw-style wool jackets that were used by drivers and a winter hat made from wool-lined canvas that resembled a traditional hunter's hat with a visor and fold-down ear flaps. A variety of knitted items completed the cold weather wear. Gloves and wrist warmers, knitted watch caps and balaclava helmets, and sleeveless pullover sweaters were all sanctioned by the AEF and either issued or made by the country's many patriotic groups and sent to soldiers.

While in the trenches, U.S. troops adopted a British item to take the place of the bulky overcoat. In the winter of 1914–1915, British troops had been issued leather and fur sleeveless jerkins. These kept the body warm without restricting movement. The Americans also adopted this practice and issued brown leather and green wool jerkins to mounted troops, military police, and tankers. They also found their way to the frontline trenches. The jerkin was sleeveless, collarless, and closed by four bone or horn buttons. It was cut loose to be worn over the uniform coat and came to about the hips or mid-thigh. The leather jerkin was lined with blanket wool.

Another innovation borrowed from the British was the rubber thigh-high "trench waders." The glutinous mud of the trenches would suck the boots off the feet of the soldiers after heavy rains or the spring thaw. These high boots were seen as a way to combat this loss and to keep feet dry, thus reducing casualties from trench foot. Made from black vulcanized rubber, they resembled a fisherman's wading boots. Troops issued with these had to be checked constantly since the boots did not allow any moisture to escape from the feet and they could, on their own, create as many problems as they were purported to solve.

The majority of American troops were equipped with the British-style "Brodie's Pattern of 1916" shrapnel helmet. This was a steel helmet that resembled a medieval helmet or, as was more commonly thought, a barber's wash basin. It had a suspension of leather straps with a felt pad at the crown and an oilcloth sweatband. The black troops of the U.S. 92d and 93d divisions (who were attached to the French Army for the duration of the war) wore the French 1915 Adrian pattern helmet. More traditional in shape, it had a deep body with a small raised crest along the top that allowed a minimum of ventilation; small visors in the front and back provided some shade and relief from the rain. The helmet had a suspension of leather pads and straps to secure it to the wearer's head.

There were several controversies regarding uniforms during World War I. Perhaps the largest and most bitter fight was over the adoption of the Sam Browne belt for officers and its unauthorized use by members of auxiliary organizations such as the Salvation Army. It was seen, by AEF GHQ, to represent a badge of commissioned rank and was not to be worn by those not holding a commission.

Another problem involved the inclusion of the 5th and 6th Marine regiments as the 4th (Marine) Brigade of the U.S. Army 2d Division. The marine uniform differed from that worn by the army. It was made from a dark forest-green wool with two box-pleated breast pockets and two bellows pockets in the skirts of the coat. It had an ornamental point on each cuff. The collar and shoulder straps were similar to the army coat; however, no insignia was worn on the collar. Likewise, the marines wore the campaign hat, but with a Marine Corps globe-and-anchor insignia on the front and no hat cords. The buttons on the coat depicted an eagle perched atop an anchor beneath thirteen stars. In an effort to present a uniform appearance of a single American army, the marines were ordered to wear the army pattern uniform with collar insignia of the globe and anchor. This decision was universally despised by the marines, who strove whenever possible to maintain their identity by keeping their uniform instead of the more common army one. Their fight was largely unsuccessful.

When the AEF went to France, it took with it a number of civilian field clerks, chauffeurs, and messengers who worked for the army but were not enlisted personnel. As early as May 23, 1917, General Pershing, in a letter to the adjutant general of the army, pointed out the need to uniform these personnel so that they would look like part of the AEF. He recommended that they be issued with the uniform of a private with bronze disks with the letters "U.S." on each side of the collar and a white brassard to be worn on the left arm, halfway between the shoulder and elbow. They would be issued a campaign hat but would not wear any hat cord. On arrival in France, they would adopt the overseas cap as well. These uniforms were to be issued to the civilians at cost by the quartermasters at embarkation depots.

The issue of insignia for different divisions within the AEF arose in 1918 when, following the example of the British Army, which had adopted formation signs in 1916, the 81st Division began to wear the silhouette of a Carolina wildcat. Initially, AEF GHQ opposed this idea of seeming to fragment the American force, but by late October 1918, GHQ authorized each division to adopt and wear a distinctive insignia on the left shoulder of the uniform coat and overcoat. In July 1918, insignia were created to signify length of service, whether that service was overseas or not, and if an individual had been wounded. Service was shown by an inverted gold chevron worn on the cuff of the left sleeve for each six months' service in the theater of operations. A blue chevron was for service of less than six months, and a silver chevron was for six months service in the United States. A gold inverted chevron on the right cuff of the coat indicated a wound received in action with the enemy.

By the time of the Armistice, the American army had taken on a unified appearance. Regimental pride was expressed in the battle honors that were represented by divisional insignia, and personal service was noted on each man's coat. The "rookies" who had answered Pershing's call were now seen not as civilian soldiers, but as a battle-tested army. Following the close of hostilities, the army moved to change and modernize the uniform, which would forever symbolize the "doughboy" of the AEF.

Michael J. Knapp

Bibliography

Mollo, Andrew, and Pierre Turner. *Army Uniforms of World War I.* New York: Arco, 1977.

Schulz, Paul, Hayes Otoupalik, and Dennis Gordon. *World War One Collectors Handbook.* 2 vols. Missoula, MT: GOS, 1977.

U.S. War Department. *Special Regulations No. 42, Specifications for the Uniform of the United States Army.* Washington, DC: Government Printing Office, 1917.

United States Coast Guard

The United States Coast Guard, a service consisting of some 4,300 officers and men who manned twenty-one seagoing cutters as well as numerous small craft of various types and shore stations, was transferred from the Treasury Department to the Navy Department when the United States declared war on April 6, 1917. This transfer was mandated by the legislation enacted on Jan. 28, 1915, which had created the Coast Guard by merging the Revenue Cutter Service and the Life Saving Service. Naval and Coast Guard officers considered the smaller service's role in wartime soon afterward, concluding that most of the larger cutters would be useful for patrol and mine laying or sweeping in coastal waters, while the personnel of lifesaving stations might serve as coast watchers and armed guards at coastal radio stations.

When war was declared, cutters and their personnel reported to the naval districts in which they were located. Most personnel and units were assigned to port security or coastal patrol, although some more traditional Coast Guard functions, such as the Bering Sea Patrol, were continued.

The Coast Guard Commandant, Capt. Ellsworth P. Bertholf, had hoped that his service's ships would continue to be manned entirely by Coast Guard personnel, but within a short time cutters found themselves performing an unanticipated function, that of training naval personnel. At first, these were officers of the Naval Reserve Force; later some enlisted men were assigned as well. In August 1917 the U.S. Navy's Bureau of Navigation asked that Coast Guard officers be ordered to yachts being converted for antisubmarine duty, and by the war's end, many were serving in a number of small combat vessels, transports, and auxiliary craft of the navy, both abroad and in home waters.

The Coast Guard also contributed to the navy's aviation endeavors. The small service's involvement in aviation had begun soon after its founding in 1915, and by April 1917, six officers and nine warrant officers had completed aviation training at the navy's Pensacola flight school. Nine more were in training, but the demands of war prevented further assignments to Pensacola. The Coast Guard aviators served at naval air stations in the United States, at least one commanding an air station, that at Chatham, Massachusetts.

The decision to adopt a system of convoys in European seas during the summer of 1917 led to orders to prepare six of the Coast Guard's larger cutters for distant service. These ranged in size and age from the 205-foot *Manning* (1897) and *Algonquin* (1898) to the 165-foot *Ossipee*, which had been commissioned in 1915. The largest and oldest vessels were also the fastest, being capable of about sixteen knots, while the 204-foot derelict destroyer *Seneca* (1908) was the slowest at eleven knots. The 191-foot *Yamacraw* (1909) could steam at thirteen knots, while the 190-foot *Tampa* (1912) and the *Ossipee* were rated at twelve knots. All had batteries of 3-inch guns and depth charges.

Whether in naval vessels or in cutters, the Coast Guardsmen ordered to the war zone experienced relatively little action. The six cutters fitted for distant service composed the Second Squadron of the Atlantic Fleet Patrol Force's Sixth Division. They were based at Gibraltar, and while some occasionally escorted vessels in the western Mediterranean Sea, they served mainly with slow convoys plying between Gibraltar and Great Britain, usually putting in at Milford Haven on the coast of Wales at the termination of the passage north. Officially, these were seven-and-one-half-knot convoys; in fact, many of the cargo ships—badly in need of overhaul—could make no more than six knots, limiting the convoys in which they sailed to that speed.

Except in the "danger zone" at either end of the passage, a cutter was the sole escort. It provided a radio link with the British Admiralty and was responsible for keeping stragglers closed up and would-be attackers at a distance. It was monotonous, arduous duty, with the threat of submarine attack ever present in clear weather—all of the cutters except the *Algonquin* reported evading torpedoes at least once, while those in the *Ossipee* and the *Seneca* thought that they had been torpedo targets on five occasions each. During periods of low visibility, the danger of collision was equally threatening.

None of the cutters sank a submarine; indeed, the *U-58* fatally damaged by the destroyers *Fanning* and *Nicholson*, was the only confirmed kill by American warships. The *Seneca*, however, gained notice by rescuing the eighty-one survivors of the British sloop *Cowslip*, torpedoed off Gibraltar in April 1918, and twenty-seven survivors from the freighter *Queen*, sunk two months later. The cutter's attempted salvage of the torpedo-damaged British collier *Wellington* in September 1918, ended in failure, with the loss of eleven Coast Guardsmen and five members of the collier's company. The *Tampa*, torpedoed and sunk with all hands in the Bristol Channel on Sept. 26, 1918, was the Coast Guard's only loss, although the larger cutters *McCulloch* and *Mohawk* were sunk in separate collisions in home waters in 1917.

Coast Guardsmen were also employed in port security and captain of the port activities, in which, if not strictly military in nature, were nevertheless of paramount importance to the war effort. A single example may illustrate this. Hundreds of munitions-laden vessels sailed from New York during the war, one of which, the French freighter *Mont Blanc*, collided with the Norwegian steamer *Imo* at Halifax, Nova Scotia, on Dec. 6, 1917. The ensuing explosion resulted in thousands of casualties and millions of dollars worth of property damage ashore. Such an occurrence in the much more congested environs of New York would have had an even more catastrophic result. Due in large part to the Coast Guard's regulation of the handling of explosive cargoes and ship movements, New York and other harbors in the United States escaped such disasters.

More than half of the Coast Guard's personnel were veterans of the former Life Saving Service. Most of these remained at their stations, rendering assistance to endangered persons and vessels on a scale quite comparable to that of peacetime. While these distress cases generally could be attributed to traditional causes—weather, accidents, and carelessness—a few resulted from the war, most notably the sinking of the *Mirlo*. This British tanker was steaming northward off North Carolina's Outer Banks when it struck a mine or was torpedoed during the afternoon of Aug. 16, 1918. The explosion alerted those at the Chicomacomico Coast Guard Station, where Keeper John A. Midgett and his crew launched a power surfboat, with some difficulty because of surf conditions. During the next six hours, the Midgetts (all but one of Keeper Midgett's boat crew were named Midgett) rescued forty-two of the *Mirlo*'s men; ten were lost. Their feat was the more remarkable because their surfboat had to brave smoke, floating wreckage, burning gas and oil to pick up a number of the survivors. Indeed, the *Mirlo* rescue would come to rank among the Coast Guard's proudest achievements.

Four of the five cutters serving in European waters returned to the United States in December 1918. The *Seneca* remained to assist various salvage operations. It steamed into New York harbor on July 1, 1919, marking the end of the Coast Guard's involvement in World War I. The service itself was returned to Treasury Department control by executive order on Aug. 28, 1919.

The Coast Guard's role in World War I seems unimpressive at first sight. None of its personnel participated in a major battle, and relatively few were involved in a military action against an enemy. Instead, they served in a variety of support functions, a number of which were undoubtedly important. Nor was the cost inconsiderable; with the possible exception of the collier *Cyclops*, which disappeared without a trace after leaving Barbados in March 1918, the 111 Coast Guardsmen and 4 U.S. Navy sailors lost in the *Tampa* constituted the U.S. Navy's greatest single personnel loss caused by enemy action.

Robert E. Johnson

Bibliography

Bell, Kensil. *"Always Ready!": The Story of the United States Coast Guard*. New York: Dodd, Mead, 1943.

Brown, Riley. *The Story of the Coast Guard: Men, Wind, and Sea*. Garden City, NY: Blue Ribbon Books, 1943.

Johnson, Robert E. "The Fifth Armed Force." *Naval History* (Spring 1990).

——. *Guardians of the Sea: History of the United States Coast Guard, 1915 to Present*. Annapolis, MD: Naval Institute Press, 1987.

Wheeler, William J. "Reminiscences of World War Convoy Work." *U.S. Naval Institute Proceedings* (May 1929).

United States Food Administration

The purpose of the United States Food Administration (USFA), established shortly after the April 6, 1917, declaration of war, was to increase food production, reduce domestic consumption, minimize war profiteering in food, and create a surplus from which to feed the European Allies. The Allies, whose normal sources of imported food from the eastern countries of Europe as well as Russia were disrupted, faced serious shortages. To head the new administration, President Wilson appointed Herbert Hoover, who had organized and directed the Commission for Relief in Belgium. Hoover quickly went to work in early May and surprised the experts by opposing both price-fixing and rationing schemes that were already commonplace in Europe. "Although Americans can be led to make great sacrifices, they do not like to be driven," he insisted. Twenty million Americans voluntarily agreed to comply with the USFA pledge: "Go back to simple food, simple clothes, simple pleasure. Pray hard, work hard, sleep hard, and play hard. Do it all courageously and cheerfully. We have a victory to win." Hoover and his top staff refused to take a salary for war work and disdained organizational charts. They insisted on a temporary and independent agency with broad powers but without any mandate to perpetuate bureaucracy after the end of the war.

A public relations campaign was organized immediately. Volunteer directors were appointed at the state and county levels. Libraries provided scientific information on nutrition and food conservation, and large numbers of women were recruited to coordinate the effort. Their slogan "Food will win the war" was widely respected. Official sanction from Congress was somewhat slower, and only in August, with the passage of the Lever Food Control Act, was the USFA properly funded and officially authorized. Hoover then set up a Grain Corporation and a Sugar Equalization Board to control these key commodities. Increasing the supply of pork at reasonable prices was also a key concern. A variety of price guarantees, taxes on excess profits, licensing schemes, and endless volunteer conferences to set prices managed the nation's supply of food and held speculation to a minimum. Hoover was able to enforce conservation and boost production without resorting to dictatorial powers. He did secure an agreement from the attorney general to waive antitrust actions against the USFA for the duration of the war. This combination of tactics enabled him to take such bold steps as purchasing the entire 1918 Cuban sugar harvest. He also directed massive shipments to Europe.

Balancing supply and demand in wartime conditions could be harrowing. Farmers were encouraged to increase production in 1918 in case war continued into the following year. With the Armistice, Hoover had to ensure that Europeans purchased American food rather than looking to other markets. In all, the USFA handled about $7 billion worth of transactions and made a substantial difference in the fighting strength of the British and French. Hoover calculated that administrative overhead to the dollar and came up with a surprisingly low figure of $7,862,669.

Elena Danielson

See also HOOVER, HERBERT CLARK; SUGAR EQUALIZATION BOARD

Bibliography

Burner, David. *Herbert Hoover: A Public Life*. New York: Atheneum, 1984.
Hoover, Herbert. *An American Epic*. 4 vols. Chicago: Regnery, 1959–1964.
———. *Memoirs of Herbert Hoover*. New York: Macmillan, 1951–1952.
Nash, George. *The Life of Herbert Hoover*. 2 vols. New York: Norton, 1983, 1988.
Smith, Richard N. *An Uncommon Man: The Triumph of Herbert Hoover*. New York: Simon & Schuster, 1984.

United States Fuel Administration

President Woodrow Wilson created the United States Fuel Administration on Aug. 23, 1917, to mobilize production and distribution of coal and oil in the furtherance of the war effort. Wilson appointed Harry A. Garfield, son of President James A. Garfield and president of Williams College, to direct the new agency. In the executive order establishing the administration, the President charged it with five functions. First, it was to encourage maximum production of fuels to exceed peacetime levels. Second, it was to restrict consumption by industries and by civilians whose activities did not directly contribute to the war effort. Third, it was to encourage voluntary conservation efforts of fuels. Fourth, the Fuel Administration was to regulate the distribution of coal by establishing a zoning system. Finally, the agency had authority to regulate fuel prices so as to curb inflationary pressures and to forestall potential shortages or rampant speculation. Within each region, the agency had the power to fix maximum prices.

Although Garfield had jurisdiction over all fossil fuels, he devoted most of his energies to bituminous coal. A firm believer in voluntary cooperation, his agency spearheaded an effective public relations campaign to persuade Americans to conserve coal. Through personal appeals and publications Garfield impressed millions of people to observe Heatless Thursdays or to skip at least one day a week in burning coal. He also urged them to keep their temperatures low in their homes so as to cut down on national bituminous coal consumption. Under the Lever Act of 1917, in which Congress granted the President virtually unlimited wartime powers, Garfield had the option of using federal sanctions whenever he deemed it necessary. More commonly, he preferred to rely on persuasion and voluntary cooperation, working closely with coal industry trade associations and major trade unions, such as the United Mine Workers of America. When necessary, however, Garfield did not shrink from using his coercive powers. When the nation's railroads became gridlocked in December 1917 and seriously impeded coal deliveries during an especially severe winter, Garfield issued a directive on Jan. 17, 1918, ordering the closing of all bituminous-coal-using industries not essential to the war effort until the railroads could resume normal operations.

But United States entry into the First World War also underscored the new importance of petroleum resources and a growing need for federal controls. By the end of 1917, Garfield became convinced that such supervision was too burdensome for him alone. He persuaded President Wilson to create an Oil Division within his agency and, on Jan. 11, 1918, to appoint Mark Requa, an experienced mining engineer and railroad executive, as its director. Requa was a protégé of Herbert Hoover and shared his belief in the need for government regulation of industry, but with a strong emphasis on joint voluntary cooperation. Given this outlook and the formal authority granted under the Lever Act, Requa worked in close collaboration with various elements in the industry. His direct contact was the Petroleum Industry War Service Committee, an emerging trade association whose members represented different segments in petroleum production and distribution. Its chairman was A.C. Bedford, head of the Standard Oil Company of New Jersey, a man of considerable influence and power. Together with Bedford, Requa established sixteen subcommittees whose members represented different regions in the United States and also different segments of the industry. Among those represented were producers of petroleum and natural gas, refiners, operators of pipelines, tank cars, and ships, and suppliers of oil well drilling equipment.

Once Requa had established an effective administrative network, he set about to implement a wide range of policies designed to increase production and to curb civilian consumption. Soon after assuming his new duties, on Feb. 11, 1918, he issued an order directing all producers on the committees to meet and plan increased production. In directing them to boost their output, he urged them to pool all of their resources and to pay little heed to prewar antitrust regulations. That led the Fuel Administration into conflicts with other federal agencies, especially the Federal Trade Commission, which Congress had established in 1914 specifically to control monopolistic business practices. Requa claimed that the wartime emergency and his authority under the Lever Act gave him primacy. Eventually, he negotiated a compromise with officials at the Federal Trade Commission and the crisis passed, but cooperation rather than trust busting became a primary emphasis of the Fuel Administration's policies.

The Fuel Administration also set prices for the industry. Requa developed specific price schedules in close consultation with the Petroleum War Service Committee. His aim was to limit spiraling prices for many petroleum products and to prevent runaway inflation.

The Fuel Administration elaborated controls over the marketing and distribution of oil and oil products. Requa used his authority to divert deliveries of oil from civilian to military or war-related uses. Sometimes he canceled oil delivery contracts of private individuals or corporations. It was within his powers to close refineries he deemed inefficient and to encourage scientific research designed to increase output. Like Garfield, Requa conducted extensive public relations campaigns. Through speakers and a wide range of publications, he persuaded civilians to conserve oil and prompted producers to adopt more careful conservation practices to eliminate waste.

On June 30, 1919, the Fuel Administration ended its operations. It had achieved considerable success in the attainment of its goals. Not only did coal and oil producers expand production, but the national spirit of cooperation also contributed to improved marketing and distribution. Although the agency went out of existence, it contributed much to greater integration in the coal and petroleum industries in succeeding years. Those who had part in the wartime experience did not forget it in the following decades. The influence of the agency could be discerned in President Coolidge's establishment of the Federal Oil Conservation Board in 1924, in the Oil Code of the National Recovery Administration in 1933, in the Petroleum Administration for War between 1942 and 1945, and the Petroleum Defense Administration during the Korean War. Thus, the U.S. Fuel Administration's impact was far greater than its short period of existence indicated.

Gerald D. Nash

Bibliography
Final Report of the U.S. Fuel Administration. Washington, DC: Government Printing Office, 1921.
Nash, Gerald D. *U.S. Oil Policy, 1890–1964.* Pittsburgh: University of Pittsburgh Press, 1968.

United States Marine Corps: Aviation
Marine Corps aviation had become a separate and distinct branch of naval aviation in 1914. At the outbreak of hostilities in 1917, marine aviation consisted of seven flying officers, forty-eight enlisted man, and four Curtiss-type AH hydroplanes. Recognizing the need for both land- and water-based operations, the Marine

Corps Aeronautic Company, under Capt. Alfred A. Cunningham, was established at the marine barracks of the Philadelphia Navy Yard on April 27, 1917. Due to an expansion in its role, the company split on Oct. 12, 1917, into the First Marine Aeronautic Company, commanded by Capt. Francis T. Evans, and the First Aviation Squadron, commanded by Capt. William M. McIlvain.

On Oct. 14, 1917, the First Marine Aeronautic Company transferred to Cape May, New Jersey, for training in seaplanes and flying boats. On December 7, the company was ordered to Naval Base 13 at Ponta Delgada in the Azores to establish a patrol base in the islands intended both to prohibit German submarines from patrolling that part of the Atlantic and to prevent the Germans from using the Azores as a refueling base for their submarines. The unit departed Philadelphia on Jan. 9, 1918, and arrived at Ponta Delgada on January 21. This unit, equipped with Curtiss R-9, N-9, and HS-2L aircraft, was the first completely equipped American aviation unit to leave the United States for service in the war.

The First Aviation Squadron was transferred to the army training field at Mineola, Long Island, also for land-plane training, on Oct. 17, 1917. On December 31, the unit was again transferred, this time to the army's facility at Gerstner Field at Lake Charles, Louisiana, for advanced training. Three months later the unit moved to the new marine flying field at Miami for further training, and on April 14, 1918, the Marine Aeronautical Detachment and the First Aviation Squadron were merged at Miami to form the 1st Marine Aviation Force, under the command of Captain Cunningham.

On Dec. 25, 1917, the Marine Aeronautical Detachment was formed at the marine barracks in Philadelphia from personnel of the First Aviation Squadron. The new unit was under the command of Capt. Roy S. Geiger. On Feb. 10, 1918, the detachment was sent to Miami to establish a marine flying field for land-plane training.

On June 16, the 1st Marine Aviation Force was split into four squadrons and a headquarters unit. A Squadron was commanded by Captain Geiger; B Squadron was under the command of Captain McIlvain; C Squadron was headed by Capt. Douglas B. Roben; and D Squadron was under the leadership of 1st Lt. Russel A. Presley. These units were to become the Day Wing of the Northern Bombing Group. On July 10, the unit

was destined for foreign expeditionary shore service. Headquarters and Squadrons A, B, and C departed from Miami for New York, where they left on July 18 for France. There the squadrons were assigned to bases at Oye and La Fresne with their headquarters at Bois en Ardes. D Squadron arrived in France on October 5.

Due to a scarcity of aircraft, marine crews rotated with No. 21 Squadron, RAF, flying D.H. 4 aircraft, and No. 218 Squadron, RAF, flying D.H. 9a aircraft. Some of the early missions flown by marine aviators did not involve bombing. On October 1 and 2, Marine Corps crews delivered 2,600 pounds of food and supplies to a French regiment surrounded by German troops near Stadenburg. The first all-marine effort was on October 14, when a morning bombing raid was made on the railway junction at Thielt, Belgium. It was on the return flight that 2d Lt. Ralph Talbot and his gunner, Captain Robinson, each won the Medal of Honor for their actions. The last raid for the unit occurred on Oct. 27, 1918. During the course of its service, the Day Wing of the Northern Bombing Group made fifty-seven raids and dropped 34,000 pounds of bombs.

During World War I, Marine Corps aviation was not limited to operations involving aircraft. The corps' sole Observation Balloon Company was in training at the army school at Fort Omaha, Nebraska, at the time of the cessation of hostilities. If war had continued, this unit would have supported combat marine forces in France.

By the end of the war, Marine Corps aviation ranks numbered 250 officers, 32 warrant officers, and 2,180 enlisted men.

Noel Shirley

Bibliography

Coletta, Paolo E., and Bauer, K. Jack, eds. *United States and Marine Bases, Domestic.* Westport, CT: Greenwood Press, 1985.

———. *United States and Marine Bases, Overseas.* Westport, CT: Greenwood Press, 1985.

Mersky, Peter B. *U.S. Marine Corps Aviation, 1912 to the Present.* Annapolis, MD: Nautical & Aviation Publishing Company of America, 1983.

Van Vleet, Clarke, and William J. Armstrong. *United States Naval Aviation, 1910–1980.* Washington, D.C. Department of the Navy, 1981.

United States Marine Corps: 4th Marine Brigade

Composed of the 5th and 6th Marine regiments and the 6th Machine Gun Battalion, the 4th Marine Brigade was an element of the U.S. Army's 2d Infantry Division. Because the Marine Corps had three other brigades on active service, the corps requested that it be numbered "4th" and retain its marine designation. Since it was one of the two brigades of the 2d Division, this request was approved. However, this created problems when army censors would not permit identification of specific units in press reports from France, But since correspondents could identify the marine brigades, this unit received much publicity, which conveyed an exaggerated sense of the corps' participation and accomplishments in France, leading many army officers to feel slighted. As a result, army personnel developed an animosity toward marines that continued into the Second World War.

The units of the 4th Marine Brigade formed between June and October 1917. Transport to France was piecemeal and was not completed until February 1918. It was detached for service with the U.S. Army's 2d Division. From February to May 1918, the brigade participated in combat training as an entire unit and entered the line near Verdun. It suffered its initial gas casualties on April 12. Between June 3 and 25, the 4th Brigade operated near Belleau Wood in the Château-Thierry area, with major defensive operations on June 3 at Les Mares Farm. On June 6, the 4th Brigade began major offensive operations, capturing Hill 142 and Bouresches. The offensive continued until Belleau Wood was secured on June 25. In mid-July, the 4th Marine Brigade participated in the Soissons offensive, followed by the St. Mihiel offensive between September 12 and 20. From September 27 until October 10, the 2d Division was under the operational command of the French Fourth Army, operating in the Champagne sector. While there, the 4th Brigade was instrumental in capturing Blanc Mont Ridge, north of Somme-Py, a position that controlled the German defenses in the sector and that, in the opinion of the French Army commander, if captured would force the Germans to retreat about nineteen miles.

Between November 1 and 11, the brigade participated in the ongoing Meuse-Argonne offensive, crossing the Meuse River against heavy enemy resistance between Mouzon and Pouilly on the night of November 10 and suffering casualties up to and beyond the official hour of the cease-fire on November 11.

Immediately after the Armistice, the 4th Brigade, as part of the 2d Infantry Division, marched over 200 miles to Germany from France via Belgium and Luxembourg. As a part of the U.S. Third Army, it participated in the occupation of the Rhineland until July 1919. Its duty there was uneventful. It did organize and operate Rhine River patrols. In July, the 4th Brigade began its return to the United States, which was completed in August. As part of the 2d Division, it paraded in New York City on August 8, then moved to Quantico that same day and reverted to the control of the Department of the Navy. On August 12, it participated in a parade in Washington, D.C., with President Woodrow Wilson reviewing it. The next day, the 4th Marine Brigade and its component units were deactivated, with the regulars transferred elsewhere and marines serving only for the duration of the war demobilized.

During World War I, the 4th Marine Brigade had an authorized strength of 258 officers and 8,211 enlisted men. Between March 15 and Nov. 11, 1918, the brigade suffered 11,968 casualties, including 2,292 battle deaths. The French Army cited its regiments three times in general orders for actions at Château-Thierry, Soissons, and Blanc Mont Ridge, while the 6th Machine Gun Battalion was likewise cited for the first two operations, and the brigade itself for Château-Thierry. In 1920, the War Department accepted the award of the French Fourragère in the colors of the Croix de Guerre for the three units of the brigade. Members of the 5th and 6th Marines still wear the French Fourragère when serving with those regiments. Also, on June 30, 1918, in recognition of the brigade's performance at Belleau Wood, the French Army published in its orders the renaming of the wood to the "Bois de la Brigade de Marine," with the new name immediately appearing on its maps.

The brigade had four commanding officers during its war service: BGen. Charles Doyen, USMC; BGen. James G. Harbord, USA; BGen. John A Lejeune, USMC; and BGen. Wendell C. Neville, USMC, plus five interim commanders, all marines.

Donald Bittner

See also Belleau Wood, Battle of; Château-Thierry; Meuse-Argonne Campaign; Soissons; United States Marine

CORPS: 5TH REGIMENT; UNITED STATES MARINE CORPS: 6TH REGIMENT

Bibliography

McClellan, Edwin N. *The United States Marine Corps in the World War*. Washington, DC: U.S. Marine Corps Headquarters, 1920.

Metcalf, Clyde H. *A History of the United States Marine Corps*. New York: Putnam, 1939.

Millett, Allan R. *Semper Fidelis: A History of the United States Marine Corps*. New York: Macmillan, 1980.

Moskin, J. Robert. *The United States Marine Corps Story*. New York: Paddington Press, 1982.

U.S. Army Center of Military History. *Order of Battle of the United States Land Forces in the World War*. Vol. 2, *American Expeditionary Force: Divisions*. Washington, DC: Government Printing Office, 1988.

United States Marine Corps: 5th Marine Brigade

Composed of the 11th and 13th Marine regiments and the 5th Machine Gun Battalion, the 5th Marine Brigade had an authorized strength of 258 officers and 8,211 men and had 2 commanders: BGens. Eli K. Cole and Smedley D. Butler. Raised in the United States at Quantico, Virginia, on Sept. 5, 1918, its elements arrived in France between Sept. 24 and Nov. 9, 1918. Although Marine Commandant George Barnett wanted to raise an all-marine division, Gen. John J. Pershing, commander of the American Expeditionary Force (AEF), opposed this. Hence, the brigade not only did not serve in combat (although individual members did as casualty replacements sent to the 4th Marine Brigade), but its units and personnel, dispersed over many locations, served in the rear area with the Service of Supply (S.O.S.). With the S.O.S., the marines provided valuable support in various capacities, such as security guards, transportation personnel, military police, stevedores, warehousemen, hospital workers, recreation aides, and interpreters. Officers were seconded to various assignments, the most notable being General Butler, who initially commanded the 13th Marine Regiment, and later the 5th Brigade. Butler assumed command of Camp Pontanezen at Brest in October 1918 and re-

tained it until July 1919. His reorganization and ensuing improvements in processing the arrival and departure of personnel were of such significance that he was awarded the Distinguished Service Medal. Butler's predecessor, BGen. Cole, eventually commanded the U.S. Army's 41st Division, a depot unit also titled the 1st Depot Division, at St. Aignan, France, between October 1918 and January 1919.

The 5th Brigade left France and arrived in the United States at the Naval Operating Base, Hampton Road, Virginia, in August 1919 and as an organized entity was disbanded shortly thereafter.

Donald Bittner

Bibliography

McClellan, Edwin N. *The United States Marine Corps in the World War*. Washington, DC: U.S. Marine Corps Headquarters, 1920.

Metcalf, Clyde H. *A History of the United States Marine Corps*. New York: Putnam, 1939.

Millett, Allan R. *Semper Fidelis: A History of the United States Marine Corps*. New York: Macmillan, 1980.

Moskin, J. Robert. *The U.S. Marine Corps Story*. New York: Paddington Press, 1982.

United States Marine Corps: 5th Regiment

One of the two infantry regiments of the 4th Marine Brigade, the 5th Marine Regiment was raised at Philadelphia and Quantico, Virginia, in May and June 1917, with Col. Charles A. Doyen commanding. With a strength of 70 officers and 2,680 enlisted men, its first units departed the United States on June 14. By July 3, the entire regiment was assembled southeast of St. Nazaire, France. Until September it was part of the U.S. Army's 1st Infantry Division. With the arrival of elements of the 6th Marine Regiment in October, a marine brigade was formed, and on October 26, 1917, the 4th Marine Brigade, with its two infantry regiments and the 6th Machine Gun Battalion, became part of the 2d Infantry Division. As such, it participated in training exercises and served in defensive positions until June 1918. From then until the Armistice, the 5th Marine Regiment participated in battle in eight separate sectors: at Verdun, the Aisne defensive, Belleau Wood area operations, the Soissons offensive, near Pont-à-Mousson, the St. Mihiel offensive, operations in Champagne, primarily the assault on Blanc Mont, and the Meuse-Argonne offensive, including the crossing of the Meuse River.

After the Armistice, the regiment moved over 200 miles into Germany for occupation duty. In late July 1919, it left France, returning to the United States on August 3. After parades in New York City and Washington, D.C., the 5th Marine Regiment was deactivated on Aug. 13, 1919.

The French Army cited the regiment three times in its army orders for its achievements in the Château-Thierry sector, the Soissons offensive, and the Meuse-Argonne campaign. The War Department, in January 1920, accepted the award of the French Fourragère in the colors of the ribbon of the Croix de Guerre, and the regiment still carries this honor on its colors. From activation in June 1917 to disbandment in August 1918, the 5th Marine Regiment had six commanding officers: Col. Charles A. Doyen, Col. Logan Feland, Col. Wendell C. Neville, Col. Harold C. Snyder, LtCol. Hiram I. Bearrs, and Maj. Frederic M. Wise.

Donald Bittner

See also BELLEAU WOOD, BATTLE OF; DOYEN, CHARLES AUGUSTUS; UNITED STATES MARINE CORPS: 4TH MARINE BRIGADE

Bibliography

U.S. Marine Corps. *A Brief History of the 5th Marines*. Washington, DC: U.S. Marine Corps Headquarters, 1963.

McClellan, Edwin N. *The United States Marine Corps in the World War*. Washington, DC: U.S. Marine Corps Headquarters, 1920.

Metcalf, Clyde H. *A History of the United States Marine Corps*. New York: Putnam, 1939.

Millett, Allan R. *Semper Fidelis: A History of the United States Marine Corps*. New York: Macmillan, 1980.

United States Marine Corps: 6th Regiment

One of the two infantry regiments of the 4th Marine Brigade, the 6th Marine Regiment was raised on July 11, 1917, at Quantico, Virginia, with Col. Albertus W. Catlin, USMC, commanding. Over half its strength of newly enlisted men were from America's colleges and universities—two-thirds of one company came from the University of Minnesota. But a core of regulars provided the leadership, including two non-commissioned officers already legends in the corps: 1st Sgt. Daniel Daly and Sgt. Maj. John Quick. The 6th Marines deployed to France between Oct. 5, 1917, and Feb. 6, 1918. Early duty there included support activities, such as unloading ships, but then the regiment, now part of the 4th Marine Brigade serving with the U.S. Army 2d Infantry Division, entered the line southeast of Verdun. There, under the tutelage of the French, the marines learned about war on the Western Front. Serving in the trenches until May 9, the regiment suffered casualties from enemy action, and endured a serious German gas attack on April 12. From then until the Armistice, the 6th Marines participated in battle in eight separate sectors: at Verdun, in the Toulon sector; the Aisne defensive, in the Château-Thierry sector; the Belleau Wood area operations in the Château-Thierry sector; the Soissons offensive; action near Pont-à-Mousson on the Moselle River in the Marbache sector; the St. Mihiel offensive; operations in Champagne, primarily the assault on Blanc Mont Ridge; and the Meuse-Argonne offensive, including the crossing of the Meuse River.

After the Armistice, the 6th Marines served as occupation troops in the Rhineland. In late July 1919, the regiment sailed for home from France. After parades in New York City and Washington, D.C., where President Woodrow Wilson reviewed it, the regiment was deactivated on Aug. 13, 1919.

The French Army cited the 6th Marine Regiment three times in its army orders for its achievements in the Château-Thierry sector, the Soissons offensive, and the Meuse-Argonne campaign. The War Department, in January 1920, accepted the award of the French Fourragère in the colors of the ribbon of the Croix de Guerre, and the regiment carries this honor on its colors to this day.

Between July 1917 and August 1919, the 6th Marines had four commanding officers: Col. Albertus W. Catlin, Maj. Frank E. Evans, LtCol. Harry Lee, and Maj. Thomas Holcomb, with Majors Evans and Holcomb essentially interim commanders.

Donald Bittner

See also BELLEAU WOOD, BATTLE OF; CATLIN, ALBERTUS WRIGHT; CHÂTEAU-THIERRY SEC-

TOR; DALY, DANIEL; UNITED STATES MARINE
CORPS: 4TH MARINE BRIGADE

Bibliography

Jones, William K. *A Brief History of the 6th
Marines*. Washington, DC: U.S. Marine
Corps Headquarters, 1987.

McClellan, Edwin N. *The United States Marine Corps in the World War*. Washington, DC: U.S. Marine Corps Headquarters, 1920.

Metcalf, Clyde H. *A History of the United
States Marine Corps*. New York:
Putnam, 1939.

Miller, William M., and John H. Johnstone.
*A Chronology of the United States Ma-
rine Corps, 1775–1934*. Washington,
DC: U.S. Marine Corps Headquarters,
1965.

Millett, Allan R. *Semper Fidelis: A History of
the United States Marine Corps*. New
York: Macmillan, 1980.

United States Naval War College

In 1917, when the United States entered World
War I, the United States Naval War College at
Newport, Rhode Island, was in its fourth decade of providing advanced education to officers of an expanding U.S. Navy. This first military school in the world to be designated a "war
college" could count some 500 graduates—officers serving in responsible assignments, afloat
and ashore. The college had been conceived and
founded by a foremost intellectual of the navy,
RAdm. Stephen B. Luce, as an institution for the
study and research on questions of war and
statesmanship connected with it and the prevention of war. Its opening in October 1884 coincided with approval by Congress of the first
modern steam and steel warships, the "New
Navy."

Luce's "war school" was not readily accepted within the U.S. Navy of the 1880s, and
its future was very much in doubt for the first
decade of summer classes in Newport. Luce was
ordered to sea early in 1886, and Capt. Alfred
Thayer Mahan, who had been chosen by Luce
to teach history, became the school's second
president. His tenure included the publication
of many articles and his most famous book—
*The Influence of Seapower on History, 1660–
1783*. This book speedily attracted worldwide
notice and led to the Naval War College becoming an internationally respected institution.

Both Luce and Mahan, after retirement from
active duty in the navy, remained as lecturers
and enthusiastic supporters of the college until
their deaths during World War I.

The brief and victorious Spanish-American
War in 1898 brought world-power status to the
United States. By this time, four-month courses
convened each summer. Luce, who had been on
duty in the Newport area before the founding
of the college, enthusiastically supported Rhode
Island's large Narragansett Bay as a summer
base for the fleet, believing also that War College students would greatly benefit by proximity of warships and their training operations.
During the administration of President
Theodore Roosevelt, additional requirements
were placed on the college faculty for war planning, designing technical characteristics of new
ships, and organizing conferences for Navy
Department leaders in the cool summer climate
of Newport. Early in the college's history war
gaming had been developed under the expertise
of retired U.S. Navy Capt. Louis McCarty
Little. The results of these games provided important information to the Navy Department in
planning ahead and to the fleet in tactics and
operations. The early twentieth century brought
growing competition between the nations for
naval power, generally measured in the strength,
size, and numbers of battleships. Great Britain
had the strongest navy, but Germany was gaining strength. In 1907, the United States paraded
its naval battle line, "The Great White Fleet,"
on a year and a half cruise around the world.
Again in 1910, many of the sixteen battleships
of that fleet and four new dreadnoughts, all in
wartime gray, made a winter cruise to British
and French ports. Each of these cruises found
a majority of the senior officers were graduates
of the college at Newport.

RAdm. Austin M. Knight assumed the
presidency of the War College late in 1913 and
held this post for three years. Courses were
lengthened to ten months with from forty to
fifty students attending. Developments in the
European war were followed closely in Newport, first by press reports and then follow-up
reports of the Office of Naval Intelligence. On
May 31, 1916, British and German fleets met
in the North Sea in the Battle of Jutland, the
major battleship action of the Great War.
Analysis and replaying of Jutland on the game
floor at the Naval War College had only started
when the United States entered World War I.
This action would remain a significant element

in future War College curricula for many years to come.

When the last prewar course at Newport was in its early stages, the German submarine *U-53* (on a shipping destruction assignment) entered Narragansett Bay in October 1916. Its commander called on Admiral Knight and Knight's aide, in return, called on the German commander on the *U-53*. Other American officers went aboard too and were shown around the ship. The Germans requested no supplies, and *U-53* sailed before the twenty-four-hour limit of a belligerent ship in a neutral port ended. Two days later several British merchantmen were sunk outside of U.S. territorial waters south of Newport. It was the first real contact the college had had with the war at sea and Germany's new, powerful, and stealthy weapon. The success of submarine warfare accelerated United States' entry into the war, but planning to combat it had hardly started at the time of *U-53*'s visit.

Admiral Knight returned to sea duty early in 1917. His relief at the college was newly promoted RAdm. William S. Sims, a graduate of the college's first ten-month course and the youngest flag officer in the navy. Sims was only in Newport briefly before being ordered to the Navy Department for temporary duty. Although not officially detached from the War College until June 1917, Sims was sent to London, where he arrived in early April to work with the British. He soon took command of the U.S. Navy forces in Europe.

Commo. Charles Eaton next took temporary command of the War College. Orders to student officers for sea duty were arriving daily, and by early April classes ceased. The Correspondence School Department continued to send courses out during the war. The college library remained open, and the secretary's office kept files open with reports and records intact. Commo. James Parker (USN ret.) was recalled to active duty as college president, but most of the college spaces were being used by the expanded naval training station, where recruits arrived by the hundreds each week for "boot training."

The most important contribution of the Naval War College in World War I was the education that its many graduates took into the wartime navy and other services. Sims, its most famous graduate of the period, attributed much of his success to his studies at the Naval War College. After the war, he requested reassignment as college president because he believed that the work of the college would shape the navy's future. Other graduates in important World War I assignments included Adm. William S. Benson, first chief of naval operations, Gen. Tasker H. Bliss, chief of staff of the U.S. Army, and VAdm. Albert Gleaves, commander, Cruiser-Transport Force, and responsible for convoying men and supplies to Europe from the United States. Fleet commanders and future fleet commanders William B. Caperton, Austin M. Knight, Hugh Rodman, and William V. Pratt and future Coast Guard Commandant H.G. Hamblett as well as future Marine Corps Commandant John H. Russell had diplomas from the War College.

Stephen Luce had founded the college to teach officers to think and plan ahead. His work was not in vain when the U.S. Navy entered a huge mobilization for World War I and conducted operations never envisioned at the time officers involved had been students. World War II would see the War College prove its worth with even greater significance, and today Luce's "war school" still stands on Coaster's Harbor Island facing the eastern passage of Narragansett Bay, a foremost senior military education institution, where all questions relating to war and the statesmanship required to prevent it are studied.

John R. Wadleigh

See also SIMS, WILLIAM SOWDEN

Bibliography

Hattendorf, John B., B. Mitchell Simpson, and John R. Wadleigh. *Sailors and Scholars, the Centennial History of the U.S. Naval War College.* Washington, DC: Government Printing Office, 1984.

Hayes, John D., and John B. Hattendorf. *The Writings of Stephen B. Luce.* Newport, RI: Naval War College Press, 1975.

Spector, Ronald. *The Naval War College and the Development of the Naval Profession.* Newport, RI: Naval War College Press, 1977.

United States Navy

From the outbreak of hostilities in late July 1914, to the Armistice on Nov. 11, 1918, the United States Navy moved from the role of interested bystander to a major participant in World War I. While not as involved as British forces, the American Navy still contributed significantly to the final victory at sea. In 1914, the existing war plans in case of a United States-German conflict envisioned British neutrality. The "Black Plan" developed in case of conflict with Germany presumed a war exclusively at sea in a classic battle between major fleets. Moreover, this theoretical confrontation would probably be waged in the Caribbean.

Despite the establishment of the Office of Chief of Naval Operations in 1915 and the passage of a 1916 Naval Appropriations Act, spurred in part by the sea battle at Jutland, the U.S. Navy remained unprepared for the approach of war and wedded to its existing plans. The 1916 appropriation emphasized a strong surface fleet including ten battleships and six battle cruisers as well as other vessels. It was a program that clearly was not tailored to meet the submarine threat, but it had received strong bipartisan Senate support, and the navy expected to commence construction of the battleships *Colorado, Maryland, Washington,* and *West Virginia* almost at once. However, the decision that same year to slice funding for this force drastically reflected congressional concerns. Even worse, a postwar congressional study found that on the day of American entry into World War I, two-thirds of the United States ships required some repair and 90 percent were undermanned.

The administration, including Secretary of the Navy Josephus Daniels, Chief of Naval Operations Adm. William S. Benson, President Wilson, and Secretaries of State William Jennings Bryan and Robert Lansing, grappled with an increasingly difficult policy aimed at maintaining neutrality while at the same time attempting to prepare for war. Although Assistant Secretary of the Navy Franklin D. Roosevelt called for increased naval activity, Daniels and the others hesitated in bringing the fleet to wartime effectiveness immediately.

American neutrality, however, faded in the face of German submarine operations. Although British naval actions also hampered U.S. merchants, U-boats meant casualties. Washington complained to Berlin when the kaiser's government proclaimed a war zone around the British Isles in February 1915. The Navy Department then proposed a series of measures in anticipation of conflict, including consultation with Allied sea powers. Wilson's reluctance to shed neutrality completely blocked the implementation of many of these plans. When the Germans torpedoed the British ship *Falaba* on

March 28, 1915, the dead included Leon Thrasher, the first American killed in the naval war. Although several other American citizens died when the U.S. merchantman *Gulflight* was torpedoed but not sunk on May 1, the sinking of the 32,000-ton British liner *Lusitania* six days later sparked American outrage. The *U-20*'s attack cost almost 1,200 lives, including 124 Americans. American literary and theater figures such as Elbert Hubbard and Charles Frohman as well as famous socialite Alfred G. Vanderbilt were among the casualties. On August 19, 1915, several Americans were killed when the *U-24* sank the British ship *Arabic* near Ireland. Over the course of the next year, Berlin agreed to limit its submarine assaults, especially emphasizing the protection of civilian lives, and turned its attention to the Mediterranean.

By 1916, German military leaders faced another crisis. In late March, mistaken identity led the *U-29* to destroy a defenseless French vessel: the *Sussex*. Several Americans were hurt in the incident. Wilson considered recalling American diplomats and severing relations with Berlin. In early May, however, Germany proclaimed the "Sussex Pledge," significantly limiting submarine activity against noncombatants.

By February 1917, the Germans again instituted full-scale submarine attacks, a move calculated to force England's surrender before U.S. mobilization could affect the European theater. Wilson severed diplomatic ties with Berlin in the same month. With hostilities imminent, the Navy Department took steps to prepare for war and to establish liaison with the Royal Navy. Admiral Benson already had enlisted outstanding scientists, including William Coolidge, Elmer Sperry, and Thomas A. Edison, to work on the Naval Consulting Board. The President called for an increase in personnel of over 85,000 men for the U.S. Navy. Wilson also issued an executive order allowing the arming of U.S. merchantmen. Nonetheless, U-boats destroyed four American ships in March. In the same month, Washington directed RAdm. William S. Sims, president of the Naval War College, to go to London to work with the British Admiralty. Sims had been in Britain in 1910 while commanding the battleship *Minnesota*. He created no small furor in a London address when he suggested that his country would support Britain in a European war. Washington officially reprimanded him for these remarks, but he never lost his admiration for England and his strong belief in Anglo-American cooperation. Chief of Naval Operations Benson, on the other hand, viewed the British with suspicion. Benson caustically commented to Sims that he should be wary of the British; the United States did not necessarily owe Britain support. Further, Benson warned, the United States might just as easily be battling England rather than Germany. Needless to say, this continuing tension affected both Sims's rapport with the Navy Department in Washington and London's view of its ally.

On March 24, 1917, the administration asked the State Department's assistance in gathering information on Triple Alliance naval strength, and the navy moved to coordinate activity with France and England. As these measures went into effect, the United States officially entered the conflict. Congress voted for war against Germany on Good Friday, April 6, 1917. The outdated and undermanned United States Navy had over 360 ships in commission, but it still needed time to overcome a significant advantage in strength enjoyed by the German High Seas Fleet which was four times its size. Given the persistent submarine threat, the navy contemplated changing its focus from capital ship construction to building several hundred destroyers. American forces at sea also required a tripling of personnel to deal with wartime responsibilities.

While the Navy Department worked furiously to upgrade the fleet, Sims received a pessimistic evaluation from the Royal Navy in London. Before his arrival, Sims believed the Triple Entente would be victorious. A meeting with then First Sea Lord Adm. Sir John Jellicoe revealed just the opposite to be not only possible but in sight. The Germans had sunk over 535,000 tons of British and neutral shipping in February; by March, the figure had reached over 600,000 tons; and the April predictions showed almost 900,000 tons going to the bottom. Unless the U-boats were stopped in the near future, Britain faced strangulation and surrender. Allied studies suggested the end could come as early as November 1917. Just as alarming, according to British sources, the Germans apparently had lost only fifty-four submarines. This statistic coupled with a construction rate of about twelve new U-boats monthly reinforced Jellicoe's pessimism. Upon hearing these figures, Sims became an ardent proponent of convoy protection as the best option to deal with this German onslaught.

Within a week of the American declaration of war, British, French, and U.S. personnel met to discuss initial cooperation. Although conflicting goals and perceptions complicated Allied efforts, these meetings did produce a number of important agreements. One of these decisions focused on the need to send American destroyers to the European theater. Sims in his communications to Washington proposed just such a move to help counter the U-boat successes. He also correctly reasoned that submarines would not be particularly effective in American home waters. Berlin shared his belief and, to avoid further antagonism, did not remove U.S. coastal waters from neutral status until late 1917.

The reinforcements for the Royal Navy sailed amid ongoing discussions regarding the best way to deal with the German menace. Sims repeated his plea for antisubmarine weapons and convoys. Despite internal Royal Navy arguments, some indecisiveness about its efficacy, and Washington's suspicion and mistrust of London, the Allied navies finally adopted the convoy system. The Royal Navy agreed to institute convoys in the spring.

Sims and his associates, Chief of Staff Capt. Nathan C. Twining, Capt. William V. Pratt, and Commo. John V. Babcock, also argued strenuously for a redirection of construction priorities. Their arguments won over Daniels, who, in July 1917, proposed an increase in the number of destroyers and an emphasis on meeting the recommendations by Sims for more antisubmarine craft as well as troopships and supply vessels.

Sims then began to build an impressive organization in London to deal with the U.S. Navy's expanded role in both convoying Atlantic merchant fleets and carrying out operations in Europe. Named naval attaché in London in 1917, he developed contacts with his British counterparts and joined the Allied Naval Council in early 1918. Adm. Henry T. Mayo, commander of the Atlantic Fleet, and Benson both visited the European theater in 1917 to get an on-site view of the conflict. For the first few months of the war, a very small group assisted Sims. By Nov. 11, 1918, however, the U.S. Navy in Europe totaled approximately 370 ships. The units ranged from Ireland to Corfu to northern Russia. The staff assigned to Sims included over 1,200 personnel.

U

In late 1917, Benson agreed to the formation of a "Planning Section" to enhance coordination with the British with whom the issue of control remained an ongoing question. While Washington committed various units to overall Royal Navy command, Sims had ultimate responsibility as commander of the U.S. Naval Forces Operating in European Waters. This thorny issue was not limited to sea power. Gen. John J. Pershing, commander of the American Expeditionary Force (AEF), adamantly opposed Sims's view that American forces should be assimilated into Allied armies. Sims did recognize the difficulties inherent in this approach but believed that this move would speed U.S. assistance to the hard-pressed Western Front. Throughout the war, and despite occasional misunderstandings, Sims and the Royal Navy cooperated as allies.

Despite these bureaucratic stumbling blocks, the convoy system gradually reduced the U-boats' effectiveness. While the Germans sank 756 merchant ships between February and July 1917, the figure dropped to 128 for August–October 1918. Moreover, the Germans lost twice as many submarines (43) in the final half of 1917 as they had in the first six months of the year. Furthermore, Germany and her allies could produce fewer than 75 submarines between January and October 1918.

The reasons for this dramatic upturn in Allied fortunes were many: convoys, better equipment, and U.S. participation. Six destroyers of Destroyer Division Eight departed Boston late on April 24 and sailed into Queenstown, Ireland, in early May, led by Commo. Joseph K. Taussig in his flagship *Wadsworth*, along with the *Conygham, Porter, McDougal, Davis,* and *Wainwright.* Within days, this squadron was participating in antisubmarine patrols. The Allies badly needed these welcome reinforcements; the Germans had sunk craft totaling almost a quarter of a million tons that very week. Throughout the war, individual ship patrols were not as effective at commerce protection as convoys, yet the Allies needed time to produce the needed ships. Adm. Sir Lewis Bayly, Royal Navy, directed overall operations in this region; though once again, U.S. naval officers exercised ultimate responsibility for American naval vessels. Capt. Joel R.P. Pringle served as Sims's liaison at Queenstown.

Within two weeks of the arrival of Taussig's flotilla, another six American destroyers steamed into Queenstown. By early July,

thirty-four U.S. destroyers were based at this port with the support vessel *Melville* as flagship. This total was particularly impressive, given the fact that only fifty-two such ships were fit for duty. In the beginning of August, eight refurbished yachts, several supporting craft, and thirty-seven destroyers comprised the United States naval forces in the European theater. By the Armistice, the U.S. Navy had approximately 7,000 personnel and almost sixty ships in Ireland alone.

While Queenstown remained the focus of early American convoy efforts, Brest, France, later assumed a significant role in this important operation, being the base for about thirty-six destroyers at the height of its use. By November 1918, RAdm. Henry W. Wilson, commander of the American naval forces in France, directed a fleet of approximately forty destroyers, along with other vessels, and 12,000 men. This squadron was responsible for protecting nearly all convoys headed for France's Atlantic bases in 1918. These two ports combined with Gibraltar and Inverness and Invergordon in Scotland were home to the bulk of American naval units committed to Europe.

The first of the convoys reached Britain on May 20, 1917. Sims, who had just been promoted to vice admiral, pointed to this event as a key to the final Allied victory because, in his view, it showed that the Entente could deal effectively with the U-boat menace. At its height, the British Admiralty's convoy center in London directed thousands of ships worldwide, using a large map to pinpoint the locations of specific convoys. Groups generally consisting of about thirty vessels left twice a month from New York and weekly from Virginia. Gibraltar, Dakar, and Halifax were other key ports. Usually merchant vessels, while traveling by convoy, did not receive escorts until they were in the so-called "danger zone" closer to England. Capt. Byron A. Long represented Sims in these operations. Sims's subordinates at Queenstown, especially the local chief of staff, Captain Pringle, and destroyer leader, Commo. David C. Hanrahan, directly assisted this successful campaign.

An example of convoy escort illustrates both the technique and approach to this important duty. Admiral Bayly ordered U.S. destroyers to protect convoy OQ 17 on its voyage back to American waters and then pick up HS 14 heading for England. OQ 17 indicated that this group was headed outward from the port at Queenstown and was the seventeenth to depart that location. Conversely, HS showed ships sailing from Sydney, Cape Breton. Queenstown functioned as an assembly point for vessels returning to the United States. The Allies later added other bases such as Milford Haven and Liverpool to this list. One specially designed British ship, whose purpose was to lure U-boats to the surface, joined eight U.S. destroyers on this mission. While several submarines were sighted, the Germans did not sink any ships in these convoys. On the return journey, the Royal Navy escorted almost two-thirds of the merchant vessels to England and the U.S. Navy led the rest to Brest.

Yet another convoy was not as lucky. In mid-October, the *Nicholson,* which came to the aid of the outgunned merchant *J.L. Luckenbach,* engaged in a three-hour gun battle with a U-boat. The enemy simply stayed beyond the surface ship's range and fired at the vessel. After an attack by the destroyer forced the submarine to submerge, the *Luckenbach* with naval assistance joined the convoy. But a U-boat then successfully fired a torpedo at the British escort *Orama* causing serious damage. The destroyer *Conyngham* depth-charged the U-boat and later helped rescue the crew of the British craft. The German vessel, apparently the *U-53,* managed to return to port.

United States naval units in Europe made almost 2,000 sorties against enemy submarines. Between four and six U-boats were known to have been sunk and seventeen others damaged. In June and July 1917, for example, the *O'Brien, Wadsworth,* and *Benham* inflicted damage on German submarines, and in November 1917, a concentrated attack near Queenstown by the *Nicholson* and *Fanning* sent the *U-58* to the bottom. A German submarine, on the other hand, damaged the *Cassin* near Ireland in mid-October 1917. When Osmond K. Ingram, a gunner's mate, noticed the torpedo wake, he attempted to release the ship's depth charges. Unfortunately, the missile hit the *Cassin.* Ingram, among the casualties, received the Medal of Honor posthumously for his attempt to save the destroyer.

The high rate of Allied success caused the U-boats to hunt elsewhere, such as the English Channel, and operations in American waters yielded meager results, sinking only 110,000 tons of shipping. The *U-151* did manage to destroy twenty-three ships during its several months off the Atlantic coast during 1918. Yet the *U-140,* in August, had to withdraw after battling the destroyer *Stringham* among others. The most significant casualty occurred when a mine from the *U-156* destroyed the *San Diego.*

The ultimate purpose of all this Allied naval deployment was clear: the transport of men and supplies safely across the Atlantic. Without a quick infusion from the United States, the war was lost. The initial problem was lack of shipping. The Emergency Fleet Corporation, established within a month of Wilson's declaration, and swift refit of German vessels seized in U.S. ports at the time of the declaration of war alleviated this shortage. Although American shipyards quadrupled output in the twelve months prior to July 1917, demand still exceeded supply. Actually, vessels belonging to the United Fruit Company took initial units of the AEF to France within months of the declaration of war. The Naval Overseas Transport Service, set up in 1917 and headed by RAdm. Albert Gleaves, directed troopship operations.

In fact, the Allied navies carried about 2 million troops to the continent without loss. The process started slowly: fewer than 10 percent of that total had reached the European theater during 1917. Early in the conflict, St. Nazaire became the landing point for American personnel. Later, the navy also used Brest and other continental ports for this purpose. The high points of these efforts involved moving over 310,000 troops in July 1918. By that summer, seven men with supplies were being put ashore per minute. Although Washington committed 450 vessels to this important operation, Berlin's forces destroyed fewer than 10. Moreover, within the first four months of American entry into the conflict, the enemy had managed to sink less than 1 percent of the thousands of vessels moving in convoy. Atlantic squadrons commanded by Admiral Mayo remained on the East Coast of the United States, and British ships carried the bulk of American military units to Europe. U.S. ships accounted for over 46 percent of this total force movement.

While Washington focused its attention primarily on the Atlantic, the navy also dispatched units to other ports. Two cruisers arrived at Gibraltar in August 1917. RAdm. Albert P. Niblack took command of American naval forces at Gibraltar which eventually totaled over 40 ships. In more than a year, Niblack's vessels worked with the Royal Navy to escort over 560 convoys, totaling well over 10,000 ships. Gibraltar stood as the gateway to the Mediterranean, and this ancient sea posed

U

special difficulties for the Allies. On the one hand, fewer than 50 enemy U-boats faced the Entente during 1917–1918. Moreover, this submarine fleet, small as it was and based primarily in Adriatic ports, sank almost 160 merchant ships during the last five months of 1917. The British Navy reported that the November 1917–June 1918 sinkings in this area totaled 34 ships monthly. Over 5,500 naval personnel and about 75 vessels constituted the American commitment in the Mediterranean. Despite internal wrangling, the Allied forces moved to close the Adriatic at the Straits of Otranto using a variety of techniques, including nets, destroyers, and American subchasers.

The sixty-ton wooden subchaser carried a normal complement of fewer than thirty officers and men, a small gun, and hydrophones designed to pick up the sound of a German submarine. These vessels were extremely effective. The U.S. Navy stationed thirty-six subchasers at Plymouth, England, and during their six-week operation, U-boats did not sink one vessel in their sector. A similar number of subchasers went to Otranto in 1918. A number of these small vessels under Capt. Charles P. Nelson joined other Allied craft in an assault on Austrian positions at Durazzo, attacking several submarines.

While destroyers, subchasers, and other smaller type vessels constituted the bulk of the United States Navy units in European waters, Washington committed other ships to the conflict. The Germans especially feared the limited number of Allied submarines. Operating in the European theater, particularly near England, these vessels, according to Sims, destroyed twenty U-boats. The American Navy stationed seven such undersea craft at Berehaven, Ireland. Because of enemy surface power, U-boats had to make sure their batteries were fully charged in case of sudden attack. The Allied submarines, on the other hand, generally did not have this problem; hence, they could submerge and surface at will. In one apparent submarine-submarine encounter, the *AL-2* commanded by Lt. Paul Foster, escaped damage when the *U-65* may have destroyed itself either by an internal explosion or errant torpedo.

As might be expected, these ships often faced danger from their own forces. Submarines were presumed to be hostile. A U.S. destroyer mistakenly shelled and depth-charged the American submarine *AL-10*. The submarine managed to convince the surface vessel it was friendly; ironically, the two commanders had roomed together at the U.S. Naval Academy.

Among other weapons to sap enemy strength were the "Q-ships." Disguised as merchant vessels these craft, which attempted to bring German submarines to the surface and close to their guns, accounted for the sinking of twelve U-boats. The contingent of Q-ships included the *USS Santee* under the command of Capt. David C. Hanrahan.

Besides ships, the U.S. Navy utilized mines in the battle against the U-boat. While Sims's immediate answer to Berlin's assaults focused on the convoy, wartime improvements enabled the Allies to develop an extensive minefield in the North Sea. Ralph C. Browne, an American scientist, helped develop the "antenna" mine. Woodrow Wilson himself thought the Royal Navy should concentrate its energy on bottling up the submarines. Although Wilson's suggestion did not result in a particular plan, Assistant Secretary of the Navy Franklin D. Roosevelt visualized a minefield in the North Sea. Approved in early November, 1917, a grandiose scheme called for a field 230 miles long and 15–20 miles wide—a distance equal to that from New York to Washington. Responding to this need, RAdm. Ralph Earle's Bureau of Ordnance supervised over 500 firms engaged in mine production.

At first the strength of Capt. Reginald R. Belknap's Mining Squadron One lay primarily in the older vessels *Baltimore* and *San Francisco*. By mid-1918, ten converted minelayers began assembling at Inverness and Invergordon. As the effort expanded, RAdm. Joseph Strauss assumed command of the squadron. Navy personnel under the overall direction of Capt. Orin G. Murfin took the final steps in putting the mines together, often up to 1,200 daily. The completion of the field required thirteen separate forays under British protection. During part of 1918, a predominantly American force led by Capt. Henry V. Butler's flagship, *San Francisco* successfully placed approximately 70,000 mines. In addition, the *Baltimore* laid mines in the channel between Scotland and Ireland, leading to the destruction of several U-boats. Ultimately, around $80 million was expended on a project hampered by enemy activity, weather, and the enormous scope of the operation. Undoubtedly, the psychological factor involved in negotiating the field had a negative impact on enemy morale, but the Allies could not gauge precisely the effectiveness of the program.

Because of the real fear of German surface raiders, Washington also dispatched three battleships, the *Nevada, Oklahoma,* and *Utah* commanded by RAdm. Thomas A. Rodgers to Berehaven, as a ready reserve in case intelligence reported the location of Berlin's surface forces. Additional surface support existed with the American battleships serving with the Grand Fleet, the Allies "force in being," beginning in December 1917. Commanded by RAdm. Hugh Rodman, these vessels included the *New York, Wyoming, Florida, Delaware, Arkansas,* and *Texas.* In the winter, both the *Florida* and *Delaware* dodged torpedoes while on convoy escort. The *New York* collided with a U-boat and also avoided underseas torpedo attack. The Allies assimilated these capital ships into the Grand Fleet as Battle Squadron Six.

With all these safeguards, loaded merchantmen generally managed to reach Europe safely, but the return voyages were not as successful. U-boats torpedoed several westbound craft in October 1917, near France. A German attack sent the *Antilles* to the bottom on October 17 with the loss of seventy men. Later the same month, the Germans damaged the larger *Finland,* also with casualties, and in February 1918, a submarine torpedo struck the 14,400-ton *Tuscania.* In May, the Germans managed to sink the *President Lincoln,* a transport.

The American naval presence in France extended beyond convoy protection. Five 14-inch guns, for example, operated by navy personnel supported Allied troops during the last months of the war. These batteries shelled enemy concentrations miles away, being particularly effective near Laon and Verdun. These huge weapons, under RAdm. Charles P. Plunkett's overall control, used ammunition weighing well over 1,000 pounds per shell with a maximum range of twenty-four miles. These guns directed their last salvo at enemy positions at 10:57 A.M. Nov. 11, 1918, just minutes before the conclusion of the conflict. General Pershing himself complimented this naval contingent's efforts.

The U.S. Marine Corps also added to its illustrious history in France. At both Château-Thierry and Belleau Wood in 1918, marine units combined with army forces to battle the Germans. Although the marines suffered casualties of over 50 percent, they were instrumental in the Allied successes of these operations.

The navy also used its newest fighting machines: airplanes. In late 1910, Eugene Ely's plane had made naval history by taking off from a cruiser. The navy, however, had fewer than 40 fully trained aviators and around 50 aircraft in April 1917. The first group of 129 officers and men went to France in early June 1917, under the leadership of Lt., later Cmdr., Kenneth Whiting. The United States naval air arm in Europe eventually grew to over 20,000 officers and men. Both sea and land targets occupied this force, which patrolled waters from the Adriatic to the North Sea.

Their missions were not easy ones. For example, enemy fire damaged Ens. George H. Hamman's plane in an attack on Pola. Yet Hammon managed a daring rescue of another pilot and headed back on the seventy-five-mile trek to his home base. Sims nominated him for the Medal of Honor. Lt. David S. Ingalls, working with the Royal Air Force, became the U.S. Navy's only ace of the conflict by knocking five enemy aircraft from the sky.

Sims also stationed several destroyers in the Azores as a contingency against U-boat attack and dispatched other units to guard against German construction of a naval facility at Murmansk. The U.S. Navy also sent forces to Russia along with other Allied personnel as the Bolshevik Revolution swept the country.

Certainly, the U.S. commitment made up only a part of the overall naval effort in World War I. Sims himself reminded the country that the Royal Navy furnished the overwhelming majority of ships engaged in the anti-U-boat battle in both the Mediterranean and Atlantic. Britain's fleet contained over four times the number of destroyers that the U.S. Navy had in Europe at the close of hostilities. The United States contributed fewer than 10 percent of the Allied units fighting the submarine. Yet the growth of Sims's staff from himself and an aide to about 1,200 officers and men, the involvement of destroyers, battleships, minelayers, planes, support vessels, and other craft, shore guns, and marines aided the weary British and helped immeasurably to provide escorts for the all-important troop convoys, reinforcements for the Grand Fleet, and assistance to the Allies in France. Thus, the United States Navy played a significant supporting role in the Allied victory at sea.

Edward J. Sheehy

See also MINES; NAVAL CONSULTING BOARD; NORTH SEA MINE BARRAGE; OTRANTO MINE BARRAGE; SIMS, WILLIAM SOWDEN; UNITED

STATES NAVY: BANTRY BAY SQUADRON; UNITED STATES NAVY: 6TH BATTLE SQUADRON, GRAND FLEET

Bibliography

Hoehling, A.A. *The Great War at Sea*. New York: Crowell, 1965.

Miller, Nathan. *The U.S. Navy: An Illustrated History*. New York: American Heritage, 1977.

Sims, William S. *The Victory at Sea*. New York: Doubleday, Page, 1920.

Trask, David F. *Captains and Cabinets: Anglo-American Naval Relations, 1917–1918*. Columbia: University of Missouri Press, 1972.

United States Navy: American Patrol Detachment

The American Patrol Detachment was the modest naval unit assigned to patrol and police the Caribbean and Gulf of Mexico during World War I. With increasing pressure to provide antisubmarine and patrol vessels for North Atlantic and European waters, the U.S. Navy withdrew all but eight warships from the Patrol Force, Atlantic Fleet and, in July 1917, designated the remaining squadron the American Patrol Detachment (AmRolDet) under the command of Capt. Edwin A. Anderson. The squadron, while technically under the organizational umbrella of Adm. Henry Thomas Mayo's Atlantic Fleet, in effect operated as a distinct naval force with the mission of guarding American and Allied shipping and interests in the Caribbean-Gulf region.

Throughout the remainder of 1917, the detachment's vessels (mostly aging cruisers and gunboats) investigated a plethora of alleged U-boat sightings and rumored clandestine submarine bases in the Caribbean. Since the Navy Department believed that U-boats might well begin operating in these tropical waters, Captain Anderson was concerned about the vulnerability of American shipping and the overall unpreparedness of his force, grown to nine vessels by January 1918, to protect it. Unable to implement a convoy system with so few escorts, Anderson routed Gulf and Caribbean maritime traffic close to shore in daylight hours under the very limited protection of naval district vessels. Merchant vessels were asked to take individual diverted routes in the evenings. Anderson also opted to concentrate his vessels at key passages into the Caribbean, particularly the Straits of Florida.

When the Germans conducted limited submarine operations off the mainland coast of the United States from May to July 1918, the navy, fully expecting the U-boats to move southward into tropical waters, expanded the American Patrol Detachment to thirteen cruisers and gunboats plus twelve wooden submarine chasers. Naval intelligence warned Captain Anderson to expect the U-boats to begin operations in his sector during the summer and fall of 1918. As his forces increased, Anderson altered his antisubmarine strategy from the hunter-killer approach of search and destroy in narrow waters to convoy routing. The war ended with the AmRolDet in heightened alert in anticipation of a U-boat threat that never materialized.

Created to meet the wartime emergency, the American Patrol Detachment was ill-suited for the postwar duties of naval diplomacy in the politically unstable Caribbean. For instance, as part of the Atlantic Fleet, the detachment was not permitted to transit the Panama Canal to meet emergencies on the Pacific coast of Central America. The squadron fell victim in 1919 to a reorganization of the navy's Caribbean patrol that culminated in September 1920 with the founding of the Special Service Squadron.

Donald A. Yerxa

Bibliography

Yerxa, Donald A. *Admirals and Empire: The United States Navy and the Caribbean, 1898–1945*. Columbia: University of South Carolina Press, 1991.

United States Navy: Aviation

At the outbreak of hostilities, United States naval aviation consisted of 48 naval aviators, 163 enlisted men, 54 aircraft, 3 balloons, 1 blimp, and 1 Aeronautic Station. Aviation operations were conducted within the office of the aide for material headed by Capt. Josiah S. McKean, USN, and were directly controlled by Lt. John H. Towers, who was an assistant for aviation to Capt. McKean. By an executive order of April 7, 1917, the Coast Guard was transferred from the Department of the Treasury to the Navy Department. The Coast Guard, of course, brought with them their small aviation unit. When the United States entered the war, the U.S. Navy was immediately faced with the multiple problems of insufficient personnel, insufficient training, insufficient aircraft, and insufficient bases from which to carry out their missions.

The personnel problem was rapidly turned around into a problem of too many volunteers for the existing facilities to handle. To deal with the influx of would-be fliers, Cmdr. Noble E. Irwin became the director of naval aviation within the U.S. Navy Bureau of Material on May 15, 1917. Lieutenant Tower, now responsible for the naval reserves, reported to Commander Irwin. It is to Tower's credit that the majority of naval aviators who served during the war came from the naval reserves. As the importance of naval aviation increased, the responsibilities of the director grew apace, and the director of naval aviation now reported directly to the chief of naval operations.

On May 1, 1917, the Navy received approval for an expanded training program for pilots and mechanics. The Aeronautic Station at Pensacola, Florida, was designated for heavier-than-air training (HTT); the Goodyear Tire and Rubber Company in Akron was to be responsible for the training of naval balloon pilots; and the Curtiss Exhibition Company at Newport News, Virginia, would provide preliminary flight training. Additional training was to be provided at the naval militia stations at Bay Shore, Long Island, and Squantum, Massachusetts. But even these facilities were inadequate to meet the navy's training needs. To relieve serious overcrowding at Pensacola, a detachment of 7 officers and 122 enlisted men commanded by Lt. Kenneth Whiting, was designated as the First Aeronautic Detachment. The detachment departed the United States from Baltimore for France in two contingents. The first left on May 23, 1917, and arrived at Brest on June 7. The second left Baltimore on May 25 and arrived at Brest on June 8. Together they became the first U.S. Navy aviation component to arrive overseas. Upon arrival in France, Lieutenant Whiting immediately left the detachment for Paris to negotiate with French authorities for coastal bases to be manned by the U.S. Navy, while enlisted personnel went into training. Mechanics were assigned to the French school at St. Raphael on the Mediterranean. Naval aviators were initially assigned to the French aviation school at Tours.

Students at various universities in the United States organized their own flight training. Using private funds with private instructors, but under U.S. naval authority, students from Yale, Harvard, Princeton, and Dartmouth began to learn to fly. This program lasted only until training facilities totally under navy auspices became available. Also, in order to meet the training demand placed upon the navy by the number of volunteers being received, the navy entered into a contract with the Royal Canadian Flying Corps wherein twenty-six cadets, under the command of an American naval officer, were to receive flight training in Canada. These men were ordered to take copious notes so that their education in Canada could be reflected in the syllabus being developed in the United States for similar training.

In addition to heavier-than-air training, the Navy also expanded into the area of lighter-than-air training. In May 1917, the U.S. Navy and the Goodyear Tire and Rubber Company contracted for the training of kite balloon and airship pilots. The school at Goodyear was commissioned on May 28, 1917, and by August 1917, dirigible pilots were being assigned to the Royal Naval air station at Cranwell, England, for advanced dirigible training. The first navy students graduated from this school in November 1917. These men, and subsequent graduates, were assigned either to British coastal bases, where they operated under British authority, or to the dirigible bases in France, which were under construction and whose operation would be under U.S. Navy command.

By the summer of 1917, the Navy Department decided to approach various educational institutions in the United States to provide facilities and faculty for the training of naval aviation cadets in the basics of military studies. Subsequently, ground schools were formed at the Massachusetts Institute of Technology (M.I.T.), the Dunwoody Institute in Minneapolis, and the University of Washington in Seattle. The first course at M.I.T. opened on July 23, 1917. Courses at Dunwoody and the University of Washington began in the summer of 1918. Training of enlisted men in the technical areas associated with aviation was likewise conducted at Dunwoody and the Great Lakes Naval Training Center.

The initial expansion of domestic patrol stations was made on June 4, 1917, when the navy arranged for the use of privately owned seaplane stations at Montauk Point, Rockaway Beach, and Bay Shore, Long Island. On Aug. 19, 1917, Secretary of the Navy Josephus Daniels approved the development of

U

eighteen air stations, both for flying boats/seaplanes and dirigibles. Temporary bases were established at East Greenwich, Rhode Island; Miami and Key West, Florida; San Diego, California; and the Curtiss Exhibition School at Newport News, Virginia. Eventually, naval air stations were built at Bay Shore; Squantum; Anacostia in Washington, D.C.; Brunswick, Georgia; Cape May, New Jersey; Chatham, Massachusetts; Norfolk, Virginia; San Diego, California; Rockaway, New York; Coco Solo, Panama Canal Zone; and Halifax and Sydney, Canada.

Very early in the war, the navy recognized the inability of the domestic aircraft industry to produce aircraft sufficient for the navy's needs. The Curtiss Company had produced the R-6 and R-9, which were suitable for training but little else. The same firm had also produced the HS series of flying boats, but they were not rugged enough to withstand the rough conditions of the North Sea. Nor did they possess the cruising range desired for long-range antisubmarine patrol. On top of this, there was an insufficient production capability of the domestic aircraft industry to manufacture the number of planes that the U.S. Navy needed. Therefore, in June, 1917, the Navy Department directed Cmdr. Frederic G. Coburn to make a survey and to report upon both the cost and suitable site for a naval aircraft factory capable of producing 1,000 seaplanes a year.

His study resulted in the construction of the Naval Aircraft Factory at the Philadelphia Navy Yard. Construction costs were estimated at $100,000. Ground was broken on August 10, and the entire plant was completed by Nov. 28, 1917. On March 28, 1918, the first plane assembled at the factory, an H-16, made its initial flight. From this point on, the factory turned out H-16, F-5-L, and N-1 aircraft.

In addition to aircraft manufacture, the navy ordered dirigibles and kite balloons from the Goodyear Tire and Rubber Company and the Connecticut Aircraft Company. The B-1, the navy's first successful dirigible, made its maiden flight in May 1917. Dirigibles manufactured by these companies were assigned to domestic coastal patrol stations designated as dirigible stations.

As noted earlier, upon his arrival in France, Lieutenant Whiting proceeded to Paris where he conducted negotiations with the French government on the selection of sites for the establishment of air stations to be operated by the U.S.

Navy. As a result of these and subsequent discussions, the navy agreed to operate facilities at L'Aber Vrach, Brest, Ile Tudy, Le Croisic, Paimboeuf, Fromentine, Rochefort, St. Trojan, Moutchic, Pauillac, Trequier, Guipavas, La Trinité-sur-Mer, La Pallice, Gujan, Arcachon, and Dunkirk. Some of these bases were intended solely for aircraft, some for balloon/dirigible (LTA) activities, and some for combined operations. Not all of these bases were operational by the time of the Armistice.

Shortly after Whiting informed Adm. William S. Sims, commander-in-chief of United States Naval Operations in European Waters, of his efforts with the French, Whiting became a member of the naval task force evaluating potential sites for naval air stations in the British Isles. On the basis of the task force's study, bases were selected at Killingholme and Eastleigh in England and Queenstown, Wexford, Lough Foyle, Whiddy Island, Lough Swilly, and Berehaven in Ireland. As with the planned stations in France, these bases were intended to function either solely with aircraft or with a combination of aircraft and balloons. Commander R. McCreary established his office as commanding officer of naval aviation in Ireland at Queenstown on Feb. 14, 1918.

On Nov. 21, 1917, the Italian government requested that the United States Navy establish air bases in Italy. LtCmdr. John L. Callan proceeded to Italy to enter into negotiations with the authorities there. Upon completion of these talks, facilities were established at Bolsena, Porto Corsini, and Pescara. Commander Callan became the commanding officer of naval aviation in Italy on April 25, 1918. It was from the naval air station at Porto Corsisi that Charles H. Hamman was to win the Medal of Honor for actions on Aug. 21, 1918, during a bombing raid on the Austro-Hungarian base at Pola.

As the level of involvement of U.S. naval aviation expanded in Europe, it was suggested that Admiral Sims add to his staff an officer to direct the aviation portion of his command. To fill this position, he selected Capt. Hutch I. Cone, a nonpilot and the former superintendent of the Panama Canal Zone. Captain Cone arrived in London on Sept. 27, 1917, and on October 24 transferred to Paris, where he replaced Lieutenant Whiting as commander, U.S. Naval Aviation, Foreign Service. In this position, the commanding officers of the stations in France as well as those of the stations in Italy reported to him. Whiting then moved to London, reported to Admiral Sims who transferred him back to the United States to coordinate and implement the plans agreed to with the French and British.

Prior to the entry of the United States into the war, many American citizens had traveled to France and had volunteered to serve in the French military. Those Americans who had volunteered for French aviation were collectively known as members of the Lafayette Escadrille. Once the U.S. Navy began to have a presence in France, several members of the Escadrille volunteered to serve with their countrymen. Eventually, some twenty-six men, all with extensive flight experience in France, were accepted into the U.S. naval aviation establishment in both France and Italy.

An additional expansion of naval aviation in France occurred with the development of the Northern Bombing Group. One of the principle objectives for naval aviation during the war was the destruction of German submarines. Based on a request of Captain Cone, the Northern Bombing Group was established as a land-based bomber organization whose targets were the German submarine bases along the Belgian coast at Zeebrugge, Ostend, and Bruges. The U.S. Navy was to supply personnel for the Night Wing of the unit, and members of the U.S. Marine Corps Air Service were to supply personnel for the Day Wing. The first aircraft for this operation was delivered on Aug. 11, 1918, but by this time, submarine menace had been drastically reduced. For its brief life, the unit functioned as a land-based bombing unit with a variety of targets.

In nineteen months, United States naval aviation grew to a force of 6,716 officers and 30,693 men, with 282 officers and 2,180 men in the Marine Corps. The force had 695 seaplanes, 1,170 flying boats, 242 land planes, 15 dirigibles, and 215 kite balloons. Of this force, about 20,000 officers and men and 570 aircraft reached foreign shores.

Noel Shirley

Bibliography

Turnbull, Archibald D., and Clifford Lord. *History of United States Naval Aviation.* New Haven: Yale University Press, 1947.

U.S. Naval Aviation, 1910–1970. Washington, DC: Government Printing Office, 1970.

United States Navy: Bantry Bay Squadron

U

The United States Navy Bantry Bay Squadron was the force of American battleships based in southern Ireland to protect Allied shipping against attack by German surface warships.

It was primarily the submarine menace that threatened to sever the Allied Atlantic supply lines that precipitated the U.S. entry into the war on April 6, 1917. After the 1916 Battle of Jutland, the British Grand Fleet had the German High Seas Fleet more or less under control, and in late 1917, a squadron of American battleships reinforced the British fleet. After a period of orientation, the Americans contributed significantly to maintaining Allied surface domination. However, there remained the possibility that a fast unit of German battlecrusiers might evade the Grand Fleet and break out into the Atlantic to menace Allied shipping. Unlike the U-boat force, such surface raiders could not cover enough territory to cut completely the Atlantic supply lines, but they could wipe out a few important convoys since no escort could resist them.

For this reason, a second American battle squadron, composed of the battleships *Nevada, Oklahoma,* and *Utah* and commanded by RAdm. Thomas S. Rodgers, was established in Bantry Bay in southwest Ireland in 1918 to guard the Atlantic convoy routes against surface attack. The 22,000-ton *Utah,* with twin 12-inch guns, was no longer a first-line battleship, but it could still deal with any German battlecrusier. The 27,500-ton *Nevada* and *Oklahoma,* each with ten 14-inch guns, were only two years old and the equal of any contemporary battleship.

The Bantry Bay Squadron kept a watchful eye on the vital Atlantic troop convoys until the end of the war, and none ever lost a ship to surface attack. The 2-million-man American Expeditionary Force arrived in France intact to decide the outcome of the land war, and the vital stream of supplies, without which the Allies could not have continued the struggle, flowed uninterrupted across the Atlantic until the end of the war.

The squadron never saw action, as the German fleet never attempted a raid of the sort feared, but the deterrent effect of the Bantry Bay battleships was great. Moreover, by lifting one major worry from the shoulders of the overburdened Grand Fleet, it permitted that fleet to carry out its other duties more effectively and efficiently. Finally, the presence of the American force in the western approaches to the British Isles helped free the Royal Navy to decommission its own old battleships guarding the English Channel and transfer the crews to chronically undermanned antisubmarine escort forces.

Two of the Bantry Bay Squadron's captains went on to important positions after the war. Charles B. McVay became commander of the Asiatic Fleet, and Mark L. Bristol commanded the U.S. naval detachment in Turkish waters in the turbulent years that immediately followed the war. Both made good use in postwar service of the diplomatic skills and relationships with the Royal Navy forged during the Great War.

David MacGregor

Bibliography

Marder, Arthur J. *From the Dreadnought to Scapa Flow.* 5 vols. New York: Oxford University Press, 1961–1970.
Sims, William S. *The Victory at Sea.* Garden City, NY: Doubleday, Page, 1920.

United States Navy: General Board

The General Board of the United States Navy, established in 1900, marks both the growth of professionalism in the American naval service and a recognition of the administrative and organizational failures of the war with Spain in 1898. Ever since the creation of the "New Navy" in the 1880s, naval reformers had searched for a solution to the problem caused by an entrenched bureaucratic system dominated by the all-powerful chiefs of the various naval bureaus. Then, when plans and strategies for the Spanish-American War had to be stitched together by an ad hoc Strategy Board, the weaknesses of existing arrangements became all too apparent.

The reformers, led by Adm. Henry C. Taylor, chief of the Bureau of Navigation and author of the basic memorandum that led to the formation of the General Board, had hoped for a naval general staff. Board members wanted an organization similar to what the army reformers sponsored by Secretary of War Elihu Root would develop, and similar to the evolving staff systems of the European Great Powers. They looked for an institution through which line officers would exercise command and control of the naval establishment. But American military tradition—the tradition of civilian supremacy and the subordination of the military

to the political—stood firmly in the way. Secretary of the Navy John D. Long was only willing to create a board that was limited to an advisory capacity, that had no operational responsibilities, and that had no authority over the various naval bureaus. Moreover, he was unwilling to seek congressional authorization for the board; instead it was created by a Navy Department order. Hence, the General Board could be changed, even abolished, by any future secretary of the navy, and was, in effect, a creature of the secretary.

The mission given the General Board was, to be sure, broad and all-inclusive. It was "to insure efficient preparation of the fleet in case of war and for the naval defense of the coast." And, from the moment of its inception, the General Board did begin to advise secretaries of the navy on naval construction, on the size, composition, and disposition of the fleet, on armaments and armor, on naval strategy, and on the need for overseas naval bases and stations. It soon developed, among other important matters, a long-range plan that called for the eventual creation of a fleet of forty-eight battleships. It recommended the concentration of the battleships in one combined fleet stationed in the Atlantic, and it developed the Black and Orange plans for possible wars with, respectively, Germany and Japan. The board also put forth a far-ranging set of recommendations for overseas naval bases in the Caribbean and the Far East, little of which was ever attained.

Yet the General Board had no authority to implement its many and varied recommendations. Secretaries of the navy were free to accept or reject its advice. Indeed, much of its prestige and influence derived from the fact that its president, from 1900 until his death in 1917, was Adm. George Dewey, the hero of Manila Bay and *the* Admiral of the Navy. Dewey, however, was no activist. He presided over rather than intervened in board discussions. He rarely, if ever, objected to the tradition that naval officers should restrict their advice to purely military matters and follow the lead of civilians who made broad policy. Moreover, as time went on, Dewey became increasingly disinterested in further attempts to turn the General Board into a genuine naval staff.

Thus, for years, the agenda of the next wave of reformers—led by William S. Sims, Albert W. Key, and Bradley A. Fiske—was thwarted. To be sure, during the Taft administration, Navy Secretary George von Lengerke Meyer established the so-called "aides system" whereby the functions of the various bureaus, the General Board, the Office of Naval Intelligence, and the Naval War College were grouped and channeled through four line officers, the "aides," who reported directly to the secretary. But even this partial reform was never approved by Congress and ended with the inauguration of Woodrow Wilson. Finally, in 1915, as a consequence of the preparedness movement and Fiske's behind-the-scenes collaboration with the House Naval Affairs Committee, Congress did create the post of "chief of naval operations" (CNO), which was to be an ex-officio member of the General Board. But Navy Secretary Josephus Daniels, afraid of "Prussianizing" the naval service, succeeded in getting the legislation watered down so that the CNO did not, in fact, become a chief of staff with full command powers. Daniels appointed William S. Benson, a moderate nonreformer, as the first CNO.

The establishment of the chief of naval operations was, to be sure, the first major step toward creating control by the line and, over time, diminishing the role of the General Board. But most of these developments occurred after the First World War. The CNO, influenced by the successful staff system that Admiral Sims had established in London in 1917 and 1918, took over the board's strategic planning functions immediately after the war. Still, the CNO did not achieve full command powers until the era of World War II, and the General Board, its responsibilities gradually diminishing in the 1920s and 1930s, survived until the massive naval reorganizations of that global conflict.

Some have seen the General Board in the years from 1900 through World War I as ineffective, especially as its aging chief, Admiral Dewey, became less and less involved in its ongoing activities. And its recommendations—for example, its early views on the significance of the submarine, its strict adherence to the sacred doctrine of Adm. Alfred T. Mahan about the role of the battleship and necessity of a unified fleet—were often conservative, not on the cutting edge of naval technology. Dewey's Germanophobia led the General Board to exaggerate the German threat to the Caribbean, while his long and unsuccessful campaign for a major naval base at Subig Bay in the Philippines (which the army determined was indefensible) diminished his and the board's standing with both Presidents Roosevelt and Taft.

The United States Navy was not prepared for war in 1917. The Black Plan, the General Board's only plan for a possible conflict with Germany, was based on the dubious proposition that the United States Navy would fight a decisive battle in the Caribbean with a German fleet that was aimed at the Caribbean and eventually the Panama Canal. Its early responses to the European war, especially to the rupture of German-American relations in 1917, emphasized parochial American interests. It should also be stressed that Wilson's long insistence on American neutrality and his opposition to military planning inhibited the General Board in preparing for possible conflict. But once the United States became a belligerent, the General Board was relatively quick to endorse convoying and, above all, to agree that the main American naval contribution to the war must be in lending all possible assistance to the antisubmarine campaign that threatened Britain's ability to remain in the war. And, over the doubts of many in the naval establishment, the board endorsed the North Sea Mine Barrage. On the other hand, the board never abandoned its insistence that the United States must continue to build battleships and strengthen its battle fleet on the assumption that new dangers as well as new responsibilities would emerge after the war. Indeed, in September 1918, on the eve of victory, it was advocating a vastly expanded building program that would, by 1925, make the United States the foremost naval power in the world. It was a recommendation that would cause Anglo-American friction at the peace conference and lead, by a circuitous route, to the Washington Naval Conference of 1921–1922.

Still, the General Board—which had brought together, under Dewey's aegis, the Office of Naval Intelligence, the Naval War College, the commandant of the Marine Corps, and various important bureau chiefs—did represent, as much by its composition as its function, the best professional opinion in the United States Navy. It also, by virtue of its participation on the Joint Army-Navy Board, established in 1903, was involved in the first tentative formal efforts to establish army-navy cooperation on issues of concern to both services. The prestige of Dewey meant that the General Board was at least listened to, even if its advice was not always taken. Theodore Roosevelt was, to be sure, his own secretary of the navy, but he did consult the General Board during the "war scare" with Japan in 1907, and on the battle fleet's famous round-the-world cruise; Josephus Daniels felt it worthwhile in 1913 to publish the General Board's long document on the naval needs of the United States. Even Woodrow Wilson, once he decided to adopt preparedness and launch his 1915 building program, consulted the General Board for the best professional advice available to him.

Richard D. Challener

See also BENSON, WILLIAM SHEPHERD; DANIELS, JOSEPHUS; NORTH SEA MINE BARRAGE; SIMS, WILLIAM SOWDEN

Bibliography

Fiske, Bradley A. *From Midshipman to Rear Admiral.* New York: Century, 1919.

Howe, M.A. *George von Lengerke Meyer: His Life and Public Service.* New York: Dodd, Mead, 1919.

May, Ernest. "The Development of Political-Military Consultation in the United States." *Political Science Quarterly* (June 1955).

Sprout, Harold, and Margaret Sprout. *The Rise of American Naval Power 1776– 1918.* Princeton, NJ: Princeton University Press, 1939.

Taylor, H.C. "Memorandum for a General Staff for the U.S. Navy." *U.S. Naval Institute Proceedings* (December 1903).

United States Navy: 6th Battle Squadron, Grand Fleet

The 6th Battle Squadron, Grand Fleet, consisted of five American battleships that served with the Royal Navy. It was the United States Navy's principal heavy combat force during the First World War.

In 1917, Adm. John R. Jellicoe, first sea lord of the British Admiralty, asked that a division of American coal-burning dreadnoughts be sent to reinforce the Grand Fleet in its mission to defend the North Sea and British coast against the German High Seas Fleet. Jellicoe wanted coal burners because there was a shortage of oil in Britain. The presence of the American vessels would allow the Royal Navy to release four battleships for service in the Strait of Dover, where they would help guard against sorties of German vessels.

Accordingly, the United States Navy dispatched Battleship Division Nine of the Atlantic Fleet, which included the dreadnoughts *New York, Florida, Delaware,* and *Wyoming,* under the command of Adm. Hugh Rodman. The vessels left the United States on Nov. 25, 1917, and arrived twelve days later at Scapa Flow in the Orkneys, where they were designated the Sixth Battle Squadron, Grand Fleet, under overall command of Adm. David Beatty, commander-in-chief of the British fleet. The 6th Battle Squadron alternated between bases in Scapa Flow and the Firth of Forth. The *Texas* arrived on Feb. 11, 1918, so that four battleships could be kept on duty while one rotated to port for repair, but occasionally all five operated together. The *Arkansas* relieved the *Delaware* on July 25, and *Nevada* joined the squadron on November 23.

The American squadron was integrated into the Grand Fleet in every way, including tactics, gunnery, methods, and signals. Within three days of their arrival the battleships took part in a full-scale Grand Fleet operation, and apparently had no difficulty in conforming to British tactical maneuvers. Within two weeks, the 6th Battle Squadron was assigned as one of the two fast wings of the British Battle Fleet.

The Americans made an excellent impression on Beatty. "They are desperately keen and are all out to make a success of the co-operation," he wrote to Jellicoe in December. "They are making every use of the [British] officers appointed to them and are quick to learn." The British, in turn, impressed Admiral Rodman, who described the Anglo-American relationship as one of "brotherhood" and "national kinship." High-ranking British representatives and officials, including King George V, frequently visited the American flagship.

The principal mission of the 6th Battle Squadron was to assist the British in containing the German High Seas Fleet in its bases and to stand ready for battle if the German fleet steamed into the North Sea. The squadron patrolled the North Sea with the Grand Fleet, participated in training exercises, escorted convoys between Britain and Norway, and supported Allied minelaying work in the North Sea.

In February, March, and April 1918, the squadron made one voyage per month from the British Isles to Norway and back again, escorting convoys with British destroyers. During the first voyage, the American battleships had their first encounter with enemy submarines. On February 8, the *Florida* and *Delaware* sighted a U-boat off the Norwegian coast. The Germans fired four torpedoes at the *Florida* and two at the

Delaware, but the dreadnoughts successfully maneuvered to avoid them. On April 17, during the third escort mission, the *Texas* sighted and fired upon a German submarine, but there was no evidence of damage.

During these missions, the officers and men endured cold, sleet, snow, high winds, and heavy seas. The ships cruised in close formation at high speed without lights during the eighteen-hour winter nights. Although the crews received no liberty or leave during their tour, morale remained high.

The 6th Battle Squadron joined British destroyers in support of minelaying operations in July and August 1918, guarding Allied vessels as they planted the North Sea Mine Barrage. During one of these operations, on July 28, the *Arkansas* sighted a submarine and opened fire. The submarine launched a torpedo, but it missed. There was no damage on either side.

The 6th Battle Squadron twice put to sea with units of the Grand Fleet in expectation of an encounter with the High Seas Fleet. On April 24, 1918, the American dreadnoughts sailed with the British 2d Battle Squadron to attack German vessels threatening an Allied convoy off Norway. Forward units caught sight of the enemy ships, but the Germans retired before they could be brought under fire. The 6th Battle Squadron sailed again on October 13, upon receiving a report that three large German warships were threatening a convoy off Scotland, but this time no enemy vessels were sighted. During the squadron's return to base, a German submarine collided with the *New York*, denting its bottom and demolishing its starboard propeller. Rodman believed that the blows of the *New York*'s spinning propeller, in turn, split the U-boat open and sank it. On October 16, on the way to the drydock for repairs, *New York* came under attack from another U-boat. The submarine launched three torpedoes, but they all missed.

On the night of Nov. 20–21, 1918, the American squadron had its only encounter with the German High Seas Fleet. That night, fourteen German capital ships steamed across the North Sea to their place of internment at Scapa Flow, to fulfill the terms of the Armistice agreement. Two lines of Allied battleships accompanied the surrendering Germans, one on each flank. The 6th Battle Squadron occupied a position in the middle of the north line.

In December 1918, the squadron performed its final European mission, serving in the honor escort for President Woodrow Wilson, who was sailing in the *George Washington* to Brest en route to the Versailles Conference. The battleships of the 6th Battle Squadron returned to New York City in late December in time to participate in the victory naval review in the North River.

Robert J. Schneller

See also NORTH SEA MINE BARRAGE

Bibliography
Marder, Arthur. *From the Dreadnought to Scapa Flow.* 5 vols. New York: Oxford University Press, 1961–1970.
Rodman, Hugh. *Yarns of a Kentucky Admiral.* Indianapolis: Bobbs Merrill, 1928.

United States Navy: Yeoman (F)

The Great War was the first paperwork war. Both sides found that they needed several soldiers or sailors in desk jobs for every fighting man sent to the front; civilians were used but were not fully trusted by the military. When the United States joined the Allies, these desk-bound men were needed at the front. Secretary of the Navy Josephus Daniels, an idealistic reformer, adopted a clever solution. When he discovered that there was no regulation that a yeoman (clerk) had to be a man, he ordered women to be enrolled in the U.S. Navy Reserve holding this administrative rating. Eventually, 11,275 women served with the U.S. Navy and 300 with the Marine Corps as yeomen (F). The "F" standing for female was added to warn personnel officials that these yeomen could not serve aboard ships. When the arm bands worn to designate rank were not enough, Daniels helped design a dark blue uniform for the women, consisting of a Norfolk jacket, skirts eight inches from the ground, high-button boots, and blue felt hats. Yeomen (F)s needed at least two uniforms (they had to wash one each night), which meant a cost of $150–$200 to outfit each woman. Reflecting thinking even more ahead of his time, Daniels insisted that yeomen (F) be paid the same as men of the same rating and rank and also receive the same subsistence allowance, medical care, war risk insurance, and other benefits. All women were enlisted; some did rise to the rank of chief petty officer.

For the majority of yeomen (F)s, the war was a sea of paperwork. Naval officers found that women could stick to tedious work better than many of the enlisted men. Jobs included serving as typists, bookkeepers, clerks, accountants, and stenographers. Some became translators, draftsmen, fingerprint experts, camouflage designers, and recruiters. A handful of women also received an electrician rating and served as telephone operators. Women between the ages of eighteen and thirty-five of "good" character and neat appearance could volunteer. No women were drafted. Local recruiters screened out anyone who might be promiscuous or lesbian. Applicants with high school diplomas or office experience were given preference. Some women applied, passed a cursory physical exam, and started typing the same day. While given no formal indoctrination, once at their duty stations, yeomen (F)s learned the rudiments of military drill and naval terminology. A few did serve in Puerto Rico, Guam, and the Panama Canal Zone and at least five went to France with naval hospital units. Fifty-one died on active duty, many from the influenza epidemic.

All the women naval reservists, as other reservists, were mustered out at the end of the war. The women received ordinary "honorable discharge" certificates and were eligible for full veteran's benefits. Several continued to work for the navy as civilian employees, taking advantage of the military preference given in civil service ratings. As late as 1943 over 100 former yeomen (F)s were serving as civilians in the U.S. Navy's Bureau of Supplies and Accounts. The admirals were proud of "their girls" and placed yeomen (F)s in visible spots for every parade or troop send-off rally. They also were asked to perform other public-relations tasks, such as working on Liberty Bond drives.

These women won high praise from their bosses and presented few disciplinary problems. Yet, after the war the loophole that had allowed women to serve as yeomen (F) was closed. The idea of women in the navy was just too radical for many, even though they were proud of individual women's contributions.

The American Legion accepted women members, although the Veterans of Foreign Wars did not until after World War II. The first all-women's chapter of the American Legion was established in Boston by 200 former yeomen (F)s.

D'Ann Campbell

Bibliography
Dessey, Eunice C. *The First Enlisted Women, 1917–1918.* Philadelphia: Dorrance, 1955.
Fournier, Donna J. "The Forgotten Enlisted Women of World War I." *Retired Officer* (October 1984).
Godson, Susan. "Womanpower in World War I." *U.S. Naval Institute Proceedings* (December 1984).
Guthrie, Lou MacPherson. "I was an Yeomanette." *U.S. Naval Institute Proceedings* (December 1984).
Hancock, Joy Bright. *Lady in the Navy.* Annapolis, MD: Naval Institute Press, 1972.

United States Railroad Administration

The railroad industry of the United States has always played a strategic role in the greater economy. Never is this more important than during wartime. Vital war materiel, troops, and foodstuffs must have an efficient and rapid transportation network. Private owners were not up to the task in 1917, forcing the federal government to step in and take control of the nation's vast railroad system. The experience proved that the government was not just able but also successful in directing a system that demanded the utmost effort and commitment.

The major turning point that led the federal government to take over the railroads was the fact that the whole system was coming to a halt. As early as 1916, there was a shortage of 115,000 cars. As one observer stated, "You may visualize these figures by imagining a freight train, made up solidly, and reaching clear across France, Belgium, Germany and Poland." What made this situation worse was that cars were accumulating at eastern terminals, leading to congestion. By late 1917, an emergency had indeed arisen: loaded cars standing idle on eastern railways totaled 180,000 above normal, and the car shortage had risen to 158,000. The transportation network on the eastern seaboard had come to a standstill. Accentuating this crisis was a railroad policy keeping empty cars at the point of unloading until freight had been accumulated for the return trip. Thus empty cars were clogging the major arteries of eastern stations.

Also causing problems was a shortage of skilled labor. Some roads were reporting a manpower shortage as high as 25 percent. The underlying reasons for this scarcity were the conscription of railroad workers into the armed forces and higher wages in other industries, which were drawing large numbers of men away from the railroads.

Central coordination, therefore, was the key to jump-starting the system. With an operational breakdown of the railway network and a vital shortage of labor, President Woodrow Wilson, on Dec. 26, 1917, took control of the nation's railroads. The new responsibility of the government was enormous: 360,000 miles of track, 2.4 million freight cars, 55,000 passenger cars, 66,000 locomotives, and over 2 million workers. The book value of the nation's railroads was $18 billion. The new agency created to oversee the country's rail system was the United States Railroad Administration (USRA) and its director general was William G. McAdoo. The USRA would become one of the most authoritative wartime government agencies, with no little credit going to McAdoo's influence. McAdoo retained his cabinet rank of Secretary of the Treasury, and thus he held an important strategic position in the country as a whole.

The first problem faced by the USRA was to relieve congestion. To coordinate the effort more easily, the country was divided into seven regions; eastern, Allegheny, Pocahontas, southern, northwestern, central western, and southwestern. To oversee operations within these regions, directors were appointed, usually presidents of principal railroads. Other company officials throughout the country were designated as federal managers, directly accountable to the director general. A "permit system" was developed to ensure that priority freight was dispatched in an efficient and speedy manner. Consolidation of terminal facilities was also addressed. Before government control, railroads had their respective terminal facilities. The government unified such facilities, thus making for more efficiency. The same procedure was applied to locomotive repair. Instead of sending locomotives to be repaired to their respective railroad shops (sometimes taking days to arrive at the shop), the USRA ordered repairs to be done at the nearest point. Aligned with the new policy, inspection reports for repairs were also standardized to ensure uniform practices. By mid-1918, the new initiatives had successfully relieved congestion and resulted in a surplus of freight cars.

To keep abreast of the vast system and its huge movement of freight and passengers, the USRA created a series of agencies. An Exports Control Committee coordinated the movement of needed war materiel with the Army and Navy departments. A Car Service Section kept track of the numbers and locations of freight and passenger cars. The railroads used on average a third of the country's bituminous coal supply as well as 45 million barrels of oil. To oversee more efficiently such a function, a Fuel Conservation Section was created. With such a vast undertaking running the whole system, the USRA needed accurate and relevant information, collected by the Operating Statistics Section.

By far one of the more important branches created was that of the Division of Finance and Purchasing. Rail traffic has a natural tendency to deplete existing equipment and materials; consequently, the railroads were constantly investing in new plants, machinery, and rolling stock. Thus the task facing the USRA was vast. Complicating the situation was the fact that wartime conditions drove prices for iron, steel, coal, and lumber to record highs. The USRA, however, used its newly found power to order suppliers to deal quickly and fairly.

It was one thing to coordinate rolling stock; it was another to retain a skilled workforce then leaving railroad employment in droves. Those who remained were increasingly frustrated with low wages and threatened strike action. One of McAdoo's first duties was to create a Railroad Wage Commission to investigate wages and to make recommendations. The commission advised across-the-board increases, and McAdoo so ordered in early 1918. The labor force was not entirely satisfied with the award and pressed for further increases. To placate the restless workforce of 2 million, McAdoo created a Division of Labor to oversee working conditions. The division was made up of equal numbers of management and union members. The division soon complained that the job of investigating the work practices and wages of over 2 million workers was too large. Thus, three Railway Boards of Adjustment were established. Number One represented the operating crafts (engineers, firemen, trainmen, and conductors); Number Two, the shopcrafts (machinists, boilermakers, blacksmiths, electricians, sheet-metal workers, and carmen); and Number Three, (clerks, telegraphers, switchmen, and maintenance-of-way employees).

The Division of Labor and the respective Boards of Adjustment gave railroad labor a voice in their industry that hitherto had been unheard of in any industry. Even more, to guarantee labor peace, the USRA, after recommendations from the Division of Labor, ordered that rail workers were entitled to trade union membership. In one fell swoop, then, the government recognized a trade union presence and bolstered the power of the already established labor organizations.

By the end of 1918, the nation's rail network was again operating in a speedy and efficient fashion. Tonnage per car had increased, terminals were unified, locomotives and car repairs standardized, orders for new rolling stock had been arranged, and the workforce had been stabilized. Just as important, 6.5 million troops—an average of 625,000 per month—had been transported. In all, 9,000 special trains had carried these troops.

By the Armistice, the USRA could well pat itself on the back. Its future was uncertain, however. A day after the end of the hostilities, McAdoo resigned and was replaced by Walker D. Hines. Dismantling the USRA was the administration's future function. President Wilson had stipulated that the railroads would be handed back to their owners once hostilities ceased. The question of how and when the return would be completed remained. In the meantime, railroad workers, mirroring those in other industries, were demanding wage increases to offset the rising cost of living. Indeed, to press their claim, a spate of unauthorized strikes broke out. Thus, the USRA consumed a great deal of its postwar life mollifying labor conflict.

After the passage of the Transportation Act in 1920, the USRA was declared superfluous. The act passed control back to the owners and disbanded the USRA. The experience of the USRA was not forgotten, however. Similar machinery to oversee labor relations was set up, and a strengthened government presence made for a keener interest in railroad operation. Even more, the USRA proved that the government, at a moment's notice, could take responsibility for the vast rail network and at the same time improve and standardize its operation.

Colin Davis

Bibliography

Cunningham, William J. *American Railroads: Government Control and Reconstruction Policies*. Chicago: Shaw, 1922.

Hines, Walker D. *War History of American Railroads*. New Haven: Yale University Press, 1928.

Kerr, K. Austin. *American Railroad Politics, 1914–1920*. Pittsburgh: University of Pittsburgh Press, 1969.

———. "Decision for Federal Control: Wilson, McAdoo, and the Railroads, 1917." *Journal of American History* (December 1967).

McAdoo, William G. *Crowded Years: The Reminiscences of William G. McAdoo*. Boston: Houghton Mifflin, 1931.

United States Supreme Court

As his administration began to amass legislation designed to increase his power to run the war effort by executive fiat, Woodrow Wilson feared for the constitutionality of those measures. He need not have worried. As it had done during the American Civil War, the United States Supreme Court proved to be the ally of the administration and a supporter of the growth of the presidential war-making and war-managing power.

On most matters, the Court that sat during World War I can safely be called conservative. Chief Justice Edward Douglas White, a Louisiana Bourbon who had been on the court since 1894 and chief justice since 1910, was a conservative on matters of federal power, but he had voted as a progressive on many social issues. A solid coalition of three conservatives—Willis Van Devanter, Mahlon Pitney, and James McReynolds—was often joined by the votes of two moderates—Joseph McKenna and William R. Day. They were opposed on most matters by three progressives, whose dissents were the true mark of the White Court. Oliver Wendell Holmes, Jr., Theodore Roosevelt's first appointee, had argued that the law could not be "dealt with as if it contained only the axioms and corollaries of a book of mathematics." His independence had infuriated Roosevelt, but Holmes had evolved into a jurist of progressive leanings, whose prose matched the force of his legal arguments. Holmes's newfound soulmate on the bench, Wilson appointee Louis D. Brandeis, had survived a brutal confirmation process, no less for his Judaism than for his liberal beliefs. Brandeis would quickly become the Court's leading dissenter on social justice issues. The junior member of the Court, John H. Clarke, was an Ohio Democrat who was noted for his stands in favor of government intervention in the economy to help the poor.

On one issue, the Court was united. Throughout World War I, the Court sided with the Wilson administration for the most part upholding legislation that expanded presidential war power. In the *Selective Draft Law Cases* (1918), the Court unanimously upheld the constitutionality of the Selective Service Act of 1917. Even the Armistice did not alter the Court's focus: in the *War Prohibition Cases* (1919), the Court reaffirmed the constitutionality of the War Prohibition Act, even though it had been passed after the cessation of hostilities. The general attitude of the Court can be found in *Northern Pacific Ry. Co. v. North Dakota* (1919), which upheld presidential seizure and operation of the railroads in wartime. Chief Justice White wrote in the unanimous opinion that "the complete and undivided character of the war power of the United States is not disputable."

Despite their unanimity on the war-making power, many expected that the Court would strike down administration-supported legislation curbing civil rights during wartime. Most agreed that some censorship of speech and even of the mails was necessary during the war. However, the Espionage Act (1918) clearly intended to punish not merely the act, but the *intent* to speak or write in a manner contrary to the war effort. Rather than challenge the law, the White Court chose to hear a case that guaranteed that the Espionage Act would be upheld. In *Schenck v. United States* (1919), a Socialist activist had been convicted of circulating antiwar leaflets to members of the army, leaflets that called for an insurrection—clearly falling within the scope of the act. Yet the Court went even further than upholding the law. Justice Holmes set the parameters for all censorship cases to follow when he wrote for an unanimous Court that "the question in every case is whether the words used are used in such circumstances and are of such a nature as to create a clear and present danger that they will bring about the substantive evils that Congress has a right to prevent. It is a question of proximity and degree."

This is not to say, however, that the Court consistently followed its own "clear and present danger" test in subsequent wartime censorship cases. Indeed, in *Peirce v. United States* (1920), the last of the cases to spring from the Espionage Act, the Court seemed to reverse itself. The case revolved around a strongly antiwar pamphlet, disseminated by three Socialist organizers. Unable to find any "clear and present danger" in the documents, the Court instead ruled that the pamphlets might have a "tendency to cause insubordination, disloyalty, and refusal of duty." Brandeis and Holmes's angry dissent was not enough to sway their fellow justices from agreeing to what became known as the "bad tendency" doctrine.

On the issue of the Sedition Act, Holmes and Brandeis were once again left to the dissent. In *Abrams v. United States* (1919), the Court heard a case dealing with the publication and dissemination of pamphlets criticizing Wilson's expeditionary force to Russia to aid the anti-Bolsheviks. The Court ruled that since the purpose of the documents was to "excite, at the supreme crisis of the war, disaffection, sedition, riots and . . . revolution," the documents fell under the umbrella of the Sedition Act. Infuriated, Holmes penned a dissent that one constitutional history textbook has called "the most eloquent and moving defense of free speech since Milton's *Areopagitica*." Dismissing the pamphlets under consideration as a "silly leaflet by an unknown man" that did not present any clear and present danger, Holmes tore into the fabric of the First Amendment: "We should be eternally vigilant against attempts to check the expression of opinions that we loathe and believe to be fraught with death, unless they so imminently threaten immediate interference with the lawful and pressing purposes of the law that an immediate check is required to save the country."

The rulings of the White Court during World War I would have wide future import. The "clear and present danger" doctrine first enunciated in *Schenck* would be revived in World War II, as the Court dealt with such free-speech cases as the *Flag Salute Cases* and later in the prosecution of Communists during the Cold War era. On a much broader scale, *Peirce* and *Abrams* particularly led to the conclusion that the Court believed that any dissent during wartime is not protected by the First Amendment. These cases would be invoked to support the actions of the government during succeeding conflicts, with mixed results.

John R. Greene

Bibliography

Kelly, Alfred H., and Winifred A. Harbison. *The American Constitution: Its Origins and Development.* New York: Norton, 1970.

Murphy, Paul L. *The Constitution in Crisis Times: 1918–1969.* New York: Harper & Row, 1972.

V

Van Kleeck, Mary (1893–1972)

Mary Van Kleeck was a social investigator and reformer. After graduating from Smith College in 1904, she began working in a settlement house on the Lower East Side of New York. Believing that reporting upon social ills was the first step to eradicating them, she investigated the conditions of working women in factories and child labor in New York tenements during the next two years. She then worked with the Alliance Placement Bureau, a New York City agency for the placement of women and girls in factories and offices. She authored a number of reports, many published by the Russell Sage Foundation, that documented the inferior working conditions in a number of female-dominated industries. Her reports were used to win court cases and to promote Progressive legislation. In 1911, she became director of the Russell Sage Foundation's Committee on Women's Work. There she compiled detailed information about women wage earners for the development of employment standards. She also lectured at the New York School of Social Philanthropy.

During World War I, Van Kleeck held various government positions relating to the employment of women in war production. She served on the War Labor Policies Board and as director of the Women's Division in the War Department's Ordnance Division. She wrote standards for the employment of women that were adopted by the War Labor Policies Board. In 1918, Van Kleeck was appointed head of the Women in Industry Division of the Department of Labor. Here she worked with employers to increase efficiency, while easing the entry of women into traditionally male occupations. She also attempted to improve conditions of labor and to ameliorate the economic positions of women workers.

Theresa McDevitt

Bibliography

Greenwald, Maurine Weiner. *Women, War and Work: The Impact of World War I on Women Workers in the United States.* Westport, CT: Greenwood Press, 1980.

Vardaman, James Kimble (1861–1930)

James Kimble Vardaman served three terms in the Mississippi legislature (1889–1895), one term as governor of Mississippi (1904–1908), and one term as United States senator (1913–1919). Throughout his career he combined appeals for racism and reform. In addition to upholding racial segregation and disenfranchisement for blacks, he also called for the abolition of public education for African Americans. But for white Americans who made their livings as farmers and laborers, Vardaman supported a wide range of programs designed to enhance their socioeconomic standing. He strongly distrusted people of great wealth as well as large corporations. As a senator, he supported every major reform passed by Congress between 1913 and 1916 and compiled a voting record that closely resembled those of midwestern Progressives as Robert M. LaFollette and George W. Norris.

From the beginning of World War I, Vardaman believed that the United States should avoid involvement in the conflict, and during the next three years he became an outspoken advocate of neutrality. Like his Progressive colleagues in the Senate, for him wars resulted from the greed of munitions makers and bankers. He wanted America to continue devoting its attention to domestic reforms and thereby set an example of a peaceful, progressive democracy for Europe to emulate.

Beginning with the Wilson administration's call for a government-operated shipping line in 1915, Vardaman became one of the harshest congressional critics of the President's foreign policy. In his opinion, the administration took too lenient a position in trying to persuade the British to recognize neutral rights because America's large businesses reaped great profit from trading with the Allies. Vardaman knew that his criticism of the administration could undermine his political support in Mississippi, but with unwavering courage he followed that unpopular course. When the President called for a declaration of war in April 1917, Vardaman was one of six senators who voted against it. After that, however, he supported most wartime legislation, but he did oppose those measures that he believed endangered free institutions at home or conceded too much to wealthy interests: conscription, the Espionage Act, the Sedition Act, and the Food Administration. He also opposed African Americans serving in the armed forces.

Vardaman's opposition to the war and his strong criticism of the President did undermine his popularity. In 1918, Congressman Pat Harrison challenged him in the Mississippi Democratic primary, basing his campaign on the importance of complete loyalty to the President during the war. During the campaign, Vardaman frequently confronted hostile audiences who heckled him with shouts of "von Vardaman," and he sometimes spoke from platforms painted bright yellow. Not surprisingly, Harrison defeated Vardaman and thereby ended his political career.

William F. Holmes

Versailles Treaty
See PARIS PEACE CONFERENCE

Victor Emmanuel (Vitorrio Emanuele) III (1869–1947)
The man who would be Italy's longest reigning monarch, Victor Emmanuel III was the son of Humbert I (then Prince of Piedmont) and Margherita de Savoia, and was thus a member of the House of Savoy-Carignan. At birth he was named Prince of Naples. Like many future

monarchs, as a young man he was taken under the wing of army officers, and grew to manhood in military service. He married Princess Elena of Montenegro, daughter of Prince Nicholas, in October 1896. Together they had five children: Jolanda, Mafalda, Humbert, Giovanna, and Maria.

Victor Emmanuel formally ascended to the Italian throne on Aug. 11, 1900, after his father's assassination the previous July 29 in Monza. Tensions within the country relaxed somewhat as he adopted a more conciliatory policy toward the Liberal Party that controlled the government. The new king was quite comfortable performing his duties as a constitutional monarch and did not necessarily wish to become more involved with the complicated and tiring process of governing. It was the Liberal administration of Giovanni Giolitti that led the country into the Tripolitan War of 1911 against the weak Ottoman Empire, which led to the Italian acquisition of Libya.

The king and his ministers had long worked at the difficult act of balancing their foreign policies between their partners in the Triple Alliance, whom they did not really care for, and Britain and France. The Italian government correctly saw that, in its vulnerable geographical position with a weak military, war against the Entente Powers in 1914 promised little gain but many costly defeats. A war against the Central Powers, on the other hand, offered the possibility of regaining lost territory now controlled by Austria-Hungary and perhaps gaining more land in the Balkans and Africa, long a focus of Italian ambitions. Italy was able to remain cautiously neutral, while negotiating with both sides for concessions, before signing the secret Treaty of London on April 26, 1915, which included the desired territorial guarantees from Britain and France.

There was great excitement in the country as bitter factional infighting and political confusion arose as to whether or not the treaty should be approved and its provisions for war against Austria-Hungary carried out. Premier Antonio Salandra resigned over a lack of public and legislative support for war, and Victor Emmanuel apparently considered abdicating. Faced with violent demonstrations and the very real possibility of civil war, the king directly involved himself in the negotiations to find a way out of the crisis. Determining that Giolitti was not ready to take over as premier, the king reappointed Salandra, his favorite, to the position. After the formal declaration of war on May 24, 1915, the king spent much of his time at military headquarters near the front lines, an environment with which he was familiar and comfortable. Victor Emmanuel was, for the most part, able to remain clear of interdepartmental squabbles. A notable exception occurred when he was called upon to mediate questions of Italian policy and actions in Albania. In general, the king did not interfere with military operations, nor did he try to exert more influence in coordinating the actions of the government. His failure to act decisively contributed to Italian difficulties and ineffectiveness during the war.

The disaster that engulfed the Italian forces at Caporetto in October 1917 provided another opportunity for the king to show his leadership skills; it would prove to be perhaps his finest hour. He worked hard to rally the retreating units, bolstering public confidence, and replace ineffective Gen. Luigi Cadorna with Gen. Armando Diaz. At a conference at Peschiera on Nov. 8, 1917, he managed to convince British Prime Minister David Lloyd George and other Allied leaders that the Italians could hold the Piave River line against the advancing Austrians. His forceful presentation convinced Britain and France to send divisions to reinforce the Italian front at this crucial time. The line was successfully held, and the Italian troops were able to advance the next year as the Austro-Hungarian forces weakened and finally collapsed.

The immediate postwar period was one of painful disillusionment for Italy. Although they had fought for over three years and suffered devastating losses, the Italians were bitterly disappointed over the way they were treated by other Allied leaders at the Paris Peace Conference. The Orlando government was unwilling to adapt to the new European political situation, where Yugoslavia was given many of the lands coveted by Rome. Only some of their territorial demands in Austria, the Adriatic, and the Aegean were met. Unilateral Italian military actions in Turkey to seize territory and gain a bargaining position only worsened relations with the other Allied powers. Rome was infuriated when President Woodrow Wilson released a statement that appealed to the Italian people over the head of their government. For a time the Italians even withdrew from the Paris Peace Conference, which further reduced their influence in Europe. The actions by Britain and France to limit Italian gains would later be used by Fascists to persuade the Italian populace that they had been robbed of an empire and that the only way to achieve colonies, economic sufficiency, and glory was to ally themselves with Nazi Germany and Japan and to take what they wanted.

In the interwar years the king was, like many others at that time, worried more about revolution from the Left than the familiar authoritarianism from the Right. While disquieted by some of Benito Mussolini's actions and statements, he, nonetheless, did not act to prevent that former Socialist from leading a Fascist takeover of the government that resulted from the famous March on Rome in October 1922. The king thus bears some responsibility for Italy's aggression in the 1930s and the catastrophe that befell the country in the Second World War. His convoluted machinations to overthrow Mussolini and switch over to the winning Allied side in the summer of 1943, culminating in the armistice of Sept. 3, 1943, were not enough to save him from the disdain of his subjects, or effect the prompt ejection of German forces from Italy. After the war he abdicated in favor of his son, Humbert II on May 9, 1946. However, Humbert was denied the chance to rule when a majority of Italians voted for a republic on June 2, 1946. Victor Emmanuel went into exile in Alexandria, Egypt, where he died at the end of the following year. While perhaps best remembered for his actions during World War II, it was during the first world conflict that he served his country best.

Daniel K. Blewett

Bibliography

Bertoldi, Silvio. *Vittorio Emanuele III*. Turin: Unione Tipografico-Editrice Torinese, 1970.

Hentze, Margot. *Pre-Fascist Italy: The Rise and Fall of the Parliamentary Regime.* New York: Octagon Books, 1962.

Mack-Smith, Denis. *Italy and Its Monarchy*. New Haven: Yale University Press, 1989.

Seton-Watson, Hugh. *Italy, From Liberalism to Fascism*. London: Methuen, 1967.

Victory Loans

See LIBERTY LOANS

Virgin Islands: United States Purchase, 1916–1917

There had been numerous proposals for the United States to purchase the Danish West Indies, or Virgin Islands, consisting of St. Thomas, St. John, and St. Croix, since the administration of Abraham Lincoln. Treaties for this purpose, in fact, had been negotiated in 1867 and again in 1902, but the first had failed to be approved by the United States Senate and the second had been rejected by the Danish Parliament. Concern that Germany might be interested in acquiring the islands for a naval base had increased the desire of the American government for their acquisition in the early twentieth century. With the outbreak of the First World War, the fear that Germany might acquire the islands through the occupation of Denmark itself made their purchase by the United States a matter of some urgency.

Maurice Francis Egan, the United States minister to Denmark, had kept the possibility of the American purchase of the islands open through quiet diplomacy since his appointment in 1907. In May 1915, he reported to Washington that Danish Foreign Minister Eric de Scavenius had indicated in an informal conversation that his government might be receptive to an American proposal to purchase the islands. In July, President Woodrow Wilson urged Secretary of State Robert Lansing to pursue negotiations for the purchase as vigorously as possible. Lansing did so. A breakthrough came as the result of a conversation in November between Lansing and Constantin Brun, the Danish minister to the United States. Brun asked whether the United States would seize the islands if Denmark refused to sell them. Lansing replied that there were no such plans at present but that such a seizure might become unavoidable if Denmark was absorbed by another nation or if Denmark transferred title to the islands to a European power. When Brun reported this conversation to Scavenius, the latter responded that Denmark clearly had no choice but to consider an American offer to purchase the islands.

From that point onward, negotiations proceeded rapidly. Denmark asked $27 million for the islands. Lansing expressed doubt about agreeing to such a huge sum, but Wilson declared on Jan. 7, 1916, that he considered the acquisition so important that Lansing should negotiate on the basis of that amount. Lansing ultimately persuaded the Danes to settle for $25 million. Lansing and Brün signed a purchase treaty on Aug. 4, 1916. The United States Senate consented to ratification of the treaty on September 7. The Danish Parliament approved ratification in December 1916, following a national plebiscite on the issue, and ratifications were exchanged on Jan. 17, 1917. The transfer of the islands to the United States took place in St. Thomas on March 31 of that year, just one week before Congress declared war on Germany.

John E. Little

Bibliography

Tansill, Charles C. *The Purchase of the Danish West Indies.* Baltimore: Johns Hopkins University Press, 1932.

Vittorio Veneto, Battle of

The Battle of Vittorio Veneto (October–November 1918) constituted the final Italian offensive of the war, which drove the Austrian Army from the Piave River front and led to Austria's surrender.

Following the collapse of the Italian Army on the Isonzo front during the Battle of Caporetto in November 1917, Italian forces retreated seventy miles southwest to the Piave River, where, with Allied support, they succeeded in halting the Austro-German advance. The Piave front, stretching for more than eighty miles from the Alps to the Adriatic Sea, settled into inactivity, and the major belligerents reduced their assistance to Italy and Austria. Germany withdrew seven divisions, and the Allies reduced their contingent to three British and two French divisions and the United States 332d Infantry Regiment. By the summer of 1918, Italian forces on the Piave totaled fifty-six infantry and four cavalry divisions.

During the summer, the Austrians transferred thousands of men from the Eastern Front to the Piave, eventually assembling a force of fifty-five infantry and eight cavalry divisions, the largest body they massed against Italy in the war. They organized their divisions into two army groups under Field Marshal Svetozar Boroević and Field Marshal Franz Conrad von Hötzendorf, formerly the Austrian chief of staff.

The Austrians made one last attempt to defeat the Italians. It was hoped that this move would also help their German ally by drawing Allied troops from the Western Front to aid Italy as had happened the previous year. The offensive envisioned a two-pronged attack on the Piave line. Conrad's army group (Tenth and Eleventh Armies) made two attacks on the central portion of the Piave front, which were quickly repulsed by French and British forces. Boroević's army group (Fifth and Sixth Armies) attacked along the lower Piave and gained a bridgehead fifteen miles long and up to five miles deep, though the defending Italian Third Army fell back in good order. Finding it difficult to maintain the bridgehead in the face of a rising river and air attacks, Boroević withdrew his forces on June 22–23. The offensive, known as the Battle of the Piave, gained little against the reorganized Italian forces and resulted in 150,000 Austrian casualties, losses the Austrians could ill-afford, particularly in light of the increasing number of desertions and political dissension within the ranks.

Although the Italian Army had only a slight numerical edge over the Austrians, Italian morale had been improving under their new commander, Gen. Armando Diaz. In view of the spirit of his troops and considerable Allied aid, General Diaz made plans for a counteroffensive. He created two new armies, the Tenth (two British and two Italian divisions and the United States regiment) under British Gen. Lord Frederic Cavan and the Twelfth (one French and three Italian divisions) under French Gen. Jean Graziani. Diaz concentrated his forces along a fifty-mile sector in the middle Piave front. The main effort was to be made by the Italian Fourth and Eighth Armies; the Fourth Army was to break through the Austrian lines and seize the town of Feltre, and the Eighth Army was to seize the town of Vittorio Veneto.

Allied forces infiltrated across the Piave River on the night of October 23 and the next morning attacked all along the front. The Austrian forces held fast and contained the initial Allied advance, successfully repulsing the Fourth Army's attack. On the night of October 26, a French division established a bridgehead over the Piave and the Twelfth Army crossed the next day. Heavy fighting erupted in the Tenth Army's sector as the British-Italian forces attacked the junction of the Austrian Fifth and Sixth Armies, securing and widening a bridgehead. By October 28, the British succeeded in breaking through the last of the Austrian defenses and Habsburg resistance began to crumble. By November 1, the entire Austrian front was in retreat, and the Allies advanced more than sixty miles before an armistice was negotiated and took effect on November 4.

Casualties in the offensive mounted to over 39,000 for the Italians, and almost 500,000 for the Austrians, including 427,000 prisoners. The Battle of Vittorio Veneto led to the collapse of the Austrian Army and was a decisive event in Austria's decision to seek an armistice. The offensive allowed Italy to end the war with a victory, which gained for them considerable influence at the Paris Peace Conference.

David Robrock

Bibliography

Coppa, Frank J. *Dictionary of Modern Italian History.* Westport, CT: Greenwood Press, 1985.

Edmonds, James E. *A Short History of World War I.* New York: Greenwood Press, 1968.

Esposito, Vincent J., ed. *The West Point Atlas of American Wars, 1900–1953.* New York: Praeger, 1959.

Falls, Cyril. *The Great War.* New York: Putnam, 1959.

Griffiths, William R. *The Great War.* Wayne, NJ: Avery Publishing Group, 1986.

Viviani, René Raphael (1863–1925)

Lawyer, journalist, and Socialist politician, René Viviani was born in French Algeria to an Italian immigrant family. He became involved in working-class politics after representing several labor unions. During the 1890s, he edited two major independent Socialist newspapers, *La Petite Republicaine* and *La Lanterne.* He was elected to the Chamber of Deputies as an independent socialist in 1893.

In 1906, Georges Clemenceau, the new French premier, chose Viviani to head the first Ministry of Labor. Although both Viviani and Clemenceau favored the moderate trade union movement and hoped to enforce existing social legislation, little progress was possible in the atmosphere of class conflict generated by the syndicalist unions. Viviani continued as labor minister under Premier Aristide Briand but eventually resigned due to Briand's hostility to labor.

In 1914, Raymond Poincaré, the conservative president of the French republic, offered to let Viviani form a ministry—if Viviani would defend the three-year term of military service against the Radical and Socialist majority of the

V

chamber. Few other politicians were willing to pay that price, but Viviani accepted—whether he did so out of patriotism or personal ambition remains unclear. His only major shortcoming in Poincaré's opinion was "a black ignorance of matters of foreign policy."

During the crisis of July and August 1914, Viviani helped to impress the British with his determination not to provoke Germany, and he directed French troops guarding the border to remain seven miles away from the frontier. This decision proved controversial when Germany attacked just a few days later. However, Viviani retained the confidence of the Chamber of Deputies until France sustained a series of military disasters in October 1915, which included the ill-fated Salonika expedition, the Austro-German and Bulgarian invasion of Serbia, and failed Franco-British offensives in the Champagne region, which brought down his government.

The French government, following Britain's lead, decided to send a commission to the United States after it declared war on Germany in April 1917. Led by Minister of Justice and Public Information René Viviani, members included Marshal Joseph Joffre, ("The Victor of the Marne"), Admiral Cocheprat (the marquis of Chambrun and Lafayette's grandson), and Joseph Simon of the Ministry of Finance, plus assorted minor diplomatic and military officials and translators. The mission sailed to Hampton Roads, Virginia, arriving on April 24. The commissioners were then taken to Washington aboard the presidential yacht the *Mayflower*.

Despite his position as the mission's nominal leader, Viviani was completely overshadowed by Marshal Joffre, and Viviani visibly resented the public adulation showered on the marshal. Like Lord Balfour, Viviani asked to address the Senate on May 1, but unlike the Briton, he spoke no English and despite the fact that no translator was available, proceeded to harangue his audience for an hour in French. When he was finished, the senators began shouting for Joffre to say a few words. The marshal, who was already on his way to the door, turned to his captive audience and said, "I do not speak English." Smiling, he added

"*Vivent les Etats-Unis!*" This, of course, brought uncontrolled cheering from the Senate in a manner that reminded reporters of a college football game. A similar scene took place the next day when Viviani addressed the House of Representatives. In Philadelphia, Joffre stepped forward to kiss the Liberty Bell, whereas Viviani not only kissed the bell, but also a very surprised Mayor Smith.

While Viviani was alienating his hosts, Joffre explained the current military situation to the U.S. Army General Staff and Col. Edward M. House in plain terms. President Wilson approved his request for the immediate deployment of a small American force to France "for morale purposes" on May 8. Both Wilson and Secretary of War Newton D. Baker believed that a truly large force would have to be sent, despite Joffre's parting observation that the Americans would not be able to send more than half a million men abroad before the end of the war.

In his meeting with the President, Viviani offended Wilson by defending the Paris Economic Conference of 1916, wherein the Allies agreed to discriminate against German commerce even after the war ended. Wilson had criticized the agreement at the time, and he still thought its terms unjust and likely to cause future conflict. The French mission departed without further incident in May. But later in July 1917, Wilson directed House to begin organizing "The Inquiry" to define American war aims—specifically citing the disagreement he had had with the French minister.

Although Viviani continued to hold minor ministerial appointments until his death in 1925, his public career was effectively over in 1917.

David Esposito

Bibliography

Halsey, Francis, ed. *Balfour, Viviani and Joffre.* New York: Funk & Wagnalls, 1917.

King, Jere C. *Generals and Politicians.* Berkeley: University of California Press, 1951.

Viviani, René. *Addresses in the United States.* Garden City, NY: Doubleday, Page, 1917.

Wald, Lillian D. (1867–1940)

A public health nurse and social reformer, Lillian D. Wald founded the Henry Street Settlement House in New York City and organized the first independent public health nursing service in the United States. Beginning in 1893, Wald established a visiting nurse service to the immigrant poor of New York's Lower East Side. Like other settlement houses of the period, her Henry Street Settlement became a center that offered educational, social, and philanthropic services to the people of the neighborhood.

As hostilities leading to World War I escalated, reformers such as Lillian Wald came to believe that war would interrupt their work of bringing humane conditions to the poor from many countries. Wald felt that war jeopardized the ideas of democracy and social progress toward which she and other social workers had been working. To show her opposition, she helped to organize, and marched in, the Women's Peace Parade in New York in August 1914. Later that year a group of antimilitarists including Wald, Jane Addams, Max Eastman, and Florence Kelley met at the Henry Street Settlement and formed the Anti-Preparedness Committee. In 1915, the group changed its name to the American Union Against Militarism, and Wald was its first president. Under Wald's leadership, the union tried unsuccessfully to get the Wilson administration to advocate their belief that the European conflict could be ended through mediation by neutral countries.

When the United States entered the war, Lillian Wald turned her energies toward filling the increased demand for nurses and protecting civil liberties on the homefront. Although some people withdrew contributions to her nursing service because of her opposition to the war, she insisted that she was willing to serve in any way, except militarily, toward home defense and the preservation of life.

Wald served on the Council of National Defense and headed its committee on home nursing. She allowed the Henry Street Settlement to be used for conscription by the local registration board. The settlement house was also involved in such wartime agency activities as the Food Council, the Red Cross, and the Baby Saving Campaign. When Spanish Influenza struck New York in the fall of 1918, Wald became the chair of the Nurses' Emergency Council, which mobilized nursing and welfare agencies and recruited volunteers to help in hospitals and homes.

Wald was a founder of the League of Free Nations Association, which grew out of the American Union Against Militarism. After the war, Wald continued her work with the Henry Street Settlement and, on a national level, pushed for social welfare legislation and promoted political candidates who supported her social welfare concerns.

Laura Kells

See also ADDAMS, JANE; AMERICAN UNION AGAINST MILITARISM

Bibliography

Duffus, R.L. *Lillian Wald: Neighbor and Crusader.* New York: Macmillan, 1938.

James, Edward T. *Notable American Women, 1607–1950.* Cambridge, MA: Belknap Press, 1971.

Wald, Lillian D. *Windows on Henry Street.* Boston: Little, Brown, 1934.

Walsh, Francis Patrick (1864–1939)

Serving as co-chairman of the National War Labor Board (NWLB) in 1918, Frank P. Walsh, a brilliant labor lawyer, played a vital role in shaping the wartime labor reforms of the Wilson administration, creating a legacy that influenced the labor legislation of the New Deal in the 1930s.

Francis Patrick Walsh was born in 1864 and raised in an Irish working-class neighborhood in St. Louis. After holding a variety of laboring jobs, the self-educated Walsh in 1885 took a position as a stenographer in a Kansas City law firm. Studying law in his spare time, Walsh eventually gained admittance to the bar. As a young lawyer, he handled a variety of cases, from defending Jesse James, Jr., on charges of train robbery to representing a wide range of corporate interests in Kansas City. On Jan. 1, 1900, however, Walsh gave up all his corporate business and embarked on a career in defense of trade unionism, a cause close to his heart since his laboring days. At the same time, Walsh became active in Missouri progressive politics. By 1912, he had developed a statewide reputation as an energetic reformer. Having supported Woodrow Wilson's 1912 presidential candidacy, Walsh was subsequently tapped by the new President to serve as chairman of the Commission on Industrial Relations in 1913. This post catapulted him into the national spotlight. Reviled by businessmen and praised by labor for his work on the commission, Walsh was identified as one of the most prominent advocates of workers' rights on the eve of World War I.

Walsh advocated American neutrality during the European war until April 1917. Thereafter, he loyally supported the United States war effort, while working to protect—both publicly and behind the scenes—the rights of those who did not. With his friend Clarence Darrow, Walsh defended suppressed newspapers in a 1917 hearing before Postmaster General Albert S. Burleson, while privately Walsh provided legal advice to the embattled leaders of the Industrial Workers of the World (IWW). When Woodrow Wilson formed the NWLB on April 8, 1918, to quell wartime labor unrest, labor leaders naturally picked the outspoken Walsh to serve as their chosen co-chair of the board. Employers chose former President William H. Taft as Walsh's counterpart.

Presiding over a quarrelsome board composed of leading representatives of business and labor, Walsh and Taft drew up a set of principles as a guide for the NWLB's settlement of wartime labor disputes. These principles clearly bore Walsh's liberal imprint. Among them were guarantees of the right of workers to organize, of women's rights to equal pay for equal work, and of the right to bargain collectively. With Walsh as the co-chair, the board proved an enormous stimulus to the wartime growth of the American Federation of Labor (AF of L). Indeed, during the brief tenure of the NWLB the AF of L saw its membership nearly double.

Days after the signing of the Armistice, however, Frank Walsh left the NWLB (which itself did not expire until June 1919). Ever the defender of the downtrodden, Walsh then successfully argued before the NWLB the case of Cleveland's women streetcar drivers, who suffered discrimination at the hands of the male-dominated union of their trade. Viewed as perhaps America's most articulate postwar Progressive leader, Walsh was approached to run as the 1920 Farmer-Labor candidate for president. He declined.

By mid-1919, Walsh had already turned his attention to another of his passions: Ireland. An ardent nationalist, Walsh led a delegation of Americans attempting to represent Ireland at the Paris Peace Conference in 1919. Walsh viewed Woodrow Wilson's actions at the conference as a betrayal of his earlier commitment to Irish self-determination. The Irish question, then, ultimately precipitated a sharp break between Walsh and the president he had recently served.

In the 1920s and 1930s, Walsh continued his relationship with the Irish Republic while returning to an active legal career in defense of workers. He represented Communists charged with sedition; he championed the cause of imprisoned labor agitator Tom Mooney; he took on numerous anti-injunction cases; he organized support for Franklin Roosevelt's 1932 presidential campaign; he fought for reform of the electric power industry; he remained active in Catholic Church efforts; and he participated in the founding of the left-leaning National Lawyers Guild. He battled for all his principles until he drew his final breath. On May 2, 1939, Frank P. Walsh died of a heart attack while en route to hearings in defense of structural iron workers in New York City.

Joseph McCartin

Bibliography

Conner, Valerie Jean. *The National War Labor Board: Stability, Social Justice, and*

the *Voluntary State in World War I*.
Chapel Hill: University of North Carolina Press, 1983.

Montgomery, David. *The Fall of the House of Labor: The Workplace, the State, and Labor Activism*. New York: Cambridge University Press, 1987.

War Brides

During World War I, approximately 10,000 members of the American Expeditionary Force (AEF) married European women. The average war bride was French, in her early twenties and of rural background. The American soldier whom she married was frequently of foreign parentage, Catholic, and from the West or Midwest.

The U.S. Army was unprepared for these marriages and failed to provide overseas commanders with an official policy or standardized procedure. AEF officials regarded the marriages between American soldiers and French civilians as prejudicial to military interest. Nevertheless, they considered marriage a personal right and privilege of the individual. Thus, American military authorities declined to give express consent to marriages or to prohibit them.

In the absence of military regulations, marriages between soldiers and civilians remained subject to French civil law. However, this caused much confusion because once the couple was married, the bride lost her French citizenship. The soldiers and their French wives and relatives were concerned about the women's citizenship status and turned to American military and government officials for advice and assistance. Faced with a growing number of inquiries concerning wartime weddings, the American government reluctantly assumed responsibility for the welfare of the brides and their transportation to the United States.

American officials issued emergency passports and travel certificates to French women who could prove that their marriages were bona fide and that their husbands had knowledge of and consented to their journey to the United States. The travel certificate entitled the French bride to overseas transportation on an army vessel. Moreover, for a fee of $1 per day, the army provided the bride with meals, transportation to the embarkation port, and railway fare in the United States.

Prior to their departure from France, the war brides were assembled in the ports of Brest, Bordeaux, and St. Nazaire. Here the AEF, in cooperation with the Red Cross and YWCA, erected Hostess Houses to provide accommodation and meals for the French women. Moreover, YWCA secretaries offered a variety of classes and programs designed to ease the brides' transition to American society. YWCA secretaries taught English-language classes and introduced the French women to American geography, culture, and cuisine until they received notice to board an army transport vessel.

Upon their arrival in the United States, the French war brides were usually greeted by their husbands or American relatives. Some husbands, however, were unable to meet their French wives because they were still in the army. Moreover, some men were reluctant to call for their brides because they had no means of supporting them, while others were already married or not naturalized citizens.

In these cases the YWCA continued to provide accommodation and meals at Hostess Houses in Newport News, Virginia, and New York City. The war brides remained at these houses until their husbands called for them or until necessary arrangements had been made to send them to their final destinations. After the couple was reunited, the YWCA often provided further assistance to the brides through its local branches.

Nina Mjagkij

Bibliography
Mjagkij, Nina. "Forgotten Women: War Brides of World War I." *Amerikastudien/American Studies* (1987).

War Camp Community Service

The War Camp Community Service (WCCS), the wartime arm of the Playground and Recreation Association of America, operated as one of the seven welfare agencies affiliated with the War Department's Commission on Training Camp Activities. Within the camps, the Commission on Training Camp Activities tried to envelop the American soldier with "invisible armor" through programs of education, health, and recreation. These programs, designed to promote cordial relations between soldiers and local civilians, targeted illicit sex and alcohol abuse as the major temptations to be overcome. To Joseph Lee, a member of the commission and president of the Playground and Recreation Association, was delegated the task of stimulating communities adjacent to the training camps to mobilize their social and recreational resources in support of the officers and soldiers streaming into the soldier-cities located throughout the nation. For the progressive reformers, urbanization and the differentiation of work and leisure time underscored the need for and restorative value of recreation and play. Social environmentalism, the notion that cultural habits shape relationships and morality, fortified the reformers' enthusiasm for a broad range of activities.

Most communities were eager to cooperate and offer services to the commission and the WCCS, especially since the War Department linked the viability of the camps to local support. Information bureaus and housing received top priority, followed by such recreational facilities and services as writing and lounging rooms, swimming pools, barber shops, cafeterias, stages for dramatics, dances, and movies. Soldiers' clubs offering many of these services were organized in every major city and in many smaller areas. Fraternal organizations and churches reached out to the soldiers, and Bible hours, dances, parades, smokers, and community sings were organized. Special recreational programs for the patients and staff of hospitals not served by the Red Cross were offered by the WCCS. Concerned with the matter of healthful relations between soldiers and local girls, the WCCS sponsored the Patriotic League, which operated programs stressing civic responsibility, social restraint, and physical fitness. The push for activities on the Sabbath often incurred the opposition of the clergy, especially in the South.

The WCCS expended approximately $4 million in over 300 communities to furnish wholesome recreation to the men in uniform. This commitment and the attendant programs must be judged a major contribution to harmonious civil-military relations and to the morale of the troops. Leisure time pursuits, for the first time, received attention as an issue worthy of social planning at the national level. Detracting from its overall success was the tendency by the commission and the WCCS to treat women as recreational objects, a view that did not advance the progressive agenda of mutual respect between the sexes and the elimination of prostitution.

Arthur P. Young

See also COMMISSION ON TRAINING CAMP ACTIVITIES

Bibliography

Allen, Edward F. *Keeping Our Fighters Fit for War and After.* New York: Century, 1918.

Bristow, Nancy K. "Creating Crusaders: The Commission on Training Camp Activities and the Pursuit of the Progressive Social Vision During World War One." Ph.D. dissertation, University of California-Berkeley, 1989.

Handbook of War Camp Community Service. New York: War Camp Community Service, 1918.

War Industries Board

The experience of World War I profoundly transformed the relationship between government and the U.S. economy. Before the conflict, government assumed a laissez-faire attitude toward the private sector despite occasional intrusions of tariff and antitrust legislation. During the war, the U.S. government reallocated some 25 percent of civilian production to war production—in some cases, taking over entire industries and firms.

From 1917 to 1918, President Wilson's War Industries Board (WIB) served as the critical institutional vehicle that centralized and directed the nation's economic output. Not unlike other agencies, the War Industries Board evolved in several stages. As early as 1916, Wilson created the Council of National Defense, a committee to coordinate possible war mobilization. The council in turn established the National Defense Advisory Committee (NDAC), which sought industry cooperation with a war conversion program.

By the summer of 1917, NDAC was deemed inadequate to the task of national mobilization. In this phase, the WIB advised the President's cabinet but possessed no independent power of enforcement. The mobilization effort of the WIB was secured by working with the United States Chamber of Commerce, volunteer industry personnel (dollar-a-year men), and some 267 industry committees.

By March 1918, the nation's mobilization effort was paralyzed by mounting orders from the War Department, a proliferation of independent government boards, and the absence of coherent economic direction. Economic gridlock prompted President Wilson to reconstitute the WIB, making the agency autonomous from the cabinet, giving it direct access to the

President, and empowering the board to reallocate the nation's productive capacity. Wilson appointed Bernard M. Baruch as "czar" of the WIB. Baruch was wealthy, was a Democrat, and had contributed $50,000 to the President's 1916 campaign.

Now reinvigorated under Baruch's leadership, the WIB bridged the gap between military demand and industrial production. A first task was to establish resource priorities. Industries were ranked and then assigned a certificate that enabled a particular company to preempt the demand for resources and raw materials. Certificates possessed by one firm thus created an incentive for other firms to convert from civilian to war production. By the fall of 1918, 73 separate industries and 7,000 individual plants enjoyed priority status.

The next task of the WIB was to establish prices on products and resources. Industry groups collaborated on setting prices—posting rates that covered production costs and generated a margin of profit. Since prices were set to cover inefficient firms, the government then penalized productive firms by invoking an excess profits tax.

In addition to priorities and price fixing, the WIB served as purchasing agent for British, French, and Russian needs. Products purchased included nitrates, tin, wool, leather, and platinum.

Finally, the WIB standardized products and materials in order to conserve scarce resources. Few products escaped this conservation effort. Even the metal stays that were removed from corsets were estimated to provide enough steel for two warships.

Resource reallocation was particularly effective in food, steel, coal, and small-arms output. The United States shipped to Britain alone 569 tons of powder and explosives, 926 million rounds of small-arms munitions, 31 million shells, 1 to 2 million rifles, 42,000 trucks, 1,400 gun carriages, and 3,400 airplane engines. France and Russia were also supplied with varying amounts of materiel.

Nevertheless, the United States Army remained heavily dependent upon Allied armaments. Almost half of U.S. troops were transported to Europe in British ships, and the American Army relied on British and French supplies of tanks, artillery, and planes. American production of war materiel was planned for the long term, and Germany collapsed before United States industries achieved their goals.

Mobilization, centralization, and government intervention did not come without some rhetorical adjustment by the Wilson administration. As a progressive, the President had campaigned against monopolies, big business, and the money trusts. His Clayton Antitrust Act and Federal Trade Commission Act were attempts to supplement the 1890 Sherman Antitrust Act. Yet Wilson's war effort rested on a cooperative business/government partnership based on a diminution of open- and free-market competition. Indeed, the WIB immunized industry from price-fixing litigation.

Despite this working arrangement, the Wilson administration still harbored populist disdain for business leaders and their commercial experience. After April 6, 1917, the administration ignored the three-year, $3 billion purchasing experience by the export division of J.P. Morgan Co.—purchases on behalf of the British government. Even Gen. Erich Ludendorff acknowledged that Morgan's director, Edward Stettinius, was worth a corps of Allied troops. Yet in 1917, the Wilson administration preferred to embark on war production and mobilization *de novo*.

Finally, the wartime experience in state economic control—priorities, allocation—and price was not without its legacy. In 1933, the WIB resurfaced as the National Recovery Administration, and price fixing was touted as the cure for what was thought to be the cause of the Great Depression, that is, excessive market competition. Franklin Roosevelt's NRA director was none other than Gen. Hugh Johnson, the 1918 liaison officer between the War Department and the War Industries Board.

Manley R. Irwin

Bibliography

Coffman, Edward M. *The War to End All Wars*. New York: Oxford University Press, 1968.

Clark, John M. *The Cost of the World War to the American People*. New Haven: Yale University Press, 1931.

Cuff, Robert D. *The War Industries Board*. Baltimore: Johns Hopkins University Press, 1973.

Tansil, Charles C. *America Goes to War*. Boston: Little, Brown, 1938.

War Labor Board

See NATIONAL WAR LABOR BOARD

War Neurosis

See SHELL SHOCK

War Risk Insurance

War risk insurance was a government-administered program that provided insurance against death or disability to soldiers, sailors, and women of the Army and Navy Nurse Corps. It grew out of the War Risk Insurance Bureau, which was established on Sept. 2, 1914, to provide insurance against loss or damage by war-related events to crews of cargo or merchant ships. Government-sponsored insurance became a necessity because of the reluctance of private firms to write policies for those considered uninsurable due to the risks posed by their involvement in the war. It was also hoped that a new system would replace the existing military pension system, which had been in place since the Civil War and was widely criticized as unfair.

The duties of the bureau were expanded at the request of Secretary of the Treasury William G. McAdoo, who worked with military leaders and insurance executives to devise a program to provide maximum benefit at minimum cost. On Oct. 6, 1917, an act of Congress established a program of allotment and allowance that compelled enlisted men to contribute a minimum of $15 or at least one half of their monthly wage for the support of their dependents. Officers were not required to send money home. It was assumed that they would eagerly provide for their families, although many did not.

The government matched contributions with an allowance that varied according to family size. This allowance also provided for compensation of up to $200 per month to veterans or their families in the event of death or disability and allowed payments for medical treatment, reeducation, and vocational training.

A second provision of the act enabled servicemen to take out additional coverage on a voluntary basis. Insurance policies could be purchased for $1,000–$10,000, in $500 increments. Unlike the allotment provision, both officers and enlisted men were encouraged to purchase policies. Rates, which varied according to age, ranged from $.63 to $1.08 per $1,000 of coverage, significantly lower than the $100/$1,000 rate charged by private insurance companies. Under this part of the program, 240 equal payments would be made to the disabled veteran or his survivors. To alleviate the fears of private insurance companies, policies were written for one year only, but they were renewable throughout the war. At war's end, they could be converted into whole life or payment life policies or into an endowment.

The response to the offering of War Risk Insurance was overwhelming, with 19,000 applications totaling $161.5 million filed in the first three weeks. By war's end, almost 90 percent of active-duty personnel had taken out policies, most for the $10,000 maximum. The low rates, which were deducted monthly from soldiers' pay, made it advantageous to take out as large a policy as possible. Ironically, both officers and enlisted men enrolled in equal numbers and for similar amounts. As a result, servicemen and their families were provided for both during and after the war and could be secure in the knowledge that their patriotism would not go unrewarded.

Jeffry Kostic

Bibliography

Douglas, P.H. "War Risk Insurance Act." *Journal of Political Economy* (May 1918).

McAdoo, William Gibbs. *Crowded Years.* New York: Houghton Mifflin, 1931.

War Savings Stamps

The War Savings Stamp program was instituted in late 1917 to raise $2 billion for the war effort. Originated by Frank A. Vanderlip, president of the National City Bank of New York, it enabled people of moderate incomes to contribute small amounts of money in support of American troops abroad. The program took the form of a five-year loan to the government, and investors earned interest on all money contributed.

Investors were encouraged to purchase a government-issued certificate with twenty spaces, upon each of which a stamp costing $4.12 would be placed. These stamps could be cashed in for $5 after five years, a return of 4 percent. A certificate containing twenty stamps cost $82.40; it returned $100 after five years. To enable people to save $4 in small amounts, a noninterest bearing "thrift stamp" costing twenty-five cents was created. Each thrift stamp was placed on a card with sixteen spaces. When the card was filled, it and twelve cents could be exchanged for an interest-bearing stamp of $5. This reflected the intention of organizers to make the program available to as many people as possible.

Organizers encouraged the purchase of War Savings Stamps by appealing to the patriotism of the American people. Both the importance of raising money to continue the war effort and the safety of lending money to the government at an attractive rate of return were stressed.

In schools, children were encouraged to purchase stamps, and essay and poster contests were held to raise students' interest in the program. Children did odd jobs, sacrificed luxuries such as gum and candy, and emptied their piggy banks in order to buy War Savings Stamps. It was hoped that by appealing to children, lessons of thrift could be taught at an early age.

Jeffry Kostic

Bibliography

"Christmas Spirit as Aid to War Savings Drive." *New York Times Magazine*, Dec. 16, 1917.

Strayer, George D. "War Savings Campaign in the Public Schools" *American Review of Reviews* (August 1918).

Vanderlip, Frank A. "Financing with War Savings Certificates." *Annals of the American Academy* (January 1918).

War Trade Board

Commercial warfare is often indistinguishable from armed conflict. Deny a nation critical resources, curtail a nation's access to products, limit availability to capital, and the machinery of war eventually withers and atrophies. It is under this logic that some historians insist the British Navy's blockade of Germany constituted a weapon more lethal than the endeavors of the Somme, Passchendaele, Château-Thierry, or Amiens campaigns.

The War Trade Board, together with sister agencies of food, fuel, shipping, etc., institutionalized the economic war policies of the United States. The board originated with Woodrow Wilson's executive order of Oct. 5, 1917. The director of the board, Vance C. McCormick, a publisher and industrialist from Harrisburg, Pennsylvania, was an early supporter of Wilson's 1912 election bid. By the time of the Armistice, McCormick directed more than 2,800 employees of the War Trade Board.

The board sought to impose an economic squeeze on the Central Powers, especially Germany and Austria. To that end, it implemented two broad programs. First was the regulation of overseas commerce by U.S. corporations; second, the monitoring and controlling, if possible, of the commercial activities of firms in neutral countries.

The pursuit of the first goal was straightforward. The board cataloged a list of 1,500 offshore firms and individuals deemed off limits to American commerce. This "blacklist," nearly all German-owned firms or individuals in Latin America, constituted the beginning of an economic embargo directed by the United States government. The board's power, derived from the Trading with the Enemy Act of 1917, denied export or import licenses to U.S. corporations. The board, in effect, regulated the buy/sell decisions of enterprises.

Imposing sanctions on foreign corporations located in neutral countries proved more illusive, though not without precedent. Britain, France, and Italy had, of course, imposed trade restrictions by blocking German access to Denmark, Sweden, and the Netherlands. The success of this Allied blockade prompted the United States to target its regulatory policy toward Central and Latin America.

In attempting to control German-owned companies in Argentina, Guatamala, Peru, or Ecuador, the War Trade Board generally assumed the following pattern. First, the board identified those concerns in the Southern Hemisphere. Second, the United States instituted an economic ban on the activities of a particular firm, that is, denial of supplies, refusal to purchase products, or curtailment of investment credits. As the economic squeeze took hold, the targeted company would reduce output, lay off workers, or curtail service to its customers. The host Latin American country would frequently issue a complaint to the U.S. government. The War Trade Board would recommend that the country create an Alien Property Custodian (APC). The APC would then seize assets of German-owned property, which would then be offered for sale. More often than not, a U.S. firm would buy the property, prompting the War Trade Board to lift its economic embargo against the new owner's commercial activities.

Individual cases varied within this general pattern of economic warfare. In some instances, the board sought outright sale of a German-owned property. In other cases, the German-owned company, cut off from crucial U.S. supplies, filed law suits against American firms. In still other instances, the neutral country prevented the repatriation of profits back to German shareholders.

Imposition of U.S. economic pressure took many forms. A U.S. oil embargo cut off nitrate production of German firms in Chile; a cutback of coal shipments curtailed electrical service by the German-held Argentine electric company; denial of bank credit squeezed revenues of a German-held sugar refinery in Peru; a refusal to sell electrical supplies to a Guatamala city power and electric company led to brownouts in Guatamala City and preceded its takeover by the country's Alien Property Custodian.

Latin American alien custody agencies often acted as an intermediary between U.S. firms and former German companies. In one case, the membership of a Latin American agency was less than subtle. Daniel B. Hodgson, an American citizen served as a member of Guatemala's customs agency.

By 1919, United States purchases of German property in South America ranged from meat-packing plants and railroad property to cacao plantations. Indeed, United States acquisition of those assets prompted Great Britain to lodge a protest with Washington that it risked being frozen out of future South American markets. The trade tension between London and Washington was such that President Wilson considered rejecting the appointment of a new British ambassador, Sir Aukland Geddes, to the United States. However, the President was advised that it would be easier to monitor Geddes in the United States than in England. Moreover, Wilson acknowledged that Britain's war indebtedness to the United States restrained any overt break with Whitehall.

As with its sister war agencies, the rationale for the War Trade Board ceased to exist after Nov. 11, 1918, and by June 1919, its personnel were transferred to the U.S. Department of State. Nevertheless, the board had, in its twenty-month life, attempted to fulfill Wilson's mandate to employ economic warfare as a "noiseless and unseen weapon." The United States had come a long way from its traditional debate over tariff policy.

Although the War Trade Board was formally dissolved in 1919, its legacy of trade regulation was to be resurrected during the Second World War and institutionalized during the Cold War that followed. True, the nomenclature of economic warfare had altered percep-

tively since 1917. Blacklists were superseded by commodities lists, dual-use commercial products, and sensitive software. But the goal of the late Cold War was not unlike that pursued by the War Trade Board in 1917—economic isolation of one's adversary.

Manley R. Irwin

Bibliography

Kennedy, David M. *Over Here*. New York: Oxford University Press, 1980.

Parrini, Carl P. *Heir to Empire*. Pittsburgh: University of Pittsburgh Press, 1969.

Paxson, Frederic L. *America at War*. Boston: Houghton Mifflin, 1939.

Tolchin, Joseph S. *The Aftermath of War*. New York: New York University Press, 1917.

Fowler, Wilton B. *British American Relations, 1917–1918: The Role of Sir William Wiseman*. Princeton, NJ: Princeton University Press, 1969.

Weaver, Erasmus Morgan (1854–1920)

Erasmus Morgan Weaver was graduated from the United States Military Academy and commissioned a second lieutenant of artillery in June 1875. He served in a variety of posts in the doldrums of the peacetime army. Weaver became a captain in the 1st U.S. Artillery on May 14, 1898. On July 1, 1898, he was promoted to lieutenant colonel of the 5th Massachusetts Infantry. After the Spanish American War, he was mustered out of volunteer service and returned to his Regular Army rank. In June 1905, Major Weaver was assigned to the General Staff. He served in that post and in the line until March 1911, when he was promoted to brigadier general and made chief of the Coast Artillery. His final promotion came on July 6, 1916, when he was made a major general.

During World War I, Weaver served on the Board of Ordnance and Fortifications, whose functions were to consider and recommend projects for fortifications and to examine and report on ordnance and other inventions submitted to the War Department. At this time, he was also a member of the War Council of the War Department. As such, he was responsible for overseeing and coordinating matters of supply for the armies in the field and for relations between the American Expeditionary Force and the War Department. He worked in these positions until May 23, 1918, when he was retired for age. Weaver died on Nov. 13, 1920.

Michael J. Knapp

Welborn, Ira C. (1874–1956)

Commissioned in the infantry after graduating from West Point in 1898, 2d Lt. Ira C. Welborn was awarded the Medal of Honor for his heroics at San Juan Hill on July 2—less than three months after his graduation.

Following the Spanish-American War, Welborn was sent to the Philippines with the 9th Infantry Regiment, fought in the Boxer Rebellion in China, and then returned to Manila for another eighteen months of campaigning against Filipino insurgents in the Viscayan Islands.

By the time America entered World War I, Welborn was a lieutenant colonel and, on Mar. 5, 1918, he was named director of the Tank Corps in the United States—a separate and distinct entity from the American Expeditionary Force Tank Corps in France.

Welborn's command became a "tank corps" in name only. His headquarters in Washington, D.C., was concerned primarily with recruiting and tank production and served as the coordinating point for stateside Tank Corps training activities. There were no tanks or weapons on hand, and Tank Corps units organized at Camps Colt, Tobyhanna, and Sommerall, Pennsylvania, and Camp Greene, North Carolina, were rushed to France as soon as they completed initial training and could be processed for overseas movement.

Welborn maintained a close relationship with LtCol. Dwight D. Eisenhower, commander of Camp Colt, the Tank Corps' largest stateside training center. He handpicked Eisenhower for the job in April 1918 because of the administrative skill Eisenhower demonstrated while coordinating the overseas movement of the army's first heavy tank battalion, in which Eisenhower was a company commander.

Following the war, Welborn returned to the infantry. He spent two years on the General Staff before moving on to command the 4th and 35th Infantry regiments and the 22d Infantry Brigade. He retired from the army in 1932.

Dale E. Wilson

Bibliography

Wilson, Dale E. *Treat 'Em Rough! The Birth of American Armor, 1917–1920.* Novato, CA: Presidio Press, 1989.

White, Henry (1850–1927)

A man of independent wealth, Henry White made a career in the American diplomatic corps, serving as the secretary of the U.S. legation in Vienna and London, 1883–1893; the secretary of embassy in London, 1897–1905; ambassador to Italy, 1905–1907; and ambassador to France, 1907–1909. President Taft requested White's resignation in March 1909, thus bringing to a close his tenure in the regular diplomatic service.

White lived in retirement in Washington, D.C., after 1911. In 1917–1918, he served as regional director of the American Red Cross and as president of the War Camp Community Service. No one was more surprised than White when Secretary of State Robert Lansing asked him on Nov. 19, 1918, on behalf of President Wilson, to be one of five American plenipotentiary commissioners to attend the Paris Peace Conference. The others were Wilson himself, Lansing, Col. Edward M. House, and Gen. Tasker H. Bliss. As a moderate Republican and a former career diplomat, White was a more acceptable choice to Wilson than prominent Republican foreign-policy leaders such as Elihu Root, William Howard Taft, or Henry Cabot Lodge.

When the peace conference got underway in January 1919, it soon became apparent that Wilson and House would be the dominant figures in the American delegation. White, Lansing, and Bliss were relegated to service on some of the many committees of the peace conference and to offering occasional advice to Wilson. White's most important assignment was to the Commission on the International Regime of Ports, Waterways, and Railways. He did maintain a cordial, if not intimate, relationship with Wilson. Though originally unenthusiastic about the League of Nations, White soon became a strong supporter of that concept. White also strongly upheld Wilson in the latter's opposition to Italy's attempts to gain control of the Adriatic port city of Fiume and to France's efforts to impose very severe peace terms on Germany. He was sharply critical of what he regarded as the President's surrender to the Japanese delegation on the Shantung question.

Without consulting Wilson or anyone else, White took upon himself the tasks of keeping his friend, Senator Henry Cabot Lodge, informed of the progress of the peace negotiations and of attempting to persuade Lodge and other Republican leaders to accept both the German peace treaty and the Covenant of the League of Nations as embodied in that treaty. However, White's efforts were doomed to failure. Lodge, from the outset sharply critical of Wilson's conduct of the peace talks and of the whole concept of the League of Nations, only grew more intransigent as the peace conference proceeded, in spite of all that White could do. With the close of the conference, White returned to his home in Washington, where he enjoyed a quiet retirement until his death in 1927.

John E. Little

Bibliography
Nevins, Allan. *Henry White: Thirty Years of American Diplomacy.* New York: Harper, 1930.

White, William Allen (1868–1944)

Between 1895 and 1944, William Allen White, editor of the *Emporia Gazette* became the Midwest's most celebrated journalist. He earned acclaim in 1896 with an editorial, "What's The Matter With Kansas?" a denunciation of the Populist Party. In his fiction—especially *Stratagems and Spoils* and *In the Heart of a Fool*—White excoriated predatory wealth and the widening gap between the social classes. The truly effective agent for change, he argued, resided among middle-class doctors, merchants, lawyers, editors, and nonunion workers. A Republican, White championed Theodore Roosevelt, especially when the former president bolted the GOP in 1912 to challenge William Howard Taft.

The outbreak of World War I horrified White, who believed America should shun involvement. Once Congress declared war, however, White rallied to Woodrow Wilson's crusade. By Christmas 1917, he boasted, "My articles reached over forty newspapers from Boston to San Diego, with a total circulation of over 5 million. Every fellow can do his damndest in the line for which he is fitted, and I am trying to do mine." The *Gazette* tolerated no dissent. It fulminated against the Nonpartisan League and suspected German Americans and those who petitioned for military exemp-

tion. In 1917, White visited France and shrilly recorded his approval of the war in *The Martial Adventure of Henry and Me*, an autobiographical novel. For the editor—as for many progressives—the war represented an opportunity, perhaps the nation's last, to construct a truly organic community. The conflict would unify Americans across all social and economic lines. Self-interest would evaporate.

White would live another twenty-five years after World War I, and in that time, the issues of the day—the New Deal and the coming of World War II—occupied his considerable energies. He was remembered as an unimpeachable interpreter of Main Street's shifting moods until his death on Jan. 29, 1944.

Richard W. Resh

Bibliography
Griffith, Sally F. *Home Town News: William Allen White and the Emporia Gazette.* New York: Oxford University Press, 1989.
Johnson, Walter. *William Allen White's America.* New York: Holt, 1947.
McKee, John D. *William Allen White: Maverick on Main Street.* Westport, CT: Greenwood Press, 1975.
Resh, Richard W. "A Vision in Emporia: William Allen White's Search for Community." *Midcontinent American Studies Journal* (Fall 1969).

Whitlock, Brand (1869–1934)

Brand Whitlock, United States minister to Belgium 1913–1921, wished to be known as a novelist. Instead, he gained fame as a reform mayor of Toledo, Ohio, and as America's representative to Belgium during World War I. Patron of the Commission for Relief in Belgium (CRB) and eloquent portrayer of the suffering of the low country under German occupation, he was later showered with honors by the Belgians. Ironically, Whitlock's most noted works, valued for their vignettes and observations, are nonfiction: *Forty Years of It,* an account of his political experiences in Illinois and Ohio; *Belgium: A Personal Record*; *La Fayette*; and *The Letters and Journal of Brand Whitlock.*

Born into the Republican household of a Methodist preacher, Whitlock struck out on his own after high school in Toledo. Rejecting family pressure to attend college, he worked as a reporter for the *Toledo Blade*, and the *Chicago*

Herald. He became a Democrat, advocated free trade, and opposed legislation backed by church moralists.

Sent by the *Herald* to the Illinois capital, Springfield, he met and married in 1892 Susan Brainerd, who died four months after their wedding. Whitlock immersed himself in the successful gubernatorial campaign of John P. Altgeld, who rewarded him with a clerkship. The post afforded him time to write, study law, and learn French. In 1894, Whitlock married Ella Brainerd, sister of his first wife.

Democratic defeats in 1896 led Whitlock to practice law in Toledo and to campaign for reform mayor Sam "Golden-Rule" Jones. After the latter's death in 1904, Whitlock was nominated for mayor on an Independent ticket and served from 1906 to 1914. Imbued with the idealism of Jones and Altgeld, Whitlock envisioned the "Free City" that could liberate and nurture the life of industrialized humankind. He challenged special interests and corporations, especially the Toledo Street Railway Company. The mayor also played a key role in winning an amendment to the Ohio constitution to allow home rule for cities.

Tired of urban politics, Whitlock declined a fifth term and sought a sinecure that would allow him to write. Through the influence of Newton D. Baker, the progressive mayor of Cleveland, on President Wilson, Whitlock became minister to Belgium in December 1913. Formal duties were few and the cultural and social life of Brussels enjoyable; as a self-taught law student, Whitlock had early adopted the immaculate dress and manners of the "gentlemanly style." A beginning was made on his best novel, *J. Hardin & Son.*

German invasion interrupted this idyll. As minister of a neutral state, Whitlock was entrusted with the interests of seven warring nations. He resisted State Department suggestions that he withdraw with the Belgian government to Antwerp. His presence in Brussels allowed him to mediate many incidents.

With the Marquis de Villalobar, minister of Spain, Whitlock persuaded King Albert and the mayor of Brussels to surrender the city without fighting, sparing it destruction. The minister's greatest concern was the feeding of the Belgian populace. The CRB consigned its relief supplies to him; their distribution was under his guardianship. Whitlock influenced the Germans to cease food requisitions in Belgium and resisted their efforts to control the supply distribution

system. He mediated innumerable quarrels among CRB staff and between its American chief, Herbert Hoover, and the Belgians and Germans. Officially neutral, Whitlock sympathized with the Belgians. At times he succeeded in softening German policies, but in such cases as the execution of Edith Cavell, his efforts were to no avail. Personal attempts to prevent deportation of Belgian laborers to Germany also met with little success, although intervention by Wilson did have some effect. After the United States declaration of war, Whitlock's refusal to depart from Belgium until all American members of the CRB were evacuated assured their safety.

Whitlock left Brussels on April 2, 1918, to join the Belgian government at Le Havre. He returned to Brussels on Nov. 21, 1918. Americans, and Whitlock as their representative, were hailed as heroes in the Belgian capital. In 1919, Whitlock accompanied King Albert, with whom he enjoyed close ties, on a tour of the United States. He accepted the ambassadorship to Italy but chose to remain in Belgium when the legation was raised to the rank of embassy. President Warren G. Harding wished the Brussels post for a Republican, and so Whitlock resigned on Dec. 31, 1921.

Estranged from America, believing it dominated by theocratic authoritarianism, and now convinced that individual creativity could best be fostered by an elite class, Whitlock remained in Europe. He died in Cannes on May 14, 1934.

Jonathan E. Helmreich

Bibliography

Anderson, David D. *Brand Whitlock.* New York: Twayne, 1968.

Crunden, Robert M. *A Hero in Spite of Himself: Brand Whitlock in Art, Politics, and War.* New York: Knopf, 1969.

Tager, Jack. *The Intellectual as Urban Reformer: Brand Whitlock and the Progressive Movement.* Cleveland: Press of Case Western Reserve University, 1968.

Wilhelm II (1859–1941)

Frederick Wilhelm Vicktor Albert of Hohenzollern, known to history at Wilhelm II, and remembered as Prussia's last king and Germany's last emperor, was born in Berlin on Jan. 27, 1859. In 1888, when death terminated his father's reign only ninety-nine days after its start, Wilhelm, as heir, succeeded to both thrones. German unification was begun with much excitement and high expectations, but the domestic and diplomatic complexities accompanying Germany's rapid transformation from a traditional to a modern society severely tested Wilhelm's abilities. The added pressures and disruption brought on by the Great War heightened still more the anomaly of a traditional monarchical institution functioning within the framework of a modernizing society. When the war ended in revolution and defeat, Wilhelm II was forced into a reluctant abdication and ignominious flight into exile. He found haven in Holland and hid there until his death on June 4, 1941, without ever having set foot on German soil again.

In the year 1888, three sovereigns ruled over Germany and Prussia. The ninety-one-year-old Emperor Wilhelm I died in March, leaving the throne to his son, Frederick, then desperately ill with the malignancy that was to claim his life just ninety-nine days later. Upon Frederick's death in June, his twenty-nine-year-old son succeeded as Wilhelm II. When the new reign began, Germany was about to begin the most critical phase in its transition toward a modern and industrial nation. A short ten years later the country was beyond a doubt the leading industrial nation in Europe. And yet, it still retained a full complement of traditional and historical institutions, values, and forms. There were, in fact, two Germanies, or at least there were two perfectly divided halves to Germany. One was modern, industrial, urban, and still growing. The other was traditional, rural, agricultural, and stagnant. Like the schizophrenic country that he now led, the new emperor was torn. He was intrigued by all that was modern. He took a keen, if superficial interest in all new inventions, in science and technology. But he also revered tradition, or believed he had to, because of his vested interest in monarchy. This medieval anachronism was the capstone of a perfectly preserved but antiquated pyramid of institutions. Germany as a whole was a country in which the old order was numerically as strong as the new. A peasantry numbering in the millions, most of them proprietors, was led by a feudal aristocracy, unwilling to yield an inch to the demands of the new times. Germany, still immaturely modern, witnessed the coronation of its new master who was still, and was destined to remain forever, in an awkward age of his own. Leader and country shared the divisive pull in opposite directions.

The accession to the thrones by Wilhelm II did not disturb the tranquility, or the work, of Imperial Chancellor Otto von Bismarck. Relations between the veteran statesman and young Wilhelm had always been close because Bismarck, in anticipation of the day when the prince would become his master, had taken special pains to cultivate them. The relationship had, in fact, been a source of great irritation between Wilhelm and his parents, both of whom disliked Bismarck and the politics he represented and blamed him for the alienation between parents and son. When Wilhelm ascended to the thrones, the elder statesman had long since convinced himself that his services were indispensable and that Wilhelm thought so too. He had every reason to believe that his position was secure. Indeed, for close to two years there was no hint of trouble. By March 1890, however, the honeymoon between Bismarck and his young master had come to an abrupt end.

Ostensibly, the conflict between Bismarck and Wilhelm was over specific political and constitutional issues. In foreign policy, for example, under the influence of advisers in his immediate circle, the emperor had begun to question the close relationship with Russia and now opposed the renewal of the Reinsurance Treaty. Bismarck favored its continuation because it kept Germany's other partner, Austria-Hungary, guessing and because he feared that without such an agreement, Russia would seek the friendship of France and put Germany precariously between them. The underlying explanation for the clash between Wilhelm II and his chancellor was the struggle for power between them. The emperor wanted to be his own man, and the prospect of personally exercising real monarchical power tantalized him. He discovered that he had his own ideas about state business and welfare. Moreover, he had highly developed notions of his royal prerogatives and even of divine sanction, as well as an inordinate confidence in his own judgment. Pride in his family's history, particularly in the traditions of Frederick the Great and of his grandfather under whose aegis Germany was united, made him think he too must fulfill some great historical mission. In short, Wilhelm wished to rule, not merely to reign. Bismarck, on the other hand, was now a curmudgeonly seventy-three. He had enjoyed the widest of discretionary powers under Wilhelm's two predecessors and was thus accustomed to handling the business of state without asking aid or advice of anyone, not even of his sovereigns. While he was still grudgingly willing to pay lip service to royal sensitivities, he drew the line at his office door. When his young master began to meddle in state affairs, which Bismarck had come to see as *his* affairs, the die was cast. In March 1890, the emperor insisted on having the old chancellor's resignation and presently received it. The era of Wilhelm's personal rule had begun.

Twenty-six years elapsed between the accession of Wilhelm II and the outbreak of World War I, ample time, one would think, for any leader to lay out and pursue an intelligible and coherent foreign policy. Yet Wilhelmian diplomacy is usually remembered for its confused, erratic, and even contradictory patterns. The record is replete with sudden and unpredictable changes of direction, with the short-lived pursuit of fatuous pet projects, with gratuitously antagonistic behavior, with quixotic adventures that led nowhere. All of this is summed up descriptively in the phrase "zig-zag course." But it is also known that Wilhelm, from the beginning to the end of his reign, was consumed with one burning and unchanging ambition—to lead Germany out of what he perceived to be the restrictive confinement of continental European politics and to win for it "a place in the sun," that is, to achieve the status of a world power. In this he differed radically from Bismarck, who, having made Prussia supreme in Germany and Germany preeminent in Europe, considered this quite enough. The preservation of his achievement was the motive behind the Junker's foreign policy after 1871. But Wilhelm did not propose to spend what might be a long reign merely maintaining the edifice erected by the Iron Chancellor. Instead, Kaiser Wilhelm was determined to make his own mark on history. That his name should be mentioned in the same breath with those of his predecessors Frederick the Great, or his grandfather Wilhelm I, was an ardent, lifelong ambition. To achieve this goal, he envisioned the construction of a great empire using the state Bismarck had built in Europe as a base. What Wilhelm had in mind as he contemplated the future Germany was an imperial establishment of global dimensions, including colonies, coaling stations, protectorates, and spheres of influence. Each outpost would fly "his" imperial flag. They would all be connected by a bridge of merchant ships carrying Germany's exports and imports and protected by a navy second to none. In short, what Wilhelm envisioned was a clone of the British Empire. It was his intention to replicate, not to replace or even necessarily to contest, the original. Some of his most cherished childhood memories were associated with Britain. Moreover, it was a country ruled by his kin, one with which he was thoroughly familiar and visited often, and one that he generally admired, if perhaps somewhat enviously. Britain was his model, not his rival.

The British, of course, never understood Wilhelm's efforts to imitate Britain to be a compliment. Instead, they regarded his aspirations at first as a gratuitous nuisance and eventually as a mortal threat. For his part, the emperor never managed to comprehend the exquisite sensitivity of the British about their supremacy on the high seas. He had read Alfred Thayer Mahan's theories about sea power and had taken them to heart. If Britain had established itself as a maritime and mercantile empire, why was it not allowable for Germany to do the same? The entire reign of Wilhelm II may be regarded as one long and unhappy declension in the relationship between the two countries. Over a period of twenty-six years, down to the day of the great collision, the relationship changed from cordial to competitive, to suspicious, to hostile. Every effort in this long period to reach agreement ended in failure.

Much has been said about the diplomatic isolation of Germany in the quarter-century before World War I, when it became acute. Not only was Germany plagued by the animosity of the two Great Powers on its eastern and western flanks, but it also had to bear the growing enmity of the great sea power, Britain. By 1900, diplomatic power on the continent of Europe was roughly balanced, with Austria-Hungary, Germany, and Italy on one side and Russia and France on the other. Britain, though still "splendidly isolated" from both blocs, was in the envious position of being wooed by both sides and thus able to name its price. The new power distribution bore no relationship to the one that had existed at the time of Bismarck's retirement. In the years before his death in 1898, the Iron Chancellor argued that Wilhelm and his epigonian diplomats had frivolously discarded Germany's priceless advantage as arbiter of the European state system. There is no question that the conclusion of the Franco-Russian alliance in 1890 radically transformed the character of European relations. In this situation, Britain could extract concessions from the two rival continental power blocs as the price for its benevolence. Austria also gained, if only passively, because it was now Germany's only ally for whose loyalty Germany could always be asked to pay a fee. The advantage gained by Russia and France through their new relationship being self-evident, it is obvious that the constellation of power in Europe had shifted in a way that provided benefits of one kind or another for four of the five Great Powers but left Germany as the sole loser, if only in a relative sense. Much of this can be attributed to the ineptitude and rashness of Wilhelm II, who insisted on setting a "new course" with himself at the helm.

In light of Germany's drastically altered and dangerous diplomatic situation after 1890, one might have expected Wilhelm and his government to conduct a cautious and circumspect foreign policy. First and foremost, this would have required the cultivation of close and friendly relations with Britain or, at the very least, one devoid of elements that might antagonize Britain. But relations between the two Great Powers deteriorated steadily over the next twenty-four years until the two finally found themselves at war. It would be a serious misreading of the record to conclude that the sole, or even major, blame for this tragedy rested on the shoulders of Wilhelm II. However, as a monarch who insisted on exercising his full constitutional prerogatives, including those in the gray areas, by playing a direct role in the management of public affairs, foreign as well as domestic, the emperor deliberately took responsibility upon himself and must be held accountable before the bar of history. Particularly in Germany's critical relationship with Britain, the record reveals a trail of blunders, missed opportunities, and even reckless folly attributable directly to Wilhelm II. By acts of commission, as well as omission, the emperor contributed to the regrettable decline in the relationship between his country and Britain that led to the Great War. As an historical figure connected to the history of that war, Wilhelm played a far more important role in the antecedents to the war than in the war itself.

The creation of a modern navy was Kaiser Wilhelm's most fervent ambition. It was also the most vexing irritant in the relationship between Britain and Germany in the quarter century before World War I. A large ocean-going fleet had been an obsession of the emperor's long before he had assumed the thrones. To Wilhelm, it represented the fulfillment of his dream to rule a mighty country whose influence and power would radiate throughout the world. He envisioned the German Navy as the herald and protector of a new dynamic Germany, a true world power, a country that had finally, under his leadership, broken out from the narrow confines and self-imposed limits of continental European politics. Colonies, industry, worldwide commerce, and a great merchant fleet were the other elements in a structure whose capstone was to be the "High Seas Fleet." Wilhelm never understood, and probably never tried to understand, why the British regarded the new German Navy as a symptom of the German problem and himself as the instigator.

The Serbian murder of the Habsburg heir and his wife in 1914 placed an unbearable load on the European diplomatic establishment. Miraculously, that establishment had succeeded in averting the great showdown in crisis after crisis—the Agadir incident, the Tangir crisis, the Bosnian annexation, the First and Second Balkan Wars, and many others. Unfortunately, however artful Europe's diplomats were in circumventing war, they had failed utterly in finding solutions to the underlying conflicts that kept producing the dangerous eruptions. The Franco-German, Austro-Russian, and Anglo-German tensions, not to mention the perennial Balkan volcano, were as menacing in 1914 as they had been in 1900. Thus, the peace of highly civilized Europe was still exposed to the whim of any malicious assassin, such as Gavrilo Princip. Once the evil deed was done, there was no buffer to protect European civilization, one of the great attainments of mankind.

It was obvious from the beginning that the Balkan crisis of 1914 threatened to overtax the flimsy peacekeeping capabilities of traditional diplomacy. Certainly at this moment only the most skillful and experienced statesman should have been involved in the conduct of international affairs. The fact of the matter was, that in Germany it was a mercurial amateur, the emperor himself, who presided over business. Nothing better illustrates the anachronistic inappropriateness of Germany's imperial constitution than that it allowed a royal amateur, particularly one of such volatile temperament, to act as his own chancellor, foreign minister, and war lord at a time like this. Wilhelm had a well-established reputation as a blunderer, but even with the highest stakes involved, nothing could be done to stop him from exercising his questionable judgment—or his unquestionable authority.

Wilhelm reacted to the news from Sarajevo with fury, concern, and genuine grief. Royal blood had been shed again. Germany's only ally was thrown into confusion. Furthermore, the emperor had lost a personal friend. A mere sixteen days had passed since he had ended an enjoyable visit to the archducal home. With his emotions about to overpower his rational faculties, Wilhelm imposed himself with characteristic volatility upon the already harried diplomats. His first action was to reject the cautious tone of his ambassador to Vienna and to insist that the day of reckoning with the Serbs was at hand. By this action he strengthened the hand of the Austrian hardliners who were calling for a military showdown with Serbia. On July 5, he let it be known, through the Austrian ambassador to Germany, that Austria could count on the full backing of Germany whatever it decided to do about Serbia.

The emperor's mood remained outraged and combative until almost the very end of the "July Crisis." The assassination, particularly since it robbed him of a friend and confidant, focused him single-mindedly on the capture and punishment of the regicides and the destruction of their Serbian refuge. He seemed to be oblivious of the danger of a general European war, believing that the Russian tsar, the very embodiment of the monarchical principle, would never allow his commitments to Serbia, or his stake in the Balkans, to override his primary interest, which was to protect monarchy itself. Thus it seemed reasonable to Wilhelm that Russia should support rather than obstruct Austria's effort to root out the regicides, even if this had to be done on Serbian soil. It confused and angered him that Russia was objecting on Serbia's behalf as the Austrians pursued the assassins. He gave little thought to the danger of a general war because he had the assurances of his chancellor, Theobald von Bethmann Hollweg, that even if should come to hostilities, it would remain a localized conflict between Austria-Hungary and Serbia. No other Great Power had a strong geopolitical motivation to involve itself in the perennial quagmire of Balkan politics. It was the chancellor who insisted, against the better judgment and wishes of Wilhelm, that his sovereign proceed on his annual cruise on the *Hohenzollern* as scheduled on July 25. In this way, the chancellor hoped to give the impression of German serenity and, at the same time,

to have the excitable emperor out of his way. With deep misgivings, the troubled kaiser sailed off.

From aboard his royal yacht, Wilhelm continued to bluster as he kept abreast of developments by dispatch. One of these informed him that the British were disturbed by the harshness of Austria's ultimatum, complaining that the time limit set for a response—forty-eight hours—was too brief and that its excessive terms made war between Austria-Hungary and Serbia inevitable. Wilhelm dismissed these points and also refused to consider British Foreign Secretary Sir Edward Grey's plea to put moderating pressure on Austria, just as he also rejected the latter's suggestion for a Great Power conference to mediate between Russia and Austria. Even when he finally learned of the actual contents of the Austrian ultimatum, long after it had been sent, he found no reason to criticize it but expressed his satisfaction instead. Apparently, Wilhelm was still more interested in limiting, rather than averting, a war between Serbia and the Habsburg Empire. Finally, on July 25, came the alarming news that Austria had rejected the Serbian reply, had broken off diplomatic relations with Serbia, and in both countries mobilization had begun. Simultaneously, word reached Wilhelm that Russia would very likely support Serbia in such a war. Now greatly agitated, Wilhelm commanded the *Hohenzollern* to head back to Germany, but not before he issued orders to the fleet to concentrate in the Baltic Sea where it would be in a position to check Russia.

What Wilhelm began to fathom upon his return to Berlin was that Germany's unconditional support of its ally was the cause of much mischief. The pledge of course, was one that he had not only endorsed, but insisted upon. Outrage and fear, two emotions that no statesman should ever allow to govern his actions, had led him to take this step immediately after the assassination. When Austria rejected Serbia's ostensibly accommodating response to the former's ultimatum, London, Paris, and St. Petersburg made the assumption that Germany had put its decrepit partner up to it. According to this line of reasoning, Germany's strong backing was not so much an expression of solidarity, but rather a bid by Germany to use the crisis, peacefully or otherwise, to change the balance of power in Europe decisively in its favor. Since all three had a negative mutuality of interest in preventing this, they decided to face off against Germany, whatever the risk of war might be.

The mercurial German emperor abruptly changed his view of the situation after reading the Serbian response to the Austrian ultimatum. He characterized the note as "a moral victory" for Austria-Hungary, asserted that it removed all cause for war, and proclaimed that he found in it the basis for a peaceful and satisfactory resolution of the crisis. When he learned of the Austrian rejection of the response as inadequate, the exasperated emperor criticized the Habsburg government for breaking diplomatic relations and for its hastiness in ordering mobilization. Wilhelm realized now that a general European war was about to break out and premonitions of an overwhelming disaster took possession of him. Frantically, he sought a way out. Reversing himself, he now ordered Bethmann to put moderating pressure on Vienna. He also exchanged a series of last-minute telegrams with Tsar Nicholas, the famous "Willy-Nicky Telegrams." It was all too late. The Dual Monarchy had already declared war on Serbia, and in the capitals of the Entente Powers, it had been decided to accept what it was imagined was Germany's challenge to the existing order of Europe.

The German public thought of their sovereign as the consummate soldier. When the Great War broke out, the reign of Wilhelm was already in its twenty-seventh year. In all that time scarcely a day had passed without the emperor's participation in some kind of military ceremony or exercise. He seldom appeared in public, or in private for that matter, in other than soldier's dress. In public addresses, he never failed to make the connection between Germany's status as a Great Power and its military prowess. Medals, weapons, uniforms, parades, maneuvers, and all the minutiae of military life fascinated and delighted him. His favorite home, the New Palace, was situated in Potsdam, which, though it is also remembered as a city brimming with architectural gems, was first and foremost a garrison town, the very birthplace and nerve center of the Prussian military tradition. The emperor's most exalted designation was "Supreme War Lord," and he gloried in the title. Unfortunately, the image of Wilhelm as a great military leader was totally misleading. In the summer of 1914, Germany entered the most demanding and challenging test of strength under a master who was as unsuited and unprepared to be a soldier as he was to be a statesman.

Wilhelm stepped into his role as Germany's Supreme War Lord on Aug. 16, 1914, as the Schlieffen Plan, the grand design for the conduct of a two-front war against France in the west and Russia in the east, was beginning to unfold. The plan was based on the premise that Germany lacked the capacity to fight offensively on two fronts simultaneously but that it could conduct an offensive operation against France while fighting defensively against Russia. It envisioned a speedy victory in the west, to be followed by a shift of the main body of German forces to the east in order then to overpower the Russians. Schlieffen's idea may have been sound enough, but of necessity it depended heavily on exact timing and, above all, on close adherence to the specified distribution of troops. The meager force in the east might be expected to withstand some punishment and perhaps even retreat on to German soil before it would be possible to reinforce it with units released by victory in the west. A leader had to understand and have faith in the Schlieffen Plan. Most of all, it required a leader who had the fortitude and steadiness of nerve to carry it out to the letter. Unfortunately, neither General Helmuth von Moltke, Chief of the General Staff, nor the Supreme War Lord was such a man.

The emperor's brittle personality obviously made him an unsuitable commander of an army faced with strenuous demands of modern war. When the unexpectedly rapid deployment of Russian forces in August 1914 confronted the light German defending screen and crossed on to German territory, Wilhelm fell to pieces. His jumpiness, and his own distress over the loss of some rural landscapes in East Prussia, unnerved von Moltke. His reaction was to detach an element of the forces critical to the quick victory in the west and send it east, along with the newly appointed team of commanders, Gens. Paul von Hindenburg and Erich Ludendorff. The result was two spectacular victories over the Russians at Tannenberg and Masurian Lakes, but at the cost of failure in the west. The Germans were stopped at the Marne, and with France undefeated, the war settled into a weary stalemate. The principles of war explain that a country such as Germany, fighting on interior lines of defense, is at a distinct disadvantage when forced to fight a prolonged war.

The next indication of flawed military leadership in Germany came in September, 1914. Just as the contest in the west was about to reach a climax, a gap opened between two elements of the German forces standing before Paris. Because of the removal of a large contingent of troops to the Russian front, no reserves were immediately available to plug the hole. The hysterical von Moltke lost his nerve and, telling the emperor that the war was lost, ordered a retreat. The move turned out to be one of the great blunders of the war. Not only did the German attack lose its momentum, but an opportunity to annihilate a British army caught between the two legs of the gap was thrown away. With Moltke rendered ineffective by his breakdown, it was obviously the Supreme War Lord's place to seize the reins. Instead, Wilhelm declined to accept the responsibility and allowed events to settle the issue by themselves. The subsequent Battle of the Marne demonstrated that the German wave had crested, that the Western Allies had weathered the first and most dangerous storm, and that the war would not be the short one projected by the Schlieffen Plan. The kaiser's only action was to relieve Moltke and to appoint Gen. Erich von Falkenhayn in his place. Between Moltke, who blundered, and Wilhelm who did nothing, Germany became mired in a long war, precisely the kind it could not win.

Wilhelm's pathetic performance during the crisis of September 1914 gave the army's senior officers a clear picture of what kind of a person they were dealing with. It must have been an unsettling and sobering experience. Their response was to take matters into their own hands and to work around their nominal leader as best they could. Many officers, Falkenhayn among them, made it obvious that they had no time to waste with an incompetent and touchy emperor. They made every effort to have as little contact with him as possible. Wilhelm found himself being humored, patronized, or ignored. Although he distracted himself with military trivialities and spent much time in his royal train traveling back and forth across Germany between his headquarters on the two fronts, the sensitive sovereign realized that these were merely compensatory activities and that he had been marginalized. He resented the way he was being treated and complained that he was being left in the dark and never asked for advice.

The German Navy never escaped from the direct control of Wilhelm II as did the German Army. Wilhelm was all the more adamant about retaining direct control of "his" navy after his experience with the generals, and he jealously guarded his authority within the naval chain of command by watching every move the admirals made. He even went so far as to keep operational control in his own hands. His notion of what to do with the navy was clear and simple: to preserve it from harm. No argument was able to weaken Wilhelm's determination to preserve his fleet. He regarded it as his own creation and the symbol of a powerful, modern, industrial Germany. Accordingly, the vaunted High Seas Fleet remained safely in port month after month as the ships and the morale of their crews both deteriorated. In the meantime, the British-German ratio of capital ships worsened steadily as the British continued with the building program, while Germany did not. This meant that the prospects for success of the Germans against the British in any sea contest declined steadily as the war dragged on.

Wilhelm's refusal to jeopardize the German Navy mystified everyone. Adm. Alfred von Tirpitz, who had done more to make Germany a modern naval power than anyone else, including the kaiser himself, was infuriated by Wilhelm's irrational forfeiture of this formidable weapon. Unlike many sycophants in the emperor's circle, Tirpitz had the courage to criticize his sovereign's decision to shield the navy. The ensuing quarrel between them began an estrangement that eventually led to the veteran sailor's early retirement. Nor was Tirpitz the only one to be confounded. The British, too, were completely baffled by the failure of their foe to use his superb fighting navy. It is ironic that the construction of the German Navy contributed more to Britain's decision to go to war against Germany than any other consideration, yet when war came, the greatly feared German fleet remained harmlessly at home. The only major contest between the two took place in 1916 at the Battle of Jutland, in which the British lost far more heavily than their opponents. Since the Germans failed to exploit their victory, the blockade continued and the strategic advantage remained with the British. The emperor, who derived great momentary satisfaction with the outcome of the engagement, refused to put his ships at risk again.

The German Navy had more than a surface fleet to fight with. Shortly before the war, a German U-boat, the *Deutschland*, made a dramatic Atlantic crossing that demonstrated to the world the feasibility of undersea navigation. Germany's more venturesome naval planners envisioned a fleet of U-boats that would one day revolutionize warfare on the high seas. A modest start in the construction of such a fighting arm was still in its infancy when the war began. The few available vessels would certainly not suffice to make a difference in the war, but a rapid expansion of the U-boat fleet was undertaken to overcome this problem. Unfortunately, submarine warfare carried with it several daunting political risks, as the sinking of the British liner *Lusitania*, in 1915, demonstrated. The loss of American lives did serious damage to Germany's image. War was averted only by a German pledge to end unrestricted submarine warfare, but the question of whether or not submarines could win the war for Germany remained unanswered.

The stalemated war and the increasingly hopeless situation in which Germany found itself in 1916 caused naval leaders to reconsider the use of the submarine. Admiral Tirpitz was among these, and with characteristic fervor, he set out to convert doubters to his view. Military professionals were generally won over, but the emperor and Bethmann Hollweg held back. Both resisted on political grounds, pointing to the damage Germany would suffer in its relations with the neutrals and that, among these, the United States would be likely to go to war. In addition, Wilhelm expressed deep reservations based on humanitarian considerations. The effort to persuade the Emperor was long and hard; finally, he accepted a proposal to reintroduce the use of U-boats, provided they were restricted to targets called "armed merchantmen." When this resulted in the sinking of the *Sussex* in April 1916, again with the loss of American lives, followed by the threat from the United States to break off diplomatic relations, Wilhelm and his chancellor again overruled the use of submarines. The vacillating emperor lost more respect among the military. In fact, Tirpitz resigned in disgust at this point, and the end of the war was as distant as ever.

By the middle of 1916, Wilhelm II was at his wit's end. His country was clearly at an impasse. The successes in the east, where Germany occupied Poland and the Baltic, where it had gained new allies in Bulgaria and Turkey, where Rumania had been quickly defeated after joining the Allies and where Serbia had been crushed, were all nullified by the reality of stalemate in the west. The Allied blockade and the impermeable front were weakening the country day by day. Submarines had accomplished nothing. All peace efforts had ended in failure.

The horrendous casualty list, the grief, deprivation, and hunger at home, all with no end in sight, steadily eroded the underpinnings of the monarchy. Clearly, the emperor had a great deal to answer for and desperately needed to find a way to extricate Germany, the monarchy, and himself from the blind alley into which he had done so much to lead them.

The desperate emperor sacrificed the discredited von Falkenhayn, author of the bloody debacle of Verdun, and replaced him with Paul von Hindenburg as chief of the General Staff. The hero of Tannenberg brought with him from the Eastern Front Erich Ludendorff, who was appointed quartermaster general. The new team received discretionary power to run the war as it saw fit, and the emperor was relegated to the position of figurehead. The chancellor, too, now found his prerogatives drastically curtailed. Should the emperor or the chancellor ever demur from a proposal made by the generals, they were quickly brought back into line by the threat of resignation. By this simple expedient, Hindenburg and Ludendorff set up a military dictatorship for themselves. Hindenburg made himself indispensable to the arrangement by lending to it his enormous prestige and popularity. Invariably, however, he deferred to Ludendorff's ideas, so that, in effect, Ludendorff held the supreme authority that had once belonged to the German emperor. The distribution of power and the political ground rules themselves had changed as though there had been a revolution. The question, of course, was whether at this late hour, the generals could still salvage Germany.

Once they were in charge of affairs, it did not take long for Hindenburg and Ludendorff to come to the conclusion that Germany's predicament offered only two alternatives. One was to follow the course preferred by Bethmann Hollweg, namely, to seek a way out of the war by negotiating a peace. This might require Germany to forgo its annexationist dreams and perhaps even to settle for the status quo antebellum. The Foreign Office, other elements of the government, the political parties of the Center and the Left, a majority of the Reichstag, as well as a large but undetermined segment of public opinion supported this dovish course of action. The emperor himself was connected with the movement by virtue of his strong and consistent support for his chancellor. For the military, the parties of the Right and Right-Center, and for all patriotic elements, such a course was unthinkable. Their solution was to pull out all the stops by thoroughly reorganizing the German war effort and then fighting on for total victory and an annexationist peace. Wilhelm's approval of this was still required, but by this time the generals knew how to deal with this perfunctory matter.

The existence of both a moderate and a war faction in Germany put the emperor on the spot. The first conflict between the two erupted over the issue of whether or not to resume unrestricted submarine warfare. Bethmann Hollweg opposed the policy, as he always had. Not only did he fear the entry of the United States into the war over the submarine issue, but he also did not wish to antagonize President Wilson just as he was being asked to use his good offices to achieve a negotiated peace. Hindenburg argued that U-boats were Germany's only hope of bringing Britain to its knees and breaking the stalemate in the west. It is significant but not surprising that the kaiser sided with the generals, even though he had well-known reservations about the use of submarines. He accepted the arguments of the High Command not because he had come to believe in them, but because the generals had the upper hand. Within two months after submarine warfare had been resumed, Germany and the United States were at war. Whether the damage inflicted on Britain by the submarines would make this negative development a real problem for Germany only time would tell. The blame or the credit would redound to Wilhelm in either case.

Hindenburg and Ludendorff had long considered Bethmann Hollweg to be a thorn in their sides. They regarded him as a defeatist and one who was ready to surrender Germany's hard-won gains in return for peace. For him, they reserved their most devastating epithet, "civilian." His promotion of a reform of the three-class voting system in Prussia and of concessions to the Socialists, with whom he had found a way to work in the Reichstag, made him anathema in their eyes. As far as they were concerned, he had to go. The difficulty was that he had the emperor's confidence and the imperial constitution was clear on this point: a chancellor was free to act as he saw fit as long as he enjoyed the confidence of the emperor. For a time, the generals decided that they had no choice but to learn to live with Bethmann Hollweg. As they grew bolder, however, and realized how weak the kaiser was, they pre-

sented Wilhelm with an alternative: dismiss the chancellor or accept the resignations of the generals. The pliant Wilhelm accommodated Hindenburg and Ludendorff, who then proposed their own man, George Michaelis, who was followed within three months by Georg von Hertling, another man with whom the High Command believed it could work. Clearly, Hindenburg and Ludendorff, if they could choose and dismiss chancellors, were now in a position to decide all important issues in Germany and Wilhelm had no grounds for complaint because he had brought himself to this point.

Having cleared a path for themselves by disposing of the most important political obstacles to their will—the chancellor, the Reichstag, and even the emperor—Hindenburg and Ludendorff now had to act and produce results on the front. Wilhelm left them to their own devices and faded meekly into the background. There his words became hollow and irrelevant and his actions ceremonial and meaningless. The generals either patronized or ignored him, even to the point of telling him occasionally that they had no time to see him. Probably, they did not, for they were prosecuting the war with new energy and vigor. The fruits of their effort were mixed. The resumption of submarine warfare, which provided Germany with a new and formidable foe, failed to bring Britain to its knees. The insertion of Lenin into the revolutionary turmoil of Russia yielded an end to hostilities in the east. In France, there was more of the same, namely, stalemate. Ludendorff's answer to this problem was yet another grand offensive, and since there was no restraint on his power, it was carried out. By July 1918, after four months of still more carnage and horror, even Ludendorff had to admit that it was just another bloody failure. At this juncture, the emperor was invited to reenter the picture.

In August, sharp setbacks and retreat followed the failure of Ludendorff's last offensive. The picture grew grimmer yet as Turkey and Bulgaria sued for peace. Austria-Hungary collapsed a short time later. In panic, Ludendorff demanded that Chancellor Hertling immediately begin armistice talks based on Wilson's Fourteen Points. Wilson's response to this stunning development was to make the creation of a parliamentary democracy a condition for further negotiation. Thereupon, Hertling resigned because he wanted no part of parliamentary government. Prince Max of Baden, long a friend of representative institutions, as well as a supporter of a negotiated peace, took his place. When the unpredictable Ludendorff began to make life difficult for the new chancellor as he began his reforms, Max had the emperor dismiss the general. It is ironic that one of the last autocratic acts of Wilhelm II was to clear the path for the constitutional reforms he had resisted for thirty years.

The changes that took place in Germany just before the end of the war were breathtaking. In less than a month, the country went through a constitutional transformation that required centuries and had cost rivers of blood in other countries. Now the chancellor and the other cabinet ministers were responsible to the Reichstag rather than to the emperor. The emperor lost his direct control of the military. In Prussia, the three-class voting system was abolished. But if Max and Wilhelm believed that they had saved the remnant of monarchy, they were mistaken. Wilson, though he had achieved everything he had originally said he wanted, suddenly raised the ante by making the removal of the kaiser a condition for peace.

The war, which cost millions of lives, was now, at the end, to cost Wilhelm II his crowns. To the kaiser's dismay and embarrassment, Wilson's insistence on abdication produced neither spontaneous outbursts of indignation nor assurances of support from the German people. On the contrary, when the disillusioned and war-weary population understood that their sovereign stood in the way of peace, revolutionary pressure for him to yield began to mount. To avoid being intimidated by staying in unruly Berlin, the emperor departed the city—for the last time as it turned out—on Oct. 29, 1918. However, on the same day mutinies broke out on board naval vessels lying in Wilhelmshafen and Kiel. The occasion for the uprising was an order to set sail for a last-ditch encounter with the British. To the sailors who knew what everyone else knew—that the war was lost—this seemed like a sacrifice of lives just for the sake of someone's conception of honor. They refused to follow orders. The uprising spread to shore, and one by one the cities of Germany fell into the hands of revolutionary workers' and soldiers' councils. These councils demanded peace, as well as the abdication of the emperor if that was what it would take to get it. Berlin was the last major city to fall, and to keep the Sparticists, soon to rename

themselves Communists, from gaining the allegiance of the masses, the chancellor appeased them by announcing that Wilhelm had resigned. Confronted with this fait accompli, the emperor flirted momentarily with the idea of leading loyal troops to Berlin to regain control. Hindenburg stepped in at this point to discourage this folly because it would surely have meant civil war. Finally, the kaiser bowed to the inevitable and boarded the train for Holland and lifelong exile. Germany thus lost a living bond to its past and presently adopted the political reforms that seemed more appropriate for a modern industrial society.

When we review the life of Wilhelm II within the context of modern German history, we come to realize that he suffered the fate of a man born into one age but fated to die in the next. Conversely, Germany was a country that experienced the great misfortune of having a leader who insisted on maintaining, and who actually embodied an antiquated ideal of government, just at the very time its economy and society were moving in the opposite direction— into the maelstrom of modernization. Wilhelm could not have been expected to see all this. For this reason, he clung tenaciously to his inheritance. He may well have been the very last person in Germany to accept as final that the time for monarchy and all it symbolized was over.

Ralph C. Walz

Bibliography

Birnbaum, Üarl. *Peace Moves and U-Boat Warfare.* Uppsala: N.p., 1958.

Kurenberg, Joachim von. *The Kaiser: A Life of Wilhelm II.* New York: Simon & Schuster, 1955.

Official German Documents Relating to the World War. The Reports of the First and Second Subcommittees of the Committee Appointed by the National Constituent Assembly to Inquire into the Responsibility for the War. 2 vols. New York: Carnegie Endowment for International Peace, 1923.

Wilhelm II. *Letters from the Kaiser to the Czar,* ed. by Isaac D. Levine. New York: Stokes, 1920.

Williams, Clarence Charles (1869–1958)

Clarence Charles Williams was born in Nacooche, Georgia. He graduated with honors from the United States Military Academy in

1894. Commissioned a second lieutenant of artillery, he was assigned to the 4th Artillery at Fort McHenry in the harbor of Baltimore, Maryland.

After a tour of duty with the 6th Artillery at Washington Barracks (now Fort McNair) in the District of Columbia, he went to the Philippines in 1898 with the Astor Battery. With that unit, he participated in the capture of Manila. In September 1898, Williams was detailed an aide-de-camp to MajGen. Arthur MacArthur at Manila.

Returning to the United States in November 1898, Williams served in various ordnance assignments at Rock Island Arsenal, Du Pont powder works, in the office of the chief of ordnance, and Watertown Arsenal.

In December 1914, he went to Germany as a military observer with the German Army. This duty gave him a keen insight into German armament and operations, which was to serve him well in the future. In May 1915, Williams returned to the United States and served on the Ordnance Board. Following a year on the board, he had various ordnance assignments culminating as a member of the Gun Board at Springfield Armory, Massachusetts. From there he was called to serve as ordnance officer of the general headquarters of the American Expeditionary Force (GHQ AEF).

LtCol. Williams sailed on the *Baltic* from New York in May 1917 with General Pershing. While at sea, he was appointed to a board of officers to study the need for artillery, assuming an AEF of half a million men. The board concluded that such a force would need a minimum of 2,500 guns, and further estimated it would be impossible to provide more than a minuscule number of these from United States sources. Thus, the AEF would have to rely on the French and British to meet its needs.

On Oct. 8, 1917, Williams was promoted to brigadier general along with the heads of all the staff departments at GHQ AEF. One of the problems with which General Williams wrestled was obtaining enough steel from the United States to keep the French arsenals supplied, so they could turn out the artillery, tanks, and munitions needed by the American forces. His success in these negotiations and his general efficiency was such that, in April 1918, he was recalled to Washington to become the chief of ordnance and was promoted to major general.

General Williams served as chief of ordnance until his retirement in 1930. With the outbreak of World War II, he was recalled to active duty in January 1942 and again retired in September 1943. He died at Woodstock, Virginia, on June 13, 1958.

James L. Collins, Jr.

Bibliography
Pershing, John J. *My Experiences in the World War*. New York: Stokes, 1931.
Smythe, Donald. *Pershing*. Bloomington: Indiana University Press, 1986.

Wilson, William Bauchop (1862–1934)

William Bauchop Wilson, labor leader, congressman, and first U.S. secretary of labor, was born in Blantyre, Scotland. In 1870, his father, a coal miner active in the union movement, decided to immigrate to the United States, and the family eventually settled in the small mining community of Arnot, Pennsylvania. As a child, Wilson received little formal education. He was forced to leave school at the age of nine to supplement the meager family income. Two years later, he joined the local labor union, became its secretary at the age of fourteen, and rose to a position of leadership when he was barely seventeen. As a union organizer, he suffered all the hardships of those who dared defy the absolute power of the coal interests. For years, he found it impossible to secure steady employment in the mines, but his experience with blacklisting, evictions, and injunctions only intensified his commitment to labor unionism and his devotion to the improvement of working-class conditions.

From 1888 to 1890, Wilson was president of the district miners' union of the National Progressive Union. As a member of its national executive board, he was instrumental in organizing the United Mine Workers of America (UMW), became the president of its central Pennsylvania division in 1899, and the secretary-treasurer of the national union one year later. Over the years, Wilson helped to shape the conciliatory and highly successful policy of the UMW, which emphasized negotiation with employers over confrontation, was willing to accept less than complete victory in order to avoid or settle a dispute, and believed in calling a strike only as the last resort. At the same time, Wilson became increasingly interested in the political aspects of organized labor's agenda. Above all, he was convinced that unions had to seek relief from judicial injunctions under antitrust legislation that was frequently employed to crush their organizing efforts. Thus, in 1906, he ran for a seat in the House of Representatives on the Democratic ticket and was elected by a slim majority.

To Wilson, his work in Congress was but an extension of his previous efforts on behalf of America's workers. Chosen by the American Federation of Labor (AF of L) as its main congressional agent, he soon became the leader of organized labor's legislative drive. However, it was not until 1911, when the Democrats won control of the House of Representatives and Wilson became chairman of the Committee on Labor, that his incessant efforts resulted in legislative gains, and, during the following two years, he managed to steer through Congress a whole series of measures long desired by the American labor movement.

To the AF of L, Wilson was thus the natural choice to head the new Department of Labor that was created in the waning days of the Taft administration in 1912. The appointment of the first secretary of labor was left to President-elect Woodrow Wilson, who had actively courted the support of organized labor in his presidential campaign. The nomination of William B. Wilson, a card-carrying union member, over fierce conservative opposition, signaled the beginning of a new relationship between organized labor and the federal government that would eventually culminate in a virtual alliance of the Wilson White House and the AF of L.

President Wilson and his secretary of labor agreed that, in addition to improving the welfare of American workers through the work of such agencies as the Bureau of Labor Statistics, the U.S. Employment Service, and the Children's Bureau, the most important task of the new department was the promotion of industrial peace and a democratization of industrial relations. Secretary Wilson made it clear that his department regarded labor and capital as equal partners in the production process, both entitled to an equal voice in determining the terms of their partnership. The workers had a right to organize and bargain collectively, and Secretary Wilson emphasized that his department would invite the cooperation and support of "responsible labor organizations." Thus, in their efforts to mediate the differences between employers and employees, the secretary and his department's Division of Conciliation tried to secure settlements that provided the foundation for stable industrial relations on the basis of the

union principles of collective bargaining and the trade agreement.

With the entry of the United States into the First World War, the prevention or adjustment of labor disputes became crucial to the mobilization of the country's industrial resources. Yet, for nine months, the Wilson administration tried to meet the wartime labor emergency by peacetime methods, relying on haphazard and piecemeal measures rather than providing a unified adjustment agency for all industries. One such ad hoc response to an emergency situation in the summer of 1917 was the creation of the so-called President's Mediation Commission, chaired by Secretary Wilson and charged with settling the industrial disputes plaguing a number of industries in the Southwest and the Pacific Northwest. While the work of the commission was only partly successful, it became a precedent for the establishment of more permanent wartime adjustment agencies.

In the first step toward a unified war labor program, Secretary Wilson was named war labor administrator in January 1918 and authorized to coordinate the labor policy of the various government departments and numerous wartime agencies. As a first step, he appointed the War Labor Conference Board, composed of an equal number of representatives of capital and labor for the purpose of drafting a comprehensive code of industrial relations. Hailed as the "Magna Carta of Labor," the code, among other things, outlawed strikes and lockouts, provided for the right of workers to organize and bargain collectively, granted the basic eight-hour day to all employees, gave women the same pay as men for equal work, and promised all workers a living wage. To implement these principles in disputes between capital and labor, Secretary Wilson named the National War Labor Board, which settled numerous controversies in industries crucial to the war effort.

Other agencies created under the umbrella of Secretary Wilson's War Labor Administration included the War Labor Policies Board, the U.S. Housing Corporation, the Division of Negro Economics, and the Woman in Industry Service. On the whole, however, they were established too late to have a major impact during the war. After the Armistice, most wartime agencies were quickly dismantled, as Americans were eager for a speedy return to normalcy. Moreover, the truce that had largely prevailed between employers and employees during the period of national crisis gave way to renewed industrial conflict. Attempts by Secretary Wilson to perpetuate the wartime understanding between capital and labor, which culminated in the convocation of two industrial conferences in the fall of 1919, failed due to the refusal of both sides to compromise their respective positions.

William B. Wilson was one of the few members of Woodrow Wilson's cabinet who stayed with the President throughout his two terms in office. On several occasions, Woodrow Wilson refused to give up his secretary of labor to the Democratic leadership of Pennsylvania, who desired to nominate him for governor of the state. The President trusted his secretary's counsel on matters concerning labor and usually followed his advice, maintaining that he had "never known a more careful or judicial mind than that of Secretary Wilson." William B. Wilson died on May 25, 1934.

Manfred F. Boemke

Bibliography

Babson, Roger W. *W.B. Wilson and the Department of Labor.* New York: 1919.

Lombardi, John. *Labor's Voice in the Cabinet: A History of the Department of Labor from its Origins to 1921.* New York: Columbia University Press, 1942.

Pritchard, Paul W. "William B. Wilson: Master Workman." *Pennsylvania History* (April 1945).

Wilhelm, Clarke L. "William B. Wilson: The First Secretary of Labor." Ph.D. dissertation, The Johns Hopkins University, 1967.

Wilson, William B. *Memories.* Washington, DC: 1916.

Wilson, Woodrow (1856–1924)

On March 4, 1913, a slender, graying man with a long face and rimless glasses entered the stands on the east front of the Capitol to take the oath of office as the twenty-eighth president of the United States. Thomas Woodrow Wilson, born on Dec. 29, 1856, at Staunton, Virginia, was the son of a prominent Presbyterian clergyman.

As a child, Wilson lived with his family in Georgia, South Carolina, and North Carolina. He was educated as an undergraduate at Davidson College and Princeton University. He later attended the law school of the University of Virginia and received a Ph.D. from Johns Hopkins University in history and political science. From 1885 to 1902, he taught at Bryn Mawr College, Wesleyan University, Johns Hopkins, and Princeton, published a large number of books and articles, and earned a national reputation as a political scientist and historian. Elected to the presidency of Princeton in 1902, he led a successful drive to modernize and strengthen the university but lost a struggle with powerful alumni over the future of the university's eating clubs and was defeated by the dean of the Graduate School over the control and location of a new graduate school.

In 1910, he left Princeton to run as a Democrat for governor of New Jersey and was elected. His success in securing adoption of an extensive reform program helped to gain for him his party's 1912 presidential nomination. In November 1912, he was elected, defeating the Republican incumbent, William Howard Taft, and the Progressive Party candidate, Theodore Roosevelt.

By the time he became prominent as a scholar, Wilson had dropped his first name and was known simply as Woodrow Wilson. He married Ellen Axson on June 24, 1885, and they had three daughters, Margaret (born April 16, 1886), Jessie (born Aug. 28, 1887), and Eleanor (born Oct. 16, 1889). Ellen died on Aug. 6, 1914. Wilson subsequently met and married Edith Bolling Galt, a wealthy widow, on Dec. 18, 1915.

During the 1912 presidential campaign Wilson concentrated on domestic issues. He promised to lower the tariff, to reform the banking and monetary system, and to adopt more effective antitrust laws. With the signing of the Underwood Tariff Act (Oct. 3, 1913), the Federal Reserve Act (Dec. 23, 1913), the Interstate Trade Commission Act (Sept. 26, 1914), and the Clayton Antitrust Act (Oct. 15, 1914), he fulfilled all of these promises. In addition, an unusual degree of cooperation between Wilson and Congress during his first administration facilitated the passage of the first national child labor law, the establishment of the Department of Labor, the creation of a banking system, a nationwide demonstration program for farmers, the implementation of an eight-hour work day for railroad employees, and the adoption of the federal income tax as the main source of governmental revenue, among other things. By the time he defeated Republican challenger Charles Evans Hughes in the 1916 presidential election, Wilson had already become one of the most successful modern presidents.

Although Wilson's main concern was with domestic reforms during his first term, he also pursued an active foreign policy, especially in Latin America. He believed that all peoples had the capacity and desire for democratic self government and that the United States had a particular mission to lead them in that direction. His Latin American policy sought to discourage revolutionary violence and to encourage constitutional order, but not to block all change. The State Department promoted American trade and investment south of the border, but it set strict rules for businessmen operating abroad as well. The administration even negotiated a treaty expressing regret for America's part in a 1903 revolution that split Panama off from Colombia. Faced with a revolution in Mexico, Wilson exerted diplomatic pressure for the restoration of order and intervened briefly in 1914 and 1916 with small military forces, but he rejected proposals for large-scale intervention and refused to block Mexican economic reforms even when they injured American interests. In Haiti (1915) and the Dominican Republic (1916), however, his impatience with incessant revolutions led to American invasions and the imposition of military governments that outlasted his presidency and contradicted his own belief in democratic self-determination.

Asia also had a important place in Wilson's foreign policy. In one of his first acts as president, he terminated American participation in an international loan program because he believed it would endanger China's sovereignty, and he was the first leader to extend diplomatic recognition to the Chinese republic in 1913. Japan's imperialism in China and a controversy between Japan and the United States over the treatment of Japanese in California, threatened Wilson's hopes for a new era of democracy and harmony in Asia, however. When World War I began in August 1914, the Japanese, who were British allies, declared war on Germany, seized German concessions in China, and demanded indirect control over much of the rest of China. American leaders were outraged but realized they could do little to influence events so far away.

Wilson was also deeply concerned about the outbreak of war in Europe but not tempted to intervene there either. Although he admired British culture and politics, he believed that all the belligerents shared responsibility for the conflict, and he hoped that a neutral United States might serve as a mediator. On Aug. 4, 1914, he issued a proclamation of neutrality and offered mediation. At the suggestion of Secretary of State William Jennings Bryan, he also announced that the government disapproved of private loans to the belligerents. He hoped to starve the war to death by cutting off the money upon which it fed.

Nevertheless, with the United States in a recession when the war began, Wilson wanted to increase, not cut off, trade with the nations at war. During the autumn of 1914, foreign sales of American products increased rapidly, especially to Britain and France, who had large merchant fleets and the British Navy to protect them. Trade with Germany, who had few merchant vessels and a small navy, declined sharply, although the administration urged the British to loosen their blockade of Europe enough to allow at least food and raw materials to pass through. By the autumn of 1915, the Allies were running out of cash with which to pay for their increasing purchases in the United States. Rather than strangle the trade that had become so important to Americans, Wilson loosened the loan ban to permit first the extension of credit and then, a year later, outright loans.

At the same time, the President tried to avoid steps that might put the nation on the side of one belligerent or the other. He resisted pressure from German Americans to ban the sale of arms and munitions to belligerents because he believed that an arms embargo would unneutrally help the Germans and injure the British and French. He also rejected demands by Theodore Roosevelt and his pro-Allied friends to begin a "preparedness" program of enlarging the army and navy because he feared that their goal was to undermine neutrality.

Wilson realized that America's economic power had become so great that neither side in the war could afford to allow the United States to trade freely with the other. To prevent this situation from forcing the nation into war, in January 1915, he sent his closest friend, "Colonel" Edward Mandell House, on a peace mission to Europe. House was to confer with leaders on both sides in hopes of defining the terms of a compromise peace.

While House was still on his way to Europe, however, the German government announced on Feb. 4, 1915, that it had established a "war zone" around the British Isles in which German submarines would sink Allied vessels. The Germans made no direct threats against neutral ships, but they warned that mistakes might be made and urged neutrals to avoid the war zone. No one outside of Germany knew that the Germans had only nine diesel submarines capable of enforcing their threat, so the German announcement not only undermined House's peace mission, but also drew a sharp response from the United States. On February 10, the State Department informed the German government that the United States would hold Germany to "strict accountability" for any damage to American lives and property. Wilson regarded the submarine blockade as illegal because fragile submarines could not save the lives of passengers and crews, or protect property, as warships had traditionally been required to do under international law.

During the early spring of 1915, minor incidents demonstrated the seriousness of the situation, but it became a crisis only on May 7, 1915, when the British passenger liner *Lusitania* was torpedoed and sunk with the loss of 1,198 lives, including 128 Americans. Theodore Roosevelt described the sinking as "piracy," and for the first time Americans began to think about the possibility of entering the war. Wilson did not want that. "There is such a thing as a nation being so right that it does not need to convince others by force that it is right," he said, and in a diplomatic note he demanded that Germany apologize for the sinking and severely limit the use of submarines. The President hoped that his strong language would force the Germans to back down without risk of war, but Secretary of State Bryan believed Wilson was leading the nation into the conflict and resigned in protest on June 9. Wilson then appointed Robert Lansing to become secretary in Bryan's place, and more and more the President and Colonel House took personal control of the nation's foreign policy.

On Sept. 1, 1915, the Germans, under heavy American pressure, promised they would not sink passenger-carrying vessels without warning and without protecting the lives of passengers. The promise eased tensions with Germany, but the *Lusitania* crisis had strengthened Republican demands for a buildup of the army and navy. On November 4, Wilson announced his support of a modest preparedness effort to prevent Congress from forcing a much larger plan on him.

During the summer of 1915 the administration's troubles had increased by a serious disagreement with England. In July, the White House learned that the British planned to place cotton on their list of contraband items that could be seized without compensation if they were being shipped to their enemies. Wilson was very concerned because his Democratic Party was dependent upon the support of the cotton-exporting South, where there was panic over the probable loss of markets. Fortunately, the British agreed to buy enough cotton to keep the price up and avert a political crisis, but Wilson could foresee trouble ahead with both Britain and Germany.

During the autumn of 1915, Wilson discussed the situation with Colonel House, and they decided to make another attempt to find a diplomatic solution to the war. On December 28, House returned to Europe, but he found that neither side was willing to offer terms the other might accept.

House had now decided that a German victory would be a disaster for Europe and the United States, and by the spring of 1916, he feared that Russian military losses and the economic exhaustion of England and France were making an Allied defeat likely. Foolishly, he promised the British, in the House-Grey Memorandum of Feb. 22, 1916, that the United States would enter the war on the Allied side if the Germans refused to attend an American-sponsored peace conference. Wilson later approved a weakened version of the memorandum in hopes of winning Allied support of a peace conference, but nothing came of the scheme. House had been wrong. The Allies did not think they were defeated and were planning a great offensive to win the war. They had no more interest in a compromise peace than the Germans did.

In the meantime, a new crisis arose when a German submarine torpedoed the French steamer *Sussex* on March 24, 1916, injuring several American passengers. Wilson threatened, on April 18, that he would break diplomatic relations unless the German government promised to stop submarine attacks on all merchant ships. In Berlin, Wilson's ultimatum strengthened the army's argument that the submarine campaign had little military value and was likely to bring the United States into the war. On May 4, 1916, therefore, the German government announced that its submarines would no longer attack merchant vessels without warning.

The Germans' *Sussex* Pledge seemed to prove the success of Wilson's policy of insisting firmly but patiently on the protection of American rights. During the presidential campaign that summer and autumn, the Democrats exploited his achievement with the campaign slogan, "He kept us out of war."

The President knew, however, how fragile American neutrality had become. On May 27, 1916, he addressed the League to Enforce Peace, a private group promoting an international peacekeeping organization. In his speech he warned that Americans had become "participants, whether we would or not, in the life of the world," and he urged that after the war the United States join with other nations in some sort of organization to make future conflicts impossible.

After the presidential election, Wilson renewed his efforts to find a negotiated solution to the war before the United States was drawn into it. On Dec. 18, 1916, he sent identical notes to both sets of belligerents, asking them to state their peace terms. By asking them to state terms publicly, he hoped that they would be forced to make reasonable proposals and that he would be able to identify the basis for a compromise. Again, neither side was interested, and their frosty responses forced the President to take another step. On Jan. 22, 1917, Wilson addressed the Senate to propose his own peace terms. He called for a "Peace Without Victory," one that would guarantee all nations security, freedom to trade, and equality of treatment. To preserve peace, he proposed the establishment of an international organization, which he believed the United States would join despite its isolationist tradition.

The President's bold overture never had a chance. The German government, having greatly increased its submarine fleet, had already decided, on Jan. 9, 1917, to resume submarine warfare with new ferocity. On January 31, Germany announced that in a war zone around the British Isles its submarines would sink all ships without warning, *whether they were belligerent or neutral*. The Germans realized that this step would probably lead to war with the United States, but they believed they would cripple the British economy and win the war before the United States could mobilize. Their move was so openly hostile that Wilson was forced to announce the termination of diplomatic relations with Germany on Feb. 3, 1917.

Three weeks later, on February 28, Wilson released to the press the Zimmermann Telegram from the German Foreign Office to the Mexican government proposing an alliance between Mexico and Germany in the event of war between Germany and the United States. The British had intercepted this bizarre offer and turned it over to the American government in hopes of shaping public opinion. Wilson published it to strengthen public support for his idea of "armed neutrality," under which American merchant vessels would be provided with guns to shoot at submarines. The House of Representatives approved his plan on March 1, but eleven senators whom Wilson called "a little group of willful men" filibustered the armed ship bill to death. The President then found authority in another law to arm the ships anyway.

The guns were useless against submerged submarines, and on March 18, Americans learned that three American ships had been sunk in the war zone, with the loss of fifteen lives. In the meantime, news arrived from Russia that the government of the tsar had been overthrown on March 12. Wilson called a special session of Congress to meet on April 2. At a dramatic joint session of the two houses that evening, he asked for a declaration of war against Germany, not only to defend American rights on the seas, but also to make the world "safe for democracy." Neutral mediation had failed, and by April, Wilson had become convinced that the United States would have a better chance to shape the peace as a belligerent than as a neutral.

The nation was little prepared for the war that was declared on April 6, 1917. Wilson had created a Council of National Defense on Aug. 16, 1916, to plan for war, but it had done little by April. The United States Army and Navy were tiny and poorly armed, the United States owned almost no merchant vessels to transport men and supplies to France, the railroad system over which men and goods would have to be moved was in chaos, and, worst of all, no one was in charge of planning and coordinating mobilization. Wilson favored conscription to raise men for the army and navy, and on May 18, 1917, he signed the draft into law. Beginning in June, about 2.7 million men were drafted, and another 2 million joined up as volunteers. The first American troops landed in France on June 26, but it would be a year before large numbers of them arrived for active service. By the end of the war in November 1918, more than 2 million American troops were in Europe.

Meanwhile, Wilson grappled with other problems. On April 14, 1917, he appointed a

Committee on Public Information headed by George Creel to censor the news and build popular support for the war. On July 28, he created a War Industries Board to manage industrial mobilization; in August, he appointed food and fuel administrations to coordinate production in those areas; and on December 26, he nationalized the railroads for the duration of the war.

In general, the agencies and boards created to run the war had little power. They were usually headed by "dollar-a-year" volunteers from business and attempted to secure voluntary cooperation rather than to control business, farmers, and labor. The administration was even reluctant to raise taxes very much for fear of alienating business, so about two-thirds of war costs were raised through Liberty Loans under which Americans loaned money to the government by buying small denomination bonds.

President Wilson generally delegated authority over both domestic mobilization and military affairs in Europe to subordinates. Most of them did their jobs remarkably well, and the size and speed of the American mobilization were nearly miraculous. A few, however, abused their powers to suppress dissent and persecute radicals. Wilson neither interfered with those who were doing well nor reined in those who were exploiting their authority in ways that violated his own standards of justice. He guarded his rather delicate health carefully and reserved his main attention for diplomacy and planning the coming peace. In September 1917, he appointed a group of experts known as The Inquiry to study the issues that would come up at the peace conference and to prepare American positions on them.

The President's own broad peace goals were set before the world in a speech to Congress on Jan. 8, 1918. In what came to be known as the "Fourteen Points" address, he proposed the open publication of all international agreements, freedom of the seas, removal of trade barriers among nations, reduction of armaments, impartial settlement of colonial claims, evacuation of Russia and self-determination for the Russian people, evacuation of other areas occupied by the Germans, self-determination for various national groups throughout Europe, and the creation of an "association of nations" to supervise the peace.

When Germany and the other Central Powers surrendered on Nov. 11, 1918, Wilson hoped that the Fourteen Points would become the basis of an armistice and a peace treaty. He had already decided in September that he would personally lead the American delegation to the peace conference to fight for his principles. The battle promised to be as fierce as those of the war. Although Wilson was enormously popular in the world because he was the leader of the nation that had finally made victory possible, he faced serious opposition at home and abroad about the specifics of the peace. In American congressional elections on Nov. 5, 1918, he urged his countrymen to elect Democrats to assure support for his program, but they rebelled and elected Republican majorities to both houses. In Europe, demands for the weakening of Germany and insistence that the defeated nations pay the vast costs of the war threatened the fair, stable peace of which Wilson dreamed.

Millions of Frenchmen turned out to cheer the President when he arrived in Paris on Dec. 14, 1918, and millions of Italians, Belgians, and Britons also cheered him on later visits to those countries. But when Wilson sat down to negotiate a peace treaty with the Allied leaders in early January 1919, the cheers were soon forgotten. British Prime Minister David Lloyd George and Italian Prime Minister Vittorio Orlando were tough, ruthless men more concerned with protecting their nations' interests than creating a new world order.

For six months, Wilson worked harder than he had ever worked before in his life, struggling to turn the Fourteen Points into the terms of the peace treaty. He had some notable successes. One of the first acts of the conference was to approve what he called the "Covenant" of a League of Nations, and in the discouraging days ahead, he took comfort in the belief that even if the rest of the treaty was imperfect, the League could later rectify mistakes. He was also pleased that the conference tried to recognize the principle of self-determination of national groups in its creation of new states in Central Europe and that it set up a mandate system that would permit the League of Nations to supervise the preparation of former German colonies for independence.

In a number of cases, however, he was forced to accept provisions in the treaty that departed from the Fourteen Points. The French wanted to detach the industrial area along the Rhine from Germany; the British wanted to inflate Germany's reparation bill by including pensions for veterans; the Italians demanded territory to which they had no real claim; the Japanese insisted on keeping the German concessions they had seized in China. In all these areas, Wilson was forced to accept compromises with which he was unhappy or risk breaking up the conference. Moreover, some of the Fourteen Points never even came up for discussion. Freedom of the seas, arms reduction (except for Germany, which was disarmed), and removal of economic barriers among nations were all left to the League of Nations to discuss. Russia, where the Bolsheviks had overthrown the democratic government in November 1917 and made a separate peace with Germany on March 3, 1918, was treated more as an enemy than a former ally and was not even invited to the peace conference.

Wilson's ability to resist compromises was weakened because he had to ask the other leaders to agree to modifications of the League of Nations Covenant after he returned from a trip to Washington in March 1919. During the trip he received from the new chairman of the Senate Foreign Relations Committee, Republican Henry Cabot Lodge of Massachusetts, a "round-robin" letter signed by more than one-third of the senators who promised to defeat the treaty unless the League Covenant was amended to protect the Monroe Doctrine and assure that the League could not interfere with tariffs or immigration. The round-robin letter suggested that Wilson's domestic support was thin and weakened his position at the peace conference. When the peace treaty was finally signed in the Hall of Mirrors at the palace at Versailles on June 28, 1919, it was not the ideal document for which Wilson had hoped, but he still believed that it was a better peace than would have been imposed on the Germans had he not been at the conference. He also believed that the one great achievement of the treaty, the creation of the League of Nations, had the potential to rectify any other mistakes that might have been made.

Wilson, exhausted from his ordeal, returned to the United States on July 8, 1919, and presented the treaty to the Senate on July 10. It was America's duty, he told the senators, to assume leadership of the League of Nations and use it to assure a stable, orderly world. Most Republicans and even some Democrats obviously did not share his opinion. Some of them argued that membership in the League of Nations would limit American freedom of action and compel the United States to uphold

European imperialism; others had more specific objections, such as the failure of the treaty to provide independence for Ireland. All of the opponents were determined that if they voted for the treaty at all, it would only be with amendments.

Through the hot Washington summer, Wilson met with undecided senators in an effort to persuade them that they should support an unmodified treaty and, on August 19, had a three-hour meeting with the full Foreign Relations Committee. By the end of the meeting, it was obvious to him that the treaty would be substantially amended or defeated unless the Senate could somehow be convinced that there was an overwhelming public demand for its approval. On September 3, he left Washington for the West in an effort to arouse enough public support to change opponents' minds. During the next three weeks he traveled almost 10,000 miles by train and delivered more than thirty-five speeches in twenty-nine cities, usually speaking to crowds of thousands without any sort of amplification and attending dinners and receptions before and after speeches.

The trip did indeed stir public support for the treaty, but it did not change any minds in the Senate, and it shattered Wilson, who had begun the ordeal against his doctor's advice. On Sept. 25, 1919, after a speech at Pueblo, Colorado, he collapsed; the rest of the trip was abruptly cancelled; and he returned to the White House. There, on October 2, he suffered a massive stroke that paralyzed his left side and left him an invalid for the remainder of his life. For several weeks after the stroke, the President saw no official visitors and did not meet with his cabinet until April 1920. His wife and doctor denied the seriousness of his illness publicly for months and shielded him from the news that might have persuaded him that an unamended treaty could not be approved in the Senate.

Ill and out of touch with reality, Wilson refused all compromise with treaty opponents, and on Nov. 19, 1919, the Senate defeated the treaty. The President's supporters, horrified that the United States might not join the League of Nations Wilson had fathered, scrambled to find some compromise that might still save the treaty, but Wilson was immovable, and a second Senate vote on March 19, 1920, confirmed the treaty's defeat.

Wilson was so out of touch with events in the spring of 1920 that he actually contemplated running for a third presidential term to seek a national referendum on the League issue. His friends quietly sidetracked the idea, and the Democrats nominated the amiable but uninspiring governor of Ohio, James M. Cox. Cox was buried in the landslide that swept Warren G. Harding into the White House. An ironic postscript to the story was that Wilson, his League of Nations dream rejected in his own country, was awarded the Nobel Peace Prize on Dec. 10, 1920. He was still too ill to attend the ceremony.

On March 4, 1921, Wilson left the White House and retired to a spacious house at 2340 S Street in Washington. There he lived quietly with Edith, occasionally seeing a few visitors, until his death on Feb. 3, 1924. He was buried in the National Cathedral in Washington on Feb. 6, 1924.

Kendrick A. Clements

See also ARMED NEUTRALITY; FOURTEEN POINTS; HOUSE, EDWARD MANDELL; LEAGUE OF NATIONS; PARIS PEACE CONFERENCE

Bibliography

Clements, Kendrick A. *Woodrow Wilson: World Statesman*. Boston: Twayne, 1987.
Devlin, Patrick. *Too Proud to Fight: Woodrow Wilson's Neutrality*. London: Oxford University Press, 1974.
Ferrell, Robert H. *Woodrow Wilson and World War I, 1917–1921*. New York: Harper & Row, 1985.
Link, Arthur S., ed. *The Papers of Woodrow Wilson*. 69 vols. Princeton: Princeton University Press, 1966–1993.
———. *Wilson*. 5 vols. Princeton: Princeton University Press, 1947–1965.

Wise, Frederic May, Jr. (1877–1940)

Frederic May ("Fritz," "Dopey") Wise, Jr., entered the Marine Corps in 1899. After a short stint at the Boston Navy Yard, he was ordered to the Philippines. He briefly served in China during the Boxer Rebellion, then returned to the Philippines to complete his tour of duty. Wise then served at the Brooklyn Navy Yard, in Puerto Rico, once more in the Philippines, and in Japan. He was ordered to Cuba in 1906 during the Second Intervention, landed at Veracruz with Marine forces in 1914, and served in the United States interventions in Haiti (1915) and the Dominican Republic (1916).

In the spring of 1917, Wise was given command of the newly formed 2d Battalion, Fifth Marines, made up of men recently returned from Haiti and the Dominican Republic. This battalion sailed for France aboard the *Henderson* on June 14, 1917, with the first contingent of the American Expeditionary Force (AEF). The battalion trained at the Gondrecourt Training Area with the French 151st Chasseurs Alpines, the "Blue Devils," until they returned to the line. Training continued throughout the remainder of 1917 and into 1918. Finally, the 2d Battalion was ordered to take over the Montgirmont-Les Eparges sector of the Verdun front.

Early in June, the battalion took part in the action in and around Belleau Wood, earning high praise from Gen. James G. Harbord, commander of the 4th Brigade to which the unit was assigned.

With his promotion to full colonel, Wise was ordered to command the 4th Division's 59th Infantry, a veteran unit that had suffered severe casualties on the Vesle and was full of green replacements. His first action with the 59th was the St. Mihiel campaign in which he and his regiment, replacements and all, showed their mettle. The 59th then moved immediately to join the Meuse-Argonne offensive, where they were instrumental in seizing the Bois de Brieulles. Casualties were severe, and on October 22, the 59th was relieved and pulled out of the Argonne.

A few weeks later the war was over and the 4th Division was selected to serve with the Army of Occupation. Wise commanded the 8th Brigade of this force.

In January 1919, Wise returned to the United States and to the Marine Corps. After a brief home leave, he reported for duty in Haiti. Subsequently, he was placed in command of the 1st Marine Regiment at Quantico, Virginia. Ill health forced him to retire in January 1926. He died in Washington, D.C., on July 24, 1940.

George B. Clark

Bibliography

Bach, Christian A. *The Fourth Division, Its Services and Achievements in the World War*. N.p.: The Fourth Division, 1920.
Wise, Frederic M. *A Marine Tells It To You*. New York: Sears, 1929.

Wise, Stephen Samuel (1874–1949)

Stephen Samuel Wise served as assistant rabbi and eventually head rabbi of B'nai Jeshrun Synagogue in New York City from 1893 to 1900. During the 1890s, Wise began to espouse the cause of Zionism, which he called "the greatest passion of my public life." He helped form the nationwide Federation of American Zionists in 1898 and served as the federation's honorary secretary until 1904, working closely with Theodor Herzl. In addition to Zionism, Wise also began to espouse social causes early in his career.

In 1900, Wise became rabbi of Temple Beth Israel in Portland, Oregon, the leading congregation of the Pacific Northwest. During his tenure there, Wise heightened Jewish awareness in the newer communities in Oregon. He also continued to render public service by advocating social and political reform. Stephen Wise returned to New York City in 1907 to found the Free Synagogue, where the pulpit was protected from any form of restriction by the temple's board of directors. For the next forty-three years, the Free Synagogue served as the principal forum for Wise's ideological expressions.

After his return to New York City, Wise became more prominently identified with the causes of organized labor. Wise campaigned for Woodrow Wilson in 1912, and from 1916 to 1919, he was an important liaison between the American Jewish community and President Wilson. Along with Louis Brandeis and Felix Frankfurter, Wise helped write the Balfour Declaration of 1917. He attended the Versailles Peace Conference of 1918–1919, where he spoke on behalf of the Zionist aspiration in Palestine.

Throughout his career, Wise maintained three constant goals: to direct American Jews toward pro-Zionist activities; to involve American Jews in liberal causes in the United States; and to democratize American Jewish life. To meet these goals, Wise helped organize the American Jewish Congress, first on a provisional basis from 1916 to 1919, then as a permanent organization in 1920. He served as vice president of the Congress from 1921 to 1925 and later as honorary president until his death in 1949.

Burton A. Boxerman

Bibliography

Voss, Carl H. *Stephen S. Wise: Servant of the People—Selected Letters*. Philadelphia: Jewish Publication Society of America, 1969.

Wise, Stephen S. *Challenging Years: The Autobiography of Stephen S. Wise*. New York: Putnam, 1949.

Wiseman, William (1885–1962)

Sir William Wiseman was a British spy, diplomatic confidante, and financier. He was the tenth holder of a baronage dating back to 1628 and son of a Royal Navy captain. He attended Cambridge University and then worked for two years as a journalist before entering a London banking house in 1908, where he secured financing for the Diaz government in Mexico. When the Great War broke out, Wiseman asked for and received an infantry commission. He was gassed in Flanders in 1915 and lost some of his eyesight. A friend of his father's arranged for his transfer to British foreign intelligence (MI-6). After training at Scotland Yard, he was sent to New York as second in command of British espionage in America. However, he and his supervisor were recalled after a few months. Thereupon Wiseman asked permission to establish an effective American section and was returned to New York in December, 1915, ostensibly as a member of the Purchasing Commission of the Ministry of Munitions, but in reality in charge of all MI-6 operations in the United States. His success as a spy master and counterespionage agent is still unknown.

Wiseman met Col. Edward M. House in December 1916, and the two grew close almost immediately. Wiseman was aware of the intimate relationship between House and President Wilson and was eager to promote an understanding between English and American leaders; House wanted a direct channel to Prime Minister Lloyd George in order to circumvent U.S. Ambassador Page in London and British Ambassador Spring-Rice in Washington, both of whom House considered partisan and unreliable. Since the British Secret Service was at this time under the Foreign Office, Wiseman offered House direct communication with Lord Arthur Balfour, the foreign minister. Wiseman proved a discrete confidante, and his liberal views impressed House. By September, he had taken an apartment in the same building as House in order to work more closely with him.

Time and again, in one crisis of misunderstanding after another, Wiseman and House eased tensions in Anglo-American relations. In the summer of 1917, they intervened to resolve a conflict between the United States Treasury and British commissioners regarding American loan policies, worked to coordinate English and American war aims, and convinced Wilson to send an American military representative to the Allied Supreme War Council. On the other hand, the President rejected their suggestion for a token American military expedition to Russia for propaganda purposes to bolster the Provisional Government. That fall, Wiseman was able to summarize Wilson's reply to Pope Benedict XV's peace proposal and forward it to Balfour before he read it in the newspapers—unlike the rest of the Allies. When Balfour intimated to Wilson that he was going to make a statement in favor of a Jewish homeland, Wiseman transmitted the President's approval so confidentially that even U.S. Secretary of State Robert Lansing was not informed. During the Allied manpower crisis in early 1918, Wiseman and House advocated the amalgamation of U.S. troops into Allied armies in France, but Gen. John J. Pershing prevailed. Efforts by House and Wiseman to have Pershing demoted for resisting amalgamation were rejected by Wilson on the advice of Secretary of War Newton D. Baker, although Baker did order Pershing to leave military diplomacy to Gen. Tasker H. Bliss, America's representative on the Supreme War Council.

After serving as an intermediary between Wilson and Lloyd George at the Paris Peace Conference, Wiseman realized that there was little future in British diplomacy for a man with his pronounced pro-American sentiments and returned to banking. He joined Kuhn, Loeb & Co. in 1921 and arranged several large financial deals for the firm.

With the advent of World War II, Wiseman helped Sir William Stevenson, the new British espionage chief in the United States, hunt Nazi spies. He also played an indirect role in establishing America's first foreign intelligence agency, the Office of Strategic Services, by arranging meetings between high-ranking British intelligence officials and President Franklin D. Roosevelt.

Wiseman once again turned his full attention to banking after the war and retired in 1958. He died in New York four years later.

David Esposito

Bibliography
Fowler, Wilton B. *British American Relations, 1917–1918: The Role of Sir William Wiseman*. Princeton, NJ: Princeton University Press, 1969.

Woman's Peace Party

The Woman's Peace Party (WPP), formed in January 1915, represented a new departure in the American peace movement. Impetus for formation of a woman's peace organization came from two European feminist pacifists, Emmeline Pethick-Lawrence of Great Britain and Rosika Schwimmer of Hungary. Their speeches channeled the horror and distress of American women over the war in Europe into a popular demand for a woman's peace movement. To get this movement off the ground, Pethick-Lawrence and Schwimmer enlisted the aid of suffragists and Jane Addams, a committed pacifist. The Hull House founder was at the peak of her prestige at the beginning of the war and only reluctantly agreed to convene a meeting in Washington, D.C., in response to the enthusiasm among women and the specific urgings of suffragist Carrie Chapman Catt.

Critical of the prewar male-dominated peace movement, the seventy-seven delegates, who represented a wide spectrum of women's organizations, elected Addams as their president and approved a platform calling for neutral mediation, limitation of armaments, democratic control of foreign policy, removal of the economic causes of war, and extension of the franchise to women, at the Jan. 9–11, 1915, organizational meeting. The preamble, written by Anna Garlin Spencer, emphasized that women felt a "peculiar moral passion of revolt" against the cruelty and waste of war because they were the "custodians of the life of the ages" and as such demanded a voice in their government.

The April 1915 International Congress of Women (ICW) at the Hague provided the first opportunity for the WPP to promote its neutral mediation plank. Addams, who was invited to be president, recognized the ICW's symbolic importance and secured a number of prestigious women to serve on the American delegation. En route to Europe, they adopted a plan by Julia Grace Wales for a conference for continuous mediation. The ICW, comprised primarily of women from neutral nations, approved the Wales Plan as well as resolutions calling for self-determination, arbitration of disputes, democratic control of foreign policy, equal political rights for women, a permanent world organization, general disarmament, freedom of the seas, abrogation of all secret treaties, and education of children in the goal of peace. The delegates voted to convene an international meeting at the end of the war, to establish a permanent organization, and to send representatives to belligerent and neutral capitols to present their resolutions to national leaders. After the U.S. delegation, which included Addams and Emily Greene Balch, met with numerous European leaders, they met with President Woodrow Wilson. Although not enthusiastic about an unofficial mediation conference, he found the resolutions of the congress the best peace proposals that had been suggested until then.

Disappointed by the lack of progress on the mediation issue and alarmed by Wilson's support of military preparedness, by the beginning of 1916, the WPP focused increasingly on antipreparedness. WPP efforts, undertaken in cooperation with the American Union Against Militarism (AUAM), included lobbying and testifying on Capitol Hill and supporting an AUAM-sponsored "Truth About Preparedness" campaign. Crystal Eastman, who was executive secretary of the AUAM and led the New York City branch of the WPP (NYC-WPP) was largely responsible for moving both organizations into the forefront of the antipreparedness movement. Although the national WPP leaders supported antipreparedness, many branches did not undertake aggressive antipreparedness activities because they did not wish to alienate those who considered it unpatriotic to challenge President Wilson.

WPP branches were allowed broad discretion, which meant that WPP programs and policies throughout the nation often lacked unity. The two strongest and most influential branches, the Massachusetts branch and the NYC-WPP, often had diametrically opposed positions. On preparedness, for example, while most Massachusetts leaders objected to an aggressive antipreparedness stance, the NYC-WPP waged an uncompromising campaign that included statehouse lobbying, parades, speakers and a "War against War" graphics exhibit.

Diversity of opinion within the organization became more pronounced as the United States moved closer to war. Following the February 1917 break in diplomatic relations with Germany, WPP board members suggested a referendum on whether or not the people wished to defend trade by war. The board also issued a statement calling on American citizens to stay out of war zones and urging arbitration of the differences between the United States and Germany. During this difficult period, some WPP members joined new emergency antiwar coalitions, some branches ceased their activities, others disbanded, and the national WPP generally avoided decisions by deferring matters to the remaining branches. Wilson's war message on April 2, 1917, brought no response from the national WPP and only the New York City branch questioned the President's message.

WPP leaders were among those who testified in opposition to the Selective Service and Espionage bills, but with their passage, WPP activities declined precipitously. While some branches became involved in war-relief activities, Eastman and others in the NYC-WPP believed it was their duty to keep the peace movement alive. Their wartime activities included publication of an irreverent antiwar journal, *Four Lights*, subsequently denied mailing privileges under the Espionage Act, and sponsorship of a series of classes on peace proposals and international organizations.

With active opposition to war far too dangerous, national WPP leaders focused on plans for an international women's peace conference after the war. The conference, held in Zurich in May 1919, attacked the vindictive Versailles peace proposal and passed a resolution that detailed the ways in which the League of Nations Covenant departed from Wilson's Fourteen Points. The delegates converted the Women's International Committee into a permanent body—the Women's International League for Peace and Freedom (WILPF)—and chose Jane Addams as its president. In November 1919, the WPP became the American section of the WILPF.

Barbara J. Steinson

See also ADDAMS, JANE; AMERICAN UNION AGAINST MILITARISM; EASTMAN, CRYSTAL; ESPIONAGE ACT; WOMEN'S INTERNATIONAL LEAGUE FOR PEACE AND FREEDOM

Bibliography

Addams, Jane. *Peace and Bread in Time of War*. New York: Garland, 1972.

Degen, Marie L. *History of the Woman's Peace Party.* Baltimore: The Johns Hopkins University Press, 1939.

Marchand, C. Roland. *The American Peace Movement and Social Reform, 1898–1918.* Princeton, NJ: Princeton University Press, 1972.

Steinson, Barbara J. *American Women's Activism in World War I.* New York: Garland, 1982.

Women in the American Expeditionary Force

Sixteen thousand American women served under the auspices of the American Expeditionary Force (AEF) in France and England. They were employed by the military and quasi-military welfare agencies in a wide range of occupations, including physical and occupational therapists, reconstruction aides, nurses' aides, dieticians, relief workers, physicians, auto and ambulance drivers, dactylographers, and librarians. The majority of women, however, served as nurses, canteen workers, telephone operators, and clerical workers. Several hundred American nurses, on loan to the British Expeditionary Force, were among the first Americans to arrive in France, within weeks of the declaration of war. The mobilization of American women by the AEF did not peak until after the Armistice, and most continued in service throughout the long and difficult demobilization period.

Underlying the mass mobilization of American women for overseas service during the First World War were vast changes in the organization of American economic life at the turn of the century. Mattie Treadwell, a pioneering historian of women's military service, has explained that the industrialization that mechanized warfare led women to work outside the home. The key factor in the military's decision to recruit women was the feminization of such service-sector jobs as nursing, telephone operation, and typing, occupations considered crucial for the modernized, bureaucratized army of World War I. Thus, AEF servicewomen were employed primarily in female-dominated occupations, while American women in the civilian workforce gained limited access to certain male-dominated jobs, such as railroad worker and streetcar conductor.

Despite the military's dependence on skilled female labor, military and civilian leaders remained deeply ambivalent about the employment of women for warfront service. Army policy in regard to the enlistment of women was therefore confused and contradictory. The creation in 1901 of the Army Nurse Corps, an all-female force headed by female superintendents drawn from the ranks of professional nursing, provided the entree for female nurses into wartime service. In the eighteen months of the war, the Army Nurse Corps and Army Nurse Corps Reserve, working closely with the American National Red Cross Nursing Service, increased from a force of less that 400 to more than 21,000, with over 10,000 in the AEF.

Though nurses were ostensibly full members of the armed services, the U.S. Army refused to uniform or equip them, leaving this task to the Red Cross. Furthermore, the exact status of Army Nurse Corps nurses was a major point of controversy between military commanders and nursing leaders. The War Department maintained that nurses were "officers without rank." Nursing critics called for equal or relative rank, insisting that War Department policy encouraged insubordination on the part of enlisted men and noncommissioned officers who worked alongside women on hospital wards. Nurses were not successful in achieving any of these goals until after the conclusion of the war, when the Army Reorganization Act of 1920 granted relative rank to members of the Army Nurse Corps.

The controversy surrounding the military employment of women overseas was most apparent in the case of office and telephone workers. Throughout the months of American involvement, the War Department was barraged by proposals and requests for the creation of an army corps of women. Pressure came from military officers, stateside and overseas, who faced a severe clerical shortage and high turnover rates among civilian workers. Army officers pointed to the British Women's Army Auxiliary Corps and the American Navy's enlisted female "Yeoman (F)"s and "Marine (F)"s as successful precedents. Secretary of War Newton Baker, however, remained adamantly opposed to the enlistment of women, insisting that such a move would be most undesirable.

An acute labor crisis for the AEF—a shortage of skilled, bilingual telephone operators—led AEF Commander-in-Chief Gen. John J. Pershing to propose a compromise. In October 1917, he cabled the War Department with a request that several units of American female telephone operators be sent over for service with the U.S. Army Signal Corps. The Signal Corps, in cooperation with the American telecommunications industry, had quickly established a communications system for the AEF, but French and American soldiers and French civilian women had all proved unable to handle the system to the satisfaction of Signal Corps commanders. Pershing believed that female employees of the Bell Telephone system would solve the problem: well-trained and ideally bilingual, they would bring natural aptitude and American efficiency to their work, and if placed until military authority, they could be kept on the job and would work and be disciplined by military standards. In November 1917, the Office of the Adjutant General approved Pershing's plan to send the operators to France as civilian contract employees of the United States Army.

Two hundred and twenty-three American operators nicknamed "Hello Girls" served with the Signal Corps. They arrived in six units beginning in March 1918. In August 1918, units of female clerical workers were brought to France under similar arrangements. These stenographers, clerks and typists, along with other American office workers hired in France, were employed by the Quartermaster Corps, Signal Corps, Medical Corps and Ordnance Corps. Despite the acclaim and approval that greeted these women workers, there was widespread confusion about their status, particularly that of the telephone operators. The swearing-in ceremony before they left the United States, the uniforms, the military transportation and housing, and the militarized work conditions and regulations led many of the women and their families, and even many of their officers, to believe that they were enlisted personnel in the armed services. Most Signal Corps women learned that this was not the case only upon their dismissal from AEF service.

In contrast to nurses, telephone operators and office workers, female canteen or welfare workers were recruited and employed by the five official civilian organizations that accompanied the AEF to France: the Young Men's Christian Association, Young Women's Christian Association, American National Red Cross, Salvation Army, and Jewish Welfare Board. The second largest group of American women with the AEF, female welfare workers, numbered approximately 6,000. The precursor to women's canteen service overseas was the

program of army "welfare work" at domestic military training bases sponsored by the War Department's Commission on Training Camp Activities, headed by attorney and reformer Raymond B. Fosdick. Concerns with doughboy morals and morale at the front led to the extension of this work with the AEF in France. Fosdick in particular promoted the recruitment of American women for overseas service, insisting that only women could create the homelike atmosphere needed to bolster the army's spirits. General Pershing and the AEF command in Paris approved Fosdick's plans, though for different reasons. Concerned with the spread of venereal disease in the AEF, Pershing believed that American women could provide the troops with a wholesome but appealing distraction from French prostitutes and lovers.

American canteen workers served in uniforms approved by the War Department but supplied by themselves or their agencies. As civilians, they were required to find their own billeting and purchase their own rations. American women ultimately staffed an elaborate network of canteens, huts, and recreation centers across the zone of American operations.

Though American women who served with the AEF were segregated in female occupations, they were not necessarily sheltered from danger. Many nurses in particular worked under combat conditions and were exposed to bombing and strafing attacks. A military hospital staffed by members of the Harvard Unit, for example, was bombed in September 1917; several enlisted men were killed and a nurse was wounded in the face while on duty. For all members of the AEF, the threat of disease was omnipresent. A total of 296 American women died in war service or as a result of injuries sustained during war service, the majority due to influenza.

American women enlisted for overseas service for a variety of reasons: altruism and patriotism, a sense of adventure, and a desire for equality with men in the public realism. After the war, women veterans of the AEF organized to fight for equal benefits. In the early 1920s, for example, ex-servicewomen lobbied for dependent care from the state, a goal accomplished in part in September 1923, when Secretary of War John W. Weeks opened veterans homes and hospitals to disabled women from the U.S. Army, Navy and Marine Corps. The most long-lasting struggle was the sixty-year fight of AEF telephone operators for military status and benefits. In 1979, the army finally granted honorable discharges to all surviving female telephone veterans, thereby acknowledging retroactively their status as full members of the armed services of World War I.

Susan Zeiger

See also COMMISSION ON TRAINING CAMP ACTIVITIES; UNITED STATES ARMY NURSE CORPS; UNITED STATES NAVY: YEOMAN (F)

Bibliography

Hillerich, Karen. "Black Jack's Girls." *Army* (December 1982).

Piemonte, Robert, and Cindy Gurney. *Highlights in the History of the Army Nurse Corps*. Washington, DC: U.S. Army Center of Military History, 1987.

Schneider, Dorothy, and Carl Schneider. *Into the Breach: American Women Overseas in World War I*. New York: Viking Press, 1991.

Treadwell, Mattie. *The Women's Army Corps*. Washington, DC: Office of the Chief of Military History, 1954.

Women's International League for Peace and Freedom

The Women's International League for Peace and Freedom (WILPF), which still exists, was officially named in 1919, although the league had been founded four years earlier. On April 28, 1915, eight months after war had broken out in Europe, women activists and suffragists from Europe and America convened in the Hague for an international conference. The meeting originally had been scheduled to promote the international women's suffrage movement, but the war drastically altered its agenda. Chaired by Dr. Aletta Jacobs of the Netherlands, the congress, convened as the International Congress of Women, discussed women's opposition to the European war, and considered strategies to oppose it. Women from twelve different nations, including the belligerent countries of Belgium and Germany, struggled to attend the meeting. Jane Addams, the American social reformer, headed the coalition delegation of forty American women at the meeting.

The conference delegates were united by their dual aims of stopping the war and promoting women's suffrage. Calling themselves the International Congress of Women for Permanent Peace (ICWPP), they drew up a constitu-

tion that reflected their conviction that programs promoting worldwide social and economic justice, combined with arbitration and mediation, would inevitably result in lasting peace based on internationalist principles. It reflected the idea that women, from their unique female perspective, should play a critical role in efforts to attain and maintain permanent world peace.

Delegates from the Hague congress met with heads of state from thirteen different neutral and warring European nations and the United States. Their aim was to persuade the neutral countries to call a conference to mediate the European conflict according to the principles of peace reflected in the constitution and the resolutions that they had passed at the Hague. The neutrals' conference did not materialize, and the war escalated with the entry of the United States in 1917.

The ICWPP was presided over by Jane Addams. During the war, thirteen national sections of the organization emerged. In the United States, the Woman's Peace Party (WPP), formed in 1915, became the U.S. branch of the International Congress. The national sections promoted the peace plan formulated at the Hague congress. Sections in neutral and warring nations alike promoted the Hague resolutions. For women from sections in warring nations, this meant that their efforts met with increasing hostility. In the United States, even prominent women like Addams were severely criticized, sometimes accused of treason, as they consistently argued for peace and arbitration. In the later years of the war, the American members focused their efforts on promoting a just peace settlement, urging the United States to take the lead in forming the League of Nations. Although section members continued to work in their separate nations for the duration of the war, maintaining an often difficult correspondence with each other, it was not until after the war's end that the ICWPP reconvened.

As world leaders met in Versailles, the ICWPP—now renamed the Women's International League of Peace and Freedom—was shocked by the harsh terms of the Versailles Treaty. The WILPF argued that there could be no permanent peace with such heavy punishments meted out to the Central Powers. The WILPF formally communicated their disapproval of the treaty's terms to the Versailles council and recommended revisions, but their views inspired no changes. Despite these disappointments, the women of the WILPF redoubled their efforts to bring lasting peace to the modern world. Electing Jane Addams as international president, WILPF committed itself to working closely with the League of Nations, making it an agency that would harbor lasting world peace.

Barbara J. Steinson

See also ADDAMS, JANE; WOMAN'S PEACE PARTY

Bibliography

Addams, Jane. *Peace and Bread in Time of War*. New York: Garland, 1972.

Bussey, Gertrude, and Margaret Tims. *Pioneers for Peace, Women's International League for Peace and Freedom, 1915–1965*. WILPF: British Section, 1980.

Foster, Catherine. *Women for All Seasons, The Story of the Women's International League for Peace and Freedom*. Athens: University of Georgia Press, 1989.

Wobblies

See INDUSTRIAL WORKERS OF THE WORLD

Wood, Leonard (1860–1927)

As a boy, Leonard Wood longed to become a soldier, but his father, a practical man, insisted that his son become a physician. Accordingly, Wood matriculated at Harvard College as opposed to the United States Military Academy and upon graduation entered Harvard Medical School. Upon completion of his requirements at age twenty-four, Wood entered private practice in the Boston area; but following his father's death, his natural inclination resurfaced, whereupon he enlisted in the Medical Corps of the United States Army as a first lieutenant and began his meteoric career.

While still in the Medical Corps, he served under Gen. William Crook in the Apache Wars and distinguished himself as a scout-combatant in the Geronimo campaign. For his service, he was awarded the Congressional Medal of Honor. He was promoted to the rank of captain in 1891. Assignment next to Washington, D.C., offered great opportunity for advancement, for he was personal physician to both President Grover Cleveland and President William McKinley. He also formed a long and fast friendship with another Harvard graduate,

Theodore Roosevelt. This association was enormously beneficial for Wood. At the beginning of the Spanish-American War in 1898, Roosevelt organized the First Volunteer Cavalry Regiment, more popularly known as the Rough Riders. Wood commanded the unit and held the rank of colonel of volunteers, gaining fame for the Rough Riders' charge at San Juan Hill. Wood led his forces on to Santiago, where he was raised to the rank of brigadier general. After the war, he was appointed military governor of Santiago. Here his medical training proved invaluable in establishing a sanitation system that was the model of efficiency. It was only a matter of time before Wood was named military governor of Cuba. In that capacity, he continued his reforms not only in medicine and sanitation but also in education, transportation, and jurisprudence.

By 1901, Wood was a brigadier general of the Regular Army and in that role he was an official visitor to the celebrated German maneuvers of 1902. In 1903, he was appointed governor of Moro Province in the Philippines and in late summer was promoted to major general, the youngest in the army at that time. His leap from captain to major general in five years was a testimony not only to his own ability but also to his friendship with President Theodore Roosevelt. In 1906 Wood commanded the entire Department of the Philippines.

In 1910, Wood was appointed to the army's most coveted post, chief of staff of the General Staff, the prize due in no small part to President William Howard Taft's attempt to ameliorate his growing difficulties with Roosevelt. The General Staff, in existence since 1903, had many problems with Congress, and Wood's tenure only exacerbated the conflict. Furthermore, Wood antagonized several general officers, chief among them Adjutant General Fred Ainsworth, ironically another medical doctor, who had many close congressional associates on the House and Senate Military Affairs Committees. Wood's insistence on merging various army posts, many of them pork barrels for congressmen, threatened his position, which surely would have been lost had it not been for the intervention of Secretary of War Henry L. Stimson and other friends.

Matters deteriorated with the new Democratic administration of Woodrow Wilson. Not only did Wilson dislike Wood, but also he nearly appointed the general's nemesis, James Slayden, to the post of secretary of war. In fairness it must be said that Wood also disliked Wilson. However, Wilson appointed Lindley M. Garrison as secretary of war, and both the secretary and General Wood pushed a program for preparedness. The key to preparedness was the Continental Army Plan, designed to raise between 400,000 and 500,000 men capable of serving the colors. It was opposed by the powerful National Guard lobby and many congressmen, and it went down to defeat with the passage of the rival National Defense Act of 1916. Wood also actively supported the Plattsburg Movement, a plan designed to raise volunteers, especially for junior officer posts, in the event of a future war. Wood left the post of chief of staff in 1914 and served as commander of the Department of the East. During the First World War, Wood was snubbed by the Wilson administration, and at the specific request of Gen. John J. Pershing, commander of the American Expeditionary Force, Wood did not receive a command in Europe. Rather, he was placed in charge of the 89th Infantry Division, a training command located in Kansas, far away from journalists and government officials.

In 1920, Wood attempted to win the presidential nomination of the Republican Party, but a deadlock developed between the general and Frank O. Lowden. As a result, Warren G. Harding was the surprise compromise candidate. Wood returned to the Philippines as governor general in 1921. He died in Boston undergoing neurosurgery in 1927.

James W. Pohl

Bibliography

Hagedorn, Hermann. *Leonard Wood.* 2 vols. New York: Harper, 1931.

Lane, Jack. *Armed Progressive.* San Raphael, CA: Presidio Press, 1978.

Nelson, Otto L. *National Security and the General Staff.* Washington, DC: Infantry Journal Press, 1946.

Weigley, Russell F. *Toward an American Army.* New York: Columbia University Press, 1962.

Wood, Leonard. *Our Military History.* Chicago: Reilly & Britton, 1916.

World Peace Foundation

Originally called the International School for Peace, the World Peace Foundation, which used practical methods to inform people about the evils of war and to promote international justice, was formally established in 1910 by Edward Ginn, the Boston publisher. He pledged contributions of $50,000 annually to the foundation until his death, when his estate provided a bequest of $1 million.

The foundation's leaders were from education, business, and the ministry. They were for the most part conservative, self-made men who advocated disarmament, the rational settlement of international conflict, and international cooperation. To carry on its educational efforts, the foundation distributed hundreds of thousands of pieces of peace literature. Prominent members, such as Edwin Mead and David Starr Jordan, delivered lectures on peace at many different organizational meetings and conferences held throughout the nation and the world. In 1913, the foundation helped sponsor an American lecture tour by Norman Angell, British author of the best-known contemporary peace publication, *The Great Illusion.*

A split soon grew between Ginn, on the one hand, and Mead and Jordan, on the other. Ginn believed that individuals would support the foundation only after they had made a tangible monetary contribution to its programs. He believed that the same methods he had followed in conducting his successful publishing house should be applied to the operation of the foundation. Mead and Jordan interpreted Ginn's penchant for financial commitment and organizational efficiency as a sharp rebuke of their own managerial abilities and accomplishments. Three tragic events, however, not only brought an end to the controversy but also portended the decline in the foundation's influence and effectiveness. Ginn died in January 1914; World War I broke out in September 1914; and Mead suffered a debilitating nervous breakdown in 1915. Under Mead's successor, Charles Levermore, the foundation worked with the Carnegie Endowment for International Peace by establishing study clubs in international relations at colleges and universities in the East and Midwest. Ginn's thrifty spirit continued to exert an influence after his death in the refusal of the foundation to provide financial support for almost any proposal. A controversial decision was made in late 1916 to provide monetary support for the influential League to Enforce Peace.

The foundation did not oppose American participation in World War I. Similar to many other "internationalist" organizations, the foundation was concerned only with the prevention of future wars.

John Imholte

Bibliography
Burns, Edward M. *David Starr Jordan: Prophet of Freedom.* Stanford, CA: Stanford University Press, 1953.
Curti, Merle. *Peace or War.* Boston: Conner, 1959.
Filene, Peter. "The World Peace Foundation and Progressivism, 1910–1918." *New England Quarterly* (December 1963).
Kuehl, Warren F. *Seeking World Order.* Nashville, TN: Vanderbilt University Press, 1969.
Patterson, David S. *Toward a Warless World.* Bloomington: Indiana University Press, 1976.

Y

Yeoman (F)

See UNITED STATES NAVY: YEOMAN (F)

York, Alvin C. (1887–1964)

In the last days of World War I, Alvin C. York came marching out of the Argonne Forest with 132 German prisoners and a tale of individual daring unsurpassed in the nation's military annals. One of the least likely heroes in our history, the Tennessee-born York spent a rowdy youth drinking and brawling but finally joined the Church of Christ in Christian Union, a deeply conservative congregation founded in reaction to the carnage of the Civil War. Its members rejected violence, and York sought deferment from military service as a conscientious objector when the United States entered World War I. His petition was rejected, but York's superiors in the 82d Division ultimately persuaded him that America was fighting God's battle in the war, an argument that transformed the pacifist from the Appalachian Mountains into a veritable soldier of the Lord.

On the smoke-shrouded morning of Oct. 8, 1918, during the battle of the Argonne Forest, Private First Class York and the rest of his patrol found themselves cut off and under fire behind enemy lines. With half of his men dead or wounded, York outshot an entire German machine gun battalion, silencing some thirty-five guns and killing approximately twenty Germans while leading his men to safety. Supreme Allied Commander Ferdinand Foch described his exploit as "the greatest accomplishment by any private soldier of all the armies of Europe." Promoted to sergeant, York received the Medal of Honor and decorations from most of the Allied nations.

On April 26, 1919, *Saturday Evening Post* correspondent George Pattullo published York's story under the title, "The Second Elder Gives Battle," an article that made York a national hero overnight. His explanation that God had been with him during the fight meshed neatly with the popular attitude that American involvement in the war was truly a holy crusade, and York returned to the United States in the spring of 1919 amid a tumultuous public welcome and a flood of business offers from people eager to capitalize on the soldier's reputation. In spite of these lucrative opportunities, York returned to his native hamlet of Pall Mall, Tennessee, where he spent the rest of his life working to bring schools and other public services to his mountain neighbors.

David D. Lee

Bibliography

Brandt, Nat. "Sergeant York." *American Heritage* (August/September 1981).

Cowan, Samuel. *Sergeant York and His People.* New York and London: Funk and Wagnalls, 1922.

Lee, David D. *Sergeant York: An American Hero.* Lexington: University Press of Kentucky, 1985.

Skeyhill, Thomas, ed. *Sergeant York: His Own Life Story and War Diary.* Garden City, NY: Doubleday, Doran, 1928.

Young Men's Christian Association/ Young Women's Christian Association (YM/YWCA)

The YM/YWCA offered a variety of activities and programs to American troops during the First World War and the period of demobilization. The YMCA constructed "Y-huts" for American soldiers in the United States and in France. In these huts "Y-secretaries" offered religious, athletic, educational, recreational, and social programs. The YWCA operated "Hostess Houses" for women visiting soldiers in American training camps and for women serving with the American Expeditionary Force (AEF) in France.

The U.S. Army welcomed the work of both associations as a means of maintaining "contentment, camp spirit, and camp morale." Military officials were concerned that the soldiers would spend their off-duty hours in the red-light districts of adjacent communities. They hoped that the supervised leisure time programs of the YM/YWCA would prevent the men from loitering in camp communities and thereby limit alcohol abuse and the spread of venereal disease.

Between April 1917 and March 1921, the YMCA's National War Work Council operated 952 Y-huts in American training camps. These buildings served as clubs, churches, schools, libraries, gymnasia, post offices, information centers, and canteens. Many of the Y-huts were equipped with shower baths, pool tables, reading and game rooms, pianos, phonographs, records, motion picture projectors, office furniture and supplies as well as theatrical and athletic equipment. During the war and the demobilization period, over 12,000 Y-secretaries, both men and women, served in the huts in the United States.

The YMCA catered to the segregated black troops in separate Y-huts. Although the YMCA promised to provide "separate but equal" services, huts for black soldiers were often ill equipped and suffered from a lack of personnel. During the war, approximately 300 black secretaries served with the nearly 400,000 black soldiers in training camps in the United States.

In addition to the YMCA's work in American training camps, Y-secretaries also served the soldiers in transit. They worked on troop trains and transport vessels carrying song sheets, religious and sex hygiene booklets, writing paper, pens, post cards, magazines, newspapers, books, small games, and first aid kits. Y-secretaries provided the men with diversion, comfort, and counsel and bolstered their morale. Nearly 400 Y-secretaries accompanied the soldiers en route to the camps and embarkation points, and 1,512 served on overseas transports.

The YMCA continued its work for American soldiers in France. On June 25, 1917, the first delegation of 27 American Y-secretaries sailed for France. During the war nearly 13,000 secretaries, both men and women, served the soldiers of the AEF. In the course of their service 6 male and 2 female secretaries were killed in action, 123 men and 5 women were wounded or gassed, and 319 secretaries received citations and decorations.

In France, the secretaries worked in huts and tents in the ports of debarkation as well as in the trenches. They tried to offer leisure time programs similar to those provided for soldiers in American camps. However, the YMCA's work in France was hampered by the constant movement of troops and the lack of adequate facilities and supplies. Thus, YMCA services for American soldiers in France were generally less sympathetic than those provided for troops in the United States.

While serving the American soldiers in France, the YMCA continued to adhere to its Jim Crow policy. The association assigned 84 black secretaries—61 men and 23 women—to work with the nearly 140,000 black troops. However, most of the black secretaries did not arrive in France until after the Armistice. Moreover, the work of the black secretaries was frequently obstructed by white opposition. Often white secretaries failed to allocate adequate supplies and equipment to black Y-huts, and white officers refused to cooperate with black secretaries.

In addition to the programs offered in the huts, the AEF asked the YMCA to provide accommodations and recreational facilities for soldiers on leave. American troops were entitled to seven-day furloughs every four months during their service in France. However, military officials were convinced that the dispersal of men on leave would make it impossible to recall them in case of a sudden German offensive. Moreover, they feared that the soldiers' ignorance of the French language and customs would lead to problems with the civilian population. In addition, the army was concerned that soldiers on leave were more likely to contract venereal diseases and thereby reduce the fighting efficiency of the troops.

Thus, the army authorized the YMCA to establish "leave areas" for the American soldiers in France. The YMCA selected resort towns with adequate hotel and recreational facilities, healthy climate, and picturesque surroundings. The first leave area opened in Aix-les-Baines on Feb. 15, 1918. By the end of the war, the YMCA operated nineteen leave areas in France, five in the Rhine Valley, two in Italy, and one in England.

In the leave areas, Y-secretaries provided educational, athletic, recreational and entertainment programs. They operated canteens, writing rooms, and libraries and organized excursions, dances, guided tours, hikes, and games. During the war and the period of demobilization, 886 Y-secretaries—477 women and 409 men—catered to 500,000 American soldiers on leave. Nearly 20,000 of these were black troops who spent their furlough in segregated leave areas in Chambery and Challes-les-Eaux. The black leave areas were staffed by 18 black Y-secretaries—8 women and 10 men.

The YMCA also operated more than 1,500 post exchanges and canteens for the AEF. Thus, YMCA secretaries in France performed a dual function. They distributed goods and provided services free of charge in the huts and leave areas. However, they charged the soldiers for goods offered in the post exchanges and canteens. This dual function caused confusion among the troops, who associated the YMCA with free services and who charged that the association was profiteering. After the war, the government investigated the YMCA and cleared the association of all charges.

The YWCA also offered special wartime services to the U.S. Army. The association operated 124 Hostess Houses in American training camps. These houses served as reception centers for women visiting soldiers in training. The Hostess Houses provided the women relatives and friends of soldiers with refreshment, rest, and shelter in a homelike atmosphere. During the war and the period of demobilization, the YWCA served black women in 17 segregated Hostess Houses.

In June 1917, the YWCA erected the first Hostess House in the Officers Training Camp in Plattsburg, New York. Initially, some officers opposed the presence of women in the camps. However, military officials soon came to view the work of the YWCA as a means of safeguarding the morals and morale of the troops. The Hostess Houses enabled soldiers to meet female visitors under the "proper" supervision of YWCA secretaries. The army hoped that this would prevent the men from leaving the camps during off-duty hours and thus help to prevent alcohol abuse as well as infection with venereal disease.

In France, the YWCA operated eighty Hostess Houses for American women serving with the AEF. The YWCA provided housing as well as recreational and social services for the 16,000 nurses, telephone operators, and women serving with the Signal Corps, Quartermaster Corps, and Ordnance Corps. Moreover, the YWCA offered lodging and meals to women in transit.

Along with the YWCA's services for American women in France, the association cared for the French brides and children of American soldiers. The YWCA provided housing and meals for the war brides and their children and helped them prepare for their departure to the United States. YWCA secretaries accompanied the women on their transatlantic journey, put them up when necessary in stateside YMCA Hostess Houses, and continued to assist them until their husbands were discharged.

Nina Mjagkij

Bibliography

Hopkins, C. Howard. *History of the Y.M.C.A. in North America.* New York: Association Press, 1951.

Lancaster, Richard C. *Serving with U.S. Armed Forces, 1861–1986: The Story of the YMCA's Ministry to Military Personnel for 125 Years.* Schaumburg, IL: Armed Services YMCA of the USA, 1987.

Mjagkij, Nina. "History of the Black YMCA in America, 1853–1946." Ph.D. dissertation, University of Cincinnati, 1990.

Sims, Mary S. *The Natural History of a Social Institution—The Young Women's Christian Association.* New York: Woman's Press, 1936.

Sprenger, James A., and Franklin S. Edmonds, eds. *The Leave Areas of the American Expeditionary Forces, 1918–1919: Records and Memoirs.* Philadelphia: Winston, 1928.

Ypres, Third Battle of

The Passchendaele campaign, also known as the Third Battle of Ypres, ranks as one of the most futile offenses undertaken in World War I. Despite the experiences of over two years of trench warfare, including the huge bloodletting at the

Somme in 1916, the British Army under Field Marshal Sir Douglas Haig persisted in the same misguided strategy and fruitless tactics, which resulted in tremendous casualties and few gains. Bogging down in the mud of Flanders, the British Army was literally bled white.

Despite their heavy losses in 1916, British and French commanders, meeting at Chantilly on Nov. 15–16, 1916, concluded that the German Army was on the verge of collapse and that the Allies should take vigorous offensive action in 1917. Plans for an offensive became even more ambitious after Gen. Robert Nivelle succeeded Marshal Joseph Joffre as French commander-in-chief in December 1916. While the British made a diversionary attack on Arras, the French were to launch the main offensive along the Aisne River between Soissons and Reims— the Chemin des Dames. Any chance for success was lost when the Germans withdrew behind the Hindenburg Line. In the aftermath of the Nivelle offensive of April 1917, a series of mutinies, beginning on May 3, broke out among the frontline troops in the French Army, leaving whole sections of trench unguarded. If the Germans had attacked at this critical juncture, they could have easily swept into Paris and ended the war.

With the French mutiny crisis, the burden of fighting the Germans shifted fully to the British. Rather than remain on the defensive until the arrival of sufficient American forces, Haig made plans for a large-scale offensive in Flanders. In seeking authorization from a reluctant British War Cabinet, Haig stressed the need to divert German attention away from the French. He also argued that a successful breakthrough in Flanders would end the German U-boat campaign by depriving them of the Belgian ports. This point alone brought the Admiralty's wholehearted endorsement. Haig further maintained that the expected Russian offensive would tie down German troops on the Eastern Front, giving operations on the Western Front a greater chance for success. As for choosing the Ypres sector for his offensive, Haig cited the necessity of widening the dangerous salient in the British lines and capturing the surrounding hills from which German artillery pounded British forces. Finally, Haig asserted, "If the fighting was kept up at its present intensity for six months, Germany would be at the end of her available manpower." To the British, therefore, would go the honors of ending the war single-handedly.

In every aspect, Haig's strategic reasoning was flawed. If the need to divert German attention away from the French was true in May, by the time the main offensive began on July 31, Pétain had succeeded in restoring French morale. Even if the British had succeeded in capturing the Belgian ports, they would not have hindered the German U-boat campaign since it was conducted primarily from German ports. While Haig counted on the Russians to tie down German forces in the east, in reality, the Russian Army, paralyzed by revolution, was clearly collapsing. Finally, even if a breakthrough had occurred, it would not have seriously threatened the German position in France because the attack diverged from the main German communications, headquarters, and forces.

Haig could not have picked a worse location than the Ypres sector. Located on the western end of a low-lying plain, which was surrounded by low, wooded hills held by the Germans, the Ypres salient was interspersed by a series of canals, a number of streams, and three large ponds. In such terrain, any disturbance of the complex drainage system, whether by heavy rains or artillery bombardment, would transform the entire battlefield into a sea of mud. Even though his own meteorological advisers gathered eighty years of weather statistics to prove the likelihood of torrential rains, even though his tank commanders warned that the drainage system would be destroyed by bombardment and make the field impassable, and even though German artillery on the surrounding hills had a commanding view of the battlefield—Haig chose this location. When his chief of staff, General Kiggell, toured the edge of the battlefield at the conclusion of the campaign, he is said to have wept and exclaimed, "Did we really send men to fight in this?" No comment better illustrates how behind-the-lines commanders were out of touch with frontline conditions.

Haig's tactics also offered little chance for success in light of previous experience and new German countermeasures. By continuing to believe that a long preliminary bombardment would weaken opposing positions and that a series of infantry frontal assaults would discover a weak link in the enemy line, penetrate it, and sweep forward to victory, Haig completely disregarded the lessons that should have been learned from earlier battles. Preliminary bombardments tipped off the enemy that an attack was coming, while making the ground almost impossible for attacking troops to advance. A few entrenched defenders, armed with machine guns, protected by barbed wire, and supported by artillery could mow down wave after wave of attackers. The Germans, moreover, had recently adopted new defensive measures that made any attack more difficult. By establishing a disconnected system of concrete pillboxes, which could withstand bombardment and which could be held by a few man armed with machine guns, the Germans were able to concentrate reserves well behind the lines for counterattacks against enemy forces that had gained positions at heavy costs. Even though air reconnaissance clearly revealed what the Germans had prepared, Haig persisted in his plans.

As a preliminary to the main offensive, the British Second Army, under the command of Gen. Sir Hubert Plumer, completed one of the most successful mining operations of the entire war by taking Messines Ridge, which was vital to protecting the right flank. Since January 1917, British tunnelers had dug some twenty miles of tunnels, sixty to ninety feet below the surface, and eventually laid twenty-four mines under Messines Ridge. Plumer assembled a total of 2,266 guns and howitzers that fired over 3.5 million shells on the German positions in a preliminary bombardment that lasted from May 26 to June 6. When nineteen of the mines went off at 3:10 A.M. on June 7, the blast was heard as far away as London. Nine British and ANZAC divisions of the Second Army met little opposition as they swarmed up what remained of Messines Ridge. They captured over 7,000 German prisoners in the first few hours and eventually inflicted well over 23,000 casualties. Although the Second Army lost only a few men in the initial advance, it eventually lost 24,562 men in the face of desperate German counterattacks. The real tragedy for the British was that Haig failed to exploit the success of the Messines Ridge operation. He inexplicably allowed six weeks to pass before the main offensive began, tipping off the Germans as to where the next blow would fall and giving them ample time to prepare for it. Indeed, Haig purposely delayed the offensive in the mistaken belief that the Germans were near collapse and that the more that could be drawn into the Ypres sector the quicker the war would end.

Haig set July 31 as the starting date for the offensive and shifted command of the main attack from Plumer to Gen. Sir Hubert Gough, commander of the Fifth Army. While Plumer's Second Army protected the right flank and the French First Army protected the left, Gough was to launch a frontal assault into the center of the German lines. Gough confidently expected the all-important Passchendaele Ridge to be in British hands on the third day of battle, August 2, before the breakthrough to the coast. Needless to say, his expectations exceeded all military reality. In fact, Passchendaele would not be taken until mid-November.

In preparation for the assault, Gough employed over 3,000 guns in one of the largest preliminary bombardments (July 22–31) that the was had seen. For ten days approximately four and three-quarter tons of shells fell on every yard of the front. Gough had expected the bombardment to soften up the German positions, but it failed miserably. Since only a direct hit by heavy howitzer could destroy German concrete pillboxes, the vast majority remained intact and protected their machine gun crews. Most of the German forces had been withdrawn behind the lines anyway. In addition, the bombardment had no effect on the German artillery on the surrounding ridges. Most important, the bombardment utterly destroyed the drainage system and transformed the ground into a morass. Indeed, of the 216 tanks the British assembled for the attack, over half slid into shell holes or became stuck in mud from which they could not be removed. Advancing infantry and field artillery likewise found the going difficult.

The so-called "Gough" phase of the Passchendaele offensive began at 3:50 A.M. on July 31, as twelve divisions advanced on an eleven-mile front. They were supported by a creeping barrage of one hundred yards every four minutes, which quickly outfaced the troops. Although 800 yards were gained in the first hour, the attack quickly became bogged down in the mud. In the initial assault of July 31–August 2, the British managed to capture Bixschoote, St. Julien, and Pilckem Ridge but failed to take the vital Menin road sector. Although they captured 6,000 prisoners and inflicted several thousand casualties, at a price of 4,000 dead and 12,000 wounded, the British were unable to advance further because of vigorous German counterattacks, the deadly German artillery, and almost continuous rain. Gough's second assault had to be postponed until August 16. Although the British gained Langemarck Ridge, the attack once more ground to a halt in impassable mud. For the

Y

remainder of August, Gough attempted a series of probing attacks but without success. As British casualties for the first four weeks approached 70,000, Haig postponed further action until September 20 in hopes that the rain would end.

Leadership of the second phase of the offensive was shifted to Plumer, whose meticulous planning proved much more successful than Gough's thrusting approach. Instead of a massive infantry assault, Plumer planned a series of shallow advances over a period of six days. Each assault was to follow an artillery barrage in short advances of 1,500 yards, use tanks and heavy howitzers to knock out pillboxes, and rely upon the artillery to deal with the inevitable German counterattacks. In major assaults on the Menin road ridge (September 20–25), Polygon Wood (September 26) and Broodseinde (Octctober 4). Plumer gained possession of the main ridge east of Ypres at relatively low cost. In each instance, the artillery, particularly the heavy howitzers, played the decisive role, while the infantry merely consolidated the ground gained and allowed the artillery to turn back the German counterattacks.

The success of Plumer's tactics created a sense of overwhelming optimism at general headquarters. Although torrential rains began on October 4, Haig determined to press on to Passchendaele Ridge over the objections of his subordinates. Haig's visions of a breakthrough to the coast and an end of the war by Christmas proved to be a nightmare of mud for his men. Assaults on Poelcapelle (October 9) and Passchendaele (October 12) failed completely because of the mud, which clogged guns, negated the impact of artillery shells, and made forward motion impossible. Soldiers literally drowned in a sea of mud. The Germans also began to rely more upon mustard gas to defend against attacks. In one last push from October 26–November 10, the Canadian 1st and 2d divisions captured Passchendaele village, leading Haig to end the campaign.

Although German commanders referred to Passchendaele as one of their worst defeats of the war, the results for the British were not much better. In over three months of fighting in horrendous conditions, the British had advanced five miles along a fifteen-mile front at a cost in casualties that ranged from the official count of 244,897 to approximately 400,000. Figures for German losses vary from under 200,000 to over 400,000. Although the British had widened the Ypres salient, they had created a more dangerous salient around Passchendaele. More important, the high morale of the British Army had been destroyed in the mud. The failure to exploit the initial breakthrough at Cambrai (Nov. 20–Dec. 5, 1917), and the utter collapse of the British Army during the Ludendorff offensive of 1918 can be traced directly to the debacle of the Third Ypres.

This campaign will always be remembered as an ill-conceived operation fought in appalling conditions. That British troops were able to endure the ghastly situation and make what gains they did is a testimony to their courage, valor, and stamina. That they were ordered to attack in such conditions and were actually expected to make greater gains is a clear indictment against their commanders.

Justin D. Murphy

See also HAIG, DOUGLAS

Bibliography

Liddell Hart, Sir Basil Henry. *History of the First World War,* rev. ed. London: Cassell, 1970.

Messenger, Charles. *Trench Fighting, 1914–1918.* New York: Ballantine Books, 1972.

Schmidt, Bernadotte E., and Harold C. Vedeler. *The World in the Crucible, 1914–1919.* New York: Harper & Row, 1984.

Warner, Philip. *Passchendaele: The Tragic Victory of 1917.* New York: Atheneum, 1988.

Z

Zimmermann Telegram

The Zimmermann Telegram played a decisive role in the United States declaration of war against Germany. By trying to bring Mexico and Japan into the conflict on its side in the event of war with the United States and offering American territory as an enticement, Germany raised the ire of the American people and forced President Wilson to revise his foreign policy. Prior to receiving the Zimmermann Telegram from the British, Woodrow Wilson believed that the United States must remain neutral if he were to craft a negotiated peace for Europe. The Zimmermann Telegram, together with Germany's resumption of unrestricted submarine warfare, pushed both Wilson and the American public toward the view that war with Germany was unavoidable.

On Jan. 9, 1917, the German High Command made the fateful decision to resume unrestricted submarine warfare effective February 1. It knew that this might bring the United States into the war against Germany, but the German government estimated that it would take over a year before the Americans could have an effective fighting force on the Western Front. Before that could happen, the expected losses in Allied shipping would have ended the war on German terms. In any event, the Germans had another card to play that they believed would keep the United States from intervening. Foreign Minister Alfred Zimmermann assured the High Command that he could embroil the United States in a war with Mexico and Japan, thereby precluding it from the war in Europe.

Zimmermann based his plan on a long-standing German policy. As early as 1906, Kaiser Wilhelm II had attempted to draw the United States into his crusade against the "Yellow Peril" by manufacturing stories of Japanese activity in Mexico, which created a stir in the American press. President Theodore Roosevelt failed to swallow the bait. In trying to delude the United States, however, German policymakers deluded themselves into believing in the possibility of a joint Japanese-Mexican action against the United States.

When the Mexican Revolution broke out in 1910, German diplomats saw an opportunity to gain naval bases in exchange for arms. German plans, however, conflicted with the United States after Woodrow Wilson assumed the presidency on March 4, 1913. The coup d'état of Gen. Victoriano Huerta and subsequent assassination of President Francisco Madero led the high-minded American President to support Huerta's chief rival, Gen. Venustiano Carranza. On April 21, 1914, Wilson ordered United States Marines to occupy Veracruz to prevent a German ship from landing arms for Huerta.

With the beginning of World War I, it became imperative for Germany to limit the flow of American munitions to the Allies, and one possibility was to create a diversion in Mexico. Although Huerta was ousted in July 1914, Germany attempted to restore him to power since this was sure to provoke Wilson. The plot was uncovered, and Huerta was arrested and imprisoned in Fort Bliss, Texas. Germany now shifted its support to the renegade Francisco ("Pancho") Villa, whose raid on Columbus, New Mexico, on March 9, 1916, killed seventeen Americans. In retaliation, Wilson sent 12,000 soldiers under Gen. John J. Pershing into Mexico to apprehend Villa. Although Carranza originally consented to the American expedition, he became increasingly resentful of its presence and eventually demanded its withdrawal. It was this situation that made Zimmermann so confident of his success.

On Nov. 12, 1916, Zimmermann sent a telegram to Heinrich von Eckhardt, the German ambassador to Mexico, hinting at an alliance with Mexico in exchange for U-boat bases. Carranza proved very receptive to Eckhardt's overtures and wrote to Zimmermann seeking closer economic, political, and military ties to Germany. Eckhardt, meanwhile, assured Zimmermann that Japan, the third party of Zimmermann's diplomatic triangle, had established closer relations with Mexico and might be drawn into an alliance. Zimmermann jumped at this opportunity, hoping to entice Japan away from the Allies and into an alliance with Germany via Mexico. If he succeeded, he not only would sever the flow of American arms to the Allies by embroiling the United States in a war with Mexico and Japan, but also would frighten Russia out of the war by bringing her foe from the Russo-Japanese war into the German camp.

The German decision to resume unrestricted submarine warfare put Zimmermann's plans into motion. He first informed Eckhardt that the U-boat campaign would begin on Feb. 1, 1917. He then suggested that in the event of a United States declaration of war against Germany, Mexico declare war on the United States in return for financial support from Germany and, most important, the recovery of Texas, New Mexico, and Arizona. In addition, Eckhardt was to urge Mexico to invite Japan into the alliance.

Had Zimmermann acted sooner, he might have found Carranza far more receptive. However, Mexican relations with the United States had become less strained after Wilson's decision on Jan. 25, 1917, to withdraw American troops from Mexico, which was completed by February 5. Although Zimmermann instructed Eckhardt on February 5 to make the alliance proposal without further delay, it was too late. The withdrawal of American forces from Mexico removed one of the best arguments that Germany could have used to pull Mexico into the war.

Ironically, it was Great Britain that discovered the Zimmermann Telegram in one of the greatest intelligence coups of the war. In the first weeks of the war, the British severed Germany's transcontinental cables, sealing it off from direct cable communication. The Germans were forced to rely mainly on their powerful wireless station at Nauen. The British, however, were able to intercept German messages, ultimately at the rate of 200 per day. To decode the transmissions, British Naval Intelligence established what was known as Room 40, which, under the direction of Adm. Sir William Reginald Hall, possessed several of the German code books, including the diplomatic code, No. 13040.

Zimmermann sent the telegram over the wireless at Nauen, through Stockholm, and via the American embassy in Berlin. The last route had been arranged by Col. Edward M. House for Germany to communicate with Ambassador Johann von Bernstorff in order to facilitate peace negotiations. The British intercepted the telegram along all three routes, and after cryptographers William Montgomery and Nigel de Grey deciphered it, Admiral Hall knew he held the key that could bring the United States into the war.

Before releasing the document to the American government, Hall arranged to keep the Germans from discovering that the British had obtained it. He ordered agents in Mexico to secure a copy of the telegram as sent by Bernstorff to Eckhardt via Western Union. By bribing a telegraph official in Mexico, British agents obtained a copy of the telegram, thus leading the Germans to believe that the United States had intercepted it in America. On February 23, Foreign Minister Arthur Balfour formally presented the Zimmermann Telegram to the United States ambassador to Great Britain, Walter H. Page, who had long worked to persuade Wilson to intervene on the Allied side. Page promptly forwarded the telegram to Wilson, who did not question its authenticity for a moment.

Almost immediately the President called upon Congress to pass the Armed Ship Bill. When ten senators, led by Robert LaFollette, attempted to filibuster the bill, Wilson released the telegram to the press and it appeared in headlines across the nation on March 1, 1917. Americans were outraged. Although a few Americans, including some senators, denounced it as a hoax, all doubts were removed when Zimmermann inexplicably admitted it was authentic. Its revelation was followed by the sinking of three American ships in the next three weeks, which brought home the German threat and led Wilson to ask Congress for a declaration of war.

Justin D. Murphy

Bibliography

Bemis, Samuel Flagg. *A Diplomatic History of the United States.* New York: Holt, 1942.

Link, Arthur S. *Woodrow Wilson and the Progressive Era, 1910–1917.* New York: Harper & Row, 1954.

Tuchman, Barbara W. *The Zimmermann Telegram.* New York: Viking, 1958.

Z

Index

The main entry for each topic is listed in boldface.

way Service Corps, 518; and H.L. Scott, 533; and Officer Acquisition, 714; and Plattsburg Movement, 717
Balfour, Arthur James, 40, 41, 61–63; and Zimmermann Telegram, 816
Balfour Declaration, 62, 103, 801
Balfour Mission, 62, 63–64
balloons, 64–65, 724–25; see also United States Air Service
Ballou, Charles Clarendon, 65, 88; commands United States Army 92d Division, 65, 688
Bandholtz, Harry Hill, 66
Barnett, George, 66–67
Baruch, Bernard Mannes, 59, 67–69, 249; relationship with W. Wilson, 68, 69; and Council of National Defense, 68, 173, 174; War Industries Board, 68, 175, 775; at Paris Peace Conference, 69
Beauvais Agreement, 1, 69–70
Belfort Ruse, in preparation for St. Mihiel offensive, 70–71, 165
Belgium. See Albert I, King of the Belgians; Commission for Relief in Belgium; Whitlock, Brand
Belknap, Reginald Rowan, 71–72; and North Sea Mine Barrage, 72, 419; design of mines by, 419
Bell, George, Jr., 72, 646
Bell, James Franklin, 73
Belleau Wood, Battle of, 73–77, 112, 130,139–40, 611, 741, 742, 743; see also Marne, Second Battle of the
Benedict XV, 77–78, 257, 801
Benes, Edvard, 78
Benson, William Shepherd, 79–80, 192, 226, 746, 747, 748, 757; relationship with W.S. Sims, 79, 553; and North Sea Mine Barrage, 79
Berchtold, Leopold, 80–81
Berger, Victor Louis, 81–82
Berkman, Alexander, 82; relationship with E. Goldman, 82
Bernstorff, Johann Heinrich von, 82–84, 478, 479; and *Arabic* and *Sussex* Pledges, 46, 83; on *Lusitania*, 83; and Black Tom explosion, 90
Bethmann Hollweg, Theobald von, 45, 46, 84–85, 788, 789; and Commission for Relief in Belgium, 157
Biddle, John, 85–86
Bisbee Deportations, 86; and Industrial Workers of the World, 86
Black Americans, 87–89; historic service in U.S. military, 87; and conscription, 88; as Army officers, 88; see also Camp MacArthur Riot; East St. Louis Riot; United States Army, 92d Division; United States Army, 93d Division
Black Tom explosion, 89–90
Blanc Mont Ridge, 90–94, 621, 656, 741, 742, 743
Bliss, Tasker Howard, 94–95, 459; U.S. representative on Supreme War Council, 41, 95, 801; a U.S. Commissioner to Paris Peace Conference, 95; and amalgamation controversy, 95
body armor, 96–97

Bolling, Raynal Cawthorne, 97; see also Bolling Mission; United States Air Service
Bolling Mission, 11, 16, 97–98; see also aircraft, Bolling, Raynal C.
Bolsheviks, Bolshevism, 98–99; see also Russia
Borah, William Edgar, 99–100
Borglum, (John) Gutzon, 100–101; see also aircraft
Bourne, Randolph Silliman, 101
Bowman, Isaiah, 102; and The Inquiry, 102, 301; at Paris Peace Conference, 102
Brandeis, Louis Dembitz, 102–103
Brent, Charles H., 103–104, 135; see also chaplains
Brest Litovsk, Treaty of, 104–105; allows transfer of German troops to western front, 104, 138; and prisoners of war, 105, 474; see also Paris Peace Conference; Russian-American relations
Brett, Sereno, 105, 215; see also tanks, United States Army Tank Corps
Bristol, Mark Lambert, 106
Bristol aircraft. See aircraft
Brittany Patrol. See Suicide Fleet
Brown, Preston, 107
Bryan, William Jennings, 39, 107–108, 145; and *Lusitania* note, 54, 107; relationship with W. Wilson, 108
Buck, Beaumont Bonaparte, 109; at Cantigny, 109, 126
Bulgaria, Salonika Armistice, 48
Bullard, Eugene Jacques, 109–110
Bullard, Robert Lee, 110–111, 372, 618; commands First Division at Cantigny, 111, 125, 126, 617
Bullitt, William Christian, 111–12, 446–47; mission to Russia, 112, 518
Bullitt Mission. See Bullitt, William Christian
Bundy, Omar, 112–13; and Belfort Ruse, 71; at Belleau Wood, 74
Bureau of Investigation, 113–14, 433; "slacker raids," 113; and Civil Liberties Bureau, 149
Burleson, Albert Sidney, 114–15; and enforcement of Espionage Act, 114; and censorship, 115, 132; and the *Masses*, 115, 132, 376
Butler, Smedley Darlington, 116
Cadorna, Luigi, 117, 202; and Battle of Caporetto, 117, 128, 129
Cameron, George Hamilton, 118, 524, 625; and Meuse-Argonne campaign, 118
camouflage, 118–19
Camp MacArthur Riot, 121; see also Black Americans
Campbell, Douglas, 120
Canada. See Canadian-American relations
Canadian-American relations, 122–24
Cantigny, 109, 124–27, 216, 282, 297, 611
cantonments, 127–28
Caporetto, Battle of, 117, 128–29, 202; leads to improved inter-Allied cooperation, 129
Carnegie Endowment for International Peace, 130
Catlin, Albertus Wright, 130–31

Catt, Carrie Clinton Lane Chapman, **131**, 396, 397; "Winning Plan," 131; *see also* Woman's Peace Party

censorship, 115, **132–33**; and *The Masses*, 115, 132, 376; and motion pictures, 132; and Committee on Public Information, 132, 164

Chafee, Zechariah, Jr., **133–34**; and censorship, 133, 134

Chamberlain, George Earle, **134–35**; and Continental Army Plan, 172

chaplains, **135–37**, 207, 481–82; rabbis as, 311

Charles I of Austria-Hungary, 55, 56, **137–38**, 246; and Sixtus Affair, 137; "People's Manifesto," 138; *see also* Austro-Hungarian-American relations

Chateau-Thierry sector, **138–41**, 372, 611, 622; and United States Air Service, 5, 6, 605; *see also* Marne, Second Battle of the

chemical warfare. *See* United States Army Chemical Warfare Service

Children's Bureau, **141–42**, 172

China. *See* Chinese-American relations,

Chinese-American relations, **142–47**; and "Twenty-One Demands," 145, 146, 600–602; *see also* Japanese-American relations

Christy, Howard Chandler, **147**

Churchill, Marlborough, **148**

Civil Liberties Bureau, 37, **148–49**; and conscientious objectors, 149, 171; *see also* American Union Against Militarism

Clark, James Beauchamp (Champ), **149–50**; on Selective Service, 149–50, 172, 541

Clemenceau, Georges ("The Tiger"), **150–53**; at Paris Peace Conference, 152, 153, 438, 439, 443, 445; and Sixtus Affair, 152; and W. Wilson, 153; relationship with F. Foch, 229; and reparations, 441, 442; on Russian situation, 446; W.G. Sharp on, 543

Coffin, Howard Earle, **153**; and Naval Consulting Board, 153, 174; and Council of National Defense, 153, 173

Collins, James Lawton, **153–54**

Commission for Relief in Belgium, **154–59**, 737, 780, 781; formed by H. Hoover, 154; *see also* Hoover, Herbert C.; Whitlock, Brand

Commission on Training Camp Activities, 31, 36, **159–61**, 234, 804; *see also* Young Men's Christian Association; Knights of Columbus; Jewish Welfare Board; Salvation Army

Committee on Patriotism Through Education, **161–62**, 406, 470

Committee on Public Information, 25, **162–64**, 275, 393, 470; and Carnegie Endowment for International Peace, 130; and censorship, 132, 164; *see also* Creel, George

Conger, Arthur Latham, Jr., **164–65**; and Belfort Ruse, 71, 165

Conner, Fox, **165–66**, 215; and St. Mihiel offensive, 166; and Sedan incident, 534

Connor, William Durward, **166–67**; and Service of Supply, 166

Conrad von Hotzendorf, Franz, 80, **167–69**, 246, 768

conscientious objectors, 60, **169–71**, 809; and Civil Liberties Bureau, 149, 171; and Selective Service, 169, 541

conscription. *See* Selective Service

Continental Army Reserve Plan, 59, **171–172**, 250, 399, 464, 533, 702; *see also* Garrison, Lindley Miller

convoys. *See* antisubmarine warfare; United States Navy

Council of National Defense, 27, 36, 57, 153, **173–75**, 261, 327, 404, 470, 710, 771; and demobilization, 198; staffed by dollar-a-year-men, 204; and National League for Woman's Service, 404; and United States Army Medical Department, 710, 713; *see also* Council of National Defense, Woman's Committee

Council of National Defense, Woman's Committee, 131, 142, **176–77**, 397, 405, 544; *see also* Council of National Defense

Craig, Malin, **177–78**

Crane, Charles Richard, **178–79**; and Root Mission to Russia 178; and King-Crane Commission, 179

Cravath, Paul Drennan, **179**

Creel, George, 132, **179–80**, 393; and Committee on Public Information, 132, 162, 163, 180, 470; and relationship with W. Wilson, 179, 180

Croly, Herbert, **180–81**; and E.M. House, 181

Crowder, Enoch Herbert, 42, 172, **181–83**; and Selective Service, 182, 541

Crowell, Benedict, **183–84**, 259

Crozier, William, **184**; and Supreme War Council, 184

Curtiss, Glenn Hammond, **184–86**; *see also* aircraft

Curtiss aircraft. *See* aircraft

Czech Legion, 2, **186–87**, 263, 514, 515, 517, 519

Czernin, Ottokar, 55, **188–89**; and Charles I, 138, 188; and Sixtus Affair, 138, 188; relationship with Franz Ferdinand, 188

Daly, Daniel, **191**

Daniels, Josephus, **191–93**, 418, 746, 757; and Naval Consulting Board, 173, 192; and B. Fiske, 191, 192, 225, 226; National Advisory Committee for Aeronautics, 192; appoints W.S. Benson as Chief of Naval Operations, 192; and W.S. Sims 193, 553, 747; and yeomen (F), 759

daylight saving time, **194**

de Havilland aircraft. *See* aircraft

Debs, Eugene Victor, 81, **194–95**

decorations, **195–97**; Medal of Honor, 195; Certificate of Merit, 195; Distinguished Service Cross, 195–96; Distinguished Service Medal, 196; Navy Cross, 196; Victory Medal, 196

demobilization, **197–99**; position of W. Wilson, 198

Denman, William, 217, 243, 259, 298, 379, 549, 550

Dernburg, Bernhard, 200, 479, 480; *see also* German-American relations; propaganda

Deutschland, 200–201

Diaz, Armando, 117, 129, 201–202, 769; *see also* Vittorio Veneto, Battle of

Dickman, Joseph Theodore, 202–203; and Sedan incident, 203, 534, 535, 536, 584; and St. Mihiel campaign, 523–24

dollar-a-year-men, 203–204

Donovan, William Joseph (Wild Bill), 204; at Meuse-Argonne campaign, 204

Doullens Conference, 1, 69, 231

Doyen, Charles Augustus, 74, 205, 620

Drum, Hugh Aloysius, 205–206; and Sedan incident, 534, 535–36

Duffy, Francis Patrick, 103, 206–207; *see also* chaplains

Dulles, John Foster, 207–208; and Paris Peace Conference, 207, 208, 445

Eagle Boats, 209; *see also* Ford Motor Company

East St. Louis Riot, 212; *see also* Black Americans

Eastman, Crystal, 210; and American Union Against Militarism, 36–37, 210; and Civil Liberties Bureau, 210; and Selective Service, 210

Eastman, Max, 126, 210–11; and *The Masses*, 211, 376; and American Union Against Militarism, 211; on Fourteen Points, 211

Edison, Thomas, 213; serves on Naval Consulting Board, 173, 213, 441

Edwards, Clarence Ranson, 213–14; and United States Army, 26th Division, 214, 537, 632

Eisenhower, Dwight David, 105, 166, 214–15; *see also* tanks; United States Army Tank Corps

Eltinge, Leroy, 215–16; and St. Mihiel offensive, 216; Service of Supply, 216

Ely, Hanson E., 92, 216–17, 631, 632; at Cantigny, 126, 216

Emergency Fleet Corporation, 217–18, 258, 379, 550, 551, 749; *see also* Shipping Board

Espionage Act of 1917, 81, 114, 132, 133, 134, 194, 219, 556; and censorship, 132; Supreme Court upholds, 219; Woman's Peace Party on, 802

Farnsworth, Charles S., 221

Federal Trade Commission, 222

Fellowship of Reconciliation, 223

Film in the First World War, 223–24; as propaganda, 223; *see also* Four-Minute Men

Fish, Hamilton, 224–25; and American Legion, 225

Fiske, Bradley Allen, 225–26, 757; relationship with J. Daniels, 191, 192, 225, 226

Fiske, Harold Benjamin, 227

flamethrowers, 228–29; used at Cantigny, 228

Foch, Ferdinand, 1, 2, 69–70, 229–32; amalgamation controversy, 1, 231; and preparation of armistice terms, 48, 49, 50, 231; and doctrine

of the offensive, 229; relationship with G. Clemenceau, 229; on J. Joffre, 230; and Paris Peace Conference, 231, 438

Food Administration. *See* United States Food Administration

Food and Fuel Control Act. *See* Lever Food and Fuel Control Act

Ford, Henry. *See* Ford Motor Company

Ford Motor Company, 232–33; and Eagle boats, 209, 232; and Liberty engine, 232; and tank production, 233; *see also* Eagle Boats; Liberty Engines

Ford Peace Ship, 2, 232, 233–34

Fosdick, Raymond Blaine, 36, 234–35; and Commission on Training Camp Activities, 159, 234; *see also* Commission on Training Camp Activities

Foulois, Benjamin Delahauf, 235, 389, 555, 605; *see also* United States Air Service

Four-Minute Men, 163, 224, 236, 393; *see also* Committee on Public Information

Fourteen Points, 41, 236–39, 426; as basis for armistice with Germany, 48, 49, 50; effect on Austria-Hungary, 55, 56; and Czech Legion, 186; impact of Russian Revolution on, 237, 238; basis for Paris Peace Conference, 239, 437; and France, 242; influence of The Inquiry on, 302; effect on Italy, 307; Sonnino's response to, 571; W. J. Stone on, 582

France. *See* Franco-American relations

Francis, David Rowland, 240, 515; *see also* Russian-American relations

Franco-American relations, 241–43

Franklin, Phillip Albright Small, 243–44, 550, 551

Franz Ferdinand, 244–45; and Conrad von Hotzendorf, 167, 168, 244

Franz Joseph, 80, 245–47

Garfield, Harry Augustus, 249–50, 738; *see also* United States Fuel Administration

Garrison, Lindley Miller, 59, 171, 172, 250, 399, 464, 533, 702; *see also* Continental Army Plan

George V of Great Britain, 251–52; *see also* Anglo-American relations

Gerard, James Watson, 252–53

German-American relations, 252, 253, 253–56

Germany, and Compeigne Armistice, 50–51, 280; *see also* German-American relations

Gibbons, Floyd, 256–57

Gibbons, James, Cardinal, 257

Gleaves, Albert, 258

Goethals, George Washington, 59, 258–60, 549, 550; serves on Emergency Fleet Corporation, 217, 258, 259, 379; and Service of Supply, 260; *see also* Emergency Fleet Corporation

Goldman, Emma, 82, 260–61

Gompers, Samuel, 25, 26, 27, 261–62; establishes American Alliance for Labor and Democracy, 25; and Council of National Defense, 27, 173, 261